THE U.S. CONSTITUTION A TO Z

THE U.S. CONSTITUTION
A TO Z

SECOND EDITION

ROBERT L. MADDEX

CQ PRESS

A Division of SAGE
Washington, D.C.

CQ Press
2300 N Street, NW, Suite 800
Washington, DC 20037

Phone: 202-729-1900; toll-free, 1-866-4CQ-PRESS (1-866-427-7737)

Web: www.cqpress.com

CQ Press gratefully acknowledges the Virginia Museum of Fine Arts for providing the image on page 120, Washington as Statesman at the Constitutional Convention, 1856 Obj. No. 50.2.1 Photo No. 51988.CT.4. Julius Brutus Stearns (American, 1810–1885). Oil on canvas (37½″H × 54″W, 95.2 × 137.1 cm). Note: Signed lower right, STEARNS. One of five original oils made for a set of colored lithographs. Gift of Edgar William and Bernice Chrysler Barbisch. Photo by Ron Jennings © Virginia Museum of Fine Arts.

Cover design: Auburn Associates, Inc.
Cover photos: Eleanor Roosevelt, Franklin D. Roosevelt Presidential Library; Bill of Rights, Getty Images; Charlton Heston (NRA), U.S. Census, male couple, and ERA protest, AP Images
Composition: Auburn Associates, Inc.

⊗ The paper used in this publication exceeds the requirements of the American National Standard for Information Sciences—Permanence of Paper for Printed Library Materials, ANSI Z39.48-1992.

Printed and bound in the United States of America

12   11   10   09   08   1   2   3   4   5

Library of Congress Cataloging-in-Publication Data

Maddex, Robert L.

   The U.S. Constitution A to Z / Robert L. Maddex. — 2nd ed.
      p. cm.
   Includes bibliographical references and index.
   ISBN 978-0-87289-764-9 (alk. paper)
   1. Constitutional law—United States—Encyclopedias. 2.
Constitutional history—United States—Encyclopedias. I. Title. II.
Title: US Constitution A to Z. III. Title: United States Constitution A to Z.

   KF4548.5.M33 2008
   342.730203—dc22

                                                        2008021902

CQ PRESS
AMERICAN GOVERNMENT A TO Z SERIES

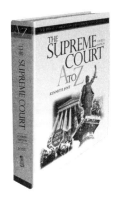

The Supreme Court A to Z, 4th Edition

This is the definitive source for information on the Court, its justices, and its impact on American democracy.

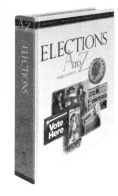

Elections A to Z, 3rd Edition

This single, convenient volume explores vital aspects of campaigns and elections, from voting rights to the current state of House, Senate, and presidential elections.

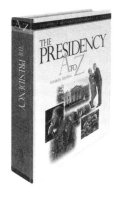

The Presidency A to Z, 4th Edition

This is an invaluable quick-information guide to the executive branch and its responses to the challenges facing the nation over time.

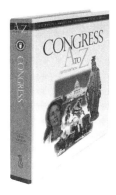

Congress A to Z, 5th Edition

No other volume so clearly and concisely explains the inner workings of the national legislature.

Contents

About the Author

Robert L. Maddex is an attorney specializing in constitutional and international law. He has served as chief counsel of the Foreign Claims Settlement Commission of the United States and as an adviser on constitutional issues to several nations. He is the author of *Constitutions of the World*, *Encyclopedia of Sexual Behavior and the Law*, *International Encyclopedia of Human Rights*, and *State Constitutions of the United States*, all published by CQ Press.

About the Book

The U.S. Constitution A to Z is part of CQ Press's five-volume American Government A to Z series, which provides essential information about the history, powers, and operations of the three branches of government; the election of members of Congress and the president; and the nation's most important document, the Constitution. In these volumes, CQ Press's writers and editors present engaging insight and analysis about U.S. government in a comprehensive, ready-reference encyclopedia format. The series is useful to anyone who has an interest in national government and politics.

The U.S. Constitution A to Z examines how the Constitution—written more than two centuries ago—continues to shape rights and issues in American society today. Its topics include the powers and constitutional checks and balances pertaining to the three branches of government; concepts such as executive privilege, judicial review, and property rights; influential constitutional law cases; profiles of individuals who have shaped American government, from James Madison to Susan B. Anthony; and key issues such as affirmative action, gun control, human rights, abortion, censorship, the death penalty, and terrorism. The entries are arranged alphabetically and are extensively cross-referenced to related information. This volume includes a detailed index, useful reference materials, and a bibliography.

The second edition of *The U.S. Constitution A to Z* has been thoroughly updated to cover contemporary events, including advances in gay marriage rights and homeland security measures stemming from the September 11 attacks. The volume contains new entries on the PATRIOT Act, sex offenders, and important recent Supreme Court cases such as *Kelo v. City of New London*. Presented in a new and engaging design, this edition contains a wealth of stimulating sidebar material, such as memorable quotations and numerous features inviting the reader to explore issues in further depth.

Preface

The framers drafted the Constitution of the United States some 220 years ago, but the document still speaks to modern issues and shapes important aspects of American life and politics. It also continues to have a profound effect on other nations. Although the Constitution is widely revered, most people have only a rudimentary knowledge or understanding of it and of the implications of its provisions on the laws and government of the United States. *The U.S. Constitution A to Z* is a comprehensive guide to the history of the supreme law of the land and the concepts that continue to influence the structure of government and the basic rights of U.S. citizens.

According to William Gladstone (1809–1898), the four-time British prime minister, the Constitution of the United States is "the most wonderful work ever struck off at a given time by the brain and purpose of man." It was not, however, a perfect work when it was drafted in 1787, nor is it today. Still a work in progress, the Constitution establishes the fundamental elements for governing the national affairs of the people of the United States. Yet it also contains gaps to be filled and language to be reinterpreted in light of the times and the needs of U.S. citizens and residents in the twenty-first century.

The U.S. Constitution is the oldest written constitution still in force. Norway's 1814 constitution is the second oldest. Both of these were preceded by the Fundamental Orders of Connecticut (1638–1639), a colonial constitution that has been called the world's first written constitution. The Massachusetts constitution of 1780 is the oldest existing state constitution and has been amended more than one hundred times.

Key Constitutional Concepts

The delegates to the Constitutional Convention of 1787 in Philadelphia came from twelve of the thirteen independent states that had evolved from British colonies during the Revolutionary War (1775–1783); only Rhode Island did not participate. At the time, these states constituted a confederacy established by the Articles of Confederation (1781). They called a convention to revise the Articles to reduce the friction among the states over interstate commerce and to strengthen the powers of the national government. James Madison, the "Father of the Constitution," realized along with other delegates that simply trying to amend the Articles would not solve the problems that had become so evident. Creating a new government acceptable to the states and the people, however, required considering and deciding on a number of concepts, including the following:

Republican Democracy. At the time of the Revolutionary War, the British monarchy ruled one of the most democratically advanced countries in the world, with a long tradition of constitutional restraints on the sovereign's absolute power. The revolutionary slogan "No taxation without representation" reflected the American colonists' awareness of the value of representation in the British Parliament. All of the colonies had experimented to some degree with democratic institutions before the Revolution and after declaring independence in 1776 had incorporated elements of representative democracy in their governments. The colonists' disappointment with the British monarch for not acting on their grievances resulted in a general agreement that any new national government must be a republic—one without a monarch and an aristocracy.

Separation of Powers. The underlying problem in creating a new government to replace the system under the Articles of Confederation concerned how to protect the rights of the states and the people from encroachment by a strong national government. Drawing on the works of earlier political theoreticians, the framers adopted the concept of the separation of powers. By preventing the legislative, executive, and judicial powers of government from falling into the hands of a few persons or even one person, the delegates to the Constitutional Convention created a system of checks and balances to protect the states and the people from tyranny.

Federalism. Ensuring that each state would retain certain basic sovereign powers over its own affairs emerged as a major consideration in getting the thirteen states to agree on a stronger national government. Federalism—a form of government that distributes political power between a national government and the constituent states that comprise the nation—solved the problem and has since been adopted by a number of other nations, including Australia, Brazil, and Germany. The line between federal and state power has shifted over the nation's two centuries, and it continues to be the subject of much debate.

Judicial Review. A significant corollary of the separation of powers principle is judicial review, which gives the judiciary—one of the three branches of government—the power to declare acts of the other branches and the states unconstitutional. Contemporaneous materials indicate that judicial review, which was commonplace in some states at the time, was an intended consequence of the Constitution's design. In addition to interpreting the provisions of the Constitution, the federal judiciary, and ultimately the Supreme Court, ensures that any major changes in the Constitution are made according to the document's amendment procedures and not by more indirect actions.

Bill of Rights. The Constitution as drafted in 1787 contained some guarantees of rights for the states and individuals—for example, a promise of a republican form of government and a prohibition against ex post facto laws. As a condition for ratification of the Constitution, however, a number of states demanded that certain rights, many of which were contained in state constitutions, be specifically guaranteed as protection against infringement by the national government. The first ten amendments, ratified in 1791, became known as the Bill of Rights and guaranteed freedom of religion, speech, and the press and safeguards for those accused of crimes. Many national constitutions, including those of Ireland (1937) and South Africa (1997), have incorporated similar guarantees of individual rights.

Understanding the Constitution

It is important for a nation's citizens and residents to understand how they are governed and what their rights are in relation to the government. A written constitution is a basic source of such information. The U.S. Constitution, including its twenty-seven amendments, is only about 8,700 words long; only so much can thus be gleaned from the document alone. Other sources of information include the laws passed to implement the provisions of the Constitution, case law through which courts interpret the Constitution's provisions, textbooks on the Constitution and government, treatises and articles by experts on the Constitution, and such reference works as this volume.

The U.S. Constitution A to Z provides a basic understanding of important aspects of the Constitution and its history as well as the law and institutions that have evolved from it. The volume offers an overview of the subject rather than exhaustive treatment; the full scope of the Constitution and constitutional law could never be reduced to a single, comprehensive work or a collection of works, for even as this book was being written, the Constitution and the law related to it were changing.

In studying the Constitution, it is always good to keep in mind the admonition of Supreme Court Justice Oliver Wendell Holmes Jr. (1841–1935): "[W]hen we are dealing with words that also are a constituent act, like the Constitution of the United States, we must realize that they have called into life a being the development of which could not have been foreseen completely by the most gifted of its begetters." Like any living organism, the Constitution is continually evolving.

A number of people have lent their time and talent to creating this reference book. I would first like to thank my wife, Diane Maddex, president of Archetype Press. David Hosansky contributed the rich new editorial features, bringing keen insight and creativity to the project. This edition also benefited from the supervision of CQ Press acquiring editor Doug Goldenberg-Hart and associate editor Anna S. Baker, who, along with development editor Anastazia Skolnitsky, thoroughly and thoughtfully reviewed the manuscript. Amy Marks edited the manuscript, and Anne Stewart handled the book's production, under the guidance of managing editor Joan Gossett.

We hope that this new edition of *The U.S. Constitution A to Z* will provide readers with easily accessible and accurate information about the United States' most important document and the underlying principles and concepts on which its government and the people's rights are based.

Robert L. Maddex
May 2008

Historic Milestones

Shaped by centuries of struggle for individual freedom and representative government, the U.S. Constitution has itself influenced countless democratic reforms around the globe since it was written in 1787. Although it is the world's oldest written constitution still in force, it has undergone numerous tests, reinterpretations, and amendments over the years. The following represent some of the major milestones in the Constitution's development:

510 B.C.E.

Cliesthenes introduces democratic reforms in Athens, extending citizenship and broadening participation in the government.

509 B.C.E.

The Romans oust their last king, after which the Senate rules the republic of Rome until 23 B.C.E., when the Roman Empire begins under Augustus Caesar.

1215

English barons force King John to accept limitations on the monarchy set forth in Magna Carta, the Great Charter of Liberties, which later kings confirmed more than thirty times, with amendments.

1407

Henry IV of England agrees that revenue measures should originate in the legislature's lower house, a practice later followed in the U.S. Constitution.

1606

The First Charter of Virginia is granted to the Jamestown settlement, guaranteeing individuals full British "liberties, franchises, and immunities."

1620

The Mayflower Compact, presaging later American documents of self-government, states that the new colony will "combine ourselves into a civil body Politik."

Pilgrims sign the Mayflower Compact.
Source: Library of Congress

1628

Charles I assents to the Petition of Right, a parliamentary declaration of the liberties of the people.

1639

The Connecticut colony adopts the Fundamental Orders of Connecticut, the world's first written constitution.

1643

The United Colonies of New England are formed as a defensive measure after the outbreak of civil war in England in 1642.

English Quaker William Penn founded the Pennsylvania colony and helped shape American principles of democracy and religious freedom.
Source: The Granger Collection, New York

1687

William Penn's commentary on Magna Carta, *The Excellent Priviledge of Liberty and Property*, is published in Philadelphia.

1688–1689

In the "Glorious Revolution" (also called the "Bloodless Revolution"), Parliament deposes James II and installs William and Mary as king and queen of England. Parliament then passes a Bill of Rights establishing its own rights, which William accepts in exchange for receiving the crown.

1735

A jury refuses to follow judges' instructions to convict New York printer Peter Zenger of seditious libel against the government, setting an early precedent for freedom of the press.

1765

The Resolutions of the Congress of 1765 are drawn up in New York and signed by nine colonies opposed to the range of duties levied by the Stamp Act imposed by the British Parliament earlier that year.

1774

The Declarations and Resolves of the First Continental Congress assert that the British have no rights to pass any laws in the colonies.

1775

The Revolutionary War begins with the "shot heard 'round the world" on April 19, 1775, in Lexington, Massachusetts. The Second Continental Congress convenes in Philadelphia.

1776

In June the Virginia Declaration of Rights, written by George Mason, is adopted by the Virginia legislature. The following month, the Declaration of Independence is issued on July 4, 1776, by the Continental Congress in Philadelphia.

1781

The Articles of Confederation and Perpetual Union for the thirteen newly independent states are declared ratified by the Continental Congress in March. They remain in effect until July 2, 1789, when Cyrus Griffin, the president of the Congress under the Articles, declares them to be abrogated by the new Constitution.

The battle at Lexington, Massachusetts, set off the Revolutionary War that eventually freed the thirteen colonies from British rule.
Source: National Archives and Records Administration

1783

The Treaty of Paris, marking the end of the Revolutionary War between the United States and Great Britain, is signed on September 3.

1786

After delegates to a special meeting in Annapolis, Maryland, discuss problems under the Articles of Confederation, some states ask the Continental Congress to revise the Articles. Shays's Rebellion begins in Massachusetts, adding impetus to the need for national power to quell such insurrections.

1787

The Constitutional Convention convenes in Philadelphia on May 25 and soon begins to draft a new constitution for the United States. Texts of the Virginia Plan and the New Jersey Plan, representing the varied concerns of larger and smaller states, respectively, are presented. On September 17 the draft of the Constitution is signed by thirty-nine of the forty-two delegates present. In October Alexander Hamilton writes the first of the Federalist Papers to support ratification; the series of eighty-five pieces is completed in May 1788. Delaware becomes the first state to ratify the Constitution on December 7.

1788

On June 21 New Hampshire becomes the ninth state needed to ratify the Constitution, allowing Congress to appoint a committee to guide the transition from a government under the Articles of Confederation to one under the new document. In September Congress resolves to fix the date for the election of a president and the organization of the government under the Constitution.

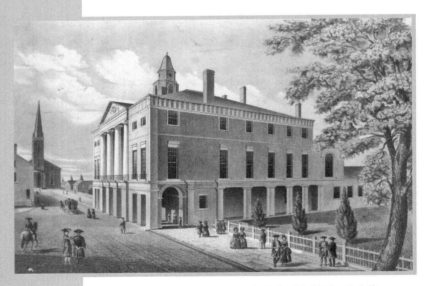

The first session of Congress convened at Federal Hall in New York City.
Source: Library of Congress

1789

The first session of Congress convenes March 4, and George Washington, who was unanimously chosen president by the electoral college, takes office on April 30. On June 8 James Madison introduces constitutional amendments in the House of Representatives that will become the Bill of Rights; Congress proposes these first twelve changes to the states in September.

1791

On February 18 Vermont is admitted to the Union under the Constitution's procedures for admission of new states. The Bill of Rights goes into effect on December 15.

1794

The Whiskey Rebellion in Pennsylvania is suppressed by a militia from four states led by the federal government.

1795

Ratification of the Eleventh Amendment limits the judiciary's power with respect to suits against the states. The Alien and Sedition Acts make it a crime to publish any "false, scandalous, and malicious" writings against the national government.

1801

The presidential election of 1800 produces an electoral college tie between Thomas Jefferson and Aaron Burr that is resolved in the House of Representatives after more than thirty ballots, setting the stage for the Twelfth Amendment (1804). John Marshall is appointed chief justice of the United States.

1803

Marbury v. Madison sets a precedent for allowing the federal courts to exercise judicial review of the constitutionality of legislative branch actions.

1804

Ratification of the Twelfth Amendment requires the electoral college to vote separately for president and vice president. No longer does the candidate who receives the second highest number of votes in the electoral college become vice president.

1810

In *Fletcher v. Peck*, the Georgia legislature's attempt to annul contracts authorized by the previous legislature is held unconstitutional by the Supreme Court under the Constitution's contract clause.

1819

In *McCulloch v. Maryland*, the Supreme Court upholds the implied power of Congress to create a national bank and assure it immunity from state taxation.

1820

The "Missouri Compromise" in Congress maintains a parity of free and slave states by admitting new states into the Union in pairs—one free state and one slave state at a time.

1824

In *Gibbons v. Ogden*, Congress's broad power to regulate interstate commerce is upheld by the Supreme Court.

1833

In *Barron v. Baltimore*, the Supreme Court refuses to make the protections of the Bill of Rights applicable to state actions.

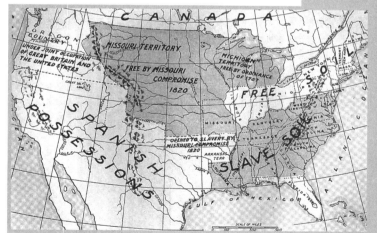

This map indicates free and slave territories at the time of the Missouri Compromise in 1820.
Source: Teaching Politics Web Site, http://teachpol.tcnj.edu/amer_pol_hist/thumbnail117.html

The Supreme Court denied freedom to Dred Scott in 1857; he was later emancipated by his original owners.
Source: Library of Congress

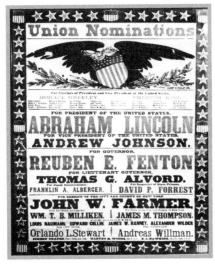

A poster from Abraham Lincoln's 1864 presidential campaign. He was reelected but assassinated shortly thereafter.
Source: Library of Congress

1850

The Fugitive Slave Act authorizes slave owners to capture runaway slaves, with few or no legal safeguards for blacks, whether fugitive or free persons.

1857

The Supreme Court rules in *Scott v. Sandford*—the Dred Scott case—that a slave or even a free black can never become a citizen of the United States.

1861

The Civil War begins when seven Southern states assert their right to secede from the Union, primarily over the issue of slavery, and form the Confederate States of America. Abraham Lincoln, elected president in 1860, vows to preserve the Union with military force.

1865

The Civil War ends with the Union restored, but Lincoln, who was reelected in 1864, is assassinated shortly after his second inauguration. The Thirteenth Amendment, abolishing slavery, is ratified.

1866

The Civil Rights Act declares equal rights under the law and equal property rights for "[a]ll persons within the jurisdiction of the United States."

1868

The Fourteenth Amendment confirms citizenship for all persons born or naturalized in the United States. It precludes the states from abridging the privileges and immunities of citizens and guarantees equal protection of the laws and due process to all persons. President Andrew Johnson is impeached by the House of Representatives but escapes conviction in the Senate by one vote.

1869

Texas v. White finds secession of states unconstitutional and upholds Congress's power to establish provisional governments in former Confederate states.

1870

The Fifteenth Amendment outlaws racial discrimination in voting.

1873

The Slaughter-House Cases limit the Fourteenth Amendment's protection to the rights of citizens of the United States and not to citizens of individual states.

1875

The Civil Rights Act prohibits racial discrimination in public accommodations, but in 1883 it is struck down by the Supreme Court, which rules that such a law lies outside Congress's power under the Thirteenth and Fourteenth Amendments.

1879

Reynolds v. United States holds that the freedom of religion guarantee in the First Amendment does not invalidate Congress's authority to ban polygamy as a "violation of social duties or subversive of good order."

1896

In *Plessy v. Ferguson*, the Supreme Court upholds "separate but equal" racial segregation in public transportation.

1908

Ex parte Young validates the use of injunctions to block the enforcement of unconstitutional state laws, allowing suits against individual state officials rather than the state itself, thus limiting the effect of the Eleventh Amendment.

1913

The Sixteenth Amendment authorizes the collection of federal income tax without the need to apportion it among the states. The Seventeenth Amendment requires the popular election of U.S. senators rather than selection by their state legislatures.

1917

The Eighteenth Amendment prohibits the sale, transportation, importation, and exportation of liquor, leading to a sixteen-year experiment in Prohibition.

Suffragists march for women's rights in front of the White House in 1917.
Source: Library of Congress

1920

The Nineteenth Amendment finally gives women the right to vote.

1931

The Supreme Court holds in *Near v. Minnesota* that the Fourteenth Amendment bars states from censoring the press before publication.

1932

In the Scottsboro Cases, the Supreme Court decides that under certain circumstances defendants must have the assistance of counsel in state murder trials to satisfy the due process requirements of the Fourteenth Amendment.

1933

The Twentieth Amendment sets January 3 for new Congresses to convene and January 20 for the inauguration of the president. The Twenty-first Amendment repeals the Eighteenth Amendment prohibiting liquor.

1951

The Twenty-second Amendment limits the president to two terms.

1954

Brown v. Board of Education of Topeka bans "separate but equal" segregation in public schools as unconstitutional under the equal protection clause of the Fourteenth Amendment.

1961

In *Mapp v. Ohio*, the Supreme Court declares that illegally obtained evidence must be excluded from state criminal trials. The Twenty-third Amendment authorizes the District of Columbia to select three electors for president and vice president.

1962

Baker v. Carr paves the way for reapportionment and redistricting by state legislatures, based on the principle of "one person, one vote."

1963

Gideon v. Wainwright requires the appointment of lawyers for indigent defendants in state as well as federal felony cases.

1964

The Civil Rights Act establishes significant protections against discrimination in public accommodations and employment. The Twenty-fourth Amendment outlaws poll taxes in federal elections. *New York Times Co. v. Sullivan* confirms constitutional protection for publications that criticize public officials.

1966

Miranda v. Arizona establishes "Miranda rules" for police to use in informing suspects of their constitutional right against self-incrimination and right to counsel.

1967

The Twenty-fifth Amendment provides for presidential succession in the event the president becomes disabled. *Katz v. United States* extends protection from government eavesdropping in locations where there is an expectation of privacy. Thurgood Marshall becomes the first African American justice appointed to the Supreme Court.

1971

The Twenty-sixth Amendment gives eighteen year olds the right to vote.

1972

The Equal Rights Amendment is proposed by Congress, but the seven-year deadline and an additional three years expire without ratification.

1973

Roe v. Wade guarantees the right to an abortion.

1976

In *Buckley v. Valeo*, the Supreme Court upholds federal limits on contributions to election campaigns but finds limits on campaign spending to be unconstitutional.

1978

Voting rights for the District of Columbia, proposed as the Twenty-third Amendment, are passed but ratified by only sixteen states

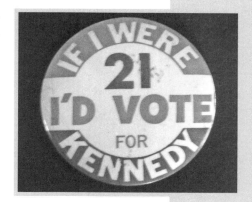

This campaign button predates the Twenty-sixth Amendment.
Courtesy of Christopher Schardt

within the specified period. *Regents of the University of California v. Bakke* prohibits the use of fixed quotas in affirmative action programs.

1981

Sandra Day O'Connor becomes the first female justice appointed to the Supreme Court.

1990

The Americans with Disabilities Act extends protection to disabled persons against discrimination in employment, public areas, and state-sponsored programs.

1992

The Twenty-seventh Amendment, drafted in 1789, is finally ratified, postponing salary increases for members of Congress until after an intervening election.

1995

United States v. Lopez limits congressional authority under the commerce clause to regulate firearms.

Bill Clinton's presidency was marred by legal trouble, including a sexual harassment suit and an impeachment trial.
Source: Library of Congress

1996

Romer v. Evans invalidates a statewide referendum banning laws to protect homosexuals from discrimination, calling it a violation of the equal protection clause of the Fourteenth Amendment.

1997

Clinton v. Jones allows a private damage suit against a sitting president to proceed while he is in office.

1998

The House of Representatives impeaches President Bill Clinton, but he avoids conviction in the Senate.

2000

After a recount of votes in Florida puts the state's twenty-five electoral votes in doubt, the Supreme Court's decision in *Bush v. Gore* decides the presidential election in favor of George W. Bush.

2001

In response to the al-Qaida attacks of September 11 on the World Trade Center in New York City and the Pentagon outside Washington, D.C., the national government begins a war against terrorism. Antiterrorism measures—additional authority to intercept communications and establishment of military tribunals in particular—draw criticism as potential infringements of constitutional rights.

2003

The Supreme Court in *Lawrence v. Texas* overturns its *Bowers v. Hardwick* (1986) decision by declaring a state statute criminalizing intimate homosexual conduct between consenting adults in the privacy of their own home to be a violation of the due process clause of the Fourteenth Amendment.

A

Abortion

Abortion (from the Latin *abortus*, meaning an untimely birth) has been practiced, often with little if any moral condemnation, since ancient times to induce premature delivery of a fetus. As with controversies over the DEATH PENALTY and the RIGHT TO DIE, no uniform agreement exists around the world on the validity of a woman's right to an abortion, and there is seemingly not much middle ground for compromise. In the United States—where abortion has been legal since 1973—the battle over abortion rights has been both divisive and deadly.

Many other countries have liberalized their abortion laws since World War II. Great Britain did so in 1967, and in 1988 Canada's highest court voided that country's restrictive abortion laws. A decade later Germany's constitutional court declared unconstitutional a Bavarian law severely limiting access to abortion. China, because of its overpopulation problem, actually encourages abortions. However, the procedure is restricted or prohibited in Latin America, Africa, and India. In some states of the United States abortions are also restricted by legislated demands such as parental notification for minors and waiting periods, controls devised to make the procedure more difficult to obtain.

The right to life is a generally acknowledged human right, but the key question in the abortion debate is exactly when human life begins. Some religious leaders such as the pope have defined human life as beginning at the moment of conception, and some legislators and jurists have emphasized the rights of an unborn child above the rights and wishes of the mother. The right to an abortion, however, has been justified by a woman's right to make important life-defining decisions with regard to reproduction and her own body and health. Proponents of choice for women also rec-

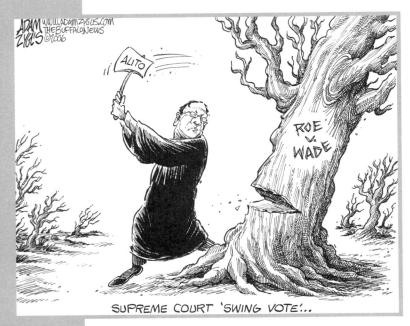

SUPREME COURT 'SWING VOTE'...

Source: © 2006, www.Adamzyglis.com, *The Buffalo News*

ognize the importance of family planning in a world experiencing rampant overpopulation (see FAMILIES; WOMEN).

Before Roe v. Wade

The Constitution does not expressly address abortion, and before 1973 a pregnant woman in the United States had no recognized constitutional right to have one. Poor women and their families were disproportionately affected by the lack of access to safe abortions. Wealthier women could afford to go abroad and pay for an abortion in countries with more liberal abortion laws or where the laws were not enforced as strictly. Poor women were forced to bear children they could not afford to raise or who were simply unwanted. Where illegal abortions could be had, conditions were often unsanitary and medically unsafe, greatly increasing the risk of harm to women seeking abortions and sometimes resulting in their death.

In its landmark decision ROE V. WADE (1973), the Supreme Court reasoned that a woman's right to an abortion during the first three months of pregnancy was a "fundamental" liberty (see FUNDAMENTAL RIGHTS). The Court's 7–2 decision was based on a woman's right of PRIVACY, a right used in GRISWOLD V. CONNECTICUT (1965) to invalidate a state law that prohibited married couples from using contraceptives. The Court held that a state law infringing a woman's right to an abortion was an unconstitutional denial of substantive DUE PROCESS of law, guaranteed by the Fourteenth Amendment (1868). In earlier cases the Court had used substantive, as opposed to procedural, due process to invalidate government action that infringed a person's right to life, LIBERTY, or PROPERTY where no legitimate government interest could be established. (In regulating private activity, courts use substantive due process to limit government powers, whereas they use procedural due process to ensure that fundamental fairness and rights are observed.)

Attempts to Limit Roe v. Wade

Although the *Roe v. Wade* decision remains the law of the land, opponents of the right to an abortion (variously labeled pro-life) continue to pursue ways to limit or nullify its constitutional protection, using such tactics as national and state legislation and regulations, a proposed federal constitutional amendment banning abortion, and court challenges. In 1977 the Hyde Amendment, named for its sponsor, Henry Hyde, Republican representative from Illinois, was enacted as part of a House of Representatives appropriations bill for Medicaid, the public health insurance program for the indigent. According to the Supreme Court in *Williams v. Zbaraz* (1980), the amendment prohibits federal funding of abortions, including in cases where an abortion would prevent "severe and long-lasting physical health damage to the mother."

The constitutionality of the Hyde Amendment was upheld by the Supreme Court in *Harris v. McRae* (1980). In the opinion of Justice Potter Stewart (1915–85), the amendment placed "no governmental obstacle in the path of a woman who chooses to terminate her pregnancy, but rather, by means of unequal subsidization of abortion and other medical services, encourages alternate activity deemed in the public interest." Different Congresses and presidents over the last several decades have also sought to keep federal foreign aid from going to family planning centers overseas that counsel patients on abortion, even if they use their own funds for this purpose.

Another contentious issue in the war between anti-abortion and pro-choice forces is late-term abortion, called partial-birth abortion by abortion opponents, a medical procedure used in the late second or third trimester of pregnancy to remove the fetus. Although rarely performed, it has drawn special attention from antiabortionists, who use the more completely developed fetus to suggest that abortion is similar to the criminal act of infanticide. In *Sternberg v. Carhart* (2000), however, the Supreme Court struck down a Nebraska law making the procedure a crime. According to the Court, criminalizing so-called partial-birth abortions places an undue burden on women seeking an abortion because it limits their options to less safe procedures and because the law in question allowed no exceptions even when the mother's health was at risk.

The law regarding abortions underwent further development in two recent Supreme Court cases: *Ayotte v. Planned Parenthood of Northern New England* (2006) and *Gonzales v. Carhart* (2007). The Court unanimously remanded the *Ayotte* case, which involved a New Hampshire statute that restricted abortion but did not contain an exception for the health of the mother, to the lower court for reconsideration as to whether the law was unconstitutional for the lack of this exception or whether a more modest remedy could be fashioned that would preserve the constitutional aspects of the law. In *Carhart*, the Court reviewed a federal law prohibiting late-term abortions passed in 2003, after the *Sternberg* decision. A divided Court upheld the law, subject to legal challenges in specific cases where the procedure was necessary to preserve the health of the woman. A dissent by Justices Ruth Bader Ginsburg, John Paul Stevens, David Souter, and Stephen G. Breyer focused on the law's interference with the right of an abortion "procedure [that had been] found necessary and proper in certain cases by the American College of Obstetricians and Gynecologists."

Terrorist Tactics

Other constitutional issues that have arisen in the abortion war involve limits on free SPEECH with respect to the First Amendment (1791) rights of antiabortion protestors near facilities in which abortions are performed. In *Hill v. Colorado* (2000), the Supreme Court upheld a Colorado law restricting demonstrators to an area at least one hundred feet from an abortion facility and barring them from approaching patients without their consent to hand them leaflets, display a sign, or orally assault them. The state's legitimate interest in protecting women entering the facility trumped the demonstrators' First Amendment rights.

Some antiabortion militants have gone so far as to use terrorist tactics such as bombings, arson, and incitements to murder doctors who perform abortions (see TERRORISM). According to the National Abortion Foundation, between 1989 and 1997, 19 murders and attempted murders were committed, together with 106 acts of clinic violence plus thousands of reports of assaults, death and bomb threats, blockades, and hate mail. In 2001 a federal appeals court panel allowed antiabortion militants to continue an Internet site featuring "wanted" posters of doctors who perform abortions. The judges ruled that the site, called the Nuremberg Files, was protected by free-

"The states are not free, under the guise of protecting maternal health or potential life, to intimidate women into continuing pregnancies."

—*Justice Harry A. Blackmun,* in *Roe v. Wade,* January 22, 1973

• • • • • • • • • • • • • • • •

"My difficulty with Roe v. Wade is a legal rather than a moral one. I do not believe— and no one believed for 200 years—that the Constitution contains a right to abortion. And if a state were to permit abortion on demand, I would and could in good conscience vote against an attempt to invalidate that law, for the same reason that I vote against invalidation of laws that contradict Roe v. Wade; namely, simply because the Constitution gives the federal government and, hence, me no power over the matter."

—*Justice Antonin Scalia,* in a 2002 speech

ABORTION RIGHTS AROUND THE WORLD

Country	To protect life of mother	To protect health of of mother	In cases of rape	For socioeconomic reasons	On request
Brazil	Yes	Yes (except for mental health)	Yes	No	No
Canada	Yes	Yes	Yes	Yes	Yes
China	Yes	Yes	Yes	Yes	Yes
England	Yes	Yes	Yes	Yes	Yes
Egypt	Restricted	No	No	No	No
France	Yes	Yes	1st trimester	1st trimester	1st trimester
Germany	Yes	Yes for physical health (just 1st trimester for mental health)	Yes	1st trimester only	No
India	Yes	Yes	1st and 2d trimesters	1st and 2d trimesters	No
Iran	Yes	No	No	No	No
Ireland	Yes	No	No	No	No
Israel	Yes	Yes	Yes	No	No
Japan	1st and 2d trimesters	1st and 2d trimesters	1st and 2d trimesters	1st and 2d trimesters	No
Nigeria	Yes	Yes	No	No	No
Pakistan	Yes	Yes	No	No	No
Russia	Yes	Yes	1st and 2d trimesters	1st and 2d trimesters	1st trimester
Sweden	Yes	Yes	Yes	Yes	Yes
Turkey	Yes	Yes	Yes	1st trimester	1st trimester
United States	Yes	Yes	Yes	Yes	Varies

SOURCE: *World Abortion Policies 2007*, United Nations, Department of Economic and Social Affairs, Population Division.

speech guarantees under the First Amendment. To counter such actions, the Freedom of Access to Clinic Entrances Act (1994) prescribes jail sentences of up to one year and fines of up to $100,000 for first-time offenders who violate the rights of clinics and their patients.

In 2006, in *Scheidler v. National Organization for Women, Inc.*, the Supreme Court was presented with a case that involved several federal laws that make extortion and racketeering a federal crime. The Court, however, in an opinion by Justice Stephen G. Breyer, found that the tactics used by anti-abortionists to hinder and delay women from gaining access to abortion clinics fell outside of the scope of the federal law. According to the decision, Congress, in enacting the Hobbs Act, did not create a freestanding physical violence offense. Rather, such law only forbids obstructing, delaying, or affecting commerce "by robbery or extortion," which is not the case with respect to the tactics of the antiabortionists.

The Court currently consists of a conservative majority, with the appointment of Chief Justice John G. Roberts Jr. and Justice Samuel A. Alito Jr. in 2005 and 2006, respectively, in addition to Justices Antonin Scalia, Clarence Thomas, and, more often than not, Justice Anthony M. Kennedy.

Therefore, abortion rights will most likely be limited, rather than expanded, in cases that come before the Court in the near future.

Access to Courts

How easy is it for the average citizen to go to court either to initiate an action to vindicate or protect his or her rights or to appeal an unjust decision? Constitutional rights do not exist in the abstract—they are meaningful only if they are observed. When rights are not observed or when an agent of the government expressly denies them, citizens must have a way to enforce their rights. To enforce the law, government agents such as prosecutors have access to COURTS as well as myriad public officials and employees. Citizens seeking help to settle a legal matter need similar access to courts to secure their rights, as do the public and the press to ensure open and fair trials.

Citizen Access

The constitutions of some countries expressly provide for access to courts. For example, South Africa's constitution (1997) states: "Everyone has the right to have any dispute that can be resolved by the application of law decided in a fair public hearing before a court or, where appropriate, another independent and impartial tribunal or forum." Some state constitutions contain a similar guarantee—New Hampshire's 1784 constitution, for one, guarantees every citizen "a certain remedy, by having recourse to the laws, for all injuries he may receive in his person, property, or character...."

The U.S. Constitution does not in so many words guarantee access to courts of law, but it does vouchsafe certain rights in judicial proceedings (see CRIMINAL LAW). Like the presumption of innocence, access to courts was assumed as a citizen's right in postcolonial America. Article III, section 2, gives the Supreme Court appellate jurisdiction, which extends the right of appeal to citizens as well as the government, and requires that the "Trial of all Crimes, except in Cases of Impeachment, shall be by Jury; and such Trial shall be held in the State where the said Crimes shall have been committed...." The BILL OF RIGHTS (1791)—in particular the Fifth and Sixth Amendments—contains a number of guarantees related to TRIALS, including the right to a speedy and public trial and the ASSISTANCE OF COUNSEL. The Seventh Amendment (1791) sets a minimum threshold for suits at COMMON LAW, extends the right of trial by jury (see JURIES), and preserves the right of the jury to be the final arbiter of the facts in such cases.

For the wealthy and politically savvy, access to courts to further or protect their interests is generally taken for granted. But for others less well off, from the poor to certain MINORITIES, access to courts and the JUSTICE that such access may afford has often been routinely denied by the legal system and the courts themselves. When Supreme Court Justice THURGOOD MARSHALL declared for the Court in *Bounds v. Smith* (1977) that there was a "fundamental constitutional right of access to the courts," it was to effective or "meaningful" access that he was referring.

Through a number of cases beginning in 1957, the Warren Court (1954–69) began expanding the rights of individuals to effective legal representation and to make effective appeals from decisions against them in lower courts, especially in the states. Such new rights included counsel for indigent defendants, free transcripts for defendants to use in seeking an appeal, and counsel for appeals. In 1971 the Court even held unconstitutional the requirement for a $60 filing fee to get into divorce court. Because the only way to obtain a divorce (see FAMILIES) was by court order, the filing fee was a bar to those who could not afford the fee.

The court went so far as to declare in *M.L.B. v. S.L.J.* (1996) that even in certain types of civil suits that are "barely distinguishable from criminal condemnation...record preparation fees" (in this case exceeding $2,300) must be waived for indigents.

The Supreme Court in *Ross v. Moffitt* (1974), over a dissent by Justices William O. Douglas, William J. Brennan Jr., and Thurgood Marshall, denied the constitutional right to court-appointed counsel in discretionary appeals. However, in *Halbert v. Michigan* (2005) the court distinguished the *Ross* case and extended the rationale in the case of *Douglas v. California* (1963) to find that the due process and equal protection clauses require appointment of counsel for defendants appealing convictions based on guilty pleas for the first time.

Public and Press Access

THE PRESS also has a constitutional right to access the courts to report on cases, a right the Supreme Court made explicit in *Richmond Newspapers, Inc. v. Virginia* (1980). The Court held for the first time that this right of access was protected. According to Chief Justice Warren E. Burger (1907–95), writing for the Court (his opinion, however, was joined by only two other justices), "[A] presumption of openness inheres in the very nature of a criminal trial under our system of justice." He continued: "[I]n the context of trials…the First Amendment guarantees of speech and press, standing alone, prohibit government from summarily closing courtroom doors which had long been open to the public at the time that amendment was adopted [1791]."

The right of the public and the press to access the courts may at times conflict with a defendant's right to a fair trial. Often the courts have to balance the competing interests (see BALANCING TESTS). In *Globe Newspapers Co. v. Superior Court* (1982), the Supreme Court invalidated a state law excluding the public and the press from a courtroom when the victim of certain sexual crimes was testifying. This does not mean, however, that under certain unique situations the court could not exclude the public or the press. In *Gannett Co., Inc. v. DePasquale* (1979), for example, the Court decided that a pretrial hearing on whether certain evidence should be suppressed could be closed to the press and the public if the prosecutor, defendant, and judge agreed to it.

Access to courts can be denied for various reasons, but for better or worse, America is a litigious nation, and access to courts is often the only possible access to justice. Any limitation on the openness of courts to citizens and the public alike must be carefully scrutinized and based on clearly overriding competing interests.

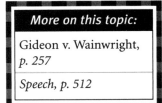

More on this topic:

Gideon v. Wainwright, *p. 257*

Speech, p. 512

Adams, John

Following GEORGE WASHINGTON as the second president of the United States was a burden for John Adams (1735–1826), Massachusetts lawyer, revolutionary, political thinker, and diplomat. His elitist views, his approval of the Alien and Sedition Acts (1798)—which attempted to narrow protections provided by the First Amendment (1791)—his appeasement of France, and a split in his own Federalist Party doomed him to a one-term presidency. However, he lived to see his son, John Quincy Adams, elected president in 1825. Adams died a year later, on July 4, exactly fifty years to the day after the DECLARATION OF INDEPENDENCE was promulgated and the same day that THOMAS JEFFERSON died.

John Adams's contributions to the development of a new national constitution included his advocacy for separation of powers and the adoption of a bicameral legislature. He became the country's first vice president and second president.
Source: Library of Congress

Born on October 30, 1735, in Braintree, Massachusetts, the eldest son of a farmer and elected town official, John Adams was graduated from Harvard College in 1755 and became a lawyer. In 1764 he married Abigail Smith (1744–1818), the daughter of a well-connected Massachusetts family, and in 1768 they moved to Boston. There he began actively opposing British oppression of the colonists, although he was not as ardent a revolutionary as his cousin Samuel Adams. In 1770 he won an acquittal for the British commanding officer and most of the soldiers implicated in the Boston Massacre, which resulted in the deaths of five colonists.

A member of the Massachusetts colonial legislature, Adams was elected a delegate to the First Continental Congress in 1774 and the following year nominated Washington as commander in chief of the fledgling colonial army. During the Revolutionary War (1775–83), Adams served as joint commissioner with Benjamin Franklin to secure an alliance with France, and after the

war was won he worked with Franklin and John Jay to help negotiate peace with Great Britain. From 1785 to 1788 he served as the first U.S. minister (ambassador) to Great Britain, where he moved with his family.

Adams made several important contributions to the development of the Constitution. He had drafted the Massachusetts state constitution (1780), which has been continuously in force longer than any other written constitution in the world. This document was considered by the delegates to the CONSTITUTIONAL CONVENTION OF 1787 and served as a model for several provisions in the new national constitution, including life appointment for federal judges and the addition of a BILL OF RIGHTS in 1791. The first volume of his three-volume work *Defence of the Constitutions of the Government of the United States of America* (1787) was also available to the convention delegates in Philadelphia. In it, Adams urged that the new government be based on the

John Adams came to prominence in 1770, when he defended British soldiers who took part in the Boston Massacre.
Source: The Granger Collection, New York

In 1780 John Adams drafted the Massachusetts constitution, which would become a model for the U.S. Constitution. Article 1 of the Massachusetts document stated: "All men are born free and equal, and have certain natural, essential, and unalienable rights; among which may be reckoned the right of enjoying and defending their lives and liberties; that of acquiring, possessing, and protecting property; in fine, that of seeking and obtaining their safety and happiness."

principle of the separation of government powers and that there be a bicameral national legislature (see CONGRESS; HOUSE OF REPRESENTATIVES; SENATE; SEPARATION OF POWERS).

After returning from England, Adams was elected the nation's first vice president under Washington and served for two terms, from 1789 to 1797. "My country has in its wisdom," he complained to Abigail, "contrived for me the most insignificant office that ever the invention of man contrived or his imagination conceived." When Washington declined to run for a third term, Adams ran, won, and in 1797 began his single term as the second president of the United States. He was a member of the Federalist Party, but the newly emerging Democratic-Republican Party, which evolved into the present-day Democratic Party (see POLITICAL PARTIES), had nominated Jefferson to oppose him. Adams prevailed by only three electoral votes (see ELECTORAL COLLEGE). Under the Constitution's presidential election scheme at the time, Jefferson became vice president.

Adams faced several crises during his administration that hindered his chances for reelection. A leader of the Federalist Party during his vice presidency, he was associated with some of his party's unpopular positions. His disdain for the French Revolution of 1789 and his fear of possible revolutionary activities by French sympathizers in America and Europe led him to take measures to prepare for a war with France that had little support among the people; he abandoned his war plans in 1799. Further adding to his unpopularity was his approval of the Alien and Sedition Acts, passed by Congress in 1798. Intended to help curtail any revolutionary activities, these laws restricted freedom of SPEECH critical of the government. It became a crime for citizens to publish "any false, scandalous, and malicious writing" aimed at the president. Before their constitutionality could be tested in court, the acts expired.

He arrived in the new capital of Washington, D.C., on November 1, 1800, to take up residence in the unfinished White House. "May none but honest and wise men ever rule under this roof," he wrote to Abigail. His loss to Jefferson later that month in the 1800 presidential election left him so bitter that he left the capital before his successor's inauguration, never to reenter political life. He died at his home in Quincy, Massachusetts, on July 4, 1826, after whispering his last words: "Thomas Jefferson survives." His former political rival, in fact, had died at Monticello several hours earlier.

Administrative Agencies

"Those democratic peoples which have introduced freedom into the sphere of politics, while allowing despotism to grow in the administrative sphere," observed Alexis de Tocqueville (1805–59) in volume two of his *Democracy in America* (1840), "have been led into the strangest paradoxes." The French visitor's view may have been skewed somewhat by the political "spoils system" introduced during the administration of President Andrew Jackson (1767–1845) from 1829 to 1837, which rewarded his Democratic supporters with plum government appointments.

For many people, America's federal bureaucracy may still conjure up the same negative connotations of a vast, unfeeling maze of offices and officials endlessly shuffling papers and producing red tape with which to ensnarl average citizens. This bureaucracy pervades CABINET departments, such as the Departments of State and Justice; independent agencies, such as the Federal Trade Commission and Central Intelligence Agency; government corporations such as the U.S. Postal Service; and presidential and congressional agencies from the Office of Management and Budget to the Library of Congress, including committees, commissions, and boards. All these types of organizations function as administrative agencies, administering the policies of the federal government created by Congress and the president.

GOVERNMENT OF THE UNITED STATES

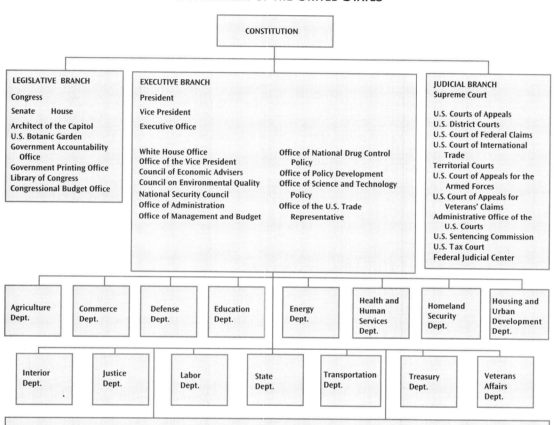

CONSTITUTION

LEGISLATIVE BRANCH

Congress

Senate   House

Architect of the Capitol
U.S. Botanic Garden
Government Accountability
   Office
Government Printing Office
Library of Congress
Congressional Budget Office

EXECUTIVE BRANCH

President

Vice President

Executive Office

White House Office
Office of the Vice President
Council of Economic Advisers
Council on Environmental Quality
National Security Council
Office of Administration
Office of Management and Budget

Office of National Drug Control
   Policy
Office of Policy Development
Office of Science and Technology
   Policy
Office of the U.S. Trade
   Representative

JUDICIAL BRANCH

Supreme Court

U.S. Courts of Appeals
U.S. District Courts
U.S. Court of Federal Claims
U.S. Court of International
   Trade
Territorial Courts
U.S. Court of Appeals for the
   Armed Forces
U.S. Court of Appeals for
   Veterans' Claims
Administrative Office of the
   U.S. Courts
U.S. Sentencing Commission
U.S. Tax Court
Federal Judicial Center

| Agriculture Dept. | Commerce Dept. | Defense Dept. | Education Dept. | Energy Dept. | Health and Human Services Dept. | Homeland Security Dept. | Housing and Urban Development Dept. |

| Interior Dept. | Justice Dept. | Labor Dept. | State Dept. | Transportation Dept. | Treasury Dept. | Veterans Affairs Dept. |

INDEPENDENT ESTABLISHMENTS AND GOVERNMENT CORPORATIONS

African Development Foundation
Broadcasting Board of Governors
Central Intelligence Agency
Commodity Futures Trading
   Commission
Consumer Product Safety Commission
Corporation for National and
   Community Service
Defense Nuclear Facilities
   Safety Board
Environmental Protection Agency
Equal Employment Opportunity
   Commission
Export-Import Bank
Farm Credit Administration
Federal Communications Commission
Federal Deposit Insurance Corp.
Federal Election Commission
Federal Housing Finance Board
Federal Labor Relations Authority
Federal Maritime Commission
Federal Mediation and Conciliation
   Service

Federal Mine Safety and Health
   Review Commission
Federal Reserve System
Federal Retirement Thrift Investment
   Board
Federal Trade Commission
General Services Administration
Inter-American Foundation
Merit Systems Protection Board
National Aeronautics and Space
   Administration
National Archives and Records
   Administration
National Capital Planning Commission
National Credit Union Administration
National Foundation on the Arts and
   the Humanities
National Labor Relations Board
National Mediation Board
National Railroad Passenger Corp. (Amtrak)
National Science Foundation
National Transportation Safety Board
Nuclear Regulatory Commission

Occupational Safety and Health Review
   Commission
Office of the Director of National
   Intelligence
Office of Government Ethics
Office of Personnel Management
Office of Special Counsel
Overseas Private Investment Corporation
Peace Corps
Pension Benefit Guaranty Corporation
Postal Rate Commission
Railroad Retirement Board
Securities and Exchange Commission
Selective Service System
Small Business Administration
Social Security Administration
Tennessee Valley Authority
Trade Development Agency
U.S. Agency for International
   Development
U.S. Commission on Civil Rights
U.S. International Trade Commission
U.S. Postal Service

The Constitution does not mention administrative agencies, and surely the FRAMERS OF THE CONSTITUTION could not have foreseen the power and influence that this "fourth branch of government" would one day wield. But certain constitutional provisions lent themselves to the growth of these agencies. For example, besides giving Congress certain express powers and areas of authority, the last paragraph of Article I, section 8, grants Congress the power "To make all Laws which shall be necessary and proper for carrying into Execution the foregoing Powers, and all other Powers vested by this Constitution in the Government of the United States, or in any Department or Officer thereof" (see NECESSARY AND PROPER CLAUSE). The appointment powers granted to the president in Article II (see APPOINTMENT AND REMOVAL POWER) and his power to "require the Opinion, in writing, of the principal Officer in each of the executive Departments, upon any Subject relating to the Duties of their respective Offices" contemplated that some federal bureaucracy would be created.

Administrative agencies bring expertise to the government's regulatory processes. The highly technical and fast-changing nature of the private sector that the government must regulate means that elected officials and judges probably lack the competence by themselves to make day-to-day decisions that affect these highly specialized activities.

ALEXANDER HAMILTON, in essay 68 of *The Federalist* (1787–88) (see FEDERALIST PAPERS), quotes an unnamed poet:

> *For forms of government let fools contest*
> *That which is best administered is best.*

THE "TYPICAL" FEDERAL EMPLOYEE

The number of civilian employees in the federal bureaucracy is over four million, located in fourteen departments and fifteen agencies. What is the typical federal employee like? The Office of Personnel Management, which oversees employment with the federal government, developed this composite portrait from 2004 data about federal civilian, permanent, non–Postal Service employees:

AGE: 46.8 years
LENGTH OF GOVERNMENT EMPLOYMENT: 16.6 years
EDUCATION: bachelor's degree or higher, 42 percent
GENDER: male, 56 percent; female, 44 percent
RACE AND NATIONAL ORIGIN: 31.4 percent minority (17 percent African American; 7.3 percent Hispanic: 5.0 percent Asian/Pacific Islander; 2.1 percent American Indian)
DISABLED: 7 percent
VETERANS: 23 percent
LOCATION OF EMPLOYMENT: inside the United States, 97 percent; inside Washington, D.C., metropolitan area, 16 percent
ANNUAL BASE SALARY: $61,714
AVERAGE GENERAL SCHEDULE GRADE: 9.8

SOURCE: The Fact Book: Federal Civilian Workforce Statistics, 2005 ed. (Washington, D.C.: Office of Personnel Management, 2006), www.opm.gov/feddata/factbook/index.asp.

Calling this "political heresy," Hamilton went on to say that "we may safely pronounce that the truest test of a good government is its aptitude and tendency to produce a good administration." When GEORGE WASHINGTON organized the first federal administration in 1789, there were several hundred workers in three cabinet departments and the office of the attorney general. Today the number of civilian employees in the federal bureaucracy is over four million, located in fourteen departments and fifteen independent agencies in most states of the Union and abroad.

Administrative Law

The body of law dealing with the activities of administrative agencies is known as administrative law. It generally includes the agency's enabling legislation, the Administrative Procedures Act (1946), and procedural rules adopted by each agency. The administrative processes to which administrative law applies generally consist of rulemaking for the activities the agency is responsible for regulating, and adjudicating complaints or disputes, which may involve informal and formal adjudication procedures.

The constitutional issues likely to arise in courts that review acts of administrative agencies include proper constitutional delegation of authority by the LEGISLATIVE BRANCH or the EXECUTIVE BRANCH and whether an agency's action may be subject to JUDICIAL REVIEW by the courts. As early as 1825, in *Wayman v. Southhard*, the Supreme Court acknowledged that Congress could delegate some of its powers with respect to overseeing the day-to-day operations of the government. But according to Chief Justice JOHN MARSHALL, Congress must establish a general outline of the regulatory program to be carried out by the agency and let the agency "fill up the details."

The Supreme Court never completely lost sight of the Constitution's Article I, section 1, which clearly vested "[a]ll legislative Powers" in CONGRESS and thus prohibited any delegation of its legislative powers. In certain cases, however, the Court would find reasons to approve some delegation to administrative agencies. A showdown came in 1935, when the Court struck down significant new delegations of authority by Congress aimed at promoting recovery from the Great Depression. At issue were laws such as the Agricultural Adjustment Act (1933) and establishment of new agencies such as the Securities and Exchange Commission in 1934. Under the National Recovery Act (1933), President Franklin D. Roosevelt (1882–1945) promulgated by executive order a Live Poultry Code, which the Court struck down in *A.L.A. Schechter Poultry Corp. v. United States* (1935) as an unconstitutional delegation of legislative power by Congress. After Roosevelt threatened to "pack the Court" with extra members who would allow the delegation of power sought by the administration and Congress, the Court began the process of reversing itself. In *National Labor Relations Board v. Jones and Laughlin Steel Corp.* (1937), the justices upheld an enforcement action by the National Labor Relations Board to avert the "catastrophic" effect a strike would have on the nation. While not expressly overruling the Court's nondelegation policy, the tide had turned and the path was clear for a proliferation of new delegations of authority to administrative agencies.

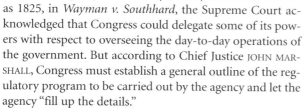

CLOSER LOOK

For many years the federal bureaucracy was influenced greatly by the "spoils system"—a practice by which the political party in power would award choice public offices to its loyal members. The term is often attributed to Sen. William Learned Marcy, who stated, "to the victor belong the spoils."

The spoils system in the national government dates back to the development of political parties, although it reached its peak during the mid-nineteenth century. It was used extensively by Thomas Jefferson and other early presidents, as well as by state leaders. President Andrew Johnson lauded the spoils system, saying the rotation of civil servants improved the government.

Over time, however, the spoils system faced growing opposition from reformers who worried that political cronies, rather than competent administrators, were being put in charge of administrating government functions. In 1871, during the scandal-plagued administration of Ulysses S. Grant, Congress took a step toward reforming the system by creating the Civil Service Commission, but did not fully fund it.

In 1881 the government was jolted into action when a spurned office seeker fatally shot President James A. Garfield. The Civil Service Act of 1883 effectively ended the spoils system by reestablishing the Civil Service Commission and creating standards for appointment to public office. States created their own civil service laws as well, thereby at least partially cushioning government agencies from political influence.

Due Process of Law

What about the fairness of this regulatory process compared to what takes place in the legislative and judicial sectors? In *Opp Cotton Mills v. Administrator* (1941), the Supreme Court held that DUE PROCESS, under the Fifth Amendment (1791), requires at a minimum a hearing for an individual or an industry before an administrative agency issues a regulatory order. Three years later, however, in *Bowles v. Willingham* (1944) the Court allowed the head of the Office of Price Administration to fix minimum rents stabilizing defense-area housing without a hearing as long as "Congress has provided for judicial review after the orders or regulations have been made effective [because] it has done all that due process under the war emergency requires." In *Wong Yang Sung v. McGrath* (1950) the Court laid down the rule that before an agency can deprive a person of life, LIBERTY, or PROPERTY, it must hold a fair hearing before an impartial hearing officer.

Enacted in 1946, the Administrative Procedures Act was intended to set standards for administrative agencies in dealing with private rights and interests of the public. The APA requires federal agencies, for instance, to publish notices of proposed rulemaking actions in the *Federal Register*, which is published daily. Agencies must make available to interested parties copies of proposed regulations and provide an opportunity for them to submit comments.

The APA also requires a fair hearing for parties aggrieved by agency actions before independent hearing officers or administrative law judges, who are assigned to various federal agencies to conduct impartial hearings on matters under the agencies' jurisdiction. The APA's judicial review section provides that a "person suffering legal wrong because of agency action, or adversely affected or aggrieved by agency action within the meaning of a relevant statute, is entitled to judicial review thereof." In *Association of Data Processing Service Org. v. Camp* (1970) and *Barlow v. Collins* (1970), the Supreme Court established a test for litigants under the APA: First, has the litigant suffered an injury-in-fact, and, second, can he or she show that the interest to be protected is arguably within the zone of interests to be protected or regulated by the agency in question? The Court also expanded the nature of the injury beyond economic injury to include "aesthetic, conservational, and recreational" interests; two years later, in *Sierra Club v. Morton* (1972), environmental interests were added as a basis for possible injury.

The Supreme Court has continued to supervise the activities of federal agencies. For example, in 2002, in *Thompson v. Western States Medical Center*, the Court declared that certain exemptions from Food and Drug Administration approval in the Food and Drug Modernization Act (1997) were an unconstitutional restriction on the freedom of commercial speech. The exemptions applied to makers of "compound drugs," on the condition that they not "advertise or promote the compounding of any particular drug, class of drug, or type of drug." But in *National Association of Home Builders v. Defenders of Wildlife* (2007), the Court reiterated its general position that administrative agencies are to be shown deference by the courts, stating that it would not vacate an agency's decision on the grounds that it was arbitrary and capricious unless the agency "relied on factors which Congress had not intended it to consider, entirely failed to consider an important aspect of the problem, offered an explanation for its decision that runs counter to the evidence before the agency, or is so implausible that it could not be ascribed to a difference in view or the product of agency expertise."

In a nation the size of the United States, at a time of tremendous technological and economic complexity, there is a delicate balance between having sufficient manpower and expertise for a government of the people, by the people, and for the people to operate effectively and justly and a bureaucratic, top-heavy government divorced from the people and the democratic institutions established by the Constitution for making government responsible to the citizens. A number of presidents have taken office vowing to reduce the federal bureaucracy or at least bring it under better control. President John F. Kennedy (1917–63) particularly wanted more direction over the Department of State, without lasting success. President Jimmy Carter (b. 1924) tried to cut the government's size but chiefly ended up merging a number of smaller agencies into larger ones. President Bill Clinton (b. 1946) put his vice president, Al Gore (b. 1948), in charge of "reinventing government," also with little long-term success. Many agencies, in fact, have developed such a rapport with the businesses and industries they are supposed to regulate and with the congressional leaders responsible for overseeing their operations that they are able to weather attempts by the chief executive to bend them to his will.

Despite the campaign promises of candidates for president to reduce the size of the federal government if elected, the size of the "fourth branch of government" seems to inevitably expand. For example, according to President George W. Bush's proposed budget for fiscal year 2008, the federal civilian workforce will grow from 1,821,100 in 2004 to 1,872,800 in 2008; this does not count military personnel, contract employees, or those who work for private employers providing goods and

More on this topic:

Judicial Branch, p. 312

Separation of Powers, p. 494

services under government contracts. Undoubtedly an important contributor to this growth are measures that have been taken to improve national security—such as the establishment of the Department of Homeland Security in 2003, in response to the terrorist acts against the United States on September 11, 2001. This gigantic federal bureaucracy, which was not specifically encompassed in the original Constitution, continues to generate myriad issues and problems for the traditional branches of government.

Admiralty and Maritime Law

"The judicial Power [of the federal courts] shall extend," Article III, section 2, of the Constitution states in part, "to all Cases of admiralty and maritime Jurisdiction." Inclusion of this provision reflected a uniform desire to give the federal government jurisdiction over this important adjunct of commerce and trade. "The most bigoted idolizers of State authority," noted ALEXANDER HAMILTON in essay 80 of *The Federalist* (1787–88) (see FEDERALIST PAPERS), "have not thus far shown a disposition to deny the national judiciary the cognizance of maritime causes. These so generally depend on the laws of nations and so commonly affect the rights of foreigners that they fall within the considerations which are relative to the public peace" (see INTERNATIONAL LAW).

Dealing with navigation, shipping, and international trade and seaports, admiralty and maritime law is a distinct body of law—admittedly a narrow field with little constitutional impact on the lives of most American citizens. It was, however, of importance to the FRAMERS OF THE CONSTITUTION, who had been called to the CONSTITUTIONAL CONVENTION OF 1787 to amend the ARTICLES OF CONFEDERATION, largely in response to problems relating to trade and COMMERCE among the states. Apparently the Committee of Detail added the admiralty and maritime provision, but nothing in the convention records indicates any significant discussion about it.

Over the centuries admiralty courts had evolved in the world's maritime cities to deal with questions of law relating to maritime commerce and navigation: shipping, navigation, commerce on the seas, seamen, wharves, piers and docks, marine insurance, liens, and recreation (private boating, swimming, surfing, fishing, and the like), not to mention piracy. In the American colonies before the Revolutionary War (1775–83), the British had maintained admiralty courts, which functioned separately from other courts of law and equity. The newly independent states themselves established admiralty courts, and the congress created under the Articles of Confederation set up a court of appeals to review admiralty court decisions.

The Judiciary Act (1789) contained a broad grant of power to the federal COURTS, including jurisdiction over "all civil causes of admiralty and maritime jurisdiction, [and] all seizures under the law of imposts, navigation or trade of the United States, where seizures are made, on waters which are navigable from the sea by vessels of ten or more tons...as well as upon the high seas...." In *New Jersey Steam Navigation Co. v. Merchants' Bank of Boston* (1848), the Supreme Court approved the broad sweep of the federal courts' jurisdiction, saying, "[W]hatever may have been in doubt, originally, as the true construction of the grant [of jurisdiction] whether it had reference to the jurisdiction in England, or to the more enlarged one that existed in other maritime countries, the question has been settled by legislative and judicial interpretation, which ought not now to be disturbed."

Much of admiralty and maritime law is based on internationally accepted principles and custom. But in *Butler v. Boston and S.S.S. Co.* (1889), the Supreme Court held that Congress had authority under the Constitution's NECESSARY AND PROPER CLAUSE to change the country's admiralty and maritime law. In deciding which acts constitute grounds for determining a matter under admiralty and maritime law, the courts look both to where the act occurred and to its connection with maritime activity, which has led to finding jurisdiction even where a bather was injured by a surfboard. In *Jerome B. Grubart, Inc. v. Great Lakes Dredge and Dock Co.* (1995), the Court held that admiralty jurisdiction applied to limit a barge owner's liability to only the value of his equipment. The barge was implicated in flooding a tunnel under the Chicago River, because it was used as a platform from which piles were driven into the riverbed above the tunnel.

Although admiralty and maritime jurisdiction is vested exclusively in the federal courts, on occasion federal and state jurisdictions collide when states enact laws that overlap with admiralty jurisdiction. After a New York longshoreman died from injuries incurred while driving a truck out of a ship's cargo hold onto a loading dock, the Supreme Court narrowly agreed in *Southern Pacific v. Jensen* (1917) that New York State could not constitutionally apply its workers' compensation protection to employees injured or killed on navigable waters. Shortly thereafter, Congress passed the Jones Act (1920), giving crew members the right to sue for negligent injury, and then the Longshoremen's and Harbor Workers' Compensation Act (1927), extending compensation to injured workers and their families. The Death on the High Seas Act (1920) makes it easier for seamen's widows to recover future earnings lost when death occurs in international waters. In 1970 the Supreme Court reversed a long line of its decisions by allowing family members to sue for wrongful death under maritime law, even though Congress had not taken any action on the matter.

Federal maritime and admiralty laws extend to many boating activities, including those involving pleasure craft. The U.S. Coast Guard patrol craft Assateague *is moored pierside in the harbor at Honolulu, Hawaii, to promote Safe Boating Week on Oahu in May 2001.*
Source: Department of Defense Photo/Don S. Montgomery

In two fairly recent cases the Supreme Court has ruled on questions of state jurisdiction and liability for wrongful death. In *Lewis v. Lewis and Clark Marine, Inc.* (2001), the Court agreed that state courts have jurisdiction over some types of admiralty and maritime claims "so long as the vessel owner's right to seek limitation of liability [to the value of the vessel or his or her interest] is protected." And in *Norfolk Shipbuilding and Drydock Corp. v. Garris* (2001), the Court found that a breach of a marine duty of care—the equivalent of negligence and similar to the duty to insure a vessel's seaworthiness—may be a valid basis for a claim for wrongful death; "[n]or is a negligence action precluded by any of the three relevant federal statutes that provide remedies for injuries and death suffered in admiralty: the Jones Act, the Death on the High Seas Act, and the Longshore[men's] and Harbor Workers' Compensation Act."

A question of the allocation of sovereign authority to deal with maritime disputes was addressed by the Supreme Court in *Federal Maritime Commission v. South Carolina State Ports Authority* (2002). The case involved a complaint made to the Federal Maritime Commission (FMC) by a cruise ship company against the South Carolina port authority for an alleged violation of the federal Shipping Act of 1984. Justice Clarence Thomas delivered the opinion for a divided Court. After noting that the Eleventh Amendment, which restricts the jurisdiction of federal courts in matters involving the states, might not be applicable because the FMC was not, in fact, exercising the "Judicial power of the United States," he concluded that the determination of the private complaint by a federal agency like the FMC violated "the sovereign immunity embedded in our constitutional structure and retained by the States when they joined the Union." The dissent by the more liberal wing of the Court emphasized the fact that the FMC is a part of the executive branch, and thus has inherent power to enforce federal law.

Cases involving a suit against a vessel or other maritime property—called *in rem* suits, because the suit is against a thing (*rem* in Latin) rather than a person—must be conducted in an admiralty court. If the case is against a person—*in personam* suits—the plaintiff has a choice of suing in admiralty or a land-based court. Admiralty courts generally do not use JURIES.

Admission of New States

The original mechanism for becoming a state of the United States of America was RATIFICATION of the ARTICLES OF CONFEDERATION (1781) by the legislatures of the original thirteen states. Maryland was the last of these former British colonies to ratify the Articles, which it did on March 1, 1781. According to JAMES MADISON, in essay 43 of *The Federalist* (1787–88) (see FEDERALIST PAPERS), the "eventual establishment of *new States* seems to have been overlooked by the compilers of [the Articles of Confederation]."

Admissions under Article VII and Article IV

The Constitution drafted in 1787 did, however, contain a provision for accepting new states into the United States. Madison, in the same *Federalist* essay, categorized the power of Congress to admit states into the Union as one of several "miscellaneous powers" granted by the Constitution, along with, among others, the power "to promote the progress of science and useful arts" through COPYRIGHT and PATENTS and the power of Congress to exercise exclusive jurisdiction over the TERRITORY of the capital (see CAPITAL, NATIONAL).

According to Article VII, "The Ratification of the Conventions of nine States, shall be sufficient for the Establishment of this Constitution between the States so ratifying the Same." Delaware was the first state to ratify the new Constitution on December 7, 1787 (see page 644), and New Hampshire was the ninth on June 21, 1788. Rhode Island became the last of the thirteen states on May 29, 1790.

ADMISSION OF STATES TO THE UNION

States	Date of Statehood	Order of Admission
Alabama	December 14, 1819	22
Alaska	January 3, 1959	49
Arizona	February 14, 1912	48
Arkansas	June 15, 1836	25
California	September 9, 1850	31
Colorado	August 1, 1876	38
Connecticut	January 9, 1788	5
Delaware	December 7, 1787	1
Florida	March 3, 1845	27
Georgia	January 2, 1788	4
Hawaii	August 21, 1959	50
Idaho	July 3, 1890	43
Illinois	December 3, 1818	21
Indiana	December 11, 1816	19
Iowa	December 28, 1846	29
Kansas	January 29, 1861	34
Kentucky	June 1, 1792	15
Louisiana	April 30, 1812	18
Maine	March 15, 1820	23
Maryland	April 28, 1788	7
Massachusetts	February 6, 1788	6
Michigan	January 26, 1837	26
Minnesota	May 11, 1858	32
Mississippi	December 10, 1817	20
Missouri	August 10, 1821	24
Montana	November 8, 1889	41
Nebraska	March 1, 1867	37
Nevada	October 31, 1864	36
New Hampshire	June 21, 1788	9
New Jersey	December 18, 1787	3
New Mexico	January 6, 1912	47
New York	July 26, 1788	11
North Carolina	November 21, 1789	12
North Dakota[1]	November 2, 1889	39
Ohio	March 1, 1803	17
Oklahoma	November 16, 1907	47
Oregon	February 14, 1859	33
Pennsylvania	December 12, 1787	2
Rhode Island	May 29, 1790	13
South Carolina	May 23, 1788	8
South Dakota[1]	November 2, 1889	40
Tennessee	June 1, 1796	16
Texas	December 29, 1845	28
Utah	January 4, 1896	45
Vermont	March 4, 1791	14
Virginia	June 25, 1788	10
Washington	November 11, 1889	42
West Virginia	June 20, 1863	35
Wisconsin	May 29, 1848	30
Wyoming	July 10, 1890	44

SOURCE: Maddex, Robert L. *State Constitutions of the United States*, 2d ed. Washington, D.C.: CQ Press, 2005.
1. North Dakota and South Dakota entered the Union on the same day.

The states that were admitted after the original thirteen states came into the Union according to varying criteria for statehood as determined by Congress; Utah's admission, for one, was held up by its practice of polygamy. "New States may be admitted by the Congress into this Union," provides Article IV, section 3, "but no new State shall be formed or erected within the Jurisdiction of any other State; nor any State be formed by the Junction of two or more States, or Parts of States, without the Consent of the Legislatures of the States concerned as well as of the Congress." West Virginia is the only new state to have been made from another state; Virginia, from whose territory it was formed, had seceded (see SECESSION) from the Union in 1861, and West Virginia was admitted in 1863.

In 1912 Arizona became the forty-eighth state of the Union. For the next four decades, until Alaska and Hawaii were admitted in 1959, the states were all located contiguously on the North American continent. Statehood ensures representation in Congress and the ability to vote for president and vice president, rights a majority of the populations in both territories desired. Statehood was also desirable from the federal government's point of view—given Alaska's enormous store of natural resources and Hawaii's strategic location out in the Pacific Ocean three thousand miles from the West Coast.

"Equal Footing" Doctrine

Although not specified by the FRAMERS OF THE CONSTITUTION, the courts have determined that once any state is admitted it is on an "equal footing" with each other state under the Constitution. According to this doctrine, property in a territory that was to become a state was treated as being owned by the federal government in trust for the future state.

An exception to the "equal footing" doctrine was permitted in accordance with the Missouri Compromise of 1820. Originally raised in the context of the enabling act in Congress to make Missouri a state, the compromise became an informal procedure of Congress to admit one slave state and one "free" state together to preserve the balance of free and slave states. In 1846 a provision introduced in Congress to prohibit SLAVERY in

A view of Harper's Ferry, West Virginia, circa 1865. West Virginia took a unique path to statehood. It became a state in 1863 when it broke away from Virginia during the Civil War and joined the North. It was the only state formed by seceding from a Confederate state.
Source: Library of Congress

new territories acquired in the Mexican War, including what would become the states of California and Nevada, broke the compromise and became a contributing factor leading to the Civil War (1861–65).

While future states were allowed to make certain binding agreements with the federal government (see FEDERALISM), such as promising not to tax certain lands held by the United States, conditions for admission that would infringe on a state's SOVEREIGNTY have not been binding. For example, in *Coyle v. Smith* (1911), the Supreme Court held that Congress, by exacting a pledge from Oklahoma not to move its capital after statehood as a condition for admission, infringed the sovereign right of any state to select its own capital. The pledge was thus ruled an improper condition that did not have to be observed by Oklahoma after it became a state on November 16, 1907.

New States on the Horizon?

The Commonwealth of Puerto Rico, which became a TERRITORY of the United States in 1898—the same year in which Hawaii was annexed by the United States—is still wrestling with the question of whether it wants to become a state, remain a territory, or seek independence. The first step in the process would be to have a conclusive referendum by the inhabitants of Puerto Rico that they want to become a state; Congress would then make the final determination of whether to grant statehood.

Another territory that would like to be a state or have key powers of a state—particularly representation in Congress—is the District of Columbia. An amendment (see AMENDMENTS) was proposed in 1978 to extend such rights to the capital's citizens, stating, "For purposes of representation in the Congress, election of the President and Vice President, and article V of this Constitution, the District constituting the seat of government of the United States shall be treated as though it were a state." The measure was ratified by only sixteen states and therefore failed to win adoption by three-fourths of the states as required under Article V of the Con-

Puerto Rico has been a territory of the United States for more than a century. Its residents are divided over whether to apply for statehood.
Source: AP Images/John McConnico

stitution. An amendment is necessary because Article I gives Congress exclusive authority over the District of Columbia given that it serves as the nation's capital.

The process through which a territory becomes a state of the Union is in some ways like an individual's application to join an exclusive club. Admission is sought by meeting certain criteria: number of citizens; a constitution that reflects a democratic, republican form of government; plus any specific preadmission criteria set by the federal government. It is not always a smooth process, however. The enabling act passed by Congress in 1910 to admit Arizona allowed the president to approve Arizona's constitution as a condition for admission. President William Howard Taft (1857–1930), later chief justice of the United States, objected to a provision allowing for the popular recall of judges (see DIRECT DEMOCRACY). So he held up statehood for Arizona for two years until the offending provision was removed.

Adoption *See* CHILDREN; FAMILIES; RATIFICATION.

Advice and Consent

Fear of a strong central government—especially a strong executive—as well as the desire to protect the federal form of government (see FEDERALISM) led the delegates at the CONSTITUTIONAL CONVENTION OF 1787 to require the "Advice and Consent" of the Senate for presidential appointments to important government offices and for approval of TREATIES. The framers considered the SENATE to be a more deliberative body and more representative of the interests of the states than the HOUSE OF REPRESENTATIVES. It was seen as a more venerable body in part because of its senior age qualification and the longer term of office and the fact that the body represented the semisovereign states as opposed to the people, who could not always be trusted to view political decisions dispassionately.

"The necessity of [the Senate's] co-operation in the business of appointments," suggested ALEXANDER HAMILTON in essay 77 of *The Federalist* (1787–88) (see FEDERALIST PAPERS), "will be a considerable and salutary restraint upon the conduct of that magistrate [the president]." Taking a contrarian position, Pennsylvania delegate James Wilson, a proponent of a strong chief executive, argued against the limitation on the president's appointment power (see APPOINTMENT AND REMOVAL POWER). "There can be no good executive," he said, "without a responsible appointment of officers to execute."

As ratified, Article II, section 2, provides that the president "shall nominate, and by and with the Advice and Consent of the Senate, shall appoint Ambassadors, other public Ministers and Consuls, Judges of the supreme Court, and all other Officers of the United States, whose Appointments are not herein otherwise provided for, and which shall be established by Law." Section 2 adds that "the Congress may by Law vest the Appointment of such inferior Officers, as they think proper, in the President alone, in the Courts of Law, or in the Heads of Departments." Jealous of its power vis-á-vis the president, Congress has not given extensive appointment powers to the president alone. Every appointment of a military officer, for example, must be confirmed by the Senate. Similar procedures for presidential appointments such as AMBASSADORS have been copied in the constitutions of other countries, including those of Argentina (1853) and Mexico (1917).

Checks and Balances

In the advice and consent procedures, the FRAMERS OF THE CONSTITUTION devised a system of checks and balances on the president. This procedure operates whether or not the president's political party holds a majority of the members in the Senate.

A parliamentary system of government has a different procedure for checking executive appointments and proposed treaties. The United Kingdom has a separate head of state and head of government: a monarch and a prime minister. Controlling the head of government's power to make appointments and treaties is solved in two ways in such a system. First, the prime minister must have the support of the majority of the elected representatives in parliament. Second, the monarch must generally countersign or approve of major appointments and treaties. Like the American advice and consent process, this form of checks and balances ensures that a legislative body approves the executive's action in both the appointment process and the making of treaties.

Consent to Appointments

The advice and consent procedure for presidential nominations is a three-step process:

(1) The president first nominates a person for a position in the executive or judicial branch. Officials a president is authorized to nominate include cabinet officers and other key officials, the heads and members of various other ADMINISTRATIVE AGENCIES, and ambassadors, as well as Supreme Court justices, other federal judges, and military officers.

(2) Then the Senate may act or not act on the nomination, as the case may be. The nomination is generally referred to the committee of the Senate that has responsibility for the related EXECUTIVE BRANCH activity—ambassadorial nominations are referred to the Foreign Relations Committee, for example, and Supreme Court nominations are referred to the Judiciary Committee. The committee may then report the nomination to the Senate based on a vote of its members. The Senate must then vote as a whole on the nomination reported out.

(3) Finally, the person confirmed must be officially appointed by the president and accept the appointment, evidenced by taking the OATH OF OFFICE. Because the U.S. president heads both state and government, no countersignature is needed once the Senate approves a nomination (or a proposed treaty).

The confirmation process in the Senate often has political and ideological overtones. Although the Senate is more likely to accept the president's personal selections for CABINET officers—because these are relatively short-term, personal appointments—the confirmation process for life-tenured federal judges, particularly justices of the Supreme Court, can become a battleground. In 1987 the Democratic-controlled Senate withheld its consent to the Supreme Court nomination of Judge Robert Bork by Republican president Ronald Reagan (1911–2004) because of his conservative views, especially on the right of PRIVACY created by the Court. The contentious confirmation proceedings gave rise to the term *borking*, meaning to savagely attack a nominee and thus thwart his or her confirmation. Bork became one of only twenty-eight Supreme Court nominees who failed to gain the Senate's consent from among 150 persons nominated by the country's presidents, not including nominations withdrawn before confirmation hearings were begun.

CLOSER LOOK

The unusually divisive battle over the nomination of Judge Robert Bork to the Supreme Court in 1987 has left ongoing scars in Congress over the process of confirming judges.

Democrats launched relentless attacks on Bork, a brilliant but controversial and highly conservative constitutional scholar. In a particularly inflammatory attack, Sen. Edward M. Kennedy (D-Mass.) said, "Robert Bork's America is a land in which women would be forced into back-alley abortions, blacks would sit at segregated lunch counters, rogue police could break down citizens' doors in midnight raids, children could not be taught about evolution."

Republicans were infuriated over the defeat of the Bork nomination. After President Ronald Reagan successfully named the more moderate Anthony Kennedy to the Supreme Court, conservatives and liberals girded up for ever-more-bitter judicial battles.

In the first few years of the twenty-first century, Senate Democrats used every legislative weapon at their disposal, including filibusters, to launch an unprecedented effort to block several conservative judicial nominations of President George W. Bush. Republicans retaliated by threatening to revamp Senate rules so that a minority party could not indefinitely block nominations. The two sides eventually compromised, and Bush got a few—but not all—of his most controversial nominees on the bench.

Cabinet appointees have fared better. When Senate Democrats voted against the nomination by President George H. W. Bush (b. 1924) of former Republican senator John Tower, citing questions about his personal fitness for the job, the rejection became the first since 1959 and only the ninth time a cabinet appointee had been turned down. More often, when the Senate's inquiries raise issues that either the administration or the nominee would rather avoid, the person's name is simply withdrawn. Several women named by Presidents Bill Clinton (b. 1946) and George W. Bush (b. 1946) came under fire and withdrew because of their questionable treatment of domestic help, including federal judge Kimba M. Wood, Clinton's first pick for attorney general in 1993. President Clinton's 1997 nomination of William Weld, a Republican from Massachusetts, to serve as ambassador to Mexico is an example of another way a nomination can fail in the Senate without a vote. Jesse Helms, a Republican from North Carolina who chaired the Senate Foreign Relations Committee, to which ambassadorial appointments are referred, refused to schedule a hearing on Weld's nomination because of the nominee's liberal position on several issues.

Consent to Treaties

Article II, section 2, of the Constitution also grants the president the "Power, by and with the Advice and Consent of the Senate, to make Treaties, provided two thirds of the Senators present concur." Again, distrust of a strong executive and national government and fear that the states' residual sovereignty might be jeopardized by the chief executive's treaty-making power led the framers to require the Senate's acquiescence for treaties as well as important nominations. The Senate seemed the proper body in which to vest the power of checking and balancing the president's treaty-making power.

In essay 64 of *The Federalist*, John Jay warned: "The power of making treaties is an important one, especially as it relates to war, peace, and commerce; and should not be delegated but in such mode, and with such precautions, as will afford the highest security that it will be exercised by men the best qualified for the purpose, and in the manner most conducive to the public good." In Great Britain at the time, Hamilton noted in essay 69, the monarch was the "sole and absolute representative of the nation in all foreign transactions." For good measure, he said, the framers added the requirement that "two thirds of the senators present concur" in the approval of a treaty.

Treaties submitted to the Senate for RATIFICATION by the president are generally first sent to the Foreign Relations Committee. They are then presented to the whole Senate and approved if two-thirds of the members present consent to them.

Not all treatylike documents are submitted to the Senate, however. Because the Constitution gives the president discretion on whether to submit a treaty to the Senate for approval, he may opt to conclude an international agreement on his own, without asking for Senate approval. Such "executive agreements" have been used increasingly to avoid having to face the Senate. The Supreme Court first approved this practice in *Tucker v. Alexandroff* (1902), involving an agreement with Mexico to allow the pursuit of marauding bands by both nations across their mutual borders.

As for the "Advice" part of the Constitution's advice and consent requirement, not since 1789—when President GEORGE WASHINGTON left the Senate chamber in a huff after his personal request for its advice

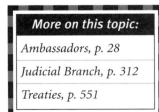

More on this topic:

Ambassadors, p. 28
Judicial Branch, p. 312
Treaties, p. 551

on a proposed Indian treaty was summarily referred to a committee—has any president attempted to avail himself of the benefits of this constitutional provision.

Affirmative Action

In the 1964 Civil Rights Act, Congress prohibited public entities and private organizations that receive federal funds from discriminating on the basis of race, sex, national origin, and religion. The national and state governments of the United States, along with a number of private businesses, have since developed various programs to give some preference in recruiting, hiring, training, and promoting certain MINORITIES that have historically suffered DISCRIMINATION, including African Americans, Hispanic-surnamed Americans, and WOMEN. Some institutions of higher learning have also adopted programs to ensure that more minority students are admitted. Because such affirmative action efforts require preferential treatment for minorities and thus may discriminate against others more qualified—a phenomenon known as reverse discrimination—they remain controversial.

The United States is not the only country that has instituted affirmative action programs. Malaysia's constitution (1957, revised 1963) reserves public service positions and business and trade permits for the *bumiputras* (Malays and other indigenous peoples). Pakistan's constitution sets aside sixty seats in the legislature's lower house for women.

History of Affirmative Action

While our own Constitution's language on its face is color neutral—it does not authorize special privileges based on race, sex, or similar minority status as do some other national constitutions— all three branches of government have authority, especially under the Fourteenth Amendment (1868), to fashion remedies for past discrimination. The problem is complicated by several issues: Who are the victims of the discrimination? Who should be compensated? And how should they be compensated?

In *BROWN V. BOARD OF EDUCATION OF TOPEKA* (1954), the Supreme Court, led by Chief Justice Earl Warren (1891–1974), declared segregation unconstitutional and invalidated "separate but equal" public schools for black and white children. The following year, in what became known as *Brown v. Board of Education II* (1955), the Court began the process of large-scale institutional reform of public school systems to remedy the injury that had been done to a large class of people for a long time. In *Green v. County School Board of New Kent County* (1968), the Warren Court found an affirmative duty to "take whatever steps might be necessary to convert to a unitary [public school] system in which racial discrimination would be eliminated root and branch."

In 1941 President Franklin D. Roosevelt (1882–1945) had signed an executive order prohibiting segregationist policies in hiring for defense-related industries, and in 1953 the Committee on Government Contract Compliance created by President Harry S. Truman (1884–1972) promoted efforts "to act positively and affirmatively to implement the policy of nondiscrimination." President Lyndon B. Johnson (1908–73), however, was the first to use the term *affirmative action* in a 1965 executive order designed to ensure that federal contractors treated job applicants and employees "without regard to their race, creed, color, or national origin."

Equal Protection

In its decision in the 1954 *Brown* case, the Supreme Court found that segregation violated the EQUAL PROTECTION provision of the Fourteenth Amendment (1868). In the same year, the Court held that exclusion of Mexican Americans from JURIES also flew in the face of equal protection. In

Califano v. Goldfarb (1977), the Court found that discrimination against female workers in the matter of Social Security death benefits—presuming that widows and not widowers are dependents—violated the equal protection clause as well.

Unlike cases involving RACIAL DISCRIMINATION, in SEX DISCRIMINATION matters the Supreme Court does not use a so-called STRICT SCRUTINY test to analyze fact patterns in particular cases, instead choosing a lower level of scrutiny based on the assumption that some sex-based differences are reasonable. The exclusion of men from an all-women nursing school, suggested the Court in *Mississippi University for Women v. Hogan* (1982), was an unconstitutional educational affirmative action plan. In *United States v. Virginia* (1996), the justices similarly found that the commonwealth had not provided an "exceedingly persuasive justification" for the all-male status of the state-funded Virginia Military Institute, and thus it had to admit women for the first time.

Reverse Discrimination

Those who oppose affirmative action often refer to the practice as reverse discrimination, an issue that arose in the first case in which the Supreme Court directly addressed the constitutionality of affirmative action programs. In *REGENTS OF THE UNIVERSITY OF CALIFORNIA V. BAKKE* (1978), a committee had selected sixteen applicants from four categories of minority groups for placement in the medical school. Alan Bakke, who is white, was denied admission among the school's one hundred new students even though he had scored higher on tests than some of the minority students admitted. Although the Court, by a 5–4 decision, found the school's affirmative action program unconstitutional and ordered Bakke to be admitted, there was some agreement among the justices that a race-conscious admissions program could be constitutional. However, they could not agree on the proper basis for such a program.

At the University of Texas, a similar policy designed to racially diversify its law school was challenged, failed to gain Supreme Court review, and has since been abandoned. Then in 2001, after a lower court had struck down the University of Michigan's admissions policy as unconstitutional, a federal appeals court upheld the use of race as one factor to be considered in the admission of students.

In *United Steelworkers v. Weber* (1979), the Supreme Court approved a private company's voluntary affirmative action plan, which was negotiated between the company and the union, to recruit more black workers. Based on the relative proportion of blacks in the community, the plan set aside 50 percent of the training program openings for black candidates. The Court would later reject plans that favored affirmative action over the rights of employees with seniority, those who had been company employees longer. Then in 1989, in *Martin v. Wilks*, the Court held that nonminority employees who are not a party to the settlement of a dispute over a voluntary affirmative action plan may go to court to challenge the plan if they are adversely af-

This cartoon reflects concerns by some civil rights advocates over the rolling back of affirmative action laws.
Source: © 2003, Mike Keefe, *The Denver Post*, and PoliticalCartoons.com

fected by it. In *Metropolitan Broadcasting v. FCC* (1990), the justices upheld the federal government's policy of preference for minority broadcasters in the allocation of broadcasting licenses—not on the grounds of remedying a specific past discrimination but because increased minority ownership would diversify the content of broadcasts, an inherently good thing.

The Supreme Court has continued to chip away at the constitutionality of affirmative action programs. In *Richmond v. J.A. Croson Co.* (1989), a majority of the Court agreed that affirmative action programs were subject to strict scrutiny, just like other forms of potentially discriminatory action based on race. Then, in *Adarand Constructors, Inc. V. Pena* (1995), the Court listed three criteria for reviewing such programs: "[a]ny preference based on racial or ethnic criteria must necessarily receive a most searching examination"; "the standard of review under the Equal Protection Clause is not dependent on the race of those burdened or benefited by a particular classification"; and "[e]qual protection analysis in the Fifth Amendment area [directed at federal action] is the same as that under the Fourteenth Amendment [directed at state action]." After upholding a narrowly tailored race-based admissions policy at the University of Michigan Law School and invalidating the use of the race-based admissions policy of the University's College of Literature, Science and the Arts as a violation of the equal protection clause of the Fourteenth Amendment in 2003, the Court, in *Parents Involved in Community Schools v. Seattle School District No. 1* (2007), reversed U.S. appeals court decisions that confirmed the constitutionality of voluntarily adopted school district plans for assigning students to high schools using racial classifications to obtain more diversity.

While the Court has left the door slightly ajar for narrowly crafted affirmative action programs to be constitutionally acceptable, there seems to be a definite trend, especially among the more conservative members of the Court, to move toward a "colorblind" or "minority-blind" Constitution in the future.

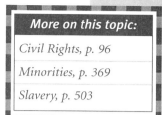

More on this topic:

Civil Rights, p. 96

Minorities, p. 369

Slavery, p. 503

Age Discrimination

In 2000, 13 percent of the U.S. population, representing thirty-five million persons, was classified as elderly (more than sixty-five years of age). By the mid-twenty-first century, twice as many elderly are expected to be living in the United States. Although older persons are typically more likely to be victims of age discrimination, those who are young and middle aged may also be affected by such DISCRIMINATION. In response to the fact that young men eighteen years of age could be drafted and asked to give their lives for their country, the Twenty-sixth Amendment to the Constitution (1971) lowered the voting age from twenty-one to eighteen.

Rationales for Differing Treatment

Recent national constitutions—for example, South Africa's (1997) and Finland's (2000)—expressly prohibit discrimination on the basis of age, whereas the U.S. Constitution does not. A number of reasonable bases exist for treating persons of different ages differently; thus the Supreme Court does not use a higher standard of STRICT SCRUTINY to review claims of age discrimination, as it does for RACIAL DISCRIMINATION, which is generally forbidden for any reason. Minor CHILDREN, for one, are not entitled to all of the same rights and privileges as adults. Laws regarding the sale of alcohol beverages and tobacco, issuance of licenses to drive, registration for voting, and eligibility for public office have validly taken age into consideration without running afoul of the Constitution, which itself sets age thresholds for the nation's top executive officers and legislators. A certain level of experience and maturity is a reasonable prerequisite for engaging in these activities.

Congress has acted to prohibit unjustifiable age discrimination as it has other forms of discrimination as far as federal government spending is concerned. The Age Discrimination Act (1975) bars discrimination on the basis of age under any program that receives federal funding. According to the act, "[n]o person in the United States shall, on the basis of age, be excluded from participation in, be denied the benefits of, or be subjected to discrimination under any program or activity receiving Federal financial assistance." The act does allow for "reasonable factors other than age" as a potential basis for different treatment, even if they "may have a disproportionate effect on persons of different ages."

Age Discrimination in Employment

Most constitutional cases brought to the Supreme Court alleging age discrimination have centered around the issue of employment. Businesses, for example, once typically required employees to retire at sixty-five years of age, whether or not they wanted to continue working. Extending a provision of Title VII of the 1964 Civil Rights Act, the Age Discrimination in Employment Act (1967) was passed to address this and related problems. It prohibits discrimination against persons who are more than forty years old and applies to both job applicants and employees. "It shall be unlawful," states the act, "for an employer...to fail or refuse to hire or to discharge any individual or otherwise discriminate against any individual with respect to his compensation, terms, conditions, or privileges of employment, because of such individual's age...." Employers are also barred from segregating or classifying employees in such a way as to deprive them of employment opportunities or otherwise adversely affect their status, as well as "to reduce the wage rate of any employee...." Employment agencies and labor organizations are also included in the act's scope. In 1978 and 1986 amendments eliminated any mandatory retirement age for most workers. The act does allow employers to set reasonable age requirements for retirement in cases where age bears a rational relationship to job qualifications or is necessary for the operation of a business.

In *Massachusetts Board of Retirement v. Murgia* (1976), the Supreme Court upheld a mandatory retirement age of fifty years of age for uniformed state police officers. For the public's safety state troopers must be in fit condition, the justices held, so the mandatory retirement age was based on a rational requirement for the job. However, in *Western Airlines v. Criswell* (1985), a unanimous Court rejected a mandatory retirement age of sixty for flight engineers, who normally are not involved in operating an airplane. The Court fashioned a two-part test for determining whether age was a "bona fide occupational qualification." Is the age limit reasonably necessary for public safety? And is the employer justified in applying the same age limit across the board to all similar types of employees, or should the employer decide each case on an individual basis? In another 1985 case, *Trans World Airlines v. Thurston*, the Court held that pilots and copilots who reached a company's mandatory retirement age of sixty years must be given the same opportunity to transfer to the position of flight engineer offered to disabled pilots under the age of sixty.

The Supreme Court has been refining the rules for proving age discrimination under the Age Discrimination in Employment Act on a case-by-case basis. In *Hazen Paper Co. v. Biggins* (1993), the Court found that an employee fired a few weeks before becoming vested in the company's pension plan, which would occur after ten years of employment, was not the victim of "disparate treatment" because of his age. The Court reasoned that the firing was not motivated by the prohibited presumptions that older workers are less productive or less competent than younger employees. The Court also found that a decision to fire a person on the basis of his or her pension status—and not because of his or her age—was not necessarily a violation of the provisions of the 1967 act.

The Supreme Court has wrestled with the question of age discrimination under the Constitution for some time now. In the case of *Kimel v. Florida Board of Regents* (2000), the Court found that the Age Discrimination in Employment Act could not be applied to the states because of their constitutionally guaranteed sovereign immunity. The act was held to have failed the congruency and proportionality test announced in *City of Boerne v. Flores* (1997). In *Boerne*, that test was applied to the Religious Freedom Restoration Act (1993), and the Court said the provisions of that federal law reflect "a lack of proportionality or congruence between the means adopted and the legitimate end to be achieved. If an objector can show a substantial burden on his free exercise, the State must demonstrate a compelling governmental interest and show that the law is the least restrictive means of furthering its interest." In *Kimel*, the Court determined that Congress did not have authority under the remedial provisions of the Fourteenth Amendment to allow state employees to sue the states for violations of the Age Discrimination in Employment Act. This denial of power to Congress to remedy age discrimination by a state, however, was cast in a new light by decisions in 2003 and 2004, so that in the future the Court may, in fact, extend the power of Congress in this area under section 5 of the Fourteenth Amendment.

Age discrimination, like SEX DISCRIMINATION, is often subtle and difficult to prove under the restrictive criteria applied by the Supreme Court justices, who themselves are guaranteed life tenure by the Constitution. Many factors go into balancing the problems of age discrimination against employees that the Court has addressed (see BALANCING TESTS), including the state of the economy—younger, lower-paid workers can replace older, higher-paid workers and improve a company's bottom line. In a society that places a premium on youth and profitability, age probably will always tend to be a liability rather than an asset.

PERCENTAGE OF TOTAL POPULATION AGED 65 AND OVER

Year	Percentage
1900	4.1
1910	4.3
1920	4.7
1930	5.4
1940	6.8
1950	8.1
1960	9.2
1970	9.9
1980	11.3
1990	12.6
2000	12.4

SOURCE: *65+ in the United States: 2005*. U.S. Census Bureau and the National Institute on Aging, 2005.
NOTE: The reference population for these data is the resident population.

The percentage of Americans aged 65 and over more than tripled over the twentieth century.
Source: U.S. Census Bureau

Aliens

In the context of the Constitution, an alien is a person who does not owe allegiance to the United States. Because aliens are thus not allied with the political jurisdiction in which they find themselves (see TERRITORY), they have been the subjects of domestic and INTERNATIONAL LAW for centuries. Aristotle, the Greek philosopher of the fourth century B.C.E., states in *The Politics*: "Resident aliens in many places do not possess even such rights completely [for example, the right to sue and be sued], for they are obliged to have a patron, so that they do but imperfectly participate in the community...." The Romans developed a law of nations (*ius gentium*) for dealing with foreigners within the empire, who could not avail themselves of the laws reserved only for CITIZENS (*ius civile*).

The rights of aliens depend on the laws of each country and the reciprocal obligations of nations under TREATIES and international law. Supreme Court decisions in the United States have generally extended to aliens DUE PROCESS and EQUAL PROTECTION as required by the Fourteenth Amendment (1868), section 1, which states in part, "...nor shall any State deprive any person of life, liberty, or property without due process of law; nor deny to any person within its jurisdiction the equal protection of the laws."

Rights and Wrongs

Aliens legally in the United States generally have most of the same rights as citizens, with the exception of certain rights that are closely associated with citizenship: the right to vote, to be elected to important public offices, and to be considered for some jobs closely linked with the community, such as police officer or public school teacher. Cases involving aliens that have come before the Supreme Court are often about the extent to which aliens may be discriminated against because they are not citizens. Illegal aliens and enemy aliens tend to have even fewer rights (see next two sections).

The rights of aliens took some time to develop. According to Article I, section 8, Congress has absolute power over the admission of aliens and the conditions by which they live or remain in the United States. In *Yick Wo v. Hopkins* (1886), the Supreme Court struck down a law that exempted laundries located in brick or stone buildings from needing a permit because it was administered in such a way as to discriminate against Chinese laundries, which for the most part were located in wooden buildings (see DISCRIMINATION; MINORITIES; RACIAL DISCRIMINATION). But in *Fong Yue Ting v. United States* (1893), the Court upheld a federal statute giving Chinese laborers lawfully in the United States one year in which to obtain certificates of residency or face deportation. The Court said that a nation's right to expel or deport foreigners who have not been naturalized or taken steps toward becoming CITIZENS is an absolute and unqualified right: "The power to exclude or to expel aliens, being a power affecting international relations, is vested in the political departments of the government, and is to be regulated by treaty or by act of Congress."

The Supreme Court expounded on the distinction between aliens and citizens in *Terrace v. Thompson* (1923). At question was the constitutionality of Washington state's Anti-Alien Land Law (1921), aimed at Japanese immigrants (see IMMIGRATION), which made it a criminal offense to sell or lease land to an alien who had not declared his or her intention to become a U.S. citizen. The Court held the law to be constitutional, saying, "It is obvious that one who is not a citizen and cannot become one lacks an interest in, and the power to effectually work for the welfare of, the state, and, so lacking, the state may rightfully deny him the right to own and lease real estate within its boundaries...."

World War II brought about more discrimination on the basis of national origin, culminating in the relocation and internment, with the Supreme Court's blessing, of American citizens of Japanese descent. After the war, however, attitudes began to change, and the Court in *Takahashi v. Fish and Game Commission* (1948) struck down a state law denying commercial fishing licenses to resident aliens. The Court reasoned that the Constitution's equal protection provision narrowly defined how STATES could treat their aliens; moreover, the fact that the federal, not the state, government had the constitutional authority for placing limitations on aliens further restricted state action. In a later case, a state's denial of welfare benefits to aliens was also declared unconstitutional.

Immigration and Naturalization Service v. Chadha (1983), an important constitutional law case, involved the U.S. Immigration and Naturalization Service's suspension of the deportation of a Kenyan citizen whose student visa had expired. Congress had passed an immigration law amendment that included a legislative VETO provision, allowing either chamber of Congress to veto an INS decision to suspend the deportation of an alien, which the House of Representatives exercised to revoke Chadha's stay of deportation. The Supreme Court ruled, however, that the legislative veto, which allows one house of Congress to act without going through the constitutional steps required for passing new legislation, was unconstitutional. The decision, while providing much grist for constitutional scholars' mills, has had little real effect. Congress continues to include legislative veto provisions in laws that go unchallenged in court because ADMINISTRATIVE AGENCIES do not want to offend the national legislature.

Generally, the Supreme Court has barred discrimination against aliens in employment (see EMPLOYMENT DISCRIMINATION). Laws requiring U.S. citizenship to practice law or civil engineering or even to hold state civil service jobs have been held to be unconstitutional. In *Sugarman v. Dougall* (1973), the Court set aside a law that totally excluded aliens from a state's competitive civil service, saying, however, that the state has power "to preserve the basic conception of a political community...to prescribe the qualifications of its officers and voters." This power, the Court continued, extends "also to persons holding state elective or important nonelective executive, legislative, and judicial positions, [because] officers who participate directly in the formulation, execution, or review of broad public policy perform functions that go to the heart of representative government." Since then, the Court has upheld laws excluding aliens from jobs such as state troopers, public school teachers, and probation officers if the state can show a rational basis for such discrimination.

Illegal Aliens

Illegal aliens are also subject to domestic and international law, but the rights to which they may be entitled may be significantly reduced. However, the Supreme Court limited the federal government's power with respect to the treatment of illegal aliens in *Wong Wing v. United States* (1896). In that case the Court held that while the government may imprison and fine persons unlawfully in the country and not entitled to remain, subjecting illegal aliens to PUNISHMENT such as hard labor or confiscating their PROPERTY without a judicial trial to establish their guilt or innocence was an unconstitutional denial of due process.

More recently, illegal aliens have been accorded even greater constitutional consideration by the Supreme Court. In *Plyler v. Doe* (1982), the Court ruled that a state could not deny free EDUCATION to school-age CHILDREN of aliens unlawfully in the United States. And in several cases the Court has upheld the due process requirement that an illegal alien receive at least a hearing before being imprisoned or deported.

One of the responses to the September 11, 2001, terrorist attacks included heightened government activity with regard to detaining aliens in and outside the United States. In *Immigration and Naturalization Service v. St. Cyr* (2001), the U.S. Supreme Court had reasoned that noncitizens in the United States have the same habeas corpus rights as citizens. And in *Rasul v. Bush* (2004), the Court reversed a ruling in *Johnson v. Eisentrager* (1950), which involved German enemy aliens tried in military courts in Germany after World War II, holding that district courts had authority to hear habeas corpus petitions from detainees at the U.S. naval station at Guantánamo Bay. But, in what is known as the REAL ID Act of 2005—named for its basic purpose of standardizing state-issued drivers licenses—Congress replaced the writ of habeas corpus for noncitizens who challenged removal orders with direct circuit court review of "constitutional claims or questions of law" stemming from such removal orders. Recently, the Supreme Court extended the right to challenge unreasonable detention by the Homeland Security Department to inadmissible aliens as well as those aliens admitted into the country, saying in *Clark v. Martinez* (2005) that habeas corpus petitions should be granted when aliens are detained unreasonably beyond the period provided under the law.

Enemy Aliens

During WAR, enemy aliens (citizens of countries with which the United States is at war) may lose nearly all constitutional protections, including JUST COMPENSATION under the Fifth Amendment (1791) for the taking of property and the right to a trial by a civilian (as opposed to a military) court, as guaranteed by the Sixth Amendment (1791). In *Ex parte Quirin* (1942), the Supreme Court held that German saboteurs set ashore in the state of New York during World War II with explosives and wearing German infantry uniforms could be tried without a jury by a military commission (see JURIES). The Court concluded that "the Fifth and Sixth Amendments did not restrict whatever authority was conferred by the Constitution to try offenses against the law of war by military commission, and [those persons] charged with such an offense [are] not required to be tried by jury at common law...."

Immigrants built the United States, and one of the reasons so many citizens of foreign countries come here is to enjoy the fairness and justice inherent in the American system of constitutional government. But until they become citizens by naturalization, aliens are subject to valid restrictions placed on them by the national and state governments. The terrorist attacks on September 11, 2001, began to call into question elements of the country's generally lenient policies toward aliens—for example, not supervising the status of student visa holders, especially those interested in learning how to fly commercial aircraft and crop dusters.

Ambassadors

Clare Boothe Luce had been a playwright and a member of Congress before being appointed U.S. ambassador to Italy in 1953.
Source: The Granger Collection, New York

Even in the fourth century B.C.E. the Greek philosopher Plato (ca. 427–347 B.C.E.) referred to the tradition of appointing and receiving ambassadors, who are public officials with diplomatic powers and immunities representing the government of one nation to the government of another. In *The Laws* Plato warns that if "a man passes himself off as an ambassador...of the state and enters into unauthorized negotiations with a foreign power..., he must be open to prosecution for violating the law."

A diplomat may be called an ambassador, a minister, or a *chargé d'affaires*. These designations indicate the rank of the diplomat but not necessarily the power he or she possesses in representing the nation to a foreign government (see FOREIGN AFFAIRS). Ambassadors and other diplomatic officials also represent nations in regional organizations such as the Organization of American States and international bodies such as the United Nations. A consul is a commercial agent in a foreign country who ordinarily does not have diplomatic powers or functions. Consuls from different countries may work in several cities of a country with major mutual trading interests, but there is only one official ambassador from one country to another.

The president is authorized under the Constitution's Article II, section 2, to "nominate, and by and with the Advice and Consent of the Senate,...appoint Ambassadors, other public Ministers and Consuls..." (see ADVICE AND CONSENT). Ambassadors historically represent their country's head of state, so that an ambassador from the United States is the personal representative of the president and generally reports to the president through the secretary of state (see CABINET). In 1855 Congress set grades and qualifications for ambassadorial appointment, but the president has great latitude in appointments to ambassadorial posts. On occasion they are made to reward political support rather than to ensure that the most qualified diplomat fills the position.

According to Title 22 of the U.S. Code (the compilation of the laws of the United States), "The President may, by and with the advice and consent of the Senate, appoint an individual as a chief of mission, as an ambassador at large, as an ambassador, as a minister, as a career member of the Senior Foreign Service, or as a Foreign Service officer." The president may also "by and with the advice and consent of the Senate, confer the personal rank of career ambassador upon a career member of the Senior Foreign Service in recognition of especially distinguished service over a sustained period." However, if the president wants to confer the rank of ambassador for "a special mission for the President of a temporary nature not exceeding six months," he must among other things transmit "to the Committee on Foreign Relations of the Senate a written report" justifying the reason "for not submitting the [proposed nomination] to the Senate," as well as providing other requested information.

Particularly prized ambassadorships include appointments to France and the United Kingdom, where ambassadors and other representatives are accredited not to England, Great Britain, or the United Kingdom but rather to the Court of St. James's, the sovereign's senior palace in London. The palace, completed by Henry VIII in 1540, now serves in part as the residence of the Prince of Wales and is used for his offices. The ambassadorship to Japan, another distinguished posting, has been held by former Speakers of the House John W. McCormack and Thomas S. Foley and former vice president Walter Mondale.

Ambassadors from foreign governments are generally accredited to a nation's head of state. Article II, section 3, indicates that the president "shall receive Ambassadors and other public Ministers." This process requires a personal presentation to the president of credentials by the foreign ambassadors or ministers for them to be officially accredited to take up residence and act on behalf of their government.

Along with the presidential power to receive foreign representatives comes the authority to recognize a new government under INTERNATIONAL LAW. In a dissent from the Supreme Court decision in *Goldwater v. Carter* (1979), which dismissed a legal challenge by five senators to this presidential authority, Justice William J. Brennan (1906–97) said that it is "firmly establish[ed] that the Constitution commits to the President alone the power to recognize, and withdraw recognition from, foreign regimes." The case grew out of the termination by President Jimmy Carter (b. 1924) of a defense pact between Taiwan and the United States as a necessary step in extending formal diplomatic relations to the government of the People's Republic of China.

Ambassadors are also mentioned in Article III, section 2, as the subjects of original jurisdiction by the Supreme Court: "In all Cases affecting

In 1949 Edward R. Dudley was named ambassador to Liberia, thereby becoming the first African American ambassador. He had previously served as a minister to Liberia. He held the position of ambassador until 1953.
Source: Arthur Brower, *New York Times*, Redux

More on this topic:

*Appointment and
Removal Power, p. 39*

Ambassadors, other public Ministers and Consuls,...the supreme Court shall have original Jurisdiction." Although the Court has never defined "other public Ministers," the term has come to mean other officers having diplomatic functions, regardless of their actual titles. For historical reasons, however, diplomatic officials do not file suits as plaintiffs, and because diplomats have legal immunity under international law, they are not liable to be sued by any person or entity in domestic courts.

Amendments

PROHIBITION ESTABLISHED — 1920
BY CONSTITUTIONAL AMENDMENT

The Eighteenth Amendment prohibited the manufacture and sale of alcohol in the United States. The law was extremely unpopular and was later repealed by the Twenty-first Amendment.
Source: The Granger Collection, New York

Every written national constitution contains procedures for amending the document—correcting, changing, or revising it for the better. Generally, amendments require several steps and often a supermajority vote to be approved. However, amendments to the constitutions of countries with unwritten constitutions, such as New Zealand (1840) and Israel (1948), in theory require only a simple majority vote of the national legislature. Tradition and custom often act as restraints on the amending process of parliaments with such supreme constitutional powers. The U.S. CONSTITUTION has been amended only twenty-seven times in more than two centuries, and only once has an amendment—the Eighteenth (1919), which prohibited the manufacture and sale of alcohol (see PROHIBITION)—been repealed by another, the Twenty-first (1933).

Modes of Amendment

Article V provides several ways to amend the Constitution: "The Congress, whenever two thirds of both Houses shall deem it necessary, shall propose Amendments to this Constitution, or, on the Application of the Legislatures of two thirds of the several States, shall call a Convention for proposing Amendments, which, in either Case, shall be valid to all Intents and Purposes, as Part of this Constitution, when ratified by the Legislatures of three fourths of the several States, or by Conventions in three fourths thereof, as the one or the other Mode of Ratification may be proposed by the Congress; Provided...that no State, without its Consent, shall be deprived of its equal Suffrage in the Senate." No constitutional convention has ever been called to propose amendments, perhaps in part because of the fear that such a convention could, like the CONSTITUTIONAL CONVENTION OF 1787 in Philadelphia, disregard its specific mandate and attempt a wholesale revision of the document.

The Constitution as ratified by the states after the 1787 convention included in Article V language regarding amendments that became obsolete after 1808, specifically: "Provided that no Amendment which may be made prior to the Year One thousand eight hundred and eight shall in any Manner affect the first and fourth Clauses [having to do with the importation of slaves and requiring that direct taxes be in proportion to the CENSUS to be conducted every ten years] in the Ninth Section of the First Article...."

According to Article V, Congress specifies the "Mode of Ratification"—either "by the Legislatures of three fourths of the several States, or by Conventions in three fourths thereof" (see RATIFICATION). Each state's convention or legislature determines how it will proceed, but states may not call a special referendum to let the citizens ratify the amendment directed to the legislatures (see DIRECT DEMOCRACY). After the last state necessary has ratified the proposed amendment, no further action is necessary except to have the amendment added to copies of the Constitution. States originally notified the secretary of state, but now they submit the information to the archivist of the United States, who is the official custodian of the Constitution.

In essay 43 of *The Federalist* (1787–88) (see FEDERALIST PAPERS), JAMES MADISON explained that the amendment procedure "guards equally against that extreme facility, which would render the Constitution too mutable; and that extreme difficulty, which might perpetuate its discovered faults. It, moreover, equally enables the general and the State governments to originate the amendment of errors, as they may be pointed out by the experience on one side, or on the other." ALEXANDER HAMILTON added in essay 85 that for him the amendment provision is "one of those rare instances in which a political truth can be brought to the test of mathematical demonstration."

The Bill of Rights

The first amendments were proposed by Madison in 1789 in the first session of CONGRESS held under the new Constitution. They were intended to answer a demand by many delegates to the state ratifying conventions who supported the Constitution but felt the need to guarantee citizens and the states protection from infringement of individual rights—from due process to freedom of the press to the right to bear arms—that had evolved in England, in the colonies, and later in the states after the Declaration of Independence in 1776. After some editing in Congress, they were approved by Congress for ratification by the state legislatures. Ten of twelve proposed amendments (Articles III through XII) were ratified in 1791 and became known as the BILL OF RIGHTS.

Two other amendments had been submitted at the same time—Articles I and II, in fact: The first, governing the apportionment of the House of Representatives, has never been ratified and is now moot; and the second, postponing the effect of any pay raise for senators and representatives until after an intervening election, was not ratified until 1992, when it became the Twenty-seventh Amendment, the Constitution's most recent addition.

Later Amendments

The Eleventh Amendment (1795) was necessary to protect the sovereign immunity of the states from legal suits, which are authorized by Article III of the Constitution. In *Hollingsworth v. Virginia* (1798), an early case challenging the validity of this amendment, the Supreme Court held that despite the president's VETO power, granted by the Constitution in Article I, section 7, amendments proposed by Congress do not have to be submitted to the president for approval.

In the so-called National Prohibition Cases (1920), the Supreme Court ruled that, assuming a quorum is present in each house of Congress, the two-thirds vote required for passage of a proposed constitutional amendment means two-thirds of the members present, not two-thirds of the total membership of each house. Beginning with the Prohibition amendment (the Eighteenth) in 1919, Congress began including a provision in the proposed amendment requiring ratification by the states within seven years of submission. According to the Court in *Coleman v. Miller* (1939), just what constituted a reasonable time frame was considered a political question to be decided by Congress, not by the courts. In a 1981 case, however, a federal judge ruled that a thirty-nine-month extension granted by Congress for ratification of the Equal Rights Amendment (1972) to guarantee equal rights for WOMEN was an unconstitutional exercise of congressional power; an appeal to the Supreme Court was dismissed when the ERA failed to get the necessary number of state ratifications even with the extension (thirty-five of the thirty-eight states necessary have ratified the amendment).

The Twelfth Amendment (1804) changed the way the president and vice president run for office and are elected. The flaws in the presidential selection process were exposed in the election of THOMAS JEFFERSON in 1800, which required thirty-six ballots in the House of Representatives. The new procedure required the presidential electors in the ELECTORAL COLLEGE to vote for president and vice president on separate ballots, thereby preventing a tie between a presidential candidate and his vice presidential running mate.

The Thirteenth (1865), Fourteenth (1868), and Fifteenth (1870) Amendments grew out of the Civil War and the need to guarantee former slaves equal rights (males only), although these amendments were not immediately successful. The Fourteenth Amendment has evolved into a key constitutional provision that allows the federal courts to extend to the states many of the fundamental guarantees of the Bill of Rights, which were originally intended only as a limitation on the national government (see DUE PROCESS; EQUAL PROTECTION).

Although the Supreme Court in 1895 struck down a personal income tax law passed by Congress, the Constitution was amended via the Sixteenth Amendment (1913) to allow such a tax. The Seventeenth Amendment (1913) provided for the direct election of senators by the voters rather than by the state legislatures, and the Nineteenth Amendment (1920) finally extended the vote to American women. The Twentieth Amendment (1933) limited lame-duck sessions—the period between the election of a new Congress and the swearing in of the newly elected members (see LAME DUCKS). After the unprecedented reelection of Franklin D. Roosevelt (1882–1945) to third and fourth terms as president, the Twenty-second Amendment (1951) was ratified to limit the president to two terms.

The Twenty-third (1961), Twenty-fourth (1964), and Twenty-fifth Amendments (1967), respectively, extended to the District of Columbia the right to three electoral votes for president and vice president (see CAPITAL, NATIONAL); abolished poll taxes that discouraged the poorest citizens from registering to vote; and, in the aftermath of the assassination of President John F. Kennedy (1917–63), established guidelines for succession to the office of president and vice president in the event of a president's disability. The Twenty-sixth Amendment (1971) lowered the voting age to eighteen, following a campaign that argued that if eighteen-year-olds were old enough to be drafted they were old enough to vote. The Twenty-seventh Amendment (1992), originally submitted in 1789 along with the rest of the Bill of Rights, prohibited senators and representatives from receiving a pay increase until after an intervening election.

A Rush to Amend

One school of thought believes that almost every ill can be cured by simply amending the Constitution. Since it went into effect in 1789, more than ten thousand amendments have been proposed in Congress, addressing everything from prohibiting misuse of the American flag to requiring a balanced federal budget, setting term limits for members of Congress, allowing school prayer, and giving Congress more authority to regulate campaign financing. Of these, however,

AMENDMENTS TO THE U.S. CONSTITUTION

No.[1]	Topic[2]	Ratified	No.	Topic	Ratified
1	Establishment of religion prohibited Freedom of speech and press Right to assemble and petition	1791	14	Citizenship rights Due process of law Equal protection of the laws	1868
2	Right to keep and bear arms	1791	15	Right to vote regardless of race, color, or previous condition of servitude	1870
3	Quartering of soldiers	1791	16	Authorization of income taxes	1913
4	Unreasonable search and seizure	1791	17	Direct election of U.S. senators	1913
5	Prosecution and due process of law Protection against double jeopardy Private property not to be taken without just compensation	1791	18	Prohibition of liquor	1919
			19	Right of women to vote	1920
			20	Presidential and vice presidential terms to begin on January 20; Congress on January 3	1933
6	Right to a speedy trial and other criminal protections	1791			
7	Right to a trial by jury	1791	21	Prohibition of liquor repealed	1933
8	Ban on excessive bail and cruel and unusual punishment	1791	22	Limitation of presidential term	1951
			23	Presidential vote for the District of Columbia	1961
9	Rights retained by the people	1791			
10	Rights reserved to the states	1791	24	Ban on poll tax in federal elections	1964
11	Suits against states restricted	1795	25	Presidential disability and succession	1967
12	Manner of choosing the president and vice president	1804	26	Lowering of voting age to 18 years	1971
			27[3]	Congressional pay	1992
13	Abolition of slavery	1865			

1. The first ten amendments are the Bill of Rights.
2. Complete text of the amendments is found on pages 635–640.
3. Originally proposed as the Second Amendment (1789).

only thirty-three (not even one percent) were passed by both houses of Congress and submitted to the states for ratification. And of these, only six have failed to become a part of the Constitution (see sidebar).

An opposite school of thought holds that the Constitution is a sacred and perfect document that needs no further amendment. An organization called Citizens for the Constitution is opposed to amending the Constitution at all, in part because amendments "have become the favored first-step panacea for all societal ills" and carry the "potential to undermine an American culture that properly treasures and reveres our Constitution." But if there are to be any amendments, this group wants its "Standards for Constitutional Amendments"—simply its own notion of what is good for the rest of us—used to measure the "correctness" of any proposed amendments. "Constitutional amendments," one of these standards mandates, "should not be adopted when they would damage the cohesiveness of constitutional doctrine as a whole."

Formal amendments are, of course, not always necessary to change the Constitution. An indirect way to alter the Constitution's effect is for the Supreme Court to simply interpret the old language in light of modern concerns. The right of PRIVACY is an example of an informal amendment, as was the abolition of segregated public schools, although some argue that the spirit of the Constitution never permitted SEGREGATION in the first place.

PROPOSED CONSTITUTIONAL AMENDMENTS NOT RATIFIED BY THE STATES

APPORTIONMENT OF THE HOUSE OF REPRESENTATIVES

1789

"After the first enumeration required by the first article of the Constitution, there shall be one Representative for every thirty thousand, until the number shall amount to one hundred, after which the proportion shall be so regulated by Congress, that there shall be not less than one-hundred Representatives, nor less than one Representative for every forty thousand persons, until the number of Representatives shall amount to two hundred; after which the proportion shall be so regulated by Congress, that there shall not be less than two hundred Representatives, nor more than one Representative for every fifty thousand persons."

[Ratified by ten states.]

TITLES OF NOBILITY FROM FOREIGN GOVERNMENTS

1810

"If any citizen of the United States shall accept, claim, receive or retain any title of nobility or honour, or shall, without the consent of Congress, accept and retain any present, pension, office or emolument of any kind whatever, from any emperor, king, prince or foreign power, such person shall cease to be a citizen of the United States, and shall be incapable of holding any office of trust or profit under them, or either of them."

[Ratified by twelve states.]

SLAVERY

1861

"No amendment shall be made to the Constitution which will authorize or give to Congress the power to abolish or interfere, within any State, with the domestic institutions thereof, including that of persons held to labor or service by the laws of said State."

The only proposed unratified amendment to the Constitution to have been signed by the president. [Ratified by two states.]

CHILD LABOR

1924

"**Section 1.** The Congress shall have power to limit, regulate, and prohibit the labor of persons under eighteen years of age.
"**Section 2.** The power of the several States is unimpaired by this article except that the operation of State laws shall be suspended to the extent necessary to give effect to legislation enacted by the Congress."

[Ratified by twenty-eight states.]

EQUAL RIGHTS AMENDMENT

1972

"**Section 1.** Equality of rights under the law shall not be denied or abridged by the United States or by any State on account of sex.
"**Section 2.** The Congress shall have the power to enforce, by appropriate legislation, the provisions of this article.
"**Section 3.** This amendment shall take effect two years after the date of ratification."

[Ratified by thirty-five states even though the seven-year deadline for ratification was extended to June 30, 1982.]

VOTING RIGHTS FOR THE DISTRICT OF COLUMBIA

1978

"**Section 1.** For purposes of representation in the Congress, election of the President and Vice President, and article V of this Constitution, the District constituting the seat of government of the United States shall be treated as though it were a State.
"**Section 2.** The exercise of the rights and powers conferred under this article shall be by the people of the District constituting the seat of government, and as shall be provided by the Congress.
"**Section 3.** The twenty-third article of amendment to the Constitution of the United States is hereby repealed.
"**Section 4.** This article shall be inoperative, unless it shall have been ratified as an amendment to the Constitution by the legislatures of three-fourths of the several States within seven years from the date of its submission."

[Ratified by sixteen states.]

Anthony, Susan B.

In 1893 New Zealand became the first country in the world to grant women the right to vote. Suffrage was not extended to American WOMEN until the Nineteenth Amendment to the Constitution was ratified in 1920, 133 years after the country's supreme law was drafted and fourteen years after the death of Susan Brownell Anthony (1820–1906). Along with Elizabeth Cady Stanton and many others suffragists, Anthony had worked so long and hard for this right.

Born in Adams, Massachusetts, on February 15, 1820, Anthony learned to read and write at the age of three. Her father was an ardent supporter of the movement to abolish SLAVERY, working closely with leaders such as Frederick Douglass. Following in her father's footsteps, Anthony supported the abolitionist movement and worked for passage of the Thirteenth Amendment (1865), which ended slavery in the United States. She also urged, unsuccessfully, that the Fourteenth (1868) and Fifteenth (1870) Amendments, dealing with citizenship rights and granting black persons the right to vote, should extend the vote to women as well.

In 1848 Anthony attended America's first women's rights convention, held in Seneca Falls, New York. The convention's statement of principles—the Seneca Falls Declaration of Sentiments and Resolutions—was drafted by Stanton, whom Anthony met in 1850 and with whom she would become closely allied in the struggle for women's rights. Although she never married, Anthony led the drive for New York State's Married Women's Property Act (1860), intended to secure economic rights for married women. She also helped organize the American Anti-Slavery Society. During the Civil War, Anthony and Stanton organized the National Women's Loyal League to promote a constitutional amendment prohibiting slavery, which became the Thirteenth Amendment.

Susan B. Anthony's static pose in this turn-of-the-century photographic portrait conceals the vocal and often combative role she played in a life-long struggle to secure voting rights for women, a battle won only after her death.
Source: Library of Congress

After the Civil War, together with Stanton, Anthony devoted herself to obtaining equal civil and political rights for women. The territory of Wyoming granted women the right to vote in 1869, and that same year the National Woman Suffrage Association was created. This organization and later the National American Woman Suffrage Association served as vehicles for Anthony's crusade. In 1872 she and fifteen colleagues became the first women to vote in a national election—and were promptly arrested. Free on bail pending her trial, Anthony traveled across the country asking the question: "Is it a crime for a U.S. citizen to

> **"For any State to make sex a qualification that must ever result in the disfranchisement of one entire half of the people, is to pass a bill of attainder, or an ex post facto law, and is therefore a violation of the supreme law of the land. By it, the blessings of liberty are forever withheld from women and their female posterity."**
>
> **—Susan B. Anthony,** in an 1873 speech

Less than a quarter-century after Susan B. Anthony's death, a woman won election to the U.S. Senate for the first time. Hattie Carraway, a Democrat, became a senator from Arkansas in 1931 when the governor named her to fill the seat of her husband, Thaddeus H. Carraway, who died in office. She made history by winning election in 1932, and was reelected six years later. In 1944, however, voters turned her out of office in favor of J. William Fulbright. Carraway supported many of President Franklin D. Roosevelt's economic proposals. Like many legislators of her era from the South, she voted against legislation that would have made lynching a federal crime.

vote?" She lost her case and, because her sentence was a nonbinding one, was denied the right to appeal to the Supreme Court, where she would have had a national audience for her arguments in favor of women's suffrage.

Anthony continued her exhausting cross-country trips in support of the franchise for women, speaking to Congress, political conventions, labor union meetings, and schools. In 1877 she began writing her *History of Woman Suffrage*, a four-volume work completed in 1902, and in 1892 became president of the National American Woman Suffrage Association. The tide began to turn worldwide, spurred on by women who marched shoulder to shoulder in Great Britain and America. New Zealand granted women the right to vote in 1893, Australia in 1902, and Finland in 1906.

Anthony died on March 13, 1906, having closed her last public speech with the words: "Failure is impossible." In honor of her tireless efforts to extend the Constitution's freedoms equally to all citizens, the U.S. government in 1979 created a coin with her image: the Susan B. Anthony dollar.

Antitrust Law

In 1776, the same year that the thirteen American colonies adopted the DECLARATION OF INDEPENDENCE and severed their ties to Great Britain, the Scottish economist Adam Smith published *The Wealth of Nations*, his treatise favoring the benefits of individual enterprise and free trade over a highly regulated economy. According to Smith, self-seeking human beings are often "led by an invisible hand…without knowing it, without intending it, [to] advance the interests of the society." The FRAMERS OF THE CONSTITUTION nonetheless were less interested in economic theory than in creating a secure and unhindered environment to promote and foster COMMERCE and trade as it was being carried on in America at the time.

Detailed provisions addressing economic policy do appear in other national constitutions. According to Paraguay's current constitution (1992), "(1) Everyone has the right to engage in any legal economic activity of his choice within a system of equal opportunities. (2) Competition at the market is hereby guaranteed…." Poland's constitution (1997) provides that the nation's economic system is a "social market economy, based on the freedom of economic activity, private ownership, and solidarity, dialogue and cooperation between social partners."

Economic competition, however, like biological evolution, can lead to the growth of entities that so dominate their environment that they significantly reduce further competition. In the case of businesses in a free market such as America's in the late nineteenth century, such growth has often led to monopolies, cartels, and trusts, which have the effect of thwarting the economic forces that tend to create greater efficiencies and lower consumer prices. A monopoly occurs when a business or a group of businesses obtain exclusive control over the means of production of goods or services. A cartel is a combination of business organizations formed to regulate the production, pricing, and marketing of goods by its members. Trusts are similar to cartels in that they consist of corporations acting in combination to reduce competition and control prices throughout a business or an industry. Other forms of trade restraint include price fixing, allocation of customers and markets among large competitors, and purposeful exclusion of potential competitors from the marketplace.

The favorable economic climate in the United States led to extensive growth of business and industry by the late nineteenth century. To protect their dominant position in the marketplace, a number of American firms in certain industries—steel, oil, sugar, leather, and tobacco, among others—combined to form trusts. These trusts made it possible for members to use their dominant market positions collectively to wring concessions from suppliers and workers, thus lowering expenses and wages. The trusts also allowed members to keep prices for their goods and services artificially high, using collective campaigns to drive their competitors from the marketplace. The resulting reduction in competition in these industries caused consumer prices to rise, which in turn led to public pressure on elected officials to restore the free-market system.

In 1890 Congress passed the Sherman Antitrust Act, which made it illegal for businesses to act in concert to restrain trade or attempt to monopolize any part of commerce. As Supreme Court Justice Hugo L. Black (1886–1971) explained in *Northern Pacific Railroad v. United States* (1958): "The Sherman Act was designed to be a comprehensive charter of economic liberty aimed at preserving free and unfettered competition as the rule of trade. It rests on the premise that the unrestrained interaction of competitive forces will yield the best allocation of our economic resources, the lowest prices, the highest quality and the greatest material progress, while at the same time providing an environment conducive to the preservation of our democratic political and social institutions."

Rule of Reason

In *United States v. Trans-Missouri Freight Association* (1897), a case brought under the Sherman Act, the Supreme Court refused to adopt a "rule of reason"—a reasonable rather than a literal interpretation of the law—and exempt "good trusts" or "reasonable restraints of trade," because the language of the statute clearly said that "every" contract, combination, and conspiracy in restraint of trade was illegal. Fourteen years later, however, in *United States v. Standard Oil of New Jersey* and *United States v. American Tobacco Co.* (both 1911), the Court reversed itself and adopted the rule of reason. The lone dissenter from these two decisions, Justice John Marshall Harlan (1833–1911), accused the majority of making judicial legislation by ignoring the clear language of the Sherman Act.

As it had done with the economic due process concept—applying the DUE PROCESS clauses of the Fifth (1791) and Fourteenth (1868) Amendments to invalidate interference by national and state legislatures in private business activities—the Supreme Court used the rule of reason to further its own ideas of economic justice. However, the Court never used the rule of reason to exempt any activities of trade UNIONS from antitrust provisions as it did for business activity. In 1914 Congress enacted both the Clayton Act and the Federal Trade Commission Act to expand and help enforce the

Many companies, from railroads to high-tech giants such as Microsoft, have faced antitrust suits for allegedly pursuing unfair business practices.
Sources: Library of Congress; Reuters/You Sung-ho

Sherman Act's prohibitions. The Clayton Act more clearly defined the types of business practices that the antitrust laws were aimed at curbing and exempted lawful labor union activities. The Federal Trade Commission Act established an administrative agency to make rules and enforce restrictions against unfair trade practices that restrain competition.

Current of Commerce

In *United States v. E. C. Knight Company* (1895), the Supreme Court rejected prosecution of the sugar trust as a monopoly on the basis that manufacturing sugar was not a part of interstate commerce and thus was not subject to the federal government's power under the Sherman Act. With the development of the "current of commerce theory" in *Swift and Co. v. United States* (1905), the so-called Beef Trust Case, the Court found the needed link with the Constitution's commerce clause. Article I, section 8, gives Congress the power to "regulate Commerce with foreign Nations, and among the several states...." Justice OLIVER WENDELL HOLMES JR. described the theory in his opinion as recognizing the general process of goods "sent for sale from a place in one State, with the expectation that they will end their transit, after purchase, in another." Thereafter, there was no question that antitrust laws could reach to any activity that might restrain competition or trade and thus affect national markets.

The number of antitrust prosecutions by the federal government has fluctuated according to the country's economic conditions and the economic goals of different government administrations. One significant antitrust case brought by the Justice Department's Antitrust Division in the late twentieth century targeted the Bell Telephone Company. Although for years Bell was considered an acceptable monopoly—akin to monopolies in urban transportation systems, mail delivery, and electrical power generation—in 1982 the company was ordered by the courts to split up its operations to increase competition in the emerging high-tech COMMUNICATIONS field.

Then in 1999, in response to another antitrust action taken by the Justice Department, a federal district court judge held that the innovative computer giant Microsoft was using its "monopoly power" to discourage its competition and hurt consumers. The specific evil of which Microsoft was accused involved requiring that its Internet Explorer browsing software be included with its Windows computer operating system, thus stifling rival browsers (see INTERNET). The judge's ruling that Microsoft should be split up to stem its monopoly was reversed by a federal appeals court, which nonetheless concluded that Microsoft had transgressed U.S. antitrust laws. At the end of 2001, with a change from a Democratic to a Republican administration, the Justice Department agreed to a court-recommended settlement of the Microsoft case that would keep the company intact. A number of state attorneys general who had joined the effort to rein in the Seattle-based company balked at the settlement, with one calling it a "license for Microsoft to use its dominance and power to crush its competition."

One factor in the government's retreat may have been the fact that between 1999 and late 2001 the national economy took a nosedive, and then the terrorist attacks of September 11, 2001, added to realistic fears of an economic recession in the United States. Although in the long term curbing monopoly power should have a salutary effect on the market and the economy, in the short term the effect of significantly restructuring a company that so dominates a portion of the market in computer software as Microsoft does could have had a negative effect.

The relaxation of the rules under the Sherman Act, however, was continued by the Supreme Court in *Leegin Creative Leather Products, Inc. v. PSKS, Inc.* (2007). The opinion by Justice Anthony Kennedy, for the conservative majority of the Court, invalidated a cardinal rule of antitrust law established in *Dr. Miles Medical Company v. John D. Park & Dons Company* (1911) to the effect that resale price maintenance agreements—that is, when manufactures and distributors agree on minimum retail prices—were per se, or by themselves, a violation of the Sherman Act. Interestingly, Justice Oliver Wendell Holmes had dissented from the holding in the *Dr. Miles* case. The Court in *Leegin* cited the fact that the current "[e]conomic literature is replete with procompetitive justifications for a manufacturer's use of resale price maintenance"; "respected economics authorities suggest that the *per se* rule is inappropriate"; and "both the Department of Justice and the Federal Trade Commission recommend replacing the *per se* rule with the rule of reason."

Appeals *See* COURTS; SUPREME COURT.

Appointment and Removal Power

A major difference between a presidential system of government like that of the United States and a parliamentary system, whose head of state is either a president or a monarch, is the personal power of the PRESIDENT to nominate and appoint key government officials who become directly responsible to him. In a parliamentary system, cabinet ministers are beholden to the parliament for their appointments and the performance of their duties. The head of state may be required to formally approve their appointments, but the cabinet, including the prime minister, is primarily a creature of the parliament. Cabinet members may lose their jobs if they lose the confidence of a majority of parliamentary members or, under most constitutions, just the lower house of the parliament.

The FRAMERS OF THE CONSTITUTION struggled with the provisions regarding the American president's appointment power, finally deciding to qualify it by requiring the ADVICE AND CONSENT of the SENATE. "There can be no good Executive without responsible appointment of officers to execute," countered Pennsylvania delegate James Wilson, a supporter of a strong presidency who was unhappy with the provisions agreed on by the CONSTITUTIONAL CONVENTION OF 1787. As ratified in 1789, the Constitution's Article II, section 2, tells the president that he may "nominate, and by and with the Advice and Consent of the Senate, shall appoint Ambassadors, other public Ministers and Consuls, Judges of the supreme Court, and all other Officers of the United States, whose Appointments are not herein otherwise provided for, and which shall be established by Law: but the Congress may by Law vest the Appointment of such inferior Officers, as they think proper, in the President alone, in the Courts of Law, or in the Heads of Departments."

In his first term of office (1789–93), GEORGE WASHINGTON eschewed partisanship and selected two members from each of the two major political factions or parties, the Federalists and the Democratic-Republicans, for the first four cabinet positions: secretaries of state, Treasury, and war and attorney general. President Andrew Jackson (1767–1845) is credited with beginning the "spoils system" of political patronage by rewarding his political supporters with appointments to government positions. Today the president's prerogative to appoint members of his own party and his own political supporters is unquestioned.

As Supreme Court Justice Noah Swayne (1808–84) explained in *United States v. Hartwell* (1868): "An office is a public station, or employment, conferred by the appointment of government. The term embraces the ideas of tenure, duration, emolument [pay], and duties." The appointment process generally begins with the president's considering several candidates for a specific position in the EXECUTIVE BRANCH or the JUDICIAL BRANCH. The White House staff and the Federal Bureau of Investigation conduct background checks to determine if the nominee is fit for the position and is not a risk to national security. After the final selection is made, the nomination is submitted to the Senate, where it is assigned to the appropriate committee with oversight responsibility for the position or agency; federal court and Supreme Court nominees are considered by the Judiciary Committee.

Once the committee votes on the nominee, the nomination is reported out to the full Senate, which then may act to confirm or reject the candidate by a majority vote. The president officially makes the appointment of the confirmed nominee. The final act giving the person authority to perform the duties of the office involves taking the OATH OF OFFICE, either in a formal ceremony or informally.

Executive Branch Appointments

Members of the president's CABINET (the department heads, usually known as secretaries) are generally chosen from members of the president's political party, although there are no set qualifications. Neither are there any constitutional qualifications for AMBASSADORS, consuls, and other public ministers. Qualifications for positions in some ADMINISTRATIVE AGENCIES are set by law; for example, some commissions and boards must have bipartisan members. In such a situation, the president may be limited to nominating someone from the opposition party. Military appointments are generally based on recommendations from the Department of Defense. The president makes only a relatively few executive branch appointments; the rest of the lower-level, nonpolitical employees are hired, generally without presidential involvement, through the federal civil service system.

After Andrew Jackson's administration, public criticism of the spoils system mounted until the assassination of President James A. Garfield (1831–81) by a disappointed office seeker led to establishment of the Civil Service Commission (now the Office of Personnel Management); its goal was to remove political influence from the growing number of non-policy-level executive office jobs. Key positions in what is known as the Excepted Service were still filled by the president. Such appointees serve either at the president's pleasure, being replaced when the new administration comes in, or for fixed terms, in which case they remain until their term expires.

The chief executive is also empowered to make what are known as recess appointments. Article II, section 2, of the Constitution grants the president "Power to fill up all Vacancies that may happen during the Recess of the Senate, by granting Commissions which shall expire at the End of their next Session." By waiting until a recess, presidents have used this authority to fill a position that became vacant even while the Senate was in session. But if the appointee is to remain in office, he or she must be confirmed by the Senate before Congress's next session. At times this power has been used to thwart the constitutionally required confirmation process and place in office a person whom the Senate might not be expected to confirm. John Rutledge (1739–1800), for example, was named chief justice by President George Washington in 1795 during Congress's August recess. Although he led the Supreme Court that month, the Senate rejected his nomination later that year because he had not favored American independence. He then tried to commit suicide by drowning.

Judicial Appointments

Unlike the president's executive branch appointments, the members of the SUPREME COURT are not responsible to the president even though the chief executive appoints them also. According to Article III, section 1, they "shall hold their Offices during good Behaviour," meaning for life unless removed by impeachment. The appointment process for members of the Court, including the CHIEF JUSTICE, is the same as for other presidential appointments that must be approved by the Senate. However, because of the Court's role in determining the constitutionality of acts of the other two branches of government (see JUDICIAL REVIEW) and the length of service possible on the bench, the appointment of a member of the Court has often become a battleground between liberals and conservatives.

"Even if he is mediocre, there are a lot of mediocre judges and people and lawyers. They are entitled to a little representation, aren't they, and a little chance?"

—Sen. Roman Hruska (R-Neb.),
defending the Supreme Court nomination of
G. Harrold Carswell in 1970

In 1969, for example, the Supreme Court nomination of Clement F. Haynesworth by Republican president Richard M. Nixon (1913–94) was rejected by the Senate, in which the Democrats held a majority, because of the nominee's generally conservative views. The specific charge that sunk Haynesworth's nomination, however, was his failure as a judge to recuse himself from taking part in a case in which he had a financial interest. Nixon's subsequent nominee for the position, G. Harrold Carswell, who was an even less distinguished jurist than Haynesworth, was similarly rejected for having opposed integration when he was a political candidate. On his third try, Nixon was able to get the Senate to approve Harry A. Blackmun (1908–99), who went on to write the Court's opinion in ROE V. WADE (1973) supporting the right to an ABORTION.

Under the Constitution the president also appoints, with the advice and consent of the Senate, all federal judges, who hold their offices during "good behaviour," meaning for life. A president who serves two terms or several presidents of the same party or political ideology who serve for consecutive terms can make a difference in the political balance of the federal court system. Ronald Reagan (1911–2004), a two-term president, deliberately set out to influence the federal courts through his appointments, supporting STATES' RIGHTS positions rather than increasing the national government's power at the expense of the states.

Removal of Appointees

Other than by IMPEACHMENT, the Constitution is silent on how appointed officials and federal jurists, including Supreme Court members, may be removed from office. Impeachment requires a majority vote in the HOUSE OF REPRESENTATIVES and conviction in the Senate by "the Concurrence of two thirds of the Members present," according to Article I, section 3. ALEXANDER HAMILTON, in essay 77 of *The Federalist* (1787–88) (see FEDERALIST PAPERS), suggested that the Senate's consent would be required to terminate a presidential appointment by means other than impeachment—for example, dismissal by the president. But this did not prove to be the case.

In *MARBURY V. MADISON* (1803)—the case that defined the Supreme Court's power to declare acts of Congress unconstitutional—Chief Justice JOHN MARSHALL addressed the problem of the extent of the president's powers to remove appointed officials not otherwise protected by the Constitution. According to Marshall, Marbury's appointment as a justice of the peace with a five-year term gave him the right to hold that position regardless of who the president was—a new president could not summarily fire him. But if the position had been one in which the incumbent served at the pleasure of the president, the manner of appointment would make no difference should the president wish to remove him. The Senate's role in appointing the official did not give it a role in removing him, except of course in the case of impeachment.

The power of the president to remove an official was involved in the impeachment of President Andrew Johnson (1808–75). The removal action was undertaken by Johnson in 1867 in defiance of the Tenure of Office Act (1867), which required approval of a successor before an office holder could be removed. In *Myers v. United States* (1926), Chief Justice William H. Taft (1857–1930), himself a former president, said that the power of removal is incidental to the power of appointment and therefore a law requiring Senate approval for the president to remove an appointee was unconstitutional. Taft added that if the president could

President Andrew Johnson was almost removed from office in 1868 when he defied Congress by firing his secretary of war.
Source: Library of Congress

not remove an appointee from office he could not be responsible for "tak[ing] Care that the Laws be faithfully executed," as charged by the Constitution's Article II, section 3.

In *Humphrey's Executor v. United States* (1935), however, the Supreme Court declared that the president has the exclusive authority to remove "purely executive officers" only. Therefore, President Franklin D. Roosevelt (1882–1945) could not remove a member of the Federal Trade Commission appointed for a seven-year term by his predecessor, Herbert Hoover (1874–1964), except for cause, which was defined by law to be inefficiency, neglect of duty, or malfeasance in of-

More on this topic:

Separation of Powers, p. 494

fice. Roosevelt had based his removal of the commissioner on policy differences, but the Court found that Congress had authority to create quasi-legislative or quasi-judicial agencies (see ADMINISTRATIVE AGENCIES) whose chief officers could act independently of executive control and be removed only for the causes prescribed by Congress.

The appointment and removal power of the president is one of the few fairly well-settled constitutional issues. Within the ambit prescribed by the Constitution, the president has great power—especially when his party holds the Senate majority—to fill key positions in the executive branch and make an impact on the character of the Supreme Court and the federal judiciary.

Apportionment *See* HOUSE OF REPRESENTATIVES; REAPPORTIONMENT.

Appropriations *See* BUDGET.

Armed Forces

In 1796 GEORGE WASHINGTON, arguably America's greatest military leader, hoped in his farewell address as president that his successors would "avoid the necessity of those overgrown military establishments, which under any form of government are inauspicious to liberty, and are regarded as particularly hostile to republican liberty." For much of its history, the United States has avoided such an "overgrown military," but because the price of LIBERTY is eternal vigilance, the armed forces have been a major component of the national government since World War II.

Democracy and a strong military are not incompatible. In ancient Athens, the cradle of DEMOCRACY, every Athenian citizen—only adult males—could expect to serve in either the army or the navy. Plato, the ancient Greek philosopher (ca. 427–347 B.C.E.), proposed in his last work, *The Laws*, that "[t]he Guardians of the Laws must compile a preliminary list of candidates, restricted to citizens, and the Generals should then be elected from this list by all those who have served in the armed forces at the proper age, or who are serving at the time."

The constitutions of most countries deal with the military to a greater or lesser degree. The constitution of Japan (1947), for example, written after the country's defeat in World War II, renounces war and declares that "land, sea, and air forces, as well as other war potential, will never be maintained." According to the German constitution (1949), "Men who have attained the age of eighteen may be required to serve in the Armed Forces, in the Federal Border Police, or in a civil defense organization."

America's Constitution refers to the military in several provisions. Article I, section 8, grants Congress the power to "declare War" and to "raise and support Armies, but no Appropriation of Money to that Use shall be for a longer Term than two Years; To provide and maintain a Navy; to make Rules for the Government and Regulation of the land and naval Forces; and To provide for calling forth the Militia to execute the Laws of the Union, suppress Insurrections and repel Invasions." Section 8 also empowers Congress to "provide for organizing, arming, and disciplining, the Militia, and for governing such Part of them as may be employed in the Service of the United States, reserving to the States respectively, the Appointment of the Officers, and the Authority of training the Militia according to the discipline prescribed by Congress."

Article II, section 2, designates the president "Commander in Chief of the Army and Navy of the United States, and of the Militia of the several States, when called into the actual Service of the

United States." The language of section 2 also authorizes the president, with the Senate's ADVICE AND CONSENT, to appoint military officers. The president's authority over the military granted by the Constitution represents the basic principle of constitutional democracy that the military should always be subordinate to civilian political authority. The president generally exercises his authority over the armed forces through the secretary of defense (see CABINET).

Separation of Powers

The monarchs of England have had the power not only to declare war but also to raise armies and direct their activities—a power that was not always exercised wisely or in the best interests of the English people. Even today, the queen is the titular head of the British armed forces. The FRAMERS OF THE CONSTITUTION were also familiar with the English Declaration of Right (1688), which made Parliament's consent a requirement for the monarch to maintain a standing army. The framers therefore split the power over the new nation's armed forces between Congress and the president, a dual responsibility that has caused tension and disputes between the two branches of government (see SEPARATION OF POWERS). In times of WAR, however, Congress tends to delegate more powers to the president than in peacetime. The Supreme Court has tried to maintain the separation of powers contemplated by the framers even during wartime.

The Supreme Court has also had to protect the fundamental rights of citizens from unconstitutional measures taken in time of war. During the Civil War (1861–65), the Court unanimously rejected the president's power to establish a military tribunal to try civilians. But when Congress was forced to make treasury notes (government IOUs called greenbacks) legal tender in order to be able to keep paying the troops during the war, the Court approved the measure when it was challenged in *Knox v. Lee* and *Parker v. Davis* (both 1871), known as the Legal Tender Cases, on the grounds that greenbacks did not have the equivalent value in gold or silver. The Court majority found that the exigencies of war made the act of Congress constitutional under the NECESSARY AND PROPER CLAUSE of the Constitution, which authorizes the legislature to "make all Laws which shall be necessary and proper for carrying into Execution...all...Powers vested by this Constitution in the Government of the United States, or in any Department or Officer thereof."

As commander in chief of the armed forces—made up of the army, navy, air force, and marines—the president may commit troops to battle without a formal declaration of war by Congress. A major showdown between the president and Congress over this provision resulted in enactment of the War Powers Act (1973) over the veto of President Richard M. Nixon (1913–94). The rancor over the Vietnam War—undeclared by Congress—moved Congress to try to limit this presidential power. As the preamble of the bill stated, its aim was "to fulfill the intent of the framers of the Constitution...and ensure that the collective judgment of both the Congress and the President will apply to the introduction of U.S. armed forces into hostilities...." The act's major provision allowed Congress at any time, by a majority vote of both houses, to order the president to disengage troops involved in an undeclared war and to require withdrawal of American armed forces from a conflict within a set number of days. Presidents continued to commit troops on their own, and only when President Ronald Reagan (1911–2004) deployed marines in Lebanon in 1982 and 1983 was it necessary for the president and Congress to negotiate the limits of the military action. The invasion of Iraq in 2003 and the ensuing military occupation of that country for a period longer than World War II at a great cost in human life and American tax dollars—without a formal declaration of war by Congress—has again raised questions concerning the proper role of Congress and the president in initiating military action under the Constitution.

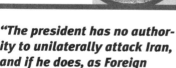

"The president has no authority to unilaterally attack Iran, and if he does, as Foreign Relations Committee chairman, I will move to impeach."

—Sen. Joseph Biden Jr. (D-Del.), warning President George W. Bush in 2007 to seek congressional approval before taking military action against Iran

Service Men and Women

The Supreme Court has generally given Congress great freedom in governing the armed services, made up of men and women who are essential to the maintenance of the freedom and democracy that citizens of the United States so highly prize. In *Parker v. Levy* (1974), the Court concluded that "[t]he military constitutes a specialized community governed by a separate discipline from that of the civilian," adding that "Congress is permitted to legislate both with greater breadth and with greater flexibility when prescribing rules by which [the military] shall be governed than when it is prescribing rules for [civilian society]." Moreover, in 2006 the Supreme Court declined to review a military court decision that confirmed that, in cases arising outside the military justice system, Supreme Court decisions interpreting the Constitution are to be applied as precedents unless such decisions can be distinguished based on unique military justice considerations.

The Court has upheld male-only registration for the draft and allowed the banning of speeches and demonstrations of a political nature and distribution without the approval of military post headquarters of literature that might endanger military personnel's loyalty, discipline, or morale. To benefit service personnel, their tangible personal property may be barred from taxation by the state in which they are stationed if they are domiciled elsewhere. Congress may allow the designation of an insurance beneficiary regardless of state law and exempt the proceeds from creditors. And Congress has moved to ban bordellos in the vicinity of places where military personnel are stationed.

The Supreme Court in *O'Callahan v. Parker* (1969) held that service personnel could not be tried by court-martial for crimes that are not "service-connected." In this case, the crime had been committed against a civilian, in peacetime, in the United States, away from the military base while the serviceman was officially off duty. But in *Solorio v. United States* (1987), the Court overruled *O'Callahan* because of confusion about the nature of "service-connected" crimes. If court-martialed, service men and women are entitled to roughly the same DUE PROCESS rights as civilians. The Uniform Code of Military Justice, however, permits superior officers to influence court-martial proceedings; unlike civilian judges, persons with judicial functions in a court-martial are appointed by their superiors and may be removed at will. Only one-third of a court-martial panel may be enlisted personnel, if requested by the accused, whereas the rest of the court is made up of officers. And because the review authority of the Court of Military Appeals is more restricted than a civilian appellate court, parties often challenge the constitutionality of court-martial proceedings in the federal courts. Not all cases involving military personnel may be so reviewable, however. In 2001 the U.S. Court of Appeals for the Eleventh Circuit held that a suit by military personnel for injunctive relief for service-connected injuries was nonjusticiable (not reviewable). The split in the federal appeals courts on this issue means that it may have to be resolved by the Supreme Court.

Discrimination in the Military

The Supreme Court's treatment of the armed forces as a specialized community with its own rules has led at various times to the virtual legalization of DISCRIMINATION against blacks, women, homosexuals, and other MINORITIES in the military services. Even though President Harry S. Truman (1884–1972) ordered the armed forces desegregated in 1948, integration did not occur until the Korean War (1950–53) (see SEGREGATION). The military has made attempts to deal with discrimination against WOMEN—admitting them into the service academies beginning in 1976—but women are still barred from combat positions. The policy toward

HOMOSEXUALS in the service of their country is described as "Don't ask, don't tell." That is, the military will not ask applicants or service personnel if they are homosexuals, but those who announce or otherwise make known their homosexuality may be discharged.

Few Supreme Court cases have addressed SEX DISCRIMINATION in the military. In *Frontiero v. Richardson* (1973), the Court held that a law allowing only the spouses of male members of the uniformed services to receive increases in some benefits (such as allowances for quarters and health benefits) unconstitutionally denied due process of law under the Fifth Amendment (1791) to a married woman air force officer. But in *Personnel Administrator of Massachusetts v. Feeny* (1979), the Court found that a state law granting an absolute lifetime preference to veterans, which a female state employee argued favored men because there were more men in the military than women, did not violate the EQUAL PROTECTION clause of the Fourteenth Amendment (1868). The military's history and methods of fighting wars have at times precluded the women and men of the armed forces from being able to enjoy the same constitutional rights and freedoms they safeguard for other citizens.

Gen. Peter Pace, then chair of the Joint Chiefs of Staff, sparked renewed debate over the military's policy on gays when he said in a 2007 interview: "I believe homosexual acts between two individuals are immoral and that we should not condone immoral acts."
Source: AP Images/Haraz N. Ghanbari

Arrest

After policemen in Lago Vista, California, pulled over the car of a woman transporting two small children, they placed her under arrest, verbally berated her, handcuffed her, put her in the police squad car, and drove her to the police station, where she was forced to remove her shoes, jewelry, and eyeglasses. The only penalty for her violation of the state's seat belt law was a fine. When the case of *Atwater v. City of Lago Vista* (2001) reached the Supreme Court, Justice David H. Souter (b. 1939) wrote in his opinion for the Court that while the woman suffered "petty humiliations," her Fourth Amendment (1791) rights against unreasonable SEARCH AND SEIZURE had not been violated. Her arrest was upheld.

To be arrested (from the Latin *ad restare*, meaning to rest or remain) is to be deprived of LIBERTY and often results in one's being placed in a hostile environment, even though under the American legal system a person is entitled to the presumption of innocence. Although the term appears in the Constitution only in the context of the privileges and immunities of members of Congress, a number of provisions address the rights of citizens relating to arrest: the seizing and detention of a person by the police or federal LAW ENFORCEMENT authorities. A citizen's constitutional rights in the event of arrest are closely related to the rights of persons accused of crimes, although arrest and the formal filing of criminal charges are two distinct actions by different government authorities, as reflected in the popular television program *Law and Order*.

Arrest is the first step in the process of criminal prosecution. According to William Blackstone (1723–80), author of *Commentary on the Laws of England* (1765–70), arrest may lead progressively to "Commitment and bail," "Prosecution," "Process," "Arraignment," "Plea," "Trial and conviction," "Judgment, and its consequences," "Reversal of judgment," "Reprieve, or pardon," and, finally, "Execution." In the United States today, an arrest may be made on the basis of an arrest warrant issued by a court because an apparent crime was committed in the presence of the arresting officer or on the arresting officer's belief that a crime was committed. After an arrest, a person must be "read his or her rights"—given the so-called Miranda warnings (see MIRANDA V. ARIZONA)—at the first practical moment. These warnings advise the detained person of his or her constitutional rights. Citizens may make an arrest if a crime is committed in their presence, but they may be sued for false arrest if they make a mistake.

Like the California woman who did not wear her seat belt, a person may be arrested for a minor violation of the law or for speeding or stealing less than fifty dollars, as well as for more serious crimes. The act of arresting an individual raises a number of constitutional questions. Procedural requirements must be followed in making an arrest, including the treatment of the accused during arrest and other conduct by the arresting officers. Additional factors are the speed with which (1) the accused is brought before a court and (2) the reasons for the arrest are made known to the detainee and his or her legal counsel. Treatment during detainment while under arrest may also raise constitutional issues, such as the right to humane treatment (see PRISONERS and ASSISTANCE OF COUNSEL).

The Fourth Amendment

Whereas the Fifth and Sixth Amendments (both 1791) address the rights of persons accused of crimes, the Fourth Amendment (1791), another BILL OF RIGHTS provision, represents the principal constitutional language regarding standards for arrests. "The right of the people to be secure in their persons, houses, papers, and effects, against unreasonable searches and seizures, shall not be violated," states the Fourth Amendment, "and no Warrants shall issue, but upon probable cause, supported by Oath or affirmation, and particularly describing the place to be searched, and the persons or things to be seized."

In *Wolf v. Colorado* (1949), the Supreme Court was still reluctant to fully extend the provisions of the Fourth Amendment applicable to the federal government to the states. But in a significant departure, the Court in MAPP V. OHIO (1961) found that the Fourth Amendment's provisions were incorporated into the Fourteenth Amendment (1868) and were therefore applicable to the states as well (see INCORPORATION DOCTRINE).

Defining Arrest and False Arrest

The U.S. Supreme Court has honed the definition of arrest in three recent cases. In *Kaupp v. Texas* (2003), the Court explained, citing *Florida v. Bostick* (1991), in which *Michigan v. Chesternut* (1988) was quoted, that the "seizure of a person within the meaning of the Fourth and Fourteenth Amendments occurs when, 'taking into account all of the circumstances surrounding the encounter, the police conduct would "have communicated to a reasonable person that he was not at liberty to ignore the police presence and go about his business."'" In *Hiibel v. Nevada* (2004), the Court upheld a state "stop and identify" statute, holding that it was not unconstitutional to arrest and convict a person for refusing to identify himself or herself to a police officer during an investigative stop involving a reported assault. The Court, in *Maryland v. Pringle* (2003), found that a Maryland law that permits police officers to execute warrantless arrests, such as the arrest of Pringle based on stopping a car for speeding and finding drugs and money in the car, did not contravene the Fourth or Fourteenth Amendments.

As for false arrest, the Court in *Wallace v. Kato* (2007) determined that the statute of limitations for bringing charges of an unlawful arrest in violation of the Fourth Amendment after a person is arrested and criminally prosecuted begins to run from the time the person becomes contained pursuant to the legal process or when he or she is arrested, and not after the prosecution drops its charges against the defendant.

Arrest Warrants

Under English COMMON LAW, an officer of the law could make an arrest if he had reasonable grounds to suspect that a felony had been committed. In the case of a lesser crime such as a misdemeanor, however, he had to have witnessed the act before he could make an arrest without a warrant. This was the law at the national and state levels at the time the Constitution was adopted in 1789.

From the beginning of the republic, the Supreme Court did not require a warrant for arrests in most cases. In *United States v. Watson* (1976), the Court explicitly rejected a mandatory requirement for an arrest warrant at least where felonies were involved. In that case, the suspect was arrested in a public place by the police on the basis of "probable cause." A year earlier, in *Gerstein v. Pugh* (1975), the Court had declared that the Fourth Amendment called for a prompt determination by a magistrate or a judge as to whether an arrest was proper on the basis of probable cause alone or whether a warrant was necessary under the circumstances. In 1991 "prompt" was defined by the Court to mean within forty-eight hours of the arrest, unless there were extraordinary reasons for a longer delay.

In *Payton v. New York* (1980), the Supreme Court upheld the requirement for an arrest warrant before the authorities could enter a person's home without consent and make an arrest. In *Ross v. United States* (1982), however, the Court found that arrests of persons in their cars did not require a warrant. Detaining a person for a short period of time, such as at a roadblock to check randomly for intoxicated drivers or stopping and questioning a person—even without probable cause—has been validated by the Court.

An arrest warrant may be issued by a judge, but unlike a search warrant, one may also be issued by a properly constituted grand jury (see JURIES). The arrest warrant must contain sufficient information to identify the person to be arrested, and it is not intended to be used as a means to simply round up a number of people suspected of a crime. Although an arrest without a proper warrant does not entitle the suspect to avoid prosecution or conviction, it may result in the exclusion of evidence, including statements made by the person arrested, under the doctrine of the "fruit of the poison tree" declared by the Supreme Court in *Wong Sung v. United States* (1963).

The conflict between the rights of persons suspected of a crime and the need for law enforcement officials to act swiftly and surely to detain lawbreakers for trial is arbitrated by the Constitution and the Supreme Court's evolving interpretation of it, particularly the Fourth Amendment.

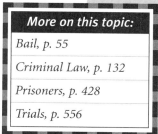

More on this topic:

Bail, p. 55

Criminal Law, p. 132

Prisoners, p. 428

Trials, p. 556

Articles of Confederation

In 1776, the year of the DECLARATION OF INDEPENDENCE, the Continental Congress appointed a committee to draft a constitution for the original thirteen colonies, which Benjamin Franklin of Pennsylvania dubbed "the Articles of Confederation and Perpetual Union." The colonies themselves had written constitutional-type documents on which their own governance was based. For example, the Fundamental Orders of Connecticut, dating from around 1638–39, has been called the world's first written constitution. New Hampshire, after declaring its independence from Great Britain, drafted the first written constitution of an independent state in 1776. These documents followed in the tradition of the ancient DEMOCRACY of Athens and the republic of Rome, whose written laws were copied down for reference by political leaders and literate citizens. At the time Britain had an unwritten constitution that combined customs and tradition with some written documents, including Magna Carta (1215), the Petition of Right (1628), and the Bill of Rights (1689).

Ratification of the Articles of Confederation by the thirteen newly independent states was officially declared by Congress on March 1, 1781, while the Revolutionary War (1775–83) was still in progress. The document was a product of radical leaders who had advocated independence from a European power, itself a strong centralized government, and were now fighting to ensure the SOVEREIGNTY and supremacy of their state governments, not a national government. The Articles served basically as an agreement to form a league of states for limited purposes, playing a key role in organizing the newly independent colonies for the successful prosecution of the Revolutionary War. But once the war was over, the states began going their own ways, which was often counterproductive to one another's interests and to those of the United States as a whole.

That the central government the document provided for after the war was weak and ineffectual might have been expected. Yet in a way the agreement reflected the philosophy of the Declaration of Independence, which concludes with the decree that the states, "as Free and Independent States,…have full Power…to do all…Acts and Things which Independent States may of right do." This issue of STATES' RIGHTS—the power of the national government vis-á-vis that of the states—is still debated today.

Sovereign States versus Central Government

The Articles of Confederation delegated only a few powers to Congress, including

THE UNITED COLONIES
AT THE
BEGINNING OF THE REVOLUTION.
SCALE OF MILES
0 50 100 150 200 250 300 350

Map of the thirteen colonies and related territories, 1775. At the time of the Articles of Confederation, many in America viewed the individual states as separate entities rather than as components of a single nation. Some of the states, such as Virginia, were considerably larger than their present-day sizes. Altogether, the states stretched about a thousand miles from north to south, which was an enormously large area for a central entity to govern.

Source: The Granger Collection, New York

control of the war effort and foreign affairs and regulation of NATIVE AMERICANS living outside the states. The document included no SUPREMACY CLAUSE making national law supreme over state laws. In fact, it stipulated that no law passed by Congress could infringe on the right of the states to pass their own laws on all other matters. Article 1 named the confederation "The United States of America," while Article 2 expressly provided: "Each State retains its sovereignty, freedom and independence, and every power, jurisdiction, and right, which is not by this confederation expressly delegated to the United States, in Congress assembled."

Delegates to Congress, according to Article 5, were to be "annually appointed, in such manner as the legislature of each State shall direct," and state delegations could consist of from two to seven members. "In determining questions in the United States, in Congress assembled," added Article 5, "each State shall have one vote." Additional powers delegated to Congress in Article 9 included determining peace and war, sending and receiving ambassadors, entering into treaties and alliances, "regulating the alloy and value of coin struck by their own authority, or by that of the respective states," and "fixing the standard of weights and measures throughout the United States...."

Article 9 also provided for "a Committee of the States," to consist of "one delegate from each State," and for the appointment of "such other committees and civil officers as may be necessary for managing the general affairs of the United States" under the direction of Congress. Congress was also authorized "to appoint one of their number to preside; provided that no person be allowed to serve in the office of president more than one year in any term of three years...." Several men served as "president" of the United States under the Articles, including Samuel Huntington (1731–1796), of Connecticut, and John Hanson (1715-1783), of Maryland.

Out of Weakness, Strength

Weaknesses of the Articles of Confederation included the fact that Congress could act only through the states and had no power to enact laws that would apply directly to the citizens of those states. Congress also was unable to check or coordinate the states' regulation of trade among themselves. In addition, Shays's Rebellion pointed up other impediments. A depression following the end of the Revolutionary War had threatened many small farmers, although some states enacted their own relief laws. But no relief was forthcoming in Massachusetts, where in 1786 a group of farmers organized by Daniel Shays marched on local courts to stop foreclosures on their property. A state of open rebellion lasted into 1787, highlighting the inability of Massachusetts alone or Congress under the Articles of Confederation to quickly quell the uprising.

Just three weeks after Shays's Rebellion ended, Congress called the CONSTITUTIONAL CONVENTION OF 1787, held in Philadelphia, ostensibly to simply revise the Articles. The Massachusetts revolt helped change the delegates' focus from simply amending the document to scrapping it altogether and beginning anew, drafting and ratifying a new federal constitution creating a strong national government. Spurring the delegates to consider relinquishing some of their states' sovereignty to a strong national government were a number of factors—for example, the needs for better security from external aggression and internal insurrection, for payment of state debts remaining from the Revolutionary War, and for uniform laws to promote economic stability. Cyrus Griffin of Virginia, president of the final Congress held under the Articles of Confederation, declared them replaced by the new Constitution on July 2, 1789. Although today little more than a historical curiosity, the Articles represent an initial, even if flawed, attempt at creating the world's first written national constitution. (For the complete text of the Articles, see pages 616–621.)

Arts *See* COPYRIGHT; PATENTS.

Assembly and Association

The First Amendment (1791) prohibits Congress from making any law "abridging…the right of the people peaceably to assemble, and to petition the Government for a redress of grievances." The right of association is not expressly mentioned but has been established as a constitutional right through a series of Supreme Court cases. The right to petition can be traced to the English Bill of Rights (1689), which mandates "the right of the subjects to petition the King…." Today the constitutions of many countries and international human rights documents such as the International Covenant on Civil and Political Rights (1966) explicitly guarantee the right of peaceful assembly and association as both political and civil FUNDAMENTAL RIGHTS of the people.

Flags unfurled, the Klu Klux Klan exercises its First Amendment right to peaceably assemble in a 1926 parade in Washington, D.C., one of many the Klan has sponsored.
Source: Library of Congress

Assembly as a Constitutional Right

The FRAMERS OF THE CONSTITUTION had direct experience with government suppression of peaceful assemblies by citizens protesting government policies and actions. Governments, however, do have legitimate concerns that an assembly that begins peacefully may quickly turn into a violent mob. William Blackstone (1723–80), the commentator on English COMMON LAW, described an unlawful assembly as three or more persons coming together to do an unlawful act.

However, popular democracy, based on the political SOVEREIGNTY of citizens, not only must condone peaceful assembly, especially for political purposes, but also must guarantee this right if the people's voices are to be heard by those elected to govern. In *United States v. Cruikshank* (1876), the first freedom of assembly case to come before the Supreme Court, the Court stated: "The very idea of a government, republican in form, implies a right on the part of its citizens to meet peaceably for consultation in respect to public affairs and to petition for a redress of grievances." In *De Jonge v. Oregon* (1937), the Court declared: "[P]eaceable assembly for lawful discussion cannot be made a crime…."

Even in the United States, government abuses of freedom of assembly have occurred. Before ratification of the Nineteenth Amendment (1920), peaceful supporters of women's suffrage were often harassed by the police or arrested simply for exercising their well-established constitutional right of assembly (see WOMEN), as were Vietnam War protesters in the 1960s and 1970s. In 2001 a group planning to protest the inauguration of George W. Bush challenged a District of Columbia law barring speech without permission from the police, and a District Court judge prohibited enforcement of the law as unconstitutional.

Association as a Fundamental Right

Freedom of association as a constitutional right is derived from both freedom of assembly and freedom of SPEECH and is recognized in two forms by the courts. Freedom of intimate association refers to relationships such as marriage, while expressive association is generally for the purposes of mutually furthering political, economic, religious, and cultural objectives. "Better use has been made of association and this powerful instrument of action has been applied to more varied aims in America than anywhere else in the world," observed Alexis de Tocqueville in his famous treatise *Democracy in America* (1835).

In *Roberts v. United States Jaycees* (1984), the Supreme Court confirmed the existence of a "freedom of intimate association," encompassing "certain kinds of highly personal relationships" such as "marriage; childbirth; the raising and education of children; and cohabitation with one's relatives"—all deserving of significant constitutional protection. In this case and a similar suit against the Rotary Club (1987), both involving alleged SEX DISCRIMINATION, the Supreme Court held that freedom of association did not protect these organizations from the reach of antidiscrimination laws. As a Supreme Court justice, Sandra Day O'Connor sought to distinguish commercial association—association primarily for the purpose of engaging in commercial or economic activity—from expressive association and allow the former less constitutional protection.

During the early days of the Cold War, members of the Communist Party and their "fellow travelers," those who associated with them or sympathized with their cause, were often subjected to attempts by Congress and the EXECUTIVE BRANCH to limit their freedom of association. In 2000 the Supreme Court in *Boy Scouts of America v. Dale* held that expressive association as guaranteed by the First Amendment allowed the Boy Scouts organization to deny membership to an avowed homosexual and gay rights activist (see HOMOSEXUALS).

Implicit in the concept of freedom of association is the right to organize and belong to POLITICAL PARTIES. In *Rutan v. Republican Party of Illinois* (1990), Justice William J. Brennan (1906–97) said that personnel decisions concerning low-level workers "based on political affiliations or support are an impermissible infringement on the First Amendment rights of public employees." And in *California Democratic Party v. Jones* (2000), the Court invalidated a California law changing primary elections from a "closed" primary (in which only party members can vote) to a "blanket" primary (in which all candidates, regardless of party affiliation, are listed and voters of any or no party are free to chose among them), ruling that it was an unconstitutional infringement of freedom of association guaranteed under the First Amendment. The Court found that whatever interest the state might have in opening up the primary process was not sufficient to trump the right of individual voters to associate by party affiliation.

A corollary to freedom of association is freedom from being forced to join or support an organization or a group against one's wishes. The courts have allowed a requirement that union dues be paid, even holding in *Abood v. Detroit Board of Education* (1977) that public employees could be forced to contribute a "service fee equal in amount to union dues" but that no portion could be

CLOSER LOOK

When Sen. Joseph R. McCarthy (R-Wis.) publicly criticized the State Department in 1950 for harboring members of the Communist Party, he gave momentum to one of the most effective attacks on freedom of association in U.S. history. McCarthy and other powerful public officials, including Federal Bureau of Investigation director J. Edgar Hoover, sought to uncover communist sympathizers and drive them out of government and private industry. Their often unscrupulous tactics and disregard for First Amendment protections became known as "McCarthyism."

The anticommunist crusade grew out of the cold war and the Soviet Union's development of an atomic bomb. It drew widespread attention in the late 1940s and early 1950s when the House Committee on Un-American Activities began investigating Hollywood. Members of the committee demanded that screenwriters, directors, and others in the movie industry answer a straightforward question: "Are you now, or have you ever been, a member of the Communist Party of the United States?"

Some movie industry witnesses refused to answer because they felt they were protected by the First Amendment's guarantee of freedom of assembly. Others cited the Fifth Amendment, saying they could not be forced to incriminate themselves. In many cases, however, people's careers were ruined because the entertainment industry would not hire them anymore.

McCarthy went on to investigate the State Department and the Army, alleging they had been infiltrated by communists. But he had little evidence for his accusations. By 1954 public sentiment had turned against McCarthy. The Supreme Court also stepped in. In several cases in the 1950s, the justices ruled that people could not be prosecuted merely for being communists, and the Court curtailed efforts to punish witnesses who declined to cooperate with government investigations into communism.

used for "ideological purposes not associated with collective bargaining" (see UNIONS). Forced political contributions and retaliation for political opposition to public officials, on the other hand, have been found to be infringements of the right of association.

However, in *Board of Regents of the University of Wisconsin System v. Southworth* (2000), the Supreme Court denied the "Abood" right to students requesting a rebate of fees used to support campus organizations that promoted politics or ideologies with which the students disagreed. In *Rumsfeld v. Forum for Academic and Institutional Rights* (2006), the Court, in a decision by Chief Justice John G. Roberts Jr. (b. 1955), upheld a federal statute that required law schools to allow military recruiters on campus at the same time as other potential employers. He reasoned: "To comply with the statute, law schools must allow military recruiters on campus and assist them in whatever way the school chooses to assist other employers. Law schools therefore 'associate' with military recruiters in the sense that they interact with them. But recruiters are not a part of the law school. Recruiters are, by definition, outsiders who come onto campus for the limited purpose of trying to hire students—not to become members of the school's expressive association. This distinction is critical. Unlike in the public accommodations in *Boy Scouts of America v. Dale* (2000), in which the Court upheld the right of the organization to refuse to allow an overt homosexual to be a scoutmaster, the statute here does not force a law school 'to accept members it does not desire.'"

Assistance of Counsel

Skillful defense lawyers can sometimes win verdicts of "not guilty" even when the evidence against their clients appears to be overwhelming. Johnnie Cochran (above, right) and a team of high-profile defense attorneys won national attention by persuading a Los Angeles jury not to convict former NFL football star O. J. Simpson (above, center) of murder in 1995.
Source: Reuters/POOL News

Without a vigorous, professional, and independent legal profession, Americans' constitutional rights and the Constitution itself would be imperiled. The intricacies of the modern U.S. legal system, combined with the formidable powers of the federal and state governments and those who command political and economic resources, can often place the average citizen at a great disadvantage—if not outright jeopardy—in confrontations with the law. Therein rests the need for all citizens to have the assistance of counsel, especially in criminal cases (see CRIMINAL LAW).

A Federal Right

"In all criminal prosecutions," states the Sixth Amendment (1791), "the accused shall enjoy [among other things] the right...to have the Assistance of Counsel for his defence." This provision was written to change the English procedure that expressly prevented accused felons from retaining their own lawyers. However, the right was not intended to require the government to provide or pay for a lawyer for a defendant who could not afford to hire one. Only in the 1930s did the federal courts begin to consider the basic issue of whether economic distinctions should determine the quality of justice a citizen receives in the American legal system.

In *Powell v. Alabama* (1932), one of the so-called Scottsboro Cases, the Supreme Court held that in view of certain factors, including the defendants' young age and illiteracy and the community's hostility, the trial judge's refusal to afford them "reasonable time and opportunity to secure counsel" in a case involving the DEATH PENALTY was a violation of DUE PROCESS of law as guaranteed by the Fourteenth Amendment (1868). And in *Johnson v. Zerbst* (1938), the Court ruled that it is a duty of a federal court in a criminal trial to protect the right of the accused to counsel. But in *Betts v. Brady* (1942), the Court refused to extend the requirement to the states.

A State Right

For the next two decades the Supreme Court required states only in "special circumstances" to provide assistance for those who could not afford counsel. These included the defendant's age (if relatively young) and immaturity, how technical the charge against a defendant was, and how potentially prejudiced the court was against the defendant. In the landmark case GIDEON V. WAINWRIGHT (1963), however, the Court finally admitted that all felony trials could be of such complexity that to require a person without legal training to defend himself or herself was tantamount to denial of a fair trial (see TRIALS). As Justice Hugo L. Black (1886–1971) wrote on behalf of a unanimous Court: "The right of one charged with crime to counsel may not be deemed fundamental and essential to fair trials in some countries, but it is in ours."

The Court has continued to delimit the nature of the right of assistance of counsel, holding that it includes, in addition to assistance at trial, the right of consultation and the right to a reasonable period of time to prepare a case for trial. Counsel must be provided at all stages of the criminal process, and it must be "effective" assistance of counsel, which means that the attorney must possess sufficient knowledge and experience to defend in a criminal case. In *Strickland v. Washington* (1984), the Supreme Court declared that if "there is a reasonable probability that, but for counsel's unprofessional errors, the result would have been different," then assistance of counsel has been ineffective. The right also extends to the first appeal of a conviction.

In several recent cases the Supreme Court has rejected claims of ineffective assistance by legal counsel for the defense. For example, in the California case *Yarborough v. Gentry* (2003), the Court reviewed in detail the summation of defense counsel to the jury in a case of assault with a deadly weapon, but found that while counsel "was no Aristotle or even Clarence Darrow," the lower federal court's conclusion that "not only [was] his performance deficient [and] that any disagreement with that conclusion would be objectively unreasonable" gave "too little deference to the state courts that have primary responsibility for supervising defense counsel in state criminal trials." The following year, in *Florida v. Nixon*, the Court held that counsel's failure to obtain the defendant's express consent to a strategy of conceding guilt in a capital trial does not automatically render his or her performance deficient.

In civil matters, in contrast, no such right of assistance applies, because the right itself arises from the imminent threat of the loss of liberty or life. Furthermore, a court cannot force a person who does not want a lawyer to accept one.

In addition to the complexity of the criminal law system and the risk of injustice for a person denied the assistance of counsel, legal counsel is considered a necessity for a number of other reasons. Indigent persons accused of crimes generally cannot investigate the charges or evidence against them because they are detained pending trial. It is also difficult for any person, rich or poor, who is under the constant threat of losing his or her liberty or life to act in the dispassionate and rational manner necessary for a thorough and logical defense.

Centuries ago justice was sometimes determined by a joust or a duel between champions of the parties or the parties themselves. In some ways, for better or worse, the modern legal system has retained the flavor of these trials-by-combat in which the well-trained knight stands a far better chance of winning than the average citizen.

Attainder, Bills of

The first bill of attainder—a legislative act to punish a person without a judicial trial—was introduced and passed in the English Parliament in 1459. Attainder was a legislative penalty for a high crime such as TREASON and stripped the condemned of all CIVIL RIGHTS, including the right to inherit or transmit PROPERTY. As JAMES MADISON noted in essay 44 of *The Federalist* (1787–88) (see FEDERALIST PAPERS), bills of attainder, along with EX POST FACTO LAWS and laws impairing the obligation of CONTRACTS, "are contrary to the first principles of the social compact and to every principle of sound legislation."

So desirous of prohibiting bills of attainder were the FRAMERS OF THE CONSTITUTION that they devoted two provisions to banning their use, one directed to the federal government and one to state governments. "No Bill of Attainder or ex post facto Law shall be passed," Article I, section 9, mandates, while section 10 commands, "No State shall...pass any Bill of Attainder, ex post facto Law, or Law impairing the Obligation of Contracts...."

On the basis of these prohibitions against bills of attainder, the Supreme Court in *Ex parte Garland* (1867) invalidated a federal law requiring attorneys to take an oath denying any part in the Confederate rebellion before they could practice law before federal courts, and in *Cummings v. Missouri* (1867), the Court struck down a similar state requirement regarding the practice of certain professions, calling both punishment without a trial. In *United States v. Lovett* (1946), the justices again relied on the prohibitions against bills of attainder to overturn a loss of pay decreed by Congress for three employees whom a congressional committee alleged to be subversives. However, in *Nixon v. Administrator of General Services* (1977), the Court held that a law giving the General Services Administration authority to take possession and control of White House records to prevent their being lost or destroyed, while directed expressly at one person—Richard Nixon—"constituted a legitimate class of one [person]" and did not impose the punishment of a bill of attainder.

But the U.S. District Court for the District of Columbia in *Morgan v. Foretich* (2003) invalidated the act passed by Congress in 1996 that permitted Elizabeth Morgan's daughter (who had been taken from the United States to New Zealand in the late 1980s to prevent contact with her father, Eric Foretich, whom her mother accused of child abuse) to decide for herself whether or not to have further contact with her father as "an unconstitutional bill of attainder." It has also been suggested that the "Palm Sunday Compromise," or the Act for the Relief of the Parents of Theresa Marie Schiavo [Terri Schiavo], passed by Congress in 2005, constituted a bill of attainder. The act moved from state court to a U.S. district court in Florida the parents' petition to prevent their daughter from being taken off life support.

Attorney General *See* CABINET; EXECUTIVE BRANCH; LAW ENFORCEMENT.

Authors *See* COPYRIGHT.

B

Bail

In the United States, a person accused of a crime is presumed innocent until he or she pleads guilty or is found guilty in a court of law. Bail is the posting of a surety, generally money, that allows a person to remain at liberty pending trial. It recognizes this presumption of innocence, which is not guaranteed in the Constitution in so many words but is nevertheless considered a fundamental right (see FUNDAMENTAL RIGHTS). "This traditional right to freedom before conviction permits the unhampered preparation of a defense, and serves to prevent the infliction of punishment prior to conviction...," declared the Supreme Court in *Stack v. Boyle* (1951). "Unless this right to bail is preserved, the presumption of innocence, secured only after centuries of struggle, would lose its meaning."

In his *Commentaries on the Laws of England* (1765–70), William Blackstone (1723–80) noted, "By the ancient common law, before and since the [Norman] Conquest [1066], all felonies were bailable, till murder was excepted by statute: so that persons might be admitted to bail before conviction almost in every case." The history of bail in England, however, was not as clear-cut as Blackstone implies. In Darnel's Case (1627), for example, English judges confirmed the monarch's right to order a person to prison without bail. In response, Parliament enacted the Petition of Right (1628), which cited Magna Carta (1215) regarding the traditional rights of those accused of a crime. After further attempts to subvert the right to bail, Parliament enacted the Habeas Corpus Act (1679), which affirmed the longstanding right of persons held in prison to be brought before a court of law to be charged with a crime or released (see HABEAS CORPUS). The English Bill of Rights (1689) admonished that "excessive bail ought not to be required...."

Source: AP Images/Journal Times, Mark Hertzberg

Judges sometimes impose high bail amounts when a defendant in considered a flight risk. Mario Sims (above), a twenty-one-year-old accused of child molestation, faced an unusually large bail of $50,000 in 2007 after he cut off his electronic monitoring bracelet in order to appear on *The Jerry Springer Show.* Wisconsin County Circuit Judge Emily Mueller, worried that Sims might try to flee again, said the bail was necessary "given the fact he absconded, admittedly for one of the more unique reasons I've heard in my time on the bench."

Bail is addressed in other national constitutions as well. The Irish constitution (1937), for example, states that "the High Court…may…at any time…allow the said person to be at liberty on such bail and subject to such conditions as the High Court may fix…." The 1982 Charter of Rights and Freedoms of the Constitution of Canada (originally 1867) provides: "Any person charged with an offense has the right…not to be denied reasonable bail without just cause."

The Right to Bail

A court grants or denies bail on the basis of whether a person charged with a crime might attempt to flee before trial. Although the accused may put up his or her own property or money (which is forfeited if the person does not appear at the time and place designated by the court), the modern procedure is to purchase a bail bond from a commercial company, which usually charges the client 10 percent of the bail amount. Because the company itself has an interest in the defendant's appearing in court—it is risking 90 percent of the bail amount—it may refuse to provide bail on the basis of its own assessment of the flight risk. The court holds the money and generally returns it when the trial is concluded.

In language echoing both the English Bill of Rights and the Virginia Declaration of Rights (1776), written by GEORGE MASON, the Eighth Amendment (1791) mandates that "[e]xcessive bail shall not be required…." Neither this provision nor the English document guarantees the right to bail, perhaps in the latter case because England's constitution is not a written constitution but consists of a mixture of tradition and some written documents of constitutional stature, including Magna Carta. The English Bill of Rights thus needed only to supplement the existing COMMON LAW right to bail, not to create it.

JAMES MADISON introduced the proposed Eighth Amendment in the House of Representatives in 1789, during the first Congress, along with other amendments to be included in the BILL OF RIGHTS. In the record of the debates, it appears that neither he nor the other representatives realized that the language might be ambiguous. At the same time Congress was working on the Judiciary Act (1789), in which the right to bail, except in capital cases (see DEATH PENALTY), was expressly stated. A statute, however, cannot create a constitutional right.

In *Carlson v. Landon* (1952), the Supreme Court held that provisions of the Internal Security Act (1950) authorizing the attorney general to hold without bail ALIENS who were members of the Communist Party, pending a determination about their deportation, were not unconstitutional. The Court emphasized the noncriminal nature of the deportation proceedings but intimated that the Eighth Amendment does not guarantee the right to bail. In *Schilb v. Kuebel* (1971), however, the Court, in finding a bail reform law constitutional, declared: "Bail, of course, is basic to our system of law…."

Whether or not bail is a fundamental constitutional right may depend on the members of the Supreme Court at any given time. The Court led by Chief Justice William Rehnquist (1924–2005) seemed disposed against it. In *United States v. Salerno* (1987), a case involving members of organized crime, the Court held that bail could be denied to prevent the accused from fleeing the court's jurisdiction and, after an adversarial hearing, to hold persons charged with serious crimes determined to be a threat to public safety. In the Court's majority opinion, Rehnquist wrote that the Eighth Amendment "says nothing about whether bail shall be available at all." In *Schall v. Martin* and *Abrams v. Martin* (both 1984), the Court had already held that bail could be denied for dangerous juveniles.

The Supreme Court in *Janklow v. Planned Parenthood, Sioux Falls Clinic* (1996) upheld the federal Bail Reform Act of 1984, which has since been amended several times. The act authorizes and sets forth the procedures for a judicial officer to order the release or detention of an arrested person pending trial, sentence, or appeal. And in *Demore v. Kim* (2003), the Court, citing *Wong Wing v. United States* (1896), ruled that although the Fifth Amendment (1791) entitles aliens to due process in deportation proceedings, detention during such proceedings, without the benefit of bail, is a constitutionally valid aspect of that process, based on evidence that a large number of deportable criminal aliens who are not detained continue to engage in crime and fail to appear for their removal hearings.

Excessive Bail

In *Stack v. Boyle* (1951), the Supreme Court defined excessive bail as bail set at an amount higher than reasonably calculated to ensure that the accused will stand trial and submit to the sentence if found guilty. A number of factors determine what such an amount is in each case, including the nature of the crime, the accused person's ties to the community, and his or her ability to leave the country. In *Pilkinton v. Circuit Court* (1963), the Court declared that "the Eighth Amendment's proscription of excessive bail has been assumed to have application to the States through the Fourteenth Amendment [1868]" (see INCORPORATION DOCTRINE).

To challenge excessive bail, an accused must file a motion for a reduction in bail. If that is denied, then appeals may be made all the way to the Supreme Court. The Eighth Amendment's prohibition against excessive bail is not available to persons after conviction while an appeal is pending, but in practice postconviction release on bail is often granted.

Whether the right to bail is guaranteed by the Eighth Amendment's language, the intent of the FRAMERS OF THE CONSTITUTION (see ORIGINAL INTENT), or as an important adjunct of the common law presumption of innocence may never be completely settled by the Supreme Court. Unlike the fundamental right to ASSISTANCE OF COUNSEL, however, the right to bail remains available only to those individuals who can afford it.

More on this topic:
Arrest, p. 45
Criminal Law, p. 132
Prisoners, p. 428
Punishment, p. 440
Trials, p. 556

Baker v. Carr

Popular SOVEREIGNTY means that a nation's political power is shared equally among all citizens. Nowhere in the Constitution does it say that citizens who live in crowded cities have one vote each and citizens in rural communities might essentially have two votes each. But this was the situation in many states at the time of the Supreme Court's decision in *Baker v. Carr* (1962). As Justice William O. Douglas (1898–1980) put it in his concurring opinion in the case: "[T]he question is the extent to which a State may weight one person's vote more heavily than it does another's."

Human nature being what it is, people who have power are reluctant to give it up unless forced to do so. For many years several state legislatures, including Tennessee's, had been reluctant to reapportion their election districts, in effect giving the less populous areas of the state proportionally more representatives than the growing population centers. Tennessee's constitution (1870) required the legislature to reapportion its representation among election districts after each census (every ten years), but rural interests had blocked such efforts since 1901. The state's supreme court refused to force the legislature to do its constitutional duty. Officials of Shelby County, which includes the city of Memphis, thus filed suit in federal court under the name of the governing body's chairman, Charles W. Baker, against Tennessee's secretary of state, Joe C. Carr, to enforce compliance with the state's constitutional provisions requiring REAPPORTIONMENT.

The suit faced an uphill battle because of a number of questions. Did the equal protection clause of the Fourteenth Amendment (1868) contemplate protecting the right to equal representation? Is how a state legislature does its job under a state constitution a political question or one that could be decided by a court under the grant of authority in Article III, section 2? Even if a court had jurisdiction to hear such a suit, did it have a way of fashioning and enforcing the remedy sought—making the legislature reapportion the state's election districts? If all these questions could be answered in the affirmative, what guidelines could the courts use to properly reapportion the districts?

> **"[T]he question is the extent to which a State may weight one person's vote more heavily than it does another's."**
>
> **—Justice William O. Douglas,** in *Baker v. Carr*

In 1959 *Baker v. Carr* was dismissed by a special three-judge panel of a federal district court in Tennessee on the basis of the Supreme Court's refusal in *Colegrove v. Green* (1946) to entertain a suit concerning congressional redistricting, but the high court agreed to hear the case. It addressed the arguments against granting judicial relief and by a 6–2 vote rejected them. The majority opinion, written by Justice William J. Brennan (1906–97), noted that for more than sixty years "all proposals in both Houses of the [Tennessee] General Assembly for reapportionment...failed to pass," even though the state's population had grown substantially albeit unevenly during that period.

As to whether redistricting was a political question, Brennan explained, "[B]ecause any reliance on the Constitution's guarantee clause [Article IV, section 4, guaranteeing to the states a republican form of government] could not have succeeded it does not follow that appellants may not be heard on the equal protection claim [under the Fourteenth Amendment]...." He concluded that "the complaint's allegations of a denial of equal protection present a justiciable constitutional cause of action upon which appellants are entitled to a trial and a decision. The right asserted is within the reach of judicial protection under the Fourteenth Amendment" (see EQUAL PROTECTION).

Perhaps the most important result of the decision in *Baker v. Carr* was summarized by Justice Douglas's majority opinion in *Gray v. Sanders* (1963): "The conception of political equality from the Declaration of Independence, to Lincoln's Gettysburg Address, to the Fifteenth, Seventeenth, and Nineteenth Amendments can mean only one thing—one person, one vote." Since 1962 the courts have had to grapple with various aspects of the problem of reapportioning state election districts to implement the "one person, one vote" principle—a difficult goal given the need especially to protect minority rights and interests. Political majorities in many places remain determined to structure the electoral system in their states in a way that ensures their continuing majority status.

More on this topic:
Elections, p. 181
Majority Rule, p. 357
Minorities, p. 369

Balancing Tests

The nature of the U.S. Constitution creates possibilities for conflict among the federal government, the state governments, and the people themselves. The Constitution describes the national government's powers and, under the Tenth Amendment (1791), reserves the remaining powers "to the States respectively, or to the people." The result is some gray areas where it is not clear whether the powers of the national government, the rights of the states, or the rights of the people take precedence (see FEDERALISM; STATES' RIGHTS). Arbitrating such disputes often falls to the SUPREME COURT, which has to weigh a number of factors and balance competing interests to settle such conflicts.

In a sense, all constitutional interpretation today involves some sort of balancing because few issues that rise to the level of Supreme Court review are clear-cut. In the early days of the Court under Chief Justice JOHN MARSHALL, who presided from 1801 until his death, many important lines were drawn to delineate the extent of the national government's power. Since then, the Court has swung back and forth, giving deference at times to states' rights and at other times to the national government. Similarly, the Court has variously expanded and curtailed individual rights vis-á-vis the national and state governments.

The balancing-test approach to analyzing constitutional questions involving states' rights vis-á-vis the national government's powers can be seen in the Supreme Court's handling of *Pike v. Bruce Church, Inc.* (1970), a case involving an order under a state law regulating the packaging and shipping of fruits and vegetables. The grower of a superior brand of cantaloupes was required to package the fruit in the state and so mark them rather than ship the fruit to the grower's regular processing plant in another state. The Court ruled that such a requirement was an unconstitutional burden on interstate COMMERCE.

In reaching its conclusion, the Supreme Court developed a balancing test to determine if a state regulation affecting commerce runs afoul of the national government's constitutional powers, under the commerce clause in Article I, section 8, to regulate commerce among the states. The test consisted of first looking to see if a state law has a legitimate state objective and operates evenhandedly or if it discriminates against interstate commerce interests. If the law is nondiscriminatory, does the state interest outweigh the law's negative effect on interstate commerce? Before *Pike*, the Court simply looked to see if the state law had a direct or an indirect effect on interstate commerce, a type of analysis called a nominalistic test, because it turned on how the state action could be defined.

Much of the language of the Constitution, while not ambiguous, has to be read in light of various contexts. For example, the Fourth Amendment (1791) prohibits "unreasonable searches and seizures." But under what circumstances is SEARCH AND SEIZURE by LAW ENFORCEMENT officers reasonable? Courts are constantly faced with new factual situations requiring a decision as to whether a violation of a law or the Constitution has occurred. To make future determinations easier, the Supreme Court sometimes tries to set out the factors it will consider in applying balancing tests to new factual situations when they are presented.

In *Pruneyard Shopping Center v. Robins* (1980), the Supreme Court said that it would weigh the "character of governmental action, economic impact, and its interference with reasonable investment-backed decisions" to determine if PROPERTY had been unconstitutionally taken by the government (see JUST COMPENSATION). And in *Mathews v. Eldridge* (1976), the Court described its balancing test for procedural DUE PROCESS of law, stating that it would look at, "[f]irst, the private interest that will be affected by the official action; second, the risk of an erroneous deprivation of such interest through the procedures used, and the probable value, if any, of additional or substitute procedural safeguards; and finally, the government's interest, including the function involved and the fiscal and administrative burden that the additional or substitute procedural requirements would entail."

Balancing has also been used by the courts in determining the government's interests as opposed to individuals' interests regarding PRIVACY. In *ROE V. WADE* (1973), the Supreme Court fashioned a remedy that allowed an ABORTION in the first three months of pregnancy as a way to balance the rights of the expectant mother and the rights of society in protecting the unborn child.

Although the balancing-test approach works well in some areas of constitutional law, in others it may simply be a way for the courts to use elastic standards to bring about justice or injustice, depending on the circumstances. The "clear and present danger" standard established by the Supreme

CLOSER LOOK

One of the Supreme Court's most difficult balancing acts in recent years has been determining the fate of so-called illegal enemy combatants—those accused of conspiring with terrorist organizations against the United States. The Bush administration, after the terrorist attacks of September 11, 2001, claimed the right to detain such individuals virtually indefinitely. Many were imprisoned in the U.S. naval base at Guantánamo Bay in Cuba.

The combatants were denied basic rights, such as meeting with their attorneys or going to court to appeal their imprisonment. Civil libertarians denounced the open-ended detentions as illegal. But Bush administration officials said they needed to take strong steps to pursue the war on terror.

Judges have struggled to balance the security needs of the nation with the rights of the accused. They have, somewhat gingerly, tended to side with the detainees. In 2004 the Supreme Court ruled that alleged terrorists could challenge their detentions in U.S. courts. When the administration set up a system of military commissions to try the detainees, the justices in 2006 ruled that the commissions did not comply with the law.

More on this topic:

Original Intent, p. 392

Strict Construction, p. 522

Court in *Schenck v. United States* (1919) to define unprotected SPEECH gave way to balancing tests in the 1950s as anticommunist fervor seized the nation and the courts sought ways to uphold laws abridging free speech.

Balancing tests are far more effective in dealing with clashes between constitutional provisions than when applied to individual constitutional rights and freedoms. For example, each instance in which the rights of a free press (see THE PRESS) or of free speech may infringe on the right to a fair trial (see TRIALS) requires a true balancing of interests to reach a just solution. In comparison, the "separate but equal" doctrine that permitted SEGREGATION of black and white schoolchildren is a classic example of the Supreme Court's giving more weight on the scales of justice to the interests of the popular majority than to the equal rights of all citizens, thereby denying EQUAL PROTECTION of the laws. If doing justice is the purpose of the Courts' constitutional interpretation, balancing tests will often be required to weigh the interests of government against the interests of citizens and the interests of some citizens against those of other citizens.

Bankruptcy

Most citizens who find themselves facing bankruptcy—without the means to pay their debts—are not dishonest but simply unable to manage their finances or unlucky in business or in their investments. While bankruptcy laws seek to protect creditors, they are also designed to some extent to keep debtors from losing everything or never being able to get out of debt, giving the bankrupt debtor a fresh start by wiping the slate clean of past debts and making it possible to begin again in business or in private life. In 1984 only some 240,000 people filed for bankruptcy; but in spite of recent measures by Congress to limit bankruptcies, according to a federal judiciary news release in 2007, nonbusiness filings for the fiscal year ending June 30, 2007, totaled 727,167, and business filings totaled 23,889.

The power to establish "uniform Laws on the subject of Bankruptcies throughout the United States" is one of several powers granted to Congress under Article I, section 8, of the Constitution. This provision has generated little controversy. JAMES MADISON, in essay 43 of *The Federalist* (1787–88) (see FEDERALIST PAPERS), written in support of RATIFICATION of the Constitution, simply argues that the "power of establishing uniform laws of bankruptcy is so intimately connected with the regulation of commerce [a power also extended to Congress by Article I, section 8], and will prevent so many frauds where the parties or their property may lie or be removed into different States, that the expediency of it seems not likely to be drawn into question" (see COMMERCE).

An End to Dickensian Practices

Congress has enacted a number of major federal bankruptcy laws, beginning with one in 1800 that generally copied the contemporaneous bankruptcy laws of England. Imprisonment for failure to repay a DEBT was standard procedure in England from the thirteenth century until around the time of Charles Dickens (1812–70), who wrote of the grim conditions of the poor and insolvent debtors and whose own father had been sent to the Marshalsea Debtors' prison in 1824. The word *bankruptcy* is derived from medieval Italian city-states' practice of literally breaking the bench of a merchant or a banker who had run off, leaving unpaid creditors. In the United States, imprisonment of debtors was abolished at the federal level in 1833 and in many states a few years later.

Although the need for uniform bankruptcy laws was behind the constitutional provision, state laws remained generally unfettered except for federal laws in effect during the periods 1800–1803, 1841–43, and 1867–78. The first permanent law was the Bankruptcy Act (1898), which remained in force, albeit with numerous amendments, until it was replaced by the Bankruptcy Reform Act

(1978). In brief, bankruptcy laws allow bankrupt debtors, including legal entities such as businesses, to discharge (cancel) their debts at less than 100 percent on the dollar and begin anew, generally free of their former debts. Federal bankruptcy laws are found in Title 11 of the U.S. Code. Chapter 7 sets forth procedures for individual and corporate debtors whose assets are to be liquidated. Chapter 11 provides primarily for corporate reorganization or restructuring short of liquidation, while chapter 13 details an alternative bankruptcy procedure for individuals with regular income.

In a bankruptcy proceeding, which is often a complex process, creditors generally receive funds from the insolvent debtor's assets to pay their claims or some portion thereof; assets such as a house may be exempted and thus protected from loss. A bankruptcy court supervises the process according to a list of priorities, which generally begin with the claims of federal and state governments for taxes due, followed by the claims of secured creditors (those such as banks and mortgage companies with rights to specific property in the event of a debtor's default), and, further down, the claims of unsecured creditors.

Rights of Debtors

In general, DUE PROCESS requires that debtors in bankruptcy have the chance to appear in court and contest a creditor's allegation of a default in payment. A creditor with a secured interest may without court authority seize the property securing the debt as long as a breach of the peace is not committed. A creditor may repossess a car, for example, but may not go into the debtor's home without the permission of the bankruptcy court. Other rights of the debtor include protection from the seizure of any tools of his or her trade, clothes, and household furnishings of little resale value. Many states also strictly limit the right of creditors to seize a debtor's paycheck and garnish wages, a process that requires employers to pay the creditor directly.

One constitutional issue relating to bankruptcy is the right of parties in a bankruptcy proceeding, usually debtors, to a trial by jury as provided for by the Seventh Amendment (1791) (see JURIES; TRIALS). The right to a jury trial, however, is complicated by the fact that bankruptcy court judges are not appointed for life like other federal judges in accordance with Article III of the Constitution. Because bankruptcy judges are not "constitutional judges," their authority to conduct jury trials has been questioned in the federal courts. The Bankruptcy Reform Act of 1978 established bankruptcy courts in each of the federal judicial districts and authorized the president to nominate the judges with Senate approval for fourteen-year terms. A ruling by the Supreme Court in *Northern Pipeline Construction Co. v. Marathon Pipe Line Co.* (1982) found unconstitutional provisions of the 1978 act investing the bankruptcy judges with "judicial power." The Court's subsequent decision in *Langenkamp v. Culp* (1990) indicated that the right to a jury trial in a bankruptcy proceeding was not yet clearly resolved.

A number of changes in the federal bankruptcy laws were codified in the Bankruptcy Abuse Prevention and Consumer Protection Act of 2005 (BAPCPA). In general the changes tightened the law and favored creditors over debtors. The bankruptcy code, as amended by the BAPCPA, was applied by the Supreme Court in *Howard Delivery Service, Inc. v. Zurich American Insurance Co.* (2006). In that case, the Court found that the insurance company's claims for unpaid workers' compensation premiums owed by the employer in bankruptcy were farther down the priority list of debtors than pension plans and group health, life, and disability insurance, which were more analogous to employee fringe benefits that are included in an employee's pay package and are given priority under the law.

Federal and State Jurisdiction

In 1819 the Supreme Court held in *Sturges v. Crowninshield* that in the absence of national bankruptcy laws, the states were free to enact laws regarding insolvency. Then in *International Shoe Co.*

More on this topic:

Federalism, p. 218

v. Pinkus (1929), the Court concluded that the states could continue to enact their own insolvency laws as long as they did not cover areas preempted by national bankruptcy laws. In several later cases, however, the Court refused to provide a general formula for what constituted national preemption of state laws.

Because some state bankruptcy laws continue to exist side by side with the federal laws, they occasionally come into conflict. In *Ohio v. Kovacs* (1985), the Supreme Court voided a state court order directing a bankrupt corporation to clean up a waste disposal site after the Court determined that the company's responsibility to clean up the site could be discharged in the bankruptcy proceeding. However, according to the Court in *Tua v. Carriere* (1886) and *Butler v. Goreley* (1892), state bankruptcy laws that are currently preempted by the federal bankruptcy laws continue to exist in a state of suspended animation, ready to spring back into life if Congress should repeal the national laws.

Bill of Rights

Although England first enacted a Bill of Rights in 1688, those rights belonged to Parliament, not to the people; their rights and their constitution itself were at the mercy of Parliament—the House of Lords, the House of Commons, and the monarch. Another more meaningful Bill of Rights, the first ten AMENDMENTS to the U.S. CONSTITUTION, was ratified in 1791, two years after the Constitution became the nation's supreme law. Together with the Declaration of the Rights of Man and of the Citizen (1789), which grew out of the 1789 French Revolution, the Bill of Rights has inspired the inclusion of guarantees of individual rights and freedoms in many national constitutions as well as in international and regional human rights documents, such as the United Nations' Universal Declaration of Human Rights (1948) and the European Convention for the Protection of Human Rights and Fundamental Freedoms (1950). Their protections for such fundamental human aspirations as the rights to speak freely and publish opinions, meet in the public arena, hold personal beliefs, and be secure in one's own home and property have become a model for the rest of the world. (British citizens finally got a bill of rights when the European Convention was incorporated into British law in 2000.)

Yet, in essay 84 of *The Federalist* (1787–88) (see FEDERALIST PAPERS), written to support RATIFICATION of the Constitution, ALEXANDER HAMILTON concluded that bills of rights "have no application to constitutions, professedly founded upon the power of the people and executed by their immediate representatives." He also pointed out that the Constitution as drafted in 1787 contained a number of guaranteed rights, including a prohibition against EX POST FACTO LAWS, safeguards for those faced with TREASON charges, and the right to a jury trial in criminal cases. Nevertheless, certain opponents of the new Constitution—Anti-Federalists who argued against a stronger central government than the one created by the ARTICLES OF CONFEDERATION—used the lack of a bill of rights as a persuasive argument that the Constitution should not be ratified.

GEORGE MASON, the author of the Virginia Declaration of Rights (1776), commented during the last days of the CONSTITUTIONAL CONVENTION OF 1787 that a bill of rights prefacing the Constitution would allay public fears, while JAMES MADISON suggested making changes to the Constitution's text rather than writing an addendum. THOMAS JEFFERSON, in an attempt to change Madison's position against the inclusion of a bill of rights, argued simply that it could do no harm. Later, when the delegates to state conventions began debating ratification of the Constitution, some states recommended a bill of rights, and proponents of the Constitution, including Madison, pledged to add a bill of rights to ensure ratification especially in battleground states such as New York, North Carolina, and Virginia, in which opposition to the Constitution was particularly strong. Madison,

BILL OF RIGHTS

I: Freedom of Speech, Press, Religion, and Petition
Congress shall make no law respecting an establishment of religion, or prohibiting the free exercise thereof; or abridging the freedom of speech, or of the press; or the right of the people peaceably to assemble, and to petition the Government for a redress of grievances.

II: Right to keep and bear arms
A well-regulated Militia, being necessary to the security of a free State, the right of the people to keep and bear Arms, shall not be infringed.

III: Conditions for quartering of soldiers
No Soldier shall, in time of peace be quartered in any house, without the consent of the Owner, nor in time of war, but in a manner to be prescribed by law.

IV: Right of search and seizure regulated
The right of the people to be secure in their persons, houses, papers, and effects, against unreasonable searches and seizures, shall not be violated, and no Warrants shall issue, but upon probable cause, supported by Oath or affirmation, and particularly describing the place to be searched, and the persons or things to be seized.

V: Provisions concerning prosecution
No person shall be held to answer for a capital, or otherwise infamous crime, unless on a presentment or indictment of a Grand Jury, except in cases arising in the land or naval forces, or in the Militia, when in actual service in time of War or public danger; nor shall any person be subject for the same offense to be twice put in jeopardy of life or limb; nor shall be compelled in any criminal case to be a witness against himself, nor be deprived of life, liberty, or property, without due process of law; nor shall private property be taken for public use without just compensation.

VI: Right to a speedy trial, witnesses, and counsel
In all criminal prosecutions, the accused shall enjoy the right to a speedy and public trial, by an impartial jury of the State and district wherein the crime shall have been committed, which district shall have been previously ascertained by law, and to be informed of the nature and cause of the accusation; to be confronted with the witnesses against him; to have compulsory process for obtaining witnesses in his favor, and to have the Assistance of Counsel for his defense.

VII: Right to a trial by jury
In Suits at common law, where the value in controversy shall exceed twenty dollars, the right of trial by jury shall be preserved, and no fact tried by a jury shall be otherwise reexamined in any Court of the United States, than according to the rules of the common law.

VIII: Excessive bail, cruel punishment
Excessive bail shall not be required, nor excessive fines imposed, nor cruel and unusual punishments inflicted.

IX: Rule of construction of Constitution
The enumeration in the Constitution, of certain rights, shall not be construed to deny or disparage others retained by the people.

X: Rights of the States under the Constitution
The powers not delegated to the United States by the Constitution, nor prohibited by it to the States, are reserved to the States respectively, or to the people.

Note: The titles are not part of the original document.

his mind changed by Jefferson and the ratification struggle, himself introduced a draft of amendments in the House of Representatives on June 8, 1789. Freedom of speech was added to the final list of rights, which in the end was written as separate amendments to the Constitution.

On September 25, 1789, the first twelve amendments were proposed to the state legislatures by the first Congress. The first one, governing the apportionment of the House of Representatives, has never been ratified; the second, governing pay raises for senators and congressmen, took effect only in 1992 as the Twenty-seventh Amendment after having been ratified by forty of the fifty states. Ten of the twelve amendments, constituting the Bill of Rights, were deemed ratified on December 15, 1791, following approval by, in order, New Jersey, Maryland, North Carolina, South Carolina, New Hampshire, Delaware, New York, Pennsylvania, Rhode Island, Vermont, and, finally, Virginia. Not until 1939 did Massachusetts, Georgia, and Connecticut follow suit and sign on to the Bill of Rights.

The First Ten Amendments

The First Amendment is often considered the most important for its guarantees of freedom of SPEECH, THE PRESS, RELIGION, and assembly. The national government's tolerance for open political debate both by the citizenry and in the press, for peaceful assembly by the citizens in order to petition the government for the redress of grievances (see ASSEMBLY AND ASSOCIATION), and for freedom of conscience as embodied in the freedom of religion guarantee was an unprecedented step for a nation to take on the road to universal human rights.

The Second Amendment—asserting a right to bear arms—remains ambiguous two centuries later because of its coupling in the document with the words "A well regulated Militia." No other major nation recognizes the right of the people to bear arms. In fact, one of the basic indicators of a sovereign authority is a monopoly on the use of force. At the end of the twentieth century the amendment gained heightened importance as a major national issue with regard to GUN CONTROL laws and the movement to keep firearms out of the hands of criminals, paramilitary organizations, and children.

The Third Amendment, dealing with quartering soldiers in private homes, is no longer relevant, but the Fourth Amendment's protection of the people's right "to be secure in their persons, houses, papers, and effects, against unreasonable searches and seizures" has been a source of much litigation (see SEARCH AND SEIZURE). LAW ENFORCEMENT officials who gather evidence against alleged criminals often come head to head with the amendment's guarantees over arrests as well as searches and seizures of evidence from automobiles, prisons, schools, and homes; at airports and border crossings; and as a result of electronic surveillance (wiretapping).

Perhaps the most famous provision in the Bill of Rights is the Fifth Amendment. WITNESSES and defendants are almost stereotypically reported to have "taken the Fifth" rather than risk testifying against themselves either in court or before congressional committees. This protection requires certain standards before one is charged with a "capital, or otherwise infamous crime" and prohibits DOUBLE JEOPARDY (being tried twice for the same offense), compelling a person "to be a witness against" himself, or depriving someone of life, LIBERTY, or PROPERTY "without due process of law...." It also bars the taking of "private property...for public use without just compensation" (see JUST COMPENSATION; PROPERTY). Many of these standards for prosecution evolved under English COMMON LAW and later in the American colonies and states. They are corollaries of the unexpressed right of any citizen charged with commission of a crime to a presumption of innocence, such that the burden of proof lies with the state to prove guilt rather than with the defendant to prove his or her innocence. The requirement for DUE PROCESS of law extends as far back as England's Magna Carta (1215).

The Sixth Amendment offers further rights to persons accused of crimes, including the right to a "speedy and public trial" (see TRIALS), an impartial jury (see JURIES), information as to the nature and cause of the accusation, the right to confront witnesses, and the right to have the ASSISTANCE OF COUNSEL.

The Seventh Amendment guarantees the right to a jury trial in civil suits and sets the standard that facts tried by a jury cannot be reviewed on appeal.

The Eighth Amendment completes the guarantees of the rights of persons accused or found guilty of crimes by prohibiting excessive BAIL and fines as well as "cruel and unusual punishments" (see CRUEL AND UNUSUAL PUNISHMENT).

The Ninth Amendment, to avoid the general rule of statutory interpretation that items not expressly included in a list of items are therefore excluded, clearly provides that the rights enumerated in the Constitution "shall not be construed to deny or disparage others retained by the people."

The Tenth Amendment similarly declares that the "powers not delegated to the United States by the Constitution, nor prohibited by it to the States, are reserved to the States respectively, or to the people." This amendment was intended to do no more than state the obvious with respect to the nature of the relationship between the federal and state governments. However, from about 1835 to 1937, the Tenth Amendment reinforced Supreme Court decisions limiting the national government's powers vis-á-vis the states (see FEDERALISM) in matters involving taxes (see TAXATION), the regulation of COMMERCE, and enforcement of the rights guaranteed under the Fourteenth Amendment (1868).

Ratified shortly after the Civil War, the Fourteenth Amendment has become a vehicle for requiring that most of the guarantees in the Bill of Rights be observed also by the states, not just the federal government, to which they were originally intended to apply exclusively (see INCORPORATION DOCTRINE). For example, between 1927 and 1979 rights guaranteed in the First, Fourth, Fifth, Sixth, and Eighth Amendments were made enforceable against the states as well as the national government. Citizens in the states thus have the right to assistance of counsel and an impartial jury and protections against cruel and unusual punishment and unreasonable searches and seizures in state as well as federal actions.

Since ratification of the Bill of Rights in 1791, only seventeen other amendments to the Constitution have been approved—including what was originally to have been the second amendment (barring senators and representatives from receiving a pay increase until after an intervening election), which was finally approved in 1992 as the Twenty-seventh Amendment.

More on this topic:
Constitution, U.S., p. 115
Criminal Law, p. 132
Human Rights, p. 283
Incorporation Doctrine, p. 297
The Press, p. 425
Religion, p. 458
Rights, p. 469
Speech, p. 512

Bills   *See* LEGISLATION.

Borrowing Power   *See* CONGRESS; DEBT.

Branches of Government   *See* EXECUTIVE BRANCH; JUDICIAL BRANCH; LEGISLATIVE BRANCH; SEPARATION OF POWERS.

Broadcasting   *See* COMMUNICATIONS.

Brown v. Board of Education of Topeka

For some delegates to the CONSTITUTIONAL CONVENTION OF 1787, drafting a new Constitution may have presented an opportunity to curb or even abolish the practice of SLAVERY, but they were inhibited by the risk of antagonizing the major slave-holding states and losing them from the Union. The problem of slavery, however, continued to fester until the Civil War (1861–65), with its tremendous loss of American lives, decisively ended it.

Adopted after the war, the Thirteenth (1865) and Fourteenth (1868) Amendments were intended to erase slavery and establish an equality of citizenship for former slaves and their families. "Neither slavery nor involuntary servitude, except as a punishment for crime whereof the party shall have been duly convicted, shall exist within the United States, or any place subject to their jurisdiction," mandated the Thirteenth Amendment. The relevant provision of the Fourteenth Amendment is section 1: "All persons born or naturalized in the United States, and subject to the jurisdiction thereof, are citizens of the United States and of the State wherein they reside. No State shall make or enforce any law which shall abridge the privileges or immunities of citizens of the United States; nor shall any State deprive any person of life, liberty, or property, without due process of law; nor deny to any person within its jurisdiction the equal protection of the laws." Despite this egalitarian language, the old practice of

The landmark decision in **Brown v. Board of Education** *paved the way for black children and white children to go to the same classes.*
Source: Library of Congress

slavery was transformed into a virulent form of government-condoned prejudice and discrimination.

In *Plessy v. Ferguson* (1896), the Supreme Court suggested that the Thirteenth and Fourteenth Amendments were not offended by "separate but equal" railroad cars for whites and "coloreds"—Plessy, a citizen of Louisiana, had "seven-eighths Caucasian and one-eighth African blood." In cases after World War II, culminating in *Sweatt v. Painter* and *McLaurin v. Oklahoma State Regents* (both 1950), the Court whittled away at the "separate but equal" principle, finding specific inequalities on the graduate school level as denials of EQUAL PROTECTION under the Fourteenth Amendment. The first case involved a black applicant's denial of admission to the University of Texas Law School, while the second took up the case of a black student segregated in a doctorate of education program at the University of Oklahoma. But the Court did not confront the principle head on until 1954, in the suit filed on behalf of Linda Brown and other black students prohibited from attending a white school in Topeka, Kansas.

In *Brown*, in a rare statement of contrition on behalf of previous members of the Supreme Court, Chief Justice Earl Warren (1891–1974) wrote for a unanimous majority, "We cannot turn the clock back to 1868 when the [Fourteenth] Amendment was adopted, or even to 1896 when *Plessy v. Ferguson* was written." Summing up the basis for striking down the "separate but equal" principle of keeping the races apart, he said: "Segregation of white and colored children in public schools has a detrimental effect upon the colored children. The impact is greater when it has the sanction of the law; for the policy of separating the races is usually interpreted as denoting the inferiority of the negro group."

After this initial decision, finding that RACIAL DISCRIMINATION in public schools was unconstitutional, often referred to as *Brown I*, the Supreme Court issued another decision the following year—in *Brown v. Board of Education of Topeka* (1955), known as *Brown II*—providing guidance for implementing the original case. Integration of the public schools did not always proceed smoothly, however, and a number of political leaders in states in the South—Governors Orval Faubus in Arkansas and George Wallace in Alabama, for example—tried to derail the federally mandated integration plans. Under the Constitution, however, the *Brown* decision was the law of the land, and it set in motion additional efforts by CIVIL RIGHTS leaders such as MARTIN LUTHER KING JR. to challenge other discriminatory policies and practices that were obstacles on the road to a truly integrated American society.

Since *Brown*, the unconstitutional status of de jure segregation—that is, segregation imposed by law—of the public schools in America has become accepted. However, the problem of de facto segregation—resulting from where people live—remains a subject of contention. The Supreme Court ruled 5–4 in *Parents Involved in Community Schools v. Seattle School District No. 1* and *Meredith v. Jefferson County Board of Education* (both 2007) that the school admission pro-

More on this topic:

grams in question, which sought to create more racially diverse public schools, violated the equal protection clause of the Constitution. Some proponents of attempts to ameliorate de facto segregation saw these rulings as an erosion of the *Brown* decision.

Buckley v. Valeo

In 1971 Congress passed and President Richard M. Nixon (1913–94) signed into law the Federal Election Campaign Act (FECA), which required political committees as well as candidates to provide information identifying contributors to election campaigns. A revenue act the same year allowed each taxpayer to contribute one dollar to finance presidential campaigns. After Nixon's 1974 resignation in the wake of the WATERGATE scandals—arising, ironically, out of his campaign abuses—FECA was amended to limit the amount of money an individual could contribute per election: $1,000 to a single candidate and a total of $25,000 to all candidates, party committees, and political action committees (PACs). Public financing of presidential ELECTIONS was also extended to party nomination campaigns.

The law was immediately challenged by James L. Buckley, Conservative Party senator from New York; the American Civil Liberties Union, which regularly challenges the constitutionality of potential infringements of individual rights; and the American Conservative Union. Their basic argument was that limits on campaign contributions and spending are an unconstitutional restriction of the right to express political ideas, a basic requirement in a democratic society (see FUNDAMENTAL RIGHTS; SPEECH).

In *Buckley v. Valeo* (1976), the Supreme Court upheld the constitutionality of the act's provisions governing public financing of presidential candidates and limiting campaign contributions. With respect to the latter, the Court reasoned that such limitations furthered the government's compelling interest in avoiding the actuality and the appearance of corruption—for example, among candidates who owe political favors to large contributors—without unnecessarily limiting the contributors' right to promote their candidates or policies. However, the Court struck down the limitations on campaign spending, reasoning that money was a form of speech and that the Constitution prohibits the government from placing "direct quantity restrictions on political communication and association."

Sen. James L. Buckley, Conservative-Republican from New York, was the lead plaintiff in the lawsuit that set the ground rules of campaign finance for more than two decades.
Source: U.S. Congress

In *Buckley* the Court thus balanced the effects of government restrictions on contributions and on spending. The burden on political expression resulting from restrictions on contributions was acceptable, it found, while the burden on political expression resulting from limitations on spending was too great. According to the Court, the "quantity of communication by the contributor does not increase perceptively with the size of his contribution"; the symbolic act of contributing is the essence of the political communication. With respect to political expenditures, however, the Court inferred that wealthy people would be discriminated against by the expenditure limitation: "[T]he concept that government may restrict the speech of some elements of our society in order to enhance the relative voice of others is wholly foreign to the First Amendment, which was designed to secure the widest possible dissemination of information."

Since the *Buckley* decision, both the courts and Congress have struggled with its implications. The current system of campaign financing, especially at the national level, seems to remain a matter of concern because of the possibility of undue influence by large contributors and the expanding amount of time and effort necessary to raise money for political campaigns. But the issue has not gained much traction, particularly among the politicians who would be most affected by additional reforms.

The Supreme Court, in *Nixon v. Shrink Missouri Government PAC* (2000), reviewed a state law that limited contributions to state candidates. In a 6–3 decision, the Court upheld the grant of considerably greater deference to legislatures in crafting limits on campaign contributions, as opposed to limits on campaign expenditures as spelled out in the *Buckley* decision. Such limitations will not run afoul of the First Amendment if they are "closely drawn" and reflect a "sufficiently important interest." But in *Randall v. Sorrell* (2006), a less cohesive Court, while not overruling *Buckley*, invalidated a Vermont campaign limitation on expenditures and, for the first time, struck down limitations on contributions for being too low—$400 for the gubernatorial race, $300 for a state senate race, and $200 for a state representatives race. Three members of the Court indicated they believed *Buckley* should be overruled: Justices Clarence Thomas and Antonin Scalia, to invalidate restrictions on contributions; and Justice Stevens, for the opposite reason, to allow limitations on expenditures.

Budget

In 2000 the overall budget for the United States for fiscal year 2001 (extending from October 1, 2000, to September 30, 2001) totaled $2.019 trillion in projected revenues and $1.835 trillion in projected outlays, resulting in a projected surplus of $184 billion. By contrast, in 2007 the figures projected for fiscal year 2008 are a total of $2.720 trillion in revenues with outlays of $2.818 trillion and a resulting deficit of $98 billion, according to the Congressional Budget Office. Although the Constitution does not mention a national budget (from a French word for a small leather bag or wallet), it clearly establishes procedures for raising revenue and spending and accounting for public funds, all of which reflect a conscious system of checks and balances.

"All Bills for raising Revenue," begins Article I, section 7, "shall originate in the House of Representatives; but the Senate may propose or concur with amendments as on other Bills...." According to section 8, CONGRESS has the power, among other things, "[t]o lay and collect Taxes, Duties, Imposts and Excises, [and] to pay the Debts...." Section 9 provides in part: "No Money shall be drawn from the Treasury, but in Consequence of Appropriations made by Law; and a regular Statement and Account of the Receipts and Expenditures of all public Money shall be published from time to time." The federal budget process has evolved from these provisions and others, including the powers granted to Congress, also enumerated in Article I, section 8, to "borrow Money on the Credit of the United States" (see DEBT) and to "coin Money, [and] regulate the value thereof..." (see CURRENCY).

A Four-Step Process

The budget process has basically four steps, although each step involves many detailed procedures.

(1) The PRESIDENT submits to Congress, usually shortly after the first of each calendar year, a proposed budget for the next fiscal year, which begins on October 1. In it he presents the Treasury Department's estimates of the expected revenues and the EXECUTIVE BRANCH's estimates of future spending, combining all the estimates of all national government obligations (activities that will require payment at some time in the future), including those for Congress and the federal courts.

(2) The two houses of Congress—the HOUSE OF REPRESENTATIVES and the SENATE—analyze the president's proposed budget and invariably make changes. Sometimes Congress drafts its own budget proposal, which presents the congressional leadership's version of revenues and expenditures. Negotiations among the members of each house, between the houses, and between Congress and the president lead to a final budget bill, with all the details approved. As with any other law (see LEGISLATION), it is then enacted by Congress and signed by the president.

(3) The third step is the execution phase. The administration, under the president's supervision, collects the revenues or borrows funds and spends the money in accordance with the budget law for the current fiscal year.

(4) Last comes the accounting phase. Although accounting is in fact a continuous process, an annual accounting for the past fiscal year, based on the figures available at the time, is presented along with the new budget submitted to Congress by the president.

The budget process was regularized by Congress through the Budget and Accounting Act (1921), under which it was formally delegated to the president, thus greatly increasing the chief executive's power. Details were handled by the executive branch's Bureau of the Budget, which in 1969 became the Office of Management and Budget with increased power over the executive departments' budget formulation process. The Budget Act (1974), anticipating the development of congressional as well as executive branch budget plans, attempted to give more control over the process to Congress. The act created permanent budget committees in each house.

On several occasions, especially during periods of large budget deficits, attempts have been made in Congress to pass a proposed balanced-budget amendment to the Constitution. The purpose of such an amendment would be to require a supermajority vote in Congress to deviate from a balanced budget, one in which projected spending would always be equal to or less than projected revenue. Arizona, California, and some other state constitutions require a balanced state budget, and the notion of a balanced national budget has been around since at least the 1930s. In 1995 a proposed constitutional amendment requiring a balanced budget lost by one vote in the Senate, a cliffhanger that was repeated in 1997. It is hard to make a case for the amendment (see AMENDMENTS). Many experts find little wrong with the government's running a deficit, especially if the programs being financed are necessary for national security or domestic economic growth. Why, they ask, should the government's hands be tied in the future in dealing effectively with crises that may require deficit spending?

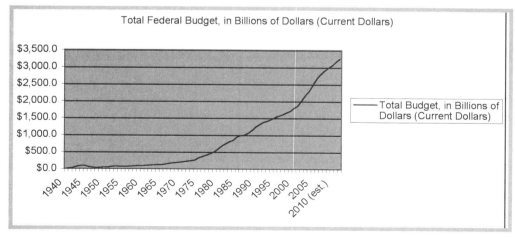

The size of the federal budget has increased exponentially since the pre–World War II era.
Source: Harold W. Stanley and Richard G. Niemi, *Vital Statistics on American Politics 2007–2008* (Washington, D.C.: CQ Press, 2008).

The "Power of the Purse"

Article I, section 9, which prohibits expenditures of funds from the Treasury except "in Consequence of Appropriations made by Law," restricts the president from using public funds not appropriated by Congress. This "power of the purse" is an important check on the executive branch (see SEPARATION OF POWERS). The Supreme Court held in *United States v. Price* (1885) that there is no check on Congress's power to direct payments from the Treasury, and neither the executive nor the judicial branch may prevent it. Congress need not expressly designate how all appropriated funds must be spent but can delegate this authority to executive branch officials.

If the Constitution restricts the president to making expenditures only on the basis of appropriated funds, can the president impound (refuse to spend) funds appropriated by Congress? Between 1969 and 1973, President Richard M. Nixon (1913–94) impounded more than $15 billion dollars in funds appropriated for domestic programs by a Democratic Party–controlled Congress. Nixon claimed the right to refuse to spend these funds, but in *Train v. City of New York* (1975), decided six months after Nixon resigned (see WATERGATE), the Supreme Court held that one of these refusals to spend appropriated funds was illegal. The decision implied that the president has no general constitutional authority to refuse to spend appropriated funds.

In 1996 Congress passed the Line Item Veto Act (see VETOES) in an attempt to delegate to the executive branch the power to strike single entries (line items) in the budget as passed by Congress. Without the line-item veto power, the president's only recourse is to veto the entire budget bill if he disagrees with any part of it. In *Clinton v. City of New York* (1998), however, the Supreme Court found the act unconstitutional, because it would allow the president to sign into law something different from what had passed the two houses of Congress. Article I, section 7, provides that to become law a bill passed by Congress must be presented to the president for his signature: "Every Bill which shall have passed the House of Representatives and the Senate, shall, before it become a Law, be presented to the President of the United States...." There is no constitutional basis for Congress's granting the president the power to change a bill after it has passed both houses. As *MARBURY V. MADISON* (1803) established, one branch of government cannot grant to another powers that are not countenanced by the Constitution.

More on this topic:

Taxation, p. 533

Bush v. Gore

The SUPREME COURT's extraordinary decision in *Bush v. Gore*, issued on December 12, 2000, a little over a month after the presidential election held on November 7, has generated dozens of books but surprisingly little concern from the American public. It may be that citizens did not understand the Court's decision, in which—for the first time in the nation's history—the unelected and virtually unaccountable JUDICIAL BRANCH of the federal government decided who the next PRESIDENT would be.

Albert Gore Jr. (b. 1948), vice president of the United States, and George W. Bush (b. 1946), governor of Texas, were the nominees of the Democratic and Republican Parties, respectively. On November 7 voters went to the polls to elect members of the ELECTORAL COLLEGE, who under Article II, section 1, of the Constitution choose the president and vice president on the basis of each state's election results. Reports on election night indicated that the presidential contest was so close that the candidate who received Florida's twenty-five electoral votes would have a majority in the electoral college, thus becoming the forty-third president.

The Florida results were extremely close—reported on November 8 to be 2,909,135 for Bush and 2,907,351 for Gore, and the state's voting procedures were later called into question for faulty ballots and potential CIVIL RIGHTS violations. Using Florida law, Gore requested recounts of the votes in some voting precincts. To summarize a complex chain of events, the recounts took a relatively long time to perform and were marked by disputes among Florida election officials and Republican and Democratic Party observers about the manner and accuracy of the recount procedures in some precincts. The word *chad*, referring to a dangling, partially punched hole in a voting card, entered the American lexicon.

On December 8 the Florida Supreme Court, after two appeals on Gore's behalf, ordered that the circuit court of Leon County tabulate by hand nine thousand ballots cast in Miami–Dade County and that other tabulated ballots be included in the official state certification of election returns. An emergency petition was immediately filed with the U.S. Supreme Court on behalf of George W. Bush and his vice presidential running mate, Dick Cheney, requesting a stay of the Florida Supreme Court's order. The Court granted the petition on December 9.

The Supreme Court's ruling in *Bush v. Gore* three days later acknowledged the role of the states in the presidential electoral process under Article II, section 1: "The individual citizen has no federal constitutional right to vote for electors for the President of the United States unless and until the state legislature chooses a statewide election as the means to implement its power to appoint members of the Electoral College." Citing *McPherson v. Blacker* (1892), the Court, in its 5–4 *per curiam* opinion ("by the court"), noted that the state legislature could select both the electors and the manner in which they are chosen. At that time the Republican Party held a majority of the seats in the Florida legislature.

Protestors line the steps to the Supreme Court, carrying large banners displaying their positions in the disputed 2000 presidential election between Bush and Gore. Five of the nine appointed justices tipped the election to Bush, who took offce by a margin of just five electoral votes.
Source: Reuters

"[T]he right to vote is protected in more than the initial allocation of the franchise," contended the decision. "Equal protection [guaranteed under the Fourteenth Amendment (1868)] applies as well to the manner of its exercise." Using this underpinning, the Supreme Court then addressed the question of "whether the recount procedures the Florida Supreme Court adopted are consistent with its obligation to avoid arbitrary and disparate treatment of the electorate." Here the Court was echoing the arguments of the two parties: Gore contended that an imperfect election process should be remedied by a recount of ballots, no matter how long such a recount took. Bush maintained that the election process had to come to a conclusion in a reasonable time, regardless of whether that meant an inaccurate count. December 18 was the date set by Congress for the electoral college delegates to meet, but a "safe harbor" provision made a state's selection of delegates "conclusive" if filed at least six days before the meeting, or December 12.

"[I]t is obvious," decided the prevailing justices, "that the recount cannot be conducted in compliance with requirements of equal protection and due process without substantial additional work" (see DUE PROCESS; EQUAL PROTECTION). The Florida election law "requires that any controversy or contest that is designed to lead to a conclusive selection of electors be complete by December 12…[and] it is evident that any recount seeking to meet the December 12 date will be unconstitutional.…" Accordingly the Court reversed the Florida Supreme Court's decision ordering a recount, thus ending the election process in Florida. Bush then became the president-elect by a margin of 271–266 electoral college votes (one more than needed to win), although he lost the nationwide popular vote to Gore.

The Constitution does not give the Supreme Court a role in the election of the president and vice president, but the winner of the 2000 U.S. presidential election was selected by the Supreme Court—or, more accurately, by five of the Court's more conservative members: William Rehnquist (1924–2005), SANDRA DAY O'CONNOR, Antonin Scalia (b. 1936), Anthony M. Kennedy (b. 1936), and Clarence Thomas (b. 1948). The dissenters—John Paul Stevens (b. 1920), Ruth Bader Ginsburg (b. 1933), Stephen G. Breyer (b. 1938), and David H. Souter (b. 1939)—focused on the deference that the Supreme Court should have given, as it generally has in other cases, to the Florida Supreme Court's efforts to accommodate the requested recount. Such deference would have avoided the need for the Supreme Court to interfere in what was constitutionally a matter for Florida to decide. Justice Souter addressed the equal protection argument, which had been used by the majority to reach its decision, to recommend that the matter be remanded to the Florida Supreme Court "with instructions to establish a uniform standard for evaluating the several types of ballots involved in the recount." This would have provided the equal protection required by the Court's majority, which Souter believed could still be accomplished by the December 18 date set for the meeting of the electoral college.

The Supreme Court's decision to accept *Bush v. Gore* and rule on the grounds it did will be debated by constitutional scholars and political activists—if not citizens—for a long time. In essence, however, whether a full and final recount of Florida's contested votes would have given Gore or Bush the presidency had the Supreme Court not intervened makes little difference. Elections, like Supreme Court decisions, are focused on giving finality to disputes. Whether elections or court decisions are right or wrong sometimes becomes not as important as the fact that they put an end to disputes and thus must be accepted by the people and the parties. Legal decisions can be reversed, and new elections can change the nation's political climate.

Recounts of the Florida vote continued informally after the election. One study by the National Opinion Research Center of the University of Chicago was commissioned by a group of major national newspapers. Its findings, made public on November 12, 2001, a year after the Supreme Court's decision, showed that the two partial recounts that were aborted would likely have let Bush's slim lead stand, while a review of all uncounted ballots or a statewide recount of all disputed ballots would likely have given the lead to Gore.

Cabinet

President William McKinley (1843–1901) (far left) meets with his cabinet around 1900. Serving as appointed advisers to the chief executive and head of their administrative agencies, the cabinet closely reflects the president's policies and agenda.
Source: Library of Congress

In England, the parliamentary cabinet evolved from the monarch's privy council, made up of advisers who often met in a small room or cabinet. In a parliamentary system of government, like the United Kingdom's, the cabinet *is* the national government. All executive decisions of importance are "taken in cabinet," meaning that the prime minister (the head of government) consults with cabinet members and obtains the majority's approval before taking action. Cabinet members, who are selected by the prime minister and approved by the parliament, are generally parliamentary members who represent it as well as their political parties and constituents.

Cabinet members, like the prime minister, are responsible to the parliament for their decisions and conduct. A parliamentary vote of no confidence in the government generally leads to new elections, in which members and supporters of that government try to make a case to the voters for why they should remain in power; if they fail, they are replaced by new leadership. An individual minister may also lose his or her cabinet position by a no-confidence vote in the parliament.

Advisory, Not Policy-Making Positions

Under the U.S. Constitution, the cabinet consists chiefly of the heads of departments in the EXECUTIVE BRANCH, who are appointed by the PRESIDENT with the ADVICE AND CONSENT of the senate (see APPOINTMENT AND REMOVAL POWER). They serve as both presidential advisers and subordinates who carry out the president's policies. In contrast to a parliamentary system, the American president does not have to consult the cabinet or obtain its approval for important policy decisions or actions.

The first cabinet—GEORGE WASHINGTON's—consisted of the secretary of state, THOMAS JEFFERSON; secretary of the Treasury, ALEXANDER HAMILTON; secretary of war (renamed secretary of defense in 1947), Major General Henry Knox; and attorney general, Edmund Randolph (the Department of Justice was established in 1870). The cabinet has since added the secretaries of the interior (1849), agriculture (1889), commerce (1913), labor (1913), housing and urban development (1965), transportation (1966), energy (1977), health and human services (1980), education (1980), veterans affairs (1989), and homeland security (2003). Cabinets since Washington's administration have tended to reflect the president's management style. Harry S. Truman (1884–1972), for instance, tried to use his cabinet like a board of directors, asking for a vote on some policy issues.

Tom Ridge is sworn in as the first secretary of the newly created Department of Homeland Security in 2003, as President George W. Bush looks on.
Source: AP Images/Ron Edmonds

The Constitution does not use the term *cabinet*, but it refers to the appointment of such officers and the requirement that they report to the president when requested. Article II, section 2, indicates that the president "shall nominate, and by and with the Advice and Consent of the Senate, shall appoint...all other Officers of the United States, whose Appointments are not herein otherwise provided for, and which shall be established by Law...." Article II, section 1, notes that the president "may require the Opinion, in writing, of the principal Officer in each of the executive Departments, upon any Subject relating to the Duties of their respective Offices...."

Although the cabinet is not explicitly a constitutional body, presidents since Washington have to a greater or lesser degree met formally with their cabinet officers. The Constitution's lack of specificity about the cabinet's role may be the result of a last-minute effort at the CONSTITUTIONAL CONVENTION OF 1787 to reject the concept of a council of state. Proposed by Gouverneur Morris, a delegate from Pennsylvania (see FRAMERS OF THE CONSTITUTION), this advisory body to the president would have included the CHIEF JUSTICE and the heads of departments appointed by the president. In essay 70 of *The Federalist* (1787–88) (see FEDERALIST PAPERS), Alexander Hamilton criticized the idea of an advisory council: "A council to a magistrate, who is himself responsible for what he does, are generally nothing better than a clog upon his good intentions; are often the instruments and accomplices of his bad [intentions], and are almost always a cloak to his faults."

Cabinet members serve at the pleasure of the president and may be dismissed as the chief executive sees fit. The first IMPEACHMENT of an American president occurred in 1868 after President Andrew Johnson (1808–75) attempted to fire the secretary of war appointed by his predecessor, ABRAHAM LINCOLN. The problem arose because Congress had passed a law over Johnson's veto unconstitutionally requiring the Senate's consent for the president to remove any officer who had been appointed with its approval (see VETOES).

Department secretaries are constitutionally bound by the doctrines of the SEPARATION OF POWERS and checks and balances that apply to the executive branch of government as a whole. In *Kendall v. United States ex rel. Stokes* (1838), the postmaster general, then a cabinet-level position, was ordered by the Supreme Court to pay out money owed by the United States as a ministerial (required) rather than a discretionary act. The Court held that the president had "no other control over the officer than to see that he acts honestly, with proper motives."

Authorization and financing of cabinet positions, the executive departments, and their programs require congressional approval. CONGRESS may also request that cabinet members appear before its budget, oversight, and investigative committees to answer questions regarding their past and proposed actions. All cabinet members function as advisers to the president when asked for their opinions either informally or as required under Article II, section 2, and as supervisors of vast departments implementing the laws of the United States and the president's policies.

Different presidents have had different relationships with their cabinets and cabinet members. Some presidents have relied heavily on their cabinets for advice and support of policy decisions; others have expected them simply to execute the administration's programs. Andrew Jackson (1767–1845) tended to rely more on his "kitchen cabinet," an unofficial advisory group of friends, than on the heads of the executive departments. Robert F. Kennedy, appointed attorney general by his brother, John F. Kennedy (1917–63), was the president's closest personal confidant; his opinion carried far more weight with the president than that of any other cabinet member.

A 1947 law, passed at the request of President Truman, who had succeeded Franklin D. Roosevelt (1882–1945), set the order of succession to the presidency in the event of the president's death or disability. After the vice president, Speaker of the House, and president pro tempore of the Senate, the line of succession passes to the cabinet secretaries in the order in which their departments were established, beginning with the secretaries of state, Treasury, and defense and the attorney general.

Secretary of State

Article II, section 2, empowers the president to "make Treaties" and "nominate...and appoint Ambassadors, other public Ministers and Consuls..." (see AMBASSADORS; TREATIES). As interpreted by the courts, these powers make the president the nation's chief public official when it comes to conducting FOREIGN AFFAIRS. The secretary of state assists the president in maintaining foreign relations and supervises the activities of the Department of State, which supports and staffs U.S. embassies in foreign countries and monitors regional and international diplomatic information.

Secretary of the Treasury

Every country has some form of treasury department or ministry responsible for managing the government's revenues and expenditures. Article I, section 9, of the U.S. Constitution provides: "No Money shall be drawn from the Treasury, but in Consequence of Appropriations made by

Law; and a regular Statement and Account of the receipts and Expenditures of all public Money shall be published from time to time." The secretary of the Treasury oversees the management of the federal government's monetary resources by regulating banks, collecting income taxes and customs duties, and producing the bills and coins of the United States. The department is also responsible for developing the nation's economic policy; reporting on national and international financial matters and transactions; and enforcing tax, tariff, and counterfeiting laws.

A number of varied agencies come under the Department of the Treasury today, including the Alcohol and Tobacco Tax and Trade Bureau, the Bureau of the Public Debt, and the Internal Revenue Service. The treasurer of the United States, originally responsible for the receipt and custody of public funds (functions now widely dispersed throughout the Treasury Department), oversees the printing and minting of money (see CURRENCY).

Secretary of Defense

Although Congress shares certain responsibilities for the nation's defense, such as declaring WAR and raising and supporting armies, the president is responsible for supervising the nation's military forces in times of peace as well as war (see ARMED FORCES; NATIONAL SECURITY). As Article II, section 2, declares: "The president shall be Commander in Chief of the Army and Navy of the United States, and of the Militia of the several States, when called into actual Service of the United States...."

From 1789 to 1949 the U.S. government had both a War Department and a Navy Department. A 1949 amendment to the National Security Act (1947) created a single Department of Defense. The Defense Reorganization Act (1958) made the secretary of defense second in command under the president and consolidated defense planning and operations of all the military services—army, navy, air force, and marines—in the office of the secretary of defense. The top military leader in the Defense Department is the chair of the Joint Chiefs of Staff.

Attorney General

Article II, section 3, requires the president to "take Care that the Laws be faithfully executed...." After the president, the attorney general, who heads the Department of Justice and provides legal advice to the president, is the nation's chief LAW ENFORCEMENT officer. The Department of Justice is responsible for, among other things, investigating federal crimes, from antitrust violations (see ANTITRUST LAW) to evasion of TAXES. The Federal Bureau of Investigation is responsible for investigating and collecting evidence in cases that come under federal legal jurisdiction. The department's lawyers represent the United States in legal matters, and the solicitor general represents the federal government before the SUPREME COURT.

According to the Presidential Succession Act of 1947, the other cabinet secretaries would rise to the presidency in this order: interior, agriculture, commerce, labor, health and human services, housing and urban development, transportation, energy, education, veterans' affairs, and homeland security. Like the other cabinet members, they head functional departments that carry out administration policies as well as advise the president and Congress on their areas of responsibility. From time to time, other federal agency heads have been accorded a seat at cabinet meetings even though they are not secretaries and heads of executive departments. President Bill Clinton (b. 1946), for example, made the administrator of the Environmental Protection Agency a member of his cabinet by EXECUTIVE ORDER, although Congress has rejected efforts to elevate the agency to cabinet-level status.

More on this topic:

Advice and Consent, p. 18

Appointment and Removal Power, p. 39

Executive Branch, p. 206

Hamilton, Alexander, p. 270

Jefferson, Thomas, p. 310

Campaign Financing

Private financing of political campaigns has always raised questions about potential corruption and influence buying in the halls of CONGRESS and the White House as well as in state legislatures. If a person or an organization gives a candidate for public office one hundred dollars in campaign contributions and another gives the same candidate one million dollars, whose telephone call does the politician take first once in office? Bribery and outright buying of votes are illegal under federal and state election laws, but spending enormous sums of money to persuade voters to vote for a particular political party or candidate is not only acceptable, it is just about the only way to get elected today.

The media's importance in modern life has driven up the cost of running for office, and campaigns last much longer, seemingly never ending. They now begin shortly after an election and extend the length of the winner's term of office—two, four, or six years in the case of candidates for the HOUSE OF REPRESENTATIVES, the presidency (see PRESIDENT), and the SENATE, respectively. Vehicles for contributing money to an American campaign have also become more complex. This is partly the result of the decreasing role of the two-party system and the rise of numerous political interest groups: from consumers and environmentalists to Christian fundamentalists, pro-choice supporters and abortion opponents, and soccer moms. Parliamentary systems do not have these problems. Their elections are usually conducted in a relatively short period of time: they are held after a vote expressing a loss of confidence in the current government or after a fairly long period of time, generally from four to five years, barring any no-confidence votes in the parliament.

Campaign Finance Reform

On the matter of campaign financing and even POLITICAL PARTIES, the Constitution is silent. In the early days of the republic, there was little public concern about campaign financing. The administration of Andrew Jackson (1767–1845), who was elected president in 1828, marked the beginning of the political patronage system (also known as the spoils system)—the practice of filling government jobs with party loyalists, regardless of their qualifications. By the end of the 1830s political parties were forcing government workers to contribute a percentage of their pay to the party in power. An 1839 proposal to prohibit campaign contributions from federal officials died in the Senate. In 1867, however, Congress did prohibit the solicitation of campaign contributions from government employees at navy yards.

The Civil Service Act (1883) curbed the spoils system by requiring competitive examinations for most federal government jobs, as well as prohibiting solicitation of political contributions from these employees. Investigations into large contributions to the campaign of President Theodore Roosevelt (1858–1919) led him to call for campaign finance reform, declaring, "There is no enemy of free government more dangerous and none so insidious as the corruption of the electorate...."

In 1906 Roosevelt asked Congress to forbid "[a]ll contributions by corporations to any political committee or for any political purpose...." Congress responded with the Tillman Act (1907), which, among other things, prohibited nationally chartered banks and corporations from making "a money contribution with any election to any political office" and made it illegal for corporations to contribute to ELECTIONS of the president or members of Congress. The law, still in effect today, has been weakened by creative fund-raising practices, including the use of "soft money" earmarked for general political activities, such as voter registration and voter turnout drives, rather than specific candidates.

The Publicity Act (1910) required committees of political parties to report contributions to and expenditures for campaigns for the House of Representatives. However, the Supreme Court in *Newberry v. United States* (1921) held that Congress's authority to regulate elections did not extend

This cartoon depicts the Teapot Dome scandal of the 1920s as having a steamrolling impact. One of the worst political scandals of the twentieth century, Teapot Dome led to a somewhat ineffectual campaign finance law.
Source: Library of Congress

to political party primaries and nomination activities. Twenty years later, in *United States v. Classic* (1941), the Court allowed regulation of primaries under certain conditions: when a state law made the primaries a part of the election process, for example, or when they in effect determined the outcome of the following election.

The Teapot Dome scandal during the brief administration of Warren G. Harding (1865–1923), involving gifts from oil developers to federal officials responsible for granting oil-leasing rights, led to enactment of the Federal Corrupt Practices Act (1925). Although it did little to curb abuses, this act was the basic national campaign finance law until 1971.

Postwar Campaign Laws

In the decades after World War II, national political campaigns changed dramatically. Costs increased exponentially, in large part because of the emergence of television and the high price of television advertising as well as the necessity of professional campaign staffs and technical equipment. "Whistle stop" campaigns, like that of President Harry S. Truman (1884–1972) during the 1948 presidential election, began to seem outmoded and almost quaint. At the same time the size of campaign contributions grew in part because of the higher cost of campaigns and the increasing importance of government to businesses and special-interest groups such as workers, minorities, and religious groups.

These developments led to the enactment of two pieces of legislation in 1971: the Presidential Election Campaign Fund Act and the Federal Election Campaign Act. The first required any committee receiving or spending more than one thousand dollars in a campaign for federal office to register with the government and publish reports of its contributions and expenditures (although some critics argued that limitations on financing are not as important as making all campaign fund raising and expenditures open to public scrutiny). The second act created a public fund for financing presidential elections, to which taxpayers could contribute a nominal amount by checking off the appropriate box on their income tax form.

In the midst of the WATERGATE scandal, which started with a break-in at Democratic National Committee headquarters, a new Federal Election Campaign Act passed in 1974 set maximum spending limits for presidential nominating and general election campaigns and also created federal matching funds for qualifying candidates in the nominating campaigns of major parties and for complete federal funding for major-party candidates in general election campaigns. The act also placed limits on the contributions of individuals, organizations, and political action committees (PACs) in national elections and established a six-member Federal Election Commission to enforce its provisions. In 2002 Congress passed the Bipartisan Campaign Reform Act to address the problem of soft money contributions, discussed below.

First Amendment Issues

Various attempts made by Congress over the years to curb campaign financing abuses have run up against the freedom of SPEECH guarantee of the First Amendment (1791). In *BUCKLEY V. VALEO* (1976), the Supreme Court faced the question of whether laws limiting campaign financing violated the Constitution's free-speech protection. The Court's ruling made a distinction between campaign contributions and campaign expenditures and the effect of the 1974 campaign law's limitations on them. Noting that the evil the law was intended to remedy or mitigate was corruption, the Court found that limitations on campaign expenditures—money used by the political parties and individual candidates to run for federal office—imposed "significantly more severe restrictions on protected freedoms" than did limitations on campaign contributions.

The Supreme Court's reasoning in *Buckley* was that the act of making a contribution to a political campaign, not the amount of the contribution, was the important element to be protected. Limiting campaign spending, on the other hand, limited the quantity of political speech the money could buy. On the issue of campaign expenditures, therefore, the Court equated dollars with political speech protected by the First Amendment, leading Justice THURGOOD MARSHALL to comment in his dissent that in any race for public office "it would appear to follow that the candidate with a substantial fortune at his disposal is off to a significant 'head start.'"

In *Federal Election Commission v. Massachusetts Citizens for Life* (1986), the Supreme Court held that provisions of the Federal Election Campaign Act prohibiting direct expenditures from corporate funds to a nonprofit political association violated the First Amendment's guarantee of free speech. But in *Austin v. Michigan Chamber of Commerce* (1990), the Court ruled that a state law barring corporations from making campaign contributions to the Michigan Chamber of Commerce, a nonprofit corporation, did not. The Court in *Federal Election Commission v. Colorado Republican Federal Campaign Commission* (2001) confirmed its stand in *Buckley*, declaring that "[p]olitical expenditure limits deserve closer scrutiny than contribution restrictions... because expenditure restraints generally curb more expressive and associational activity than contribution limits."

Since the decision in *Buckley* permitted limits on campaign contributions, the process of developing loopholes, such as generating soft money and switching to issue advertising as opposed to candidate advertising, led to the passage of the Bipartisan Campaign Reform Act of 2002 (BCRA). The act was sponsored by Sen. John McCain, a Republican, and Sen. Russ Feingold, a Democrat. Soft money includes political contributions to influence state or local elections that were considered to be in addition to the limited contributions to federal candidates. Issue advertising involves contributions not used directly to elect or defeat a named candidate and thus were also considered outside of the limitations of the Federal Election Campaign Act of 1971. BCRA, or the McCain-Feingold law as it is sometimes called, imposed new restrictions on soft money and issue advertising.

In *McConnell v. Federal Election Commission* (2003), the Supreme Court found that most of the provisions of BCRA passed constitutional muster. Then, in *Federal Election Commission v. Wisconsin Right to Life, Inc.* (2007), the Court revisited BCRA and specifically section 203, which makes it a federal crime for any corporation to broadcast shortly before an election any communication that names a federal candidate for an elected office and is directed to the electorate.

More on this topic:

Buckley v. Valeo, *p. 67*

Elections, p. 181

Political Parties, p. 403

Watergate, p. 578

During the election period proscribed in 2004, the right-to-life organization in Wisconsin ran several broadcast ads urging constituents to "call Senator Feingold" to protest the filibuster in the Senate regarding certain judicial nominees. In the decision, announced by Chief Justice John G. Roberts (b. 1955), the Court noted that it had focused objectively on the substance of the communication, rather than its intent and effect, and concluded that the ads did not constitute express advocacy to vote for or against a particular candidate. Therefore, because the ads were not express advocacy or its functional equivalent and because there was no government interest sufficiently compelling to justify burdening the organization's right of free speech, section 203 of BCRA was held to be unconstitutional as applied to the ads in question.

Capital, National

Many national capitals such as Jerusalem, Rome, Paris, and London have ancient origins predating the current boundaries of their countries, but the United States, like a number of New World nations, had to create a capital when it was formed. Because of the federal nature of the U.S. government, representing its semisovereign component states, the FRAMERS OF THE CONSTITUTION decided to set aside a separate territory for the capital. Several other countries, including Australia, the Federative Republic of Brazil, and the Federated States of Micronesia, have since similarly created a separate territory for their national capital. Most capital cities are the location of major government offices, although South Africa and Switzerland have dispersed some branches throughout several cities.

Article I, section 8, of the Constitution, which lists a number of the powers delegated to Congress, provides: "The Congress shall have Power…To exercise exclusive Legislation in all Cases whatsoever, over such District (not exceeding ten Miles square) as may, by Cession of Particular States, and the Acceptance of Congress, become the Seat of the Government of the United States…." Northern and southern states, willing to give up their own territory to obtain the honor, contended for the prize; when the North's war debts were assumed by the federal government, the South got the capital, which was to be placed along an eighty-mile area of the Potomac River north of its junction with the Anacostia River. Speculators, envisioning riches from a commercial metropolis, pressured Washington to choose their land. In the end, Virginia gave up territory from its city of Alexandria, not far from the president's Mount Vernon, and Maryland ceded Georgetown to help form the new seat of government.

"No nation perhaps had ever before the opportunity offered them of deliberately deciding on the spot where their capital city should be fixed…."

—*Pierre Charles L'Enfant,* designer of Washington, D.C.

The three commissioners appointed to oversee development of the capital in 1791 informed Pierre Charles L'Enfant, the new city planner, that it was to be called the "Territory of Columbia" in honor of Christopher Columbus "and the City of Washington" in honor of George Washington. Andrew Ellicott got to work surveying the chosen diamond-shaped location on the Potomac, and L'Enfant began laying out a city of classical grace and symmetry. Not long after a run-in with one of the commissioners, Daniel Carroll of Maryland, who was also one of the framers of the Constitution, L'Enfant was dismissed in 1792. (Carroll had started to build his home on the hill the Frenchman had reserved for the U.S. Capitol.) Ellicott finished the plan, and the government moved to the still-raw capital territory in 1801.

The framers apparently never considered that the District of Columbia would have a large permanent population, larger than that of four individual states by 1980. Except for a brief period of

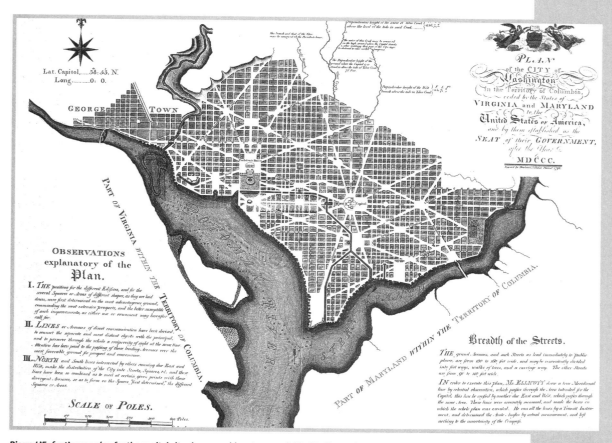

Pierre L'Enfant's 1791 plan for the capital city shows a grid system overlaid with diagonal avenues radiating from important sites. He included locations for the executive and legislative branches and a national church but not for the Supreme Court.
Source: Library of Congress

home rule between 1871 and 1874, it was governed by appointed commissioners until passage of the District of Columbia Government Reorganization Act (1973). The adoption of a city charter the following year provided for a new government consisting of an elected mayor and city council. Congress still approves the District's BUDGET and has VETO power over legislation.

Because the capital city belongs to all the states and the entire populace of the United States, the status of the citizens of the District of Columbia has been uncertain at times, although the Fourteenth Amendment (1868) makes them citizens of the United States. Citizens of the District of Columbia share the limited citizenship of the inhabitants of U.S territories and possessions such as Guam and Puerto Rico (see TERRITORY), which are governed under Article IV, section 3, granting Congress the power "to dispose of and make all needful Rules and Regulations respecting the Territory and Property belonging to the United States" and which also have no voting representation in that body.

The Twenty-third Amendment (1961) authorizes residents of the District of Columbia to choose three electors for the president and vice president of the United States (see ELECTORAL COLLEGE). Otherwise, residents of the District of Columbia have no national voting representation. And only since 1970 have they been permitted to elect one nonvoting delegate to the House of

Representatives; American Samoa, Guam, and Puerto Rico also have nonvoting delegates in the House. The desires of D.C. residents—a largely African American population and predominantly supporters of the Democratic Party—for greater autonomy and representation in Congress have generally fallen on deaf ears. In 1978, however, Congress passed a constitutional amendment that would treat the District of Columbia as a state for purposes of congressional and presidential ELEC- TIONS. The amendment failed to obtain the required ratification by the states in the seven-year time limit set by Congress—most likely because it would have added three black Democratic members to Congress.

Local activists, thwarted in their longtime efforts to obtain statehood or gain full voting representation in Congress like their fellow Americans, have begun taking their campaign to international forums. The United Nations has been asked to hold that the denial of voting rights violates the International Convention on the Elimination of All Forms of Racial Discrimination (1969), while the Organization of American States has been beseeched to find a violation of the American Declaration of the Rights and Duties of Man (1948). Today the inhabitants of Washington, D.C., the "capital of the free world," remain second-class citizens of the United States and drive cars whose license plates bear the motto "Taxation Without Representation." In 2001, however, shortly after taking office, President George W. Bush ordered the "Taxation without Representation" motto removed from the license plates on the presidential limousine, telegraphing his lack of sympathy for the expansion of voting rights in D.C. In the same year, a new initiative was introduced in Congress; and in 2003, legislation to grant the District full voting representation in the national legislature advanced as far as being approved 9–0 by the Senate Governmental Affairs Committee. No Republican members attended the committee meeting.

Capital Punishment   *See* DEATH PENALTY.

Caucuses   *See* CONGRESS; POLITICAL PARTIES

Censorship

Unfortunately, censorship is alive and well in the United States. In 2001 a librarian in Oskaloosa, Oklahoma, was coerced into removing the popular Harry Potter books from the reading program because a few citizens thought they contained an "evil factor." And in New York City, an advertisement promoting a free health service for homosexuals was removed by the advertising company awarded a city contract to place the ads at bus stops. Other efforts to enlist government support for censorship in recent years include attempts to clean up the language in popular music and, with renewed vigor after September 11, 2001, violence portrayed by the motion picture and television industry.

Censorship is the review of material before it is disseminated in forums such as books, newspapers, magazines, advertisements, movies, television, plays, music, and the Internet with the intent of banning anything objectionable. To a great extent, government censorship is banned by the First Amendment (1791) guarantee of freedom of SPEECH and THE PRESS. But like other individual rights, these freedoms are not absolute. Even in a free, open, democratic, and pluralistic society such as America's, limitations on freedom of expression are constitutionally permissible.

Limitations on freedom of speech and the press may take either of two forms: punishment after the fact or prior restraint. According to William Blackstone (1723–80) in his *Commentaries on the Laws of England* (1765–70), "The liberty of the press is indeed essential to the nature of a free state; but this consists in laying no previous restraints upon publications, and not in freedom from censure for criminal matter when published."

The desire by people in authority to proscribe what other people may read or view has been pervasive throughout history. In *The Republic*, in which he describes his ideal state, the ancient Greek philosopher Plato (ca. 427–347 B.C.E.) declares: "[T]he first thing will be to establish a censorship of the writers of fiction, and let the censors receive any tale of fiction which is good and reject the bad." The British also had censors, including the English poet John Milton (1608–74), who both advocated freedom of the press and served as a censor of a major newspaper in 1651.

Prior restraint of expression has been tried unsuccessfully by all three branches of the government. In 1789 Congress passed the Sedition Act, which was formally titled "An Act for the Punishment of Certain Crimes against the United States." Among other things, it authorized a huge fine of $2,000 and two years in prison for "publishing any false, scandalous and malicious writing" against the government or the president. Fortunately, the law expired automatically after three years and before the Supreme Court could pass judgment on it. But many Americans at the time agreed with THOMAS JEFFERSON, who declared the law "to be a nullity as absolute and as palpable as if Congress had ordered us to fall down and worship a golden image."

In the case of *Near v. Minnesota ex rel. Olson* (1931), the Supreme Court struck down a state law that authorized a permanent court injunction against any newspaper or magazine that published an "obscene, lewd and lascivious" or a "malicious, scandalous and defamatory" issue. Any future publication of the newspaper or periodical had to be cleared by the judge. Noting that the great struggle for freedom of the press was for the right to publish without a license from the government, the Court also found that court-ordered injunctions are a form of prior restraint that are subject to close judicial scrutiny.

Many states nevertheless sponsored censorship boards that, on the basis of even a single offensive passage, would ban works such as books by Stephen Crane (1871–1900), who wrote *The Red Badge of Courage* (1895); Walt Whitman (1819–92), who wrote *Leaves of Grass* (1855); and Sigmund Freud (1856–1939), the father of modern psychoanalysis—as well as movies on just about any religious or moral grounds. One important case curtailed such censorship but did not reach the Supreme Court. In *United States v. One Book Called "Ulysses"* (affirmed by the U.S. Court of Appeals for the Second Circuit in 1934), the judge held that "we believe that the proper test of whether a given book is obscene is its dominant effect. In applying this test, relevancy of the objectionable parts to the theme, the established reputation of the work in the estimation of approved critics, if the book is modern, and the verdict of the past, if it is ancient, are persuasive pieces of evidence; for works of art are not likely to sustain a high position with no better warrant for their existence than their obscene content." In *A Book Named "John Cleland's Memoirs of a Woman of Pleasure" [Fanny Hill] v. Attorney General of Commonwealth of Massachusetts* (1966), the Supreme Court finally created a test for censorship. To be obscene, it ruled, the dominant theme of a work must appeal to a prurient interest in sex, be "patently offensive because it affronts contemporary community standards relating to the description of sexual matters," and be "utterly without redeeming social value." This decision virtually ended censorship except for hardcore pornography (see OBSCENITY).

Although Walt Whitman is now regarded as one of the nation's greatest poets, censors tried to ban his verses on the grounds that they were obscene.
Source: Library of Congress

More on this topic:

Communications, p. 104

The Supreme Court decided in *New York Times Co. v. United States* (1971), the PENTAGON PAPERS CASE, that an attempt by the EXECUTIVE BRANCH to restrain the publication of classified information about the Vietnam War was unconstitutional, because the government had not met "the heavy burden of showing justification" for the restraint. The Court's decision makes it clear, however, that censorship under certain circumstances—for example, serious impairment of national security—might be justified. The terrorist attacks on the United States in 2001 raised the specter of new censorship measures by the government.

The advent of the INTERNET has provided a new battleground between censorship and constitutionally protected freedom of expression. In 1996 Congress tried to censor material on the Internet through the Communications Decency Act (1996), but the Supreme Court in *Reno v. American Civil Liberties Union* (1997) held the act to be unconstitutionally broad in the scope of its censorship. Among other things, the act made the knowing transmission of obscene or indecent material to anyone under the age of eighteen years a felony. Congress struck back in 1998 with the Child Online Protection Act (COPA), devised to keep children from viewing pornographic Web sites. That attempt to rely on "community standards" of decency was challenged at the Supreme Court in 2001 by the American Civil Liberties Union, which prefers that parents rather than the government choose which sites children visit online. A basic problem with Internet censorship is that attempts to apply "community standards" to determine which content is harmful must take place in the nongeographic realm of cyberspace.

In *Ashcroft v. American Civil Liberties Union* (2002), the Supreme Court rejected the argument that COPA was unconstitutional because of its reliance on "community standards" to define "material that is harmful to minors" and remanded the case. The U.S. Court of Appeals for the Third Circuit then confirmed the lower court's preliminary injunction against enforcing COPA. In *Ashcroft v. American Civil Liberties Union* (2004), the Supreme Court affirmed that decision, 5–4, on the grounds that the law was unconstitutional under the First Amendment, because the government had failed to demonstrate that less restrictive measures would be less effective. Another basic problem with Internet censorship is that in banning what appear to be objectionable words or symbols, socially acceptable material is also removed. For example, blocking the word *breast* may keep out important information about breast cancer.

Some legitimate reasons can be cited for censorship of adult-oriented materials, such as limiting their accessibility to young children. However, we live in a pluralistic society, one in which information that some parents would find objectionable others might not. The courts have told public officials at all levels that they may take community standards into account in deciding which materials should be censored but that they may not censor generally acceptable publications—neither J. K. Rowling's Harry Potter books nor literary classics such as *Tom Sawyer* (1876) or *The Adventures of Huckleberry Finn* (1884) by Mark Twain (1835–1910)—simply to please a small minority of the community.

Some classrooms and school libraries have banned the bestselling Harry Potter books because of concerns that they promote witchcraft.
Source: Danny Lawson/PA Wire (Press Association via AP Images)

Census

For purposes of taxation, both the citizens of ancient Rome and their property were registered in a census, an official enumeration of persons in a nation or another political subdivision. In England, the revenue of the Crown was based on the *census regalis* (royal census). Today nearly all countries provide for some regular means of counting their population.

The U.S. Constitution specifies in Article I, section 2, that a census "shall be made within three Years after the first Meeting of the Congress of the United States [1789], and within every subsequent Term of ten Years, in such Manner as they shall by Law direct." The accuracy of the census was originally important for ensuring both fair proportional taxation of the STATES and fair proportional representation in the HOUSE OF REPRESENTATIVES (see REAPPORTIONMENT). Today census data are constitutionally required only for the latter purpose. The U.S. Census Bureau, an agency within the Department of Commerce, bears the primary responsibility for conducting the census at the start of each decade.

At the time the Constitution was written, the purpose and extent of the census were stated in Article I, section 2: "Representatives and direct Taxes shall be apportioned among the several States which may be included within this Union, according to their respective Numbers, which shall be determined by adding to the whole Number of free Persons, including those bound to Service for a Term of Years, and excluding Indians not taxed, three fifths of all other persons [slaves]." This provision was af-

In this 1870 engraving from **Harper's Weekly,** *a census taker collects information from a diverse group of people, including an African American. Two years earlier, the Fourteenth Amendment allowed former slaves to be counted as individuals for the first time.*
Source: Library of Congress

fected by two subsequent constitutional amendments. The Thirteenth Amendment (1865) prohibited SLAVERY, and the Fourteenth Amendment (1868) changed the language of Article I, section 2, so that former slaves were thereafter to be counted as single persons. According to section 2 of the amendment, "Representatives shall be apportioned among the several States according to their respective numbers, counting the whole number of persons in each State, excluding Indians not taxed."

JAMES MADISON, in essay 54 of *The Federalist* (1787–88) (see FEDERALIST PAPERS), pointed out one of the clever checks and balances built into the census provisions. "As the accuracy of the census to be obtained by the Congress will necessarily depend, in a considerable degree, on the disposition, if not the co-operation of the States," he wrote, "it is of great importance that the States should feel as little bias as possible to swell or to reduce the amount of their numbers. Were their share of representatives alone to be governed by this rule, they would have an interest in exaggerating their inhabitants. Were the rule to decide their taxation alone, a contrary temptation would prevail. By extending the rule to both objects, the States have opposite interests which will control and balance each other and produce the requisite impartiality."

PROFILE OF GENERAL DEMOGRAPHIC CHARACTERISTICS

Subject	Number	Percent
Total population	**281,421,906**	**100.0**
Sex and Age		
Male	138,053,563	49.1
Female	143,368,343	50.9
Under 5 years	19,175,798	6.8
5 to 9 years	20,549,505	7.3
10 to 14 years	20,528,072	7.3
15 to 19 years	20,219,890	7.2
20 to 24 years	18,964,001	6.7
25 to 34 years	39,891,724	14.2
35 to 44 years	45,148,527	16.0
45 to 54 years	37,677,952	13.4
55 to 59 years	13,469,237	4.8
60 to 64 years	10,805,447	3.8
65 to 74 years	18,390,986	6.5
75 to 84 years	12,361,180	4.4
85 years +	4,239,587	1.5
Median age (years)	35.3	n.a.
18 years +	209,128,094	74.3
Male	100,994,367	35.9
Female	108,133,727	38.4
21 years =	196,899,193	70.0
62 years =	41,256,029	14.7
65 years =	34,991,753	12.4
Male	14,409,625	5.1
Female	20,582,128	7.3
Race		
One race	274,595,678	97.6
White	211,460,626	75.1
Black or African American	34,658,190	12.3
American Indian and Alaska Native	2,475,956	0.9
Asian	10,242,998	3.6
Asian Indian	1,678,765	0.6
Chinese	2,432,585	0.9
Filipino	1,850,314	0.7
Japanese	796,700	0.3
Korean	1,076,872	0.4
Vietnamese	1,122,528	0.4
Other Asian	1,285,234	0.5
Native Hawaiian/Other Pacific Islander	398,835	0.1
Native Hawaiian	140,652	0.0
Guamanian or Chamorro	58,240	0.0
Samoan	91,029	0.0
Other Pacific Islander	108,914	0.0
Some other race	15,359,073	5.5
Two or more races	6,826,228	2.4
Race alone or in combination with one or more other races		
White	216,930,975	77.1
Black or African American	36,419,434	12.9
American Indian and Alaska Native	4,119,301	1.5
Asian	11,898,828	4.2
Native Hawaiian/Other Pacific Islander	874,414	0.3
Some other race	18,521,486	6.6

Subject	Number	Percent
Hispanic or Latino and Race		
Total population	**281,421,906**	**100.0**
Hispanic or Latino (of any race)	35,305,818	12.5
Mexican	20,640,711	7.3
Puerto Rican	3,406,178	1.2
Cuban	1,241,685	0.4
Other Hispanic or Latino	10,017,244	3.6
Not Hispanic or Latino	246,116,088	87.5
White alone	194,552,774	69.1
Relationship		
Total population	**281,421,906**	**100.0**
In households	273,643,273	97.2
Householder	105,480,101	37.5
Spouse	54,493,232	19.4
Child	83,393,392	29.6
Own child under 18 years	64,494,637	22.9
Other relatives	15,684,318	5.6
Under 18 years	6,042,435	2.1
Nonrelatives	14,592,230	5.2
Unmarried partner	5,475,768	1.9
In group quarters	7,778,633	2.8
Institutionalized population	4,059,039	1.4
Noninstitutionalized population	3,719,594	1.3
Household by Type		
Total households	**105,480,101**	**100.0**
Family households (families)	71,787,347	68.1
With own children under 18 years	34,588,368	32.8
Married-couple family	54,493,232	51.7
With own children under 18 years	24,835,505	23.5
Female householder, no husband	12,900,103	12.2
With own children under 18 years	7,561,874	7.2
Nonfamily households	33,692,754	31.9
Householder living alone	27,230,075	25.8
Householder 65 years +	9,722,857	9.2
Households: individuals under 18 years	38,022,115	36.0
Households: individuals 65 years +	24,672,708	23.4
Average household size	2.59	n.a.
Average family size	3.14	n.a.
Housing Occupancy		
Total housing units	**115,904,641**	**100.0**
Occupied housing units	105,480,101	91.0
Vacant housing units	10,424,540	9.0
Seasonal/recreational/occasional use	3,578,718	3.1
Homeowner vacancy rate (percent)	1.7	n.a.
Rental vacancy rate (percent)	6.8	n.a.
Housing Tenure		
Occupied housing units	**105,480,101**	**100.0**
Owner-occupied housing units	69,815,753	66.2
Renter-occupied housing units	35,664,348	33.8
Average household size/owner-occupied units	2.69	n.a.
Average household size/renter-occupied units	2.40	n.a.

SOURCE: U.S. Census Bureau, Census 2000.

Census information collected today, far exceeding simply the number of inhabitants in each state, includes data about the minority status of those enumerated as well as the nature and number of persons making up the households canvassed. The 2000 census, for example, found that the U.S. population had exceeded 281 million persons, that their average age was 35.3 years, that more than half were females, that the average family size was 3.14 persons, that 66.2 percent lived in housing they owned themselves (see sidebar). The Supreme Court implied its approval of this extended scope for the census in *Knox v. Lee* (1871), one of the Legal Tender Cases (see CURRENCY).

Accuracy of the census information is extremely important to the states, their citizens, and their representatives in Congress because it is used to determine how many members each state can send to the House of Representatives as well as states' eligibility for federal funding and grants. In Supreme Court decisions, the federal government has been granted wide latitude as to how it implements the census every ten years and uses it to apportion seats in Congress. For example, in *Utah v. Evans* (2002), the Court found that "hot-deck imputation," a method by which the Census Bureau increased the total population count artificially by about 0.4 percent in 2000 to account for uncertain data collected, did not violate the Census Clause of the Constitution. The method resulted in North Carolina being eligible for one additional representative and Utah being eligible for one less representative. The Court noted that the "actual Enumeration" to be made under the Constitution "in such Manner as [Congress] shall by Law direct" referred to the counting process, and therefore Congress was permitted wide latitude in prescribing the methodology to be used in obtaining the data for such enumeration.

The 435 seats in the House of Representatives are reapportioned (reallocated) every ten years on the basis of the new census figures if any state records a sufficient increase or decrease in population. Although some states, such as Alaska, Wyoming, and Delaware, do not warrant more than one representative, most states have two or more. When population changes occur, congressional election districts may have to be redrawn (known as redistricting) to reflect the new census figures. If a state gains a seat or seats in the House, its election districts must be redrawn to provide a geographic area from which the new member or members will be elected. Changes in the size and redistribution of population uncovered in the census may also require similar reapportionment and redistricting of seats in state legislatures.

MINORITIES have often been undercounted by the census for various reasons, from failure to receive returned census forms to census workers' inability to verify information in some minority communities. (The 2000 census showed that approximately 75 percent of the population regarded themselves as white, 12.5 percent as Hispanic or Latino, 12–13 percent as African American, and 3–4 percent as Asian.) In *Wisconsin v. City of New York* (1996), the Supreme Court found that the secretary of commerce's decision not to statistically adjust the census figures to compensate for the minority undercount was well within the executive branch's discretion in matters involving the census. And in *Department of Commerce v. United States House of Representatives* (1999), the Court held that a statistical adjustment could not be made for the purpose of altering the apportionment of seats in Congress. Where DISCRIMINATION has been alleged, the Court has tended to use the lowest level of analysis, the so-called rational basis standard of review, rather than the STRICT SCRUTINY used in cases of RACIAL DISCRIMINATION or heightened scrutiny as used in sex discrimination cases.

Census information has played an important role in the federal courts' enforcement of the "one man, one vote" rule of electoral reapportionment first articulated by the Supreme Court in *Gray v. Sanders* (1963) (see BAKER V. CARR) and in subsequent reapportionment cases and redistricting efforts. In fact, in *Reynolds v. Sims* (1964), the Court declared, "Population is, of necessity, the starting point for consideration and the controlling criterion for judgment in legislative apportionment controversies." However, computer technology soon made it all too easy, regardless of actual census

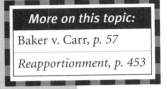

More on this topic:

Baker v. Carr, *p. 57*

Reapportionment, p. 453

figures, to generate just about any configuration to shape electoral districts to the advantage of the majority political interests.

The information obtained by the U.S. Census every decade is not a perfect reflection of the country's population and its distribution among the states. But the traditional use of census information is important in effecting the constitutional mandate of apportioning congressional seats among the states as well as determining the extent of federal benefits to the states.

Certiorari, Writs of   *See* CRIMINAL LAW; SUPREME COURT.

Checks and Balances   *See* SEPARATION OF POWERS.

Chief Justice

Although he served as president of the United States from 1909 to 1913, William Howard Taft (1857–1930) apparently thought that he had attained a more desirable station when he was appointed chief justice of the United States in 1921. Not as visible or as political as the PRESIDENT or the SPEAKER OF THE HOUSE, the chief justice is recognized as the highest officer in the coequal JUDICIAL BRANCH of the federal government.

A court of law invariably has a presiding officer called the chief judge, chief justice, or president. Even the American colonies had courts with presiding officers, as did the states formed later. By the time the Constitution was drafted in 1787, the need for a presiding member of the SUPREME COURT was clearly understood by the FRAMERS OF THE CONSTITUTION.

The president's authority to appoint the chief justice is found in Article II, section 2, of the Constitution, which states that the chief executive "shall nominate, and by and with the Advice and Consent of the Senate, shall appoint Ambassadors, other public Ministers and Consuls, Judges of the supreme Court, and all other Officers of the United States, whose Appointments are not herein otherwise provided for...."

The Constitution mentions the office of chief justice only once and then only in regard to presiding over the Senate in an IMPEACHMENT trial of the president. The reference appears in Article I, section 3: "The Senate shall have the sole Power to try all Impeachments.... When the President of the United States is tried, the Chief Justice shall preside...."

Like the Constitution itself, the role of the chief justice has evolved over the past two centuries. Only sixteen men have held the position of chief justice; they have served under forty-three presidents. President GEORGE WASHINGTON was not impressed with the first chief justice, John Jay (1745–1829), or the Court's other members. Some chief justices have had more impact on the Court, the Constitution, and constitutional law than others.

The third chief justice, JOHN MARSHALL, significantly raised the level of competence and respect for the office and the Supreme Court during his tenure from 1801 until his death in 1835. By giving the Constitution an expansive reading when it came to the powers of the national government vis-á-vis the states, Marshall's impact on the development of constitutional law and the nation was profound. His opinion in *MARBURY V. MADISON* (1803) established the federal judiciary as a coequal branch of government and the Court as the guardian of the Constitution through its power of judicial review over national and state government actions.

Chief Justice Roger B. Taney (1777–1864), who served from 1836 to 1864, however, had the dubious distinction of writing the majority opinion in *Scott v. Sandford* (1857), the Dred Scott case.

Chief Justice Roger B. Taney in 1857 wrote one of the most infamous opinions in the history of the Supreme Court in the case of *Scott v. Sandford*. Better known as the Dred Scott case, the dispute involved a Missouri slave who moved with his owner to the free state of Illinois and the free territory of Wisconsin in the 1830s before being taken back to the slave state of Missouri. The slave, Dred Scott, turned to the courts to gain his freedom. He argued that he had been legally free in Illinois and Wisconsin, and he could not be reenslaved.

In a sweeping opinion, Taney said that Scott did not have the right to file a lawsuit. He wrote that slaves and their descendants "are not included, and were not intended to be included, under the word 'citizens' in the Constitution." Taney went even further, saying that Congress did not have the authority to prohibit slavery in a territory.

The decision undermined years of political compromises between slave and free states. Heavily criticized in the North, it helped spark the Civil War. After the war, Taney's decision was overturned by the Thirteenth Amendment, which prohibited slavery, and the Fourteenth Amendment, which extended citizenship to all people who are born or naturalized in the United States, regardless of their race.

Taney's reputation was forever tarnished by his opinion in that case. But many legal historians believe that, on balance, Taney was an insightful judge and capable administrator. Despite his ruling in Dred Scott, Taney personally opposed slavery. He freed his own slaves before the 1857 case.

Source: Library of Congress

This decision barred slaves from becoming members of the political community created by the Constitution and therefore denied them entitlement to any of the rights and privileges guaranteed to citizens.

The names of chief justices who provide strong leadership or under whose leadership the Supreme Court takes on a distinct legal direction have become associated with various eras—for example, Earl Warren, head of the so-called Warren Court from 1953 to 1969 (appointed by President Dwight Eisenhower [1890–1969]), and William H. Rehnquist, head of the Rehnquist Court from 1986 to 2005 (appointed by President Ronald Reagan [1911–2004]).

Earl Warren (1891–1974) led the Court in reversing support for second-class citizenship for African Americans by writing the majority opinion in BROWN V. BOARD OF EDUCATION OF TOPEKA (1954), declaring "separate but equal" schools—SEGREGATION—unconstitutional (see RACIAL DISCRIMINATION). Warren was a controversial figure on the Court. Although a Republican appointee, he became a strong advocate for liberal rulings that led some conservatives to mount an unsuccessful campaign in the 1950s and 1960s to have him impeached. (No justice of the Supreme Court has ever been removed from office by impeachment.)

William H. Rehnquist (1924–2005), having served as an associate justice for fifteen years before rising to chief justice in 1986, was a leading conservative on the Court, often joining with four other similarly minded justices to reach 5–4 majority decisions on important cases involving individual rights and STATES' RIGHTS. Since replacing Rehnquist in 2005, Chief Justice John G. Roberts Jr. (b. 1955), who was a law clerk for his predecessor during the 1980 term of the Court, has continued his conservative leadership.

In addition to having the same responsibilities as the associate justices—hearing cases, voting in decisions, and writing opinions or dissents from majority opinions—the chief justice presides at oral hearings before the Court and in closed meetings with the other justices to discuss the disposition of cases. He also determines which justice will write the Court's opinion in a particular case when he has voted with the majority. Only two chief justices have presided over impeachment

CHIEF JUSTICES OF THE UNITED STATES

Name	Years Served	Appointed By	Home State
John Jay	1789–1795	Washington	New York
John Rutledge[1]	1795	Washington	South Carolina
Oliver Ellsworth	1796–1800	Washington	Connecticut
John Marshall	1801–1835	Adams	Virginia
Roger B. Taney	1836–1864	Jackson	Maryland
Salmon P. Chase	1864–1873	Lincoln	Ohio
Morrison R. Waite	1874–1888	Grant	Ohio
Melville W. Fuller	1888–1910	Cleveland	Illinois
Edward D. White	1910–1921	Taft	Louisiana
William Howard Taft	1921–1930	Harding	Ohio
Charles Evans Hughes	1930–1941	Hoover	New York
Harlan Fiske Stone	1941–1946	Roosevelt	New York
Fred M. Vinson	1946–1953	Truman	Kentucky
Earl Warren[2]	1953–1969	Eisenhower	California
Warren E. Burger	1969–1986	Nixon	Minnesota
William H. Rehnquist	1986–2005	Reagan	Arizona
John G. Roberts Jr.	2005–	G. W. Bush	Maryland

1. Rutledge accepted a recess appointment and presided over the Supreme Court at its August 1795 term, during which two cases were decided. In December 1795, however, the Senate refused, 10–14, to confirm him.
2. Warren accepted a recess appointment as chief justice in September 1953 and was confirmed by the Senate in March 1954.
Source: Jost, Kenneth, ed. *The Supreme Court A to Z*, 4th ed. Washington, D.C.: CQ Press, 2007.

trials of a president in the Senate: Salmon P. Chase (1808–73) in 1868 (for Andrew Johnson) and Rehnquist in 1999 (for Bill Clinton), both of whom were acquitted.

The chief justice is also responsible for the general administration of the Supreme Court and presides over the Judicial Conference of the United States, which is composed of the chief judge and a justice from each of the nine federal circuit courts of appeal and is responsible for setting policy for the administration of the entire federal judicial system. In addition, the chief justice supervises the Administrative Office of the U.S. Courts, which provides administrative support for the federal judiciary. Like his fellow justices, the chief justice is appointed for life and has four law clerks, but he receives a higher salary and the use of a car. The chief justice also traditionally administers the OATH OF OFFICE to incoming presidents.

Children

Despite much rhetoric about "family values," the rights and welfare of children in the United States—apart from occasional debates over public, private, and parochial EDUCATION—are far from the center of America's political agenda. Currently about thirteen million children in the United States live in poverty, and a similarly large number lack adequate health care. In addition to malnutrition and disease, children are vulnerable to physical and mental abuse, neglect, exploitation, DRUGS, crime, and gun violence (see GUN CONTROL).

The Twenty-sixth Amendment (1971) gave eighteen-year-olds the right to vote, but the Constitution has nothing to say specifically about young children. (Ireland's 1937 constitution is rare in addressing the education, employment, and state guardianship of children as well as the duties of parents, calling for "a certain minimum education, moral, intellectual and social.") Even today the Senate, which is constitutionally charged with approving TREATIES, cannot bring itself to ratify the United Nations' Convention on the Rights of the Child (1989), as all but one other (Somalia) UN-member nations have done; this international agreement urges adults to take into account what is best for children and consider their views, to guarantee them the right of survival and healthy development, and to ensure equal opportunity for boys and girls.

The legal definition of *children* includes both the young offspring of parents and unborn progeny as well as adopted and illegitimate children and stepchildren. Although the Supreme Court's decision in *ROE V. WADE* (1973) may have set the first three months after conception as the lower limit on the time when a child has the status of a human being and thus the right to life, some people opposed to ABORTION declare that they are fighting for the rights of the "unborn child." The age at which a person ceases to be a child and legally becomes an adult is set by the states.

A person under eighteen cannot vote, of course, and most are at the mercy of the FAMILIES into whose care they are entrusted until they reach adulthood. These families—varying from caring to abusive, from wealthy to poverty-stricken—as well as public and private institutions charged with looking after abandoned and neglected children often have their own ideas as to what constitutes their rights and their charges' rights. In *Parham v. J. R.*

In 1915 Lewis Hine found a seven-year-old topping sugar beets near Sterling, Colorado. The Fair Labor Standards Act (1938) finally contained a provision regulating child labor, which was upheld by the Supreme Court in 1941.
Source: Library of Congress

(1979), the Supreme Court held that parents may commit their child to a mental institution without any hearing, as would be required for an adult under the Constitution's DUE PROCESS provisions. And in *Santosky v. Kramer* (1982), the Court ruled that the Constitution does not require a state to prevent parental abuse of a child, although it may remove the child from the parents on a showing of clear and convincing evidence of actual abuse. Increasingly, however, the needs and rights of children are becoming focal points for social and political concern.

Child Labor

Child labor gained the public's attention at the beginning of the twentieth century. In *Hammer v. Dagenhart* (1918), the Supreme Court, using unusually contorted logic, struck down as unconstitutional a 1916 act of Congress prohibiting interstate shipments of products made using child labor. The Court distinguished lottery tickets—specifically banned by Congress from being sent through the mail and interstate commerce, a ban the Court upheld in *Champion v. Ames* (1903), The Lottery Case—as being evil in themselves, whereas child labor was called an evil before their products were transported in interstate commerce and therefore constitutionally permissible. Justice OLIVER WENDELL HOLMES JR., seeing through the majority's sophistry, dissented, saying that when Congress finds a practice to be a moral evil, it can implement its policies regardless of any indirect effect they may have on the activities of the states. "[I]f there is any matter upon which civilized countries have agreed," he added, "it is the evil of premature and excessive child labor."

In 1924 Congress again tried to curb child labor by offering an amendment to the Constitution (see AMENDMENTS). Opposed by farmers and businesses using cheap child labor, it failed to receive sufficient state ratification for approval. The Supreme Court's philosophy with respect to the federal government's attempt to deal with health and welfare concerns resulting from the crisis of the Great Depression began to change in 1937. The Fair Labor Standards Act (1938), which contained prohibitions against child labor, was therefore allowed to stand. It set fourteen as the minimum age for nonfarm work, barred employment for unlimited hours as well as for hazardous work by those under the age of eighteen, and restricted fourteen- and fifteen-year-olds to working only outside school hours.

Children and Pornography

Pornography (written, graphic, or other forms of COMMUNICATIONS intended to excite lascivious feelings) can adversely affect both the children depicted in such material and those exposed to it. Whereas adult pornography has proven difficult to deal with legally because of the constitutional guarantee of free SPEECH and freedom of THE PRESS, the constitutionality of laws designed to curb pornography that may affect or involve children has been well established by the Supreme Court (see CENSORSHIP; OBSCENITY).

Laws banning the sale of obscene material to minors under the age of seventeen were upheld by the Supreme Court in *Ginsberg v. New York* (1968) as long as it is "utterly without redeeming social importance for minors." In *New York v. Ferber* (1982), the Court held unanimously that the visual depiction of children engaged in sexual activity is not speech protected by the Constitution. And in *Osborn v. Ohio* (1992), the Court determined that a state law making it a crime to possess child pornography even in the PRIVACY of the home was not unconstitutional; such laws help curb the abuse of children forced to participate in the production of pornographic materials and also help protect a victim's privacy.

Recent attempts by Congress to protect children from pornography on the Internet have been struck down by the Supreme Court. In *Ashcroft v. Free Speech Coalition* (2002), the Supreme Court held that the Child Pornography Prevention Act of 1996, which aimed to prohibit virtual child pornography, went beyond the constitutional bounds set by the Court in *Ferber*. Then, in two decisions in *Ashcroft v. American Civil Liberties Union* (2002 and 2004), the Court struck down the Child Online Protection Act of 1998, because the law's content-based restrictions on free speech violated the First Amendment (1791). A law requiring public libraries that receive federal funds—which most do—to use Internet filters to block depictions of obscenity or child pornography, however, was upheld by the Court in *United States v. American Library Association* (2003). A new federal law, the Prosecutorial Tools to End Exploitation of Children Today (PROTECT), enacted in 2003, was struck down by a U.S. court of appeals in 2007 for being a vague and overly broad infringement of free speech. It will be interesting to see if the Supreme Court will let this ruling stand.

Adoption and Custody

Adoption and child custody are generally determined under state law. The Supreme Court has extended EQUAL PROTECTION of the law to unwed fathers when decisions are made about placing an illegitimate child for adoption. But a father's attempt to prevent adoption of his illegitimate child by the child's natural mother and her husband was denied in *Lehr v. Robertson* (1983), in large part because he had made no attempt ever to see or support the child.

A basic principle in reaching legal decisions involving children is whether the outcome is in the best interest of the child. The Supreme Court in *Palmore v. Sidoti* (1984) overruled a judge's decision removing a daughter from the custody of her mother, who was white, when the mother married an African American man, saying, "The effects of racial prejudice, however real, cannot justify…removing an infant child from the custody of its natural mother found to be an appropriate person to have such custody." In *Reno v. Flores* (1993), however, the Court denied an alien juvenile any constitutional right to a custody arrangement that is "in the best interest of the child" and refused to find that an alien child has any right to appeal federal custody or detention.

Juvenile Offenders

Legally, a juvenile is a young person who has not yet attained the age at which he or she would be treated as an adult under CRIMINAL LAW. A juvenile as defined by the Juvenile Delinquency Prevention Act (1972) (enacted originally in 1968 as the Juvenile Delinquency and Control Act) is a person not yet eighteen years of age. The rights of juveniles are often established by state law and may include access to juvenile court, in which the rules of law and evidence are not strictly adhered to. The basis for a separate court is to treat juvenile offenders not as adult criminals but as troubled youths for whom adult procedures and PUNISHMENT would be counterproductive to their proper social and moral development.

A seminal children's rights case was *In re Gault* (1967), involving a fifteen-year-old boy charged with making an obscene phone call. His sentence—six years in an "industrial school"—was meted out in a juvenile proceeding conducted without benefit of legal counsel (see ASSISTANCE OF COUNSEL) or DUE PROCESS procedures and thus, the Supreme Court ruled, was invalid. Justice Abe Fortas (1910–82), writing for the majority, declared: "Under our Constitution, the condition of being a boy does not justify a kangaroo court." Three years later, in *In re Winship* (1970), the Court added that criminal charges against a juvenile, as against adults, must be proven beyond a reasonable doubt.

In *Breed v. Jones* (1975), the Supreme Court found that juveniles are protected by the prohibition in the Fifth Amendment (1791) against DOUBLE JEOPARDY. However, according to the Court's ruling in *McKeiver v. Pennsylvania* (1971), a juvenile does not have a right to a jury trial (see JURIES; TRIALS). Furthermore, under the Court's decision in *Stanford v. Kentucky* (1989)—in which a juvenile sixteen and a half years old at the time a murder was committed was certified for trial as an adult—sixteen-year-olds are subject to the DEATH PENALTY for capital crimes just like adults.

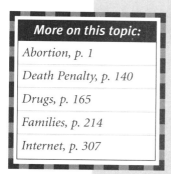

More on this topic:

Abortion, p. 1

Death Penalty, p. 140

Drugs, p. 165

Families, p. 214

Internet, p. 307

Children are not simply little adults. Depending on their age and their physical, social, and intellectual maturity, they often require special protection, at times even from close relatives. The issue of children's rights is fraught with obstacles, but so far neither the Constitution nor the Supreme Court appears very helpful in navigating around them safely.

Church and State   *See* RELIGION.

Citizens

In ancient Athens, citizenship conferred the right to participate in the world's first DEMOCRACY. In the Roman republic, a citizen (from the Latin *civitas*, meaning citizenship) was entitled to participate in certain decisions related to governance of the republic. Citizenship, however, was limited to free adult males.

The word *citizen* appears eleven times in the Constitution as drafted in 1787. Article IV, section 2, for example, provides: "The Citizens of each State shall be entitled to all Privileges and Immunities of Citizens in the several States." The term was not defined in the document until the

Fourteenth Amendment (1868) was ratified. Section 1 of the amendment begins: "All persons born or naturalized in the United States and subject to the jurisdiction thereof, are citizens of the United States and of the State wherein they reside."

An Evolving Concept

The concept of citizenship contemplated under the 1787 document represented a break with the notion of what it meant to be a subject of the British Crown or even a citizen of one of the thirteen colonies or states that would become the United States. According to English law at the beginning of the seventeenth century, being a subject involved a perpetual, immutable relationship of allegiance in return for protection by the sovereign or monarch. The colonies, to quickly assimilate new colonists and thus increase the population and the work force, found a more liberal interpretation expedient.

In the new states and new nation, however, the definition of citizenship was unclear. JAMES MADISON, in essay 42 of *The Federalist* (1787–88) (see FEDERALIST PAPERS), written in support of RATIFICATION of the Constitution, pointed out the problem under the ARTICLES OF CONFEDERATION (1781). "In the fourth article…it is declared 'that the *free inhabitants* of each of these States, paupers, vagabonds, and fugitives from justice excepted, shall be entitled to all privileges and immunities of *free citizens* in the several States; and *the people* of each State shall, in every other, enjoy all privileges of trade and commerce….' There is a confusion of language here which is remarkable," Madison concluded. The FRAMERS OF THE CONSTITUTION might be excused their imprecision about a concept that was still evolving and that meant one thing at the state level and another at the national level. The decision of Robert E. Lee at the beginning of the Civil War to honor his obligations to the Commonwealth of Virginia over those to the nation exemplifies the dichotomy.

Unlike other national constitutions, the Constitution requires of U.S. citizens no express duties of citizenship. In light of the theory that the document represents a grant of powers by the states and the citizens to the national government, they had no reason to place duties on themselves.

The idea expressed in Article IV, section 2—that all citizens share the same "Privileges and Immunities"—is continued in the Fourteenth Amendment (1868), section 1: "No State shall make or enforce any law which shall abridge the privileges or immunities of citizens of the United States; nor shall any State deprive any person of life, liberty, or property, without due process of law; nor deny to any person within its jurisdiction the equal protection of the laws" (see DUE PROCESS; EQUAL PROTECTION). On the surface, the Constitution treats citizens equally, although certain qualifications regarding citizenship are required for certain offices. The Constitution requires a specific number of years of citizenship for candidates for Congress—seven for representatives and nine for senators—and requires that a person be a natural-born citizen to be president.

The actual history of the United States belies the Constitution's promise of truly equal treatment for all Americans. For example, slaves (see SLAVERY) and WOMEN were denied citizenship rights for too long, and during World War II Americans of Japanese descent living on the West Coast were considered a threat to national security and forced to relocate (see DISCRIMINATION). Today limitations persist on the rights of citizens of the District of Columbia (see CAPITAL, NATIONAL) and U.S. territories and possessions (see TERRITORY), including the lack of voting representation in Congress, and on the rights of homosexuals serving in the military.

The terrorist attacks on the United States on September 11, 2001, have resulted in a number of efforts by Congress and the executive branch to improve intelligence regarding activities related to potential new terrorist attacks. These efforts, such as surveillance and intelligence gathering (including wiretapping), are ostensibly directed at foreigners and noninternal communications, but officials in the government, legal scholars, and citizen groups have expressed concerns that some measures may infringe on the constitutional guarantees for U.S. citizens regarding search and seizure and privacy. As a balance is struck between the definition of these rights and the legitimate need for national security, the relationship between American citizens and their government will undoubtedly undergo further evolution. However, in HAMDI V. RUMSFELD and *Rumsfeld v. Padilla* (both 2004), the Supreme Court, by less than an absolute majority in the first case and by 5–4 in the second, upheld the basic rights of U.S. citizens seized and detained in the war on terror. In the first case the American citizen was seized on the battlefield in Afghanistan and declared to be an enemy combatant; in the second case the citizen was seized in the United States and detained in connection with an investigation into the September 11 attacks.

Acquiring Citizenship

The federal government has bestowed citizenship on groups as well as on individuals. Such citizenship can be granted by treaty—for example, the Louisiana Purchase (1803), which conferred citizenship on the eligible inhabitants in the Louisiana Territory—or by law, as in the annexations of Texas and Hawaii, which made residents of those states U.S. nationals and later citizens.

British law determining how an individual person acquired citizenship or became a subject of the Crown, inherited by the United States at its inception, required only that a person be born on British soil. This *jus soli* method, based on where a person is born, may be distinguished from the *jus sanguinis* method, based on the nationality of the parents. Today the United States and a number of other countries still extend citizenship to people born in their territory, regardless of the nationality of the parents, with the exception of children of foreign diplomats and enemy ALIENS.

The Constitution does, however, address the process of naturalization, in which a noncitizen may become a citizen of the United States. Article I, section 8, expressly gives Congress the power to "establish an uniform Rule of Naturalization...." Individual naturalization usually requires the filing of a petition by a person of lawful age who has been a lawful resident of the United States for at least five years. The U.S. Citizenship and Immigration Services (formerly the Immigration and Naturalization Service) investigates to determine if the applicant has a good command of English and knowledge of the government and history of the United States. After a hearing before a court, the applicant must take an oath of allegiance to the United States. As of March 1, 2003, the service and benefits functions of the INS were transferred to the U.S. Citizenship and Immigration Services. The other functions went to the Department of Homeland Security.

Juan Escalante reacts as he holds his new certificate of citizenship and a U.S. flag following his swearing in as a naturalized U.S. citizen. Escalante was born in Mexico and used a false green card to join the U.S. Army and fight in the Iraq War.
Source: AP Images/Elaine Thompson

Loss of Citizenship

The Supreme Court's about-face within ten years on the question of Congress's power to strip a citizen of U.S. citizenship is a good example of the evolution of constitutional law. In *Perez v.*

More on this topic:

Immigration, p. 286

Privileges and
Immunities, p. 432

Terrorism, p. 543

Brownell (1957), the Court decided that Congress's power over foreign affairs under the Nationality Act (1940) allowed it to make voting in a foreign election a basis for losing one's citizenship. But in the landmark decision *Afroyim v. Rusk* (1967), a new five-member majority on the Court found that pursuant to the Fourteenth Amendment Congress did not have authority to strip away citizenship without the citizen's consent. As Justice Hugo Black (1886–1971) wrote for the Court: "Citizenship in this Nation is a part of a cooperative affair. Its citizenry is the country and the country is its citizenry."

The Supreme Court has continued to look carefully at provisions that may constitute grounds for loss of citizenship. In *Rogers v. Bellei* (1971), it allowed Congress to impose subsequent conditions on the retention of citizenship acquired at birth where a person was born abroad to parents, one or both of whom were U.S. citizens, because he or she would not meet the definition of a citizen under the Fourteenth Amendment: being born or naturalized in the United States.

Civil Forfeiture   *See* JUST COMPENSATION.

Civil Rights

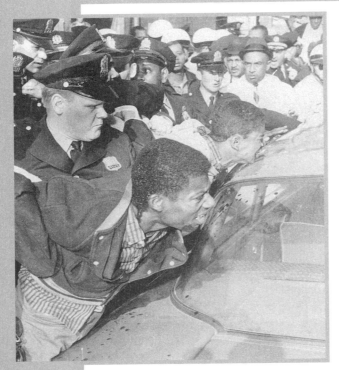

Resistance to desegregation marked the civil rights protests of the 1950s and 1960s. The strong arm of vigilantism, as well as reactionary police power, helped push the nation toward legislative solutions to the problem of inequality.
Source: Library of Congress

The International Covenant on Civil and Political Rights (1966), adopted by the United Nations, went into force in 1976 after being ratified by thirty-five countries, including the United States. The rights recognized in the document, including the right to LIBERTY, freedom of movement and residence, equality in the courts, and recognition as a person before the law, are to be protected, according to part II, article 2, "without distinction of any kind such as race, color, sex, language, religion, political or other opinion, national or social origin, property, birth or other status." Underlying the concept of civil rights is the notion that each person is a unique individual who is politically equal to any other person and entitled to equal treatment by government authorities but who should be allowed every opportunity to maximize his or her potential as a human being.

In the United States, civil rights became synonymous in the 1950s and 1960s with freedom from DISCRIMINATION, especially with regard to MINORITIES, particularly African Americans. If there is any truth to the proclamation in the DECLARATION OF INDEPENDENCE (1776) that "all Men are created equal," all CITIZENS of the United States (including women, despite the document's language) are entitled to equal and fair treatment regardless of race, sex, social status, national origin, or other incidents of birth. Discrimination on the basis of age, disability, language, religion, sexual orientation, and economic status might also be added to the list.

The concept of civil liberties implies a freedom to be let alone by the government; freedom of SPEECH and RELIGION and the right of PRIVACY all address what the government should not do to repress or insinuate itself into the ordinary private and social lives of the citizenry. The concept of civil rights, on the other hand, implies that the government in certain situations should use its power to ensure equality of treatment for all citizens.

Government versus Private Discrimination

But what constitutes government discrimination, and what constitutes private discrimination? Obviously, a court may not automatically find a person guilty of a crime simply because he or she is a member of an ethnic, a racial, or a religious minority. On the other hand, the government has no right to force citizens to socialize with or invite into their homes members of any particular minority. Somewhere in between these two extremes lies the proper balance of government treatment of and assistance to minorities who are often discriminated against in American society.

On its face the Fourteenth Amendment (1868) appears to guarantee all citizens—at the time, all male citizens—equal treatment by state governments. The difficulty arose in determining the extent to which a state must go to ensure equality of treatment for all citizens. In the so-called Civil Rights Cases (1883), the Supreme Court selected certain cases representative of asserted violations of civil rights under the Civil Rights Act of 1875 and the Fourteenth Amendment. To the dismay of recently freed slaves, who had been made citizens of the United States, the Court held that the Fourteenth Amendment does not require private businesses to refrain from practicing discrimination. Frederick Douglass (1817–95), spokesman for the rights of former slaves and a former slave himself, decried the Court's decision, saying that it "has inflicted a heavy calamity…upon seven millions of people of this country, and left them naked and defenceless against the action of a malignant, vulgar, and pitiless prejudice."

The Supreme Court's decision in *Plessy v. Ferguson* (1896) institutionalized the SEGREGATION of African Americans by declaring constitutionally acceptable the doctrine of "separate but equal" facilities for blacks and whites. This principle remained substantially intact until the Court's decision in BROWN V. BOARD OF EDUCATION OF TOPEKA (1954), in which the "separate but equal" doctrine was finally declared to be an unconstitutional violation of the EQUAL PROTECTION clause of the Fourteenth Amendment. The civil rights movement that followed the *Brown* decision resulted in a number of laws to implement equality of treatment and make up for past discrimination. Among them were the Civil Rights Act (1964), Voting Rights Act (1965), Equal Employment Opportunity Act (1968), and Fair Housing Act (1968).

The civil rights struggle led by MARTIN LUTHER KING JR. did not end with his assassination in 1968. New programs were implemented with varying degrees of success, from AFFIRMATIVE ACTION, requiring a special effort to hire and train minority workers and assist minority businesses, to forced busing of schoolchildren to create a racial balance in public schools. However, ridding American society of prejudice, discrimination, and hatred of minority citizens is an unfinished process. Perhaps the nation as a whole has come a long way since the Civil War (1861–65), but as individuals some Americans exhibit an astonishing degree of discrimination against and intolerance of those who are different from themselves. For example, in *Virginia v. Black* (2003), in which the defendants had been convicted of violating a Virginia statute that made it a felony "for any person…, with the intent of intimidating any person or group…, to burn…a cross on the property of another, a highway or other public place," the Supreme Court held that such a law did not offend the First Amendment's guarantee of free speech. The Court noted that the law was a permissible means of protecting civil rights because cross burning was a particularly virulent form of intimidation that had a long and pernicious history as a signal of impending violence. On the other hand, at the national level, the Employment Non-Discrimination Act, which first was introduced in Congress in the mid-1970s to provide civil rights protection for homosexuals and other gender minorities, has still not been enacted into law.

Civil Disobedience

Civil disobedience is a method of bringing about social change that emphasizes the willingness of people of conscience to disobey unjust laws. The concept originated with Socrates, the Greek philosopher of the fifth century B.C.E., who was sentenced to death for teaching his students to question authority, and drew on the works of St. Thomas Aquinas (ca. 1224–74), who argued that the law of temporal rulers should be judged against divine law, and Henry David Thoreau (1817–62), who spent a night in jail for refusing to pay taxes to support a government that condoned SLAVERY and an imperialistic war against Mexico. In 1913 WOMEN suffragists picketed the White House in a lawful protest against being denied the vote but were arrested by police disdainful of their cause. In the twentieth century civil disobedience was used effectively by Mahatma Gandhi (1869–1948) to gain India's complete independence from Great Britain (achieved in 1950) and by Martin Luther King shortly thereafter to further the civil rights movement in the United States.

Demonstrators opposed to the impacts of global trade denounce the World Trade Organization in Washington, D.C., in 2003.
Source: AP Images/Ron Edmonds

Because of its potential legal consequences, including imprisonment, civil disobedience is not to be undertaken lightly. But in some cases challenging government authorities to enforce an unjust law is the only way to bring nationwide or worldwide attention to a just cause. Today activists have begun rallying against various perceived wrongs: protesting adverse economic and social effects of globalization by causing civil disturbances during World Trade Organization meetings in Seattle, Washington, D.C., and Genoa, Italy; calling for an end to use of populated areas as military testing grounds by holding sit-ins and being arrested in Puerto Rico. If enough people disobey unjust laws often enough, those who make the laws and policies are generally forced to rethink the need to keep them on the books.

More on this topic:
Age Discrimination, p. 23
Disabled Persons, p. 156
Employment Discrimination, p. 192
Homosexuals, p. 275
Sex Discrimination, p. 497

Clear and Present Danger *See* SPEECH.

Cloning *See* GENETICS.

Coinage *See* CURRENCY.

Commander-in-Chief *See* PRESIDENT.

Commerce

In *The Laws*, a dialogue about constructing a constitution for a new colony, Plato, the Greek philosopher of the fourth century B.C.E., devoted an entire section to commercial law. Aristotle, his younger contemporary, also addressed commerce but concluded that in the best governed state, whose men are absolutely just "and not merely relative to...the constitution, the citizens must not lead the life of artisans or tradesmen...." By the eighteenth century, commerce and trade were more respectable endeavors. William Blackstone (1723–80), in his *Commentaries on the Laws of England* (1765–70), declared offenses against public trade to be one of the five major categories of crime and misdemeanors.

From the beginning of England's colonization of North America, trade and commerce were important activities. According to ALEXANDER HAMILTON in essay 7 of *The Federalist* (1787–88) (see FEDERALIST PAPERS), "The spirit of enterprise, which characterizes the commercial part of America, has left no occasion of displaying itself unimproved." JAMES MADISON noted in essay 42 that the perceived lack of power to regulate commerce between the states was a major defect in the ARTICLES OF CONFEDERATION (1781) and was the primary reason for calling the CONSTITUTIONAL CONVENTION OF 1787.

> **"The spirit of enterprise, which characterizes the commercial part of America, has left no occasion of displaying itself unimproved."**
>
> **—Alexander Hamilton**

The Commerce Clause

The Constitution's commerce clause, included in Article I, section 8, declares: "The Congress shall have Power...To regulate Commerce with foreign Nations, and among the several States, and with the Indian Tribes...." This language is significant because it encouraged a nationwide policy governing commercial activity, thus fostering free trade among the states, and it provided a tool for extending the national government's power into the states. The commerce clause and the cases relating to it that have come before the Supreme Court are also particularly helpful in understanding the evolution of FEDERALISM in the United States. Although the FRAMERS OF THE CONSTITUTION clearly intended to charge the national government with the regulation of commerce with foreign nations and NATIVE AMERICANS, the extent of its power to regulate interstate and even intrastate commerce has often been the subject of great controversy.

Two ferry operators in New York first brought the issue to the Supreme Court in 1824. Licensed by a firm granted a monopoly by a 1798 state law, Aaron Ogden operated a steam-driven ferry between New Jersey and New York City. Thomas Gibbons had a permit under the federal Coastal Licensing Act (1793) for his own two boats, which he defiantly ran to New York despite Ogden's license. After New York courts granted Ogden an injunction against his rival, Gibbons appealed to the Supreme Court. On the question of whether New York could grant such exclusive rights and thus exclude Gibbons from New York's waters, Chief Justice JOHN MARSHALL, writing in *GIBBONS V. OGDEN*, determined that it could not because Congress's regulating power over commerce among the states does not stop at the state lines but may be exercised within a state.

Another important case, *Cooley v. Board of Wardens* (1851), however, allowed state regulation of commerce in purely local matters. A Pennsylvania statute required that vessels entering or leaving the port of Philadelphia have local pilots, whose specialized knowledge was necessary to safely navigate the port's waters. The Supreme Court upheld the state statute on the grounds that unless the subject to be regulated required a uniform national policy, states were permitted to regulate local commerce as long as the federal government had not enacted a preemptive law concerning it.

Congress did not begin actively regulating the national economy until passage of the Interstate Commerce Act (1887) and the Sherman Antitrust Act (1890) (see ANTITRUST LAW). At this point the Supreme Court, in what is called its economic due process of law phase, began to take a restrictive view of Congress's commerce power. In *United States v. E. C. Knight Co.* (1895), the Sugar Trusts Case, the Court found that the federal government's antitrust power under the commerce clause did not permit an antitrust action against a company with 98 percent of the nation's sugar-refining capacity because the production was a local activity and that it could not intervene until the final movement of the goods into interstate commerce.

Soon, however, the Supreme Court began upholding antitrust actions based on an activity's direct effect on interstate commerce. In *Swift and Co. v. United States* (1905), Justice OLIVER WENDELL HOLMES JR. proposed a "current of commerce" theory that extended the reach of government antitrust enforcement even further. But the Court was reluctant to use the commerce power to extend the federal government's regulation of business to further an enlightened social policy. Thus, in *Hammer v. Daganhart* (1918), the Court struck down an attempt by Congress to curtail child labor abuses (see CHILDREN).

By the 1940s the Supreme Court's composition had changed, and it began upholding Congress's HEALTH and safety legislation on the basis of the laws' effect on commerce. Even a law penalizing a farmer for growing and consuming on his own property more wheat than allowed by a government allotment was upheld for its effect on the total supply and demand for wheat throughout the country. Congress was given wide latitude until 1995, when in *United States v. Lopez* the Court struck down the lawmakers' attempt to criminalize possession of a gun within one thousand feet of a school (see GUN CONTROL). The Court's opinion emphasized that the relationship between the possession of a gun within one thousand feet of a school and its effect on commerce was so tenuous that upholding the constitutionality of the law would permit Congress to regulate any activity of citizens related to economic production, including "marriage, divorce, and child custody" (see FAMILIES).

Although Congress enacted a less sweeping gun control law regulating only guns having some connection with interstate commerce, the current Supreme Court may have reached the limit of how far it will extend the federal government's commerce power. In *Jones v. United States* (2000), for example, the Court held that arson of an owner-occupied private residence is not a federal crime under a statute covering fire damage or destruction of any property used in interstate commerce because the property in question was not used for commercial purposes. But in *Circuit City Stores, Inc. v. Adams* (2001), the Court upheld Congress's reliance on the commerce clause, saying that the Court had interpreted the statutory language "involving commerce" in the Federal Arbitration Act (1925, as amended) to mean Congress's intent to "exercise [its] commerce power to the full."

Following its line of reasoning in *Lopez*, the Supreme Court in *United States v. Morrison* (2000) again found the power of Congress under the commerce clause to be unconstitutional with regard to the Violence Against Women Act of 1994. In his decision for the Court—with one concurring opinion and four dissents—Chief Justice William H. Rehnquist (1924–2005), the author of the *Lopez* decision, concluded that Congress did not have the power under the commerce clause to "regulate noneconomic, violent criminal conduct based solely on that conduct's aggregate effect on interstate commerce." This decision to curtail federal power in this area of law enforcement was interesting given that the National Association of Attorneys General unanimously supported it, as did the attorneys general of thirty-eight states. But in *Gonzales v. Raich* (2005), in an opinion delivered by Justice John Paul Stevens (b. 1920), the Court upheld the power of the federal government to prohibit the local cultivation and personal use of marijuana, even if done in compliance with state law. Citing *National Labor Relations Board v. Jones & Laughlin Steel Corp.* (1937), the Court declared that Congress has a constitutional right to regulate local activities when they are a part of an economic class of "activities that substantially affect interstate commerce."

The Doctrine of Preemption

Because the Constitution's commerce clause simply allows the federal government to regulate interstate commerce when Congress sees a need to be addressed, state regulation has taken place in many areas where Congress has not yet acted. The inchoate power of Congress to regulate interstate commerce—often referred to as the "dormant commerce clause"—raises the question of whether some aspects are inherently off limits to the states. The Supreme Court has struck down state regulation in the absence of congressional action in two situations: (1) where the state regulation discriminates against interstate commerce and (2) where it places a burden on interstate commerce that is clearly excessive in relation to the local benefits obtained by the state regulation.

When Congress does initiate regulation of some aspect of interstate commerce, the Supreme Court may find that its attempts preempt any state attempts to regulate the same activity. In *Rice v. Santa Fe Elevator Corp.* (1947), the Court listed three criteria for finding preemption: (1) if the national regulatory scheme is "so pervasive as to make reasonable the inference that Congress left no room for the States to supplement it"; (2) if the federal interest in the subject matter is "so dominant that the federal system will be assumed to preclude enforcement of state laws on the same subject"; and (3) if the policy by the state "may produce a result inconsistent with the objective of the federal statute." The Court held that although the U.S. Warehouse Act (1916) made state regulations regarding grain warehousing preeminent over federal regulations on the same subject, subsequent amendments terminated the dual system of regulation. The act's creation of an exclusive federal system, said the Court, meant that it was no longer necessary for warehouses to comply with state regulations that were superseded by federal law.

An example often used to explain chaos theory in mathematics (the random and unpredictable behavior of a deterministic system such as weather patterns) is that a tornado in Kansas may have

More on this topic:

Admiralty and Maritime Law, p. 13

Federalism, p. 218

Gibbons v. Ogden, p. 256

Travel, p. 548

its origins in the beating of a butterfly's wings in South America. The federal government's power to regulate commerce taking place wholly within a single state is similar, because nearly every local transaction has at least a minute effect on interstate commerce. A farmer in Iowa who does not plant an additional acre of corn one year affects, in an infinitesimal way, the future price of grain on the world market. In 1787 the framers of the Constitution were seeking a solution to the problem of trade restrictions imposed by thirteen individual states, so it is not surprising that over the last two centuries Congress and the Supreme Court have been able to expand the federal government's power to regulate nearly all aspects of commerce throughout the United States.

Commercial Speech   *See* SPEECH.

Committees   *See* HOUSE OF REPRESENTATIVES; SENATE.

Common Defense   *See* ARMED FORCES.

Common Law

A nation's legal system is generally based on one of two types of law: code law or common law. Code law is law that has been promulgated by some authority or enacted by a legislature to be used by judges in deciding cases. One country that uses code law is France, which has adopted the Code Napoleon—a civil law code written by a commission of jurists and promulgated in 1804. This code became influential in many European countries during Napoleon's rule over the French Empire in the early nineteenth century. France's influence in Louisiana, especially before the Louisiana Purchase in 1803, has made it the only state in the United States that relies on code law.

The type of law that influenced the thirteen original states of the United States and the Constitution drafted in 1787 was England's common law. Even today the Anglo-American legal system and the laws of many of Great Britain's other former colonies, such as Canada and New Zealand, are rooted in the rules and principles of common law. Rather than having been enacted by a legislature like code law (sometimes called statute law), English common law has been created over centuries by judges' decisions in cases brought before them.

Common law has come to be relied on as authoritative because of the principles of *stare decisis* ("to stand by decided cases") and precedent, which requires a court to apply the same law as was applied in the past in similar cases. This reliance on precedent means that the outcomes in similar factual situations should always be the same. A person who trespasses on another person's land, for example, should receive the same treatment at the hands of a court as in previous cases involving this same transgression. Under code law, courts look first to the provisions of the enacted law to discover what the outcome of a particular case should be.

The legal definition of the term *common law* is law that derives its authority solely from usages and customs of immemorial antiquity or from judgments and decrees of the courts that recognize, affirm, and enforce such usages and customs. It has been characterized as law so ancient that "the mind of man runneth not to the contrary." In some other contexts, however, the term may simply refer to a general law common to a particular people, a country, or a group of countries. In the United States, *common law* originally referred to all statutory and judge-declared law in effect before the American Revolution.

Common law was not expressly incorporated into the law of the United States by the Constitution. The only explicit references to common law in the document appear in the Seventh Amendment (1791): "In Suits at common law, where the value in controversy shall exceed twenty dollars, the right of trial by jury shall be preserved, and no fact tried by a jury, shall be otherwise re-examined in any Court of the United States, than according to the rules of the common law." A number of the rights guaranteed in the Constitution, however, especially the rights of persons accused of crimes, reflect accepted common law principles.

Some states, unlike the federal government, have specifically adopted common law. The California Civil Code, section 22.2, provides that the "common law of England, so far as it is not repugnant to or inconsistent with the Constitution of the United States, or the Constitution or laws of this State, is the rule of decision in all the courts of this State." States have a general power to enact, in accordance with their own constitutions, laws that affect their citizens across a broad spectrum of activities, excluding those areas of law delegated exclusively to the federal government, such as foreign affairs and national defense. Many areas of law under the states' legal jurisdiction, such as property rights, contract law, and inheritance law, have in fact developed through court decisions rather than by statutes enacted by the state legislatures. The states were expected to continue to develop their own common law through judgments of their courts, whereas the federal courts were to rely for guidance only on the Constitution and laws enacted by Congress.

However, the Supreme Court under its power of diversity jurisdiction to hear cases between citizens of different states and between citizens of a state and foreigners, under often conflicting laws, began developing its own common law. In *Swift v. Tyson* (1842), Justice Joseph Story (1779–1845) ruled that state court decisions, unlike state constitutions and statutes, were not laws within the meaning of the Judiciary Act (1789), section 34; therefore, while such decisions were entitled to respect, they were not binding on federal courts. Story's ruling opened the door for federal courts to develop a federal common law parallel to common law in the states, which had been developing for nearly one hundred years.

In a strong dissent in *Black and White Taxicab and Transfer Co. v. Brown and Yellow Taxicab and Transfer Co.* (1928), Justice OLIVER WENDELL HOLMES JR. indicated his belief that *Swift* had been wrongly decided but that it was not necessary to overrule it. The Supreme Court, as it has done on other occasions, changed course, adopting Holmes's position in its decision in *Erie Railroad Co. v. Tompkins* (1938). In a unique act of contrition, the Court acknowledged that it had been acting unconstitutionally in allowing the development of a separate federal common law; "there is no general federal common law," it proclaimed. From then on, federal courts could not fashion their own remedies in diversity cases but had to apply the common law of the state involved as well as its statutory and constitutional law.

In another sense, however, common law principles are alive and well in the federal judiciary. Justice Louis D. Brandeis (1856–1941), the author of the *Erie* opinion, acknowledged in a second majority opinion on the same day that a question in *Hinderlider v. La Plata River and Cherry Creek Ditch Co.* (1938) turned on "federal common law." In this context Brandeis was referring to the general principles of common law that the federal courts continue to develop as they interpret the Constitution and the laws enacted by Congress.

Code law starts from a premise that wise minds can create rules for all future situations. Common law is based on the incremental evolution of rules that have been applied in actual situations for many years. Both have their strengths and weak-

More on this topic:

Federalism, p. 218

International Law, p. 304

Law, p. 336

Legislation, p. 343

William Blackstone compiled English common law in the eighteenth century.
Source: Library of Congress

nesses. The Constitution itself was created using both concepts: applying great principles learned from past experiences with governments in other countries and also prescribing rules for operating a new form of government in the future.

Attorneys and judges still use the common law to bolster arguments and decisions. For example, as recently as 2005, in *Deck v. Missouri*, Supreme Court Justice Stephen G. Breyer (b. 1938) referred to common law principles to underscore the impropriety of shackling a criminal defendant during the sentencing phase of the court proceedings. "The rule [that a prisoner may not be visibly shackled during the guilt phase of the trial] has deep roots in the common law." Citing the compiler of the English common law, William Blackstone (1723–80), he continued: "Blackstone wrote that 'it is laid down in our antient [sic] books, that, though under an indictment of the highest nature,' a defendant 'must be brought to the bar without irons, or any manner of shackles or bonds; unless there be evident danger of an escape.'"

Communications

The ability to use complex language distinguishes humans from other animals, making communication the glue of human culture, religion, and social and political organization. In a democracy, communication plays an especially important role. Through the free exchange of ideas, unhampered by government CENSORSHIP or control, an informed electorate can make the decisions required under the Constitution. In 1787 the FRAMERS OF THE CONSTITUTION addressed communications only once—in Article I, section 8, when they gave Congress the power "To establish Post Offices and post Roads." Several years later the First Amendment (1791) took up the important communications methods of the times, stating, "Congress shall make no law respecting an establishment of religion, or prohibiting the free exercise thereof; or abridging the freedom of speech, or of the press; or the right of the people peaceably to assemble, and to petition the Government for a redress of grievances."

Today the constitutions of many nations specifically address freedom and PRIVACY of communications. Two of Sweden's four constitutional documents concern communications: the Freedom of Expression Act (1992) and the Freedom of the Press Act, as amended in 1992, which provides that every Swedish citizen is free to "publish his thoughts and opinions in print…and to make statements and communicate information on any subject whatsoever." Romania's constitution (1991) states in article 28: "Secrecy of letters, telegrams and other postal communications, of telephone conversations and of any other legal means of communication is inviolable."

Traditional forms of communication in the United States, such as RELIGION, SPEECH, THE PRESS, and ASSEMBLY AND ASSOCIATION, are constitutionally guaranteed. The Supreme Court has held in several cases, including *Martin v. City of Struthers* (1943) and *Capitol Square Review and Advisory Board v. Pinette* (1995), that the First Amendment gives broad protection to communication of religious beliefs against government censorship. Similarly, speech in a secular context is protected, especially where it can be defined as political speech—the *sine qua non* of a DEMOCRACY. Freedom of the press and freedom of assembly and association also involve traditional ways of communicating politically in a free, open, and democratic society and therefore generally receive broad protection under the Constitution.

However, the invention of radio and television, the telephone, and the Internet has raised new questions regarding the constitutionality of government interference in or regulation of communications.

Broadcasting

Under the power granted by the COMMERCE clause in Article I, section 8, of the Constitution, Congress in 1934 passed the Communications Act, in which the electromagnetic spectrum (the wavelengths used to broadcast radio and later television programs) was established as a national resource. The act required businesses that wanted to use the public airwaves for communications, including broadcasting commercial and public programming, to be regulated and licensed by the Federal Communications Commission. In *Metropolitan Broadcasting v. FCC* (1990), the Supreme Court validated the government's policy of allocating broadcasting licenses on the basis of increasing minority ownership of broadcasting stations (see MINORITIES), stating that it would diversify the content of such communications media, an inherently good objective.

Because the Constitution does not expressly grant the national government the power to regulate communications but does prohibit government interference with certain types of communications, there have been a number of challenges to and changes in federal government communications policies. For example, the FCC's "fairness doctrine" in effect from 1949 to 1987 required broadcasters to grant equal time for replies to controversial messages aired by their stations. In *Columbia Broadcasting System v. Democratic National Committee* (1973), the Supreme Court rejected claims that the Constitution required broadcasters to sell air time for the presentation of views on controversial issues. Congress, which had enacted the fairness doctrine into law, repealed it, thus terminating the policy.

Other FCC regulations have prohibited obscenity in broadcasting. In *Federal Communications Commission v. Pacifica Foundation* (1978), the Supreme Court decided that the First Amendment affords radio and television less protection than the other media and confirmed the FCC's authority to regulate "indecent" language. This particular case arose from a radio monologue by the comedian George Carlin on the topic of "filthy words." In his opinion for the Court, Justice John Paul Stevens (b. 1920) said that "the individual's right to be left alone [in the home] plainly outweighs the First Amendment rights of [the broadcaster]."

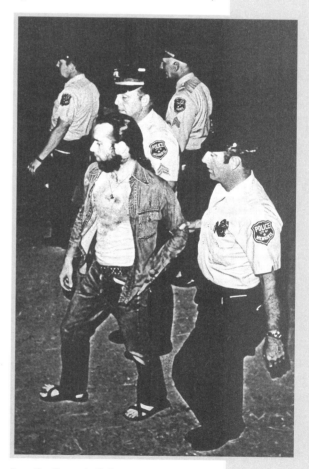

Comedian George Carlin is arrested in 1972 for using allegedly profane language during a performance in Milwaukee, Wisconsin. His act covered "seven dirty words" that could not be used on television. Carlin inadvertently sparked a Supreme Court case over federal regulation of indecent language after a radio station broadcast one of his monologues.
Source: AP Images

The rationale in *Pacifica* was rejected by the Supreme Court in the dial-a-porn case of *Sable Communications, Inc. v. Federal Communications Commission* (1989), because, unlike broadcasting, which can "intrude on the privacy of the home without prior warning as to program content," the telephone allows an alert listener "to take steps to receive the communication," rather than being subjected to an unexpected message. The Court applied some of the *Pacifica* reasoning in its decision in *Denver Area Educational Telecommunications Consortium v. Federal Communications Commission* (1996). In that case, a plurality of the justices found that two of three sections of the Cable Television Consumer Protection and Competition Act of 1992 were unconstitutional. The provision that cable operators could prohibit descriptions or depictions of patently offensive material "as measured by contemporary community standards" was allowed to stand. The decision for the Court, written by Justice Stephen G. Breyer (b. 1938), noted that changes "in the law, the technology, and the industrial structure related to telecommunication" were taking place rapidly, but an important interest at stake in the decision was "protecting children from exposure to patently offensive depictions of sex."

Wiretapping

Communications via the telephone, another invention that could not have been anticipated in 1787, are also protected by the First Amendment. Its guarantees formed the basis for the Supreme Court's decision in KATZ V. UNITED STATES (1967), in which the WIRETAPPING of a public telephone without a warrant was invalidated. One element in the *Katz* case was what the Court referred to as legitimate expectations of privacy, a right the Court has found in the Constitution in the nature of several provisions, including the Fourth Amendment's protection against unreasonable searches and seizures (see SEARCH AND SEIZURE).

Under the Fourth Amendment, wiretapping and other types of electronic eavesdropping now generally require warrants. However, in *United States v. Knotts* (1983), the Supreme Court upheld putting a tracking device on a car to follow it on the road without obtaining a warrant. Nevertheless, according to the ruling in *United States v. Karo* (1984), a warrant is required to put a similar device on an object in a person's house.

Internet

Communications took on a new dimension with the advent of the INTERNET, a vehicle for transmitting not only valuable information but also material that some people may find indecent. In 1996, alarmed by the availability of sexually explicit material on various Web sites and the easy access to it by children and adults who would be offended by it (see OBSCENITY), Congress passed the Communications Decency Act (CDA). In *Reno v. American Civil Liberties Union* (1997), the Supreme Court found the act to be an unconstitutional abridgement of the First Amendment's guarantee of free speech. The Court's decision turned on the act's overly broad proscriptions that were based on content and "suppresse[d] a large amount of speech that adults have a constitutional right to receive and to address to one another."

In 2002 and 2004 the Supreme Court reviewed the Child Online Protection Act passed by Congress in 1998 to remedy defects of the CDA and struck down it, too, as unconstitutionally restrictive under the protections of the First Amendment. In *National Cable & Telecommunications Association v. Brand X Internet Services* (2005), the Court upheld the FCC's interpretation of the language in the Federal Communications Act of 1934, as amended in 1996, and allowed the agency to define "cable internet service providers" in such a way as to exempt them from compulsory "common carrier" regulation by the FCC. The FCC had based its definition on the finding that cable broadband is utilized for "internet access" and not for its "ability to transmit information." The Act requires that all providers of "telecommunications service" are subject to compulsory regulation.

Comparable Worth *See* SEX DISCRIMINATION; WOMEN.

Compensation of Officials

The constitutions of many countries address the matter of compensation for key government officials. Malaysia's constitution (1957, revised 1963), as amended, states: "Parliament shall by law provide for the remuneration of members of each House [of Parliament]." The constitution of Ireland (1937) provides: "The President shall receive such emoluments and allowances as may be determined by law. [They] shall not be diminished during his term of office." And India's constitution (1950) directs that "[t]here shall be paid to the Judges of the Supreme Court such salaries as may be determined by Parliament by law,…[but] neither the privileges nor the allowances of a Judge nor his rights in respect of leave of absence or pension shall be varied to his disadvantage after his appointment."

Congress

The U.S. Constitution addresses compensation for the members of Congress in Article I, section 6: "The Senators and Representatives shall receive a Compensation for their Services, to be ascertained by Law, and paid out of the Treasury of the United States" (see HOUSE OF REPRESENTATIVES; SENATE). Members of Congress are currently paid an annual salary of $169,300; in addition, they receive allowances for offices, staff, and travel. The salary of the SPEAKER OF THE HOUSE is $217,400, and other officers receive compensation over and above their base salary. House majority and minority political party leaders, for example, are paid $188,100.

The Twenty-seventh Amendment (1992), originally proposed with the first amendments that became the BILL OF RIGHTS in 1791, adds a limitation on when these salaries can be raised: "No law, varying the compensation for the services of the Senators and Representatives, shall take effect, until an election of Representatives shall have intervened." The obvious purpose of this amendment is to give citizens a way to voice their approval or disapproval of any salary increase that representatives and senators award themselves—at the polls: legislators not returned to office cannot benefit from the increase. Congress has recently taken to awarding itself automatic cost-of-living increases that do not require passage of any "law," thus skirting the amendment's intent.

The President

The Constitution also directly provides for compensation for the PRESIDENT of the United States. According to Article II, section 1, "The President shall, at stated Times, receive for his Services, a Compensation, which shall neither be encreased nor diminished during the Period for which he shall have been elected, and he shall not receive within that Period any other Emolument [payment for services rendered] from the United States, or any of them." This provision insulates the president from action by Congress to either punish the chief executive or link his actions to the possibility of a reward. "The legislature, on the appointment of a President, is once for all to declare what shall be the compensation for his services during the time for which he shall have been

● CLOSER LOOK

When President Clinton went house hunting in his last year in office, he had little money for a down payment. Even though Clinton earned $200,000 a year as president, he owed several million dollars in legal fees.

But Clinton and his wife, Hillary, were able to qualify for a large bank loan that enabled them to buy a spacious house in an exclusive section of Westchester County, New York. The reason: the former president had the potential to earn millions of dollars from speeches, book contracts, and possible service on corporate boards.

Many prominent politicians, like Clinton, make far more money in retirement than while in office because of their worth as speakers and authors. Some politicians leave office while still at the peak of their influence to become lobbyists—a profession that can pay millions of dollars. In 2007 the number-two Republican in the Senate, Trent Lott of Mississippi, surprised some of his colleagues by stepping down from office to pursue opportunities in the private sector.

elected," as ALEXANDER HAMILTON explains in essay 73 of *The Federalist* (1787–88) (see FEDERALIST PAPERS). "This done, they will have no power to alter it,…[and therefore] [t]hey can neither weaken his fortitude by operating on his necessities, nor corrupt his integrity by appealing to his avarice." The president's salary was raised from $200,000 per year during the administration of President Bill Clinton, which ended in 2000, to $400,000 per year beginning with President George W. Bush, who took office in 2001.

Compensation for other executive branch officials and employees must be approved each fiscal year in the BUDGET law passed by Congress. Executive salary levels, as published by the Office of Personnel Management (OPM), which implements the Civil Service System, range from $136,200 for key lower-level officials to $186,600 for agency heads. Other salaries are set by OPM, subject to approval by the Office of Management and Budget and Congress.

The Judiciary

Compensation for judges is also expressly provided for by the Constitution. Article III, section 1, states: "The Judges, both of the supreme and inferior Courts, shall hold their Offices during good Behaviour, and shall, at stated Times, receive for their Services, a Compensation, which shall not be diminished during their Continuance in Office." The importance of JUDICIAL INDEPENDENCE is evidenced in the Constitution by both the life tenure of federal judges and the protection against any diminution of salary while in office. The yearly salary of the first CHIEF JUSTICE, John Jay (1745–1829), was $4,000 in 1789 and that of the first associate justices was $3,500. The salary of the SUPREME COURT justices today is $203,000 per year, although the chief justice is paid $212,100.

More on this topic:

Just Compensation,
p. 323

In *Evans v. Gore* (1920) and *Miles v. Graham* (1925), the Supreme Court declared that federal judges, even those appointed after the federal income tax law went into effect under the Sixteenth Amendment (1913) (see TAXATION), were exempt from paying income taxes because such a tax diminished their salaries. But in *O'Malley v. Woodrough* (1939), the Court reversed its position and declared that taxes on judges—as well as on citizens—did not diminish their compensation.

Concurrent Powers

The government of the United States is based on the principles inherent in FEDERALISM, which requires a delegation of POWERS from the constituent STATES and the CITIZENS to a national government and the retention of certain powers and rights by the states and the people. The Constitution grants certain exclusive powers to the federal government, a number of which—such as the power to declare WAR and exercise authority over the territory set aside for the nation's capital (see CAPITAL, NATIONAL)—are set forth in Article I, section 8.

Other powers expressly granted to the national government in Article I, section 8, including the power to tax (see TAXATION), to regulate COMMERCE, and to establish uniform rules regarding BANK-

RUPTCY, are concurrent powers—powers that may be exercised by both the states and the national government at the same time. To a limited extent, states also extend COPYRIGHT protection, and both state and federal governments have inherent POLICE POWER. The concept of concurrent powers is not cited in the main body of the Constitution, although the Eighteenth Amendment (1919), which established PROHIBITION, uses the term in section 2: "The Congress and the several States shall have concurrent power to enforce this article by appropriate legislation." The amendment was repealed by the Twenty-first Amendment (1933).

Referring to the allocation of powers then existing under the ARTICLES OF CONFEDERATION (1781–89), JAMES MADISON, in essay 44 of *The Federalist* (1787–88) (see FEDERALIST PAPERS), wrote: "The right of coining money, which is here [in the proposed Constitution] taken from the States, was left in their hands by the Confederation as a concurrent right with that of Congress, under an exception in favor of the exclusive right of Congress to regulate the alloy and value [of the coinage]." ALEXANDER HAMILTON, in essay 32, added: "[A]s the plan of the convention aims only at a partial union or consolidation, the State governments would clearly retain all the rights of sovereignty which they before had, and which were not, by that act, *exclusively* delegated to the United States" (see SOVEREIGNTY; STATES' RIGHTS). In those cases where the grant of power to the federal government was not exclusive, he further noted, "the exercise of a concurrent jurisdiction might be productive of occasional interferences in the *policy* of any branch of administration, but would not imply any direct contradiction or repugnancy in point of constitutional authority."

For the most part, the body of constitutional law relating to concurrent powers has been developed by the courts when faced with conflicts between national and state attempts to legislate in the same areas. In the area of taxation, Chief Justice JOHN MARSHALL, speaking for the Supreme Court in *MCCULLOCH V. MARYLAND* (1819), recognized the concurrent power of the state of Maryland and the federal government to levy taxes. In light of the national government's constitutional supremacy, a state's power to tax stops when it attempts to tax a federal instrumentality—in this case, a nationally chartered bank located in the state.

In a succession of cases beginning with *GIBBONS V. OGDEN* (1824), the Supreme Court has mapped out spheres of authority for the national government and the states with regard to their concurrent powers to regulate commerce. Although Article I, section 8, gives Congress the power to regulate interstate commerce, conflicts have arisen from the continuing encroachment of national regulation on state power and from the effect of state regulation of intrastate commerce on interstate commerce.

In addition to concurrent federal and state powers, there exists what EDWARD S. CORWIN, in *The President: Office and Powers* (1957), referred to as "the doctrine of 'concurrent' or 'co-ordinate' powers.'" This is the doctrine that "neither Congress nor the Senate can be *constitutionally* bound...by anything done previously by the President in his capacity as [the principal actor in] foreign relations." For example, although the PRESIDENT may enter into a treaty with another nation—which, according to the Constitution, becomes the supreme law of the land—Congress's exclusive power to appropriate funds leaves it in control of implementing such a treaty or refusing to do so (see FOREIGN AFFAIRS; TREATIES).

Recently the Supreme Court has begun reining in the expansion of concurrent powers exercised by the national government at the expense of state powers. In *United States v. Lopez* (1995), which invalidated the federal government's attempt to make possession of a gun within one thousand feet of a school a federal offense, Chief Justice William H. Rehnquist (1924–2005) commented that to do otherwise "would bid fair to convert congressional authority under the Commerce Clause to a general police power of the sort retained by the States" under the Tenth Amendment (1791).

Although the September 11, 2001, terrorist attacks in the United States have created an atmosphere in which the concept of concurrent power may have to be reexamined in light of the over-

More on this topic:

Federalism, p. 218

Separation of Powers,
p. 494

arching concern for national security, the U.S. Supreme Court relied on this doctrine in its decision in *Rhines v. Weber* (2005). The opinion, written by Justice Sandra Day O'Connor, cited *Rose v. Lundy* (1982) to the effect that the "doctrine 'teaches that one court should defer action on causes properly within its jurisdiction until the courts of another sovereignty with concurrent powers and already cognizant of the litigation have had an opportunity to pass on the matter.'"

Confirmation Process   *See* ADVICE AND CONSENT; APPOINTMENT AND REMOVAL POWER.

Congress

The word *Congress* (from the Latin *congressus*, meaning meeting) appears twenty-seven times in the Constitution, in six articles. The importance of Congress and the fact that it plays a significant role in how the Constitution functions and whether and how it is amended (see AMENDMENTS) is evidenced by its being addressed in the first article of the Constitution. In many cases it, rather than the SUPREME COURT, is the final arbiter in matters involving the Constitution. For one, the Senate has a key role in the approval process for all federal judges, including those on the Supreme Court. Congress's political philosophy can influence the selection process and thus the determinations made by the approved appointees. Second, many issues that come before the Court involve laws passed by Congress, and the way a law is written—narrowly or broadly, for example—may determine its constitutionality. Third, Article V gives Congress the power, along with the as-yet-unused state convention method, to propose amendments to the Constitution.

Although this engraving of the East Front of the remodeled U.S. Capitol, published in the 1859 London Illustrated News, *shows the iron dome in its finished state, Thomas U. Walter's design was not completed until five years later. Continuation of the work on the dome during the Civil War symbolized that the Union itself would persevere. The House of Representatives moved into its new space in December 1857 and the Senate in January 1859.*
Source: Library of Congress

A number of nations, especially those in the Western Hemisphere, such as Bolivia and Mexico, have followed the American example and used the name *congress* for their national legislature. In international affairs, a congress is an assembly of representatives from various sovereignties. It was thus not surprising that the sovereign American states that declared their independence from Great Britain in 1776 chose this name for their own assembly of representatives. Since the U.S. Constitution was adopted, having a congress has come to imply a government structure with three major coequal branches and a PRESIDENT who is head of both state and government. In contrast, a parliament generally is chosen for a government that has either a monarch or a president as head of state plus a prime minister, who is responsible to the legislature, as head of government.

The U.S. Congress is a direct descendant of the First Continental Congress (1774), called by American colonial leaders in response to the brutal British retaliation for the Boston Tea Party in December 1773. Revolutionary conventions and committees in twelve of the thirteen British colonies that later formed the United States of America chose the fifty-five delegates to this congress, which convened in Philadelphia on September 5, 1774. During the Revolutionary War (1775–83), the congress functioned as the "federal government" for the colonies and, after 1776, for the states.

The first constitution of the United States, the ARTICLES OF CONFEDERATION (1781–88), vested in a new congress the few powers of governing delegated by the states. ALEXANDER HAMILTON, in essay 22 of *The Federalist* (1787–88) (see FEDERALIST PAPERS), noted that under the Articles "[t]he organization of Congress is itself utterly improper for the exercise of those powers which are necessary to be deposited in the Union." Hamilton was referring to the lack of national power to regulate COMMERCE among the states and to raise an army without having to ask the states, as well as the lack of a supreme tribunal to ensure consistent interpretation of national laws (see SUPREME COURT). The country's new Constitution, drafted in 1787 and adopted in 1789, was intended to correct this and similar defects in the Articles.

A Bicameral National Legislature

Article I, section 1, of the Constitution declares: "All legislative Powers herein granted shall be vested in a Congress of the United States, which shall consist of a Senate and House of Representatives." Bicameralism—the use of an upper house, the SENATE, and a lower house, the HOUSE OF REPRESENTATIVES—is also the system used by all the state governments except one (Nebraska) as well as by many national legislatures of unitary (nonfederal) governments, such as those of France and the United Kingdom. The president, through his veto power over bills passed by Congress (see VETOES), plays a role in the legislative process—one of the constitutional checks designed to balance the powers of the LEGISLATIVE BRANCH and the EXECUTIVE BRANCH.

Structurally, Congress reflects the country's federal nature—administered by both national and state governments. The Senate is composed of one hundred members, two from each state regardless of population. The presiding officer is the VICE PRESIDENT of the United States rather than one of the Senate members, who might show favoritism to his or her own state. Originally senators were elected by their respective state legislatures, but since ratification of the Seventeenth Amendment (1913) it has been required that they be elected at large by the people in their states for six-year terms; one-third are chosen every two years at the same time as the members of the House.

Whereas the Senate represents the states, the 435-seat House of Representatives is considered the more egalitarian body because membership is based on population and representatives are accountable to the people in elections every two years rather than every six years as are senators. Members are elected by voters in each state's designated congressional districts, which undergo periodic REAPPORTIONMENT based on changing census figures. Because more members come from the more populous states and the size of the delegations may change following each census, the House attains a closer approximation of MAJORITY RULE than the Senate. Although these state delegations do not play as strong a role in the daily operation of Congress as do POLITICAL PARTIES, they have an important function, however, on those rare occasions when the ELECTORAL COLLEGE is deadlocked over a presidential election.

The Legislative Process

The major responsibility of both houses of Congress is passing legislation, which is generally accomplished by a majority vote in each house. The House of Representatives, because it is more representative of the citizens, takes the lead with respect to money bills. "All Bills for raising Revenue," states Article I, section 7, "shall originate in the House of Representatives; but the Senate may propose or concur with amendments as on other Bills." One of the galvanizing issues of the Revolutionary War was "taxation without representation," and the FRAMERS OF THE CONSTITUTION wanted to ensure that raising revenues through TAXATION would have popular approval.

Laws enacted by the Senate and House begin as bills introduced in either house by a member or members. Bills are generally referred to committees on the relevant topic and are acted on by each house only after the committee issues a report. Measures may be debated before a vote is taken, and then a bill passed by one house must be passed by the other before being sent to the president for signature, which is required for the bill to become law. As set forth in Article I, section 7, the president may also veto any act of Congress, but a veto can be overridden by a vote of at least two-thirds of the members of each house.

In addition to bills, Article I, section 7, also requires that "[e]very Order, Resolution [joint resolution], or Vote to which the Concurrence of the Senate and House of Representatives may be necessary (except on a question of Adjournment) shall be presented to the President" for approval; if vetoed it, like any other bill, must be "repassed by two thirds of the Senate and the House...."

Article 1, section 5, requires each house to "keep a Journal of its Proceedings, and from time to time publish the same" unless secrecy is approved by a vote of the members. A majority of the members of each house constitute a quorum to do business, although not every national legislature follows this fairly standard parliamentary procedure. Japan's constitution (1947), for example, requires only one-third of the members of either house for a quorum, and the House of Commons in the United Kingdom requires only forty out of well over six hundred members.

Other Powers of Congress

A long list of the powers granted to Congress in its capacity as the national legislature is given in Article I, section 8, including the following responsibilities:

Taxation. "To lay and collect Taxes."
Borrowing. "To borrow Money on the credit of the United States."
Commerce. "To regulate Commerce with foreign Nations, and among the several States, and with the Indian Tribes."
Citizenship. "To establish an uniform Rule of Naturalization."
Bankruptcy. "To establish...uniform Laws on the subject of Bankruptcies."
Currency. "To coin Money, regulate the Value thereof...and fix the Standard of Weights and Measures; To provide for the Punishment of counterfeiting."
Postal service. "To establish Post Offices and post Roads."
Copyrights and patents. "To promote the Progress of Science and useful Arts."
Judiciary. "To constitute Tribunals inferior to the Supreme Court" (also under Article III, section 1).
Admiralty and international law. "To define and punish Piracies and Felonies committed on the high Seas, and Offences against the Law of Nations."
War. "To declare War."
Defense. "To raise and support Armies...; To provide and maintain a Navy; To make Rules for [governing and regulating] the land and naval Forces; To provide for calling forth the Militia to execute the Laws of the Union, suppress Insurrections and repeal Invasions; To provide for organizing, arming, and disciplining, the Militia."

National capital. "To exercise exclusive Legislation in all Cases whatsoever, over such District (not exceeding ten Miles square) as may, by Cession of particular States, and the Acceptance of Congress, become the Seat of the Government of the United States...."

The houses of Congress are given additional powers under other provisions of the Constitution:

Customs. To "lay any Imposts or Duties on Imports or Exports...." (Article I, section 10).

Advice and consent by the Senate. To ratify "Treaties, provided two thirds of the Senators present concur"; and to approve "Ambassadors, other public Ministers and Consuls, Judges of the supreme Court, and all other Officers of the United States, whose Appointments are not herein otherwise provided for, and which shall be established by Law" (Article II, section 2).

Impeachment. To impeach the "President, Vice President and all civil Officers of the United States...[for] Treason, Bribery, or other high Crimes and Misdemeanors" (Article II, section 4).

Treason. "[T]o declare the Punishment of Treason" (Article III, section 3).

Admission of new states. To admit "[n]ew States...into this Union" (Article IV, section 3).

Territory. To "dispose of and make all needful Rules and Regulations respecting the Territory or other Property belonging to the United States" (Article IV, section 3).

To ensure that Congress can fully exercise the powers expressly assigned to it by the Constitution, Article I, section 8, grants Congress authority "To make all Laws which shall be necessary and proper for carrying into Execution the foregoing Powers and all other Powers vested by this Constitution in the Government of the United States, or in any Department or Officer thereof" (see NECESSARY AND PROPER CLAUSE).

Certain limitations are placed on the powers of Congress, including, in Article I, section 9, prohibitions against suspending the writ of HABEAS CORPUS except when "in Cases of Rebellion or Invasion the public Safety may require it"; enacting any "Bill of Attainder or ex post facto Law" (see ATTAINDER, BILLS OF; EX POST FACTO LAWS); or granting any "Title of Nobility" (see NOBILITY, TITLES OF). This article also mandates that any direct tax must be "in Proportion to the Census"; that "[n]o Tax or Duty shall be laid on Articles exported from any State"; that "[n]o preference shall be given...to the Ports of one State over those of another..."; and that "[n]o money shall be drawn from the Treasury, but by...Appropriations made by Law; and a regular Statement and Account of the Receipts and Expenditures of all public Money shall be published from time to time."

To an extent, the federal courts give deference to congressional enactments. For example, the general principle that within the context of the proper exercise of its powers Congress may to some degree restrict freedom of speech and the press was confirmed in the 2003 U.S. Court of Appeals decision *Elsinore Christian Center v. City of Lake Elsinore*. The law under review, the Religious Land Use and Institutionalized Persons Act of 2000, redefined the right of free speech.

Privileges, Immunities, and Compensation

Like most other national constitutions, the U.S. Constitution extends privileges and immunities to members of Congress during the performance of their duties. This follows the tradition of the British Parliament, where such protections reflect attributes of monarchical sovereignty and serve as a bar to harassment during legislators' tenure in office. Article I, section 6, exempts members of Congress from arrest "during their Attendance at the Session of their respective Houses, and in going to and returning from the same," except in cases of "Treason, Felony and Breach of Peace." Similarly, the same article provides members immunity from libel or slander suits by stipulating that "for any Speech or Debate in either House, they shall not be questioned in any other Place." Senators and representatives are prohibited from holding any other "civil Office under the Authority of the United States...."

Congressional immunity regarding speech and debate applies to other work generally done in Congress, including writing committee reports, introducing resolutions, and voting. In *Gravel v.*

United States (1972), the Supreme Court extended this immunity to congressional aides. The Court also held that Sen. Mike Gravel of Alaska, who served from 1969 to 1981, had immunity with respect to his involvement in releasing classified material about the Vietnam War that became involved in the PENTAGON PAPERS CASE, but that he did not have immunity for later arranging for their publication in book form.

Article I, section 6, provides for the compensation of members of Congress "to be ascertained by Law, and paid out of the Treasury of the United States." The Twenty-seventh Amendment (1992), originally introduced in Congress in 1789 by JAMES MADISON along with other proposed amendments that became the BILL OF RIGHTS, limits when increases in compensation become effective: "No law, varying the compensation for the services of the Senators and Representatives, shall take effect, until an election of Representatives shall have intervened" (see COMPENSATION OF OFFICIALS).

The Dominance of Political Parties

Congress, by its rules, political organization, and committees, affects the basic operation of the national government to a degree that would no doubt astound the nation's founders. Madison, called the "Father of the Constitution," warned against "factions" or what in his day approximated special-interest groups like modern political parties. But today both houses of Congress are totally dominated by party organizations, from the SPEAKER OF THE HOUSE to committee heads (who set schedules and agendas) to majority and minority party leaders (who largely control the operations of their respective houses). Members of each party meet outside Congress in party caucuses to organize and coordinate their actions for the formal sessions. A feature of a two-party political system is the working majority of one or the other party that allows it to control the operations of a house or the entire Congress when it is in the majority. Having an odd number of members in the House and the stipulation that a tie in the Senate is broken by the vice president facilitates majority-party rule.

Sam Rayburn, who became Speaker of the House in 1940, is regarded as one of the most powerful men in the history of Congress.
Source: The Granger Collection, New York

Special-interests groups, primarily through the work of lobbyists, have also come to play a significant role in Congress, almost to the extent of constituting a "shadow" staff, drafting legislation and mobilizing constituent support for laws favoring their clients. What began as a legislature composed of citizens to represent all of their constituents and the interests of the national and state governments in general today more resembles a machine for translating the interests of powerful factions into law.

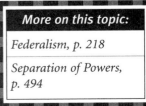

More on this topic:

Federalism, p. 218

Separation of Powers, p. 494

Conscience, Freedom of *See* RELIGION.

Conscientious Objection *See* RELIGION.

Constitution, U.S.

The Constitution of the United States, drafted by the CONSTITUTIONAL CONVENTION OF 1787 in Philadelphia, was the first written national constitution in the world. Since it went into effect in 1789, hundreds of written national constitutions have been debated, gone into effect, been revised, and some suspended, but the American document remains the oldest continuously in existence (Norway's 1814 constitution is the second oldest). As unique as it was at the time, the document was not cut from whole cloth. The Constitution that has served the people of the United States so well for more than two hundred years is deeply rooted in centuries of world political history.

Some of the FRAMERS OF THE CONSTITUTION seemed especially aware of the historical importance of their task. According to the notes of the convention made by JAMES MADISON, Gouverneur Morris, a delegate from Pennsylvania, divulged that in some degree he felt that he represented the whole human race at the convention. ALEXANDER HAMILTON, in essay 1 of *The Federalist* (1787–88) (see FEDERALIST PAPERS), declared: "It has been frequently remarked that it seems to have been reserved to the people of this country, by their conduct and example, to decide the important question, whether societies of men are really capable or not of establishing good government from reflection and choice, or whether they are forever destined to depend for their political constitutions on accident and force."

> **"The Constitution of the United States was made not merely for the generation that then existed, but for posterity—unlimited, undefined, endless, perpetual posterity."**
>
> **—Henry Clay**

A "Most Wonderful Work"

Although William Gladstone (1809–98), who served as British prime minister four times in the late nineteenth century, called the U.S. Constitution "the most wonderful work ever struck off at a given time by the brain and purpose of man," the framers had a vast reservoir of history and personal experience to draw on during their labors of drafting a constitution for the new nation. On the whole they were well educated in political history, and Great Britain's in particular. Under the banner "No taxation without representation," revolutionaries in Britain's thirteen American colonies had separated themselves from the mother country with their DECLARATION OF INDEPENDENCE (1776) and the long Revolutionary War (1775–83). Britain's government was (and is) a monarchy, albeit limited to some degree by the country's constitution, led by a Parliament in which the colonists had no representation when it came to unwelcome taxes or other matters.

Democratic experiments—in ancient Greece, the Roman Republic, the confederacy of Switzerland, and particularly European models of political organization—informed the delegates in Philadelphia in 1787 (see DEMOCRACY). *The Federalist Papers* (1787–88) indexes references to Germany, Ireland, Scotland, Spain, France, Italy, and the Netherlands. The works of the English philosophers John Locke (1632–1704) and David Hume (1711–76) and the French philosophical historian and jurist Charles-Louis de Secondat, Baron de La Bréde et de Montesquieu (1689–1755), among many others, also provided guidance in their deliberations. The delegates knew about Isaac Newton's success in formulating the laws of gravity and motion, making sense of the orbits of the planets around the sun. The many lawyers at the convention were undoubtedly aware of William Blackstone's (1723–80) monumental work *Commentaries on the Laws of England*

(1765–70), which reduced the vast body of English law into an organized and comprehensible entity. If such complexities as the solar system and a nation's hundreds of years of judicial opinions and statutes could be reduced to basic concepts and organized into a meaningful whole, why then, they thought, could not a nation's political organization be amenable to rational description and understanding?

Of even greater importance in guiding the delegates to the Constitutional Convention was the practical experience the thirteen states had acquired since declaring their independence from Britain. Each state had written a constitution; Massachusetts's 1780 constitution remains the oldest of any state's written constitution still in effect. The states had also experimented with different types of legislatures, chief executives, and judicial systems before and during their preconstitutional union under the ARTICLES OF CONFEDERATION (1781–89)—itself a model perhaps of what not to do the second time around.

After RATIFICATION, the Constitution went into operation in 1789 with the convening of the first Congress on March 4, the installation of the first president, GEORGE WASHINGTON, on April 30 (postponed from March 4 because the House of Representatives lacked the quorum needed to count the votes), and the confirmation by the Senate of the first appointments to the SUPREME COURT on September 26. The BILL OF RIGHTS, the first ten amendments, was added in 1791, and the last of the seventeen remaining amendments was ratified in 1992 after taking more than two centuries to make it through the approval process.

A Government's Blueprint

A constitution is simply a description of how the government of a political jurisdiction works. All of the world's approximately 192 nations have a constitution, and most have a written constitution—a single document in which the institutions and procedures for the government's operation are set forth. Written constitutions contain a country's supreme laws, indicating the institutions and rules that regulate the acquisition, use, and transfer of political power as well as limitations on that power. These limitations often include checks and balances within the government—IMPEACHMENT procedures, for example—and limitations that CITIZENS can exercise, such as regular ELECTIONS and individual RIGHTS that they can enforce against the government through the courts. The United Kingdom, New Zealand, and Israel have unwritten constitutions that consist of a number of basic constitutional documents and laws, together with customs and traditions that reach constitutional status.

The U.S. Constitution contains both specific procedures on how the national government works and individual rights of citizens. Because the United States is a federal government, the Constitution also addresses the powers specifically delegated by the states and the citizens to the national government and the limitations on those powers. Only CONGRESS, for example, can declare WAR, but the members of Congress represent their states and can vote against a declaration of war, and the citizens, if they wish, may vote in regularly scheduled elections against members of Congress who voted for an unpopular war. Individual rights are also limitations on the powers of government at the national and state levels. Such rights include the right to a trial by jury in criminal cases, guaranteed in Article II, section 2, and the prohibition against laws abridging freedom of speech, guaranteed in the First Amendment (1791). With its reserved powers and rights of the states and the people, the Constitution strikes what has been called "a delicate balance" between the need of a national government to have sufficient power to protect the nation and promote its prosperity but not so much as to destroy the citizens' SOVEREIGNTY and LIBERTY.

In addition to the written document and its twenty-seven amendments, the Constitution includes a number of customary and traditional aspects. For example, not mentioned in the Constitution itself is the presumption of innocence for those persons accused of a crime (see CRIM-

INAL LAW); nevertheless, this is a fundamental right as inalienable as any expressly mentioned in the Bill of Rights. The role played by POLITICAL PARTIES in organizing elections and the government's LEGISLATIVE BRANCH and EXECUTIVE BRANCH after elections is a part of our own unwritten constitutional traditions and of immense significance in the operation of our national government.

Congress, the president, and, most important, the federal COURTS constantly tinker with the way the written document impacts the nation. Laws are passed, executive actions taken, and court decisions issued that confirm, augment, or restrict the scope of the Constitution at any given time. A relatively straightforward document, the Constitution is really only a bare skeleton on which the entire "constitution" of the United States hangs.

About the Document

One of the shortest constitutions in the world, the U.S. Constitution required only some 8,700 words, including its amendments, beginning with this now world-famous PREAMBLE:

"We the People of the United States, in Order to form a more perfect Union, establish Justice, insure domestic Tranquility, provide for the common defence, promote the general Welfare, and secure the Blessings of Liberty to ourselves and our Posterity, do ordain and establish this Constitution for the United States of America."

The document is divided into major subject areas called articles, followed by subsections as well as paragraphs, usually called clauses, that are not numbered in the original document but are often enumerated for ease of study and reference.

Articles I, II, and III, respectively, address the functions and powers of the legislative, executive, and judicial branches of government. Congress is given authority to enact laws, with the chief executive's approval, regarding specific subjects such as taxes and naturalization of new citizens. The PRESIDENT, as head of the executive branch, is empowered to nominate and appoint, with the Senate's approval, key government officials and is made commander in chief of the ARMED FORCES. The JUDICIAL BRANCH is given original jurisdiction over national types of cases—AMBASSADORS and ADMIRALTY AND MARITIME LAW, for example—and appellate jurisdiction over other cases "with such Exceptions, and under such Regulations as the Congress shall make." Although each of these first three articles deals with a separate branch of government, many areas of interaction occur between them as well.

Article IV deals with aspects of the federal relationship between the STATES and the national government as well as the relationship among the states; each state, for instance, is required to give "[f]ull faith and Credit" to the acts and records of the others (see FULL FAITH AND CREDIT), recognize "all Privileges and Immunities of Citizens of the United States," and grant Congress power over the ADMISSION OF NEW STATES and the TERRITORY and PROPERTY of the national government. Article IV also guarantees the states a "Republican form of Government" and protection "against Invasion" (see DOMESTIC TRANQUILITY; REPUBLICAN FORM OF GOVERNMENT).

Article V sets out the procedures for amending the Constitution (see AMENDMENTS).

Article VI contains certain general provisions, including that the government's DEBT under the Articles of Confederation would be valid against the new government, that the Constitution and laws and TREATIES made thereunder would be the "supreme Law of the Land," that all state and national officials must take an oath to support the Constitution (see OATH OF OFFICE), and that religious tests for office are prohibited (see QUALIFICATIONS FOR OFFICE).

The last article, Article VII, establishes the procedure for ratifying the document and acknowledges its adoption by the convention on September 17, 1787.

Where a provision appears in the Constitution may provide a clue as to the ORIGINAL INTENT of the framers. The importance of the three branches is indicated by the fact that the legislative branch is dealt with first, the executive second, and the judicial third and last of the branches. A provision's placement in the document may also help in judicial interpretation. In *Ex parte Merryman* (1861), the Supreme Court concluded that the fact that authorization to suspend the writ of HABEAS CORPUS appears in Article I, dealing with Congress, means that the president was not intended to exercise this power. Other clues to the importance attached by the framers to some aspect of the Constitution are reflected in the number of times a topic is addressed. Checks and balances are found in nearly thirty places (see SEPARATION OF POWERS), while six references are made to IMPEACHMENT.

The original Constitution is in the custody of the National Archives and Records Administration and is generally on display in a protective case at the National Archives building located at Pennsylvania Avenue and Seventh Street, N.W., in Washington, D.C.

Worldwide Influence

For more than two centuries the Constitution has been an important symbol of people's ability to intellectually and deliberately organize themselves politically—rather than to simply acquiesce in living under a government based on the historical legitimization of a ruling class or one imposed by conquerors. The French Revolution that began in 1789 led to a constitution for the first French Republic in 1791, after which other nations, starting with Sweden in 1809 and Norway in 1814, began following suit. As the colonies in the New World obtained their independence from European powers, all of these new governments, from Canada to Mexico and Bolivia, turned to written constitutions, many of which were based directly on the U.S. model. Other newly independent nations around the world, many imitating the British or the French parliamentary models, also wrote constitutions following America's lead. Cambodia, for example, became a constitutional monarchy in 1947, and Chad became a presidential-style republic in 1959.

Even communist countries and other dictatorships felt the need to write constitutions to emulate the growing number of true democracies in the world. The Soviet Union, for example, had constitutions under Joseph Stalin in 1936 and Leonid Brezhnev in 1977, which were significantly amended under Mikhail Gorbachev between 1988 and 1990. When the Soviet empire collapsed in 1991, Russia adopted a new constitution for its fledgling democracy, influenced greatly by its new president, Boris Yeltsin.

Today almost all the major countries of the world have written national constitutions. (The 1995 constitution of Bosnia and Herzegovina, annexed to the peace accords drafted in Dayton, Ohio, follows the structure of the U.S. Constitution.) The United Kingdom, New Zealand, and Israel are unusual in having unwritten constitutions, and Saudi Arabia stands alone as an absolute monarchy. Pakistan's constitution (1973) was suspended in 1999 with the takeover of a military leader.

The U.S. Constitution has also influenced the constitutions of the American states, many of which have been rewritten and significantly amended a number of times. Some state constitutions incorporate provisions similar to those in the national document, while others have experimented with different concepts. Minnesota and Tennessee, for example, allow election of judges, rather than appointment with life tenure, and Colorado and South Dakota, among others, permit DIRECT DEMOCRACY procedures such as popular initiatives and referendums on legislation and amendments to their state constitutions.

The Constitution, like a nation or an individual life, is always a work in progress. As social and political realities change, the way a nation's government works must also change. The U.S. Constitution—whether spelled with a capital *C* or a lower case *c*—will undoubtedly evolve in the future as it has in the past. The hope is always that the changes are for the better.

Several years ago, pursuant to the Constitution Heritage Act (1988), the National Constitution Center was opened at 525 Arch Street in Philadelphia.

(For the complete text of the Constitution, see pages 627–634.)

Constitutional Convention of 1787

"The men who founded your republic," observed the twentieth-century British philosopher and mathematician Alfred North Whitehead, "had an uncommonly clear grasp of the general ideas that they wanted to put in [the Constitution], then left the working out of the details to later interpreters, which has been, on the whole, remarkably successful. I know of only three times in the Western world when statesmen consciously took control of historic destinies: Periclean Athens, Rome under Augustus, and the founding of your American republic." As Whitehead alludes, trust in those who would govern under the Constitution probably best characterizes the FRAMERS OF THE CONSTITUTION. At the Constitutional Convention of 1787, held in Philadelphia, they set the system in motion, trusting to those who would follow to make it work without destroying their ORIGINAL INTENT.

Members of a constitutional convention are authorized to amend, revise, rewrite, or draft a new constitution for a political jurisdiction. They may be empowered to draft and adopt measures themselves or to draft a proposal that is to be submitted for ratification by others, including eligible voters. The power of such bodies lies in their ability to fashion the supreme laws of a state or a nation. Members of the Israeli constitutional convention who met in 1949 to draft a constitution for the new state of Israel instead declared themselves to be a supreme legislative body—a parliament—and decided to make laws gradually to form a constitution. The 1787 Constitutional Convention in America similarly abandoned its mandate to revise the ARTICLES OF CONFEDERATION and instead drafted a new constitution.

The Articles of Confederation

The 1787 Constitutional Convention was not the first constitutional convention in America; New Hampshire had held a state constitutional convention in June 1778. What were the reasons for calling a national convention?

The Revolutionary War that began in 1775 had been sparked by Great Britain's treatment of the American colonies. "The colonies must either submit or triumph," George III of England wrote to his prime minister following the Boston Tea Party of 1773, in which colonists disguised as Indians dumped 342 large chests of tea into Boston Harbor to protest exorbitant taxes levied by the British Parliament. Then in April 1775 an "unprovoked" attack by British soldiers on peaceful farmers at Concord, Massachusetts—"the shot heard 'round the world," as described by the nineteenth-century American poet Ralph Waldo Emerson—impelled the Second Continental Congress of delegates from the colonies to issue a Declaration on the Causes of Taking Up

---

THE CALL FOR THE FEDERAL CONSTITUTIONAL CONVENTION

RESOLUTION OF CONGRESS

February 21, 1787

WHEREAS there is provision in the Articles of Confederation & Perpetual Union for making alterations therein by the Assent of a Congress of the United States and of the legislatures of the several States; And whereas experience hath evinced that there are defects in the present Confederation, as a means to remedy which several of the States and particularly the State of New York by express instruction to their delegates in Congress have suggested a convention for the purposes expressed in the following resolution and such Convention appearing to be the most probable means of establishing in these states a firm national government.

Resolved that in the opinion of Congress it is expedient that on the second Monday in May next a Convention of delegates who shall have been appointed by the several states be held at Philadelphia for the sole and express purpose of revising the Articles of Confederation and reporting to Congress and the several legislatures such alterations and provisions therein as shall when agreed to in Congress and confirmed by the states render the federal constitution adequate to the exigencies of Government & the preservation of the Union.

In a posthumous group portrait from 1856, Julius Brutus Stearns depicts General Washington addressing members of the Constitutional Convention of 1787. Washington acted as a unifying presence rather than as a debater during the proceedings.

Arms, written by John Dickinson and THOMAS JEFFERSON. On June 23, 1775, General GEORGE WASHINGTON took command of the Continental Army (such as it was) to prepare for war with Britain. The Rubicon had not yet been crossed, however, and on July 8, 1775, the Continental Congress adopted the Olive Branch Petition, begging the king not to provoke a war and to repeal onerous laws passed by Parliament regarding the colonies. Instead, in retribution Parliament passed an act in December prohibiting all trade and intercourse by Britain with the thirteen colonies.

The DECLARATION OF INDEPENDENCE, adopted by the Continental Congress on July 4, 1776, resulted in the former British colonies' becoming independent states with their own governments and constitutions. While simultaneously coordinating the war effort, the delegates adopted a constitution of sorts on November 15, 1777. These Articles of Confederation, in which the sovereign thirteen states delegated some powers to create a government for the federation of the new United States of America, were ratified by the states and became effective in 1781. Under them, the sovereignty of the states could not be compromised, each state had one vote in Congress, and any amendments to the Articles had to be agreed to by all thirteen states.

After the war, officially concluded on February 3, 1783, a number of problems with the Articles of Confederation became apparent, among them the lack of strong executive leadership: Congress selected a president who held office for only one year and was responsible to it. Other major problems included Congress's inability to regulate commerce among the states and defend them from internal or external aggression. Of particular concern was Shays's Rebellion in Massachusetts beginning in the fall of 1786, which demonstrated the difficulties a single state faced in dealing on its own with large-scale mob lawlessness and rebellion.

A New Constitution

Conflicts among the states over trade and COMMERCE led Virginia, which had its own share of trade problems, particularly with Maryland, to suggest a meeting of delegates from the states in Annapolis, Maryland, in September 1786. Only five states sent delegates, but among them were ALEXANDER HAMILTON and JAMES MADISON, who urged a broader-based meeting "to devise such further provisions as shall appear…necessary to render the constitution of the federal government adequate to the exigencies of the Union." On February 21, 1787, on the basis of the report from the Annapolis meeting, the Congress established by the Articles of Confederation called for a convention in Philadelphia that began on May 25 and ended on September 17, 1787, "for the sole and express purpose of revising the Articles of Confederation."

In 1776 the Declaration of Independence had boldly declared, "Governments are instituted among Men, deriving their just Powers from the Consent of the Governed, that whenever any form of Government becomes destructive of these Ends, it is the Right of the People to alter or to abolish it, and to institute new Government, laying its Foundation on such Principles, and organizing its Powers in such Form, as to them shall seem most likely to effect their Safety and Happiness." The fifty-five delegates to the convention were now to embark on such an exercise.

Nearly all the delegates had experience in colonial and state legislatures, and twenty-eight had been members of the various continental congresses and the national Congress under the Articles of Confederation, of which some delegates were still members. Five delegates were younger than thirty years old, and Hamilton was only thirty-two. There were two college presidents, three professors, and an additional twenty-six who were college graduates. Many were lawyers, four of whom had studied law at the Inns of Court in London. They chose Washington president of the convention and elected to conduct their deliberations in secret.

Besides Washington, the most illustrious and oldest citizen present was Benjamin Franklin. Three political luminaries unable to attend were Jefferson, JOHN ADAMS of Massachusetts, and John Jay of New York. Several members of the Virginia delegation, which from the beginning was inclined to form a stronger national government, met informally with several like-minded members of the Pennsylvania delegation and decided at the outset to abandon the mandate to amend the Articles of Confederation and instead to begin writing an entirely new constitution. According to Madison's notes, Gouverneur Morris of Pennsylvania, an irrepressible wit, announced on July 5 that "he flattered himself he came here in some degree as a Representative of the whole human race; for the whole human race will be affected by the proceedings of this Convention."

A Great Compromise

On the convention's third day Edmund Randolph of Virginia presented an outline of a new national government known as the Virginia Plan. It included a bicameral legislature, with membership in both houses apportioned by population; an executive; and a judiciary, appointed by the legislature. After much debate, William Paterson created a stir by introducing the New Jersey Plan, which basically endorsed a one-state, one-vote system of government, more like the Articles of Confederation. The New Jersey Plan was soon defeated and the Virginia Plan (see pages 622–623) amended to change "national government" to the "Government of the United States."

Hot weather brought hot tempers, but the deadlock over what form the new government would take was broken on July 16 with a plan offered by Roger Sherman, a delegate from Connecticut.

Called the "Connecticut Compromise," it later became known as the "Great Compromise." The lower house of the new national legislature, the House of Representatives, would be popularly elected, and the number of members from each state would be apportioned on the basis of the number of free inhabitants plus three-fifths of the slaves. The upper house, the Senate, would have two members from each state, chosen by the state legislatures.

Other issues—the chief executive and the judiciary—still had to be addressed, but the main obstacle had been overcome. Written sources on the convention's activities are limited. The convention secretary, William Jackson, was less than diligent in taking notes, but journals and notes by Madison and Hamilton, among others, have supplemented the official record. Issues that were debated included PROPERTY ownership as a qualification for public officials, the federal government's power to pay the national debt, and SLAVERY. Although Abigail Adams admonished her husband to "Remember the Ladies," they did not (see WOMEN).

The final method of choosing the PRESIDENT was a compromise. The framers, believing that each state would back its "favorite son" as a candidate (they could not foresee the rise of national parties), expected that the House of Representatives would be the final arbiter of presidential ELECTIONS. Because they assumed that Washington would be the first president, no limitation was placed on the number of terms.

Another important issue was whether the new national government's laws would be effective only on the states as political entities, as under the Articles of Confederation, or whether they would apply directly to individuals as citizens of the United States. Perhaps the convention's greatest achievement was finding ways of giving the national government power directly over the citizenry and bypassing the states. The SUPREMACY CLAUSE in Article VI, section 2, and the jurisdiction of federal judges laid out in Article III, section 2, were key to this important aspect of the new constitution.

Finishing their work at 4 P.M. on September 17, 1787, the members of the Constitutional Convention, as noted in the convention records, "adjourned to the City Tavern, dined together, and took cordial leave of each other." On the same day a resolution signed by Washington and Jackson was transmitted to Congress, together with a letter, signed by Washington, that begins: "WE HAVE now the honor to submit to the consideration of the United States in Congress assembled, that Constitution which has appeared to us the most advisable.... In all our deliberations on this subject we kept steadily in our view, that which appears to us the greatest interest of every true American, the consolidation of our Union, in which is involved our prosperity, felicity, safety, perhaps our national existence...."

The new constitution became valid on June 21, 1788, when New Hampshire became the ninth state, as required by Article VII, to ratify it. The other six states followed, with Rhode Island last in 1790. Congress, still operating under the Articles of Confederation, declared the Constitution duly ratified, set the first presidential and congressional elections, and set March 4, 1789, as the beginning of the first term of the presidency.

Since 1787 hundreds of constitutional conventions have been held in individual states and in other nations. The democratic form of government crafted at the 1787 Constitutional Convention has had an exceptional impact throughout the world, and the constitutional convention has become a standard forum for shaping democracy the world over.

The impetus for the Constitutional Convention of 1787 was not altruism or utopianism but simply the need to promote better trade and commercial relations between the states. Nevertheless, a century later William Gladstone, the British prime minister, declared the product of the convention "the most wonderful work ever struck off at a given time by the brain and purpose of man."

Contracts

Although the Constitution does not endorse any economic theory, the United States since its inception has never abandoned the capitalist economic system based on free trade and a free market extolled by the Scottish economist Adam Smith (1723–90) in *The Wealth of Nations*, published in 1776, the year the DECLARATION OF INDEPENDENCE was adopted. A decade later the CONSTITUTIONAL CONVENTION OF 1787 was called to overhaul the ARTICLES OF CONFEDERATION (1781–89), principally because they hindered free COMMERCE across the new nation. Although most citizens at the time were farmers, business and commerce were on the increase, and the sanctity of contracts (agreements between two parties to participate in or abstain from some action) was of great importance in transacting business of all kinds.

The Contract Clause

Contracts may create legal obligations that are enforceable under the law, a fact recognized by the Constitution's contract clause, found in Article I, section 10: "No State shall…pass any…Law impairing the Obligation of Contracts…."
The English philosopher John Locke (1632–1704) had linked personal LIBERTY with the right to PROPERTY, which is often secured by contracts. As ALEXANDER HAMILTON pointed out in essay 7 of *The Federalist* (1787–88) (see FEDERALIST PAPERS), the FRAMERS OF THE CONSTITUTION feared—based on past experience in Connecticut and Rhode Island—that state legislatures might incite their citizens to violence if private contracts were easily violated. The Constitution's checks and balances and its limited powers apparently did not produce similar fears. The sanctity of contracts was generally held to be a moral and social obligation that ensured the protection of private property and the accumulation of wealth acquired from one's talent and labor.

The Supreme Court's first case under the contract clause was *FLETCHER V. PECK* (1810). Here the Court found that a state legislature could not rescind an executed contract that was made under a law passed by a previous legislature. After the New Hampshire legislature passed a law that would reorganize Dartmouth College, thereby impairing the terms of the school's charter, the Court, in *Dartmouth College v. Woodward* (1819), upheld a private contract chartering the college. The Court's decisions in later cases toward the end of the nineteenth century, however, found some limitations on the contract clause—for example, where protection would hinder the government's "power of improvement and public accommodation" and where it threatened to diminish the government's POLICE POWER.

Unfortunately, the constitutional protection for private contractual obligations gave the Supreme Court a rationale for striking down various state legislative measures to protect workers at the beginning of the twentieth century. In *Lochner v. New York* (1905), the Court voided a state law that limited bakery workers' hours of employment and was intended as a health protection measure, alleging that such laws were a "meddlesome interference with the rights

Source: Courtesy of the Collection of Joseph Lochner Jr. by Dante Tranquille

Joseph Lochner, a baker from New York, won a major Supreme Court case in 1905 when he challenged a state law that limited bakery workers to no more than ten hours a day or sixty hours a week. The Supreme Court justices sided with Lochner, therefore limiting the power of states to regulate working hours. Bakery workers and labor unions assailed the decision, fearing that it would lead to the overturning of other laws regulating labor.

of the individual" to contract for his or her labor. This line of reasoning was finally abandoned in 1937, and since then the contract clause has been used sparingly to challenge state legislation.

The law does not protect all types of contracts, however. Contracts that have been entered into fraudulently or obtained by duress or that contravene public policy may be found by the courts to be illegal and therefore unenforceable. Moreover, in *Tenet v. Doe* (2005), the U.S. Supreme Court, citing *Totten v. United States* (1875), which prohibits suits against the United States based on covert espionage agreements, held that the plaintiffs could not sue the U.S. government—in this case, the Central Intelligence Agency—for financial assistance promised them for espionage that they engaged in during the cold war between the communist countries and the western nations after World War II.

Contractual Theory of Government

The notion of a contract between a ruler and those ruled has a long and multicultural history. In German mythology, Wotan, king of the gods, was supposed to have ruled by contract with the other gods, and the biblical God of the Israelites is said to have entered into a covenant, a form of contract, with Abraham.

In *The Social Contract* (1762), the French philosopher Jean-Jacques Rousseau (1712–78) provided a theoretical foundation asserting that all government is dependent on the consent of the governed—as declared in the Declaration of Independence in 1776—rather than on the legitimacy of a monarch's right to rule. Popular SOVEREIGNTY means that individual citizens in a civil society theoretically enter into a social contract with one another to allow some to rule the rest. Rousseau suggested that the people should both create laws and follow them, with government being the instrument through which their collective will is translated into action.

In some ways the U.S. Constitution can be considered a contract, drafted by the framers, ratified by the citizens in state conventions, and continually approved thereafter by generations of Americans who tacitly accept the basis and form of government it creates. In essay 78 of *The Federalist*, Alexander Hamilton referred to the notion of the social contract in the context of the proposed Constitution: "Until the people have, by some solemn and authoritative act, annulled or changed the established form [of government], it is binding upon themselves collectively, as well as individually; and no presumption, or even knowledge of their sentiments, can warrant their representatives in a departure from it prior to such an act."

Constitutional protection for contractual obligations is of paramount importance to the efficiency and stability of both everyday commercial transactions and the national economy as a whole. Being able to rely on the rights and interests established by contracts allows Americans to take risks and reap the rewards of the American system of private enterprise that has become the envy of the world.

Copyright

A creator's right in a literary work or another original product executed in a tangible medium of expression is recognized and enforceable under the law as a copyright. Copyright law can be traced back to England's Statute of Anne (1710), which acknowledged the royal prerogative to bestow a monopolistic privilege on the authors of books, thus granting them the sole right to publish their works for a designated period of time. Today most nations, in addition to the United States, have constitutional provisions or other laws regarding copyrights; both Germany's constitution (1949) and Ethiopia's (1996), for example, have such provisions. Copyright laws have also been the subject of some regional and international agreements, including the Universal Copyright Convention (1952), which was revised in 1971 and entered into force in 1974.

"The Progress of Science and Useful Arts"

At the time the U.S. Constitution was drafted in 1787, copyright privileges in the United States, as in Great Britain, were rooted in COMMON LAW. However, the FRAMERS OF THE CONSTITUTION gave to the federal government the power to make consistent and effectual laws regarding copyrights and PATENTS. Article I, section 8, provides that Congress has the power, among other responsibilities, "[t]o promote the Progress of Science and useful Arts, by securing for limited Times to Authors and Inventors the exclusive Right to their respective Writings and Discoveries." In essay 43 of *The Federalist* (1787–88) (see FEDERALIST PAPERS), JAMES MADISON defended this change, noting that under the ARTICLES OF CONFEDERATION (1781–89) individual states were unable to "make effectual provision" for either copyrights or patents. Nearly two centuries later the Supreme Court in *Mazer v. Stein* (1954) reaffirmed that the purpose of this provision was to encourage "individual effort by personal gain [and] to advance public welfare through the talents of authors."

The nature of copyright laws under the new Constitution was the subject of a significant early Supreme Court case, *Wheaton v. Peters* (1834), which involved two reporters of Supreme Court decisions. Wheaton accused Peters of infringing his copyright in twelve volumes of his reports, but Peters argued that Wheaton had not complied with all the federal copyright law requirements to secure his copyright in those volumes. Wheaton's defense was that common-law copyright still obtained and that any laws passed by Congress only added rights to the common-law rights he already possessed. The Court found for Peters on the basis that no federal common law of copyright existed at the time and that whatever rights Wheaton might be entitled to had to be secured according to Article I, section 8, solely under the acts of Congress.

Walt Disney with his creation, Mickey Mouse, in the 1940s. In 1998 Congress added twenty years to the copyright limit, extending protection for any work created in or after 1923, which just happens to be the year of Mickey's "birth."
Source: Rue des Archives/The Granger Collection, New York

Intellectual Property

Copyright protection in the United States extends to various types of original works, including literary, musical, dramatic, choreographic, pictorial, graphic, architectural, and sculptural creations, as well as recordings and photographs. Despite the language in the Constitution regarding "Discoveries," some things—ideas, procedures, principles, and even discoveries—may not be copyrighted according to the Copyright Act (1976, revised 1978). This act set the length of a copyright generally at the life of the author plus fifty years. In 1998 Congress added the Sonny Bono Copyright Term Extension Act (CTEA), which extended the copyright period for another twenty years. This extension was challenged in the U.S. Court of Appeals for the District of Columbia on the grounds that it keeps copyrighted materials out of the public domain for too long, but a three-judge panel disagreed. The Supreme Court, in *Eldred v. Ashcroft* (2003), also found that CTEA did not go beyond the language in the Constitution that provides that copyrights and patents may be granted "for limited Times" and, thus, was not unconstitutional.

Copyright is one form of intellectual PROPERTY, which also includes PATENTS and trademarks. The differences among the three types can be explained by analogy to a modern personal computer. The computer's hardware and software may be protected by a patent, the user's manual by a copyright, and the commercial name or identification of the computer by a trademark. Unlike private works, information and inventions created by the government or at taxpayer expense are excluded from copyright or patent protection, although some may be restricted from the public domain and subject to nondisclosure for NATIONAL SECURITY reasons. Although copyright protection arises at the time a work is created, it should be registered with the Copyright Office of the Library of Congress if the owner wishes to sue for infringement.

Intellectual property protections for creators generally place restrictions on freedom of SPEECH and information by others, especially students and scholars who may wish to use copyrighted material. Thus the government's interest in protecting intellectual property, theoretically to encourage its production, must be balanced with the public's right to know and make use of information. This conflict between the copyright laws and the First Amendment (1791) surfaced in *Harper and Row v. Nation Enterprises* (1985). The Supreme Court held, however, that although the copyright law does not restrict ideas or facts, verbatim excerpts of several hundred words from yet-to-be-published material—in this case, the memoirs of President Gerald Ford (1913–2006)—did not constitute "fair use" and thus was an infringement of Harper and Row's copyright interest.

According to U.S. copyright law, factors that will be considered in determining whether the fair use exception is applicable include "(1) the purpose and character of the use, including whether such use is of a commercial nature or is for nonprofit educational purposes; (2) the nature of the copyrighted work; (3) the amount and substantiality of the portion used in relation to the copyrighted work as a whole; and (4) the effect of the use upon the potential market for or value of the copyrighted work." Nonetheless, the concept of what constitutes fair use of copyrighted material in criticism, parody, scholarly research, or journalism remains a gray area of constitutional law.

Internet Protection

The advent of the Internet has raised new challenges for copyright laws, which have not yet been fully tested in the courts (witness one federal court ruling barring the free downloading of copyrighted music through Napster, an online music-swapping company). A poem is protected equally on a hard drive or on paper, and creators of e-mail lists and Web pages have the same right as similar artists to exclude others from using their works. Although Webmasters have rights in their creations, works placed on the Internet generally carry an implied license to make copies; use beyond that may be a violation of the author's rights. The fair use exception applies to the Internet, but one organization, the Online Freedom Foundation, argues that some copyrighted material on Web sites maintained by fans or followers, as opposed to competitors or businesses, also comes under the fair use exception. Many

Rocker Jon Bon Jovi performs in New Jersey in October 2007. The rise of the Internet has spawned court battles over the free downloading of music that is copyrighted, and artists are divided as to whether online distribution channels help or hurt their record sales.

Source: AP Images/The Prudential Center, Jennifer Graylock

Web pages now carry a copyright license that allows unlimited copying if the copyright notice remains attached, no commercial profit is made from the copying, and the author is notified of any variance from the license requirements. In *Metro-Goldwyn-Mayer Studios, Inc. v. Grokster, Ltd.* (2005), the Supreme Court, in a decision written by Justice David H. Souter (b. 1939), held that one who distributes a device—in this case, file-sharing computer networking software—with the object of promoting its use to infringe copyright, as shown by clear expression or other affirmative steps to foster infringement, is liable for the resulting acts of infringement by third parties.

Copyright laws, like BANKRUPTCY laws, are not exclusive to the federal government, according to the decision of the Supreme Court in *Goldstein v. California* (1973). The states may extend additional copyright protection within their jurisdiction, but for all intents and purposes this area has been preempted by federal law.

More on this topic:
Common Law, p. 102
Patents, p. 396

Corwin, Edward S.

Edward Samuel Corwin (1878–1963) is considered one of the foremost twentieth-century authorities on the Constitution. A philosopher rather than a legal scholar (he was not a lawyer), Corwin outlined the two great constitutional challenges of his time: the balance between liberty and government restrictions and the development of a welfare state under a chief executive who had come to dominate the other two coequal branches of government (see PRESIDENT). Often cited in Supreme Court opinions, he once observed: "If judges make law, so do commentators."

Born in Plymouth, Michigan, on January 19, 1878, Edward Corwin was graduated in 1900 from the University of Michigan, where he was chosen class president and inducted into Phi Beta Kappa. He received his Ph.D. in history from the University of Pennsylvania in 1905. That same year Woodrow Wilson (1856–1924), then president of Princeton University, selected Corwin to participate in a new special postgraduate program as one of the school's first preceptors (assistant professors who led small discussion groups with students). With Corwin's strong interest in American history—his doctoral dissertation focused on the American and French alliance during the Revolutionary War (1775–83)—the course he taught in constitutional interpretation became a favorite of the students despite its acknowledged difficulty.

In 1911 Corwin was made a full professor of politics at Princeton and in 1918 became McCormick Professor of Jurisprudence, a position formerly held by Wilson. Corwin—called "The General" for his erect bearing—later assumed the chairmanship of the university's Department of Politics. He was appointed an adviser to the Public Works Administration in 1935 and during the following two years was a special assistant for constitutional matters to the attorney general of the United States, Homer S. Cummings. After retiring from Princeton in 1946, he taught at Columbia University, the University of Virginia, New York University School of Law, Emory University, the University of Minnesota, and the University of Washington. Corwin's classes were considered both hard and rewarding by his students, who included the two-time Democratic presidential candidate Adlai E. Stevenson (1900–65).

The breadth of Corwin's involvement in political science and constitutional development was impressive. In addition to teaching and writing, between

"The proper point of view from which to approach the task of interpreting the Constitution is that of regarding it as a living statute, palpitating with the purpose of the hour, reenacted with every waking breath of the American people, whose primitive right to determine their institutions is its sole claim to validity as a law and as the matrix of laws under our system."

—*Edward S. Corwin,* in the *American Political Science Review,* 1925

Source: Princeton University Library

1949 and 1952 he edited for the Library of Congress *The Constitution Annotated: Analysis and Interpretation*. President of the American Political Science Association in 1931 and a member of the American Philosophical Society (which bestowed on him its Benjamin Franklin Medal) and the American Historical Association, among other organizations, he received honorary degrees from Princeton and Michigan.

During his lifetime, Corwin wrote more than twenty books, including *John Marshall and the Constitution* (1919), *The Commerce Power Versus States' Rights: Back to the Constitution* (1936), *Liberty Against Government* (1948), and *A Constitution of Powers in a Secular State* (1951). An important collection of his essays, *Corwin on the Constitution*, was published by Cornell University Press in 1981. The titles of the essays range from "The Worship of the Constitution" and "The Constitution as Instrument and as Symbol" to "The Spending Power of Congress" and "The President's Power of Removal." The Supreme Court cited Corwin and his works in at least nineteen cases decided in the twentieth century. Most quoted from and cited was *The President: Office and Powers* (1940, revised 1957). His ability to put constitutional interpretation into a historical context and to frame the important debates over constitutional issues had an impact on how constitutional interpretation was taught in the classroom as well as on how cases were decided in the courts.

Perhaps because he was not a lawyer, Corwin brought political, social, and philosophical insights to the interpretation of the Constitution. He identified two competing grounds in American political theory for constitutional interpretation. The first was based on natural law, which according to St. Thomas Aquinas (ca. 1224–74) was derived from God and therefore higher than man-made law. The second theory was based on the theory of evolution formulated by Charles Darwin (1809–88), in which natural selection would determine the political organization best fitted to the human environment. Corwin believed that Darwinian political theory led political reformers to abandon the basic concepts of government intended by the FRAMERS OF THE CONSTITUTION (see ORIGINAL INTENT). But his defense of natural law as used by the founders failed to rout arguments made by proponents of positive (man-made) law, such as Supreme Court Justice OLIVER WENDELL HOLMES JR., who characterized the law as a triumph of experience over logic. In the realm of constitutional politics, Corwin tended to favor congressional over presidential power (see CONGRESS), criticizing the opinion of Chief Justice William H. Taft (1857–1930) in *Myers v. United States* (1926), in which he supported the president's unconditional power to remove appointees such as cabinet members (see APPOINTMENT AND REMOVAL POWER).

More than a scholar, Edward Corwin laced his comments on the Constitution with humor, characterizing JUDICIAL REVIEW as "American democracy's way of covering its bets" and proposing that the CABINET be replaced by a legislative council "whose daily salt does not come from the Presidential table." Corwin proved over his lifetime that the study of the Constitution need not be a dry and dusty undertaking.

Counterfeiting *See* CURRENCY.

Courts

Any state "without duly established courts," concluded the ancient Greek philosopher Plato (ca. 427–347) in *The Laws*, "simply ceases to *be* a state." In England, courts of law evolved from the courts of monarchs and feudal lords, where they or their representatives dispensed justice. Since then, the term *court* has come to refer to the officials, generally called judges or justices, who carry out judicial functions in the name of the sovereign or the people.

Federal Courts

The federal judiciary consists of courts established under the authority of the Constitution. At the top of the national court system is the SUPREME COURT. The Constitution's provisions regarding the JUDICIAL BRANCH are contained in Article III, section 1 of which declares: "The judicial Power of the United States, shall be vested in one supreme Court, and in such inferior Courts as the Congress may from time to time ordain and establish."

Under Article I, section 8, the Constitution also grants Congress "Power...To constitute Tribunals inferior to the supreme Court...." In addition to the Supreme Court, the federal judiciary currently includes thirteen courts of appeal and ninety-four district courts, each of which hears cases

Clarence Darrow, the noted attorney and social reformer, rests against his desk in the Dayton, Tennessee, district courtroom during the Scopes "monkey trial" of 1925. Defending the right to teach evolution in the schools, he went up against the famous orator William Jennings Bryan, representing the prosecution in his last public appearance.
Source: Library of Congress

in designated geographic regions of the United States. Eighty-nine district courts are located in the fifty states; the rest serve the District of Columbia and the territories.

Administration. The federal court system is a pyramid, with the Supreme Court at the top, the courts of appeals at the next level, and the district courts below that. The CHIEF JUSTICE of the United States, in addition to presiding over the Supreme Court, supervises the Administrative Office of the U.S. Courts, which provides administrative support for all federal courts. He also serves as chair of the Judicial Conference of the United States, which determines policies for administering the federal court system.

The Judicial Conference was created by Congress in 1922 to make "a continuous study of...the general rules of [judicial] practice and procedure" and to recommend "such changes in and addition to those rules as the Conference may deem desirable" to Congress, which has constitutional authority for regulating the Supreme Court's appellate jurisdiction under Article III, section 2. The conference originally consisted of the chief justice, the chief judges of the courts of appeal, and the attorney general (see CABINET). Since the 1950s, a district court judge from each circuit has been included.

Tenure and Compensation of Judges. All justices of the Supreme Court, including the chief justice, and all judges of all the federal courts are appointed by the president with the ADVICE AND CONSENT of the Senate. Article II, section 2, gives the president this power to "nominate, and by and with the Advice and Consent of the Senate,...appoint...Judges of the supreme Court, and all other Officers of the United States, whose Appointments are not herein otherwise provided for, and which shall be established by Law." Section 2 also provides that "Congress may by Law vest the Appointment of such inferior Officers as they think proper, in the President alone, in the Courts of Law, or in the Heads of Departments" (see APPOINTMENT AND REMOVAL POWER).

Throughout the nation's history there has been a difference of opinion as to whether judges, especially at the state level, should be appointed for life or whether they should be elected, as are officials in the legislative and executive branches. In Article III, section 1, the Constitution mandates:

"The Judges, both of the supreme and inferior Courts, shall hold their Offices during good Behaviour…," which essentially means for life; involuntary removal is possible only by IMPEACHMENT.

Valid arguments can be made for either electing or appointing judges. The security of a lifetime appointment may allow judges to make decisions based on the law and their conscience, rather than on what might appeal to the voters at the polls. Others ask, however, whether all public officials in a democracy should not regularly be held accountable to the citizens. If an incompetent or egregiously prejudicial judge has support in the legislature and is thus insulated from impeachment, how can he or she be removed except by the people at an election?

In 1803 President THOMAS JEFFERSON instigated the impeachment by the House of Representatives of a district judge who was subsequently convicted by the Senate. Several months later the House impeached Justice Samuel Chase (1741–1811), also at Jefferson's urging, but he was acquitted. Three district judges were removed from office during the 1980s on the basis of criminal charges. And then in 1969 Justice Abe Fortas (1910–82) resigned from the Supreme Court after the House began looking into charges of mismanagement of funds. In 1953 and 1970 Justice William O. Douglas (1898–1982) was twice the subject of a House investigation aimed at bringing impeachment charges.

Federal judges, according to Article III, section 1, "shall, at stated Times, receive for their Services, a Compensation, which shall not be diminished during their Continuance in Office." This prohibition is a protection against punishment for unpopular decisions or the threat of punishment by Congress through its power to enact appropriations for all government offices, including the courts (see COMPENSATION OF OFFICIALS).

Jurisdiction. The FRAMERS OF THE CONSTITUTION attempted to place two types of cases under federal jurisdiction: those of a national character, such as conflicts relating to AMBASSADORS and ADMIRALTY AND MARITIME LAW, and those involving controversies between states, such as border disputes. Article III, section 2, states: "The judicial Power shall extend to all Cases, in Law and Equity, arising under this Constitution, the Laws of the United States, and Treaties made, or which shall be made, under their Authority;—to all Cases affecting Ambassadors, other public ministers and Consuls;—to all Cases of admiralty and maritime Jurisdiction;—to Controversies to which the United States shall be a Party;—to Controversies between two or more States;—between a State and Citizens of another State;—between Citizens of different States;—between Citizens of the same State claiming Lands under Grants of different States, and between a State, or the Citizens thereof, and foreign States, Citizens or Subjects." The terms *cases* and *controversies* have been interpreted to mean real disputes between parties that have a real stake in the outcome, not test cases or requests only for an advisory opinion. (In some states, such as Maine, New Hampshire, and Rhode Island, and some countries, such as Germany and India, the highest courts are authorized to give such advisory opinions.)

The Eleventh Amendment (1795) removed some jurisdiction from the federal courts, stating, "The Judicial power of the United States shall not be construed to extend to any suit in law or equity, commenced or prosecuted against one of the United States by Citizens of another State, or by Citizens or Subjects of any Foreign State." The purpose of the amendment was to protect the sovereign immunity of the states, which would be lost if litigants could plead cases against states in federal courts. But Chief Justice JOHN MARSHALL read the amendment in such a way as to allow federal review of state decisions in such cases, because, as he noted, they were not "commenced or prosecuted" originally in a federal court (see JUDICIAL REVIEW). He further gutted the amendment by excluding from its scope cases in which an officer of the state and not the state itself was the party of record. As Marshall put it in *Osborn v. Bank of the United States*: "If the person who is the real principal, the person who is the true source of the mischief…be exempt from all judicial process [via state sovereign immunity], it would be subversive of the best established principles…."

The Constitution grants the Supreme Court both original and appellate jurisdiction, a distinction made in Article III, section 2: "In all Cases affecting Ambassadors, other public Ministers and Consuls, and those in which a State shall be a Party, the supreme Court shall have original Jurisdiction." The SOVEREIGNTY of a foreign state and of the STATES of the Union requires that the nation's highest court alone hear and determine such cases.

Appeals. Regarding appeals, Article III, section 2, continues: "In all the other Cases before mentioned, the supreme Court shall have appellate Jurisdiction, both as to Law and Fact, with such Exceptions, and under such Regulations as the Congress shall make." Appeals can come to the Supreme Court from inferior federal courts—a U.S. court of appeals or, in some cases, directly from a U.S. district court—or from state courts. Most cases arrive at the Supreme Court on a writ of certiorari (Latin for "to be more fully informed"), which allows the Court to select the appeals it will formally review. Appeals of decisions of federal ADMINISTRATIVE AGENCIES may also be taken by the Supreme Court after a lower federal court has heard them. As Marshall explained in MARBURY V. MADISON (1803), the Constitution allows Congress to add to the Court's appellate jurisdiction but not to its original jurisdiction.

The appellate court system originally consisted of three circuit courts including two Supreme Court justices and one district court judge. Today the system is much larger, and each appellate court has its own judges. The U.S. Court of Appeals for the First Circuit, covering Maine, New Hampshire, and Massachusetts, has six judges, while the Ninth Circuit, encompassing California and six other western states, has twenty-eight. These courts hear appeals from decisions of the U.S. district courts, which are courts of first instance (trial courts), as well as appeals from decisions of federal agencies directly and on appeal from the district courts.

Trial Courts. Federal TRIALS are held only in U.S. district courts, although district court judges may appoint magistrates to try minor cases or handle preliminary matters; bankruptcy judges (who are not appointed for life and thus are not considered "Article III" judges) decide BANKRUPTCY cases. At trial, a civil or a criminal matter is heard in the first instance. Such a trial may have a jury (see JURIES) and may take place over a number of days. Appeals of trial courts decisions, in contrast, are generally held in a shorter time, and only the attorneys for the parties appear before the court of appeals.

District courts are situated in a single state, and no district court's jurisdiction extends beyond one state, although some states have more than one federal district court. These courts began with only limited jurisdiction—the Judiciary Act of 1789 gave them original jurisdiction only in matters of admiralty and maritime law. Their current jurisdiction includes cases involving federal civil and criminal law and disputes between citizens of different states or between citizens of a state and foreigners.

State Courts

Because the U.S. government is based on the principle of FEDERALISM, the country has a dual system of courts: federal courts and state courts. Each state has its own court system, including courts of first instance, which conduct trials and other types of hearings, such as divorce or juvenile proceedings; state courts of appeal; and state supreme courts, which may be known by another name (in Maryland and New York the supreme court is called the court of appeals).

Unlike the appointive federal court system, well over half of the states have some elected judgeships, although many of these states, such as Alaska and Wyoming, also have some appointed judges (generally at the higher level), typically appointed by the governor. Many state jurists serve for a set number of years or have a mandated retirement age.

Cases in state courts involving the U.S. Constitution or federal issues, such as the interpretation of TREATIES, may end up going to the Supreme Court on appeal. Through the process of judicial review of state court decisions, established by Marshall's opinions in *FLETCHER V. PECK* (1810) and *MARTIN V. HUNTER'S LESSEE* (1816), the Supreme Court may reverse state supreme court decisions and declare state government actions unconstitutional, just as it does federal actions and laws.

The evolution of the federal courts' jurisdiction—and the Supreme Court's claim to be the final arbiter of the Constitution through its power to review state and federal actions—has been a force for welding a vast and diverse territory of semisovereign states into a nation. The dynamics of the American federal system of government vary, alternating between periods when STATES' RIGHTS dominate and periods when individual rights do so. In the long run, however, the tendency has been toward far greater central authority and power in the national government than might have been envisioned by most of the framers of the Constitution in 1787.

Credit   *See* CURRENCY; DEBT.

Criminal Law

Criminal laws are enacted by legislatures or derived from COMMON LAW, enforced by the EXECUTIVE BRANCH of government, and interpreted and applied in particular cases by the JUDICIAL BRANCH. The Constitution empowers the three branches of government to perform their roles and guarantees citizens certain rights when they are accused, arrested, tried, and convicted of an offense against the government and the people represented by that government. Their crimes may be overt acts, such as robbery or murder, or omissions, such as failure to stop at a red traffic light or pay income taxes.

At the time the Constitution went into effect in 1789, much of the criminal law in America was derived from English law. In his *Commentaries on the Laws of England* (1765–70), William Blackstone (1723–80) explained that "both crimes and misdemeanors,...properly speaking, are mere synonymous terms; though in common usage the word 'crimes' is made to denote offences [that] are deeper and more atrocious..., while smaller faults and omissions of less consequence, are comprised under the gentler name of 'misdemeanors' only." A felony, he noted, was an offense that "occasions a total forfeiture of either lands or goods, or both, at the common law; and to which capital or other punishment may be [added], according to the degree of guilt."

The term *felony* appears three times in the U.S. Constitution. Article I, section 6, provides that members of Congress are immune from ARREST during congressional sessions except in cases of "Treason,

Bobby Seale is forcibly silenced in this 1969 courtroom drawing by David Brodie, made during the infamous "Chicago Eight" conspiracy trial. Despite this drastic judicial restraint, he was found not guilty of violating the Civil Rights Act during the 1968 Democratic Convention.
Source: **Howard Brodie, Library of Congress**

Felony and Breach of the Peace," and section 8 states that Congress has the power to punish "Piracies and Felonies committed on the high Seas." Article IV, section 2, provides for the EXTRADITION of "[a] Person charged in any State with Treason, Felony, or other Crime...." In American law, however, *felony* is not consistently defined, although many state constitutions and statutes classify felonies as crimes punishable by death or by imprisonment in a federal penitentiary or a state prison, thus distinguishing them from lesser crimes called misdemeanors.

The U.S. Constitution addresses a number of subjects related to criminal law—for example, excessive BAIL (Eighth Amendment [1791]), HABEAS CORPUS (Article I, section 9), and PUNISHMENT (Eighth Amendment [1791]). Article I, section 8, and Article III, section 3, expressly authorize Congress to enact laws regarding a few specific crimes, such as counterfeiting (see CURRENCY), piracy and felonies committed on the high seas (see ADMIRALTY AND MARITIME LAW), offenses against the law of nations (see INTERNATIONAL LAW), and TREASON. It also provides, in Article II, section 4, for IMPEACHMENT of high government officials: "The President, Vice President, and all civil Officers of the United States, shall be removed from Office on Impeachment for, and Conviction of, Treason, Bribery, or other high Crimes and Misdemeanors." Congress's authority to legislate with respect to a much broader range of criminal laws, however, is provided under the NECESSARY AND PROPER CLAUSE of Article I, section 8.

Criminal Procedure

The rules governing the apprehension, prosecution, trial, and sentencing of persons accused and convicted of crimes are collectively called criminal procedure. Most criminal law matters come under the jurisdiction of the STATES, although the Supreme Court often hears appeals from state criminal cases and has extended to the states many of the rights of persons accused of federal crimes. Such rights, for example, include indigent defendants' right to ASSISTANCE OF COUNSEL and the accused's right to confront adverse WITNESSES.

The DUE PROCESS clause of the Fifth Amendment (1791) is the vehicle by which the Supreme Court enforces the rules of criminal procedure at the federal level, whereas it uses the due process clause of the Fourteenth Amendment (1868) to enforce these rules in the states. The Court's role includes determining the constitutionality of laws regarding punishment (by voiding overly vague laws, for example), the methods used by the police to identify suspects, how prosecutors seek indictments and plea bargains (accepting guilty pleas in exchange for reduced sentences), the conduct of TRIALS, and the imposition of sentences for persons found guilty of crimes.

Investigation. Investigation is the first phase of the government's involvement in criminal acts. The RIGHTS of those suspected of a crime are guaranteed in the Fourth Amendment (1791), which prohibits "unreasonable searches and seizures" and requires that warrants for searches, seizures, and arrests (seizures of persons) be based on "probable cause, supported by Oath or affirmation, and particularly describing the place to be searched, and the person or things to be seized" (see SEARCH AND SEIZURE).

Arrest. The Fifth Amendment (1791) contains rights for arrested persons: the right to DUE PROCESS of the law, protection from SELF-INCRIMINATION (being coerced into giving a confession), and the right to bail (not expressly guaranteed in the Constitution, but excessive bail is prohibited in the Eighth Amendment [1791]). According to the Fifth Amendment, "No person...shall be compelled in any criminal case to be a witness against himself, nor deprived of life, liberty [which includes arrest and preconviction detention], or property, without due process of law...." The protection for life, LIBERTY, or PROPERTY guards a suspect against unnecessary force during arrest, inhumane treatment, or any action that inflicts punishment before an accused's guilt has been established in court according to the law. It also includes unlawful arrest or imprisonment, whereby a person's liberty is threatened or taken away by persons acting outside the scope of the law. In

MIRANDA V. ARIZONA (1966), the Supreme Court mandated that all suspects be informed—using the so-called Miranda warnings—about their constitutional rights, including the right to remain silent and to have a lawyer present during interrogation.

In recent years, federal courts have been circumscribing the effect of *Miranda*. For example, in *Chavez v. Martinez* (2003), the Court held that a confession obtained against the suspect's will was not a violation of the Constitution if it was not used in a criminal proceeding. And in 2004 a U.S. Court of Appeals found in *United States v. Beard* that the defendant was not "in custody" in the sense required under the *Miranda* decision; therefore, the incriminating statements he made without being read his Miranda rights could be used against him.

Indictment. The next step in the process of bringing an accused person to trial for a crime is the indictment, a charge by the government before a court or by a grand jury that requires the accused to stand trial and defend himself or herself against the case to be brought by the prosecution (see COURTS; JURIES; TRIALS). The Fifth Amendment provides, among other things: "No person shall be held to answer for a capital, or otherwise infamous crime, unless on a presentment or indictment of a Grand Jury, except in cases arising in the land and naval forces, or in the Militia, when in actual service in time of War or public danger...." The amendment also mandates that no person shall "be subject for the same offence to be twice put in jeopardy of life and limb," a provision known as the prohibition against DOUBLE JEOPARDY. Simply put, this means that the prosecution gets only one chance to convict a person of a crime.

Trial. Article IV, section 2, requires the EXTRADITION of fugitives from one state to another to stand trial; extradition between nations is usually based on a bilateral treaty (see TREATIES), and Article III, section 2, provides for trial by jury. The Sixth Amendment (1791) guarantees a fair trial, including the right to "a speedy and public trial," the right "to be informed of the nature and cause of the accusation," and the rights "to be confronted with the witnesses against him; to have compulsory process for obtaining witnesses in his favor, and to have Assistance of Counsel for his defence." These Sixth Amendment guarantees are supplemented by the due process clauses of the Fifth and Fourteenth Amendments and the latter's EQUAL PROTECTION clause.

Punishment. A number of provisions of the Constitution relate to punishment for crimes (see PRISONERS; PUNISHMENT). Under Article I, section 8, the Constitution prohibits certain types of punishment, such as bills of attainder (see ATTAINDER, BILLS OF) and EX POST FACTO LAWS. The Eighth Amendment prohibits excessive fines and CRUEL AND UNUSUAL PUNISHMENT, although the Supreme Court has not found the DEATH PENALTY to be cruel and unusual.

Sentencing. Sentencing, the final stage in a criminal prosecution, is generally left to the discretion of the judge and jury. The Supreme Court has indicated that the Constitution's requirement of due process does not overly restrict a judge's discretion in meting out a sentence to a person convicted of a crime. However, the U.S. Code, in Crimes and Procedures, Title 18, requires that "a defendant who has been found guilty of an offense described in any Federal statute...shall be sentenced in accordance with the provisions" of chapter 227—Sentences. The U.S. Sentencing Commission has issued new sentencing guidelines, as amended, that became effective November 1, 2001.

Appeal. After being convicted of a crime, a state or federal defendant has the right to appeal to a higher court. Article III, section 2, of the Constitution provides that, except in certain cases, "the supreme Court shall have appellate Jurisdiction, both as to Law and Fact, with such Exceptions, and under such Regulations as the Congress shall make." It was 1889, however, before Congress gave the Supreme Court jurisdiction to hear appeals in criminal cases.

The Federal Rules of Appellate Procedure, contained in Title 28 of the U.S. Code, address how appeals are to be made and what is required for a reversal of a lower court's decision. Most appeals come to the Supreme Court by a writ of certiorari (Latin for "to be more fully informed"), which allows the Court to select which cases it will hear and decide. Important considerations in the selection process include whether a U.S. court of appeals has entered a decision that is in conflict with another on a significant matter, whether a state court of last resort has decided a significant federal question that is in conflict with other state or federal court decisions, and whether a state or federal court of appeals has decided a significant question of federal law that should be reviewed by the Court.

Pardon. If an appeal is unsuccessful in overturning a conviction, Article II, section 2, authorizes the PRESIDENT "to Grant Reprieves and Pardons for Offences against the United States, except in Cases of Impeachment." Most state constitutions similarly empower the governor to grant PARDONS for criminal offenses. Pardons are relatively rarely granted by presidents, but the power is available to prevent grave injustices. In his two terms in office, President Bill Clinton (b. 1946) granted 456 pardons; Woodrow Wilson (1856–1924), in contrast, offered 2,480. But according to congressional testimony of the U.S. pardon attorney, when Clinton left office on January 20, 2001, well over three thousand clemency requests were pending for action by his successor.

More on this topic:
Arrest, p. 45
Assistance of Counsel, p. 52
Bill of Rights, p. 62
Due Process, p. 168
Habeas Corpus, p. 266
Justice, p. 325
Punishment, p. 440

The American criminal law system does not always work perfectly, but the aim of the system in each and every case is justice. When guilty verdicts are overturned on appeal because the government has violated a defendant's constitutional rights, the system is working as the framers intended. As Justice William O. Douglas (1898–1980) said in his dissent in *Couch v. United States* (1973): "We should not be swayed by the popular cry for a formalistic and narrow interpretation of those provisions which safeguard our fundamental rights. It is a Constitution we are construing, not a legislative-judicial code of conduct that suits our private value choices or that satisfies the appetite of prosecutors for more and more shortcuts that avoid constitutional barriers."

Cruel and Unusual Punishment

All governments sanction some kind of PUNISHMENT to penalize people who violate their laws. In ancient Athens, the birthplace of democratic government, punishment ranged from fines to execution in rare cases such as the murder of an Athenian by a foreigner. For much of human history, national rulers have subjected their people to a varied lot of cruel and inhumane punishments, such as burning them alive or disemboweling them alive for treason in eighteenth-century England and beheading suspected adulterers in twenty-first-century Afghanistan.

Punishment Proportionate to the Crime

Movement toward a more rational and humane theory of punishment, at least in some parts of Europe, was launched by Cesare Beccaria (1738–94), an Italian jurist and economist who wrote *Treatise on Crimes and Punishment* (1764). Based on the utilitarian proposition that government should aim to achieve the greatest good for the greatest number of people, Beccaria contended that a punishment's severity should depend on the extent to which the crime endangers society—and should be no more severe than needed to deter crime. His ideas persuaded the British reformer Jeremy Bentham (1748–1832) and made their way to America as well.

As the Constitution's Eighth Amendment (1791) mandates: "Excessive bail shall not be required, nor excessive fines imposed, nor cruel and unusual punishments inflicted." This language was picked up almost verbatim from the ninth clause of the Virginia Declaration of Rights (1776), written by GEORGE MASON, who heavily influenced the national BILL OF RIGHTS as well. A century earlier, the English Bill of Rights (1689) included a virtually identical provision, demanding "[t]hat excessive bail ought not to be required, nor excessive fines imposed; nor cruel and unusual punishments inflicted." William Blackstone (1723–1780), in his *Commentaries on the Laws of England*, said that "'[f]ormerly' some offenses, though rarely, occasioned a mutilation or dismembering, by cutting off the hands or ears"; but as for torturing of prisoners before conviction, which was considered "a species of trial in itself," when it was proposed by the royal privy counsel to put the assassin of a nobleman on the rack, "the judges, being consulted, declared unanimously, to their own honour and the honour of the English law, that no such proceeding was allowable by the laws of England."

The Supreme Court has not often used the "cruel and unusual" clause to invalidate punishment. In *In re Kemmler* (1890), the Court defined "cruel and unusual punishments" as "such punishment as would amount to torture or barbarity, and any cruel and degrading punishment not known to the common law, and also any punishment so disproportionate to the offense as to shock the moral sense of the community." In *Weems v. United States* (1910), decided when the United States had possession of the Philippines, the Court held that a punishment applied in the Philippines—fifteen years in chains at hard labor for making a false but harmless entry in a public record—was unconstitutional. And in *Trop v. Dulles* (1958), the Supreme Court overturned a military court's ruling that stripped a deserter of his U.S. citizenship. According to Chief Justice Earl Warren (1891–1974), the Eighth Amendment "must draw its meaning from the evolving standards of decency that mark the progress of a maturing society."

Since World War II the international community has addressed the problem of excessive punishment in international human rights documents. The Declaration on the Protection of All Persons from Being Subjected to Torture and Other Cruel, Inhuman or Degrading Treatment or Punishment (1975) calls torture and "cruel, inhuman or degrading treatment or punishment...an offense to human dignity," condemning it as a violation of fundamental human rights (see HUMAN RIGHTS). The declaration was backed up in 1987 with a UN convention committing signatory nations to ban torture and cruel punishment in their own countries. A number of nations limit excessive punishment in their constitutions; Nicaragua's (1987), for example, declares that its "penitentiary system is humane," while Poland's (1992) prohibits "the application of corporal punishment."

Since the terrorist attacks against the United States on September 11, 2001, cruel and unusual punishment has become a part of the national debate about the treatment of terrorists and terrorist suspects by the government. In March 2008 President George W. Bush exercised one of his very infrequent vetoes to quash legislation that would have banned the use by the Central Intelligence Agency of extreme interrogation procedures, including a torture technique called "waterboarding," whereby a person is strapped down face up and subjected to a simulation of drowning.

The Death Penalty and Other Extreme Cases

"When a juvenile commits a heinous crime, the State can exact forfeiture of some of the most basic liberties, but the State cannot extinguish his life and his potential to attain a mature understanding of his own humanity."

—*Justice Anthony Kennedy,* in *Roper v. Simmons*

The DEATH PENALTY is prohibited in many national constitutions and a number of international human rights documents. When capital punishment as it was then being imposed in America was invalidated by the Supreme Court in *Furman v. Georgia* (1972), the justices relied on the Constitution's cruel and unusual clause. In a bitter 5–4 decision, the Court found that judges and juries had insufficient guidance in sentencing to death a person convicted of murder and that their unfettered discretion in sentencing had led to palpable discrimination in some cases. In *Furman*, however, the Court did not say that the death penalty itself was unconstitutional. Rather, in a series of court cases beginning in 1976, the justices laid out guidelines for its imposition. As a result of fine-tuning the sentencing process, the Court has been deluged with petitions to review death sentences that are still legal in many states and under federal law.

The cruel and unusual clause has come up in recent Supreme Court cases, for example, in the application of the death penalty to mentally retarded persons. In another case, *Roper v. Simmons* (2005), the Court declared that both the Eighth (1791) and Fourteenth (1868) Amendments forbid the imposition of the death penalty on offenders who were under the age of eighteen when the crime was committed. And in *Nelson v. Campbell* (2004), the Court reviewed the use of a "cut-down" procedure to access severely compromised veins due to drug abuse in order to facilitate administering a lethal injection to carry out an execution. The Court, in reversing the lower court's dismissal of the claim and remanding the case for further findings, referred to a statement in the record by a physician to the effect that the procedure was "dangerous and antiquated" and that the only reason for employing the procedure was "to render [it] more painful and risky than it otherwise needs to be."

In other cases involving the Constitution's cruel and unusual clause, the Court held in *Ingraham v. Wright* (1977) that it did not apply to the corporal punishment of schoolchildren but only to people convicted of crimes. In *Youngblood v. Romero* (1982), the Court ruled that the clause did not apply to people being held for treatment such as in a mental institution. A year later, however, in *Solem v. Helm*, addressing the "three strikes and you're out" laws in some states, the Court overturned a life sentence without the possibility of parole for a person who had passed a bad check for $100 and whose two former convictions were for nonviolent crimes against property.

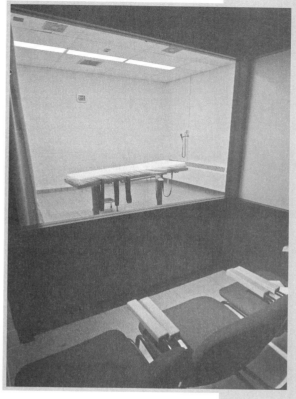

The death chamber at an Ohio corrections facility as seen from the witness room. Lethal injection procedures have been pushed into the national spotlight in recent years, as courts have considered their constitutionality.
Source: AP Images/Kiichiro Sato

Although more than two centuries ago Beccaria argued for proportionality in sentencing—making the punishment fit the crime—Chief Justice William Rehnquist (1924–2005) and Justice Antonin Scalia (b. 1936) advocated abandoning JUDICIAL REVIEW of proportional sentencing. They argued that the Eighth Amendment prohibits only extreme forms of punishment, such as drawing and quartering or other punishments not expressly prescribed by law. Using this logic, Scalia wrote the opinion of the Court in *Harmelin v. Michigan* (1991) upholding a sentence of life imprisonment without the possibility of parole for a person found in possession of 650 grams of cocaine.

The Supreme Court has also had to grapple with the issue of RACIAL DISCRIMINATION in sentencing, especially when a death sentence is imposed. Although acknowledging a study showing that in Georgia in the 1970s the death sentence was imposed 4.3 more times in cases where the victim was white than in cases where the victim was black, in *McCleskey v. Kemp* (1986) the Court did not agree that there was any significant racial bias in Georgia's sentencing procedures. The death penalty, especially in the cases of minors (see CHILDREN) and the mentally disabled (see DISABLED PERSONS), will probably continue to be challenged under the Constitution's prohibition of "cruel and unusual punishments," but this ultimate punishment does not seem in danger of being declared unconstitutional in the United States.

More on this topic:

Death Penalty, p. 140

Human Rights, p. 283

Judicial Review, p. 318

Prisoners, p. 428

Currency

One of the principal indicators of SOVEREIGNTY is the power to issue and control currency—any form of money in actual use as a medium of exchange, including coins and paper money. In his *Commentaries on the Laws of England* (1765–70), William Blackstone (1723–80), speaking of crimes relating to coins, said that counterfeiting money is "a species of high treason; as being a breach of allegiance, by infringing the royal prerogative, and assuming one of the attributes of the sovereign, to whom alone it belongs to set the value and denomination of coin made at home, or to fix the currency of foreign money."

The constitutions of federal countries often lodge this power in the national government (see FEDERALISM). Both Austria's (1934) and Switzerland's (2000) do so, as does the U.S. Constitution, which states in Article I, section 8: "The Congress shall have Power...To coin Money, regulate the Value thereof, and of foreign Coin...[and] provide for the Punishment of counterfeiting the Securities and current Coin of the United States...." Article I, section 10, also mandates, among other things: "No State shall...coin Money; emit Bills of Credit [paper money]; make any Thing but gold and silver Coin a Tender in Payment of Debts...."

In essay 44 of *The Federalist* (1787–88) (see FEDERALIST PAPERS), JAMES MADISON commented: "The right of coining money, which is here taken from the States, was left in their hands by the Confederation [under the ARTICLES OF CONFEDERATION] as a concurrent right with that of Congress, under an exception in favor of the exclusive right of Congress to regulate the alloy and value." He continued: "The extension of the prohibition to bills of credit [to the states] must give pleasure to every citizen in proportion to his love of justice and his knowledge of the true springs of public prosperity."

The FRAMERS OF THE CONSTITUTION did not hand Congress the power to "emit Bills of Credit." But in *MCCULLOCH V. MARYLAND* (1819), the Supreme Court upheld Congress's establishment of a national bank, which could issue paper money. It based its decision on the powers expressly granted to Congress, such as the power to lay and collect taxes, borrow money (see DEBT), and regulate COMMERCE, among others, as well as on the doctrine of IMPLIED POWERS reflected in the Constitution's NECESSARY AND PROPER CLAUSE.

The evolution of the federal government's power to issue paper currency demonstrates one of the ways in which the ORIGINAL INTENT of the framers can be changed by necessity and interpretation. At the CONSTITUTIONAL CONVENTION OF 1787, the draft language giving Congress the power "to borrow money and emit bills on the credit of the United States" was changed by striking out the phrase "and emit bills," because many delegates feared that giving the national government the power to issue paper money would tempt it to simply print more money to pay its debts rather than adopt more prudent measures. The decision in *McCulloch*, however, cleared the way for Congress to establish a national bank that could do just that: issue non-interest-bearing paper notes that would be legal tender for the payment of private debts.

The need to pay soldiers in the field during the Civil War (1861–65) forced Congress for the first time to authorize the printing of paper money called "greenbacks." In *Veazie Bank v. Fenno* (1869), the Supreme Court upheld the national government's power to tax state bank notes so highly that they could not profitably compete with the national currency. The Court in *Hepburn v. Griswold* (1870) temporarily prohibited the issuance of national notes not redeemable in specie (the equivalent sum in coin), but in *Knox v. Lee* (1871) *and Julliard v. Greenman* (1884), known as the Legal Tender Cases, the Court confirmed the federal government's currency power and its right to issue paper money.

In 1863 the office of the comptroller of the currency was set up as a bureau of the Department of the Treasury. Today its examiners conduct onsite reviews of national banks and supervise bank-

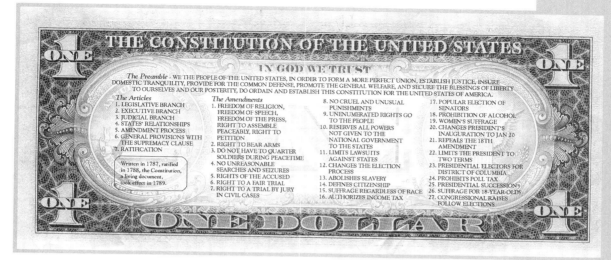

The Constitution of the United States

IN GOD WE TRUST

The Preamble - WE THE PEOPLE OF THE UNITED STATES, IN ORDER TO FORM A MORE PERFECT UNION, ESTABLISH JUSTICE, INSURE DOMESTIC TRANQUILITY, PROVIDE FOR THE COMMON DEFENSE, PROMOTE THE GENERAL WELFARE, AND SECURE THE BLESSINGS OF LIBERTY TO OURSELVES AND OUR POSTERITY, DO ORDAIN AND ESTABLISH THIS CONSTITUTION FOR THE UNITED STATES OF AMERICA.

The Articles
1. LEGISLATIVE BRANCH
2. EXECUTIVE BRANCH
3. JUDICIAL BRANCH
4. STATES' RELATIONSHIPS
5. AMENDMENT PROCESS
6. GENERAL PROVISIONS WITH THE SUPREMACY CLAUSE
7. RATIFICATION

Written in 1787, ratified in 1788, the Constitution, a living document, took effect in 1789.

The Amendments
1. FREEDOM OF RELIGION, FREEDOM OF SPEECH, FREEDOM OF THE PRESS, RIGHT TO ASSEMBLE PEACEABLY, RIGHT TO PETITION
2. RIGHT TO BEAR ARMS
3. DO NOT HAVE TO QUARTER SOLDIERS DURING PEACETIME
4. NO UNREASONABLE SEARCHES AND SEIZURES
5. RIGHTS OF THE ACCUSED
6. RIGHT TO A FAIR TRIAL
7. RIGHT TO A TRIAL BY JURY IN CIVIL CASES

8. NO CRUEL AND UNUSUAL PUNISHMENTS
9. UNENUMERATED RIGHTS GO TO THE PEOPLE
10. RESERVES ALL POWERS NOT GIVEN TO THE NATIONAL GOVERNMENT TO THE STATES
11. LIMITS LAWSUITS AGAINST STATES
12. CHANGES THE ELECTION PROCESS
13. ABOLISHES SLAVERY
14. DEFINES CITIZENSHIP
15. SUFFRAGE REGARDLESS OF RACE
16. AUTHORIZES INCOME TAX

17. POPULAR ELECTION OF SENATORS
18. PROHIBITION OF ALCOHOL
19. WOMEN'S SUFFRAGE
20. CHANGES PRESIDENT'S INAUGURATION TO JAN 20
21. REPEALS THE 18TH AMENDMENT
22. LIMITS THE PRESIDENT TO TWO TERMS
23. PRESIDENTIAL ELECTORS FOR DISTRICT OF COLUMBIA
24. PROHIBITS POLL TAX
25. PRESIDENTIAL SUCCESSION
26. SUFFRAGE FOR 18-YEAR-OLDS
27. CONGRESSIONAL RAISES FOLLOW ELECTIONS

ONE DOLLAR

In 1998 a middle school teacher and his students in Ashland, Virginia, proposed a design for paper currency featuring the Constitution on the reverse. Congress has not approved the design, although some members of Congress and civic groups have endorsed it.
Source: Liberty Middle School in Ashland, VA

ing operations; it also approves or rejects applications for bank charters and issues regulations governing bank practices, including investment and lending activities. In *First National Bank v. Fellows* (1917), the Supreme Court upheld the creation of the Federal Reserve System to control the currency supply and national monetary policy.

In 1933 Congress nullified "gold clauses" in contracts that required payment in gold coin of the United States. The Supreme Court in *Norman v. Baltimore and Ohio Railroad Co.* (1935) found that such nullification was not unconstitutional because the obligations in the contracts were for the payment of money and not a specific number of grains of gold. Although the gold clauses were obviously an attempt to avoid receiving payment in devalued currency, the Court explained that Congress had the power to devalue the currency whenever it saw fit. To require payment in gold would then place an unjust burden on corporations, municipalities, and other entities whose revenue base was the devalued dollar; they would be obligated to pay many of their debts in gold, which might then have a different standard of value than the dollar at the time the contracts were signed.

U.S. currency is used in many countries around the world as a primary or secondary medium of exchange. Even the communist country of Cuba has special stores where Cuban citizens can purchase a greater variety of high-quality goods only with American "greenbacks."

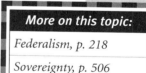

More on this topic:

Federalism, p. 218

Sovereignty, p. 506

Taxation, p. 533

Customs *See* CABINET; CONGRESS.

Death Penalty

According to Amnesty International, 86 percent of all government executions worldwide in 1998 took place in four of the ninety countries that still allow it: China, the Democratic Republic of Congo, Iran, and the United States. After 1976, when capital punishment was reinstated in the United States, the number of persons executed annually reached a peak of ninety-eight in 1999, including thirty-five in Texas and fourteen in Virginia; however, the numbers declined in 2000 to eighty-five and then in 2001 still further to sixty-six. As the leading state, Oklahoma, with eighteen executions, replaced Texas, which carried out seventeen in 2001. These states were followed by Missouri, with seven, North Carolina, with five, and Georgia, with four; no other state had more than two executions. According to estimates by the NAACP Legal Defense Fund, in 2005 some 3,452 PRISONERS were on death row throughout the country, only 53 of whom were women; of the total, 1,572 were white, 1,440 black, 359 latino or latina, 40 Native American, 40 Asian, and one of unknown origin.

Perhaps the most vexing moral question in America, the death penalty is rooted in English law as it stood at the time the Constitution was written in 1787. The document does not prohibit or limit this ultimate PUNISHMENT, except to the extent that the "cruel and unusual punishments" clause of the Eighth Amendment (1791) may be interpreted to apply to the death penalty (see CRUEL AND UNUSUAL PUNISHMENT). The Constitution merely alludes to capital punishment in the Fifth Amendment: "No person shall be held to answer for a capital, or otherwise infamous crime, unless on a presentment or indictment of a Grand Jury...." A capital crime then was one whose punishment was loss of the offender's head (capital comes from the Latin *caput*, meaning head).

DEATH PENALTY POLICIES IN SELECTED NATIONS

Nation	Most Recent Execution	Policy
Afghanistan	2007	Permitted in cases of murder, child smuggling in order to use the victim's body parts, and apostasy
Argentina	1916	Prohibited
Australia	1967	Prohibited
Austria	1950	Prohibited
Brazil	1855	Prohibited
Britain	1964	Prohibited
Canada	1962	Prohibited
China	2007	Permitted in cases of murder, embezzlement, child rape, fraud, bombing, trafficking in people, piracy, theft, corruption, arson, terrorism, and endangering national security
Egypt	About 2004	Permitted in cases of murder, treason, drug trafficking, and rape when accompanied by kidnapping of victim
France	1977	Prohibited
Germany	1956 (West Germany) 1981 (East Germany)	Prohibited
Japan	2007	Permitted in cases of mass murder, or murder with aggravating circumstances
Kenya	1984	Permitted in cases of murder and armed robbery
India	2004	Permitted in cases of murder, treason, terrorism, instigating a child's suicide, and a second conviction for drug trafficking
Iran	2007	Permitted for murder, rape when accompanied by kidnapping, sodomy, armed robbery, terrorism, drug trafficking, and apostasy
Israel	1962	Crimes against humanity and high treason
Mexico	1937	Prohibited
Nigeria	2001	Permitted in cases of sodomy
Russia	1999	Permitted in cases of murder with aggravating circumstances, attempted assassination of a prominent figure or law enforcement official, and genocide
Saudi Arabia	2005	Permitted for many offenses, including murder, apostasy, drug offenses, witchcraft, and sexual misconduct
South Africa	1991	Prohibited
South Korea	1997	Permitted in cases of murder
Turkey	1984	Prohibited

SOURCE: Amnesty International.

NOTE: Nations have differing approaches to the death penalty. Some nations have formally abolished the death penalty, or they rarely or never impose it. Others, like the United States, continue to execute people convicted of certain crimes.

William Blackstone (1723–80), the eighteenth-century commentator on the laws of England, recorded that in capital cases the grim sentence " 'let him be hanged by the neck' " was written opposite the prisoner's name and that "this [notation] is the only warrant that the sheriff has for so material an act as taking away the life of another." In the same century the French philosopher Jean-Jacques Rousseau (1712–78) contended that capital punishment is justified because if people are willing to have soldiers, for example, risk their lives for the sake of others, they must risk losing their own lives should they commit serious crimes. The Italian jurist Cesare Beccaria (1738–94)

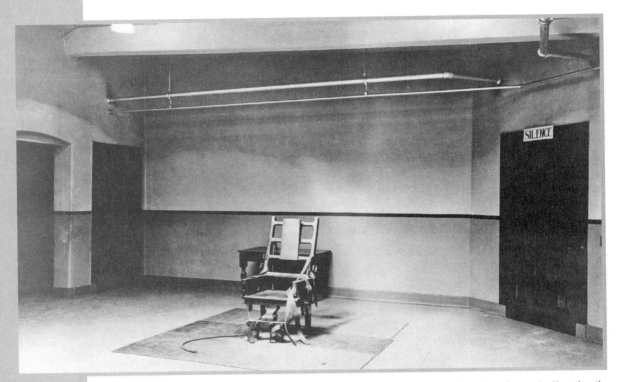

The stark presence of an electric chair dominates the death chamber of New York's Sing Sing prison about 1965. Since then the majority of states, including New York, have adopted lethal injection as the preferred method of carrying out the death penalty, although even that procedure has been increasingly scrutinized as cruel and unusual punishment.
Source: AP Images

took the opposite side—arguing in his *Treatise on Crimes and Punishment* (1764) against the use of torture by law enforcement officers as well as the death penalty.

Today the nations of the world are about evenly divided on whether a sentence of death for any crime, no matter how heinous, is a violation of HUMAN RIGHTS. The death penalty is denounced in international human rights documents such as the International Covenant on Civil and Political Rights (1966) and its Second Optional Protocol Aiming at the Abolition of the Death Penalty (1989), both adopted by the UN General Assembly. The American Convention on Human Rights (1969) mandates that in countries in the Americas that have not abolished the death penalty "it may be imposed only for the most serious crimes...and in accordance with a law establishing such punishment...." The constitutions of some nations, including Brazil (1988) and Mozambique (1990), prohibit or limit the death penalty. In 1995 ten of eleven judges of South Africa's constitutional court held that it constituted "cruel, inhuman or degrading treatment or punishment." Because feelings in other parts of the world run strongly against the American use of the death penalty, some countries refuse to extradite wanted criminals for trial in the United States if they would face capital punishment; alternatively, they demand a guarantee that the defendants will not be put to death.

A Matter for the States

Criminal laws are generally matters for the states (see CRIMINAL LAW). Questions regarding the death penalty, however, are sometimes raised in federal courts under the Constitution's HABEAS CORPUS guarantee and DUE PROCESS clause, as well as its ban on cruel and unusual punishment.

Unfettered by any prohibition in the federal Constitution, states have treated the death penalty as it suits them. Thirty-eight states, the U.S. government, and the U.S. military (see ARMED FORCES) make the death penalty mandatory for certain serious crimes (see sidebar); in 2000 the Illinois governor suspended all state executions in the face of serious error found in many of the state's capital convictions, and Nebraska's legislature also declared a moratorium on the death penalty. States that do not allow imposition of the death penalty are Alaska, Hawaii, Iowa, Maine, Massachusetts, Michigan, Minnesota, North Dakota, Rhode Island, Vermont, West Virginia, and Wisconsin, as well as the District of Columbia. The number of homicides per 100,000 residents in states with the death penalty is 9.3, although the average for all states is only 9 percent.

Crimes that warrant the death penalty vary from state to state. In Pennsylvania, for example, the sentence is limited to first-degree murder with aggravating circumstances, while in New Jersey it was used, until abolished in 2007, for purposeful murder by one's own conduct, contract murder, and solicitation by command or threat in furtherance of a narcotics conspiracy. Federal laws authorize the death penalty in about forty instances, including homicides related to kidnappings and child molestation, aircraft and automobile hijackings, drive-by drug shootings, the smuggling of aliens, murder of high government and foreign officials, transportation or mailing of explosives, destruction of government property, and uniquely federal crimes such as espionage and treason.

All but one of the states that permit the death penalty and the federal government use lethal injection as the primary method of carrying out the death penalty. A number of states also allow electrocution, the gas chamber, hanging, and a firing squad. Since 1976 some 927 lethal injections were used as opposed to 154 electrocutions, 11 deaths by gas chamber, 3 hangings, and 2 deaths by firing squad. All of the 2001 executions were carried out by lethal injection. In 2007 the U.S. Supreme Court halted the planned execution of a Virginia inmate by lethal injection, signaling that the Court may want to rule on the constitutionality of this procedure. The Court has also granted stays of execution in several other cases and agreed in September 2007 to hear a Kentucky case— *Baze v. Rees*—on the subject. Fourteen of the thirty-eight states that use lethal injections are holding up further executions using this method pending legal review of the procedure. The basic problem, however, is this: By what test will the courts determine if lethal injections constitute cruel and unusual punishment? For example, in *Glass v. Louisiana* (1985), dissenters Justices William J. Brennan Jr. (1906–97) and THURGOOD MARSHALL posited that "the Eighth Amendment requires that, as much as humanly possible, a chosen method of execution minimize the risk of unnecessary pain, violence, and mutilation." Therefore, if any "unnecessary cruelty inheres in [such a] method...the method violates the Cruel and Unusual Punishments Clause" of the Constitution.

Sometimes JURIES take the matter of capital punishment into their own hands. Even if jurors believe that a defendant is guilty of a capital crime, in a process termed jury nullifaction they may avoid having the death penalty imposed in favor of life imprisonment or even acquittal. During the nineteenth century a number of states began implementing discretionary sentencing, which permits a guilty verdict but without mandatory capital punishment for specified crimes. One criticism of the death penalty has been that black males receive this sentence far more often than white males. Nevertheless, in *McGautha v. California* (1971) the Supreme Court decided that discretionary sentencing procedures did not violate the due process clause of the Fourteenth Amendment (1868).

The justices did an about-face the following year in *Furman v. Georgia* (1972), and by a 5–4 vote the Supreme Court found that capital punishment violated the Eighth Amendment's prohibition against cruel and unusual punishment. Many states responded by requiring a separate hearing in which juries consider the sentence. In decisions on five cases in 1976, the Court upheld the new discretionary scheme but struck down statutes requiring mandatory sentencing. The following year capital punishment came back to life in the United States. But at the end of 2007 the New Jersey legislature voted to become the first state since 1976 to officially repeal the death penalty.

JURISDICTIONS ALLOWING THE DEATH PENALTY

Jurisdiction	Crimes	Method of Execution
Alabama	Intentional murder with at least one of eighteen aggravating circumstances	Lethal injection; electrocution
Arizona	First-degree murder with at least one of fourteen aggravating factors	Lethal injection; gas chamber
Arkansas	Capital murder with at least one of ten aggravating circumstances; treason	Lethal injection; electrocution
California	First-degree murder with special circumstances; train wrecking; treason; perjury causing execution	Lethal injection; gas chamber
Colorado	First-degree murder with at least one of seventeen aggravating excluded factors; first-degree kidnapping resulting in death; treason	Lethal injection
Connecticut	Capital felony with eight categories of aggravated homicide	Lethal injection
Delaware	First-degree murder with at least one aggravating circumstance	Lethal injection; hanging
Florida	First-degree murder; felony murder; capital drug trafficking; capital sexual battery	Lethal injection; electrocution
Georgia	Murder; kidnapping with bodily injury or ransom where the victim dies; aircraft hijacking; treason	Lethal injection
Idaho	First-degree murder with aggravating factors; aggravated kidnapping; perjury resulting in death	Lethal injection; firing squad
Illinois	First-degree murder with at least one of twenty-one aggravating circumstances (suspended in 2000)	Lethal injection
Indiana	Murder with at least one of sixteen aggravating circumstances	Lethal injection
Kansas	Capital murder with at least one of eight aggravating circumstances	Lethal injection
Kentucky	Murder with aggravating factors; kidnapping with aggravating factors	Lethal injection; electrocution
Louisiana	First-degree murder; aggravated rape of victim under the age of thirteen; treason	Lethal injection
Maryland	First-degree murder (premeditated or during the commission of a felony, with certain requirements) (suspended in 2002)	Lethal injection
Mississippi	Capital murder; aircraft piracy	Lethal injection
Missouri	First-degree murder	Lethal injection; gas chamber
Montana	Capital murder with at least one of nine aggravating circumstances; capital sexual assault	Lethal injection
Nebraska	First-degree murder with at least one statutorily defined aggravating circumstance (suspended in 2000)	Electrocution
Nevada	First-degree murder with at least one of fifteen aggravating circumstances	Lethal injection
New Hampshire	Six categories of capital murder	Lethal injection; hanging
New Jersey	Murder by one's own conduct, by solicitation, committee in furtherance of a narcotics conspiracy, or during commission of a crime of terrorism	Lethal injection
New Mexico	First-degree murder with at least one of seven aggravating circumstances	Lethal injection
New York	First-degree murder with at least one of thirteen aggravating factors	Lethal injection
North Carolina	First-degree murder	Lethal injection
Ohio	Aggravated murder with at least one often aggravating circumstances	Lethal injection
Oklahoma	First-degree murder with at least one of eight statutorily defined aggravating circumstances; sex crimes against a child under fourteen	Lethal injection; electrocution; firing squad
Oregon	Aggravated murder	Lethal injection
Pennsylvania	First-degree murder with at least one of eighteen aggravating circumstances	Lethal injection
South Carolina	Murder with at least one of twelve aggravating circumstances; criminal sexual conduct with a minor with one of nine aggravating circumstances	Lethal injection; electrocution
South Dakota	First-degree murder with at least one of ten aggravating circumstances	Lethal injection
Tennessee	First-degree murder with one of fifteen aggravating circumstances	Lethal injection; electrocution

JURISDICTIONS ALLOWING THE DEATH PENALTY (CONTINUED)

Jurisdiction	Crimes	Method of Execution
Texas	Criminal homicide with at least one of nine aggravating circumstances	Lethal injection
Utah	Aggravated murder	Lethal injection; firing squad
Virginia	First-degree murder with at least one of thirteen aggravating circumstances	Lethal injection; electrocution
Washington	Aggravated first-degree murder	Lethal injection; hanging
Wyoming	First-degree murder	Lethal injection; gas chamber
U.S. Government	Homicides involving federal officials and facilities, genocide, civil rights offenses, kidnapping, terrorism, weapon of mass destruction, etc., as well as espionage, treason, and drug trafficking	Lethal injection
U.S. Military	Fifteen offenses (many, such as desertion and disobeying a superior's order, applicable only in time of war)	Lethal injection

SOURCES: Bureau of Justice Statistics, *Capital Punishment 2006*. Criminal Justice Project, NAACP Legal Defense and Education Fund. *Death Row U.S.A.*, Fall 2001. Death Penalty Information Center (viewed at www.deathpenaltyinfo.org/article.php?did=180).

Eighth Amendment Due Process

The Supreme Court has continued to develop the constitutional law of capital punishment through what is known as Eighth Amendment due process, extending to capital defendants in the sentencing phase many of the same rights allowed persons accused of crime. These include the right of confrontation to rebut evidence, compulsory process to produce mitigating evidence, the ASSISTANCE OF COUNSEL, and the prohibition against SELF-INCRIMINATION and DOUBLE JEOPARDY. In *Lockett v. Ohio* (1978), the Court went so far as to allow mitigating evidence to be presented in a death penalty hearing, seemingly coming full circle from demanding uniform treatment of capital defendants to basing each determination on the defendant's unique circumstances. Where life imprisonment without parole is available, the Supreme Court reaffirmed in *Kelly v. South Carolina* (2002) that courts must tell jurors that this alternative sentence can be imposed to keep especially dangerous criminals away from the public. And in the same year, in *Atkins v. Virginia*, the Court broke new ground by acknowledging that the Eight Amendment permits evolution of the law such that a mentally retarded defendant convicted of murder may not be sentenced to death.

On appeal, serious error has been found in 68 percent of death penalty sentences; 5 percent of the defendants convicted have later been found not guilty. The increasing use of DNA evidence (see GENETICS) to make exacting genetic identifications has led to the release of death-row inmates and suspension of the death penalty in some cases where convictions for capital crimes are proved erroneous.

Since *Lockett*, the Supreme Court has faced a number of habeas corpus petitions from death-row inmates seeking to have their sentences reexamined. (The average time between sentencing and execution is a little more than ten years.) The mere assertion of innocence as the basis for a new trial has been rejected, as have other habeas corpus appeals on the grounds that in determining a matter under habeas corpus rules, a court may not apply new rules favoring the defendant. Congress, in the Antiterrorism and Effective Death Penalty Act (1996), weighed in on the side of reducing the number of habeas corpus petitions; the act calls for limiting how many times such petitions may be filed with the Supreme Court and imposing a statute of limitations on the filings. A reevaluation of the constitutionality of the death penalty may not be undertaken until there is a significant change in the Supreme Court's membership.

The arguments for and against the death penalty, like arguments for and against ABORTION, seem to allow no compromise or common ground. Opponents argue that the death penalty is a violation of a basic and fundamental right to life, while proponents counter that simple JUSTICE condones treating a person who viciously and callously takes another person's life no better than his victim was treated. In resolving this moral dilemma, the Constitution provides little guidance.

Debt

On January 1, 1791, according to the U.S. Treasury Department's Bureau of Public Debt, the national debt was $75,463,476.52; and as of October 15, 2007, it had risen to $9,042,951,429,732.49. Currently, with the U.S. population numbering approximately 303 million persons, each American's share of the national debt is approximately $30,000. Although the debt, just over nine trillion dollars, is large, its significance to the American economy is not clear. Throughout its history, the United States has generally had an outstanding national debt. Yet such debt has not caused the economy to collapse or hampered long-term progress, at least compared with other countries.

In contrast, until 2001 the national BUDGET had been running a surplus in recent years. The deficit is the difference between the government's receipts (what it takes in from taxes and other types of revenues) (see TAXATION) and its outlays (the amount it spends) in any one fiscal year (from October 1 to September 30). It is computed using on-budget items including tax revenues but excluding surpluses that come into the Treasury from various off-budget funds, such as Social Security trust funds, old-age and survivors insurance and disability insurance, and the Postal Service fund. The national debt is the total accumulated deficits in relation to on-budget items plus the surpluses in the Treasury from off-budget items.

All national governments have to finance their activities from their tax revenues, by borrowing (through the sale of bonds, for example), and from other sources, including gifts to the government from citizens and other nations. Switzerland's constitution (2000) mandates that "[t]he Confederation shall keep its long term expenditure and receipts in balance...[and] shall reduce the federal debt." Similarly, Columbia's constitution (1981, as amended) provides: "The domestic and foreign indebtedness of the nation and the territorial entities may not exceed their capacity of repayment. The law will regulate this matter."

NATIONAL DEBT AS PERCENT OF GDP, 1940–2012

The national debt, which totaled about $43 billion (in current dollars) in 1940, is projected to reach $5.7 trillion in 2012. As a percentage of the nation's gross national product, however, that portion of the national debt is declining from 44 to 32 percent.

Source: U.S. Office of Management and Budget, *Budget of the United States Government, Fiscal Year 2008*, Historical Tables (Washington, D.C.: Government Printing Office, 2007), 126–127.

Note: Amounts are in current dollars. Figures reflect debt held by the public and do not include debt held by federal government accounts. 2007–2012 percentages are estimates.

Of the several powers delegated by the U.S. Constitution to the federal government, set forth in Article I, section 8, the first two relate directly to money and debt. Section 8 begins: "The Congress shall have Power To lay and collect Taxes, Duties, Imposts and Excises, to pay the Debts and provide for the common Defence and general Welfare of the United States…[and] To borrow Money on the credit of the United States." The Constitution places no limit on the amount of indebtedness the United States can incur. The government's debt is owned by various investors who have lent money to the government through the purchase of U.S. government securities: the general public (through savings bonds, for example), federal reserve banks, foreign investors, and corporations.

Incurring debt, which is expressly authorized by the Constitution, has not in itself raised a constitutional problem. However, the government's deficit and its borrowing power have come before the Supreme Court. The Balanced Budget and Emergency Deficit Control Act (1985), popularly known as the Gramm-Rudman-Hollings Act, attempted to balance the annual budget and thus eliminate annual deficits by delegating to the comptroller general of the United States the authority to make budget cuts. The Court struck down this act as an unconstitutional delegation of Congress's authority.

Other tangential cases include the Legal Tender Cases—*Knox v. Lee* and *Parker v. Davis* (both 1871)—in which the Supreme Court upheld the issuance of paper money based only on the credit of the United States and not redeemable in coins. In *Norman v. Baltimore and Ohio Railroad Co.* (1935), the Gold Clause Case, the Court affirmed the Constitution's grant to Congress of the power to devalue the CURRENCY. Here it upheld Congress's invalidation of clauses in CONTRACTS of corporations, municipalities, and other organizations requiring repayment in gold on the grounds that their income would be in devalued dollars while their debts would be repayable in the higher valued gold.

The federal government's ability to go into debt is necessary to meet emergency needs resulting from national disasters, such as the ten-year-long Great Depression, or wars, such as the war on TERRORISM. Obviously, borrowing money for priorities—combating a long-term economic depression or waging a major WAR—takes precedence over balancing the budget when there is no compelling need to do so. Apart from emergencies, however, the option to incur large deficits may encourage unnecessary government spending.

Declaration of Independence

The American rebellion against British colonial rule that began in 1775 picked up steam as the result of two events in early 1776. The first was the publication of an incendiary pamphlet, *Common Sense*, written by a recent immigrant from England, Thomas Paine (1737–1809). In it Paine made the logical argument that to change the harsh treatment by the British it was time to move beyond protest and rebellion to revolution and independence. Around the same time, at the beginning of 1776, news reached America about the British Act of December 22, 1775, which prohibited all trade and intercourse with the thirteen colonies.

On January 31, 1776, GEORGE WASHINGTON, a still-loyal subject of the Crown, wrote: "A few more of such flaming arguments [for example, the burning of Norfolk, Virginia, blamed on the British], added to the sound doctrine and unanswerable reasoning contained in the pamphlet *Common Sense*, will not leave numbers at a loss to decide upon the propriety of a separation."

In early May 1776, after hearing that George III was sending twelve thousand German mercenaries to quell the rebellion, a Virginia convention instructed its delegates to the Continental Congress "to declare the United Colonies free and independent states." And on June 7, 1776, Richard Henry Lee of Virginia introduced in the Continental Congress a resolution declaring that the colonies "are, and of right ought to be, free and independent states, [and that] they are absolved

The signers of the Declaration of Independence, as depicted in this early nineteenth-century painting by John Trumbull. The painting features the members of the committee that drafted the document—John Adams, Roger Sherman, Robert Livingston, Thomas Jefferson (presenting the declaration), and Benjamin Franklin—standing in front of John Hancock, who was president of the Continental Congress.

Source: Library of Congress

from all allegiance to the British Crown..." (see LIBERTY).

On the basis of Lee's resolution, seconded by JAMES MADISON, also of Virginia, a committee of five members headed by THOMAS JEFFERSON was appointed to craft the sentiments contained in the resolution into a declaration of independence. The other committee members, who reviewed and edited Jefferson's draft, were JOHN ADAMS of Massachusetts, Benjamin Franklin of Pennsylvania, Robert R. Livingston of New York, and Roger Sherman of Connecticut. Among the changes to the draft was the deletion of Jefferson's condemnation of the slave trade, which he called "an abominable commerce" (see SLAVERY).

The resolution for independence was adopted by the Continental Congress on July 2, 1776, which became the effective date of separation from Great Britain. The vote was twelve for and none against, with only New York abstaining. Two days later the Congress adopted the Declaration of Independence. The document was signed first by John Hancock of Massachusetts, president of the Congress, and Charles Thomson, its secretary. In all, fifty-eight colonists committed treason against the British Crown by signing the Declaration of Independence, which concludes, "we mutually pledge to each other our lives, our Fortunes, and our sacred Honor." Six signers, including Franklin and Sherman, later signed the Constitution (see FRAMERS OF THE CONSTITUTION).

While much of the language of the Declaration is directed at making the case for the colonies' independence from the government of Great Britain—in particular, George III—the enduring concepts with which the document begins have inspired generations the world over. Of the greatest significance is the second sentence: "We hold these Truths to be self-evident, that all Men are created equal, that they are endowed by their Creator with certain unalienable Rights, that among these are Life, Liberty, and the Pursuit of Happiness—That to secure these Rights, Governments are instituted among Men, deriving their just Powers from the Consent of the Governed, that whenever any Form of Government becomes destructive of these Ends, it is the Right of the People to alter or to abolish it, and to institute new Government, laying its Foundation on such Principles, and organizing its Powers in such Form, as to them shall seem most likely to effect their Safety and Happiness." Thus the document not only provided a basis for separating the thirteen colonies from Great Britain; it also sounded a clarion call for creating a new form of government such as that created by the Constitution a decade later.

Broadside editions of the Declaration, printed by Congress's official printer, were ready on the morning of July 5 and sent to various committees. The full text appeared on the front page of the *Pennsylvania Evening Post*, and it was read aloud to an enthusiastic crowd in the yard of the State House in Philadelphia. The news spread quickly throughout the colonies. On August 2 the actual signing of the official document, elegantly printed on a single large sheet of parchment, began.

Eventually there were fifty-six signers, all of them risking their lives for the crime of high TREASON against the British Crown.

Following the lead of the United States, other nations have adopted declarations of independence. Israel's (1948) has even been accorded quasi-constitutional status. The U.S. declaration, in contrast, has no constitutional or legal status domestically, but the political theory it enunciates influenced the framers of the Constitution, and its avowed principles of the equality of all people and their "unalienable rights" have provided the philosophical context for many constitutional developments, from the abolition of slavery to extending to WOMEN the right to vote. (For the complete text of the Declaration, see pages 613–615.)

> **More on this topic:**
>
> *Framers of the Constitution, p. 230*
>
> *Jefferson, Thomas, p. 310*

Defense *See* ARMED FORCES; NATIONAL SECURITY.

Deficit *See* DEBT.

Democracy

"In Europe it is hard for us to judge the true character and permanent instincts of democracy," comments Alexis de Tocqueville, the French politician and political scientist, in *Democracy in America* (1835). "[But t]hat is not the case in America. There the people prevail without impediment; there are neither dangers to fear nor injuries to revenge. Therefore in America democracy follows it own inclinations." Americans, who sometimes take for granted their more than two hundred years of democratic GOVERNMENT, tend to have simplified the concept of democracy, thinking that there is only one type or that its principles are always obvious and easily grasped. Only when something goes wrong, as in the 2000 presidential election contest in Florida (see BUSH V. GORE), do American citizens reexamine their democracy with renewed interest.

Greek and Roman Precedents

Democracy—government by the many as opposed to government by the few or rule by a single person—began in ancient Athens and is generally dated from the democratic reforms introduced by Cleisthenes in 510 B.C.E. The Greek experiment with democracy, in which adult male citizens made decisions about the city-state and voted for public officials in regularly held elections, lasted with brief interruptions until 322 B.C.E., a year after Alexander the Great died.

The Republic of Rome, which began around the same time as Greek democracy in 509 B.C.E., similarly included some degree of citizen participation in making political decisions and selecting public officials. However, the republic was dominated by an aristocratic body called the Senate. Banners carried by the Roman legions proclaimed "S.P.Q.R." (The Senate and the People of Rome). The Roman Republic ended around 27 B.C.E., when Octavian Caesar was given the honorary title of Augustus and in effect became the emperor of the Roman world, beginning a long succession of Roman emperors.

The democracy of the ancient Greeks was a DIRECT DEMOCRACY: all citizens could participate in discussions on important political issues and vote on important issues such as war and peace. The concept of democratic government reasserted itself in the tenth century in the form of representative, instead of direct, democracy in Iceland, where the first parliament, the Althing, began meeting to make laws and judge disputes (albeit without a chief executive or a monarch). A parliament that included representatives of the common people, the aristocracy, and the monarch developed later in England. There, together with written constitutional limitations on the monarch's power, such as Magna Carta (1215) and the Bill of Rights (1689), representative democracy evolved. When English colonists came to North America in the seventeenth and eighteenth centuries, they brought with them the rights and principles embodied in this then-unique form of democratic government.

Representative democracy, in which CITIZENS elect from among themselves representatives to act on their behalf in making laws and policy, had several important advantages over the Greeks' direct democracy: (1) It was not necessary to gather all of the citizens of a political jurisdiction in one place to determine government policies. (2) It permitted the rise of a class of politicians who could develop an expertise in various areas of government concern. (3) Every citizen did not have to be an expert on all subjects relating to government decision making; only those chosen as representatives needed to be so informed (see REPRESENTATIVE GOVERNMENT).

The FRAMERS OF THE CONSTITUTION in 1787 deliberately created a purely representative form of democratic government with no elements of direct democracy. Since the beginning of the twentieth century, however, a number of states have experimented with direct democracy procedures to supplement our basic representative form of government. Such procedures include popular initiatives, in which citizens can propose LAWS and AMENDMENTS to the Constitution; referendums, in which citizens can vote to approve or disapprove laws and amendments; and recall, in which citizens can oust elected officials from office before their legal term of office expires.

Elements of Democracy

The constitutions of most countries create democratic governments, even if they do not use the term *democracy*. Germany's constitution (1949) declares: "Any person who has attained the age of eighteen shall be entitled to vote; any person who has attained the age of majority may be elected." The People's Republic of China, a nondemocratic country, describes itself in its constitution (1982) as "a socialist state under the people's *democratic* dictatorship" [emphasis added]; it further provides that "[t]he state organs...apply the principle of *democratic* centralism [the Communist Party makes all political decisions]." The constitutions of several democratic countries also incorporate direct-democracy procedures. Switzerland's new constitution (2000), adopted by referendum in 1999, contains a chapter on direct democracy, including articles on initiative and referendum.

According to Winston Churchill (1874–1965), "Democracy is the worst form of government, except all others." It may also be the form most difficult to operate and maintain. Key elements of a viable democracy include (1) an informed and motivated citizenry, (2) contested elections in which multiple political parties propose candidates, (3) a free and aggressive press, (4) an open society, (5) the rule of law, and (6) a commitment by those elected to office not to subvert the political system. Not all of these elements are mandated by the Constitution, but all are at least indirectly provided for and protected.

Informed citizens. The citizens of a democracy cannot simply leave the running of their government to others. They have a responsibility to themselves and their posterity to actively participate in ELECTIONS and other methods of holding elected officials accountable for the stewardship of their public office. Citizens must keep abreast of local, state, national, and international events that may influence decision making about candidates and polices. They must convey to their children the importance of maintaining the democratic processes and institutions that have served them well. Above all, they must actively criticize officials and policies that are against their interests and the interests of the nation, as they see it. To accomplish this, citizens must have freedom of information and freedom of SPEECH, both guaranteed by the BILL OF RIGHTS.

Political parties. The role of POLIT-ICAL PARTIES in organizing national elections, the national legislature (see CONGRESS), and the EXECUTIVE BRANCH is extremely important. Whether the political system is a parliamentary one, in which the majority party or coalition of parties elected to the legislature governs, or one with separate but equal executive, legislative, and judicial branches of government, as in the United States, political parties are necessary to ensure that there are always real choices among policies and candidates. A nation that has only one party or elects only one party to run the government—such as Mexico, a democratic country that until 2000 returned the same political party to power for nearly seven decades—loses an important benefit of democracy: the ability to be innovative and evolve.

Delegates wave signs in support of President George W. Bush's candidacy for reelection at the 2004 Republican National Convention. Political parties play an essential role in most democratic nations, although battles between opposing parties can lead to gridlock.
Source: Reuters/Rick Wilking

Political parties are not cited by name in the Constitution, but the right of such parties to exist and actively carry on in the democratic process is guaranteed by the Bill of Rights, particularly the First Amendment (1791), which protects freedom of ASSEMBLY AND ASSOCIATION.

A free press. A free press and its multifaceted media outgrowths (see THE PRESS), guaranteed in the First Amendment (1791), ensure an authoritative voice providing to the electorate information that is neither the propaganda of the public officials in power nor self-serving criticism by candidates who seek to replace them in office. A dictator's first act is always to shut down the free press. The government that governs best is one whose acts are always liable to public scrutiny, and the press and other media outlets provide informed and motivated critics to help keep the people in power honest and accountable for their actions.

An open society. Hand in hand with a free press goes the need for an open society, in which the uncensored exchange of ideas allows the people to select from the marketplace of ideas the best polices for governing (see CENSORSHIP). The Bill of Rights similarly protects and promotes free social discourse by prohibiting the government from closing down avenues of information and expression.

Rule of law. The Constitution does not mention the RULE OF LAW but does mandate, through the Fifth (1791) and Fourteenth (1868) Amendments, DUE PROCESS and EQUAL PROTECTION of the laws. These guarantees create a framework of legal rights and protections that help ensure that all citizens receive equal treatment under the law. Democracy, constitutionalism, and the rule of law are the triumvirate of a good system of government.

Abuse of power. The one factor in any democracy that may be beyond the control of any government founders is the willingness of those entrusted with power not to abuse it or subvert the principles by which it was conferred on them. In ancient Greece a person who became too popular for the good of the democracy

More on this topic:

Citizens, p. 93

Elections, p. 181

Representative Government, p. 464

Republican Form of Government, p. 467

could be ostracized (voted into exile). In the United States, after President Franklin D. Roosevelt (1882–1945) ran for and was elected to unprecedented third and fourth TERMS OF OFFICE, the Twenty-second Amendment (1951) was ratified to prohibit anyone from holding the office for more than two terms, regardless of how popular or effective a chief executive he or she might be.

There can be no single blueprint for democracy. It is a principle for organizing a form of government based on the equality of all citizens and the SOVEREIGNTY of the people. Its benefits seem to far outweigh the price people have to pay to attain it and make it work. In any democracy, whatever its specific procedures, the citizens' commitment to its principles ensures its success.

Democratic Party *See* POLITICAL PARTIES.

Departments *See* ADMINISTRATIVE AGENCIES; CABINET; EXECUTIVE BRANCH.

Deportation *See* IMMIGRATION.

Die, Right to

Can or should the law prohibit a person from taking his or her own life with or without the assistance of others under all circumstances? Plato, the Greek philosopher of the fourth century B.C.E. accepted suicide with certain conditions, although his student, Aristotle, declared that it was cowardly and "treats the state unjustly." Seneca, the first-century Roman Stoic, set his own course: "Just as I choose a ship to sail in or a house to live in, so I choose a death for my passage from life."

The right to die encompasses a number of methods for terminating life, including suicide, assisted suicide, and euthanasia. Suicide is the act of killing oneself; if suicide were not given the status of a crime under state systems of criminal justice, no one could legally stop people from attempting to end their own lives. Assisted suicide is help given by one person, often a physician or other medically trained individual, to another who wishes to die. Jack Kevorkian, a seventy-year-old retired doctor, was convicted of second-degree murder in Michigan in March 1999 for administering a lethal injection at the request of a fifty-year-old man. In late 2001 Kevorkian's conviction was upheld by the Michigan Court of Appeals, which rejected his argument that euthanasia is legal and that his conviction was unconstitutional.

Euthanasia (from the Greek *eu*, meaning good, and *thanos*, meaning death) is the act of inducing a painless death, presumably for reasons of mercy, but it may also conjure up images of Nazi death camps and gas chambers. Simply withholding certain necessities can end the life of a dying person who relies on medicine, drugs, or machinery to stay alive. Food can be withheld from persons who cannot eat for themselves but rely on intravenous or tubal feeding. The issue of the right to die came under the national spotlight when Karen Ann Quinlan, the subject of a since-famous New Jersey court case, suffered brain damage and fell into a "persistent vegetative state" after taking tranquilizers and alcohol at a party in 1975. Although her parents finally won court permission to remove her from life-supporting equipment, she continued living in a coma for nearly ten years.

Although medical treatments in certain situations may reduce the chances of survival, the absolute right to take one's own life or legally assist someone else—unlike the DEATH PENALTY and ABORTION, two similarly controversial issues—has not yet been read into the Constitution by the courts. Although the Constitution is silent on any right to die, persons claiming the right to take their own life or assist in an act of suicide generally base their claims on the right of PRIVACY or the DUE PROCESS clause of the Fourteenth Amendment (1868).

Cruzan v. Director, Missouri Department of Health (1990) relied more on due process than the right of privacy. Nancy Cruzan suffered a brain injury in an automobile accident and spent seven years in a vegetative state; although she was able to ingest food on her own, a feeding tube was inserted into her stomach to make her care easier. Her parents sought to have the tube removed, arguing that she had indicated before the accident that she would not want to be kept alive under such conditions. A trial court approved the parents' request, but the Missouri Supreme Court overturned the ruling and the Supreme Court, by a 5–4 decision, agreed. Chief Justice William H. Rehnquist (1924–2005) reasoned in his opinion that the state has a right to keep a physically able-bodied person from voluntarily starving herself to death but cannot require a person needing artificial life support such as tube feeding to continue living under such conditions. The question was how this distinction affected Nancy Cruzan. Agreeing with the Missouri Supreme Court that there was insufficient evidence to ascertain Cruzan's wishes, the Court indicated, however, that if Cruzan, when she was competent, had properly appointed a representative with the authority to speak on her behalf and express her wishes, the Court's decision might have been different. "[F]or purposes of this case," said the Court, "we assume that…a competent person [has] a constitutionally protected right to refuse life-saving hydration and nutrition."

More recently, in the case of Terri Schiavo, a Florida woman who had survived in an unconscious state for fifteen years, a state court contest ensued between the woman's parents, who wanted to keep her on life support in the hospital, and her husband as her legal guardian, who indicated it was her wish to have the life support removed. In 2003, when the matter became of national interest, Florida passed "Terri's Law" to grant the state's governor the power to intervene. After the state law was declared unconstitutional, Terri's husband prevailed in state court, but Congress got into the act early in 2005 by passing a law to have the case transferred to a federal district court in Florida. The U.S. Supreme Court, however, on several occasions refused to intervene on behalf of the parents' plea to keep their daughter on life support, and Terri died on March 31, 2005, at the age of forty-one.

The states of the United States are able to enact legislation allowing physicians to prescribe lethal medication requested by terminally ill but competent persons diagnosed to have six months or less to live. In 1997 Oregon, following the approval of voters in 1994 and lifting of a U.S. circuit court of appeals injunction blocking it, became the first and only state to declare the right to die. (The Netherlands, goes further, extending the right to die even to persons who are not terminally ill.) On November 6, 2001, however, Attorney General John Ashcroft, in a communication to the chief of the Drug Enforcement Administration (DEA), stated that assisting in a suicide has no "legitimate medical purpose" and ordered the DEA to revoke the drug licenses of Oregon doctors who help patients commit suicide. This action was an attempt to overrule the will of the Oregon people and legislature on the question of assisted suicide and thwart any possible efforts to extend the right to die to other states.

In 1997 the Supreme Court overturned the decisions of two separate federal appeals courts upholding laws permitting physician-assisted suicide in Washington and New York states. In *Washington v. Glucksberg* (1997), the lower court found that there is a FUNDAMENTAL RIGHT to control one's bodily integrity, a right akin to abortion discerned in ROE V. WADE (1973). In the New York case, *Vacco v. Quill* (1997), the lower court

Living wills, or advance health care directives, have become widespread since being introduced in the 1960s. A living will is a legal document that enables a person to outline what types of treatment should and should not be allowed in the event of incapacitation.

Many people say they would not want life-sustaining treatment if they were in a permanent unconscious state with no hope of recovery. Typically they designate a relative or friend to make certain medical decisions for them in the event that they become so ill or injured that they cannot communicate.

State legislatures in the 1960s began debating whether to allow the use of living wills. In 1976 California became the first state to legally sanction them. Other states soon followed, and by the early 1990s they were recognized in every state and the District of Columbia.

Courts have agreed that people have the right to refuse live-saving measures. Less clear, however, is whether treatment can be withdrawn from a person in a permanently unconscious state who does not have a living will. For that reason, lawyers and patient advocates generally urge people to draw up living wills while they are still healthy to avoid legal battles if they become incapacitated.

rejected that ground but found that New York would have acted irrationally if it required physicians to respect a patient's refusal of life-sustaining treatment but also required them to ignore a patient's request for assistance with hastening death. In unanimous decisions the Supreme Court reversed the lower courts, basing its rulings on the distinction between a physician's passive assistance in the death of a person requiring life support and a physician's active participation in assisting in the death of an otherwise viable patient—that is, one who can live on one's own under normal conditions.

The government has a legitimate interest in ensuring that the lives of citizens are protected to the greatest extent possible. However, the development of personal rights in the United States has been toward extending to individuals freedom of choice over the quality and direction of their lives with little interference by the government. After all, among the rights enumerated in the DECLARATION OF INDEPENDENCE (1776) are the rights to life, LIBERTY, and the pursuit of happiness. For some people, death with dignity—with control over how their lives will end—represents a form of liberty and the pursuit of happiness. In the near future, however, there seems little chance that the right to die will come to be recognized as a constitutionally guaranteed right on a par with such rights as abortion and privacy.

Direct Democracy

The world's first DEMOCRACY, which originated in Athens in 510 B.C.E., was a direct democracy. Much of the city-state's day-to-day public business was conducted by elected officials, but its major policy decisions—whether to go to war or to declare peace, for example—were debated and voted on by the citizens themselves (free adult males only), assembled together.

The form of democracy developed in the thirteen British colonies that became the United States of America was a representative democracy, without any provisions for direct democratic procedures (see REPRESENTATIVE GOVERNMENT). Under the Constitution, every decision of the federal government is made by someone chosen to represent CITIZENS and not by the citizens themselves. Laws are passed by representatives elected to the two houses of CONGRESS, and executive decisions are made by the PRESIDENT or those acting under his authority. Only in the case of some TRIALS of first instance, in which JURIES (representing a community's citizens) determine the facts in dispute, is there a semblance of direct democracy. The process of proposing and approving AMENDMENTS to the Constitution is kept out of the hands of the people, although all states except Delaware require direct voter ratification of amendments to their constitutions by referendum. Of course, the nation's representatives may take polls of citizens' opinions before making important decisions, but such polls are not binding and therefore may be ignored by decision makers.

Supplementing Representative Democracy

Concepts that today would be regarded as direct democracy have been around since the ancient Greeks, so it is not surprising that in 1775 THOMAS JEFFERSON proposed that the voters themselves approve Virginia's constitution, but his suggestion arrived after the delegates to the drafting convention had already approved it and adjourned. In 1857 Congress mandated that state constitutions be approved directly by the voters in each state rather than by the legislatures or conventions. Forty years later in 1897 Nebraska became the first state to allow its cities to include initiative and referendum provisions in their charters.

The rise of the Populist Party at the end of the nineteenth century spurred the movement to incorporate direct democracy procedures into the American system of representative government, at least in the states. The party's platform in 1892 included public ownership of railroads, a graduated income tax (see TAXATION), direct elections to the U.S. SENATE (originally senators were chosen by the state legislatures), and direct democracy tools such as the initiative and the referendum. In 1898 South Dakota became the first state to adopt initiative and referendum procedures statewide, and in 1904 Oregon put the use of statewide initiative on the ballot, but, ironically, the citizens defeated it.

The movement to supplement representative democracy institutions and procedures in some states grew out of the popular distrust of and dissatisfaction with elected state officials, who are often perceived as being interested only in serving the special-interest groups that help them get elected and not the average citizen. In many states, however, the direct democracy process has been co-opted by those same groups and used to further their own interests. Such groups can pay people to collect the necessary signatures to get their initiatives on the ballot and then can mount expensive campaigns to persuade voters to support their proposal.

Today nearly forty states, including California and Oregon, and the District of Columbia, have some form of direct democracy. In most cases states adopt direct democracy provisions by amendment to their constitutions (Arizona and Colorado, for example) or by statute (Connecticut and Georgia, for example). These direct democracy procedures take the form of popular initiative, referendum, and recall.

Popular initiative. The right of popular initiative allows citizens to bypass their legislature or other bodies such as city councils and place proposed laws or amendments on the ballot to be voted on at an election. To get a measure on the ballot in those states that allow initiative, a designated, relatively small percentage of the voters must sign a petition requesting it. In California, valid signatures representing 8 percent and 5 percent of the votes cast in the last election for governor are required to bring up a constitutional amendment and a proposed law, respectively.

Referendum. A referendum is a measure that requires approval by the citizens rather than the vote of a representative body such as a legislature. The measure to be voted on may be either an amendment to the state constitution or a law. Arizona's constitution (1912, as amended), for example, in addition to requiring referendums on "any measure" and "any amendment to the constitution" that are proposed by 10 and 15 percent of the qualified electors, respectively, allows "the legislature or five percentum of the qualified electors [to submit] to the people at the polls...any measure, item, section, or part of any measure, enacted by the legislature... "

Recall. Recall refers to the right of the people to vote to remove elected officials before the end of their legally established TERMS OF OFFICE. Arizona's constitution provides that "[e]very public officer in the state...holding an elective office, either by election or appointment [temporarily to fill a vacancy in an elective office], is subject to recall from such office by the qualified electors of the electoral district from which the candidate is elected...." A recall vote requires a petition by at least 25 percent of the number of votes cast in the preceding election.

California governor Arnold Schwarzenegger suffered a stinging setback when state voters rejected all four referendums he backed in 2005, including one that would have limited state spending.
Source: CQ Photo/Scott J. Ferrell

Supreme Court Rulings

Direct democracy has its opponents, although in legal challenges the Supreme Court has generally found that such procedures do not infringe any constitutional provisions. In *Pacific States Telephone and Telegraph Co. v. Oregon* (1912), the Court was asked to declare that Oregon's use of the initiative to approve a tax proposal was a violation of the Constitution's Article IV, section 4, which guarantees the states a REPUBLICAN FORM OF GOVERNMENT. The Court simply held that what constitutes a republican form of government was a political and not a judicial question.

In *Hunter v. Erikson* (1969), however, the Supreme Court struck down an initiative to require voter approval of open housing laws. The majority of the justices held that any barriers to the enactment of such legislation, among them requiring popular approval, would prejudice ethnic and religious MINORITIES and thus violated the EQUAL PROTECTION clause of the Fourteenth Amendment (1868). Certain other types of DISCRIMINATION have been acceptable to the Court. Proposition 13, a California initiative that established a tax system prejudicial to future property owners, was upheld in *Nordlinger v. Hahn* (1992). By refusing to hear an appeal from a federal appeals court, the Supreme Court also allowed the state's Proposition 209 to stand; the initiative had been approved by Californians in 1996 to end state AFFIRMATIVE ACTION programs. According to the lower court's decision, it was a general rule of American constitutional democracy that the judgment of a federal court should not be used to "trump self-government."

In a related issue—gathering voters' signatures to get an initiative measure placed on the ballot—the Supreme Court in *Buckley v. American Constitutional Law Foundation* (1999) ruled against state requirements such as having signature gatherers wear badges and prohibiting nonresidents from soliciting signatures. The Court found that such requirements served no compelling state interest in view of the importance of the First Amendment (1791) protection for "core political speech" (see SPEECH).

Many of the FRAMERS OF THE CONSTITUTION, particularly JAMES MADISON, feared the "public passions" and therefore saw representative democracy as a check on momentary popular follies. The French philosopher Jean-Jacques Rousseau (1712–78), on the other hand, observed that British citizens were sovereign only on election day, because thereafter Parliament exercised supreme sovereignty for them.

The evidence so far in the United States, however, is that direct democracy procedures are neither better nor worse than representative democracy as far as bad laws or corruption by special-interest groups are concerned. New methods of communications now made possible by modern technology (see SCIENCE AND TECHNOLOGY), such as e-mail and the INTERNET, and even newer innovations in the future that could protect against voting fraud in electronic voting may allow for even greater expansion of direct democracy procedures.

More on this topic:

Democracy, p. 149

Jefferson, Thomas, p. 310

Republican Form of Government, p. 464

Disabled Persons

The condition of being handicapped or disabled is addressed by the constitutions of most countries. An exception is South Africa's constitution (1997), which declares: "The state may not unfairly discriminate directly or indirectly against anyone on one or more grounds, including race, gender, sex, pregnancy, marital status, ethnic or social origin, colour, sexual orientation, age, disability, religion, conscience, belief, culture, language and birth." The Declaration on the Rights of Disabled Persons, adopted by the General Assembly of the United Nations in 1975, defines a disabled person as "any person unable to ensure by himself or herself, wholly or partly, the necessities of [an able-bodied] individual and/or social life, as a result of a deficiency, either congenital or not, in his or her physical or mental capabilities."

Accommodation under the Constitution

Under the law in the United States, disabled persons are those who lack the legal capacity to act on their own behalf or who are physically or mentally unable to act on their own behalf or to pursue their normal occupations. *Disabled*, however, has come to refer more generally to those who require assistance or accommodation, such as ramps or other special facilities, to enjoy the same opportunities and benefits as able-bodied persons.

The Constitution's only references to disability are found in the Twenty-fifth Amendment (1967), which sets forth procedures in the event of the disability of the PRESIDENT. The Supreme Court, however, has found constitutional grounds for adjudicating issues relating to the rights of disabled persons, or the lack thereof. An early case, *Buck v. Bell* (1927), involved a state-ordered sterilization of Carrie Buck, an inmate of the "State Colony for Epileptics and Feeble Minded." The operation was proposed because Carrie, her mother, and her child were all diagnosed as "feeble-minded." In a decision immortalized by the conclusion of Justice OLIVER WENDELL HOLMES JR. that "three generations of imbeciles is enough," the Supreme Court upheld the forced sterilization.

The Supreme Court's decision in *Buck v. Bell* is now considered not just paternalistic but inhumane. Mentally handicapped persons have rights that must be respected. In fact, what may appear to be mental deficiencies may be the result of learning disabilities or even simply a lack of education or proper nutrition. The emergence of the CIVIL RIGHTS movement in the United States following the Supreme Court's decision in BROWN V. BOARD OF EDUCATION OF TOPEKA (1954), which declared that separate-but-equal public schools for black and white students were unconstitutional, inspired efforts to increase understanding and appreciation of the rights of disabled persons as well.

By the 1970s the Supreme Court and perhaps the nation as a whole were becoming more enlightened. Although the states were still considered to have the power of *parens patria* (state guardianship of persons under a disability), the Court found in *O'Connor v. Donaldson* (1975), among other cases, that retarded or handicapped individuals have a right to freedom from confinement and personal restraint, a right protected under DUE PROCESS of law. Even if properly committed to an institution, these individuals still have substantive rights in reducing the degree of confinement. Earlier, in *Jackson v. Indiana* (1972), the Court had ruled that "due process requires that the nature and duration of commitment bear some reasonable relation to the purpose for which the individual is committed." And in *Cleburne v. Cleburne Living Center, Inc.* (1985), the Court applied the so-called rational basis test rather than the more stringent STRICT SCRUTINY or heightened scrutiny tests used for RACIAL DISCRIMINATION and SEX DISCRIMINATION cases, respectively. Nevertheless, it concluded that a city ordinance requiring a special permit for a group home for the mentally retarded was unconstitutional because it appeared to result from an "irrational prejudice against the mentally retarded."

Antidiscrimination Laws

The Rehabilitation Act (1973) and a 1988 amendment to the Fair Housing Act (1968) banned DISCRIMINATION against the disabled in federally funded programs and housing. In *School Board of Nassau County, Florida v. Arline* (1987), the Supreme Court held that the Rehabilitation Act prohibited firing someone simply because he had a contagious disease—in this case, tuberculosis.

Additional protections in employment (see EMPLOYMENT DISCRIMINATION), business establishments that cater to the public, and state-sponsored programs and services were extended to the disabled through the Americans with Disabilities Act (ADA), signed into law on July 26, 1990. In *Bragdon v. Abbott* (1998), one of the first cases under the act to come before the Supreme Court, the justices held that HIV, the basic cause of AIDS, constituted a disease from the moment of infection, thereby establishing a case for discrimination when a dentist refused to treat a person who had tested HIV-positive.

Casey Martin won a Supreme Court case enabling him to use a golf cart in PGA tournaments because of his disability.
Source: Reuters/Sam Mircovich

In *PGA Tour, Inc. v. Martin* (2001), a case that attracted national attention, a talented golfer who suffered from a degenerative circulatory disease sued the Professional Golf Association to use a cart in PGA tournaments. The Supreme Court upheld a lower court ruling that, under the ADA, the plaintiff's disease specifically constituted a disability and the PGA's enforcement of its rule against using carts in its tournaments was unconstitutional. Noting that the act specifically covered golf courses as well as other recreational areas such as gymnasiums and bowling alleys, the majority opinion held that allowing a disabled golfer to use a cart while able-bodied golfers walked the course would not "fundamentally alter the nature" of the PGA's competition and therefore must be permitted.

Ella Williams, a former worker at an automobile assembly plant, was not so lucky after she developed carpal tunnel syndome. In *Toyota v. Williams* (2002), SANDRA DAY O'CONNOR writing for the Supreme Court, narrowed the act's scope by concluding that an impairment must have a substantial effect on a person's daily life to be termed a disability under the ADA. The decision could make it more difficult for similar workers to prove that they are disabled and thus entitled to accommodation by their employers.

Justice John Paul Stevens (b. 1920), writing for a 5–4 majority in *Tennessee v. Lane* (2004), however, upheld the scope of title II of the ADA, which states: "No qualified individual with a disability shall, by reason of such disability, be excluded from participation or denied the benefits of the services, programs or activities of a public entity, or be subjected to discrimination by any such en-

"No qualified individual with a disability shall, by reason of such disability, be excluded from participation or denied the benefits of the services, programs or activities of a public entity."

—Americans with Disabilities Act

tity." This case involved a paraplegic who had to crawl up the stairs of a county courthouse to the second floor to appear in court. Earlier, in *Board of Trustees of the University of Alabama v. Garrett* (2001), the Court had held that states are exempt from title I of the ADA, which prohibits employers from discriminating against qualified individuals because of a disability and requires them to make "reasonable accommodations to the [physical] or mental limitations of [otherwise] qualified" disabled workers except in cases of "undue hardship," and authorizes money damages for violations. In that case, the Court explained that the act could not be applied to state employers because they had sovereign immunity under the Eleventh Amendment, and the Fourteenth Amendment not would support enforcement of the act's provisions against a state so long as the state's actions toward disabled persons are rational.

The range of human disabilities is great. Eye glasses, hearing aids, and special telephones can compensate for some minor disabilities. Ramps, special restroom facilities, and the use of Braille can open up a whole new world for others more seriously impaired. The rights sought by the disabled are those that will allow them to participate in society as active and useful citizens—in other words, exactly what most citizens want the Constitution to guarantee for them.

Discrimination

In its nonpejorative sense—the simple recognition of differences—discrimination is not all bad. It can even be positive in that it can lead to the granting of privileges based on differences. Following the precedent of the British Parliament, for example, the U.S. CONSTITUTION grants members of CONGRESS special privileges. Article I, section 6, makes them, with certain exceptions, "privileged from Arrest during their Attendance at the Session of their respective Houses, and in going to and returning from the same; and for any Speech or Debate in either House, they shall not be questioned in any other Place."

Today, however, discrimination is more commonly associated with its negative connotation: the failure to treat all persons equally where no reasonable distinction can be found between those favored and those not favored. Discrimination in this negative sense is not expressly mentioned in the U.S. Constitution. This is partly a reflection of the era in which the document was drafted, when discrimination was acceptable and SLAVERY was legal, and partly because of its general underlying premise that all citizens are to be treated equal. However, the constitutions of many other nations—including Japan (1889, rewritten 1947) and Kenya (1964), for example—specifically denounce government discrimination on the basis of race, color, sex, religion, and national origin, among other factors, as do many regional and international human rights documents.

Article IV, section 2, extends to citizens of each state the PRIVILEGES AND IMMUNITIES of all the states, which, according to the Supreme Court's ruling in *Paul v. Virginia* (1869), means that a state may not discriminate against nonresidents when they come within its jurisdiction. Article VI prohibits any religious test for public office, thus prohibiting discrimination on the basis of religion. The Fifth Amendment (1791) requires DUE PROCESS of law for all people, and the Fourteenth Amendment (1868) reiterates the privileges and immunities of citizens of the United States and requires states to provide due process of the law and equal protection of the laws to all persons. The Thirteenth (1865) and Fourteenth Amendments address the question of discrimination against African Americans held in slavery and their descendents, and the Nineteenth Amendment (1920) remedies the denial of women's political rights, notably the right to vote.

Even so, discrimination has become an insidious legacy that still prevents many U.S. citizens from enjoying equal opportunity in employment and education as well as housing, recreation, and social opportunities. The question of civil and political rights for MINORITIES has been resolved, at least in theory, by such national and state legislation as the Voting Rights Act (1965). AFFIRMATIVE ACTION programs at the state and national levels have attempted to make amends for past discrimination and level the playing field for the younger generations of minority citizens. But it is doubtful that constitutional provisions or laws will ever entirely erase the unfair treatment of people of a different race, gender, or religion by some in positions of power. In fact, according to the U.S. Equal Employment Opportunity Office (EEOC), racial harassment in the workplace complaints have risen in the past seventeen years from 3,075 in fiscal year 1991 to some 7,000 in fiscal 2007. Since fiscal year 2001 the EEOC has filed more than thirty lawsuits that involve the display of a noose—the symbol of lynching of blacks—in the workplace.

Dealing with discrimination under the Constitution has been a challenge for the executive, legislative, and judicial branches, themselves composed primarily of the United States' historically white male Christian political majority. For example, in *Ledbetter v. Goodyear Tire & Rubber Co., Inc.* (2007), the U.S. Supreme Court squelched a sexual discrimination lawsuit related to unfair compensation for a female employee because the claim of discrimination was untimely filed—not because of the merits of the claim. But a year later, in *Sprint/United Management Co. v. Mendelsohn* (2008), the Court agreed that in a case of age discrimination in employment, evidence of other similar discrimination against coworkers was not to be automatically excluded. Writing for the Court, Justice Clarence Thomas (b. 1948) said that the relevance of evidence of similar discrimination by other supervisors in the company "depends on many factors, including how closely related the evidence is to the plaintiff's circumstances and theory of the case."

The basic areas of discrimination with constitutional implications include race, sex, age, and disability. While the tendency of national and state governments has been to deal with these areas separately, some cases involve allegations of discrimination on more than one ground—for example, by African American women who may be discriminated against on the basis of race and sex. Other cases have alleged discrimination against ALIENS, illegitimate CHILDREN, and adherents of certain religions. Moreover, discrimination may be subtle, as in the case of the percentage of convictions of minorities for similar crimes or the severity of punishments meted out to minorities for similar crimes, such as the harsher sentences given for the possession of crack cocaine, a drug used more often by black Americans, as opposed to regular cocaine, a drug used more by white Americans.

National Origin

Although the Constitution does not expressly ban discrimination on the basis of a citizen's national origin, the Supreme Court as early as 1880 in *Strauder v. West Virginia* held that exclusion from a jury because of national origin was unconstitutional. However, in *Korematsu v. United States* (1944), the Court did uphold as constitutional removing Americans of Japanese ancestry from the West Coast, segregating them, and interning them during World War II. This particular act of discrimination has come to be viewed as a wartime aberration that could not occur again.

IMMIGRATION is another area in which U.S. laws and government policies sometimes have discriminated on the basis of national origin. In *Chae Chan Ping v. United States* (1889), the Supreme Court confirmed the constitutionality of the Chinese Exclusion Act (1882), which banned all Chinese immigration for ten years and denied U.S. citizenship to resident Chinese aliens. More recently, however, in *Landon v. Plasencia* (1982), the Court, while acknowledging Congress's power to deny aliens admission to the United States, did find that a legal resident alien could not be denied entry after leaving the country for a short period of time without at least a hearing to contest the grounds for the exclusion.

Hate Crimes

Hate crimes, an extreme form of discrimination committed by private individuals, illustrates the conflict between freedom of thought, which should not be punishable by the government, and the legislature's power to enhance the punishment of a crime because of the motive for committing it. If a person simply hates people sharing a certain characteristic—people of a certain race, for example—and does not act on that hatred, no crime has been committed because under the law a crime requires both the intent to commit a criminal act (*mens rea*) and the commission of the act itself (*actus reus*). On the other hand, a person who is hit on the head may find irrelevant the question of whether the assault was a consequence of being robbed or of being hated; the physical injury is the same.

The U.S. Supreme Court, however, in *Wisconsin v. Mitchell* (1993) unanimously reversed a Wisconsin supreme court ruling

More on this topic:
Age Discrimination, p. 23
Civil Rights, p. 96
Disabled Persons, p. 156
Racial Discrimination, p. 449
Sex Discrimination, p. 497
Women, p. 589

that found increasing the punishment for a hate crime was an unconstitutional attempt by the legislature to punish thought with which it disagreed. The Supreme Court opinion distinguished the act of selecting a victim of a crime from hate speech, which is covered by the First Amendment guarantee of free SPEECH. Hateful thoughts and even speech may be constitutionally protected, but criminal acts motivated by hate or bigotry may be punished more severely than similar acts motivated for other reasons.

District of Columbia   *See* CAPITAL, NATIONAL.

Divorce   *See* FAMILIES.

Domestic Relations   *See* FAMILIES.

Domestic Tranquility

Among the reasons to "ordain and establish" the Constitution, as stated by the FRAMERS OF THE CONSTITUTION in the PREAMBLE, is to "insure domestic Tranquility." Article IV, section 4, provides that "[t]he United States…shall protect each [state] against Invasion; and on Application of the Legislature, or of the Executive (when the Legislature cannot be convened) against domestic Violence." The Constitution's concept of domestic violence predates the modern legal concept, which refers to violence within the home or among family members, including abuse of spouses, children, and the elderly (see FAMILIES).

Protection of the states from domestic violence constitutes one of the principal purposes of a national government: to maintain the security of its citizens and their property from internal or external attack (see NATIONAL SECURITY). Because the original thirteen states were to retain some elements of SOVEREIGNTY despite the Constitution's grant of powers to the national government, the founders were careful to include in this provision the requirement that the national government not interfere unless a state formally requests its assistance.

JAMES MADISON, in essay 43 of *The Federalist* (1787–88) (see FEDERALIST PAPERS), pointed to the Swiss confederation as an example of mutual aid among the cantons, Switzerland's political subdivisions, in the event of domestic violence. Even today, as Switzerland's recent constitution (2000) states, "The Confederation and the Cantons ensure…the security of the country and the protection of the population. They coordinate their efforts in the field of internal security." He also alluded to Shays's Rebellion in Massachusetts in 1786. In that revolt, less than a year before the CONSTITUTIONAL CONVENTION OF 1787, farmers rose up in arms to try to prevent the courts from enforcing foreclosures. Referring to insurrections in the states, Madison suggested that "[i]t will be much better that the violence in such cases should be repressed by the superintending power [the federal government], than that the majority [the people] should be left to maintain their cause by a bloody and obstinate contest. The existence of a right to interpose will generally prevent the necessity of exerting it."

In 1795 Congress gave the president the authority to respond to requests from the states to assist in quelling domestic violence, and this authority remains the president's today. It has been exercised sparingly, however.

In 1841 small freeholders led by Thomas Wilson Dorr called for the repeal of Rhode Island's constitution, which strictly limited the right to vote, and for the extension of suffrage to all white adult males. In an uprising known as Dorr's Rebellion, they bypassed the state's legislature, called their own "people's convention," and drafted a new constitution that provided for universal suffrage. Claiming that this constituted an insurrection, the Rhode Island government asked President John Tyler (1790–1862) to declare martial law (see EMERGENCY POWERS). Tyler pleaded for a calm resolution of the issue, no federal forces actually entered the state, and the state government, conceding that changes were in order, produced a new state constitution, which was approved by the voters and went into effect in 1843. The matter, however, came before the Supreme Court in *Luther v. Borden* (1849). The Court refused to decide whether the 1841 "people's" constitution was legitimate. However, on the related question of whether the courts can guarantee a REPUBLICAN FORM OF GOVERNMENT under Article IV, section 4, it ruled that determining when the federal government should respond to a request for federal assistance under the domestic violence clause is purely a political matter, not a judicial question (see SEPARATION OF POWERS).

In 1877 President Rutherford B. Hayes (1822–93) did respond to a request by the governor of West Virginia to help put down a riot by railroad workers who were stopping trains in Martinsburg. Fearing a loss of life and property, Hayes sent federal troops from Fort McHenry in Baltimore, Maryland, via the railroad (which charged the government for their fares) to assist in quelling the strike.

In addition to the power granted by the domestic violence clause, the PRESIDENT, of course, has authority under Article II—which charges him to "take care that the Laws be faithfully executed"—to enforce federal law and federal court decisions in the states without waiting for a state to request help. After the Supreme Court's decision in BROWN V. BOARD OF EDUCATION OF TOPEKA (1954) declaring "separate but equal" schools unconstitutional, President Dwight D. Eisenhower (1890–1969) sent troops to enforce the law and maintain order in Little Rock, Arkansas, when state authorities refused to integrate the public schools there (see SEGREGATION).

One argument supporting the domestic violence clause is that it precludes the federal government from "invading" the states to punish a crime without a state's permission. This line of argument resurfaced during the early debates in the 1960s over CIVIL RIGHTS legislation designed to enforce the EQUAL PROTECTION provisions of the Fourteenth Amendment (1868). Today, however, the states and the federal government cooperate in many LAW ENFORCEMENT operations, including efforts against organized crime, drug trafficking (see DRUGS), and TERRORISM.

More on this topic:

Federalism, p. 218

Framers of the Constitution, p. 230

Madison, James, p. 355

States' Rights, p. 520

Double Jeopardy

In law, jeopardy is the danger of conviction and PUNISHMENT faced by a person who has committed a crime after a valid indictment has been brought, a jury has been impaneled to try the case, and a guilty verdict has been reached in a court of competent jurisdiction. Double jeopardy would place a person on trial twice for the same crime.

The constitutions of some countries, including the United States, prohibit double jeopardy to a greater or a lesser degree. Albania's constitution (1998), for example, provides: "No one may be sentenced more than once for the same criminal offense or be tried again, except for cases when the re-adjudication of the case is ordered by a higher court, in the manner specified by law." Russia's constitution (1993), in contrast, simply states: "No person may be tried twice for the same crime."

According to the Fifth Amendment (1791) of the U.S. Constitution, "nor shall any person be subject for the same offence to be twice put in jeopardy of life or limb." The history of the double jeopardy clause extends back to the laws of ancient Greece and Rome and then England. In his

Commentaries on the Laws of England (1765–70), William Blackstone (1723–80) noted that "in many instances, where contrary to evidence the jury have found the prisoner guilty, their verdict has been mercifully set aside, and a new trial granted by the Court of King's Bench,…[b]ut there has yet been no instance of granting a new trial, where the prisoner was *acquitted* upon the first."

The English rule regarding retrials was that a person accused of the same crime a second time could appeal either his conviction or his acquittal, thus avoiding a new trial and the possibility of a second conviction and additional punishment. In the United States, the rule was expanded to bar a retrial even if the first trial had not resulted in a verdict of either guilty or not guilty. But a retrial may be held if there is a hung jury, meaning that the jurors are deadlocked and cannot reach a unanimous verdict of either guilty or innocent. As with the other rights guaranteed in the BILL OF RIGHTS (1791), this rule initially afforded protection only against charges brought by the federal government, although some states also had similar protections in their own constitutions.

In *Palko v. Connecticut* (1937), the Supreme Court held that the constitutional protection against double jeopardy was not so fundamental a right that it should be incorporated through the DUE PROCESS clause of the Fourteenth Amendment (1868) to apply to the states (see FUNDAMENTAL RIGHTS; INCORPORATION DOCTRINE). Finally, in *Benton v. Maryland* (1969), the Court declared that "the double jeopardy prohibition…represents a fundamental ideal in our constitutional heritage," and since then it has applied to both the national and state governments.

The basic rationale behind the double jeopardy clause is that the government, in charging a person with a crime, should get only one chance. As Justice Hugo L. Black (1886–1971) explained in *Green v. United States* (1957): "The underlying idea, one that is deeply ingrained in at least the Anglo-American system of jurisprudence, is that the state with all its resources and power should not be allowed to make repeated attempts to convict an individual for an alleged offense.…" Double jeopardy, he added, forces the individual to face additional embarrassment and expense and live in a continual state of anxiety and insecurity; it enhances the possibility that a defendant, even if innocent, will eventually be found guilty.

> *"[T]he state with all its resources and power should not be allowed to make repeated attempts to convict an individual for an alleged offense."*
>
> **—Justice Hugo L. Black**

As a rare exception to the rule that an appeal may be made only after a trial and verdict, an appeal based on a claim of double jeopardy may be made to a higher court before a verdict has been handed down. According to the Supreme Court's rulings in *United States v. Perez* (1824) and *Crist v. Bretz* (1978), the double jeopardy rule comes into play any time after a jury is impaneled or evidence is introduced. A defendant thus may not be retried unless he or she requests a mistrial or one is granted for reasons beyond the prosecutor's control. Nonetheless, if a conviction is overturned on appeal on the basis of errors made during the trial, a defendant may generally be retried.

Retrial after Acquittal or Conviction

"[T]he most fundamental rule in the history of double jeopardy jurisprudence," the Supreme Court ruled in *United States v. Martin Linen Supply Co.* (1977), is that a defendant may not be retried following an acquittal, no matter how egregiously erroneous the first trial was. This is the case whether a defendant is acquitted by a jury or a judge alone. When a judge allows the case to go to a jury and the jury finds the defendant guilty, and then the judge, believing that the evidence does not support the verdict, enters an acquittal, the prosecution has the right to appeal on the basis that if the appeal is successful there will not be a new trial, only a reinstatement of the guilty verdict. Moreover, in *Smith v. Massachusetts* (2005), the Court, citing *Martin*, held that when a judge had ruled during a trial that the evidence produced by the prosecution was insufficient to sustain a conviction but later allowed the question to go to the jury, double jeopardy applied as to the charge previously ruled on. The Court said that the double jeopardy clause forbade the judge from reconsidering the acquittal later in the trial.

A defendant who appeals a conviction and is successful in having the conviction set aside because of errors committed during the trial may still be retried, but he or she cannot be convicted of a greater offense on retrial. As the Supreme Court ruled in *Green v. United States* (1957), if the original conviction was for a lesser crime—for example, second-degree rather first-degree murder—and the conviction is reversed, the defendant cannot be retried for a more serious crime because conviction for second-degree murder implies acquittal for first-degree murder.

Trials for Multiple Offenses

In *Blockburger v. United States* (1932), the Supreme Court ruled that in cases where a single act constitutes separate violations of law, to avoid double jeopardy the prosecution must show that "each provision requires proof of a fact which the other does not." In *United States v. Felix* (1992), the Supreme Court allowed a second trial of an illegal drug producer for the same act committed in two states. The Court rationalized that prosecution in one state for illegal manufacturing of drugs did not bar prosecution for attempted manufacturing in the second state, where the defendant was planning to move his operations.

An act that crosses state lines, such as kidnapping, may be prosecuted by each state involved, according to the Supreme Court's decision in *Heath v. Alabama* (1985). And under the ruling in *United States v. Lanza* (1922), both federal and state governments may prosecute certain single criminal acts, such as robbing a federally insured bank. But in *Department of Revenue of Montana v. Ranch* (1994), the Court found that a tax levied on the possession and storage of drugs, for which the defendant was tried and convicted, was a successive criminal punishment prohibited by the Constitution's double jeopardy clause.

Determining what is and what is not the same offense can be difficult. The Supreme Court decided in *Brown v. Ohio* (1977) that a person convicted of joyriding may not be tried again for stealing the vehicle, because the proof of both offenses is the same (joyriding being a lesser-included offense of auto theft); under the criteria of the *Blockburger* decision, a second trial was thus barred. But in *Illinois v. Vitale* (1980), the Court found that a conviction on the charge of failing to reduce speed did not preclude a trial for manslaughter, because failure to reduce speed is not an element in the statutory definition of manslaughter.

Perhaps the most difficult determinations involve multiple offenses that arise out of the same act or transaction. In *Ashe v. Swenson* (1970), the Supreme Court held that the defendant, after being acquitted of robbing one of seven poker players, could not be tried again for robbing another at the same time. Using the principle of collateral estoppel (the basic facts alleged in the first instance have been adjudicated by a court of competent jurisdiction and may not be raised again in a second venue), the Court held that the defendant would face double jeopardy if the facts on which the robbery charge was based were relitigated with respect to each possible victim.

More on this topic:

Criminal Law, p. 132

Fundamental Rights, p. 247

Trials, p. 556

During the 1990s the Supreme Court was generally more circumspect in extending the protections of double jeopardy, with the result that civil and criminal prosecutions arising out of the same act have been upheld. For example, the fact that O. J. Simpson was acquitted in a notorious criminal trial in California did not preclude relatives of the victims from bringing a civil action for wrongful death against him in 1997, which resulted in a verdict requiring the former football player to pay them monetary damages of $33.5 million, most of which remains unpaid. In *Nichols v. Oklahoma* (2002), the Supreme Court also turned aside an allegation of double jeopardy raised by Timothy McVeigh's associate Terry Nichols in the bombing of the Alfred P. Murrah Federal Building in Oklahoma City.

Although Nichols had already been convicted of federal conspiracy and involuntary manslaughter charges and sentenced to life in prison, the justices' refusal to hear his appeal meant that a subsequent state trial was not viewed as double jeopardy. Whereas the federal case centered on the eight federal agents killed in the April 19, 1995, terrorist attack, Oklahoma's charges against Nichols relate to the premeditated murder of the remaining 160 persons.

Dred Scott Case *See* SLAVERY.

Drugs

In the benign definition of the term, *drugs* are substances used in the diagnosis, cure, mitigation, treatment, and prevention of disease in humans and animals. Some drugs are also controlled substances—products whose abuse can be harmful and even deadly—and thus their sale and use may be regulated by the government. The Drug Enforcement Administration of the Department of Justice maintains schedules of drugs and other controlled substances. Listed in schedule I are drugs or other substances that have a high potential for abuse and no currently accepted medical use for treatment in the United States, including heroin, marijuana, and methaqualone. Schedule II contains substances that have a high abuse potential but are currently accepted in medical treatment, such as morphine, cocaine, and methamphetamine. Schedule V, the last schedule, includes over-the-counter cough medicines with codeine that have a low potential for abuse and are currently accepted for use in medical treatment. Criminal charges may be brought against persons who illegally traffic in proscribed drugs.

The illicit production, transportation, distribution, sale, possession, and abuse of drugs have been addressed at national and international levels for nearly two centuries. The British East India Company, for example, monopolized the trade in opium in 1779, and at the beginning of the next century China unsuccessfully tried to ban the importation of opium because it was draining the country's economy. Singapore's constitution (1963) makes specific reference to the "misuse of drugs or intoxicating substances." And in 1984 the UN General Assembly issued a Declaration on the Control of Drug Trafficking and Drug Abuse and in 1988 adopted the Convention against Illicit Traffic in Narcotic Drugs and Psychotropic Substances.

Although the drug problem gives rise to many constitutional issues—from the balance between the states' POLICE POWER to the federal government's authority to tax and regulate COMMERCE to personal PRIVACY rights—the Constitution does not directly address drugs or controlled substances. But any attempts to curtail or prohibit illicit drugs through a constitutional amendment have no doubt been made more difficult by the country's failed effort to prohibit the manufacture, sale, and transportation of "intoxicating liquors" under the Eighteenth Amendment (1919), which was subsequently repealed by the Twenty-first Amendment (1933) (see PROHIBITION). The reports from the front in the war on drugs conjure up the vision of Canute, the eleventh-century king of England, Denmark, and Norway, who tried to command the ocean tides to recede.

Regulation of Drugs

Until the twentieth century, the fight against illicit drugs and drug trafficking relied on the police power of the states. The first antidrug law in the country was an 1875 San Francisco ordinance targeting opium dens in Chinatown; later the city banned opium smoking for white persons "under penalty of a heavy fine or imprisonment, or both." In 1886 the police raided an opium den in Denver. After that, the national government's involvement began to expand. In *Champion v. Ames*

(1903), also known as the Lottery Case, the Supreme Court ruled that Congress, under its power to regulate commerce, could attempt to suppress lottery traffic—a vice akin to drug abuse—to protect the people from the "widespread pestilence of lotteries." In 1914 the Opium Registration Act was passed to regulate the drug's possession as part of a clearly designated revenue law. Within two years, in *United States v. Jin Fuey Moy* (1916), the Court upheld the act even though it had generally struck down congressional attempts to usurp state police power in the guise of a revenue or tax law (see TAXATION). Twenty years later Congress passed the Marijuana Tax Act (1937), which set as stiff a penalty for the possession of marijuana as for heroin and cocaine; alcohol, however, was not treated as a drug and thus escaped criminalization again four years after Prohibition ended.

A number of provisions of the BILL OF RIGHTS (1791) have posed obstacles to the enforcement of drug laws. Freedom of RELIGION and drug enforcement clashed in a 1964 California state case, which involved the use of peyote by NATIVE AMERICANS in religious ceremonies. The Supreme Court had already declared that only a compelling state interest based on a substantial threat to public safety, peace, or order could justify infringement of religious freedom. In this case, however, the supreme court of California granted a new trial to determine if the religious belief was genuine. Six years later the Comprehensive Drug Abuse Prevention and Control Act (1970) (also referred to as the Controlled Substances Act) exempted the sacramental use of peyote, making the issue moot for a while. Then the Supreme Court, in *Employment Division, Department of Human Resources of Oregon v. Smith* (1990), tackled the question of the use of peyote in religious ceremonies under an Oregon statute criminalizing its possession and concluded that religious activities need not be exempted from otherwise valid criminal laws.

A few years later, however, in *Gonzales v. O Centro Espirita Beneficente Uniao Do Vegtal* (2006), the Supreme Court affirmed a preliminary injunction against the federal government to stop the prosecution of a Christian sect of thirty members who receive a form of communion using a tea brewed from hallucinogenic plants.

Relying on Congress's power over commerce rather than on its power to tax, the Controlled Substances Act repealed earlier drug laws based on the taxing power. The Supreme Court has since taken a hard line with respect to cases involving controlled substances. In *United States v. Oakland Cannabis Buyers' Cooperative* (2001), the Court held that the act allowed only one exception—government-approved research projects—and therefore the use of marijuana, even for valid medical purposes, is illegal. This decision invalidated a California law permitting the use of marijuana for medical purposes. Following the decision, the Drug Enforcement Administration raided the Los Angeles Cannabis Resource Center, which provided marijuana to patients with doctors' prescriptions for use in reducing pain. The Court affirmed its stand against the use of marijuana for medical purposes even when authorized by state law in *Gonzales v. Raich* (2005).

The Drug Enforcement Administration came into existence in 1973 as the successor to the Justice Department's Bureau of Narcotics and Dangerous Drugs, established in 1968. As early as 1915 drug regulation and control had been placed under the purview of the Treasury Department, whose Bureau of Narcotics was active from 1930 to 1968. U.S. Customs and Border Protection, part of the Department of Homeland Security, still has drug investigation responsibilities, and the Bureau of Alcohol, Tobacco and Firearms enforces laws and regulations with respect to those products as well as explosives. The Justice Department administers several other drug-related offices, while the Narcotics Advance Research Management team and the "drug czar," who heads the Office of National Drug Control Policy, are located in the president's office. Created in 1931, the Food and Drug Administration, which is a part of the U.S. Department of Health and Human Services, is responsible, among other things, for ensuring the safety, efficacy, and security of legal human and veterinary drugs. Its mission includes product approval, over-the-counter and prescription drug labeling, and standard setting for the manufacturing of legal drugs.

Drug Testing

In the 1980s drug testing by employers raised several constitutional issues that came before the Supreme Court. Urine testing programs by public and private employers to identify drug users have raised issues regarding SEARCH AND SEIZURE addressed by the Fourth Amendment (1791). Such testing in individual cases was considered reasonable even without a search warrant if based on probable cause, but could employers conduct random or universal testing of employees?

In two cases in 1989—*National Treasury Employees Union v. Von Raab* and *Skinner v. Railway Labor Executives' Association*—the Supreme Court upheld testing programs for Customs Service agents and railroad employees, respectively, because of the sensitivity and safety requirements of their work. But that same year a federal district court rejected random testing of Antitrust Division attorneys in the Justice Department. And in *Chandler v. Miller* (1997), the Supreme Court invalidated a Georgia law requiring all candidates for public office to be tested for drug use, noting that there was no indication of a drug abuse problem among the candidates and no public safety considerations. In 2002, however, the Court in *Board of Education of Independent School District No. 92 v. Earls* held that the Fourth Amendment (1791) does not prevent school districts from conducting random drug testing of any student involved in competitive extracurricular activities.

In *Kyllo v. United States* (2001), another case involving the Fourth Amendment's prohibition against unreasonable searches and seizures, the Supreme Court ruled that police officers must obtain a search warrant before using heat-sensing technology to identify houses in which "grow lights" were being used to produce marijuana. The Court also invalidated, in *Ferguson v. City of Charleston* (2001), a procedure by which tests of pregnant women indicating drug use were forwarded to the police; the justices called this an unreasonable search because the patient did not consent to the procedure.

Efforts to attack the drug problem in the United States have ranged from the "Just say no" slogan promoted during the administration of President Ronald Reagan (1911–2004) to direct assistance to countries such as Colombia, a major drug exporter, to cut off the source of the drug supply. The death toll, wasted lives, and criminal activities resulting from the illegal importation, manufacturing, distribution, sale, and use of narcotics is staggering, but critics of recent government policies to counteract this scourge note the hypocrisy in the treatment of alcohol compared to marijuana. Proposals have been made to decriminalize drug use in the same manner as gambling and to treat drugs—at least the less harmful ones such as marijuana—like alcohol. As the American experiment with Prohibition proved, it is difficult to legislate morality.

The nation's drug laws have occasionally ensnared well-known public figures, such as conservative radio talk show host Rush Limbaugh. In 2003 Limbaugh admitted to being addicted to prescription painkillers. He was subsequently investigated by prosecutors in Florida and agreed to undergo random drug testing. Some commentators noted the irony of Limbaugh's addiction in light of earlier comments in which he called for strong penalties against drug addicts. But Limbaugh's lawyers said he was being singled out for investigation because of his high public profile.

Source: CARLSON © *Milwaukee Sentinel*. Reprinted with permission of UNIVERSAL PRESS SYNDICATE. All rights reserved.

Due Process

The keystone of a government of laws—in contrast to a government of arbitrary rulers—is the concept of due process of law, embodied, if not always in so many words, in more than twenty provisions of the Constitution. The concept predates England's Magna Carta (1215), in which due process is phrased as "the law of the land." To understand the importance of due process, it must be remembered that for much of human history the vast majority of humankind was subject to the arbitrary and capricious judgments of their rulers.

A uniquely Anglo-American legal concept, due process encompasses determinations that are made in the regular course of the administration of JUSTICE by the COURTS. The core of the concept is that government should not have the power to deprive a person of life, LIBERTY, or PROPERTY except by procedures that have been previously established by law and that are applicable to all CITIZENS alike.

"The Law of the Land"

Like Magna Carta, the first American state constitutions as well as the Northwest Ordinance (1787), which applied to governance of U.S. territories (see TERRITORY), referred to due process as "the law of the land." But the original Constitution drafted in 1787 did not contain either that phrase or the phrase "due process of law," although certain provisions—including the prohibition against EX POST FACTO LAWS, bills of attainder (see ATTAINDER, BILLS OF), and interference with CONTRACTS as well as guarantees of trial by jury (see JURIES), HABEAS CORPUS, and equal status for all citizens in the several states—reflect the concept. Due process was finally explicitly guaranteed in both the Fifth (1791) and the Fourteenth (1868) Amendments. "No person shall be...deprived of life, liberty, or property, without due process of law...," declares the Fifth Amendment. The Fourteenth Amendment states in part: "nor shall any State deprive any person of life, liberty, or property, without due process of law...." In general, due process in the earlier amendment was to apply to the federal government, whereas in the later amendment it was to be extended to the states.

The evolution of the Constitution's due process provisions through court decisions is analogous to the growth of a tree. The roots are embedded in the COMMON LAW of England and the early English colonies in America. The trunk represents the CONSTITUTION, and its major branches are the rights guaranteed by the BILL OF RIGHTS (1791), with the Fifth Amendment and later the Fourteenth Amendment significant offshoots. Grafted onto the Fourteenth Amendment limb are portions of the due process guarantees in the Bill of Rights.

In *Murray's Lessee v. Hoboken Land and Improvement Co.* (1855), the Supreme Court defined *due process* to include legal procedures that did not conflict with the Constitution's prohibitions or with the accepted practices in England at the time the colonies were established. Although the Court had earlier reasoned that the guarantees of the Bill of Rights were not applicable to the states, ratification of the Fourteenth Amendment in 1868 changed that view. In *Allgeyer v. Louisiana* (1897), the Court held that a state law fining anyone for insuring property in the state with a company that had not complied with state law—in this case, a New York company—was an unconstitutional interference with the Fourteenth Amendment's protection of liberty. "The liberty mentioned in [the Fourteenth Amendment]," noted the Court, "means not only the right of the citizen to be free from the mere physical restraint of his person, as by incarceration, but the term is deemed to embrace the right of the citizen to be free in the enjoyment of all his faculties, to be free to use them in all lawful ways; to live and work where he will; to earn his livelihood by any lawful calling; to pursue any livelihood or avocation, and for that purpose to enter into all contracts which may be proper, necessary and essential to his carrying out to a successful conclusion the purposes above mentioned."

The courts have used the concept of due process to greatly expand citizens' protection from arbitrary and unjust actions of the government that may infringe individual liberties. Two major ways in which the courts analyze due process have evolved: procedural and substantive. Procedural due process relates to protection of citizens' rights in any procedure, such as a trial, conducted by authorities and that threatens their life, liberty, or property; substantive due process relates to how laws and regulations impinge on a person's basic RIGHTS and liberties.

Procedural Due Process

Procedural due process emphasizes the judicial process or procedures by which rights are determined in individual cases; civil or criminal procedures may be involved. Although criminal charges may jeopardize life and liberty as well as property—through fines and other forfeitures, for example—civil law actions too may involve large and devastating property losses. Such civil actions occur when the government sues a person, a person sues the government (assuming sovereign immunity is waived), or one person sues another in a court of law or when government administrative proceedings are carried out, entitlements such as Social Security are created by the government, or actions are taken against students by public school officials. All require a certain level of due process to give aggrieved parties a chance to defend themselves before forfeiting a benefit or receiving punishment. Under "self-help" laws, the government may additionally authorize private individuals to seize people or their property, such as when creditors repossess property for an overdue debt.

In *Mathews v. Eldridge* (1976), the Supreme Court fashioned a three-part test balancing private and government interests (see BALANCING TESTS) for cases involving civil due process procedures. After analyzing the private interest at risk, the Court looks first at the possibility of a loss of such interest under the procedures being used and then at the burden any additional procedural safeguards will cause government authorities. In balancing interests when private property is taken with the government's aid, as in the case of "self-help" laws, the Court has held that at a minimum a hearing is required before property can be seized.

If sufficient due process is not granted, an injured party has several options. A federal civil rights action, claiming a violation under the Fifth Amendment, can be brought against the officials involved. Under certain circumstances, state laws may have been violated as well. But the Supreme Court has held that only deliberate—not merely negligent—state actions resulting in a deprivation of property warrant due process protections.

Procedural due process in criminal actions involves all the aspects of ARREST, detention, trial (see TRIALS), and PUNISHMENT (see CRIMINAL LAW). These include the rights of an accused to ASSISTANCE OF COUNSEL, notification of the charges, a fair and speedy trial, and prohibition against SELF-INCRIMINATION. Originally guaranteed at the federal level by the Fifth Amendment, many of these rights were subsequently extended to the states after the Civil War under the Fourteenth Amendment.

The INCORPORATION DOCTRINE, urged as early as 1892 in dissenting opinions by the first John Marshall Harlan (1833–1911) to serve on the Supreme Court, resulted in extending to the states the federal rights guaranteed under the Fifth Amendment. *Adamson v. California* (1947) provides an example of how the process worked. Clearly, under the Fourteenth Amendment's due process clause, a state must provide a defendant a fair trial. But what if the defendant stands on his Fifth Amendment right not to testify against himself? Is the trial fair if the prosecutor or the judge makes an adverse comment to the jury on the defendant's failure to testify? In a federal trial such a comment would violate the Fifth Amendment's due process clause. In *Griffin v. California* (1965), the Court held that neither the prosecutor nor the judge may comment to the jury in a state trial on the defendant's failure to testify on his or her own behalf. The Court said that such a comment would be a "penalty imposed by the courts for exercising a constitutional privilege," one that reduces the privilege "by making its assertion costly."

Since *Adamson v. California,* a number of Supreme Court cases—among them, MAPP V. OHIO (1961), GIDEON V. WAINWRIGHT (1963), and MIRANDA V. ARIZONA (1966)—have extended due process rights to those accused of crimes at the state level. These cases involved, respectively, exclusion of evidence gained by an illegal search of the defendant's home (see SEARCH AND SEIZURE), failure to provide an indigent person accused of a serious crime with legal counsel, and failure of police officers (see LAW ENFORCEMENT) to advise the accused of his rights, specifically his right against self-incrimination, before taking his confession. The Court's zealous extension mostly in the 1960s of rights to persons accused of crimes, who are innocent until proven guilty, resulted in a popular backlash led by conservatives, who argued that guilty criminals were getting off on "mere technicalities." In recent years the Court has been less likely to expand constitutional due process in state cases, especially where the justices believed that the state has in place adequate remedies after conviction. For example, in *Zinermon v. Burch* (1990), the Court found no constitutional denial of due process in the case of an allegedly incompetent person's admission to a state mental facility without the benefit of the state's involuntary placement procedures, noting that the state's postdeprivation remedies provided Burch with all the process that was due him. Similarly, in *Duesenbery v. United States* (2002), the Court held that the Federal Bureau of Investigation's procedures in attempting to give a prisoner notice of the agency's intent to effect a forfeiture of money seized at the time of arrest was all that was required to comply with the Fifth Amendment's due process clause. Actual notice, in fact, was not necessary.

Substantive Due Process

Substantive due process goes beyond procedures for arriving at a determination that affects a person's rights. It addresses the substance of a law, rule, or regulation itself as it impinges on constitutional guarantees. A state or federal law may be enacted in complete accordance with the Constitution and legislative procedures yet violate fundamental constitutional restraints. Around the turn of the twentieth century, for example, state legislatures began to enact economic regulation of business activities, and the Supreme Court, as exemplified by *Lochner v. New York* (1905), began finding such legislation unconstitutional as an infringement of the due process protection of liberty and property rights under the Fourteenth Amendment (1868). Later, when the federal government began passing legislation to combat the effects of the Great Depression in the 1930s, the Court also at first struck down these laws on the grounds that they infringed due process rights. In the late 1930s the Court abandoned its reliance on substantive due process and thus validated federal economic

An abandoned farmhouse in North Dakota, circa 1930. During the Great Depression, the court changed its views of substantive due process to validate key laws that were intended to help the nation regain its economic strength.

Source: The Granger Collection, New York

recovery legislation. In *Ferguson v. Skrupa* (1936), Justice Hugh L. Black (1886–1971) explained the Court's new understanding of substantive due process: "We have returned to the original constitutional proposition that courts do not substitute their social and economic beliefs for the judgment of legislative bodies, who are elected to pass laws."

The basis for substantive due process comes from the notion, proclaimed in the DECLARATION OF INDEPENDENCE (1776), that "Governments are instituted among Men, deriving their just Powers from the Consent of the Governed...." Therefore, in a society based on equality and popular sovereignty, laws that infringe on citizens' basic and fundamental liberties are suspect for being unfair or unjust and may be invalidated as unconstitutional. As the Supreme Court explained in *Hurtado v. California* (1884), to hold to only the traditional forms of procedural due process "would be to deny every quality of the law but its age, and to render it incapable of progress or improvement." The Court must examine, said the opinion, "not [only] particular forms of procedures, but the very *substance* of individual rights to life, liberty, and property [emphasis added]."

Substantive due process was used again by the Supreme Court in *ROE V. WADE* (1973). In that case the Court invalidated ABORTION laws in forty-six states as infringements of a woman's fundamental right to decide, together with her doctor, whether to terminate a pregnancy, at least during the first three months. Personal autonomy and PRIVACY rights also played a key role in that decision. Since then, the Court has been refining—some might say limiting—those rights. In 1997, for example, the justices refused to invalidate laws in forty-nine states that make physician-assisted suicide a crime (see DIE, RIGHT TO).

Economic Due Process

The extension of substantive due process under the Fourteenth Amendment to property and contract rights is sometimes referred to as economic due process (see ECONOMIC LIBERTY). In 1897 the Supreme Court equated the concept of liberty contained in the Fourteenth Amendment's due process clause—no "State shall deprive any person of life, liberty, or property, without due process of law"—with the right to contract in the *Allgeyer* case. The Court's love affair with the since-discredited concept of economic due process culminated in 1905 in *Lochner v. New York*, in which the justices struck down a perfectly reasonable exercise of the state legislature's discretion—a law limiting working hours for bakers as a HEALTH regulation—on the grounds that it was an infringement of a person's "right to purchase or to sell labor... protected by [the Fourteenth] Amendment."

In *Lochner*, the majority of the Supreme Court took an amendment designed to extend rights to minorities—former slaves, in particular—and used it to prohibit legislative efforts to protect individuals from economic oppression and health and safety hazards. Justice OLIVER WENDELL HOLMES JR. dissented from the Court's economic due process decisions, reasoning that the majority will as expressed by the legislature must be affirmed "unless it can be said that a rational and fair man necessarily would admit that the statute proposed would infringe fundamental principles as they have been understood by the traditions of our people and our law." As a consequence of the economic due process rationale, the Supreme Court struck down some two hundred state and federal laws until in *Nebbia v. New York* (1934), by a 5–4 majority, it upheld a state law regulating the price of milk. Justice Owen Roberts (1875–1955) sounded the death knell for economic due process by declaring that the states were "free to adopt whatever economic policy may reasonably be deemed to promote public welfare."

Thus, until the Great Depression in the 1930s, when national and state government action became necessary to ameliorate the nation's economic problems, the courts used substantive due process to thwart many reasonable federal and state attempts to provide for the general WELFARE

More on this topic:

Bill of Rights, p. 62

Death Penalty, p. 140

Fundamental Rights, p. 247

Habeas Corpus, p. 266

Justice, p. 325

Rule of Law, p. 475

and promote economic and social justice. The Supreme Court finally got the message and in *West Coast Hotel v. Parrish* (1937) upheld a minimum wage law to protect WOMEN, who were particularly vulnerable to economic exploitation.

Due process of law as required by the Fifth and Fourteenth Amendments and as developed by the courts is a potent weapon in the fight of individuals against government oppression and tyranny. The simple logic that citizens should not forfeit their life, liberty, or property except by laws and procedures that are constitutional, known beforehand, and applicable to all persons is finally beginning to prevail in one small corner of human history.

Economic Liberty

Written constitutions can be broadly interpreted simply in terms of their economic policies. In his *Economic Interpretation of the Constitution* (1913), Charles A. Beard (1874–1948), a teacher and historian, went so far as to propose that the U.S. Constitution was the work of a few wealthy men who wanted to advance certain economic interests to the detriment of others. His thesis has since been discredited on empirical grounds: the FRAMERS OF THE CONSTITUTION were not as wealthy or as single-minded as Beard portrayed them. Nevertheless, had poor and landless citizens called their own constitutional convention in 1787, the result no doubt would have been a different document.

Because constitutions set the overarching rules for determining how a nation's political power can be acquired, used, protected, and transferred, they also affect the rules of economic competition. They determine what government taxing and spending policies will prevail and under what circumstances force will be used to protect the wealth of a nation's citizens and opportunities for acquiring it. A constitution with effective checks and balances (see SEPARATION OF POWERS) can also keep those to whom political power is entrusted from siphoning off national wealth through corrupt practices—as is done by many dictators, such as Ferdinand Marcos (1917–89) of the Philippines and Manuel Noriega (b. 1934) of Panama—adversely impacting honest economic competition and citizens' economic WELFARE.

When THOMAS JEFFERSON wrote in the DECLARATION OF INDEPENDENCE (1776) of the people's "unalienable rights" to "life, liberty, and the pursuit of happiness," he altered the basic rights enunciated earlier by the English philosopher John Locke (1632–1704)—life, LIBERTY, and PROPERTY—linking happiness with the ownership of property. After the Revolutionary War (1775–83), COMMERCE and trade grew rapidly in the newly independent thirteen states. In fact, much of the impetus for abandoning the ARTICLES OF CONFEDERATION (1781) and drafting a new constitution in 1787 came from problems associated with the weak national government's inability to regulate commerce among the states. In essay 13 of *The Federalist* (1787–88) (see FEDERALIST PAPERS), entitled "Advantage of the Union in Respect to Economy in Government," ALEXANDER HAMILTON addressed the many economic benefits of having a strong national government rather than thirteen loosely confederated states. In essay 11 he promoted the idea of a national economy, arguing that a strong union would improve commerce and trade with foreign nations.

Today economics (from the Greek word *oikonomia*, meaning one who manages a household) encompasses macroeconomics and microeconomics, the managing of supply and demand at the national as well as the individual levels. Modern constitutions of many nations devote whole sections to economic rights and development. Brazil's constitution (1988) has a portion entitled "The Economic and Financial Order" (Title VII), which begins: "The economic order, founded on the appreciation of human work and on free enterprise, is intended to ensure everyone a life with dignity, in accordance with the dictates of social justice...." Similarly, Italy's constitution (1948) has a section entitled "Economic Relations" (Title III); it begins: "The Republic protects work in all its forms and applications. It takes care of the training and professional elevation of workers."

A Capitalist System

The U.S. Constitution, although it does not mention economics or the economy, encourages private entrepreneurship while providing the national government with sufficient power to regulate important aspects of the economy. Over two centuries the country's capitalist system has been modified through fiscal and monetary policies used, among other things, to stimulate and dampen the national economy when needed, redistribute wealth, provide social programs, and sanction government-run monopolies such as the postal service.

Article I, section 8, provides copyright and patent protection for authors and inventors (see COPYRIGHT; PATENTS) and authorizes uniform laws on BANKRUPTCY, while section 10 prohibits state laws that impair CONTRACTS. Section 8 also gives Congress the power to regulate commerce with foreign nations and among the states as well as the power to tax (see TAXATION) and to coin money and regulate its value (see CURRENCY). In *Corfield v. Coryell* (1823), Supreme Court Justice Bushrod Washington (1762–1829) stated that the PRIVILEGES AND IMMUNITIES of U.S. CITIZENS cited in Article IV, section 2, included "the right to acquire and possess property of every kind." More than a century later Justice Robert H. Jackson (1892–1954) commented in *H. P. Hood and Sons v. DuMond* (1949): "Our system...is that every farmer and every craftsman shall be encouraged to produce by the certainty that he will have free access to every market in the nation...."

"Our system...is that every farmer and every craftsman shall be encouraged to produce by the certainty that he will have free access to every market in the nation...."

—Justice Robert H. Jackson

In addition to balancing economic growth against economic regulation, the Supreme Court has also had to balance the national government's role against that of the states in cases involving economic issues. In *GIBBONS V. OGDEN* (1824), the Court found that the Constitution gives Congress broad power to regulate interstate commerce and that a state monopoly is inconsistent with the free-market principles embodied in the document. Over the years the Court has dealt with the Constitution's economic implications with respect to economic discrimination, economic due process, public taking of private property, and monopolies and antitrust laws.

Economic Discrimination

When state laws seem to favor one type of business or industry at the expense of another, the Supreme Court has generally rejected appeals that such acts violate the EQUAL PROTECTION clause of the Fourteenth Amendment (1868) as long as, according to *McGowan v. Maryland* (1961), "any state of facts reasonably may be conceived to justify it." In *Williamson v. Lee Optical Co.* (1955), the Court upheld an Oklahoma law requiring opticians to obtain a prescription before replacing old eyeglass lenses, while exempting from the same requirement merchants who sold ready-to-wear eyeglasses. Then in *McGowan*, the Court refused to find unconstitutionally discriminatory a Maryland law that prohibited some stores from opening on Sundays while allowing others to do so. In *Allegheny Pittsburgh Coal v. Webster County* (1989), however, the Court found that "intentional systematic undervaluation" of only some property by the state of West Virginia for tax purposes was not constitutionally permissible.

Economic Due Process

Beginning in the 1890s, the Supreme Court used the DUE PROCESS clauses of the Fifth Amendment (1791) as well as the Fourteenth Amendment to declare unconstitutional many state laws that adversely affected private property or contractual obligations. This idea of "economic due process" (finding state restrictions on business activities unconstitutional) had been rejected by the Court in the Slaughter-House Cases (1873), in which New Orleans was allowed to create a monopoly in the slaughtering business. Eventually, however, the Court accepted the idea of economic due process, in effect allowing public policy to be decided by a majority of the justices rather than by elected representatives of the people. In the leading economic due process case, *Lochner v. New York* (1905), the Court elevated the right to contract for one's own labor over the state legislature's desire to protect the health of bakery workers by prohibiting their employment for more than ten hours a day.

The demise of economic due process is reflected in *Nebbia v. New York* (1934), in which the Supreme Court let stand a milk pricing law in New York. Leo Nebbia, a grocer, refused to obey a state law, passed in response to the hardship many citizens suffered in the Great Depression, setting a maximum price for milk. Ignoring past economic due process arguments that such regulations interfered with business rights, the Court took the position that a state "may regulate a business in any of its aspects, including the prices to be charged...." The Depression and the threat by President Franklin D. Roosevelt (1882–1945) to "pack" the Court with additional members more sympathetic to his economic recovery program undoubtedly influenced the Court's change of direction.

The concept of economic due process is a reminder of the power of unelected jurists to thwart the will of the majority expressed through their elected representatives (see MAJORITY RULE; REPRESENTATIVE GOVERNMENT). The system of constitutional checks and balances devised in 1787 is not perfect: it allows the government and the courts a great deal of leeway in setting economic policy, but a policy for a period of economic boom may be wrong for a period of economic depression.

Taking of Private Property

Capitalist economics in a nation such as the United States differ markedly from communist economics, under which the government may nationalize private property, taking it without compensation. The Fifth Amendment (1791) provides in part that "private property [shall not] be taken for public use, without just compensation" (see JUST COMPENSATION). This takings clause is applicable to the federal government and, through the Fourteenth Amendment, to the states. The problem for the Supreme Court, however, has been defining what constitutes the government's taking of property.

In *Pennsylvania Coal Co. v. Mahon* (1922), the Supreme Court held that although property may be regulated to a certain extent, "if regulation goes too far it will be recognized as a taking" and the government must compensate for its loss. Even a temporary or a partial deprivation of property may be considered a taking requiring compensation. *Lucas v. South Carolina Coastal Council* (1992) involved a state regulation banning construction on beachfront property. The plaintiff had purchased a portion of the property for real estate development. Even though the nature of the regulation was for a worthy public purpose—preservation of the state's beaches—the Court held that the state by regulating the beneficial use of property had effected a "total taking" from a private owner that, according to the Constitution, required compensation.

In another beach-front property case, *Nollan v. California* (1987), the Nollans wanted to build a larger house on their property but were told that only by granting public access to the beach would the enlargement be approved. The U.S. Supreme Court, by a 5–4 decision, held that the requirement of the easement to the beach was, in fact, a taking by the government. The Court would explain in *Lingle, Governor of Hawaii, v. Chevron U.S.A., Inc.* (2005) that a party alleging a taking may proceed on one of four grounds—"a 'physical' taking, a *Lucas*-type total regulatory taking, a *Penn Central* taking (see JUST COMPENSATION), or a land-use extraction violating the *Nollan* standards."

A recent controversial decision by the Supreme Court in *Kelo v. City of New London, Conn.* (2005) extended the limits of the definition of "public use" to include a city's taking of private property to give to a private developer in pursuance of an approved economic development plan. Critics of the 5–4 decision predicted it would lead to a rash of takings of private property from one citizen to give to another, but so far, few serious consequences, if any, have resulted.

Monopolies and Antitrust Laws

Under the regulatory power of the commerce clause in Article I, section 8, the federal government can try to level the economic playing field for businesses. Market competition theoretically maximizes the choices and benefits for the consumer, but a company or a group of companies that has a dominant share of the market may limit production and raise prices arbitrarily, to consumers' disadvantage. The government, however, wants to ensure, to the extent possible, the ability of new businesses to enter the marketplace and make a reasonable return on their investments.

The Sherman Antitrust Act (1890) made illegal "every contract, combination in the form of trust or otherwise" and "conspiracy in restraint of trade and commerce" (see ANTITRUST LAW). In *United States v. E. C. Knight* (1895), the Sugar Trusts Case, the Supreme Court found that the prosecution of major sugar producers located in a single state exceeded Congress's power under the commerce clause. After the beginning of the twentieth century, however, the Court adopted the theory propounded by Justice OLIVER WENDELL HOLMES JR. that there was a "stream" or "current" of commerce such that a restraint of trade caused in one place by a trust or combination of businesses could have an effect in another. This theory, which meant that an action in one state could affect commerce in other states, allowed the Court to validate legislation by Congress, under its power to regulate interstate com-

A businessman with a good idea can make a lot of money in the United States because the government tends to encourage entrepreneurs. Ray Kroc took over the McDonald's Corporation in 1955 and changed American dining habits by creating the most successful fast food chain in the world.
Source: AP Images

merce, that extended commerce regulation back to the source of a product or a service. Thus government suits against businesses that acted illegally to restrain trade and commerce—antitrust suits—were more likely to be upheld by the Court.

The recent antitrust prosecutions of Microsoft Corporation by the Department of Justice attest to businesses' continuing ability to monopolize the market to the potential detriment of free competition and consumer interests. Both federal and state governments seek to encourage entrepreneurship and profit making by individuals and businesses in order to increase economic wealth and thus the tax base that fuels the operation of government. If a business like Microsoft becomes too large or too successful, it can have a negative effect on the rest of the business environment for others and on the economy as a whole when it engages in monopoly practices, price fixing, and restraint of trade. The government continually attempts to balance these interests, sometimes resulting in extremes of overregulation or too little regulation.

Education

The key to an informed electorate in a democracy, believed THOMAS JEFFERSON, is free public education. As he wrote to a correspondent in 1818, "If the condition of man is to be progressively ameliorated, as we fondly hope and believe, education is to be the chief instrument in effecting it." For much of American history, however, education was not a subject given much national attention. The U.S. Department of Health, Education, and Welfare was not created until 1953, and the U.S. Department of Education was established as a separate entity in 1979. Reacting to the changed emphasis, recent candidates for the presidency have often made education a top campaign priority.

The Constitution does not specifically refer to education, but the constitutions of many other countries, including those of Belgium (1831, significantly amended 1970–93), Iceland (1944), and Panama (1972), address the education of their citizens. In addition, the United Nations' Universal Declaration of Human Rights (1948) proclaims: "Everyone has the right to education. Education shall be free, at least in the elementary and fundamental stages."

Public schools in the United States to a great extent come under the authority of the STATES and local jurisdictions, whose policies are generally directed by appointed or elected boards of education. Because Article I, section 8, of the Constitution gives Congress the power to tax (see TAXATION) and spend, the courts have allowed the federal government to impose conditions on state and local educational institutions that receive federal funds. In addition, the Fourteenth Amendment (1868), which requires the states to provide DUE PROCESS and EQUAL PROTECTION of the laws to those under their jurisdiction, protects the rights of parents and CHILDREN vis-á-vis the rights of states regarding education. Section 5 provides that "Congress shall have power to enforce, by appropriate legislation, the provisions of [the amendment]." The federal government is also involved in setting education policy, which obviously affects the nation's economic development, through both the LEGISLATIVE BRANCH, in laws passed by Congress, and the EXECUTIVE BRANCH, under the Department of Education. For example, since the Bush administration took office in 2001, there has been an emphasis on faith-based programs sponsored by the federal government that promote abstinence-only sex education through, among other avenues, the U.S Department of Education.

Unequal Education

Perhaps the Supreme Court's most famous decision regarding education was *BROWN V. BOARD OF EDUCATION OF TOPEKA* (1954), which declared that SEGREGATION in public schools was unconstitutional and put an end to separate but allegedly "equal" schools for different races. In *REGENTS OF THE*

UNIVERSITY OF CALIFORNIA V. BAKKE (1978), the Court narrowly held that a university medical school could not admit a set number of students solely because they were MINORITIES, thus denying entry to better-qualified applicants who were not minorities. This "reverse discrimination" case did not prohibit educational institutions from taking into consideration the minority status of applicants in their admissions policy (see AFFIRMATIVE ACTION).

State methods for funding education were addressed by the Supreme Court in *San Antonio Independent School District v. Rodriguez* (1973). Because Texas funded schools on the basis of taxes collected in individual school districts, the claim was made that the education provided in the poorer districts was of a lower quality than that provided in the wealthier districts; the funding disparity between the wealthiest and poorest districts was $594 to $356 per pupil per year. The Court rejected this claim, however. "The undisputed importance of education," said Justice Lewis F. Powell Jr. (1907–98), speaking for the majority, "will not alone cause this Court to depart from the usual standard for reviewing a State's societal and economic legislation." He concluded that the state's use of local property taxes to pay for schools was "not so irrational as to be invidiously discriminatory."

Inequities in educational funding in Michigan and New Hampshire, however, have led to reform efforts. In New Hampshire the state's supreme court, after noting a disparity of some 400 percent in the tax rates of two school districts, said that such taxes were not in fact local taxes but state taxes required to fulfill "the State's duty to provide a constitutionally adequate public education."

Religion in the Schools

The facts that America was founded on principles of religious freedom and that children of families of various religious faiths, as well as nonbelievers, are required by law to attend school makes it especially important that the school system, like other government institutions, remains neutral concerning competing systems of belief. In *Engel v. Vitale* (1962), the Supreme Court held that under the First Amendment (1791), which forbids any law "respecting an establishment of religion," it was unconstitutional for New York state to require a prayer written by the state board of regents, even though nondenominational, to be read in the public schools. A Kentucky law requiring that the Ten Commandments be posted on classroom walls in public schools was invalidated in *Stone v. Graham* (1980), but the outcome might have been different if the Ten Commandments were part of the school curriculum relating to the study of history, ethics, or comparative religion. In *Good News Club v. Milford Central School* (2001), the Court weighed the right of a religious student group to use public school facilities, which were open to nonreligious groups, against the separation of church and state doctrine. It ruled that the religious group must be accorded the same privileges as any other group.

Parents' Rights

It is not unconstitutional for states to compel children to attend public school, but parents are generally permitted to choose public or private schooling for their children. According to the Supreme Court's ruling in *Wisconsin v. Yoder* (1972), parents—Amish in this case—may remove their children from public school before the end of the period required for compulsory education. In making this narrow exception to compulsory attendance laws, the majority of the Court did not address whether the child's interests may be different from the parents' and thus did not discuss a child's right to education.

The Supreme Court decision in *Zelman v. Simmons-Harris* (2002) has implications for both parental rights and religion in education. In that case, the Court upheld a school voucher program in

Ohio that permitted low-income and minority parents to send their children to either private schools, including religious schools, or public schools against a challenge that the program violated the establishment clause of the First Amendment (1791) of the Constitution. Chief Justice William H. Rehnquist (1924–2005) noted in his opinion for the Court that the Court has "repeatedly recognized that no reasonable observer would think a neutral program of private choice, where state aid reaches religious schools solely as a result of the numerous independent decisions of private individuals, carries with it the *imprimatur* of government endorsement. [Any] objective observer familiar with the full history and context of the Ohio program would reasonably view it as one aspect of a broader undertaking to assist poor children in failed schools, not as an endorsement of religious schooling in general."

The Supreme Court in 1972 agreed that Amish parents could have a rare exemption from compulsory education laws.
Source: AP Images/The Alliance Review, Kyle Lanzer

Students' Rights

According to Supreme Court decisions, students have a right to attend public schools and may not be suspended arbitrarily without a hearing. The Court also upheld, in *West Virginia Board of Education v. Barnette* (1943), the right of a student, a Jehovah's Witness, not to participate in the salute to the American FLAG.

As early as 1923 the Supreme Court upheld the right to teach and learn foreign languages in school. Where students cannot speak English, the Supreme Court held in *Lau v. Nichols* (1974) that they must be schooled in their own language or taught to speak English. The Constitution does not mandate an official language, but the constitutions of some states, including those of Nebraska (1875) and Arizona (1912), make English their official state language; Hawaii's constitution (1959) designates both English and Hawaiian.

In *Tinker v. Des Moines Independent School District* (1969), the Supreme Court upheld limitations on a student's freedom of expression (see SPEECH), saying that "[i]n our system, state-operated schools may not be enclaves of totalitarianism. School officials do not possess absolute authority over their students. Students in school as well as out of school are 'persons' under our Constitution. They are possessed of fundamental rights which the State must respect, just as they themselves must respect their obligations to the State." But in *Morse v. Frederick* (2007), the Supreme Court, while acknowledging the principle established in *Tinker* that young people do not give up all of their First Amendment rights when they enter school, found that the principal of a high school had not violated a student's right of free speech when she confiscated a banner he held at a school-sanctioned and school-supervised event that read: "Bong Hits 4 Jesus." After the decision, the student—by this time an English teacher in China—said: "I find it absurdly funny. I was not promoting drugs[,]…I assumed most people would take it as a joke."

Although education traditionally has been guided by officials at the state level, Congress passed a sweeping bill in 2002 to increase public school standards. The bill, known as No Child Left Behind, also gave parents more flexibility over choosing the schools for their children.

No Child Left Behind marked a major change in the delicate balance of rights between Washington and the states, and between parents and teachers. The law penalizes schools whose students fail to do well on standardized tests in reading and math. States that fail to comply with the law face the loss of federal funding for their schools.

Almost from its inception, the law has proven highly controversial. State officials chafe over the imposition of federal goals, and some states even have debated whether to give up federal funds in order to remove themselves from the law's requirements. Many teachers also are critical because they have to teach subjects covered by standardized tests instead of tailoring their lessons to the needs of individual students.

But President George W. Bush, who signed the bill into law, praised it as an important step toward forcing low-performing schools to improve their standards or face consequences. Supporters of the law also say it gives parents more opportunity to move their children to higher-performing schools.

Somewhat ironically, Bush came to office on a conservative platform espousing states' rights. Yet No Child Left Behind gives Washington unprecedented power over the nation's system of public education.

Other rights of students, such as PRIVACY and protection from unreasonable searches and seizures of student property on school premises (see SEARCH AND SEIZURE), raise special constitutional issues for students and administrators. Searches conducted without a warrant generally must be based on probable cause—there must be sufficient evidence to indicate a reason to forego obtaining a legal warrant. But the Supreme Court has gone further by balancing the need to maintain discipline in the school environment against a student's expectation of privacy (see BALANCING TESTS). In *New Jersey v. T.L.O.* (1985), the Court found that search warrants were not required for searches on school property under certain circumstances. For example, if there were reasonable grounds that evidence would be produced, if the measures used were reasonably related to the search objectives, and if they were not intrusive given the student's age and sex and the nature of the suspected offenses, no warrant would be required.

Teachers' Rights

Do teachers have the right to freedom of expression in the classroom? Public schools have no definitive rule with respect to academic freedom, the right of free and unfettered discourse and exchange of ideas by students and teachers in a school setting. However, the courts appear willing to allow school authorities in elementary and secondary schools to teach community values through lesson materials and therefore to deny individual teachers the right to teach independently. As for a teacher's freedom of expression outside the classroom, the Supreme Court in *Perry v. Sindermann* (1972) held that a teacher could not be fired for exercising First Amendment rights.

In *Ingraham v. Wright* (1977), the Supreme Court confirmed the right of teachers and other school officials to administer corporal punishment without holding a hearing because if excessive force or wrongful punishment were proven, it could be dealt with afterward in a lawsuit. The Court noted, however, that the practice of corporal punishment did raise issues concerning protection of the student's LIBERTY but that the teacher's ability to observe the misbehavior directly, the openness of the school environment such that the punishment could be witnessed by students and other faculty members, and the parents' ability to judge the results reduced the chances of improper or excessive punishment.

Where public education is concerned, the goals of parents, students, teachers, and the community are continually being balanced against the goals of local, state, and national governments—a constant challenge in the context of the Constitution, especially its First and Fourteenth Amendments.

> **More on this topic:**
>
> *Racial Discrimination,*
> *p. 449*

Eighteenth Amendment See PROHIBITION.

Eighth Amendment *See* BAIL; CRUEL AND UNUSUAL PUNISHMENT.

Elections

One of the possible ways of selecting government officials is through an election (from the Latin *electus*, meaning choice). In ancient Athens, where DEMOCRACY and MAJORITY RULE began, CITIZENS were allowed to vote for public officials, although some element of chance was often introduced to allow the gods to influence the outcome. In a sense, an election or a vote in which the majority of the votes cast determines a policy or a political leader can be viewed as a substitute for a physical fight in which the strongest side wins and enforces its will on the losers. In a democracy, elections determine rulers and political policy by "ballots, not bullets," as the saying goes.

Fair, honest, regular, and open elections by secret ballot for political leaders are the hallmark of a true constitutional democracy, although most modern democracies also have some indirect election provisions—such as the ELECTORAL COLLEGE used for election of the U.S. PRESIDENT and VICE PRESIDENT and the election of most prime ministers by the members of parliament—and some appointive offices. "As it is essential to liberty that the government in general should have a common interest with the people," commented JAMES MADISON in essay 52 of *The Federalist* (1787–88) (see FEDERALIST PAPERS), "so it is particularly essential that the branch of it under consideration [the House of Representatives] should have an immediate dependence on, and an intimate sympathy with, the people. Frequent elections are unquestionably the only policy by which this dependence and sympathy can be effectually secured." In a constitutional monarchy, the head of state is not elected but is chosen generally under a constitutional act of succession based on heredity or in some cases by a constitutional body that selects from persons of a certain lineage.

The Constitution contains a number of provisions regarding the election of representatives, senators, and the president and vice president. In addition, a number of constitutional AMENDMENTS address the right to vote. The Fifteenth Amendment (1870), for one, prohibits the United States or any state from denying the right to vote to any person on account of race, color, or previous condition of servitude (see SLAVERY). The Nineteenth Amendment (1920) grants WOMEN the right to vote. The Twenty-third Amendment (1961) extends the right to vote for president and vice president to the citizens of the District of Columbia (see CAPITAL, NATIONAL). The Twenty-fourth Amendment (1964) bars a poll tax, and the Twenty-sixth Amendment (1971) lowers the voting age to eighteen years.

The Constitution requires that the federal and state governments share the responsibilities associated with na-

A jubilant Harry S. Truman proves the editors wrong. The front page went to press on election night, when Thomas E. Dewey had been projected to win the 1948 presidential race.
Source: St. Louis Mercantile Library

tional elections, and to a large extent states bear most of this burden. States and their counties are responsible for voter registration, operation of polling stations, vote counting, and certification of the results. State laws, as long as they are constitutional, determine the qualifications for voting in the general election and the primaries usually held by POLITICAL PARTIES. The federal government's role involves regulating CAMPAIGN FINANCING of federal elections and some state and local campaign fund raising, enforcement of the right to vote, setting the time for federal elections, and determining the winners of contested or challenged presidential, House, and Senate elections. In *Foster v. Love* (1997), the Supreme Court said that the election clause in Article I, section 4, "invests the States with responsibility for the mechanics of congressional elections, but only insofar as Congress declines to preempt state legislative choices."

Election of U.S. Representatives

As Article I, section 2, of the Constitution specifies: "The House of Representatives, shall be composed of members chosen every second year by the people of the several states, and the electors in each state shall have the qualifications requisite for electors of the most numerous branch of the state legislature." All states except Nebraska have a bicameral legislature. The same section also prescribes the qualifications for persons who stand for election to the HOUSE OF REPRESENTATIVES: "No person shall be a representative who shall not have attained to the age of twenty-five years, and been seven years a citizen of the United States, and who shall not, when elected, be an inhabitant of that state in which he shall be chosen."

The number of representatives who may be elected from each state is related to the population of that state. As set forth in Article I, section 2, the number is to be determined every ten years and based on the CENSUS (see REAPPORTIONMENT). The original basis for apportioning seats in the House of Representatives was changed by the Fourteenth Amendment (1868) just after the Civil War. The relevant provision, in section 2 of the amendment, provides: "Representatives shall be apportioned among the several states according to their respective numbers, counting the whole number of persons in each state, excluding Indians not taxed." (Even today some NATIVE AMERICANS and tribal activities are not taxed.) The amendment also denies the right to vote to people "for participation in rebellion, or other crime" and prohibits those who have engaged "in insurrection or rebellion against" the United States from holding office.

⊙ **CLOSER LOOK**

When Abraham Lincoln ran for the Illinois Senate against Stephen A. Douglas in 1858, he won over many voters through his eloquence in a series of closely watched debates. But he failed to win the Senate seat because the Constitution at the time called for state legislators, not voters, to pick senators—and Douglas had more support in the legislature.

Election of U.S. Senators

Article I, section 3, provides for the selection of two senators from each state and for one-third of the total number to be selected every two years. The original method of selection—by the state legislatures—was changed by the Seventeenth Amendment (1913), which states in part: "The Senate of the United States shall be composed of two Senators from each state, elected by the people thereof, for six years; and each Senator shall have one vote." According to the same section, "No Person shall be a Senator who shall not have attained to the Age of thirty Years, and been nine Years a Citizen of the United states, and who shall not, when elected, be an Inhabitant of that State for which he shall be chosen."

"The Times, Places, and Manner of holding Elections for Senators and Representatives," notes Article I, section 4, "shall be prescribed in each State by the Legislature thereof; but the Congress may at any time by Law make or alter such Regulations, except as to the Places of chusing Senators." And section 5 states in part: "Each House shall be the Judge of the Elections, Returns, and Qualifications of its own Members..." (see also SENATE).

Election of President and Vice President

Article II, section 1, of the Constitution directs that the president "shall hold his Office during the Term of four Years"; the vice president is chosen for the same term. They are elected as follows: "Each State shall appoint, in such Manner as the Legislature thereof may direct, a Number of Electors, equal to the whole Number of Senators and Representatives to which the State may be entitled in the Congress: but no Senator or Representative, or Person holding an Office of Trust or Profit under the United States, shall be appointed an Elector." Under the Twenty-third Amendment, the District of Columbia also selects "in such manner as the Congress may direct: A number of electors of President and Vice President equal to the whole number of Senators and Representatives in Congress to which the District would be entitled if it were a State, but in no event more than the least populous State...."

The qualifications for president and vice president are set forth in Article II, section 1: "No Person except a natural born Citizen, or a Citizen of the United States, at the time of the Adoption of this Constitution, shall be eligible to the Office of President; neither shall any Person be eligible to that Office who shall not have attained the Age of thirty-five Years, and been fourteen Years a Resident within the United States." The Twenty-second Amendment (1951) also limits eligibility for the presidency: "No person shall be elected to the office of the President more than twice, and no person who has held the office of President, or acted as President, for more than two years of a term to which some other person was elected President shall be elected to the office of the President more than once." The amendment was enacted to constitutionally enshrine the precedent set by GEORGE WASHINGTON, who refused to run for a third term; Franklin D. Roosevelt (1882–1945) disregarded the precedent when he ran for and was elected to not just a third but also a fourth term in 1940 and 1944.

"The Congress may determine the time of chusing the Electors [for president and vice president], and the Day on which they shall give their Votes; which Day shall be the same throughout the United States," provides Article II, section 1. This has now been set as the first Tuesday after the first Monday in November of even years. Before ratification of the Twelfth Amendment (1804), the person receiving the ELECTORAL COLLEGE's second highest number of votes became vice president. Now the president and vice president run together on the same party ticket and are voted for together.

All states and the District of Columbia select electors who collectively constitute the electoral college and who are pledged to vote for president and vice president. This indirect method—electors, elected by the people, actually cast the ballots to elect the president and vice president—contrasts with most other presidential elections in democratic republics. In others the president is generally elected at large, although he or she may be required to obtain an absolute majority of the votes; and if no candidate receives an absolute majority, a runoff is then held between the two candidates receiving the most votes.

Political Parties

Technically, anyone who meets the qualifications for the office set forth in the Constitution can be a candidate for a national political office. (The word *candidate* comes from the Latin *candidus*, meaning white, because Roman candidates wore white togas; the word also means being candid or open and honest.) The reality, however, is that to have any hope of being elected to national office a person requires the support of a large number of people and organizations.

For most of the history of the United States, political parties have provided the base of support for candidates at the state and national levels. The nomination process conducted by the political parties generally determines which candidates will have a chance to vie successfully for political office. Since George Washington was unanimously elected the first president of the United States by the electors of the first electoral college, every successful candidate for president has had the support of a political party. The Constitution does not address political parties, which have evolved since its adoption, but they have become traditional constitutional institutions and are the subject of national and state election laws.

Primary Elections

The Constitution does not address primary elections, which are held in many states to determine the candidates to be placed on the ballot for the general election. Political parties generally use primaries to determine their candidates, although other methods may be used, such as party caucuses that bring together registered voters of a particular party. Some states have allowed "open" primaries, in which voters from any party may vote to nominate candidates. In *Foster v. Love* (1997), a unanimous Supreme Court invalidated Louisiana's open primary system that in effect determined the winner of the general election in October, whereas a federal statute passed under Congress's authority in Article I, section 4, specified that elections for congressional candidates are to be held in November. The justices explained that the earlier election might influence later voters. But that same year the Court upheld a "jungle" (wide-open) primary used in several states, including Alaska, California, and Washington, in which voters can pick and choose among the parties, office by office, on a single ballot.

The Ballot

In U.S. elections a ballot (from the Italian *ballota*, meaning a round bullet or ball used to choose or draw lots) refers to a number of methods of actually recording a citizen's vote. For many years paper ballots were standard, and in early elections voters were required to sign their names to the ballot as a measure to prevent fraud or double voting. Britain's Ballot Act of 1872 introduced the so-called Australian, or secret, ballot, and the United States followed suit. By 1888 all states were using the secret ballot prepared at government expense.

More recently, voting machines of various designs have taken the place of paper ballots, which must be counted by hand, a lengthy process, and are not completely safe from being tampered with. Voter registration, the presence of poll watchers—members of the major parties who supervise the voting process to keep each side honest—and mechanical and electronic voting machines help ensure that elections are relatively honest. However, the close 2000 presidential election between George W. Bush (b. 1946) and Al Gore (b. 1948) brought the balloting process under sharp criticism. A 2001 study by several universities has determined, among other findings, that punch-card ballots like those used in the 2000 presidential election in some voting precincts in Florida have an error rate of 2.5 percent, higher than any other method used.

Absentee ballots—votes cast by mail by certain citizens who are unable to get to the polls on election day—are legal exceptions to the general rule that voting must be done in person at the polls. Absentee ballots also came in for criticism after the 2000 presidential election when it was alleged that vote counters used subjective reasons to determine whether the ballots met the legal criteria for inclusion in the official tally. Some absentee ballots in Florida, for example, were not postmarked by the date required, had no postmark, or did not indicate the ballot number assigned when application was made as required by absentee ballot law.

Voter Identification

As of 2007, some seventeen states require some sort of identification at the polls, although it may not necessarily be a photo ID. The use of photo IDs has been promoted as a means of precluding voter fraud, but opponents of such requirements argue that they just restrict poor and minority voters who often do not have a driver's license or a passport. The U.S. Court of Appeals for the

Seventh Circuit recently upheld an Indiana voter photo ID law as constitutional; but the U.S. Supreme Court has agreed to review this issue involved in the combined cases of *Crawford v. Marion County Election Board* and *Indiana Democratic Party v. Rokita.*

Elections serve a variety of functions in a democracy in addition to selecting officials and determining policy issues. They provide the mechanism for the voters—the popular sovereigns—to hold their officials accountable for actions taken on their behalf. Moreover, election campaigns educate the voters and provide a forum for individuals to participate in the process of governing. Elections legitimize the policy decisions and authority of elected officials because the voters have had an opportunity to be heard and participate in the process. By the same token, the voters may bear responsibility for bad policies and bad elected officials. Democracy is, among other things, a way to spread the blame for political blunders.

More on this topic:

Baker v. Carr, *p. 57*

Campaign Financing, p. 77

Civil Rights, p. 96

Reapportionment, p. 453

Representative Government, p. 464

Although the Supreme Court in the case of BUSH V. GORE (2000) seemed to emphasize the need for finality in the election process over the right of every voter to have his or her vote properly counted, the Court has on numerous occasions indicated that the right to vote and the equality of every person's vote is fundamental under America's constitutional democracy (see BAKER V. CARR). After the 2000 election problems in Florida and elsewhere, a private commission recommended a number of reforms, including federal standards for voter registration, provisional balloting, voting equipment designed to minimize errors, and uniform statewide definitions of what constitutes a vote for each type of voting machine. A nation that can send people into space and that perceives itself as the world's leading democracy ought to be able to conduct elections accurately and efficiently.

Electoral College

The term *electoral college*, although not found in the Constitution, is used to describe the body of electors who are chosen by the citizens of each state every four years and who in turn elect the PRESIDENT and VICE PRESIDENT of the United States. The number of presidential electors each state is entitled to equals the state's total number of senators and representatives in Congress.

Most other nations choose their president in direct, popular ELECTIONS. Some exceptions, in addition to the United States, are Indonesia and Switzerland. Indonesia's constitution (1995) states that the president is to be elected to a five-year term by the people's consultative assembly, which includes the legislature and delegates from territorial regions and other groups. Switzerland's constitution (2000) provides that the president of the Swiss confederation is elected for a one-year term by the national legislature from the members of an executive body called the federal council.

Alexis de Tocqueville (1805–59), author of *Democracy in America* (1835), wryly observed that the founders of the United States had "only to choose the least dangerous of the various modes of election [for selecting the president]; the rules they laid down in this respect admirably complete the guarantees already provided by the physical and political structure of the country." Article II, section 1, of the Constitution mandates that presidential electors be chosen by each state "in such Manner as the Legislature thereof may direct." In essay 68 of *The Federalist* (1787–88) (see FEDERALIST PAPERS), entitled "The Mode of Electing the President," ALEXANDER HAMILTON noted that "[t]he mode of appointment of the Chief Magistrate [president] of the United States is almost the only part of the system, of any consequence, which has escaped without severe censure or…the slightest mark of approbation from its opponents." Even so, the system of electing the president underwent a radical change fairly soon.

The FRAMERS OF THE CONSTITUTION devised the electoral college system to establish a balance between popular democracy and aristocratic elements as well as between the interests of the large and small states. They expected that GEORGE WASHINGTON would be the first president of the United States, and he was—chosen unanimously by the electoral college—but the framers feared that succeeding candidates would never command such unanimity and that state electors would rarely muster a majority for any one candidate. Thus the framers provided that if no candidate receives a majority of the electoral college vote the House of Representatives is to decide the election. The Constitution also originally specified that the candidate with the greatest number of votes became president and the one with the second-greatest number became vice president.

In the 1800 presidential election, THOMAS JEFFERSON and Aaron Burr received an equal number of electoral votes. As called for, the matter went to the House of Representatives, where more than thirty ballots were required before one candidate—Jefferson—eventually received a majority. To prevent similar problems in the future, the Twelfth Amendment was adopted in 1804, providing that electors vote separately for president and vice president, "one of whom, at least, shall not be an inhabitant of the same state with themselves." If a majority is not reached, then the House chooses the president, with each state delegation casting one vote. After the amendment, the only time the House chose the president was in 1824, when it selected John Quincy Adams. The amendment also changed the Constitution's original provision making the candidate with the second-highest vote total vice president, which had resulted in a president and a vice president from different political parties. If no vice presidential candidate receives a majority, the Senate is to select one.

The emergence of strong POLITICAL PARTIES and the development of the two-party political system led by 1836 to the requirement by all states except one that the winner of a statewide popular election for president be accorded all the state's electoral votes. In this winner-take-all system, also referred to as "unit voting," citizens in each state vote not for the president and vice president but for a slate of party electors who then serve as delegates to the electoral college and who are pledged to vote for their party's presidential and vice presidential candidates. The president and vice president, although voted on separately by the electors, run together on a single-party ticket, so that whichever candidate is elected president will have as vice president the person who ran on the same ticket.

The electoral college, as amended by the Twelfth Amendment and supplemented by the traditionally accepted two-party system, has worked relatively well, generally ensuring that even if two presidential tickets receive nearly equal popular votes, the margin in the electoral college is more decisive. This is important because even in a democracy clear-cut majority elections tend to give greater legitimacy to the winners. In the 1960 presidential election, for example, John F. Kennedy (1917–63) received 34,221,344 popular votes and Richard M. Nixon (1913–94) received 34,106,671; however, Kennedy won the electoral college vote by 303 to 219.

The indecisive results of the 2000 presidential election between George W. Bush (b. 1946) and Al Gore (b. 1948), involving an extremely close national popular vote and a disputed vote in Florida—which had a sufficient number of electoral votes to swing the election either way—almost led to a constitutional crisis. Gore's requests for recounts in key voting precincts resulted in decisions by Florida's supreme court and the U.S. Supreme Court, whose ruling in BUSH V. GORE (2000) rendered moot questions about the Florida election results and ensured Bush's election even though Gore won the popular vote nationwide. The crisis led initially to public reexamination of the electoral college system, but the focus later shifted to improving election procedures, particularly in Florida.

Relying on the electoral college can lead to the election of a president like Bush who does not receive a majority of the popular vote. In 1876 Rutherford B. Hayes (1822–93) defeated Samuel J. Tilden (1814–86) by one electoral vote (185 to 184), although he lost the popular vote by a wide margin (4,034,311 to 4,288,546). In 1888 Benjamin Harrison (1883–1901) over-

More on this topic:

Bush v. Gore, *p. 70*

Elections, *p. 181*

Political Parties, *p. 403*

whelmingly won the electoral vote 233 to 168, while losing the popular vote to Grover Cleveland (1837–1908) by 5,443,892 to 5,534,488. Nevertheless, the electoral college plays an important role in the government's federal structure (see FEDERALISM). States, through the votes of their citizens, have the final say in who is to be elected president of the United States. If the Constitution were ever amended to provide for the direct election of the president, the federal nature of the U.S. system of government would not be completely changed, but it would be diminished.

An interesting proposal, which would require states entering into an interstate compact to agree to cast their electoral votes for the winner of the popular vote in a presidential election, was adopted by the state of

The nine Colorado presidential electors cast their ballots for President George Bush and Vice President Dick Cheney in Denver's state capital after the 2004 elections. Donetta Davidson, Colorado's secretary of state, observes in the background.
Source: AP Images/Ed Andrieski

Maryland in 2007. The Constitution gives the states the power to decide how their electors are chosen, so any state can have its electoral votes cast as it pleases. If all the states and the District of Columbia entered into the compact, it would effectively create a national election for president and vice president, which would avoid the possibility of a candidate who received fewer votes taking office. It would also nullify the effect of third-party candidate spoilers, who siphon off votes from one of the two major-party candidates. Of course, a state would still be able to withdraw from the compact even after an election and change the way it would cast its votes. A recent proposal in California to have proportional electoral voting based on the percentage of votes presidential candidates received in the state seems to have lost steam.

Electors   *See* ELECTIONS; ELECTORAL COLLEGE.

Eleventh Amendment   *See* IMMUNITY; SOVEREIGNTY; *YOUNG, EX PARTE.*

Eligibility for Office   *See* QUALIFICATIONS FOR OFFICE.

Emergency Powers

"There are certain emergencies of nations in which expedients that in the ordinary state of things ought to be forborne become essential to the public weal," commented ALEXANDER HAMILTON in essay 36 of *The Federalist* (1787–88) (see FEDERALIST PAPERS). "And the government, from the possibility of such emergencies, ought ever to have the option of making use of them."

MILITARY ORDER: DETENTION, TREATMENT, AND TRIAL OF CERTAIN NON-CITIZENS IN THE WAR AGAINST TERRORISM (EXCERPTS)

By the authority vested in me as President and as Commander in Chief of the Armed Forces of the United States by the Constitution and the laws of the United States of America, including the Authorization for Use of Military Force Joint Resolution (Public Law 107–40, 115 Stat. 224) and sections 821 and 836 of Title 10, United States Code, it is hereby ordered as follows:

Section 1. Findings.

(a) International terrorists, including members of al Qaida, have carried out attacks on United States diplomatic and military personnel and facilities abroad and on citizens and property within the United States on a scale that has created a state of armed conflict that requires the use of the United States Armed Forces.

(b) In light of grave acts of terrorism and threats of terrorism, including the terrorist attacks on September 11, 2001, on the headquarters of the United States Department of Defense in the national capital region, on the World Trade Center in New York, and on civilian aircraft such as in Pennsylvania, I proclaimed a national emergency on September 14, 2001 (Proc. 7463, Declaration of National Emergency by Reason of Certain Terrorist Attacks).

(c) Individuals acting alone and in concert involved in international terrorism possess both the capability and the intention to undertake further terrorist attacks against the United States that, if not detected and prevented, will cause mass deaths, mass injuries, and massive destruction of property, and may place at risk the continuity of the operations of the United States Government.

(d) The ability of the United States to protect the United States and its citizens, and to help its allies and other cooperating nations protect their nations and their citizens, from such further terrorist attacks depends in significant part upon using the United States Armed Forces to identify terrorists and those who support them, to disrupt their activities, and to eliminate their ability to conduct or support such attacks.

(e) To protect the United States and its citizens, and for the effective conduct of military operations and prevention of terrorist attacks, it is necessary for individuals subject to this order pursuant to section 2 hereof to be detained, and, when tried, to be tried for violations of the laws of war and other applicable laws by military tribunals.

(f) Given the danger to the safety of the United States and the nature of international terrorism, and to the extent provided by and under this order, I find consistent with section 836 of Title 10, United States Code, that it is not practicable to apply in military commissions under this order the principles of law and the rules of evidence generally recognized in the trial of criminal cases in the United States district courts.

(g) Having fully considered the magnitude of the potential deaths, injuries, and property destruction that would result from potential acts of terrorism against the United States, and the probability that such acts will occur, I have determined that an extraordinary emergency exists for national defense purposes, that this emergency constitutes an urgent and compelling government interest, and that issuance of this order is necessary to meet the emergency.

Section 2. Definition and Policy.

(a) The term "individual subject to this order" shall mean any individual who is not a United States citizen with respect to whom I determine from time to time in writing that:

(1) there is reason to believe that such individual, at the relevant times,

(i) is or was a member of the organization known as al Qaida;

(ii) has engaged in, aided or abetted, or conspired to commit, acts of international terrorism, or acts in preparation therefore, that have caused, threaten to cause, or have as their aim to cause, injury to or adverse effects on the United States, its citizens, national security, foreign policy, or economy; or

(iii) has knowingly harbored one or more individuals described in subparagraphs (i) or (ii). . . .

Section 3. Detention Authority of the Secretary of Defense.

Any individual subject to this order shall be—

(a) detained at an appropriate location designated by the Secretary of Defense outside or within the United States;

(b) treated humanely, without any adverse distinction based on race, color, religion, gender, birth, wealth, or any similar criteria;

(c) afforded adequate food, drinking water, shelter, clothing, and medical treatment;

(d) allowed the free exercise of religion consistent with the requirements of such detention; and

(e) detained in accordance with such other conditions as the Secretary of Defense may prescribe.

Section 4. Authority of the Secretary of Defense Regarding Trials of Individuals Subject to this Order.

(a) Any individual subject to this order shall, when tried, be tried by military commission for any and all offenses triable by military commission that such individual is alleged to have committed, and may be punished in accordance with the penalties provided under applicable law, including life imprisonment or death. . . .

(c) Orders and regulations issued . . . shall include, but not be limited to, rules for the conduct of the proceedings of military

MILITARY ORDER: DETENTION, TREATMENT, AND TRIAL OF CERTAIN NON-CITIZENS IN THE WAR AGAINST TERRORISM (EXCERPTS) (CONTINUED)

commissions, including pretrial, trial, and post-trial procedures, modes of proof, issuance of process, and qualifications of attorneys, which shall at a minimum provide for—

(1) military commissions to sit at any time and any place . . . as the Secretary of Defense may provide;

(2) a full and fair trial, with the military commission sitting as the triers of both fact and law;

(3) admission of such evidence as would, in the opinion of the presiding officer of the military commission . . . have probative value to a reasonable person;

(4) in a manner consistent with the protection of [classified] information . . .

(A) the handling of, admission into evidence of, and access to materials and information, and

(B) the conduct, closure of, and access to proceedings;

(5) conduct of the prosecution by one or more attorneys designated by the Secretary of Defense and conduct of the defense by attorneys for the individual subject to this order;

(6) conviction only upon the concurrence of two-thirds of the members of the commission present at the time of the vote, a majority being present;

(7) sentencing only upon the concurrence of two-thirds of the members of the commission present at the time of the vote, a majority being present; and

(8) submission of the record of the trial, including any conviction or sentence, for review and final decision by me or by the Secretary of Defense if so designated by me for that purpose.

Section 7. Relationship to Other Law and Forums.

. . . (b) With respect to any individual subject to this order—

(1) military tribunals shall have exclusive jurisdiction with respect to offenses by the individual; and

(2) the individual shall not be privileged to seek any remedy or maintain any proceeding, directly or indirectly, or to have any such remedy or proceeding sought on the individual's behalf, in

(i) any court of the United States, or any State thereof,

(ii) any court of any foreign nation, or

(iii) any international tribunal. . . .

George W. Bush
The White House
November 13, 2001

A government's special requirements during an emergency are addressed in the constitutions of most countries. The Netherlands' constitution (1814, as revised through 1989), states: "The cases in which a state of emergency, as defined by Act of Parliament, may be declared by Royal Decree in order to maintain internal or external security shall be specified by Act of Parliament. The consequences of such a declaration shall be governed by Act of Parliament." Armenia's constitution (1995) provides that "in the event of an armed attack against or of an immediate danger to the Republic, or a declaration of war" by the legislature, the president of the republic "shall declare a state of martial law [temporary military rule as opposed to civilian rule] and may call for a general or partial mobilization [of the armed forces]."

Of the five reasons for writing the U.S. Constitution set forth in the document's PREAMBLE, two concern possible emergency situations: (1) to "insure domestic Tranquility," and (2) to "provide for the common defence."

DOMESTIC TRANQUILITY was on the minds of many FRAMERS OF THE CONSTITUTION when they met in Philadelphia in 1787. They had just witnessed the difficulties encountered by the commonwealth of Massachusetts and the country as a whole, under the ARTICLES OF CONFEDERATION (1781), in dealing with the emergency caused by Shays's Rebellion. This uprising, which began in 1786 and ended early the following year, was ignited by the Massachusetts legislature's failure to provide debt relief for small farmers caught in the depression after the Revolutionary War (1775–83). Daniel Shays, a farmer and former military officer, had organized a military attempt to force reform of the legal system and stem the tide of foreclosures on small farms.

Providing for the common defense—maintaining internal order and protecting the nation from external attack—is the most basic of government functions.

Providing for the common defense—maintaining internal order and protecting the nation from external attack—is the most basic of government functions. The massive response by the federal and state governments in the wake of the terrorist attacks on September 11, 2001, are ample evidence of the importance of being able to anticipate, avoid, and ultimately respond to emergency situations (see TERRORISM). Although Congress plays an important role in planning and financing actions required to respond to emergencies, the nation's main focus during emergencies is on the PRESIDENT. Rebellion and riots, economic crises, natural disasters, WAR, and terrorist attacks generally call for a rapid assessment and response, which is not the strong point of deliberative bodies like Congress.

Domestic Crises

The emergency powers of the national government and the president in particular come into play during times of domestic crisis. President GEORGE WASHINGTON confronted an emergency situation in 1792—the Whiskey Rebellion—when whiskey manufacturers in western Pennsylvania refused to pay federal taxes on their products. In a show of strength and decisiveness, Washington rode into the area at the head of fifteen thousand militia troops supplied by four states, including Pennsylvania. The rebellion was quelled without any soldiers being ordered into combat.

During times of domestic unrest, the president can call on the states' national guard units as well as federal troops to maintain order. As Article II, section 2, provides: "The President shall be Commander in Chief of the Army and Navy of the United States, and of the Militia of the several States, when called into the actual Service of the United States." Under Article IV, section 4: "The United States shall…protect each [state] against Invasion; and on Application of the Legislature, or of the Executive (when the Legislature cannot be convened) against domestic Violence."

In 1877, at the request of the West Virginia governor, President Rutherford B. Hayes (1822–93) sent in federal troops to keep striking railroad workers from disrupting train service. President Dwight D. Eisenhower (1890–1969) sent troops into Little Rock, Arkansas, in 1957 to enforce desegregation, which was required by the Supreme Court's decision in BROWN V. BOARD OF EDUCATION OF TOPEKA (1954) (see SEGREGATION). Declaring a state of national emergency in 1970, President Richard M. Nixon (1913–94) ordered federal troops to take over and keep running the New York postal system when a strike threatened to disrupt mail service nationally.

Beginning in 1917, presidents have had a strong tool to use in intervening in economic crises. That year, in the Trading with the Enemy Act, Congress granted the president authority to regulate aspects of the economy during wartime and other national emergencies. Because this authority was not revoked after World War I, presidents have continued to rely on it to take steps to stabilize the economy. During the Great Depression, President Franklin D. Roosevelt (1882–1945) used the act to justify closing the banks and thus averted financial disaster from the pending collapse of the nation's financial system.

Congress has also given the president statutory authority to declare states of emergencies in areas of the United States hard hit by natural disasters such as floods, hurricanes, tornadoes, earthquakes, and fires. A declaration of a state of emergency qualifies affected citizens and businesses for disaster relief through a number of federal funding programs as well as federally guaranteed home and business loans.

Wars, Declared and Undeclared

The first war declared under the new constitution was the War of 1812. President JAMES MADISON asked Congress for a formal declaration of war against the British as a result of Britain's capture of American commercial vessels and its arming of hostile Indian tribes, among other actions. According to Madison, going to war was a "solemn question which the Constitution wisely confides to the legislative department of the Government." According to Article I, section 8: "The Congress shall have Power...To declare War...."

Before the Civil War (1861–65), presidents relied on their power as commander in chief and sparingly used other emergency powers. But when hostilities began in 1861, President ABRAHAM LINCOLN, on his own, declared a blockade of southern ports, mobilized state militias, and took other measures to begin the prosecution of the war while Congress was out of session. Lincoln justified his actions on the basis of his INHERENT POWERS as president and as commander in chief, and Congress retroactively approved them. The Supreme Court, however, in *Ex parte Merryman* (1861), declared Lincoln's emergency suspension of the writ of HABEAS CORPUS unconstitutional. And in *Ex parte Milligan* (1866), the Court held that the president lacked constitutional authority to use military courts behind the lines of the Union Army, where civilian courts were available.

During the two world wars, Congress delegated broad powers to the presidents. During World War I, President Woodrow Wilson (1856–1924) was given the power, among others, to seize defense-related facilities and regulate and censor external communications. Before the United States officially entered World War II, President Franklin D. Roosevelt (1882–1945), relying on his emergency powers, took a number of steps to prepare for war, including creating wartime executive agencies and coordinating private industry without express congressional approval.

Reacting to the Japanese bombing of Pearl Harbor in Hawaii on December 7, 1941, the United States also ordered Japanese Americans out of their homes along the West Coast and into relocation camps. Civilian Exclusion Order no. 34, issued by military authorities in California pursuant to an act of Congress, met with some resistance, and the case of one citizen charged with noncompliance ended up at the Supreme Court. In *Korematsu v. United States* (1944), the Court upheld his conviction, saying that "because Congress, reposing its confidence in this time of war in our military leaders—as inevitably it must—determined that they should have the power to do just this.... We cannot—by availing ourselves of the calm perspective of hindsight—now say that at that time these actions were unjustified." Recognizing the questionable constitutionality of the relocation order, a federal district court in the 1980s set aside the conviction of Toyosaburo Korematsu and others who had refused to leave their homes.

The president's designation as commander in chief of the ARMED FORCES confers certain powers that can be used in other constitutional emergencies short of war. The Korean War (1950–53), an undeclared war, resulted in the significant Supreme Court case *YOUNGSTOWN SHEET AND TUBE CO. V. SAWYER* (1952). Fearing that an announced strike of steelworkers would disrupt the supply of ammunition for American soldiers helping South Korea defend itself against the communist invasion from the north, President Harry S. Truman (1884–1972) ordered the federal government to seize the steel mills to keep them running. The Court, however, held that his action was unconstitutional because it relied neither on

President Clinton presents Fred Korematsu with a Presidential Medal of Freedom during a White House ceremony in 1998. Korematsu had challenged a World War II order to relocate Japanese Americans.

Source: AP Images/Dennis Cook

congressional authorization—in fact, Congress had earlier voted against granting the president this very power—or on powers found in the Constitution.

The federal government's emergency powers, especially the powers of the president, tend to expand with the seriousness of the emergency. "If the Union's existence were constantly menaced," wrote the French politician and political scientist Alexis de Tocqueville (1805–59) in *Democracy in America* (1835), "one would see the prestige of the executive growing, because of what was expected from it and of what it did." As many framers of the Constitution were aware, the English philosopher John Locke (1632–1704), in describing the English constitution, commented on the residual well of executive power that could be tapped by the monarch during times of emergency.

The terrorist attacks on America of September 11, 2001, and the ensuing war on terrorism forced President George W. Bush (b. 1946) to dip into a similar well of constitutional authority. As the U.S. Code provides in Title 50, chapter 34, subchapter II, section 1621, "With respect to Acts of Congress authorizing the exercise, during the period of a national emergency, of any special or extraordinary power, the President is authorized to declare such national emergency." By presidential proclamation on September 14, 2001, Bush issued a Declaration of National Emergency by Reason of Certain Terrorist Attacks. The next month Congress enacted the USA PATRIOT ACT of 2001. The act, which was reauthorized, as amended, by Congress in 2006, expanded a number of LAW ENFORCEMENT powers, including surveillance and border protection measures that might infringe individual constitutional rights such as PRIVACY, freedom of SPEECH, the right to TRAVEL, and freedom from unreasonable SEARCH AND SEIZURE.

Eminent Domain   *See* ECONOMIC LIBERTY; JUST COMPENSATION.

Employment Discrimination

Throughout American history, discrimination in employment has taken many forms and affected many groups. Employment discrimination extends to hiring and firing employees, job assignments, training, promotion, pay, and fringe benefits such as leave, insurance coverage, unemployment compensation, and retirement. Groups that have been most severely affected include blacks, WOMEN, ethnic MINORITIES, religious groups, people of various national origins, older persons, and DISABLED PERSONS.

The Constitution does not guarantee a right to work (see LABOR), although the constitutions of some other countries, including those of Honduras (1982), Italy (1948), and Ukraine (1996), do. The United Nations' Universal Declaration of Human Rights (1948) guarantees the right to work, prohibits any kind of job discrimination, and mandates equal pay for equal work. The capitalist economic system embraced by the United States basically rejects all government interference in private business activity except what is absolutely necessary, which sometimes makes it more difficult for the U.S. government to monitor and enforce its antidiscrimination laws.

Types of Discrimination

Racial. The CIVIL RIGHTS movement that began after the Supreme Court's decision in *BROWN V. BOARD OF EDUCATION OF TOPEKA*(1954), which called for an end to SEGREGATION in the public schools, set in motion a closer scrutiny by legislators and courts of other areas of discrimination, including job discrimination. A decade earlier, when an all-white union sided with a railroad to terminate black firemen, the Supreme Court in *Steele v. Louisville and Nashville Railroad Co.* (1944) declared that federal labor laws required UNIONS to represent all employees fairly "without hostile discrimination."

Although the Constitution does not in so many words forbid discrimination on the basis of race, sex, national origin, religion, disability, or age, such discrimination often violates federal laws, including Title VII of the Civil Rights Act of 1964. This act was passed by Congress to prohibit discrimination in many areas, including public accommodations (Title II), federally funded programs (Title VI), and employment (Title VII). In addition, in *Johnson v. Railway Express Agency, Inc.* (1975), the Supreme Court found that a surviving section of the Civil Rights Act of 1866 was still applicable to employment discrimination by race in the private sector.

The Supreme Court in *Fitzpatrick v. Bitzer* (1976) upheld the extension of Title VII of the 1964 act to the states against a challenge that it violated the Eleventh Amendment (1795), which prohibits suits against a state by a citizen of another state or of a foreign country. The Court found the amendment of the 1964 act to be a constitutionally proper exercise by Congress of its power, granted by the Fourteenth Amendment (1868), section 5, "to enforce, by appropriate legislation, the provisions of [the amendment]."

Earlier, in *Griggs v. Duke Power Co.* (1971), the Supreme Court in an 8–0 decision upheld an allegation of discrimination against black applicants for jobs by a North Carolina power company, which required them to have a high school diploma or pass an intelligence test for jobs where such requirements bore no relation to successful job performance. The Court declared that the 1964 Civil Rights Act required "the removal of artificial, arbitrary, and unnecessary barriers to employment when the barriers operate invidiously to discriminate on the basis of racial or other impermissible classification."

Religious. In *Braunfield v. Brown* (1961), the Supreme Court indicated that a state law requiring stores to be closed on Sundays was not a violation of the Constitution's freedom of RELIGION provision even though such a law inconvenienced and reduced profits for persons whose religion required them to observe the Sabbath or Saturday as a day of rest. Two years later, in *Sherbert v. Verner* (1963), however, the Court upheld an appeal by a person who was denied state unemployment compensation because her religion forbade her from working on Saturdays, which reduced her ability to seek new employment as required to be entitled to benefits. In this case the Court found that the disqualification from compensation imposed a burden on the person's right to the free exercise of her religion and was not justified by any compelling state reason. In *McDaniel v. Paty* (1978), the justices found unconstitutional a state law barring members of the clergy from holding certain public offices.

In an unusual religious discrimination case also involving unemployment compensation, *Employment Division, Department of Human Resources of Oregon v. Smith* (1990), the Supreme Court found no infringement of religious freedom in the denial of unemployment compensation to drug and alcohol abuse counselors who were fired by the state for the work-related "misconduct" of taking peyote in a Native American religious ceremony. Justice Antonin Scalia (b. 1936), in a technically crafted opinion for the five-member Court majority (there was one concurring opinion and three dissenters), concluded that religious freedom could not be asserted in order to evade an otherwise proper state law unless some other important right such as freedom of SPEECH or assembly (see ASSEMBLY AND ASSOCIATION) were also infringed. According to Scalia, "The only decisions in which we have held that the First Amendment bars application of a neutral, generally applicable law to religiously motivated action have involved not the Free Exercise [of Religion] Clause alone, but the Free Exercise Clause in conjunction with other constitutional protections...."

National Origin. In *Graham v. Richardson* (1971), a case involving the denial of welfare benefits, the Supreme Court held that ALIENS are "a prime example, of a single 'discrete and insular' minority for whom...heightened judicial solicitude is appropriate." Such heightened judicial solicitude (see STRICT SCRUTINY) has led the Court to strike down state statutes that bar aliens from competitive civil service positions in state governments, as in *Sugarman v. Dougall* (1973), and that

Myra Bradwell, founder of the **Chicago Legal News,** *passed the bar in 1869 but was denied admission. She later pressured Illinois to give everyone access to a profession.*
Source: Library of Congress

prohibit aliens from practicing professions such as law, as in *In re Griffiths* (1973). It is not unconstitutional, however, for states to bar aliens from some jobs that are of a political nature or that relate to community values, such as public school teachers and police officers.

Sex. Perhaps the most condescending and egregious example of the Supreme Court's support for discrimination against women in employment was uttered by Justice Joseph P. Bradley (1813–92) in *Bradwell v. Illinois* (1873). In a Court decision denying the right of the noted Myra Bradwell (1831–94) to practice law, he pronounced that "[t]he natural and proper timidity and delicacy which belongs to the female sex evidently unfits it for many of the occupations of civil life.... This is the law of the Creator."

The change in the constitutional grounding of equal opportunity for women began in earnest in the 1970s, in the wake of the civil rights movement. While attempts to ratify the Equal Rights Amendment between 1972 and 1982 failed (see AMENDMENTS), they nevertheless resulted in a heightened awareness of women's employment rights at the national level—under the Civil Rights Act of 1964, as amended, for example—and in the states. The majority of the states have constitutional provisions prohibiting discrimination on the basis of sex, or they have similar statutory provisions, as do Tennessee and South Dakota. In 1971 the Supreme Court rejected an employer's policy of refusing to hire women who had preschool children, although it hired men with young children. But in *Personnel Administration of Massachusetts v. Feeny* (1979), the Court concluded that a state law granting preferences in employment decisions to veterans, who overwhelmingly happened to be males, did not irrationally disadvantage women.

Equal Employment Opportunity Commission

The U.S. Equal Employment Opportunity Commission was established by Congress under Title VII of the Civil Rights Act of 1964. Headquartered in Washington, D.C., the agency has fifty field offices throughout the country. The commission's main purpose is to enforce the act's Title VII, which prohibits discrimination in employment on the basis of race, color, sex, or national origin, as well as violations under provisions of the Equal Pay Act (1963); Age Discrimination Act (1967); Rehabilitation Act (1973), which prohibits employment discrimination against federal employees with disabilities; Americans with Disabilities Act (1990); and Civil Rights Act of 1991, which provides monetary damages in cases of intentional discrimination.

The EEOC, which reported receiving 75,428 private sector charges of discrimination in fiscal year 2005 and 75,768 in fiscal year 2006, investigates charges of discrimination and attempts to settle valid claims; it may also become involved in litigating private-sector discrimination charges. In *Espinoza v. Farah Manufacturing Co. Inc.* (1973), a case alleging employment discrimination by a private employer who failed to hire a person because she was a Mexican citizen, the Supreme Court rejected the EEOC's discrimination guideline that "discrimination on the basis of citizenship is tantamount to discrimination on the basis of national origin." Instead, the Court found that Title VII of the Civil Rights Act of 1964 "does not proscribe discrimination on the basis of [being an alien]."

For most people jobs are crucial for their livelihood. When the playing field is unequal for either applicants or employees, the victims of employment discrimination can legitimately question the underlying premise of the American legal and economic system: that the United States is a land of opportunity for all. The pursuit of happiness sanctioned by the DECLARATION OF INDEPENDENCE (1776) includes the right to work on equal terms with others and to receive equal pay, training, promotion consideration, and other job benefits based on equal work and ability, regardless of race, religion, sex, national origin, or other irrelevant considerations. The system still needs fine tuning, however, before the Constitution's potential for ensuring equality for all is fulfilled.

Enumerated Powers *See* POWERS.

Enumeration *See* CENSUS; REAPPORTIONMENT.

Environment

"We must acknowledge that uncertainty is inherent in managing natural resources, recognize [that] it is usually easier to prevent environmental damage than to repair it later, and shift the burden of proof away from those advocating protection toward those proposing an action that may be harmful," warned Christine Todd Whitman in an October 2000 speech during her tenure as governor of New Jersey, before she was named to head the U.S. Environmental Protection Agency under President George W. Bush (b. 1946).

The environment—the physical and cultural conditions under which humans live—is not limited to the air, land, and water necessary for our survival. It includes biodiversity, the wide range of plants and animals needed for a balanced and viable environment, recreational facilities, natural resources, and historic artifacts. Some of the earliest cases relating to the environment that came before the Supreme Court involved state game protection laws. In *New York ex rel. Silz v. Hesterberg* (1908), the Court upheld a ban on the possession of protected wildlife even in the case of a dealer of imported game who possessed "one dead body of an imported grouse...taken in Russia." With respect to the preservation of historic landmarks, the Court in *Penn Central Transportation Co. v. City of New York* (1978) upheld New York City's landmarks ordinance, under which the owners of Grand Central Terminal were denied the right to build a fifty-three-story office building on top of the historic train station, thus losing millions of dollars in potential revenue.

Protecting the General Welfare

The environment was not a specific concern of the FRAMERS OF THE CONSTITUTION in 1787 except as encompassed in the phrase "general Welfare," used in the PREAMBLE and in Article I, section 8. English law dealt with offenses against public HEALTH, including nuisances and noxious trades. In his *Commentaries on the Laws of England* (1765–70), William Blackstone (1723–80) referred to "those acts of omission which consist of allowing any premises to remain uncleansed,...or in permitting any pool, ditch, gutter, water-course, privy, urinal, cesspool, drain, or ashpit, to be so foul...as to be injurious to health."

Today, however, the range of possible pollutants of the environment is far greater and the scope of their effects extends worldwide, as in the case of global warming. In addition to industrial waste, emissions from burning fossil fuels, extensive deforestation, overcultivation of farmland, and

Clear-cut timber chokes a river in Michigan at the turn of the twentieth century. Extensive logging in the absence of environmental controls destroyed this natural resource, ending the state's leading position in the lumber industry by 1910.
Source: Library of Congress

nuclear waste resulting from the ordinary lawful conduct of human activities, the earth's citizens confront threats of biological, chemical, and nuclear pollution of the environment from terrorist attacks, wars, accidents, and natural disasters. All of these potential environmental hazards make protection of the environment a major concern for all countries.

A number of national constitutions today include express language addressing the environment. "Everyone has the right to be informed about the status of the environment and its protection," states Albania's constitution (1998). Thailand's constitution (1997) acknowledged the "right of a person to share with the State and communities in the preservation and exploitation of natural resources and biological diversity and in the protection, promotion and preservation of the quality of the environment...."

Constitutional Bases

Although the Constitution does not specifically mandate that citizens are entitled to a safe and clean environment, it does provide some mechanisms for the federal government to regulate aspects of the environment. One important source of federal power is the COMMERCE clause in Article I, section 8, which states: "The Congress shall have Power...To regulate Commerce with foreign Nations, and among the several States, and with the Indian Tribes." On the basis of this clause, the Supreme Court has in fits and starts gradually expanded Congress's power to deal with activities that can be described as affecting commerce inside and outside the country.

SIGNIFICANT FEDERAL ENVIRONMENTAL LEGISLATION

Year	Act	Purpose
1864	Yosemite Land Grant Bill	Granted Yosemite Valley and Mariposa Big Tree Grove to California for preservation as a public park
1872	Yellowstone Act	Established Yellowstone National Park as the world's first national park
1890	Yosemite Act	Established Yosemite National Park
1891	Forest Reserve Act	Authorized the president to set aside forests as public reservations
1897	Forest Management Act	Regulated cutting and provided protection for forests
1900	Lacey Act	Supported state laws against commercial hunting of wildlife
1906	Antiquities Act	Authorized the president to designate national monuments
1913	Weeks-McLean Act	Gave the federal government responsibility for migratory game birds
1916	National Park Service Organic Act	Established the National Park Service to conserve scenery and wildlife in national parks
1918	Migratory Bird Treaty Act	Set hunting limits for migratory birds and banned trade in birds and bird parts
1929	Migratory Bird Conservation Act	Created a national system of waterfowl refuges
1935	Historic Sites Act	Declared historic preservation to be a national policy and set up a landmarks program
1955	Air Pollution Control Act	Declared air pollution to be a national problem
1956	Fish and Wildlife Act	Established a national fish and wildlife policy and sanctioned the development of refuges
1960	Multiple Use Sustained Yield Act	Established a policy of promoting multiple uses in the national forests, including recreation, wildlife, fishing, and hunting as well as logging
1963	Clean Air Act	Set emission standards for power plants and steel mills
1964	Wilderness Act	Created the National Wilderness Preservation System
1965	Land and Water Conservation Act	Authorized acquisition of land for recreation and park use as well as conservation
1966	Endangered Species Act	Supported discretionary federal protection of endangered and threatened species
1966	National Historic Preservation Act	Required that federal agencies consider impacts on historic properties and created the Advisory Council on Historic Preservation
1966	National Wildlife Refuge System Administration Act	Established the National Wildlife Refuge System
1968	National Trails Act	Established the National Trails System
1968	National Wild and Scenic Rivers Act	Established the National Wild and Scenic Rivers System
1969	National Environmental Policy Act	Created the Council on Environmental Quality and required that federal agencies assess the impact of major projects on the environment
1970	Clean Air Act	Strengthened automobile emission standards
1971	Alaska Native Claims Settlement Act	Earmarked Alaskan lands for preservation and settled native land claims
1972	Clean Water Act	Set objectives for restoring and maintaining clean water
1972	Water Pollution Control Act	Regulated the discharge of pollutants into U.S. waters
1973	Endangered Species Act	Created the Endangered Species List, encompassing federal, state, and private lands
1974	Archaeological and Historic Preservation Act	Required that federal construction projects protect archaeological sites
1977	Clean Air Act Amendments	Addressed air quality and visibility in national parks and wilderness areas
1980	Alaska National Interests Lands Conservation Act	Designated more than 100 million acres of parks, wildlife refuges, and wilderness areas in Alaska
1980	"Superfund" Act	Taxed chemical and petroleum industries to promote clean air and water
1990	Clean Air Act	Set national air quality standards, delegating major control efforts to the states
1990	Oil Pollution Act	Strengthened the ability of the Environmental Protection Agency to respond to oil spills
1990	Pollution Prevention Act	Made preventing or reducing pollution at its source a national policy
1990	Great Lakes Critical Programs Act	Set cleanup deadlines for the Great Lakes
1994	California Desert Protection Act	Created Mojave National Preserve; increased National Wilderness Preservation System
1997	National Wildlife Refuge System Improvement Act	Made wildlife conservation a major priority and encouraged science-based management

SOURCE: Carley, Rachel. *Wilderness A to Z: The Essential Guide to the Great Outdoors.* New York: Fireside, Simon and Schuster, 2001. As updated by the author.

The courts justify environmental regulations partly on the basis that sources of environmental pollution include automobiles and ships, both of which may be involved in interstate commerce, as well as agricultural products, livestock, and many chemical products, such as oil and gasoline, which can cause pollution if mishandled or spilled in transit. The National Environmental Policy Act (1969), which went into effect on January 1, 1970, and was amended in 1975 and 1982, and the Clean Air Act (1990) have been upheld by federal courts on the basis of the commerce clause. One purpose of the 1969 act was to "declare a national policy which will encourage productive and enjoyable harmony between man and his environment...." The Clean Air Act, among other requirements, gives the federal government authority to set "national ambient air quality standards."

The treaty power of the United States is another source of constitutionality for federal environmental regulations (see TREATIES). In the landmark case *Missouri v. Holland* (1920), the Supreme Court held that although Congress might not have power under the Constitution to directly protect migratory birds in the states, when the power was exercised in accordance with the provisions of a valid treaty between the United States and Canada, as in this case, the exercise of such power was constitutional.

Congress also has explicit power, granted in Article IV, section 3, "to dispose of and make all needful Rules and Regulations respecting the Territory or other Property belonging to the United States..." (see TERRITORY). The Supreme Court has ruled that when Congress acts pursuant to this constitutional provision, its legislation overrides conflicting state laws. In *Kleppe v. New Mexico* (1976), the Court unanimously upheld a federal regulation protecting wild-roaming horses and burros on federal lands. The taxing power found in Article I, section 8 (see TAXATION), permits Congress to set fees for emissions and effluents that may affect the environment. Article I, section 10, which requires Congress's consent to any interstate compacts, as cited by the Supreme Court in *West Virginia ex rel. Dyer v. Sims* (1951), permits the federal government to influence interstate agreements regarding the environment.

A relatively recent decision by the Supreme Court in *Department of Transportation v. Public Citizen* (2004), however, illustrates the limitations of the federal government's ability to deal effectively with environmental issues. In that case, the Court found that because the Federal Motor Carrier Safety Administration lacked authority to prevent cross-border operations of Mexican carriers, neither the Clean Air Act of 1990 nor the National Environmental Policy Act of 1969 required the agency to evaluate the environmental impact of such crossings. Another decision by the Court in 2004, in *Bates v. Dow AgroSciences LLC*, halted the lower federal courts' practice of broadly interpreting federal statutes to preempt state remedies for harm done by pollutants—in this case, by a weed killer that stunted the growth of peanut plants.

Environmental Protection Agency

The national importance of environmental protection led to the creation of the Environmental Protection Agency in 1970 by consolidating parts of five departments and agencies into a single, independent agency (see ADMINISTRATIVE AGENCIES). The EPA's administrator and deputy administrator are appointed by the president, confirmed by the Senate, and serve at the pleasure of the president.

The EPA makes regulations and administers environmental programs enacted by Congress. It has enforcement authority to impose fines and institute criminal proceedings against polluters. The agency also promotes environmental safety and protection and negotiates compliance with polluters to accomplish its goals without unduly disrupting or damaging businesses. The EPA's responsibilities have increased with the passage of environmental legislation by Congress, such as the "Superfund" law, the Comprehensive Environmental Response, Compensation, and Liability Act (1980), intended to assist in cleaning up pollution; the Clean Water Act (1987); and the Clean Air Act (1990). The Supreme Court in *Whitman, Administrator of Environmental Protection Agency v. American Trucking Association, Inc.* (2001) declared in part that the Clean Air Act does not permit the EPA administrator to take into consideration the cost that might be incurred as a result of setting national ambient air quality standards.

A decision in the same vein, in *Alaska Department of Environmental Conservation v. Environmental Protection Agency* (2004), held that the Clean Air Act authorizes the EPA to stop construction of a major polluting facility allowed under state authority when the EPA determines that the state's conclusion as to whether the facility was equipped with the "best available [pollution] control technology" was unreasonable under the applicable federal law. But in *Rapanos v. United States* (2006), the Court defined the scope of the act narrowly to preclude the U.S. Army Corps of Engineers from preventing the backfilling, and thus the destruction of, three wetland areas adjacent to navigable waters of the United States, over which the federal government claimed to have jurisdiction.

President George H. W. Bush (b. 1924) attempted to raise the EPA to a cabinet-level department (see CABINET), but Congress has not approved this change. President Bill Clinton (b. 1946) also supported making the EPA a cabinet-level department, allotting a seat at his cabinet meetings for the EPA administrator.

In his six years in office, President Richard M. Nixon supported a number of landmark environmental bills, including the creation of the Environmental Protection Agency.
Source: Library of Congress

Protecting the nation's environment is a concern at all levels of government: local, state, and federal. The basic problem for the federal government, however, often has been finding constitutional grounds for enforcing national environmental laws at the state and local levels without overstepping the bounds between state and federal jurisdiction created by the Constitution (see FEDERALISM). In *Solid Waste Agency of Northern Cook County v. U.S. Army Corps of Engineers* (2001), the Supreme Court declared that STATES' RIGHTS trumped the national interest in environmental protection. In this instance the Court concluded that the Constitution does not give the federal government authority to regulate nonnavigable bodies of water located wholly within one state. But in *Massachusetts v. Environmental Protection Agency* (2007), by a 5–4 decision, the Court found, based on scientific evidence—some of which the EPA itself supplied—that Massachusetts and other states were experiencing the deleterious effects of global warming and that the EPA had the authority to redress the situation, despite claiming that it did not. It is perhaps too early to predict the direction the Court will go in future cases involving national and state interests in protecting the environment and citizens from the harmful effect of changes in the environment caused by human activity. The current trend in public opinion, as encouraged by many members of the scientific community and former vice president Al Gore, seems to be that much more can and should be done in this area.

Equal Protection

The notion of equality of all citizens, or at least those persons eligible to participate in a DEMOC-RACY, predates the American experiment in self-government. Discussing how to preserve a constitution, Aristotle, the Greek philosopher who lived in the fourth century B.C.E., argued that rulers "should never wrong the ambitious in a matter of honour, or the common people in a matter of money; and they should treat one another and their fellow-citizens in a spirit of equality. The equality which the friends of democracy seek to establish for the multitude is not only just but likewise expedient among equals."

Both the social compact theory of democracy—that there is a tacit agreement between the rulers and the ruled that legitimizes democratic governments—and the notion that SOVEREIGNTY in a democracy is vested in the citizens lead to the logical conclusion that all citizens of a democracy are equal with respect to their constitution and the laws enacted pursuant to it. In looking to the intent of the FRAMERS OF THE CONSTITUTION for guidance in matters concerning equality, it must be remembered that in 1789 WOMEN and slaves (see SLAVERY) were denied the rights of citizenship granted to adult white males. Although no aristocracy or class distinctions existed as in England (Article I, section 9, prohibited titles of nobility), equality was recognized to exist only among white adult male owners of PROPERTY.

The first constitutional effort to expand equality was the Thirteenth Amendment (1865), prohibiting slavery. The Civil Rights Act of 1866 guaranteed that all citizens, "of every race and color [including former slaves but not women], shall have the same right...as is enjoyed by white citizens...." Two years later the Fourteenth Amendment (1868) was approved to ensure the act's constitutionality, providing in part: "No State shall make or enforce any law which shall abridge the privileges and immunities of citizens of the United States; nor shall any State deprive any person of life, liberty, or property, without due process of law; nor deny to any person within its jurisdiction the equal protection of the laws."

The constitutions of a number of other countries, including Germany (1949) and Colombia (1991), guarantee their citizens similar equality before the law or equal protection of the law. Many also include a list of types of DISCRIMINATION—for example, sex, race, and national origin—that may not be used to deny equal protection. How all these equal protection guarantees are applied raises a number of questions: What constitutes equal treatment? When is equal treatment unjust rather than just? And what government interests can override equal treatment?

"Separate but Equal"

Even at the time of the Fourteenth Amendment's ratification, the term *citizens of the United States* was not intended by the male legislators who approved it to fully include women. Black males who were formerly slaves—supposedly the direct beneficiaries of the equal protection clause—were still considered outside its scope because of decisions by the courts, including the SUPREME COURT, restricting its effect. In addition, de facto discrimination against African Americans by persons in positions of economic and political power, particularly in the South, significantly limited the effect of the equal protection clause (see RACIAL DISCRIMINATION).

A case in point is *Plessy v. Ferguson* (1896). The Supreme Court decided that the equality meant by the Fourteenth Amendment was political and not social equality. Therefore, "separate but equal" train accommodations restricting to "Negro" railroad cars those with as little as one-eighth African blood—a practice, the Court said, that had been established by custom and tradition to preserve peace and public order—was deemed constitutionally acceptable. The "separate but equal" principle on which this ruling was based, which perpetuated the treatment of a large segment of American citizens as second-class citizens, would stand for sixty years until *BROWN v. BOARD OF EDUCATION OF TOPEKA* (1954).

Because all the rights and privileges guaranteed under the Fourteenth Amendment were not spelled out in detail, state officials and the courts were free to limit them. In addition to the "separate but equal" interpretation, the Supreme Court also began to use the "state action" doctrine, asserting that the Constitution applies only to government action and not to actions of individuals. By 1927 Justice OLIVER WENDELL HOLMES JR. declared this reasoning to be the "last resort of constitutional arguments."

"Suspect Classifications"

After World War II, the booming economy, the aftermath of Nazi Germany's insidious racial discrimination, and new members on the Supreme Court led to a new era of expansion and protection of rights using the Fourteenth Amendment's equal protection clause. Under Chief Justice Earl Warren (1891–1974), appointed by President Dwight D. Eisenhower (1890–1969) in 1953, the Supreme Court ended school segregation in 1954 with *Brown v. Board of Education of Topeka*. The Warren Court relaxed reliance on "state action" and heightened the standard of review for legislation. "Suspect classifications" on the basis of race or sex were carefully considered by the Court, as were attempts to discriminate against citizens' fundamental interests under the Constitution. The government had a new burden to prove that any actions infringing the rights of citizens or groups of citizens were justified.

The CIVIL RIGHTS movement that gained momentum after the *Brown* decision brought the Civil Rights Act of 1964, which statutorily extended many of the rights, especially to African Americans, that the Court had found in the equal protection clause, such as equality in public accommodations, restaurants, and hotels. Full equality of citizenship became the goal. AFFIRMATIVE ACTION—requiring race-conscious preferences to offset entrenched political, economic, educational, and social discrimination—became the farthest reach of the idea of equality of citizenship. State and national governments also began to take steps to assist other MINORITIES who had historically been discriminated against, such as women and Hispanic Americans.

Retrenchment

Since 1985 the Supreme Court has been pulling back on the previous decades' expansion of equality and equal rights. Courts including the Supreme Court generally give deference to the government's laws and actions. This means that they begin any inquiry into allegations of discrimination by assuming that the legislature—being an elected representative body—acts constitutionally. But in reviewing the Court's history of dealing with equal protection of the laws, Justice THURGOOD MARSHALL found that a sliding scale had been devised to deal with cases involving various degrees

CLOSER LOOK

In the decades following the Civil War, courts weighed in on a number of cases that determined whether blacks should have the same rights as whites. One of the most famous of these legal battles took place when the state of Louisiana passed a law requiring blacks and whites to ride in separate, but equal, railroad cars. A man named Homer Plessy, who was one-eighth black, was arrested after he tried to board a Louisiana railroad car that had been designated for use by white passengers only. He went to court, arguing that his civil rights had been violated.

The case, *Plessy v. Ferguson* (1896), wound through the Louisiana courts and eventually reached the Supreme Court. In a 7–1 decision, the justices sided with the state of Louisiana. They wrote that states could segregate public accommodations as long as facilities for both races were equal.

In fact, the justices at the time did not believe that segregation disadvantaged blacks. They wrote, "We consider the underlying fallacy of the plaintiff's argument to consist in the assumption that the enforced separation of the two races stamps the colored race with a badge of inferiority. If this be so, it is not by reason of anything found in the act, but solely because the colored race chooses to put that construction upon it."

The lone justice who dissented, John Marshall Harlan (1833–1911), was a former slaveholder who had become a supporter of civil rights after viewing the effects of discrimination firsthand. "Our Constitution is color-blind, and neither knows nor tolerates classes among citizens," Harlan wrote in one of the most famous dissents in Supreme Court history. "In respect of civil rights, all citizens are equal before the law."

Almost sixty years later, the Supreme Court revisited the issue and took Harlan's side. In 1954 the justices unanimously overturned the separate but equal doctrine, ordering an end to school segregation in the landmark case *Brown v. Board of Education of Topeka.*

<table>
<tr><td colspan="2">More on this topic:</td></tr>
<tr><td>Civil Rights, p. 96</td></tr>
<tr><td>Discrimination, p. 159</td></tr>
<tr><td>Minorities, p. 369</td></tr>
<tr><td>Women, p. 589</td></tr>
</table>

of infringement of equal protection. In some cases in which laws enacted by a legislature were alleged to be discriminatory, the Court would find a rational basis for the discrimination and thus uphold their constitutionality. There may be a rational reason, for example, for treating women and men differently with respect to pregnancy—a condition to which only women are subject.

The sliding scale was also applicable to laws or other government actions that called for heightened scrutiny or a somewhat lower level of scrutiny—intermediate scrutiny—by the Supreme Court (see STRICT SCRUTINY), because the unequal treatment involved suspect classifications. In *Cleburne v. Cleburne Living Center* (1985), for instance, the Court found a denial of equal protection in a municipality's refusal to grant a zoning variance for a home for the mentally retarded, using an even lower level of scrutiny because the case involved the disabled. In *Craig v. Boren* (1976), the Court moved the review of allegations of unequal treatment by the government in SEX DISCRIMINATION cases from the "rational basis" test to the higher level of examination, intermediate scrutiny.

In other more recent cases the Supreme Court has held that a military academy could not constitutionally exclude women, that discrimination against children of unmarried parents—including denying welfare benefits—is unconstitutional, and that discrimination against HOMOSEXUALS solely on the basis of their sexual orientation is unconstitutional even under the "rational basis" standard of review. But in *Nguyen v. Immigration and Naturalization Service* (2001), the Court rejected a claim that discriminating against children born out of wedlock overseas to fathers who are U.S. CITIZENS—as opposed to mothers who are U.S. citizens—is a violation of the equal protection clause; the Court hinged its distinction on the fact that a father's parentage is harder to establish than a mother's.

Chief Justice William H. Rehnquist (1924–2005), in his opinion for the Court in *Board of Trustees of the University of Alabama v. Garret* (2001), cited *Cleburne* to the effect that the classification of a person as mentally retarded "incurs only the minimum 'rational-basis' review [rather than] a 'quasi-suspect' classification under our equal protection jurisprudence." *Garret* involved a suit by employees of Alabama under Title I of the Americans with Disabilities Act of 1990, which the Court ultimately rejected as being barred by the Eleventh Amendment (1798). But Justice Sandra Day O'Connor, in her concurring opinion in LAWRENCE V. TEXAS (2003), said that she based her decision to strike down a state law against homosexual sodomy between consenting adults on the equal protection clause, because "[w]hen a law exhibits such a desire to harm a politically unpopular group, we have [in the past] applied a more searching form of rational basis review to strike down such laws under the equal protection clause." Justice O'Connor is no longer on the bench, and only the future will tell if the equal protection clause will reemerge as a significant basis for protecting against discrimination in America.

That a nation catapulted into existence with the ringing words "all Men are created equal,... [and] are endowed by their Creator with certain unalienable Rights" could condone unequal citizenship has no rational basis. Individuals will always be unequal in as many ways as there are individuals. But for purposes of living and working in a political democracy based on popular SOVEREIGNTY, constitutionalism, the RULE OF LAW, and equal protection of the laws, every citizen, whether among the governing or the governed, should, as Aristotle put it nearly twenty-five hundred years ago, "treat one another and their fellow-citizens in a spirit of equality."

Equal Rights Amendment   *See* AMENDMENTS; WOMEN.

Equity *See* COMMON LAW.

Establishment Clause *See* RELIGION.

Evidence *See* SEARCH AND SEIZURE.

Ex Post Facto Laws

An ex post facto law (Latin for "made after the occurrence") is one promulgated as PUNISHMENT for acts not punishable at the time they were committed. (It gives new meaning to the warning "Ignorance of the law is no excuse," because it requires foreknowledge of what will be a law in the future.) Ex post facto laws are generally criminal, not civil (see CRIMINAL LAW); they may make a formerly lawful act unlawful as well as increase the punishment for an existing crime.

Such laws are a clear violation of DUE PROCESS and, like BILLS OF ATTAINDER, are twice prohibited by the Constitution. Article I, section 9, pertaining to CONGRESS, states: "No...ex post facto Law shall be passed." And section 10 declares: "No state shall...pass any...ex post facto Law...." Many other countries, including India (1950) and Bolivia (1967), prohibit retroactive criminal laws.

ALEXANDER HAMILTON in essay 84 of *The Federalist* (1787–88) (see FEDERALIST PAPERS) comments on the Constitution's prohibition against ex post facto laws. "The creation of crimes after the commission of the fact, or, in other words, the subjecting of men to punishment for things which, when they were done, were breaches of no law, and the practice of arbitrary imprisonments, have been, in all ages, the favorite and most formidable instruments of tyranny."

In the SUPREME COURT's decision in *Calder v. Bull* (1798), Justice Samuel Chase (1741–1811) gave the ultimate definition of ex post facto laws: "1. Every law that makes criminal an action done before the passing of the law and which was innocent when done, and punishes such an action. 2. Every law that aggravates a crime, or makes it greater than it was, when committed. 3. Every law that changes punishment, and inflicts a greater punishment, than the law annexed to the crime when committed. 4. Every law that alters the legal rules of evidence, and receives less or different testimony than the law required at the time of the commission of the offense, in order to convict the offender." As the first definition indicates, the prohibition against ex post facto laws was interpreted as applicable only to criminal law and not to civil law.

The Supreme Court, however, has relaxed the prohibition against ex post facto laws in instances where changes in the rules of evidence had no substantial impact on a defendant's rights—for example, in *Beazell v. Ohio* (1925), in which the Court held that changes in trial procedures or rules of evidence that "do not deprive the accused of a defense and [that] operate only in a limited and unsubstantial manner are not prohibited." It has also exempted judicial decisions that change the law as opposed to statutory changes made by legislation; in *Powell v. Nevada* (1994), the Court decided that any constitutional rule of procedure that had an impact on criminal prosecutions had to be applied retroactively to all cases that were not yet final when the new rule was announced. Further, in *Carlson v. Landon* (1952), the Court upheld the deportation of ALIENS for acts committed before the applicable law was passed.

"The creation of crimes after the commission of the fact, or, in other words, the subjecting of men to punishment for things which, when they were done, were breaches of no law, and the practice of arbitrary imprisonments, have been, in all ages, the favorite and most formidable instruments of tyranny."

—Alexander Hamilton

Avtex textile plant in Front Royal, Virginia, was shut down by the EPA in the late 1980s because its toxic waste was being dumped in the Shenandoah River. Under the nation's Superfund law, a company can be found liable for dumping toxic waste even if it broke no law at the time.
Source: CQ Photo/Scott J. Ferrell

The Supreme Court has also upheld a number of retroactive laws, including tax laws, that restrict PROPERTY or legal rights that vested before the laws were passed. In *Usery v. Turner Elkhorn Mining Co.* (1976), the Court held that mining companies have to pay disability benefits even to workers who had quit their jobs before the law requiring such payments was passed. When Ohio's supreme court failed to apply a Supreme Court rule announced in *Bendix Autolite Corp. v. Midwesco Enterprises, Inc.* (1988) to a case that arose out of a 1984 incident, the Court unanimously held that the Ohio court had violated the supremacy clause of the Constitution by not giving its ruling retroactive effect. In *Stogner v. California* (2003), however, the Court, in a 5–4 decision, found that a California law in 1993 that allowed criminal prosecutions to be brought after the previously applicable statute of limitations had expired violated the Constitution's ex post facto provision when applied to sex-related child abuse crimes committed between 1955 and 1973.

> **More on this topic:**
>
> *Rule of Law, p. 475*

Exclusionary Rule *See* SEARCH AND SEIZURE.

Exclusive Powers

The Constitution grants or delegates POWERS to the federal government, while, in accordance with the principles of FEDERALISM, other powers, such as the power to tax (see TAXATION), are shared with the STATES as CONCURRENT POWERS. Still others, such as state PROPERTY laws and state POLICE POWER, are left exclusively to the states. How these powers interact has been a problem of interpretation for the Supreme Court almost from the Republic's beginning.

In *GIBBONS V. OGDEN* (1824), Chief Justice JOHN MARSHALL laid down certain ground rules concerning the grants of exclusive powers to the national government. "These delegated powers," he wrote, "whether express or implied, are, (1.) those which are exclusively vested in the United States; and, (2.) those which are concurrent in the United States and the respective States." According to the eminent jurist, "The powers vested exclusively in Congress are, (1.) Those which are granted in express terms. (2.) Those which are granted to the United States, and expressly prohibited to the States. (3.) Those which are exclusive in their nature."

Marshall went on in the opinion to say that "[a]ll powers, exclusive in their nature, may be included under two heads: (1.) Those which have their origin in the constitution, and where the object of them did not exist previous to the Union. These may be called strictly national powers. (2.) Those powers which, by other provisions in the constitution, have an effect and operation, when exercised by a State, without or beyond the territorial limits of the State."

As an example of the federal government's exclusive powers that originated in the Constitution and did not previously exist, Marshall cited the power to borrow money set forth in Article I, section 8 (see DEBT). As an example of the second class of exclusive national powers, he cites the power of Congress, set out in the same section of the Constitution, to establish uniform rules of naturalization (see CITIZENS; IMMIGRATION). That power, which was a state power under the ARTICLES OF CONFEDERATION (1781), now runs concurrent with the states, but they are unable to exercise it because of the provisions in Article IV, section 2, that grant to the "Citizens of each State...all the Privileges and Immunities of Citizens in the several States."

The exclusive powers of the federal government are therefore those which it alone may exercise under the Constitution, whether solely—because the states have no such power—or to the exclusion of any similar power of the states. The power to make TREATIES with a foreign government is one. The power to regulate COMMERCE granted to Congress in Article I, section 8, however, was characterized by the Supreme Court as having the quality of selective exclusiveness. In *Cooley v. Board of Wardens* (1851), the Court devised what became known as the *Cooley* Doctrine, saying: "Whatever subjects of this [commerce] power are in their nature national, or admit only of one uniform system, or plan of regulation, may justly be said to be of such a nature as to require the exclusive legislation of Congress." The *Cooley* Doctrine was later supplanted by a modern balancing approach that allows for state regulation where it is nondiscriminatory against interstate commerce and the state's interests are sufficient to override any adverse effect on interstate commerce. Other exclusive powers of the federal government include the power to declare WAR and make peace, raise and command the ARMED FORCES, conduct FOREIGN AFFAIRS, legislate with respect to the nation, and make final determinations on federal and constitutional questions.

Within the federal government, under the SEPARATION OF POWERS doctrine, each of the three branches of government—the EXECUTIVE BRANCH, LEGISLATIVE BRANCH, and JUDICIAL BRANCH—are considered to have exclusive power or authority within their respective spheres under the Constitution. But the countervailing requirement of checks and balances ensures that any one branch has few exclusive powers, which helps prevent corruption and abuse. CONGRESS may choose its own officers, but LEGISLATION must be signed by the president and pass constitutional muster in the courts. The PRESIDENT may unilaterally terminate CABINET members (see APPOINTMENT AND REMOVAL POWER), but even as commander in chief he requires Congress's approval to fund his actions. Similarly, the judiciary is independent in making its decisions (see JUDICIAL INDEPENDENCE) but needs the executive branch to enforce them.

Federalism requires a constant fine-tuning of the relationship between the national government and the states. The federal government's exclusive powers represent ones that the FRAMERS OF THE CONSTITUTION and the Supreme Court have believed are required to make fifty states and several territories one nation, while the exclusive powers of the government's separate branches are tempered by overlapping checks and balances. Moreover, according to the principle of INHERENT POWERS, there may be an enlargement or expansion of executive power in cases of national emergency. For example, the powers of the president asserted after the terrorist attacks on the United States on September 11, 2001, have been justified on the basis of the inherent power of the president to respond to such situations. As long as the additional powers are not checked by the legislature, the courts, or the people at the polls, they may remain in effect until such time as the national emergency is over.

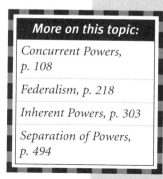

More on this topic:

Concurrent Powers,
p. 108

Federalism, p. 218

Inherent Powers, p. 303

Separation of Powers,
p. 494

Executive Agreements *See* TREATIES.

Executive Branch

In *The Spirit of the Laws* (1748), the French jurist and legal scholar Charles-Louis de Secondat, Baron de La Bréde et de Montesquieu (1689–1755), identified three separate branches in the British government: the legislative, executive, and judicial. When such powers were combined rather than kept separate, he argued, tyranny might result. The SEPARATION OF POWERS of government, along with checks and balances, was a basic principle accepted by the FRAMERS OF THE CONSTITUTION in creating a new system of government for the United States.

The U.S. Constitution and many other national constitutions, including those of Chile (1981, significantly amended 1989), Slovakia (1993), and Poland (1997), have incorporated Montesquieu's principle and created at least three major branches of government. While the LEGISLATIVE BRANCH enacts laws and the JUDICIAL BRANCH interprets and applies the laws in individual disputes, the executive branch implements and enforces the laws. The basic provisions of the U.S. Constitution that relate to the executive branch are found in Article II.

"The administration of government, in its largest sense," noted ALEXANDER HAMILTON in essay 72 of *The Federalist* (1787–88) (see FEDERALIST PAPERS), "comprehends all the operations of the body politic, whether legislative, executive, or judiciary; but in its most usual and perhaps in its most precise signification, it is limited to executive details, and falls peculiarly within the province of the executive department."

The Federal Bureaucracy

The sheer size of the federal government's executive branch today is staggering. It encompasses fifteen CABINET-level departments, including the Department of Defense and all U.S. military personnel (see ARMED FORCES), as well as smaller departments, independent ADMINISTRATIVE AGENCIES, and other specialized bodies such as administrations, commissions, councils, and offices (see chart, page 9). According to the president's budget for fiscal year 2008, executive branch civilian employees in 2006 numbered approximately 2.6 million persons, compared to approximately 63,000 employees in the other two branches combined; the annual payroll in 2006 for the executive branch was then more than $177 billion.

The cabinet secretaries, as heads of the executive departments, and some other administrative bodies, such as the Office of Management and Budget and the National Security Council, are directly responsible to the president. Other independent bodies, including the Federal Trade Commission and the Federal Communications Commission, are not directly supervised by the president. These bodies have statutory authority to perform certain functions that require a relative balance of political interests; in addition, their heads serve set terms of office and therefore may not be summarily removed by the president (see APPOINTMENT AND REMOVAL POWER).

The federal bureaucracy, as the executive branch is sometimes referred to, can be a source of strength to a president in carrying out his policies, but it can also be a hindrance and frustration. The nation's first PRESIDENT, GEORGE WASHINGTON, had only three executive departments and an attorney general, along with a few hundred civilian employees. But the executive branch could cause headaches for the chief executive even then. Washington's secretary of state, THOMAS JEFFERSON, had his own political philosophy and agenda, which often brought him into conflict with the secretary of the Treasury, ALEXANDER HAMILTON. The thirty-ninth president, Jimmy Carter (b. 1924), once reflected, "I...was warned that dealing with the federal bureaucracy would be one of the worst problems I would have to face. It has been worse than I had anticipated."

Defining an "Officer"

One issue that has arisen is just who, under the Constitution, is an "officer" of the executive branch. This branch has four types of employee, three of which are expressly mentioned in the Constitution: the president and vice president, who are elected by the people; officials appointed by the president with the ADVICE AND CONSENT of the Senate, such as cabinet members and heads of agencies; and, as provided in Article II, section 2, "such inferior Officers" as "Congress may by Law vest the Appointment...in the President alone, in the Courts of Law, or in the Heads of Departments." The vast majority of other executive branch employees, including civil servants, are not mentioned.

> "I...was warned that dealing with the federal bureaucracy would be one of the worst problems I would have to face. It has been worse than I had anticipated."
>
> —President Jimmy Carter

In *BUCKLEY V. VALEO* (1976), the Supreme Court defined an "officer of the United States" as "any appointee exercising significant authority" under federal law. The Court, however, has not been very clear as to who are "officers" and who are "inferior officers" under the Constitution. In *Edmond v. United States* (1997), it said that in general "the term 'inferior officer' connotes a relationship with some higher ranking officer or officers below the President.... [W]e think it evident that 'inferior officers' are officers whose work is directed and supervised at some level by others who were appointed by presidential nomination with the advice and consent of the Senate."

Constitutional Issues

To further the principle of separation of powers, Article I, section 6, mandates: "No Senator or Representative shall, during the Time for which he was elected, be appointed to any civil Office under the Authority of the United States, which shall have been created, or the Emoluments whereof shall have been encreased during such time; and no Person holding any Office under the United States, shall be a member of either House during his Continuance in Office." There is no similar prohibition with respect to judicial officers, and for about a week in 1801 JOHN MARSHALL served as both secretary of state and chief justice of the United States.

In *MARBURY V. MADISON* (1803), an important early Supreme Court case whose opinion was written by Marshall, the Court concluded that executive branch officials were not immune from legal suits against them in their official capacities but could be ordered by the courts to perform ministerial, in contrast to discretionary, acts. Jefferson, then president, denounced that decision. In *Mississippi v. Johnson* (1867), the Court held that a suit could not be filed to stop the president from acting in his official capacity. In that case the state of Mississippi sought to prevent President Andrew Johnson (1808–75) and his generals from enforcing the Reconstruction Acts of 1867. In *Clinton v. Jones* (1997), however, the Court concluded for the first time that the president, even while in office, was not immune from a civil suit for misconduct unrelated to his official duties. Immunity for other officers in the executive branch with regard to their official duties is handled by the courts on an ad hoc basis. For example, an interesting law suit has been filed by convicted terrorism conspirator Jose Padilla, the subject of the U.S. Supreme Court's decision in *Rumsfeld v. Padilla* (2004), against John Yoo, a former senior official in the U.S. Department of Justice for his role in writing several legal memorandums that resulted in the president's declaring Padilla, a U.S. citizen, to be an enemy combatant in the war on terror. Padilla was arrested in 2002 at Chicago's O'Hare International Airport based on allegations that he took part in a plot by the terrorist group al Qaeda. He was detained for three and a half years at a U.S. Navy facility.

The constitutional protection against libel suits extended to members of Congress under Article I, section 6, the Supreme Court has declared, does not include all executive branch officials. In *Doe v. McMillan* (1973), a suit based on a libelous report of a congressional committee that had been

More on this topic:

Administrative Agencies, p. 8

Cabinet, p. 73

Judicial Branch, p. 312

Legislative Branch, p. 346

printed by the superintendent of documents, the Court ruled that the superintendent, an executive branch official, was not immune to legal action.

Because the INDEPENDENT COUNSEL is a unique position—appointed by a special division of the U.S. Court of Appeals for the District of Columbia, assigned to work in the executive branch, but removable only for good cause by the attorney general—provisions in the Ethics in Government Act (1978) setting up the office have been challenged. In its decision in *Morrison v. Olson* (1988), the Supreme Court upheld the office's constitutionality on three grounds: (1) The independent counsel was an "inferior officer" under the Constitution because the nature of the office was to perform limited duties of investigation and prosecution for a term limited to the completion of the task and not to make general policy. (2) Article II, section 2, authorizes "Courts of Law" to make such appointments. (3) The president's lack of control over the office was deemed not "so central to the functioning of the executive branch" that the president had to have the power to fire the independent counsel.

The separation of powers principle that led to the creation of three coequal branches of the federal government does not preclude some overlap of functions, such as the president's power to veto legislation (see VETOES) and the Senate's role in presidential appointments. As Justice OLIVER WENDELL HOLMES JR. put it in his dissent in *Springer v. Government of the Philippine Islands* (1928): "[H]owever we may disguise it by veiling words we do not and cannot carry out the distinction between legislative and executive action with mathematical precision and divide the branches into watertight compartments, were it ever so desirable to do so, which I am far from believing that it is, or that the Constitution requires." But where the Constitution clearly intends that one branch have exclusive authority in some area of government—the president's authority as commander in chief, for instance, or the Supreme Court's authority to judge cases and controversies—the line is clear, and any infringement is unconstitutional.

Executive Orders

Throughout history monarchs and dictators have ruled directly and absolutely by decrees that have the force of law. The constitutions of some countries still provide for rule by decree under certain circumstances. Paraguay's constitution (1992) states that "[d]uring the time a state of exception [a state of emergency] is in force, the executive branch may order, by decree and on a case-by-case basis,…[t]he detention of people suspected of participating in [such] events [giving rise to the state of emergency]…." Armenia's constitution (1995) authorizes the president to "issue orders and decrees which shall be executed throughout the Republic, [but they] shall not contravene the Constitution and the laws."

The U.S. Constitution does not expressly give the PRESIDENT the power to issue orders or decrees. The president nonetheless often manages the operations of the EXECUTIVE BRANCH by issuing executive orders, which are official government documents that direct this branch—but not the nation as a whole. Around fifteen thousand of them, numbered consecutively since 1907, have been issued to date.

Most executive orders emanate from specific authorization by Congress. Others, however, derive from the president's own authority as chief executive pursuant to Article II, section 1, of the Constitution. On April 7, 1917, the day after the United States declared WAR on Germany during

World War I, President Woodrow Wilson (1856–1924) issued an unnumbered executive order authorizing the heads of departments and independent offices (see ADMINISTRATIVE AGENCIES) in the executive branch to "forthwith remove any employee…[if] the retention of such employee would be inimical to the public welfare by reason of his conduct, sympathies or utterances, or because of other reasons growing out of the war." Executive Order 9066 (1942), which permitted military commanders in the United States to relocate citizens of Japanese ancestry on the West Coast, was issued under the War Powers Act (1918) and a specific grant of authority under Public Law 503 (1942).

On March 21, 1947, in an attempt to root out communists in the government, President Harry S. Truman (1884–1972) issued Executive Order 9835, the "Loyalty Order." The order sought, among other things, to deny government employment to and dismiss from government employment any person when it was determined that "on all the evidence, reasonable grounds exist for belief that the person involved is disloyal to the Government of the United States." This order placed many federal employees at serious risk without recourse to DUE PROCESS standards or other legal protections. At the time the courts looked on government employment primarily as a privilege and not a right, so employees were at the mercy of their superiors. Regarding Executive Order 9835, EDWARD S. CORWIN commented in *The President: Office and Powers* (1957) that it "marked the close of an epoch, the Age of Innocency of a democratic faith still untainted by European revolutionary nihilism and its mordant class hatreds."

In 1952 Truman used an executive order to direct the secretary of commerce to seize steel mills after a threatened strike by steelworkers, thus ensuring that ammunition would continue to be produced for the Korean War effort. In *YOUNGSTOWN SHEET AND TUBE CO. V. SAWYER* (1952), the Supreme Court held that the president's action in this instance was an unconstitutional exercise of presidential authority because Congress had refused to give the president such power when it passed the Taft-Hartley Act in 1947.

In the wake of the September 11, 2001, terrorist attacks on the United States, President George W. Bush (b. 1946) issued Executive Order 13228 on October 8 to establish a new Office of Homeland Security and the Homeland Security Council (see pages 544–545). Bush's controversial authorization of military tribunals to try noncitizens in the war against TERRORISM, however, was accomplished not by an executive order but by a military order issued on November 13, 2001 (see pages 188-189), which relied on his powers as commander in chief rather than as head of the executive branch.

The president's power to use executive orders to direct government actions is a two-edged sword. Although it provides a means of swiftly communicating policy throughout the executive branch, it nonetheless contains the seeds of despotism. If unchallenged, an executive order, as in the *Youngstown* case, can authorize illegal or unconstitutional actions.

Signing Statements

A presidential signing statement—an official document in which the president sets forth his interpretation of an act of Congress that he has just signed into law—differs from an executive order in that the statement relates to the new law and, in effect, gives the president an opportunity to waive the application of the law in certain situations. There has been criticism of the many signing statements issued by President George W. Bush, particularly that they put him above the law. But Vice President Dick Cheney has stated: "I believe in a strong, robust executive authority [and] that the [use of signing statements is] totally

> **The president's power to use executive orders to direct government actions is a two-edged sword. Although it provides a means of swiftly communicating policy throughout the executive branch, it nonetheless contains the seeds of despotism.**

More on this topic:

Executive Branch, p. 206

President, p. 417

Youngstown Sheet and Tube Co. v. Sawyer, p. 594

appropriate and consistent with the constitutional authority of the president." The majority in *Hamdan v. Rumsfeld* (2006) held that the use of military commissions to try prisoners in the war on terror detained at Guantanamo Bay, Cuba, was unconstitutional insofar as it violated both the Uniform Code of Military Justice and the Geneva Conventions. In his dissent, Justice Antonin Scalia (b. 1936) chided the majority for consulting the legislative history of the Detainee Treatment Act of 2005, while "wholly ignor[ing] the President's signing statement, which explicitly set forth *his* understanding" of the Act.

Executive Powers *See* PRESIDENT.

Executive Privilege

"This is not a monarchy," declared Rep. Dan Burton (R-Ind.), chair of the Committee on Government Reform of the House of Representatives, at the end of 2001 when he was informed that President George W. Bush (b. 1946) refused to provide requested information on the grounds of executive privilege; at issue was the Federal Bureau of Investigation's handling of informants in Boston. By asserting executive privilege, the EXECUTIVE BRANCH and its officers exempt themselves from having to provide information or evidence to either of the other two branches of government, the LEGISLATIVE BRANCH and the JUDICIAL BRANCH. Executive immunity, which is similar to executive privilege, is the claim of high government officials, including the PRESIDENT and state governors, that they should be immune from prosecution under certain circumstances.

Executive privilege—the term itself was not coined until the administration of President Dwight D. Eisenhower (1890–1969)—has been claimed by presidents from GEORGE WASHINGTON to Richard M. Nixon (1913–94), Bill Clinton (b. 1946), and George W. Bush. Washington refused to provide Congress with information relating to the Jay Treaty (1794) between the United States and Great Britain, which set out various territorial and commercial boundaries. A problem with executive privilege is that it is not expressly provided for in the Constitution, as are legislative PRIVILEGES AND IMMUNITIES in Article I, section 6.

According to a dissent by Chief Justice Earl Warren (1891–1974) in *Barr v. Mateo* (1959), "Absolute legislative privilege dates back to at least 1399 [and]…absolute immunity arising out of judicial proceedings existed at least as early as 1608 in England." Warren explained that executive privilege in England was confirmed in the case *Chatterton v. Secretary of State for India* (1895), in which the court cited a learned treatise: "For reasons of public policy the same protection would, no doubt, be given to anything in the nature of an act of state, e.g., to every communication relating to state matters made by one minister to another, or to the Crown." Of course, in Britain the monarch is immune from any judicial process or suit, and the prime minister and cabinet members, as members of Parliament, have the immunities and privileges of any other parliamentary member.

In the 1974 case *United States v. Nixon*, a landmark constitutional decision, the Supreme Court voting 8–0 ordered President Nixon to give up evidence requested by the special prosecutor (see INDEPENDENT COUNSEL) in the WATERGATE investigation, despite Nixon's claim of executive privilege. As grounds for the privilege, he had asserted "the valid need for protection of communications between high Government officials" and the "doctrine of separation of powers…[that] insulates the

President [and] protects confidential Presidential communications" (see SEPARATION OF POWERS). The opinion, delivered by Chief Justice Warren Burger (1907–95), went to great lengths to emphasize the basic presumption favoring executive privilege, citing Chief Justice JOHN MARSHALL in *United States v. Burr* (1807) for the proposition that presidential accountability to the legal system does not mean that the courts may proceed against the president as against any other citizen. In the 1974 case, however, the special prosecutor had a specific need for evidence that related to the credibility of witnesses and the alleged crime of obstructing justice.

In *Nixon v. Fitzgerald* (1982)—a suit brought by an Air Force management analyst who became a government whistle-blower—a 5–4 Supreme Court majority held that the former president enjoyed absolute immunity from damages resulting from acts lying in the "outer perimeter" of his official responsibilities while in office. The Court also said that presidential privilege is rooted in the separation of powers doctrine, and although some interests might call for judicial action, "merely private suit[s] for damages based on a President's official acts" do not serve this "broad public interest."

> *"From Watergate we learned what generations before us have known; our Constitution works. And during Watergate years it was interpreted again so as to reaffirm that no one—absolutely no one— is above the law."*
>
> **—Watergate special prosecutor Leon Jaworski**

The Supreme Court went even further in *Clinton v. Jones* (1997), a suit by Paula Jones alleging sexual harassment by Bill Clinton when he was the governor of Arkansas in 1991. The justices declared that the office of president did not confer any special privilege allowing a president in office to avoid a civil suit. They noted that an important distinction between the *Jones* case and the *Fitzgerald* case was that in *Jones* the suit involved unofficial actions when Clinton was not president. The government did not expressly raise the executive privilege defense in *Cheney v. United States District Court for the District of Columbia* (2004), and the case was decided on other grounds, but the Supreme Court discussed such a defense in its decision on the civil suit to obtain information about the National Energy Policy Group set up by President George W. Bush after taking office in 2001. Vice President Cheney was made the head of this group to advise the president on energy policies. Citing the decision in *Clinton v. Jones*, the Court noted that "[s]pecial considerations control when the Executive's interests in maintaining its autonomy and safeguarding its communications' confidentiality are implicated."

The FRAMERS OF THE CONSTITUTION in 1787 rejected making the chief executive a creature of the national legislature, as the United Kingdom's prime minister is beholden to Parliament—a privileged member responsible to that body for his or her actions. But the separate and coequal status of the president under the U.S. Constitution gives rise to legitimate as well as self-serving claims of executive privilege that become grist for the mill of justice. The civil suit that was allowed to proceed against President Clinton in 1997 was viewed by many as part of a campaign of political harassment that culminated in his IMPEACHMENT in 1998. Politicians and legal scholars at the time debated a related issue that remains unresolved by the courts: whether a criminal action—in Clinton's case for lying under oath in a deposition—also could be brought against a sitting president.

> **More on this topic:**
>
> *National Security, p. 375*

Export Duties *See* CONGRESS; STATES.

Extradition

The federal nature of the national government (see FEDERALISM), which allows each state to retain its own legal system and criminal jurisdiction, required the FRAMERS OF THE CONSTITUTION in 1787 to include a provision for returning criminals from one state of the Union to another through the process of extradition (from the Latin *ex*, meaning out, and *tradere*, meaning to deliver up). "A Person charged in any State with Treason, Felony, or other Crime, who shall flee from Justice, and be found in another State," mandates Article IV, section 2, "shall on Demand of the executive Authority of the State from which he fled, be delivered up, to be removed to the State having Jurisdiction of the Crime." The last paragraph of section 2, dealing with persons "held to Service or Labour in one State...escaping into another...," was rendered void by the Thirteenth Amendment (1865), which abolished SLAVERY after the Civil War.

The constitutional provision regarding fugitives from justice was not without precedent. The New England Confederation of English colonies in 1643 required the surrender of fugitives when a demand was made by two magistrates of the colony from which they had fled. A provision nearly identical to that in the 1787 constitution also appeared previously in the ARTICLES OF CONFEDERATION (1781).

Seeing That Justice Is Done

To implement the fugitive clause, which encompasses any act forbidden by a state's laws, Congress in 1793 passed "An Act respecting fugitives from justice, and persons escaping from the service of their masters"; it was upheld by the Supreme Court in *Prigg v. Pennsylvania* (1842). But in *Taylor v. Taintor* (1873), the Court explained that a state's duty to surrender a fugitive is not absolute and unqualified. For example, if the fugitive is subject to the laws of the state to which he or she has fled and is imprisoned there for another crime, that state's laws may be satisfied before the fugitive is extradited to the requesting state.

In *Kentucky v. Dennison* (1861), the Supreme Court ruled that only after a person had been formally charged with a crime in the regular course of a judicial proceeding is the governor entitled to demand that a fugitive be returned from another state. In the same decision the Court found that the federal government could not force a state governor to honor a request for extradition. Therefore, Congress made it a federal crime in 1934 for a person to flee the jurisdiction of one state to avoid prosecution in certain cases.

All the states have a mutual interest in seeing justice done throughout the nation. The process of interstate extradition is routinely supervised by the Supreme Court to ensure that the letter and the spirit of the Constitution are complied with.

International Extradition

International extradition is directly addressed in some countries' constitutions. Jordan's constitution (1952), for example, provides that the "[e]xtradition of ordinary criminals [as opposed to political refugees] shall be regulated by international agreements and laws." In addition, some regional documents, including the European Convention on Extradition (1957) and the Inter-American Convention on Extradition (1981), deal with extradition across national borders.

Although the U.S. Constitution does not address international extradition, it authorizes the United States to enter into TREATIES, prescribes how treaties are to be made, and, in Article 6, section 2, makes treaties a part of "the supreme Law of the Land" (see SUPREMACY CLAUSE). Moreover, the SUPREME COURT has ruled on cases involving international extradition under the jurisdiction conferred on it by Article III, section 2 (see COURTS).

In *Terlinden v. Ames* (1902), the Supreme Court interpreted extradition under INTERNATIONAL LAW as "the surrender by one nation to another of an individual accused or convicted of an offense outside of its own territory, and within the territorial jurisdiction of the other...." In *Factor v. Laubenheimer* (1933), the Court explained that "[w]hile a government may, if agreeable to its own constitution and laws, voluntarily exercise the power to surrender a fugitive from justice to the

More on this topic:

Criminal Law, p. 132

Travel, p. 548

country from which he has fled, and it has been said that it has a moral duty to do so…the legal right to demand his extradition and the correlative duty to surrender him to the demanding country exist only when created by treaty."

The United States has entered into bilateral extradition treaties with most of the countries of the world, from Albania to Zambia. There are two basic types of extradition treaties. Enumerative treaties list and define the crimes for which extradition will be granted. Eliminative ("no list") treaties define extraditable offenses in terms of whether, according to the laws of the two countries party to the treaty, they are punishable on the basis of a minimum standard of severity. Under both types of treaty, however, no extradition will take place unless the act constitutes a crime according to the laws of both nations.

International extradition law differs from interstate extradition law in one important respect. According to the Supreme Court in *United States v. Rauscher* (1886), when a fugitive is surrendered by a foreign government pursuant to an extradition treaty, the offender may be tried only "for the offense with which he is charged in the proceedings for his extradition, until a reasonable time and opportunity have been given him, after his release or trial upon such charge, to return to the country from whose asylum he had been forcibly taken under those proceedings." In interstate extraditions, in contrast, once a fugitive is returned to a state, whether by lawful extradition or any other means, he or she may be tried and punished for other offenses even though extradited for a specific crime.

It is becoming increasingly difficult for a person to commit a crime in one country and then flee to another to avoid lawful prosecution. Bilateral international extradition treaties and cooperation among national and state law enforcement officials as well as a growing perception that the countries of the world constitute an international community are making international extradition the rule rather than the exception. In addition to traditional bilateral agreements for extradition, many nations have also entered into judicial assistance and cooperative agreements for the enforcement of drug laws and international interdiction of drug trafficking (see DRUGS) and other related crimes, such as smuggling and money laundering. Issues such as political refugees seeking asylum and international disagreement over whether the DEATH PENALTY should be imposed on extradited felons, however, can complicate the extradition process.

Extraterritoriality *See* TERRITORY.

CLOSER LOOK

In a high-profile criminal case, former NatWest bankers David Bermingham, Giles Darby, and Gary Mulgrew were extradited from Britain in July 2006 to face charges in the United States. Known as the "NatWest Three," the men were charged with engaging in fraudulent dealings with the Enron Corporation, and subsequently contributing to the company's downfall. Corrupt financial practices left the American energy company suddenly bankrupt in late 2001; shareholders became penniless and thousands of employees lost their jobs and benefits.

The bankers' extradition was controversial, as it was governed by the British Extradition Act of 2003, thought to be reserved for the most serious of international crimes. Critics of the law also indicate that the United States' provisions do not reciprocate those of Britain—that is, extraditing an American to Britain is much more difficult than extraditing a British citizen to the United States.

F

Fair Trial *See* CRIMINAL LAW; JURIES; TRIALS.

Fairness Doctrine *See* COMMUNICATIONS.

Families

For far longer than recorded history, the family has been the basic unit of human social organization. The traditional concept of a family is the nuclear family, composed of parents and their children; the extended family encompasses grandparents, grandchildren, and other close relatives. Aristotle (383–322 B.C.E.), the ancient Greek philosopher, acknowledged the family as the fundamental social unit in civilized society and concluded in *The Politics* that the family was a basic unit of the state. A number of national constitutions, including those of Italy (1948), Egypt (1971), and Brazil (1988), expressly refer to the family; the Italian constitution, for example, provides: "The Republic acknowledges the rights of the family as a natural society founded on marriage." At the international level, the Universal Declaration of Human Rights (1948) addresses rights of the family, asserting, "The family is the natural and fundamental group unit of society and is entitled to protection by society and the State."

Under the U.S. Constitution, however, the theory of popular SOVEREIGNTY and the political equality of all citizens make the individual—rather than the family—the basic unit of political organization. As Alexis de Tocqueville (1805–59), the French political scientist, observed in *Democracy in America* (1835), "In America, the family, if one takes the word in its Roman and aristocratic sense, no longer exists." Indeed, the 2000 U.S. Census indicated that only 23.5 percent of American households consist of married couples with children, down from 45 percent in 1960. This trend, which is due at least in part to the growing number of households consisting of older couples whose children have left home, is slowing, but the decline in the number of traditional family households is real.

Although the U.S. Constitution does not expressly mention families, the constitutional rights of individuals to participate in family relationships, such as marriage and raising children, have been confirmed in decisions of the Supreme Court. In *Roberts v. United States Jaycees* (1984), the Court for the first time declared a "freedom of intimate association" (see ASSEMBLY AND ASSOCIATION). According to the

Although the post–World War II idealization of the basic family unit centered around a married couple and their offspring, the definition of what constitutes the American family continues to evolve. Today this traditional family represents less than a quarter of all households.
Source: AP Images

opinion, there are "certain kinds of highly personal relationships [such as] marriage; childbirth; the raising and education of children and cohabitation with one's relatives" that are constitutionally protected (see CHILDREN; EDUCATION). Family or domestic relations law also addresses the dissolution of families through divorce, as well as adoption, paternity, and child custody and support.

Another decision by the Supreme Court in 2003 furthered the rights of families. In *Nevada Department of Human Resources v. Hibbs,* the Court upheld the power of Congress under the Fourteenth Amendment (1868) to abrogate the Eleventh Amendment (1795) insofar as it would bar state employees from recovering damages for violations of the Family and Medical Leave Act of 1993. The act entitles eligible employees to take up to twelve work weeks of unpaid leave annually for one of a number of family-related reasons, including a "serious health condition" in an employee's spouse, child, or parent. The Court distinguished the situation in this case from the opposite outcome regarding the power of Congress to make state employers liable for violations of federal laws regarding discrimination in *Board of Trustees of the University of Alabama v. Garrett* (2001) and *Kimel v. Florida Board of Regents* (2000).

Marriage

The basis of the traditional nuclear family is marriage, although in 2006 a milestone was reached when, for the first time in the United States, the number of nonmarried couples surpassed the number of married couples. This trend is continuing to widen the gap. In *Skinner v. Oklahoma* (1942), a criminal sterilization case, Justice William O. Douglas (1898–1980) characterized marriage as "one of the basic civil rights of man...fundamental to the very existence and survival of the race." Two decades later, in the important case GRISWOLD V. CONNECTICUT (1965), Douglas further defined marriage as "a coming together for better or for worse, hopefully enduring, and intimate to the degree of being sacred. It is an association...for as noble a purpose as any involved in our prior decisions [upholding freedom of association]." Eventually, in *Zablocki v. Redhail* (1978), the Supreme Court went so far as to categorize the right to marry as a "fundamental interest"

A gay couple with their adopted son. Courts have gradually extended more rights to gay couples.
Source: Reuters/Mike Segar

requiring a "critical examination" of any government restrictions that "interfere directly and substantially" with it. However, a person does not have an unfettered right to marry just anyone. As Justice Potter Stewart (1915–85) explained in a concurring opinion in *Zablocki*, no one may legitimately marry a sibling or a person who already has a living spouse.

In *Loving v. Virginia* (1967), the Supreme Court found that state laws barring marriage on the basis of race, religion, or national origin violate both the DUE PROCESS and the EQUAL PROTECTION clauses of the Fourteenth Amendment. Speaking for the Court, Chief Justice Earl Warren (1891–1974) said: "The freedom to marry has long been recognized as one of the vital personal rights essential to the orderly pursuit of happiness by free men. Marriage is one of the 'basic civil rights of man,' fundamental to our existence and survival" (see FUNDAMENTAL RIGHTS).

Although the Supreme Court disclaimed any constitutional right of homosexuals to be legally married in its decision in *Bowers v. Hardwick* (1986), in LAWRENCE V. TEXAS (2003), the Court overruled *Bowers*, at least to the extent of recognizing a constitutional right for adult homosexuals to engage in consensual sexual relations in the privacy of their own home. Some other countries, including Canada and South Africa, allow same-sex marriages. Massachusetts is the only state that permits same-sex marriages, and several states, including Connecticut and Vermont, have legalized civil unions and domestic partnerships that extend some of the rights and privileges of marriage to homosexual couples. While New York state does not permit homosexual marriage, the state's appellate court ruled early in 2008 that valid out-of-state same-sex marriages must be recognized by the state.

Divorce

Divorce, the judicial termination of a marriage, may be accomplished by a decree that dissolves or nullifies the marriage, thus allowing the parties to remarry, or by a decree of separation that only partially terminates the marriage and precludes remarriage. Before its decision in *Haddock v. Haddock* (1906), the Supreme Court treated a divorce proceeding as a suit against the status of the marriage itself rather than as a suit by one partner in the marriage against the other. This early type of proceeding—called *in rem* (Latin for "against the thing"), in contrast to *in personam* (Latin for "against the person")—allowed either party to bring a divorce suit in good faith in any state where he or she was domiciled and not residing simply for the purpose of obtaining the divorce. But this approach could mean that the man and woman were considered married in one state but divorced in another—for example, if the state in which one party resided refused to recognize the legality of a divorce granted in another state that had different requirements for obtaining a divorce.

The major difficulty posed by the *Haddock* decision was that the postdivorce possibility of the parties' different status—married or not married—in different states flew in the face of the Supreme Court's declaration in *Atherton v. Atherton* (1901) that "a husband without a wife, or a wife without a husband, is unknown to the law." Article IV, section 1, of the Constitution also requires: "Full Faith and Credit shall be given in each State to the public Acts, Records, and judicial Proceedings of every other State" (see FEDERALISM; FULL FAITH AND CREDIT). In 1942 a majority of the justices overruled *Haddock* in the first of two *Williams v. North Carolina* cases. A man and a woman, both of whom lived in North Carolina and were married to other people, established the required six-weeks residency in Nevada and were granted divorces there. The same day they married each other. Their spouses, who had remained in North Carolina, were served notices of the divorces there. North Carolina refused to recognize the Nevada divorces and subsequent marriages and prosecuted the woman for bigamy. When the case reached the Supreme Court, the justices assumed that the six-week domicile in Nevada was undertaken in good faith and was not merely a sham—although in fact it was—and required North Carolina to recognize the Nevada divorce decree.

The *Williams v. North Carolina* precedent surfaced again in 1945. This time the Supreme Court reversed its earlier ruling by allowing a collateral attack in North Carolina—that is, an attack on the question of whether the Nevada domicile was in fact undertaken in good faith or just for the purpose of obtaining the divorce. Lack of good faith was established, and the Court ruled that North Carolina did not have to recognize the Nevada divorce, thus providing the deserted spouses a remedy against out-of-state "quickie" divorces.

Since the *Williams* cases, divorce laws in most states have been liberalized, and today fewer divorce issues come before the courts. However, in *Sosna v. Iowa* (1975), the Supreme Court upheld an Iowa law requiring a one-year residency for couples moving to the state before a divorce can be granted. Justice William H. Rehnquist (1924–2005) commented that a state like Iowa "may quite reasonably decide that it does not wish to become a divorce mill."

Children

For most of the country's history, the Constitution has had little to do with the relationship of children to families. This relationship has generally been held to be private and outside government interference except when there is sufficient proof of abuse or neglect. In *Michael H. v. Gerald D.* (1989), for example, the Supreme Court concluded that it was valid to presume that a woman's husband was the father of her child in spite of evidence proving that the child was fathered by another man.

In *Belle Terre v. Boraas* (1974), the Supreme Court upheld an ordinance restricting occupancy in a one-family dwelling to traditional family members or to groups of not more than two unrelated people. The Court found that six unrelated college students leasing the premises was not a traditional family. But in *Moore v. City of East Cleveland* (1977), the Court invalidated a ZONING ordinance that would not permit a woman to live with her son and two grandchildren. Rejecting the town's argument that only a nuclear family—a mother, father, and children—has a constitutional right to live together, the Court declared that the Constitution prohibits a municipality "from standardizing its children—and its adults—by forcing all to live in certain narrowly defined family patterns."

Given the Constitution's emphasis on the individual as the basic unit of political organization, it is not surprising that the traditional family structure has lost some of its historical relevance in America after more than two hundred years of constitutional democracy. Still, the Supreme Court has found opportunities to extend the Constitution's protections to marriage, divorce, and children, all important aspects of the family.

Federalism

Federalism is the principle of political organization by which a nation contains both a central government and semisovereign states or provincial governments. France has a unitary government—in which all of its subdivisions are created by the national government itself—while a number of nations, including Germany, Australia, and Argentina as well as the United States, are constitutionally organized according to various types of federalism. In Austria and Germany, as in the United States, the constituent political units are called states, whereas in the confederations of Canada and Switzerland, the semisovereign units are called provinces and cantons, respectively.

The FRAMERS OF THE CONSTITUTION in 1787 were well aware of the history of federations and confederations, from the ancient Greek leagues to the Swiss confederated system of government with its cantons. In 1643 the four colonies of Plymouth, Connecticut, New Haven, and Massachusetts had formed an early league called the New England Confederation that dealt with boundary matters and joint military operations, among other things. The early colonies, being far from England, had relatively broad autonomy, so the colonial administrations of the thirteen colonies developed along different lines until in 1763 Britain began centralizing its power by levying new taxes and reforming the governments.

The ARTICLES OF CONFEDERATION (1781), adopted by the new states toward the end of the Revolutionary War (1775–83), provided for a type of federative system that did not work well. Under the Articles the national government had no power to tax the states, to uniformly regulate COMMERCE among the states—over which they were constantly bickering—or to quickly come to the aid of states in cases of insurrection. When the CONSTITUTIONAL CONVENTION OF 1787 was convened, the delegates had extensive experience on which to base an improved federal system for the new government of the United States, one that JAMES MADISON, called "the Father of the Constitution," would describe as "a novelty and a compound." By this he meant that it contained features of a unitary system of government, such as Great Britain's, with centralized power over the military and foreign affairs, combined with the states' residual SOVEREIGNTY regarding such things as civil and CRIMINAL LAW, PROPERTY laws, and TAXATION. This federal system is evident in the overall structure of the Constitution itself, but the Tenth Amendment (1791) expresses it best: "The powers not delegated to the United States by the Constitution, nor prohibited by it to the States, are reserved to the States respectively, or to the people" (see EXCLUSIVE POWERS).

The Constitution's federalism functions on several levels. The most obvious is the relationship that continues to evolve between the national government and the STATES. This relationship was not meant to always be cooperative but rather to embody a dynamic tension between the demands of the sovereign national government and the semisovereign state governments. For example, in MCCULLOCH V. MARYLAND (1819), the U.S. Supreme Court drew the line by precluding states from taxing instrumentalities of the federal government within their territorial jurisdiction. In U.S. Term Limits, Inc. v. Thornton (1995), the Court declared that the states have no reserve powers over the composition or operations of the national government, which in this case involved imposing term limits on members of Congress. A second level of federalism is the relationship among the states as they vie with each other and the national government for power and resources to satisfy the demands of their governments and citizens. A third level involves each state's role as "a laboratory" of "social and economic experiments," as Justice Louis D. Brandeis (1856–1941) dubbed it—tinkering with political and legal solutions to problems that all governments often face and making adjustments that can be shared with one another and the national government. At the same time, the states can be proving grounds for political leaders and movements, as reflected in the fact that many governors go on to be president and in concepts such as social security and popular election of senators, which began in the states but later became the national model as well.

A major benefit of federalism, which is derived from a basic distrust of government in general and centralized government in particular, is that it serves as an extension of the doctrine of the SEPARATION OF POWERS and the checks and balances embodied in the Constitution. By analogy with the solar system, the central government—like a sun—is ringed by large and small states—planets—gravitationally keeping the whole system in check and in harmony. As Chief Justice Salmon P. Chase (1808–73) described it in *Texas v. White* (1869): "The Constitution in all its provisions looks to an indestructible Union composed of indestructible states."

The theory of dual federalism, coined by the constitutional scholar EDWARD S. CORWIN, was reflected in many decisions of the Supreme Court before the 1930s. This concept, which viewed the central government and the states as both sovereign and therefore equal, took a back seat during Franklin D. Roosevelt's New Deal beginning in 1933, when the Constitution's provisions granting powers to the national government in the areas of COMMERCE, contracts, and taxing (see TAXATION) and spending were used to centralize the nation's efforts to recover from the Great Depression.

Although the Rehnquist Court of the 1990s again began relying on the doctrine of state sovereignty—also called STATES' RIGHTS—to invalidate some national legislation, in *Reno v. Condon* (2000) the Supreme Court found that the Driver's Privacy Protections Act (1994), which restricts a state's ability to disclose personal information about a driver without his or her consent, does not violate either the Tenth Amendment (1791) or the Eleventh Amendment (1795), which states that the "[j]udicial power of the United States shall not be construed to extend to any suit in law or equity, commenced or prosecuted against one of the United States by Citizens of another State, or by Citizens or Subjects of any Foreign State."

The continuing evolution of the nature of constitutional federalism is reflected in the issue of migratory birds and a state's rights regarding its wetlands, home to such birds. In *Missouri v. Holland* (1920), the Supreme Court relied on the national government's power under Article VI to enact supreme laws of the land pursuant to "Treaties made…under the Authority of the United States" (see TREATIES). It upheld the constitutionality of national legislation that forbid the killing, capturing, or selling of certain migratory birds, a law that was attacked as an infringement of the states' residual rights under the Tenth Amendment. Eighty years later, however, in *Solid Waste Agency of Northern Cook County v. U.S. Army Corps of Engineers* (2001), the Court limited the federal government's authority to deal with national environmental issues by holding that the term *navigable waters*, found in Article I, section 8, did not apply to "isolated ponds, some only seasonal, wholly located within two Illinois counties." Unlike in the 1920 case, the federal government thus was precluded from extending its authority to deal with some environmental problems, which can often involve many states and require concerted efforts across state lines. Although the Supreme Court's more recent decisions have not always supported federal intervention to address far-reaching environmental problems, in *Alaska Department of Environmental Conservation v. Environmental Protection Agency*

CLOSER LOOK

One of the most important aspects of a federalist system is that a single state or province has the capability of transforming national policy. A famous instance of this occurred in Canada in the mid-twentieth century, when a socialist named Tommy Douglas won election as premier of the sparsely settled province of Saskatchewan and set into motion a series of policies that would fundamentally change the entire country.

Douglas instituted a number of changes after his 1944 election, including the nation's first program to offer free hospital care to all residents and a bill of rights that protected fundamental freedoms. With the new programs popular in Saskatchewan, Canadians began a national debate over adopting them for the entire country.

Douglas was initially rebuffed in his call for a national bill of rights in 1950. (Canada, unlike the United States, did not have a bill of rights.) But the nation would eventually adopt the Canadian Charter of Rights and Freedoms.

Douglas scored another triumph in 1962 when, although no longer premier, he helped guide Saskatchewan in the adoption of a public health care program for its residents. Just four years later, the nation adopted a similar plan for all Canadians.

Although Douglas never became prime minister of Canada, his power as a provincial leader was recognized in 2004 when he was voted "The Greatest Canadian" of all time in a national contest organized by the Canadian Broadcasting Corporation.

More on this topic:

Due Process, p. 168

Secession, p. 482

Supremacy Clause, p. 526

(2004), the Court upheld the federal Clean Air Act of 1990 as a basis for federal curtailment of major pollutant-emitting facilities in states. And in *Massachusetts v. Environmental Protection Agency* (2007), the Court went so far as to permit states to force the federal government to take action to curb the effects of greenhouse gases on global warming.

Federalist Papers

Following adjournment of the CONSTITUTIONAL CONVENTION OF 1787 on September 17, 1787, eighty-five essays under the title *The Federalist* appeared in New York newspapers between October 27, 1787, and August 16, 1788, all under the name Publius ("lover or cherisher of the people"), a political figure in the ancient republic of Rome. Written by ALEXANDER HAMILTON, JAMES MADISON, and John Jay, the essays were intended to secure ratification of the CONSTITUTION. Hamilton, a New Yorker and signer of the Constitution, instigated the endeavor. He is believed to have written fifty-one of the essays plus three in conjunction with Madison, who was also a signer of the Constitution and probably wrote twenty-six on his own. Jay, who served as the first chief justice of the United States from 1789 to 1795 and was also a New Yorker, penned five essays. These pieces were directed primarily at the people of New York state and the delegates who would be chosen to vote on whether or not to ratify the Constitution.

There is obvious value in having contemporaneous writings addressing the philosophy behind the constitutional provisions and discussing their advantages, especially over the unsatisfactory ARTICLES OF CONFEDERATION (1781). From the beginning the essays have provided great insight for constitutional lawyers, scholars, and public officials who must interpret the document. THOMAS JEFFERSON called them "the best commentary on the principles of government which ever was written." The essays contain references to

Writing under the pseudonym Publius, Alexander Hamilton, James Madison, and John Jay published a series of newspaper articles on the Constitution known as the Federalist Papers. They appeared in 1787–88, shortly after the Constitutional Convention, and were designed to persuade the states, particularly New York, to adopt the document.

Source: U.S. Senate Historical Office

TOPICS ADDRESSED BY ALEXANDER HAMILTON, JAMES MADISON, AND JOHN JAY IN *THE FEDERALIST* (1787–88)

Number	Topic	Author
1	General Introduction	Hamilton
2–5	Dangers from Foreign Force and Influence	Jay
6–7	Dangers from Dissensions between the States	Hamilton
8	Consequences of Hostilities between the States	Hamilton
9–10	The Union as a Safeguard Against Domestic Faction and Insurrection	Hamilton, Madison
11	Utility of the Union in Respect to Commercial Relations and a Navy	Hamilton
12	Utility of the Union in Respect to Revenue	Hamilton
13	Advantage of the Union in Respect to Economy in Government	Hamilton
14	Objections to the Proposed Constitution from Extent of Territory	Madison
15–20	Insufficiency of the Present Confederation to Preserve the Union	Hamilton, Madison
21–22	Other Defects of the Present Confederation	Hamilton
23	Necessity of an Energetic Government to the Preservation of the Union	Hamilton
24–25	Powers Necessary to the Common Defense	Hamilton
26–28	Restraining Legislative Authority in Regard to the Common Defense	Hamilton
29	The Militia	Hamilton
30–36	General Power of Taxation	Hamilton
37–38	Difficulties of the Convention in Devising a Proper Form of Government	Madison
39	Conformity of the Plan to Republican Principles	Madison
40	Powers of the Convention to Form a Mixed Government	Madison
41–43	Powers Conferred by the Constitution	Madison
44	Restrictions on the Authority of the States	Madison
45	Alleged Danger of the Union to the State Governments	Madison
46	Comparative Influence of the State and Federal Governments	Madison
47	Structure of the New Government and the Distribution of Power	Madison
48	Constitutional Control of Departments Over Each Other	Madison
49	Guarding Against the Encroachments of Any One Department by Appealing to the People Through a Convention	Madison
50	Periodical Appeals to the People	Madison
51	Proper Checks and Balances Between the Departments	Madison
52–53	House of Representatives	Madison
54	Apportionment of Members Among the States	Madison
55–56	Total Number of the House of Representatives	Madison
57	Elevation of the Few at the Expense of the Many	Madison
58	Augmentation of the Number of Members Based on Population	Madison
59–61	Congress's Power to Regulate the Election of Members	Hamilton
62–63	Senate	probably Madison
64–65	Powers of the Senate	Jay, Hamilton
66	Objections to the Senate's Power to Sit as a Court for Impeachments	Hamilton
67	Executive Department	Hamilton
68	Election of the President	Hamilton
69	The Real Character of the Executive	Hamilton
70	Executive Department Further Considered	Hamilton
71–72	Executive's Duration in Office	Hamilton
73	Veto Power	Hamilton
74	Command of the Military and Pardon Power	Hamilton
75	Treaty-making Power	Hamilton
76–77	Appointment Power	Hamilton
78–79	Judiciary Department	Hamilton
80–82	Powers of the Judiciary	Hamilton
83	Trial by Jury	Hamilton
84	Miscellaneous Objections to the Constitution	Hamilton
85	Concluding Remarks	Hamilton

countries and regions around the world—France, Germany, Canada, and Asia—as well as citations to great scholars and philosophers, including the ancient Greek philosopher Plato (ca. 427–347 B.C.E.), Hugo Grotius (1583–1645) of the Netherlands, Montesquieu (1689–1755) of France, and David Hume (1711–76) of Scotland.

> **"The federal Constitution forms a happy combination in this respect; the great and aggregate interests being referred to the national, the local and particular to the State legislatures."**
>
> **—James Madison**

At the time the *Federalist* essays were published, a strong faction known as the Anti-Federalists opposed adoption of the new Constitution on a number of grounds. Citing Montesquieu themselves, the Anti-Federalists insisted that only small countries could benefit from a republic and that large countries ruled by monarchs enjoyed a distinct advantage in foreign affairs. In essay 10 Madison rebutted such arguments. Making a distinction between a pure DEMOCRACY and a republic, he pointed out that even a small republic needs a sufficient number of elected representatives "in order to guard against the cabals of the few; and that however large it may be they must be limited to a certain number in order to guard against the confusion of the multitude." The only difference between the small and the large nation is that "each representative will be chosen by a greater number of citizens in the large than in the small republic...." "The federal Constitution," he concluded, "forms a happy combination in this respect; the great and aggregate interests being referred to the national, the local and particular to the State legislatures."

Other important arguments for ratifying the new constitution included support for a strong union of the states instead of the loose confederation created by the Articles of Confederation; the necessity for a strong, effective, and "energetic" central government; the ability of a republican form of government to maintain liberty as well as stability; and the advantages of a federal government, in which individual states retain some sovereign powers of government. Essay 78 by Hamilton had an impact on the development of the concept of JUDICIAL REVIEW, which is not expressly mentioned in the Constitution but was enunciated by the Supreme Court in *MARBURY V. MADISON* (1803). As Hamilton argued, the Supreme Court's power to declare laws and actions of the other two branches of government unconstitutional has played a key role in the protection and expansion of individual liberties.

More on this topic:

Federalism, p. 218

Hamilton, Alexander, p. 270

Madison, James, p. 355

Ratification, p. 451

For well over two centuries, the Constitution has answered the question posed by Hamilton in the very first essay of *The Federalist*: "whether societies of men are really capable or not of establishing good government from reflection and choice, or whether they are forever destined to depend for their political constitutions on accident and force."

Fifteenth Amendment *See* CIVIL RIGHTS; ELECTIONS; RACIAL DISCRIMINATION; SLAVERY.

Fifth Amendment *See* CRIMINAL LAW; DOUBLE JEOPARDY; DUE PROCESS; JUST COMPENSATION; PROPERTY; WITNESSES.

Filibusters *See* MAJORITY RULE; SENATE.

First Amendment   *See* ASSEMBLY AND ASSOCIATION; THE PRESS; RELIGION; SPEECH.

The Flag

A country's flag is an icon, a symbol of patriotism, sacrifice, and heroism and of the nation itself, or as Justice John Paul Stevens (b. 1920) in his decision for the U.S. Supreme Court in *Elk Grove Unified School District v. Newdow* (2004) put it, citing *Texas v. Johnson* (1989): "'The very purpose of a national flag is to serve as a symbol of our country' and its proud traditions 'of freedom, of equal opportunity, of religious tolerance, and of good will for other peoples who share our aspirations.'" America's national anthem, *The Star-Spangled Banner*, is a paean to the American flag, whose significance as a symbol is further reinforced by the ritual of the pledge of allegiance; the codified rules for handling, flying, and otherwise displaying the flag; and indelible images etched in the national consciousness—U.S. Marines raising the flag on Mount Suribachi to mark the capture of the island of Iwo Jima during World War II and U.S. astronauts displaying the flag on the moon. Certain basic principles of the government of the United States, such as freedom of SPEECH and RELIGION, the right—and, some might argue, the obligation—to criticize the government, and freedom of THE PRESS and artistic expression, however, can come in conflict with the reverence often accorded the flag.

Some national constitutions, such as those of Austria (1920) and the Czech Republic (1991), mention their flags in their constitutions. According to the Austrian constitution, its "flag consists of three identically broad horizontal stripes of which the intermediate is white, the upper and the lower are red." In the Czech Republic, the state symbols mentioned are "the large and small state emblems, the state colors, the state flag, the banner of the president of the republic, the state seal and the state anthem." In contrast, the U.S. Constitution makes no mention of a national flag or any other symbol. However, a number of issues regarding the flag—including symbolic speech (communication using symbols rather than words), the flag's alleged desecration by protesters, and state-sponsored reverence—have found their way into the courts.

"Dread" Scott Tyler's 1988 installation What Is the Proper Way to Display the U.S. Flag? invited viewers to sign an open book by stepping on the national symbol, inspiring outrage and legislation in Congress against flag desecration.
Source: Courtesy of Wessel & O'Connor Fine Art, Brooklyn, NY

Desecration of the Flag

In *Halter v. Nebraska* (1907), a case tried before free speech was deemed applicable to the states through the Fourteenth Amendment (1868) (see INCORPORATION DOCTRINE), the Supreme Court upheld a state law prohibiting desecration or commercial use of the flag. In a series of cases beginning in 1931, the Court recognized that most expression involves more than mere words; conduct too, including use of the flag as a symbol, can communicate ideas. Justice Abe Fortas (1910–82) summed up the issue in *Brown v. Louisiana* (1966): "As this Court has repeatedly stated, these rights are not confined to verbal expression. They embrace appropriate types of action which certainly include the right in a peaceable and orderly manner to protest by silent and reproachful presence, in a place where the protestant has every right to be…" (see ASSEMBLY AND ASSOCIATION).

In *United States v. O'Brien* (1968), the Supreme Court upheld a federal statute prohibiting the burning of draft cards, affirming that it was a valid government regulation unrelated to free-speech issues that arose when protesters burned their draft cards as a symbol of protest against the draft and the Vietnam War. But in *Smith v. Goguen* (1974), the Court reversed a person's conviction, under a Massachusetts flag desecration law, for wearing the flag on the seat of his pants. The statute, the Court held, was void as being too vague. The following year the justices set aside another conviction, under a Washington state law, for placing a peace symbol on the flag. In *Sutherland v. Illinois* (1976), however, the Court upheld a conviction for flag burning because such laws, according to the Court, represented a valid government interest unrelated to freedom of expression such as "the prevention of breaches of the peace and the preservation of public order."

The Supreme Court again did an about-face in *Texas v. Johnson* (1989), holding that burning a flag to protest the Republican Party's renomination of Ronald Reagan (1911–2004) as president, in an incident where no breach of the peace occurred, was not punishable under a Texas desecration law because it was protected as political speech. Justice William J. Brennan (1906–97), writing for the 5–4 majority, noted that the Court had already found a number of nonspeech means of communication protected under the freedom of speech provision of the First Amendment (1791), in-

> **"If there is a bedrock principle underlying the First Amendment, it is that the Government may not prohibit the expression of an idea simply because society finds the idea offensive or disagreeable."**
>
> **—Justice William J. Brennan**

cluding sit-ins and picketing. By punishing a person for burning the flag, Brennan concluded, the state was prohibiting free expression through conduct: "If there is a bedrock principle underlying the First Amendment, it is that the Government may not prohibit the expression of an idea simply because society finds the idea offensive or disagreeable." Chief Justice William H. Rehnquist (1924–2005), who dissented in the *Johnson* case, argued that flag burning did not express an idea but was "the equivalent of an inarticulate grunt or roar… indulged in…to antagonize others." The dissenters wanted the flag held up as "a symbol of freedom, of equal opportunity, of religious tolerance, and of goodwill for all other peoples."

The Flag Protection Act (1989), an attempt by Congress to prohibit flag burning without involving free speech issues, was nullified when a federal district court dismissed charges against persons who had burned the flag in a political demonstration minutes after the act became law. Although ardent patriots still attempt to rewrite the First Amendment's freedom of speech provisions by adding essentially "except in the case of the American flag," the U.S. courts seem to understand that the primary objects of constitutional protection are the U.S. system of government and the individual rights and freedoms for which the flag stands, not a tangible piece of colored cloth.

Salute to the Flag

In *Minersville School District v. Gobitis* (1940), the Supreme Court sanctioned the expulsion from public school of two students—a brother and a sister who as Jehovah's Witnesses were forbidden to worship any graven images—for refusing to join in the daily salute to the flag. In a lone dissent, Chief Justice Harlan Fiske Stone (1872–1946) denounced the state's effort to coerce "these children to express a sentiment which, as they interpret it,…violates their deepest religious convictions."

Three years later the Supreme Court reversed itself. In *West Virginia State Board of Education v. Barnette* (1943), a landmark case in the Court's quest for rational reasoning, the Court concluded:

"Symbolism is a primitive but effective way of communicating ideas. The use of an emblem or flag to symbolize some system, idea, institution, or personality, is a short cut from mind to mind.... [But] if there is any star in our constitutional constella-tion, it is that no official, high or petty, can prescribe what shall

More on this topic:
Censorship, p. 82

be orthodox in politics, nationalism, religion, or other matters of opinion or force citizens to con-fess by word or act their faith therein. If there are any circumstances which permit an exception, they do not now occur to us." Thus, the Court's opinion in *Gobitis* was overruled.

Despite the majority opinions in the *Burnette* and *Johnson* cases, in summer 2001, for the fourth time since 1995, the House of Representatives made yet another attempt to protect the American flag from desecration by constitutionally protected protesters of government policies. Members passed an amendment to the Constitution (see AMENDMENTS) banning flag burning, this time by a vote of 298 to 125, but the measure failed to pass in the Senate. And more recently, in June 2006, during the Republican-controlled 109th Congress, a proposed constitutional amendment to pro-hibit the desecration of the U.S. flag was narrowly defeated in the Senate by a vote of 66–34, which was closer than the four previous votes by the upper house.

Fletcher v. Peck

If a foolish consistency is the hobgoblin of small minds, JOHN MARSHALL, chief justice of the United States, was a genius. In *Fletcher v. Peck* (1810), ostensibly a question regarding a state legislature's power to abrogate the contractual obligation of a preceding legislature, Marshall—as in MARBURY V. MADISON (1803)—produced an opinion that further expanded the role of the Supreme Court in JUDICIAL REVIEW of legislative acts.

The state of Georgia had laid claim in 1785 to an extensive tract of land to its west known as the Yazoo territory, which would ultimately become part of Alabama and Mississippi. Four land companies bribed members of the Georgia legislature to pass a bill on January 7, 1795, selling two-thirds of the land to these companies. A subsequent legislature in the winter of 1795–96 repealed the earlier body's sale of the land but did not return the money paid for it.

In 1802 Georgia again sold its western territory, this time to the federal government, for $1.25 million. Some of the speculators, however, wanted to proceed against Georgia for the loss of their title. Because a direct suit against a state is barred by the Eleventh Amendment (1798), a collusive suit (one in which the parties are not actually adversaries) was filed by John Peck and Robert Fletcher to address the question of Georgia's obligation to those injured in what had become known as the Yazoo land scandal. Peck, a citizen of Massachusetts, had sold 15,000 acres of Yazoo land to Fletcher, so Fletcher sued basically to test whether his title to the land was good or void be-cause of the repeal of the sale.

The difficulty in determining what the Constitution allowed in this case stemmed from the fact that the contract clause found in Article I, section 10, provides, "No state shall...pass any Bill of Attainder, ex post facto Law, or Law impairing the Obligation of Contracts...," while an elemen-tary rule of government precludes any legislature from binding a future legislature. In other words, the legislative repeal of the sale of the Yazoo land to speculators was valid, yet it seemed to violate the Constitution's prohibition against impairing contractual obligations. In his opinion Marshall addressed a number of other, somewhat tangential issues: the distinction between public and pri-vate CONTRACTS and between executory and executed contracts as well as EX POST FACTO LAWS.

In the end Marshall based the Supreme Court's decision on both the Constitution and extra-constitutional principles in a vague and general way. Encompassing both executory and executed as well as public and private contracts, the Court found that state legislatures may not disturb

More on this topic:

Contracts, p. 123

Ex Post Facto Laws, p. 203

Judicial Review, p. 318

Marshall, John, p. 362

vested rights—ones that citizens have come to rely on as valid—and therefore the subsequent legislature's repeal of the earlier sale of Yazoo land was invalid. The ruling's chief importance, however, was that the notion of vested rights was now incorporated into the Constitution. This expanded protection for PROPERTY rights simultaneously broadened the Court's role in the judicial review of state legislation.

Fletcher v. Peck, the Supreme Court's first decision on the Constitution's contract clause, highlights the Court's refusal to look at the motives behind state legislative acts, such as whether the Georgia legislature's initial act in selling the land had been furthered by bribery. More important, in making decisions on the limitations of government, the case represents the Court's reliance for guidance not only on the Constitution itself but also on "general principles which are common to our free institutions." Such principles may present a fundamental inconsistency for a government based on a written constitution. But just as an unwritten constitution contains documents of constitutional stature—Magna Carta (1215), for example, is a part of the United Kingdom's unwritten constitution—a written constitution such as America's may have unwritten constitutional elements alongside it.

In 1814 Congress compensated the Georgia speculators whose title to the land was nullified by repeal of the legislature's sale. Their take: $5 million in return for their initial purchase price of $525,000—a penny and a half per acre for thirty-five million acres (plus the bribes paid).

Foreign Affairs

"If we are to be one nation in any respect, it clearly ought to be in respect to other nations," wrote JAMES MADISON in essay 42 of *The Federalist* (1787–88) (see FEDERALIST PAPERS). The national government's power to "regulate the intercourse with foreign nations" is second only to the power to provide for NATIONAL SECURITY, he noted, and this "*second* class of powers" includes the constitutional authority, as Madison outlined, "to make treaties; to send and receive ambassadors, other public ministers, and consuls; to define and punish piracies and felonies committed on the high seas, and offenses against the law of nations; to regulate foreign commerce, including a power to prohibit, after the year 1808, the importation of slaves...." Concluded Madison, "This class of powers forms an obvious and essential branch of the federal administration."

The constitutions of most nations vest primary responsibility for the conduct of foreign affairs in the chief executive and the executive branch of government. Portugal's constitution

President Richard M. Nixon shakes the hand of China's Communist Party leader, Mao Zedong, in 1972. Nixon's historic visit to China launched a closer political and economic relationship between the United States and the powerful Asian nation.

Source: The White House

(1976), for example, provides: "The President of the Republic shall be competent in international relations to: a. Appoint ambassadors...and accept the credentials of foreign diplomatic representatives; b. Ratify international treaties once they have been duly approved [by the parliament]; c. Declare war in the case of actual or imminent aggression and make peace, at the proposal of the Government...."

The Executive Branch

The role of the PRESIDENT in foreign affairs has evolved since the Constitution went into effect in 1789. Article II, section 2, gives the nation's chief executive the "Power, by and with the Advice and Consent of the Senate, to make Treaties, provided two thirds of the Senators present concur; and he shall nominate, and by and with the Advice and Consent of the Senate, shall appoint Ambassadors, other public Ministers and Consuls...[and] he shall receive Ambassadors and other public Ministers..." (see ADVICE AND CONSENT; AMBASSADORS; TREATIES).

President GEORGE WASHINGTON, on behalf of the EXECUTIVE BRANCH, unilaterally declared the nation's neutrality in the war between Britain and France in 1793, but CONGRESS nevertheless passed a neutrality act in 1794, superceding the president's declaration and asserting the role of the LEGISLATIVE BRANCH under Article I, section 8, to declare WAR. THOMAS JEFFERSON, the third president, refused to accept the appointment of a consul from France because his commission was addressed to Congress. The president, so Jefferson maintained, was "the only channel of communication between the United States and foreign nations, [and] it was from him alone 'that foreign nations or their agents are to learn what is or has been the will of the nation....'" The president also has the power to recognize or not recognize the legitimacy of foreign governments, a problem that might arise after a revolution or a dispute over a de jure or a de facto government.

The tension and cooperation between the president and Congress over foreign policy is a natural result of the SEPARATION OF POWERS and the principle of checks and balances on which the Constitution is based. Depending on the circumstances, the process may help or hinder foreign policy initiatives. After World War I, President Woodrow Wilson (1856–1924), a Democrat, proposed the League of Nations as an organization that could play a significant role in reducing the potential for international conflict. The Republican-dominated Senate, however, refused to approve U.S. participation in the League. It was only after World War II that a similar organization, the United Nations, was finally launched with the United States a charter member.

The U.S. president is both the head of state and the head of government. In contrast, in a parliamentary government such as the United Kingdom's, the monarch is the head of state and the prime minister is the head of government. As head of state, the president is required to ceremonially represent the nation, receiving visiting dignitaries and making state trips to other countries. As head of government, the chief executive is also responsible for developing and executing the nation's foreign policy. Justice Stephen G. Breyer (b. 1938), in his opinion for the Supreme Court in *Zadvydas v. Davis* (2001), confirmed the president's role in foreign affairs by noting that the "[o]rdinary principles of judicial review in this area...recognize Executive Branch primacy in foreign policy matters."

The secretary of state, a position in the first presidential CABINET of 1789, heads the U.S. Department of State. The State Department assists the president in developing and implementing foreign policy through its information resources and its staff in the more than 160 U.S. diplomatic missions around the world. In addition to intergovernmental affairs, the State Department also has a Bureau of International Organization Affairs, which deals with the United Nations and its programs and agencies.

The Legislative Branch

Although the president and the executive branch have become the primary instrument of foreign affairs, the president cannot declare war, and treaties are negotiated by the executive branch but ratified by the SENATE, thus ensuring a continuing role for Congress in certain areas of foreign affairs (see LEGISLATIVE BRANCH). The Constitution, in Article I, section 8, also grants Congress the power "To regulate Commerce with foreign Nations...; [and] To define and punish Piracies and Felonies committed on the high Seas, and Offences against the Law of Nations..." (see INTERNATIONAL LAW).

Most clashes between the president and Congress over their respective constitutional powers have resulted in a victory for the president. *Goldwater v. Carter* (1979), for example, was a challenge by members of Congress—including Sen. Barry Goldwater (R-Ariz.) (1909–98)—to the unilateral abrogation of a U.S.-Taiwan mutual defense treaty by President Jimmy Carter (b. 1924). The Supreme Court held that although the Constitution required Senate approval of this treaty, as for any other treaty, it does not require Senate approval of its abrogation; the president alone may cancel a treaty on behalf of the nation. In a concurring opinion, four of the justices stated that the question posed was a political question, which the Constitution leaves to the branches involved to settle and which is therefore not justiciable by the courts.

The Judicial Branch

The Supreme Court's role in foreign affairs stems from the Constitution's grant of jurisdiction to it under Article III, section 2, which extends "to all Cases, in Law and Equity, arising under this Constitution, the Laws of the United States, and Treaties made...;—to all Cases affecting Ambassadors, other public ministers and Consuls;—to all Cases of admiralty and maritime Jurisdiction;—to Controversies...between a State, or the Citizens thereof, and foreign States, Citizens, or Subjects" (see JUDICIAL BRANCH). The Supreme Court also has final legal authority on the application of international law in the United States.

The way in which the Supreme Court can influence foreign affairs through its decisions and interpretation of international law is demonstrated by its ruling in *The Appollon* (1824). In that case, the Court determined that the maritime jurisdiction of the United States—its territorial waters—extended three miles off its coast, because, as Justice Joseph Story (1779–1845) put it, that was "within the range of a cannon shot from our shores." The jurisdiction asserted over territorial waters (see TERRITORY) has had an impact on relations with other nations, especially with respect to seagoing traffic (see ADMIRALTY AND MARITIME LAW).

Five years after the *Appollon* decision, Chief Justice JOHN MARSHALL explained in *Foster v. Neilson* (1829), a case involving a dispute between the United States and Spain over title to a portion of the

> **"The President, both as Commander in Chief and as the Nation's organ for foreign affairs, has available intelligence services whose reports are not and ought not be published to the world."**
>
> **—Justice Robert H. Jackson**

Louisiana Purchase: "The judiciary is not that department of the government to which the assertion of its interests against foreign powers is confided.... A question like this...is...more political than a legal question." And in *Chicago and Southern Airlines v. Waterman S.S. Corp.* (1948), a case involving applications by national carriers to engage in foreign air transportation, Justice Robert H. Jackson (1892–1954) wrote on behalf of the Court: "The President, both as Commander in Chief and as the Nation's organ for foreign affairs, has available intelligence services whose reports are not and ought not be published to the world. It would be intolerable that courts, without the relevant information, should review and perhaps nullify actions of the Executive taken on information properly held secret."

However, the Supreme Court still has a role to play in determining the constitutionality of the government's foreign affairs actions. In YOUNGSTOWN SHEET AND TUBE CO. V. SAWYER (1952), it held that the attempt by President Harry S. Truman (1884–1972) to seize U.S. steel mills on the eve of an impending union strike, citing national needs during the Korean War, was an unconstitutional exercise of executive power. Had Congress concurred in the action, Truman's executive order might not have been overturned (see EMERGENCY POWERS; EXECUTIVE ORDERS).

Act of State Doctrine

What became known as the Act of State Doctrine was first articulated by Chief Justice Melville W. Fuller (1833–1910) in the Supreme Court's decision in *Underhill v. Hernandez* (1897): "Every sovereign State is bound to respect the independence of every other sovereign State, and the courts of one country will not sit in judgment on the acts of the government of another done within its own territory. Redress of grievances by reason of such acts must be obtained through the means open to be availed of by sovereign powers as between themselves." In other words, because under international law sovereigns speak only to sovereigns, the proper channel for an American citizen's claim of injuries against a foreign government is through the executive branch, led by the head of state, the traditional representative of a nation's SOVEREIGNTY.

The Act of State Doctrine, which is similar to the legal concept of sovereign IMMUNITY, was used by the Supreme Court in *Banco Nacional de Cuba v. Sabbatino* (1964) to decide not to rule on a foreign government's action—in this case, Cuba's taking of PROPERTY belonging to U.S. citizens without JUST COMPENSATION—even when it was a clear violation of international law. A number of exceptions to the doctrine were provided for in the Foreign Sovereign Immunities Act (1976). In response to the *Sabbatino* decision, for example, the act authorized the courts to determine claims of foreign sovereign immunity and claims based on the taking of certain property rights in violation of international law. In addition, the act mandated that a foreign country be denied immunity when the act in question involves a commercial activity or when it is sued for certain types of injuries.

States and Foreign Affairs

One of the basic powers of sovereignty delegated to the national government by the STATES is the power over foreign affairs. This power is inherent in the national sovereignty of the United States and does not depend on any specific language in the Constitution. In *Chae Chan Ping v. United States* (1889), the Supreme Court upheld Congress's power to regulate IMMIGRATION as a right of national sovereignty. And in *United States v. Curtiss-Wright Export Corp.* (1936), the Court ruled that "the investment of the federal government with the powers of external sovereignty did not depend upon the affirmative grants of the Constitution. The power to declare and wage war, to conclude peace, to make treaties, to maintain diplomatic relations with other sovereignties, if they had never been mentioned in the Constitution, would have vested in the federal government as necessary concomitants of nationality...."

This does not mean, however, that states may not have relationships with other countries. In some areas, such as under the COMMERCE clause in Article I, section 8, states can interact with foreign governments as long as the national government has not indicated its intention to preempt the field (see EXCLUSIVE POWERS). Article I, section 10, provides that a state may enter into an agreement with a foreign power as long as it has "the Consent of the Congress."

The states may have direct relations with foreign governments regarding commercial interests, including promoting tourism, attracting international business, and expanding the sale of state products and services. However, the states may not conduct commercial activities that interfere with the national government's policies or actions. In *Crosby et al. v. National Foreign Trade Council* (2000), the Supreme Court held that a Massachusetts law barring companies in the state from conducting business with Burma (now Myanmar), which is ruled by a military junta bent on quashing attempts to restore democracy, had to yield to congressional foreign policy decisions, as required by both the Constitution's commerce clause and its SUPREMACY CLAUSE. Congress had delegated

More on this topic:

Advice and Consent, p. 18

Ambassadors, p. 28

Terrorism, p. 543

Treaties, p. 551

power to the president to lift sanctions if Myanmar made progress in human rights and democracy. Massachusetts's absolute ban conflicted with the national policy of encouraging a change in the Myanmar government's policies.

The states' relations with foreign governments are limited primarily to commercial interests. In *Zschernig v. Miller* (1968), the Supreme Court reviewed a state law that denied an alien's inheritance of property unless a state court was satisfied that the alien's country of origin reciprocated by allowing U.S. citizens to inherit property (see ALIENS); the Court found that the state law was improper because it permitted a state court to rule on the acts of a foreign government.

Even in a federal system of government (see FEDERALISM), it is desirable that as far as possible a nation speak with one voice in international affairs. The Constitution, while expressly assigning certain aspects of foreign affairs to the legislative and judicial branches, is structured to allow the president and the executive branch to have the primary role, especially in times of emergency such as war or, more recently, the nation's response to the terrorist attacks of September 11, 2001 (see TERRORISM).

Founding Fathers   *See* FRAMERS OF THE CONSTITUTION.

Fourteenth Amendment   *See* REAPPORTIONMENT; CITIZENS; CIVIL RIGHTS; DEBT; DUE PROCESS; ELECTIONS; EQUAL PROTECTION; RACIAL DISCRIMINATION; SECESSION.

Fourth Amendment   *See* SEARCH AND SEIZURE.

Framers of the Constitution

The fifty-five delegates who attended the CONSTITUTIONAL CONVENTION OF 1787 at the State House in Philadelphia did not set out to create a utopian state. They simply wanted to provide a means for securing the internal order and defense of the United States, removing trade barriers between the states, and ensuring a fiscally sound national government with limited powers that would not threaten the residual sovereignty of the states and the citizens.

On February 21, 1787, the Continental Congress invited the states to send delegates, who were chosen by various means, to the convention. Well educated for their time, they were knowledgeable about the history of Great Britain and the other major nations of the world. Many of them were financially well off, but some had suffered setbacks from the Revolutionary War (1775–83), postwar speculation, and the new nation's uncertain economy under the ARTICLES OF CONFEDERATION (1781), which had been adopted as a basis for running the new confederation of the thirteen former British colonies. Most of the delegates owned considerable property, and thirty-five owned slaves.

Delegations came from twelve of the thirteen states to attend the four-month convention in Philadelphia beginning on May 25, 1787. Only Rhode Island, notorious for having a state government rife with corruption, did not send any delegates because it did not relish having a national government that would force it to put its political house in order. The framers signed the CONSTITUTION on September 17, 1787, according to state delegations in the order discussed, except for

Howard Chandler Christy's 1940 painting captures the signing of the Constitution on September 17, 1787. In front of George Washington, Benjamin Franklin is flanked by Alexander Hamilton and the "Father of the Constitution," James Madison.
Source: Library of Congress

GEORGE WASHINGTON of Virginia, who as the president of the convention signed first. Delegates who did not sign the Constitution for political reasons or because they had to leave on personal business are indicated by an asterisk (*) after their name. Six delegates—George Clymer, Benjamin Franklin, Robert Morris, and James Wilson of Pennsylvania; George Read of Delaware; and Roger Sherman of Connecticut—were signers of both the DECLARATION OF INDEPENDENCE (1776) and the Constitution.

After thirty-nine of the fifty-five delegates signed the document, Washington sent a resolution transmitting the new document to the Congress, which on September 28 then transmitted it to the state legislatures so that the nation's new Constitution could be debated and approved by special conventions in each state. Delaware became the first state to ratify the Constitution on December 7, 1787, followed by Pennsylvania on December 12, New Jersey on December 18, Georgia on January 2, 1788, Connecticut on January 9, Massachusetts on February 6, Maryland on April 28, and South Carolina on May 23. When New Hampshire became the ninth state to ratify on June 21, 1788, the document had obtained the sanction of three-fourths of the states as required under Article VII. Four days later Virginia gave its assent, followed by New York on July 26. The next year, North Carolina ratified the Constitution on November 21, 1789, and Rhode Island added its approval on May 29, 1790 (see RATIFICATION).

New Hampshire

John Langdon (1741–1819). The former president of his state and speaker of its legislature, John Langdon was a mercantile businessman who owned considerable property. He served as a colonel in the army during the Revolutionary War and as a member of the Continental Congress from 1777 to 1781. Langdon was the chairman of the two-person New Hampshire delegation sent to Philadelphia in 1787 (two other delegates declined to attend) and personally helped defray its expenses. A Federalist in favor of a strong national government, he supported a congressional veto over state legislation, among other measures, and took an active part in the convention proceedings, serving on three committees. Afterward, Langdon worked for the RATIFICATION of the CONSTITUTION and served in the Senate (1789–1801), becoming the first president pro tempore. He later served as governor of New Hampshire in 1805–09 and 1810–12.

Nicholas Gilman (1755–1814). The son of a general store owner and the brother of John Taylor Gilman, who was elected governor of New Hampshire several times, Nicholas Gilman was a captain in the army by the end of the Revolutionary War in 1783. At the CONSTITUTIONAL CONVENTION OF 1787, he played a supporting role to John Langdon, the delegation's chairman. Gilman was a moderate Federalist and after the convention worked actively in New Hampshire for RATIFICATION of the CONSTITUTION. Elected to the House of Representatives in the first Congress under the new Constitution, he served from 1789 until 1797, becoming disenchanted with the prospect of a strong national government promoted by the Federalist Party. Switching to the Democratic-Republican Party, he was appointed by President THOMAS JEFFERSON to the position of bankruptcy commissioner in 1802.

Massachusetts

Nathaniel Gorham (1738–96). Apprenticed to a merchant in Connecticut until 1759 and not well educated, Nathaniel Gorham returned to the place of his birth—Charlestown, Massachusetts—and became a successful merchant. Having served in the Massachusetts colonial legislature (1771–75), including as speaker of its lower house for three years, he represented his home state in the Congress convened under the ARTICLES OF CONFEDERATION in 1782–83 and again in 1785–87, serving as president for a little more than half a year. A supporter of a strong national government, Gorham was among the most active delegates to the CONSTITUTIONAL CONVENTION OF 1787. He chaired the Committee of the Whole, in which the delegates sat as a body to consider measures, and also served on the Committee of Detail, which produced a rough draft of the CONSTITUTION. A businessman who saw America's role as being whatever was good for business, Gorham tended to vote with fellow delegate Rufus King and against the other two Massachusetts delegates. After the convention, he served until 1796 as a judge in Massachusetts (although he was not a lawyer).

Rufus King (1755–1827). One of the youngest delegates, Rufus King was a graduate of Harvard. An attorney who was first elected to the Massachusetts legislature in 1783, he was sent in 1784 as a delegate to the Congress under the ARTICLES OF CONFEDERATION. King helped write the Northwest Ordinance to govern the territory of the United States—especially its provisions prohibiting SLAVERY and impairment of the obligations of CONTRACTS—but had not supported the calling of the CONSTITUTIONAL CONVENTION OF 1787 to change the Articles. An advocate of a strong central government, he opposed equal representation of the states in the Senate. King supported the election of the president by popular vote instead of the electoral system ultimately agreed on by a majority of the delegates. However, the contract clause and the provision admitting new states on an equal footing, which he urged, were included in the document's final draft. After the convention he moved to New York and served as U.S. senator from that state from 1789 to 1796, supporting ALEXANDER HAMILTON, his political patron. King also helped write the 1821 constitution of New York and after being reelected served in the Senate until retiring in 1825 and becoming minister to Great Britain until his health failed in 1826.

Elbridge Gerry* (1744–1814). The man who would lend his name to the lizardlike configuration of a voting district created to favor one political party over another—the Gerrymander—was an Anti-Federalist. Having worked in his father's dried-fish shipping business, Elbridge Gerry was graduated from Harvard and in 1772 won election to the Massachusetts legislature. He was also elected to the Second Continental Congress in 1776 and signed the ARTICLES OF CONFEDERATION in 1781. From 1779 to 1785 Gerry represented Massachusetts in the Congress held under the Articles. Although he favored republicanism, he nevertheless opposed "an excess of democracy." Gerry was the chairman of the committee that proposed the "Great Compromise" to satisfy both large and small states—giving the large states representation by population in the House of Representatives and the smaller states equal representation in the Senate—but he could not support the final draft of the CONSTITUTION because there was no BILL OF RIGHTS and too much power was concentrated in the national government. Elected a member of the first Congress under the new Constitution in 1789, he was later elected governor of his home state as a Republican in 1810 and 1811. During his second term the state legislature created new districts so contorted to maintain Republican voting strength that a political cartoon of the day likened one to a salamander, dubbing it a "Gerrymander" (see REAPPORTIONMENT). Gerry served as the nation's vice president under JAMES MADISON from 1813 until his death.

Caleb Strong* (1745–1819). Of Puritan heritage, Caleb Strong was a pragmatic Federalist who supported the CONSTITUTION but doubted whether the expanding new nation could long endure united. Strong was blessed with common sense, which he displayed at the CONSTITUTIONAL CONVENTION OF 1787. Because of an illness in his family, he was not able to sign the document. His personality and character, however, helped him persuade the Massachusetts RATIFICATION convention to adopt the Constitution. Afterward he served as one of the state's first senators from 1789 to 1793, helping frame the Judiciary Act (1789). He defeated Elbridge Gerry to become governor of Massachusetts in 1800 and won reelection annually until 1807 but then regained the post in 1812, again over Gerry, serving until retiring in 1816.

Connecticut

William Samuel Johnson (1727–1819). William Samuel Johnson, a descendant of one of the founders of New Haven, Connecticut, was held in high esteem by his fellow citizens, even though he had remained neutral during the American Revolution. Admitted to the Connecticut bar in 1749, Johnson, a state legislator and judge, played the role of conciliator at the CONSTITUTIONAL CONVENTION OF 1787. He formally proposed the "Great Compromise" (also called the "Connecticut Compromise") by which the large states gained representation by population in the House of Representatives and the smaller states received equal representation in the Senate. Also instrumental in writing the CONSTITUTION's judicial article (Article III), he is credited with adding the requirement that judicial power extend to "all Cases arising under the Constitution and laws of the United States." Johnson was the chairman of the convention's Committee on Style and served as a U.S. senator from 1789 to 1791.

> *Instrumental in writing the Constitution's judicial article (Article III), William Samuel Johnson is credited with adding the requirement that judicial power extend to "all Cases arising under the Constitution and laws of the United States."*

Roger Sherman of Connecticut, a signer of three seminal American documents, opposed a strong national government but supported the "Great Compromise," which struck a balance of power between the large and small states.
Source: Library of Congress

Roger Sherman (1721–93). A skilled politician who was the oldest delegate after Benjamin Franklin, Roger Sherman supported the Federalist aims with respect to commerce, but otherwise he feared a strong national government. He studied law with William Samuel Johnson and was elected to the colonial legislature in 1755. In 1766 he began a twenty-three-year career as a judge of the Connecticut Superior Court and in 1776 signed the DECLARATION OF INDEPENDENCE, later also signing the ARTICLES OF CONFEDERATION. At the CONSTITUTIONAL CONVENTION OF 1787, Sherman helped secure the adoption of the "Great Compromise" to satisfy large and small states' demands for representation in Congress.

*Oliver Ellsworth** (1745–1807). A moderate Federalist and an active delegate at the CONSTITUTIONAL CONVENTION OF 1787, Oliver Ellsworth later became the second CHIEF JUSTICE of the United States. Born into a successful Connecticut farming family, he attended Yale but was expelled because of disciplinary problems. After graduation from Princeton in 1766, Ellsworth studied law and was admitted to the bar in 1771. A delegate to the Continental Congress from 1778 to 1783 and a judge on his state's highest court, he was an influential delegate at the Philadelphia convention, serving on the Committee of Detail, which produced a rough draft of the CONSTITUTION. Admired by a congressional colleague for the "neatness and accuracy of his mind," Ellsworth was elected in 1789 to the first Congress as a senator from Connecticut. He served as chief justice from 1796 to 1800.

New York

Alexander Hamilton (1757–1804). ALEXANDER HAMILTON possessed a brilliant mind and extreme views on the benefits of strong, centralized government. During the CONSTITUTIONAL CONVENTION OF 1787, his call for a virtual dissolution of the states placed him at ideological odds with the two other New York delegates, John Lansing and Robert Yates, and at the political fringe. Hamilton nonetheless was the only delegate from his state to sign the document and always maintained that he was in agreement with "the strict theory of Government purely Republican." He also vigorously pressed for RATIFICATION at the New York state convention in 1788 and organized publication of *The Federalist Papers* (1787–88) (see FEDERALIST PAPERS), to which he contributed fifty-one of eighty-five essays. As the first secretary of the Treasury in 1789, Hamilton defended his Report on the National Bank by citing the theory of IMPLIED POWERS and the NECESSARY AND PROPER CLAUSE contained in the CONSTITUTION. His arguments still guide the interpretation of legislative powers under the Constitution.

*John Lansing** (1754–1829). John Lansing was chosen as a delegate to represent New York's Anti-Federalist leanings. An upper-class slaveholder and lawyer who had studied for the bar with fellow delegate Robert Yates, he opposed creating a strong national government. On July 10, 1787, he and Yates withdrew from the convention on the grounds that it was exceeding its mandate to simply amend the ARTICLES OF CONFEDERATION. Lansing worked to defeat New York's RATIFICATION of the CONSTITUTION, but after approval seemed certain he urged a number of conditions for ratification, including the addition of a BILL OF RIGHTS.

Robert Yates* (1738–1801). An ardent Anti-Federalist, Robert Yates withdrew from the CONSTITUTIONAL CONVENTION OF 1787 in July with John Lansing, declaring that he disagreed with every step taken to draft the CONSTITUTION and with every "sentence in it." A lawyer who was admitted to the bar in 1760, he served as an alderman in Albany and as a member of the committee that drafted New York's first constitution in 1777. The notes Yates kept on the convention are considered second only to JAMES MADISON's with regard to the early proceedings. After the convention, Yates published letters under the pseudonym "Brutus" that set forth alleged dangers in adopting the Constitution. (The letters of ALEXANDER HAMILTON, James Madison, and John Jay, all Federalist supporters of RATIFICATION, were published in *The Federalist* (1787–88) [see FEDERALIST PAPERS] under the name "Publius.") At New York's convention to approve the Constitution, Yates voted against it.

Robert Yates claimed he disagreed with every step taken to draft the Constitution, and with every "sentence in it."

New Jersey

William Livingston (1723–90). As a boy, William Livingston had lived with missionaries among the Mohawk people. Educated at Yale, he became a successful lawyer and was elected to the New York legislature in 1759. After a political falling-out over how best to resist the British, Livingston moved to New Jersey to become a gentleman farmer. A delegate to the First and Second Continental Congresses in 1774 and 1775–76, he left to lead the New Jersey militia in 1776. Livingston spoke little at the CONSTITUTIONAL CONVENTION OF 1787 but was instrumental in forging the compromise on SLAVERY. A moderate Federalist, he helped win New Jersey's RATIFICATION of the CONSTITUTION. Livingston died in office in 1790, having served as governor of New Jersey for fourteen years.

David Brearley (1745–90). Educated at the College of New Jersey (later Princeton), David Brearley began the practice of law in New Jersey before 1770. A colonel in the New Jersey infantry during the Revolutionary War and a member of New Jersey's constitutional convention in 1776, Brearley became the state's chief justice in 1779. Like his fellow delegate William Paterson, he supported the small states' position at the convention. A man of modest means, Judge Brearley presided over New Jersey's ratifying convention, where he eloquently led the fight for RATIFICATION. President GEORGE WASHINGTON named him a judge on the federal district court for New Jersey in 1789, a position he held until his death a year later.

William Paterson (1745–1806). After coming to New Jersey from Ireland at the age of two, William Paterson graduated from Princeton and became a member of the New Jersey bar in 1768. He helped draft the state's first constitution in 1776 and served as the state attorney general from 1776 to 1783. At the CONSTITUTIONAL CONVENTION OF 1787, Paterson was influential in determining the final composition of Congress. His plan—the New Jersey Plan—was in opposition to the Virginia Plan urged by JAMES MADISON and a majority of the other delegates. His suggestion that equal votes be given to all states in a unicameral legislature led to the "Great Compromise," which produced a bicameral Congress consisting of a Senate with two senators from each state and a House of Representatives with proportional representation based on population. Satisfied that he had gotten the concessions he wanted for his state, Paterson left the convention in July but returned in September to sign the document. He later became a U.S. senator in 1789 and then governor of New Jersey in 1790. President GEORGE WASHINGTON appointed him to the U.S. Supreme Court in 1793, a position he held until his death.

William Paterson's suggestion that equal votes be given to all states in a unicameral legislature led to the "Great Compromise," which produced a bicameral Congress consisting of a Senate with two senators from each state and a House of Representatives with proportional representation based on population.

Jonathan Dayton (1760–1824). At twenty-seven the youngest signer of the CONSTITUTION, Jonathan Dayton served as a delegate in place of his father,

General Elias Dayton of Elizabethtown, New Jersey. Educated at Princeton, he was promoted to the rank of captain in the Continental Army at the age of nineteen. Dayton was concerned particularly with the rights of smaller states. As a slaveholder, he opposed the compromise of counting slaves as three-fifths of a person for purposes of congressional representation and taxation and wanted a simple majority for Senate approval of TREATIES instead of the two-thirds finally agreed on. First elected to the House of Representatives in 1791, Dayton served as SPEAKER OF THE HOUSE in 1797–99. He was arrested in 1807, but not convicted, for conspiring with Aaron Burr to take over Mexico and parts of Florida and Louisiana.

William Churchill Houston* (1746–88). An attorney from Trenton, New Jersey, and a second-level leader during his time, William Churchill Houston was dying of tuberculosis when he arrived at the CONSTITUTIONAL CONVENTION OF 1787 in Philadelphia. He contributed little to the debates during his two weeks at the convention and never signed the document.

Pennsylvania

The oldest delegate to the Constitutional Convention, Benjamin Franklin had been an active legislator in the Second Continental Congress and signed both the Declaration of Independence and the Constitution.
Source: Library of Congress

Benjamin Franklin (1706–90). The first president of Pennsylvania and the oldest and most famous delegate to the CONSTITUTIONAL CONVENTION OF 1787, Benjamin Franklin added his prestige to the undertaking and helped ease tensions among the other delegates. Born in Boston, he moved to Philadelphia in 1723, where he was employed as a printer. After spending two years in England, he returned and published *The Pennsylvania Gazette* from 1730 to 1748. His *Poor Richard's Almanac*, published from 1733 to 1758, became a big hit in America and Europe. In addition to publishing and scientific pursuits—Franklin's experiments with electricity using a kite became world famous—he was active before and during the Revolutionary War in Pennsylvania politics and government and the nascent union of the thirteen former British colonies. In 1754 Franklin was a delegate to the Albany Congress, where he proposed the Albany Plan of a colonial union. At the Second Continental Congress in 1775 he suggested articles of confederation and served the following year on the committee with THOMAS JEFFERSON and three others to draft the DECLARATION OF INDEPENDENCE, which he signed as well. Franklin was a notable minister to France from 1776 to 1785 and was also accredited to several other countries. Although he did not play a leading role at the Constitutional Convention, he facilitated much of its work, sometimes with a joke or a homily to ease tensions or to bring contending parties together in compromise. His own proposals for a unicameral legislature, a plural executive, and an elected judiciary did not find support among the delegates. Nonetheless, upon leaving the convention, he is alleged to have said, when asked what the delegates had created: "A republic, if you can keep it."

Upon leaving the Constitutional Convention, Benjamin Franklin is alleged to have said, when asked what the delegates had created: "A republic, if you can keep it."

Thomas Mifflin (1744–1800). A former president of the United States under the ARTICLES OF CONFEDERATION in 1783 and speaker of the Pennsylvania legislature, Thomas Mifflin attended the CONSTITUTIONAL CONVENTION OF 1787 as the chairman of his state's delegation. Born into a well-to-do Philadelphia family, Mifflin was graduated from the College of Philadelphia at the age of sixteen. A successful businessman, he fought in the Revolutionary War—against the tenets of his Quaker faith—becoming a general in 1776. He was elected to the Pennsylvania legislature in 1778 and served as a delegate to the Continental Congress in 1782. Although Mifflin regularly attended the sessions of the Constitutional Convention, he played only a marginal role in its deliberations. He continued in politics afterward, succeeding Benjamin Franklin as the chief executive of Pennsylvania and later becoming governor of the state from 1790 to 1799.

Robert Morris (1734–1806). Robert Morris, like Roger Sherman, signed the DECLARATION OF INDEPENDENCE, ARTICLES OF CONFEDERATION, and CONSTITUTION. Born in England, he joined his father in Maryland at the age of thirteen. Morris rose from humble beginnings to learn the banking and trading business as a young man in Philadelphia, becoming a member of the Pennsylvania legislature and the Continental Congress in 1775. Under his stewardship the finances of the Continental Congress were saved in 1781 by a loan that allowed him to create the Bank of North America. Regularly in attendance at the CONSTITUTIONAL CONVENTION OF 1787, he spoke only twice in debates. After turning down President GEORGE WASHINGTON's offer to serve as the first secretary of state, Morris was elected to the Senate in 1789. Plagued by financial difficulties in later life, he wound up in debtors' prison in 1798 and died in relative obscurity in Philadelphia.

George Clymer (1739–1813). At the CONSTITUTIONAL CONVENTION OF 1787, George Clymer played a small but effective role as a conscientious delegate and a member of the committees on state debts and the slave trade. An orphan, he was raised by a wealthy uncle who groomed him for his mercantile business in Pennsylvania. Hurt by the harsh British policies against trade in the colonies, he was one of the first people to support independence and also signed the DECLARATION OF INDEPENDENCE. A three-term member of the Continental Congress (1776–77, 1780–82, 1784–88) and a state legislator, Clymer supported a bicameral national legislature and argued against the DEATH PENALTY. At the convention he regularly attended the sessions, speaking seldom but effectively. Elected in 1789 as one of Pennsylvania's first representatives to the new Congress, he was later appointed in 1795 as a commissioner to negotiate a treaty between the Cherokee and Creek peoples in Georgia.

George Clymer of Pennsylvania was another signer of both the Declaration of Independence and the Constitution. He supported a bicameral legislature and went on to become an early state representative in the new Congress.
Source: Library of Congress

Thomas FitzSimons (1741–1811). An aristocratic merchant, Thomas FitzSimons favored a strong national government for commercial reasons. Born in Ireland, he was one of two Roman Catholics at the CONSTITUTIONAL CONVENTION OF 1787. He was a founder of the Bank of North America and one of its directors from 1781 to 1803, and he served as a state legislator from 1785 to 1789. Active in the Philadelphia convention, FitzSimons supported restrictions on the right to vote and making wealth a qualification for high office. He nonetheless generally followed Robert Morris and the Federalists in his voting at the convention. A supporter of ALEXANDER HAMILTON's views of the role of the national government, FitzSimons served in the House of Representatives from 1789 to 1795. Later he returned to

Philadelphia, becoming the president of its chamber of commerce. After going bankrupt in 1805, he recovered some of his wealth although not his prestige.

Jared Ingersoll (1749–1822). The son of a British colonial official, Jared Ingersoll was born in Connecticut. After graduation from Yale in 1766, he studied law and was admitted to the bar of Pennsylvania, continuing his legal education in London. In 1780 he was elected to the Continental Congress before becoming a delegate to the CONSTITUTIONAL CONVENTION OF 1787. Seldom speaking at the sessions, which he faithfully attended, Ingersoll supported revising the ARTICLES OF CONFEDERATION. Afterward he held a number of public offices in Pennsylvania, but his campaign to be elected vice president under the Federalist Party banner failed in 1812. He appeared in important cases before the U.S. Supreme Court and represented William Blount of North Carolina, another signer of the CONSTITUTION, in his defense against IMPEACHMENT.

James Wilson (1742–98). One of the six men to have signed both the DECLARATION OF INDEPENDENCE and the CONSTITUTION, James Wilson was an influential delegate at the CONSTITUTIONAL CONVENTION OF 1787, speaking more than anyone except his fellow Pennsylvania delegate Gouverneur Morris. Born in Scotland, Wilson came to America in 1765. Two years later, after studying with John Dickinson of Delaware, he became a member of the Pennsylvania bar. A delegate to the Second Continental Congress in 1775, he was wary of independence from Britain but voted for the 1776 declaration anyway. His contributions to the deliberations at the 1787 convention rank second only to those of the "Father of the Constitution," JAMES MADISON. However, Wilson disagreed with Madison's basic distrust of the citizens and the need for elaborate constitutional mechanisms to protect the people from themselves. Wilson believed that "no government could long subsist without the confidence of the people" and that the new national government should be given "as broad a basis as possible." His arguments that both houses of Congress should be elected by the people finally bore fruit with the ratification of the Seventeenth Amendment in 1913, which required that senators be chosen in popular elections rather than by the state legislatures. Wilson also argued

> **Wilson believed that "no government could long subsist without the confidence of the people" and that the new national government should be given "as broad a basis as possible."**

for a strong federal judiciary to defend the principles enshrined in the CONSTITUTION. Like ALEXANDER HAMILTON, he did not believe that a BILL OF RIGHTS was necessary. Wilson went on to help write Pennsylvania's 1790 constitution and was appointed one of the six original members of the U.S. Supreme Court. Having developed his own theory of government and law, he gave lectures at what would become the University of Pennsylvania.

Gouverneur Morris (1752–1816). Responsible to a large extent for the final wording of the CONSTITUTION, Gouverneur Morris was a leading member of the CONSTITUTIONAL CONVENTION OF 1787, giving 173 speeches during the session. Born in New York into a wealthy family of mixed French and English ancestry, he was graduated at the age of sixteen from what would become Columbia University. After being admitted to the bar three years later, he served in a revolutionary provincial congress in New York in 1775. In 1776 he joined the militia and helped draft New York's first state constitution the following year. A member of the New York state legislature and the Continental

Gouverneur Morris of Pennsylvania led the Committee of Detail in shaping the final wording of the Constitution. Although his proposal for life-long presidential tenure failed, Morris's concept of a decimal system of coinage is still in use.
Source: Library of Congress

Congress, he signed the ARTICLES OF CONFEDERATION. Morris relocated to Philadelphia after losing reelection to Congress in 1779. Two years later he became the assistant to Robert Morris, superintendent of finance for the United States. His proposal for a decimal system of coins, as modified by THOMAS JEFFERSON, resulted in the type of coins we use today. Although Gouverneur Morris personally wanted the president to have lifelong tenure in office and senators to be appointed by the president, as chairman of the Committee of Detail he hammered out the final draft of the Constitution as adopted by a majority of the delegates. He changed the beginning of the preamble from "We, the People of the [enumerated states]…" to "We, the People of the United States…" and added the list of reasons for the new Constitution stated in the PREAMBLE. Although Morris undertook a failed diplomatic mission to London in 1790, he was appointed ambassador to France by President GEORGE WASHINGTON in 1792, replacing Jefferson.

Delaware

George Read (1733–98). Another signer of both the DECLARATION OF INDEPENDENCE and the CONSTITUTION, George Read led the Delaware delegation at the CONSTITUTIONAL CONVENTION OF 1787 with John Dickinson and argued for a unitary, rather than a federal, government through the abolition of state boundaries. Read was born in Maryland but subsequently moved with his well-off family to Delaware and went to school in Pennsylvania. He began studying law at the age of fifteen, was admitted to the bar in 1753, and began a practice in New Castle, Delaware, the following year. Read acted as attorney general for the Crown from 1763 to 1774. That year he became a member of the Continental Congress and signed the Declaration of Independence in 1776 even though he had voted against it. The presiding officer at the Delaware constitutional convention, Read also chaired the drafting committee. He spoke often at the convention in Philadelphia, especially in favor of the rights of the smaller states. Afterward he led the fight for RATIFICATION by Delaware—which became the first state to do so—and served as U.S. senator from Delaware from 1789 to 1793, resigning to become chief justice of his home state.

Gunning Bedford Jr. (1747–1812). A roommate of JAMES MADISON's at what would become Princeton University, Gunning Bedford was a fierce advocate for Delaware's interests at the CONSTITUTIONAL CONVENTION OF 1787. Born in Philadelphia, Bedford was graduated from the College of New Jersey (later Princeton) in 1771 and was admitted to the Pennsylvania bar. He later moved to Wilmington, Delaware. Having been a member of the Delaware state legislature and the Continental Congress from 1783 to 1785, Bedford was chosen a delegate to the 1786 convention in Annapolis, Maryland, that preceded the 1787 Constitutional Convention, but he did not attend. Once in Philadelphia, however, he championed the interests of the smaller states, arguing for their equal representation, as well as for efficient procedures for removing the president. Bedford also protested the proposal to allow Congress to veto state legislation. A delegate to the Delaware ratifying convention and twice a presidential elector, he held no major political posts after the adoption of the CONSTITUTION.

John Dickinson (1732–1810). Born into a wealthy Quaker family, John Dickinson studied law in England and became a successful lawyer in Philadelphia. As a delegate to the Congress convened in response to the British Stamp Act (1765), he drafted the statement called the Declaration of Rights and Grievances (1765), which petitioned George III for relief from the act's onerous provisions. Dickinson was an expert on the constitutional relations between the colonies and Britain, writing in 1774 that while George III was king of the American colonies, Parliament's power to legislate for the colonies was "equally contradictory to humanity and the Constitution [of Great Britain], and illegal." The principal author of the ARTICLES OF CONFEDERATION, he was called the "Penman of the Revolution." Dickinson represented Delaware at the 1786 Annapolis convention that recommended the CONSTITUTIONAL CONVENTION OF 1787, and he was again chosen to represent

Delaware at the convention. Although he did not play a major role there, he was the first to propose a bicameral Congress with equal representation of the states in one house and proportional representation in the second. Dickinson wrote articles under the name of "Fabius" in support of RATIFICATION of the CONSTITUTION but declined to hold any public office in the new government. Earlier he had served as president of both Delaware (1781–82) and Pennsylvania (1782–85).

Richard Bassett (1745–1815). Born in Maryland, Richard Basset inherited a large estate near Delaware and was admitted to the practice of law there in 1770. A Revolutionary War leader, Basset was a member of the Delaware state constitutional convention (1776) and the state legislature. A follower of the delegate John Dickinson, he played no major role at the convention but helped get the document ratified in his home state. A devout Methodist and a loyal Federalist, he became a U.S. senator from Delaware in 1789 and later chief justice of the Delaware Court of Common Pleas. He served as governor from 1799 to 1801, but his appointment by JOHN ADAMS to the federal district court failed when the opposition party in Congress, the Democratic-Republicans, abolished his seat on the court.

Jacob Broom (1752–1810). The son of a blacksmith, Jacob Broom became a farmer, merchant, and banker in Delaware. A member of the state legislature in 1784–87 and 1788–89, he was chosen a delegate to the 1786 convention held in Annapolis that led directly to the CONSTITUTIONAL CONVENTION OF 1787 in Philadelphia. A supporter of the interests of the smaller states, Broom feared a strong national executive. His major contribution to the proceedings was to argue against terminating the convention over the issue of whether the people or the states should be represented in Congress. Broom pushed for Delaware's early RATIFICATION of the CONSTITUTION, giving it the status of the "First State" in the union.

Maryland

James McHenry (1753–1816). General GEORGE WASHINGTON's secretary toward the end of the Revolutionary War and later assigned to the staff of the Marquis de Lafayette, James McHenry took valuable notes at the CONSTITUTIONAL CONVENTION OF 1787. Born in Ireland and trained in medicine in Philadelphia, McHenry entered the Continental Army in 1775, and after leaving the service in 1781 he was elected to the Maryland senate. A representative from Maryland to the Congress under the ARTICLES OF CONFEDERATION from 1783 to 1785, he was chosen to represent the commercial community at the convention in Philadelphia. However, McHenry was unable to attend during the first two months, and when he was present he spoke little. He later served as secretary of war in President Washington's administration.

Daniel of St. Thomas Jenifer (1723–90). A wealthy aristocrat, Daniel Jenifer had little personal impact on the CONSTITUTIONAL CONVENTION OF 1787. The owner of a large estate near Annapolis, he was a commercial agent and became a member of a provincial court and the royal governor's council in Maryland. Having profited from his relationship with the British Crown, he was slow to embrace the movement for independence. Although Jenifer envisioned the nation's full attainment of liberty only as a future prospect, he served as president of the Maryland senate in 1777–80 and as a delegate to the Continental Congress in 1778–82. As a friend of GEORGE WASHINGTON's, he followed the lead of Washington and JAMES MADISON at the convention. He died three years later.

Daniel Carroll (1730–96). The brother of the Catholic archbishop of Baltimore, Daniel Carroll signed both the ARTICLES OF CONFEDERATION and the CONSTITUTION. A man of wealth and influence who had been educated by Jesuits in Flanders, he used slaves to grow tobacco on his land. Not an avid revolutionary, he was nevertheless a member of the Maryland Council of Safety (a body charged with organizing the defense of the state), and he later served in the Maryland senate and in the Congress under the Articles from 1781 to 1783. Chosen after other Marylanders refused appointment to the CONSTITUTIONAL CONVENTION OF 1787, Carroll became the authoritative spokesman for the Maryland delegation. He favored a strong national government—the better to protect the value of currency and property—spoke often, and served on three committees. Elected to the House of Representatives in 1789, Carroll supported the BILL OF RIGHTS. A friend of President GEORGE WASHINGTON's, he was appointed as one of the three commissioners chosen to establish the District of Columbia (see CAPITAL, NATIONAL).

*Luther Martin** (1748–1826). Luther Martin opposed the encroachment on the rights of sovereign states by a strong national government, nearly destroying the CONSTITUTIONAL CONVENTION OF 1787 in Philadelphia with his opposition to proportional representation in the House of Representatives. Born into a New Jersey farming family, he was graduated in 1766 from the College of New Jersey (later Princeton) and moved to Maryland to be a teacher. He began studying law there and then moved to Virginia, where he continued his studies and took the bar examination given by George Wythe, later a Virginia delegate to the Constitutional Convention. He returned to Maryland to practice law. Becoming friends with Samuel Chase, a future justice of the U.S. Supreme Court, he was appointed Maryland attorney general in 1778, serving until 1805. In favor of JUDICIAL REVIEW but opposed to the establishment of federal COURTS, Martin served on the committee that brought about the "Great Compromise" that settled the struggle between the small and large states over representation in Congress. Although he was personally against proportional representation, he supported the committee's recommendation endorsing it. Still he opposed the final document, later switching his position and becoming a staunch Federalist. A brilliant lawyer, Martin appeared before the Supreme Court in such important cases as FLETCHER V. PECK in 1810 and MCCULLOCH V. MARYLAND in 1819.

*John Francis Mercer** (1759–1821). Attending the CONSTITUTIONAL CONVENTION OF 1787 for just two weeks, two and one-half months after it had started, John Mercer nevertheless spoke often in opposition to the document. Born in Virginia, he studied law under THOMAS JEFFERSON. Mercer moved to Maryland to live on the estate of the wealthy heiress he had married. Only after other prominent men had declined to serve was he selected to represent his adopted state at the Philadelphia convention. There he declared: "It is a great mistake to suppose that the paper we propose will govern the United States." In 1801 he was elected governor of Maryland by his fellow members in the state legislature and served two consecutive one-year terms.

Virginia

George Washington (1732–99). General GEORGE WASHINGTON led the CONSTITUTIONAL CONVENTION OF 1787 by the sheer force of his presence. Encouraged by JAMES MADISON, Washington agreed to head the contingent of delegates from Virginia. His involvement helped spur the participation of the other twelve states, and once in Philadelphia he was unanimously chosen president of the convention. Although Washington spoke only one time during the four-month session, he acted as a catalyst for the agreement on the final document and assisted in obtaining RATIFICATION by distributing copies of *The Federalist Papers* (1787–88) (see FEDERALIST PAPERS), essays composed by ALEXANDER HAMILTON, James Madison, and John Jay that supported adoption of the CONSTITUTION. In 1789 Washington was elected the first president of the United States under the document he helped usher into the world.

John Blair (1732–1800). One of the three Virginia delegates to the CONSTITUTIONAL CONVENTION OF 1787 to sign the document, John Blair helped draft the Virginia Declaration of Rights (1776) (see MASON, GEORGE) and the Virginia state constitution (1776). A lawyer and a reluctant Federalist who had studied at the College of William and Mary and in England, he was chosen for his legal abilities to represent Virginia's old ruling class at the convention. There is no record of his having ever spoken there, and on occasion he voted against proposals by his Virginia colleagues, including the Virginia Plan for Congress. Blair was a delegate to the Virginia ratifying convention and was appointed by President GEORGE WASHINGTON to be one of the first justices of the U.S. Supreme Court, on which he served until 1796.

James Madison (1751–1836). Known as the "Father of the Constitution," JAMES MADISON played a pivotal role in creating the CONSTITUTIONAL CONVENTION OF 1787 and in shaping its defining document. Intellectual, pragmatic, and politically astute, Madison spoke 161 times, covering almost every topic of importance. He held that the people, rather than an intervening body of electors, should elect one branch of the national legislature, and his concept of encouraging opposing factions in a framework of checks and balances became a fundamental principle of government (see SEPARATION OF POWERS). As the main author of the Virginia Plan, which served as the framework for restructuring the federal system, he also advocated giving real power to the national government (see FEDERALISM). Madison helped promote RATIFICATION of the CONSTITUTION by writing twenty-nine of the eighty-five essays that composed the Federalist Papers (1787–88) (see FEDERALIST PAPERS). As a member of the first House of Representatives in 1789, he sponsored the Constitution's first ten AMENDMENTS, the BILL OF RIGHTS.

George Mason* (1725–92). Although he wrote Virginia's first constitution (adopted on July 5, 1776), GEORGE MASON's greatest constitutional achievement was the drafting of the Virginia Declaration of Rights (1776). This document's written guarantees of liberty, the right to property, and the pursuit of happiness elevate it to a historical importance shared by Magna Carta (1215) and the BILL OF RIGHTS. Mason carried his deep concern for HUMAN RIGHTS to the CONSTITUTIONAL CONVENTION OF 1787. Although he influenced a number of final provisions, his opposition to the slave trade (see SLAVERY) kept him from signing the final draft. Only after approval in 1791 of the Bill of Rights did Mason give his full support to the new CONSTITUTION.

James McClurg* (1746–1823). A supporter of a strong central government, James McClurg's inclusion as a delegate to the CONSTITUTIONAL CONVENTION OF 1787 was promoted by JAMES MADISON. Born in Virginia, McClurg was graduated from the College of William and Mary in 1762 and received a degree in medicine from the University of Edinburgh, Scotland, in 1770. Perhaps out of his depth at the convention, he took the floor to speak only twice and supported the unadopted proposals to give Congress a veto over state laws and to allow the president to serve effectively for life. McClurg was made a director of the Bank of the United States in President GEORGE WASHINGTON's administration and was mayor of Richmond for three terms beginning in 1797.

Edmund Jennings Randolph* (1753–1813). Edmund Randolph, the youngest member of Virginia's constitutional convention in 1776, supported a less extensive revision of the ARTICLES OF CONFEDERATION than the majority at the CONSTITUTIONAL CONVENTION OF 1787 in Philadelphia. Born into a family of considerable distinction—his grandfather was the first native Virginian to receive a knighthood from the British Crown—Randolph studied at the College of William and Mary and his father's law offices. Appointed attorney general in the Virginia government after the state's independence in 1776, he was first elected to the Continental Congress in 1779 and struck up a friendship with JAMES MADISON. Randolph headed the Virginia delegation to the Constitutional Convention but would not sign the final product because he believed that it made the presidency too monarchical. Nevertheless, he supported Virginia's RATIFICATION of the CONSTITUTION. President GEORGE WASHINGTON appointed him the new nation's first attorney general in 1789, and he later succeeded THOMAS JEFFERSON as secretary of state. Although charges of treason and bribery ended his political career, he won acquittal in 1807 of the treason charge lodged against Aaron Burr.

George Wythe* (1726–1806). A distinguished jurist and teacher of law—his students included THOMAS JEFFERSON, JOHN MARSHALL, James Monroe, and Henry Clay—George Wythe would undoubtedly have had a greater impact on the CONSTITUTIONAL CONVENTION OF 1787 had he not left early to return to Virginia; before that he acted as chairman of the convention's rules committee.

From 1755 to 1775, Wythe was a delegate to Virginia's legislative council, the House of Burgesses, and was one of the signers of the DECLARATION OF INDEPENDENCE in 1776. During his term in the Continental Congress (1775–76), he supported his fellow Virginian Richard Henry Lee in the latter's stand against making compromises with the British. Wythe designed the Virginia state seal, which contains the motto *Sic Semper Tyrannis* ("thus [opposition] always to tyrants") and opposed SLAVERY, freeing the slaves he had inherited. Wythe was appointed to the Virginia Court of Chancery in 1778; his opinion affirming the judiciary's power to check unconstitutional acts of the legislature was declared by Chief Justice John Marshall in *MARBURY V. MADISON* (1803) to be a precursor to JUDICIAL REVIEW at the federal level.

North Carolina

William Blount (1749–1800). William Blount, an aristocratic republican, had no strong interest in the work of the CONSTITUTIONAL CONVENTION OF 1787 and signed the document only to recognize "the fact that the plan was the unanimous act of the States." A plantation owner and land speculator, Blount did not believe that North Carolina would accept any great change in the ARTICLES OF CONFEDERATION. Having enlisted during the Revolutionary War, he was elected to the North Carolina legislature's lower house in 1780 and to its upper house in 1788, representing his state in 1782–83 and 1786–87 in the Congress held under the Articles. Blount was not surprised when North Carolina first refused to ratify the CONSTITUTION (it later approved the document on November 21, 1789). Defeated in his bid for a seat in the first U.S. Senate, he was appointed in 1790 by President GEORGE WASHINGTON as governor of the territory that included the future state of Tennessee. In 1796 Blount was elected one of the first senators from that new state. An attempt to help the British seize Spanish territory in Florida and Louisiana got him expelled from the Senate, although the subsequent effort to impeach him failed.

Richard Dobbs Spaight (1758–1802). Richard Spaight favored a strong national government at the CONSTITUTIONAL CONVENTION OF 1787 and championed the CONSTITUTION'S RATIFICATION in North Carolina, only to become disillusioned, especially with the northern states, after the document went into effect. Orphaned at age eight, Spaight was sent from North Carolina to be educated in Ireland and later in Scotland at the University of Glasgow. After returning to North Carolina in 1778, he joined the fight for independence and was elected to the state legislature, becoming speaker of the lower house in 1785. Only twenty-nine when he was selected as a delegate to the Constitutional Convention, he spoke little but attended every session. He suggested that the convention had produced "a system…that has not Occurred in the History of men." Spaight lost his bid for the governorship of his home state in 1787 and for the Senate in 1789. He was elected governor in 1792 and a member of the House of Representatives in 1798. He died in a duel with a political rival.

Hugh Williamson (1735–1819). A man of many talents—preacher, physician, essayist, businessman, scientist, and politician—Hugh Williamson played a vital role on behalf of his adopted state at the CONSTITUTIONAL CONVENTION OF 1787. Born in Pennsylvania, Williamson became a licensed Presbyterian minister and in 1764 traveled to Europe to study medicine. After returning to America, he was admitted to the American Philosophical Society and became a friend of Benjamin Franklin's, assisting him in his experiments with electricity. Williamson served as surgeon general for the North Carolina troops in the Revolutionary War and was elected to the state legislature and to the Continental Congress in 1782; he was a member of the Congress again from 1787 to 1789. As a delegate to the Philadelphia convention he served on five committees and proved to be a skillful debater on behalf of North Carolina's interests. He worked for RATIFICATION of the CONSTITUTION by his home state and later served two terms in the House of Representatives beginning in 1789. In 1793 Williamson moved to New York City, where he continued his educational and scientific pursuits.

*William Richardson Davie** (1756–1820). Although he did not sign the CONSTITUTION, William Davie cast a crucial vote for the "Great Compromise," creating the bicameral Congress with a Senate and a House of Representatives, and he seconded the proposal to remove the president by IMPEACHMENT. Born in England of Scottish ancestry, Davie was educated in North Carolina and New Jersey. Wounded in the Revolutionary War, he was admitted to the bar in North Carolina in 1780. A lukewarm Federalist, Davie argued for the South's position on apportionment for the lower house of Congress, which was based on the inclusion of slaves. After the 1787 convention he worked for RATIFICATION of the Constitution in his home state, and in 1798 he was elected governor by the legislature. Both presidents JOHN ADAMS and THOMAS JEFFERSON appointed Davie to ad hoc federal positions. In 1811 he received the first doctorate of laws awarded by the University of North Carolina, an institution he had helped establish.

*Alexander Martin** (1740–1807). One of five delegates from North Carolina to the CONSTITUTIONAL CONVENTION OF 1787, Alexander Martin left no record of any contribution, and he departed before the document was signed. Born in New Jersey, he moved to North Carolina and was admitted to the bar in 1772. Tried for and acquitted of cowardice during the Revolutionary War, Martin later held a number of state and national government offices. He was elected to the Congress in 1786 under the ARTICLES OF CONFEDERATION but resigned without attending any sessions. Elected to the U.S. Senate in 1792, he worked to make that body's sessions open to the public.

South Carolina

John Rutledge helped draft South Carolina's state constitution (1776). A promotor of slavery and an advocate of states' rights at the Philadelphia convention, he briefly served as chief justice of the United States in 1795.
Source: Library of Congress

John Rutledge (1739–1800). A wealthy lawyer, John Rutledge represented South Carolina in 1765 at the congress called to respond to the Stamp Act (1765) levied by Great Britain on the colonies; later he served in the First and Second Continental Congresses in 1774–76 and 1782–83. Having studied law in England, Rutledge was named royal attorney general of the colony of South Carolina before passage of the Stamp Act. Together with his brother Edward, a signer of the DECLARATION OF INDEPENDENCE, Rutledge feared the antiaristocratic philosophies of New Englanders as much as British troops. He helped draft South Carolina's 1776 state constitution and was elected the state's first president. Rutledge's role at the Philadelphia convention included protecting STATES' RIGHTS and the rights of the southern slaveholding aristocracy (see SLAVERY). After RATIFICATION of the CONSTITUTION, he served in an unofficial capacity, pending confirmation by the Senate, as CHIEF JUSTICE of the United States in 1795. However, the Senate did not confirm him for that office in light of his outspoken criticism of the Jay Treaty (1794), which was negotiated by Chief Justice John Jay and thought by some to have gone too far in appeasing the British.

Charles Cotesworth Pinckney (1746–1825). A cousin of Charles Pinckney III, another delegate to the CONSTITUTIONAL CONVENTION OF 1787, and possibly a descendant of one of the barons who forced King John of England to accept Magna Carta in 1215, Charles Cotesworth Pinckney studied at Oxford with the noted English legal scholar William Blackstone (1723–80). A southern aristocrat, he was a member of the Congress created under the ARTICLES OF CONFEDERATION in 1777–78 and 1784–87 and proposed amendments to strengthen its provisions for the national government. Like his cousin, he came to the Philadelphia convention convinced that only a strong federal government could defend the fledgling nation and relieve the debts that South Carolina had amassed during the Revolutionary War. A leader of the southern Federalists, he declined President GEORGE WASHINGTON's offer of a seat on the U.S. Supreme Court, choosing instead to run, unsuccessfully, for vice president in 1800 and for president in 1804 and 1808.

Charles Pinckney III (1757–1824). One of the youngest delegates to the CONSTITUTIONAL CONVENTION OF 1787, Charles Pinckney III was a lawyer and wealthy planter who would eventually own hundreds of slaves. A proponent of a strong national government, he brought a draft version of a revised ARTICLES OF CONFEDERATION with him to the convention. Although Pinckney drafted a bill of rights and talked about equality, he also defended SLAVERY as a positive moral good. An admirer of the British constitution, he believed that the draft of the U.S. Constitution made the president too weak and dependent on the legislative branch. Nevertheless, he signed the document along with his cousin Charles Cotesworth Pinckney and continued to defend the right to own slaves. Pinckney served as governor of South Carolina numerous times (1789–92, 1796, and 1806–8) and won a seat in the U.S. Senate in 1798. THOMAS JEFFERSON appointed him minister to Spain from 1801 to 1805, where he dealt with issues relating to the acquisition of Florida and Louisiana. He later served in both the state legislature and the House of Representatives, where he fought against the Missouri Compromise, retiring from politics in 1821.

Pierce Butler (1744–1822). Born in Ireland, Pierce Butler became wealthy and influential in his adopted state of South Carolina, after serving in Canada as a major in the British army. Finally settling down in South Carolina after his marriage to the daughter of a landowner, he immediately took up the cause for independence from Britain. Elected to the state legislature in 1778, he was appointed adjutant general of South Carolina the following year. At the CONSTITUTIONAL CONVENTION OF 1787, he spoke often and was addressed as "the Major." A proponent of SLAVERY and a weak national government, he was the first delegate to suggest that the convention's sessions be conducted in secret. Butler later became a U.S. senator from South Carolina in 1789.

Georgia

William Few (1748–1828). Mostly self-taught, William Few basically took his cue at the CONSTITUTIONAL CONVENTION OF 1787 on issues such as SLAVERY, retirement of the state's debts, and the need for a strong national defense from his fellow Georgia delegates. The son of a poor farmer, Few was born in Maryland, but ten years later his family moved to North Carolina. There their opposition to the royal governor of the colony resulted in the hanging of Few's brother and the ruin of the family's farm. After moving to Georgia, Few was admitted to the bar. He joined the Georgia dragoons at the beginning of the Revolutionary War and then served in the local legislature off and on beginning in 1776 and in the Continental Congress in 1780–88. He did not make any speeches at the Constitutional Convention and missed a great deal of the proceedings, but he voted at critical stages for the new national government. Few was elected one of Georgia's first U.S. senators and served from 1789 to 1793. He resigned a federal judgeship to relocate to New York City, where he became president of the City Bank in 1814.

Abraham Baldwin (1754–1807). A minister, educator, lawyer, and politician, Abraham Baldwin facilitated the compromises on SLAVERY and equal representation of the states in the Senate. Born in Connecticut and a graduate of Yale, Baldwin was admitted to the bar in 1783. A year later he moved to Georgia, where he obtained permission to practice law. In 1785 he became a member of the Georgia Assembly and the Continental Congress. A moderate Federalist and a believer in caution and restraint, Baldwin, who served as a member of the Committee on Postponed Matters, was a quiet influence at the CONSTITUTIONAL CONVENTION OF 1787. A close affiliation with the Connecticut delegation helped persuade him to drop his support for representation in the Senate based on property holdings and to support the final version calling for equal state representation in the Senate. Baldwin later served in Congress as a representative in 1789–99 and then as a senator in 1799–1807, and he helped found the college that became the University of Georgia.

William Houstoun* (1757–1812). A reluctant revolutionary but an advocate for a stronger national government, William Houstoun served in the CONSTITUTIONAL CONVENTION OF 1787 only from May 31 to July 26. A wealthy man with extensive land holdings, Houstoun was admitted to the bar in 1782 and served in the Georgia legislature beginning in the same year and in the Congress set up under the ARTICLES OF CONFEDERATION in 1784–86. At the convention he generally supported the Federalists and the position of the southern states on issues such as SLAVERY, but he recommended federal review of state constitutions as they were drafted. After the convention he led a quiet, private life divided between New York and his home state.

William Leigh Pierce* (1740–89). A distinguished veteran of the Revolutionary War and a self-made, successful merchant, William Pierce supported the major features of the draft constitution but thought that Senate terms should be three years instead of six. Considering himself a Virginian, Pierce excelled at the College of William and Mary and in 1780 joined the revolutionary forces. In 1783 he settled as a merchant in Savannah, Georgia, and in 1786 was elected to the Georgia state legislature. From 1786 to 1787 Pierce was a delegate to the Congress under the ARTICLES OF CONFEDERATION. He spoke four times at the CONSTITUTIONAL CONVENTION OF 1787, where he was considered a "military Federalist" because he favored a strong, protective national government based on the experiences of war. Pierce left the convention in July for business reasons but wrote literary sketches of its members, which he called "the wisest Council in the World."

Fruit of the Poison Tree   *See* SEARCH AND SEIZURE.

Full Faith and Credit

The federal system of government devised by the FRAMERS OF THE CONSTITUTION (see FEDERALISM) creates the potential for two major areas of conflict: between acts of the nation and those of the STATES, and between acts of one or more states and those of the other states. The Constitution's SUPREMACY CLAUSE, found in Article VI, helps resolve conflicts between POWERS of the nation and those of the states, but how are conflicts between states resolved? Alexis de Tocqueville (1805–59), the French political scientist, answered that question in *Democracy in America* (1835), noting that "the federal system rests on a complicated theory which, in application, demands that the governed should use the lights of their reason every day."

Similar to language in the ARTICLES OF CONFEDERATION (1781), the Constitution's Article IV, section 1, reads: "Full Faith and Credit shall be given in each State to the public Acts, Records, and judicial Proceedings of every other State. And the Congress may by general Laws prescribe the Manner in which such Acts, Records and Proceedings shall be proved, and the Effect thereof." This full faith and credit provision "is an evident and valuable improvement on the clause relating to this subject in the Articles of Confederation," suggested JAMES MADISON in essay 43 of *The Federalist* (1787–88) (see FEDERALIST PAPERS). "The power here established may be rendered a very convenient instrument of justice, and be particularly beneficial on the borders of contiguous States, where the effects liable to justice may be suddenly and secretly translated in any stage of the process within a foreign jurisdiction."

In 1790 Congress enacted a law implementing the full faith and credit provision for records of state legislatures and judicial proceedings, specifying that "the said records and judicial proceedings shall have such faith and credit given to them in every court of the United States, as they have by law or usage in the courts of the State from whence the said records are or shall be taken." In 1804 full faith and credit was extended to any TERRITORY under U.S. jurisdiction. Even though the Constitution refers to "Acts," however, state statutes—in contrast to court judgments—are not entitled to full faith and credit recognition, because each state's SOVEREIGNTY requires the laws of another state to be treated as foreign law—the way a national court treats the laws of a foreign country. This interpretation was upheld by the U.S. Supreme Court in *Franchise Tax Board of California v. Hyatt* (2003), which held that the full faith and credit clause does not require Nevada to give full faith and credit to California's statutes providing its tax agency with immunity from suit. The Court noted that the full faith and credit language in the Constitution "is exacting" and refers only to a final judgment of a court with adjudicatory authority over the subject matter and persons governed by the judgment.

Without the full faith and credit provision, a divorce recognized as legal in one state might not be recognized as such in another, for example, and a judgment against a debtor in one state might not be enforceable in another. And after recognizing one state's official act, the other state must then enforce it. In one 1948 case, *Sherrer v. Sherrer*, a woman who had been living in Massachusetts received a divorce in Florida after complying with the relatively short ninety-day residency requirement. She then remarried and returned to Massachusetts, because her first spouse had had an opportunity to contest the divorce proceedings in court. The Supreme Court held that Massachusetts must recognize the Florida divorce according to the Constitution's full faith and credit provision.

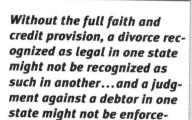

Forum shopping (to find a sympathetic legal jurisdiction) is also used to solve other legal problems. In *Sun Oil Co. v. Wortman* (1988), which arose over interest owed to the owners of mineral rights under a contract governed by Texas law, the Supreme Court ruled that the Kansas courts did not have to recognize the shorter statute of limitations applicable in Texas.

> *Without the full faith and credit provision, a divorce recognized as legal in one state might not be recognized as such in another...and a judgment against a debtor in one state might not be enforceable in another.*

The courts have generally maintained that the full faith and credit provision requires that a judgment rendered in one state in accordance with constitutional DUE PROCESS of law be recognized in courts in all the other states and that a controversy settled judicially in one state may not be reopened in another. State courts may choose whether or not to recognize foreign (non-U.S.) judgments, and a state does not have to enforce the judgment of another court that is subject to modification, as in the case of alimony and child support decrees. The latter rule has been changed by recent national legislation to implement the full faith and credit language in the specific cases of child custody and support.

> **More on this topic:**
>
> *Privileges and Immunities, p. 432*

Fundamental Rights

Fundamental rights, or fundamental interests as they are sometimes called, have been defined by one state court as those RIGHTS whose origin lies in the language of the Constitution or those which are implied from its terms. The FRAMERS OF THE CONSTITUTION in 1787, however, most likely had a different notion of fundamental rights. After all, the DECLARATION OF INDEPENDENCE (1776) proclaimed "Life, Liberty and the pursuit of Happiness" as "unalienable Rights" bestowed on "all men...by their Creator."

At the time the Constitution was written, fundamental rights and principles were deemed to exist before any constitutional framework of government devised by mere mortals. ALEXANDER

THE FOUR FREEDOMS: PRESIDENT FRANKLIN D. ROOSEVELT'S ADDRESS TO CONGRESS, JANUARY 6, 1941

In the future days, which we seek to make secure, we look forward to a world founded upon four essential human freedoms.

The first is freedom of speech and expression—everywhere in the world.

The second is freedom of every person to worship God in his own way—everywhere in the world.

The third is freedom from want—which, translated into world terms, means economic understandings which will secure to every nation a healthy peacetime life for its inhabitants—everywhere in the world.

The fourth is freedom from fear—which, translated into world terms, means a world-wide reduction of armaments to such a point and in such a thorough fashion that no nation will be in a position to commit an act of physical aggression against any neighbor—anywhere in the world.

That is no vision of a distant millennium. It is a definite basis for a kind of world attainable in our own time and generation. That kind of world is the very antithesis of the so-called new order of tyranny which the dictators seek to create with the crash of a bomb.

To that new order we oppose the greater conception—the moral order. A good society is able to face schemes of world domination and foreign revolutions alike without fear.

Since the beginning of our American history, we have been engaged in change—in a perpetual peaceful revolution—a revolution which goes on steadily, quietly adjusting itself to changing conditions—without the concentration camp or the quick-lime in the ditch. The world order which we seek is the cooperation of free countries, working together in a friendly, civilized society.

This nation has placed its destiny in the hands and heads and hearts of its millions of free men and women; and its faith in freedom under the guidance of God. Freedom means the supremacy of human rights everywhere. Our support goes to those who struggle to gain those rights or keep them. Our strength is our unity of purpose.

To that high concept there can be no end save victory.

SOURCES: www.ukans.edu/carrie/docs/amdocs_index.html; www.wwnorton.com/college/history/ralph/workbook/ralprs36b.htm.

HAMILTON in essay 78 of *The Federalist* (1787–88) (see FEDERALIST PAPERS) underscored "that fundamental principle of republican government which admits the right of the people to alter or abolish the established Constitution whenever they find it inconsistent with their happiness...." Fundamental rights were thus seen as based on natural rights or natural law, which was God given, not made by humans. As the Declaration of Independence stated, "[I]t is the Right of the People to alter or abolish" any government unable or unwilling "to secure these Rights."

The term *fundamental rights* today often refers to various basic rights on which constitutional government and individual participation in government and civil society are based—for example, the right to vote and hold public office and the right of free speech and assembly. In this regard, a citizen's political and CIVIL RIGHTS are generally considered fundamental rights, also called first-generation rights. Economic and social rights, such as the right to work and receive welfare assistance, tend to be considered, at least in the United States, as less than fundamental rights and are known as second-generation rights. While fundamental rights are basic to a free society and a democratic government, other less fundamental rights are contingent on the nation's political and social will and its economic ability to provide them. For example, in *Lindsey v. Normet* (1972), the U.S. Supreme Court refused to acknowledge the need for "decent shelter" or the right to retain peaceful "possession of one's home" as a fundamental right or interest; and in *Dandridge v. Williams* (1970), the Court refused to interfere in a state's formulation for welfare benefits even though it "result[ed] in some disparity in grants of welfare payments to the largest [needy] families."

The Constitution does not explicitly describe any rights as "fundamental." Rather, that designation has been enunciated in decisions of the Supreme Court. As early as 1823, in *Corfield v. Coryell*, Justice Bushrod Washington (1762–1829), speaking about the PRIVILEGES AND IMMUNITIES of U.S. CITIZENS referred to in Article IV, section 2, said that they embodied principles "which are, in their nature, fundamental; which belong, of right, to the citizens of all free governments...." These include, he continued, "[p]rotection by the Government; the enjoyment of life and liberty, with the right to acquire and possess property of every kind, and to pursue and obtain happiness and safety.... The right of a citizen of one State to pass through, or to reside in any other State, for purposes of trade, agriculture, professional pursuits, or otherwise; to claim the benefits of the writ of habeas corpus; to institute and maintain actions of any kind in the courts of the State...." (see HABEAS CORPUS; LIBERTY; PROPERTY; TRAVEL).

In *Palko v. Connecticut* (1937), the Supreme Court rejected the argument that all of the guarantees of the first eight amendments included in the BILL OF RIGHTS (1791) were encompassed in the DUE PROCESS clause of the Fourteenth Amendment (1868) and were thus applicable to the states as well as the national government. But it did rule that some guarantees of the Bill of Rights were so fundamental that, in the words of Justice Benjamin N. Cardozo (1870–1938), they are

"of the very essence of the scheme of ordered liberty" and "neither liberty nor justice would exist if they were sacrificed." The Court in this case, however, found that the Fifth Amendment's prohibition against DOUBLE JEOPARDY was not such a fundamental right, although Justice Felix Frankfurter (1882–1965) raised a dissenting voice, characterizing the concept of due process of law as embracing "a system of rights based on moral principles so deeply embedded in the traditions and feelings of our people as to be fundamental to a civilized society...." As a result of an evolutionary process in the Supreme Court's decision making, most of the guarantees of the Bill of Rights are now viewed as applicable to both the national and state governments (see INCORPORATION DOCTRINE).

According to Supreme Court decisions, fundamental rights generally include freedom of RELIGION, SPEECH, THE PRESS, and assembly and the right to petition the government for redress of grievances (see ASSEMBLY AND ASSOCIATION), as well as due process rights, such as the right to a fair trial. Other rights that the Court has referred to on occasion as "formal" rights are less than fundamental rights; these include the procedural rights guaranteed by the Fourth, Fifth, Sixth, Seventh, and Eighth Amendments, such as the right to a jury trial (see JURIES; TRIALS). Much of the distinction be-

The right to assemble and protest is generally viewed as a fundamental right. In this photo, demonstrators in 1998 call for an end to impeachment proceedings against President Bill Clinton.
Source: Reuters/Larry Downing

tween fundamental and formal rights has been blurred, however, especially as the Supreme Court began to incorporate Bill of Rights guarantees into the Fourteenth Amendment between the 1920s and the 1960s. Certain rights not mentioned in the Constitution, such as the right of PRIVACY and marriage, have been described in Court opinions as fundamental rights. In *Meyer v. Nebraska*

More on this topic:

Assembly and Association, p. 50

Bill of Rights, p. 62

The Press, p. 425

Religion, p. 458

Rights, p. 469

Speech, p. 512

(1923), for example, the Court announced the fundamental right to marry and educate one's CHILDREN (see EDUCATION; FAMILIES).

Although there is perhaps no single list of fundamental rights that judges, constitutional scholars, and practitioners of the law may agree on, the nature of such rights reaches far back into the history of English law to the evolution of the principles of the writ of habeas corpus and due process of law. Yet a worldwide consensus is growing as to what constitutes fundamental rights, principles proclaimed in such human rights documents as the Universal Declaration of Human Rights (1948) and the International Covenant on Civil and Political Rights (1966).

Gays *See* HOMOSEXUALS.

Gender *See* SEX DISCRIMINATION.

General Welfare *See* WELFARE.

Genetics

The brave new world of genetic engineering and testing, stem cell research, and the cloning of life forms is creating moral and ethical as well as legal and constitutional conundrums. Genetics, which may be defined as the science or study of variations in the characteristics of organisms and their hereditary transmission, is not a traditional field of legal or constitutional analysis. This relatively new subject is not addressed in the U.S. Constitution or in most other national constitutions. But Switzerland's constitution (2000), article 119, provides in part: "a. all forms of cloning and interference with genetic material of human reproductive cells and embryos are prohibited; [and] b. non-human reproductive genetic material may not be introduced into or combined with human reproductive materials."

At the international level, the Universal Declaration on the Human Genome and Human Rights (1997), adopted by the International Bioethics Committee of the United Nations Educational, Scientific and Cultural Organization (UNESCO), states: "Everyone has a right to respect for their

During a 2001 meeting President George W. Bush heard Pope John Paul II's views on the debate over stem-cell research. At home Bush proposed a political compromise, barring federal funds for research using human embryos.
Source: Reuters

dignity and for their rights regardless of their genetic characteristics.... [Such] dignity makes it imperative not to reduce individuals to their genetic characteristics and to respect their uniqueness and diversity."

Undoubtedly, as disputes arise over government and private policies toward genetic experimentation, the Constitution will be used both to try to justify expanding this new realm of biological knowledge and to curtail it. Some constitutional issues related to genetics include discrimination, evidence in criminal and some civil cases, privacy, freedom of information, and intellectual property.

Discrimination

Neither the Americans with Disabilities Act, Title I (1990), nor the Rehabilitation Act (1973) expressly addresses the potential problems of discrimination based on genetic information, but they do prohibit DISCRIMINATION on the basis of a disability and protect persons with genetic disabilities (see DISABLED PERSONS; EMPLOYMENT DISCRIMINATION). The U.S. Equal Employment Opportunity Commission declared in 1995 that entities that discriminate on the basis of a genetic predisposition are in effect treating such individuals as impaired and therefore such persons are covered by the Americans with Disabilities Act. The facts that the DNA, which contains genetic information, of any two people is only about 99 percent identical and that the genome of an individual can now be easily and quickly analyzed have led to fears that just as race was once used as a way of stereotyping individuals, the unique DNA of individuals may be used to link genetic makeup to race or to other bases for discrimination such as linking certain genetic markers to high or low IQ potentials.

A presidential executive order (see EXECUTIVE ORDERS) issued in early 2000 banned all federal departments and ADMINISTRATIVE AGENCIES from using genetic information in their own hiring and promotions. Federal employers may not request genetic tests as a condition of being hired or receiving benefits, for example, and they may not deny employees a promotion or an assignment to overseas jobs because of a genetic predisposition to certain illnesses.

In the private sector there is apprehension that genetic information about predispositions to diseases may induce insurance companies to deny, limit, or cancel insurance policies or lead employers to make discriminatory decisions about workers or potential employees. Moreover, the fact that DNA can be kept indefinitely has led to concerns that even if collected for one purpose it could later be used for other purposes.

Evidence

In recent years DNA profiling, also called genetic fingerprinting, has become an important tool in convicting the guilty and freeing the innocent. A perpetrator's hair, blood, or semen (in cases of rape) left at the crime scene can be matched with DNA samples from an accused person to determine with fairly high accuracy the probability of guilt. DNA testing has also been used in civil suits to determine the paternity of CHILDREN. "It's the most significant advancement in investigative tools at least in this century," observed a U.S. Department of Justice official in 1999.

In what is believed to be the first reported criminal case in which DNA testing was used in New York, a state court said in 1988: "DNA fingerprinting, if accepted, will revolutionize the disposition of criminal cases…[and] can constitute the single greatest advance in the 'search for the truth,' and the goal of convicting the guilty and acquitting the innocent, since the advent of cross-examination." On appeal by the defendant in that case, who had been convicted of several charges including murder and rape, the U.S. Court of Appeals in 1994 said that DNA testing, when properly performed, generated results that were accepted as reliable within the relevant scientific community and that the procedure thus met the "Frye test" for admissibility at the time, established in *Frye v. United States* (1923), a federal court of appeals case.

All fifty states now have laws that require DNA profiling—the keeping of DNA records on some offenders—and some LAW ENFORCEMENT officials want to extend the profiling to persons arrested as well as those tried or convicted of a crime. Like fingerprints, DNA samples can be kept on file and then compared to the DNA of suspects months and even years after a crime is committed. DNA samples, however, may contain information collected for one purpose that could be used for another—for example, to influence personnel or health insurance coverage decisions.

A major new development has resulted from the use of DNA evidence found at a crime scene to identify a person with extreme precision—the exoneration of individuals falsely accused or convicted of the crime. For example, the Innocence Project, founded in 1992 at the Benjamin N. Cardoza School of Law to assist prisoners who can be proven innocent through DNA testing, reported recently that some 208 people, including 15 on death row, have been set free based on tests of DNA evidence. The Supreme Court weighed in on the issue in its decision in *House v. Bell* (2006), allowing a HABEAS CORPUS action to proceed in a case where, in direct contradiction of evidence presented at trial, DNA testing established that the semen on the victim's clothes was that of her husband and not the defendant. Over the claims by the state that the evidence of sexual contact between the victim and the defendant was immaterial, the Court declared that it found this new disclosure to be of central importance.

> *A major new development has resulted from the use of DNA evidence found at a crime scene to identify a person with extreme precision—the exoneration of individuals falsely accused or convicted of the crime.*

Privacy

Before ordering DNA testing, courts generally try to balance the issues, including the rights of persons accused of crimes (see CRIMINAL LAW). Primary among these rights is the PRIVACY of the person to be tested, such as the constitutional protections against unreasonable SEARCH AND SEIZURE and the disclosure of personal or medical information to third parties (employers or health insurance companies) that could use it in a discriminatory manner.

The Supreme Court in *Schmerber v. California* (1966) held that taking a blood sample when probable cause exists that the person committed a crime does not unduly intrude on a suspect's right of privacy; neither does it violate the constitutional guarantees of DUE PROCESS of law or unreasonable search and seizure or the protection against SELF-INCRIMINATION guaranteed in the Fifth Amendment (1791). In another case that supports the principles behind DNA testing and record keeping, *Whalen v. Roe* (1977), the Court found that for the state to maintain records of patients who take drugs and of the physicians who prescribe them was not an invasion of privacy. However, in *Ferguson v. City of Charleston* (2001), the Court found that an unreasonable search and seizure occurred when hospital drug tests on pregnant women were forwarded to the police to serve as evidence of drug law violations (see DRUGS).

Freedom of Information

Stem Cells. Proposed scientific research using stem cells and human embryos has become a controversial moral and political issue. An embryo is an agglomeration of cells resulting from the union of a sperm cell and an egg cell. A human embryo, given the proper environment—ideally, the mother's womb—has the capacity to develop into a human being. Embryonic stem cells are the inner layer of cells at the earliest stage of embryonic development. An outer layer of cells will develop into the placenta, through which the embryo will be nourished by the mother. At this early stage the cells have not yet differentiated into specific cells such as nerve or muscle cells. Many medical researchers predict that stem cells could be used to cure a number of ailments, including Parkinson's and Alzheimer's diseases and diabetes. Other possible uses for stem cells include tissue replacement for damaged heart muscles.

The arguments on both sides of the question are similar to those with regard to ABORTION, in which a woman's right, in consultation with her doctor, to choose to have an abortion competes with the right to life of the fetus. With respect to stem-cell research, women of child-bearing age regularly discharge unfertilized eggs and males produce far more sperm cells than necessary to fertilize eggs. A blastula—the early stages of a fertilized egg, when it consists of a few divided but undifferentiated embryonic stem cells—cannot become a child unless placed in a woman's womb.

In August 2001 President George W. Bush (b. 1946) barred the use of federal funds for research involving stem cells derived from embryos, exempting only those stem-cell cultures already in existence. However, despite the denial of federal funding, the issue retains its currency. The right to conduct research and develop cures for medical problems without government interference is not clearly protected under the Constitution. A final decision on the constitutionality of stem-cell research will thus undoubtedly have to be made by the Supreme Court in some case in which the rights of medical researchers, doctors, and patients to use stem cells are tested against the government's interests in denying such rights. A 2007 breakthrough that allowed adult skin cells to mimic embryonic stem cells genetically identical to the donors has raised hopes that the ethical concerns limiting progress in stem cell therapy could be satisfied.

Cloning. In 2000 the United Kingdom tried unsuccessfully to amend its Human Fertilization and Embryology Act (1990) to allow therapeutic, as opposed to reproductive, cloning. And in the United States, the president and others urged the Senate in November 2001 to pass a sweeping ban, already approved by the House of Representatives, on both therapeutic and reproductive cloning. The U.S. Food and Drug Administration has asserted regulatory authority over cloning efforts under the Public Health Service Act (1912), which gives the agency power to regulate "biological products" that are used to treat medical conditions.

The Supreme Court has not yet spoken on whether the right to cloning—the asexual reproduction of a living human being from only one

These three female dogs were cloned by a South Korean researcher in 2006. Such advances in cloning are stirring speculation that scientists will one day be able to clone human beings.

Source: AP Images/Seoul National University

reproductive cell without the union of a male and a female reproductive cell—stands on an equal footing with the right to sexual reproduction. In *Meyer v. Nebraska* (1923) and other cases, the Court asserted that the guarantee of liberty in the Fourteenth Amendment (1868) included the right to marry, establish a home, and bring up children (see FAMILIES). According to the Court, the right to procreation is one of an individual's FUNDAMENTAL RIGHTS. If a family can include adopted children as well as children conceived by fertilization outside the womb (*in vitro* fertilization), could it not also include children produced by cloning? In *Eisenstadt v. Baird* (1972), the Supreme Court opined that if the right of privacy means anything, it is the right of the individual, married or single, to be free from unwarranted government intrusion into matters so fundamentally affecting a person as the decision to have a child.

Whether attempts at cloning human beings should or can be banned is becoming one of the great debates of the twenty-first century. The process by which we are conceived, born, and reared in a family contributes to the definition of who we are as human beings. However, human life and the processes of living are far more complex and at times more wondrous than imagined. Perhaps humanity can arrive at some consensus that neither demeans the dignity of the individual nor precludes the development of medical science to serve future human needs.

Intellectual Property

Since 1980 the U.S. Patent and Trademark Office, according to a 2001 interview with one of its officials, has granted "more than 20,000 patents on genes or other gene-related molecules [for humans and other organisms]" and had "more than 25,000 applications outstanding [of the same type]." Patent protection for biotechnological innovations has thus become another intellectual property issue (see PATENTS).

Innovations in the field of biotechnology range from technical equipment and processes to genetically engineered organisms. The potential to exclude competitors from using these new discoveries makes the patent the preferred form of protection, even though the patent procedure requires disclosure of the new process or product. Disclosure is helpful, however, because others may use this knowledge as a starting point for further innovations.

Since 1980 the federal government has encouraged the patenting of research discoveries as part of the general wave of privatizing formerly government-sponsored activities and research. Article I, section 8, of the Constitution empowers Congress to promote science by giving those responsible for discoveries or inventions exclusive rights to the commercial exploitation of their patents for a limited period of time, originally seventeen years; in 1995 Congress extended the period to twenty years from the date of application. The Supreme Court weighed in on the question of patenting biological discoveries in *Diamond v. Chakrabarty* (1980) by affirming that living organisms are patentable. In 1988 a patent was issued for a transgenic mammal (with genetic material introduced from another species) known as the "Harvard mouse."

The relationship between genetics and the law is in its infancy, and the Supreme Court has issued no definitive opinions on many of these issues. Public debate and action by national and state legislatures and the courts will begin to define the policies that permit or restrict the development and use of genetic information, especially in the area of human genetics. The Constitution may yet be interpreted to limit government restrictions on the search for scientific truths and better medical treatment.

More on this topic:
Discrimination, p. 159
Health, p. 271
Privacy, p. 430
Property, p. 436
Science and Technology, p. 477

Gerrymander   *See* REAPPORTIONMENT.

Gibbons v. Ogden

The opinion of Chief Justice JOHN MARSHALL in *Gibbons v. Ogden*, decided by the Supreme Court in 1824, ranks alongside his opinions in *MARBURY V. MADISON* (1803) and *MCCULLOCH V. MARYLAND* (1819) as another foundation stone in the development of the national government's broad powers under the Constitution. The decision, which was well received at the time, prompted a senator from New York—whose state granted a monopoly to Robert Fulton (credited with inventing the steam-powered boat) and his partner, Robert R. Livingston, that the Court invalidated in *Gibbons*—to call Marshall "the ablest Judge now sitting upon any judicial bench in the world."

Under the monopoly granted by New York state to Fulton and Livingston, Aaron Ogden had been assigned rights to operate a steamboat line between New York City and ports in New Jersey. Thomas Gibbons operated his own two steamboats between towns in New Jersey and New York City, licensed under a 1793 act of Congress "for controlling and licensing ships and vessels to be employed in the coasting trade and fisheries, and for regulating the same." Ogden sought an injunction against Gibbons to stop him from running his steamships in New York waters in defiance of the monopoly rights granted by the state. The question presented to the Supreme Court was this: Could a state grant exclusive rights to navigate its waters in spite of the power granted to Congress in the Constitution's Article I, section 8, to regulate COMMERCE among the states?

Before Marshall's opinion in *Gibbons*, the federal government's power to regulate commerce was believed to be quite narrow. President JAMES MADISON had declared in 1817 that "the power to regulate commerce among the several states cannot include a power to construct roads and canals, and to improve the navigation of water courses." Commerce, in fact, was considered trading or buying and selling and was not concerned with transportation and navigation.

Marshall, however, found that because Gibbons was operating under an act of Congress, his right trumped the power of the state of New York to exclude his boats to protect Ogden's monopoly rights. As the jurist argued in his opinion, "We do not find, in the history of the formation and adoption of the constitution, that any man speaks of a general concurrent power, in the regulation of foreign and domestic trade, as still residing in the states. The very object intended, more than any other, was to take away such power" (see CONCURRENT POWERS).

The opinion points out that "from the very nature of the case, these powers [to regulate commerce] must be exclusive; that is, the higher branches of commercial regulation must be exclusively committed to a single hand. What is it that is to be regulated? Not the commerce of the several states, respectively, but the commerce of the United States.... [T]herefore the words [of the commerce clause] must have a reasonable construction, and the power should be considered as exclusively vested in Congress, so far, and so far only, as the nature of the power requires."

The outcome of this first Supreme Court case under the commerce clause is that the power of Congress to regulate commerce is viewed as unlimited except by the Constitution. Commerce is deemed not just trade; it includes intercourse among the states that is subject to rules prescribed by Congress. According to *Gibbons*, federal regulation does not stop at state lines, but it does not reach to commerce wholly within a state—a conclusion that would later be modified.

Marshall's bold ruling provided the basis, via the commerce clause, for the expansion of federal power over many previously exclusive areas of state jurisdiction, including economic recovery measures in the 1930s and enforcement of CIVIL RIGHTS in the 1950s. Justice Robert H. Jackson (1892–1954), however, accurately stated in 1941 that "Marshall described the federal commerce power with a breadth never exceeded."

More on this topic:

Commerce, p. 99

Concurrent Powers, p. 108

Federalism, p. 218

Marshall, John, p. 362

Gideon v. Wainwright

If a cat can dare to speak to a king, can a petty thief teach the Supreme Court about the meaning of the Constitution? In 1963 Clarence Earl Gideon, charged with stealing coins from a vending machine along with a bottle of wine, dared to confront the nine berobed Supreme Court justices and challenge them on whether the Constitution guarantees the ASSISTANCE OF COUNSEL to all citizens tried for a felony. "Although he did not know it, Clarence Earl Gideon was calling for one of those great occasions in legal history," wrote Anthony Lewis in *Gideon's Trumpet*. "He was asking the Supreme Court to change its mind."

"In all criminal prosecutions," states the Sixth Amendment (1791), "the accused shall enjoy the right...to have the Assistance of Counsel for his defence." Since ratification of the Fourteenth Amendment (1868), the provisions of the BILL OF RIGHTS (1791)—originally applicable only to the national government—have been gradually incorporated by the Supreme Court to apply to the states as well through the amendment's DUE PROCESS clause (see INCORPORATION DOCTRINE). *Gideon v. Wainwright* (1963) represents the incorporation of the Sixth Amendment's right of counsel into the Fourteenth Amendment, making it applicable to the states for felonies.

Looking back over the cases that led up to *Gideon*, it is difficult to understand why the Supreme Court had such a hard time extending the right of counsel to all persons charged with possible loss of their life or liberty. In *Powell v. Alabama* (1932), the first of the two Scottsboro Cases, the Court held that due process of law required at the least a hearing to provide an opportunity to present both sides of a controversy for an impartial determination on the evidence. In his opinion for the Court in this case, Justice George Sutherland (1862–1942) went so far as to say that the presence of counsel is fundamental to any meaningful hearing (see FUNDAMENTAL RIGHTS). And in *Johnson v. Zerbst* (1938), the Court concluded that under the Sixth Amendment indigent felony defendants in federal cases must be provided with counsel. However, the Supreme Court was still reluctant to extend to criminal defendants in the states the Sixth Amendment's guarantee of assistance of counsel. In *Betts v. Brady* (1942), the Court defended its action by contending that the states should not be "straitjacketed" and that only where denial of counsel demonstrated a fundamental lack of fairness would the justices overturn a conviction.

In a Florida court in 1961, Clarence Gideon, a poor man, was convicted of a felony: breaking and entering a poolroom to commit a misdemeanor. His request for court-appointed counsel was denied because state law provided for appointment of counsel only in cases involving the DEATH PENALTY. Although Gideon defended himself as best he could, he was sentenced to five years in prison. His personally prepared petition requesting a federal court to overturn his conviction on the grounds that he was denied the assistance of counsel in violation of the Sixth Amendment was taken up by the Supreme Court. Abe Fortas (1910–82), who a few years later became a Supreme Court justice, was appointed to represent Gideon.

The Court's opinion was written by Justice Hugo L. Black (1887–1971), who had dissented in *Betts v. Brady* twenty years earlier. An ardent supporter of the absoluteness of the guarantees in the Bill of Rights, Black believed that the Constitution meant what it said and that no deviation from its stated freedoms should be tolerated. In perhaps his most famous opinion, Black summed up by saying that the precedents, reason, and reflection "require us to recognize that in our adversary system of criminal justice, any person haled into court, who is too poor to hire a lawyer, cannot be assured a fair trial unless counsel is provided for him. This seems to us to be an obvious truth." Granted a new trial in Florida, in which he was represented by a court-appointed attorney, Gideon was acquitted by a jury (see JURIES).

Hugo Black
Source: Collection of the Supreme Court of the
United States

Hugo Black, who wrote the landmark ruling in *Gideon v. Wainwright*, was one of the most influential justices of the twentieth century—and also one of the more difficult to typecast. Neither a liberal nor a conservative, his strict reading of the Constitution led him to support civil rights and a strong federal government.

But he parted ways with liberal justices on such issues as privacy. In the 1965 case GRISWOLD V. CONNECTICUT, Black was one of just two justices who voted to uphold the right of a state government to bar the use of contraceptives.

Black became especially noteworthy for his support of First Amendment rights. He was one of the few justices in the nation's history who believed that First Amendment freedoms, such as speech and assembly, were so absolute that they could not be curtailed. When the government after World War II began prosecuting members of the Communist Party, Black claimed that the laws were a violation of the right to free speech. In a famous dissent in 1951 (*Dennis v. United States*), Black wrote:

"Public opinion being what it now is, few will protest the conviction of these Communist petitioners. There is hope, however, that, in calmer times, when present pressures, passions and fears subside, this or some later Court will restore the First Amendment liberties to the high preferred place where they belong in a free society."

Black was vindicated by the end of the decade, when the justices began reining in government efforts to prosecute leading communists.

In the same year as its decision in *Gideon*, the Supreme Court in *Douglas v. California* (1963) required the states to provide counsel for defendants in their first appeal of a conviction, and in *In re Gault* (1967) the right to the assistance of counsel was extended to indigent juvenile defendants. The Court subsequently emphasized that the right to court-appointed counsel meant effective counsel, and in *Scott v. Illinois* (1979) the justices granted the right to counsel to persons accused of misdemeanors if a jail sentence is involved.

In a truly egalitarian society, JUSTICE should not depend on a person's wealth. The Supreme Court took a significant step toward that goal in its decision in *Gideon v. Wainwright*.

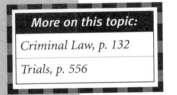

More on this topic:

Criminal Law, p. 132

Trials, p. 556

Good Behavior   *See* COURTS.

Government

Anarchy—the chaos that results from the absence of government authority—occurs between the collapse of one form of government and the establishment of another, such as during the French Revolution of 1789 and the subsequent Reign of Terror (1793–94). In the general lawlessness of such periods, people are forced to protect themselves and their property without the aid of government, which represents LAW and order and may be defined as the political organization within a territorial jurisdiction that governs by fundamental rules, principles, and institutions.

The Evolution of Government

Government was not so much invented, like the wheel, or discovered, like fire; rather, it evolved in response to the needs of humans living in groups larger than a single nuclear family and later in much larger permanent settlements made possible by the development of agriculture. The governments of the first great civilizations in the Middle East, India, China, and the Western Hemisphere shared several features. All were hierarchical: rulers ruled from the top down. They tended to be dynastic; barring conquests from outside or coups from within, the right to rule descended generally from father to son or to another family member. Finally, all rulers were in some way connected with the spirit world, seen as intercessors between the people and the gods or as having divine powers attributed to them.

Two new forms of government, significantly different from the standard monarchical model, began around the end of the sixth century B.C.E. Democracy in ancient Athens (ca. 510–322 B.C.E.) placed government in the hands of adult male citizens, who could vote on government decisions, elect public officials to serve for set TERMS OF OF-FICE, and hold public office by appointment or election (see ELECTIONS). The republic of ancient Rome (ca. 509–27 B.C.E.) was established when the last Roman king was expelled. There government became the business of the public (in Latin, *res publica*) directed by an aristocratic senate, to which government officials were responsible; major decisions required approval by political bodies that represented elements of the citizenry. Greece's democracy and Rome's republic each lasted several hundred years.

The government model for the modern state developed in Europe at the beginning of the Renaissance in the fourteenth century. The foundations were laid by St. Augustine (354–430), an early Christian scholar who wrote of the spiritual and temporal realms of authority that set the stage for the development of the secular state. In the thirteenth century, St. Thomas Aquinas (ca. 1224–74) drew on the works of Aristotle to conclude that secular government was necessary but asserted that it should be based on the superior morality and wisdom of the ruler for the benefit of those ruled. He also developed the concept of natural law given by God, by which the competence of secular rulers could be judged.

Jean Bodin (1530–96), a French political philosopher, contributed to the theoretical development of modern government by identifying and describing the concept of national SOVEREIGNTY, which in his day resided in the person of the monarch. In Bodin's idealized government, subjects owed obedience to the sovereign ruler. The international implications of national governments vis-á-vis one another were further developed by the Dutch jurist Hugo Grotius (1583–1645) in his work *On the Law of War and Peace* (1625), in which he maintained that the law of nations is a "law which is broader in scope than [the law of each individual state]" (see INTERNATIONAL LAW).

The U.S. Government

At the time of the CONSTITUTIONAL CONVENTION OF 1787, most of the governments in the world were monarchies, each having greater or lesser constitutional limitations. The FRAMERS OF THE CONSTITUTION were aware of how these countries were governed, as ALEXANDER HAMILTON pointed out in essay 19 of *The Federalist* (1787–88) (see FEDERALIST PAPERS). Switzerland, although a loose confederation of individual provinces called cantons, had no great common sovereignty and no national monarchy, he observed. The Netherlands, as he noted in essay 20, was united and its sovereignty represented by a parliament called the States-General, whose members were appointed by the seven coequal sovereign states. Germany had an emperor and a diet (council) representing its member states, but the emperor could veto any of its decrees (see VETOES). Spain, Portugal, France, and the Scandinavian countries were monarchies, with few if

"The only sure bulwark of continuing liberty is a government strong enough to protect the interests of the people, and a people strong enough and well enough informed to maintain its sovereign control over the government."

—Franklin D. Roosevelt

"It may be a reflection on human nature, that such devices [constitutions] should be necessary to control the abuses of government. But what is government itself but the greatest of all reflections on human nature. If men were angels, no government would be necessary."

—**James Madison** in essay 51 of *The Federalist*

any constitutional restraints. In 1814 Norway adopted a constitution that, after the U.S. Constitution, has become the second oldest written constitution still in effect.

Although the framers knew that they wanted a stronger form of government than the ARTICLES OF CONFEDERATION (1781) had provided, they did not know exactly which type. "Nothing is more certain than the indispensable necessity of government," wrote John Jay (1745–1829) in essay 2 of *The Federalist*, "and it is equally undeniable that whenever and however it is instituted, the people must cede to it some of their natural rights, in order to vest it with requisite powers." The only question was what form of government to create.

The American colonists' unfortunate experiences with the British monarchy—although a more constitutional one than perhaps any other at the time—predisposed most delegates at the 1787 convention toward a REPUBLICAN FORM OF GOVERNMENT, which is government in which the head of state is not a monarch. The STATES that had formed from the earlier British colonies after the DECLARATION OF INDEPENDENCE (1776) and the Revolutionary War (1775–83) generally wanted a government strong enough to provide for the common defense and to ensure uniform regulation of COMMERCE and trade but not so strong as to extinguish their residual sovereign powers, such as their POLICE POWER, judicial systems, and laws regarding PROPERTY. One suggestion that would have greatly curtailed the power of the states—that Congress be given the power to veto state legislation—was voted down. The states had previously written their own constitutions after declaring their independence from Great Britain, and the new United States had struggled since 1781 to govern itself under the imperfect Articles of Confederation. The failure of the Articles to forge a strong nation was the primary reason the delegates had gathered in Philadelphia to draft a new constitution.

The type of government the delegates finally agreed on was a constitutional democratic federal republic (see FEDERALISM). It is constitutional in that, unlike an absolute monarchy, its rulers are limited by a constitution (see CONSTITUTION, U.S.). It is democratic in that the most powerful public officials—the PRESIDENT and members of the HOUSE OF REPRESENTATIVES and the SENATE—are elected. It is federal in that the constituent states have retained some of their sovereignty (in unitary nations such as Great Britain, subsidiary levels of government are created and can be abolished by the national government). In the new U.S. government, the states and CITIZENS delegated certain powers to the federal government and retained the rest, as guaranteed by the Ninth and Tenth Amendments (1791). The government agreed on was a republic because no monarchy or hereditary right to rule was established by the Constitution.

Our Constitution's major contributions to the theory and practice of government around the world were, first, the fact that it was written (Britain's is unwritten), and, second, its dependence on the nation's citizens for its legitimacy. Government, for the first time, became the creature of the people—a great beast chained and trained to do their bidding rather than the other way around. As JAMES MADISON commented in essay 51 of *The Federalist*: "It may be a reflection on human nature, that such devices [constitutions] should be necessary to control the abuses of government. But what is government itself but the greatest of all reflections on human nature. If men were angels, no government would be necessary." For all the technological achievements of humankind, such as putting astronauts on the moon, developing the global Internet, and harnessing the power of the atom, perhaps good government—government of the people, by the people, and for the people—is an even greater achievement.

Grand Juries *See* JURIES.

"Great Compromise" *See* CONSTITUTIONAL CONVENTION OF 1787.

Grievances *See* ASSEMBLY AND ASSOCIATION.

Griswold v. Connecticut

The right of PRIVACY is not expressly mentioned in the Constitution but has nevertheless been found by the Supreme Court in the penumbra—the shadows—of other expressly guaranteed rights. In a decision that developed the Court's ability to reason outside the limited framework of the rights explicitly guaranteed in the Constitution, the Court in *Griswold v. Connecticut* (1965) found state laws banning the use of contraceptives by married couples to be an unconstitutional invasion of protected natural and FUNDAMENTAL RIGHTS.

Privacy as a right did not spring fully formed as Athena did, according to Greek mythology, from the mind of Zeus. As so often happens, a dissent set the stage for a turnaround by the Court. In his dissenting opinion in *Adamson v. California* (1947), Supreme Court Justice Frank Murphy (1890–1949) argued that under the doctrine of the incorporation of federal rights (see INCORPORATION DOCTRINE) contained in the BILL OF RIGHTS (1791), which makes some of these rights applicable to the states through the DUE PROCESS clause of the Fourteenth Amendment (1868), other fundamental rights in addition to those expressly found in the Bill of Rights might also be protected by that clause. But attempts to invalidate state laws against the use of contraceptives were denied by the Supreme Court on various grounds in *Tileston v. Ullman* (1943) and then in *Poe v. Ullman* (1961).

In a major due process ruling, the Supreme Court in *Griswold v. Connecticut* voided the convictions of an officer of the Planned Parenthood League of Connecticut and its medical director, a licensed physician, for giving married people advice on how to prevent conception and, following an examination, prescribing a contraceptive device. The opinion, written by Justice William O. Douglas (1898–1980), developed the concept of the right to privacy from several perspectives.

The decision begins by refusing to be guided by *Lochner v. New York* (1905), a case that struck down a New York law regulating the working hours of bakers for health reasons on the basis that it violated the right of contract (see CONTRACTS) under the Fourteenth Amendment's due process clause. *Lochner* had come to symbolize the Court's substitution of its own social policy for that of elected legislatures. After declaring that the Court is not a "super-legislature" bent on substituting its own views on "economic problems, business affairs, or social conditions," Douglas pointed out that the anticontraceptive law in question "operates directly on an intimate relation of husband and wife and their physician."

The logic of the decision is then built on a foundation of prior cases that developed rights associated with those expressly set forth in the Constitution. For example, the right of association (see ASSEMBLY AND ASSOCIATION), of parents to educate their children in the manner of their own choice (see EDUCATION), and even the right to study a foreign language are derived from other express rights. In an earlier case—*NAACP v. Alabama* (1958)—the Supreme Court had already declared that "freedom to associate and privacy in one's associations" are protected by the Constitution. According to Douglas, the Bill of Rights has "penumbras, formed by emanations from those guarantees that help give them life and substance." Privacy, one such penumbral right, is created by other rights in the First, Third, Fourth, Fifth, and Ninth Amendments (all 1791).

To some, the derivation of a right of privacy from the Constitution is just another example of an overzealous court rewriting the actual text of the framers. To others, however, it represents the way the FRAMERS OF THE CONSTITUTION provided for the document's growth and expansion as times and the understanding of human rights change. ALEXANDER HAMILTON hinted at this in essay 85 of *The Federalist* (1787–88) (see FEDERALIST PAPERS), the last essay. He quoted the Scottish philosopher David Hume (1711–76) as stating that creating a government is "so great a difficulty that no human genius, however comprehensive, is able by mere dint of reason and reflection to effect it.... Experience must guide their labor; Time must bring it to perfection, and the Feeling of inconvenience must correct the mistakes which they *inevitably* fall into in their first trials and experiments."

After *Griswold*, the Supreme Court, relying on experience and time, went even further. The right of privacy with respect to the distribution of contraceptives was extended to unmarried persons in *Eisenstadt v. Baird* (1972), and in *ROE V. WADE* (1973) the right of privacy was stretched to include the right of a woman to have an ABORTION. Furthermore, in *LAWRENCE V. TEXAS* (2003), the Court expanded the original right of privacy acknowledged in *Griswold* to include the right of consenting adult homosexuals to have sexual relations in the privacy of their own home.

Supreme Court Justice William O. Douglas supported the right to privacy in his opinion in Griswold v. Connecticut.
Source: Library of Congress

Guarantee Clause *See* REPUBLICAN FORM OF GOVERNMENT.

Gun Control

The U.S. Constitution is the only national constitution that guarantees its citizens the right to possess firearms. "A well regulated Militia, being necessary to the security of a free State," the Second Amendment (1791) enigmatically provides, "the right of the people to keep and bear Arms, shall not be infringed." However, a state's right to regulate the use of force within its territorial jurisdiction is integral to the concept of SOVEREIGNTY.

Before the Revolutionary War (1775–83), each American colony had militia units for self-defense. As relations between Great Britain and the colonists deteriorated, they began taking control of these militias, made up of fellow colonists. Following the signing of the DECLARATION OF INDEPENDENCE (1776), the thirteen colonies, which became states, adopted constitutions. Those for North Carolina (1776), Pennsylvania (1776), Virginia (1776), and Massachusetts (1780), as well as Vermont (1777 and 1786) (which would become a state in 1791, the same year the BILL OF RIGHTS was ratified), contained language allowing the citizenry to bear arms.

The FRAMERS OF THE CONSTITUTION did not include a bill of rights in the Constitution itself, and it soon became evident to those supporting RATIFICATION of the Constitution that one would be

On May 14, 2000, a Million Mom March on the National Mall promoted support for stronger gun control laws. Attempts to restrict the use of firearms have faced powerful opposition from the National Rifle Association and other gun advocates.
Source: Reuters

necessary to win over doubters. The first twelve proposed amendments constituting a Bill of Rights were introduced in Congress in 1789 by JAMES MADISON. The last ten, including the one ensuring the right to bear arms, were ratified in 1791.

Exactly why the framers included the right to bear arms in the Bill of Rights is uncertain. One reasonable theory is that after having fought a war to throw off the tyranny of Britain, Americans wanted to be able again to take up arms against any new tyranny that might arise. Moreover, the United States and its territory on a newly discovered continent was not a completely safe environment. Having citizens armed and trained would help ensure a readily available defense force in the event of attacks from British Canada, Spanish Florida, French Louisiana, or hostile Native Americans. And many Americans, especially on the frontier, relied on hunting for survival.

Given the Second Amendment, do the states and the national government have constitutional authority to limit or prohibit citizens' possession of guns? This has become one of the most divisive questions in the United States. At one end of the spectrum are those who advocate that no citizen not engaged in LAW ENFORCEMENT or the ARMED FORCES should be allowed to possess a gun. At the other end are those who believe that every citizen should be armed for self-protection.

Although the number is declining, each year nearly thirty thousand persons die, and many more are wounded, by firearms in the United States, far exceeding that of any other nation. According to the National Crime Victimization Survey in 2005, as reported by the Bureau of Justice Statistics of the U.S. Department of Justice, some 477,040 victims of violent crimes faced an offender with a firearm, and firearms were involved in nine percent of the 4.7 million violent crimes in the United States, including rape, sexual assault, and robbery. According to the Federal Bureau of Investigation, 66 percent of the 16,137 murders in 2004 were committed by people with firearms. Moreover, in spite of the number of violent crimes involving guns, in 2004 Congress failed to renew a ban on semiautomatic assault weapons and ammunition clips holding more than ten rounds, except for military and police use, which was put in place in 1994.

The Supreme Court has provided only limited guidance on the extent to which the Second Amendment allows the government to restrict gun possession. The Court has generally held that the amendment applies only to the federal government and thus is not applicable to the states, as was originally intended for all the guarantees in the Bill of Rights. Many other provisions of the Bill of Rights, however, have been extended to the states through the Court's interpretations of the Fourteenth Amendment (1868) (see INCORPORATION DOCTRINE). In any case, today the constitutions of forty-four states guarantee the right to bear arms, and two others allow citizens to defend "life and liberty" as self-protection. New Hampshire's constitution (1784) sanctions the right to "keep and bear arms," but it also states: "No person, who is conscientiously scrupulous about the lawfulness of bearing arms, shall be compelled thereto."

In *United States v. Miller* (1939), however, the Supreme Court confirmed the constitutionality of a law requiring federal registration of sawed-off shotguns. The Court explained that a militia was composed of "citizens primarily, soldiers on occasion…[who] when called for service…were expected to appear bearing arms supplied by themselves and of the kind in common use at the time." The justices concluded that shotguns with a barrel of less than eighteen inches were not "part of ordinary military equipment" and thus had no "reasonable relationship to the preservation or efficiency of a well-trained militia."

In the 1990s the Supreme Court struck down two federal gun control laws enacted by Congress. In *United States v. Lopez* (1995), the Court declared unconstitutional the provision of the Gun-Free School Zones Act (1990) that made it a federal crime for "any individual knowingly to possess a firearm" within one thousand feet of a school. The decision was based on the Constitution's COMMERCE clause, which gives Congress the authority to "regulate Commerce with foreign Nations, and among the several States, and with the Indian Tribes," as set forth in Article I, section 8. Speaking for the majority, Chief Justice William H. Rehnquist (1924–2005) stated that the law did not attempt to regulate interstate commerce or "an activity that substantially affects interstate commerce."

Two years later, in *Printz v. United States* (1997), the Court by a bare 5–4 majority invalidated a major provision of the Brady Act (1993), named for Jim Brady, press secretary to President Ronald Reagan (1911–2004), who was severely injured in the 1981 assassination attempt on the president. In throwing out the requirement that local law enforcement officials conduct background checks of prospective gun buyers, Justice Antonin Scalia (b. 1936) wrote in the majority opinion: "[T]he Federal Government may not compel the States to implement, by legislation or executive action, federal regulatory programs."

Perhaps a sense of where the Supreme Court stands on the gun control issue can be gleaned from three cases the justices declined to review in 2001. In one, Louisiana's supreme court upheld the constitutionality of a state law that retroactively prohibited New Orleans from suing gun manufacturers to hold them liable for gun violence. The second and third cases involved challenges to laws banning assault weapons in California and New Jersey. There appears to be a limit on the type of firearm protected by the Second Amendment, but from the Court's point of view, people—not guns—kill people. However, the Supreme Court has recently agreed to review a Second Amendment case that raises the issue of whether the Constitution protects an individual's right to own a gun or only grants a collective civic right related to maintaining a state militia. The case has been filed on appeal under the title *District of Columbia v. Dick Anthony Heller*. This will be the first time that the Supreme Court has ruled on a crucial gun control issue since the *Miller* case in 1939.

Unlike other divisive constitutional issues—such as ABORTION and the DEATH PENALTY—a constitutionally acceptable and reasonable common ground likely could be found for limiting possession of firearms through national and state measures. A major obstacle, however, remains the powerful National Rifle Association, which lobbies on behalf of gun owners as well as firearms manufacturers and related commercial interests. As with measures to prevent TERRORISM, however, a free society must be able to balance the desire of law-abiding and safety-conscious citizens to possess firearms against the need to protect citizens, especially children, from accidents and from the dangers of readily available guns used for criminal purposes.

More on this topic:

Bill of Rights, p. 62

States' Rights, p. 520

Terrorism, p. 543

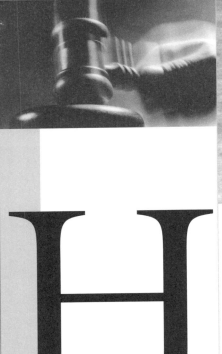

Habeas Corpus

Confinement of a person "by secretly hurrying him to jail, where his sufferings are unknown and forgotten, is a less public, a less striking, and therefore a *more dangerous engine* of arbitrary government" than sentencing a person without a trial, wrote William Blackstone (1723–80) in his *Commentaries on the Laws of England* (1765–70). Habeas corpus (Latin for "thou shalt have the body") evolved as a powerful tool with which individuals could challenge detention in the absence of a judicial proceeding. Under this principle, a person in government custody has the right to be brought before a court, where the authorities must show cause why he or she should be legally held.

The importance of the writ of habeas corpus to the FRAMERS OF THE CONSTITUTION is highlighted by ALEXANDER HAMILTON, who quoted Blackstone's point in essay 84 of *The Federalist* (1787–88) (see FEDERALIST PAPERS). In this essay, a defense of the Constitution's original lack of a bill of rights, Hamilton included the writ of habeas corpus in a list of civil protections that did not have to be spelled out in a bill of rights, among them the prohibition against EX POST FACTO LAWS and the guarantee of a trial by jury (see JURIES). Hamilton also concurred with Blackstone's praise of Britain's Habeas Corpus Act (1679) as "the Bulwark of the British Constitution," calling habeas corpus "a remedy for this fatal evil" of unauthorized detention.

In Article I, section 9, the Constitution directs: "The Privilege of the Writ of Habeas Corpus shall not be suspended, unless when in Cases of Rebellion or Invasion the public Safety may require it." Its use in the United States has been greatly expanded to include challenging the constitutionality of criminal trials and convictions by courts of law.

The constitutions of a number of other countries incorporate the Anglo-American concept of the writ of habeas corpus. Brazil's constitution (1988) guarantees that habeas corpus "shall be granted whenever a person suffers or is in danger of suffering violence or coercion against his freedom of locomotion, on account of illegal actions or abuse of power." The habeas corpus provision of the Philippines constitution (1987), adopted two centuries after the U.S. Constitution, uses the same wording as the 1787 document.

The Supreme Court Weighs In

According to English COMMON LAW, a writ of habeas corpus could be used to challenge confinement by an executive order before or in the absence of a trial but not after conviction by a court with proper jurisdiction. Chief Justice JOHN MARSHALL in *Ex parte Bollman* (1807) found that the Judiciary Act (1789) authorized federal courts to issue writs of habeas corpus but only in cases where the confinement was under federal authority. However, in 1867 Congress passed the Habeas Corpus Act, which empowered the federal courts to inquire into the circumstances of imprisonment of persons under state authority as well.

At the beginning of the Civil War (1861–65), President ABRAHAM LINCOLN suspended the writ of habeas corpus, but in *Ex parte Merryman* (1861), the Supreme Court declared the suspension unconstitutional. In an example of what is called structural analysis (an approach to resolving questions based on the placement of provisions in the Constitution itself), the Court carefully scrutinized the habeas corpus provision (see STRICT SCRUTINY). Because suspension of the writ of habeas corpus was incorporated in Article I, the article relating to Congress, the Court reasoned that only Congress, not the president, could exercise this power.

In *Frank v. Mangum* (1915), the owner of a pencil factory was convicted of killing a thirteen-year-old female worker, but a mob was alleged to have dominated the state court proceedings. The Supreme Court agreed to base its review of the conviction on habeas corpus grounds, because if DUE PROCESS had been denied, the state court's jurisdiction could be questioned. The Court found that the state's appeal process had given the defendant an adequate opportunity to challenge the trial. Justice OLIVER WENDELL HOLMES JR., in a dissent, argued that the trial had been far from fair, despite the state appeals court's decision to the contrary. In a similar case, *Moore v. Dempsey* (1923), the Court sent the matter back to the district court for a finding as to whether that trial had been unfairly influenced by mob action.

In the case *Brown v. Allen* (1953), the Supreme Court concluded that it could rehear habeas corpus claims of PRISONERS and set forth rules for habeas corpus cases: (1) Any federal constitutional question may be raised by state prisoners. (2) The Supreme Court is not bound by state court judgments even where there has been full and fair consideration of the issues. (3) A federal court may rely on habeas corpus to inquire into issues of fact as well as law. (4) A new evidentiary hearing must be held if the state proceedings show any unusual circumstances or a "vital flaw" or if the state court record is incomplete or inadequate.

> *"The Privilege of the Writ of Habeas Corpus shall not be suspended, unless when in Cases of Rebellion or Invasion the public Safety may require it."*
>
> —Article I, section 9, of the Constitution

CLOSER LOOK

When President Abraham Lincoln suspended the writ of habeas corpus in 1861, he precipitated one of the sharpest battles between the executive and judicial branches in the nation's history.

Chief Justice Roger Taney ruled in *Ex parte Merryman* that the president had far exceeded his authority by allowing his generals to arrest citizens without formal charges. In a particularly fiery opinion, Taney warned that "the people of the United States are no longer living under a government of laws, but every citizen holds life, liberty and property at the will and pleasure of the army officer in whose military district he may happen to be found."

Lincoln, however, refused to back down. He believed that the government, threatened by the growing Civil War, could collapse if his military officers could not arrest those who they suspected of subversive activities. "Are all the laws, but one, to go unexecuted, and the government itself go to pieces, lest that one be violated?" he asked.

Several lower courts supported Taney, ruling that only Congress—not the president—could suspend habeas corpus. With the Civil War continuing to engulf the nation, Congress finally stepped in, passing a bill to suspend habeas corpus in 1863.

In the 1970s the Supreme Court began restricting the relief it would provide in habeas corpus requests. In *Wainwright v. Sykes* (1977), the justices decided that a failure to assert a federal issue at the state level would bar habeas corpus relief unless there was a good reason for the omission or actual prejudice resulted from a violation of the defendant's rights. The Rehnquist Court also began limiting prisoners to a single habeas corpus petition even if new evidence was discovered that their rights had been violated.

In recent years the number of Supreme Court decisions involving habeas corpus petitions has increased markedly, undoubtedly due to the detention of prisoners in the war on terror and the renewed concerns over aspects of the DEATH PENALTY. For example, a total of 15 decisions dealt with habeas corpus issues in the 2000, 2001, and 2002 terms, whereas in the most recent four terms the collective number is 49.

Petitions from Death Row

Many of the habeas corpus petitions seeking Supreme Court review have come from prisoners who have been condemned to death. In *Payne v. Tennessee* (1991), a challenge to the DEATH PENALTY, the Court agreed to allow victim-impact statements during death-penalty sentencing hearings, and in two other death-penalty cases that year the Court further limited habeas corpus review. In *Delo v. Blair* (1993), Chief Justice William H. Rehnquist (1924–2005) stated that "in a capital case a truly persuasive demonstration of 'actual innocence' made after trial would render the execution of a defendant unconstitutional, and warrant federal habeas [corpus] relief if there were no state avenue open to process such a claim."

The Supreme Court's attempts to limit habeas corpus relief for death-row inmates led to enactment of the Antiterrorism and Effective Death Penalty Act (1996), which attempts to statutorily reduce the habeas corpus appeals to just one. It requires that a second petition be dismissed if the same claim was raised in the previous proceeding. If not, the second petition must show that the prisoner relies on a "new rule of constitutional law," which the Court has made retroactive in habeas corpus cases (see EX POST FACTO LAWS). Alternatively, it must show that the facts on which the new petition is based could not have been discovered previously and that they establish by clear and convincing evidence that "but for constitutional error, no reasonable fact-finder would have found the applicant guilty of the underlying offense." Not surprisingly, the Court in *Felker v. Turpin* (1996), in an opinion by Chief Justice Rehnquist, had no difficulty upholding the constitutionality of the 1996 act.

Key recent U.S. Supreme Court cases involving the writ of habeas corpus include *Rasul v. Bush* (2004) and *HAMDI V. RUMSFELD* (2004). These two cases basically upheld the right of habeas corpus for alien and enemy combatant detainees. In another major case, *Hamdan v. Rumsfeld* (2006), the Court found that the president, as commander-in-chief, lacked congressional authority to try detainees by military commissions. The Court, however, began revisiting in the 2007 term the question of the rights of detainees in the war on terror in two cases consolidated by the Court—*Boumediene v. Bush* and *Al Odah v. United States*.

Hamdi v. Rumsfeld

On September 11, 2001, the al Qaeda terrorist network hijacked several commercial airliners in order to destroy prominent targets in the United States. Some three thousand people lost their lives in the attacks. A week later Congress passed a resolution authorizing the president to "use all necessary and appropriate force against those nations, organizations, or persons he determines planned, authorized, committed, or aided the terrorist attacks [or] harbored such organizations or persons, in order to prevent any future acts of international terrorism against the United States...." Based on this "Authorization for Use of Military Force" (AUMF), the president ordered U.S. military forces into Afghanistan to conquer al Qaeda operatives and any of their supporters, such as the Taliban—a group of Islamic "holy warriors" who ruled Afghanistan from 1996 to 2001.

Yaser Esam Hamdi was born an American citizen in Louisiana in 1980 and moved with his family to Saudi Arabia as a child. Later, having moved to Afghanistan by 2001, he was captured by local militiamen as a terrorist sympathizer and turned over to the U.S. military. After interrogating Hamdi, the military transferred him to the United States for further detention. In June 2002 Hamdi's father filed a petition of habeas corpus—a request for a judicial writ that orders the prisoner to be brought to court so that those holding him may explain why he is lawfully being detained—in a U.S. district court. The particular petition in question also asked the court, among other things, to appoint legal counsel for Hamdi; order that he no longer be interrogated; declare that he is being held in violation of the Fifth and Fourteenth Amendments; schedule an evidentiary hearing; and order Hamdi's release.

The district court ordered additional material regarding the detainee's status; but on review, the U.S. Court of Appeals for the Fourth Circuit found that Hamdi could be held as an enemy combatant and that his status as an American citizen did not change this conclusion. The government had alleged that Hamdi had been affiliated with a Taliban unit in Afghanistan, had received military training, and had "remained with his Taliban unit following the attacks of September 11"; and, therefore, the president had authority under Article II of the Constitution to detain him, or, in the alternative, that Congress, in fact, had authorized such detentions through the AUMF.

The plurality opinion of the Supreme Court, which was announced by Justice Sandra Day O'Connor, concluded that due process required that a U.S. citizen being held as an enemy combatant must be given a meaningful opportunity to contest the factual basis for his or her detention. After agreeing that the president was authorized by AUMF to detain individuals such as Hamdi, the Court cited the test articulated in *Matthews v. Eldridge* (1976) "for balancing serious competing interests," in this case Hamdi's "most elemental of liberty interests...in being free from physical detention by [his] own government" and the "sensitive governmental interests in ensuring that those who in fact fought with our enemy during a war do not return to battle against the United States."

Concluding that "it is during our most challenging and uncertain moments that our Nation's commitment to due process is most severely tested...and it is in those times that we must preserve our commitment at home to the principles for which we fight abroad," the Court went on to "hold that a citizen-detainee seeking to challenge his classification as an enemy combatant must receive notice of the factual basis for his classification, and a fair opportunity to rebut the Government's factual assertions before a neutral decision maker." The Supreme Court vacated the lower court's ruling and remanded the case for a determination on the question of whether or not Hamdi is an enemy combatant.

Justices Antonin Scalia, John Paul Stevens, and Clarence Thomas dissented. In Scalia's dissent, in which Justice Stevens joined, he took the plurality to task for "distorting the Suspension Clause [Article I, section 9 of the Constitution that permits Congress to suspend the writ of habeas corpus "when in Cases of Rebellion or Invasion the public Safety may require it"] and for disposing of the present habeas petition by remanding for the District Court to 'engage in a factfinding process that is both prudent and incremental.'" He goes on to argue that "[i]f Hamdi is being imprisoned in violation of the Constitution (because without due process of law), then his habeas petition should be granted." Justice Thomas also wrote a dissent saying that the president,

> "It is during our most challenging and uncertain moments that our Nation's commitment to due process is most severely tested."
>
> —Justice Sandra Day O'Connor

More on this topic:

Aliens, p. 25

National Security, p. 375

Terrorism, p. 543

"acting pursuant to the powers vested in [him] by the Constitution and with explicit congressional approval, has determined that [Hamdi] should be detained. This detention falls squarely within the Federal Government's war powers, and we lack the expertise and capacity to second-guess that decision."

In another enemy combatant case, *Rumsfeld v. Padilla* (2004), in which an American citizen was arrested by federal law enforcement officers at Chicago's O'Hare Airport for allegedly participating in a plot to set off a "dirty" bomb, the Supreme Court in a 5–4 decision found on jurisdictional grounds that Padilla had filed his habeas corpus petition in a federal district court in New York against the secretary of defense, Donald Rumsfeld, by mistake and should have filed it in the district court for South Carolina, where he was being incarcerated. Justice Stevens, in his dissenting opinion, noted that the four dissenters believed that the "protracted, incommunicado detention of American citizens arrested in the United States" was illegal.

Hamilton, Alexander

After the Constitution was adopted by the CONSTITUTIONAL CONVENTION OF 1787, Alexander Hamilton (1755–1804) commented: "The new constitution has in favour of its success these circumstances—a very great weight of influence of the persons who framed it, particularly in the universal popularity of General Washington,—the good will of the commercial interest throughout the states which will give all its efforts to the establishment of a government capable of regulating, protecting and extending the commerce of the Union—the good will of most men of property in the several states who wish a government of the union able to protect them against domestic violence and the depredations which the democratic spirit is apt to make on property...."

Hamilton, who was the lone New York delegate to the convention to sign the document, would soon join with John Jay and JAMES MADISON to write *The Federalist* (1787–88) (see FEDERALIST PAPERS), a series of newspaper articles prepared in support of the Constitution's RATIFICATION. Appointed by President GEORGE WASHINGTON to be the new nation's first secretary of the Treasury, Hamilton became the leader of the Federalist Party, the country's first political party (see POLITICAL PARTIES).

The illegitimate son of a Scotsman and a mother whose father was a French Huguenot doctor, Alexander Hamilton was born on the island of Nevis in the British West Indies on January 11, 1755. After working as a clerk in a trading firm between the ages of eleven and thirteen, he immigrated to New York City in 1773 and attended what would become Columbia University. Hamilton was active in supporting the cause of the American Revolution and then joined the Continental Army. An aide-de-camp to General Washington, he became the head of a line regiment at the decisive Battle of Yorktown in 1781.

An unapologetic Federalist, Alexander Hamilton was the only member of the New York delegation to sign the Constitution, and afterward he was the major contributor to The Federalist *(1787–88), promoting its ratification.*
Source: Library of Congress

After serving in the Continental Congress, both Hamilton and JAMES MADISON urged the delegates to attend a conference in Annapolis, Maryland, in September 1786, on interstate trade problems. He wanted to recommend to the Congress that a national meeting be held to address the inadequacies of the ARTICLES OF CONFEDERATION (1781). At the Constitutional Convention held beginning in Philadelphia on May 25, 1787, Hamilton's own proposal based on the British model of government found little support. As soon as the draft document was approved, however, he became an ardent proponent of its ratification by the thirteen states.

As the nation's first secretary of the Treasury, Hamilton created the First National Bank of the United States to strengthen the country's credit. THOMAS JEFFERSON questioned the constitutionality of the new bank, and the two men would continue a philosophical rivalry until a duel with another political rival, Aaron Burr, ended Hamilton's life on July 12, 1804.

> **"Were the people of America, with one voice, to ask, What shall we do to perpetuate our liberties and secure our happiness? The answer would be, 'govern well.'"**
>
> **—Alexander Hamilton,** in Letter from Phocion, January 1–27, 1784

Hamilton's vision for the United States, in contrast to Jefferson's view that it was a nation of farmers, pictured a major commercial and trading country (see COMMERCE). It would be this vision, grounded as he said in "an eternal and immutable law, which is indispensably, obligatory upon all mankind," that would lead the United States to become the greatest economic and commercial power in the world.

More on this topic:
Federalist Papers, p. 220
Framers of the Constitution, p. 230

Handicapped Persons *See* DISABLED PERSONS.

Hate Crimes *See* DISCRIMINATION; SPEECH.

Health

The constitutions of a number of countries expressly address health care for their citizens. The Netherlands constitution (1814, as amended) states, "Rules to protect health, in the interest of traffic and to combat or prevent disorders, may be laid down by Act of Parliament," and Ukraine's constitution (1996) provides: "Every person has the right to health protection, medical care, and medical insurance." The U.S. Constitution, however, does not mention health, and the U.S. courts have not recognized a constitutional right of American citizens to health care. As a result, constitutional law on the subject has developed piecemeal.

Police Power v. Economic Due Process

Under their POLICE POWER, states generally have the authority to enact laws to safeguard public health, safety, and morals. Short of contravening the Constitution, they may take whatever steps are necessary to effect their health policies. As early as the turn of the twentieth century, in *Jacobson v. Massachusetts* (1905), the Supreme Court affirmed a state's authority to enact a statute making smallpox vaccination mandatory and imposing a fine of five dollars on those who refused. Justice John Marshall Harlan (1833–1911), writing for the Court, stated that the Court "has distinctly recognized the authority of a state to enact quarantine laws and 'health laws of every description....'"

However, the Supreme Court, citing economic due process (see ECONOMIC LIBERTY), has not always upheld legislation aimed at protecting the health of the American public. In *Lochner v. New York* (1905), the justices invalidated a state law designed to protect bakery workers' health by limiting how long they could work. The Court found that such a law was an unreasonable government interference with the right of contract—the bakers' right to contract out their labor regardless of the number of hours to be worked—and violated the DUE PROCESS provision of the Fourteenth Amendment (1868). The Court also held that the statute had not been proven necessary to safeguard the public health or the health of bakers in general. The Court's tendency to strike down public health laws on the grounds of economic due process ended in the 1930s.

Even then, however, the Supreme Court did not completely abandon its economic analysis of health measures or its standards of reasonableness. In *Dean Milk Co. v. Madison* (1951), the Court invalidated a Wisconsin municipality's provision forbidding the sale of pasteurized milk processed beyond five miles from the city center. The decision stated that "[e]ven in the exercise of its unquestioned power to protect the health and safety of its people, a municipality may not erect an economic barrier" to competition. "In view of the reasonable and adequate alternatives...available for [such protection]," it added, "the discrimination against interstate commerce inherent in the ordinance violates the Commerce Clause" (see COMMERCE).

Federal Steps toward Health Care

The Public Health Service was created by Congress in 1912 to administer national health programs. In 1953 Congress established the CABINET-level Department of Health, Education, and Welfare, which in 1979 was split into the Department of Health and Human Services and the Department of Education (see EDUCATION). The Department of Health and Human Services is now chiefly responsible for administering national health programs, although other ADMINISTRATIVE AGENCIES, such as the Food and Drug Administration and the Occupational Health and Safety Administration in the Department of Labor, have some related functions.

In 1965 Congress amended the Social Security Act (1935) to create Medicare, a limited national health insurance program for citizens at least sixty-five years old. The program covers a major portion of health-care costs of eligible elderly citizens and is financed by Social Security taxes deducted regularly from citizens' paychecks during their working years. The act was also amended that same year to create the Medicaid program for needy citizens of all ages who cannot afford to pay for private health care. The federal and state governments jointly fund the Medicaid program.

A number of cases relating to Medicare have come before the Supreme Court. In *Bowen v. Michigan Academy of Family Physicians* (1986), the Court confirmed its power of JUDICIAL REVIEW over the actions of agencies such as the Department of Health and Human Services. As the Court noted, based on the program's legislative history, "There is a strong presumption that Congress intends judicial review of administrative action" taken by the secretary of health and human services. In other words, substantive and constitutional challenges can be made to various provisions.

The Supreme Court has also heard a number of cases relating to Medicaid. Under the so-called Hyde Amendment (1977), Congress barred the use of federal Med-

Rep. Henry Hyde (R-Ill.) successfully prevented the use of Medicaid funds for abortions.
Source: CQ Photo/Scott J. Ferrell

icaid funds for abortions. In *Harris v. McRae* (1980), a case challenging the ban, the Court held that Congress had not violated the Constitution or run afoul of its landmark decision in ROE V. WADE (1973), which validated a woman's right to an ABORTION.

More recently, the Supreme Court addressed the scope of the federal government's involvement in health care in *Aetna Health v. Davila* (2004). The opinion for the Court, written by Justice Clarence Thomas (b. 1948), declared that participants and beneficiaries under an employee benefit plan governed by the federal Employee Retirement Income Security Act of 1974 were precluded from bringing an action under a state health care liability law for injuries resulting from the plan's administrator and their health maintenance organization's (HMO's) refusal to cover treatment recommended by their physician. The decision reasoned that in enacting the federal law Congress had intended to preempt any other type of enforcement action.

Patients' Rights

In the 1970s the Supreme Court took on several cases involving the rights of mental patients. In *O'Connor v. Donaldson* (1975), as well as in some other cases, the Court declared that each person has a right, protected by due process of law, to freedom from confinement and personal restraint even if he or she is properly committed to a hospital or another institution. *O'Connor* set the principle that a state "cannot constitutionally confine without…[sufficient evidence] a nondangerous individual who is capable of surviving safely in freedom by himself or with the help of willing and responsible family members or friends."

In the 1990s, however, the Supreme Court affirmed in *Washington v. Harper* (1990) that a prisoner could be forced to take a psychotropic medication without a judicial hearing or determination of the prisoner's competency to refuse the medication (see PRISONERS). *Cruzan v. Director, Missouri Department of Health* (1990) held that a patient in a "persistent vegetative state" and incompetent to make a decision on her own could not be taken off medical life support without "clear and convincing" evidence of the patient's will (see DIE, RIGHT TO).

In 1999 a Patients' Bill of Rights was introduced in the Senate. The proposed law addressed such issues as access to emergency health services, specialty medical care, necessary drugs, nondiscrimination in the delivery of health care services, quality assurance programs, patient information and protection of patient confidentiality, grievance and appeal procedures, protection of the doctor-patient relationship, patient advocacy, and promotion of good medical practices. A version of the bill passed the Senate in 2001, but for various reasons, including its possible adverse impact on HMOs, the bill was not enacted into law.

A number of nations, including Canada and the United Kingdom, have national health care programs that cover their citizens. The goal of providing national health care in the United States came to a head in the early 1990s, when the administration of President Bill Clinton (b. 1946) proposed steps in this direction. However, Congress rejected the idea, and the issue of national health care became overshadowed by other concerns, such as maintaining the viability of the Social Security trust fund and NATIONAL SECURITY.

> **More on this topic:**
>
> *Abortion, p. 1*
>
> *Welfare, p. 582*

Holmes, Oliver Wendell, Jr.

Oliver Wendell Holmes Jr. (1841–1935) has been acknowledged as the supreme U.S. jurist of the twentieth century. Appointed to the SUPREME COURT in 1902 by President Theodore Roosevelt (1858–1919), he served on it for thirty years. Excepting JOHN MARSHALL, Holmes probably had the greatest impact on constitutional law of any American justice.

A brilliant and eloquent jurist, Oliver Wendell Holmes Jr. devised a notion of "clear and present danger" in Schenck v. United States (1919) that became a hallmark of free speech. His minority views were often adopted years later.
Source: Library of Congress

"The law embodies the story of a nation's development through many centuries, and it cannot be dealt with as if it contained only the axioms and corollaries of a book of mathematics. In order to know what it is, we must know what is has been, and what it tends to become."

—Oliver Wendell Holmes Jr. in The Common Law (1881)

Born in Boston, Holmes was the son of the famous writer Oliver Wendell Holmes, also a medical doctor who was known to his readers as "the autocrat of the breakfast table." After graduating from Harvard College in 1861, he joined the Northern Army during the Civil War (1861–65), serving three years with the Massachusetts volunteers. He was wounded three times, a fact in which he took great personal pride. He would later often draw on his war experience and profess the need to commit oneself to great causes.

After the war Holmes attended Harvard Law School. He practiced law in Boston for fifteen years, taught constitutional law at Harvard, and edited the *American Law Review*. *The Common Law* (1881)—a compilation of his lectures, in which he argued that "the law" represented pragmatic solutions to social problems and not esoteric legal logic—opened the door for the development of sociological jurisprudence in the United States. "The life of the law," Holmes wrote in the first paragraph of the first of these lectures, "has not been logic: it has been experience." He served on the Massachusetts Supreme Judicial Court, becoming a justice in 1883 and chief justice in 1899, before being appointed to the U.S. Supreme Court.

Whereas Marshall's legacy as a Supreme Court justice consists primarily in establishing the Court's authority as an equal branch of the federal government, Holmes's major contribution was to define the CONSTITUTION as a "living document" that could evolve and grow to deal effectively with the needs of a changing nation. As he wrote in *Gompers v. United States* (1914): "[T]he provisions of the Constitution are not mathematical formulas having their essence in their form; they are organic living institutions transplanted from English soil. Their significance is vital not formal; it is to be gathered not simply by taking the words and a dictionary, but by considering their origin and the line of their growth."

Although Holmes was often in the minority in his early days on the Supreme Court, some of his dissenting opinions would later become the basis for majority opinions. His dissent in *Lochner v. New York* (1905), for example, was vindicated thirty years later with the demise of economic due process, whereby the Court would substitute its social and economic theories for those of elected representatives (see ECONOMIC LIBERTY). In *Lochner* he said that the majority will should prevail through laws passed by the legislature "unless it can be said that a rational and fair man necessarily would admit that the statute proposed would infringe fundamental principles as they have been understood by the traditions of our people and our law."

In perhaps his most famous opinion, *Schenck v. United States* (1919), Holmes set the limit for constitutional tolerance of free SPEECH. "The most stringent protection of free speech would not protect a man in falsely shouting fire in a theatre and causing a panic.... The question in every case is whether the words used are used in such circumstances and are of such a nature as to create a clear and present danger that they will bring about the substantive evils that Congress has a right to prevent." The best writer ever to sit on the Supreme Court, he could state his case in timeless prose even when wrong. In *Buck v. Bell* (1927), a case permitting involuntary sterilization by a state, he declared: "Three generations of imbeciles are enough."

In recent years Holmes has been criticized for his relatively small number of written dissents and the perceived inconsistency in his opinions supporting social justice. He could just as well be praised for selecting only cases where his reasoning was sufficiently sound to warrant a written dissent and for not having some grand social design that would predetermine his decisions on varied facts. In the end, however, Holmes's deference to the democratic process and the will of the majority—except in clear cases of infringement of FUNDAMENTAL RIGHTS—exercised through elected representatives, rather than the courts, cannot be disparaged.

Homosexuals

"A considerable portion of the population," reported Alfred Kinsey in *The Sexual Behavior of the Human Male* (1948), "has had at least some homosexual experience between adolescence and old age." Homosexual behavior (*homo* is derived from the Greek word meaning same), the opposite of heterosexuality, has been recorded in many cultures throughout history. Homosexual men, or gays, and homosexual women, or lesbians, are attracted to members of their own sex.

Homosexuality is not addressed in most national constitutions, although South Africa's constitution (1997) states in its bill of rights, under the heading Equality, that the "state may not unfairly discriminate directly or indirectly against anyone on one or more grounds, including race, gender, sex, pregnancy, marital status, ethnic or social origin, color, [or] sexual orientation...." The U.S. Constitution makes no reference to sex, except in the Fourteenth Amendment (1868), which refers to "male citizens," and the Nineteenth Amendment (1920), which extended to WOMEN the right to vote. Technically, the Constitution is color blind as well as blind to sex and sexual orientation, but the moral implications of homosexual behavior for some people have made it difficult for Congress and the federal courts to accord homosexuals the same rights as heterosexuals in spite of the Constitution's DUE PROCESS and EQUAL PROTECTION clauses.

By 1961 all fifty states had outlawed sodomy, and homosexual conduct is still a criminal offense in some states, although such laws are no longer strictly enforced and have been repealed in many states. Cases before the Supreme Court in the 1960s that extended the constitutional protection of PRIVACY to heterosexual adults and married couples legitimized nonreproductive sexual relationships, thus opening the door for the legitimization of sexual relations between consenting adult homosexuals. But in *Bowers v. Hardwick* (1986), a 5–4 majority of the Court upheld a Georgia law prohibiting sodomy. In a rare moment of candor, however, one of the justices in the majority, Justice Lewis F. Powell Jr. (1907–98), indicated to a group of law students at New York University in 1990 that he might have made a mistake. Although Powell had retired from the Court, in 2003 the justices took the opportunity to overrule *Bowers* in their decision in LAWRENCE V. TEXAS, which struck down a similar Texas law prohibiting homosexual sodomy as an unconstitutional violation of the right of privacy guaranteed by the due process clause of the Fourteenth Amendment (1868).

The Netherlands—admittedly an avant-garde nation with respect to many issues, from the use of DRUGS to the right to die (see DIE, RIGHT TO)—recognizes same-sex marriages among homosexuals, as do a number of other countries. In the United States, currently all states except Massachusetts prohibit same-sex marriage, but Vermont and Connecticut permit civil unions for homosexual couples that provide many of the same benefits as marriage. Some states, including California, and some municipalities and businesses recognize domestic partnerships between members of the same sex for

Spurred by the ravages of the AIDS epidemic, gays and lesbians have used rallies sponsored by Act Up and other organizations to demand greater recognition of their constitutional rights in areas such as association, privacy, employment, and civil unions. In an August 1992 protest outside the Republican National Convention in Houston, demonstrators perform a die-in symbolizing people dying from AIDS.
Source: AP Images/Tim Johnson

the purpose of extending certain rights and benefits usually reserved to married heterosexual couples. (Heterosexual marriage, in contrast, has been held by the Supreme Court to be a right of intimate association, meaning that the state must prove a strong interest before interfering with it.)

In another case involving the right of association, *Boy Scouts of America v. Dale*, the Supreme Court in 2000 held that "expressive" association, which has been found by the Court to be guaranteed by the First Amendment (1791), allowed the Boy Scouts to reject as a leader an avowed homosexual adult who was a gay rights activist. The rights of homosexuals in the military have since 1993 been limited to a "don't ask, don't tell" policy, which permits the ARMED FORCES to discharge persons who overtly identify themselves as homosexuals. In 2001 a federal district court upheld the right of the Air Force to recover medical education benefits from an officer who was considered voluntarily separated from the service for declaring that he was gay. In *Hurley v. Irish-American Gay Group of Boston* (1995), the Supreme Court refused to force the organizers of Boston's St. Patrick's Day Parade to include a homosexual group, saying that to do so would force the organizers to appear to support a message with which they did not agree. That would violate the organizers' right of free SPEECH and their right not to be forced to speak.

Reviewing a voter-approved Colorado constitutional amendment that would bar any state or local agency from offering special protection to homosexuals, the Supreme Court ruled in *Romer v. Evans* (1996) that the amendment was unconstitutional. The justices' rationalization was that the amendment classified homosexuals not to further a proper legislative end but to make them unequal to everyone else. "[W]e cannot accept the view," wrote Justice Anthony M. Kennedy (b. 1936) for the majority, "that [the]… prohibition on specific legal protections does no more than deprive homosexuals of special rights. To the contrary, the amendment imposes a special disability upon those persons alone."

Justifying their dissent in the Colorado case, Justice Antonin Scalia (b. 1936), joined by Chief Justice William H. Rehnquist (1924–2005) and Justice Clarence Thomas (b. 1948), wrote: "[The amendment] is not the manifestation of a 'bare… desire to harm' homosexuals…but is rather a modest attempt by seemingly tolerant Coloradans to preserve traditional sexual mores against the efforts of a politically powerful minority to revise those mores through use of the laws." Some civil libertarians would note that SLAVERY and inequality for women were also once part of the traditional mores of many Americans. In 2007 the U.S. House of Representatives passed the Employment Non-Discrimination Act that would make it illegal for employers to fire, refuse to hire, or fail to promote an employee because of the person's real or perceived sexual orientation. The initiative for this type of employment protection for homosexuals began in Congress in 1974. There remains little hope today that the measure will be passed in the Senate or, if passed by Congress, would survive a veto by President George W. Bush.

More on this topic:
Assembly and Association, p. 50
Discrimination, p. 159
Families, p. 214
Minorities, p. 369
Privacy, p. 430

House of Representatives

The House of Representatives is the most democratic of all the national government institutions because it is the most accountable—its members are elected directly by the people every two years. While the "principle of state independence prevailed in the shaping of the Senate," observed the French political scientist Alexis de Tocqueville (1805–59) in *Democracy in America* (1835), "the dogma of national sovereignty [prevailed] in the composition of the House of Representatives." The power and superiority of the lower house of CONGRESS were also asserted by JAMES MADISON in essay 63 of *The Federalist* (1787–88) (see FEDERALIST PAPERS). In the event of any attempted usurpation of power by the upper house, the SENATE, said Madison, "[T]he House of Representatives, with the people on their side, will at all times be able to bring back the Constitution to its primitive form and principles."

The term *house* to indicate a legislative body in England dates at least from the sixteenth century. Britain's national legislature, known collectively along with the English monarch as Parliament, consists of an upper chamber, the House of Lords, and a lower chamber, the House of Commons. The House of Representatives is similar to the British House of Commons in that it includes representatives elected from electoral districts. It is dissimilar, however, in that the House of Commons selects the prime minister, who is the British head of government, and the cabinet, which together perform the executive functions for the government of the United Kingdom.

> "[T]he House of Representatives, with the people on their side, will at all times be able to bring back the Constitution to its primitive form and principles."
>
> —James Madison

The House and the Senate constitute congress, the coequal LEGISLATIVE BRANCH that works in concert with the EXECUTIVE BRANCH, headed by the PRESIDENT, and the JUDICIAL BRANCH, headed by the SUPREME COURT, to form the federal government (see SEPARATION OF POWERS). Signifying Congress's importance, the Constitution details the nation's legislative framework in Article I.

Specialized duties for the House of Representatives are set forth there, most important being the power to initiate revenue bills, to bring charges of impeachment against government officials,

Special constitutional responsibilities of the House of Representatives include initiating revenue bills, bringing impeachment charges against government offcials, and electing the president when the electoral college fails to produce a majority vote.
Source: Library of Congress

and to elect the president when the electoral college fails to confer a majority. Members of the House are also mentioned in Article II with respect to the electors of the president and VICE PRESIDENT, whose numbers mirror the total of each state's representatives plus two senators to which each state is entitled. Like senators, however, representatives are excluded under Article II from being electors of the president and vice president in the electoral college. Several constitutional AMENDMENTS also address the House of Representatives.

Structure of the House

"All legislative Powers herein granted," states Article I, section 1, "shall be vested in a Congress of the United States, which shall consist of a Senate and House of Representatives." As section 2 provides in the first clause, "The House of Representatives shall be composed of Members chosen every second Year by the People of the several States, and the electors in each State shall have the qualifications requisite for electors of the most numerous Branch of the State Legislature."

The character of the House and the Senate resulted from the "Great Compromise" at the CONSTITUTIONAL CONVENTION OF 1787 in Philadelphia. Edmund Randolph of Virginia had proposed a bicameral legislature in which representatives in the lower house would be elected directly by the people but members of the upper house would be chosen by the lower house from lists of candidates. To counteract this Virginia Plan (see pages 622–623), which favored the states with large populations, William Paterson then presented the New Jersey Plan (see pages 624–626), which proposed a unicameral body in which all states would be represented equally.

The "Great Compromise" proposed by Roger Sherman of Connecticut became the basis for Congress as adopted at the Philadelphia convention. This compromise allowed the delegates to have the best of both plans. James Madison in essays 52 through 58 and ALEXANDER HAMILTON in essays 59 through 61 of *The Federalist* explained and defended the creation by the FRAMERS OF THE CONSTITUTION of a lower house consisting of representatives elected by the inhabitants of the states whose number was to be based on the relative population of each state. "The House of Representatives," Madison also noted in essay 39, "will derive its powers from the people of America; and the people will be represented in the same proportion and on the same principle as they are in the legislature of a particular State."

Qualifications of Representatives. Article I, section 2, of the Constitution sets forth the qualifications of a member of the House. "No person shall be a Representative who shall not have attained to the Age of twenty-five Years, and been seven Years a Citizen of the United States, and who shall not, when elected, be an Inhabitant of that State in which he shall be chosen." As Madison contended in *The Federalist*, "Under these reasonable limitations, the door of this part of the federal government is open to merit of every description, whether native or adoptive, whether young or old, and without regard to poverty or wealth, or to any particular profession of religious faith."

Apportionment. The first sentence of Article I, section 2, was changed by section 2 of the Fourteenth Amendment (1869) to read: "Representatives shall be apportioned among the several States according to their respective numbers, counting the whole number of persons in each State, excluding Indians not taxed." The framers originally created a special relationship between representation in the House and the basis for TAXATION by making both related to state population. This linkage gave the number of people counted in the CENSUS both a positive and a negative outcome, therefore denying the states an incentive to purposely increase or decrease the population count. The greater a state's population, the greater its representation in the House could be but, by the same token, the higher its possible tax burden. Although the relationship to taxes is no longer of any significance, the size of a state's population does have an impact on some benefits to the states, such as federal grants.

According to section 2, "The Number of Representatives shall not exceed one for every thirty Thousand, but each State shall have at Least one Representative...." The Constitution called for a census (an "actual Enumeration") to be conducted "within every subsequent Term of ten Years, in such Manner as they [Congress] shall by Law direct." The number of representatives originally established was sixty-five. Currently there are 435 members of the House, the number having been set by Congress with the admission of Arizona and New Mexico in 1912. On the basis of the 2000 Census, each House district from which a member is elected had an average of 646,952 constituents. California has the most representatives (fifty-two), and a number of states, including Alaska and Delaware, have only one representative. The 2000 census resulted in some changes in the distribution of House seats beginning with the election of 2002 (see REAPPORTIONMENT). In addition to the representatives from the states, the House has five nonvoting delegates, one each representing the District of Columbia, Puerto Rico, Guam, the Virgin Islands, and American Samoa.

Elections. "The Times, Places and Manner of holding Elections for Senators and Representatives," Article I, section 4, provides, "shall be prescribed in each State by the Legislature thereof; but the Congress may at any time by Law make or alter such Regulations, except as to the Places of chusing Senators." As section 5 indicates, "Each House shall be the Judge of the Elections, Returns and Qualifications of its own Members...." After the Civil War, the House refused to seat some representatives from the South because of how House seats were apportioned when former slaves were fully counted.

Nancy Pelosi became the first woman Speaker of the House in 2007.
Source: CQ Photo/Scott J. Ferrell

Section 2 addresses vacancies: "When vacancies [such as death, resignation, or expulsion] happen in the Representation from any State, the Executive Authority thereof [the governor] shall issue Writs of Election to fill such Vacancies."

Officers. Section 2 also indicates that the House "shall chuse their Speaker and other Officers...." Many national legislatures have a presiding officer with various powers and duties who is often called the speaker. The British Parliament's speaker is elected by and from the members of the House of Commons and literally sits on a throne between the majority party and the opposition party or parties. In the United States, the SPEAKER OF THE HOUSE is elected by the members of the House of Representatives along party lines, annointing a member of the majority party. According to the Twenty-fifth Amendment (1967), it falls to the Speaker to declare the president "unable to discharge the powers and duties of his office," and the Speaker, who is elected by a majority of the nation's elected representatives, is next in the line of succession to the presidency after the vice president. In 2007 Nancy Pelosi became the first woman Speaker of the House, making her the highest elected female official in the national government in U.S. history. Over the years the Speaker has acquired many other duties that are not spelled out in the Constitution.

Other House officers include the leaders of the majority and minority parties and the party whips, who serve as liaisons between the party leaders and their members. Among the unelected officers are the chief administrative officer, clerk of the House, inspector general, and chaplain.

Quorum and Rules. Congress is required to "assemble at least once in every Year," and pursuant to section 2 of the Twentieth Amendment (1933), "such meeting shall begin at noon on the 3d day of January, unless they shall by law appoint a different day."

"[A] Majority of each [house] shall constitute a Quorum to do Business; but a smaller Number may adjourn from day to day, and may be authorized to compel the Attendance of absent Members, in such Manner, and under such Penalties as each House may provide," states Article 1, section 5. Regarding adjournment, the Constitution further mandates: "Neither House, during the Session of Congress, shall, without the Consent of the other, adjourn for more than three days, nor to any other Place than that in which the two Houses shall be sitting."

Each house is permitted to determine its own rules of procedure and to punish "Members for disorderly Behaviour, and, with the Concurrence of two thirds, expel a Member." In 1969 the Supreme Court ruled that the House had unconstitutionally excluded one of its members, Adam Clayton Powell Jr., from the 90th Congress in 1967.

Section 5 also states that each house is required to keep a "Journal of its Proceedings, and from time to time publish the same," although they may vote to keep some parts secret.

Compensation and Immunity. For their services, Article I, section 6, provides that members of both houses receive compensation; currently the pay is $169,300 (see COMPENSATION OF OFFICIALS). They are also to be granted certain privileges and immunities: "They shall in all Cases, except Treason, Felony and Breach of the Peace," the section continues, "be privileged from Arrest during their Attendance at the Session of their respective Houses, and in going to and returning from the same; and for any Speech or Debate in either House, they shall not be questioned in any other Place" (see IMMUNITY).

COMMITTEES OF THE HOUSE OF REPRESENTATIVES

STANDING COMMITTEES

Standing committees generally have legislative jurisdiction. Their subcommittees are responsible for specific subject areas. The chairs and a majority of members are appointed by the majority party.

Agriculture
Appropriations
Armed Services
Budget
Education and Labor
Energy and Commerce
Financial Services
Foreign Affairs
Homeland Security
House Administration
Judiciary
Natural Resources
Oversight and Government Reform
Rules
Science and Technology
Small Business
Standards of Official Conduct
Transportation and Infrastructure
Veterans' Affairs
Ways and Means

SELECT COMMITTEES

Select and joint committees conduct primarily oversight or housekeeping responsibilities.

Energy Independence and Global Warming
Intelligence

JOINT COMMITTEES WITH THE SENATE

Economic
Printing
Taxation

AD HOC COMMISSIONS

Commission on Security and Cooperation in Europe
   (Helsinki Commission)
Congressional-Executive Commission on China

SOURCES: *The World Almanac and Book of Facts.* New York: World Almanac Books, 2002. Information Resources, U.S. House of Representatives.

Also according to section 6, "No Senator or Representative shall, during the Time for which he was elected," hold any other federal government position created or whose salary was increased "during such time; and no Person holding any Office under the United States, shall be a Member of either House during his Continuance in Office."

Committees. Much of how the House of Representatives does business is not expressly set forth in the Constitution but has become a part of its written and unwritten rules. The major structural innovation is the use of permanent committees, of which the House now has twenty. Standing committees are assigned specific legislative jurisdiction, while their multiple subcommittees handle work in specific areas. Select committees, such as the House Select Committee on Intelligence, provide oversight of targeted government endeavors. Committees review and approve legislation, hold oversight hearings to provide accountability for operations of the executive and judicial branches, and decide initially on budget requests for the activities under their jurisdiction. The House and Senate also cooperate on a number of joint committees dealing with topics such as printing and taxation.

Committee chairs are delegated significant power, which can lead to occasional abuses. Daniel Rostenkowski (D-Ill.), for example, became chair of the powerful House Ways and Means Committee in 1981 but was convicted in 1996 of mail fraud stemming from his misuse of public funds (to pay employees who did little work). After serving time in prison, he was pardoned by President Bill Clinton (b. 1946) at the end of his term.

Political Parties and Caucuses. The framers did not anticipate the role that POLITICAL PARTIES would play in electing and organizing the members of both houses of Congress. The majority party, Democratic or Republican, in effect runs the House administration and controls the flow of legislation during each two-year congressional session because it can count on its members to vote in favor of fellow party members for key positions such as Speaker of the House and chairs of the standing committees. This leaves the minority party to look for defectors in order to defeat measures sponsored by the majority party leadership. When the president is of the same party that controls both houses of Congress, that party's legislative agenda has a good chance of being enacted.

Additional informal creations of the House, such as party caucuses, are special affiliations of other House members. These include the Black Caucus and the Hispanic Caucus, which meet often to discuss and develop voting positions on various proposals that affect their particular constituencies.

Legislation

Article I, section 7, sets forth basic procedures for the passage of LEGISLATION in both the House and the Senate. The first clause, however, requires that "[a]ll Bills for raising Revenue [taxes] shall originate in the House of Representatives; but the Senate may propose or concur with Amendments as on other Bills." The framers believed that the members of the House would be more closely in touch with the voters and therefore would also be more accountable to the people for tax increases. This power also balances to some degree the EXCLUSIVE POWERS given to the Senate with respect to appointments (see ADVICE AND CONSENT; APPOINTMENT AND REMOVAL POWER) and RATIFICATION of TREATIES.

The House has an equal role with the Senate in the enactment of legislation. According to Article I, section 7, "Every Bill which shall have passed the House of Representatives and the Senate, shall, before it become a Law, be presented to the President…." All bills generally must be passed by a majority of the members present and voting. If the language of a bill passed by the House is not exactly the same as a similar measure passed by the Senate, then a conference committee is appointed to meet with its Senate counterpart to try to resolve the differences.

Presidential Elections

The other unique power of the House of Representatives is found in the Twelfth Amendment (1804), which sets out the procedure by which the president and vice president are elected. First, the ballots of the ELECTORAL COLLEGE are to be certified and sent sealed to the president of the Senate. "The President of the Senate shall, in the presence of the Senate and House of Representatives, open all the certificates and the votes shall then be counted;—The person having the greatest number of votes for President, shall be the President, if such number be a majority of the whole number of Electors appointed; and if no person have such majority, then from the persons having the highest numbers not exceeding three on the list of those voted for as President, the House of Representatives shall choose immediately, by ballot, the President. But in choosing the President, the votes shall be taken by states, the representation from each state having one vote; a quorum for this purpose shall consist of a member or members from two-thirds of the states, and a majority of all the states shall be necessary to a choice." The framers believed that in the case of a tie in the electoral college, the House of Representatives was the body that most closely reflected the will of the people, and therefore it was the body best suited to elect the president on behalf of the people.

In the 1800 presidential election, THOMAS JEFFERSON and Aaron Burr received an equal number of electoral votes, so the decision devolved on the House of Representatives, where members needed more than thirty ballots to find a majority for one candidate—Jefferson. After the Twelfth Amendment was ratified in 1804, the only time the House has chosen the president was in 1824, when it selected John Quincy Adams.

The Twentieth Amendment (1933) gave Congress the authority to "provide for the case of the death of any of the persons from whom the House of Representatives may choose a President whenever the right of choice shall have devolved upon them...." And the Twenty-fifth Amendment (1967) mentions both houses of Congress in setting the procedure for filling a vacancy in the vice president's office, requiring "confirmation by a majority vote of both Houses of Congress" of a candidate nominated by the president.

Impeachment

The IMPEACHMENT powers of the House of Representatives are set forth in Article I, section 2: "The House of Representatives shall...have the sole Power of Impeachment." This role is similar to that of the British Parliament, in which charges of impeachment against a government official are brought by the House of Commons and tried in the House of Lords. The House of Representatives has formally brought impeachment charges against a president only twice: against Andrew Johnson (1808–75) in 1868 and Bill Clinton in 1998. In both cases the Senate did not convict the president. President Richard M. Nixon (1913–94) resigned after a committee of the House voted to recommend that impeachment charges be brought against him.

Essentially a redesign of the British House of Commons, the House of Representatives has been copied in various renditions in many countries, especially in the Western Hemisphere. Although its size makes it difficult for the hoped-for accountability to be focused on any one member, the House remains a government instrument for change; it can act quickly to implement good policies—as well as bad ones. The framers thus believed it important to balance the House with a more deliberative and thus more conservative body, the Senate.

> **More on this topic:**
>
> *Impeachment, p. 293*
>
> *Legislative Branch, p. 346*
>
> *Political Parties, p. 403*
>
> *Reapportionment, p. 453*

Housing *See* DISCRIMINATION.

Human Rights

Human rights have been defined as those rights an individual acquires solely by reason of being a human being. The former secretary-general of the United Nations, Boutros Boutros-Ghali, referred to them at the World Conference on Human Rights held in Vienna in 1993 as "the quintessential values through which we affirm together that we are a single [world] community."

The DECLARATION OF INDEPENDENCE (1776) espouses basic human rights in the language, "We hold these truths to be self-evident, that all men are created equal, that they are endowed by their Creator with certain unalienable Rights, that among these are Life, Liberty and the pursuit of Happiness." Although some national constitutions expressly refer to human rights—Portugal's constitution (1976), for example, provides that "[i]n international relations, Portugal is governed by the principles of national independence [and] respect for human rights...."—the U.S. Constitution does not contain the term *human rights*. This is not surprising, because the term became significant only after British prime minister Winston Churchill called for "the enthronement of human rights" in the wake of the Nazi atrocities committed before and during World War II.

International Human Rights

Prepared under the direction of Eleanor Roosevelt (1884–1962), then chair of the Commission on Human Rights, the Universal Declaration of Human Rights was adopted by the United Nations in 1948. This seminal human rights document forbids discrimination on the basis of "race, color, sex, language, religion, political or other opinion, national or social origin, property, birth or other status" and declares that "[e]veryone has the right to recognition everywhere as a person before the law" and "an effective remedy…for acts violating the fundamental rights granted him by the constitution or by law." In consonance with the U.S. Constitution, the declaration forbids slavery and cruel and inhuman punishment and declares

Eleanor Roosevelt displays a copy of the Universal Declaration of Human Rights after its approval by the United Nations in 1948. The former first lady was appointed U.S. representative to the UN's Commission on Human Rights by President Harry S. Truman in 1945.
Source: UN Photo

that everyone is entitled to a fair trial, privacy, freedom of religion, peaceful assembly and association, freedom of opinion and expression, and the right to take part in the government of one's country. Since the declaration's adoption, an international movement has grown up to create a standard of treatment for all people based on international agreement as to what constitutes universal human rights.

International declarations and treaties regarding human rights represent goals that national governments agree to strive for. Although highly developed, such rights are difficult to enforce in international and regional institutions. There is no real threat, for example, that leaders of nations will be held responsible for human rights violations, except in some isolated cases such as the trial of Serbian leader Slobodan Milosevic (1941–2006) for attempts at ethnic cleansing (a form of genocide) in Kosovo. Many more cases go unprosecuted and unpunished.

"America did not invent human rights. In a very real sense it's the other way around. Human rights invented America. Ours is the first nation in the history of the world to be founded explicitly on such an idea."

—President Jimmy Carter

Human Rights in America

According to President Woodrow Wilson (1856–1924), "The history of liberty is a history of limitations on governmental power, not the increase of it." Through its national and state constitutions, the United States approaches human rights from a direction opposite from that of the international community. Whereas under INTERNATIONAL LAW, nations—not their CITIZENS—are sovereign (see SOVEREIGNTY), the theory underlying American government is that all government power resides first and foremost in the nation's individual citizens. They delegate to government the power to accomplish certain objectives, including the security of the nation, the people, and their property; enactment and enforcement of laws that are in their best interests; and resolution of disputes under a system of law. A free people need a government they can control.

By creating a democratic federal government, the Constitution set up a system of checks and balances (see SEPARATION OF POWERS) to protect citizens' inherent sovereignty and freedom. Human rights are not a condition subsequent (coming after the creation) of government; they are, as President Carter noted, a condition precedent to government. Government in the United States cannot require citizens to justify their freedom and rights; the citizens must always be able to require the government to justify any infringement or violation of them.

As early as 1887, in *Runkle v. United States*, the Supreme Court used the term *human rights* with respect to "the most sacred questions…that are ever placed on trial in a court of justice." Speaking of the right to the ASSISTANCE OF COUNSEL guaranteed by the Sixth Amendment (1791), Justice Hugo L. Black (1886–1971) declared in *Johnson v. Zerbst* (1938): "This is one of the safeguards…deemed necessary to insure [the] fundamental human rights of life and liberty…[and one of the] essential barriers against arbitrary or unjust deprivation of human rights." In *Skinner v. Oklahoma* (1942), Justice William O. Douglas (1898–1980) said that a case involving enforced sterilization for habitual criminals "touches a sensitive and important area of human rights."

References to human rights became more routine in later cases. In a dissent in *Williams v. Zuckert* (1963), Justice Douglas, joined by Justice Black, decried the majority's failure to review a claim that the right of cross examination (see CRIMINAL LAW) had been denied a veteran challenging his dismissal from the federal government. "To be sure," said Douglas, "[the request to cross examine] was not phrased in constitutional terms. But administrative procedures are not games in which rights are won or lost on the turn of a phrase…. [I]t is unhealthy to let [strict formalities] take root in administrative hearings where human rights are involved that are as precious to 'liberty,' within the meaning of the Fifth Amendment, as a person's right not to be fined or imprisoned unless prescribed procedures are followed."

Later, in *Astoria Federal Savings and Loan Association v. Solimino* (1991), the Supreme Court decided not to preclude review under the Age Discrimination in Employment Act (1967) (see EMPLOYMENT DISCRIMINATION) of an appeal by a dismissed employee, even though the matter had been decided against the former employee by the New York State Division of Human Rights. But not all human rights cases are justiciable for the Court. In *Saudi Arabia v. Nelson* (1993), the Court held that "[h]owever monstrous [the] abuse [of Nelson by the Saudi government] may be, a foreign state's exercise of that power has long been understood…as peculiarly sovereign in nature." Thus, the Foreign Sovereign Immunities Act (1976), under which Nelson sought redress for violations of his human rights, was held not to confer jurisdiction on the Court, because such violations were not "based upon a commercial activity," although Nelson had argued that the abuses stemmed from his report of on-the-job hazards at a Saudi hospital.

> **More on this topic:**
>
> *Fundamental Rights,*
> *p. 247*

Based as it is on the rights guaranteed by the Constitution, U.S. constitutional law has been slowly assimilating human rights concepts into the fabric of state and national government policy. Human rights nonetheless remain far more relevant today in the international than in the domestic arena.

Illegal Aliens   *See* ALIENS; CITIZENS; IMMIGRATION.

Immigration

Throughout human history people have migrated from one place to another and from one country to another. The constitutions of a number of nations, including those of Argentina (1853) and Austria (1920, restored 1945), address the process of immigration (settling in a new country with the intention to stay). Immigration can have important implications for a nation by increasing its population and, by extension, demands for housing, food, health care, welfare, and other goods and services.

America has long been eager to receive, as Emma Lazarus's memorable poem inscribed on the Statue of Liberty expressed it, the world's "huddled masses yearning to breathe free." As GEORGE WASHINGTON characterized the new country's view of immigration, "The bosom of America is open to receive not only the opulent and respectable stranger, but the oppressed and persecuted of all Nations and Religions; whom we shall welcome to a participation of all our rights and privileges, if by decency and propriety of conduct they appear to merit the enjoyment." Many immigrants to the United States have been refugees from WAR, famine, and religious or political persecution, including its earliest European colonists.

In 2001 the Census Bureau reported that one in five Americans—56 million persons—were born in another country or have at least one parent who was. Although these numbers, fueled by immigration law changes since the 1970s, represent the highest such count in the nation's history, at the turn of the twentieth century the proportion was even greater: one in three U.S. residents was of foreign origin. According to current census figures, a record number of immigrants are living in the United States. Of these approximately 40 million people not born in the United States, some 22 million are not naturalized citizens and, of them, at least 12 million are estimated to be in the United States illegally.

Formulating an Immigration Policy

Immigration in a federal nation like the United States has implications for both the federal and state governments, yet the Constitution does not directly address immigration policy. Its only immigration-related provisions are found in Article I, section 9, and Article V, both concerning the importation of slaves (see SLAVERY). For most of the nation's first century, Congress actually had little to say about immigration policy.

With regard to state regulation of immigration, the Supreme Court in *New York City v. Miln* (1837) determined that a state statute requiring masters of vessels to report on the passengers they brought into port was a valid exercise of the state's POLICE POWER and not an attempt to unconstitutionally regulate COMMERCE. In *Henderson v. New York* (1875), the Court confirmed the national government's exclusive power (see EXCLUSIVE POWERS) to set immigration policy, holding that a state's own limits on immigration were unconstitutional because its regulation was a national power resulting from national SOVEREIGNTY. Congress had already acted to place national restrictions on immi-

An immigrant family arrives at Ellis Island in the early 1900s. The 1924 Immigration Act set quotas that have since been eliminated in favor of less rigid immigration policies.
Source: Library of Congress

gration in 1875 by forbidding convicts and prostitutes to enter the country. The Court thus relied on the Constitution's commerce clause in Article I, section 8, granting Congress the authority to "regulate Commerce with foreign Nations, and among the several States, and with the Indian Tribes."

In its decisions on immigration, the Supreme Court also came to rely on the power over FOREIGN AFFAIRS entrusted to the federal government by the Constitution in a number of provisions, including Article I, sections 8, 9, and 10, and Article II, section 2. In *Chae Chan Ping v. United States* (1889), known as the Chinese Exclusion Case, the Court affirmed Congress's right to reject a noncitizen with a valid entry permit, saying that the right to determine admittance or rejection of ALIENS seeking admission into the country is a privilege of national sovereignty. Entry certificates, on which returning aliens relied to reenter the country, were deemed merely licenses that could be revoked at will by the government. The Court concluded that Congress's power to exclude aliens and prevent their return to the United States is legitimate during war or in peacetime. The Supreme Court in *Demore v. Kim* (2003) noted that "[i]n the exercise of its broad power over naturalization and immigration, Congress regularly makes rules that would be unacceptable if applied to citizens."

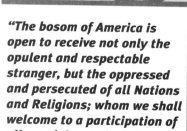

"The bosom of America is open to receive not only the opulent and respectable stranger, but the oppressed and persecuted of all Nations and Religions; whom we shall welcome to a participation of all our rights and privileges, if by decency and propriety of conduct they appear to merit the enjoyment."

—President George Washington

Beginning in the late nineteenth century, Congress began to regulate immigration in a piecemeal fashion, excluding, for example, "all idiots, insane persons," professional beggars, paupers, polygamists, epileptics, and "persons afflicted with a loathsome or with a dangerous contagious disease," under the Act to Regulate the Immigration of Aliens into the United States (1903). The new wave of immigration around the turn of the century, especially from eastern and southern Europe, resulted in further restrictions on immigration. The Immigration Act (1924) set annual ceilings—for example, no more than 150,000 immigrants were to be allowed into the United States in 1929—as well as quotas on the number of immigrants of certain national origins, based on the origins of people already living in the United States in 1920. The quota system was abolished in 1968 and the basis for admission changed to first-come, first-served; the annual ceiling was set for no more than 170,000 immigrants with visas for nations beyond the Western Hemisphere, with a maximum of 20,000 from any one nation, and a ceiling of 120,000 for the Western Hemisphere.

The Supreme Court's decision in BROWN V. BOARD OF EDUCATION OF TOPEKA (1954), in which it held that SEGREGATION in public schools was unconstitutional, led to a government review of immigration policies to determine if they could result in RACIAL DISCRIMINATION. The Court was still reluctant to constitutionally curb Congress's immigration policies or actions. In *Landon v. Plasencia* (1982), however, the justices upheld the DUE PROCESS rights of a resident alien attempting to be readmitted into the country after a brief sojourn in Mexico. And in *Jean v. Nelson* (1985), the Court determined that detained Haitian aliens who had entered the country illegally had to be treated individually rather than by race or national origin.

Illegal Immigration

The Immigration Reform and Control Act (1986) placed sanctions on employers who hire aliens not authorized to work in the United States and provided amnesty (the right to apply for legal resident status) to illegal aliens who had lived continuously in the country since before January 1, 1982. The act also increased enforcement to keep out illegal aliens. Ten years later Congress enacted the Illegal Immigration Reform and Immigrant Responsibility Act (1996), which contained provisions authorizing expedited deportation procedures and limitations on JUDICIAL REVIEW of orders to remove criminal aliens. The Supreme Court addressed congressional limits on judicial review in 2001, in two related cases decided together: *Zadvydas v. Davis* and *Ashcroft v. Kim Ho Ma*. The Court held in *Zadvydas* that statutory changes in the immigration laws did not affect its review of the continued custody of unadmitted aliens after a deportation order becomes final, nor were limitations on judicial review applicable in these two cases. The second case involved Kim Ho Ma, a Cambodian citizen convicted of manslaughter and incarcerated for two years, who was turned over to the Immigration and Naturalization Service and held pending deportation. The statutory period for removal was thirty days, but because there was no possibility of repatriation to Cambodia, Kim continued to be held in custody. In *Ashcroft* the Court held that it was unconstitutional for the federal government to indefinitely hold Kim, even if the country of his origin refused to take him back.

More on this topic:
Aliens, p. 25
Citizens, p. 93
Terrorism, p. 543
Travel, p. 548

Since the terrorist attacks on the United States on September 11, 2001 (see TERRORISM), the Department of Homeland Security has been given certain authority to oversee immigration and customs law enforcement. And in *Clark v. Martinez* (2005), citing *Zadvydas*, which dealt with admitted aliens, the Court held that the secretary of homeland security may detain inadmissible aliens beyond the statutory ninety-day limit, but only for as long as is reasonably necessary to achieve removal.

Immunity

According to the Supreme Court in *Long v. Converse* (1875), immunity is an exemption, such as from performing duties that the law generally requires other citizens to perform. An exemption from military service, for example, allows a citizen to avoid being drafted and serving in the ARMED FORCES. Types of immunity include sovereign immunity, immunity of government officials, immunity of citizens, and immunity from criminal prosecution.

Sovereign Immunity

Federal Government. Under INTERNATIONAL LAW all nations are sovereign (equal and independent) and may not be subjected involuntarily to the laws of another country (see SOVEREIGNTY). This immunity stems from the days when sovereign monarchs were considered the embodiment of all the powers, privileges, and immunities of their countries. Sovereigns made the law and were therefore considered to be above those laws and immune from their application. William Blackstone (1723–80) in his *Commentaries on the Laws of England* (1765–70) spoke of "the sovereign; who, by virtue of his royal prerogative is not under the coercive power of the law; which will not suppose him capable of committing a folly, much less a crime."

Even today the queen of England, for example, is not subject to the laws of the United Kingdom, as are other citizens—her subjects. The Jordanian constitution (1952) declares: "The king is the head of state and is immune from any liability and responsibility." Monarchs are also immune "from arrest or detention within a foreign territory," according to Chief Justice JOHN MARSHALL in *The Schooner Exchange v. McFaddon* (1812).

Modern governments, even republics without monarchs such as the United States, continue to possess sovereign immunity. "It is inherent in the nature of sovereignty," wrote ALEXANDER HAMILTON in essay 80 of *The Federalist* (1787–88) (see FEDERALIST PAPERS), "not to be amenable to the suit of an individual *without its consent*. This is the general sense and the general practice of mankind…." The U.S. government is immune from being sued unless it waives its sovereign immunity, as it has, for example, in the Federal Tort Claims Act (1946), which allows certain suits against the government to recover for injuries caused by the actions of government personnel.

Diplomats. The immunity of AMBASSADORS and other diplomats, who represent the sovereign or a sovereign nation in a foreign country, is even older than the concept of sovereign immunity for heads of state. Diplomatic immunity protects U.S. representatives from having to be defendants in lawsuits (civil and most criminal suits) while performing their duties in a foreign country.

Although Article III, section 2, of the Constitution grants federal courts jurisdiction to hear "Cases affecting Ambassadors, other public Ministers and Consuls," immunity for diplomats serving in the United States is based on laws passed by Congress and interpretation by the courts of the principles of international law. Many diplomatic immunity questions are decided by state courts, because they never reach the Supreme Court on appeal. A New York county court in 1959, for example, held that the chauffeur of the Indonesian ambassador to Canada had no diplomatic immunity from a charge of speeding even though a "person of high diplomatic standing" was being driven in the car.

CLOSER LOOK

The extent of diplomatic immunity became a much-discussed issue in 1997, when a diplomat who was driving while intoxicated plowed into three other vehicles in Washington, D.C. The accident killed a sixteen-year-old girl.

The driver, Gueorgui Makharadze of the nation of Georgia, was immune from prosecution because of his diplomatic status. The case caused a furor. Makharadze had been driving almost 75 miles per hour in a 25 mph zone after consuming six alcoholic drinks.

Under pressure from the U.S. government, President Eduard A. Shevardnadze of Georgia lifted Makharadze's immunity and allowed him to be tried in U.S. court. Makharadze faced up to seventy years in prison; his lawyers argued that he should get no more than a few years. After Makharadze pleaded guilty, the judge sentenced him to seven to twenty-one years. The judge said he did not want to impose such a harsh sentence that other countries would be discouraged from lifting immunity for their diplomats.

State Governments. According to JAMES MADISON, who set out his own theory in essay 39 of *The Federalist*, "Each State, in ratifying the Constitution, is considered as a sovereign body independent of all others, and only to be bound by its own voluntary act. In this relation, then, the new Constitution will…be a federal and not a national constitution." Since the Constitution went into effect in 1789, debate has continued as to exactly what extent the states gave up their inherent sovereign powers by ratifying the document or later joining the Union.

State sovereign immunity, like federal sovereign immunity, is the rule rather than the exception. Because of the Constitution's supremacy clause and Supreme Court decisions, however, the states are subject to more exceptions, in addition to any specific waivers of immunity they may agree to.

In *Chisholm v. Georgia* (1793), the Supreme Court was forced to hold that the language of Article III, section 2, which mandates that the "judicial Power shall extend…to Controversies…between a state and Citizens of another State…," precluded any state immunity from a suit of this type. As a result of this decision, the Eleventh Amendment was proposed and ratified in 1798 to restore to the states their sovereign immunity from being sued. This amendment did not completely insulate states from suits, however. In *Osborne v. Bank of the United States Bank* (1824), Chief Justice John Marshall concluded that the Eleventh Amendment did not bar suits against state officials, as opposed to actions against the state itself. And in *Ex parte Young* (1908), the Court also ruled that under certain circumstances a citizen could go into federal court to protect a constitutional right where infringement by a state was alleged (see YOUNG, EX PARTE).

State sovereign immunity is still an issue in cases that come before the Supreme Court. Under the Indian commerce clause in Article I, section 8 (see NATIVE AMERICANS), Congress provided for gambling activities by Indian tribes as long as they had an agreement with the state in which they were to be conducted. Congress also allowed the tribes to sue the state in federal court to compel the state's performance under such an agreement. In a victory for STATES' RIGHTS proponents, a 5–4 majority of the Supreme Court in *Seminole Tribe of Florida v. Florida* (1996) asserted that Congress did not have power under the Indian commerce clause to circumvent the Eleventh Amendment's grant to the states of immunity from lawsuits. The Court extended sovereign immunity to states from federal administrative as well as judicial proceedings in *Federal Maritime Commission v. South Carolina State Ports Authority* (2002). In his opinion for the Court, Justice Clarence Thomas (b. 1948) declared that "the preeminent purpose of state sovereign immunity is to accord States the dignity that is consistent with their status as sovereign entities."

Intergovernmental Immunity

FEDERALISM, which recognizes the sovereignty of both the national and state governments, creates areas in which each type of sovereignty is immune from any action by the other. As Chief Justice John Marshall declared in MCCULLOCH V. MARYLAND (1819), a state may not tax an instrumentality of the federal government in its territory, because the power to tax involves the power to destroy. The nation's sovereignty, therefore, may not be compromised by state intrusion. Reciprocally, in *Collector v. Day* (1871), the Supreme Court held that the federal government could not tax a state judge's salary. This form of state immunity was later overruled in *Graves v. New York ex rel. O'Keefe* (1939).

As part of the general trend since the beginning of the Republic toward greater federal power at the expense of the states, the sphere of state intergovernmental immunity has shrunk. The national government's immunity is bolstered by the SUPREMACY CLAUSE in Article VI, while state power relies on the less effective Tenth Amendment (1791), which protects the "powers not delegated [by the states] to the United States by the Constitution, nor prohibited by it to the States." But Justice SANDRA DAY O'CONNOR, who was often a proponent of states' rights, found in *Gregory v. Ashcroft* (1991) that a federal law—the Age Discrimination in Employment Act (1967 as amended), barring mandatory retirement—did not apply to state judges. (Missouri's state constitution [1945] sets mandatory retirement for judges at seventy years of age.) Such a ban, she wrote, would "upset the usual constitutional balance of federal and state powers."

In a 5–4 decision in *Granholm v. Heald* (2005), the Supreme Court held, in a widely followed case, that New York and Michigan state laws regarding in-state and out-of-state wine sales discriminated against interstate commerce in violation of the commerce clause of the U.S. Constitution. The Court noted that the court of appeals had rejected the argument that the Twenty-first Amendment (1933)—repealing Prohibition—immunizes state liquor laws from the federal grant of power in the commerce clause. Again, in *Central Virginia Community College v. Katz* (2006), the Court found that federal bankruptcy authority trumped state sovereign immunity.

Immunity of Government Officials

Article I, section 6, states that senators and representatives "shall in all Cases, except Treason, Felony and Breach of the Peace, be privileged from Arrest during their Attendance at the Session of their respective Houses, and in going to and returning from the same; and for any Speech or Debate in either House, they shall not be questioned in any other Place" (see HOUSE OF REPRESENTATIVES; SENATE). Their immunity from arrest for debts in civil suits was upheld by the Supreme Court in *Long v. Ansell* (1934). But in *Williamson v. United States* (1908), the Court found that the language "Treason, Felony and Breach of the Peace" meant that members of Congress were not immune from being arrested for criminal acts. In contrast, the immunities of members of Congress under the speech and debate clause have been interpreted more broadly by the Court. In *Kilbourn v. Thompson* (1881), the justices concluded that a member could not be held liable for an erroneous vote holding a witness in contempt. Congressional committees are similarly immune from court process.

Executive immunity (see EXECUTIVE PRIVILEGE) is not mentioned in the Constitution, but the Supreme Court has nonetheless extended to federal officials immunity from civil suits based on COMMON LAW principles. In *Spalding v. Vilas* (1896), the Court held that CABINET officials could not be sued for libel relating to acts connected with their official duties; and in *Barr v. Mateo* (1959), this protection was extended to lower-level administrative officials.

EXECUTIVE BRANCH officials, however, do not enjoy immunity if they violate constitutional rights. Officials may be sued for damages for constitutional torts such as infringing a citizen's rights under the Fourth Amendment (1791) by breaking into the wrong house even with a search warrant (see SEARCH AND SEIZURE). The Supreme Court has said that government officers have a qualified immunity that extends only to actions done in good faith.

Immunity is also accorded to judges. In *Bradley v. Fisher* (1871), the Supreme Court held that federal judges could not be sued for damages caused by their decisions unless they clearly had no jurisdiction over the matter. And in *Stump v. Sparkman* (1978), this principle was affirmed even in the case of a judge who approved a mother's petition to have her daughter sterilized without granting a hearing or giving notice to the daughter.

Privileges and Immunities of Citizens

Article IV, section 2, of the Constitution provides that "Citizens of each State shall be entitled to all Privileges and Immunities of Citizens in the several States" (see PRIVILEGES AND IMMUNITIES). According to Justice Bushrod Washington (1762–1829) in *Corfield v. Coryell* (1823), the privileges and immunities referred to include protection by the government, the enjoyment of life and LIBERTY, and the rights to acquire and possess PROPERTY, TRAVEL through or reside in a state, work at an occupation (see LABOR), and claim the benefit of the writ of HABEAS CORPUS. He went on to say that "we cannot accede to the proposition…that, under this provision of the Constitution, the citizens of the several States are permitted to participate in all the rights which belong exclusively to the citizens of any particular State, merely upon the ground that they are enjoyed by those citizens.…" The right to sue in a state court, with reasonable restrictions, has also been upheld under the privileges and immunities clause, and a state may not substantially discriminate between residents and nonresidents with respect to TAXATION.

Although the Fourteenth Amendment (1868) provides "No State shall make or enforce any law which shall abridge the privileges or immunities of citizens of the United States," the Supreme Court, with a bare majority, gutted this provision's power in the Slaughter-House Cases (1873). The Court found that any reading of the amendment as intending "to transfer the security and protection of all the civil rights…to the Federal Government,…[or] to bring within the power of Congress the entire domain of civil rights heretofore belonging to the States [would be] to fetter and degrade the State governments by subjecting them to the control of Congress.… We are convinced that no such results were intended.…"

Through the INCORPORATION DOCTRINE, however, the Supreme Court has extended to the states a number of the protections in the BILL OF RIGHTS (1791). But the Fourteenth Amendment's privileges and immunities clause has only rarely been relied on by the Court. In fact, in *Dennis v. Higgins* (1991), it declared that the "Commerce Clause confers 'rights, privileges, or immunities'…" (see COMMERCE).

Immunity from Prosecution

In 1710 the British Parliament passed the first law granting immunity to persons who gave useful but self-incriminating evidence against another. Congress, however, did not get around to passing such a law until 1857, immunizing a person who testified before a congressional committee as far as the subject matter of the testimony was concerned. Then, in *Counselman v. Hitchcock* (1892), the Supreme Court held that despite a federal law granting immunity to a witness for his or her testimony, such a witness could not be forced to testify because of the prohibition against SELF-INCRIMINATION in the Fifth Amendment (1791). Although the immunity grant under the statute in question banned the use of the testimony in any federal proceedings, it did not bar use of that testimony to search for other incriminating evidence. But in *Kastigar v. United States* (1972), the Court decided that an immunity statute did not have to absolutely protect WITNESSES before testimony could be compelled; rather, it ruled, such immunity requires that the prosecution, in order to later convict a witness, "prove affirmatively that the evidence used comes from a wholly independent source."

In a system of government based on popular sovereignty and political equality of all citizens, immunity is a special exception that should be carefully weighed. But government officials must be free to act on their own best judgment, as long as they act within the scope of their duties and do not violate the legal rights of others. And grants of immunity from prosecution given to persons who have committed offenses require great care on the part of prosecutors and judges in view of the basic premise of the RULE OF LAW that no one should be above the law and everyone should be equal before the law.

Impeachment

To impeach a witness (see WITNESSES) is to call into question his or her truthfulness by introducing contradictory evidence in a court of law. But in constitutional law, and as used in the Constitution, impeachment means to charge a public official with an offense before a quasi-political court, the punishment for which generally includes removal from office. The constitutions of most other countries, including Bulgaria, Finland, and the United Kingdom, also include provisions for impeachment of government officials.

Radical Republicans' unsuccessful impeachment attempt against Democratic President Andrew Johnson in 1868 was likened in the press to a dead horse beginning to smell. Seven Republican senators voted to acquit the beleaguered Johnson, shown at right.
Source: Library of Congress

In the United Kingdom, impeachment is a prosecution by the House of Commons, the elected lower house of Parliament, before the House of Lords, the hereditary, appointed upper house of Parliament, of a person for TREASON or other high crimes and misdemeanors. William Blackstone (1723–80), in his *Commentaries on the Laws of England* (1765–70), explained that "an impeachment before the lords by the commons of Great Britain, in parliament, is a prosecution of the already known and established law, and has been frequently put in practice; being a presentment to the most high and supreme court of criminal jurisdiction by the most solemn grand inquest of the whole kingdom."

IMPEACHMENT TRIALS IN THE SENATE, 1798–2007

Year	Official	Position	Outcome
1798–1799	William Blount	U.S. senator	Charges dismissed
1804	John Pickering	District court judge	Removed from office
1805	Samuel Chase	Supreme court judge	Acquitted
1830–1831	James H. Peck	District court judge	Acquitted
1862	West H. Humphreys	District court judge	Removed from office
1868	Andrew Johnson	President	Acquitted
1876	William Belknap	Secretary of war	Acquitted
1905	Charles Swayne	District court judge	Acquitted
1912–1913	Robert W. Archbald	Commerce court judge	Removed from office
1926	George W. English	District court judge	Charges dismissed
1933	Harold Louderback	District court judge	Acquitted
1936	Halsted L. Ritter	District court judge	Removed from office
1986	Harry E. Claiborne	District court judge	Removed from office
1989	Alcee L. Hastings	District court judge	Removed from office
1989	Walter L. Nixon Jr.	District court judge	Removed from office
1999	Bill Clinton	President	Acquitted

SOURCE: *Congress A to Z*, 5th ed. Washington, D.C.: CQ Press, 2008.

"High Crimes and Misdemeanors"

These same bases for impeachment—treason or other high crimes and misdemeanors—are reflected in the language of the U.S. Constitution. Article II, section 4, directs: "The President, Vice President and all civil Officers of the United States, shall be removed from Office on Impeachment for, and Conviction of, Treason, Bribery, or other high Crimes and Misdemeanors."

Other provisions of the Constitution relate to impeachment. Article I, section 2, states: "The House of Representatives shall...have the sole Power of Impeachment," while section 3 mandates: "The Senate shall have the sole Power to try all Impeachments. When sitting for that Purpose, they shall be on Oath or Affirmation. When the President of the United States is tried, the Chief Justice shall preside: And no Person shall be convicted without the Concurrence of two thirds of the Members present. Judgment in Cases of Impeachment shall not extend further than to removal from Office, and disqualification to hold and enjoy any Office of honor, Trust or Profit under the United States: but the Party convicted shall nevertheless be liable and subject to Indictment, Trial, Judgment and Punishment, according to Law."

ALEXANDER HAMILTON devoted essays 65 and 66 in *The Federalist* (1787–88) (see FEDERALIST PAPERS) to the Senate's impeachment powers. In essay 69 he compared the impeachment of the PRESIDENT with the inviolability of the person of the British monarch, who is accordingly not subject to impeachment, and with the impeachment processes prescribed by some of the state constitutions of his day. Hamilton also pointed out the limitation on the power of presidential PARDONS found in Article II, section 2: "The President shall...have Power to grant Reprieves and Pardons for Offenses against the United States, except in Cases of Impeachment."

The FRAMERS OF THE CONSTITUTION obviously had no idea in 1787 of the extent to which the impeachment provisions would be used. Only two presidents have had impeachment charges voted against them by the House of Representatives, but in both cases—Andrew Johnson (1808–75) in 1868 and Bill Clinton (b. 1946) in 1999—the Senate refused to convict them. In 1974 Richard M. Nixon (1913–94) resigned the presidency when threatened with impeachment over the WATERGATE scandal. Several federal judges, however, have been successfully impeached, although Supreme Court Justice Samuel P. Chase (1741–1811) was acquitted of impeachment charges in 1805 and Justice William O. Douglas (1898–1980) survived an impeachment investigation by Congress in 1970.

Checks and Balances

The procedures for impeachment established by the Constitution were not immediately obvious to the delegates to the CONSTITUTIONAL CONVENTION OF 1787. A Virginia delegate proposed giving this power to the national judiciary, and a New Jersey delegate also suggested a role for the federal courts and, in addition, removal of the president by Congress in response to a request by a majority of state governors. In the end, however, the delegates chose a procedure that placed the responsibility totally in the hands of the national legislature—with the exception that the chief justice of the United States presides over the Senate during an presidential impeachment trial. This was seen as being more accountable to the people in return for the extreme step of impeaching federal officials, including the president.

One of the most severe of the checks and balances (see SEPARATION OF POWERS) built into the Constitution, impeachment is probably more effective as a threat than as a PUNISHMENT. As evidenced in the cases of Presidents Johnson and Clinton, impeachment has not been untainted by partisan political interests. Following closely after the Civil War and the assassination of ABRAHAM LINCOLN, the "Reconstruction" Congress was strongly opposed to Johnson's less punitive policies toward former Confederate states. In the case of the impeachment charges against Clinton, the fact that both houses of Congress were controlled by the Republican Party, which had not held such power for many years, was reflected in the largely partisan voting. Such partisanship had not been the case in the later stages of the development of impeachment charges against Nixon.

Some commentators have criticized impeachment provisions as being too drastic to be of much use. However, a congressional resolution censuring the president for perceived violations of his constitutional duties or other acts that negatively reflect on his stewardship of the office would be of no constitutional effect. Another criticism is that the type of acts that constitute a finding of "high Crimes and Misdemeanors" are nowhere else defined, so the legislators are free to fit a wide variety of presidential actions—both official and personal—into a set of articles of impeachment.

Although the impeachment process may not be perfect, the very fact that the Constitution places no one above accountability for his or her acts as a government official represents a giant step forward from the days of absolute monarchies and the inviolability of heads of state. The lesson has been learned around the world, as evidenced by the many constitutional democracies that today similarly provide for the head of state's removal by impeachment-like procedures.

CLOSER LOOK

Impeachment proceedings against Supreme Court justices are few and far between. But in 1970 House members briefly weighed impeaching Justice William O. Douglas.

Douglas had long drawn the ire of conservatives, because of both his liberal rulings and an unconventional lifestyle that included four marriages. House minority leader Gerald R. Ford (R-Mich.) went further, charging Douglas with improperly conducting outside legal work and failing to disqualify himself from cases in which he had a particular interest. The justice had accepted money from a number of outside sources, including a foundation with ties to Las Vegas gambling.

A special House subcommittee investigated the charges. But members concluded that there was no evidence of actual wrongdoing, and the House never took a vote on the matter.

The controversy marked an escalation in partisan battles over judges. It is also remembered because Ford delivered a famous speech about impeachment. Noting that the Constitution does not define which offenses are punishable by impeachment, Ford said, "[A]n impeachable offense is whatever a majority of the House of Representatives considers to be at a given moment in history."

Implied Powers

The NECESSARY AND PROPER CLAUSE of the Constitution, in Article I, section 8, grants Congress the power "To make all laws which shall be necessary and proper for carrying into Execution the foregoing Powers, and all other Powers vested by this Constitution in the Government of the United States, or in any Department or Officer thereof." It was "only declaratory of a truth which would have resulted by necessary and unavoidable implication from the very act of constituting a federal government and vesting it with certain specified powers," wrote ALEXANDER HAMILTON in essay 33 of *The Federalist* (1787–88) (see FEDERALIST PAPERS). By this Hamilton meant that any power necessary and proper to the exercise of the Constitution's express grants of power should be implied, even if there were no necessary and proper clause. Implied powers have thus come to mean those POWERS necessary to carry out the responsibilities entrusted to a government agency or official, even though such powers may not have been expressly granted in the Constitution.

"We must never forget that it is a constitution that we are expounding."

—Chief Justice John Marshall

Chief Justice JOHN MARSHALL noted in *MCCULLOCH V. MARYLAND* (1819)—the leading case expounding the principle of implied constitutional powers—that the Constitution was a general outline of the new federal government's structure and powers and that "we must never forget that it is a constitution that we are expounding." As he concluded, "Let the end be legitimate, let it be within the scope of the constitution, and all means which are appropriate, which are plainly adapted to that end, which are not prohibited, but consist[ent] with the letter and spirit of the constitution, are constitutional."

Among the express powers delegated to CONGRESS in Article I, section 8, are the authority to "establish an uniform Rule of Naturalization" and to "establish Post Offices...." These express powers give rise to implied powers of Congress, such as the power to regulate immigration and to punish mail fraud. By the same token, the express power of appointment granted to the PRESIDENT in Article II, section 2, carries with it the implied power to terminate such appointees (see APPOINTMENT AND REMOVAL POWER).

COURTS also have implied powers. In *United States v. Hudson* (1812), for example, the SUPREME COURT noted that it was the only federal court that derived powers directly from the Constitution. "All other Courts created by the general Government possess no jurisdiction but what is given them by the power that creates them [Congress]...." Then, in rejecting the argument that it could exercise criminal jurisdiction in all COMMON LAW cases, the Court said: "Certain implied powers must necessarily result to our Courts of justice from the nature of their institution. But jurisdiction of crimes against the state is not among those powers."

In *Bivens v. Six Unknown Named Agents of the Federal Bureau of Narcotics* (1971), the Supreme Court found that it had an implied power to grant a remedy for federal officers' violation of the Fourth Amendment (1791) even though Congress had not expressly granted the Court such power. In his concurring opinion Justice John Marshall Harlan (1899–1971), said, "I do not think that the fact that the interest is protected by the Constitution rather than statute or common law justifies the assertion that federal courts are powerless to grant damages in the absence of congressional action authorizing the remedy." In this case federal narcotics officers searched a house and arrested Bivens without a search warrant, employing unreasonable force in the process (see SEARCH AND SEIZURE).

In a government of laws and not individuals, implied powers are used only when the intent of lawmakers—either the FRAMERS OF THE CONSTITUTION or modern-day legislators in Congress—would fail if the relevant power were not implied. For one to imply powers that were not intended violates the RULE OF LAW and the principles of constitutional government.

More on this topic:

Immunity, p. 289

Inherent Powers, p. 303

Incorporation Doctrine

The first ten amendments to the Constitution—the BILL OF RIGHTS, ratified in 1791—were intended to serve as limitations on the federal government and not on the states. This intention is underscored by the fact that a proposal by JAMES MADISON, who introduced the first draft of the Bill of Rights in Congress in 1789, to require the states to respect individuals' right of conscience, freedom of speech and the press, and right to trial by jury was defeated by that first Congress.

Following the DECLARATION OF INDEPENDENCE (1776), the thirteen former British colonies had created their own state governments, with constitutions and in some cases—in Virginia, for example—their own declarations of rights. When the states ratified the federal Bill of Rights, they were seeking protection only for the sovereign powers they retained after delegating some powers to the national government, along with protection for their citizens from possible infringements of liberties by the new federal government. If the citizens of a state believed that their rights were being infringed by their state government, their recourse was to amend their state constitution or otherwise change the laws or the officials responsible for enforcing the laws.

According to the Supreme Court in *Barron v. City of Baltimore* (1833), the protections in the Bill of Rights did not apply to state and local governments—meaning that these guarantees were not viewed as being incorporated into state law. By criminalizing criticism of SLAVERY in the 1830s, for example, the southern states ignored the right of free speech contained in the federal Constitution. The Civil War (1861–65) and then the ratification of the Fourteenth Amendment in 1868, however, changed the dynamics of FEDERALISM in the United States. The amendment elevated citizenship in the United States over citizenship in the states, guaranteeing, at least in its wording, that the PRIVILEGES AND IMMUNITIES of citizens of the United States may not be abridged by a state, nor may a state deny a citizen DUE PROCESS of law or EQUAL PROTECTION of the laws.

Rights Applicable to the States

By 1897 the Supreme Court, in *Chicago, Burlington and Quincy Railway v. Chicago*, had held that the Fourteenth Amendment's due process clause required that a state pay JUST COMPENSATION for a taking of PROPERTY as guaranteed by the Fifth Amendment. It was not until 1927, in *Fiske v. Kansas*, however, that the Court first incorporated freedom of speech, using the Fourteenth Amendment's due process clause, to declare a state law unconstitutional. The justices struck down a law making it a crime for "[a]ny person who, by word of mouth, or writing, advocates, affirmatively suggests or teaches the duty, necessity, propriety or expediency of crime,…or sabotage.…"

Two years earlier, in *Gitlow v. New York* (1925), a Supreme Court majority had suggested that freedom of expression was protected against infringement by the states under the Fourteenth Amendment's due process clause. But in that case the Court's 7–2 majority—the dissenters were Louis D. Brandeis (1856–1941) and OLIVER WENDELL HOLMES JR.—nevertheless had upheld a state law suppressing utterances that might incite the overthrow of the government by unlawful means. The practical effect was that the Court had to wait until *Fiske* in 1927 to make freedom of speech applicable to the states.

Other guarantees of the Bill of Rights followed, including freedom of THE PRESS in *Near v. Minnesota ex rel. Olson* (1931), freedom of assembly in *De Jonge v. Oregon* (1937), and freedom of association in *NAACP v. Alabama* (1958) (see ASSEMBLY AND ASSOCIATION). The free exercise of RELIGION and the prohibition against laws "respecting an establishment of religion" were incorporated in *Cantwell v. Connecticut* (1940) and *Everson v. Board of Education of Ewing Township* (1947), respectively. Fourth Amendment rights regarding unreasonable SEARCH AND SEIZURE and the exclusion of illegally obtained evidence were extended to the states in *MAPP V. OHIO* (1961) and

Wolf v. Colorado (1949). The Fifth Amendment prohibition against SELF-INCRIMINATION was extended in *Malloy v. Hogan* (1964) and against DOUBLE JEOPARDY in *Benton v. Maryland* (1969).

ASSISTANCE OF COUNSEL guaranteed by the Sixth Amendment was incorporated in capital cases in *Powell v. Alabama* (1932), the right to assistance of counsel in all felony cases in GIDEON V. WAINWRIGHT (1963), and the right to counsel in misdemeanor cases involving imprisonment in *Argersinger v. Hamlin* (1972). That amendment's rights to a public trial and to a speedy trial (see JURIES; TRIALS) were incorporated in *In re Oliver* (1948) and *Klopfer v. North Carolina* (1967), and the rights to a trial by an impartial jury, to a jury trial in significant criminal cases, and to a unanimous verdict when only six jurors are sitting were added in *Parker v. Gladden* (1966), *Duncan v. Louisiana* (1968), and *Burch v. Louisiana* (1979), respectively. Other Sixth Amendment rights—to compulsory process to obtain WITNESSES for the defense, to confront adverse witnesses, and to receive notice of the nature of an accusation—were made applicable to the states in *Washington v. Texas* (1967), *Pointer v. Texas* (1965), and *Rabe v. Washington* (1972), respectively. The Eighth Amendment prohibition against CRUEL AND UNUSUAL PUNISHMENT was incorporated to apply to the states in *Robinson v. California* (1962).

Beyond the Bill of Rights

Even though a particular guarantee in the Bill of Rights has not been extended to the states under the Fourteenth Amendment through case law, a similar provision may be available under the state's own constitution. In any case, the national guarantees represent minimum standards, which the states can enhance under their own laws. The California constitution (1879), for example, prohibits "cruel *or* unusual" punishment (rather than "cruel *and* unusual," as in the national document), language the state's supreme court in 1972 interpreted to mean that the death penalty was unconstitutional in California.

Incorporation of the few remaining guarantees that have not yet been made applicable to the states—such as the right to bear arms (Second Amendment) (see GUN CONTROL), the provision against quartering soldiers in the home (Third Amendment), the right to a grand jury indictment (Fifth Amendment), the right to a jury trial in civil cases (Seventh Amendment), and the prohibition against excessive BAIL and fines (Eighth Amendment)—is unlikely in the near future. Not the least of the reasons is the conservative nature of the present Supreme Court majority. In addition, quartering of soldiers is not an important issue today, and bail is not clearly admitted by the Court to be one of a citizen's FUNDAMENTAL RIGHTS.

The march toward making the Bill of Rights guarantees applicable to the states as well as to the national government can be viewed as a part of an overall trend that started at the beginning of the Republic. The goal has been to increase the national character of government in order to secure the rights and privileges of all citizens at the expense of the original concept of federalism conceived by the FRAMERS OF THE CONSTITUTION in 1787. State laws still have a lot of room left to grow along their separate paths, but the development of the doctrine of incorporation has circumscribed divergences in the extent to which citizens' constitutional rights are guaranteed.

More on this topic:

Criminal Law, p. 132

Due Process, p. 168

Federalism, p. 218

States' Rights, p. 520

Independent Counsel

"[Y]ou must first enable the government to control the governed," said JAMES MADISON, "and...next, oblige it to control itself." In 1787 the FRAMERS OF THE CONSTITUTION set about organizing the new national government to do just this. The Constitution created three separate but coequal branches of government—the LEGISLATIVE BRANCH, EXECUTIVE BRANCH, and JUDICIAL BRANCH—to avoid a concentration of power in a few hands and to encourage interaction to check and balance each branch's powers (see SEPARATION OF POWERS). Periodic ELECTIONS also act as checks on two of the federal branches, the legislative and the executive.

In 1973 the evolving WATERGATE scandal brought into sharp focus the difficulty of having the officers of the executive branch—many of whom were personal friends and political allies of President Richard M. Nixon (1913–94)—investigate alleged illegal or unconstitutional acts. To avoid the appearance of bias, the attorney general appointed a special prosecutor to investigate the circumstances surrounding the break-in at the offices of the Democratic Party in the Watergate office building in Washington, D.C., not far from the White House. A condition of the position was that the special prosecutor could "not be removed from his duties except for extraordinary improprieties."

In spite of the protection against arbitrary removal, the special prosecutor, Archibald Cox, was fired by the solicitor general, Robert Bork, who held the number-three position at the Department of Justice after the attorney general and the deputy attorney general, both of whom resigned rather than carry out the dismissal order from President Nixon. After what became known as "the Saturday night massacre," Nixon was pressured to reestablish the office, and Cox's successor, Leon Jaworski, prosecuted the case before the Supreme Court to obtain relevant presidential records for his investigation. The Court held that as long as the special prosecutor's office was in existence, the incumbent could oppose the president before the Court, even though his office was in the government's executive branch. The climax of the special prosecutor's investigation came when the Supreme Court, in a unanimous 8–0 ruling in *United States v. Nixon* (1974), held that tapes of private conversations in the president's office had to be turned over to the prosecutor. This was the "smoking gun" evidence that led a committee of the House of Representatives to recommend IM-PEACHMENT charges against Nixon. Faced with certain impeachment by the House and conviction by the Senate, Nixon resigned in August 1974.

Special prosecutors were not born with Watergate. In 1972 Governor Nelson Rockefeller of New York created an office of special prosecutor to investigate charges of corruption in New York City's criminal justice system. But because of the difficulties engendered by the ad hoc establishment of a special prosecutor's office in the executive branch, Congress passed the Ethics in Government Act (1978) to authorize the appointment of an independent counsel whenever there were reasonable grounds for suspecting that a high-level executive branch official had committed a crime. Under the act, the Division for the Purpose of Appointing Independent Counsel of the U.S. Court of Appeals for the District of Columbia, a three-judge panel, made the appointment of independent counsels who were removable only for "good cause." Eight independent counsels were appointed in the first ten years.

Only a few of these counsels investigated presidential actions. One of the most noted was independent counsel Lawrence E. Walsh, who was hired in 1986 to look into two operations coordinated by National Security Council staff in the White House, one designed to obtain the release of American hostages in the Middle East through the sale of weapons to Iran and the other involving secret government support of military activities in Nicaragua despite congressional prohibition. Walsh filed his official report on the Iran-contra investigation in 1993, concluding in part that "sales of arms to Iran contravened United States Government policy and may have violated the Arms Export Control Act," that "the Iran operations were carried out with the knowledge of, among others, President Ronald Reagan [and] Vice President George Bush," and that "the policies behind both Iran and contra operations were fully reviewed and developed at the highest levels of the Reagan administration." The report noted that "Reagan Administration officials deliberately deceived Congress and the public about the level and extent of official knowledge of and support for these operations."

The most expensive independent counsel investigation was led by Kenneth Starr in pursuit of President Bill Clinton, his wife, and associates.
Source: Reuters

Kenneth Starr, a former Republican solicitor general, was appointed by the appeals court in 1994 to investigate President Bill Clinton (b. 1946). Four years later, as required by a 1994 law directing that the "independent counsel shall advise the House of Representatives of any substantial and credible information …that may constitute grounds for an impeachment," Starr issued a report to the House addressing, among other actions, the president's sexual relations with a White House intern. The Starr report led to President Clinton's impeachment by the House in 1998, although the Senate failed to convict him of the charges, which included the allegation that he lied under oath in a deposition regarding an earlier alleged sexual encounter when he was governor of Arkansas (see EXECUTIVE PRIVILEGE).

A constitutional attack on the independent counsel law, in *Morrison v. Olson*, was rejected by the Supreme Court in 1988. The basic argument made on behalf of the president was that his constitutional right to appoint and remove senior government officials (see APPOINTMENT AND REMOVAL POWER) was infringed by the 1978 act and that the independent counsel's autonomy violated the separation of powers enshrined in the Constitution, especially the power of the PRESIDENT to enforce the law. The Court determined that the independent counsel's narrow role made the office an "inferior" one in the Constitution's definition. It also held that the executive branch had sufficient control to avoid the separation of powers challenge because the attorney general made the triggering decision to appoint an independent counsel and he had the right of removal for good cause.

Toward the end of Clinton's second term, Congress let the independent counsel law lapse in 1999 essentially because after twenty years of experimentation, the law had not worked as well as expected. It is possible that any future allegations of wrongdoing at the highest levels of the executive branch may awaken interest in reestablishing the position. In the absence of such a law, executive branch wrongdoing can still be investigated through such devices as congressional oversight, ad hoc special prosecutors, and the constitutionally mandated impeachment process.

A form of check and balance that was not foreseen or intended by the framers of the Constitution, the extraconstitutional device of the independent counsel has been criticized by some as creating an unnecessary and intrusive institution. However, such a device may be the only way to uncover the truth when government transgressions are potentially being covered up by those officials responsible under the Constitution for investigating crimes and enforcing the laws.

More on this topic:

Executive Privilege, p. 210

Impeachment, p. 293

Watergate, p. 578

INDEPENDENT COUNSEL INVESTIGATIONS, 1978–2007

Subject	Date	Counsel	Allegations	Outcome	Cost
Hamilton Jordan (White House)	1979–80	Arthur Hill Christy	Drug use	No charges	$182,000
Timothy Kraft (White House)	1980–81	Gerald J. Gallinghouse	Drug use	No charges	$3,300
Raymond A. Donovan (secretary of labor)	1981–82	Leon Silverman	Organized crime	No charges	$326,000
Edwin Meese III (attorney general–designate)	1984	Jacob A. Stein	Financial	No charges	$312,000
Theodore B. Olson (assistant attorney general)	1986–89	Alexia Morrison	Lying to Congress	No charges	$2.1 million
Michael Deaver (White House)	1986–89	Whitney North Seymour	Illegal lobbying	Perjury	$1.6 million
Iran-contra (Oliver North, National Security Council; Caspar Weinberger, secretary of defense; other Reagan Administration officials)	1986–94	Lawrence E. Walsh	Obstruction of justice, lying to Congress, destruction of documents	14 indictments; 7 guilty pleas; 4 convictions after trial; 2 convictions overturned on appeal (Oliver North, John Poindexter); 1 dismissal; 4 convictions or pleas; 2 indictments nullified by pardons	$48.5 million
Lawrence Wallace (assistant attorney general)	1986–87	James R. Harper	Tax irregularities	No charges	$50,000
Wedtech (Edwin Meese III, Lyn Nofziger, White House)	1987–90	James C. McKay	Lobbying activities	2 indictments; 1 conviction overturned on appeal (Lyn Nofziger); 1 acquittal (Edwin Meese)	$2.8 million
Confidential	1989	Not identified	Not disclosed	13 indictments; No charges	$15,000
Samuel Pierce (secretary of Housing and Urban Development)	1990–96	Arlin M. Adams, Larry D. Thompson	Official misconduct, misuse of funds, perjury, obstruction of justice	12 guilty pleas; 4 convictions after trial; 1 acquittal	$29.5 million

(continues)

INDEPENDENT COUNSEL INVESTIGATIONS, 1978–2007 (CONTINUED)

Subject	Date	Counsel	Allegations	Outcome	Cost
Confidential	1991–92	Donald Bucklin	Not disclosed	No charges	$93,000
Clinton Passport Search (White House)	1992–95	Joseph E. diGenova, Michael Zeldin	Violation of Privacy Act	No charges	$3.5 million
Whitewater (Bill and Hillary Clinton)	1994–2000	Robert Fiske, Kenneth W. Starr, Robert Ray	Financial improprieties, official misconduct	12 convictions; 2 acquittals; Bill and Hillary Clinton not charged; Bill Clinton impeached by House but not convicted in Senate	$64.3 million
Michael Espy (secretary of agriculture)	1994–98	Donald E. Smaltz	Illegal gratuities	6 convictions (1 reversed on appeal); 4 acquittals (including Espy)	$24.2 million
Henry G. Cisneros (secretary of Housing and Urban Development)	1995–99	David M. Barrett	False statements	3 guilty pleas (including Cisneros)	$15.6 million
Ronald H. Brown (secretary of commerce)	1995–96	Daniel S. Pearson	Financial improprieties	No charges (closed after Brown's death)	$1.3 million
Eli Segal (chief, Americorps)	1996–98	Curtis von Kann	Financial conflict of interest	No charges	$465,000
Bruce Babbitt (secretary of the interior)	1998–99	Carol Elder Bruce	Lying to Congress	No charges	$7 million
Alexis Herman (secretary of labor)	1998–2000	Ralph E. Lancaster Jr.	Kickbacks, illegal campaign contributions	No charges	$5.8 million

SOURCES: CQ Researcher, May 7, 1999. Kathleen Clark, "Targets, Dates, and Costs of Independent Counsel Investigations," retrieved from http://law.wustl.edu/Publications/ic.cost7.html. Government Accountability Office, Offices of the Independent Counsels. Senate Governmental Affairs Committee.

Inherent Powers

"A government ought to contain in itself every power requisite to the full accomplishment of the objects committed to its care, and to the complete execution of the trusts for which it is responsible…," declared ALEXANDER HAMILTON in essay 31 of *The Federalist* (1787–88) (see FEDERALIST PAPERS). The Constitution, however, is one of the shortest written constitutions in the world, and in addition to being only a general framework for the national government, it can be ambiguous in its disposition of POWERS. Occasions thus arise when the question of whether a particular power is entrusted to the federal government or one of its branches must be determined by more than a simple examination of the document's words.

Nothing in the Constitution requires a STRICT CONSTRUCTION or a literal interpretation of its text, and there is every reason to believe that the FRAMERS OF THE CONSTITUTION wanted it, above all, to work not merely as they wrote it but as they intended it to work. It was inevitable that courts would end up having to consider what constitutes the government's inherent powers in order to resolve specific questions regarding the extent of the power of the federal government and its instrumentalities.

Inherent powers are those that go beyond the power expressly granted in the Constitution or reasonably implied (see IMPLIED POWERS) from its explicit grants of power. No express grant of power is made for the federal government and the PRESIDENT to conduct FOREIGN AFFAIRS, for example, but in *United States v. Curtiss-Wright Export Corp.* (1936), the Supreme Court found that because "the powers of external sovereignty passed from" Great Britain to the independent colonies after the DECLARATION OF INDEPENDENCE (1776), "It results that the investment of the Federal Government with the powers of external sovereignty did not depend upon the affirmative grants of the Constitution" (see SOVEREIGNTY). These powers, in other words, are inherent in the nature of the federal government.

Courts also have inherent powers or those necessary to carry out the duties entrusted to them by the Constitution and the laws passed by Congress. In *Abraham v. Ordway* (1895), the Supreme Court held that "it is now well settled that, independently of any limitation prescribed for the guidance of courts of law, equity [as opposed to stricter rules at COMMON LAW] may, in the exercise of its own inherent powers, refuse relief where it is sought after undue and unexplained delay, and when injustice would be done, in the particular case, by granting the relief asked." But in *Carlisle v. United States* (1996), the Court rejected a request that it exercise its "inherent supervisory power" over a federal district court. "Whatever the scope of federal courts' inherent power to formulate procedural rules not specifically required by the Constitution or the Congress, it does not include the power to develop rules that circumvent or conflict with the Federal Rules of Criminal Procedure," replied the Court.

Inherent power is not to be lightly inferred under the Constitution. It is basically a last resort for the courts, enabling them to preserve the framers' plan when specific language does not exist to justify an obvious conclusion.

> **More on this topic:**
>
> Federalism, p. 218
>
> Federalist Papers, p. 220
>
> Implied Powers, p. 296
>
> Strict Construction, p. 522

Income Tax *See* TAXATION.

Initiatives *See* DIRECT DEMOCRACY.

Insular Cases *See* TERRITORY.

Intellectual Property *See* COPYRIGHT; INTERNET; PROPERTY.

International Law

Only once does the Constitution refer specifically to international law (the law governing the legal relations among nations), in Article I, section 8: "The Congress shall have Power…To define and punish Piracies and Felonies committed on the high Seas, and Offences against the Law of Nations…." But the Constitution's grant to the national government of its exclusive role in FOREIGN AFFAIRS, including appointing and recalling AMBASSADORS and making and abrogating TREATIES, expands the Constitution's international law implications for the national government. As JAMES MADISON commented in essay 42 of *The Federalist* (1787–88) (see FEDERALIST PAPERS): "The power to define and punish piracies and felonies committed on the high seas and offenses against the law of nations belongs with equal propriety [along with the power to make treaties and send and receive ambassadors] to the general government…."

The American colonies, subject as they were to Great Britain, were not responsible for international affairs. After their declaration of independence, the states conducted foreign affairs through the Continental Congress and the congress established under the ARTICLES OF CONFEDERATION (1781). According to the Articles, no state "without the consent of the United States in Congress assembled" could send or receive ambassadors or enter into any treaty or alliance with a foreign power or with one another. The Constitution drafted in 1787, however, grants expressly and exclusively to the national government the power to appoint and receive ambassadors and make treaties. "If we are to be one nation in any respect," warned Madison in the same *Federalist* essay, "it clearly ought to be in respect to other nations."

Consensual Law

The United States and its form of constitutional government do not exist in a vacuum but rather in a community of nations under international law, which is a body of consensual law—there is no international legislature or police force to make and enforce it—that has evolved from customs and practices of civilized nations and carries great moral and reciprocal force. Nations tend to obey established international law principles not only because it is customary to do so but also because it is in the general interest of each nation to act in accordance with such principles. Much of international law has been codified in United Nations treaties such as the International Covenant on Civil and Political Rights (1966) and other multilateral documents such as the Geneva Conventions, which relate to rules of warfare among other principles, and confirmed in decisions of national and international courts and tribunals (see HUMAN RIGHTS). As stated in the Declaration on Principles of International Law Concerning Friendly Relations and Co-operation Among States in Accordance with the Charter of the United Nations (1970), "[T]he faithful observance of the principles of international law…and the fulfillment in good faith of obligations assumed by States…is of the greatest importance for the maintenance of international peace and security…."

The United States and its form of constitutional government do not exist in a vacuum but rather in a community of nations under international law.

Some national constitutions, such as those of Portugal (1976) and Bosnia and Herzegovina (1995), expressly incorporate international law provisions or treaties. For example, Portugal's constitution, Article 8, section 1, states: "The norms and principles of general or customary international law are an integral part of Portuguese law." Bosnia and Herzegovina's supreme law, in Article

II, paragraph 2, states that the "rights and freedoms set forth in the European Convention for the Protection of Human Rights and Fundamental Freedoms [1950] and its Protocols shall apply directly in Bosnia and Herzegovina. These shall have priority over all other law." The U.S. Constitution does not incorporate the body of customary international law in so many words, but, as the Supreme Court confirmed in *The Paquete Habana* (1900), "International law is part of our law, and must be ascertained and administered by the courts…as often as questions of right depending upon it are duly presented for their determination."

The Supreme Court often has to interpret treaties in light of international and domestic law. For example, in 2004, the Court in *Olympic Airways v. Husain* found that the defendant airline was liable for the death of an international passenger because the conduct of one of its employees—a flight attendant who refused to seat an asthmatic passenger away from a smoking section—constituted an "accident" under article 17 of the Warsaw Convention. And in 2006 the Court, in *Sanchez-Llamas v. Oregon*, found that it was not necessary to suppress evidence in a trial simply because the defendant, who was a foreign national, was not advised of his rights under the Vienna Convention on Consular Relations to notify his country's consulate of his detention by law enforcement officials. With respect to legal actions against a foreign government, in *Republic of Austria v. Altman* (2004), the Supreme Court declared that the Foreign Sovereign Immunities Act of 1976 applies to conduct prior to its adoption. Therefore the heir of the owner of paintings taken by the Nazis in violation of international law could sue in the United States to recover the paintings from the Austrian government and a state-owned gallery where the paintings were housed.

Federal and State Relations

Because of the U.S. government's federal nature and the states' individual judicial systems, issues involving the rights of foreign citizens, businesses, and even governments can come before state courts in criminal, tax, and property matters. The case of MARTIN V. HUNTER'S LESSEE (1816), which involved the inheritance of Virginia property by a British subject and the interpretation of a 1794 treaty, was pending in Virginia's court of appeals when it came before the Supreme Court on a writ of error. Whereas the subjects of most international law are nations, not citizens, a branch of international law called "private international law" or "conflicts of laws" deals with determinations of jurisdiction in cases involving parties from different nations, which can arise in state as well as federal courts.

In the landmark case *Missouri v. Holland* (1920), the Supreme Court affirmed that the federal government's powers, specifically the power to regulate COMMERCE, may be broader when they are exercised in accordance with a valid international treaty. In this case, which involved a treaty between the United States and Great Britain to protect migratory birds, Justice OLIVER WENDELL HOLMES JR. said on behalf of the Court: "It is obvious that there may be matters of the sharpest exigency for the national well-being that an act of Congress could not deal with, but that a treaty followed by such an act could."

Federal and state courts generally applied customary international law until the Supreme Court declared in *Erie Railroad v. Thompkins* (1938): "There is no federal general common law"—law that, like international law, has evolved through usage and custom (see COMMON LAW). But in *Banco Nacional de Cuba v. Sabbatino* (1964), the Court found that customary international law was a part of federal common law and that it thus will preempt or supercede inconsistent state law in the same manner that a treaty or a federal statute does under the SUPREMACY CLAUSE in Article VI, section 2.

In many ways, however, both the national and state governments are inconsistent in their application and respect for international requirements. In 1998 the federal government and the commonwealth of Virginia both opposed a stay of execution for an alien who was convicted of a crime without being provided the opportunity to speak with a diplomatic representative from his country. The matter involved Mir Aimal Kansi, a Pakistani citizen who had killed two persons and wounded three others with an AK-47 assault rifle at a traffic light outside the main entrance to the Central Intelligence Agency; he had fled the country but was apprehended and returned to Virginia by Federal Bureau of Investigation agents to stand trial. Neither government enforced international law standards that the federal government would demand be recognized by other countries with respect to American citizens abroad (see ALIENS).

The President as Enforcer

As commander in chief of the nation's military forces, the PRESIDENT is the main instrument under the Constitution for the conduct of foreign affairs. "If the president is of the opinion that the relations of this country with foreign nations are, or are likely to be endangered by action deemed by him inconsistent with a due neutrality [the U.S. position during World War I at that time]," an attorney general's opinion stated in 1914, "it is his right and duty to protect such relations...."

In his role as chief treaty negotiator, the president, through the Department of State, plays the major role with regard to international and regional relations. Such relations, conducted through organizations such as the United Nations, Organization of American States, and North Atlantic Treaty Organization, often lead to the development of international law principles and actions supporting provisions of international law. International treaties such as the Charter of the United Nations (1946) require UN members, including the United States, to act to preserve peace or oppose aggression. For example, although the United States never formally declared WAR before it entered the Korean War (1950–53), the military nevertheless conducted it as if it were a declared war under the authority of the president with the support of Congress. The war, in which the U.S. military played a major role, was called a "police action" because it was undertaken in response to a UN Security Council call for assistance by all members to halt the invasion of South Korea by North Korean troops.

NATO soldiers have served in Kosovo since 1999, when they were deployed to end ethnic cleansing.
Source: AP Images/Zvezdan Djukanovic

Even though no mechanism exists to enforce international law principles and rules, from time to time members of the international community—as in the Korean War (1950–53)—take it upon themselves to enforce them. To end ethnic cleansing in Kosovo in 1999, North Atlantic Treaty Organization (NATO) forces took military action against Serbia, and multinational forces led by the United States following the September 11, 2001, attack began a war in Afghanistan to root out international terrorism. These actions represent efforts to enforce certain principles of international law such as the right of free peoples to self-determination, the prohibition of genocide, and the right of all nations to defend themselves against aggression.

More on this topic:

Admiralty and Maritime Law, p. 13

Sovereignty, p. 506

International Relations   *See* FOREIGN AFFAIRS.

Internet

"When the courts find themselves as not the arbitrators but the victims…, all of a sudden you find judges saying 'this could very well be a violation of…our rights,'" contends the Internet attorney Robert Hamilton, referring to many employers' policy of routinely monitoring their employees' Internet use. To protest this practice, judges on the U.S. Circuit Court of Appeals for the Ninth Circuit in San Francisco had disabled the monitoring software in their office computers.

As with the legal issues relating to GENETICS and modern biotechnology, those involving the Internet are just beginning to surface and be addressed. PRIVACY and eavesdropping are two of the many constitutionally charged issues being raised by the COMMUNICATIONS revolution the Internet has engendered; others include freedom of SPEECH and PROPERTY rights.

When it officially began in 1969, the Internet was called Arpanet by its founders, who successfully linked computers at the University of California at Los Angeles, Stanford Research Institute, University of California at Santa Barbara, and University of Utah. Academic researchers and the U.S. Department of Defense quickly saw the benefits of linking computers and using the system to communicate. Soon private companies began to participate in setting up and managing the Internet. Today hundreds of millions of persons and computers have access to each other through this basically unregulated medium of global communications. In the United States, more than half the population now uses the Internet, the Department of Commerce reported in 2002. Nine out of ten school-age children can use computers at home or in school.

The Internet has two major components: communication by e-mail and the World Wide Web. E-mail allows about 45 percent of the U.S. population to send and receive communications on the Internet. Because it involves active commercial and noncommercial communications among individual users, e-mail is analogous to the postal and telephone systems. The Web, in contrast, creates sites at which information is posted and permits interaction in many cases, commercial or private, between the site sponsors and users of a particular Web site. A person visiting the Amazon.com Web site, for example, can purchase books and other items through the Internet, but the merchandise must be delivered via "snail mail": the old-fashioned way. Art, literature, and entertainment are also available on Web sites, thus making this form of communication analogous in some ways to the earlier forms of communication: books, newspapers, magazines, movies, videos, and radio.

> *"The Internet has been the most fundamental change during my lifetime and for hundreds of years. Someone the other day said, 'It's the biggest thing since Gutenberg,' and then someone else said 'No, it's the biggest thing since the invention of writing.'"*
>
> **—Rupert Murdoch**

The First Amendment

Because the Internet is basically a means of communication—relying on telephone, cable, and satellite transmission—users turn primarily to the First Amendment for constitutional protection. Radio and television, by comparison, require a finite band or spectrum of radio-wave lengths. To parcel out the limited broadcast frequencies and regulate the manner and content of broadcasting, the Federal Communications Commission was established in 1934. The Internet depends on no such limitations and thus is not as easily amenable to government regulation.

In 1996 Congress passed the Communications Decency Act in part to make the knowing transmission of obscene or indecent material to anyone under the age of eighteen years a felony. The

American Civil Liberties Union lodged a First Amendment complaint alleging that the act was unconstitutionally broad. The Supreme Court, in *Reno v. American Civil Liberties Union* (1997), agreed with the ACLU and found that while Congress could have carefully crafted a law to address access to Internet pornography, it did not do so in this act and thus it went too far and infringed the right of free speech. "[T]he level of discourse reaching [a computer] simply cannot be limited to that which would be suitable for a sandbox," said the opinion. In 1998 Congress tried again with the Child Online Protection Act, an attempt to keep children from viewing pornographic Web sites by relying on "community standards" of decency. Although in *Ashcroft v. American Civil Liberties Union* (2002) the Supreme Court refused to find the act unconstitutional simply because of the reliance on community standards for a medium that had a much broader scope, in *Ashcroft v. American Civil Liberties Union* (2004) the Court concluded that the government had alternatives to the restrictions on free speech in the act that could be just as effective in protecting children from online pornography. In *U.S. v. American Library Association* (2003), however, the Court, by 6–3, upheld the Children's Internet Protection Act of 2001, which requires pubic libraries receiving federal funds to install software to block material that might be harmful to minors (see CENSORSHIP).

Privacy

Spam and cookies may sound like an unappetizing combination for lunch, but in the Internet world they represent two forms of potential invasions of privacy. Spam is junk e-mail, unasked-for solicitations or commercial offers; cookies are methods of identifying, retaining, and ultimately making use of information about a Web site user. Spam is a nuisance like telemarketers, while cookies are more insidious, like mail-order companies that sell a consumer's name and address to commercial enterprises and charities without permission.

Many states have enacted antispam laws, and the Federal Trade Commission, which is charged with enforcing fair trade practices, is also looking into the practice. In 2001 the FTC filed charges against a company for "harvesting" consumers' personal information from a competitor's Web site and sending spam solicitations for business. In another case, the FTC alleged that a company used cookies to create profiles of Internet users in violation of the company's stated privacy policy.

Although the Supreme Court has not yet directly addressed such questions, a federal circuit court of appeals in 2000 held that a government employee charged with violating federal child pornography laws did not have a reasonable expectation of privacy with respect to documents on his computer where the government agency had notified employees of computer-use limitations and conducted regular audits to determine compliance with agency policy. The following year, the same court, the U.S. Court of Appeals for the Ninth Circuit, withdrew an opinion in which it had sided with the plaintiff, who alleged that his employer, an airline company, had improperly accessed his secure Web site in violation of the Electronic Communications Privacy Act (1986) and other federal laws. The act updated legislation passed in 1968 to clarify what constitutes invasion of privacy when electronic surveillance involves computers and innovations in electronic communications.

Since the terrorist attacks on the United States on September 11, 2001, the federal government has increased its efforts to identify potential future terrorist activities in the United States in some ways that have raised concerns about the constitutionality of the methods used. For example, telephone, Internet, and public library records have been accessed in some cases without the individuals whose records are involved being notified. Google, Inc., the online search engine company, was required by a federal court in 2006 to turn over some information in response to subpoenas issued by the U.S. Justice Department. It is likely that the Supreme Court will have to rule on the legality of some of these attempts by the government to invade the privacy of citizens in the near future.

Intellectual Property

Article I, section 8, of the Constitution empowers Congress to make laws regarding COPYRIGHT and PATENTS, which are vehicles by which individuals can protect their rights and interests in intellectual property such as written articles and books, music, and other forms of art and communication. The Internet, like recording devices and copying machines available to the public, provides a means for users to download, store, and reproduce information of various types without obtaining copyright permission. One recent important federal court ruling barred the free downloading of copyrighted music through Napster, an online music-swapping company.

In *New York Times v. Tasini* (2001), the *New York Times* appealed a federal appeals court ruling that the copyrights of authors for newspapers and magazines published by the *Times* and others had been infringed by placing their work products in an electronic database without their consent. The Supreme Court tested the facts of the case against the 1976 Copyright Act, which says: "Copyright in each separate contribution to a collective work is distinct from copyright in the collective work as a whole, and vests initially in the author of the contribution. In the absence of an express transfer of the copyright or of any rights under it, the owner of copyright in the collective work is presumed to have acquired only the privilege of reproducing and distributing the contribution as part of that particular collective work...." The Court thus held that the publishers' use of the authors' works infringed the authors' copyright because they were used in databases that "reproduce and distribute articles standing alone and not in context, not as part of that particular collective work to which the author contributed [such as the newspaper or magazine], as part of any revision thereof, or as part of any later collective work in the same series."

> **More on this topic:**
>
> *Censorship, p. 82*
>
> *Communications, p. 104*
>
> *Copyright, p. 124*

The Internet will undoubtedly continue to raise constitutional questions as it expands and evolves into a wider and more powerful form of communication. Just as undoubtedly, the use of this new medium of communication by those who want to commit crimes, including sexual predators, con artists, and even terrorists, will renew efforts to regulate it—which may lead to clashes with the constitutional rights of law-abiding citizens.

Interstate Commerce *See* COMMERCE.

Invasions *See* NATIONAL SECURITY.

Inverse Condemnation *See* JUST COMPENSATION.

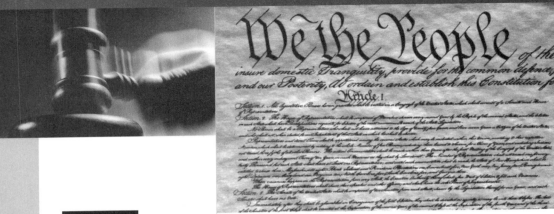

J

Jefferson, Thomas

Thomas Jefferson was serving as the U.S. minister to France during the Constitutional Convention, but the views of the author of the Declaration of Independence influenced key delegates such as James Madison and Alexander Hamilton.

Source: Library of Congress

At a 1962 White House dinner honoring forty-nine Nobel Prize winners, President John F. Kennedy (1917–63) paid tribute to a person not present: "This is the most extraordinary collection of talent, of human knowledge, that has ever been gathered in the White House—with the possible exception of when Thomas Jefferson dined alone." The author of the DECLARATION OF INDEPENDENCE (1776), the third president of the United States (1801–9), and the force behind the Louisiana Purchase in 1803, Jefferson (1743–1826) more than anyone else continues to epitomize the quintessential American.

Born on April 13, 1743, in Albemarle County, Virginia—his father was one of the early settlers in the area—Thomas Jefferson entered the College of William and Mary at the age of seventeen. Having developed a special interest in the English constitution, he later studied law with George Wythe, who also taught him history, culture, and ethics. Admitted to the bar in 1767, Jefferson became a member of the Virginia legislature two years later. In addition to pursuing a career in politics, Jefferson became an accomplished musician, scientist, agriculturist, amateur architect, and philosopher, having developed for himself a philosophy centered on reason, progress, and improvement that was derived especially from the works of the Englishmen Francis Bacon (1561–1626), Isaac Newton (1642–1727), and John Locke (1632–1704).

Along with Benjamin Franklin (1706–90), Jefferson was among those who spearheaded the Enlightenment movement in America. In his first published work, *A Summary View of the Rights of America* (1774), he argued against Great Britain's hegemony over the colonies. The following year he was made a delegate to the Second Continental Congress, where in 1776, as a member of a committee of five, he wrote the first draft of the Declaration of Independence. Jefferson was familiar with the Virginia Declaration of Rights (see pages 000–000), drafted by GEORGE MASON and adopted on June 12, 1776. Jefferson later also drafted the Statute of Virginia for Religious Freedom, enacted after much debate in 1786.

Jefferson served as governor of Virginia from 1779 to 1781, thereafter returning to the Congress, where he helped draft the Northwest Ordinance to guarantee political freedoms and eventual statehood for settlers in the country's Northwest Territory, the sparsely settled upper region between the Ohio and Mississippi Rivers. Serving as the U.S. minister (ambassador) to France during the CONSTITUTIONAL CONVENTION OF 1787, he was neither a drafter nor a signer of the Constitution it produced. But his discussions with ALEXANDER HAMILTON and his close friendship with JAMES MADISON, delegates to the convention from New York and Virginia, respectively, ensured that his ideas influenced the shape of the new government. In a November 13, 1787, letter to the secretary of JOHN ADAMS, Jefferson responded from France to the news of Shays's Rebellion, a farmers' uprising in Massachusetts that illustrated the need for a strong central government. "God forbid," said the author of the Declaration of Independence, "we should ever be twenty years without rebellion....[T]he tree of Liberty must be refreshed from time to time with the blood of patriots & tyrants."

Once the Constitution went into effect in 1789, Jefferson played leading roles in the new government, serving as the nation's first secretary of state under GEORGE WASHINGTON. By 1796 Jefferson had become the leader of the newly emergent Democratic-Republican Party, which became the present-day Democratic Party (see POLITICAL PARTIES). He won the election in 1800 as the country's third president in a bitter contest with JOHN ADAMS. In a letter to Dr. Benjamin Rush (1745–1813) in September, during the bitterly fought contest with Washington's vice president, who was the Federalist Party candidate, Jefferson wrote: "I have sworn upon the altar of God, eternal hostility against every form of tyranny over the mind of man." Because of a flaw in the early Constitution regarding the method of selecting the president, however, he was initially denied a victory over Adams when the majority Democratic–Republican Party presidential electors, trying to ensure the election of both Jefferson as president and Aaron Burr as vice president, awarded them both an equal number of votes. The matter was then thrown into the House of Representatives. After thirty ballots and the urging of Alexander Hamilton—a Federalist and no supporter of either Jefferson or Burr—Jefferson prevailed. The problem with this election led to the ratification of the Twelfth Amendment in 1804 (see ELECTIONS).

> *"[Ours is] a constitution of government destined to be the primitive and precious model of what is to change the condition of man over the globe."*
>
> —*Thomas Jefferson,* Letter to Edward Livingston, 1824

The Sage of Monticello was responsible for the addition to the new nation of the Louisiana Territory's vast land and resources, which would play a key role in helping the United States reach across the continent to the Pacific Ocean. To apprise the nation of the extent and nature of the Louisiana Purchase, he lost no time in sending a two-year expedition across the continent led by Captain Meriwether Lewis (1774–1809) and Lieutenant William Clark (1770–1838) beginning in 1804.

More on this topic:

Declaration of Independence, p. 147

Hamilton, Alexander, p. 270

Madison, James, p. 355

Jefferson wanted to be remembered especially for establishing the University of Virginia and asked that his tombstone read simply: "Here was buried Thomas Jefferson, Author of the Declaration of American Independence, of the Statute of Virginia for Religious Freedom, and the father of the University of Virginia." Nearby, at his innovative, self-designed hilltop estate, Monticello, he grew experimental vegetables and made wine. Jefferson died there on July 4, 1826, on the fiftieth anniversary of the Declaration of Independence—the same day that his political rival, John Adams, died believing that Jefferson had outlived him.

Jefferson's immortal Declaration of Independence laid the foundations for the Revolutionary War and the framing of the Constitution. Today it remains a symbol of hope for people around the world who struggle against tyranny for the right of self-determination. His vision of a basically agricultural nation of well-educated, politically active citizens lost out to Hamilton's plan for a commercial nation with a powerful central government. But as a creative force who could inspire a nation and the world at an important time in America's history, Jefferson has no peer.

Joint Resolutions *See* CONGRESS.

Journal *See* CONGRESS.

Judges *See* COURTS; SUPREME COURT.

Judicial Branch

"The judicial organization of the United States," observed the French political scientist Alexis de Tocqueville (1805–59) in *Democracy in America* (1835), "is the hardest thing there for a foreigner to understand. He finds judicial authority invoked in almost every political context, and from that he naturally concludes that the judge is one of the most important political powers in the [country]. But when he then begins to examine the constitution of the courts, at first glance he sees nothing but judicial attributes and procedures. The judges seem to intervene in public affairs only by chance, but that chance recurs daily."

De Tocqueville's confusion about the role of the judicial branch in America is understandable. Of the federal government's three branches—the LEGISLATIVE BRANCH, EXECUTIVE BRANCH, and judicial branch—the judicial branch is both the weakest but at times the strongest. Its weaknesses stem from the fact that it has neither the power of the purse (to raise and spend money), as the legislative branch does, nor the power of enforcement (to command armies and federal law enforcement agencies), as does the executive branch.

The federal judicial branch has many strengths, however. One of these, as de Tocqueville also recognized, lies in its lack of accountability to any particular political entity. Judges on all the courts established under Article III of the Constitution are appointed for life, although, like any other national government official, they are subject to IMPEACHMENT. The Constitution additionally protects their salary from diminishment, which helps ensure JUDICIAL INDEPENDENCE. Another strength lies in the national courts' power to arbitrate constitutional disputes and declare the acts of the other two branches unconstitutional and therefore null and void.

The constitutions of many countries divide the national government into three major branches, including a judicial branch. Sri Lanka's constitution (1978), for example, states: "The Sovereignty of the People shall be exercised [through] the legislative power…, the executive power. …, [and] the judicial power.…" Poland's constitution (1997) declares that the government "shall be based on the separation of and balance between the legislative, executive and judicial powers."

The U.S. Constitution's Article III, which pertains to the judiciary (from the Latin *judicium*, meaning court), similarly establishes the judicial branch as the coequal of the other two branches. While the principle of the SEPARATION OF POWERS in a government protects against the accumulation of powers in too few hands, the principle of checks and balances among those powers protects against the domination of one branch over another.

Judicial Power

"The judicial Power of the United States," Article III, section 1, declares, "shall be vested in one supreme Court, and in such inferior Courts as the Congress may from time to time ordain and establish.…" Included in the judicial branch are the federal courts—the SUPREME COURT, courts of appeal, district courts, and territorial courts—as well as such specialized courts and agencies as the Court of International Trade, Court of Federal Claims, Court of Appeals for the Armed Forces, Court of Veterans Appeals, Administrative Office of the Courts, Federal Judicial Center, and Sentencing Commission (see COURTS).

Judicial power was one of the three basic powers of government identified by the French jurist Charles-Louis de Secondat, Baron de La Bréde et de Montesquieu (1689–1755) in *The Spirit of the Laws* (1748), a work familiar to many of the delegates to the CONSTITUTIONAL CONVENTION OF 1787. The FRAMERS OF THE CONSTITUTION were also aware of the history of the judicial system in Great Britain and the colonies, as well as the various systems that developed in the thirteen states after the DECLARATION OF INDEPENDENCE (1776). The British judicial system had on occasion provided some balance against the excesses of the monarch and Parliament, but as Parliament's supremacy became a principle of the unwritten British constitution, the judicial branch, at least in theory, remained at its mercy. The judicial systems in the American states, especially in Massachusetts, served as models for the framers to consider when devising the plan of the national judicial branch.

Because the major officials in the legislative and executive branches were to be elected, some of the framers feared that they might act in accordance with their constituencies' passions rather than reason. The judicial branch was thus meant to be a counterpoise to the other two branches, but the judicial power evolved away from the framers' concept and even the intentions of Congress when it passed the first Judiciary Act (1789), which established a six-member Supreme Court and lower federal courts with limited federal jurisdiction.

The judiciary's powers began expanding early in the nation's history, largely as a result of the able direction of Chief Justice JOHN MARSHALL, who served on the Supreme Court from 1801 to 1835. Its original jurisdiction, as opposed to its appellate jurisdiction, was limited to the express language in the Constitution and could not be augmented or diminished without a constitutional amendment. In such key decisions as *MARBURY V. MADISON* (1803) and *MARTIN V. HUNTER'S LESSEE* (1816), however, the Supreme Court began extending its appellate jurisdiction to include JUDICIAL REVIEW of acts of the other two federal branches to determine if they were unconstitutional and therefore void, as well as decisions of state courts involving the Constitution and federal law.

Today the federal judiciary's power with respect to the balance between the powers of the federal government and the states (see FEDERALISM) and the often precarious rights of the citizens vis-á-vis the government—for example, regarding ABORTION—is crucial. As a result, any new appointment to the Supreme Court that might sway the Court to one side or the other in controversial areas is of great importance to the American people.

Scope of Power

The scope of the judicial branch's power is the narrowest of the three branches. The proportion of the national budget and the number of federal personnel devoted to this branch has always been far smaller than that of the other two. Courts cannot initiate judicial action but must rely on interested parties to bring cases before them. And enforcement of their decisions ultimately rests with the executive branch. When the Supreme Court invalidated "separate but equal" public schools for white and black children in BROWN V. BOARD OF EDUCATION OF TOPEKA (1954), assistance from the Justice Department was needed to enforce the Court's decision, and federal troops including National Guardsmen were required to supervise integration in some southern states.

As Article III, section 2, mandates: "The judicial Power shall extend to all Cases, in Law and Equity, arising under this Constitution, the Laws of the United States, and Treaties made, or which shall be made, under their Authority" (see TREATIES). Section 2 then specifies the types of cases that fall under the Supreme Court's original jurisdiction: only those "affecting Ambassadors, other public ministers and Consuls" (see AMBASSADORS) and cases in which "a State shall be a party." All other cases fall under the Court's appellate jurisdiction: "In all the other cases before mentioned, the supreme Court shall have appellate Jurisdiction, both as to Law and Fact, with such Exceptions, and under such Regulations as the Congress shall make."

The judicial branch's scope with respect to original jurisdiction is very narrow, and although it has broad powers with respect to appellate review, Congress retains its own power to check and balance. Some of the federal courts' authority over suits against states that infringe on their right of sovereign immunity (see IMMUNITY; SOVEREIGNTY) was removed by the Eleventh Amendment (1798). In addition, through a number of judiciary acts—in 1789, 1801, 1837, 1869, 1875, 1891, 1911, and 1925 and in the Judiciary Reform Act (1937)—Congress manipulated the judicial branch's jurisdiction and structure. As recently as 1996, in the Antiterrorism and Effective Death Penalty Act, Congress restricted the Supreme Court's ability to hear HABEAS CORPUS petitions from persons regarding a DEATH PENALTY sentence.

The Supreme Court, however, guards its role under the Constitution jealously. For example, in *Zadvydas v. Davis* (2001), the Court rejected the government's argument that just "because Congress has plenary power to create immigration law, the Judicial Branch must defer to the Executive and Legislative Branch…in that area…because that power is subject to constitutional limits." And in an important case involving the power of the executive branch to hold detainees in the war on terror indefinitely, HAMDI V. RUMSFELD (2004), the Court noted that even the war power does not remove constitutional limitations safeguarding essential liberties, and that "the Great Writ of habeas corpus allows the Judicial Branch to play a necessary role in maintaining [the] delicate balance of governance, serving as an important judicial check on the Executive's discretion in the realm of detentions."

Limitations on Judicial Power

A number of quasi-judicial bodies exist outside the judicial branch. Some commissions, panels, and boards that perform judicial-type functions in limited areas are under the aegis of the executive branch. The Social Security Administration, for one, adjudicates benefit claims. Often the decisions of such bodies are reviewable by the federal court system, but in some cases review is limited or prohibited by Congress. In addition, the system of BANKRUPTCY courts is considered outside the federal court system established by Article III, in part because bankruptcy judges are appointed for set TERMS OF OFFICE rather than for life.

The Supreme Court concluded in *Thomas v. Union Carbide Agricultural Products Co.* (1985) that "Congress, acting for a valid legislative purpose pursuant to its constitutional powers under Article I, may create a seemingly 'private' right that is so closely integrated into a public regulatory scheme as to be a matter appropriate for agency resolution with limited involvement by the Article III judiciary." As Justice SANDRA DAY O'CONNOR explained in *Commodities Futures Trading Commission v. Schor* (1986), in such cases the Court has to weigh "a number of factors including...the extent to which the 'essential attributes of judicial power' are reserved to Article III courts, and, conversely, the extent to which the non-Article III forum exercises the range of jurisdiction and powers normally vested only in Article III courts, the origins and importance of the right to be adjudicated, and the concerns that drove Congress to depart from the requirements of Article III."

The role of the judicial branch is also circumscribed by certain informal judicial policies. These include the Supreme Court's stated refusal to decide "political questions"—issues that the Court believes the Constitution does not intend the courts to settle—as well as judicial restraint, a conscious effort to refrain from going beyond what is absolutely necessary to determine cases and controversies. Such judicial conservatism is sometimes leavened with judicial activism, a conscious desire to reach out and tackle new problems or change existing law.

Both independent of and interactive with the other two branches, the judicial branch at times serves as a check on abuses by the other two branches and on state governments by reviewing their actions against both the letter and the spirit of the Constitution. This branch can be an active force in guaranteeing rights spelled out in the Constitution to protect the basic liberties of the American people and those, like PRIVACY and abortion rights, that are found between the lines.

CLOSER LOOK

In 1956 the influential American Bar Association (ABA) began to evaluate nominations to the Supreme Court and other federal judgeships. Its closely watched assessments gradually became controversial, with conservatives charging that the ABA has a liberal bias.

The ABA committee on the federal judiciary has usually been unanimous in rating Supreme Court nominees as well-qualified, which is its highest rating. However the committee split on the nominations of two controversial conservatives: Robert H. Bork in 1987 and Clarence Thomas in 1991. The Senate rejected Bork and narrowly approved Thomas, with the ABA's vote apparently giving ammunition to opponents of the nominations.

In 2001 the administration of President George W. Bush announced that it would no longer submit candidates for judgeships to the ABA's committee. Nevertheless, the committee has continued to evaluate candidates. It gave unanimous, well-qualified ratings to both of Bush's Supreme Court nominees: John G. Roberts Jr. and Samuel A. Alito Jr.

Judicial Independence

In a letter to JAMES MADISON dated March 15, 1789, THOMAS JEFFERSON offered one argument in support of adding a bill of rights to the Constitution: "the legal check which it puts into the hands of the judiciary." Independent COURTS, Jefferson believed, would be able to declare unconstitutional any legislative or executive acts that violated such a statement of individual rights. In the first session of Congress several months later, Madison introduced a draft of the BILL OF RIGHTS, which since its ratification in 1791 has been a continual source of Supreme Court cases.

An inevitable result of creating a national government based on the SEPARATION OF POWERS of government—legislative, executive, and judicial—was an independent judiciary. In the United Kingdom, Parliament was and still is supreme, able to overrule decisions of the judiciary and take away its powers. Parliament may also function as the highest court of the realm, and the judiciary is bound by its decisions. In France also, the courts, never greatly trusted by the French people, take a back seat to the other branches of government.

Article III: The Judiciary

The Constitution ensures the independence of the national court system in several ways. It devotes an entire section to each branch of government, addressing the LEGISLATIVE BRANCH in Article I, the EXECUTIVE BRANCH in Article II, and the JUDICIAL BRANCH in Article III. Article III, section 1, provides in part: "The judicial Power of the United States, shall be vested in one supreme Court, and in such inferior Courts as the Congress may from time to time ordain and establish." Thus in a single sentence the Constitution establishes the independence of the judiciary while maintaining the check and balance of Congress with respect to the number of courts to be established under it.

The independence of the federal courts is buttressed by the fact that justices and judges have life tenure and may be removed only by IMPEACHMENT. "The Judges, both of the supreme and inferior Courts," section 1 states, "shall hold their Offices during good Behaviour, and shall, at stated Times, receive for their Services, a Compensation, which shall not be diminished during their Continuance in Office." The phrase prohibiting diminution of the judges' salaries further enhances their independence—their pay cannot be reduced in retaliation for unpopular decisions—and also prevents the threat of such an act from affecting their judgments.

Section 2 outlines the jurisdiction of the federal court system, including the SUPREME COURT's original jurisdiction and its appellate jurisdiction. Further checks and balances with the legislative branch are erected by the phrase subjecting the Court's appellate jurisdiction to "such Exceptions, and under such Regulations as the Congress shall make."

Checks and Balances

More checks and balances come from the Constitution's requirement that federal judges, including Supreme Court justices, be nominated by the PRESIDENT (the executive branch) and approved by the SENATE (the legislative branch). The constitutions of some other countries allow members of the judiciary a role in the process of selecting new members. Poland's constitution (1992) provides for judges to be "appointed for an indefinite period by the President...on the motion of the National Council of the Judiciary," while Syria's constitution (1973) specifies that judges are appointed by a supreme judicial council, presided over by the president of the republic. Although such provisions may emphasize an even greater independence for the judiciary, they also may lead to inbreeding. Incumbent judges may tend to promote the selection of those who agree with their judicial philosophy, thus insulating the judiciary from the changes necessary to reflect a pluralistic and evolving society.

In addition to the constitutional nomination and approval process (see APPOINTMENT AND REMOVAL POWER), other checks that counterbalance the basic independence of the federal judiciary are the BUDGET process, which requires legislation by CONGRESS with the approval of the president to finance its activities, and the power of impeachment, which the Constitution has entrusted to Congress.

An important benefit of an independent judiciary is its ability in turn to act as a check on actions of the executive and legislative branches as well as on actions of the state governments that may contravene provisions of the Constitution. Members of the judiciary, like all officers of the national and state governments, are sworn to uphold the Constitution (see OATH OF OFFICE). Moreover, through the process of JUDICIAL REVIEW, the courts can declare as void and without effect any act not consistent with the Constitution. Strictly speaking, the federal judiciary is the least democratic of the three branches of government because its members are appointed and

not responsible to the electorate. However, it reflects the intent of the FRAMERS OF THE CONSTITU-
TION to create an impartial and nonpolitical institution that would maintain the consistency of
the laws throughout the nation and act as a check on the possible excesses of popular democracy.
A number of state constitutions do permit judges to be selected in contested elections or approved at the polls.

Judicial Restraint

The philosophy of judicial restraint—refraining from exercising judicial powers to show deference
to the other branches of government and sometimes to state supreme courts—has been espoused
by some Supreme Court justices throughout the Court's history,
among them Louis D. Brandeis (1856–1941) and Wiley B. Rutledge
(1894–1949). At the root of this philosophy is the notion that the
Court's authority is less likely to erode or be threatened by the other
branches if it exercises that authority in a restrained manner, thus
ensuring its judicial independence. Judicial restraint is the opposite
of judicial activism, in which a court reaches out to make new law or
issue opinions based on its views of social or economic policy rather
than sticking strictly to its legal role (see STRICT CONSTRUCTION).

Some rules the Supreme Court has developed to enforce judicial
restraint were set forth in *Ashwander v. Tennessee Valley Authority*
(1936). A concurring opinion by Justice Brandeis specified that these
rules include avoiding passing judgment on the constitutionality of
laws in a nonadversarial or friendly proceeding or on any question of
constitutionality unless it is absolutely necessary to a case's determination. Restraint also includes restricting any determination to the
most narrow constitutional basis possible and construing statutes
passed by Congress to avoid finding them unconstitutional, "even if
a serious doubt of constitutionality is raised" by one of the parties in
the case.

*Justice Wiley B. Rutledge, who
served on the Court from 1943 to
1949, was a proponent of judicial
restraint.*
Source: Collection of the Supreme Court
of the United States

Judicial restraint, like judicial activism, depends to a large extent
on the predisposition of each justice and on the nature of the cases
that come before them for consideration, although the Warren Court
(1954–69) could be called generally activist and the Rehnquist Court
(1986–2005) relatively restrained. However, in the unprecedented
case of *BUSH V. GORE* (2000), in which a decision of five members of the Supreme Court virtually
ensured the election of George W. Bush (b. 1946) as president, there was little evidence of judicial
restraint. Rather than rely on its own precedents to give deference to state supreme court decisions
on matters within their jurisdiction, the Rehnquist Court actively sought to make the final decision itself.

The rule of law includes the right of all citizens to be tried by an independent and impartial
court or tribunal. In many countries, especially those with dictators or those dominated by a single political party, the courts are only extensions of the government's leaders; they see their role as
primarily protecting the prerogatives and often the abuses of the executive branch. The French political scientist Alexis de Tocqueville (1805–59) pointed out in *Democracy in America* (1835) "that
among a free people such as the Americans all citizens have the right to prosecute public officials
before the ordinary judges and that all judges have the right to condemn public officials." It is the
independence of the judiciary under the Constitution that makes de Tocqueville's observation possible and still relevant today.

Judicial Review

A basic tenet of constitutionalism is that government, whether a monarchy, a DEMOCRACY, or something in between, must be limited if individual LIBERTY and other RIGHTS are to be protected. One way to try to ensure limitations on GOVERNMENT, particularly one with a written constitution, is to separate government powers among several institutions or officials (see SEPARATION OF POWERS). An additional precaution is to give one institution the power to declare acts by the others to be unconstitutional.

At the time the Constitution was drafted in 1787, the British Parliament's overriding supremacy meant that the nation's executive and judicial branches were always, in theory at least, at Parliament's mercy on constitutional matters because the legislators could always pass a law overriding any action of another branch. Judicial review—the power of COURTS in the regular course of business to judge the constitutionality of acts of other government officials and institutions—was therefore not a part of Great Britain's unwritten constitution. In the thirteen former British colonies that made up the new United States, however, courts did declare acts of other government branches unconstitutional.

"The complete independence of the courts of justice is particularly essential in a limited Constitution," wrote ALEXANDER HAMILTON in essay 78 of *The Federalist* (1787–88) (see FEDERALIST PAPERS), presaging judicial review by the SUPREME COURT. "Limitations...can be preserved in practice no other way than through the medium of courts of justice, whose duty it must be to declare all acts contrary to the manifest tenor of the Constitution void. Without this, all the reservations of particular rights or privileges would amount to nothing." Although the Supreme Court is the final judicial authority concerning violations of the Constitution when cases raising such questions come before it, lower federal courts and state courts also rule on constitutional matters in the course of their determinations. One of the functions of the Supreme Court, as the nation's highest court, however, is to ensure a uniformity in the Constitution's application nationwide.

Today national constitutions from Norway (1814) to Australia (1901, significantly amended 1986) provide for some form of judicial review. Other nations, especially in Europe, have adopted constitutional review procedures whereby the constitutionality of laws and government actions is reviewed by a special constitutional court, rather than the regular courts. A few countries, including France, have a constitutional council that can review laws before they go into effect to ensure that they comply with the constitution.

An important distinction between judicial review by regular courts, as practiced in the United States, and constitutional review by special constitutional courts in other nations is that a regular court's authority arises from an actual case, although both the EXECUTIVE BRANCH and the LEGISLATIVE BRANCH can and do file suits with the Supreme Court to test the constitutionality of controversial issues. Any decision in a case where judicial review is exercised is technically limited to the parties involved, except that the legal practice of *stare decisis* (the application of precedent to subsequent similar cases) generally ensures that Supreme Court decisions will be followed in future cases.

The very nature of the Constitution—which creates limited national powers separated among three branches and contains built-in procedural checks and balances—requires that each branch of government individually uphold the document's language and principles. Although the Supreme Court in *MARBURY V. MADISON* (1803) officially took it on itself to declare an act of Congress unconstitutional and thus set the precedent for judicial review by the federal courts, Congress and the president are also responsible under the Constitution for determining the constitutionality of their own actions and that of the other branches.

The Supreme Court can also declare state government laws and actions unconstitutional when pertinent cases are brought before it. Between 1791 and 1799 federal courts had begun striking down state laws. In FLETCHER V. PECK (1810), the Supreme Court found a state statute unconstitutional under the Constitution's contract clause in Article I, section 10 (see CONTRACTS). Six years later, in MARTIN V. HUNTER'S LESSEE (1816), the Court used its authority to review constitutional implications of state court decisions. The Constitution grants the Supreme Court original jurisdiction, which was the basis of the *Marbury* decision. It also sets forth the Court's appellate jurisdiction "with such Exceptions, and under such Regulations as the Congress shall make." In the Judiciary Act (1789), Congress elaborated on the Court's appellate jurisdiction. In *Martin* the Court dismissed the argument that its appellate jurisdiction was limited to cases on appeal from lower federal courts. In the words of Justice Joseph Story (1779–1845): "It is the *case*, then, and not the *court*, that gives the jurisdiction."

With respect to the standing of a party to seek judicial review, article III, section 2 of the Constitution states that the "judicial power shall extend [to certain] cases [and] controversies." As recently as 2007, the Supreme Court confirmed its bases for determining standing in *Massachusetts v. Environmental Protection Agency*. In its decision in that case, the Court cited *Lujan v. Defenders of Wildlife* (1992) for the proposition that "a litigant must demonstrate that it has suffered a concrete and particularized injury that is either actual or imminent, that the injury is fairly traceable to the defendant, and that it is likely that a favorable decision will redress that injury." In this case, the Court, noting that a sovereign state has special rights "for the purposes of invoking federal jurisdiction," found that Massachusetts had standing to seek judicial review.

The practice of judicial review in the United States has become well accepted, even though Congress, the president, and large segments of the public may at times disagree with specific outcomes, and the Court's ruling that a law or an action is unconstitutional can essentially be overturned. If the matter turns on a technicality—for example, if a law improperly relied on taxing power but would be constitutional if it was based on the commerce clause—Congress can correct the error. Another congressional weapon is the power to limit which matters may be appealed to the Supreme Court, as Congress did recently in the Antiterrorism and Effective Death Penalty Act (1996) by limiting HABEAS CORPUS appeals by PRISONERS facing the DEATH PENALTY. Also, if Congress and the president are in philosophical or political disagreement with a series of decisions, the members of the Supreme Court can be replaced over time. A more direct route, if the mood of the country is behind it, is to amend the Constitution (see AMENDMENTS).

Some critics of judicial review argue that it is basically undemocratic to give appointed officials not directly responsible to the electorate the power to void the actions of duly elected representatives. However, both an absolute monarchy and an absolute democracy are capable of great injustices, especially when it comes to the rights of MINORITIES. All forms of government can be corrupted, but the process of judicial review tries to balance the power of the majority (see MAJORITY RULE) with the power of an independent and nonpolitical judiciary (see JUDICIAL INDEPENDENCE). A similar criticism in a different guise is that the courts may try to legislate rather than interpret the law, thus violating the separation of powers doctrine.

The judiciary is the weakest of the three branches of government (see JUDICIAL BRANCH), with neither an army to command nor the power of the purse. That courts can reach out to prevent injustice condoned by the majority is often the only way that justice will ever be done.

More on this topic:
Judicial Independence, p. 315
Marbury v. Madison, p. 360
Separation of Powers, p. 494
Supreme Court, p. 527

Juries

Panels of CITIZENS charged with passing judgment on a fellow citizen accused of breaking the LAW were used in ancient Greece, the cradle of DEMOCRACY. The U.S. jury system, however, had its origins in the legal system that evolved in England. Magna Carta (1215), the charter of liberties forced on King John by his barons, provides in chapter 29: "No freeman shall be taken or imprisoned,…nor will we not pass upon him, nor [condemn him] but by lawful judgment of his peers, or by the law of the land."

As Article III, section 2, of the Constitution requires, "The Trial of all Crimes, except in Cases of Impeachment, shall be by Jury…." The Sixth Amendment (1791) provides that "[i]n all criminal prosecutions, the accused shall enjoy the right to a speedy and public trial, by an impartial jury of the State and district wherein the crime shall have been committed…." In addition, the Seventh Amendment (1791) guarantees: "In Suits at common law, where the value in controversy shall exceed twenty dollars, the right of trial by jury shall be preserved, and no fact tried by a jury, shall be otherwise re-examined in any Court of the United States, than according to the rules of the common law" (see COMMON LAW).

The jury system is an important aspect of guaranteeing the impartiality of TRIALS. An affirmation of the use of juries that became a landmark in England's legal history was *Bushell's Case* (1670). William Penn, a Quaker who later founded the Pennsylvania colony in America, was arrested with an associate for preaching outside the Quaker meetinghouse in London, which had been officially closed. They were tried before a jury on the spurious charge of inciting a riot. Although the judge had threatened the jurors and detained them without food or heat to coerce a guilty verdict, Penn was acquitted by the jury, led by Edward Bushell. The judge fined and imprisoned the jurors for their obstinace. Eventually England's lord chief justice intervened, saying that a judge "may try to open the eyes of the jurors, but not to lead them by the nose." The 1735 case of

In the nation's early years, female defendants were denied the constitutional right to a jury of their "peers" because women were barred from jury service. About 1902 Charles Dana Gibson captured the new jury system, complete with "Gibson Girls."
Source: Library of Congress

Peter Zenger (see ZENGER'S CASE) in New York is a similar example of a resolute jury's refusal to return a guilty verdict despite threats by the judge.

Jurors

As used in Magna Carta, the term *peers* originally referred to people of equal social status who knew the accused and his or her character. In today's more populous and anonymous society, this principle has taken a 180-degree turn: juries are instructed to be as impartial as possible, and anyone who personally knows the defendant is precluded from serving on a jury.

The Supreme Court has held that jurors must represent a cross section of the community and that DISCRIMINATION is unconstitutional. In an early case, *Strauder v. West Virginia* (1880), the Court, relying on the EQUAL PROTECTION clause of the Fourteenth Amendment (1868), overturned the conviction of an African American because a state law precluded blacks from serving on juries. A century later, in *Peters v. Kiff* (1972), the Court reversed the conviction of a white person because African Americans had been excluded from the jury, thus denying the defendant an impartial trial by a cross section of the community.

The preliminary examination of potential jurors to ascertain their fitness to serve at a trial is called *voir dire* (from the Latin *verus dicere* and the Old French, meaning to speak the truth). Both parties are entitled to a certain number of preemptory challenges of jurors, which require no explanation, but they can also make as many challenges as necessary "for cause," based on a perception that a juror is biased or otherwise unable to render a fair verdict. Although questions can be raised about a juror's racial prejudice, according to the Supreme Court's ruling in *Ristaino v. Ross* (1976), just because the accused and the victim are of different races or ethnic backgrounds does not constitutionally require a special inquiry into racial prejudice. The Court also held in *Witherspoon v. Illinois* (1968) that a person with doubts about the DEATH PENALTY could not be excluded from a jury if he indicated that he could impose it under appropriate circumstances.

The Supreme Court in *Snyder v. Louisiana* (2007) reversed the conviction of a man sentenced to death because the prosecution had unconstitutionally excluded African Americans from the jury. Citing their precedent decision in *Batson v. Kentucky* (1986), the Court noted that a prosecutor may not use preemptory challenges to exclude jurors based on their race. The ruling in *Batson* applies only to the prosecution, only to criminal trials, and only to challenges where the excluded juror is the same race as the defendant.

Types of Juries

Petit Juries. The Constitution does not mandate that juries be composed of a specific number of persons, but the most common panel used to judge the facts and determine the outcome of criminal and civil trials is a petit (from the French, meaning small) or petty jury, generally twelve in number. In *Maxwell v. Dow* (1900), the Supreme Court upheld the use of an eight-person jury in Utah, stating that "[t]rial by jury has never been affirmed to be a necessary requisite of due process of law" (see DUE PROCESS). And in *Williams v. Florida* (1970), the Court affirmed that as few as six jurors could be used in felony cases.

For federal criminal cases, however, the Supreme Court has held that a twelve-person jury is required, and a guilty verdict must be unanimous. State verdicts in criminal cases need not be unanimous. The Supreme Court has upheld verdicts of 9–3 by state juries, saying that they do not violate the due process clause of the Fourteenth Amendment, but it has reserved judgment on closer ratios. In *Burch v. Louisiana* (1979), the Court found that a 5–1 verdict of a six-person jury violated the constitutional guarantee of a trial by jury.

Grand Juries. "No person shall be held to answer for a capital, or otherwise infamous crime," mandates the Fifth Amendment (1791), "unless on a presentment or indictment of a Grand

Jury...." A grand (French for large) jury consists of from twelve to twenty-three people who are called together to decide if there is probable cause to place the accused on trial. Their decision is based on evidence presented by government prosecutors.

The Right to a Jury Trial

Before 1968 the Supreme Court had not held that under the Fourteenth Amendment a jury was required in state court trials (see INCORPORATION DOCTRINE). In *Duncan v. Louisiana* (1968), the Court reversed itself and invalidated a conviction without the benefit of a jury that resulted in a two-year prison sentence for a Louisiana man. In the Court's decision the justices declared that the right to a jury trial was "fundamental to the American scheme of justice" and mandated that jury trials be extended in all cases in which they would be required in federal cases under the Sixth Amendment (1791): "In all criminal prosecutions, the accused shall enjoy the right to a speedy and public trial, by an impartial jury of the State and district wherein the crime shall have been committed...."

In federal civil actions, the courts have tried to make a meaningful distinction between suits for damages under common law and for injunctive relief (a court order to do or not to do something). The latter type of case does not require a jury. The Supreme Court has upheld some grants of authority by Congress to government agencies to award monetary damages without the use of a jury, even though such cases are similar to COMMON LAW suits. The Supreme Court in *Blakely v. Washington* (2004) held that the right to a trial by jury guaranteed under the Sixth Amendment extends not only to the guilt phase of a trial but also to the sentencing phase. The Court noted that the constitutional right to a trial by jury is no mere procedural formality, but rather it is a fundamental reservation of power in our constitutional structure meant to ensure the people's ultimate control in the judiciary. A year later, in *United States v. Booker*, the Court extended the ruling in *Blakely* to cover the Federal Sentencing Guidelines, as amended since being issued in 1994.

Jury Nullification

In a criminal case a jury's refusal to convict a person despite the presentation of evidence beyond a reasonable doubt is called jury nullification. Such nullification generally occurs when the jurors believe that the penalty is unfair—for example, the possibility of a harsh sentence for small-time gambling or overly restrictive liquor laws. Jury nullification is also likely to occur in cases where the DEATH PENALTY is mandated but is deemed too severe a PUNISHMENT. Because some jurors have personal convictions against capital punishment, they would rather have a defendant go free than be given the death penalty even when the evidence of guilt is conclusive. Some recent cases resulting in jury nullification have involved disproportionately harsh penalties for the possession of small amounts of drugs.

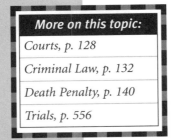

More on this topic:

Courts, p. 128

Criminal Law, p. 132

Death Penalty, p. 140

Trials, p. 556

A fundamental aspect of American democracy, juries represent all citizens in deciding if the government has presented sufficient evidence to warrant punishing a fellow citizen or resident for breaking the law. At the same time, jurors can put themselves in the defendant's shoes. If they conclude that his or her treatment is unjust or prejudicial, they act as a check on unfair laws or prosecution. However, jurors bring with them their own prejudices and misconceptions, which may also influence their decision.

Jurisdiction *See* COURTS; SUPREME COURT.

Jury Nullification *See* DEATH PENALTY; JURIES.

Just Compensation

In *The Communist Manifesto* (1848), published in English in 1888, Karl Marx (1818–83) and Friedrich Engels (1820–95) explained that "the theory of the Communists may be summed up in the single phrase: Abolition of private property." The experiment of vesting ownership of all PROPERTY, or at least income-producing property, in government instead of in individual citizens was tried in many communist countries in the twentieth century and found to be woefully wanting. To make the communist system work initially, private property that the state wanted to control for economic reasons in nations such as the Soviet Union and Cuba had to be confiscated and made state-owned property. After being nationalized in the name of the people or the common good—taken generally without just or fair compensation to the owner—the property was managed by government authorities or transferred to others whom the communist dictatorship determined to be worthy of it.

Even in the United States the concept of eminent domain—the right of the government to acquire private property for public use—is recognized as constitutional. What is unconstitutional, however, according to the Fifth Amendment (1791), is the government's failure to pay just, fair, and prompt compensation to the owner. As the Fifth Amendment states: "...nor shall private property be taken for public use, without just compensation." The constitutions of many other democracies contain a similar guarantee. The 1917 constitution of Mexico and the 1987 constitution of the Philippines, for example, have similar provisions guaranteeing compensation or indemnity for the taking of private property.

Using the Fourteenth Amendment (1868), the just compensation requirement was extended by the Supreme Court in *Chicago, Burlington and Quincy Railway Co. v. Chicago* (1897) to the states, even though most state constitutions have similar provisions. Federal and state courts, however, do not always agree on which factual situations trigger a finding that a taking or regulation of property calls for just compensation.

A Balancing Test

The definition of public use generally is liberally construed by the courts so that even if the government takes private property and turns it over to a private developer, the action may be upheld. A taking, to be compensable, must be at least a nearly complete loss of the use of the property in question. In a 1946 case, *Causby v. United States*, the Supreme Court said that a taking by inverse or indirect condemnation had occurred when farmland at the end of an airport runway was made unusable by frequent low-flying planes; compensation was thus required. Other lesser inconveniences, such as noise from a nearby airport or a busy highway, do not generally constitute a taking under the Fifth Amendment.

Justice OLIVER WENDELL HOLMES JR. explained the problem in an opinion for the Supreme Court in *Pennsylvania Coal Co. v. Mahon* (1922). According to Holmes, there must be a balance (see BALANCING TESTS) between the government's right to regulate property that falls short of a taking under the Fifth Amendment and the private owners' rights to be compensated for those losses when they benefit the public. The public as a whole in those cases must pay just compensation. The factors in Holmes's balancing test include the extent of the owners' loss and their ability to receive some benefit from the property afterward. The amount of compensation now considered just is based on the same factors that set the market price of property—what a willing seller would obtain from a willing buyer—absent the government's involvement.

Former first lady Jacqueline Kennedy Onassis (left) and Bess Myerson, former consumer advocate for New York City, were among the many New Yorkers who battled the construction of a high-rise building over Grand Central Station in the 1970s.
Source: AP Images

In an important case, *Penn Central Transportation Co. v. City of New York* (1978), the Supreme Court upheld New York City's landmarks law, under which the owners of Grand Central Terminal were barred from building a high-rise building over the historic railway station. Although the owners alleged that the historic preservation regulation resulted in a taking without just compensation, the lower court had found that private property owners are due only a "reasonable return" and that society "is also entitled to its due": an unsullied landmark structure that adds vitality to the urban environment. In a more conservative decision, *Lucas v. South Carolina Coastal Council* (1992), the Court found that a land-use regulation denying any economic benefit to an owner who wanted to develop beach-front property went too far and thus ran afoul of the Fifth Amendment's prohibition against a taking of private property without payment of just compensation.

The Supreme Court, in *Lingle v. Chevron U.S.A., Inc.* (2005), retreated somewhat from extending the scope of the Fifth Amendment provisions by refusing to use a formula for determining if a government regulation effects a taking of property requiring just compensation. The Court ruled that the regulation—in this case, a Hawaii statute that limits the rent oil companies may charge dealers leasing company-owned service stations—did not substantially advance the state's asserted interests—in this case, controlling retail gas prices. The Court reiterated that the primary model for a compensable taking by the government is a direct government appropriation or physical invasion of private property and concluded that the "substantially advances" test is inappropriate because it reveals nothing about the magnitude or character of the burden a particular regulation imposes on private property rights or how any regulatory burden is distributed among property owners.

Civil Forfeiture

Property implicated in criminal activity may be seized by the government without compensation; for example, houses, cars, and boats may be taken because of the owners' alleged drug activities. A person found guilty of a crime may also have to forfeit property as a part of his or her PUNISHMENT. In 1993 the Supreme Court began to take a hard look at civil forfeitures with respect to the prohibition in the Eighth Amendment (1791) against "excessive fines" but later backed off. In *Bennis v. Michigan* (1996), the Court upheld the seizure of property even though the owner had no knowledge that it was being used in criminal activities. And in *United States v. Ursery* (1996), the Court held that a person may be prosecuted for a crime and have his or her property seized by the government without running afoul of the constitutional prohibition against multiple punishments.

Outside the constitutional protection of the Fifth Amendment, civil forfeiture often requires a costly private lawsuit to recover property wrongly or mistakenly seized by LAW ENFORCEMENT authorities as property involved in a crime. If property is damaged, the owners may never be compensated. The courts have generally held that under a legal fiction the property itself may be sued as if it had consciously participated in a crime. In 1966, for example, the government sued the weapon used in the assassination of President John F. Kennedy (1917–63) in *The United States v. One 6.5 mm. Mannlicher-Carcano Military Rifle.*

Damages

The monetary amount claimed as compensation for some injury caused by a wrongful act or negligence is called damages. Any such payment recovered in a lawsuit may compensate for a financial loss or for pain and suffering caused by the defendant. Damages may also be exemplary, punitive, and vindictive when they exceed the actual losses claimed and are imposed as a punishment for fraud, actual malice, or violence.

In *Browning-Ferris Industries v. Kelco Disposal, Inc.* (1989), the Supreme Court declared that the Eighth Amendment prohibition against excessive fines did not apply to punitive damages in a civil case between private litigants. Several years later, the Court held that JURIES have wide discretion in setting damages but that there can be a limit to punitive damage awards. In 1996, for the first time, the Supreme Court found in *BMW of North America, Inc. v. Gore* that punitive damages awarded by a state jury were so excessive as to violate the DUE PROCESS clause of the Fourteenth Amendment.

Because justice seeks to make a person whole for a loss caused by another, compensation for a loss of property or for more personal forms of damage is an attempt to do justice. The right to acquire and own property and to be secure in one's person were important to the FRAMERS OF THE CONSTITUTION and they still are to citizens today. Although the American legal system has been criticized as overly litigious and the capitalist economic system as overly materialistic, the alternative of a state-regulated system of property ownership and distribution has been proven to be far less just in the long run.

> **More on this topic:**
>
> *Economic Liberty, p. 173*
>
> *Environment, p. 195*
>
> *Zoning, p. 598*

Justice

"Justice is the end of government," declared JAMES MADISON in essay 52 of *The Federalist* (1787–88) (see FEDERALIST PAPERS). "It is the end of civil society. It ever has been and ever will be pursued until it be obtained, or until liberty be lost in the pursuit." If justice is the goal of any good GOVERNMENT, then it must also be the goal of any good constitution and of those citizens who live under such a constitution. In jurisprudence, justice is defined as the constant and perpetual disposition to render every person his or her due.

One of the Constitution's six goals, stated in the PREAMBLE, is to "establish Justice." The only other place the word *justice* appears in the document is in Article IV in relation to EXTRADITION. Many other national constitutions also include some references to justice. Italy in its constitution (1948) declares that it "repudiates war as an instrument of offense…[and] agrees…to the sovereignty limitations needed by a system which assures peace and justice between nations…." Paraguay's constitution (1992) mentions justice in its preamble and designates the nation's highest court the "Supreme Court of Justice."

> **"Justice…ever has been and ever will be pursued until it be obtained, or until liberty be lost in the pursuit."**
>
> **—James Madison**

The nature of justice—exactly what it means and how it can be obtained—has been debated at least as far back as the fifth century B.C.E. In *The Republic*, written by the Greek philosopher Plato (ca. 428–347 B.C.E.), Socrates is quoted as saying that justice is "sometimes spoken of as the virtue of an individual, and sometimes as the virtue of a State." One of the goals of the delegates to the CONSTITUTIONAL CONVENTION OF 1787 was to create a government that personified the concept of justice as they perceived it.

The Constitution has numerous mechanisms for ensuring justice by curbing the injustices that have plagued people in nations governed by tyrants and despots: the SEPARATION OF POWERS and built-in checks and balances; the specific guarantees of RIGHTS; restrictions on the national and state governments including the BILL OF RIGHTS (1791); regular elections of key public officials; and the accountability of officials through the IMPEACHMENT process.

The Judicial Branch

One of the most important mechanisms for fostering justice throughout the republic was the creation of the SUPREME COURT and the federal judicial system (see JUDICIAL BRANCH). Even if these bodies have not ensured perfect justice, they have evolved to at least reduce the injustices that could be done at the national and state levels of government. The FRAMERS OF THE CONSTITUTION intended that both of the other branches pursue justice in their own spheres of authority. However, the HOUSE OF REPRESENTATIVES, because of its popular, democratic nature, is often viewed as susceptible to the sometimes fickle popular will, and the PRESIDENT, who must act to maximize the government's effectiveness, is viewed as susceptible to overzealously pursuing national goals, such as NATIONAL SECURITY, at the expense of justice for all.

Justice as meted out by the Supreme Court has both an abstract and a concrete quality. In its decision in *Hawkins v. Barney's Lessee* (1831), an example of the former, the Court noted: "It is not to be questioned, that laws limiting the time of bringing suit, constitute a part of the [laws] of every country: they are laws for administering justice; one of the most sacred and important of sovereign rights and duties...." As to the more practical implications of justice, in *Weems v. United States* (1910)—a case in the Philippines involving a sentence of fifteen years' incarceration at hard labor while chained by the ankles, loss of all civil rights, and perpetual surveillance by the police after release for falsifying public documents—the Court declared that such a CRUEL AND UNUSUAL PUNISHMENT "exhibits a difference between unrestrained power and that which is exercised under the spirit of constitutional limitations formed to establish justice."

The Executive Branch

While the courts, in interpreting the laws, can help achieve the Constitution's goal of establishing justice, the EXECUTIVE BRANCH bears the responsibility for administering justice in accordance with the Constitution and the law. Article II, section 3, charges the president to, among other things, "take Care that the Laws be faithfully executed." Justice here is administered mainly through the Department of Justice, headed by the attorney general (see CABINET). Nine Supreme Court justices were attorneys general before joining the Court, and ten others—including one recent member, William H. Rehnquist (1924–2005), and four current members, Chief Justice John G. Roberts, Jr (b. 1955), and justices Samuel A. Alito, Jr (b. 1950), Stephen G. Breyer (b. 1938), and Antonin Scalia (b. 1936)—once served in the Justice Department. The attorney general supervises the national government's various LAW ENFORCEMENT activities, including the Federal Bureau of Investigation and the Drug Enforcement Administration, and issues opinions that guide the executive branch in administering justice. Many other agencies, offices, bureaus, commissions, and boards (see ADMINISTRATIVE AGENCIES) have the power to issue rules and regulations and to hear disputes that affect rights and benefits of citizens and businesses, from the Social Security Administration to the Securities and Exchange Commission.

The Legislative Branch

The LEGISLATIVE BRANCH also plays a role in administering justice. The Constitution in Article VI requires: "The Senators and Representatives...and the Members of the several State Legislatures, and all executive and judicial Officers, both of the United States and of the several States, shall be bound by Oath or Affirmation, to support this Constitution...." Like other public officials, legislators are thus pledged to "establish Justice" as mandated in the preamble of the Constitution. Some laws passed by Congress address justice in specific areas, such as the Equal Access to Justice Act of 1980, which encourages cost reductions in order to obtain justice from the government, and the Juvenile Justice and Delinquency Prevention Act of 1974.

More on this topic:
Courts, p. 128
Criminal Law, p. 132
Juries, p. 320
Trials, p. 556

Justice is not an absolute concept. The Constitution calls not for absolute justice but for the constant pursuit of greater justice.

Justices *See* CHIEF JUSTICE; SUPREME COURT.

Juveniles *See* CHILDREN.

K

Katz v. United States

"I will not distort the words of the [Fourth] Amendment in order to 'keep the Constitution up to date' or 'to bring it into harmony with the times,'" said Justice Hugo L. Black (1886–1971) in *Katz v. United States* (1967). "It was never meant that this Court have such power, which in effect would make us a continuously functioning constitutional convention." Black, a staunch defender of the literal language of the BILL OF RIGHTS (1791) (see STRICT CONSTRUCTION), dissented from the Supreme Court's 7–1 ruling in the case. If the First Amendment, analogized Black, said that "Congress shall make no law…," then there could be no exceptions.

The problem for Justice Black in the *Katz* case was that it involved modern electronic devices: public telephones. In *Olmstead v. United States* (1928), the Supreme Court had upheld WIRETAPPING of telephones in spite of prohibitions against unreasonable searches and seizures in the Fourth Amendment (1791) (see SEARCH AND SEIZURE). In *Olmstead* the Court found that there was no search and no seizure, reasoning that telephone lines extend from a person's house around the world, making them outside the Fourth Amendment's protection, unlike the home itself. Said Chief Justice William Howard Taft (1857–1930), speaking for the Court: "A standard which would forbid the reception of evidence if obtained by other than nice ethical conduct by government officials would make society suffer and give criminals greater immunity than has been known heretofore."

When Katz was tried for gambling, the prosecution introduced evidence obtained without a search warrant from an electronic listening and recording device placed on the public telephone booth he regularly used for "transmitting wagering information." The key question for the Court

was whether the Fourth Amendment's protection against unreasonable searches and seizures extends beyond the home to a public telephone booth.

Justice Black looked to the Fourth Amendment and saw that it prohibited unreasonable searches and seizures of "persons, houses, papers, and effects." The amendment does not mention public telephone booths. The opinion of the Court, delivered by Justice Potter Stewart (1915–85) (Justice THURGOOD MARSHALL did not participate in the decision), said that the government's eavesdropping activities violated the defendant's PRIVACY, which he had justifiably relied on while using a public telephone booth.

Then the Court answered two questions concerning the privacy afforded by a public telephone booth. First, was a public telephone booth a constitutionally protected area, such that an eavesdropping device violated the user's privacy? Second, was physical penetration of a constitutionally protected area necessary to constitute a violation of privacy as guaranteed under the Fourth Amendment? The answer to the first question was yes and to the second, no.

Obviously the FRAMERS OF THE CONSTITUTION and those who proposed and ratified the Bill of Rights could not have anticipated the invention of the telephone or the nature and use of a public telephone booth. But the Supreme Court reasoned that the same considerations governing a citizen's expectation of privacy at home must be "transferred from the setting of a home, an office, or a hotel room to that of a telephone booth. Wherever a man may be, he is entitled to know that he will remain free from unreasonable searches and seizures. The government agents here ignored 'the procedure of antecedent justification' [obtaining a judicial warrant before using the eavesdropping device]…that is central to the Fourth Amendment…."

In the same year that *Katz* was decided, the Supreme Court in *Berger v. New York* struck down a state eavesdropping statute that unconstitutionally permitted eavesdropping "without requiring belief that any particular offense has been or is being committed; nor that the 'property' sought, the conversations, be particularly described."

As the surveillance capabilities of LAW ENFORCEMENT become more sophisticated, the courts—despite Justice Black's fear that the Supreme Court may become a "continuously functioning constitutional convention"—continuously review the reasons behind particular constitutional rights to ensure that certain ones are not infringed simply because of new technology. In *Kyllo v. United States* (2001), for example, the Court held that the warrantless use from the air of heat-sensing devices such as a thermal imager to detect marijuana plants being grown inside a home violated the Fourth Amendment.

National Security

Citing its decision in *United States v. United States District Court* (1972)—"a logical extension…of the ruling in Katz"—for the conclusion that that the Fourth Amendment does not permit warrantless wiretaps in cases involving domestic threats to the

> **"I will not distort the words of the [Fourth] Amendment in order to 'keep the Constitution up to date' or 'to bring it into harmony with the times.'"**
>
> **—Justice Hugo L. Black**

CLOSER LOOK

When Roy Olmstead was convicted in the 1920s of selling alcohol illegally, he appealed his case all the way to the Supreme Court. The police had wiretapped his private telephone conversations without obtaining a warrant, which Olmstead claimed violated such constitutional guarantees as the Fourth Amendment's ban on "unreasonable searches and seizures."

In a 5–4 decision, the justices upheld the conviction in 1928. They reasoned that law enforcement agents merely listened to conversations but did not seize anything.

But the Court's decision in *Olmstead v. United States* is most remembered for the dissenting opinion of Justice Louis Brandeis (1856–1941). "The makers of our Constitution…conferred, as against the Government, the right to be let alone—the most comprehensive of rights, and the right most valued by civilized men," Brandeis wrote. "To protect that right, every unjustifiable intrusion by the Government upon the privacy of the individual, whatever the means employed, must be deemed a violation of the Fourth Amendment."

Almost forty years later, Brandeis was vindicated when the Court ruled in *Katz v. United States* that Fourth Amendment protections extend to conversations in public telephone booths. Search and seizure issues aside, Brandeis's dissent also became highly influential in legal debates over the right to PRIVACY.

More on this topic:

Communications, p. 104

Drugs, p. 165

Science and Technology, p. 477

national security, the U.S. Supreme Court in *Mitchell v. Forsyth* (1985) nevertheless held that the attorney general of the United States was entitled to qualified immunity from a lawsuit for his authorization of a wiretap for the purpose of gathering intelligence regarding activities that threatened the nation's security notwithstanding his action violated the Fourth Amendment. After the *Mitchell* decision, in 1986 roving wiretaps were regularly used to track suspected drug dealers. After the terrorist attacks in the United States on September 11, 2001, Congress passed the PATRIOT ACT, which specifically authorizes roving wiretaps under the Foreign Intelligence Surveillance Act of 1978.

Kelo v. City of New London

The framers of the Constitution did not expressly address the legal concept of eminent domain, the right a government retains to take private PROPERTY for public use. But the concept of the right of individuals to own and use their own property was of foremost interest to them. The "unalienable Rights [of] Life, Liberty, and the pursuit of Happiness" in the DECLARATION OF INDEPENDENCE (1776), in fact, paraphrased an earlier declaration by the English philosopher John Locke (1632–1704) of the rights to life, liberty, and property. Moreover, in the essays in *The Federalist* (1787–88) by Alexander Hamilton, John Jay, and James Madison (see FEDERALIST PAPERS) in support of adoption of the draft U.S. Constitution, the "public good" is often equated with "happiness."

The notion of eminent domain, however, is directly implicated in the language of the Fifth Amendment (1791) to the Constitution and later in the Fourteenth Amendment (1868) in what are known as the due process clauses, which guarantee that neither the federal or a state government "shall deprive any person of life, liberty, or property, without due process of law." The relevant text in the Fifth Amendment reads, "nor shall private property be taken for public use, without just compensation." Two separate questions usually arise in cases involving eminent domain: Is the government's action in taking private property permitted by the Constitution, and if so, is the compensation offered just? (See JUST COMPENSATION.)

In *Kelo v. City of New London, Conn.* (2005), the SUPREME COURT addressed the question of how far a state agency may go to take "private property...for public use." In 2000 the city of New London, Connecticut, approved a plan to revitalize its economy. In implementing the plan, the city purchased a number of privately owned properties from willing sellers. However, several owners were unwilling to sell their properties. The city's development agent brought condemnation actions in state court to compel the recalcitrant owners to transfer their property for just compensation. The property acquired by the city's agent would be transferred to a private developer to build a $300 million dollar research facility, which was expected to help rejuvenate the economically depressed area of the city. The owners who did not wish to sell brought an action in state court to halt the condemnation proceedings. They alleged that the planned state taking of their property violated the public use requirement of the Fifth Amendment because the properties were not going to be used for a public facility such as a park or a fire station, but were going to other private parties that would stand to gain economically from the petitioners' loss of their property.

The Supreme Court, in what would turn out to be a highly controversial 5–4 decision written by Justice John Paul Stevens (b. 1920), with one concurring opinion and four dissents, held that the city's proposed disposition of the holdout owners' property did qualify as a "public use" within the meaning of the takings clause of the Fifth Amendment. Citing Justice Oliver Wendell Holmes Jr.'s opinion in *Strickley v. Highland Boy Gold Mining Co.* (1906), in which he highlighted "the inadequacy of use by the general public as a universal test" of "public use" as used in the Constitution,

Justice Stevens went on to say that "[p]romoting economic development is a traditional and long accepted function of government." While there may not be a "bright-line rule" for all cases, should an attempt be made by a state agency to simply transfer property owned by one citizen to another outside of a similar "integrated development plan" as in the present case, it "would certainly raise a suspicion that a private [an unconstitutional] purpose was afoot."

A dissenting opinion, which was joined in by Chief Justice William H. Rehnquist and Justices Antonin Scalia and Clarence Thomas, was written by Justice Sandra Day O'Connor. A separate dissenting opinion was also written by Justice Thomas. In her opinion, Justice O'Connor warned that because of the Court's decision "[t]he specter of condemnation hangs over all property," and thus the value of all property is downgraded. "Nothing," she continues, "is to prevent the State from replacing any Motel 6 with a Ritz-Carlton, any home with a shopping mall, or any farm with a factory."

Immediately after the *Kelo* decision public opinion polls registered strong disapproval of it, and President George W. Bush issued an executive order directing that the federal government restrict its use of eminent domain where economic development issues were involved. Some states also took steps to limit the extent of government takings of private property permissible under *Kelo*. But in 2006 California voters turned down a proposed constitutional amendment that would limit government taking of private property to only where it was for occupation by a government agency or government-regulated entity.

To date, however, state authorities have not made a wholesale rush to upgrade private properties to higher economic use by condemning and transferring them from one citizen to another. The extent to which the government may go under the Constitution to transfer wealth from one group of citizens to another remains an ongoing one that encompasses other questions including earmarked appropriations by Congress, no-bid government contracts, TAXATION, and WELFARE, to name just a few. The preamble to the Constitution sets the nation's sights on the creation of a "more perfect Union," but the methods governments choose to reach this goal are constantly being debated. How government must treat private property is a key concern in that debate.

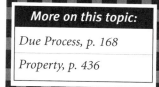

More on this topic:

Due Process, p. 168

Property, p. 436

King, Martin Luther, Jr.

Struck down by an assassin's bullet at the height of his career, Martin Luther King Jr. (1929–68) left the world a legacy of leadership in the field of CIVIL RIGHTS, HUMAN RIGHTS, and constitutional rights. King, born in Atlanta, led a nonviolent revolution aimed at bringing the Constitution's promise of equality closer to reality. Educated at Morehouse College and Crozer Theological Seminary, he received a Ph.D. in theology from Boston University in 1955. A Baptist minister beginning in 1947, he became an active member of the National Association for the Advancement of Colored People (NAACP) and the Alabama Council for Human Relations.

The pernicious practice of SLAVERY and the slave trade are a part of American history and are reflected in the Constitution as drafted in 1787. Article I, section 2, counted slaves as "three fifths of all other Persons" for the purposes of apportioning representatives in Congress and direct taxes. Article IV, section 2, required the return of escaped slaves, and Article V gave Congress until 1808 before acting to abolish the importation of slaves. Many of the delegates to the CONSTITUTIONAL CONVENTION OF 1787 were opposed to slavery, but to maintain the Union of the thirteen states, compromises were made. After the Civil War (1861–65) and the enactment of the Thirteenth (1865), Fourteenth (1868), and Fifteenth (1870) Amendments, the Constitution held out a new promise that freed slaves would be equal citizens under federal and state laws.

Even so, after the Civil War southern states passed so-called Jim Crow laws segregating and generally making former slaves second-class citizens (see SEGREGATION). In *Plessy v. Ferguson* (1896),

Following the model of the pacifist Mahatma Gandhi, the Reverend Martin Luther King Jr. in the 1960s fashioned a nonviolent movement to make the Constitution work for all Americans regardless of their race. Calling himself a "drum major for justice," King spoke out and led boycotts and marches that called attention to civil rights violations suffered by the nation's black citizens.
Source: The Granger Collection, New York

More on this topic:

Racial Discrimination,
p. 449

the Supreme Court confirmed the constitutionality of the discriminatory doctrine of "separate but equal" public facilities. The Supreme Court's decision in BROWN V. BOARD OF EDUCATION OF TOPEKA (1954), which declared this doctrine unconstitutional and directed that public schools be desegregated, ushered in a new era of promise for a colorblind American society. However, there were still many discriminatory holdovers of segregation in the South, for example, separate seating for blacks and whites on public transportation, in public accommodations, and in commercial businesses.

After a black woman, Rosa Parks, was arrested in 1955 for refusing to sit at the back of a public bus in Montgomery, Alabama, King and other black leaders in Alabama organized a boycott that ended the discriminatory practice and led to the hiring of black bus drivers. In 1956 the Supreme Court confirmed the unconstitutionality of segregated buses. An admirer of the Indian civil and human rights leader Mahatma Gandhi (1869–1948), King adopted Gandhi's nonviolent methods of confronting and challenging racially discriminatory practices and soon became the acknowledged leader of the civil rights movement in the United States.

In 1963 King and a black college student civil rights organization, the Student Nonviolent Coordinating Committee, held mass demonstrations in Birmingham, Alabama, where police officials were known for their strong opposition to integration. The violence that occurred between the police and the civil rights demonstrators became world news and led President John F. Kennedy (1917–63) to submit a legislative proposal that became the Civil Rights Act of 1964, banning DISCRIMINATION in public accommodations, federally funded programs, and employment. The Voting Rights Act of 1965 then protected the right of suffrage for African Americans—all tangible results of the civil rights movement for which King had worked so tirelessly and effectively. On August 28, 1963, after a civil rights march, King delivered his now-famous "I Have a Dream" speech at the Lincoln Memorial in the nation's capital. King also played a role in an important Supreme Court decision, NEW YORK TIMES CO. V. SULLIVAN (1964), in which the Court held that an advertisement in the *New York Times* seeking support for King's civil rights activities did not libel a Montgomery, Alabama, city commissioner by falsely portraying police conduct.

In 1964 King was awarded the Nobel Peace Prize for his nonviolent civil rights crusade. Having achieved a number of substantial goals in the movement toward equality for African Americans in the United States, he began speaking out against the Vietnam War and in 1967 undertook planning for a "Poor Peoples' March" on Washington, D.C., in support of the plight of people of all races. His life, however, was ended on April 4, 1968, in Memphis, Tennessee, after he was shot by James Earl Ray, who was later convicted of murder. To commemorate the achievements and sacrifices of King's life, his birthday, January 15, has been designated a national holiday.

L

Labor

In *The Laws*, Plato, the Greek philosopher of the fourth century B.C.E., praised "the class of crafts-men who have enriched our lives by their arts and skills," yet he recommended harsh PUNISHMENT for work not accomplished in the amount of time stipulated. And in ancient Rome the plebeians (common workers) would occasionally stage a strike to protest their ill treatment by the patricians (upper class).

This struggle between employees and their employers over wages, working conditions, and benefits of employment has endured since the first large-scale human settlements, when a class of free persons emerged to produce goods and services for those who could pay for them. "In the constant struggle about wages between these two classes," observed Alexis de Tocqueville (1805–59) in *Democracy in America* (1835), "power is thus divided, and success goes first to one, then to the other." As the French political scientist noted, however, "It even seems probable that in the long run the workers' interest should prevail. For the high wages they have already gained make them daily less dependent on their masters, and in proportion, as they are more indepen-dent, it is easier for them to obtain higher wages." When the supply of labor is plentiful in relation to the demand, employers are in the driver's seat, but of course the opposite is true when the re-verse conditions prevail.

Although the U.S. Constitution does not address the rights of workers, modern constitutions of other nations do. For example, Hungary's constitution (1949, revised 1972 and 1989) provides that "everyone shall have the right to work, to freedom of choice of employment and occupation." It also guarantees "equal pay for equal work," along with the right to fair compensation for labor per-formed and the "right to rest and leisure and to regular holidays, with pay." Greece's constitution

A Labor Day parade in New York City in the early 1900s provides an opportunity for the Women's Auxiliary Typographical Union to promote the American labor movement, whose goals have included better working conditions, benefits, and fair wages for all workers.
Source: Library of Congress

(1975) states: "General working conditions shall be determined by law, supplemented by collective labour agreements contracted through free negotiations and, in case of the failure of such, by rules determined by arbitration."

Labor Policy before the New Deal

In the nineteenth century, international labor conventions were held in Europe to address the industrial revolution's pernicious effects on workers, and then in 1919 the International Labor Organization was founded as an autonomous intergovernmental organization to promote the rights and interests of workers around the world. The growth of and support for labor UNIONS beginning in the first half of the twentieth century played an important role in establishing the rights and protections of workers in America.

However, until the Great Depression in the 1930s triggered the New Deal programs of President Franklin D. Roosevelt (1882–1945), the nation's courts, including the Supreme Court, were generally more supportive of flexibility in private labor arrangements than of broader protections for workers.

In a series of cases—*Allgeyer v. Louisiana* (1897), *Lochner v. New York* (1905), *Adair v. United States* (1908), and *Coppage v. Kansas* (1915)—the Supreme Court struck down legislative attempts by the states and the federal government to promote better working conditions and relations between employers and employees. In *Lochner v. New York* (1905), the justices ruled that employees' ECONOMIC LIBERTY was infringed by regulations setting the maximum number of hours that they could work in a day.

The Supreme Court not only opposed the regulation of workers' conditions in general, but in *Hammer v. Dagenhart* (1918) it also struck down laws to curb the abuses of child labor (see CHILDREN). In addition, a constitutional amendment proposed in 1926 to grant Congress "power to limit, regulate, and prohibit the labor of persons under eighteen years of age" has never been ratified by the states (see AMENDMENTS).

During this period the use of court-ordered injunctions was commonly used to stop workers and union activists who were picketing or organizing boycotts of businesses that refused to negotiate or meet the workers' demands. In *Truax v. Corrigan* (1921), the Supreme Court said that a provision in an Arizona statute permitting peaceful picketing (see ASSEMBLY AND ASSOCIATION) deprived an owner of his property and thus violated the EQUAL PROTECTION clause of the Fourteenth Amendment (1868). It was not until 1937 that the Supreme Court in *Senn v. Tile Layers Protective Union* upheld a state statute—not appreciably different from the statute it had invalidated in the *Truax* case—banning such injunctions.

In *Dorchy v. Kansas* (1924), the Supreme Court ruled that a state statute requiring employers and employees to submit wage and hour disputes to state arbitration was unconstitutional. And by a 5–4 vote in 1936, in *Carter v. Carter Coal Co.*, the Court invalidated a federal act, the Bituminous Coal Conservation Act of 1935, that sought to regulate wages and hours of work in the coal industry, relying on a STRICT CONSTRUCTION of Congress's enumerated powers in the Constitution—in this case the COMMERCE clause in Article I, section 8—and the reserve powers of the STATES under the Tenth Amendment (1791).

The New Deal

The tide turned the following year when the Supreme Court upheld the National Labor Relations Act (1935) in *National Labor Relations Board v. Jones and Laughlin Steel Corp.* (1937). The case was argued before the Court less than a week after Roosevelt announced his "court-packing" plan to create new seats on the Supreme Court and appoint members who would find constitutional his New Deal legislative program aimed at ameliorating the effects of the Depression. That plan undoubtedly had an impact on the Court's 5–4 decision upholding the act and actions taken by the board under it against the Jones and Laughlin Steel Corporation. In an abrupt reversal of the Court's long-term leanings, Chief Justice Charles Evans Hughes (1862–1948) declared that the "fundamental principle is that the power to regulate commerce is the power to enact 'all appropriate legislation' for its protection or advancement...; to adopt measures 'to promote the growth and insure its safety'...[and] 'to foster, protect, control and restrain.... That power is plenary and may be exerted to protect interstate commerce 'no matter what the source of the dangers which threaten it.'"

> "[T]he power to regulate commerce is the power to enact 'all appropriate legislation' for its protection or advancement...."
>
> —**Chief Justice Charles Evans Hughes**

With some minor exceptions—for example, the Supreme Court's decision in *National League of Cities v. Usery* (1976) striking down a 1974 federal law extending maximum-hour and minimum-wage provisions of the Fair Labor Standards Act (1938) (sometimes called the Wages and Hours Act)—the Court has continued to uphold the extension of federal labor laws to the states. In *Garcia v. San Antonio Metropolitan Transit Authority* (1985), it abandoned the position it took in *Usery*, once again freeing Congress from any restrictions on its commerce power under the Constitution and upholding the application of federal minimum-wage and maximum-hour regulations to a city-owned and -operated transportation system.

More recently, however, the Supreme Court has ruled against union activities in terms of the First Amendment's guarantee of freedom of association and the right to petition the government. In *BE Construction Co. v. National Labor Relations Board* (2002), the Court overruled the NLRB's determination that unions could file a grievance with the board to protest an unmeritorious and harassing lawsuit by employers in retaliation for the unions' going on strike. In its decision the Court noted that the right to petition is one of the most precious liberties safeguarded by the Bill of Rights (1791). Then, in *Davenport v. Washington Education Association* (2007), the Court ruled against public-sector unions' use of common funds for political campaigns supported by the union leadership, holding that a state law that required the unions, which collected agency fees from nonmembers, to receive affirmative authorization from such nonmembers before their fees could be spent on election-related activities did not violate the expressive or associational rights of the unions.

The regulation of working conditions in the United States is still less extensive than that of most other major industrial and postindustrial nations, and the Constitution holds little promise for workers seeking protection of their rights apart from state and national legislation that passes constitutional muster according to the courts. America has traditionally been considered a land of opportunity—not of social guarantees—partly because of the strong commitment of many of its political leaders to the capitalist economic system (see ECONOMIC LIBERTY) and the long-held fear of communism, which is often equated with socialist policies that strengthen the rights of workers at the expense of free enterprise. However, a balance can be struck between the power of employers to hire and fire employees to ensure the survival and profitability of their businesses and the right of employees to strike and boycott to ensure decent wages, benefits, and working conditions.

Lame Ducks

A lame duck is a wounded bird that does not have long to live. In Great Britain the term refers to a bankrupt business person, while on Wall Street it denotes someone who is unable to meet his or her financial commitments. In politics and government, however, a lame duck is an office holder whose authority is due to expire in the near future.

The Twentieth Amendment (1933) is referred to as the "Lame Duck Amendment." "The terms of the President and Vice President shall end at noon on the 20th day of January," states section 1, "and the terms of Senators and Representatives at noon on the 3rd day of January, of the years in which such terms would have ended if this article had not been ratified; and the terms of their successors shall then begin." According to section 2, "The Congress shall assemble at least once in every year, and such meeting shall begin at noon on the 3rd day of January, unless they shall by law appoint a different day."

Before the amendment, these officials had taken office on March 4 of the year following an election. Because Congress had set the date of federal ELECTIONS as Tuesday after the first Monday in November, an incumbent may have been defeated at the polls in November but could continue to vote in CONGRESS until March. In Congress the long period in between became known as the lame-duck session.

The problem with lame-duck sessions was exacerbated when a different party was about to control the incoming Congress. It was just such a lame-duck session that created havoc in 1801. Congress, controlled by the Federalist Party—which was voted out of power in November 1800—confirmed the appointment by a fellow Federalist Party member, President JOHN ADAMS, who had been defeated at the polls, of William Marbury to be a justice of the peace. The stage was thus set for the landmark Supreme Court decision in the case of MARBURY V. MADISON (1803), establishing the Court's power of JUDICIAL REVIEW to declare acts of Congress unconstitutional.

Presidents have also been referred to as lame ducks, including Lyndon B. Johnson (1908–73), who decided not to seek reelection in 1968, and Jimmy Carter (b. 1924), who lost his bid for a second term in 1980. In addition, the Twenty-second Amendment (1951) prohibits the PRESIDENT from serving a third term, making even two-term presidents essentially lame ducks at the end of their second term. A lame duck in this case is a person holding an office of great power whose power is about to expire and who thus becomes weaker by the day.

CLOSER LOOK

Lame-duck sessions—congressional sessions held after an election—became more common as political rancor increased in the latter decades of the twentieth century. A lame-duck session was held in every even-numbered year from 1998 through 2006.

Law

"The prophecies of what the courts will do in fact, and nothing more pretentious," explained Supreme Court Justice OLIVER WENDELL HOLMES JR., "are what I mean by the law." Another definition is a command that is enforced by the paramount authority in a political society. Constitutions, judicial precedent, legislation, and custom create law. The term *law* appears in the Constitution more than twenty times. Article VI, for example, provides: "This Constitution, and the Laws of the United States which shall be made in Pursuance thereof; and all Treaties made, or which shall be made, under the Authority of the United States, shall be the supreme Law of the Land…" (see TREATIES).

Constitutional Law

A constitution is the supreme law of a political jurisdiction such as a nation or a state. It may be written, like the U.S. Constitution, or it may be unwritten—not contained in a single authoritative document but based on generally accepted customs and traditions, like the constitution of the United Kingdom. A constitutional law is one that is valid according to a particular constitution.

Constitutional law is the branch of law that deals with the organization and framework of government. In the United States, it relates particularly to the decisions of the SUPREME COURT that interpret and apply the provisions of the Constitution and that review laws and actions of the federal and state governments in light of the grants and limitations spelled out in the Constitution (see JUDICIAL REVIEW). States and several territories of the United States—American Samoa, the Commonwealth of the Northern Mariana Islands, and Puerto Rico—also have constitutions and their own bodies of constitutional law.

Statutory Law

Statutory laws are enacted by constitutionally authorized legislatures or otherwise promulgated constitutionally. In the United States, bills passed by Congress and state legislatures are statutory laws (see LEGISLATION). Statutes may be public (applying in general to all cited) or private (having special application to particular persons or places). All such laws or statutes must be in consonance with the provisions of the constitution under whose authority they are made. In *MARBURY V. MADISON* (1803), the Supreme Court held that a law passed by Congress could not enlarge the scope of the Court's own powers as set forth in the Constitution.

Common Law

COMMON LAW is a system of law that derives its authority from the decisions of COURTS rather than from any statute passed by a legislature. The Seventh Amendment (1791) recognized common law. "In Suits at common law, where the value in controversy shall exceed twenty dollars [then a considerable amount], the right of trial by jury shall be preserved…" (see JURIES; TRIALS). Like the Second Amendment (1791), however, this amendment has never been incorporated into the Fourteenth Amendment (1868) (see INCORPORATION DOCTRINE) as have most other provisions of the BILL OF RIGHTS, and thus it is not applicable to the STATES.

A parallel system called equity law developed in the English courts to allow new remedies for which common law and statutory law were inadequate. Equity is a method by which courts can judge which of two parties is entitled to a remedy. For example, according to equitable principles of law, a plaintiff cannot seek help from an equity court unless he has "clean hands" (has acted correctly with respect to the subject matter of his suit). The separate common and equity law systems are recognized in the Eleventh Amendment (1798): "The Judicial power of the United States shall not be construed to extend to any suit in law or equity, commenced or prosecuted against one of the United States by Citizens of another State, or by Citizens or Subjects of any Foreign State."

International Law

The Constitution refers to international law in Article I, section 8: "The Congress shall have Power…To define and punish Piracies and Felonies committed on the high Seas, and Offences

CLOSER LOOK

Congress passes dozens or hundreds of new laws every year. But those represent just a fraction of the number of bills that are introduced.

For a bill to become a law, it must be passed in identical form by both the House of Representatives and the Senate and signed by the president. The process typically takes at least several months. Opponents have many opportunities to derail a bill, including defeating it in a committee or on the House or Senate floor, weakening it through amendments, or simply creating so many procedural obstacles that Congress runs out of time to pass it.

In the 109th Congress, which served from 2005 to 2007, lawmakers introduced 10,703 bills and resolutions. Only 396 were ultimately enacted.

against the Law of Nations [international law]" (see ADMIRALTY AND MARITIME LAW). INTERNATIONAL LAW refers to the accepted practices among nations in dealing with one another and with problems of a regional or a worldwide nature (see FOREIGN AFFAIRS). Unlike domestic or municipal law—the law used internally in nations—international law is obeyed by nations only on a voluntary basis. There is no mechanism for enforcing it on a par with the LAW ENFORCEMENT capabilities within nations.

Federal and State Law

Under the federal system of government in the United States (see FEDERALISM), each semisovereign state and the national government have separate legal systems and laws made up of both laws enacted by legislatures and law developed through judicial decisions of federal and state courts. The Constitution requires, however, that all laws must be in consonance with its provisions and the interpretation of those provisions by the federal courts and ultimately the Supreme Court.

More on this topic:

Admiralty and Maritime Law, p. 13

Common Law, p. 102

Criminal Law, p. 132

International Law, p. 304

Legislation, p. 343

The *Marbury* case confirmed the power of the Supreme Court to determine the constitutionality of national laws, and in *MARTIN V. HUNTER'S LESSEE* (1816), the Court held that it could determine on appeal cases pending before state courts as well, thus giving it power to ensure that state court decisions were uniformly in accord with the Constitution. And in *MCCULLOCH V. MARYLAND* (1819), the Court held that the Constitution and the national laws made pursuant to it are supreme laws and cannot be otherwise affected by the states. The separate national and state legal systems provide a rich supply of potential constitutional conflicts for the Supreme Court to address and settle.

Law is the primary means by which a nation or another political jurisdiction maintains order and creates rights and responsibilities for its CITIZENS. Laws are imperfect, but they are necessary in any ordered human society to protect life, LIBERTY, and PROPERTY.

Law Enforcement

The LEGISLATIVE BRANCH makes the laws, and the JUDICIAL BRANCH interprets and applies them to cases and controversies that come before the COURTS, but it is the EXECUTIVE BRANCH that has the primary responsibility under the Constitution for enforcing the laws. After Chief Justice JOHN MARSHALL, on behalf of the Supreme Court, struck down a state law in *Worcester v. State of Georgia* (1832), President Andrew Jackson (1767–1845) is reported to have replied in anger: "John Marshall has made his decision, now let him enforce it."

Enforcement of the LAW is basic to the internal security of a nation and its citizens (see NATIONAL SECURITY) and derives from the government's inherent SOVEREIGNTY, which gives it a monopoly on such power within its territorial jurisdiction. Enforcement by private individuals—vigilantes—is a characteristic of lawlessness.

State Law Enforcement

When the Constitution went into effect in 1789, state and local governments had the primary responsibility for law enforcement. While this is still the case, the Supreme Court has generally upheld congressional efforts to expand the federal government's law enforcement jurisdiction and has increased its own power to strike down state laws as unconstitutional (see JUDICIAL REVIEW).

As an example of the former, the Supreme Court in *Champion v. Ames* (the Lottery Case) in 1903 upheld congressional legislation making the conduct of interstate lotteries a criminal offense, saying that just as states may ban lotteries to protect the morals of their own people, so Congress could protect interstate COMMERCE from the "widespread pestilence of lotteries." As an example of the latter type of case, in *Dombrowski v. Pfister* (1965), the Court upheld an injunction prohibiting the enforcement of state criminal laws that constituted "overly broad and vague regulations of expression" such that criminal prosecution under them could inhibit freedom of SPEECH under the First Amendment (1791).

Presidential Powers

National constitutions generally vest the power to enforce the laws in a chief executive. The constitution of the Philippines (1987) states that its president "shall have control of all the executive departments, bureaus, and offices. He shall ensure that the laws are faithfully executed." The Greek constitution (1975) provides: "The President of the Republic shall issue the decrees required for the execution of laws; he may never suspend the application of laws nor exempt anyone from their execution."

Article II, section 3, of the U.S. Constitution mandates that the PRESIDENT "shall take Care that the Laws be faithfully executed." Other provisions give the chief executive the power to appoint key national law enforcement officials (see APPOINTMENT AND REMOVAL POWER), among them the attorney general of the United States (see CABINET), and to command the military and state militias to enforce the laws if need be (see ARMED FORCES). Article IV, section 4, further authorizes the federal government to protect the STATES from domestic violence. President Grover Cleveland (1837–1908), for example, ordered federal troops to Chicago in 1894 to prevent striking workers from interfering with railroad transportation.

Enforcement Acts. In a precedent-setting case, *Martin v. Mott* (1827), the Supreme Court upheld an order by President JAMES MADISON pursuant to the Enforcement Act of 1795, calling out the state militias in the face of an imminent invasion by the British during the War of 1812. At the beginning of the Civil War (1861–65), President ABRAHAM LINCOLN relied on this case for the extraordinary measures he took on his own authority, such as blockading the South, doubling the size of the armed forces, and suspending the writ of HABEAS CORPUS—unconstitutionally, as the Supreme Court later held. However, in a Louisiana case that arose during the postwar Reconstruction era, *United States v. Cruikshank* (1876), the Court refused to uphold the criminal prosecution of an armed band of white men who killed more than one hundred black men in the Colfax Massacre, a dispute over the election of the governor. The justices based their rejection of federal jurisdiction in the case on the grounds that no denial of federal rights was alleged, in spite of the provisions of the Enforcement Act of 1870 prohibiting conspiracies to deny citizens their constitutional rights.

Justice Department. The executive branch's main agency for enforcing the law is the Department of Justice, headed by the attorney general. The Justice Department includes the Federal Bureau of Investigation, Drug Enforcement Administration, and U.S. Marshals Service. The FBI is responsible for investigating federal crimes, while the Marshals Service—the nation's oldest law enforcement agency, founded in 1789—provides protection to the federal judiciary, transports prisoners, and protects endangered WITNESSES, among other responsibilities.

Other Executive Branch Law Enforcement Activities. The Department of the Treasury includes the Internal Revenue Service, which enforces the federal tax laws (see TAXATION). The U.S. Customs Service is responsible for enforcing laws regarding the importation of items from other countries and is the principal agency charged with guarding the borders of the United States. The U.S. Secret Service was created to enforce laws against counterfeiting and also provides protection for the president. The Treasury Department runs the interagency Federal Law Enforcement Training Center. Many other executive branch agencies (see ADMINISTRATIVE AGENCIES) have some law enforcement

The Federal Bureau of Investigation (FBI) helped protect the nation's aviation system after the September 11, 2001, terrorist attacks.
Source: AP Images/Stephen J. Boitano

powers in the specific areas of their expertise, among them the Securities and Exchange Commission and the Federal Trade Commission.

Pardons. Another aspect of the president's law enforcement authority is vested in him by Article II, section 2, which states: "The President...shall have Power to grant Reprieves and Pardons for Offences against the United States, except in Cases of Impeachment" (see PARDONS). The president may pardon a person any time after a crime has been committed or alleged to have been committed. A reprieve simply reduces the severity of the PUNISHMENT without removing the legal finding of guilt.

Supreme Court Supervision

The judicial branch monitors federal law enforcement activities for their compliance with the law and the Constitution. In *Rea v. United States* (1956), for example, the Supreme Court asserted its authority by enjoining a federal agent from testifying in a state court on the basis of evidence that was obtained without a valid search warrant and was not admissible in a federal court (see SEARCH AND SEIZURE). According to Justice William O. Douglas (1898–1980), the case "raises not a constitutional question but one concerning our supervisory powers over federal law enforcement agencies." More recently with respect to search and seizures by law enforcement officials, in *Muehler v. Mena* (2005), the Supreme Court reconfirmed its decision in *Michigan v. Summers* (1981), in which it had "posited three legitimate law enforcement interests that provide substantial justification for detaining [the] occupant" of premises to be searched: "preventing flight in the event that incriminating evidence is found"; "minimizing the risk of harm to the [law enforcement] officers"; and facilitating "the orderly completion of the search," as detainees' "self-interest may induce them to open locked doors or locked containers to avoid the use of force."

In *Department of Justice v. Landano* (1993), the FBI withheld information under an exemption in the Freedom of Information Act (1966), which was passed to facilitate public access to government information, for records "compiled for law enforcement purposes." The Supreme Court held that the government was not entitled to a presumption that all sources supplying information to the FBI in a criminal investigation are confidential within the meaning of the FOIA exemption, but it suggested that affidavits might be offered to a court in camera (nonpublicly) to establish whether or not disclosure could compromise legitimate interests of the law enforcement agency.

Law enforcement officials from the local police force to the state police to national law enforcement agencies have both a duty and a responsibility under the Constitution. The duty to enforce laws carries with it the responsibility of obeying the letter and the spirit of the Constitution and all other laws to be enforced.

More on this topic:
Criminal Law, p. 132
Domestic Tranquility, p. 161
Emergency Powers, p. 187
Police Power, p. 401

Law of the Land   *See* DUE PROCESS.

Law of the Sea   *See* ADMIRALTY AND MARITIME LAW; INTERNATIONAL LAW.

Lawrence v. Texas

Following the reasoning developed in several earlier cases involving the right of PRIVACY, such as *GRISWOLD V. CONNECTICUT* (1965) and *ROE V. WADE* (1973), the U.S. Supreme Court in *Lawrence v. Texas* (2003) overruled *Bowers v. Hardwick* (1986) and declared that state laws prohibiting intimate sexual relations between consenting homosexual adults were unconstitutional under the due process clause of the Fourteenth Amendment (1868).

Much like the ABORTION issue in the United States, the rights of homosexuals, as well as of others whose sexual orientation deviates from strict heterosexuality, has resulted in a pitched battle between various factions of the citizenry. Religious, moral, and human rights arguments have been bandied about on both sides of the questions regarding the extent to which homosexual behavior should be condoned by society and the law and the extent to which homosexuals should be considered a protected class like ethnic, religious, and racial minorities.

In *Bowers*, the Supreme Court considered a Georgia law that made sodomy a felony that could result in up to twenty years in prison for conviction. The defendants were homosexuals, and the Court addressed only that aspect of the law and gave no opinion as to heterosexual acts of sodomy also covered by the Georgia law. In 1961 all fifty states had laws making sodomy a crime, but as of 1986 only twenty-four states and the District of Columbia still had such laws on the books. The opinion of the Court, upholding the constitutionality of the law, focused on the difficulty of the majority justices concluding that the conduct at issue could be considered "deeply rooted in [the] Nation's history" or "implicit in the concept of ordered liberty" and therefore worthy of the constitutional protection that had been extended by the Court in previous cases involving family, marriage, and procreation.

The *Lawrence* case involved a Texas law similar to the Georgia law in *Bowers*, except that it made it a crime for any two persons of the same sex to engage in "deviant sexual intercourse," or sodomy, which was defined as "any contact between any part of the genitals of one person and the mouth or anus of another person; or the penetration of the genitals or the anus of another person with an object." The defendants, John Geddes Lawrence and Tyrone Garner, purposely allowed them-

When voters in statewide elections weigh in on the issue of gay marriage, they almost invariably choose to ban it. State courts, however, have taken a variety of positions.

Less than a year after *Lawrence v. Texas*, Massachusetts became the first state in the nation to sanction gay marriage. A divided Massachusetts Supreme Judicial Court concluded there was no reason for the state to "deny the protections, benefits and obligations conferred by civil marriage to two individuals of the same sex who wish to marry."

Other courts have moved more cautiously. The top court in New York, for example, ruled in 2006 that the legislature should decide the issue, concluding, "It is not for us to say whether same-sex marriage is right or wrong."

The same year, the New Jersey Supreme Court gave legislators 180 days to grant same-sex couples the same rights as opposite-sex couples. However, the judges left it up the legislature to decide whether to sanction gay marriage or civil unions. "Although we cannot find that a fundamental right to same-sex marriage exists in this state, the unequal dispensation of rights and benefits to committed same-sex partners can no longer be tolerated under our state constitution," the court ruled.

selves to be caught by the police while engaging in the proscribed activity and then set out to challenge the constitutionality of the Texas law as a violation of their protected right of privacy and on the grounds that the law treated homosexuals in an unequal manner compared to heterosexuals, who were not covered under the law.

The Supreme Court was, in essence, being asked to arbitrate between two powerful social concepts: the political ideal of individual liberty protected by the Constitution and the traditional religious and moral belief that sodomy was an abomination. After all, according to the Bible, God destroyed the cities of Sodom and Gomorrah to put an end to the immorality of their inhabitants. From this, *sodomy* came to mean anal intercourse, or more generally now, any type of supposedly unnatural sex act or perversion.

The opinion for the Court was delivered by Justice Anthony M. Kennedy (b. 1936). Justice SANDRA DAY O'CONNOR wrote a concurring opinion, and Chief Justice William H. Rehnquist (1924–2005) and Justices Antonin Scalia (b. 1936) and Clarence Thomas (b. 1948) dissented. After generally surveying the development of the right of privacy in Supreme Court decisions, Justice Kennedy focused on the *Bowers* decision, noting that it missed the point by not recognizing the important issue involved. He explained that the "laws involved in *Bowers* and here…[touch] upon the most private human conduct, sexual behavior, and in the most private of places, the home. The statutes do seek to control a personal relationship that, whether or not entitled to a formal recognition in the law, is within the liberty of persons to choose without being punished as criminals."

After reviewing the manner in which many European nations treat the right of adult homosexuals to engage in intimate sexual conduct, Justice Kennedy found that the decision in *Bowers* could not withstand careful analysis. Citing language in the Court's decision in *Planned Parenthood of Southern Pennsylvania v. Casey* (1992) declaring that it was the Court's duty "to define the liberty of all, not to mandate our own moral code," he went on to conclude that "the Due Process Clause gives [homosexuals] the full right to engage in their conduct without intervention of the government."

Justice O'Connor's concurring opinion made the case for grounding the decision in the equal protection clause of the Fourteenth Amendment (1868), because the Texas statute "makes sodomy a crime only if a person 'engages in deviate sexual intercourse with another individual of the same sex.'" Justice Scalia, joined by Chief Justice Rehnquist and Justice Thomas, argued that the question of whether sodomy should be a right should be left up to the legislative branch of government. Justice Thomas, in a separate dissenting opinion, found "the law before the Court today [to be] 'uncommonly silly,'" and he declared that he could not find in the Constitution any such right of privacy as the majority relied on for its ruling.

Perhaps the Court's decision in *Lawrence* has emboldened the homosexual community and its supporters to press for even more equality, although it may have inspired those opposed to such extension to redouble their efforts, too. The conflict over extending or limiting the rights of homosexuals to be married or to enter legally into civil unions, or otherwise obtain benefits that have traditionally been reserved for married couples, has not abated. As of 2005, all but nine states had legally defined marriage as the union of one man and one woman, while only a few of the nine have legally extended the right to marry or enter into civil unions to homosexuals. In 2007 a bill was passed in Congress by a vote of 235 to 184 to protect homosexuals in the workplace, but it is doubtful the measure will pass in the Senate.

Legislation

Legislation is the primary way in which new laws are made and existing laws are amended or abrogated. In a representative democracy like that of the United States (see REPRESENTATIVE GOVERNMENT), elected representatives in CONGRESS and the state legislatures legislate—make statutory law. Such laws must be constitutional under the federal and state constitutions and must be enforced by the EXECUTIVE BRANCH of government and interpreted and applied by the JUDICIAL BRANCH.

Legislative Power

The power to make laws for the national government is vested by Article I, section 1, of the Constitution "in a Congress of the United States, which shall consist of a Senate and House of Representatives" (see HOUSE OF REPRESENTATIVES; SENATE). The legislature's power to enact laws was a basic assumption of the FRAMERS OF THE CONSTITUTION. Unlike the unique creation of the presidency and the federal judiciary, the starting point for the creation of Congress was the historic role of the British Parliament as a supreme constitutional body. One major difference was that in Britain the electorate who periodically chose the members of the House of Commons, Parliament's lower house, had only one function: to elect representatives to a legislative body in which all of the nation's SOVEREIGNTY resided.

Even in 1888 lobbyists—in this case women meeting with senators in the Capitol's Marble Room—attempted to sway votes on legislation. Today thousands of paid professionals work on behalf of their clients to influence bills in Congress.
Source: Library of Congress

In the United States, in contrast, the framers wanted the nation's sovereignty to reside in the people, who delegated power first to those who ratified the Constitution and then, on a regular basis through the system created by the Constitution, to some of their fellow citizens to exercise the nation's sovereignty on behalf of all citizens. The distinction is crucial, because Parliament in Britain is the final arbiter of that country's unwritten constitution, whereas in the United States the three branches of government are each responsible for complying with the Constitution, with the judicial branch serving as the final interpreter of the document.

Congress's many legislative powers are itemized in Article I, section 8, followed by the license "To make all Laws which shall be necessary and proper for carrying into Execution the foregoing Powers, and all other Powers vested by this Constitution in the Government of the United States, or in any Department or Officer thereof" (see NECESSARY AND PROPER CLAUSE). The list begins with the power to "lay and collect Taxes, Duties, Imposts and Excises, to pay the Debts and provide for the common Defence and general Welfare of the United States" and enumerates other specific subjects for legislation: borrowing and coinage of money (see CURRENCY), counterfeiting, BANKRUPTCY, weights and measures, post offices (see POSTAL POWER), roads, COPYRIGHT and PATENTS, establishment of federal COURTS, declaration of WAR, support of the ARMED FORCES, naturalization, and supervision of the seat of government.

The Constitution places some limits on which laws Congress may pass: (1) Because the federal government is based on specific powers authorized by the Constitution and ultimately determined

As chair of the Senate Appropriations Committee, Robert S. Byrd of West Virginia has wielded far-reaching power over the nation's spending.
Source: CQ Photo/Scott J. Ferrell

by the Supreme Court, Congress cannot make laws in areas reserved to the STATES, such as inheritance of estates and distribution of PROPERTY, or laws infringing STATES' RIGHTS. (2) The Constitution prohibits Congress from passing certain laws such as EX POST FACTO LAWS and bills of attainder (see ATTAINDER, BILLS OF). (3) Congress is also prevented from enacting legislation that infringes on rights guaranteed by the Constitution to the CITIZENS, such as laws abridging freedom of RELIGION, SPEECH, ASSEMBLY AND ASSOCIATION, or THE PRESS.

The Legislative Process

In the United States, only members of Congress can introduce a bill to enact a law. Even the PRESIDENT must have a member of Congress introduce a bill on behalf of the executive branch—which is where most bills in fact originate. A bill must pass both houses of the bicameral Congress in identical form to become law and must also be signed by the president. During the legislative process a bill may be amended, but only the Senate permits riders (nongermane amendments) to be attached to legislation.

Before a bill is voted on, however, it must first be considered by the appropriate committee or committees of the house in which it was introduced. These committees reflect the majority political party (see POLITICAL PARTIES) in the House and Senate, with the chairperson and more members coming from that party. Relying to a great extent on their staffs, committees analyze proposed legislation and may hold hearings to clarify issues and hear from interested parties, both public and private, who may be affected by it or have particular related expertise. After a committee issues a report recommending that a bill be voted on and giving its views on it, the measure is placed on the legislative agenda and voted on. If passed, the bill is then introduced in the other house and the committee process takes place there as well.

Once a bill has passed both houses, it is sent to the president for signature. If the president VETOES it, then the bill, according to Article I, section 7, is returned "with his Objections to that House in which it shall have originated, who shall...proceed to reconsider it." If that house passes it again, this time by at least a two-thirds majority, "the Bill...shall be sent, together with the Objections, to the other House, by which it shall likewise be reconsidered, and if approved by two thirds of that House, it shall become a Law."

Laws go into effect when signed by the president or when the president's veto has been overridden, unless some other date is specified in the law itself. If the president neither signs nor vetoes a proposed law, it goes into effect, according to section 7, "within ten Days (Sundays excepted) after it shall have been presented to him...unless the Congress by their Adjournment prevent its Return, in which Case it shall not be a Law."

Federal and State Spheres

Given that the United States is a federal republic (see FEDERALISM), the constituent states retain their own legislative authority to act in certain areas not exclusively reserved by the Constitution to Congress. Legislation levying taxes, for instance, may be enacted by the national and state legislatures (see TAXATION), but no state legislature can enact a law regarding the District of Columbia (see CAPITAL, NATIONAL) or U.S. territories (see TERRITORY).

In the Republic's early days, Chief Justice JOHN MARSHALL, through a number of his decisions for the Supreme Court, expanded the power of the federal government and its institutions in cases such as *MARBURY V. MADISON* (1803) and *GIBBONS V. OGDEN* (1824). The Court relied on certain provisions of the Constitution, among them the COMMERCE clause and the Fourteenth Amendment (1868), to allow Congress power to enact legislation that broadly affects citizens' daily lives—often at the expense of the states' residual legislative power. The nation today is bound together by national legislation on matters that can affect the country as a whole.

Legislative Intent

Once enacted into law, legislation must be applied by the courts and executed by executive branch officials. If a law is ambiguous, jurists may have to interpret it to determine how it is to be applied in certain situations. Legislative intent has been used to varying degrees by judges to try to understand the purpose of a particular law when it was enacted. This involves reviewing reports of congressional committees and debates by the legislators at the time of passage.

If a bill's proponent is asked on the floor of the House or Senate if the legislation will cover a certain type of situation and the response is no, then that is some evidence of the legislative intent. During the debate over the Taft-Hartley Act (1947), for example, a provision authorizing seizure of property such as steel mills in a national emergency was rejected. Five years later President Harry S. Truman (1884–1972) ordered the seizure of the nation's steel mills the day before a proposed strike. When the president's move was challenged at the Supreme Court in the case *YOUNGSTOWN SHEET AND TUBE CO. V. SAWYER* (1952), the fact that Congress's intent was clearly otherwise—it had specifically rejected such a unilateral action—influenced the Supreme Court's decision finding the president's directive unconstitutional.

Legislative Veto

The legislative veto is a means used to draft legislation so that Congress retains some control over a law's implementation after it is enacted. But the Supreme Court ruled in *Immigration and Naturalization Service v. Chadha* (1983) that such a move is unconstitutional when one house of Congress alone could overturn an executive branch action. The Court prohibited any measure that has the "purpose and effect of altering the legal rights, duties, and relations of persons outside the legislative branch."

The two major problems the Supreme Court saw were that such laws violated the bicameral structure of the legislature created by the Constitution and avoided the requirement that legislation be presented to the president. Congress thus cannot act to change an aspect of a law already in effect without following explicit procedures in the Constitution regarding the enactment of laws. However, it has continued to exercise some control over authority it has delegated—for example, by conditioning certain executive branch actions on a joint resolution of Congress or by using congressional power to reduce or eliminate funding for executive branch activities that it dislikes.

Citizen-Made Law

The traditional system of having laws handed down by elected legislatures is not the only way a DEMOCRACY can work. In ancient Greece, where democracy was invented, the citizens participated directly in making laws and voting on important issues such as war and peace. In an effort to revive citizen participation in the legislative

> **More on this topic:**
> *Legislative Branch*, p. 346

process, as of 2005 some thirty-seven states, California and Colorado among them, have adopted DIRECT DEMOCRACY procedures, by which citizens are empowered to initiate and enact laws using the referendum procedure. So far the jury is out on whether citizen-made laws are any improvement on the legislative system devised by the country's founders in 1787.

Legislative Branch

Nowhere in the Constitution are the concepts of DEMOCRACY and MAJORITY RULE more evident than in its framework for the legislative branch of government, which consists primarily of the SENATE and the HOUSE OF REPRESENTATIVES, both together making up CONGRESS. "In the legislature," said ALEXANDER HAMILTON in essay 70 of *The Federalist* (1787–88) (see FEDERALIST PAPERS), "promptitude of decision is oftener an evil than a benefit. The differences of opinion, and the jarring of parties in that department of the government, though they may sometimes obstruct salutary plans, yet often promote deliberation and circumspection, and serve to check excesses in the majority. When a resolution too is once taken, the opposition must be at an end."

The FRAMERS OF THE CONSTITUTION in 1787 had a number of models for the legislative branch, whose primary task is to make, amend, and abrogate laws (see LEGISLATION). One example was the British Parliament, which Congress superficially resembles—having two houses, an upper and a lower house, one of which (the House of Representatives) was popularly elected in the beginning (senators were originally chosen by the state legislatures), and a system of enacting laws requiring the approval of both houses and the chief executive, the monarch in the case of Britain and the PRESIDENT in the United States.

The framers also had the history of the British colonies and later the independent states to draw on. In 1700 every British colony in America had an elected assembly and, except for South Carolina, some form of local self-government. Virginia had a statewide assembly called the House of Burgesses, while New England had its township governments, in which matters were debated and voted on. From the continental congresses, beginning with the first one that met in Philadelphia on September 5, 1774, came experience in organizing a legislative body consisting of delegates from the colonies and states during the Revolutionary War (1775–83). The "Congress of the United States assembled" created under the ARTICLES OF CONFEDERATION (1781) became a model of the type of deliberative body that most of the framers agreed did not work very well.

First among Equals

Congress was established by Article I of the Constitution. Section 1, furthering the principle of the SEPARATION OF POWERS, declares: "All legislative Powers herein granted shall be vested in the Congress of the United States." While the separation of major government powers into a legislative branch, an EXECUTIVE BRANCH, and a JUDICIAL BRANCH is designed to prevent the accumulation of power in too few hands, the purpose of the checks and balances built into the Constitution is to ensure that each branch has some responsibility for curbing the excesses of the others. Congress in the legislative branch, for example, has the sole authority to appropriate funds for the activities of all the branches of government, yet the Supreme Court, as confirmed in *MARBURY V. MADISON* (1803), has the power to declare acts of Congress unconstitutional and therefore void.

Although the Constitution created three coequal branches of government, the legislature—by its nature and the fact that it is addressed in the first article—was intended to be the most important branch, as it should be in a democracy. As JAMES MADISON put it in essay 48 of *The Federalist*: "The legislative department derives a superiority in our governments from…[the fact of its] constitutional powers being at once more extensive, and less susceptible of precise limits [and therefore] it can, with the greater facility, mask under complicated and indirect measures, the encroachments which it makes on the co-ordinate departments."

Other Legislative Branch Institutions

Architect of the Capitol. The responsibility for the maintenance, operation, development, and preservation of the U.S. Capitol Complex, including the Capitol building and the congressional office buildings, Library of Congress buildings, Supreme Court building, and U.S. Botanic Garden, is entrusted by Congress to the architect of the Capitol.

Congressional Budget Office. The Congressional Budget Office was created so that the annual federal budget request can be considered as a whole. The budget sent to Congress by the president is divided among the various congressional committees responsible for the government's functional areas. Only after each appropriations committee has made its report is the budget voted on, and then in a piecemeal fashion by department or program. (It is not unusual for some agencies to have budget approval for a new fiscal year while others are awaiting action on theirs.) In 1974 Congress created the House and Senate Budget Committees and the Congressional Budget Office. The CBO's role is to give Congress data relevant in analyzing the budget request independently of the Office of Management and Budget, which may be biased because it is located in the executive branch.

Government Accountability Office. The largest congressional support agency, GAO monitors the spending of the executive branch by conducting investigations, performing audits, and providing legal opinions in financial disputes. The office was created in 1921 when the Bureau of the Budget (now the Office of Management and Budget) was established in the executive branch.

Government Printing Office. The Government Printing Office is a public printing operation that produces, among other things, bills, public laws, committee reports, the *Congressional Record* (a daily digest of the proceedings of Congress as required by Article I, section 5, of the Constitution), the Congressional Directory (a listing of the members of Congress and the congressional committees), legislative calendars, records of hearings, and franked (free postage) envelopes.

Library of Congress. A congressional library was established when Congress moved the federal government to Washington, D.C., in 1800 with 740 volumes obtained from booksellers in London. Most of the books were burned during the War of 1812, but President THOMAS JEFFERSON agreed to sell Congress his library of some six thousand volumes after he retired. Today the library has more than 134 million items, a number that increases each year by over two million. Although the Library of Congress is available to the public, its main role is to answer some 500,000 inquiries a year from Congress. It also assists the research of scholars from all over the world.

The legislative branch has both strong and weak points. The two-party political system (see POLITICAL PARTIES) makes Congress's role depend to a great extent on which party is in power in each of its two houses as well as in the executive branch. It can act in concert with the president, or it can act as a brake on the president's policy goals. But because Congress's members are chosen by popular election directly by the people, the legislative branch remains the most democratic—if not the most efficient—of our federal institutions.

CLOSER LOOK

All of the state legislatures, except Nebraska's, have two chambers. Nebraska has a single-chamber, or unicameral, legislature.

The name of the chamber is the Nebraska Legislature. Its members are known as senators. The unicameral system came about in the 1930s, when Nebraska voters abolished the two-chamber system. They were concerned about legislators from each chamber meeting in secret to hammer out final versions of bills, and they also wanted to make the legislative process more efficient.

The other unique characteristic of the Nebraska Legislature is that it is nonpartisan. Instead of holding separate primaries to choose Republican and Democratic nominees, Nebraska has a single nonpartisan primary. The two top vote-getters advance to run in the general election, regardless of their party affiliations.

Legislative Power   *See* CONGRESS; LEGISLATION; LEGISLATIVE BRANCH.

Legislative Vetoes   *See* LEGISLATION; SEPARATION OF POWERS; VETOES.

Libel   *See NEW YORK TIMES CO. V. SULLIVAN;* SPEECH.

Liberty

Liberty is both the beginning and the end of constitutional democracy. Free people create their own government to protect and foster freedom in perpetuity. As the Greek philosopher Aristotle (384–322 B.C.E.) described it in *The Politics*: "The basis of a democratic state is liberty, which, according to the common opinion of men, can only be enjoyed in such a state—this they affirm to be the great end of every democracy." John Winthrop (1588–1649), the first governor of the Massachusetts Colony, defended himself from virtual impeachment with these words, as repeated by Alexis de Tocqueville (1805–59) in *Democracy in America* (1835): "[T]here is a civil, a moral, a federal *liberty*, which is the proper end and object of *authority*; it is a *liberty* for that only which is just and good; for this *liberty* you are to stand with the hazard of your very *lives*...."

The word *liberty* (from the Latin *libertas*, referring to the status of a freed slave) appears in the Constitution three times. The PREAMBLE states that one of the document's goals is to "secure the Blessings of Liberty to ourselves and our Posterity." The Fifth Amendment (1791) asserts that "no person shall be...deprived of life, liberty, or property, without due process of law." And the Fourteenth Amendment (1868) similarly states, "No State shall...deprive any person of life, liberty, or property without due process of law." Now an international concept, the term is used in many national constitutions, including those of Cuba (1976) and Liberia (1986), and in many international human rights documents. The African Charter on Human and Peoples' Rights (1981), for example, guarantees: "Every individual shall have the right to liberty and to the security of his person."

Criminal Procedures

Being deprived of one's liberty, in the narrow legal sense of the term, refers to the criminal process (see CRIMINAL LAW), particularly ARREST and incarceration. Constitutional rights and protections against loss of an individual's liberty include the right to ASSISTANCE OF COUNSEL, to a speedy and fair trial (see TRIALS), to a trial by jury (see JURIES), and to DUE PROCESS of the law by the federal government, as guaranteed in the Fifth Amendment, and by the states, as guaranteed in the Fourteenth Amendment.

The Supreme Court has not always been consistent in defining an unconstitutional deprivation of liberty. In *Robinson v. California* (1962), the Court held that a state's sentence of ninety days in jail for drug addiction was CRUEL AND UNUSUAL PUNISHMENT under the Eighth Amendment (1791), but in *Powell v. Texas* (1968) the Court upheld a criminal conviction for chronic alcoholism (see DRUGS). The minority in *Powell* argued that no one should be deprived of liberty for a condition that he is powerless to change.

The Supreme Court has also found that one's liberty is affected when physical freedom is restricted by imprisonment or commitment or when bodily integrity is impaired, including corporal PUNISHMENT administered by teachers. Once a person is lawfully imprisoned, however, the Court found in *Kentucky Department of Corrections v. Thompson* (1989) that the suspension of visitation privileges did not affect a prisoner's liberty (see PRISONERS). In *Sandin v. Conner* (1995), the justices held that a person's liberty is not necessarily infringed when restraints are placed on prisoners for violating a prison disciplinary code.

The war on terror that followed in the wake of the terrorist attacks on the United States on September 11, 2001, has given rise to new questions regarding the constitutionality of certain types of detention by the military and other government agencies. For example, in *HAMDI V. RUMSFELD* (2004), the Court noted that Hamdi, the individual whose detention was at issue, has a "'private interest...affected by the official action' [of the government that] is the most elemental of liberty interests—the interest in being free from physical detention by one's own government."

GIVE ME LIBERTY OR GIVE ME DEATH (EXCERPTS)

Patrick Henry, March 23, 1775

…This is no time for ceremony…. For my own part, I consider it as nothing less than a question of freedom or slavery; and in proportion to the magnitude of the subject ought to be the freedom of the debate…. Should I keep back my opinions at such a time, through fear of giving offense, I should consider myself as guilty of treason towards my country, and of an act of disloyalty toward the Majesty of Heaven, which I revere above all earthly kings.

Mr. President, it is natural to man to indulge in the illusions of hope. We are apt to shut our eyes against a painful truth, and listen to the song of that siren till she transforms us into beasts. Is this the part of wise men, engaged in a great and arduous struggle for liberty? Are we disposed to be of the number of those who, having eyes, see not, and, having ears, hear not, the things which so nearly concern their temporal salvation? For my part, whatever anguish of spirit it may cost, I am willing to know the whole truth; to know the worst, and to provide for it.

I have but one lamp by which my feet are guided, and that is the lamp of experience. I know of no way of judging of the future but by the past. And judging by the past, I wish to know what there has been in the conduct of the British ministry for the last ten years to justify those hopes with which gentlemen have been pleased to solace themselves and the House. Is it that insidious smile with which our petition has been lately received? Trust it not, sir; it will prove a snare to your feet. Suffer not yourselves to be betrayed with a kiss. Ask yourselves how this gracious reception of our petition comports with those warlike preparations which cover our waters and darken our land. Are fleets and armies necessary to a work of love and reconciliation? Have we shown ourselves so unwilling to be reconciled that force must be called in to win back our love? Let us not deceive ourselves, sir. These are the implements of war and subjugation; the last arguments to which kings resort…. Has Great Britain any enemy, in this quarter of the world, to call for all this accumulation of navies and armies? No, sir, she has none. They are meant for us: they can be meant for no other. They are sent over to bind and rivet upon us those chains which the British ministry have been so long forging. And what have we to oppose to them? Shall we try argument? Sir, we have been trying that for the last ten years…. Shall we resort to entreaty and humble supplication? … Sir, we have done everything that could be done to avert the storm which is now coming on. We have petitioned; we have remonstrated; we have supplicated; we have prostrated ourselves before the throne, and have implored its interposition to arrest the tyrannical hands of the ministry and Parliament. Our petitions have been slighted; our remonstrances have produced additional violence and insult; our supplications have been disregarded; and we have been spurned, with contempt, from the foot of the throne! … If we wish to be free—if we mean to preserve inviolate those inestimable privileges for which we have been so long contending—if we mean not basely to abandon the noble struggle in which we have been so long engaged, and which we have pledged ourselves never to abandon until the glorious object of our contest shall be obtained—we must fight! …

They tell us, sir, that we are weak; unable to cope with so formidable an adversary. But when shall we be stronger? Will it be the next week, or the next year? … The millions of people, armed in the holy cause of liberty … are invincible by any force which our enemy can send against us…. The battle, sir, is not to the strong alone; it is to the vigilant, the active, the brave…. There is no retreat but in submission and slavery! Our chains are forged! Their clanking may be heard on the plains of Boston! The war is inevitable—and let it come! …

… The war is actually begun! The next gale that sweeps from the north will bring to our ears the clash of resounding arms! Our brethren are already in the field! Why stand we here idle? … Is life so dear, or peace so sweet, as to be purchased at the price of chains and slavery? Forbid it, Almighty God! I know not what course others may take; but as for me, give me liberty or give me death!

SOURCE: The Avalon Project at Yale Law School, Eighteen Century Documents. Retrieved from www.yale.edu/lawweb/avalon/18th.htm.

Liberty in Other Guises

Constitutional protections of liberty are continually being refined. The Supreme Court has determined that there is a liberty component in the rights in the BILL OF RIGHTS (1791) that is incorporated into the Fourteenth Amendment (see INCORPORATION DOCTRINE), as well as in other rights found indirectly in the Constitution, such as the rights of association (see ASSEMBLY AND ASSOCIATION) and PRIVACY. In *Fiske v. Kansas* (1927), a case involving a conviction based solely on proscribed language in the constitution of an organization to which the defendant belonged, the liberty interest was found to be of sufficient importance that the Court was emboldened to incorporate the First Amendment (1791) guarantee of free SPEECH into the Fourteenth Amendment and free the defendant.

ECONOMIC LIBERTY has been a source of constitutional controversy. At the end of the nineteenth century, the Supreme Court began finding grounds to overturn government attempts to protect working people, ruling that employees' economic liberty was infringed by regulations setting minimum wages and governing the maximum number of hours that they could work in a day. The Court identified another type of liberty in *Meyer v. Nebraska* (1923). Here the Court struck down a law prohibiting the teaching of modern languages other than English to children who had not passed the eighth grade. Finding that the law violated the liberty protected by the Fourteenth Amendment's due process clause, the Court said that liberty "denotes not merely freedom from bodily restraint but also the right of the individual to contract, to engage in any of the common occupations of life, to acquire useful knowledge, to marry, to establish a home and bring up children, to worship God according to the dictates of his own conscience and generally to enjoy those privileges long recognized as essential to the orderly pursuit of happiness by free men."

With respect to the right of privacy under the Constitution, beginning with *GRISWOLD V. CONNECTICUT* (1965), through *ROE V. WADE* (1973), and ending with *LAWRENCE V. TEXAS* (2003), the Supreme Court has also developed a concept of liberty protected by the "penumbra," or overlapping shadows, of several provisions of the Bill of Rights (1791) that relates to sexual behavior and reproduction. In these cases, the Court has supported the right of individuals to make decisions regarding these intimate concerns without interference by the government.

Procedural Protections

Liberty depends on due process of law, especially with regard to personal autonomy and choice—for example, a prisoner's desire not to take antipsychotic drugs or a student's wish to remain in school. Due process essentially seeks to prevent government from depriving a person of life, liberty, or property except by constitutionally acceptable procedures. In *Board of Regents v. Roth* (1972), the Supreme Court found that government action preventing access to common occupations of a community may infringe both liberty and PROPERTY interests protected by the due process clause. But the Court has set a limit to this argument: in *Paul v. Davis* (1976), Justice William H. Rehnquist (1924–2005) contended that constitutionally protected liberty or property interests are attained "by virtue of the fact that they have been initially recognized and protected by state law," such as a child's right to attend school but not a person's right to enjoy a good reputation. Such an argument comports with the Rehnquist Court's relatively active support for state interests vis-á-vis the federal government (see STATES; STATES' RIGHTS).

In *Mathews v. Eldridge* (1976), the Supreme Court set out a number of procedural protections to consider when liberty has been denied, including the extent of the private interests that may be affected by official action, the risk of error in depriving a person of such interests under the procedures in place, the probable value of additional or different procedures to safeguard against error, and the government's interest, such as the financial or administrative burden that new procedural safeguards might impose (see BALANCING TESTS).

As the English philosopher John Locke (1632–1704) wrote in 1690: "The Idea of Liberty is the Idea of a Power in any Agent to do or forbear any particular Action." Most people probably long to be totally free of all restraints, but such freedom is more likely to lead to the excesses present in failed states than to a utopia. The Constitution, more realistically, creates a system for maximizing liberty within the context of an orderly and just system of government.

More on this topic:
Criminal Law, p. 132
Due Process, p. 168
Economic Liberty, p. 173
Punishment, p. 440

Lincoln, Abraham

In an 1862 letter to Horace Greeley (1811–72), the founder of the *New York Tribune* who similarly opposed SLAVERY, Abraham Lincoln (1809–65), the sixteenth president of the United States, explained: "As to the policy 'I seem to be pursuing,' as you say, I have not meant to leave any one in doubt. I would save the Union. I would save it in the shortest way under the Constitution."

The country's leader during the Civil War (1861–65), Lincoln is second only to GEORGE WASHINGTON in the esteem in which he is held by the American people. Presiding over a nation torn apart by slavery and WAR, he had one guiding constitutional principle: states once united into a nation under the Constitution cannot unilaterally secede.

Abraham Lincoln, shown here reading his 1863 Emancipation Proclamation to his cabinet, presided over the nation during the Civil War, which was fought over the question of slavery and the right of states to secede from the Union.
Source: Library of Congress

Born in a log cabin in Kentucky on February 12, 1809, Lincoln and his family moved to Illinois after his mother died and his father had remarried. Largely self-taught—his total schooling amounted to about one year—he liked to read. One book he enjoyed was *The Life and Memorable Actions of George Washington* (ca. 1800) by Mason Locke "Parson" Weems, complete with its story about George and the cherry tree. Six feet four inches tall at twenty-one years of age, Lincoln worked as a storekeeper, postmaster, and surveyor until the Black Hawk War in 1832. Having volunteered to fight, he was elected captain of his unit, but he suffered defeat in his first bid for the Illinois state assembly when he returned. Running as a Whig, he prevailed in 1834 and thereafter was reelected as a state legislator to serve four terms even while studying law.

Lincoln began his legal practice in 1836, moving to the new state capital of Springfield a year later. Continuing his interest in politics, he was elected to Congress in 1846. There he incurred criticism for his opposition to the Mexican War and slavery in the District of Columbia (see CAPITAL, NATIONAL). After turning down an appointment as governor of the Oregon Territory (see TERRITORY), he returned to the practice of law.

When Stephen A. Douglas (1813–61), a Democrat from Illinois, began campaigning to extend slavery into the nation's western territories, Lincoln felt it his duty to oppose him. Failing to be nominated by the Whig Party as a candidate for the Senate, he switched to the Republican Party. With what some have called his greatest speech, opposing the further spread of slavery, in 1856 he became the leader of his newly adopted party at its state convention. In 1860 he was named the party's presidential candidate, and because of the split in the Democratic Party and the formation of a new third party, his election was assured.

> **"I have never had a feeling, politically, that did not spring from the sentiments embodied in the Declaration of Independence."**
>
> **—Abraham Lincoln** in *Speech at Independence Hall, Philadelphia,* 1861

Once Lincoln was elected president, however, seven southern states seceded from the Union and formed the Confederate States of America. In his inaugural address in 1861, Lincoln claimed that SECESSION was anarchy and that the nation could not be legally separated because the STATES were not sovereign; only the nation was sovereign (see SOVEREIGNTY; STATES' RIGHTS). America's laws were the supreme laws of the land, he asserted, and could not be disobeyed simply because the citizens of some states disagreed with the candidate elected as PRESIDENT.

During the Civil War, President Lincoln took steps to abolish slavery, including issuing the Emancipation Proclamation (see page 504), which took effect on January 1, 1863. Although not effective in the secessionist states, it gave substance to his conviction that the nation was "conceived in liberty and dedicated to the proposition that all men are created equal," as he put it in his world-renowned address at the Gettysburg battlefield in 1863. The president's action at the beginning of the war in suspending the writ of HABEAS CORPUS, however, was ruled unconstitutional by the Supreme Court in *Ex parte Merryman* (1861) because such power was vested only in Congress. A military officer had arrested Merryman for treason and refused to honor a court-ordered writ of habeas corpus on the grounds that the president, as a security measure in time of war, had authorized the writ's suspension.

Just as the war was being won for the Union—General Robert E. Lee surrendered on behalf of the Confederate States on April 9, 1865—Lincoln was assassinated on April 14, 1865, early in his second term. He did not live to see the Thirteenth (1865), Fourteenth (1868), and Fifteenth (1870) Amendments, respectively, prohibiting slavery, extending the rights of DUE PROCESS and EQUAL PROTECTION of the law to all CITIZENS, and guaranteeing the right to vote (see ELECTIONS).

Abraham Lincoln's most important contribution to the Constitution's strength was his unshakable belief in its continuing supremacy over the states and its intrinsic promise of equality for all. His vision for the future, as expressed in a speech at Independence Hall in Philadelphia in 1861, was just as unshakable. "I have often inquired of myself what great principle or idea it was that kept this [union] so long together. It was not the mere matter of the separation of the colonies from the motherland, but that sentiment in the Declaration of Independence which gave liberty, not alone to the people of this country, but, I hope, to the world, for all future time" (see LIBERTY).

Line-Item Vetoes   *See* SEPARATION OF POWERS; VETOES.

Local Government

In *Democracy in America* (1835), the French political scientist Alexis de Tocqueville (1805–59) said in reference to the New England township—one of the oldest forms of self-government in America—that "not only do municipal institutions exist [in America], but there is also a municipal spirit which sustains and gives them life." Local government is addressed by the constitutions of a number of countries, even those with federal forms of government whose major political subdivisions are free to create their own local entities. Brazil's constitution (1988), for one, provides: "Municipalities shall be governed by organic law, voted in two readings...and approved by two-thirds of the members of the Municipal Chamber, which shall promulgate it...."

State Constructs

The U.S. Constitution is silent on cities, towns, municipalities, counties, and districts—political subdivisions of state government. STATES, like unitary national governments (France, for example), do not share SOVEREIGNTY with any political subdivisions within their territorial jurisdictions, as the federal government does with the states themselves in accordance with the principles of FEDERALISM contained in the Constitution and as interpreted by the Supreme Court. In *Hunter v. City of Pittsburgh* (1907), the Court declared that "political subdivisions of the State [are] created as convenient agencies for exercising such of the powers of the State as may be entrusted to them."

As far as individuals are concerned, there is no national constitutional right to any particular form of local government. The creation of local governments is a matter for the states, not the federal government, although a state may not do indirectly through one of its political subdivisions what the Constitution forbids it to do directly. Local governments are created by state legislatures and have no powers or rights of their own. In disputes between local and state authorities, courts generally side with the state. But more than half of the fifty states, including Alaska, Illinois, and West Virginia, have now added home-rule provisions to their constitutions. Before home rule, state legislatures granted, amended, and rescinded city charters, established and determined counties and their government structure, and even passed ordinances for their political subdivisions. The home-rule provisions authorize certain local governments to conduct their own affairs and limit the state's power to interfere, making them more "federal" in nature than before.

Local Elections

Various experiments with the structure and voting methods of local governments have brought several cases before the Supreme Court. In *City of Rome v. United States* (1980), the Court reviewed a Georgia city's attempt to change its electoral system from a plurality method, as used generally throughout the United States (see MAJORITY RULE), to an absolute majority system. To prevent actions that might be construed as RACIAL DISCRIMINATION, the Voting Rights Act of 1965 required preclearance for the change by the attorney general of the United States. The Court found that the review requirement did not go beyond the scope of congressional enforcement power regarding voting rights under the Fifteenth Amendment (1870).

In *New York Board of Estimate v. Morris* (1989), the Supreme Court declared unconstitutional the composition of New York City's Board of Estimates, ruling that it was inconsistent with the EQUAL PROTECTION clause of the Fourteenth Amendment (1868) because each of the city's five boroughs had widely disparate populations but were each equally represented on the board. The Court noted that board membership elections are local elections subject to review under prevailing REAPPORTIONMENT doctrine, which can be traced back to *BAKER V. CARR* (1962) and the Supreme Court's standard of "one person, one vote."

Other State and Local Issues

In *San Antonio Independent School District v. Rodriguez* (1973), the Supreme Court found that state reliance on local school districts to fund a substantial portion of the cost of local schools—even though the districts varied widely in their taxable resources and how much they spent on each pupil—did not violate the Constitution's equal protection clause of the Fourteenth Amendment (1868) (see EDUCATION). In New Hampshire, however, the state's supreme court noted that there was a disparity of about 400 percent in the tax rates of two school districts, saying that such taxes were not in fact local taxes but state taxes required to fulfill "the State's duty to provide a constitutionally adequate public education."

In spite of the language in the Eleventh Amendment (1795) prohibiting suits against a state, they may be brought against municipalities in federal courts. In addition, the Supreme Court in *Community Communications Co. v. City of Boulder* (1982) held that federal ANTITRUST LAW, not applicable to states because of their sovereign IMMUNITY, was nevertheless applicable to cities and other municipalities. The question of whether states or their political subdivisions are engaged in government or private commercial activity was addressed earlier by the Court. In *New York and Saratoga Springs Commission v. United States* (1946), the Court found that a state engaged in commercial activity—selling water from the Saratoga Springs—was not exempt from paying federal taxes, as it would be if the state were engaged in a purely governmental activity.

Supreme Court cases in the 1970s upheld Congress's general power to impose duties and standards on state subdivisions, despite the Tenth Amendment (1791) provision reserving the powers not delegated to the United States "to the States respectively, or to the people." However, in *National League of Cities v. Usery* (1976), the Court barred Congress from directly impairing a state's ability to structure its traditional government functions, only to overturn this ruling in *Garcia v. San Antonio Metropolitan Transit Authority* (1985), saying that traditional government functions could not be defined by the Court and should therefore be left up to Congress.

Local governments are varied and range in size from cities more populous than some states to unincorporated wide spots in the road. While communities need to have some autonomy in local affairs, they should not be able to escape the state and federal constitutional requirements for good government and protection of the rights of all citizens—raising a perpetual challenge for citizens, lawmakers, and the courts.

More on this topic:

Federalism, p. 218

Sovereignty, p. 506

States' Rights, p. 520

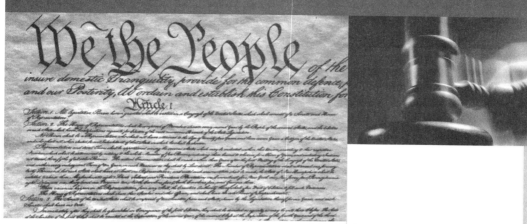

Madison, James

Perhaps the quintessential American pragmatist, James Madison (1751–1836)—who would become known as the "Father of the Constitution"—contributed mightily to the foundation of the government of the United States, including the drafting of the CONSTITUTION itself. Madison was born on March 16, 1751, in Port Conway, Virginia, the son of a landowner with significant holdings near the Blue Ridge Mountains. A frail boy, he entered the College of New Jersey (later Princeton University) in 1769, gaining an education in Enlightenment principles and a degree in just two years. He soon became interested in revolutionary politics.

In 1776 Madison was elected a delegate to the Virginia constitutional convention, which supported independence and wrote a constitution for the commonwealth. He urged a strong religious freedom provision, proclaiming "liberty of conscience for all." In 1780 he began four years' service in the Continental Congress, where the studious legislator and orator favored a strong national government, a view that would come to shape the new United States of America.

In 1786 a meeting of representatives from Virginia, Delaware, New York, New Jersey, and Pennsylvania was held in Annapolis, Maryland, to wrestle with interstate COMMERCE problems that had arisen under the ARTICLES OF CONFEDERATION (1781). Among these problems were retaliatory taxation measures by the states and disagreement over oyster fisheries and transportation of goods through adjacent states. Along with ALEXANDER HAMILTON and several other delegates, Madison urged that a constitutional convention be held, ostensibly to revise the woefully inadequate Articles by strengthening the powers of the federal government (see FEDERALISM).

In preparation for the CONSTITUTIONAL CONVENTION OF 1787, Madison studied the histories of other nations, in particular the problems of confederations such as those of ancient Greece and

An active proponent of the new Constitution before and during the Constitutional Convention of 1787, James Madison's contributions earned him the title "Father of the Constitution." His essays in The Federalist (1787–88) helped secure the document's ratification, and later, as a representative, he sponsored the Bill of Rights (1791).
Source: Library of Congress

Switzerland. He compared their problems to America's contemporary ills under the Articles in order to give direction to the assemblage of delegates who were to meet in Philadelphia in 1787. Madison corresponded with fellow delegates, including GEORGE WASHINGTON and Edmund Randolph of Virginia and Rufus King of New York (see FRAMERS OF THE CONSTITUTION). He also wrote to THOMAS JEFFERSON, who was in France and was not a delegate, about the goals of the convention as Madison saw them. For eleven days in May immediately before the convention got under way, Madison brought together his fellow Virginia delegates to set the stage for what he believed was the momentous task that lay ahead.

"I am afraid you will think this project, if not extravagant, absolutely unattainable and unworthy of being attempted," he wrote to Randolph on April 8. "I hold it for a fundamental point that an individual independence of the States, is utterly irreconcilable with the idea of an aggregate sovereignty. I think at the same time that a consolidation of the States into one simple republic is not less unattainable than it would be inexpedient. Let it be tried then whether any middle ground can be taken which will at once support a due supremacy of the national authority, and leave in force the local authorities so far as they can be subordinately useful."

One outcome of Madison's persistence with his own delegation was the Virginia Plan as a model for a new government (see pages 622–623), which he drafted but which was presented at the convention on May 29 by Randolph as the head of Virginia's delegation. The Virginia Plan virtually consigned the Articles to history by serving as the catalyst for earnest discussions about a new federal constitution for America.

Madison was a conscientious delegate, taking extensive notes that today provide insight into the convention's otherwise closed sessions. In fact, many original papers were destroyed by the convention's secretary (not a delegate), so what is known of many of them—for example, the Virginia Plan itself—comes from Madison's "Notes on Debates."

To see the job of shepherding the new constitution through to its successful completion, Madison joined with Alexander Hamilton and John Jay (later the first CHIEF JUSTICE of the United States) to explain in detail the draft of the Constitution in a series of essays collectively referred to as the FEDERALIST PAPERS, which were published in newspapers to promote the Constitution's ratification by the states. Madison also led the fight to adopt the Constitution in Virginia's ratifying convention.

Madison's contribution to the government created by "his" constitution continued even after it was ratified and went into effect in 1789. A close friend of George Washington, Madison drafted portions of the first president's inaugural speech. As an elected member of the HOUSE OF REPRESENTATIVES in the first CONGRESS, he introduced a draft of what would become the BILL OF RIGHTS (1791), the first ten AMENDMENTS to the Constitution. In 1794 Madison married a widow, Dolly Todd, who, after Madison assumed the presidency in 1809, became perhaps the most popular of any first lady.

A tireless campaigner for the presidency of his friend Thomas Jefferson in 1800, he was appointed secretary of state by Jefferson after the election. Madison was instrumental in bringing about the Louisiana Purchase (1803) and suppressing the Barbary Coast pirates (1803–05), who were endangering American trade. His influence in Jefferson's administration (1801–09) was so great that several senators and the foreign minister of France believed that he actually governed the president as the power behind the throne.

Twice elected president in his own right beginning in 1808, Madison had to defend the nation from the British during the War of 1812. In 1814 he lowered the average age of his generals from sixty to thirty-six years; the ensuing victories reversed Britain's policy of belligerency toward its former colonies. To his credit, Madison did not resort to wartime aggrandizement of his power and was justly proud upon leaving office for having defeated the British without infringing the political, religious, or CIVIL RIGHTS of the people.

Outliving all of the other signers of the Constitution, Madison died on June 28, 1836, at his home, Montpelier, in Orange County, Virginia, refusing attempts to prolong his life until July 4—the memorable day of the year on which both JOHN ADAMS and Jefferson died. After his death, Madison's *Advice to My Country* was opened. In it he offered these words: "The advice nearest my heart and deepest in my convictions is, *that the union of the states be cherished and perpetuated.*"

> "[W]hat is government itself, but the greatest of all reflections on human nature? If men were angels, no government would be necessary. If angels were to govern men, neither external nor internal controls on government would be necessary. In framing a government which is to be administered by men over men, the great difficulty lies in this: you must first enable the government to control the governed; and in the next place oblige it to control itself."
>
> —*James Madison,* in *The Federalist,* No. 51, February 8, 1788

Majority Leader
See CONGRESS; HOUSE OF REPRESENTATIVES; POLITICAL PARTIES; SENATE.

Majority Rule

The concept of majority rule lies somewhere between the extremes of rule by a single person and rule by consensus of all citizens. Since the birth of DEMOCRACY in ancient Greece more than 2,500 years ago, the foundation of democratic government has been majority rule, whereby public officials are selected and decisions are made on the basis of a majority of the votes cast in ELECTIONS and in legislative assemblies.

The constitutions of all modern democratic countries incorporate some aspects of majority rule in their procedures for electing officials and enacting laws as well as for other decision-making processes, such as judicial proceedings. The Twelfth Amendment (1804) of the U.S. Constitution states in part: "The person having the greatest Number of votes for President, shall be the President, if such number be a majority of the whole number of Electors appointed...." The constitution of Indonesia (1955), written nearly two centuries later, similarly provides that the "president and the vice president shall be elected by...a majority vote."

Absolute and Supermajorities

An absolute majority means that half of all the votes cast plus at least one additional vote are necessary for a candidate to be elected or a proposal to be approved. If two candidates are running for an office, one must receive more than half of the votes, unless there is a tie vote, in which case some other method of determining a winner must be used. For example, under the Constitution

President Woodrow Wilson
Source: Library of Congress

In eighteen presidential elections, the winner has failed to get a majority of the popular vote. This means that many occupants of the White House, despite having enormous influence, were actually elected by fewer than fifty percent of the voters.

Woodrow Wilson failed to surpass the fifty-percent mark in both his initial election and his reelection because strong third-party candidates split the popular vote. Similarly, Bill Clinton won both his elections with less than fifty percent because third-party candidate Ross Perot won enough popular votes to prevent any candidate from gaining a majority.

Other well-known presidents who never got fifty percent of the popular vote include Grover Cleveland, Harry S. Truman, and John F. Kennedy.

Regardless of whether they were elected by a minority or a majority, presidents in general have not hesitated to assert themselves. Abraham Lincoln won the 1860 election with less than forty percent of the popular vote and then assumed emergency powers to lead the nation through the Civil War.

a tie vote for PRESIDENT in the ELECTORAL COLLEGE sends the process to the HOUSE OF REPRESENTATIVES. If more than two candidates are running, it is possible that no candidate will receive an absolute majority of the votes cast. Then the winner may be determined by a runoff election between the two candidates with the most votes. One way to avoid the possibility of a runoff in this case is to simply select the candidate who receives the highest number of votes—a plurality—whether or not that number represents an absolute majority. Congressional elections in the United States are won on the basis of a plurality of the votes cast.

Most constitutions also require a supermajority of the votes, such as two-thirds or three-fourths, for some decisions or actions. Article I, section 7, provides that a veto by the president may be overturned "if approved by two thirds of" each house of CONGRESS (see VETOES), while Article II, section 2, requires that "two thirds of the Senators present" concur in TREATIES submitted by the president for their approval (see RATIFICATION). A supermajority is also required for conviction after IMPEACHMENT of public officials such as judges and the president. According to Article I, section 3: "[N]o Person shall be convicted [of impeachment] without the Concurrence of two thirds of the Members [of the Senate] present." Article V requires several supermajorities for proposal and ratification of constitutional AMENDMENTS: two-thirds of both houses of Congress must propose amendments or two-thirds of the state legislatures must call for a constitutional convention, and three-fourths of the state legislatures or state conventions must ratify amendments.

Majority Rule in the Three Branches

In a parliamentary system of government, the prime minister must have the continuing support of the cabinet and of a majority of the members of the lower house of parliament to remain in office and to gain support for his or her decisions. The American president, in contrast, is not required to rely on a continuing legislative majority to support decisions that the Constitution entrusts to his discretion alone. The president need not even consult cabinet members and other EXECUTIVE BRANCH officers, let alone obtain majority approval, for any decision. In important matters, a president may consult with advisers or examine public opinion polls before determining what moves to make. If a possible course of action requires Congress's cooperation, the president may informally determine the members' majority sentiment.

In each house of the LEGISLATIVE BRANCH, decisions are generally made (assuming there is a quorum to do business) by a simple majority vote of those members present and voting. Article I, section 5, requires a majority of the members of each house for a quorum. This approach makes sense because theoretically one-half plus one of all the members in either house of Congress (as long as they all agreed) could vote and pass any measure requiring an absolute majority vote. Under the Constitution, however, in the SENATE certain decisions, such as treaty ratification and conviction after impeachment, can be approved only by a supermajority vote. Moreover, by the Senate's own rules, ten more members than an absolute majority—a total of sixty senators—are required for cloture (to close debate). This practice has led to the use of the filibuster, in which one or more senators in the minority on an issue speak continuously on the floor in order to delay or thwart a vote on a disliked measure.

In the JUDICIAL BRANCH, the SUPREME COURT also generally makes decisions on the basis of a majority vote. The Court is composed of nine members, so five votes out of the nine are usually required for the Court to change a lower court decision. However, in some cases justices who have a conflict of interest may recuse themselves (withdraw from taking part in deciding a case), thus reducing the number of votes needed for a majority, or there may be a vacancy on the Court. In deciding whether or not to accept a case submitted by a petitioner using a writ of certiorari (requesting the Supreme Court to hear an appeal), by tradition only four of nine votes are required. The Court takes a small number of other cases without voting—for example, cases based on the Court's original jurisdiction authority or on certification by a lower court.

Majoritarianism

Recently fifty-one percent of Americans polled agreed that government officials should use their own judgment when they believe that a majority of citizens may be wrong on an issue, although forty percent thought that these officials should follow the majority. Strict adherence to the principle of majority rule is known as majoritarianism, a practice that would prevent unelected judges from thwarting the will of the majority by declaring certain laws passed by elected representatives to be unconstitutional.

Majoritarianism is thus a position that runs counter to the many checks and balances built into constitutional democracies to guard against popular but perhaps erroneous, unjust, or even disastrous decisions. The majority of U.S. citizens apparently saw no injustice in the SEGREGATION of black students in the public schools before the Supreme Court's ruling in BROWN V. BOARD OF EDUCATION OF TOPEKA (1954), which declared "separate but equal" schools unconstitutional (see MINORITIES; RACIAL DISCRIMINATION).

More recently, the two major issues that have divided Americans are ABORTION and homosexual rights (see HOMOSEXUALS). Because politicians have to pander to activists on both sides of these issues, it has become difficult to resolve the conflicts over these issues by majoritarian principles. Thus the judicial branch, which is insulated to a large extent from political pressure, was presented the opportunity in ROE V. WADE (1973) and LAWRENCE V. TEXAS (2003) to vindicate the rights of certain citizens who traditionally have been oppressed by the institutions that operate under the principles of majority rule.

The tyranny of the majority can be as unjust as the tyranny of an absolute dictator. To avoid the consequences of what some have called "mobocracy" (rule based solely on the passions of the people), the Constitution provides for both majority rule and checks and balances among the branches of government. Good government requires the proper mix of democracy and protections for minority rights.

More on this topic:
Electoral College, p. 185
Representative Government, p. 464
Separation of Powers, p. 494

Mapp v. Ohio

With its decision in *Mapp v. Ohio* (1961), the Supreme Court fully extended to the states the federal rule that evidence seized in violation of the Fourth Amendment (1791) must be excluded from a trial (see SEARCH AND SEIZURE). The Court declared that this so-called exclusionary rule is the "most important constitutional privilege" of the Constitution's prohibition against unreasonable searches and seizures and "an essential part of the right of privacy" (see PRIVACY).

On the pretext of looking for a fugitive and gambling equipment, police officers entered Dolly Mapp's house in Cleveland without a search warrant. Instead they found and seized materials used to convict her of possession of obscene books and pictures (see OBSCENITY). Beginning with *Boyd v. United States* (1886), the Supreme Court had held that evidence compelled from a defendant must be excluded from his or her trial primarily because of the guarantee against SELF-INCRIMINATION in the Fifth Amendment (1791). *Boyd* was a federal case, so the rule did not apply to the states because the Court had held in *Barron v. Baltimore* (1833) that the BILL OF RIGHTS (1791) was intended to be a protection only against the federal government and not against the STATES.

Beginning in 1927, however, with *Fiske v. Kansas*, the Supreme Court began incorporating protections of the Bill of Rights into the Fourteenth Amendment and making them applicable also to the states (see INCORPORATION DOCTRINE). *Mapp v. Ohio* is the case the Court used to extend to the states the exclusionary rule developed in the federal COURTS. The groundwork for the *Mapp* decision had been laid in *Wolf v. Colorado* (1949), in which the Court held unanimously that freedom from unreasonable searches and seizures prohibited by the Fourth Amendment was so fundamental a right that it was applicable to the states. However, the Court in *Wolf* stopped short of requiring the exclusion of illegally obtained evidence, because it was not the only way for the states to enforce the Fourth Amendment prohibition. And then in *Mapp* the Court—with three dissents, two concurring opinions, and one separate opinion—concluded that evidence obtained in violation of the Fourth Amendment search and seizure provisions must be made inadmissible as evidence in state courts.

The exclusionary rule has been criticized by some legal experts, including Justice Benjamin N. Cardozo (1870–1938), who said: "The criminal is to go free because the constable has blundered."

An imperfect solution to the problem of providing court supervision for LAW ENFORCEMENT activities, the exclusionary rule is similar to the "fruit of the poison tree" rule. Articulated in *Nardone v. United States* (1939), this principle holds that any evidence obtained illegally may be ruled inadmissible in court unless other circumstances intervene, such as a showing that the police would have discovered the evidence independently or that there was an intervening act of free will by the accused, such as a legally admissible confession, to cure the illegality of the earlier evidence. Both rules place the burden on law enforcement officials to act constitutionally and legally at all times—a reasonable expectation.

But in part because even the exclusionary rule does not always work to curb illegal searches and seizures, the Supreme Court in *Bivens v. Six Unknown Named Agents of the Federal Bureau of Narcotics* (1971) opened the door for suits against law enforcement officials who violate citizens' Fourth Amendment rights.

More on this topic:

Bill of Rights, p. 62

Criminal Law, p. 132

Incorporation Doctrine, p. 297

Search and Seizure, p. 479

Trials, p. 556

Marbury v. Madison

The Supreme Court's decision in *Marbury v. Madison* (1803) defined the nature of JUDICIAL REVIEW: the power of the federal courts to declare acts of CONGRESS or the EXECUTIVE BRANCH unconstitutional and therefore void and unenforceable. But the famous opinion on the matter rendered by Chief Justice JOHN MARSHALL was, in fact, a tactical political maneuver to save face with his own party—the Federalists—and perhaps save himself from IMPEACHMENT by the opposition party, the Democratic–Republicans (later renamed the Democrats).

William Marbury was one of forty-two justices of the peace for the District of Columbia nominated on March 2, 1801, by the lame-duck administration of the Federalist president JOHN ADAMS (see LAME DUCKS). The Senate confirmed the nominees the next day, making the appointment process complete except for delivery of the appointment commissions (official documents) to the appointees before Adams's successor, THOMAS JEFFERSON, took office on March 4. However, Jefferson, a member of the opposition party, ordered his secretary of state, JAMES MADISON, to withhold delivery of the four commissions that had not yet been delivered to appointees, including Marbury's. In 1789 Congress had passed the Judiciary Act, giving the Supreme Court authority to issue writs to officers of the federal government. Marbury thus sought the Court's help in obtaining his commission, asking the justices to issue a writ of mandamus directing Madison to deliver it.

Marshall, whom Adams had appointed chief justice in January 1801, decided first that Marbury indeed had a legal right to his commission. Further, he pronounced, one general and indisputable rule of law is that where there is a legal right there is also a legal remedy, so Marbury was due his remedy under the laws of the United States. However, he found that the Constitution did not give the SUPREME COURT original jurisdiction under Article III to enforce Marbury's right and remedy. And just as important, the Constitution did not give Congress the power to confer additional original—as opposed to appellate—jurisdiction on the Court (see FLETCHER V. PECK).

> "It is a proposition too plain to be contested, that the Constitution controls any legislative act repugnant to it; or that the legislature may alter the constitution by ordinary acts. Between these two alternatives there is no middle ground. The constitution is either a superior, paramount law, unchangeable by ordinary means, or it is on a level with ordinary legislative acts, and like other acts, is alterable when the legislature shall please to alter it."
>
> —Chief Justice John Marshall, in *Marbury v. Madison*, 1803

This was Marshall's way out of the dilemma he faced. Either he could enforce Marbury's right to the commission and thus anger the new Democratic–Republican Party–dominated Congress, or he could deny enforcement and anger his Federalist Party colleagues. By declaring void the Judiciary Act provision giving the Supreme Court the power to issue writs to government officials, on the basis that Congress had no such authority under the Constitution, Marshall sidestepped the responsibility. In effect he said that his hands were tied by the Constitution itself. "The particular phraseology of the Constitution," Marshall went on to declare, "confirms and strengthens the principle, supposed to be essential to all written constitutions, that a law repugnant to the constitution is void, and that courts, as well as other departments, are bound by that instrument."

Marshall's opinion was a brilliant ploy to avoid offending either his own party, under whose administration the appointments had been made, or the opposition party's new administration, which might try to impeach him if the case went the other way. The following year Justice Samuel Chase (1741–1811) was impeached by the Democratic–Republican-controlled House of Representatives for his partisan Federalist activities, but he was acquitted in the Senate. At the time of the *Marbury* decision, the politics of the matter was the primary focus of the parties, and the precedent under which judicial review was established by Marshall's now-famous opinion would not be used until the Dred Scott case, *Scott v. Sandford* (1857), more than fifty years later.

More on this topic:

Appointment and Removal Power, p. 39

Judicial Review, p. 318

Marshall, John, p. 362

Marriage   *See* FAMILIES.

Marriage, Same-Sex   *See* FAMILIES; HOMOSEXUALS.

Marshall, John

John Marshall's tenure as CHIEF JUSTICE of the United States from 1801 to 1835 came during a period of unsurpassed development in American constitutional law. The author of several key majority opinions on important national issues, Marshall (1755–1835) set the course for the continuing evolution of the Constitution, the federal government, and the United States as a nation.

Marshall was born in a log cabin in Virginia. His father worked for GEORGE WASHINGTON as a surveyor, and Marshall fought in the Revolutionary War. After studying law at the College of William and Mary, Marshall was admitted to practice in 1780. A member of Virginia's House of Delegates, he helped persuade the state to ratify the Constitution. Marshall turned down several positions within the federal government, including attorney general, minister to France, and secretary of war. In 1799 he won a seat in the House of Representatives, where he became a leader of the Federalist Party.

In 1800 President JOHN ADAMS appointed Marshall secretary of state, and when Adams returned to Massachusetts for several months Marshall virtually ran the government. The following year, after Oliver Ellsworth, the nation's second chief justice, resigned and John Jay, the first chief justice, declined the post, Adams nominated Marshall, who was confirmed on January 27, 1801.

More than a thousand cases came before the SUPREME COURT during Marshall's service on it, and he wrote more than five hundred opinions. Perhaps the most well known is his opinion in *MARBURY V. MADISON* (1803), which established the Court's right to review legislative acts and declare them unconstitutional (see JUDICIAL REVIEW). *MCCULLOCH V. MARYLAND* (1819) validated the theory that Congress held implied powers, extending federal power beyond the Constitution's strict enumeration of powers. And in *GIBBONS V. OGDEN* (1824), Marshall wrote an opinion that confirmed Congress's extensive power vis-á-vis the states under the Constitution's COMMERCE clause, setting an outer limit that would not be pushed further for more than a hundred years.

With his landmark decision in **Marbury v. Madison (1803)**, *confirming the Supreme Court's power of judicial review to declare congressional legislation unconstitutional, Chief Justice John Marshall strengthened the federal judiciary.*
Source: Library of Congress

Marshall helped shape the law of the new nation in many other important cases. The Supreme Court's decision in *United States v. Burr* (1807) narrowed the definition of TREASON as used in the Constitution, making prosecution more difficult. Regarding the Constitution's prohibition against

impairment of CONTRACTS, in *FLETCHER V. PECK* (1810) Marshall's opinion for the Court declared unconstitutional an attempt by a state legislature to rescind contractual rights granted earlier by the same body, and his opinion in *Sturges v. Crowninshield* (1819) limited the standards for absolving a bankrupt of his debts. In *Dartmouth College v. Woodward* (1819), the Court in an opinion written by Marshall again upheld the sanctity of contractual obligations.

More than merely doing justice within the letter and spirit of a new and untested Constitution in individual cases, Marshall used his position on the Supreme Court to enforce his vision of the federal government it created for the new nation. To him the Constitution was a radical departure from the ARTICLES OF CONFEDERATION, which had governed the United States of America between 1781 and 1789. The new government possessed both judicial and political powers, but these powers were intended to have their effect directly on the citizens of the United States and not through the states, which had relinquished some of their sovereignty for the sake of a stronger Union.

A Federalist, Marshall became troubled by the excesses of democratic majorities begun in the administration of THOMAS JEFFERSON and greatly extended during Andrew Jackson's (1829–37). Although a champion of federal power, he nevertheless feared—as did the FRAMERS OF THE CONSTITUTION—"legislative omnipotence." He therefore positioned the Supreme Court as the guardian of the Constitution's principles and as a check on the excesses of the other branches of government. As he put it in *Marbury v. Madison*, "The particular phraseology of the Constitution…confirms and strengthens the principle, supposed to be essential to all written constitutions, that a law repugnant to the constitution is void, and that courts, as well as other departments, are bound by that instrument."

> *"I ask you if your House of Representatives would be better than it is, if a hundredth part of the people were to elect a majority of them? If your Senators were for life, would they be more agreeable to you? If your President were not accountable to you for his conduct; if it were a constitutional maxim that he could do no wrong, would you be safer than you are now? If you can answer yes to these questions, then adopt the British constitution. If not, then good as that government may be, this is better."*
>
> **—John Marshall,** in a speech at the Virginia Constitutional Ratification Convention (1788)

Marshall, Thurgood

In response to a request from Justice Felix Frankfurter (1882–1965) for a definition of *equal*, Thurgood Marshall, appearing as legal counsel before the Supreme Court, answered succinctly: "Equal means getting the same thing, at the same time and in the same place." Much of Marshall's life was devoted to the pursuit of just this kind of equality for all Americans.

Born on July 2, 1908, in Baltimore, Maryland, young Thurgood Marshall was required to read the Constitution as punishment in school. After graduating from Lincoln University in Pennsylvania in 1930, he was barred because of his race from enrolling in the University of Maryland's law school and instead went to Howard Law School in Washington, D.C., from which he was graduated first in his class in 1933. While practicing law in Baltimore, Marshall worked to develop the local branch of the National Association for the Advancement of Colored People, becoming the director of the NAACP Legal Defense Fund in 1940.

> *"Equal means getting the same thing, at the same time and in the same place."*
>
> **—Justice Thurgood Marshall**

After Marshall's success with the case of *Sweatt v. Painter* (1950), in which the Supreme Court agreed that Texas's law school for blacks was not equal to the school established for white law students, he assembled a team of lawyers to attack the constitutionality of the "separate but equal" doctrine approved by the Court in *Plessy v. Ferguson* (1896). His crowning achievement as a lawyer was his victory in BROWN V. BOARD OF EDUCATION OF TOPEKA (1954), in which the Supreme Court ended the segregation of black and white students in public schools.

Until his 1961 nomination by President John F. Kennedy (1917–63) to be a judge on the Second Circuit Court of Appeals for New York was confirmed, Marshall continued to work to end DISCRIMINATION against blacks in education, housing, public accommodations, and voting. A group of southern senators delayed his appointment, so he was finally given a recess appointment. None of his 112 opinions on the court was overturned. In 1965 President Lyndon B. Johnson (1908–73) appointed Marshall to be solicitor general of the United States, the number three position in the Department of Justice (see CABINET). The unexpressed understanding was that he would soon be nominated as the first African American justice on the SUPREME COURT, which happened in 1967.

The Supreme Court he joined was the Warren Court (1954–69), dominated by relatively liberal justices who felt little compunction in using the power of the Court and the Constitution to support social change and the extension of RIGHTS to historically disadvantaged MINORITIES such as blacks and WOMEN. Generally siding with the Court majority in the beginning, by the end of his twenty-four-year term he was more often writing dissents from majority opinions as the composition of the Court gradually changed with the addition of more conservative members appointed by Presidents Richard M. Nixon (1913–94) and Ronald Reagan (1911–2004) in the 1970s and 1980s.

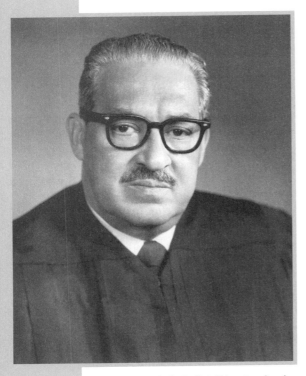

Thurgood Marshall, the first African American justice on the Supreme Court—a steadfast liberal and a champion of equal rights—retired in 1991 from a court increasingly dominated by more conservative members.
Source: Library of Congress

Besides blazing a trail for African Americans, Marshall made important contributions to the development of constitutional law, including a consistent championing of the promise of the rights guaranteed by the Constitution against assaults by the national and state governments. Whether siding with the majority or in dissents, Marshall spoke plainly of his dissatisfaction with government policies that forced members of the PRESS to reveal their sources to grand juries, limited busing of school children to achieve racial integration, provided no support for the right to EDUCATION, or condoned the use of the DEATH PENALTY.

In his dissents in *Dandridge v. Williams* (1970) and *San Antonio Independent School District v. Rodriguez* (1973), Marshall made an important contribution to constitutional analysis, noting that two types of judicial scrutiny were being used by the Supreme Court in reviewing laws under the EQUAL PROTECTION clause of the Fourteenth Amendment (1868). On the upper level were suspect classifications based on race or other fundamental interests; on the lower level were laws in which there was some possible rational basis for discrimination by the legislature. The laws with suspect classifications on the first tier were subjected to a standard of STRICT SCRUTINY by the Court and were generally struck down as unconstitutional. Laws with a rational basis for discrimination—for example, with respect to pregnancy,

More on this topic:

Civil Rights, p. 96

Racial Discrimination, p. 449

Segregation, p. 484

which affects only women—were subjected to a lower standard of scrutiny and generally upheld. Instead of the strict two-tier approach, Marshall offered a sliding scale of analysis and scrutiny that was never expressly adopted by the Court.

Thurgood Marshall resigned from the Court in 1991—undoubtedly frustrated in his role as the liberal dissenter in the Court's later decisions—and died of heart failure two years later on January 24, 1993. To honor him, on October 1, 2005, the Baltimore/Washington International Airport was renamed the Baltimore/ Washington International Thurgood Marshall Airport.

Martin v. Hunter's Lessee

In the nation's early years under the Constitution, federal institutions including the Supreme Court were testing the scope of their new authority. *Martin v. Hunter's Lessee* (1816) is the first case in which the Court declared that it had appellate jurisdiction over cases pending in state courts.

In Article III, section 2, the Constitution grants the Supreme Court two types of jurisdiction: original and appellate. Original jurisdiction means that cases based on the subject matters set forth in the Constitution—"Cases affecting Ambassadors, other public Ministers and Consuls, and those in which a State shall be a Party"—must be decided initially and exclusively by the Supreme Court. All other cases come to the Court on appeal from a lower court decision, based on its appellate jurisdiction granted in the same article and section: "In all the other Cases before mentioned, the supreme Court shall have appellate Jurisdiction, both as to Law and Fact, with such Exceptions, and under such Regulations as the Congress shall make." It was clear that the Supreme Court had appellate jurisdiction over cases in inferior federal courts, but in the U.S. government did the Court have similar authority under the Constitution to review state court decisions?

This question was answered in the affirmative in *Martin v. Hunter's Lessee*, which arose from a dispute over title to PROPERTY in Virginia formerly owned by Lord Fairfax, a citizen and inhabitant of Virginia until his death in 1781.

Lord Fairfax bequeathed a tract of land to Denny Fairfax (previously Denny Martin), a native-born British subject and enemy alien (see ALIENS) during the Revolutionary War (1775–83). In 1785 the Commonwealth of Virginia took the property under a state law confiscating enemy property and four years later made a grant of some of it to David Hunter. Not long afterward, peace treaties with Great Britain in 1793 and 1794 protected the American property of British subjects. In protest, Martin sued in state court, questioning whether the property was subject to such a confiscation by the state. A Virginia court upheld his title against Hunter's. In 1810, however, the Virginia Court of Appeals decided in Hunter's favor.

Section 25 of the Judiciary Act (1789) authorized appeals from certain state court decisions, including those in which a state court upheld a state statute against a claim that it was repugnant to the Constitution, treaties, or laws of the United States. In an appeal to the Supreme Court brought on behalf of claimants under Martin's interest—one of whom was Chief Justice JOHN MARSHALL's brother James—the Court reversed the state appeals court and held in favor of Martin's interest. (John Marshall did not take part in the decision.)

The key question before the Court was whether the appellate power of the United States extends to cases in state courts. This was an important question for the future relationship between the federal government and the states under the Constitution. The Court held that state judges are required in

> **More on this topic:**
>
> *Federalism, p. 218*

Justice Joseph Story wrote the historic decision in Martin v. Hunter's Lessee.
Source: Portrait by Alexander Healy, Collection of the Supreme Court of the United States

their official capacity to determine cases in accordance with the "supreme law of the land": the Constitution, laws, and treaties of the United States. According to the Constitution, the Supreme Court's judicial power—appellate jurisdiction, not original jurisdiction—extends to all such cases. The noted Justice Joseph Story (1779–1845), who served on the Court from 1811 to 1845, wrote the opinion of the Court, saying, "It is the case, then, and not the court, that gives the jurisdiction."

Justice Story's opinion in *Martin v. Hunter's Lessee* has been ranked by some legal scholars as one of the great Supreme Court decisions and an important step in the development of the federal judicial system and federal JUDICIAL REVIEW. For Virginia, the decision was a hard pill to swallow. The constitutionality of section 25 of the 1789 Judiciary Act would be debated until the outbreak of the Civil War in 1861.

Mason, George

If JAMES MADISON can be called the "Father of the Constitution," then George Mason (1725–92) can be considered the document's godfather. Mason, an American patriot, drafted the Virginia Declaration of Rights, which was adopted by the Virginia Assembly in June 1776, less than a month

George Mason's estate, Gunston Hall, is now a national historic landmark in Fairfax County, Virginia.
Source: Library of Congress

before the Continental Congress issued the DECLARATION OF INDEPENDENCE for the new United States of America. The first written guarantee of the rights citizens expect from their government, the Virginia document became a link between England's Magna Carta (1215) and the BILL OF RIGHTS (1791), not to mention the many national and international declarations and bills of rights adopted since then.

Born in 1725 in Dogue's Neck along the Potomac River in Virginia, where his ancestors had lived for close to 150 years, George Mason became a neighbor and mentor of GEORGE WASHINGTON. Even before the Declaration of Independence was signed, the thirteen British colonies along the Atlantic coast from Massachusetts to Georgia were making important decisions

that would lead to revolution and self-government. After Washington became commander of the continental armies in 1775, Mason took his place in the Virginia Assembly in 1776. Together with Washington, he had written the Fairfax Resolves, widely published resolutions containing revolutionary slogans and bywords for the colonists. Incorporating such language as "We can not be con-

VIRGINIA DECLARATION OF RIGHTS

June 12, 1776
Drafted by George Mason

I That all men are by nature equally free and independent, and have certain inherent rights, of which, when they enter into a state of society, they cannot, by any compact, deprive or divest their posterity; namely, the enjoyment of life and liberty, with the means of acquiring and possessing property, and pursuing and obtaining happiness and safety.

II That all power is vested in, and consequently derived from, the people; that magistrates are their trustees and servants, and at all times amenable to them.

III That government is, or ought to be, instituted for the common benefit, protection, and security of the people, nation or community; of all the various modes and forms of government that is best, which is capable of producing the greatest degree of happiness and safety and is most effectually secured against the danger of maladministration; and that, whenever any government shall be found inadequate or contrary to these purposes, a majority of the community hath an indubitable, unalienable, and indefeasible right to reform, alter or abolish it, in such manner as shall be judged most conducive to the public weal.

IV That no man, or set of men, are entitled to exclusive or separate emoluments or privileges from the community, but in consideration of public services; which, not being descendible, neither ought the offices of magistrate, legislator, or judge be hereditary.

V That the legislative and executive powers of the state should be separate and distinct from the judicative; and, that the members of the two first may be restrained from oppression by feeling and participating the burthens of the people, they should, at fixed periods, be reduced to a private station, return into that body from which they were originally taken, and the vacancies be supplied by frequent, certain, and regular elections in which all, or any part of the former members, to be again eligible, or ineligible, as the laws shall direct.

VI That elections of members to serve as representatives of the people in assembly ought to be free; and that all men, having sufficient evidence of permanent common interest with, and attachment to, the community have the right of suffrage and cannot be taxed or deprived of their property for public uses without their own consent or that of their representatives so elected, nor bound by any law to which they have not, in like manner, assented, for the public good.

VII That all power of suspending laws, or the execution of laws, by any authority without consent of the representatives of the people is injurious to their rights and ought not to be exercised.

VIII That in all capital or criminal prosecutions a man hath a right to demand the cause and nature of his accusation to be confronted with the accusers and witnesses, to call for evidence in his favor, and to a speedy trial by an impartial jury of his vicinage, without whose unanimous consent he cannot be found guilty, nor can he be compelled to give evidence against himself; that no man be deprived of his liberty except by the law of the land or the judgement of his peers.

IX That excessive bail ought not to be required, nor excessive fines imposed; nor cruel and unusual punishments inflicted.

X That general warrants, whereby any officer or messenger may be commanded to search suspected places without evidence of a fact committed, or to seize any person or persons not named, or whose offense is not particularly described and supported by evidence, are grievous and oppressive and ought not to be granted.

XI That in controversies respecting property and in suits between man and man, the ancient trial by jury is preferable to any other and ought to be held sacred.

XII That the freedom of the press is one of the greatest bulwarks of liberty and can never be restrained but by despotic governments.

XIII That a well regulated militia, composed of the body of the people, trained to arms, is the proper, natural, and safe defense of a free state; that standing armies, in time of peace, should be avoided as dangerous to liberty; and that, in all cases, the military should be under strict subordination to, and be governed by, the civil power.

XIV That the people have a right to uniform government; and therefore, that no government separate from, or independent of, the government of Virginia, ought to be erected or established within the limits thereof.

XV That no free government, or the blessings of liberty, can be preserved to any people but by a firm adherence to justice, moderation, temperance, frugality, and virtue and by frequent recurrence to fundamental principles.

XVI That religion, or the duty which we owe to our Creator and the manner of discharging it, can be directed by reason and conviction, not by force or violence; and therefore, all men are equally entitled to the free exercise of religion, according to the dictates of conscience; and that it is the mutual duty of all to practice Christian forbearance, love, and charity towards each other.

Adopted unanimously by the Virginia Convention of Delegates

SOURCE: The Avalon Project at Yale Law School, Eighteen Century Documents. Retrieved from www.yale.edu/lawweb/avalon/18th.htm.

More on this topic:

*Framers of the
Constitution, p. 230*

sidered as a conquered Country" because we are "Descendants not of the Conquered, but the Conquerors," the Resolves invoked saber rattling by the Virginia colonists in the face of their perceived unconstitutional treatment—such as taxation without representation—by Britain.

In the crucial year of 1776, after Virginia committed itself to independence from Great Britain, Mason wrote the draft of the Virginia Declaration of Rights, which was adopted on June 12, 1776, with only minor changes. Praised as one of the world's most influential documents of freedom, along with Magna Carta and the English Bill of Rights (1688), it proclaimed: "[A]ll men are by nature equally free and independent, and have certain inherent rights, of which…they cannot, by any compact, deprive or divest their posterity; namely, the enjoyment of life and liberty, with the means of acquiring and possessing property, and pursuing and obtaining happiness and safety." Much of this language is similar to that found in the Declaration of Independence, adopted on July 4, 1776, based on the draft by THOMAS JEFFERSON, a fellow Virginian. Immediately after drafting the Virginia declaration, Mason set his hand to outlining Virginia's first constitution (1776), which had a significant impact on constitutions around the world. Written eleven years before the groundbreaking federal constitution, Virginia's constitution provided that the "legislative, executive, and judiciary departments, shall be separate and distinct," that there should be a bicameral legislature whose upper house is called the Senate, and that judges would have lifetime appointments.

A delegate to the CONSTITUTIONAL CONVENTION OF 1787 in Philadelphia, Mason influenced a number of the final provisions, such as the requirement that revenue bills must originate in the HOUSE OF REPRESENTATIVES. An opponent of SLAVERY—his attack on the slave trade proved that his concerns for HUMAN RIGHTS could transcend his loyalty to his native state—he refused to sign the draft constitution. After adoption of the Bill of Rights in 1791, which he had urged be added to the Constitution, he commented that now he could "chearfully" put his "hand & heart to the new government." He died at Gunston Hall, his plantation home, on October 7, 1792.

McCulloch v. Maryland

McCulloch v. Maryland (1819) confirmed—some might say it created—the IMPLIED POWERS doctrine. It is one of the trilogy of great decisions by Chief Justice JOHN MARSHALL that, along with *MARBURY V. MADISON* (1803) and *GIBBONS V. OGDEN* (1823), extended the scope of the national government under the Constitution. Relying on the NECESSARY AND PROPER CLAUSE in Article I, section 8, Marshall reasoned that as long as a power (see POWERS) was not expressly denied by the Constitution and it was reasonably related to the general nature of the federal government's enumerated powers, then the exercise of such a power was not unconstitutional. As the chief justice himself put it: "Let the end be legitimate, let it be within the scope of the Constitution, and all means which are appropriate, which are plainly adapted to that end, which are not prohibited, but consist [are consistent] with the letter and spirit of the Constitution, are constitutional."

This case involved Congress's incorporation of the Bank of the United States. Under Maryland law a bank not chartered in the state had to pay a tax on the bank notes it issued. McCulloch, a cashier, issued bank notes without paying the Maryland tax, and the state sued to recover the tax due. The two key questions before the Supreme Court were: (1) Is it constitutional for Congress to incorporate a bank (incorporation of legal entities is normally a state function)? and (2) Can a state tax a nationally incorporated bank?

The Supreme Court's decision on the first issue was based on a broad reading of the powers delegated to CONGRESS by the Constitution. Referring to the legislature's list of powers enumerated in Article I, section 8, the Court noted that these powers include the power to lay and collect taxes (see TAXATION), borrow money (see DEBT), regulate COMMERCE, declare and conduct WAR, and raise and support armies and navies (see ARMED FORCES). Taken together with the power to "make all Laws which shall be necessary and proper for carrying into Execution the foregoing Powers," these directives implied to the Court that the incorporation of a national bank was not an unconstitutional exercise of power by Congress.

Regarding the state's power to tax the nationally chartered bank, Marshall simply pointed out that the power to tax includes the power to destroy. Thus, were the state permitted to tax a national bank or another federal activity, it could thwart the national purpose simply by raising the level of taxation to make the activity prohibitively expensive. Such a tax was therefore found to be unconstitutional and void.

The doctrine enunciated by Chief Justice Marshall in *McCulloch* that the federal government has implied powers has had significant implications for later Supreme Court decisions. The same broad interpretation of Congress's power under the commerce clause, also enumerated in Article I, section 8, would be used by the Court, for example, to countenance the extension of federal power to local commercial activity within the states. Legal scholars have praised Marshall's opinion in *McCulloch* on behalf of a unanimous Court, with one going so far a century afterward as to say that it is "among the very first of the greatest judicial utterances of all time."

The *McCulloch* decision figured prominently in the 1995 case of *U.S. Term Limits, Inc. v. Thorton* (1995). In that case the Supreme Court was presented with the question of whether the states could set term limits for members of Congress. The Court's opinion referred to Chief Justice Marshall's rejection in *McCulloch* of the argument that the Constitution's silence on the subject of the powers of the states to tax implies that they have a reserve power under the Tenth Amendment (1791) to tax federal instrumentalities. Similarly, the Court in *Thorton* held that just as the states never had the power to tax federal instrumentalities before the Constitution went into effect and therefore such power could not have been reserved to them, there could be no power reserved to the states to set term limits on members of Congress because they had no such power before the national government was formed.

> **"If any one proposition could command the universal assent of mankind, we might expect it would be this—that the government of the Union, though limited in its powers, is supreme within its sphere of action."**
>
> **—Chief Justice John Marshall,** in *McCulloch v. Maryland*

Military *See* ARMED FORCES; PRESIDENT.

Militia *See* ARMED FORCES; PRESIDENT.

Minorities

"If all mankind minus one, were of one opinion, and only one person were of the contrary opinion," suggested John Stuart Mill (1806–73), the English philosopher and champion of individual LIBERTY, "mankind would be no more justified in silencing that one person, than he, if he had the power, would be justified in silencing mankind." The great strength of DEMOCRACY is that today's minority views can become tomorrow's majority views. Governments based on a single ideology or party line cannot adapt as easily as a nation that always has a loyal opposition offering an alternative to the political party in power (see POLITICAL PARTIES).

In the context of the Constitution, the term *minorities* has two meanings: (1) Minorities may be persons who lose in voting contests, such as in an election, a vote on a measure in CONGRESS, or a controversy that reaches the SUPREME COURT. (2) Minorities are also particular groups of citizens who may be classified and treated as separate and not members of a larger or more politically potent group constituting the majority.

The rights of the first type, voting minorities, are determined by the procedures set forth in the Constitution for ELECTIONS as well as other procedures prescribed by law or put in place by constitutionally authorized institutions. The rights of individuals in the second category, class minorities (persons who belong to a specific demographic group), are determined under the Constitution just as all other CITIZENS' rights are determined in accordance with constitutional guarantees, laws enacted to implement those guarantees, and interpretation by the COURTS.

Voting Minorities

Constitutional democracies like the United States are predicated on the two key principles of political equality of all citizens and MAJORITY RULE as the preferred method of making political decisions. Equality of citizenship is derived from the notion of popular SOVEREIGNTY, which holds that the political power of a territorial jurisdiction—once considered to reside in the person of the monarch—is equally divided among all citizens in a democratic republic (see REPUBLICAN FORM OF GOVERNMENT). Majority rule, used since the ancient Greeks invented democracy some 2,500 years ago, is considered the logical method of determining political decisions in a democracy in which sovereignty is shared among the citizens.

The Constitution creates a number of procedural safeguards to protect voting minorities. The SEPARATION OF POWERS and checks and balances built into the federal government's structure require that all laws be passed by both houses of Congress and be approved by the PRESIDENT (see LEGISLATION). Thus a majority in a single house or even in both houses is procedurally unable to act with impunity. The independence of the judiciary (see JUDICIAL INDEPENDENCE) and its power of JUDICIAL REVIEW are additional checks on a legislative majority bent on undermining the principles of constitutional democratic government. And when it comes to changing the Constitution itself, Article V requires that an amendment be proposed by a supermajority—two-thirds of both houses of Congress or two-thirds of the state legislatures—and ratified by three-fourths of the state legislatures or state conventions (see AMENDMENTS).

Class Minorities

Just as majority rule can be destructive of democratic principles if unchecked by a separation of powers and constitutional procedures, it can also be as tyrannical as any absolute monarchy or dictatorship with respect to the rights of minority groups. What, for instance, is to stop a majority of Congress from passing a law that strips some ethnic or religious minority of its RIGHTS?

The United States prides itself on being a melting pot for people of many races and cultures, and almost every American can claim to be a member of some definable group or class minority— the elderly (see AGE DISCRIMINATION), CHILDREN, DISABLED PERSONS, WOMEN, HOMOSEXUALS, ALIENS, NATIVE AMERICANS, African Americans (see RACIAL DISCRIMINATION), Hispanic Americans, Asian Americans, Catholics, Jews, and Muslims, even, on occasion, white males. Classification as a minority group may also be ad hoc, such as employees who are not members of a union representing a majority of workers at a plant.

The Constitution ratified in the eighteenth century was hardly neutral toward disenfranchised groups, such as slaves, Native Americans, and women.

Slaves. Slaves (see SLAVERY) were excluded from citizenship by implication and common agreement among the FRAMERS OF THE CONSTITUTION, although they were to be counted, according to Article I, section 2, as "three fifths of all other Persons" in the census of the states' population. The rights of slaves varied in the states. In the northern (free) states, slavery was illegal, while in the

South before the Civil War (1861–65), it was legal. After the war, the Thirteenth (1865), Fourteenth (1868), and Fifteenth (1870) Amendments attempted to extend the same citizenship rights of whites to former slaves.

Native Americans. By giving Congress power to regulate COMMERCE with the "Indian Tribes" as well as "among the several States" and "with foreign Nations," Article I, section 8, intended Native Americans, for the most part, to remain a separate minority of noncitizens. Their treatment was changed somewhat by legislation and Supreme Court decisions but not expressly in the Constitution. Government protection was gradually extended to Native Americans living in tribal communities, and U.S. citizenship was granted, although at first only on a tribe-by-tribe basis.

Although an often impoverished minority, Native Americans enjoy certain rights, including electing tribal leaders. Here, President Bill Clinton (left) talks with Navajo Nation president Kelsey Begaye in 2000. Clinton was the first president to visit the Navajo Reservation.
Source: AP Images/Matt York

Women. Although not denied citizenship, women were by custom not entitled to political rights on a par with male citizens. They were not allowed to vote, to pursue certain occupations, or in many cases to manage their own PROPERTY. Political rights—to vote and to be elected to public office—were extended to women by the Nineteenth Amendment (1920).

Protection of Minority Rights

The Supreme Court has not always been in the forefront of protecting the rights of minorities, as evidenced by decisions in such cases as *Plessy v. Ferguson* (1896), which denied full citizenship rights to blacks, and *Bradwell v. Illinois* (1873), which denied an otherwise well-qualified lawyer admission to a state bar solely because she was a woman. But on the basis of the Fourteenth Amendment's EQUAL PROTECTION clause, the Supreme Court eventually struck down state laws that discriminated on the basis of race in *BROWN V. BOARD OF EDUCATION OF TOPEKA* (1954), finding unconstitutional the "separate but equal" principle of separating black and white public school students.

After the *Brown* decision, government actions that might involve DISCRIMINATION against members of groups classified as minorities began coming under closer scrutiny. For cases creating certain suspect categories of minorities, the Supreme Court has in fact begun to apply a STRICT SCRUTINY test, bringing the highest level of judicial oversight to laws passed by legislatures. For example, in *Dunn v. Blumstein* (1972), the Court held that when a law is based on racial or ethnic classifications the government must prove that it is "necessary to promote a compelling state interest."

Federal and state AFFIRMATIVE ACTION programs that attempt to remedy the effects of past discrimination against minorities, especially blacks, are also subject to strict scrutiny to determine if they go too far and violate the Constitution, according to the Supreme Court in *Richmond v. J. A. Croson Co.* (1989) and *Adarand Constructors, Inc. v. Pena* (1995). In *Morton v. Mancari* (1974), however, the Court did not find that the Indian Preference Act (1934), which gave Native Americans preference in employment in the Department of the Interior's Bureau of Indian Affairs, unconstitutionally discriminated against other racial minorities. In a number of cases involving affirmative action plans relating to school admission from REGENTS OF THE UNIVERSITY OF CALIFORNIA V. BAKKE (1978) to *Parents Involved in Community Schools v. Seattle School District No. 1* (2007), the Supreme Court has tried to determine exactly what types of affirmative action programs will pass constitutional muster.

Alleged discrimination against women and disabled persons has not been accorded this strict scrutiny test by the Supreme Court, receiving only a lower level of review such as "heightened scrutiny" or the "rational test" analysis. The latter simply looks to see if there is a rational basis for treating members of the classified minority group differently without actually discriminating. In *Craig v. Boren* (1976), using the heightened scrutiny test, the Court said that a classification based on sex must "serve important governmental objectives and must be substantially related to those objectives" (see SEX DISCRIMINATION). And in *McGowan v. Maryland* (1961), a case asserting discrimination against a religious minority, the Court found that a "statutory discrimination will not be set aside if any state of facts reasonably may be conceived to justify it" (see RELIGION).

The Supreme Court's special attention to laws affecting minorities in the second half of the twentieth century was presaged by a footnote in the opinion of Justice Harlan F. Stone (1872–1946) in *United States v. Carolene Products Co.* (1938). Justice Stone contended that the Court's presumption that legislation is constitutional might be abandoned "when legislation appears on its face to be within a specific prohibition of the Constitution, such as those of the first ten Amendments [the BILL OF RIGHTS (1791)], which are deemed equally specific when held to be embraced within the Fourteenth…[or when such laws are] directed at particular religious, or national, or racial minorities, [or when] prejudice against discrete and insular minorities…tends seriously to curtail the operation of those political processes ordinarily to be relied upon to protect minorities."

In any democracy a balance must be struck between the rules allowing the will of the majority to prevail and the rules ensuring that the majority will does not destroy the system itself or the constitutional rights of minorities. As Justice William O. Douglas (1898–1980) reiterated in a dissent in *Fortson v. Morris* (1966), "A citizen's constitutional rights can hardly be infringed simply because a majority of the people choose that it be."

In any democracy a balance must be struck between the rules allowing the will of the majority to prevail and the rules ensuring that the majority will does not destroy the system itself or the constitutional rights of minorities.

Minority Leader   *See* CONGRESS; HOUSE OF REPRESENTATIVES; POLITICAL PARTIES; SENATE.

Miranda v. Arizona

Persons accused of crimes are guaranteed three important constitutional rights. The Fifth Amendment (1791) prohibits SELF-INCRIMINATION: "No person…shall be compelled in any criminal case to be a witness against himself…." The Sixth Amendment (1791) provides for ASSISTANCE OF COUNSEL, stating, "In all criminal prosecutions, the accused shall enjoy the right…to have the Assistance of Counsel for his defence." A third right not expressly stated in the Constitution is the COMMON LAW presumption of innocence until an accused is proven guilty in a court of law.

A theme running through these rights is that the government has the burden of proving guilt beyond a reasonable doubt on the basis of evidence produced in court. The confession of a person accused of a crime is evidence, but it is not independent evidence obtained by the prosecution. Coming from the mouth of the defendant, it relieves LAW ENFORCEMENT authorities and government prosecutors of the burden of obtaining other evidence to establish the defendant's guilt. "Upon a simple and plain confession," wrote William Blackstone (1723–80) in his *Commentaries on the Laws of England* (1765–70), "the court has nothing to do but to award judgment: but it is usually very [reluctant] in receiving and recording such confession ('especially in capital felonies,' out of tenderness to the life of the subject), and will generally advise the prisoner to retract it, and plead to the indictment."

Voluntary vs. Involuntary Confessions

The *Miranda* rules, now a staple of police and courtroom dramas, evolved from Supreme Court decisions in four separate cases, including *Miranda v. Arizona* (1966). They require law enforcement authorities, before interrogation, to inform suspects taken into custody for questioning that they have certain rights, including the right to remain silent, derived from the Fifth Amendment's guarantee against self-incrimination, and the right under the Sixth Amendment to assistance of counsel during interrogation, either of a suspect's own choosing or appointed by the court. Moreover, suspects must be warned that anything they say may be used against them in a court of law. These *Miranda* warnings are aimed at ensuring that those accused of crimes are aware of their constitutional rights and are not intimidated by law enforcement authorities into confessing to a crime.

Using the DUE PROCESS clause of the Fourteenth Amendment (1868), in *Brown v. Mississippi* (1936) the Supreme Court held the Fifth Amendment applicable to the states (see INCORPORATION DOCTRINE) to bar the admission of an involuntary confession. In this case, the accused was beaten with ropes and studded belts until he confessed. Other "voluntary" confessions were still admissible as evidence even if the accused persons had not been expressly warned that they had the constitutional right to remain silent.

As with the Supreme Court's gradual development of the right to the assistance of counsel, which extended on a case-by-case basis a suspect's right to be represented by an attorney, the Fifth Amendment's protection against self-incrimination underwent a similar evolution. In *Culombe v. Connecticut* (1961), for example, the Court began looking at cases and weighing the individual circumstances to determine if a confession had been coerced or had in fact been given voluntarily (see BALANCING TESTS). In *Escobedo v. Illinois* (1964), the justices held that the police's refusal to allow a suspect to speak to his lawyer after repeated demands to do so during interrogation—even though the lawyer was present in the police station—made his confession involuntary.

Evolution of Miranda Warnings

Ernesto Miranda was convicted of kidnapping and rape after being picked out of a police line-up and signing a confession. The prosecution asserted that the suspect had voluntarily given the confession and completely understood his rights. Miranda, however, had not been advised of his Fifth Amendment right to remain silent or that he could have a lawyer present during his interrogation. The Supreme Court reversed Miranda's conviction, even though, as the Court admitted, it had no way of knowing what happened during the suspect's interrogation. However, the circumstances surrounding the interrogation—Miranda was not advised of his Fifth Amendment right to remain silent and was denied assistance of legal counsel, which he requested—created an "interrogation environment" that could have compelled him to make a confession against his will.

In his opinion for the five-member Court majority, Chief Justice Earl Warren (1891–1974) announced that rules regarding the admission of confessions into evidence were "an absolute prerequisite to interrogation." "The [Miranda] warnings required and the waiver [of the suspect's constitutional rights] necessary in accordance with our opinion today are prerequisites to the admissibility of any statement made by a defendant." The dissenting justices balked at the rules'

Television police shows like "NYPD Blue" and "Law & Order" have popularized the phrase: "You have the right to remain silent."
Source: Corbis/Albane Navizet

strictness, stating that they would prefer a more "pliable" standard as had been used in the Court's earlier analyses of the admissibility of confessions under the Fourteenth Amendment's due process clause.

Since the *Miranda* decision, the Supreme Court has carved out a number of exceptions that lessen the strict nature of the *Miranda* rules. For example, the warnings must be given only when a suspect is in custody—defined as any time a person is held against his or her will, even if in one's own home—and when there is an actual interrogation. In *Rhode Island v. Innes* (1980), the Court defined interrogation as an "express questioning or its functional equivalent," including "any words or action on the part of the police...reasonably likely to elicit an incriminating response from the subject." A suspect's second confession after being informed of his or her rights, however, is admissible as evidence, as is a confession obtained without the warnings if a reasonable concern for public safety precludes giving the warnings. In *New York v. Quarles* (1984), the Court found that asking a suspect immediately after taking him into custody where he may have disposed of a gun was not unconstitutional even though the suspect was not read his *Miranda* rights.

The requirement that the government bear the burden of proving—by a preponderance of the evidence at the federal level—that a confession was given voluntarily may be somewhat onerous for law enforcement officials. If a constitutional right is to have any meaning, however, it must be available to people at the time they most need it: when they are arrested and interrogated by the police. Despite an initial outcry from some critics about criminals being allowed to escape through technicalities and dire predictions about how the Supreme Court was tying the hands of law enforcement officials, the *Miranda* warnings have entered the pantheon of basic constitutional rights. In 2000 the rules survived a legal attack after they were challenged by a federal law that reduced admissibility of a suspect's statement to a question of whether it was voluntary or not. The Supreme Court in *Dickerson v. United States* held that "*Miranda* and its progeny in this Court govern the admissibility of statements made during custodial interrogations in both state and federal courts." But in *United States v. Patane* (2004), the Court made it clear that *Miranda* does not require the suppression of the physical fruits, for example, in this case a gun, obtained as a result of the suspect's unwarned but voluntary statements.

More on this topic:

Criminal law, p. 132

Monetary Power *See* CURRENCY.

Movement *See* TRAVEL.

National Powers *See* FEDERALISM; SEPARATION OF POWERS.

National Security

The German philosopher Immanuel Kant (1724–1804) characterized the role of the state most simply as securing an internal "system of right" and providing protection against external enemies. "The rights of man," he wrote, "are more important than order and quiet peace." All nations have some form of national security activities even if they are based on alliances with other nations to provide for their defense. For example, the Federated States of Micronesia, while maintaining its own internal security, relies on the United States, by treaty, for its external defense.

The U.S. Constitution's PREAMBLE proclaims that the document is intended, among other things, to "establish Justice, insure domestic Tranquility, [and] provide for the common defence…." According to Article IV, section 4, "The United States shall guarantee to every State in this Union a Republican Form of Government, and shall protect each of them against Invasion; and on Application of the Legislature, or of the Executive (when the Legislature cannot be convened) against domestic Violence" (see DOMESTIC TRANQUILITY; REPUBLICAN FORM OF GOVERNMENT). These provisions, together with the powers of CONGRESS and the PRESIDENT with respect to WAR, the ARMED FORCES, and FOREIGN AFFAIRS, give the national government the authority and the responsibility for taking measures to implement national security.

The nation's security is an ongoing operation whose mission is to thwart the possibility of war or other national emergency but also to be prepared to respond effectively if such exigencies occur. The primary instruments of national security are found in the government's EXECUTIVE

BRANCH. General responsibility for national security falls to the president, whose White House staff includes a group of close advisers called the National Security Council. Major roles in the nation's security are played by the Homeland Security Department, Defense Department, State Department, and Federal Bureau of Investigation in the Department of Justice (see CABINET), as well as the Central Intelligence Agency and the National Security Administration.

War and Other Emergencies

Constitutional issues regarding national security can arise in times of war or during other emergency situations (see EMERGENCY POWERS), as well as in periods of relative peace. During the Civil War (1861–65), President ABRAHAM LINCOLN instituted a number of measures aimed at bolstering national security, including establishing military commissions to act as courts. In *Ex parte Milligan* (1866), however, the Supreme Court found unconstitutional the use of such a commission to try, convict, and sentence to death a civilian who had never been in the military service. "The Constitution of the United States," the Court declared, "is a law for rulers and people, equally in war and in peace, and covers with the shield of its protection all classes of men, at all times, and under all circumstances. No doctrine involving more pernicious consequences, was ever invented by the wit of men than that any of its provisions can be suspended during any of the great exigencies of government."

Another Supreme Court decision addressed the detention, under the guise of national security, of U.S. citizens of Japanese ancestry during World War II. In *Korematsu v. United States* (1944), the Supreme Court upheld this detention as a valid exercise of the war powers conferred on the national government by the Constitution. The justices found that the action was taken not to discriminate against Japanese Americans but as a security measure for such persons residing on the West Coast. The same day as the decision in *Korematsu* came down, however, the Court's decision in *Ex parte Endo* (1944) released another Japanese American on the grounds that "[l]oyalty is a matter of the heart and mind, not of race, creed or color." After finding out that the military had presented false information about the security risk involved in *Korematsu*, the Court later vacated the decision. In 1998 Congress formally apologized for the internment of Japanese Americans during World War II, granting each living survivor $20,000 in compensation.

Subversive Activities

To protect the country from subversive activities in anticipation of war with France, Congress in 1798 passed the Alien and Sedition Acts, which banned the publication of false and malicious writings against the government and incitement of opposition to any acts of Congress or the president. Although the acts generally met with popular approval, some people thought that they were unconstitutional infringements on freedom of SPEECH and other constitutional rights. After the threat of war passed, the laws expired or were repealed within a few years.

Security fears during World War I led Congress to enact new espionage and sedition laws. The Espionage Act (1917), for one, barred anyone from obtaining information about national defense "with intent or reason to believe that it is to be used to the injury of the United States...." The Sedition Act (1918) made it a crime to "willfully utter, print, write, or publish any disloyal, profane, scurrilous, or abusive language about the form of government of the United States, or the Constitution of the United States...." During the Cold War following World War II, the communist threat brought about the Internal Security Act (1950)—passed over the veto of President Harry S. Truman (1884–1972)—which established the Subversive Activities Control Board to assist the attorney general with registering communist organizations and exposing subversive organizations.

At first the courts upheld some of these acts, weighing the magnitude of the harm against the infringement of such freedoms as speech and association (see ASSEMBLY AND ASSOCIATION). In

Rosenberg v. United States (1953), the Supreme Court in a 6–3 decision allowed to stand a DEATH PENALTY verdict against Julius and Ethel Rosenberg under the Espionage Act (1917) for giving atomic secrets and military information to the Soviet Union. The execution of the Rosenbergs took place on the same day that the Court's decision was handed down.

But in *Albertson v. Subversive Activities Control Board* (1965), the Supreme Court in an 8–0 decision held that the requirement that communist organizations register and thus be exposed to possible criminal sanctions amounted to SELF-INCRIMINATION in violation of the Fifth Amendment (1791). The Supreme Court later decided in *Hess v. Indiana* (1973) that only speech urging immediate lawless action could be punished and that the "advocacy of illegal action at some indefinite future time" is protected by the Constitution.

Vietnam War

The Vietnam War (1955–75)—an undeclared war—also raised constitutional issues with respect to national security. In the famous PENTAGON PAPERS CASE, *New York Times Co. v. United States* (1971), the Supreme Court refused to permit the government to restrain the publication in the *New York Times* of articles based on a classified government study of U.S. involvement in the war, which had been leaked to THE PRESS. The Court, however, did not say that under certain circumstances national security might not take priority over freedom of speech and the press, only that prior restraint of a publication is an extraordinary measure that was not proven to be necessary for national security in this particular case (see CENSORSHIP).

In *United States v. U.S. District Court* (1972), the Supreme Court rejected the president's assertion that in the name of national security he could authorize domestic WIRETAPPING without a judicial warrant (see SEARCH AND SEIZURE). Two somewhat unsettled constitutional questions remain concerning the extent of the executive branch's power to authorize electronic surveillance of foreign nationals, including foreign embassies, and to what degree Americans overseas are protected by the Constitution.

The War on Terror

The war on terror declared by the executive branch following the terrorist attacks on September 11, 2001, has raised a number of new constitutional issues regarding the president's power under the Constitution to take unilateral steps to defend the nation from further attack. Examples of such issues include the detention of prisoners, both citizens and noncitizens, captured or arrested for alleged terrorist activities; warrantless surveillance of potential terrorists; the use of torture to attempt to gain information regarding possible terrorist activities; and the leaking of information about U.S. intelligence staff for political purposes. In the last case, the identity of Central Intelligence Agency operative Valerie Plame was leaked by members of the executive branch, for which I. "Scooter" Libby, an aide to Vice President Dick Cheney, was convicted of obstruction of justice, lying to the Federal Bureau of Investigation, and perjury in 2007. (See *HAMDI V. RUMSFELD*; PRESIDENT; SEARCH AND SEIZURE; TERRORISM; WAR; WIRETAPPING.)

Need to Protect, Need to Know

In an open democratic system of government (see DEMOCRACY), a continuing tension is the proper balance between citizens' need to know information about their government in order to make

More on this topic:

Armed Forces, p. 42

Emergency Powers, p. 187

Terrorism, p. 543

War, p. 573

informed judgments, especially at the polls, and the government's need for secrecy in certain exceptional situations. Article I, section 5, of the Constitution provides a way for Congress to make some of its proceedings secret, but for the executive branch—in particular with respect to its role in conducting foreign affairs, making TREATIES, and maintaining a military force—there will always be a need for a delicate balance.

The chief advisor to King Louis XIII, Cardinal Richelieu (Armand Jean du Plessis de, 1585–1642) opined that "secrecy is the first essential in affairs of state." Too often, however, the cloak of secrecy is used on the pretext of national security in an attempt to unconstitutionally cover up mistakes and wrongdoing by government officials. Even legitimate secrecy then becomes more suspect.

Native Americans

"If it be true that the Cherokee Nation have rights, this [the Supreme Court] is not the tribunal in which those rights are to be asserted. If it be true that wrongs have been inflicted, and that still greater are to be apprehended, this is not the tribunal which can redress the past or prevent the future," declared Chief Justice JOHN MARSHALL in *Cherokee Nation v. Georgia* (1831). A year later, in *Worcester v. State of Georgia* (1832), he distanced himself from the earlier decision and wrote: "The Constitution, by declaring treaties already made, as well as those to be made, to be the supreme law of the land, had adopted and sanctioned the previous treaties with the Indian nations, and consequently admits their rank among those powers who are capable of making treaties" (see TREATIES).

A treaty signing at Prairie du Chien, Wisconsin, in September 1825 was attended by almost five thousand Indian warriors from nine tribes, as well as by U.S. commissioners, Michigan governor William Cass, and William Clark of Missouri.
Source: Library of Congress

The United States is not unique in having aboriginal or indigenous peoples living within its territory—for example, the Maori people live in New Zealand, the aborigines in Australia, and the Sami (Laplanders) in several Scandinavian countries. It is not unusual for the constitutions of such countries to refer to their indigenous population. The Charter of Rights and Freedoms (1982), which is a part of the Canadian constitution, provides in part I, section 25: "The guarantee of this Charter of certain rights and freedoms shall not be construed so as to abrogate or derogate from any aboriginal treaty or other rights or freedoms that pertain to the aboriginal peoples of Canada.…"

The major legal problem posed by indigenous peoples, including Native Americans, Alaska Natives, and Hawaiian Natives, is to what extent they may continue to live in their own societies and cultures apart from a nation's dominant—and generally more technologically advanced—society and culture, as well as the extent to which they can be integrated into that society and culture.

Before World War II the international community tended to favor integration. Because of changes in humanitarian and social philosophy, however, today there is greater emphasis on helping indigenous peoples maintain their traditional culture, while allowing individual members to opt to integrate into mainstream society to the extent that they wish to or are able to do so.

In *Rice v. Cayetano* (2000), the Supreme Court determined that a provision in the Hawaiian constitution that limited the right to vote for the trustees or members of the governing body of the state Office of Hawaiian Affairs to certain defined "native Hawaiians" violated the Fifteenth Amendment (1870) of the U.S. Constitution. That amendment prohibits denying the right to vote "on account of race, color, or previous condition of servitude." After skeletal remains of the approximately 9,000-year-old "Kennewick Man" were found in 1996 on the banks of the Columbia River, the U.S. Department of the Interior ordered that the remains be returned to tribal lands under the Native American Grave Protection and Repatriation Act of 1990. A U.S. court of appeals held in *Bonnischen v. United States* (2004) that only remains related to currently existing tribes must be repatriated and there was no evidence that any existing tribes or cultures could trace their lineage back 9,000 years.

> *Today there is greater emphasis on helping indigenous peoples maintain their traditional culture, while allowing individual members to opt to integrate into mainstream society to the extent that they wish to or are able to do so.*

Coexistence and Hostilities

The English colonists who founded the original thirteen states interacted in various ways with Native Americans (called Indians presumably because Christopher Columbus mistakenly thought he had sailed east from Europe to India). By turns, Native Americans and colonists coexisted and fought. As the population of European settlers increased, Native Americans more and more found themselves being driven from lands valued by the settlers. At the time of the CONSTITUTIONAL CONVENTION OF 1787, Native American hostilities were an important issue. John Jay, in essay 3 of *The Federalist* (1787–88) (see FEDERALIST PAPERS), asserted: "Not a single Indian war has yet been produced by aggressions of the present federal government, feeble as it is; but there are several instances of Indian hostilities having been provoked by the improper conduct of individual States...."

The ARTICLES OF CONFEDERATION (1781), under which the nation first governed itself, did not deal effectively with the regulation of COMMERCE with the Indian tribes, as pointed out by JAMES MADISON in essay 42 of *The Federalist*. The language in the new constitution thus gave Congress the power "To regulate Commerce with foreign Nations, and among the several States, and with the Indian Tribes." In this context, Native American tribes were to be treated as separate sovereign entities similar to foreign nations and the STATES of the United States (see SOVEREIGNTY). Relations between the U.S. government and Native Americans living in tribal communities were governed by treaties.

The Constitution originally also mentioned Native Americans in Article I, section 2—excluding them from congressional apportionment—and this language was later incorporated into the Fourteenth Amendment (1868), section 2 of which provides: "Representatives shall be apportioned among the several States according to their respective numbers, counting the whole number of persons in each State, excluding Indians not taxed." Native Americans were not taxed as long as they were living within a tribe or a community apart from other U.S. citizens. As such, they were not considered U.S. CITIZENS and were deemed outside federal and state legal jurisdictions.

Inherent Tribal Sovereignty

Gradually, however, the status of Native Americans has changed. Today the federal government does not tax tribal government revenues, just as it does not tax state and LOCAL GOVERNMENT revenues. Individual Native Americans, however, pay taxes like everyone else (see TAXATION), unless the source of income is directly from a treaty or a trust.

Congress's power to regulate commerce with Native American tribes nonetheless remains in force, and its power under Article IV, section 3, to regulate "the Territory or other Property belonging to the United States" still applies to federal lands held in trust for Native Americans (see TERRITORY). Such lands include reservations created by treaties or EXECUTIVE ORDERS of the president. According to *Maryland v. Louisiana* (1981), in cases of conflict between state and federal laws, the Supreme Court starts with a presumption that Congress did not intend to oust the state law. But according to *New Mexico v. Mescalero Apache Tribe* (1983), in cases relating to Native Americans and Indian tribes the presumption is reversed.

In an earlier case, *Johnson and Graham's Lessee v. McIntosh* (1823), the Supreme Court declared that the right of conquest gave the government control over all lands within the United States. And in *Cherokee Nation v. Georgia*, Chief Justice John Marshall in 1831 dismissed a suit by the Cherokee Nation on the grounds that it was not a foreign country but a dependent nation under the protection of the United States. In fact, the United States has seldom protected Native American tribes, and the Court has sanctioned Congress's power to simply break treaties with them.

Congress banned new treaties with Native American tribes in 1871, relying after that on its commerce power to enact legislation regarding them. The Supreme Court held in *Elk v. Wilkins* (1884) that the Fourteenth Amendment, making former slaves citizens of the United States, did not automatically extend citizenship to Native Americans born in the United States because the tribes were "an alien though dependent power." Citizenship was later extended to particular tribes and their members by law until 1924, when all Native Americans were declared to be citizens. In *United States v. Nice* (1916), the Court held that Native Americans who become U.S. citizens do not lose their tribal citizenship and are therefore entitled to dual citizenship.

The Supreme Court has acknowledged that Native American tribes have the power of self-government based on their inherent tribal sovereignty. But this has not always benefited individual members of a tribe. In *United States v. Wheeler* (1978), the Court held that DOUBLE JEOPARDY would not ensue if a Native American were tried in federal court for the same crime for which he had been tried and convicted in a tribal court, contending that the trials were in separate sovereign jurisdictions.

More recently, the unique status of Native American tribes has fueled a debate over gambling casinos run on reservations. Without the consent of Congress, states generally cannot tax commercial activities conducted on reservations or individual income from such sources. The untaxed casinos have raised questions about such exemptions for Native Americans. In *Nevada v. United States* (1983), the Supreme Court declared that "the United States owes a strong fiduciary duty" to Native Americans, although in *Menominee Tribe v. United States* (1968), the Court had held that the government may unilaterally end its trust relationship with any tribe.

The nation's history with respect to the treatment of Native American peoples is a chronicle of many tragic episodes, such as the Trail of Tears—the name given to the forced march of Cherokees in 1838–39 from Georgia to Oklahoma, during which some four thousand persons died. It is said that whenever an American diplomat protested the inhumane policies of the Soviet dictator Joseph Stalin (1879–1953), he would simply ask: But what about the Indians? The Constitution provides little special protection for Native Americans, and it is doubtful that their rights will be expanded in the near future.

More on this topic:

Drugs, p. 165

Minorities, p. 369

Religion, p. 458

Treaties, p. 551

Naturalization   See CITIZENS.

Necessary and Proper Clause

The Constitution, even with all twenty-seven AMENDMENTS, is one of the world's shortest written constitutions, containing only some 8,700 words overall. The FRAMERS OF THE CONSTITUTION realized that many of its principles would have to be fleshed out by the three branches of government, especially by the legislature in fulfilling its responsibility for making the nation's laws. Because the national government was to be a limited government of specific delegated powers, however, the framers felt the need to ensure that CONGRESS would have the necessary authority to carry out its intended functions.

Their solution was to include what has become known as the "necessary and proper" clause in the Constitution's first article. Article I, section 8, states: "The Congress shall have Power…To make all Laws which shall be necessary and proper for carrying into Execution the foregoing Powers, and all other Powers vested in this Constitution in the Government of the United states, or in any Department or Officer thereof." The Supreme Court in *MCCULLOCH V. MARYLAND* (1819) elaborated on the meaning of "necessary," concluding that to use the means necessary to an end is generally understood as using any means calculated to produce the end. It is not limited to any single means without which the end would be entirely unattainable.

Both JAMES MADISON and ALEXANDER HAMILTON discussed the necessary and proper clause at some length in *The Federalist* (1787–88) (see FEDERALIST PAPERS). Madison placed it in the last category of six types of power found in the Constitution, under "Provisions for giving efficacy to all [the other] powers." Although the clause was "the source of much virulent invective and petulant declamation against the proposed Constitution," he wrote in essay 44 that "[n]o axiom is more clearly established in law, or in reason, than that whenever the end is required, the means are authorized; whenever a general power to do a thing is given, every particular power necessary for doing it is included." Hamilton agreed, concluding that even without the necessary and proper clause, the same power would be a "necessary and unavoidable implication from the very act of constituting federal government and vesting it with certain specified powers."

THOMAS JEFFERSON, who opposed the establishment of a bank of the United States, argued with Hamilton in 1791 over whether "necessary" meant "absolutely necessary." In *McCulloch*, Chief Justice JOHN MARSHALL sided with Hamilton and upheld the power of Congress to establish a national bank. In 1869 the Supreme Court went on to uphold the power of Congress to tax state and private bank notes, because having "undertaken to provide a currency for the whole country, it cannot be questioned that Congress may constitutionally secure the benefits to the people by appropriate legislation" (see CURRENCY). In 1904 the Court upheld the extension of federal power over COMMERCE, stating that challenged revenue acts were within "their necessary scope and operation" and that therefore "the acts are within the grant of power [to Congress]." Later the Court sanctioned the use of the taxing power to attack drug abuse (see DRUGS) and the commerce power to combat other vices, including gambling and prostitution.

In a more recent case, however—*Printz v. United States* (1997)—the Supreme Court decided that it has to look not only at the "necessary" part of the clause but also at the requirement that acts be "proper." In striking down a legislative provision requiring states to conduct background checks on handgun purchasers, Justice Antonin Scalia (b. 1936) wrote that it was not "proper" if a federal statute infringed on state sovereignty. Scalia called up the language of Madison in *The Federalist* to shore up his finding that the states retained "a residuary and inviolable sovereignty," which Congress could not trespass on simply by relying on the necessary and proper clause. He further elaborated on the role of the necessary and proper clause in his concurring opinion in *Gonzales v. Raich* (2005), to bolster the Court's conclusion that Congress had suffi-

The Supreme Court has ruled that the necessary and proper clause prohibits the federal government from imposing certain requirements on handgun purchases.
Source: AP Images/Donna McWilliam

cient constitutional authority, under the commerce clause, to regulate and even prohibit the purely local cultivation and use of marijuana—in this case for state-permitted medical purposes on the advice of a physician. Undoubtedly, differences of opinion over the extent of the necessary and proper clause's power to justify congressional actions—which has been going on for more than two centuries—will continue into the foreseeable future.

New Jersey Plan   *See* CONSTITUTIONAL CONVENTION OF 1787.

New States   *See* ADMISSION OF NEW STATES.

New York Times Co. v. Sullivan

Freedom of THE PRESS, guaranteed by the First Amendment (1791), benefited indirectly from the CIVIL RIGHTS movement. In *New York Times Co. v. Sullivan* (1964), the Supreme Court strengthened the protections of a free press and free SPEECH by refusing to permit a libel suit against the *New York*

Times for publishing an advertisement by the Committee to Defend Martin Luther King and the Struggle for Freedom in the South. In its decision the Court held that freedom of expression on public questions is protected by the First Amendment and that criticism of the conduct of government officials does not lose such protection because it is effective and diminishes their reputations.

The advertisement in question, placed in the *New York Times* on March 29, 1960, by a group of entertainers and civil rights activists to solicit support for MARTIN LUTHER KING JR. and his civil rights crusade, accused unnamed Montgomery, Alabama, officials of causing Alabama State College students who were followers of King to be expelled, ringing the campus with armed police, barring students from the dining hall, bombing King's home, assaulting him, and arresting him seven times on trumped-up charges. City Commissioner L. B. Sullivan filed suit in state court against the paper, alleging that he had been libeled—he was responsible for supervising the Montgomery police—and that the advertisement contained factual errors (King had been arrested four times, not seven, and police had been ordered into the area of the campus but had not "ringed" it). He asked that he be compensated for damage to his professional reputation.

Although Sullivan had not been named in the advertisement, a jury found that he could be identified by inference and awarded him $500,000. This was one of several libel suits pending against the *Times* in Alabama, where such actions were seen as a vehicle for punishing the newspaper and threatening other publishers who might want to aid the civil rights struggle in the South. Together the awards against the *Times* amounted to more than $5 million when the U.S. Supreme Court agreed to review the case in 1964.

Three justices seemed willing to accept the *Times*'s argument that use of the state's libel laws to attack civil rights activists was itself tantamount to seditious libel (the criminalization of criticism of the government) and similar to the questionably constitutional Alien and Sedition Acts (1798). The majority, however, agreed to a somewhat less drastic finding: the Alabama libel law making the publication of words that injured or imputed misconduct to public officials in their office libelous *per se* was inconsistent with the First Amendment (1791) as well as the Fourteenth Amendment (1868), which makes certain guarantees in the BILL OF RIGHTS applicable to the states, even though a defense could be made based on the truth of the statement. The Court held further that constitutional protections for speech and the press require that a public official be barred from recovering damages for a defamatory falsehood relating to official conduct unless he or she proves that the statement was made with "actual malice"—with reckless disregard for whether it was false or not. Writing for the Court, Justice William J. Brennan Jr. (1906–91) said that "a profound commitment to the principle that debate on public issues should be uninhibited, robust, and wide open" was more important than requiring a degree of accuracy that could lead to self-censorship and a stifling of debate. The Court continued to expand the rationale for this decision in later cases to cover minor public officials, candidates for public office, and public figures in general.

In *New York Times Co. v. Sullivan*, the Supreme Court made the point that in a democracy people who hold or aspire to public office or who are otherwise public figures cannot insulate themselves from public criticism by using libel laws. People who willingly place themselves in the public forum may not hide from being criticized in that forum. The Court has drawn a line between public and private citizens, however, and has narrowly defined those who can be considered public figures and who thus have less protection from libel.

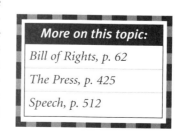

More on this topic:

Bill of Rights, p. 62

The Press, p. 425

Speech, p. 512

Nineteenth Amendment   *See* ANTHONY, SUSAN B.; WOMEN.

Ninth Amendment *See* BILL OF RIGHTS; PRIVACY.

Nobility, Titles of

A number of the world's democratic nations, notably constitutional monarchies, still maintain class distinctions between the royal family and titled aristocrats on one hand and commoners on the other. Such distinctions run contrary to internationally accepted principles such as those contained in the Universal Declaration of Human Rights (1948) and the International Covenant on Civil and Political Rights (1966), which emphasize the equality of all persons. As the Universal Declaration declares, "All human beings are born free and equal in dignity and rights."

By definition a republic (see REPUBLICAN FORM OF GOVERNMENT) is a country that is not governed by a monarch who is a titular figurehead—for example, the Queen of England is the titular head of state of Australia and Canada—or by an absolute ruler or despot. Class distinctions, based on family connections and wealth, nonetheless occur in many republics. The Roman Republic was divided into the upper class, called patricians, and the lower class, called plebeians; only after several centuries were the plebeian citizens given the right to participate meaningfully in governing the republic.

Article I, section 9, of the U.S. Constitution barred such class distinctions in the newly republican United States, stating: "No Title of Nobility shall be granted by the United States: And no Person holding any Office of Profit or Trust under them, shall, without the Consent of the Congress, accept of any present, Emolument, Office, or Title, of any kind whatever, from any King, Prince, or foreign State." In essay 84 of *The Federalist* (1787–88) (see FEDERALIST PAPERS), ALEXANDER HAMILTON referred to this prohibition as one of the "greater securities to liberty and republicanism.... Nothing need be said," he continued, "to illustrate the importance of the prohibition of titles of nobility. This may truly be denominated the cornerstone of republican government; for so long as they are excluded there can never be serious danger that the government will be any other than that of the people."

No important disputes have occurred over this provision of the Constitution, which bars any federal—not state—official from accepting a title from a foreign government without the consent of Congress. Under Article I, section 10, states are similarly prohibited from granting any title of nobility. In 1871 the attorney general of the United States determined that a "minister of the United States abroad [may render] a friendly service to a foreign power...provided he does not become an officer of that power" (see AMBASSADORS), adding that Article I, section 9, prohibits "the acceptance of a formal commission [that] creates an official relation between the individual thus commissioned and the government which in this way accredits him as its representative."

A proposed constitutional amendment was approved by Congress in 1810 to strip a person of U.S. citizenship for accepting a foreign title of nobility without the consent of Congress. "If any citizen of the United States," it reads, "shall accept, claim, receive or retain any title of nobility or honour, or shall, without the consent of Congress, accept and retain any present, pension, office or emolument of any kind whatever, from any emperor, king, prince or foreign power, such person shall cease to be a citizen of the United States, and shall be incapable of holding any office of trust or profit under them, or either of them." This "missing Thirteenth Amendment" was approved by twelve states but was never certified as having been ratified. Controversy has swirled around it through the years, and as recently as 1993 some citizens requested that the National Archives and Records Administration certify that the amendment had in fact received the required number of state ratifications. The Department of Justice concluded that the agency lacked the authority to make such a determination in this case because it had not received official notification from three-quarters of the states as required by the Constitution (see AMENDMENTS).

Congress has allowed honorary U.S. citizenship to be conferred on some foreigners, including Winston Churchill (1874–1965), the prime minister of the United Kingdom during most of World War II; Raoul Wallenberg (1912–47?), the Swedish diplomat who helped save many Jews in Hungary from Nazi atrocities during World War II; and Mother Teresa (1910–97), the Roman Catholic nun who ministered to the poorest of the poor in India.

Inherent in the concept of popular SOVEREIGNTY is the idea that all citizens have equal political and legal rights. Not every U.S. citizen is qualified under the Constitution to become president—by being born in the United States, being thirty-five years of age, and not having been previously elected twice to the position—but no hereditary transfer of power takes place in this republic. The Constitution's prohibitions against granting titles of nobility are a reminder that an individual's respect and political power must be merited and not simply conferred or inherited.

Mother Teresa is one of the few foreigners who have been named honorary U.S. citizens by Congress. Here she receives the Medal of Freedom from President Ronald Reagan and his wife, Nancy, in 1985.
Source: Courtesy Ronald Reagan Library

More on this topic:

Rule of Law, p. 475

Nominations *See* ADVICE AND CONSENT; APPOINTMENT AND REMOVAL POWER; POLITICAL PARTIES; PRESIDENT.

Oath of Office

ALEXANDER HAMILTON, in essay 27 of *The Federalist* (1787–88) (see FEDERALIST PAPERS), commented that "all officers, legislative, executive, and judicial in each State will be bound by the sanctity of an oath [to the observance of the supreme law of the land enacted by the national government]. Thus the legislatures, courts, and magistrates, of the respective members will be incorporated into the operations of the national government *as far as its just and constitutional authority extends....*"

Oaths (a word derived from Teutonic and Germanic languages) have been used for many reasons throughout history to swear allegiance or fealty to a feudal lord or king, to attest to the truth of a statement, or to promise to perform an act in good faith. Most national constitutions require the president and other public officials to take an oath of office. Bolivia's constitution (1967), for example, mandates: "Upon taking possession of their offices, the President and the Vice President...shall take a solemn oath of loyalty to the Republic and the Constitution before Congress." Some constitutions prescribe the language of the oath to be taken. The constitution of Egypt (1971) calls for this presidential oath: "I swear by Almighty God to uphold the Republican system with loyalty, to respect the Constitution and the law, and to look after the interests of the people fully and to safeguard the independence and territorial integrity of the motherland."

The U.S. Constitution also prescribes the language of the oath to be taken by the PRESIDENT. The last paragraph of Article II, section 1, states: "Before he [the president] enter on the Execution of his Office, he shall take the following Oath or Affirmation:—'I do solemnly swear (or affirm) that I will faithfully execute the Office of President of the United States, and will to the best of my Ability, preserve, protect and defend the Constitution of the United States.'" Taking the oath of office during inauguration ceremonies is considered a formality and not a legal requirement for exercising the powers of the office of president. In fact, if a president dies in office, the vice president (who has already sworn to uphold the Constitution) does not have to wait for a swearing-in ceremony but is immediately vested with the powers of the presidency. The CHIEF JUSTICE of the United States traditionally administers the oath of office to the president, although the Constitution is silent on this.

All federal and state officers are also bound by oath or affirmation to support the Constitution. According to the last clause of Article VI, "The Senators and Representatives before mentioned, and the Members of the several State Legislatures, and all executive and judicial Officers, both of the United States and of the several States, shall be bound by Oath or Affirmation, to support this Constitution; but no religious Test shall ever be required as a Qualification to any Office or public Trust under the United States." Persons whose religious beliefs prohibit them from swearing oaths, such as Quakers, may affirm the oath.

House Speaker Nancy Pelosi administers the oath of office to Rep. Keith Ellison (D-Minn.), the first Muslim member of Congress, in January 2007. Ellison's wife Kim holds Thomas Jefferson's Quran, which was provided by the Library of Congress for the occasion.
Source: Reuters/Jim Young

The Supreme Court has considered several cases involving oaths. After the Civil War, Congress and some states required a "test oath" for lawyers to prove that they had not participated in the Confederate rebellion. In *Ex parte Garland* and *Cummings v. Missouri* (both 1867), however, the Supreme Court held that such oaths were a form of a bill of attainder (a law punishing a person without a court trial; see ATTAINDER, BILLS OF) and thus prohibited by the Constitution. But in 1890, in *Davis v. Beason*, the Court sanctioned an oath by which Idaho's territorial legislature required that voters swear that they did not support polygamy. More recently, in *Bond v. Floyd* (1966), the Supreme Court held that the Georgia legislature could not refuse to seat Julian Bond because it believed that his criticism of the Vietnam War prevented him from honestly taking the oath of office. Bond's remarks were protected under the freedom of SPEECH guarantee of the First Amendment (1791), the Court said, and did not preclude him from validly swearing to uphold the Constitution.

In spite of the Constitution's prohibition of any religious test for office, GEORGE WASHINGTON established the precedent that the incoming president place his left hand on a Bible while taking the oath of office. He also added the phrase, "so help me God."

Obscenity

Obscenity and pornography have long been notoriously difficult to define, but legal scholars such as the British authority William Blackstone (1723–80) have tried to do so. In his *Commentaries on the Laws of England* (1765–70), Blackstone denounces "the sale of immoral pictures and prints" as

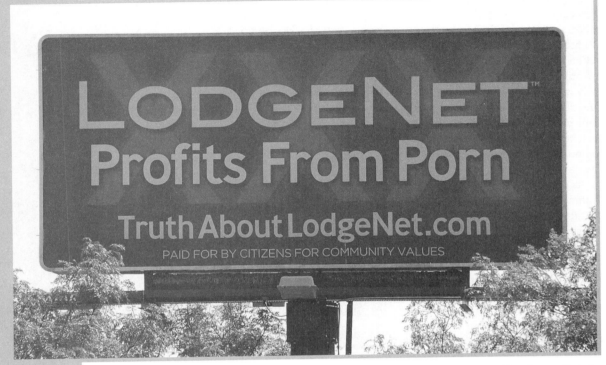

A billboard in Sioux Falls, S.D., paid for and sponsored by Citizens for Community Values, a Cinncinnati-based group, illustrates the group's attempt to pressure LodgeNet Entertainment Corporation to stop offering pornographic titles through its in-room pay-per-view service. The difficulty of defining what constitutes pornography led Justice Potter Stewart to admit in 1964 only that "I know it when I see it."
Source: AP Images/Dirk Lammers

a "grossly scandalous and public indecency," noting that "the punishment 'at common law' is by fine and imprisonment." Or, as Supreme Court Justice Potter Stewart (1915–85) famously retorted in *Jacobellis v. Ohio* (1964), "I know it when I see it," adding that the motion picture involved in this case "is not that."

Until the Supreme Court began wrestling with the scope and definition of these terms after World War II, the traditional legal definition of obscenity was conduct tending to corrupt the public morals by its indecency or lewdness. A great many types of activity can be viewed as obscene or pornographic, including printed matter, photographs, art, speech, and live or recorded performances in any medium. The problem the government often faces with respect to prohibiting or regulating obscenity is the risk of infringing upon the constitutionally guaranteed right to free SPEECH. For example, in 2006 a U.S. appeals court panel unanimously struck down a Portland, Oregon, city ordinance that allowed the ejection of disagreeable hecklers from events authorized by permit held in public areas. The panel ruled that the ordinance was an infringement of freedom of speech, even though in this case the heckler referred to women who supported abortion rights as "whores," "sluts," and "prostitutes."

The federal government is acknowledged to have the power to ban obscene or pornographic material sent through the mail, as well as its importation into the country or transportation through interstate COMMERCE. The legal question then becomes how obscenity is defined. The government's recent foray into prohibiting indecency on the INTERNET, under the Communications Decency Act (1996), was struck down by the Supreme Court. In *Reno v. American Civil Liberties Union* (1997), the Court termed the act overly broad and therefore an unconstitutional infringement of the right of free speech guaranteed by the First Amendment (1791).

"Appeals to Prurient Interest"

The first Supreme Court case to determine what constitutes obscenity under federal constitutional law was *Roth v. United States* (1957). Since the early nineteenth century, laws had banned the sale or distribution of obscene literature, but before *Roth* no case had reached the Court to test the enforcement of those laws against First Amendment guarantees of free speech and freedom of THE PRESS. A New York publisher of magazines, photographs, and sexually explicit books by authors such as James Joyce and D. H. Lawrence, Sam Roth was convicted under a federal law that made it a crime to mail material that is "obscene, lewd, lascivious, or filthy…or other publications of an indecent character." In his opinion for the Court, Justice William J. Brennan (1906–97) defined obscenity as whether "to the average person, applying contemporary community standards, the dominant theme of the material taken as a whole appeals to prurient interest." Justices Hugo L. Black (1886–1971) and William O. Douglas (1898–1980) dissented on the basis that the material was protected speech under the First Amendment.

After *Roth*, the Supreme Court justices began defining obscenity in their own terms and reversing lower court convictions under obscenity laws whenever a majority, each member using his own criteria, agreed. In *Ginzburg v. United States* (1966), Justice Brennan added that in close cases, where the distinction between "obscene" and "nonobscene" was difficult, the Court would consider whether the seller "pandered" the material to the customers or audience in such a way as to be catering to prurient interests. In *Stanley v. Georgia* (1969), the Court ruled that having obscene material in one's private possession could not be punished (see PRIVACY).

Contemporary Community Standards

In *Miller v. California* (1973), the Supreme Court set new rules for determining obscenity using a three-part test: (1) Would the average person, applying contemporary community standards, find that the work taken as a whole appeals to the prurient interest? (2) Does the work depict or describe, in a patently offensive way, sexual conduct specifically defined by the applicable state law? (3) Does the work, taken as a whole, lack serious literary, artistic, political, or scientific value? Miller had been convicted under a California statute for mailing unsolicited sexually explicit material, and the trial court instructed the jury to evaluate the allegedly obscene materials in light of contemporary community standards in California. The Supreme Court, while acknowledging that obscene material is not protected by the First Amendment—as established in *Roth*—tried to limit its role as national censor by approving the local determination of what constitutes obscenity. The Court also held in *Paris Adult Theatre I v. Slaton* (1973) that the First Amendment's freedom of speech guarantee does not protect consenting adults viewing films in an adult movie theater.

With respect to nude dancing, in *Schad v. Mount Ephraim* (1981) the Supreme Court invalidated a ZONING ordinance as an overbroad infringement of the First Amendment because it banned all live entertainment, including nude dancing that was not obscene, but permitted other kinds of commercial activity. However, in *New York State Liquor Authority v. Bellanca* (1981), the Court found that nude dancing and other types of nudity were entitled to some degree of First Amendment protection, except that a ban on nude dancing in places that sold liquor was a valid exercise of the state's POLICE POWER, in order to prevent disturbances.

Pornography

Like obscenity, pornography (from the Greek word *pornai*, meaning a prostitute) has not been easy for lawmakers or the courts to define. A basic concern raised in the modern feminist movement is the extent to which pornography exploits and degrades WOMEN (see SEXUAL DISCRIMINATION). The Supreme Court in *American Booksellers v. Hudnut* (1985) affirmed a federal appeals court decision accepting evidence of the harm pornography may cause to women, but it decided that this harm was outweighed by the First Amendment's guarantee of free speech.

Child pornography has even less of a claim to First Amendment protection than hard-core adult pornography. In *Ginsberg v. New York* (1968), the Supreme Court allowed the state to forbid sales to minors of material that was obscene for them but not obscene for adults. The Court held in *New York v. Ferber* (1982) that the First Amendment does not protect material in which CHILDREN were shown engaged in sexual activity, even if the material would not be considered obscene under the three-part test devised in the *Miller* decision. The Court has also distinguished visual depiction of children, as in the *Ferber* case, from verbal descriptions, which may not be banned under *Ferber*. In that case the Court acknowledged that the law in question was broad enough to ban pictures of children in foreign cultures of the type seen in *National Geographic* magazine. A state law banning mere possession of child pornography in the privacy of one's own home was upheld in *Osborne v. Ohio* (1990). Yet in *Ashcroft v. Free Speech Coalition* (2002), the Supreme Court rejected a federal ban on computerized "virtual" child pornography, calling the Child Pornography Protection Act (1996) so broad that it would also prohibit legitimate artistic or political expression. More recently, in *Ashcroft v. American Civil Liberties Union* (2002 and 2004), the Court struck down the Child Online Protection Act of 1998, which was aimed at keeping obscene materials available online away from children. Again, the question did not involve the definition of obscenity, but rather the concern that the measures used by Congress were too restrictive in view of the constitutional guarantee of freedom of expression under the First Amendment.

The basic premise of a democratic government is that a free and unhampered exchange of ideas and information, including ideas and information that some citizens may find offensive, can serve a valuable purpose by enriching life through entertainment and the arts. Falsely shouting fire in a crowded theater has the potential to cause real physical harm to people and thus is a valid exception to the constitutional guarantee of free speech. Nude dancing and pictures of sexual activity do not pose such a direct physical threat.

More on this topic:

The Press, p. 425

Privacy, p. 430

Search and Seizure, p. 479

Speech, p. 512

O'Connor, Sandra Day

Nominated by President Ronald Reagan (1911–2004) to be the first woman on the SUPREME COURT, Sandra Day O'Connor (b. 1930) testified at her Senate confirmation hearing in 1981: "My experience as a state court judge and as a state legislator has given me a greater appreciation of the important role the States play in our federal system, and also a greater appreciation of the separate and distinct roles of the three branches of government at the state and federal levels. Those experiences have strengthened my view that the proper role of the judiciary is one of interpreting and applying the law, not making it." True to her word, during more than two decades on the Court Justice O'Connor played a key role in the conservative coalition that decided many important cases by a 5–4 majority.

Born in the border town of El Paso, Texas, on March 26, 1930, Sandra Day grew up on her family's ranch in Arizona and graduated from high school at the age of sixteen. After obtaining an undergraduate degree in economics from Stanford University in 1950, two years later she graduated third in her law school class at Stanford, behind William H. Rehnquist (1924–2005)—the former CHIEF JUSTICE of the United States and her colleague on the Court—who graduated first in the class. Day was turned down for an attorney's position by several California law firms because she was a woman and then was offered only a position as a legal secretary in the Los Angeles law firm of Gibson, Dunn, and Crutcher. One of the firm's partners, William French Smith, would later be appointed attorney general by President Reagan and have the job of contacting her regarding her appointment to the High Court.

Day began her legal career as a deputy county attorney for San Mateo County, California, in 1952. After marrying John J. O'Connor III that year, she worked as a civilian legal officer for the U.S. Army in Germany, where her husband was stationed. Before being appointed assistant attorney general for Arizona in 1965, she practiced law while raising three children. Active in the Republican Party, she served as a state senator in Arizona from 1969 to 1975, cochaired President Richard M. Nixon's (1913–94) reelection committee in Arizona in 1972, was named senate majority leader shortly afterward (the first such woman in the nation), and then was elected a judge of the Maricopa County Superior Court in 1974. In 1979 Democratic governor Bruce Babbitt named her to the state's court of appeals. Two years later she had all the right credentials to help Reagan make good on his pledge to appoint a woman to the Supreme Court in return for his opposition to the Equal Rights Amendment (see AMENDMENTS).

In 1981 President Ronald Reagan appointed Sandra Day O'Connor the first woman justice to sit on the Supreme Court. Pictured (at right) with fellow justice Ruth Bader Ginsburg, O'Connor generally staked out centrist positions.
Source: Photograph by Ken Heinen, Collection of the Supreme Court of the United States

During her tenure on the Supreme Court, Justice O'Connor did not fit into any easy ideological mold. Basically conservative, she nevertheless showed limited support for measures to overcome racial discrimination and voted in favor of upholding ABORTION rights for women won in ROE V. WADE (1973). In Hodgson v. Minnesota (1990), she voted against a state law forcing minors to notify both parents before obtaining an abortion, and in Planned Parenthood of Southeastern Pennsylvania v. Casey (1992), she disapproved a similar state law requiring women to notify their husbands. She also served as an important link between the relatively liberal four-member faction and the relatively conservative four-member faction of the Court, although she tended to vote more often with the conservatives. Her centrist position, however, made her perhaps the most powerful member of the Court during the last few years of her tenure there. Justice O'Connor, citing her husband's medical problems as the impetus, retired in 2006.

Even though she was the first female associate justice of the Supreme Court—she was joined by Justice Ruth Bader Ginsburg (b. 1933) in 1993—and was clearly a victim of SEX DISCRIMINATION in the early days of her legal career,

"Thomas Jefferson and James Madison would be turning over in their graves right now, but let's hope Abigail Adams would be pleased."

—Justice Sandra Day O'Connor, at her celebration banquet, September 1981

O'Connor eschewed the notion that women are somehow different from men when it comes to the legal profession. According to her, "[T]he question whether women are different merely by virtue of being women recalls the old myths we have struggled to put behind us."

One Person, One Vote *See* BAKER V. CARR; REAPPORTIONMENT.

Original Intent

The CONSTITUTION, asserted Chief Justice Roger B. Taney (1777–1864) in *Scott v. Sandford* (1857), the infamous Dred Scott case holding that slaves were property, "speaks not only in the same words, but with the same meaning and intent with which it spoke when it came from the hands of its framers." Speaking to the American Bar Association 128 years later, Attorney General Edwin Meese III similarly called for the courts to return to a "jurisprudence of original intent."

The notion that court decisions interpreting the Constitution should be based solely on the original intent of the delegates to the CONSTITUTIONAL CONVENTION OF 1787 (see FRAMERS OF THE CONSTITUTION) has become a litmus test for conservative and liberal legal philosophies. Reverence for a timeless and eternal prescription for the structure of government and the rights of citizens has some appeal. Under this scenario, when new questions arise regarding the interpretation of the Constitution, the decision maker simply looks back into history and determines what was intended at the moment the document's words were committed to paper. Of course, disputes may arise over whether the intent was that of the original drafters, the body that adopted the language, or the bodies that ratified it.

Yet, the arguably greater intellectual challenge is to continually reinterpret not just the words but also the meaning of the Constitution in every new case. As Justice OLIVER WENDELL HOLMES JR. reminded us in *Missouri v. Holland* (1920): "[W]hen we are dealing with words that also are a constituent act, like the Constitution of the United States, we must realize that they have called into life a being the development of which could not have been foreseen completely by the most gifted of its begetters. It was enough for them to realize or to hope that they had created an organism; it has taken a century and has cost their successors sweat and blood to prove that they created a nation. The case before us must be considered in the light of our whole experience and not merely in that of what was said a hundred years ago."

The absolutist concept of original intent has not been relied on to any great extent by the Supreme Court, although some of the more conservative members of the Rehnquist Court (1986–2005) often used historical analysis to bolster their opinions. In fact, in perhaps the most important case of the second half of the twentieth century, *BROWN V. BOARD OF EDUCATION OF TOPEKA* (1954), the Court in overturning the legal basis for SEGREGATION of black and white students in public schools said that history was "inconclusive" on the question of whether the authors of the Fourteenth Amendment (1868) intended it to allow racially segregated schools. The increased importance of public EDUCATION in modern society nonetheless required that the Court's decision be made in a new context.

The words "We the People of the United States" in the Constitution's PREAMBLE can be read as referring either to those relatively few citizens alive in 1787 and long since dead or encompassing those who lived afterward and those who are now living under the government established by the Constitution. The world at the end of the eighteenth century was one of legalized SLAVERY, disenfranchised WOMEN, and little access to JUSTICE except for those few who were sufficiently educated and wealthy. One would hope that were the framers called on to remake the Constitution today, they would, in their genius, fashion an even more perfect document.

One legal adage holds that when the reason for a rule ceases to exist, the rule should cease to exist as well. Examining the history of how a constitutional provision came to be or what it was originally intended to do is not wrong. But to continue to cling to the original intent of the authors of a provision when the basis for it has changed or no longer exists is to risk a constricted vision that does not match that of the nation's founders.

More on this topic:

Constitution, p. 115

Framers of the Constitution, p. 230

Original Jurisdiction *See* SUPREME COURT.

P

Pardons

"If neither pregnancy, insanity,…nor other plea, will avail to avoid the judgment, and stay the execution consequent thereupon," noted William Blackstone (1723–80) in his *Commentaries on the Laws of England* (1765–70), "the last and surest resort is in the sovereign's most gracious *pardon*; the granting of which is the most amiable prerogative of the Crown." The power to relieve a person of the PUNISH-MENT imposed for illegal conduct originated with absolute monarchs, who, having the power to make laws, also had the power to forgive offenses against those laws. The constitutions of most countries in which the head of state is the president—from Argentina (1853, significantly amended 1994) to France (1958)—vest the president with the power to grant pardons.

The U.S. Constitution likewise provides in Article II, section 2, that the PRESIDENT "shall have Power to Grant Reprieves and Pardons for Offences against the United States, except in Cases of Impeachment" (see IMPEACHMENT). A reprieve differs from a pardon in that it only suspends the execution of a sentence rather than completely voids it. "Humanity and good policy conspire to dictate that the benign prerogative of pardoning should be as little as possible fettered or embarrassed," argued ALEXANDER HAMILTON in essay 74 of *The Federalist* (1787–88) (see FEDERALIST PAPERS). "The criminal code of every country partakes so much of necessary severity that without an easy access to exceptions

> *"The criminal code of every country partakes so much of necessary severity that without an easy access to exceptions in favor of unfortunate guilt, justice would wear a countenance too sanguinary and cruel."*
>
> **—Alexander Hamilton,** in essay 74 of *The Federalist*

in favor of unfortunate guilt, justice would wear a countenance too sanguinary and cruel."

The FRAMERS OF THE CONSTITUTION were not completely at ease in vesting the president with the power to pardon. After all, they had only recently fought a war against England's monarch, who, although constitutionally limited, had many prerogatives, including the right to issue pardons. But a majority of the delegates to the CONSTITUTIONAL CONVENTION OF 1787 believed that this power might help maintain order in the new nation by allowing the president to offer pardons to quell insurrection or rebellion (see DOMESTIC TRANQUILITY). Confidence that GEORGE WASHINGTON, in whom the delegates had great trust, would be the first president perhaps made the decision easier. During his presidency Washington did use this

President Gerald R. Ford announced the pardon of President Richard M. Nixon on September 8, 1974. The American public responded with mixed but generally favorable reaction to his decision allowing Nixon, the only president ever to resign from office, to avoid criminal charges stemming from the Watergate scandal.
Source: Courtesy Gerald R. Ford Library

power in 1795 to stop the Whiskey Rebellion, a revolt by farmers in western Pennsylvania who objected to an excise tax on whiskey, granting them an amnesty, which is a general pardon.

In the first court case involving a presidential pardon, *United States v. Wilson* (1833), Chief Justice JOHN MARSHALL declared that a pardon, according to English law, was "an act of grace," a private yet official act that a person must accept for it to have any effect. In 1915 a grand jury witness, George Burdick, the city editor of the *New York Tribune*, refused to testify about his editorial policies and sources for newspaper articles concerning a customs fraud investigation conducted by the government. President Woodrow Wilson (1856–1924) offered him a pardon to obtain his testimony, but Burdick refused it, fearing that accepting the pardon would make him appear guilty. The Supreme Court, in *Burdick v. United States* (1915), held that a witness could not be forced to accept the pardon or to testify against himself (see SELF-INCRIMINATION; WITNESSES).

The Supreme Court has used several other cases to address the president's pardon power, which extends to federal criminal offenses but not to state crimes or civil liabilities. After the Civil War (1861–65), the Court in *Ex parte Garland* (1867) struck down the requirement of a loyalty oath (see OATH OF OFFICE) for former Confederates but acknowledged that a pardon granted to Augustus Garland would exempt him from the oath requirement anyway. In addition, in *United States v. Klein* (1872), the Court upheld a wartime pardon by President ABRAHAM LINCOLN to Confederates that offered to restore their property if they swore allegiance to the Union. Although a pardon does not necessarily expunge the crime from the record, the Court held in *Garland* that if a pardon is granted before conviction, "in the eye of the law the offender is as innocent as if he had never committed the offense."

The president's power to pardon is one of the checks and balances built into the Constitution (see SEPARATION OF POWERS). It provides a procedure for righting injustices and preventing intractable conflict between the government and citizens, as well as allowing the nation to heal after times of crisis. Still, presidential pardons are often controversial. In 1974 President Gerald R. Ford

More on this topic:

Criminal Law, p. 132

(1913–2006) granted what was perhaps the most notorious pardon, absolving former president Richard M. Nixon (1913–94) from liability for all federal offenses he may have committed during his presidency. The pardon came one month after Nixon resigned from the presidency rather than face inevitable conviction on impeachment charges growing out of the WATERGATE scandal. Pardons granted by President Bill Clinton (b. 1946) at the end of his second term in 2001 also caused a great deal of controversy because of the relatively large number awarded and some of the cases' apparent political motivation. Like the presidential veto power (see VETOES), the pardoning power may be more appropriate for a monarchy than for a democratic republic like the United States because it conveys the possibility of unequal treatment based on political or personal favoritism.

In addition to commuting five sentences since taking office in 2001, President George W. Bush granted 142 pardons by the end of 2007, significantly fewer than most of his predecessors.

PARDONS

Presidential Clemency Actions, 1789–2007

George Washington	16	Grover Cleveland	1107[1]
John Adams	21	Benjamin Harrison	613
Thomas Jefferson	119	William McKinley	918[1]
James Madison	196	Theodore Roosevelt	981[1]
James Monroe	419	Woodrow Wilson	2480
John Quincy Adams	183	Warren G. Harding	800
Andrew Jackson	386	Calvin Coolidge	1545
Martin Van Buren	168	Herbert Hoover	1385
William Henry Harrison	0	Franklin D. Roosevelt	3687
John Tyler	209	Harry S. Truman	2044
James K. Polk	268	Dwight D. Eisenhower	1157
Zachary Taylor	38	John F. Kennedy	575
Millard Fillmore	170	Lyndon B. Johnson	1187
Franklin Pierce	142	Richard M. Nixon	926
James Buchanan	150	Gerald R. Ford	409
Abraham Lincoln	343	Jimmy Carter	566
Andrew Johnson	654	Ronald Reagan	406
Ulysses S. Grant	1332	George H. Bush	77
Rutherford B. Hayes	893	Bill Clinton	456
James Garfield	0	George W. Bush	142[2]
Chester Arthur	337		

1. Estimated actions
2. As of December 12, 2007, according to Justice Department spokesperson Erik Ablin, quoted by the Associated Press.

Patents

Included in the list of Congress's enumerated powers in Article I, section 8, of the Constitution is the power "To promote the Progress of Science and useful Arts, by securing for limited Times to Authors and Inventors the exclusive Right to their respective Writings and Discoveries." Authors are typically granted a COPYRIGHT, while inventors receive a patent.

As intended in the Constitution, a patent is a grant made by the government giving an individual inventor or a business the exclusive right to make, use, and sell an invention for a term of years. Patents are issued for four general types of invention or discovery: machines, human-made products, compositions of matter, and processing methods, as well as for design and plants. Before June 8, 1995, a patent for an invention ran for a nonrenewable period of seventeen years from the date of issuance. Currently, however, the period is twenty years from the date of the application.

In a recent interview the director of biotechnology for the U.S. Patent and Trademark Office said: "Genes are complex organic molecules, and when you isolate and purify them from the chromosomes where they reside, they are eligible to be patented as chemical compounds." Whatever the delegates to the CONSTITUTIONAL CONVENTION OF 1787 in Philadelphia may have debated about the patent clause, it is fairly certain that there were no discussions about the patentability of microorganisms or genetic material. (In *Diamond v. Chakrabarty* [1980], the Supreme Court held that live, genetically altered strains of microorganisms could be patented.) The FRAMERS OF THE CONSTITUTION did have available for their review the English Statute of Monopolies (1623), which, while outlawing monopolies, made an exception for letters patent (another term for patent rights in Anglo-American law) of fourteen years' duration to the "true and first inventors" of "new manufactures."

JAMES MADISON explained in essay 43 of *The Federalist* (1787–88) (see FEDERALIST PAPERS) that copyright was recognized under COMMON LAW and that "the right to useful inventions seems with equal reason to belong to the inventors. The public good fully coincides in both cases with the claims of individuals." Several of the states already had procedures for granting patents to inventors. But, as Madison pointed out, "The States cannot separately make effectual provision for either of the cases [copyright or patents], and most of them have anticipated the decision of this point by laws passed at the instance of Congress."

One of the framers of the Constitution was a renowned scientist and inventor himself—Benjamin Franklin (1706–90). His inventions and discoveries ranged from the lightning rod to bifocal glasses and the Franklin stove, still produced today. America's free society would spawn many more great inventors who gave the world inventions such as the electric light, the telephone, and the airplane.

The first Congress enacted a patent law in 1790, which was revised in 1836 when the Patent Office was created. Supreme Court rulings in the cases *Hotchkiss v. Greenwood* (1850) and *Funk Bros. Seed Co. v. Kalo Co.* (1948) held that patents may be issued only for new and useful inventions and that the discovery of a law of nature cannot be patented. According to the Court in *James v. Campbell* (1881), the government gets no benefit from a patented invention without compensating the inventor, and under its ruling in *Bonito Boats v. Thunder Craft Boats* (1989), states may not prevent competitors from making or using anything that is ruled not eligible for a patent under federal law.

In *Graham v. John Deere Co. of Kansas City* (1966), the Supreme Court propounded the conditions for obtaining a patent: the invention must be novel, useful, and not obvious. The Court, in *Festo Corp. v. Shoketsu Kinzoku Kogyo Kabushiki Co.* (2002), reaffirmed its doctrine of equivalents, which permits protection beyond the literal terms of the patent description. The federal COURTS have exclusive jurisdiction over patent infringement cases.

Several recent cases, including *Medimmune, Inc. v. Genentech, Inc.* and *Microsoft Corp. v. AT & T Corp.*, both decided in 2007, as well as a settlement of a trademark dispute, also in 2007, between

> *"The American lives in a land of wonders; everything around him is in constant movement, and every movement seems an advance. Consequently, in his mind the idea of newness is closely linked with that of improvement."*
>
> **—Alexis de Tocqueville,** in *Democracy in America* (1835)

More on this topic:

Common Law, p. 102

Copyright, p. 124

Property, p. 436

Cisco Systems and Apple, Inc. over the use of the name "iPhone," have led to calls for a reform of the patent laws. Patent reform bills have been introduced in Congress, but the difference in investment and production strategies between technology firms and drug companies has set the two industries at odds over possible patent law reforms. For instance, the tech companies need cheap, reliable access to new software and components whereas drug companies have a high front-end investment in medicines that can take years to get to market.

PATRIOT Act

The USA PATRIOT Act (Uniting and Strengthening America by Providing Appropriate Tools Required to Intercept and Obstruct Terrorism Act) was passed by Congress just 45 days after the terrorist attacks on America on September 11, 2001, and it was signed into law by President George W. Bush (b. 1946) on October 26, 2001. A controversial measure to enhance a number of aspects of the nation's ability to detect and combat terrorist activities, it was reauthorized by Congress in 2006. Several provisions of the act have drawn criticism from a number of individuals and organizations, including the American Civil Liberties Union, the Electronic Frontier Foundation, and the Electronic Privacy Information Center, for being unconstitutional. Although the U.S. Supreme Court has not yet ruled on these provisions, a U.S. appeals court at the end of 2007 ruled that some portions of the measure related to dealing with foreign terrorist organizations violate the Constitution because of the vague language concerning training, expert advice or assistance, personnel, and service to such organizations.

In general, the PATRIOT Act mandates the following: expansion of federal authority to track and intercept communications to aid law enforcement and foreign intelligence gathering; creation of new crimes and penalties; streamlining of procedures for prosecution; a grant of new powers to the secretary of the Treasury to regulate U.S. financial institutions with respect to foreign money laundering; new measures for tightening immigration and border crossing laws; and provision of new tools regarding the detention and removal of suspected terrorists in the United States.

More specifically, Title I of the act enhances the ability of internal security services, including the Federal Bureau of Investigation, to prevent terrorism. Title II addresses enhanced surveillance procedures relating to suspected terrorists and other clandestine activities. Title III is directed at improving the government's ability to deal with money-laundering to prevent terrorism. Title IV beefs up the law enforcement and investigative operations of the Department of Justice and U.S. Citizenship and Immigration Services with respect to border security. Title V enlarges the government's ability to investigate terrorism activities by, among other things, permitting the attorney general to pay rewards for assistance. Title VI changes the Victims of Crime Act of 1984 with regard to funding and managing the U.S. Victims of Crime Fund. Title VII improves the ability of U.S. law enforcement related to counterterrorism activities that cross jurisdictional lines through information sharing. Title VIII redefines domestic terrorism to include mass destruction and activities that are dangerous to human life and are intended to intimidate or coerce a civilian population. Title IX amends the National Security Act of 1947 by requiring the director of central intelligence to set priorities for foreign intelligence gathered under the Federal Intelligence Surveillance Act of 1978 and to provide assistance to the U.S. attorney general to ensure that information obtained from electronic surveillance or physical searches is disseminated for efficient and effective foreign intelligence purposes. Finally, Title X contains a number of miscellaneous laws that did not logically fit under other sections of the act. For example, hazmat (hazardous material) driver's licenses are restricted to drivers who pass background security checks, and the definition of "electronic surveillance" is amended to exclude the interception of communications done through or from a protected computer where the owner allows the interception or is lawfully engaged in an investigation.

Congress changed the PATRIOT Act in 2005 after a federal judge ruled in 2004 that the federal government's practice under the law of issuing national security letters amounted to an unreasonable search and seizure under the Fourth Amendment (1791). These letters are an investigative tool used by the Federal Bureau of Investigation to compel businesses to turn over customer information without an order from a judge or a subpoena from a grand jury. In 2007 a federal judge again struck down parts of the revised act because they did not allow for the courts to supervise cases where the federal government orders Internet providers to turn over records to the government without notifying customers. The American Civil Liberties Union had contended that the revisions of the act had not gone far enough, and the judge noted that "[i]t is axiomatic that in our system of government it is the province of the courts to say what the law is" and "[w]hen Congress attempts to curtail or supersede this role, it jeopardizes the delicate balance of powers among the three branches of government and endangers the very foundations of our constitutional system."

> **More on this topic:**
>
> *Law Enforcement, p. 338*
>
> *National Security, p. 375*
>
> *Terrorism, p. 543*

Patronage   *See* POLITICAL PARTIES.

Peace   *See* WAR.

Pentagon Papers Case

"The greater the importance of safeguarding the community from incitements to the overthrow of our institutions by force and violence," declared Chief Justice Charles Evans Hughes (1862–1948) in *De Jonge v. Oregon* (1937), "the more imperative is the need to preserve inviolate the constitutional rights of free speech, free press, and free assembly in order to maintain the opportunity for free political discussion, to the end that government may be responsive to the will of the people and that changes, if desired, may be obtained by peaceful means. Therein lies the security of the Republic, the very foundation of constitutional government."

On June 13, 1971, the *New York Times* published its first installment of a 7,000-page classified document commissioned by the secretary of defense to trace American policy in prosecuting the Vietnam War (1955–75). The material was given to the newspaper by Daniel Ellsberg, who had assisted in the report's preparation but later became an antiwar activist. Two days afterward a federal district court issued a temporary restraining order sought by the government to prohibit further publication of the material. And then on June 18 the *Washington Post* began publishing the report. The following day the district court judge refused to grant the government a permanent restraining order. After the order was reinstated by the U.S. Court of Appeals, the matter was scheduled for hearing by the Supreme Court on June 26.

On June 30 the Supreme Court handed down its opinion in the Pentagon Papers Case, *New York Times Co. v. United States* (1971), concluding that the government had not met the "heavy burden of showing justification for the imposition of such a restraint." The restraining orders of the court of appeals were reversed, and the district court's judgment refusing to grant a permanent injunction against further publication was affirmed.

The Supreme Court's decision was issued *per curiam* (representing the whole Court, as opposed to a majority opinion written by an individual justice), with each of the nine justices writing separate

Daniel Ellsberg speaks to reporters during the Penatgon Papers trial.
Source: AP Images

opinions, three of them dissents. According to the opinion of Justice Hugo L. Black (1886–1971), with whom Justice William O. Douglas (1898–1980) concurred, "In the First Amendment the Founding Fathers gave the free press the protection it must have to fulfill its essential role in our democracy. The press was to serve the governed, not the governors. The Government's power to censor the press was abolished so that the press would remain forever free to censure the Government. The press was protected so that it could bare the secrets of government and inform the people. Only a free and unrestrained press can effectively expose deception in government. And paramount among the responsibilities of a free press is the duty to prevent any part of the government from deceiving the people and sending them off to distant lands to die of foreign fevers and foreign shot and shell. In my view, far from deserving condemnation for their courageous reporting, the New York Times, the Washington Post, and other newspapers should be commended for serving the purpose that the Founding Fathers saw so clearly. In revealing the workings of government that led to the Vietnam war, the newspapers nobly did precisely that which the Founders hoped and trusted they would do."

The three dissenters complained about the rush to judgment in the matter. One of them, Chief Justice Warren E. Burger (1907–95), expressed his view that the publishers of the Pentagon Papers should be prosecuted for violation of NATIONAL SECURITY laws that prohibit printing classified information, but he did not support any prior restraint of publication.

The Vietnam War divided the country as no other war since the Civil War (1861–65), and some Americans who supported it considered the activities of the more strident dissenters to be unpatriotic and even treasonous. During times of war or other national emergencies (see EMERGENCY POWERS), there is a great temptation on the part of those who govern to withhold evidence of their failures to act responsibly. The decision in the Pentagon Papers case advanced the proposition that in a democracy, especially in extreme circumstances, the people need timely and accurate information on which to judge whether those they have entrusted with the power to govern them are acting responsibly and in good faith. Nevertheless, some Americans continued to argue that the release of the Papers constituted a genuine and irresponsible breach of national security.

More on this topic:

Censorship, p. 82

The Press, p. 425

Perez v. Brownell   See CITIZENS.

Petitions   See ASSEMBLY AND ASSOCIATION.

Picketing   *See* ASSEMBLY AND ASSOCIATION.

Police Power

The underlying basis of all government is SOVEREIGNTY. In domestic and INTERNATIONAL LAW, sovereignty includes the unfettered right of every nation to make and enforce laws with respect to all elements affecting the political organization of its citizens. Police power is the power of any sovereign or semisovereign political jurisdiction, such as the STATES of the United States, to make laws for the protection and WELFARE of that jurisdiction. In an absolute monarchy or a dictatorship, such power rests in the monarch or the dictator, who may delegate some aspects of it to others. In a constitutional monarchy or a DEMOCRACY, however, the CITIZENS delegate the police power to political offices and institutions established in their constitutions.

In U.S. law, *police power* has two meanings: (1) the power vested in Congress or a state legislature to make laws for the welfare of the nation, state, and the people; and (2) the general power vested in each state to maintain and regulate its police force—the administrative arm of government charged with preserving public order, promoting public HEALTH, safety, and morals; and preventing, detecting, and punishing crimes (see CRIMINAL LAW; PUNISHMENT). "By the public police and economy," wrote William Blackstone (1723–80) in his *Commentaries on the Laws of England* (1765–70), "I mean the due regulation and domestic order of the kingdom; whereby the individuals of the state, like members of a well-governed family, are bound to conform their general behaviour to the rules of propriety, good neighbourhood, and good manners; and to be decent, industrious, and inoffensive in their respective stations."

Although the term *police power* does not appear in the Constitution, Chief Justice JOHN MARSHALL in *GIBBONS V. OGDEN* (1824) recognized an "immense mass" of power in the states that could be used for the protection of citizens and the promotion of local interests. Then in *Brown v. Maryland* (1827), Marshall focused more specifically on this theme, declaring: "The power to direct the removal of gunpowder is a branch of the police power, which unquestionably remains, and ought to remain, with the States [as is] the removal or destruction of infectious or unsound articles."

State Police Power

In *Brown v. Maryland*, the Supreme Court equated a state's legislative power with its police power. That power is broad enough to encompass laws promoting "public convenience or the general welfare and prosperity," according to *Chicago and Alton Railroad v. Tranbarger* (1915). And in *Barnes v. Glen Theater* (1991), a case involving a state statute prohibiting anyone from knowingly or intentionally appearing nude in public, the Court confirmed that state police power has historically been considered to extend to matters involving public health, safety, and morals.

State police power is not unlimited, however, especially when it comes in conflict with the powers delegated to the federal government by the Constitution, such as the COMMERCE clause in Article I, section 8; the contract clause in Article I, section 10 (see CONTRACTS); and the DUE PROCESS clause of the Fourteenth Amendment (1868). In such cases the state power generally gives way to the federal government's powers and protections.

States may not delegate or bargain away their police power either, according to the Supreme Court's decision in *Boston Beer Co. v. Massachusetts* (1877). Under a charter granted in 1828, the beer company had the right to manufacture and sell malt liquors, but its products were seized on the basis of a Massachusetts law known as the Prohibitory Liquor Law (1869). The Court held that the exercise of the state's police power did not infringe the contract clause of the Constitution: "Whatever differences of opinion may exist as to the extent and boundaries of the police power…, there seems to be no doubt that it does extend to the protection of the lives, health, and property of the citizens, and to the preservation of good order and the public morals. The legislature cannot, by any contract, divest itself of the power to provide for these objects."

Regarding the extent to which state police power is limited by the Constitution, Supreme Court Justice OLIVER WENDELL HOLMES JR. drew the line in *Pennsylvania Coal Company v. Mahon* (1922). In this case, a statute designed to protect the safety of area residents prohibited a coal company from exercising its subsurface mining rights, even though the company had reserved such rights in the deeds given to the homeowners. Holmes found that the statute went "too far" because it effectively took the coal company's rights, which had been openly bargained for with the homeowners, without compensating it for its loss, as required by the Fifth Amendment (1791) (see JUST COMPENSATION).

In a concurring opinion in *Dartmouth College v. Woodward* (1819), Justice Joseph Story (1779–1845) concluded that a corporate charter granted by a state could not be changed by the state unless the charter contained a clause reserving that option. States thus began adding such a reserve clause to charters they granted. But in *Home Building and Loan Association v. Blaisdell* (1934), the Supreme Court held that state laws may modify or abrogate contracts because "the reservation of essential attributes of sovereign power [such as the right to pass laws that may be inconsistent with existing contracts] is also read into contracts."

The authority of every state to maintain a police force is important for promoting public safety. In this photo, California Highway Patrol officers aim their guns at a suspect after a high-speed chase.
Source: AP Images/Damian Dovarganes

National Police Power

In addition to the conflicts that can arise from the overzealous use of state police power, resulting in denial of constitutional rights, in a federal system of government (SEE FEDERALISM) there is the constant threat of conflicts between state police power and the powers delegated to the federal government.

Strictly speaking, no national police power exists, but the term is used to refer to Congress's authority under the Constitution's delegated powers to enact laws regarding public health, safety, and morals, as well as antidiscrimination, environmental, and criminal laws. The Supreme Court in *United States v. Carolene Products Co.* (1938), in language that mirrors that used to uphold state police power, said that Congress is free to exclude from interstate commerce articles whose use may be injurious to public health, morals, or welfare or that contravene the policy of the state of their destination.

In the sense of having authority to enforce laws in the states, there is also no national police power. The closest agency to a national police force is the Federal Bureau of Investigation in the Department of Justice, which has limited jurisdiction in certain areas of criminal activities under federal law, including espionage, international crime, and TERRORISM. Other federal agencies have limited powers to enforce specific laws in areas such as TAXATION, DRUGS, customs, and financial wrongdoing, among them the Treasury Department, Justice Department, Labor Department, and Securities and Exchange Commission.

More on this topic:
Discrimination, p. 159
Environment, p. 195
Law Enforcement, p. 338

Political Parties

In any large group of people, there will be factions—groups with similar interests or goals that differ from the interests and goals of others. In the democracy of ancient Athens (510–322 B.C.E.), wealthier persons often opposed war because of the risk of losing their wealth in defeat. Poorer citizens, in contrast, tended to support the idea of going to war because victory might produce gains for them. Factions also existed in the ancient republic of Rome (509–27 B.C.E.); and in Italy, at the time of Dante Alighieri (1265–1321), the Guelph and Ghibelline families each had their own supporters in their quests for power.

At the time of the American Revolution, the major factions—political parties—in Great Britain were the Tories (from an Irish term for a papist outlaw), who supported the hereditary right of James II (reigned 1685–88) to succeed to the throne even though he was a Catholic, and the Whigs (from a Scottish term for a thief), who opposed James II. Some of the FRAMERS OF THE CONSTITUTION, however—JAMES MADISON among them—were leery of factions, which had not yet become political parties as we know them today. In his essay 10 in *The*

"A LIVE JACKASS KICKING A DEAD LION."
And such a Lion! and such a Jackass!

Thomas Nast's illustration for Harper's Weekly *on January 15, 1870, helped to popularize the donkey as a symbol for the Democratic Party.*
Source: Library of Congress

The Republican elephant made its first appearance in a Thomas Nast illustration for Harper's Weekly *on November 7, 1874.*
Source: Library of Congress

Federalist (1787–88) (see FEDERALIST PAPERS), the "Father of the Constitution" cited evidence of his fears. "Complaints are everywhere heard from our most considerate and virtuous citizens…that our governments are too unstable, that the public good is disregarded in the conflicts of rival parties, and that measures are too often decided, not according to the rules of justice and the rights of the minor party, but by the superior force of an interested and overbearing majority." The French political observer Alexis de Tocqueville (1805–59) agreed, saying in *Democracy in America* (1835) that political "[p]arties are an evil inherent in free governments.…" He added that "great political parties are those more attached to principles than to consequences, to generalities rather than to particular cases, to ideas rather than to personalities."

The role played by political parties in governing the United States is based on tradition and custom; they are not mentioned in the written Constitution. However, the constitutions of a number of other nations, including Egypt (1971, as revised), Portugal (1976), and Tunisia (1959), expressly address the relationship of political parties to the government. The Tunisian constitution, for example, provides that political parties must observe a number of principles and restrictions and are subject to laws that set "the rules governing the establishment and organization of parties."

The right to have ELECTIONS in which several political parties vie for public office is especially important for a strong constitutional DEMOCRACY. The Communist Party and other dictatorial systems instead generally attempt to maintain their domination through a single party. But even among multiparty democracies there is a distinction between the two-party system such as America's, which may be a carryover from the system the colonists knew in Britain, and one that embraces a number of minority parties that form coalitions in order to put together a viable government after elections.

Organizing the Government

Even though political parties are not expressly mentioned in the U.S. Constitution, they play an important role in how the government operates. Although the heyday of the two-party system in the United States is over—many citizens no longer identify themselves as belonging to one party or the other—the basic system remains intact despite several attempts since World War II to create a significant third party to rival the traditional Democratic and Republican Parties. Among the third parties that have tried to gain a toehold are the Free Soil Party, which supported Martin Van Buren (1782–1862) as its presidential candidate in 1848; the Progressive (Bull Moose) Party, whose candidate in 1912 was Theodore Roosevelt (1858–1919); the Progressive Party, whose candidate in 1924 was Robert M. La Follette (1855–1925); and the Reform Party, whose candidate in 1992 and 1996 was Ross Perot (b. 1930). The Socialist, Communist, and Libertarian Parties also unsuccessfully sought to shape the nation's agenda at various times during the twentieth century.

After a presidential election, the party whose candidate wins gains control of the process of selecting the heads of federal departments and their key policy makers (see ADMINISTRATIVE AGENCIES; APPOINTMENT AND REMOVAL POWER; CABINET) and fills vacancies in the federal COURTS, with the ADVICE AND CONSENT of the Senate. Most important, the majority party has the opportunity to set the agenda for the nation in domestic policy and FOREIGN AFFAIRS.

Following congressional elections, the majority party in each house of CONGRESS—and they may be different parties—organizes the SENATE and the HOUSE OF REPRESENTATIVES and selects the SPEAKER OF THE HOUSE. Members of Congress from the majority party hold the preponderance of seats on congressional committees and the leadership roles on those committees.

Organizing Elections

Even before elections, the two major parties have the opportunity to frame debate on the national political agenda and to select the candidates who will run for public office. The party out of power at any given time in the EXECUTIVE BRANCH or the LEGISLATIVE BRANCH also acts as a check on the party in power (see SEPARATION OF POWERS), bringing to the attention of the media and the public the failures of its policies and leaders.

Primary elections have become an important part of the process by which political parties select candidates to put up for general elections. These are preferential contests in which members of a party determine who will represent it in national and state elections. In *Nixon v. Herndon* (1927), the Supreme Court found that because primary elections are held under state auspices, they are subject to the prohibition in the Fourteenth Amendment (1868) against excluding minority voters, as are selections of candidates by party committees. But in *Grovey v. Townsend* (1935), where the membership of a state political party voted to include only white citizens in its deliberations, the Supreme Court said that this constituted a substantial difference from an action by an executive committee of the party and upheld the exclusion of blacks on the basis of the right of association under the Constitution (see ASSEMBLY AND ASSOCIATION). It distinguished earlier cases requiring inclusion of MINORITIES as those involving some state action, as opposed to actions by an association of private citizens.

In 1941, in *United States v. Classic*, the Supreme Court brought primary elections under the supervision of Congress. The Court concluded that while a state government has the power to regulate primary elections, it is the duty of Congress to ensure the integrity of such elections. In effect,

CLOSER LOOK

The two-party system almost broke down in 1912. The unusual three-way election featured a clash between two former presidents, neither of whom could muster the needed votes to return to the White House.

William Howard Taft, the incumbent president, won the Republican nomination despite fierce opposition from Theodore Roosevelt, his progressive predecessor. Roosevelt formed his own party, known as the Bull Moose Party, and ran in the general election.

The Democrat, Woodrow Wilson, garnered just 42 percent of the popular vote. But that was enough to win the election because of the split in the Republican ranks.

Although Roosevelt finished second—a remarkable feat for a third-party candidate—the Bull Moose Party failed to remain competitive. Its candidates won little support in 1914, and the party disappeared shortly after.

the right to vote in a primary election is therefore incorporated under Article I, sections 2 and 4, which prescribe procedures for general elections. And in *Terry v. Adams* (1953), the last of the so-called White Primary Cases, the Supreme Court extended the voting rights guarantees in the Fifteenth Amendment (1870) even to a straw vote paid for and conducted by a local group calling itself the Jaybird Democratic Association.

Because of the central role played by the political parties in elections and the formation of the government afterward, the Supreme Court has tended to be deferential to them. In fact, in *Renne v. Geary* (1991) it refused to decide a California dispute involving a state constitutional provision banning parties from actively campaigning for or against candidates for nonpartisan offices. But in *California Democratic Party v. Jones* (2000), the Court entered the fray and invalidated as an unconstitutional infringement of freedom of association a California law changing primary elections from "closed," in which only party members can vote, to "blanket" primaries, in which candidates regardless of political party affiliation were listed and voters were free to choose among them. In its decision the Court noted that "[s]tates play a major role in structuring and monitoring the primary election process, but the processes by which political parties select their nominees are not wholly public affairs." Therefore, it concluded, "States must act within the limits of the Constitution when regulating parties' internal processes." The Court, by a 6–3 vote, ruled in *Clingman v. Beaver* (2005) that an Oklahoma law that allowed a political party to invite registered independent voters to participate in the party's primary did not violate the Constitution's freedom of association guarantee, unlike the Connecticut law struck down by the Court in *Tashjian v. Republican Party of Connecticut* (1986) that prohibited independent voters from participating in a major party's primaries when invited to do so.

The large amounts of money required to run major election campaigns today mean that candidates must have either great personal wealth or access to effective fund raising by associations such as the political parties and interest groups that support a party, its candidates, or its agenda (see CAMPAIGN FINANCING). Even though not contemplated by the framers of the Constitution, the two-party system has served the nation reasonably well, and it is doubtful that a better system will take its place in the near future.

> **More on this topic:**
>
> *Majority Rule, p. 357*

Poll Tax   *See* RACIAL DISCRIMINATION.

Popular Sovereignty   *See* SOVEREIGNTY.

Pornography   *See* OBSCENITY.

Postal Power

A postal system was vital to the sprawling American colonies that became independent states following their DECLARATION OF INDEPENDENCE in 1776. A monthly post (mail) run had been set up

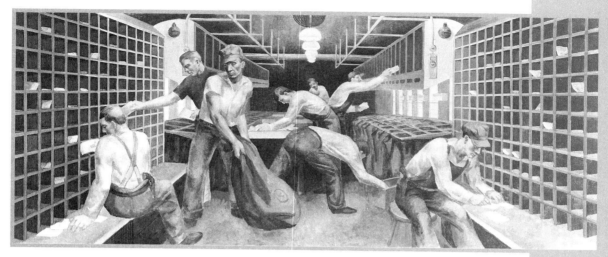

This 1930s mural by Frank Long in Hagerstown, Maryland, depicts the arduous job of hand-sorting the mail. The power to establish post offces was given by the framers to Congress in Article I of the Constitution.
Source: Library of Congress

between New York and Boston as early 1673, and ten years later William Penn (1644–1718) established the first post office in Pennsylvania. In 1753 Benjamin Franklin (1706–90) became deputy postmaster general, responsible for the mail in all of the northern colonies. His experience with the relationships among the colonies gave him a broad perspective on the new nation and no doubt impelled him the following year to propose a Plan of Union to provide for the colonies' common defense and to oversee relations with the various Native American tribes (a plan that was, however, a little ahead of its time). Two decades later, on July 26, 1775, the Continental Congress appointed Franklin the first postmaster general.

When Franklin became one of the delegates to the CONSTITUTIONAL CONVENTION OF 1787 (see FRAMERS OF THE CONSTITUTION), he brought with him personal knowledge of the country's postal needs. The Constitution, in Article I, section 8, provides specifically for them, stating: "The Congress shall have Power…To establish Post Offices and post Roads." According to JAMES MADISON in essay 42 of *The Federalist* (1787–88) (see FEDERALIST PAPERS), the "power of establishing post roads must, in every view, be a harmless power and may, perhaps by judicious management become productive of great public conveniency. Nothing which tends to facilitate the intercourse between the States can be deemed unworthy of public care."

After the Constitution went into effect in 1789, the Office of Postmaster General of the United States was established with some seventy-five post offices and two thousand miles of post roads. Acts of Congress in 1790 and 1791 provided details for running the federal post office. Then in 1872 Congress officially established the Post Office Department in the EXECUTIVE BRANCH.

In *Kohl v. United States* (1876), the Supreme Court resolved the question of whether the words "To establish" in the Constitution meant that the federal government could only identify or designate places to become post offices and routes serving as post roads, or whether it could take PROPERTY and construct post offices and post roads on them. A lower federal court in 1855 had concluded that the government's postal power "has generally been considered as exhausted in the designation of roads on which the mails are to be transported." But in *Kohl* the Supreme Court found that the United States could appropriate property for a post office and a courthouse in Cincinnati, Ohio.

In the modern era of overnight mail and text messaging, it seems remarkable that it used to take up to two weeks to send a letter from Philadelphia to New York. But that was the situation in the mid-eighteenth century before Benjamin Franklin took over the postal service.

Letters used to be carried by ship captains, friends, and other travelers, who dropped off the correspondence in taverns and other gathering places. Roads were poorly marked and maintained. Postal fees were based on a confusing system of weight and distance, often provoking arguments between clerks and customers.

Franklin, who became deputy postmaster general for the crown in 1753, made sweeping reforms. He toured major postal offices, set up more direct routes, and established faster service by having mail carriers travel by both night and day.

By the time he was appointed the first postmaster general in 1775 by the Continental Congress, Franklin had done as much as anyone to unite the colonies—simply by improving the communication among them.

Protecting the Mail

Congress's postal power, according to the Supreme Court in *Ex parte Jackson* (1878), extends to taking the measures required to ensure the safe and speedy delivery of the mail. In *Jackson* the Court upheld a ban on literature relating to lotteries—a form of gambling—on the grounds that "the right to designate what shall be carried necessarily includes the right to determine what shall be excluded." In later cases, however, the Court qualified the broad scope of that decision, ruling in *Lamont v. Postmaster General* (1965) that Congress could not hold up the mail to check it for "communist political propaganda." The Court explained that a postal law could not violate citizens' First Amendment right to receive any information they wished to receive. Under the ruling in *Rowan v. U.S. Post Office Department* (1970), however, post office customers may refuse delivery of offensive mail, and the post office may keep a list of those who do not wish to receive obscene or sexually oriented mail.

State Interference

In *Pensacola Telegraph Co. v. Western Union Telegraph Co.* (1878), the Supreme Court invalidated Florida's grant of an exclusive right to operate an in-state telegraph business because federal law gave telegraph companies the right to construct telegraph lines on post roads. The Court concluded that the state monopoly was an improper interference with Congress's powers over COMMERCE and post roads. The Court in *Illinois Central Railroad v. Illinois* (1896) also invalidated a state law that required an interstate mail train to detour seven miles to stop at a specified station, but it upheld a state requirement in *Gladson v. Minnesota* (1897) that required intrastate trains to stop at county seats. As far as states' authority to punish postal employees is concerned, the Court in *United States v. Kirby* (1869) condoned the arrest for murder of a postal employee while on duty, but, according to *Johnson v. Maryland* (1920), a state cannot punish a mail truck driver for driving without a valid state license.

Franking Privilege

One of the fringe benefits that grew out of the Constitution's vesting of the postal power in Congress is the franking privilege, the right of members of Congress to send material through the mail without paying postage; they merely affix a facsimile of their signature in the upper right-hand corner where a stamp is usually placed. First extended to members of the Continental Congress in 1775, franking encourages members of Congress to keep their constituents fully informed about congressional decisions and federal activities of special interest to them.

A postal reform law in 1970 changed the Post Office Department into the United States Postal Service, an independent organization still under the executive branch. The law also removed the postmaster general from the president's cabinet, making the position more akin to the chief operating officer of a private company under a board of governors. Other changes included an end to political recommendations of employees, a traditional practice, and authorization for collective bargaining, although a ban on the right of employees to strike remained in place (see UNIONS).

The spread of anthrax through the U.S. mail following the September 11, 2001, terrorist attacks on America brought home the nation's dependency on the Postal Service and the mail's vulnerability. Despite the technological advances in COMMUNICATIONS from the telephone to cellular phones, satellite transmission, e-mail, and the proliferation of private delivery services, the mail service operated under the auspices of the federal government remains vitally important to the country.

Poverty

Looking for causes behind the "great convulsions in the world" when he came to America early in the new nation's history, the French political scientist Alexis de Tocqueville (1805–59) observed that "you will almost always find that equality was at the heart of the matter." As he wrote in *Democracy in America* (1835), "Either the poor were bent on snatching the property of the rich, or the rich were trying to hold the poor down. So, then, if you could establish a state of society in which each man had something to keep and little to snatch, you would have done much for the peace of the world."

Nearly two centuries later, poverty—primarily an economic rather than a legal or constitutional term, although it does have political implications—remains a problem in America. In 2001 some federal agencies were still struggling just to define poverty in the United States. A family of four in 2000 with a household income of $17,604 was considered impoverished. But the overall poverty rate had dropped from 11.8 percent of the population to 11.3 percent, a result of a strong economy and the success of federal and state welfare reform programs (sometimes called "workfare"). By the calculation of others, using disputed criteria such as the rising costs of housing and child care, the 2000 figure for an impoverished family could have been significantly higher.

An 1876 cover of **Harper's Weekly** *calls attention to the rampant socioeconomic disparity in the nation's cities at the time, contrasting the prosperous with the poor.*
Source: Library of Congress

Few national constitutions address the problem of poverty, although many contain provisions concerning social welfare and economic policy (see ECONOMIC LIBERTY). In the U.S. Constitution, only the PREAMBLE and Article I, section 8, speak of promoting and providing for the general WELFARE. National and state legislatures and on occasion the courts have nonetheless undertaken to alleviate some of the deleterious effects of poverty in this country. Even if often unacknowledged, socialism and the welfare state—along with capitalism—are concepts that have influenced legislators and judges who shape the constitutional law of the United States.

Access to Justice

"The mere state of being without funds is a neutral fact—constitutionally an irrelevance, like race, creed, or color," said Supreme Court Justice Robert H. Jackson (1892–1954) in a concurring opinion in *Edwards v. California* (1941). Later, however, in cases such as *Griffin v. Illinois* (1956) and *Douglas v. California*

> **"The mere state of being without funds is a neutral fact—constitutionally an irrelevance, like race, creed, or color."**
>
> —*Justice Robert H. Jackson,* in *Edwards v. California*

(1963), the Court began addressing poorer citizens' economic obstacles to criminal and civil justice, using the EQUAL PROTECTION clause of the Fourteenth Amendment (1868) (see ACCESS TO COURTS). In *GIDEON V. WAINWRIGHT* (1963), the Court extended to indigents the right to assistance of counsel in all felony cases. And in 1971, in *Boddie v. Connecticut*, the Supreme Court granted access to divorce courts to persons unable to pay the filing fees.

Civil Rights

Rich and poor citizens alike are guaranteed by the Constitution access to the nation's political processes, as both voters and candidates for office. In *Harper v. Virginia State Board of Elections* (1966), the Supreme Court held that a state poll tax of $1.50 levied as a precondition to vote in a state election was unconstitutional under the Fourteenth Amendment's equal protection clause. The Twenty-fourth Amendment (1964) banned poll taxes or any other taxes on the right to vote "for President or Vice President, for electors for President or Vice President, or for Senator or Representative in Congress." Other Supreme Court decisions have invalidated state laws that require indigent candidates for public office to pay filing fees.

Welfare Assistance

Although people in need have no constitutional right to economic assistance from the government, national and state laws can provide some help. But measures of relative wealth and poverty are imprecise at best, and opportunities for abusing the welfare system abound. Because there is no constitutional mandate to provide welfare assistance, however, the Supreme Court has been reluctant to hold the government to a strict standard with respect to implementation of welfare programs.

In *Dandridge v. Williams* (1970), for example, the Supreme Court refused to declare unconstitutional a state law setting a monthly income cap of $250 on financial assistance regardless of the size of the family or its actual need. In upholding the validity of Maryland's method for reconciling the demands of the needy with the state's finite resources to meet those demands, the Court, referring to an earlier case, declared: "In the area of economics and social welfare, a State does not violate the Equal Protection Clause merely because the classifications made by its laws are imperfect. If the classification has some 'reasonable basis,' it does not offend the Constitution simply because the classification 'is not made with mathematical nicety or because in practice it results in some inequality.'" In *Jefferson v. Hackney* (1972), the Court also upheld regulations that favor the aged (see AGE DISCRIMINATION) and infirm (see DISABLED PERSONS) over families with dependent CHILDREN.

The Supreme Court, however, in *Department of Agriculture v. Moreno* (1973) invalidated a federal welfare program law, finding that it violated the DUE PROCESS clause of the Fourteenth Amendment because the Court thought that Congress had been motivated by improper purposes. The offensive law, the Food Stamp Act (1971), disqualified from participation in the food stamp program any household containing an individual unrelated by birth, marriage, or adoption to any other member of the household. The Court found that the disqualification in fact excluded "not those who are 'likely to abuse the program,' but, rather, only those who so desperately need aid that they cannot even afford to alter their living arrangements so as to retain their eligibility." In *Goldberg v. Kelly* (1970), the Court admitted that welfare benefits "are a matter of statutory entitlement," declaring that an evidentiary hearing for recipients is required under the due process clause before such benefits may be terminated. In *Zelman v. Simmons-Harris* (2002), the Court held that state tuition aid to poor children that permitted students to attend religious as well as nonreligious schools does not offend the establishment clause of the First Amendment (1791).

The recurring clashes between liberal and conservative philosophies regarding the extent to which the nation should be committed to social and economic welfare attest to the fact that there is no consensus as yet on a single theory of economic rights.

Powers

Any constitution is fundamentally about power, specifically political power, although many other forms of power—military, police, economic, religious, and social—may be encompassed under it. Absolute monarchs and dictators jealously protect against any loss or diminution of their power, but political power obtained through constitutional procedures is temporary by nature, being subject to regular ELECTIONS and legal proceedings such as IMPEACHMENT when abuses are alleged. For a constitutional democracy to work successfully, limitations on political power like these are part of the rules by which the political power game is played.

Under the principles of FEDERALISM on which the GOVERNMENT of the United States is based, political power begins with the CITIZENS as the basic element of popular SOVEREIGNTY. As the DECLARATION OF INDEPENDENCE (1776) states, "Governments are instituted among Men, deriving their just Powers from the Consent of the Governed." At the time of the CONSTITUTIONAL CONVENTION OF 1787, there were thirteen sovereign STATES of the United States, each with its own constitutional government that had joined in a confederacy under the ARTICLES OF CONFEDERATION (1781). The sovereign power of the people was exercised through these state governments.

Enumerated Powers

When each state ratified the Constitution, some of the powers originally delegated to the state governments by their citizens were transferred to the new U.S. government—for example, the power to make TREATIES and to regulate COMMERCE among the states. Under the newly ratified Constitution beginning in 1789, power was shared further: among the citizens, the states, and the national government. The citizens of the states believed that the best way to protect against a loss of their residual sovereignty was to limit the new federal government to expressly enumerated powers. If the Constitution said, in other words, that the national government could do A, B, and C, then it could not do X, Y, and Z. This was an accepted rule followed in interpreting any legal document: that which is not included in a list of items is by definition excluded.

The Constitution enumerates, or lists, different powers and levels of power. Articles I, II, and III, respectively, address the three major powers of government: legislative, executive, and judicial (see SEPARATION OF POWERS). In addition to these general grants of power, the Constitution also makes express grants of more specific powers, such as IMPEACHMENT (assigned to the LEGISLATIVE BRANCH), PARDONS (assigned to the EXECUTIVE BRANCH), and the power to determine legal disputes arising under the Constitution (assigned to the JUDICIAL BRANCH).

The major powers of CONGRESS are enumerated in Article I, section 8. They include the "Power To lay and collect Taxes…; borrow Money on the Credit of the United States; coin Money…; [and] establish Post Offices and post Roads." Article II, section 2, contains certain enumerated powers of the PRESIDENT, such as to serve as "Commander in Chief of the Army and Navy of the United States, and of the Militia of the several States, when called into the actual Service of the United States;…to grant Reprieves and Pardons;…by and with the Advice and Consent of the Senate, make Treaties, provided two thirds of the Senators present concur;…[and] nominate, and by and with the Advice and Consent of the Senate,…appoint Ambassadors…, Judges of the supreme Court," and certain other "Officers of the United States." Article III, section 2, sets forth the powers of the federal COURTS, including deciding "all Cases, in Law and Equity, arising under this Constitution, the Laws of the United States, and Treaties made, or which shall be made, under their Authority…."

Limitation on Powers

The FRAMERS OF THE CONSTITUTION devised a second method to ensure against encroachment on the powers left to the states and the citizens. Included in the original document and later amendments

are express prohibitions on the federal government's powers. For example, Article I, section 9, declares: "No Tax or Duty shall be laid on Articles exported from any State"; and according to the First Amendment (1791): "Congress shall make no law respecting an establishment of religion...."

As a final bulwark against the national government's arrogating additional power to itself, the Tenth Amendment (1791) guarantees that "[t]he powers not delegated to the United States by the Constitution, nor prohibited by it to the States, are reserved to the States respectively, or to the people."

> *"The Americans believe that in each state supreme power should emanate directly from the people.... But once this power has been constituted, they can hardly conceive any limits to it. They freely recognize that it has the right to do everything."*
>
> **—Alexis de Tocqueville,** in *Democracy in America* (1835)

Implied Powers

While the Constitution intended to limit the national government to the confines of the enumerated powers, the history of constitutional interpretation by the Supreme Court, although uneven, has nonetheless generally tended to uphold the extension of power to the federal government at the expense of the states, if not of the citizens. In *MCCULLOCH V. MARYLAND* (1819), Chief Justice JOHN MARSHALL, taking the enumerated powers together with the NECESSARY AND PROPER CLAUSE, broadly construed federal power to mean all those powers necessary to carry out government responsibilities even if they may not have been expressly granted in the Constitution (see IMPLIED POWERS). The last clause of Article I, section 8, grants Congress the power "To make all Laws which shall be necessary and proper for carrying into Execution the foregoing Powers, and all other Powers vested by this Constitution in the Government of the United States, or in any Department or Officer thereof." In an eloquent statement in support of the national government's implied powers, Marshall wrote: "Let the end be legitimate, let it be within the scope of the constitution, and all means which are appropriate, which are plainly adapted to that end, which are not prohibited, but consist [are consistent] with the letter and spirit of the constitution, are constitutional."

Implied powers tend to be linked to a seemingly limited power. For example, Congress's power to punish those who rob the mail is implied in the enumerated power in Article I, section 8, to "establish Post Offices." An implied power may also be derived from the nature of the Constitution itself, as in the case of JUDICIAL REVIEW, whereby the courts in the regular course of business may declare acts of the other two branches unconstitutional.

Narrowing the scope of federal powers on the basis of a literal reading of each enumerated power in the Constitution and the Tenth Amendment would require scrapping nearly two hundred years of constitutional evolution. The early proponents of a strong national government, Federalists such as ALEXANDER HAMILTON and John Marshall, had no qualms about using the notion of implied powers of Congress to broaden the Constitution's scope, as they perceived it necessary. Yet the Republican candidate for president in 1996, Bob Dole, let it be known that he always carried with him a copy of the Tenth Amendment, indicating his commitment to STATES' RIGHTS as opposed to a powerful, centralized federal government.

Exclusive Powers

Expressly enumerated powers and express prohibitions are the primary basis of the Constitution. But the fact that a power is expressly granted to the federal government

⊙ CLOSER LOOK

Libertarians believe in limiting the power of government in order to maximize individual liberties. The Libertarian Party in the United States generally opposes regulations that could interfere with free markets, while supporting civil liberties. It would do away with government programs such as food stamps.

Although political conservatives are sympathetic to some libertarian ideals, they would not go as far in weakening the powers of government. Conservatives, for example, tend to be more supportive of using America's clout, including its military, to resolve overseas threats.

In 2008 Rep. Ron Paul of Texas ran for the Republican presidential nomination on a largely libertarian platform. He opposed the war in Iraq and called for an end to the federal income tax. Although he enjoyed considerable fund-raising success, he won few delegates needed for the nomination.

does not always mean that it is exclusively a federal power. For example, the national and state governments both have the power to levy taxes (see TAXATION).

The power to make a treaty with a foreign government is an exclusive federal power (see EXCLUSIVE POWERS), partly because of monarchs' historically exclusive role in FOREIGN AFFAIRS—sovereigns speak only to other sovereigns—and because of positive and negative language in the Constitution. Article II, section 2, speaking of the president, says: "He shall have Power, by and with the Advice and Consent of the Senate, to make Treaties...." To emphasize the exclusivity of this power, Article I, section 10, mandates: "No State shall enter into any Treaty, Alliance, or Confederation." The nature and extent of the federal government's exclusive treaty power (see TREATIES) was expounded on by the Supreme Court in *Missouri v. Holland* (1920). In this case the Court found that a treaty made under the authority of the United States gave Congress the power, based on the necessary and proper clause, to enact laws that it might not otherwise have the power to do.

While some powers, like the treaty-making power, are exclusive to the federal government, the power of Congress under the commerce clause in Article I, section 8, came to be treated by the Supreme Court beginning in 1851 as having "selective exclusiveness." According to what is known as the Cooley Doctrine, first articulated by the Supreme Court in *Cooley v. Board of Wardens* (1851), "Whatever subjects of this [commerce] power are in the nature of national, or admit only of one uniform system, or plan of regulation, may justly be said to be of such a nature as to require the exclusive legislation of Congress." The Cooley Doctrine, however, has been supplanted by a modern balancing approach (see BALANCING TESTS) that allows for state regulation where it is nondiscriminatory against interstate commerce and where the state's interests override any adverse effect on interstate commerce.

Concurrent Powers

Just as, in accordance with the principles of federalism, some government powers are assigned to the national government and the rest to the states, in some circumstances state and federal governments both have jurisdiction (such as with taxation). The term *concurrent power* is used only in the Eighteenth Amendment (1919, repealed 1933). The difficulties in concurrent (joint) state and federal LAW ENFORCEMENT of the PROHIBITION experiment contributed to its repeal.

Other areas of overlapping federal and state powers (see CONCURRENT POWERS) include commerce, especially in the relationship between intrastate and interstate commerce; TAXATION; and BANKRUPTCY laws. Regulation of interstate commerce by the federal government often affects intrastate commerce; likewise, regulation of intrastate commerce by the states can have an impact on interstate commerce. In the case of taxation, both the federal and state governments have concurrent taxing powers, although the federal taxing power is limited in some respects by the Constitution. Furthermore, federal and state bankruptcy laws can vary widely.

Inherent Powers

Implied and INHERENT POWERS are similar. Justice Robert H. Jackson (1892–1954) commented in a concurring opinion in *YOUNGSTOWN SHEET AND TUBE CO.* v. Sawyer (1952) that "'inherent' powers, 'implied' powers, [and] 'incidental' powers, [among others,] are used, often interchangeably and without fixed or ascertainable meanings." Inherent powers resemble implied powers in that they are not expressly stated in the Constitution, except in the broadest terms. For example, whereas the powers of Congress are enumerated in detail in Article I, section 8, the Constitution states simply in Article II, section 1: "The executive Power shall be vested in a President of the United States of America." Although in section 2 a number of specific powers and duties of the president are enumerated, the general grant of "executive Power" includes powers that are inherent in being the chief executive of a nation.

The president's inherent powers include such responsibilities as assigning bodyguards to federal judges and using great latitude in conducting foreign affairs, including arranging meetings with international leaders and sending officials to other nations for various reasons to further national and international interests. The president's inherent powers may expand during a time of emergency or crisis, such as during wartime. But a president who goes too far—such as when Harry S. Truman (1884–1972) attempted to take over steel mills to avert negative effects from a proposed strike by steelworkers during the Korean War—may find that the Supreme Court has a narrower definition of his inherent powers, as the justices concluded in *Youngstown Sheet and Tube Co. v. Sawyer*.

Resulting Powers

Taking a number of provisions of the Constitution together, it can be concluded that the federal government has resulting powers that are not literally expressed in the document. In one of the Legal Tender Cases, *Knox v. Lee* (1871), the Supreme Court held that "it is not indispensable to the existence of any power claimed for the federal government that it can be found specified in the words of the Constitution…. Its existence may be deduced fairly from more than one of the substantive powers expressly defined, or from them all combined…. [Such powers] are called by Judge [Joseph] Story [1779–1845] in his *Commentaries on the Constitution of the United States* [1833], resulting powers, arising from the aggregate powers of the government."

Police, Emergency, and War Powers

POLICE POWER is the power of government to enact laws for the HEALTH, safety, morals, and general WELFARE of the public. The Constitution does not give the national government police powers in so many words. In general, police power resides in the states, although Congress can enact similar laws under its enumerated powers such as the powers to regulate commerce and to tax and to exercise its POSTAL POWER.

EMERGENCY POWERS are those powers that can be called on during a national crisis. Article I, section 9, permits the suspension of the writ of HABEAS CORPUS, and section 8 provides for "calling forth the Militia to execute the Laws of the Union, suppress Insurrections and repel Invasions." The president has inherent emergency powers that allow him to take measures for the nation's protection that in normal times would be questionable under the Constitution, such as declaring martial law or restricting TRAVEL.

The power to declare WAR is expressly granted to Congress under Article I, section 8. But in practice the implied war powers of the president as commander in chief of the ARMED FORCES and as the leader in conducting the nation's foreign affairs make the executive branch, and the Department of Defense in particular, the principal wielder of the war powers.

Power is to government as fuel is to an engine: it is necessary for it to run, but it must be strictly controlled. "Happy it is when the interest which the government has in the preservation of its own power coincides with a proper distribution of the public burdens and tends to guard the least wealthy part of the community from oppression!" asserted Alexander Hamilton in essay 36 of *The Federalist* (1787–88) (see FEDERALIST PAPERS). The federal government created by the Constitution may not always be a well-oiled machine, but it has satisfactorily controlled the republic's raw power for more than two centuries. As MARTIN LUTHER KING JR., the American CIVIL RIGHTS

Power is to government as fuel is to an engine: it is necessary for it to run, but it must be strictly controlled.

More on this topic:
Emergency Powers, p. 187
Federalism, p. 218
Implied Powers, p. 296
Inherent Powers, p. 303
Separation of Powers, p. 494

leader, phrased it, "Power…is the strength required to bring about social, political, and economic changes. In this sense power is not only desirable but necessary in order to implement the demands of love and justice."

Prayer in School *See* RELIGION.

Preamble

A preamble (from the Latin *pre*, meaning before, and *ambulo*, meaning to walk) is an introduction to a document's basic text. In legal documents, a preamble is an opening clause that explains the reasons for the document's enactment and what it seeks to accomplish. In constitutions, a preamble is an introductory statement that precedes the document's operational and legally effective provisions. It should be noted, however, that other language in a constitution may sometimes be considered a preamble. For example, in *Eldred v. Ashcroft* (2003), the unpersuasive argument was

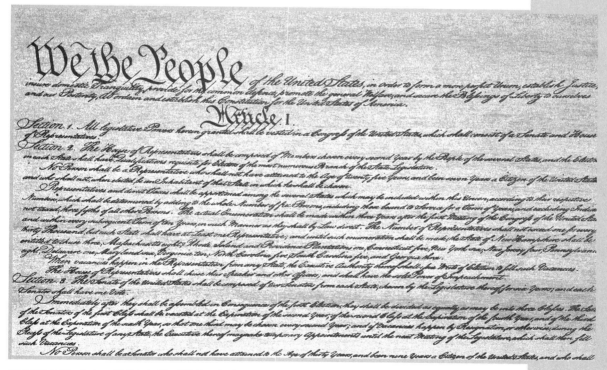

Preamble and beginning of Article I of the U.S. Constitution.
Source: The Granger Collection, New York

made that the preamble (that is, "To promote the Progress of Science and useful Arts") to the power of Congress to secure "for limited Times to Authors and Inventors the Exclusive Right to their respective Writings and Discoveries" under section 8 of Article I of the Constitution somehow placed a "substantive limit on Congress' legislative power." Preambles to national constitutions vary widely in length and purpose. A few constitutions, such as those of the Netherlands

(1814) and Italy (1948), do not even have a preamble. In the constitutions of countries dominated by the Communist Party, such as North Korea's (1972, revised 1998) and China's (1982), the preambles often provide some political and ideological insight into the countries themselves. The constitutions of Croatia (1990) and Chad (1996) each bear a preamble stating their national history leading up to the adoption of the constitution.

RELIGION or a deity are referred to in the constitutions of many nations and many states of the United States. The preamble to the constitution of the Philippines (1987) begins: "We, the sovereign Filipino people, imploring the aid of the almighty God...." According to the preamble of Louisiana's state constitution (1974): "We, the people of Louisiana, grateful to Almighty God for the civil, political, economic, and religious liberties we enjoy...." The preamble to the West Virginia constitution (1872), which was added by amendment in 1960, proclaims: "Since through Divine Providence we enjoy the blessings of civil, political and religious liberty, we, the people of West Virginia, in and through the provisions of this constitution, reaffirm our faith in and constant reliance upon God and seek diligently to promote, preserve and perpetuate good government in the state of West Virginia for the common welfare, freedom and security of ourselves and our posterity."

In contrast, the relatively short preamble of the U.S. CONSTITUTION, drafted in 1787 and adopted in 1789, contains no religious references, stating in its entirety: "We, the People of the United States, in Order to form a more perfect Union, establish Justice, insure domestic Tranquility, provide for the common defence, promote the general Welfare, and secure the Blessings of Liberty to ourselves and our Posterity, do ordain and establish this Constitution for the United States of America."

Although it comes at the beginning of the Constitution, the preamble was the last part of the document written at the CONSTITUTIONAL CONVENTION OF 1787. The task fell to Gouverneur Morris (1752–1816), a Pennsylvania delegate (see FRAMERS OF THE CONSTITUTION), who was largely responsible for the final wording of the Constitution. He was specifically responsible for changing the proposed opening phrase "We, the People of the United States" from "We, the people of the states of [the thirteen states, listed in order from north to south]." Morris also added the Constitution's list of purposes ("in Order to form a more perfect Union..."), which are in harmony with the language of the DECLARATION OF INDEPENDENCE (1776).

In essay 84 of *The Federalist* (1787–88) (see FEDERALIST PAPERS), ALEXANDER HAMILTON analyzed one of the intentions of the Constitution set forth in the preamble: "We, the People of the United States, [...] to secure the Blessings of Liberty to ourselves and our Posterity, do *ordain* and *establish* this Constitution for the United States of America." This single statement, he noted, is "a better recognition of popular rights than volumes of those aphorisms which make the principal figure in several of our State bills of rights and which would sound much better in a treatise of ethics than in a constitution of government." Hamilton was referring to the unalienable power of the people—the consent of the governed—for the creation of the Constitution, a power that the people retain even though they delegate specific powers to the national GOVERNMENT. The constitutional scholar EDWARD S. CORWIN has pointed out that the use of the active voice—"*do* ordain and establish this Constitution"—reflects the continuing act of constituting the government and not merely a completed act that occurred at a point in the past.

The preamble does not have the legal effect that the rest of the Constitution's text does, because it neither grants nor limits government powers, a point confirmed by the Supreme Court in *Jacobson v. Massachusetts* (1905). "Although that preamble indicates the general purposes for which the people ordained and established the Constitution," said the justices, "it has never been regarded as the source of any substantive power conferred on the government of the United States, or on any of its departments." The opinion added that even though "one of the declared objects of the Constitution was to secure the blessings of liberty to all..., no power can be exerted to that end by

the United States, unless, apart from the preamble, it be found in some express delegation of power, or in some power to be properly implied therefrom."

Yet the preamble provides important insight into the aspirations of the convention delegates (see ORIGINAL INTENT). Today the words "We, the People" signify that no matter how diverse the people of the United States may be, they agree on the blueprint for a national government based on the consent of the governed. The preamble's language remains an important guide for interpreting the Constitution's provisions and, like the language in the Declaration of Independence, has inspired peoples around the world to establish constitutional democracies of their own.

Preemption   *See* COMMERCE; SUPREMACY CLAUSE.

> *Today the words "We, the People" signify that no matter how diverse the people of the United States may be, they agree on the blueprint for a national government based on the consent of the governed.*

President

The president of the United States is one of the greatest inventions of the FRAMERS OF THE CONSTITUTION in 1787. In a world that at the time was filled with monarchs, emperors, and other potentates, the office of chief executive created to head the EXECUTIVE BRANCH of the new federal government was a strange hybrid of public servant and sovereign head of state. Yet today nearly every nation without a monarch who serves as the head of state has a position entitled president for either the head of state or, as in the United States, the combined head of state and government. Every government in the Western Hemisphere, excluding Canada (nominally a monarchy), has a president as the nation's highest executive official, as do most other countries, among them France, Russia, and South Africa.

The president of the United States is now in some ways even more powerful abroad than at home. As the head of the nation with the largest and most influential economy, one that is the world's only military superpower, he commands respect from other nations regardless of his own personal qualities or even the strength of his political support in the United States.

Domestically, however, the president must contend with a variety of constituencies: the citizens of the United States as a whole, the voters who voted him into office, other leaders of his own political party—some of whom may be his rivals—as well as the leaders in CONGRESS, who may represent a different political party. If the president was elected by a large majority and if his political party is in the majority in Congress, his path may be a little smoother, but he will still not be able to implement his own agenda all the time. In addition to the external factors that may help or hinder a president's exercise of power, his own attributes contribute to his ability to get things done. How well he makes the case for his agenda to the people and Congress often determines his success or failure.

There were high hopes for the office when it was created. According to ALEXANDER HAMILTON in essay 68 of *The Federalist* (1787–88) (see FEDERALIST PAPERS), "It will not be too strong to say that there will be a constant probability of seeing the station filled by characters pre-eminent for ability and virtue. And this will be thought no inconsiderable recommendation of the Constitution by those who are able to estimate the share in which the executive in every government must necessarily have in its good or ill administration." Since these words were published, there has been an enduring tendency to view the fortunes of the nation as riding on the ability of the incumbent president.

A New Type of Leader

The well-known models on which the framers of the Constitution could draw in designing the office of the president were the English monarch, colonial governors, and the chief executives of the

PRESIDENTS OF THE UNITED STATES

No.	Name	Politics	Born	State	Inaug.	Died
1.	George Washington	Federalist	February 2, 1732	Virginia	1789	December 14, 1799
2.	John Adams	Federalist	October 30, 1735	Massachusetts	1797	July 4, 1826
3.	Thomas Jefferson	Democratic-Republican	April 13, 1743	Virginia	1801	July 4, 1826
4.	James Madison	Democratic-Republican	March 16, 1751	Virginia	1809	June 28, 1836
5.	James Monroe	Democratic-Republican	April 28, 1758	Virginia	1817	July 4, 1831
6.	John Quincy Adams	Democratic-Republican	July 11,1767	Massachusetts	1825	February 23, 1848
7.	Andrew Jackson	Democrat	March 15, 1767	South Carolina	1829	June 8, 1845
8.	Martin Van Buren	Democrat	December 5, 1782	New York	1837	July 24, 1862
9.	William Henry Harrison	Whig	February 9, 1773	Virginia	1841	April 4, 1841
10.	John Tyler	Whig	March 29, 1790	Virginia	1841	January 18, 1862
11.	James Knox Polk	Democrat	November 2, 1795	North Carolina	1845	June 15, 1849
12.	Zachary Taylor	Whig	November 24, 1784	Virginia	1849	July 9, 1850
13.	Millard Fillmore	Whig	January 7, 1800	New York	1850	March 8, 1874
14.	Franklin Pierce	Democrat	November 23, 1804	New Hampshire	1853	October 8, 1869
15.	James Buchanan	Democrat	April 23, 1791	Pennsylvania	1857	June 1, 1868
16.	Abraham Lincoln	Republican	February 12, 1809	Kentucky	1861	April 15, 1865
17.	Andrew Johnson[1]	Democrat	December 29, 1808	North Carolina	1865	July 31, 1875
18.	Ulysses Simpson Grant	Republican	April 27, 1822	Ohio	1869	July 23, 1885
19.	Rutherford Birchard Hayes	Republican	October 4, 1822	Ohio	1877	January 17, 1893
20.	James Abram Garfield	Republican	November 19, 1831	Ohio	1881	September 19, 1881
21.	Chester Alan Arthur	Republican	October 5, 1830	Vermont	1881	November 18, 1886
22.	Grover Cleveland	Democrat	March 18, 1837	New Jersey	1885	June 24, 1908
23.	Benjamin Harrison	Republican	August 20, 1833	Ohio	1889	March 13, 1901
24.	Grover Cleveland	Democrat	March 18, 1837	New Jersey	1893	June 24, 1908
25.	William McKinley	Republican	January 29, 1843	Ohio	1897	September 24, 1901
26.	Theodore Roosevelt	Republican	October 27, 1858	New York	1901	January 6, 1919
27.	William Howard Taft	Republican	September 15, 1857	Ohio	1909	March 8, 1930
28.	Woodrow Wilson	Democrat	December 28, 1856	Virginia	1913	February 3, 1924
29.	Warren Gamaliel Harding	Republican	November 2, 1865	Ohio	1921	August 2, 1923
30.	Calvin Coolidge	Republican	July 4, 1872	Vermont	1923	January 5, 1933
31.	Herbert Clark Hoover	Republican	August 10, 1874	Iowa	1929	October 20, 1964
32.	Franklin Delano Roosevelt	Democrat	January 30, 1882	New York	1933	April 12, 1945
33.	Harry S. Truman	Democrat	May 8, 1884	Missouri	1945	December 26, 1972
34.	Dwight David Eisenhower	Republican	October 14, 1890	Texas	1953	March 28, 1969
35.	John Fitzgerald Kennedy	Democrat	May 29, 1917	Massachusetts	1961	November 22, 1963
36.	Lyndon Baines Johnson	Democrat	August 27, 1908	Texas	1963	January 22,1973
37.	Richard Milhous Nixon[2]	Republican	January 9, 1913	California	1969	April 22, 1994
38.	Gerald Rudolph Ford	Republican	July 14, 1913	Nebraska	1974	December 26, 2006
39.	James Earl Carter	Democrat	October 1, 1924	Georgia	1977	
40.	Ronald Wilson Reagan	Republican	February 6, 1911	Illinois	1981	June 5, 2004
41.	George Herbert Walker Bush	Republican	June 12, 1924	Massachusetts	1989	
42.	William Jefferson Clinton	Democrat	August 19, 1946	Arkansas	1993	
43.	George Walker Bush	Republican	July 6, 1946	Connecticut	2001	

Source: *The World Almanac and Book of Facts*. New York.: World Almanac Books, 2002. As updated by the author.

1. Nominated vice president by Republicans and elected with Lincoln on National Union Party ticket.
2. Resigned August 9, 1974.

thirteen states after their independence from Great Britain. Important theorists they looked to included the English philosopher John Locke (1632–1704), the commentator on English law William Blackstone (1723–80), and the French jurist and legal scholar Charles-Louis de Secondat, Baron de La Brède et de Montesquieu (1689–1755).

The many constitutional prerogatives of the British monarch George III and his ability to dominate Parliament argued for limitations on the American chief executive. The colonial governors—who, even though appointed by the king, had tended to become more and more dependent on the colonial assemblies for men, material, and financing, especially in time of war—influenced the creation of the new state chief executives, some of whom were called president. The first presidents of the nation itself under the ARTICLES OF CONFEDERATION (1781), who were chosen for one-year terms by the Continental Congress, were mere instruments of that body and had no independent power or privileges.

New York's governor under its constitution of 1777, however, was not a creature of the legislature but was directly elected by the people. And under the 1780 constitution of Massachusetts, the commonwealth's governor had an effective veto over legislation. Reflecting the principle of SEPARATION OF POWERS and checks and balances in government, both these attributes—popular election and veto power—were not wasted on the delegates to the Constitutional Convention who wished to create a balanced constitution.

A balanced constitution was one that incorporated principles identified by Locke and Montesquieu. The latter, after rediscovering the works of Aristotle, wrote: "In every government there are three sorts of power: the legislative; the executive in respect of things dependent on the laws of nations; and the executive in regard to matters that depend on the civil law...." Whereas Blackstone had emphasized the "omnipotence of Parliament," there was ample evidence in the new president's powers of the English monarch's prerogatives in the areas of FOREIGN AFFAIRS and command of the military. From Locke the framers took the notion of a residual well of executive power that could be tapped especially during times of emergency, when a single leader as the head of state can marshal the nation's forces more quickly than a deliberative body like a legislature. From Montesquieu they took the concept of the separation of powers, making the executive separate from the legislature.

At the convention in Philadelphia, one of the two major proposals submitted for consideration in structuring the new government, the Virginia Plan (see pages 622–623), used the term *national executive* for the future president. Roger Sherman, a delegate from Connecticut, argued for a national executive who was appointed by and accountable to the legislature. James Wilson, from Pennsylvania, argued instead for a single magistrate who would be independent of the legislature. These two delegates reflected the larger debate between the need for a strong executive to deal with events such as the insurrection known as Shays's Rebellion in Massachusetts (1786–87) and the need to quiet widespread popular fears that the convention might create a monarchy.

Sherman's concept of a chief executive was similar to that of the prime minister in a parliamentary system of government, who is chosen by the legislature and is accountable to it. A major problem with his proposal was the need to have simultaneous elections to ensure that the president represented the majority in the legislature, as in a parliamentary system. The staggered elections of senators (see SENATE), the two-year elections of members of the HOUSE OF REPRESENTATIVES, and the four-year term of the chief executive made Sherman's CABINET system of government impractical. And with the need for checks and balances on the new chief executive—for example, Senate approval of TREATIES and appointments—to allay fears of monarchical powers, Wilson's vision of an even more powerful president than the one that finally emerged from the convention was also doomed.

Qualifications

Article II, section 1, of the Constitution sets out simple qualifications for the nation's president: "No Person except a natural born Citizen, or a Citizen of the United States, at the time of the Adoption of this Constitution, shall be eligible to the Office of President; neither shall any Person be eligible to that Office who shall not have attained to the Age of thirty five Years, and been fourteen years a Resident within the United States." Article VI adds that "no religious Test shall ever be required as a Qualification to any Office or public Trust under the United States" (see QUALIFICATIONS FOR OFFICE). The youngest person to hold the office of president was Theodore Roosevelt (1858–1919), who succeeded to the presidency at the age of forty-two, on the assassination of William McKinley (1843–1901). John F. Kennedy (1917–63) was the youngest person elected president at age forty-three in 1960.

Under the Twenty-second Amendment (1951), anyone who has been elected president twice is not eligible to hold the office again, and a person who has held the office or acted as president for more than two years of another's term is not eligible to be elected more than once. The first president, GEORGE WASHINGTON, established the precedent of not seeking a third four-year term, perhaps to allay the fears that Hamilton mentioned. Franklin D. Roosevelt (1882–1945), however, ignoring precedent, sought and won reelection to a third in 1940, and then a fourth term in 1944 but died before completing it.

Grover Cleveland is the only president ever elected to two nonconsecutive terms. Cleveland won the elections of 1884 and 1892.
Source: Library of Congress

Election

The American procedure for electing the president is unique. Most constitutions of countries that elect a president require him or her to be elected by the people with an absolute majority of the votes cast (see ELECTIONS; MAJORITY RULE). Article II, section 1, of the U.S. Constitution instead sets up an ELECTORAL COLLEGE, providing that the president "together with the Vice President, chosen for the same term, [is to] be elected, as follows: Each State shall appoint, in such Manner as the Legislature thereof may direct, a Number of Electors, equal to the whole Number of Senators and Representatives to which the State may be entitled in the Congress: but no Senator or Representative, or Person holding an Office of Trust or Profit under the United States, shall be appointed an Elector."

The third paragraph of Article II, section 1—setting out a complicated mechanism for awarding the two highest vote getters the presidency and the vice presidency—was replaced by the Twelfth Amendment (1804). This amendment was added in response to the election of THOMAS JEFFERSON in 1800 after difficulties encountered in the original electoral process required more than thirty votes in the House of Representatives before a president was finally chosen. Because there was no distinction between votes for president and VICE PRESIDENT, electors favoring one political party could cast an equal number of votes for both of their party's candidates, resulting in a tie vote. Now, according to the Twelfth Amendment: "The Electors shall meet in their respective states, and vote by ballot for President and Vice-President, one of whom, at least, shall not be an inhabitant of the same state with themselves; they shall name in their ballots the person voted for as President, and in distinct ballots the person voted for as Vice-President....." Under the original procedure, the electors were to vote by ballot for two persons, with the person having the greatest number of votes being named president and the next highest becoming vice president.

The electoral college was supposed to provide a check against the possibility that a popular but unworthy candidate might become president. Favoring the STATES with a small population by guaranteeing them no fewer than three electors (two senators plus one representative), the electoral college also represented a compromise between direct election by the people and election by Congress. The presidential election system generally works well, although it has been criticized as not being as democratic as having a direct popular election for president. The contested presidential election in 2000 (see *BUSH V. GORE*), in which Al Gore won the popular vote but lost the electoral college vote, renewed concerns about the unique method the framers devised for selecting the most powerful chief executive in the world.

Installation and Compensation

Once elected by the electoral college after national elections every four years, held on the first Tuesday after the first Monday in November, the president-elect takes office, according to the Twentieth Amendment (1933), "at noon on the 20th day of January" (see LAME DUCKS).

Traditionally the new president is sworn in by the CHIEF JUSTICE of the United States on the steps of the U.S. Capitol, symbolizing—as least for that moment—the unity of the three branches of government. Article II, section 1, prescribes the OATH OF OFFICE: "Before he enter on the Execution of his Office, he shall take the following Oath or Affirmation:—'I do solemnly swear (or affirm) that I will faithfully execute the Office of President of the United States, and will to the best of my Ability, preserve, protect and defend the Constitution of the United States.'"

Section 1 also provides remuneration for the chief executive: "The President shall, at stated Times, receive for his Services, a Compensation, which shall neither be encreased nor diminished during the Period for which he shall have been elected, and he shall not receive within that Period any other Emolument from the United States, or any of them." As of the presidential term beginning in 2001, the salary of the president is $400,000, having been doubled by Congress from $200,000.

Powers and Duties

The president's responsibilities are addressed second in the Constitution, in Article II, following those of Congress in Article I.

Executive Branch. "The executive Power," begins Article II, section 1, "shall be vested in a President of the United States of America," making the president the chief executive and administrative officer of the national government. Article II, section 3, charges him to "take Care that the Laws be faithfully executed." Congress enacts the LAW, the COURTS interpret and apply it, and the president is responsible for executing or carrying it out. In *Wilcox v. McConnel* (1839), the Supreme Court affirmed that the president himself did not have to act at all times but could delegate his authority to administrative officers. And in *Kendall v. United States ex rel. Stokes* (1938), the Court held that the president's power over executive officers was not exclusive and that Congress could direct executive branch officials as to how laws were to be carried out.

CLOSER LOOK ◉

The enormous powers of the presidency came into focus after Republicans swept to victory in the 1994 congressional elections. The new conservative leadership began pressing an ambitious agenda to cut federal spending and pare back regulations.

The Democratic president, Bill Clinton, found himself so weakened that he memorably tried to remind reporters at a 1995 press conference, "The president is still relevant here."

Nevertheless, Clinton vetoed several Republican bills. A charismatic leader, he denounced Congress in a series of much-publicized speeches.

In the end, Congress was forced to back down on many of its top priorities. A resurgent Clinton, very much relevant again, won reelection in 1996.

Article II, section 2, sets out the president's responsibilities, declaring: "The President shall be Commander in Chief of the Army and Navy of the United States, and of the Militia of the several States, when called into the actual Service of the United States." In keeping with a basic principle of constitutionalism that the military be subordinate to the civilian government, the president, as the highest civilian executive, is also the highest military authority. Directly under the president militarily is the secretary of defense (see CABINET), the second-highest-ranking civilian authority over the military. The highest-ranking military authority is the chairman of the joint chiefs of staff, representing the various ARMED FORCES—the army, navy, marines, and air force.

The powers of the president during a time of war have been the subject of much analysis and criticism throughout the history of the Republic. Highly ranked commanders-in-chief, including Abraham Lincoln (1809–1865) and Franklin D. Roosevelt (1882–1945), have been faulted for overreaching their constitutional powers during the Civil War (1861–1865) and World War II (1939–1945), respectively. President George W. Bush (b. 1946), who has garnered little consensus on his success as a commander-in-chief to date, has also been criticized as exceeding the limits of his wartime authority under the Constitution. Civil rights groups have found cause for concern in his purported authorization of torture for prisoners taken in the wars in Afghanistan and Iraq, the use of military tribunals to try suspects in the war on terror, and government authorization of wiretapping in alleged violation of the Constitution's guarantee of protection against unreasonable SEARCH AND SEIZURE.

President Clinton vetoes two spending bills in 1995 as Vice President Al Gore looks on.
Source: AP Images/J. Scott Applewhite

As the chief executive officer of the United States, the president appoints (see APPOINTMENT AND REMOVAL POWER) and supervises the heads of the executive departments and ADMINISTRATIVE AGENCIES. The heads of the executive departments, called secretaries, comprise the president's cabinet. Members are personally responsible to the president, unlike in a parliamentary form of government, where cabinet members and the prime minister are responsible to the parliament. Article II, section 2, adds that the president "may require the Opinion, in writing, of the principal Officer in each of the executive Departments, upon any Subject relating to the Duties of their respective Offices."

Article II, section 2, also gives the president the power to appoint, with the ADVICE AND CONSENT of the Senate, AMBASSADORS and other diplomatic officials "and all other Officers of the United States, whose Appointments are not herein otherwise provided for, and which shall be established by Law; but the Congress may by Law vest the Appointment of such inferior Officers, as they think proper, in the President alone, in the Courts of Law, or in the Heads of Departments." The president is also "to make Treaties, provided two thirds of the Senators present concur."

Under Article II, section 2, the president is empowered "to grant Reprieves and Pardons for Offenses against the United States, except in Cases of Impeachment."

CLOSER LOOK

An important recent Supreme Court case on the wartime powers of the president, *Hamdan v. Rumsfeld* (2006), which reprises the ruling of Chief Justice John Marshall in *Little v. Barreme* (1804), held that the president may not constitutionally disregard valid substantive limitations placed on his authority by Congress—even during wartime.

According to Chief Justice JOHN MARSHALL in *United States v. Wilson* (1833), pardoning is a private although official act similar to the English monarch's power to pardon as an "act of grace," requiring no justification to anyone else (see PARDONS).

The president's specific powers have given the office a virtual monopoly on setting policy in several areas, including foreign affairs and the conduct of WAR—whether declared by Congress or undeclared, as well as during times of emergency (see EMERGENCY POWERS).

Judicial Branch. The Constitution in Article II, section 2, grants the president the power to appoint, with the Senate's advice and consent, the justices of the Supreme Court, including the CHIEF JUSTICE, and all other judges of the federal courts. This power might seem somewhat insignificant because after their appointment, judges are totally independent and beyond the president's control (see JUDICIAL BRANCH; JUDICIAL INDEPENDENCE). But, in fact, because the appointments are for life and because the Supreme Court has extensive powers of JUDICIAL REVIEW over legislation and the president's actions, this power is of great significance with respect to contentious issues such as STATES' RIGHTS, ABORTION, and even election procedures, as evidenced in the case of *Bush v. Gore*, in which the Supreme Court virtually decided the presidential election in 2000.

Legislative Branch. Because only members of Congress are authorized to introduce LEGISLATION, when the president wants a bill to be considered a member of Congress must introduce it on behalf of the executive branch. As stated in Article II, section 3, "He shall from time to time give to the Congress Information of the State of the Union, and recommend to their Consideration such Measures as he shall judge necessary and expedient...." After a bill passes both houses of Congress in identical form, it must also be signed by the president to become law.

The Constitution also gives the president the power to veto legislation. But Article I, section 7, which sets forth the president's veto power, also authorizes Congress to override such VETOES by a two-thirds vote in each house. Such an override does not require a presidential signature. The veto power is more effective when the president's political party is slightly in the minority in Congress and can thus be used to thwart the legislative agenda of the other party that is barely in control of Congress. Sometimes the mere threat of a presidential veto forces modifications in the laws considered by Congress.

On "extraordinary Occasions," notes Article II, section 3, the president may "convene both Houses, or either of them, and in Case of Disagreement between them, with Respect to the Time of Adjournment, he may adjourn them to such Time as he shall think proper." From time to time, the president has called both houses into special session to get a bill passed, and the Senate has been summoned to consider nominations and treaties. No president, however, has yet exercised his privilege to adjourn either house.

Accountability

The president, although nominated by a political party and assisted in campaigning for office by a political party (see POLITICAL PARTIES), becomes the president of the nation and all its citizens on taking office. Nevertheless, the opposition party, the news media, and many special-interest groups whose interests are not aligned with the president's can unofficially criticize the president's actions. Under the Constitution's guarantees of free SPEECH and freedom of THE PRESS, the president must accept being constantly held accountable for his stewardship in office.

In addition to these popular means, constitutional methods for holding the president accountable include his ability to stand for—and his likely desire for—a second term of office, congressional action to defeat the administration's legislative proposals, and congressional investigations, including IMPEACHMENT. In addition, the Supreme Court can invalidate any presidential actions that it finds unconstitutional. One example of the Supreme Court's role in holding the president accountable came in *YOUNGSTOWN SHEET AND TUBE CO. V. SAWYER* (1952). Here the Court held that

Theodore Roosevelt used the powers of the presidency to set aside large regions of American wilderness. In 1908 he designated the Grand Canyon as a national monument, thereby protecting it from development.
Source: National Park Service

the president exceeded his constitutional authority by trying to seize steel mills in order to maintain production needed for the Korean War (1950–53).

Succession

Of the more than forty presidents elected to office, eight died in office and one resigned rather than face impeachment. The vice president in each case assumed the office of president, but it was not until the Twenty-fifth Amendment (1967) that the vice president was expressly acknowledged as the first in line of SUCCESSION to the presidency.

According to the Succession Act (1792), if the offices of the president and vice president became vacant at the same time, the president pro tempore of the Senate would serve as president until a special election could be held. Congress changed the law in 1886, making the second in line after the vice president the secretary of state and after that the secretaries of the cabinet offices in order of their creation.

In 1947 the law was again changed at the insistence of President Harry S. Truman (1884–1972). He thought that in a democracy elected officials, rather than appointed ones such as the cabinet secretaries, should be the first to succeed to the presidency. The next in line after the vice president would be the SPEAKER OF THE HOUSE and the president pro tempore of the Senate, and then the secretaries of the cabinet departments, beginning with the secretary of state, then Treasury, defense, and so forth. This order of succession remains in effect today.

In *The President: Office and Powers, 1787–1957* (1957), the noted constitutional scholar EDWARD S. CORWIN quoted Secretary of State William H. Seward (who served 1861–69, originally under President ABRAHAM LINCOLN), speaking of the American president: "We elect a king for four years, and give him absolute power within certain limits, which after all he can interpret for himself." Writing after the extraordinary presidency of Franklin D. Roosevelt, Corwin himself observed, "Taken by and large, the history of the presidency has been a history of aggrandizement." Yet the president's power under the Constitution is expandable and contractible depending on many factors, including the personality of the incumbent. Perhaps that as much as anything reflects the genius of the framers: that the presidency can accommodate many styles of governing as long as they all serve the ends of the Constitution.

> **More on this topic:**
>
> *Executive Orders, p. 208*
>
> *Legislative Branch, p. 346*

President of the Senate *See* VICE PRESIDENT.

President Pro Tempore *See* SENATE.

The Press

"The time, it is to be hoped, is gone by, when any defence would be necessary of the 'liberty of the press' as one of the securities against corrupt or tyrannical government," wrote the British philosopher John Stuart Mill (1806–73) in 1859 in his essay *On Liberty*. Even earlier, the English jurist William Blackstone (1723–80) stressed in his *Commentaries on the Laws of England* (1765–70), "The liberty of the press is indeed essential to the nature of a free state; but this consists in laying no *previous* restraints upon public actions, and not in freedom from censure for criminal matters published. Every free man has an undoubted right to lay what sentiments he pleases before the public; to forbid this is to destroy the freedom of the press."

Printing was invented by the Chinese, who began printing books as early as the seventh century. In Europe, Johannes Gutenberg built a printing press about 1452 that used movable metal type for the first time and revolutionized mass COMMUNICATIONS in Europe and the world. The word *press* comes from the Latin *presso* (to press), which refers to how a sheet of paper is pressed against an inked plate or die, thus transferring the inked impression to paper. Thousands of exact duplicates of printed materials could thereafter be made and placed in the hands of people in a short period of time.

A Print Revolution

Undoubtedly the American Revolution that began in 1775 and the French Revolution of 1789 would not have been possible without the printing press. The power of the press was recognized several decades previously, in the 1735 trial of Peter Zenger in New York (see ZENGER'S CASE), in which a jury acquitted this printer of libel against the colonial government—defying the presiding judge's direction to return a guilty verdict. Benjamin Franklin, a signer of both the DECLARATION OF INDEPENDENCE (1776) and the Constitution (1789), made his early fortune and reputation as a printer and publisher in Pennsylvania.

In Peter Green's 1970s cartoon parody of First Amendment violations, policemen arrest founding father Ben Franklin and prepare to haul him away from his printing press.
Source: Peter Green, Politicards.com

At the time of the CONSTITUTIONAL CONVENTION OF 1787 in Philadelphia, the FRAMERS OF THE CONSTITUTION opted first to get the Constitution ratified and then draft a bill of rights and present it for ratification also. The First Amendment, contained in that BILL OF RIGHTS (1791), attests to the importance that Americans place on a free press. "Congress shall make no law…," it states, "abridging the freedom of…the press…." Enshrined in the First Amendment as one of four basic freedoms, along with freedom of RELIGION, SPEECH, and assembly (see ASSEMBLY AND ASSOCIATION), freedom of the press was never intended to be an absolute right. Although this freedom can be abused and misused like other rights, citizens of a constitutional DEMOCRACY are far safer with a vigorous and aggressive free press and its occasional mistakes than without it.

Before the Constitution was even a decade old, however, Congress in 1798 enacted the Alien and Sedition Acts—laws that permitted prosecution of editors for false and malicious writings against the government and for inciting opposition to any act of Congress or the president. These acts, whose constitutionality was questionable from the beginning, were strongly criticized by THOMAS JEFFERSON, and were allowed to lapse after two years.

A Bundle of Rights

Freedom of the press includes the right of citizens to disseminate information in print, a form of the more general right of free expression. However, in *Schenck v. United States* (1919), the Supreme Court set a limit on the right to disseminate printed information. The defendant had distributed a circular that urged young men to oppose the World War I draft and was indicted under the Espionage Act (1917) for obstructing the draft. Justice OLIVER WENDELL HOLMES JR. concluded for the Court that when circulated material presents a "clear and present danger," the First Amendment's protection could be lost, especially in time of WAR. The example he gave was of a man "falsely shouting fire in a theatre and causing a panic."

Freedom of the press also refers specifically to publishing and news institutions—from newspapers and magazines to television and radio—that hire reporters and editors and are produced on a regular basis. It is a popular fallacy that the press has any duty to be objective or to publish or broadcast both sides of an issue. The media are profit-making businesses that, as long as they avoid publishing legally libelous or defamatory items, can print what they and their readers want and like.

The first significant freedom of the press case to reach the Supreme Court came in 1931 with *Near v. Minnesota ex rel. Olson*. The *Saturday Press* of Minneapolis had published charges of neglect and misconduct against certain public officials, after which the county brought action against the publication under a statute that permitted closing down a "malicious, scandalous and defamatory newspaper, magazine, or other periodical." In a showdown between the POLICE POWER of the STATES and freedom of the press, the Supreme Court held that liberty of the press is applicable to the states under the Fourteenth Amendment (1868) (see INCORPORATION DOCTRINE). As the Court went on to point out trenchantly, "The fact that the liberty of the press may be abused by miscreant purveyors of scandal does not make any the less necessary the immunity of the press from previous restraint in dealing with official misconduct. Subsequent punishment for such abuses as may exist is the appropriate remedy, consistent with constitutional privilege."

Five years after *Near*, the Supreme Court declared that a tax levied only on thirteen newspapers in Louisiana—twelve of which openly opposed the state's senator and political kingpin, Huey Long—was an unconstitutional abridgment of freedom of the press. In the PENTAGON PAPERS CASE (1971), the Court concluded that the United States had not met the heavy burden of proving that NATIONAL SECURITY concerns outweighed the right of newspapers to publish a top-secret Defense Department history of the Vietnam War (1955–75).

Another issue that has been around since the Zenger trial concerns the Supreme Court's power to compel a member of the press to disclose information or sources of information relevant to a criminal prosecution (see WITNESSES). In 1972 the Court held in a 5–4 decision in *Branzburg v. Hayes* that it could not "seriously entertain the notion that the First Amendment protects a newsman's agreement to conceal criminal conduct of his source" from a grand jury. The dissenters were concerned that such a ruling would hinder reporters' ability to obtain information if they could not guarantee protection for their sources. A concurring opinion by Justice Lewis F. Powell Jr. (1907–98), calling for a "proper balance between freedom of the press and the obligations of all citizens to give relevant testimony," was seized on by supporters of the media to claim a right of confidentiality for members of the press. This dubious analysis was punctured, however, in 2003 by U.S. Court of Appeals Judge Richard A. Posner, who noted that the decision in *Branzburg* did not, in fact, extend the privilege of confidentiality to reporters. In 2007 the House of Representatives passed a bill for the Free Flow of Information Act to provide a federal version of a reporter "shield" act to grant confidentiality akin to that provided lawyers, doctors, and the clergy. Thirty-two states have similar laws in place.

Fair Trial and the Press

The notion of a fair trial (see TRIALS) includes judicial proceedings that are open to the public and the press and in which JURIES are fair and impartial. "[F]ree speech and fair trial," as Supreme Court Justice Hugo L. Black (1886–1971) once put it, "are two of the most cherished policies of our civilization, and it would be a trying task to choose between them." In 1980 the Supreme Court held that the public and the press have a constitutional right to attend judicial proceedings unless a compelling reason for secrecy can be shown. The Court has also upheld the press's right to cover proceedings involving minor victims' testimony about sexual attacks and lawyers' examinations of jurors in trials involving rape and murder, as well as its right to transcripts of preliminary hearings that all parties and the court want to remain confidential. To lessen publicity in the press that may be prejudicial to a defendant, the Court has sanctioned a number of measures, such as sequestering jurors so that they have no access to the news, but it has ruled out a court injunction against publishing articles that might prejudice the jury because this would constitute prior restraint of the press, which was prohibited by the decision in the *Near* case.

Although freedom of expression now encompasses many ways in which we can communicate—through speech, writing, nonverbal speech, artistic expression, newspapers, magazines, books, radio television, and the INTERNET—the press retains a special niche in the pantheon of forms of human expression. Like a free and vigorous legal profession, the press remains a bulwark guarding against infringement of the government's constitutional structure and our individual constitutional rights.

Prior Restraint   *See* CENSORSHIP; THE PRESS.

Prisoners

A person convicted of a crime may expect to forfeit many rights—LIBERTY, PROPERTY, protection against unreasonable SEARCH AND SEIZURE, and the right to vote, not to mention one's reputation and

Rows of cots and bedding fill a prison dorm in Leavenworth, Kansas, circa 1910.
Source: Library of Congress

possibly one's life. But there is a common humanitarian view that PUNISHMENT should fit the crime and that a person should not lose the right to humane treatment even if he or she is accused of or has committed the most heinous crime. In his *Treatise on Crimes and Punishment* (1764), Cesare Beccaria (1738–94), an Italian jurist and economist, argued for proportionality in the punishment of crimes, ideas that initiated a reevaluation of the treatment of prisoners in Western Europe. And William Blackstone (1723–80), in his *Commentaries on the Laws of England* (1765–70), alluded to a fundamental right of prisoners: "The justice before whom [a] prisoner is brought, is bound immediately to examine the circumstances of the crime alleged."

Some national constitutions, including Italy's (1948) and Nicaragua's (1987), call for humane treatment of prisoners. The International Covenant on Civil and Political Rights (1966), sponsored by the United Nations, requires that "[a]ll persons deprived of their liberty shall be treated with humanity and with respect for the inherent dignity of the human person." Other international HUMAN RIGHTS documents also address prisoners' rights, including the Declaration on the Protection of All Persons from Being Subjected to Torture and Other Cruel, Inhuman, or Degrading Treatment or Punishment (1975) and the Body of Principles for the Protection of All Persons under Any Form of Detention or Imprisonment (1988).

Obviously, many lapses in granting rights to prisoners and other detainees have occurred in countries around the world, including in the United States. State and federal systems have varied greatly over the centuries in how they have treated prisoners. The Supreme Court and state supreme courts have generally given short shrift to complaints by prisoners about their treatment or living conditions. "Federal courts sit not to supervise prisons but to enforce the constitutional rights of all 'persons,' including prisoners," said the Supreme Court in *Cruz v. Beto* (1972), citing *Johnson v. Avery* (1969). "We are not unmindful that prison officials must be accorded latitude in the administration of prison affairs, and that prisoners necessarily are subject to appropriate rules and regulations." However, nearly two centuries after the Constitution was drafted, the Supreme Court confirmed in *Hutto v. Finney* (1978) that conditions in the Arkansas prison system were so appallingly inhuman that they constituted "a dark and evil world completely alien to the free world."

The FRAMERS OF THE CONSTITUTION were well aware that without guarantees of humane treatment for prisoners, JUSTICE may be corrupted and the rights of those being held on criminal charges infringed. The BILL OF RIGHTS (1791) grants a number of specific rights to prisoners. Many of these are procedural, such as the right to be informed of the government's charges, the requirement for a speedy and public trial by an impartial jury (see JURIES; TRIALS), and access to the ASSISTANCE OF COUNSEL. The right to test the legality of detention by government authorities by filing a writ of HABEAS CORPUS, found in Article I, section 9, is another constitutional measure safeguarding prisoners and detainees. The Eighth Amendment (1791) contains prohibitions against excessive BAIL, excessive fines, and "cruel and unusual punishments" (see CRUEL AND UNUSUAL PUNISHMENT). Some state constitutions, including California's (1879), prohibit "cruel *or* unusual punishment," and such a distinction can make a difference in judicial rulings.

According to the Supreme Court's decision in *Pell v. Procunier* (1974), prison inmates are entitled to First Amendment rights that are consistent with the status of being prisoners and with the objectives of the correction system. The Court thus found it unconstitutional for prison authorities to delay or censor mail simply because it contained complaints about prison conditions. Prisoners generally have the right, according to the Court, to be free from racial SEGREGATION, except as necessary for security and discipline; to petition for redress of grievances; and to bring actions in federal court for wrongful damage caused by prison administrators. They also are entitled to minimal conditions necessary for survival: food, clothing, shelter, adequate medical care, and a secure environment. In *Wolff v. McDonnell* (1974), the justices declared that there "is no iron curtain drawn between the Constitution and the prisons."

For a while, however, the Supreme Court seemed little inclined to extend further rights to prisoners. They held, for example, that, in general, a prisoner had no right to be incarcerated in the facility of his or her choice or to be housed in an uncrowded prison. The Court held in *Bell v. Wolfish* (1979) and *Rhodes v. Chapman* (1981) that "double celling," or requiring two or more prisoners to share a cell designed for one, does not violate the Constitution's "cruel and unusual punishments" clause. The rights of prisoners to vote is not clear, although in *Richardson v. Ramirez* (1974) the Court upheld a state law disqualifying convicted felons from voting, even after they had served their prison terms. Reporters have no right to designate particular prisoners to interview, the Court held in *Saxbe v. Washington Post* (1974), but they can communicate with specific inmates by mail and talk with them during prison visits.

Blatant cases sometimes impel the Supreme Court to react. In 1992 a court of appeals found that a Louisiana prisoner who had been handcuffed, shackled, and beaten mercilessly by a prison guard, all while the prison supervisor advised against having "too much fun," had suffered no Eighth Amendment violation; however, on appeal in *Hudson v. McMillian* (1992), the Supreme Court ruled that the beating violated "contemporary standards of decency." In *Helling v. McKinney* (1993), the justices held that prisoners might have a right to be protected from secondhand tobacco smoke. However, in *Lewis v. Casey* (1996), the Court denied prisoners the right to effectively litigate their cases—beyond affording a prisoner the opportunity to file a petition or a claim, it held that there is no further constitutional requirement for prison authorities to assist in the matter. The Prison Litigation Reform Act of 1995 represented Congress's attempt to curb the filing of frivolous lawsuits by prisoners. Interestingly, in recent cases, for example, *Hope v. Pelzer* (2002), *Muhammad v. Close* (2004), *Nelson v. Campbell* (2004), *Wilkinson v. Austin* (2005), and *Jones v. Bock* (2007), the Supreme Court has ruled more favorably on issues related to prisoners' rights.

As for young prisoners, the Constitution does not give children and juveniles rights of their own. Those who have not reached the age of majority are the responsibility of their parents, guardian, or the state; therefore, they are largely dependent on others for protection of their rights, even though they are entitled like all other persons to EQUAL PROTECTION and DUE PROCESS of the law, as provided by the Constitution. Between 1989 and 1998 the number of delinquency cases handled by juvenile courts increased forty-four percent; in 1998 these courts handled some 4,800 delinquency cases every day.

In *In re Gault* (1967), the Supreme Court declared that juveniles had such constitutional rights as the assistance of counsel and due process before being committed to a juvenile detention facility.

There, said Justice Abe Fortas (1910–82), a young prisoner's "world becomes 'a building with whitewashed walls, regimented routine and institutional hours.' …Instead of mother and father, sisters and brothers and friends and classmates, his world is peopled by guards, custodians, state employees, and 'delinquents' confined with him for anything from waywardness to rape and homicide."

The number of prisoners in the United States has grown dramatically in recent years. The Justice Department's Bureau of Justice Statistics announced that as of the end of 2006 there were 2,258,983 prisoners being held in federal and state prisons or in local jails and that the average annual increase in prisoners has been 3.4 percent since 1995. More recently, at the beginning of 2008, it was estimated that approximately 1 out of every 100 Americans was incarcerated. The projected growth in the prison population by 2010 is 13 percent. Many federal and state prisons have been operating far above capacity. Regular professional inspections by human rights organizations, combined with opportunities for inmates and others acting on their behalf to file legitimate complaints without the possibility of reprisals, could ameliorate some problems faced by this expanding population.

> ### More on this topic:
>
> *Criminal Law, p. 132*
>
> *Cruel and Unusual Punishment, p. 135*
>
> *Death Penalty, p. 140*
>
> *Habeas Corpus, p. 266*

Privacy

Plato, the Greek philosopher of the fourth century B.C.E., warned in *The Laws* that a citizen's private life was a proper subject for legislation. But today most nations recognize various aspects of an individual's right of privacy. English courts, for example, have held that if no COMMON LAW remedy for an invasion of privacy exists, then courts of equity—a more flexible branch of English jurisprudence—may be invoked for protection. The constitutions of many other nations, Israel (1948) and Croatia (1990) among them, expressly guarantee their citizens the right of privacy. The U.S. Constitution does not directly address such a right, but the Supreme Court has derived it by implication from other language in the document.

In 1890 Louis D. Brandeis (1856–1941) coauthored an article in which the phrase "the right to be let alone" appeared. Thirty-eight years later, in a dissent in *Olmstead v. United States* (1928) when he was a justice on the Supreme Court, Brandeis expounded on the meaning of the DECLARATION OF INDEPENDENCE's famous phrase, "Life, Liberty and the pursuit of Happiness": "The makers of our Constitution," he said, "…sought to protect Americans in their beliefs, their thoughts,

their emotions and their sensations. They conferred, as against the Government, the right to be let alone—the most comprehensive of rights and the right most valued by civilized men."

This right to be left alone—the right of privacy—was finally recognized by the Supreme Court in the landmark case GRISWOLD V. CONNECTICUT (1965). In his decision for the Court, which struck down a state criminal law prohibiting the use of contraceptives, Justice William O. Douglas (1898–1980) emphasized that the contested law "operates directly on an intimate relation of husband and wife and their physician's role" in that relationship. The right of privacy, Douglas explained, exists in the penumbras (secondary shadows) and emanations of the First, Third, Fourth, Fifth, and Ninth Amendments of the BILL OF RIGHTS (1791). The First Amendment's right of association (see ASSEMBLY AND ASSOCIATION) protects the marital relationship, while a basis for a right of privacy can be found in the Third and Fourth Amendment guarantees against invasions of one's home (see SEARCH AND SEIZURE) and in the Fifth Amendment's concern for DUE PROCESS of law before citizens are deprived of their liberty; the Ninth Amendment underscores that all residual rights are retained by the people.

> "[If] the right of privacy means anything, it is the right of the individual, married or single, to be free from unwarranted governmental intrusion into matters so fundamentally affecting a person as the decision whether to bear or beget a child."
>
> —Justice William J. Brennan, in *Eisenstadt v. Baird*

The newly acknowledged right of privacy led to another landmark decision of the Supreme Court—ROE V. WADE (1973), which upheld a woman's right to an ABORTION and a number of cases stemming from that decision. Expanding on *Griswold* in a case in which Massachusetts prohibited the distribution of contraceptives to unmarried persons, Justice William J. Brennan (1906–97) declared in *Eisenstadt v. Baird* (1972) that if "the right of privacy means anything, it is the right of the individual, married or single, to be free from unwarranted governmental intrusion into matters so fundamentally affecting a person as the decision whether to bear or beget a child."

In KATZ V. UNITED STATES (1967), the Supreme Court created the "reasonable expectation of privacy" test and found that WIRETAPPING a public telephone booth was unconstitutional. In 1977 the Court explained that privacy rights involve two types of interests: those of individuals who want to make important decisions about their own lives (as in *Griswold* and *Roe*) and those of individuals in avoiding personal disclosures (as in *Katz*). The right of privacy is thus sometimes a personal right and sometimes related to a place, such as the home or a public telephone booth. With respect to sexual privacy, for example, the Supreme Court in LAWRENCE V. TEXAS (2003) overruled *Bowers v. Hardwick* (1986), which had upheld a Georgia law that made sodomy a crime applicable to consenting homosexual adults (see HOMOSEXUALS), by striking down a similar Texas law on the grounds that it constituted an unconstitutional invasion of privacy.

Confidentiality, like privacy, is not directly addressed in the Constitution, but some COMMON LAW rules apply to the confidentiality of relationships such as between husband and wife, priest and penitent, doctor and patient, and lawyer and client. In *United States v. Dege* (1960), the Supreme Court refused to allow the traditional right of confidentiality between spouses to thwart a federal criminal conspiracy statute. According to the Court, Congress would not have been concerned that joint participation by a married couple in a conspiracy "would make for marital disharmony" or would have presumed that the wife must be acting "under the coercive influence of the husband…[which] implies a view of American womanhood offensive to the ethos of our society."

In another type of confrontation over confidentiality, Justice Douglas criticized the government's refusal to make draft-board documents available to a defendant's counsel on the grounds that they contained confidential information; as he pointed out in his dissent in *Weintraub v. United States* (1971), the names could simply have been masked out to protect confidentiality. More recently, a U.S.

More on this topic:

Censorship, p. 82

Civil Rights, p. 96

Telemarketing calls can conflict with the right to privacy.
Source: AP Images/Minot Daily News, Jill Schramm

Court of Appeals in 2006 refused to grant immunity to a police officer who violated a woman's right of privacy by releasing to a television reporter a videotape—of the woman allegedly being raped—that the reporter aired on a local news broadcast. And in *Ferguson v. City of Charleston* (2001), the Supreme Court found that public hospitals cannot send positive results of drug tests administered to a pregnant woman to the police without her consent. Although using DRUGS is not a constitutional right, the Court believed that it had to extend the same protection of confidentiality to pregnant women's drug tests as to other private medical records.

Ever since Judge Robert H. Bork's 1987 nomination to the Supreme Court was defeated in the Senate, in part because he criticized the right of privacy as an example of unwarranted, judge-made law, subsequent Court nominees have been quick to express their belief in the unenumerated constitutional right of privacy as basic to the American way of life. In 2003 the Federal Trade Commission created a "do-not-call" registry to allow citizens to avoid unwanted telemarketing calls. Saying the list would not hamper businesses' free SPEECH rights, as some of them contended, the FTC suggested that it would instead add to individuals' right to privacy—their right to be left alone at dinnertime.

Privileges and Immunities

The federal nature of the U.S. government creates two types of citizenship: national and state. In the country's early days, many Americans felt a stronger allegiance to their states than to the nation. For example, Robert E. Lee (1807–70), who commanded the army of the Confederate States of America during the Civil War (1861–65), believed that his duty as a soldier lay first with Virginia rather than with the Union. But just as the federal government has accrued power at the expense of the states over the past two centuries, national citizenship has risen in importance over state citizenship as far as constitutional rights are concerned.

Article IV, section 2, of the Constitution provides: "The Citizens of each State shall be entitled to all Privileges and Immunities of Citizens in the several States." Although ALEXANDER HAMILTON, in essay 80 in *The Federalist* (1787–88) (see FEDERALIST PAPERS), called this guarantee "the basis of the Union," the privileges and immunities clause has not figured all that prominently in the Constitution's evolution.

Interpreting Article IV

From the beginning there have been differences of opinion as to what was intended by the clause's language. One theory, now obsolete, is that the privileges and immunities clause was intended to be an EQUAL PROTECTION clause, guaranteeing equal treatment by Congress for the CITIZENS of different states. Another since-rejected theory is that the clause allows a citizen of one state while in another state to be accorded all the rights to which he or she was entitled in his or her home state. Yet another theory is that it was intended to guarantee certain natural and FUNDAMENTAL RIGHTS to all citizens of a free society, ones that no state could deny to the citizens of another state when they came within its jurisdiction. The most accepted interpretation, however, is that the clause simply prohibits one state from discriminating against the citizens of another state in favor of its own citizens, except in some minor economic distinctions between residents and nonresidents.

In *Corfield v. Coryell*, a case heard by Supreme Court Justice Bushrod Washington (1762–1829) on circuit in 1823, the natural rights theory was adopted, only to be later rejected by the Court in *McKane v. Durston* (1894). Had his view been accepted, the process of incorporating most of the guarantees in the BILL OF RIGHTS (1791) into the Fourteenth Amendment (1868) to make them applicable to the states—which began only in 1927 in a piecemeal manner—could have been speeded up. Justice Washington's theory, in other words, could have formed a basis for the Supreme Court to review state legislation that restricted rights, analogous to the power that has developed under the DUE PROCESS and equal protection clauses of the Fourteenth Amendment (1868).

The prevailing theory of the clause's meaning and scope was confirmed in *Paul v. Virginia* (1869), in which the Supreme Court concluded: "It was undoubtedly the object of the clause in question to place the citizens of each State upon the same footing with citizens of other States, so far as the advantages resulting from citizenship in those States are concerned. It relieves them from the disabilities of alienage in other states; it inhibits discriminatory legislation against them by other States; it gives them the right of free ingress into other States, and egress from them; it insures to them in other States the same freedom possessed by the citizens of those States in the acquisition and enjoyment of property, and in the pursuit of happiness; and it secures to them in other States the equal protection of their laws."

In *Baldwin v. Montana Fish and Game Commission* (1978), the Supreme Court elaborated on the nature of the privileges and immunities clause. "Some distinctions between residents and nonresidents," the Court said, "merely reflect the fact that this is a Nation composed of individual States, and are permitted; other distinctions are prohibited because they hinder the formation, the purpose, or the development of a single Union of those States. Only with respect to those 'privileges' and 'immunities' bearing upon the vitality of the Nation as a single entity must the State treat all citizens, resident and nonresident, equally." The *Baldwin* case involved a challenge to Montana's statutory elk-hunting license scheme, which required nonresident hunters to pay a license fee some seven and one-half times higher than that paid by residents. The Court upheld the fee as a rational economic means to protect a valuable resource and not a violation of the

The Constitution's privileges and immunities clause has been invoked in lawsuits over fees for such activities as hunting elk.
Source: Minnesota Historical Society/Kenneth Melvin Wright

privileges and immunities clause, concluding that access to Montana elk is not basic to the well-being of the Union.

The ruling in *Baldwin* had been presaged by Chief Justice Frederick M. Vinson (1890–1953), who wrote in *Toomer v. Witsell* (1948), a similar case of higher fees for out-of-state fishermen: "The primary purpose of [the privileges and immunities] clause, like the clauses between which it is located [the FULL FAITH AND CREDIT clause and the EXTRADITION clause] was to help fuse into one Nation a collection of independent sovereign States."

While the privileges and immunities clause has generally been narrowly interpreted by the courts, the federal government has been able to use other avenues—among them the COMMERCE clause and the Fourteenth Amendment—to expand citizens' privileges and immunities despite the residual SOVEREIGNTY of the individual STATES recognized in the Tenth Amendment (1791). Today the distinctions between the ways state and out-of-state citizens are treated tend to reflect economic considerations, such as preserving state resources and ensuring residents' access to state educational institutions by charging higher fees for out-of-state students. For example, in *Hillside Dairy Inc. v. Lyons* (2003), the Supreme Court, in an opinion written by Justice John Paul Stevens (b. 1920), held that a claim of economic discrimination under a state law that is based on the privileges and immunities clause may not be dismissed simply because the state law does not expressly identify "out-of-state citizenship as a basis for disparate treatment." The case involved a complex California law, as amended in 1997, that required out-of-state milk producers who sold to in-state processors to contribute to a "price equalization pool" the same as in-state producers.

Interpreting the Fourteenth Amendment

The Fourteenth Amendment contains a "privileges *or* immunities" clause: "No State shall make or enforce any law which shall abridge the privileges or immunities of citizens of the United States." Like the clause in the original document, however, this language has not figured prominently in the development of constitutional law. In the Slaughter-House Cases (1873)—three cases including *Butchers Benevolent Association v. Crescent City Live-Stock Landing and Slaughter-House Co.*— the Supreme Court ruled that the privileges or immunities clause referred to national and not to state citizenship. And according to *Twining v. New Jersey* (1908), the rights encompassed, including the right to TRAVEL and vote (see ELECTIONS), are not extensive.

Supreme Court Justice Hugo L. Black (1886–1971) wanted to use the clause in the Fourteenth Amendment to incorporate the first eight amendments of the Bill of Rights, thus making them applicable to the states (see INCORPORATION DOCTRINE). But the clause was found relevant only in *Oyama v. California* (1948) to uphold the right of a six-year-old American-born citizen, whose Japanese father was ineligible for U.S. citizenship, to own land in California. The Court found that only the most exceptional circumstances could excuse discrimination against an American citizen, albeit a minor, under a state law that forbade the ownership or transfer of agricultural property by ALIENS ineligible for citizenship.

The privileges and immunities of American citizens have grown extensively since the Constitution's inception but not through the application of either the privileges *and* immunities clause in Article IV or the privileges *or* immunities clause in the Fourteenth Amendment.

Prohibition

Alcoholism is a serious problem in many countries, particularly Iceland and Russia. Although cultures and countries worldwide have tried to ban or prohibit the manufacture, sale, and use of al-

On May 23, 1923, offcers enforcing Prohibition stage a lunch-room raid on Pennsylvania Avenue in Washington, D.C., as by-standers watch. Ratified in 1919, the unpopular Eighteenth Amendment banning liquor was repealed fourteen years later.
Source: Library of Congress

cohol beverages, few have been successful. Both Finland and the United States tried Prohibition beginning in 1919, and both repealed it—Finland in 1931 and the United States in 1933. The Prohibition movement in America was fueled in the first half of the nineteenth century by a revival of religious fervor that equated the perfection of humankind with the practice of temperance and the abolition of SLAVERY.

Factors contributing to the Prohibition movement included population increases in urban centers, where alcohol was most visibly consumed; the relative overrepresentation of rural areas in state legislatures, where proposed constitutional AMENDMENTS have to be ratified; and the clash of evangelical Protestants, who viewed alcohol as evil, with Roman Catholics, who were not adverse to drink. The National Women's Christian Temperance League was launched in 1874 and the World's Women's Christian Temperance Union in 1883, the latter founded by Frances Willard, who also started the Prohibition Party in 1882. The Anti-Saloon League was established in 1893. In 1917 the matter came to a head: A temporary Wartime Prohibition Act (1917) reserved all grain for food rather than allow any for alcohol production, thirty-three states with more than sixty percent of the nation's population had adopted Prohibition measures, and then Congress proposed a constitutional amendment banning alcohol nationwide.

The Eighteenth Amendment (1919) consisted of three sections. Section 1, the major section, provided: "After one year from the ratification of this article the manufacture, sale, or transportation of intoxicating liquors within, the importation thereof into, or the exportation thereof from the United States and all territory subject to the jurisdiction thereof for beverage purposes is hereby prohibited." The amendment gave Congress and the states concurrent power to enforce Prohibition and made RATIFICATION dependent on the state legislatures within a seven-year period. It took only thirteen months for thirty-six of the forty-eight states to agree, and the amendment was declared by the secretary of state to be ratified on January 29, 1919. Nine other states subsequently added their approval, but Rhode Island rejected it.

America's experiment with banning alcohol bolstered the old argument that morality cannot be legislated effectively. Other human vices have been treated differently by Congress and state legislatures. Today, for example, gambling is not merely condoned but officially sponsored by many states through lotteries and is used to pay for state programs, including education. Prostitution, while not widely legalized except in certain Nevada counties, is not strictly enforced in many jurisdictions. Tobacco products are still sold freely, except to minors, despite their proven consequences to health. DRUGS, in contrast, constitute a vice that the government still aims to eradicate, although there is some support for legalizing drugs so that the drug trade can be controlled and taxed by the government.

Guidelines to enforce Prohibition were established under the National Prohibition Act (1920), which became known as the Volstead Act after its congressional sponsor, Rep. Andrew J. Volstead (R-Minn.). This ushered in the infamous era of bootleggers and speakeasies, Al Capone, and the St. Valentine's Day Massacre. Both the Eighteenth Amendment and the Volstead Act were upheld by the Supreme Court in a series of seven cases in 1920, the lead case being *Rhode Island v. Palmer*.

In a fast turnabout, after the stock market crash in 1929 and the ensuing economic depression, politicians soon proposed that one way to stimulate the economy would be through the legal manufacture and sale of alcohol beverages. In 1932, when Franklin D. Roosevelt (1882–1945) ran for president the first time, the Democratic Party's platform included repeal of the Eighteenth Amendment. The text of the amendment to repeal the liquor ban specified that ratification had to be by conventions in the states rather than by the state legislatures, which were dominated by the rural interests that had supported Prohibition in the first place.

The Twenty-first Amendment was proposed on February 20, 1933, and quickly ratified by December 5, 1933, when Utah became the thirty-sixth state to approve the change. The Supreme Court ruled in *United States v. Constantine* (1935) that Prohibition ceased as of that date and that any prosecutions or appeals pending or begun afterward had to be dismissed. Final convictions while the Volstead Act was still in force were unaffected. Although Prohibition was repealed at the national level, it was left up to the states whether to allow the sale of alcoholic beverages within their jurisdictions. A few states continued to prohibit alcohol, but by 1966 all had repealed outright bans on liquor. Today some "dry" counties still enforce their own versions of Prohibition.

Property

William Blackstone (1723–80), the eighteenth-century commentator on the laws of England, called property the "third absolute right [after life and liberty], inherent in every Englishman." It "consists in the free use, enjoyment and disposal of all his acquisitions, without any control or diminution, save only the laws of the land." Both life and liberty can in fact be equated in some sense with property. Without sufficient property in the form of food and shelter, life cannot be sustained, and without even greater resources, liberty—the freedom to live as one wishes—is nugatory.

A person's right to create or otherwise obtain exclusive rights to property is the cornerstone of civil society. Governments are constituted to a large extent to determine and enforce rules relating

Residents of New London, Connecticut, protest the city's attempt to use its eminent domain powers to evict them.
Source: AP Images/Steve Miller

to the ownership, use, and transfer of property. The communist theory that the state owns all property produced under the direction of the state, to be doled out by the government rather than exchanged in a relatively free market economy, has been proved unworkable. The Greek philosopher Aristotle predicted this in the fourth century B.C.E. when he observed that "there is always a difficulty in men living together and having all human relations in common, but especially in their having common property."

Property and the Constitution

The issue of property and laws regarding property was of great concern to the FRAMERS OF THE CONSTITUTION and is an important subtext of the document. The PREAMBLE, which states the document's aims to "provide for the common defence, promote the general Welfare, and secure the Blessings of Liberty to ourselves and our Posterity," embraces the idea of protecting property, promoting the greater acquisition of property, and transmitting property to one's heirs. The impetus for the CONSTITUTIONAL CONVENTION OF 1787 itself was not altruism or utopianism but the need to promote better trade and commercial relations among the states. A number of delegates to the convention supported property requirements for eligibility to government positions, particularly for senators. Property ownership was a qualification for voting during the early days of the Union, and for many years some states required voters to pay a poll tax for the privilege of voting, often a subterfuge to discourage some types of voters, particularly African Americans (see RACIAL DISCRIMINATION).

A number of provisions in the Constitution address the relationship between the government and individuals regarding property and property rights. Article I, section 8, sets forth Congress's power with regard to property interests relating to TAXATION, COMMERCE, BANKRUPTCY, the valuation of CURRENCY, and PATENTS and COPYRIGHT laws, for example. Section 10 prohibits the states from several property-related activities, including issuing "bills of credit" (paper money) and passing laws "impairing the Obligation of Contracts."

The most overt constitutional provision dealing with property is perhaps in the Fifth Amendment (1791), which states in part: "...nor shall any person...be deprived of life, liberty, or property, without due process of law; nor shall private property be taken for public use, without just compensation." The Fourteenth Amendment (1868) extends to the states the DUE PROCESS protection for property. The Fourth Amendment (1791) protects people from unreasonable searches and seizures of their property (see SEARCH AND SEIZURE). The Seventh Amendment (1791) guarantees the right to a jury trial in controversies that "shall exceed twenty dollars" (see JURIES), and the Eighth Amendment (1791) prohibits excessive BAIL or fines.

Evolving Concepts of Property

The economics of property relationships has been important to the Supreme Court in reaching decisions in many cases. When the Constitution was drafted in 1787, some people—slaves, for example—were treated as property (see SLAVERY). In the infamous Dred Scott case of 1857, the Supreme Court held that a slave could not become free simply by being taken into a part of the United States where slavery was outlawed. According to the Court, such a ruling would deprive the slave owner of his constitutionally protected property right without due process of law. On the other hand, in compensation disputes the Court initially took a narrow view of what constituted property, thus not requiring compensation where government regulation of property merely interfered with use of that property. Beginning around the turn of the twentieth century, the Court adopted the economic due process principle: that the due process clauses of the Fifth Amendment (1791) and the Fourteenth Amendment (1868) required the courts to invalidate laws interfering with private property. Using this principle, the courts could determine whether laws interfering with the rights of private businesses were unreasonable, unnecessary, or arbitrary and therefore unconstitutional.

In the 1930s, however, the Supreme Court retreated from the economic due process concept and virtually gave the national and state legislatures carte blanche to regulate business activity. During the last quarter of the twentieth century, the Court extended the definition of *property* to state employment and welfare benefits that may not be taken away without due process, such as a hearing and a right of appeal.

Another area addressed by the Supreme Court in the 1990s involved the civil and punitive forfeiture of property—property used in the commission of a crime or taken as a punishment for a crime. Here the Court has by narrow margins been inconsistent in deciding whether individual property rights trump the rights of the government. In *Eastern Enterprises v. Apfel* (1998), however, a bare majority of the Court did agree that the definition of property does not include intangible general liabilities to pay money but is limited to specific identifiable property interests. And, by a larger majority, the Court in *Castle Rock Co. v. Gonzales* (2005) ruled that a person "who has obtained a state-law restraining order has [no] constitutionally protected property interest in having the police enforce the restraining order when they have probable cause to believe it has been violated." In his opinion for the Court, Justice Antonin Scalia (b. 1936) explained "that a benefit is not a protected entitlement if government officials may grant or deny it at their discretion." In essence, there are just too many laws and too many circumstances to believe that the police will always have the resources to be able to enforce them.

The law today recognizes many forms of property, including intellectual and artistic property that may be covered by copyright. In addition, a person whose fame makes his or her name and likeness a valuable commodity has a property right in them. Courts have also recognized property rights in human embryos. In 2001 the New Jersey Supreme Court ruled that a man and his ex-wife had equal rights in their embryos, which had been frozen, so that the man could not unilaterally have the embryos implanted in another woman over his ex-wife's objection.

The growing medical industry in human body parts for transplantation and other uses is also generating new laws and new constitutional issues. In addition to the moral implications of using human genetic material, stem cells, and information based on the human genome (see GENETICS) for scientific and medical purposes, significant new legal and constitutional property rights issues are likely to surface as well.

More on this topic:
Copyright, p. 124
Economic Liberty, p. 173
Genetics, p. 251
Just Compensation, p. 323
Kelo v. New London, p. 330
Patents, p. 396
Zoning, p. 598

Public Forums

The *agora* of ancient Athens, the city's public marketplace and ad hoc civic center, was where DEMOCRACY began. The gathering place for public discussion, it was also the focal point for decision making by the assembly, open to all male Athenians older than eighteen years of age. In Roman law a *forum* (Latin for marketplace) was a paved court where public business was transacted and elections and trials were held. Thus a place in which to make and listen to political speeches and to voice complaints about the government—a public forum—has been essential since the beginning of democracy.

At the time of the CONSTITUTIONAL CONVENTION OF 1787 in Philadelphia, the United States already encompassed an extensive amount of territory, making impractical a single public forum for political debate accessible to all citizens. The idea of REPRESENTATIVE GOVERNMENT that had developed in England allowed some citizens to be chosen by the rest of the citizenry to meet in one place—the nation's capital (see CAPITAL, NATIONAL)—to carry out the decision-making functions on their behalf. But the concept of public forums for the exchange of political ideas and information was still important at the national, state, and local levels to further the American form of representative democracy established by the Constitution.

Public places—streets, municipal buildings, and public parks—are traditional forums where people may assemble and discuss and protest government policy. The First Amendment (1791) rights of free SPEECH and assembly (see ASSEMBLY AND ASSOCIATION) by those who wish to use public spaces as public forums must be balanced against the legitimate needs of the government and the rights of the public at large, a basic conflict resolved on a case-by-case basis.

In *Davis v. Massachusetts* (1897), the Supreme Court affirmed a Massachusetts Supreme Court decision in which Justice OLIVER WENDELL HOLMES JR. said that banning or limiting public speaking in a highway or public park "is no more an infringement of the rights of a member of the public than for the owner of a private house to forbid it in his house." This deference to government ownership of public PROPERTY lasted until 1939, when in *Hague v. CIO* the Court struck down a New Jersey ordinance that prohibited public assemblies "in or upon public streets, highways, public parks, or public buildings" without a permit. Using the DUE PROCESS clause of the Fourteenth

CLOSER LOOK ◉

Art is not protected as much as speech under the public forum tests. In *National Endowment for the Arts v. Finley* (1998), the Supreme Court allowed the National Endowment for the Arts, at the instigation of Congress, to take "into consideration general standards of decency" in judging the artistic merits of grant applications.

CIVIL LIBERTIES IN WAR TIMES

By Max Lerner

CITY WIDE FORUM

ROOSEVELT HIGH

JAN. 24TH — 8: P.M.

IOWA ART PROGRAM WPA

Crises have always generated public forums. This WPA poster from January 1940 advertises a lecture on the outbreak of war in Europe and its effect on individual rights at home.
Source: Library of Congress

Amendment (1868) to extend protection of the right to use public property as a public forum, the Court indicated that U.S. citizenship would have little meaning if natural persons—not artificial or legal entities—could be denied the right to discuss national legislation and its benefits, advantages, and opportunities.

In *Cornelius v. NAACP Legal Defense and Educational Fund, Inc.* (1985), the Supreme Court denied the National Association for the Advancement of Colored People the right to solicit contributions from federal employees through the Combined Federal Campaign, a vehicle for charity contributions approved by the federal government for its employees and devised to exclude any soliciting, particularly separate soliciting. The 4–3 majority declared that neither the federal workplace nor the campaign had been designated as a public forum. The Court did remand the case for a determination of whether the NAACP had been excluded because the government disagreed with the NAACP's particular viewpoint.

In addition to the type of place designated a public forum—and thus available with minimal restrictions—an important consideration for the courts has been government regulation of the content of speech in those public forums. As Justice Byron R. White (1917–93) expressed it for the Supreme Court in *Perry Education Assn. v. Perry Local Educators Assn.* (1983), restrictions on the use of a public space such as to the time, place, or manner of the use must be "content-neutral,…narrowly tailored to serve a significant government interest, and leave open ample alternative channels of communication."

The world's major public forums, even in the INTERNET age, will most likely still be public spaces where citizens can air their views with other citizens and confront those in power. The electronic media do not create the same immediate impact as a massive rally or march by citizens showing their support for, or displeasure about, government policies.

Public Safety   *See* POLICE POWER.

Public Use   *See* JUST COMPENSATION; PROPERTY.

Punishment

Punishment of crime has been a basis of civil society for at least as long as recorded history. Both the Code of Hammurabi, who was the king of Babylon from 1792 to 1750 B.C.E., and the Bible's Old Testament demand an "eye for an eye, a tooth for a tooth," as a way of having the punishment fit the crime. In his *Commentaries on the Laws of England* (1765–70), William Blackstone (1723–80) described punishment as "evils or inconveniences consequent upon crimes and misdemeanors; being devised, denounced, and inflicted by human laws, in consequence of disobedience or misbehavior in those, to regulate whose conduct such laws were respectively made." But the ancient Greek philosopher Aristotle (384–322 B.C.E.) argued in *The Politics* that "just punishments and chastisements do indeed spring from a good principle, but they are good only because we cannot do without them—it would be better that neither individuals nor states need anything of the sort...."

Punishment is addressed in many national constitutions. For example, Singapore's constitution (1963) guarantees that "no person shall suffer greater punishment for an offense than was prescribed by law at the time it was committed." The Nicaraguan constitution (1987) declares: "In Nicaragua the penitentiary system is humane, and it has as a fundamental objective the transformation of the interned in order to reintegrate him or her into society."

The Power to Punish

The power to impose punishment for wrongdoing is a basic right of SOVEREIGNTY for any government. In an enlightened society, that power should not include the power to inflict inhuman, brutal, or, in the words of the Eighth Amendment (1791), "cruel and unusual punishments." Dissenting from the Supreme Court's rejection in *Sweeney v. Woodall* (1952) of a HABEAS CORPUS appeal

At the beginning of the twentieth century, when this photograph of inmates at a Delaware prison was taken, some states still officially practiced corporal punishment, including the use of pillories and whipping posts.
Source: Library of Congress

in which a prisoner alleged, among other things, that he had been beaten frequently by his jailers with a nine-pound strap bearing five metal prongs, Justice William O. Douglas (1888–1980) said: "I rebel at the thought that any human being should be forced to run a gamut of blood and terror in order to get his constitutional rights."

The Constitution expressly grants the power to punish for a number of transgressions.

Counterfeiting. Article I, section 8, authorizes Congress "To provide for the Punishment of counterfeiting the Securities and current Coin of the United States" (see CURRENCY). In *United States v. Marigold* (1850), the Supreme Court upheld Congress's power to criminalize the circulation or importation of counterfeit money. And in *Atlantic Coast Line Railroad v. City of Goldsboro* (1914), the Court confirmed the authority of Congress to make it illegal to possess counterfeiting tools and dies.

Piracy and Offenses under International Law. Congress is also empowered under Article I, section 8, "To define and punish Piracies and Felonies committed on the high Seas, and Offences against the Law of Nations" (see ADMIRALTY AND MARITIME LAW; INTERNATIONAL LAW). The Supreme Court approved an act of Congress punishing "the crime of piracy, as defined by the law of nations," in *United States v. Smith* (1820). The same year in *United States v. Furlong*, the Court broadly interpreted "high Seas" to cover crimes committed on U.S. vessels docked in foreign ports. In

United States v. Arjona (1887), the Court validated a law punishing counterfeiting of foreign securities in the United States under international law.

Treason. "The Congress shall have Power," states Article III, section 3, "to declare the Punishment of Treason, but no Attainder of Treason shall work Corruption of Blood, or Forfeiture except during the Life of the Person attainted." The limitation imposed here by the Constitution is meant to ensure that punishment affects only the person convicted of TREASON and not his or her heirs (see ATTAINDER, BILLS OF). During the Civil War (1861–65) Congress passed the Confiscation Act (1862) "to suppress Insurrection, to punish Treason and Rebellion, [and] to seize and confiscate the Property of Rebels." In order to comply with Article III, section 3, however, the takings were limited to a life estate in the offender's PROPERTY, so that the remainder could be inherited by his children when he died.

Members of Congress. According to Article I, section 5, "Each House may determine the Rules of its Proceedings, punish its Members for disorderly Behavior, and, with the Concurrence of two thirds, expel a member." CONGRESS can punish a member by a vote to censure or reprimand or by a fine. Expulsion is rarely used, but the first case occurred in 1797, when for the first and only time the House of Representatives voted to impeach a member of Congress—a senator who was charged with inciting NATIVE AMERICANS to attack Spanish Florida and Louisiana—but the Senate voted simply to expel him. During the Civil War (1861–65) Southerners loyal to the Confederacy were expelled from Congress.

In 1967 the House of Representatives refused to allow Adam Clayton Powell Jr. to take the seat to which he had been elected, despite a House select committee's recommendation of a lesser punishment. Allegations against Powell, perhaps the most politically powerful African American in the country at the time, included such charges as income tax evasion, unnecessary trips at government expense, and employment of his wife on his staff although she lived in Puerto Rico. After Powell was reelected in 1968 and allowed to take his seat in 1969, the Supreme Court held in *Powell v. McCormack* (1969) that his rejection by the House had been unconstitutional, in part because the SPEAKER OF THE HOUSE had advised members that the vote was only to exclude and not to "expel"—the language of the Constitution—and that only a majority vote was necessary rather than the two-thirds required by Article I, section 5.

Impeachment. Article I, section 3, provides: "Judgment in Cases of Impeachment shall not extend further than to removal from Office, and disqualification to hold and enjoy any Office of honor, Trust or Profit under the United States: but the Party convicted shall nevertheless be liable and subject to Indictment, Trial, Judgment and Punishment, according to Law." No president, member of Congress, or Supreme Court justice has been convicted of IMPEACHMENT charges, but several judges have. Three district court judges were removed from office in the 1980s on charges including lying under oath, tax fraud, and conspiracy to accept a bribe. Two presidents and one Supreme Court justice have had impeachment charges voted against them by the House of Representatives, but they were not convicted by the Senate as required under the Constitution.

Involuntary Servitude. The Thirteenth Amendment (1865) permits involuntary servitude "as a punishment for crime whereof the party shall have been duly convicted." This part of the amendment, which also prohibits SLAVERY, has been used mainly to challenge private actions under state laws, such as compelling a person to labor against his will to pay off a debt. In *Bailey v. Alabama* (1911), the Supreme Court invalidated a state statute that made the refusal to perform labor called for in a written contract prima facie evidence of fraud and therefore punishable as a criminal offense. In other similar cases of "peonage" (requiring a person to work off a debt or obligation), the Court has held that laws creating conditions of private involuntary servitude as punishment are unconstitutional.

Prohibited Punishments

The Constitution contains several provisions that prohibit or limit punishment. Perhaps the most well known is in the Eighth Amendment (1791), which states: "Excessive bail shall not be required, nor excessive fines imposed, nor cruel and unusual punishments inflicted."

Bills of Attainder and Ex Post Facto Laws. Article I, sections 9 and 10, respectively, prohibit the federal and state governments from passing bills of attainder (see ATTAINDER, BILLS OF), which are special laws that extinguish a person's CIVIL RIGHTS after a death sentence or conviction of treason or a felony, or EX POST FACTO LAWS, which criminalize an action after it has been committed or increase its punishment.

Excessive Fines. The Supreme Court has been reluctant to declare fines levied as a punishment to be excessive under the Eighth Amendment even when the excessiveness is apparent on its face. As recently as 1989, the Court found in *Browning-Ferris Industries v. Kelco Disposal, Inc.* that punitive damages of $6 million awarded by a jury in a case in which the compensatory damages were only $51,146 was not so disproportionate as to be constitutionally excessive. But in *Philip Morris USA v. Williams* (2007), the Supreme Court said that while a plaintiff may show harm to other victims to prove that the conduct complained of was more reprehensible than just the damage to the plaintiff, a jury may not go so far as to award punitive damages to punish the defendant directly on account of harm allegedly done to others not a party to the litigation.

In *Austin v. United States* (1993)—a case involving the forfeiture of PROPERTY that was to be used to facilitate drug-related crimes—the Supreme Court announced that the crucial question was whether the forfeiture was in fact a monetary punishment rather than a government action to recover property related to illicit activity. The Court found that forfeitures of property can be considered a punishment by a fine and that the Eighth Amendment prohibition against excessive fines must be considered by the courts. Civil forfeiture is a claim by the government against property related to illicit activity and not against the suspect. The procedural safeguards extended to those accused of crimes thus do not generally apply to such civil actions against the property itself.

Cruel and Unusual Punishment. In *Wilkerson v. Utah* (1878), the Supreme Court admitted that what constituted CRUEL AND UNUSUAL PUNISHMENT was not easy to define, "but it is safe to affirm that punishments of torture [such as drawing and quartering, disemboweling alive, beheading, public dissecting, and burning alive], and all others in the same line of unnecessary cruelty, are forbidden by that amendment to the Constitution." The Court held in *Trop v. Dulles* (1958) that divesting a natural-born citizen of his citizenship was an unconstitutionally cruel punishment. In *Hope v. Pelzer* (2002) the Court found, by a 6–3 vote, that chaining a prisoner to a hitching post shirtless in the sun for approximately seven hours with no bathroom breaks as punishment for bad behavior violated the "'basic concept underlying the Eighth Amendment[, which] is nothing less than the dignity of man.'" More recently, in *Erickson v. Pardus* (2007), the Court ruled that a civil suit by a prisoner complaining that the termination of treatment for hepatitis by prison officials endangered his life could involve a violation of the Eight Amendment right against cruel and unusual punishment.

In *Furman v. Georgia* (1972), the Supreme Court found that the DEATH PENALTY—at least as it was being imposed at the time—violated the Eighth Amendment. Later changes in procedures, including standards to guide judges and juries in applying capital punishment and separate hearings to isolate the

> *"It is safe to affirm that punishments of torture [such as drawing and quartering, emboweling alive, beheading, public dissecting, and burning alive], and all others in the same line of unnecessary cruelty, are forbidden...."*
>
> —Supreme Court decision, 1878

conviction portion of the trial from the sentencing portion, led the Court to again permit the death penalty in cases involving certain very serious crimes.

Sentencing

The Supreme Court has let judges and juries have broad discretion in handing down sentences, but federal and state sentencing guideline laws at least provide a range from which a sentence must be selected. Obviously improper sentences, however, can trigger a reversal by the Court. In *Townsend v. Burke* (1948), the Court overturned a judge's sentence for a defendant who had not had the ASSISTANCE OF COUNSEL, noting that the judge made errors and facetious remarks about the defendant's record.

In *Williams v. New York* (1949), however, the Supreme Court let stand the imposition of the death penalty even though the judge disregarded the jury's recommendation of mercy and based his sentence on information that was undisclosed to the defendant or his counsel. This ruling was limited when the Court found in *Gardner v. Florida* (1977) that because the death penalty is a special type of sentencing, then at the least any information available to the judge imposing it should be made a part of the record and available to the defense.

The Supreme Court has placed some limitations on sentencing. According to *North Carolina v. Pearce* (1969), a judge may not show vindictiveness by imposing a harsher penalty after a second trial because the defendant appealed the first trial. Nonetheless, penalties for some types of convictions can be enhanced if the person has been convicted before of crimes involving violence or drug offenses. In 2001, finding a violation of the Eighth Amendment's ban on cruel and unusual punishment, a federal appeals court struck down a long sentence meted out under California's 1994 "Three Strikes and You're Out" law, which imposes harsh sentences for habitual criminals after the third conviction. Forty states have adopted similar measures to lock up recidivists for life or lengthy terms.

The Sentencing Reform Act (1984) established the U.S. Sentencing Commission as an independent agency in the JUDICIAL BRANCH. In addition to other functions such as collecting data about crime and sentencing, the commission develops guidelines for sentencing in the federal courts for cases such as bank robberies, drug trafficking, fraud, and immigration offenses. Its guidelines take into account factors such as a defendant's prior criminal record, if any, and the severity of the offense. For example, firing a gun during the commission of a crime brings a harsher sentence than mere possession of a gun during the crime, and embezzlement of $100 is treated less severely than embezzlement of $30,000. In *Mistretta v. United States* (1989), the Supreme Court gave its approval to the act, saying that placing the commission in the judicial branch did not violate the SEPARATION OF POWERS principle and that its mission to develop sentencing guidelines was an "essential neutral endeavor" in which judicial participation was "peculiarly appropriate." But, with regard to the 100:1 ratio for the length of sentences for crimes involving crack cocaine—a drug far more likely to be used by minorities—and powdered cocaine, guidelines that originated in the Anti-Drug Abuse Act of 1986, the Court held, in *Kimbrough v. United States* (2007), that federal district judges are empowered to use their discretion in arriving at sentences in criminal cases. In this particular case, a U.S. district court judge had imposed a relatively light sentence on a crack cocaine distributor. Immediately after the decision in *Kimbrough*, the U.S. Sentencing Commission voted unanimously to give federal inmates incarcerated for crack cocaine offenses—nearly 3,800 prisoners—the opportunity to have their sentences reduced.

Pardons

Article II, section 2, declares that the president "shall have Power to grant Reprieves and Pardons for Offences against the United States, except in Cases of Impeachment." Reprieves suspend the execution of a punishment validly imposed by a federal court, while PARDONS void a crime, thus eliminating a basis for punishment. The president's pardon power is derived from similar power held by an absolute monarch, who, as the source of all law, is above it and may exempt anyone he chooses from its effect. A major reason why the Constitution includes this power, which Chief Justice JOHN MARSHALL in *United States v. Wilson* (1833) described as akin to "an act of grace," was to allow the nation's chief executive to defuse rebellion and insurrection by offering to pardon rebels.

Today the rules for determining which punishment can be meted out and how punishments are affected by the constitutional prohibitions are, unfortunately, extremely complex and no doubt will only become more so as the government and the courts attempt to bring more rationality and scientific study to bear on the subject. Among the problems that call for review are the imposition of the death penalty in the face of statistics that show it is imposed disproportionately on blacks and used for minors and mentally handicapped persons, as well as the inhumane treatment of many PRISONERS in the United States documented by international HUMAN RIGHTS organizations.

More on this topic:
Criminal Law, p. 132
Immunity, p. 289
Just Compensation, p. 323

Qualifications for Office

Although in a republic all citizens are theoretically equal, the FRAMERS OF THE CONSTITUTION set certain qualifications that limit the field of those eligible for high government office. Other national constitutions similarly set forth qualifications for the elected head of state and other elected government officials, and qualifications may also be given for appointees. The Honduran constitution (1982), in addition to requiring that the president be a Honduran by birth, more than thirty years of age, a citizen, and a "layman," precludes from election, among other persons, "[s]enior officers of the armed services and the police and security forces," the "spouse and relatives of military commanders…," and "[r]elatives of the president…within the fourth degree of relationship by blood or the second degree of relationship by marriage."

General Qualifications

The U.S. Constitution states one overriding requirement for each national or state public office holder and prohibits use of one specific qualification. According to Article VI, "The Senators and Representatives…, and the Members of the several State Legislatures, and all executive and judicial Officers, both of the United States and of the several States, shall be bound by Oath or Affirmation, to support this Constitution; but no religious Test shall ever be required as a Qualification to any Office or public Trust under the United States."

The OATH OF OFFICE is required so that the supremacy of the Constitution as well as TREATIES and laws written under it will be upheld throughout the nation (see SUPREMACY CLAUSE). The prohibition against religious tests stems from the fact that the American colonies had to a great extent been settled by members of various religious sects—Protestants, Catholics, and Quakers, for example—who had fled religious persecution overseas. Although a religious tolerance law had been enacted in England in 1696, anyone who renounced the Protestant faith was excluded from holding public office. Most of the colonies followed suit, requiring profession of faith in God or a specific religious sect to obtain the rights of citizenship or to hold public office.

The Virginia Statute for Religious Freedom (1786), written by THOMAS JEFFERSON, officially separated church and state, a concept endorsed by JAMES MADISON and other delegates to the CONSTITUTIONAL CONVENTION OF 1787 (see RELIGION). But many states continued the practice of requiring a religious test for public office. The last of these tests was struck down by the Supreme Court in *Torasco v. Watkins* (1961), which involved a requirement that notary publics in Maryland affirm a belief in God. The Court said that considering the prohibition against religious oaths in Article VI and the religious freedom espoused by the First Amendment (1791), it is impossible "for government, state or federal, to restore the historically and constitutionally discredited policy of probing religious beliefs by test oaths or limiting public offices to persons who have, or perhaps more properly, profess to have a belief in some particular kind of religious concept." In *McDaniel v. Paty* (1978), the Court also invalidated a state law excluding ministers and priests from serving in a constitutional convention and, by inference, any similar laws that would ban them from serving in the legislature.

Qualifications for Legislators

According to Article I, section 2, "No person shall be a Representative who shall have not attained to the Age of twenty five Years, and been seven Years a Citizen of the United States, and who shall not, when elected, be an Inhabitant of that State in which he shall be chosen." Section 3 sets qualifications for senators: "No Person shall be a Senator who shall not have attained to the Age of thirty Years, and been nine Years a Citizen of the United States, and who shall not, when elected, be an Inhabitant of that State for which he shall be chosen" (see CONGRESS; HOUSE OF REPRESENTATIVES; SENATE).

Some states have tried to establish term limits for their members of Congress (see TERMS OF OFFICE). In a 5–4 decision in *U.S. Term Limits, Inc. v. Thornton* (1995), however, the Supreme Court held that such limitations were unconstitutional because the qualifications set out in the Constitution were fixed and could not be modified by any state.

Disqualifications for being a member of Congress are given in Article I, section 6, which says that "no Person holding any Office under the United States, shall be a Member of either House during his Continuance in Office." This provision stems from the principle of SEPARATION OF POWERS of government; it differs markedly from a parliamentary system of government, in which the prime minister and the other cabinet members are elected members of the parliament.

Section 5 authorizes the members of each house of Congress to "be the Judge of the Elections, Returns and Qualifications of it own Members." In contested elections the nod usually goes to the candidate of the party in power.

John Henry Eaton
Source: U.S. Senate Historical Office

Even though the Constitution says a senator must be at least thirty years old, senators apparently never asked John Henry Eaton of Tennessee how old he was before seating him in 1818. At the time, birth records were not well kept, and it is possible that Eaton did not know he was just twenty-eight.

It may have been only later that Eaton determined his birth date, which was eventually engraved on his tombstone.

Prior to Eaton's election, at least two other senators were seated in violation of the Constitution's age requirement. Both Henry Clay and Armistead Mason were just a little older than Eaton when they took office.

Eaton is believed to be the youngest U.S. senator in history, and his record is unlikely to be broken. A few years after he took office, the Senate began paying closer attention to the ages of newly elected members.

CLOSER LOOK

In early 2008, after John McCain (b. 1936) became the presumptive Republican Party nominee for president, the question arose as to whether the fact that he was born a citizen but outside of the United States in the Panama Canal Zone disqualified him from office. While acknowledging that there is no controlling legal precedent, it was the consensus of a number of lawyers and government officials that McCain met the Constitution's "natural born Citizen" requirement.

In 1870 the Fifteenth Amendment opened up both the voting rolls and access to public office, allowing black men to join the white males who had originally been envisioned as the nation's voters and office holders. Not until 1920, when the Nineteenth Amendment was ratified, were women finally accorded this right of citizenship as well. The Twenty-sixth Amendment (1971) lowered the age limit of voters to eighteen years.

Qualifications for President

According to Article II, section 1: "No Person except a natural born Citizen, or a Citizen of the United States, at the time of the Adoption of this Constitution, shall be eligible to the Office of President; neither shall any Person be eligible to that Office who shall not have attained to the Age of thirty five Years, and been fourteen Years a Resident within the United States." Because the framers worked under the assumption for most of the convention that the PRESIDENT would be elected by Congress, these qualifications were a last-minute addition.

The age requirement was chosen to ensure that a candidate had developed a reputation by which his character and ability could be assessed, not to mention the notion that age brings maturity. The residency requirement was added because at the time there were fears that former British sympathizers who had fled the country might return and attempt to run for president.

The original draft of the Constitution does not mention any qualification for the office of VICE PRESIDENT, but the Twelfth Amendment (1804), which established the current procedures for the election of the president and vice president, requires that one of the two candidates "shall not be an inhabitant of the same state...." In 2000 the vice presidential candidate Dick Cheney (b. 1941) had to change his residency to Wyoming from Texas—where he lived at the time—before he could qualify to run with George W. Bush (b. 1946), who was also from Texas. The amendment additionally provides that "no person constitutionally ineligible to the office of President shall be eligible to that of Vice-President of the United States."

In creating the ELECTORAL COLLEGE, Article II, section I, provides: "Each State shall appoint, in such Manner as the Legislature thereof may direct, a Number of Electors, equal to the whole Number of Senators and Representatives to which the State may be entitled in the Congress: but no Senator or Representative, or Person holding an Office of Trust or Profit under the United States, shall be appointed an Elector."

Qualifications for Judges

Of the three branches of government created by the Constitution, the JUDICIAL BRANCH is the least described. No qualifications are expressly mentioned for judges, so they do not have to be lawyers or have any legal training whatsoever. This lack of specificity about judicial qualifications is based on the fact that federal justices and judges are appointed by the president and approved with the ADVICE AND CONSENT of the Senate, thus ensuring, in the minds of the delegates to the 1787 convention, that their qualifications would be addressed at a stage in the appointment process by both of the other branches (see APPOINTMENT AND REMOVAL POWER).

That the Constitution does not provide extensive qualifications for the important public offices in the federal government reflects its deference to the judgment of the electorate and the officials charged with making appointments to office.

More on this topic:

Courts, p. 128

Executive Branch, p. 206

Legislative Branch, p. 346

Quorum *See* CONGRESS.

Racial Discrimination

The DECLARATION OF INDEPENDENCE (1776) boldly states that "all Men are created equal," and the Universal Declaration of Human Rights, adopted by the United Nations in 1948, echoes this sentiment, proclaiming: "All human beings are born free and equal in dignity and rights." Many national constitutions likewise prohibit discrimination on the basis of race, among other bases. For example, the Japanese constitution (1947) declares: "All of the people are equal under the law and there shall be no discrimination in political, economic, or social relations because of race, creed, sex, social status, or family origin."

Felix M. Keesing, a Stanford University professor who is coauthor of *New Perspectives in Cultural Anthropology* (1971), explains that the term *race* "in popular usage is emotionally charged and imprecise [but] it has a straightforward and important meaning in evolutionary biology. A race is a geographically separated, hence genetically somewhat distinctive, population within a species." The term has been used in English since at least the sixteenth century and may have been derived from *raza* (Spanish for clan or breed).

Attempts to Correct Slavery

In the United States racial discrimination has its roots in the institution of SLAVERY. After the Civil War (1861–65), three amendments were made to the Constitution to give the federal government the power to protect the RIGHTS of the newly freed black slaves, especially in the former states of the Confederacy. The Thirteenth Amendment (1865) abolished slavery, except in the case of PUNISHMENT for crime. The Fourteenth Amendment (1868), among other things, conferred citizenship rights on former slaves and mandated that "[n]o State shall make or enforce any law which shall abridge the privileges or immunities of citizens of the United States; nor shall any State deprive any person of life, liberty, or property, without due process of law; nor deny to any person within its jurisdiction the equal protection of the laws." The Fifteenth Amendment (1870) provides that "[t]he right of citizens of the United States to vote shall not be denied or abridged by the United States or by any State on account of race, color, or previous condition of servitude."

On the surface, these amendments would seem to create an atmosphere in the letter and spirit of the Constitution that would preclude racial discrimination. In fact, however, with the support of the Supreme Court, DISCRIMINATION against blacks continued. In *United States v. Cruikshank* (1876), the Court found that the indictments of three white men who participated in the murder of more than one hundred black men in a dispute over a gubernatorial election in Louisiana—the Colfax Massacre—were insufficient to uphold their convictions. The decision came despite the constitutional amendments and the Enforcement Act (1870), which prohibited conspiracies to deny the constitutional rights of any citizen.

The landmark case in the sad history of confirming the constitutionality of racial discrimination is *Plessy v. Ferguson* (1896). Here the Supreme Court upheld the blatantly discriminatory "separate but equal" doctrine that legalized SEGREGATION of whites and blacks in public schools, accommodations, and transportation, as well as in private business establishments. Not until 1954, in BROWN V. BOARD OF EDUCATION OF TOPEKA, was the doctrine found unconstitutional by a different Supreme Court.

Civil Rights Acts

Congress passed CIVIL RIGHTS acts in 1866, 1871, and 1875. The 1866 act, which is still in force, sought to counter the so-called black codes used in some states to deny legal rights to blacks. The purpose of the 1871 act, known as the Ku Klux Klan Act, was to help enforce the Fourteenth Amendment. And in the 1875 act Congress prohibited private discrimination with respect to public accommodations such as theaters, restaurants, and railroads. As the *Plessy* case illustrates, however, these laws were far from successful.

In the wake of the *Brown* decision and others, Congress enacted the Civil Rights Act of 1964, Voting Rights Act of 1965, and Civil Rights Act of 1968. The 1964 act prohibited discrimination in public accommodations (Title II), federally funded programs (Title VI), and employment (Title VII) (see EMPLOYMENT DISCRIMINATION). The 1965 act added to the federal government's power to guarantee blacks the right to vote. (In spite of the Fifteenth Amendment, a number of procedures had been developed especially in the South to disenfranchise blacks, including imposition of poll taxes and discriminatory literacy tests.

As this 1877 cartoon indicates, Chinese workers faced severe discrimination in the United States.
Source: The Granger Collection, New York

Enacted after the death of the civil rights leader MARTIN LUTHER KING JR., the 1968 law, also called the Fair Housing Act, prohibited racial discrimination in transactions involving buying and selling housing.

Enforcement

In 1957 President Dwight D. Eisenhower (1890–1969) had to send troops to Little Rock, Arkansas, to desegregate the public schools, as required by the *Brown* decision. The Justice Department also had to help enforce desegregation in some of the recalcitrant southern states. And in a number of cases in the wake of *Brown*, the Supreme Court had to fashion remedies for ongoing racial discrimination practices and desegregation efforts.

AFFIRMATIVE ACTION plans were adopted by governments and private institutions and businesses to make up for many years of past discrimination against African Americans and other vulnerable groups such as Hispanic Americans and WOMEN. In upholding a reverse discrimination claim in *REGENTS OF THE UNIVERSITY OF CALIFORNIA V. BAKKE* (1978), the Supreme Court concluded that states may not deny anyone the EQUAL PROTECTION of the laws guaranteed by the Fourteenth Amendment. However, the Court also upheld affirmative action programs for these groups, including racial minorities, if they are crafted in such a way as to avoid setting racial quotas. In *Wygant v. Jackson Board of Education* (1986), the Court found unconstitutional a plan to give minorities "preferential protection against layoffs." A plan that did pass constitutional muster to remedy past discriminatory hiring practices was accepted in *United States v. Paradise* (1987), involved hiring one black person for every white employee hired by the Alabama Department of Public Safety.

The Rehnquist Court all but decided that the government could never take race into consideration to remedy social inequality. Justices Antonin Scalia (b. 1936) and Clarence Thomas (b. 1948), the only black member on the Court, urged their colleagues to move toward a totally "colorblind" stance. Thomas, contrary to some observers' expectations, has said that there is "a 'moral and constitutional equivalence' between laws designed to subjugate a race and those that distribute benefits on the basis of race in order to foster some current notion of equality." In two cases, *Miller-El v. Dretke* and *Johnson v. California* (both 2005), the Court ruled favorably on challenges by defendants that there was racial discrimination in the jury selection process. But in *Domino's Pizza, Inc. v. McDonald* (2006), the Court, now headed by Chief Justice John G. Roberts Jr. (b. 1955), agreed (8–0) that, to bring a claim based on racial discrimination in contractual dealings, the claimant had to be party to the contract and not merely a shareholder in a corporation that allegedly had been injured by the racial animus of the other party to the contract.

In an ideal world, all humans would be treated equally regardless of race, sex, sexual orientation, RELIGION, national origins, age, disability, social status, wealth, or political views. But in the obviously imperfect world we live in, the solution to the problem of long-standing grievances by some American citizens is more complicated than wiping the slate clean and starting all over again. Fortunately the Supreme Court has periodically interpreted the Constitution in ways that redress some of these historic wrongs.

More on this topic:
Due Process, p. 168
Privileges and Immunities, p. 432

Ratification

The CONSTITUTION uses the terms *ratification* and *ratify* in several places, including in Article VII, governing the number of states originally required to ratify the Constitution, and in Article V, relating to procedures for amending the Constitution. In law, *ratification* means the adoption or confirmation of an act or a contract made by another party who lacks complete authority. For example, a person who is incompetent at the time a contract is made can later ratify the document when he or she is competent. Unlike the term *adoption*, *ratification* refers to final approval of a transaction that otherwise is voidable.

The Constitution

The PREAMBLE to the Constitution, adopted at the CONSTITUTIONAL CONVENTION OF 1787, begins with the words "We the People of the United States." JAMES MADISON, the "Father of the Constitution," suggested in essay 39 of *The Federalist* (1787–88) (see FEDERALIST PAPERS) that "it appears, on one hand, that the Constitution is to be founded on the assent and ratification of the people of America, given by deputies elected for the special purpose; but, on the other, that this assent and ratification is to be given by the people, not as individuals composing one entire nation, but as composing the distinct and independent States to which they respectively belong." Further, he wrote, "[i]t is to be the assent and ratification of the several States, derived from the supreme authority in each State—the authority of the people themselves. The act, therefore, establishing the Constitution will not be a *national* but a *federal* act."

The procedure for ratifying the new document after it was adopted on September 17, 1787, was provided in Article VII: "The Ratification of the Conventions of nine States, shall be sufficient for the Establishment of this Constitution between the States so ratifying the Same." Under the ARTICLES OF CONFEDERATION (1781), which had been in effect since 1781, any revision of the Articles required unanimous agreement by the Continental Congress and confirmation by the legislatures of every state. By proposing to draft a wholly new document and having it sent by the Congress to be ratified by "assemblies of Representatives...expressly chosen by the people," Madison hoped to get around the requirement contained in the Articles and to bypass the state legislatures, which had a vested interest in maintaining their state independence. GEORGE MASON, Madison's fellow delegate from Virginia, reasoned that because nine out of thirteen votes—a two-thirds majority—"had been required in all great cases under the Confederation," that was as good a number as any to require for ratification of the Constitution.

The first state to ratify the Constitution was Delaware; the delegates to its ratification convention, held on December 7, 1787, did so unanimously. The other states that gave their assent, in order of the date of ratification, were Pennsylvania on December 12, New Jersey on December 18, Georgia on January 2, 1788, Connecticut on January 9, Massachusetts on February 6, Maryland on April 28, South Carolina on May 23, and New Hampshire on June 21. With ratification certified by the first nine states, the Constitution was adopted according to its terms for those states.

Virginia subsequently ratified the Constitution on June 25, 1788, New York on July 26, North Carolina on November 21, 1789, and Rhode Island on May 29, 1790. Vermont was the first state to be admitted under the terms of Article IV, section 3, as all other new states have been (see ADMISSION OF NEW STATES). In *Owings v. Speed* (1820), the Supreme Court held that even though the Constitution was ratified in 1788 by the requisite nine states, it did not go into effect until the first Wednesday in March 1789, the date appointed by Congress "for commencing proceedings under the Constitution."

Amendments

AMENDMENTS to the Constitution are also ratified by the states, according to procedures prescribed in Article V. Proposed amendments become a part of the Constitution "when ratified by the Legislatures of three fourths of the several States, or by Conventions in three fourths thereof, as the one or the other Mode of Ratification may be proposed by the Congress." The Eleventh Amendment (1795) was declared to have been ratified in a message by President JOHN ADAMS to Congress on January 8, 1798, but in fact the necessary number of state legislatures had ratified it on February 7, 1795, which has retroactively been made the official date on which it became part of the Constitution.

The ratification of the Fourteenth Amendment (1868), which in part sought to correct the discriminatory effects of SLAVERY, did not go smoothly. Congress adopted the proposed amendment on June 13, 1866. The approval of twenty-eight of the thirty-seven states was required for ratification, which took place when the last two states, North and South Carolina, gave their assent on July 4 and 9, 1868, after previous legislatures in those states had rejected it. Congress passed a resolution declaring the amendment a part of the Constitution on July 21, 1868, and the secretary of state declared the amendment officially ratified on July 28. Other states, some of which had previously rejected the amendment, came on board later. Delaware finally ratified the amendment in 1901, Maryland and California in 1959, and Kentucky in 1976; New Jersey, whose original approval was rescinded twice, including once over the governor's veto, finally expressed its support for the amendment in 1980.

The Twenty-seventh Amendment, which was proposed by Congress in 1789 along with eleven others—ten of which were ratified and became the BILL OF RIGHTS in 1791—was finally ratified in 1992. It prevents CONGRESS from increasing its members' salaries without an intervening election (see COMPENSATION OF OFFICIALS).

More on this topic:
Amendments, p. 30
Constitution, U.S., p. 115
Constitutional Convention of 1787, p. 119
Framers of the Constitution, p. 230
Treaties, p. 551

Treaties

The ratification of TREATIES is a formal procedure sometimes spelled out in the treaty itself. To be valid, ratification must generally comply with the constitutional requirements of the countries that are party to the agreement. The PRESIDENT of the United States or another official delegated this authority can negotiate and sign a treaty, but if it involves a major commitment or is of special importance or controversial, it is presented to the SENATE as required under Article II, section 2, of the Constitution. In such cases ratification of the treaty takes place as soon as the Senate has given its ADVICE AND CONSENT.

Reapportionment

In a representative democracy like the United States, one fundamental constitutional question is how public officials are to be selected for office. When population changes in electoral districts call into question the basis for this selection, legislative representation should be similarly redistributed by a process called reapportionment. Redistricting is the redrawing of boundaries of these electoral or administrative districts. Reapportionment takes place on the national and state levels, while redistricting is done within STATES.

National Reapportionment

To reflect the federal nature of the government (see FEDERALISM), the delegates to the CONSTITUTIONAL CONVENTION OF 1787 created the HOUSE OF REPRESENTATIVES as the lower house of CONGRESS to represent the people and the SENATE as the upper house to represent the states. Article I, section 2, of the Constitution, as amended by section 2 of the Fourteenth Amendment (1868), addresses the reapportionment of the House. The seats in the Senate are fixed for each state at two senators who run for at-large seats and are not subject to reapportionment.

In the Constitution as ratified in 1789, in Article I, section 2, slaves were counted for purposes of representation in the House as "three fifths of all other persons." After the Civil War (1861–65),

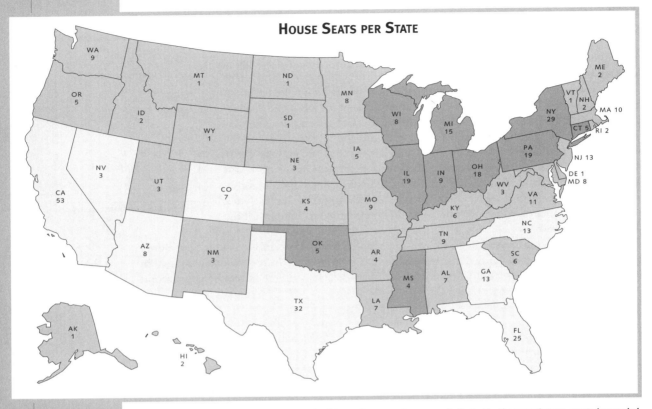

HOUSE SEATS PER STATE

Changes in population distribution in the United States from 1990 to 2000, as indicated by the 2000 Census, created a new balance of regional power at the start of the 108th Congress in 2003. Reapportionment of seats in the House of Representatives favored states in the South and Southwest at the expense of the Northeast. Numerical values in the map represent reapportioned seat totals for each state. Light gray indicates states that gained seats; dark gray indicates states that lost seats; medium gray indicates no change.

Source: Inter-University Consortium for Political and Social Research (http://www.icpsr.umich.edu/CENSUS2000/apportion.html).

SLAVERY was abolished by the Thirteenth Amendment (1865). To reflect the fact that former slaves were from then on to be counted as one person, section 2 of the Fourteenth Amendment (1868) provided in part: "Representatives shall be apportioned among the several States according to their respective numbers, counting the whole number of persons in each State, excluding Indians not taxed."

The portion of Article I, section 2, that remains unaffected by the Fourteenth Amendment states: "The actual Enumeration shall be made within three Years after the first Meeting of the Congress of the United States, and within every subsequent Term of ten Years, in such Manner as they shall by Law direct." Apportionment of representatives in the House of Representatives is based on each state's population, as determined by the latest CENSUS taken every ten years. Thus every ten years states that lose a sufficient number of residents will lose one or more representatives in the House and states that gain in population will receive an additional seat or seats.

But the number of seats in the House of Representatives—435—remains the same, as set by law in 1912. Every state, no matter how small its population—including Vermont, Delaware, North and South Dakota, Wyoming, Montana, and Alaska—is guaranteed at least one seat in the House.

The remaining 385 seats are the ones that get reapportioned every ten years, based on a formula set by law.

Four different formulas have been used since 1790 for reapportioning the seats in the House of Representatives. After the 1930 census and a report made by the National Academy of Sciences, Congress chose the "method of equal proportions." This formula is complicated but results in the smallest relative difference between any pairs of states when comparing any district's population and the number of people per representative—which obviously has increased as the nation's population has increased. As a result of the 2000 census, the average number of constituents for each member of the House is 646,952.

Whereas members of the House of Representatives in states with one representative are elected at large, like U.S. senators, by the state's whole population, states that are entitled to more than one representative divide themselves into congressional districts. Residents of each district vote for the member of the House from that district. Redistricting becomes necessary when a state records a sufficient population change to lose or gain representatives after each census.

State Redistricting and Reapportionment

In addition to congressional election districts, states also create election districts for members of the state legislature, generally a responsibility of the legislatures themselves. Because the size and shape of a district can clearly affect the outcome of state legislative elections, there is a tendency for the legislature's majority party (see POLITICAL PARTIES) to create districts that favor candidates from their party. For example, as the population increases in a state's urban areas and remains the same or decreases in rural areas, the party that represents the rural areas will want to keep the apportionment unchanged. Fewer rural voters—with interests that differ from those of the urban dwellers—would thus have a greater number of representatives in the legislature per voter than those constituents living in the city. One result of this inequality may be an unequal allocation of government spending to the two constituencies.

Inequality in voter representation began increasing rapidly in a number of states after the turn of the twentieth century, and efforts to force the state legislatures to reapportion their districts to more fairly approximate the population changes were generally unsuccessful. Even where state constitutional requirements mandated reapportionment on a regular basis, legislatures did not do it, and state courts held that they could not force their legislature to act.

The Supreme Court finally acted in BAKER V. CARR (1962) to remedy the problem. After first determining that the question of state reapportionment in Tennessee was a legal and not a political question—which would have meant that the courts were constitutionally barred from deciding it—the Court ruled that states' failure to reapportion their voting districts in the face of population shifts was a violation of the EQUAL PROTECTION clause of the Constitution. This decision was followed by *Gray v. Sanders* (1963), which declared that the goal of reapportioning and redistricting in the states was to approximate as closely as possible "one person, one vote," so that every citizen was equally represented in the state legislatures.

In a series of six cases in 1964 regarding challenges to apportionment in Alabama, New York, Maryland, Virginia, Delaware, and Colorado, the Supreme Court similarly found the apportionment by the state legislatures to be unconstitutional. Thus began a long process of supervision by the federal courts of the reapportionment schemes in these states to remedy inequalities in voter representation. By the 1970s most states had complied well enough to pass constitutional muster. More recently, when a Mississippi state court's plan for reapportionment, required after the state lost a seat in Congress due to the 2000 census, was not approved by the U.S. Department of Justice in time for the next election, as mandated by the Voting Rights Act (1965), the Supreme Court

Before the Massachusetts election of 1812, Gov. Elbridge Gerry signed a bill redrawing the state senatorial districts so that his party, the Democratic-Republicans, would be likely to win more seats than their actual numbers warranted. One of the new districts looked like a salamander and was quickly dubbed a "gerrymander," a term that continues to be used to describe a redistricting plan designed to benefit one party.
Source: Library of Congress

The word *gerrymander* combines the name of Elbridge Gerry, an early governor of Massachusetts, with the word "salamander."

In 1812 the Massachusetts legislature passed a redistricting bill intended to favor the party of Jeffersonian Democrats in upcoming elections. Even though the bill was mocked in a cartoon that likened the new districts to a salamander-like creature, Gerry signed it into law.

Gerry was one of the most distinguished political leaders of his time, becoming vice president under James Madison. But he is best known for the tortuous approach to redistricting that is named after him. After signing the controversial districting bill, he lost his bid to win reelection as governor.

unanimously agreed in *Branch v. Smith* (2003) that a federal district court's "alternative" ruling that the plan was unconstitutional had to be dismissed as premature. As Justice Anthony M. Kennedy (b. 1936) wrote in his concurring opinion, "the district courts should not entertain constitutional challenges to non-precleared voting changes and in this way anticipate a ruling not yet made by the Executive [branch]."

Gerrymandering

The use of creative configurations for election districts in order to improve the electability of a candidate or a party has a long history. The most famous of these districts was called the gerrymander, after Elbridge Gerry (see FRAMERS OF THE CONSTITUTION), the Massachusetts governor who in 1812 created a district so oddly shaped that it resembled a salamander. More recently, the fourth congressional district in Chicago was redrawn to connect two largely Hispanic American sections; as a result, it nearly surrounds a district with an African American majority. The obvious purpose was to favor candidates who would represent the interests of the different minority populations.

In *Davis v. Bandemer* (1986), the Supreme Court agreed to decide cases where political partisanship in state legislatures adversely affects apportionment. The 6–3 decision found that challenges to political gerrymandering can be brought to the courts where there is "continued frustration of the will of the majority of the voters or a denial to a minority of voters of a fair chance to influence the political process." The Court concluded, however, that the 1981 redistricting in Indiana at issue had not caused the continued minority status of the minority party. Finally, in *Vieth v. Jubelirer* (2004), the Court, by one less than a majority, agreed to consider all claims of political gerrymandering to be nonjusticiable political questions. Justice Antonin Scalia (b. 1936), joined by Chief Justice William H. Rehnquist (1924–2005) and Justices SANDRA DAY O'CONNOR and Clarence Thomas (b. 1948), said that there were no judicially discernible and manageable standards for judging such claims. Justice Anthony M. Kennedy (1936), in his concurring opinion rejecting the claim in this case, said he would not, however, "foreclose all possibility of judicial relief if some limited and precise rationale were found to correct an established violation of the Constitution in some redistricting cases."

Discrimination

With respect to racial or other types of DISCRIMINATION against MINORITIES, the Supreme Court in *Gomillion v. Lightfoot* (1960) concluded that drawing an election district with twenty-eight sides to effectively exclude black residents from the town of Tuskegee, Alabama, violated the EQUAL PROTECTION clause of the Fourteenth Amendment. The Court tends to focus on any inequality between white and black voters rather than the effect of the redistricting on other voter minorities. For example, in *United Jewish Organizations v. Carey* (1977), the Court upheld a redistricting scheme to ensure black voter representation in the state legislature, even though in the process it meant splitting up white communities, including Hasidic Jewish residents.

In a series of cases from North Carolina, the Supreme Court decided that where political rather than racial concerns were the prime motivation behind a redistricting effort, it was not unconstitutional.

In *Shaw v. Reno* (1993), the Court first addressed a charge that a North Carolina congressional district had been drawn by the state legislature "for race-based reasons," which, if true, would indicate that the legislature had violated the Fourteenth

Amendment's equal protection clause. In *Shaw v. Hunt* (1996), the Court reversed a three-judge district court's decision that the redistricting in question did not violate the Constitution. And then in *Hunt v. Cromartie I* (1999), the Court addressed the question of whether the same newly redrawn district was based on race or was in fact intended to create a safe voting district for the Democratic Party, which it indicated would not be unconstitutional. In *Hunt v. Cromartie II* (2001), the Court found that the evidence of the relationship between the voting behavior of the district's mainly black residents and the fact that they overwhelmingly voted for Democratic candidates was insufficient to conclude that the legislature had violated the equal protection clause in redrawing the boundaries of the congressional district.

More on this topic:
Elections, p. 181
Representative Government, p. 464

Trying to balance the constitutional requirements of equal voter representation and minority political rights without discriminating against any political party will undoubtedly keep the courts busy for years to come. To add to the existing controversies, in *Rodriguez v. Popular Democratic Party* (1982) the Supreme Court even suggested that "the right to vote, *per se*, is not a constitutionally protected right." Although there may be no constitutional requirement that a legislator be chosen by election, the Court has found that when there is an election the right to vote must be open equally to all eligible voters.

Recall *See* DIRECT DEMOCRACY.

Redistricting *See* REAPPORTIONMENT.

Referendums *See* DIRECT DEMOCRACY.

Regents of the University of California v. Bakke

Since the Supreme Court's ground-breaking decision in BROWN V. BOARD OF EDUCATION OF TOPEKA (1954), which declared unconstitutional the "separate but equal" doctrine on which SEGREGATION was based, a number of steps have been taken to promote AFFIRMATIVE ACTION in both public and private educational facilities. Affirmative action policies attempt to make amends for the long history of DISCRIMINATION against blacks, women, and other MINORITIES. In the reverse discrimination case of *Regents of the University of California v. Bakke* (1978), the Supreme Court held that the school could take race into consideration in its admissions process as long as it did not use fixed quotas for minority applicants.

In 1973 and 1974 there were two admissions procedures for students applying for the one hundred openings at the Medical School of the University of California at Davis. Regular students were admitted after an admissions committee interviewed the applicants and made recommendations based on criteria such as undergraduate grade-point averages and scores on the Medical College Admissions Test. Another special committee, most of whom were members of minority groups, focused on applicants who wanted to be considered economically or educationally disadvantaged and members of minority groups such as "blacks, Chicanos, Asians, and American Indians." Sixteen places were set aside for these applicants, who were not ranked on the basis of the same standards as the regular applicants. Allan Bakke, a white male who applied twice, was processed through the regular admissions procedure but was denied admission even though special minority applicants with significantly lower scores were accepted. He then challenged the school's admissions policy, alleging that it operated to exclude him from the school on the basis of his race in violation of the EQUAL PROTECTION clause of the Fourteenth Amendment (1868).

In holding that the university could not use fixed quotas, the Supreme Court affirmed the lower court's judgment ordering Bakke's admission to the school in part because the university did not prove that Bakke would not have been admitted if the affirmative action program had not been in place (his scores were lower than the cutoff for the other regular candidates). The decision, however, allowed the university to take race into account in future admissions decisions. Although the Court found that Bakke was the victim of reverse discrimination (discrimination against a person who was not a member of a historically disadvantaged group), the justices' reasoning varied. The decision was 5–4, but four of them focused on the language of Title VI of the Civil Rights Act of 1964 (see CIVIL RIGHTS), which prohibits the exclusion of any individual on racial grounds from publicly funded programs. Another four justices concluded that as long as the admissions policy served an important state purpose and did not unduly burden "those least well represented in the political process," it was acceptable.

> **"The file of a particular black applicant may be examined for his potential contribution to diversity without the factor of race being decisive...."**
>
> —*Justice Lewis P. Powell Jr.,* in *Regents of the University of California v. Bakke*

Justice Lewis P. Powell Jr. (1907–98), often identified as politically moderate, was the fifth and deciding vote. The problem he saw with the university's special admissions procedure was that it "totally foreclosed" Bakke from competing with the special admissions applicants for the 100 openings. He agreed, however, that race could be fairly taken into account in trying to achieve a "diverse student body." According to Powell, "The file of a particular black applicant may be examined for his potential contribution to diversity without the factor of race being decisive.... Such qualities could include exceptional personal talents, unique work or service experience...demonstrated compassion, a history of overcoming disadvantage, [or] ability to communicate with the poor...."

More on this topic:
Affirmative Action, p. 21
Brown v. Board of Education of Topeka, p. 65
Civil Rights, p. 96
Discrimination, p. 159
Minorities, p. 369
Racial Discrimination, p. 449
Sex Discrimination, p. 497

More problems with affirmative action programs arose after the *Bakke* case, but such efforts to right past wrongs have generally been upheld by the Supreme Court. Strong criticism of affirmative action nonetheless continues in some sectors, often under the guise of calling for a truly colorblind Constitution. In *Adarand Constructors, Inc. v. Peña* (1995), the Court said that affirmative action programs must pass a STRICT SCRUTINY test to be constitutional; in other words, no presumptions in favor of such programs will be allowed, and proof will be needed to show that they do not infringe the constitutional rights of others. In 1997 the Court also let stand a lower court ruling upholding a California referendum that banned racial or gender affirmative action policies in certain state activities such as employment and public contracting.

The *Bakke* case and subsequent cases before the Supreme Court involving the same issue, including *Gratz v. Bollinger* (2003) and *Parents Involved in Community Schools v. Seattle School District No. 1* (2007), indicate just how difficult it is to level the playing field for all citizens when it has been unfairly tilted in favor of some and against others for a long time.

Religion

Religious liberty and freedom of conscience have been fundamental human aspirations throughout history, often resulting in conflict between religious beliefs and government—church and state. Seeking religious freedom, English settlers called Puritans sailed across the Atlantic Ocean and landed on Plymouth Rock in 1620, soon establishing the Massachusetts Bay Colony. By the time the CONSTITUTIONAL CONVENTION OF 1787 was held in Philadelphia, numerous Christian religious sects could be found in the first thirteen states, including Catholics, Calvinists, and Quakers.

"In a free government the security for civil rights must be the same as that for religious rights," wrote JAMES MADISON, the "Father of the Constitution," in essay 52 of *The Federalist* (1787–88) (see FEDERALIST PAPERS). "It consists in the one case in the multiplicity of interests, and in the other in the multiplicity of sects." Convention delegates represented a wide spectrum of Christianity, although several of the FRAMERS OF THE CONSTITUTION were Deists, a philosophy that was about as close to atheism as a person dared to be in the eighteenth century. A Deist who did not attend the convention, THOMAS JEFFERSON—author of the DECLARATION OF INDEPENDENCE (1776) and the third president of the United States—believed that it was important to the government's integrity for "a wall of separation" to be erected between church and state. As he wrote in a letter in 1802, after he had become president, "Believing with you that religion is a matter which lies solely between man and his God; that he owes account to none other for his faith or his worship; that the legislative powers of the government reach actions only, and not opinions, I contemplate with sovereign reverence that act of the whole American people which declared that their legislature should 'make no law respecting an establishment of religion, or prohibiting the free exercise thereof,' thus building a wall of separation between church and State."

Thomas Nast's 1871 drawing for* Harper's Weekly *addresses the First Amendment guarantee of religious freedom, depicting sundry religious sects demanding entry to the hall of "State."
Source: Library of Congress

Madison agreed with Jefferson, but on the grounds that separation was necessary to maintain the integrity of religions. Delegates from Virginia and others were familiar with the Virginia Statute for Religious Freedom (1786), drafted by Jefferson and adopted by Virginia's legislature with Madison's help. It represented the first time a Western government had guaranteed freedom of religion and separation of church and state. Both men considered it among their proudest achievements, one that Jefferson asked to have noted on his tombstone.

Following ratification of the first ten AMENDMENTS to the CONSTITUTION in 1791, freedom of religion took its place in the BILL OF RIGHTS alongside freedom of SPEECH, THE PRESS, and assembly (see ASSEMBLY AND ASSOCIATION) as the first four freedoms guaranteed—the first one, in fact. "Congress shall make no law respecting an establishment of religion, or prohibiting the free exercise thereof...," begins the First Amendment, recalling the ideals expressed in the Virginia Statute for Religious Freedom. This provision has two distinct parts: the establishment clause and the free exercise clause. The establishment clause was intended to prevent the federal government from designating an official religion or favoring one religion over another, whereas in Great Britain at the time the British monarch was (and still is) the titular head of the Church of England in addition to being head of the secular government. The freedom of exercise clause was included in the First Amendment to prohibit the federal government from passing laws that interfered with one's right to practice a religion.

Separation of Church and State

Two years before the 1787 Constitutional Convention, Madison and Jefferson spearheaded an effort in Virginia to oppose the use of public taxes to support the state's established church, arguing that any true religion does not need the support of the law and that the people—whether believers or nonbelievers—should not be taxed to support any religious institution. Over the nation's history, however, the Supreme Court has been inconsistent in dealing with the question of the separation of church and state required by the establishment clause.

In *Reynolds v. United States* (1879), the nation's highest court acknowledged that the establishment clause creates a "wall of separation" between church and state. But in *Zorach v. Clauson* (1952), the Supreme Court declared that this constitutional language did not express "a philosophy of hostility to religion." Then in *Lynch v. Donnelly* (1984), the Court suggested that the wall of separation was "not a wholly accurate description of the practical aspects of the relationship that in fact exists between church and state," claiming that the Constitution "affirmatively mandates accommodation, not merely tolerance, of all religions and forbids hostility towards any."

In *Everson v. Board of Education of Ewing Township* (1947), a case that extended to the STATES (see INCORPORATION DOCTRINE) the First Amendment prohibition against the establishment of religion, Justice Hugo L. Black (1886–1971) noted in his opinion for the Court: "Two great drives are constantly in motion to abridge, in the name of education, the complete division of religion and civil authority which our forefathers made. One is to introduce religious education and observances into public schools. The other, to obtain public funds for the aid and support of various private religious schools...." As for the latter, the Court permitted government reimbursement for parents who used public transportation to get their children to accredited schools, even religious schools, ruling that the expenditure was primarily secular and only incidentally aided religion. Two decades later, in *Board of Education v. Allen* (1968), the Court extended this First Amendment exception to include loans of secular textbooks to private school students, including those attending parochial schools.

The Supreme Court finally fashioned a test for analyzing the constitutionality of state assistance to parochial schools and students in *Lemon v. Kurtzman* (1971). The Court said that it would consider the type of aid, how much it would help further the aims of religion, whether the aid is administered by the schools or the state, and whether the aid is provided in private or publicly owned facilities. Then, in *Wolman v. Walter* (1977), the Court barred public schools from lending instructional materials such as maps and tape recorders and from using public transportation for field trips for sectarian school students because of "the impossibility of separating the secular education function from the sectarian." In the Court's opinion, state aid in such cases created a danger of furthering religious teaching. In *McCreary County v. American Civil Liberties Union* (2005), finding wall displays of the Ten Commandments in schools to be unconstitutional, the Court rejected an invitation to abandon the requirement of a "secular purpose" for any government support of religious activities, which it set forth in *Lemon*. But, in *Van Orden v. Perry* (2005), the Court ignored the test in allowing the Commandments on a monument on the grounds of the Texas state capitol.

The *Lemon* test has not always been followed. For example, in *Larson v. Valente* (1982), the Supreme Court substituted STRICT SCRUTINY—the highest level of judicial analysis as to a law's constitutionality—in striking down a state law that required disclosure of information from only those religious institutions that solicited more than fifty percent of their funds from nonmembers. The justices reasoned that the law discriminated against nontraditional religions, which was prohibited by the establishment clause.

In *Lee v. Weisman* (1992)—a case involving a middle school's invitation to members of the clergy to say prayers at graduation ceremonies—the Supreme Court ignored the *Lemon* test. Instead it found the practice so obviously an infringement of the establishment clause—because school children were involved—that no deeper analysis or BALANCING TESTS were required. Speaking for the Court, Justice Anthony M. Kennedy (b. 1936) said that the government has a "duty to guard and respect the sphere of inviolable conscience and belief which is the mark of a free people." In *Locke v. Davey* (2004), the Court upheld a ban by Washington state on the use of state tax funds to help pay for a degree in "devotional theology," although the two dissenters, Justices Antonin Scalia (b. 1936) and Clarence Thomas (b. 1948), asked whether the ruling would lead to denying "priests and nuns their prescription-drug benefits on the ground that taxpayers' freedom of

Advocates of allowing public displays of the Ten Commandments kneel in prayer in front of the Supreme Court.
Source: AP Images/J. Scott Applewhite

conscience forbids medicating the clergy at public expense?" And, in the same year, the Court avoided ruling on a challenge to requiring the recitation of "under God" in the pledge of allegiance in public schools on the technicality that the plaintiff lacked sufficient legal standing to bring the suit in *Elk Grove Unified School District v. Newdow.*

Despite the Supreme Court precedents and the unambiguous language of the First Amendment, governments throughout the United States have continually sought ways to finance or aid the establishment of a particular religion or religions in general. Congress has made and continues to make laws appropriating funds for religious chaplains for both houses of Congress and for chaplains in the ARMED FORCES; in 1983 the Supreme Court confirmed the constitutionality of a similar practice by the Nebraska legislature. Soon after taking office as president in 2001, George W. Bush (b. 1946) followed suit, launching a new effort to channel federal financial support to religious charitable institutions in lieu of direct federal funding to provide for citizens' general WELFARE.

Free Exercise of Religion

Governments may also discriminate against a particular religion by banning or otherwise interfering with its practices. In *Reynolds v. United States* (1879)—the case that confirmed the wall of separation between church and state—the Supreme Court upheld the prosecution of Mormons for bigamy in spite of the argument that polygamy was a religious practice protected by the First Amendment. But in later years the Court began to carefully analyze religiously neutral laws that might place an undue burden on the practice of a religion.

By relying on the First Amendment's freedom of the press provisions, the Supreme Court in *Lovell v. City of Griffin* (1938) upheld the right of Jehovah's Witnesses to proselytize their religion through the sale and distribution of printed matter without first obtaining written permission from the city manager. And in *Cantwell v. Connecticut* (1940), which extended the free exercise of religion clause to the states, the Court, citing that clause, affirmed the right of a Jehovah's Witness to proselytize from door to door without having to get the required government approval. The First Amendment freedom of religion language, the Court said, guarantees both the freedom to believe and the freedom to act on that belief.

Jehovah's Witnesses later asserted that a state law requiring public school children to salute the American flag was, according to their faith, a violation of the Bible (see THE FLAG). In *West Virginia Board of Education v. Barnette* (1943), in an opinion by Justice Robert H. Jackson (1892–1954), the Supreme Court agreed, holding that the Constitution prohibited the government from prescribing for citizens what was orthodox in politics, nationalism, or religion. Although the decision rested mainly on the right of free speech, the implications for religious freedom were apparent.

In *Braunfeld v. Brown* (1961), the Supreme Court declared forthrightly: "The freedom to hold religious beliefs and opinions is absolute." This case involved state blue laws (Sunday closing laws), which the Court upheld because they only indirectly burdened the practice of religion for some persons. Such laws were not unconstitutional, said the justices, unless the state could accomplish its secular purpose by other, less burdensome means. Then, in *Sherbert v. Verner* (1963), the Court found that the denial of unemployment benefits to a Seventh Day Adventist whose religion kept her from working on Saturdays was an infringement of the free exercise of religion clause. Using the strict scrutiny test—requiring a compelling state interest for upholding the constitutionality of the state's policy—the Court found that forcing a person to choose between forfeiting her religious principles or benefits to which she was entitled violated the free exercise clause. Justice John Marshall Harlan (1899–1971), in a dissent, saw no real distinction between the *Braunfeld* and *Sherbert* cases.

In *Employment Division, Department of Human Resources of Oregon v. Smith* (1990), however, the Supreme Court upheld the denial of unemployment benefits to a person dismissed from his job for using the drug peyote in a religious ritual in a Native American church. In his opinion for the Court, Justice Antonin Scalia (b. 1936) abandoned the requirement that the state must prove a compelling interest before a law infringing the exercise clause would be held constitutional. Then, in *Church of the Lukumi Babalu Aye, Inc. v. City of Haileah* (1993), the Court unanimously found that city ordinances banning the sacrificial slaughtering of animals were directed primarily at restricting such religious practices and were therefore unconstitutional under the free-exercise clause.

In response to the Supreme Court's ruling in the *Smith* case, Congress passed the Religious Freedom Restoration Act (1993) as an attempt "to restore the compelling interest test" used by the Court in *Sherbert*. The act banned any government action that would "substantially burden" the exercise of religion without a compelling government interest. But in *City of Boerne v. Flores* (1997), the Court held the act to be unconstitutional as an attempt to determine constitutional interpretation—the prerogative of the federal COURTS.

The right of conscientious objectors to be exempted from military combat has been upheld by the Supreme Court, but in *Gillette v. United States* (1971), it required that such an objection be to all wars and not just selectively to a particularly unjust war. Conscientious objectors are exempted only from combat; they must perform alternative noncombat roles in the military. As for prisoners, in *Cutter v. Wilkinson* (2005), the Supreme Court unanimously rejected a challenge to the Religious Land Use and Institutionalized Persons Act of 2000, which, among other things, prohibits state and local governments from "impos[ing] a substantial burden on the exercise of religion by a person residing in or confined in an institution." The suit was brought by state prison officials who contended that the law violated the establishment clause of the Constitution.

School Prayer

For many years, religious activists have attempted to interject prayer and religious teaching into public schools under various guises, not the least of which entails beginning each school day with a "moment of silence." The problem of allowing school prayers raises two questions: (1) whether permitting praying aloud constitutes government promotion of religion, a violation of the First Amendment's establishment clause, and, if allowed, (2) whether the prayers of one religion will infringe the free exercise of other religions or the beliefs of nonreligious persons. In *Engel v. Vitale* (1962), the Supreme Court found unconstitutional a nondenominational prayer written by the New York Board of Regents that a local school board required be read in each classroom every day.

The following year, in *Abington School District v. Schempp* (1963), the Supreme Court invalidated a Pennsylvania requirement that public schools begin each day with a reading of Bible verses, fashioning a standard for reviewing such cases. Validity under the establishment clause would turn, it said, on whether the activity has "a secular legislative purpose and a primary effect that neither advances nor inhibits religion." In *Stone v. Graham* (1980), the Court further found that placing copies of the Ten Commandments in school classrooms had no secular purpose, and in *Santa Fe Independent School District v. Doe* (2000), the Court held that a prayer given by a public high school student council chaplain over the school intercom before a football game was unconstitutional. It is unlikely, however, that this is the Court's last word on this prickly issue.

Religion vs. Free Speech

Toward the end of the twentieth century, the Supreme Court began dealing with clashes between the First Amendment's clauses governing free speech and the establishment of religion. In *Capitol Square Review and Advisory Board v. Pinette* (1995), the Court held that a ten-foot-high cross

More on this topic:

Assembly and
Association, p. 50

Bill of Rights, p. 62

Education, p. 177

Employment
Discrimination, p. 192

The Press, p. 425

Speech, p. 512

erected by the Ku Klux Klan on a public square next to the state capitol in Columbus, Ohio, was constitutionally protected. In another 1995 case, *Rosenberger v. University of Virginia,* the Court again found that the free speech clause trumped the First Amendment prohibition against the establishment of religion, striking down as unconstitutional a state university's refusal to fund student publications that had a religious viewpoint. Continuing this line of reasoning, in *Good News Club v. Milford Central School* (2001), the Court allowed the use of public school facilities for an after-school Christian children's club, reasoning that to exclude the club when other nonreligious clubs were permitted to use the facility amounted to discrimination on the basis of religious viewpoint. The reasoning in this case was similar to that used in *Lamb's Chapel v. Center Moriches Union Free School District* (1993), in which the Court held unanimously that if a school permitted its facilities to be used by other groups that were not affiliated with a school, it could not deny the same right to a church organization activity.

Religious Tests

In 1787 no single religious group could lay claim to being a nationally sponsored religion, and the framers of the Constitution wanted to be sure that religious belief would never be a barrier to anyone's serving in the government. They thus added in Article VI that "no religious Test shall ever be required as a Qualification to any Office or public Trust under the United States" (see QUALIFICATIONS FOR OFFICE). A state requirement that a prospective notary public swear to a belief in God was rejected by the Supreme Court in *Torcaso v. Watkins* (1961). In *McDaniel v. Paty* (1978), the Court later invalidated a reverse religious test: a Tennessee law barring members of the clergy from holding state office. The decisions in both cases relied on the First Amendment, however, rather than Article VI's prohibition against religious tests.

The Constitution reflects the notion that less interference by government in religion is better, and that Jefferson's concept of a "wall of separation between church and State" is in everyone's best interests—the religious and nonreligious alike.

Representative Government

JAMES MADISON, the "Father of the Constitution," had a deep-seated fear of the disruptive power of what he called factions—contentious minorities. "If a faction consists of less than a majority, relief is supplied by the republican principle, which enables the majority to defeat its sinister views by regular vote," he warned in essay 10 of *The Federalist* (1787–88) (see FEDERALIST PAPERS). "[I]t may be concluded," he added "that a pure democracy, by which I mean a society consisting of a small number of citizens, who assemble and administer the government in person, can admit of no cure for the mischiefs of faction."

Madison's fear of factions may have been unwarranted, but there is no doubt that a pure DEMOCRACY of the type invented and practiced by the ancient Greeks in Athens and elsewhere would not have been suited for the sprawling territory of America at the time of the CONSTITUTIONAL CONVENTION OF 1787. His solution? "A republic, by which I mean a government in which the scheme of representation takes place, opens a different prospect and promises the cure for which we are seeking." The convention delegates (see FRAMERS OF THE CONSTITUTION) did not seriously consider any other type of government, although the proposal by ALEXANDER HAMILTON that a chief executive serve during good behavior—essentially for life, as federal judges do—came close to a monarchy or a dictatorship.

Early Representative Governments

Around the same time that the Athenians were becoming a DIRECT DEMOCRACY in 510 B.C.E., the Romans were driving out their last king and declaring themselves to be a republic—a state without a single head or ruler. The primary new ruling body was called the Senate, representing the upper-class citizens (the patricians). Later, the lower-class Romans (the plebeians) would be allowed to share political power with the patricians through representative political institutions of their own. One indication of the representative character of postmonarchial Rome was the banners carried into battle by the Roman soldiers that bore the motto "SPQR" (the Senate and People of Rome).

Representative government reappeared in Iceland in 930 with the establishment of the Althing, the grandmother of all parliaments, which consisted of representatives with legislative and judicial functions but no chief executive. The mother of all parliaments, the English Parliament, developed as constitutional limitations were placed on English monarchs beginning in 1215 with Magna Carta, the great charter of English liberties forced on King John at Runnymede by his belligerent barons. The process culminated in the Glorious Revolution of 1688, in which Parliament solidified its power over the monarchy. But even in the mother of parliaments, only the lower house, the House of Commons, included democratically elected representatives. The membership of the upper house, the House of Lords, was limited to high-level members of the church and hereditary members of the aristocracy.

In 1787, when the framers of the Constitution began to determine which type of representative government they would create for the new nation, they had as models the British Parliament, the various colonial assemblies, and the subsequent legislatures of the thirteen independent states, as well as historic and contemporary predecessors from other nations.

Government by Representatives

In theory, democratic representative government at the national level in the United States provides a way for each individual citizen, who shares political power equally with all other citizens, to transfer that power to someone who will represent his or her interests in the operation of the GOVERNMENT. Through a system of regular ELECTIONS and political party organizations (see POLITICAL PARTIES), citizens authorize a few among themselves to act on their behalf. Such representatives are then accountable at the next election for their stewardship of the power entrusted to them by a majority of the electorate.

> *In theory, democratic representative government at the national level in the United States provides a way for each individual citizen to transfer that power to someone who will represent his or her interests in the operation of the government.*

The Constitution reflects the representative government principle most completely in the LEGISLATIVE BRANCH. Members are elected to the HOUSE OF REPRESENTATIVES every two years and must be accountable to the citizenry to be reelected. Whether representative government is really effective is a debatable issue, because in polls CITIZENS often register general dissatisfaction with CONGRESS but, inconsistently, also indicate satisfaction with their particular representative. This contradiction is borne out by the generally high reelection rate of incumbents.

The Constitution make senators generally less accountable to their constituents, given that they have to face reelection only every six years (see SENATE). But this lack of accountability is purposefully built into the system because of the Senate's role in checking both the lower house and the PRESIDENT (see SEPARATION OF POWERS). Frequent reelection might influence senators to act more in accordance with the wishes of the voters than would be good for the nation as a whole.

The president's indirect election by the delegates chosen for the ELECTORAL COLLEGE every four years makes the office, at least theoretically, less representative and less democratic than would be the case if the chief executive were directly elected by the citizens. George W. Bush (b. 1946) won election in 2000 in the electoral college, but he did not win a majority or even a plurality of the votes of all citizens who voted for president that year (see *BUSH V. GORE*).

The JUDICIAL BRANCH, including the SUPREME COURT, is the least representative of the three branches, as all federal judges are appointed for life, rather than elected, and thus are not accountable as representatives of the citizens. Just as the Senate was created with less frequent accountability than the House of Representatives—in order to act as a check on the House in legislative matters and on the president regarding TREATIES and appointment of key government officials (see APPOINTMENT AND REMOVAL POWER)—the Supreme Court's insulation from any form of direct accountability to the electorate ensures that it can act impartially on cases that come before it and in generally interpreting the Constitution.

Each state has a representative government. Vermont's House of Representatives is shown in session above.
Source: AP Images/Alden Pellett

Representative Government in the States

In Article IV, section 4, the Constitution guarantees to every state a REPUBLICAN FORM OF GOVERN-MENT. It is nowhere spelled out what constitutes a republican form of government, but it does not include a monarchy or a dictatorship. But neither the Constitution nor the Supreme Court requires that a state's chief executive be elected by the people. In 1966 the Supreme Court in *Fortson v. Morris* upheld the election of the governor of Georgia by the state legislature when the gubernatorial election failed to produce a winner. The U.S. president in fact is elected by an electoral college rather than by the people, and the Constitution also provides for the House of Representatives to select the president when no candidate receives a majority of votes in the electoral college.

One obstacle to be overcome in reaching truly representative government is ensuring that each person's vote counts equally in an election. To help solve this problem, the Constitution requires in Article I, section 2, and the Fourteenth Amendment (1868) that "Representatives shall be apportioned among the several States" every ten years after a national CENSUS. The Fifteenth Amendment (1870) also prohibits abridging the right to vote "on account of race, color, or previous condition of servitude." But to override attempts made by some STATES over the years to deny citizens living in electoral districts with an increasing population the right to equal representation with those living in districts with smaller populations, the Supreme Court in BAKER V. CARR (1962) began the process of forcing state legislatures to reapportion their voting districts to reflect population changes. The aim is to have roughly the same number of people represented by each representative (see REAPPORTIONMENT). The Court continued the process in *Reynolds v. Sims* (1964) by enunciating the goal of "one person, one vote."

> **More on this topic:**
>
> *Majority Rule, p. 357*

After more than two hundred years, even with many states experimenting with procedures such as the initiative, referendum, and recall to supplement representative state government, direct democracy has made no formal inroads on the framework of the representative government set out in 1787.

Representatives   *See* HOUSE OF REPRESENTATIVES.

Reprieves   *See* PARDONS.

Republican Form of Government

A republic is a political system without a monarch that is governed by the people, or at least some of them. In *The Republic*, the ancient Greek philosopher Plato (ca. 427–347 B.C.E.) suggested that an ideal city-state or republic be ruled by wise elders or "philosopher kings." For Aristotle (384–322 B.C.E.), Plato's student, republicanism depended on CITIZENS who act as free agents but saved a role for a meritorious aristocracy that serves the many and is constrained by them.

THOMAS JEFFERSON defined a pure republic—which he called the system most practicable for a large population—as one where divided powers are exercised by representatives for a short period of time to ensure that they express the will of their constituents. His drafts of the 1776 Virginia constitution and the Northwest Ordinance (1787) for governing the American territories, as well as other early state constitutions, all required a republican form of government, one without a monarch or an aristocracy. For JAMES MADISON, writing in essay 39 of *The Federalist* (1787–88) (see FEDERALIST PAPERS), a republic was "a government which derives all its powers

directly or indirectly from the great body of the people, and is administered by persons holding their offices...for a limited period, or during good behavior." Republicanism during the American Revolution, in contrast, included a sense of responsibility for governing the people's affairs and a willingness to sacrifice for the good of the community.

"What is meant by 'republic' in the United States is the slow and quiet action of society upon itself. It is an orderly state really founded on the enlightened will of the people. It is a conciliatory government under which resolutions have time to ripen, being discussed with deliberation and executed only when mature."

—*Alexis de Tocqueville,* in *Democracy in America* (1835)

Guarantee Clause

According to Article IV, section 4, of the Constitution, "The United States shall guarantee to every State in this Union a Republican Form of Government...." The introduction of this provision, often referred to as the guarantee clause, at the CONSTITUTIONAL CONVENTION OF 1787 has been attributed to Madison. According to ALEXANDER HAMILTON in essay 21 of *The Federalist*, because history was replete with tyrants such as Julius Caesar (102–44 B.C.E.) and Oliver Cromwell (1599–1658), the national government had to be able to protect the republican form of government at the state as well as the federal level. The convention delegates, fearing that external threats or internal rebellion could threaten the stability of the republican institutions that ensured REPRESENTATIVE GOVERNMENT and individual RIGHTS, thus linked this clause with another in the same section guaranteeing that the national government will protect the states against invasion and domestic violence (see DOMESTIC TRANQUILITY).

Although the Supreme Court held as early as 1798, in *Calder v. Bull*, that "[t]here are certain vital principles in our free Republican governments, which will determine and overrule an apparent and flagrant abuse of legislative power," in *Luther v. Borden* (1849) the Court declared that the question of what constitutes a republican form of government is a political question for Congress—not the COURTS—to decide. Chief Justice Roger B. Taney (1777–1864) added that "the sovereignty in every State resides in the people of the State, and...they may alter and change their form of government at their own pleasure."

Defining "Republican" Government

In later cases the Supreme Court has continued to dodge the question of what constitutes a republican form of government, saying in *Minor v. Happersett* (1875) that "no particular government is designated as republican, neither is the exact form to be guaranteed, in any manner especially designated." In 1911 President William Howard Taft (1857–1930) vetoed statehood for Arizona and New Mexico (see ADMISSION OF NEW STATES) because the bill admitting them provided for recall, a DIRECT DEMOCRACY procedure by which voters can remove a public official from office before his term expires. But the following year in *Pacific States Telephone and Telegraph Co. v. Oregon* (1912), the Supreme Court found that other direct democracy provisions such as popular initiative (proposing legislation) or referendums did not violate the guarantee clause.

When the Supreme Court ordered Tennessee to reapportion its electoral districts in BAKER V. CARR (1962), it based its decision not on the state's denial of a republican form of government—by failing to properly apportion voting districts, thus allowing some citizens' votes to count more than others—but on the EQUAL PROTECTION clause of the Fourteenth Amendment (1868) (see REAPPORTIONMENT). The framers envisioned a republican form of government based on popular SOVEREIGNTY that required that the vote of each eligible voter have equal value. Any apportionment of electoral districts that gives the votes of some voters more weight or influence than others leans toward a class society, in which some members have more power than others. Requiring the electoral system to reflect to the greatest extent possible the principle of "one person, one vote" restores the basis of the republican form of government.

If a state were to abandon elections altogether and set up a hereditary monarch in place of the governor, citizens living there would be denied a republican form of government. But because the STATES are, in a sense, laboratories of DEMOCRACY—experiments in better government—variations taken by the forms of republican democracy can be countenanced. The governor of New Hampshire, for example, is elected for two years rather than for four years as are the other governors and the president. Some states, including Washington and West Virginia, have elected rather than appointed judges. And Nebraska is unique in having a unicameral rather than a bicameral legislature. The Constitution's guarantee clause apparently can accommodate many types of such experiments.

> **More on this topic:**
>
> Democracy, p. 149
>
> Majority Rule, p. 357
>
> Representative Government, p. 464
>
> Separation of Powers, p. 494

The strength and the weakness of a republican form of government, as de Tocqueville pointed out, is that it moves more slowly and deliberately than a government headed by an absolute ruler, who can give orders to be obeyed immediately. Yet only a republic that requires the involvement in its decision-making processes of citizens through elections and whose opinions must be canvassed and considered by their elected representatives—as slow and cumbersome as those processes may be—can ensure the protection of LIBERTY and individual RIGHTS.

Republican Party *See* POLITICAL PARTIES.

Reverse Discrimination *See* AFFIRMATIVE ACTION; DISCRIMINATION; REGENTS OF *THE UNIVERSITY OF CALIFORNIA V. BAKKE.*

Riders *See* LEGISLATION.

Rights

The CITIZENS of the world's first DEMOCRACY in ancient Athens enjoyed certain rights, among them the freedom to vote, hold public office, and have disputes settled according to prescribed legal procedures. Women, slaves, and children had no rights of their own but were dependent on an adult male citizen for their status and enforcement of any rights they might claim. Foreigners within the city-state's jurisdiction had no rights except by treaty (see ALIENS).

U.S. citizens, in contrast, have a constitution that is a form of contract in which rights, duties, and POWERS are divided between the governors and the governed. This idea first gained credence with Thomas Hobbes (1588–1679), who argued in *The Leviathan* (1651) for an implied contractual relationship between the ruler and the ruled. "It is a contract amongst the potential subjects to yield up their rights in favour of a sovereign. Indeed since the original contract takes place in the state of nature (in which all men have a right to all things) there are no rights which the subject could give to the sovereign, since he, in common with them, until the moment of contract, has a right to all: the right of nature."

Two types of rights can be identified: (1) human rights that are recognized in international documents and by international courts and tribunals, and (2) domestic legal rights that are enforceable under a nation's constitution and laws. Some rights may be recognized in both contexts.

HUMAN RIGHTS are rights that a person is entitled to by virtue of being a human being in a human society. These rights have been expressed in some national documents, such as the DECLARATION OF INDEPENDENCE (1776) and France's Declaration of the Rights of Man and of the Citizen (1789). More recently they have been set forth in international and regional documents such as the Universal Declaration of Human Rights (1948), American Declaration of the Rights and Duties of Man (1948), European Convention for the Protection of Human Rights and Fundamental Freedoms (1950), and African Charter on Human and Peoples' Rights (1981). Rights cited in such documents, many of which are also guaranteed in national constitutions, generally include freedom from DISCRIMINATION on the basis of race, sex, ethnic background, color, language, or RELIGION; equality before the law and EQUAL PROTECTION of the law; freedom of conscience, expression, and movement; and equal access to participation in the GOVERNMENT and public service.

Domestic legal rights are natural, civil, political, and personal rights that can be enforced by the COURTS. Constitutional guarantees are legal rights, as are rights contained in laws enacted by legislatures and other laws recognized by courts of law, such as COMMON LAW rights and rights based on precedent or prior court decisions. Natural rights include the right to life, LIBERTY, PRIVACY, and a good reputation. CIVIL RIGHTS include the right to own PROPERTY, to marry (see FAMILIES), legal protection of CONTRACTS, and trial by jury (see JURIES; TRIALS). Political rights include the power to participate directly or indirectly in government, from voting to holding public office.

Although civil, political, and property rights have been recognized to some degree in all human civilizations, in most cases only a select few people had any real or enforceable rights. More often than not, a right depended on power—the power of the person asserting the right or the power of someone acting on his or her behalf. Enforcement of rights also generally depended on power. The closer a person's relationship to those wielding power, the more likely he or she was able to enforce the rights claimed. In an absolute monarchy, all power was vested in the monarch, who might personally grant a right, recognize an asserted right, or delegate to others the authority to grant and enforce rights.

Constitutional Rights

Most written constitutions contain two parts: (1) a description of how the government works and (2) a list of rights guaranteed to the people and, in the case of federal nations, to their semisovereign political subdivisions such as the American STATES. Because governments have a monopoly on the use of force within their territorial jurisdictions, constitutional rights represent one form of limitation on the government's power to coerce those under its control. For such rights to be effective, however, the constitution must offer enforcement mechanisms, which have to be independent of government officials and institutions that may be liable to infringe those rights. Under most constitutions, the LEGISLATIVE BRANCH is responsible for enacting laws to enforce rights, the EXECUTIVE BRANCH is responsible for enforcing the laws, and the independent JUDICIAL BRANCH is responsible for determining and punishing infringement of rights (see JUDICIAL INDEPENDENCE).

A constitutional right is one a person is entitled by a constitution to have, to do, or to receive from others. It may be expressed in the negative—for example, the First Amendment (1791) injunction that "Congress shall make no law respecting an establishment of religion..."—or in the positive—for example, the Sixth Amendment (1791) mandate that "[i]n all criminal prosecutions, the accused shall enjoy [among other things] the right...to have the Assistance of Counsel for his defence." Such rights, like these two, may be expressly stated in the Constitution or inferred by the courts, such as the right of privacy.

The right to a trial by jury is guaranteed in the main body of the Constitution, as are other rights such as the writ of HABEAS CORPUS; protection against bills of attainder (see ATTAINDER, BILLS OF), EX POST FACTO LAWS, and the impairment of CONTRACTS; and entitlement to "all the Privileges and Immunities of Citizens in the several States" (see PRIVILEGES AND IMMUNITIES). Numerous other constitutional rights are guaranteed in the BILL OF RIGHTS (1791), the first ten amendments to the Constitution, from freedom of SPEECH and THE PRESS to peaceable assembly (see ASSEMBLY AND ASSOCIATION) and the rights of those accused of crimes (see CRIMINAL LAW). Some of the seventeen later amendments also extended rights, among them the right of black men to vote, granted by the Fifteenth Amendment (1870); the right of WOMEN to vote, granted by the Nineteenth Amendment (1920); and the right of citizens eighteen years of age or older to vote, granted by the Twenty-sixth Amendment (1971). In contrast, the presumption of innocence is recognized by the courts even though it is not mentioned in the Constitution.

Just as the national constitution guarantees certain rights, so too do state constitutions. Many national constitutional rights have been made applicable to the states by the INCORPORATION DOCTRINE, under which most of the rights guaranteed in the Bill of Rights have been gradually incorporated into the DUE PROCESS clause of the Fourteenth Amendment (1868). State constitutions may provide rights in addition to the U.S. Constitution's; for example, unlike the federal constitution, the Illinois constitution (1971) guarantees that equal protection of the laws will not be denied on account of sex (see SEX DISCRIMINATION). Sometimes a state's constitutional rights are simply expressed a little differently than those in the national document. California's constitution (1879), for one, prohibits "cruel *or* unusual" punishment rather than "cruel *and* unusual" punishment, a semantic difference that can lead to different outcomes in state judicial proceedings (see CRUEL AND UNUSUAL PUNISHMENT). In 1972 the California supreme court used this distinction as the basis for invalidating the state's DEATH PENALTY. In general, state constitutions may extend rights but cannot reduce rights below the minimum guaranteed by the U.S. Constitution if such national rights are applicable to the states.

Rights and privileges are sometimes confused. In 1892, while serving on the Massachusetts Supreme Judicial Court, OLIVER WENDELL HOLMES JR., later a justice of the U.S. Supreme Court, made the distinction. To hold a government job, he said, was considered a privilege rather than a right, and thus a public employee could be fired even for exercising his or her constitutional rights. A government employee, as Holmes put it, "may have a constitutional right to talk politics, but he has no constitutional right to be a policeman," and thus he could be fired for expressing his political views. In more recent cases the distinction between rights and privileges has become blurred. While there is no constitutional right to a government job or a government benefit, such as a WELFARE payment, the Supreme Court held in *Perry v. Sindermann* (1972) that the government may not fire a government employee or deny a person a government benefit on certain constitutionally protected grounds. Concluded the Court: "For if the government could deny a benefit to a person because of his constitutionally protected speech or association, his exercise of those freedoms would in effect be penalized and inhibited.... Such interference with constitutional rights is impermissible...."

Rights during Wartime

Governments around the globe have used wars and other emergency situations as excuses for curtailing citizens' rights (see EMERGENCY POWERS; WAR). In anticipation of such emergencies, the constitutions of some countries—those of Poland (1992) and South Africa (1997), for example—refer to some rights as "nonderogable," meaning that they are so fundamental that they cannot be limited or suspended even under extreme emergency conditions, including wartime.

During the Civil War (1861–65), President ABRAHAM LINCOLN tried to suspend the right of HABEAS CORPUS—as allowed under Article 1, section 9, during times of "Rebellion or Invasion"—but was thwarted by the Supreme Court in *Ex parte Milligan* (1866). "The Constitution of the United States is a law for rulers and people, equally in war and in peace, and covers with the shield of its protection all classes of men, at all times, and under all circumstances," the Court stated. During World War II, however, in *Korematsu v. United States* (1944), the Court sustained the relocation of Japanese Americans to internment camps as a valid wartime measure. This decision has since been discredited as an improper curtailment of the rights of minority citizens, and it is doubtful that measures infringing the rights of citizens to this extent would be found constitutional today. The issue of protection of individual rights has come before the Supreme Court in several key cases since the war on terror was initiated following the terrorist attacks on the United States on September 11, 2001. The Court has generally upheld individual constitutional rights in the face of the executive branch's claims for extraordinary powers to deal with persons suspected of involvement in terrorist activities (see HAMDI V. RUMSFELD; NATIONAL SECURITY; EXECUTIVE BRANCH; WAR).

> **"The Constitution of the United States is a law for rulers and people, equally in war and in peace, and covers with the shield of its protection all classes of men, at all times, and under all circumstances."**
>
> —Supreme Court, in *Ex parte Milligan*, 1866

Waiver of Rights

A person does not have to take advantage of all the rights to which he or she is entitled. For example, someone accused of a crime may waive the right to a jury trial (see TRIALS) or even the presumption of innocence by pleading guilty. Failure to appear in court or to take advantage of the ASSISTANCE OF COUNSEL provided may also constitute a waiver of rights.

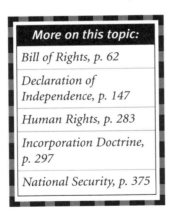

More on this topic:
Bill of Rights, p. 62
Declaration of Independence, p. 147
Human Rights, p. 283
Incorporation Doctrine, p. 297
National Security, p. 375

But in *Brady v. United States* (1970), the Supreme Court held that rights could not be inadvertently waived, noting that a waiver must be voluntary and "knowing, intelligent [and] done with sufficient awareness of the relevant circumstances and likely consequences." Yet in *United States v. Gagnon* (1985), the Court upheld a waiver of rights based on a defendant's failure to object to an overt denial of DUE PROCESS. The defendant did not demand to be present when a judge declared in court his intention to privately speak to a juror about the juror's objectivity, a silence that was held to constitute a waiver of his right to due process.

As Alexis de Tocqueville (1805–59), the French political observer, declared in *Democracy in America* (1835), "No man can be great without virtue, nor any nation great without respect for rights; one might almost say that without it there can be no society...." The evolutionary path from "might makes right" to "rights make might" has been a long and arduous one. Among the foundations of a constitutional democracy based on popular SOVEREIGNTY such as that of the United States are mutual respect for individuals' rights and the government's obligation to protect and equally enforce the rights of all citizens under the law.

Roe v. Wade

Roe v. Wade (1973) was perhaps the most controversial case decided by the Supreme Court in the twentieth century. It continues to be the focus of almost daily political, religious, and legal debates, and both supporters and critics of the decision—which struck down state laws criminalizing

ABORTION—urge that nominees for any Supreme Court vacancy be screened carefully to determine if they support the decision or want to overturn it.

Norma McCorvey, identified in the case as Jane Roe for her protection, was an unmarried woman who had an abortion in Texas, where it was prohibited except to save a pregnant woman's life. A companion case, *Doe v. Bolton*, challenged a less-restrictive ban on abortions in Georgia. Initially McCorvey asserted that her pregnancy was the outcome of a gang rape but later admitted that it resulted from consensual sexual relations. Although both women were pregnant at the time their cases were initially filed in 1970, they were no longer pregnant when the Supreme Court heard their appeals. The Court agreed that because the condition of pregnancy is repeatable, the case was not moot simply because the women were no longer pregnant. As Justice Harry A. Blackmun (1908–99) said for the Court, "[Although] pregnancy is a significant fact in the litigation, the normal 266-day human gestation period is so short that the pregnancy will come to term before the usual appellate process is complete.... Pregnancy provides a classic justification," he said, for not holding such cases to be unjusticiable.

Joining Justice Blackmun in the Supreme Court's 7–2 decision were Chief Justice Warren E. Burger (1907–95) and Justices William O. Douglas (1898–1980), Potter Stewart (1915–85), William J. Brennan Jr. (1906–97), Lewis F. Powell Jr. (1907–98), and THURGOOD MARSHALL concurring opinions were filed by Chief Justice Burger and Justices Douglas and Stewart. Justices Byron R. White (1917–2002) and William H. Rehnquist (1924–2005) wrote dissenting opinions.

The decision was grounded on the right of PRIVACY developed by the Supreme Court and recognized earlier in *GRISWOLD V. CONNECTICUT* (1965). Because this right of privacy rests on citizens' fundamental LIBERTY, as protected by the DUE PROCESS clause of the Fourteenth Amendment (1868), the state was required to show that it had a compelling interest in infringing McCorvey's privacy by banning abortion.

According to the opinion, the two state interests involved were the protection of the health of the mother and the protection of the life of the unborn child. The case was argued twice before the Supreme Court, an unusual occurrence due in part to the fact that some of the justices found unacceptable Justice Blackmun's first draft of the opinion, in which he argued that the laws were unconstitutionally vague. During the interval, Justice Blackmun, who had served as legal counsel for the Mayo Clinic in Minnesota, did extensive medical research on abortion. The major breakthrough in his analysis came with the recognition that a nine-month pregnancy could be divided into three trimesters. The Court would allow women the right, in consultation with their physicians, to an abortion during the first trimester, the first three months of pregnancy. An abortion could also be obtained during the second trimester, but states could pass laws to regulate abortion during this period to protect the woman's health. The Court held that even during the third trimester, states could permit an abortion to save the mother's life.

The Supreme Court found that the medical evidence and opinion were so unsettled as to when human life might begin during pregnancy that states could not adopt an arbitrary time in order to ban abortion based on the right to life of the fetus. The dissenters, however, portrayed the trimester analysis as arbitrary and rejected the adoption of a right not expressly found in the Constitution. Alluding to the ORIGINAL INTENT argument—that a woman's right to have an abortion could not have been contemplated by the framers of the Fourteenth Amendment (1868)—they concluded that the abortion statutes in question were no more restrictive than other statutes in force when that amendment was ratified.

As the constituency on the Supreme Court changed after *Roe* from relatively liberal to relatively conservative, the Court began to find opportunities to restrict this decision. In *Maher v. Roe* (1977), the Court held that states did not have to fund abortions for poor women, and in *Harris v. McRae*

Norma McCorvey, the successful plaintiff in **Roe v. Wade,** subsequently became an activist in the anti-abortion movement.

Source: AP Images/Tony Gutierrez

"Childbirth may deprive a woman of her preferred lifestyle and force upon her a radically different and undesired future"

—Justice William O. Douglas

• •

"It is a poverty to decide a child must die so that you may live as you wish."

—Mother Teresa

(1980), it sanctioned the government's right to withhold nontherapeutic federal Medicaid funding for abortions for poor women.

A major challenge to the *Roe* decision was presented in *Planned Parenthood of Southeastern Pennsylvania v. Casey* (1992), in which the Supreme Court by a 5–4 decision upheld state restrictions on access to abortion but left intact the right of abortion itself. Justice SANDRA DAY O'CONNOR, then the only woman on the Court, along with Justices Anthony M. Kennedy (b. 1936) and David Souter (b. 1939), recognized a woman's constitutional right to have an abortion before a fetus becomes viable (able to live on its own), about the first six months. Since then, the Supreme Court has heard a number of cases attempting to limit the scope of the *Roe* decision.

A majority of Americans continue to support limited abortion under some circumstances. In 2005 a Gallup poll found that 26 percent of Americans thought abortion should always be legal, 56 percent said it should be legal in certain cases, and only 16 percent said the procedure should be totally banned. Many state legislators and antiabortion groups in particular still seek to stop or limit abortions and thus curtail *Roe v. Wade.* Interestingly, Norma McCorvey, the Jane Roe in *Roe v. Wade,* subsequently became an abortion opponent; but her attempt to have the 1973 decision overturned was rejected by the Supreme Court in 2005.

Abortion proponents argue that if American society is to be truly equal, then women should be as unfettered in making their choices of how they wish to live their lives as men have been throughout history. Abortion opponents counter that the state cannot know when human life begins and thus cannot authorize termination of a fetus, privileging the woman's right to manage her life choices over the rights of the unborn.

This view has been rejected by justices such as Justice William O. Douglas, who argued in his concurring opinion in the companion *Doe* case, after citing a litany of earlier cases supporting the principles on which the right of abortion rests: "The Georgia statute—banning abortions—is at war with the clear message of these cases—that a woman is free to make the basic decision whether to bear an unwanted child. Elaborate argument is hardly necessary to demonstrate that childbirth may deprive a woman of her preferred lifestyle and force upon her a radically different and undesired future."

Rule of Law

"When we say that the supremacy or the rule of law is a characteristic of the English constitution," wrote the British constitutional scholar Albert V. Dicey in *Law of Constitution* (1885), "…[we] mean, in the first place, that no man is punishable…except for a distinct breach of law established in the ordinary legal manner before the ordinary courts of the land." Nearly two centuries earlier, the English philosopher John Locke (1632–1704) explained in his *Second Treatise* (his *Two Treatises on Government* was published in 1690) that "*Allegiance* being nothing but an *obedience according to Law*, which when he [the monarch] violates, he has no right to Obedience." In other words, even the English monarch was not above the law, and subjects of the Crown owed no personal feudal allegiance to the monarch—only allegiance to the sovereign as the constitutional head of state.

The opposite of *the* rule of law—as opposed to merely *a* rule of law—is arbitrary and capricious rule by an absolute monarch or a dictator. It was in part the seemingly arbitrary and capricious acts of the British king and Parliament that sparked the movement for independence in the thirteen original American colonies and led to the Revolutionary War (1775–83). In his incendiary pamphlet *Common Sense* (1776), Thomas Paine, a recently arrived British subject, declared that "in America, *the law is king.*"

Some national constitutions enshrine adherence to the rule of law. The Bulgarian constitution (1991), for example, provides: "The Republic of Bulgaria is a state based on the rule of law." Although the U.S. Constitution does not expressly refer to the rule of law, by its nature it incorporates the concept. Election of the PRESIDENT every four years (see ELECTIONS) and the IMPEACHMENT process to remove the president from office both provide checks on any arbitrary and capricious use of power that the chief executive might attempt. The independent JUDICIAL BRANCH and its inherent power of JUDICIAL REVIEW (see JUDICIAL INDEPENDENCE) represent other elements of the Constitution that are calculated to ensure adherence to the rule of law by the U.S. government.

A handful of Supreme Court cases decided since the 1970s illustrate the application of the rule of law. The first case, *United States v. Nixon* (1974), grew out of the WATERGATE scandal, which centered around allegations of the president's involvement in covering up a break-in at Democratic Party headquarters in 1972. The special prosecutor (see INDEPENDENT COUNSEL) appointed to investigate the charges sought the Court's assistance in obtaining what turned out to be incriminating tape recordings made under the direction of Richard M. Nixon (1913–69). In denying the president's assertion of executive privilege to withhold the evidence (see IMMUNITY), the Supreme Court confirmed the principle of the rule of law: that no one is above the law, not even the president. In this case the coequal judicial branch enforced the LAW against the president.

This theme was expanded on in the case of *Clinton v. Jones* (1997). Here the Supreme Court went so far as to say—although THOMAS JEFFERSON had argued otherwise in his day—that "it is…settled that the President is subject to judicial process in appropriate circumstances." President Bill Clinton (b. 1946) was seeking to avoid having to respond during his term to a civil suit filed against him for sexual harassment. The Court noted that the suit involved unofficial acts. A similar question came up during the impeachment proceedings against Clinton in 1999 as to whether criminal charges arising out of the impeachment investigation could be brought against a sitting president, but no attempt was made to formally file such charges while he was in office.

More recently, however, in *Cheney v. United States District Court for the District of Columbia* (2004), the Court found in favor of executive privilege with respect to a claim for information concerning meetings on national energy policy that had been chaired by Vice President Dick Cheney several years earlier. The ruling was made while noting the Nixon case and the Court's "'historic[al] commitment to the rule of law.'"

In *Romer v. Evans* (1996), the Supreme Court articulated another aspect of the rule of law. A statewide referendum (see DIRECT DEMOCRACY) in Colorado had prohibited any government action designed to protect persons on the basis of their sexual orientation or lifestyle preference (see HOMOSEXUALS). In ruling on the case, Justice Anthony M. Kennedy (b. 1936) wrote: "Central both to the idea of the rule of law and to our own Constitution's guarantee of equal protection is the principle that government and each of its parts remain open on impartial terms to all who seek its assistance.... A law declaring that in general it shall be more difficult for one group of citizens than for all others to seek aid from the government is itself a denial of equal protection in the most literal sense."

The rule of law cannot be expressed in a few words. Rather, like constitutionalism, it is a concept with many principles, among them rule by law and not individuals, equal access to JUSTICE for all, equal application of the laws to all citizens, even-handed and fair enforcement of the law, and prohibitions against EX POST FACTO LAWS that punish an act that was not a crime when it was committed. Not least is the principle that no one is above the law. While no system of justice is perfect, the more a government is rooted in the rule of law, the more just it will become.

S

School Busing *See* SEGREGATION.

Schools *See* EDUCATION; RELIGION.

Science and Technology

Many of the FRAMERS OF THE CONSTITUTION were aware of contemporary science and the technology of their day, including the advances in physics made by the English mathematician Sir Isaac Newton (1642–1727). Benjamin Franklin, a delegate from Pennsylvania, was a world-renowned scientist and inventor, credited with inventing the lightning rod and a wood-burning stove named after him. Those framers familiar with the LAW no doubt knew about the *Commentaries on the Laws of England* (1765–70), written by the English jurist William Blackstone (1723–80)—a monumental work organizing the nation's laws and legal principles spanning many centuries. At the time, as many copies of Blackstone's tomes were sold in America as in England.

Although the disciplines of science and engineering on one hand and the law and constitutions on the other are distinct and at times in conflict, the Constitution, drafted in 1787, can be considered the first scientific effort to create a national government using logic and reason. In consideration of the benefits to be gained from science and technology, the founders included among the powers of CONGRESS in Article I, section 8, the authority "To promote the Progress of Science and useful Arts, by securing for limited Times to Authors and Inventors the exclusive Right to their respective Writings and Discoveries."

Sending a man to the moon in 1969 represented one of the nation's most spectacular technological accomplishments.
Source: The Granger Collection, New York

The American system of government fostered by the Constitution has led to an unprecedented era of scientific and technological discoveries, from the steamboat, electric light, and telephone to skyscrapers, nuclear power, and men on the moon. In addition to constitutional questions relating to PATENTS—the primary point of interface between constitutional law and science and technology—the Supreme Court has faced other issues raised by the explosion of knowledge and inventions in recent years.

In the field of COMMUNICATIONS, for example, the definition of what constitutes a performance of a copyrighted work (see COPYRIGHT) has been changed by the invention of the radio. In *Twentieth Century Music Corp. v. Aiken* (1975), the Supreme Court affirmed a lower court ruling that refused to hold businesses that played radio broadcasts for their customers to strict copyright protections, concluding that such use was simply unenforceable—short of mandating that they keep the radio turned off. The old concept of a performance before a paying audience had to be discarded in the new era of mass communications.

Medical technology has been responsible for a number of cases involving removal of life-support systems for terminally ill or incurable patients (see DIE, RIGHT TO). In the significant case *Cruzan v. Director, Missouri Department of Health* (1990), the parents of a woman rendered permanently unconscious by a car accident sought to terminate the use of artificial means to keep her alive. The state's supreme court refused the parents' request on the grounds that the patient's wishes were unclear on the question, even though there was evidence that she had informally indicated that she would not wish to be kept alive under such circumstances. The U.S. Supreme Court, in a 5–4 decision that made no distinction regarding the types of medical technology used, held that a state may reasonably require clear evidence of the patient's wishes before granting a request by relatives to have medical life-support devices withdrawn. In 2005 the U.S. Supreme Court refused to grant the plea of the parents of Terri Schiavo to have her feeding tube reinserted after it had been removed by court order in response to a request by her husband that she be allowed to die. She had been in an unconscious state for years and was being kept alive by modern medical technology.

The federal government has an interest in protecting classified scientific and technological data or sensitive information it may have developed (see PENTAGON PAPERS CASE). In 1979 a federal district court enjoined the publication of instructions on how to build a hydrogen bomb on the grounds that such information was a threat to NATIONAL SECURITY, but the case became irrelevant before an appeal could be taken to the Supreme Court when the material was published elsewhere.

Science and technology have contributed to new methods of obtaining and introducing evidence into the legal process. High-tech surveillance devices provide LAW ENFORCEMENT officials with powerful new tools for gathering evidence against persons suspected of committing a crime (see PRIVACY; SEARCH AND SEIZURE; WIRETAPPING).

In *Frye v. United States* (1923), the U.S. Court of Appeals for the District of Columbia established the rule that scientific evidence presented in court had to be generally accepted by scientists in that field. But in *Daubert v. Merrell Dow* (1993), after the Supreme Court's adoption of new federal rules of evidence in 1975, Justice Harry A. Blackman (1908–99) concluded for the majority that the *Frye* rule was no longer applicable and that scientific evidence was admissible just as long as it was based on scientifically valid principles and was both reliable and relevant. A recent result of the increased use of scientific forensic evidence in court is the "CSI effect," or the concern that the popular television show "CSI: Crime Scene Investigation," which has attracted a great number of viewers since it debuted in 2000, may influence jurors in criminal trials. As of 2007, however, studies seem to indicate that the effect is negligible in influencing jurors to acquit or convict, either because insufficient scientific forensic evidence, such as DNA comparisons, is presented, or because such evidence, if presented, is considered infallible.

A number of federal ADMINISTRATIVE AGENCIES have responsibilities relating to science and technology, including the Department of Energy, National Aeronautics and Space Administration, Federal Aviation Administration, National Science Foundation, and Nuclear Regulatory Commission. The National Science and Technology Council was established by presidential order in 1993 as the principal body to assist the president in coordinating the related functions of science, space, and technology.

In contrast to the law, which develops in slow increments, science and technology change at lightning speed—one need look no further than the modern revolution in computers, INTERNET communication, and GENETICS. Viewed as a living document that can evolve with the times, the Constitution may be able to cope with twenty-first century issues involving science and technology. But if it is interpreted as a stagnant document that can be applied only by delving into the ORIGINAL INTENT of the framers, the Constitution is likely to fail to provide the answers required by a democracy hurtling toward an ever more complex and dangerous future.

More on this topic:
Copyright, p. 124
Genetics, p. 251
Internet, p. 307
Patents, p. 396

Scott v. Sandford See SLAVERY.

Search and Seizure

The fire of rebellion in the American colonies was fueled in part by British actions such as the hated Townshend Acts (1767), named for the British chancellor of the exchequer, Charles Townshend. One of these acts set duties on imports into the American colonies, including tea from the British East India Company, leading to the 1773 conflagration known as the Boston Tea Party. Another act, intended to reorganize the collection of customs duties in the colonies, allowed British agents to resort to the hated writs of assistance, which permitted wholesale searches of homes and businesses and the seizure of PROPERTY suspected of having been obtained without payment of required duties. Although the economic effect of the acts was to exacerbate the depression already sweeping the colonies, their political effect was far greater.

The authors of the BILL OF RIGHTS (1791) thus had immediate experience to draw on when drafting the Fourth Amendment, which declares: "The right of the people to be secure in their persons, houses, papers, and effects, against unreasonable searches and seizures, shall not be violated, and no Warrants shall issue, but upon probable cause, supported by Oath or affirmation, and particularly describing the place to be searched, and the persons or things to be seized." In its simplest terms, the Fourth Amendment—a reaction to the general warrants and warrantless searches of

The Constitution places limits on police searches of private residences.
Source: AP Images/AJ Mast

colonists' homes before the Revolutionary War (1775–83)—guarantees to all persons that their home is their castle, a principle of English law at least as old as *Semayne's Case* (1603), in which the right to defend one's home against the unlawful entry of even the king's agents was assured. A corollary provision is the Fifth Amendment's prohibition against giving up self-incriminating evidence: "...nor shall any person be compelled in any criminal case to be a witness against himself..." (see SELF-INCRIMINATION).

In its first case to look at the Fourth Amendment in detail, *Boyd v. United States* (1886), the Supreme Court, relying on a 1765 English opinion, ruled: "Breaking into a house and opening boxes and drawers are circumstances of aggravation; but any forcible and compulsory extortion of a man's own testimony or of his private papers to be used as evidence to convict him of crime or to forfeit his goods, is within the condemnation of that [English] judgment. In this regard, the Fourth and Fifth Amendments run almost into each other."

"Fruit of the Poison Tree"

Later cases would prove more complicated than *Boyd*. In fact, the Fourth Amendment's language regarding what constitutes "unreasonable" search and seizure brought almost ad hoc Supreme Court opinions based on the facts of each case. The remedy suggested in *Boyd* for an unreasonable warrantless search was adopted in *Weeks v. United States* (1914), in which the Court declared that the private papers belonging to a person accused of a crime and obtained by an unconstitutional search could not be used against him in a federal court. Thus was born the exclusionary rule, also known as the "fruit of the poison tree" principle.

The Supreme Court has continued to rethink, expand, and refine the exclusionary rule—the inadmissibility in court of illegally seized evidence. In *Gouled v. United States* (1921), subsequently overturned, the Court held that even with a valid warrant the government could take only stolen property or other property related to criminal activity, such as goods concealed to avoid taxes, but it could not take property merely because it could be used as evidence against a person in court. The Court required that warrantless searches and seizures be based on a valid probable cause. The exclusionary rule was later extended to the states through the DUE PROCESS clause of the Fourteenth Amendment (1868) in the Court's landmark decision in MAPP V. OHIO (1961). In that case, police officers broke into a home on the pretext of looking for gambling equipment and a fugitive from justice but seized books and pictures later used in court as evidence of possession of obscene materials (see OBSCENITY).

The Supreme Court has been concerned with applying the exclusionary rule in many subsequent cases, including *Terry v. Ohio* (1968), in which a police officer patted down and removed weapons from suspects. The Court upheld the officer's actions as reasonable procedures under the Fourth Amendment for protecting himself and others, and thus the weapons seized could be properly admitted in evidence. The pat-down search was upheld by a U.S. court of appeals as recently as 2007; and the Supreme Court in *Hiibel v. Sixth Judicial District Court of Nevada* (2004), citing the decision in *Terry*, went so far as to uphold a conviction of a person who refused to identify himself to a police officer under a state "stop and identify" law, rejecting arguments that the requirement violated the unreasonable search and seizure provision of the Fourth Amendment or the prohibition against self-incrimination in the Fifth Amendment. A sharply divided Court in *Hudson v. Michigan* (2006) also found that officers violating the "knock and announce" requirement established in *Wilson v. Arkansas* (1995) before executing a search warrant did not violate the Fourth Amendment such that evidence obtained had to be suppressed.

Constitutionally Protected Places

Two important cases regarding search and seizure are *Warden v. Hayden* and KATZ V. UNITED STATES (both 1967). In the former the Supreme Court ruled that certain types of physical evidence could be seized for use in convicting a person, as long as the evidence was not "testimonial" or "communicative" in nature and thus would not run afoul of the Fifth Amendment's prohibition against self-incrimination. The latter case overruled a 1928 opinion that had focused on government agents' trespassing into constitutionally protected physical places. In *Katz*, which involved WIRETAPPING of a public telephone booth, the court changed the focus of the Fourth Amendment from a place such as a home or an office (traditionally held to be entitled to protection under the Fourth Amendment) to any place, such as a telephone booth, where a person today would have a reasonable expectation of PRIVACY.

In *California v. Ciraolo* (1986), the Supreme Court refused to extend Fourth Amendment protection to the backyard of a home under aircraft surveillance. The view of the marijuana plants growing there, the Court said, "took place within public navigable airspace in a physically nonintrusive manner." But in *Kyllo v. United States* (2001), the justices found that the use of thermal imaging to "see" the heat of lights used to grow marijuana indoors constituted an unconstitutional search.

Warrantless Searches

In the 1914 *Weeks* case, the Supreme Court concluded that the physical search of an arrested person to check for concealed weapons or evidence constituted an exception to the Fourth Amendment's search warrant requirement. The extent of the area that could be searched at the time of arrest was later expanded by the Court. Its decision in *Harris v. United States* (1947) validated the search of an entire apartment, and in *Washington v. Chrisman* (1982), the Court held that as long as police officers were legally in a place where evidence of criminal activity was in "plain view," they could seize it without a warrant. The Court later tried to strike a happy medium by allowing only a search of a person arrested and anything in his or her immediate control. A search of an arrested person's clothing has been upheld, and any property in his or her possession may be inventoried and safeguarded at the police station.

Many other questions incidental to search and seizure may arise, such as what constitutes probable cause for a search warrant or what conditions justify a warrantless search. The basic problem of how to balance citizens' privacy rights, including the rights of those accused of crimes—such as the presumption of innocence and the prohibition against self-incrimination—has been made more difficult by the Supreme Court's finding of a basic constitutional right of privacy and by technological advances that give LAW ENFORCEMENT officers new tools to use in the search for incriminating evidence (see BALANCING TESTS).

The automobile has posed new challenges regarding search and seizure. In deciding more than ninety cases relating to evidence found in cars, the Supreme Court has generally held that there is a diminished expectation of privacy with respect to a car as opposed to a home. A valid probable

More on this topic:

Criminal Law, p. 132

cause by the police can result in a warrantless search of a vehicle and containers in it. But the passengers in the vehicle may not be searched unless there is an independent basis for doing so. Stopping a vehicle for a traffic violation and ordering the people in it to get out is generally constitutional, as is a search of the vehicle in the face of a probable cause, such as observing a container of DRUGS.

"The makers of our Constitution undertook to secure conditions favorable to the pursuit of happiness...," explained Justice William O. Douglas (1898–1980) in his dissenting opinion in *On Lee v. United States* (1952). "They sought to protect Americans in their beliefs, their thoughts, their emotions and their sensations. They conferred, as against the Government, the right to be let alone—the most comprehensive of rights and the right most valued by civilized men. To protect that right, every unjustifiable intrusion by the Government upon the privacy of the individual, whatever the means employed, must be deemed a violation of the Fourth Amendment."

Secession

In a speech on March 6, 1860, ABRAHAM LINCOLN identified the cause of the impending secession of the nation's slave-owning states in the South the following year. "What ever endangered this Union save and except slavery? Did any other thing cause a moment's fear? All men must agree that this thing alone has ever endangered the perpetuity of the Union" (see SLAVERY). The South's secession from the Union and the formation of the Confederate States of America brought on the Civil War (1861–65), the most destructive WAR on American soil.

Most national constitutions, even those of federal nations like the United States, do not raise the specter that states or provinces will separate themselves from the federal system of government (see FEDERALISM). In fact, the constitutions of many federal governments emphasize just the opposite. Australia's (1901), for example, begins: "Whereas the people of New South Wales, Victoria, South Australia, Queensland, and Tasmania...have agreed to unite in one indissoluble federal commonwealth." In contrast, the constitution of the Soviet Union (1977), before its dissolution in 1991, contained a unique provision permitting secession.

The U.S. Constitution speaks of the "Union" of the states of the United States (in Article I, section 2, for example) and addresses the ADMISSION OF NEW STATES but is silent regarding whether states might withdraw from the Union. Movements that contemplated secession began in America as early as 1794, after the signing of the Jay Treaty (1794) patching up differences with the British. Before the Civil War, when the slave states decided to secede, some abolitionists (antislavery activists) themselves argued for "disunion," or the withdrawal of the free states from the slave states.

For many political leaders in the slave states of the South, the American Union was merely a voluntary association of sovereign STATES (see SOVEREIGNTY). They even pointed to the language of the DECLARATION OF INDEPENDENCE (1776), which validated the right of the people to alter or abolish a form of government that was destructive of their rights—in this case, the right to own slaves. John C. Calhoun (1782–1850)—a South Carolina U.S. representative, senator, cabinet officer, and vice president of the United States—argued for the concepts of "interposition" and "nullification" by states when faced with what were viewed as unconstitutional acts of the federal government. For example, in 1832 South Carolina's legislature objected to national tariffs by passing a "nullification ordinance" that allowed damages to be claimed by any person arrested by federal officials for failing to pay the tariff. According to Calhoun, because the Constitution was merely a compact among the sovereign states, they could interpose their authority between the people and the national government and nullify federal legislation within their territory.

The acid test of whether states could withdraw from the Union occurred when seven southern states—South Carolina, Mississippi, Florida, Alabama, Georgia, Louisiana, and Texas—seceded after Lincoln's election to the presidency in 1860, making their announcements between December 24, 1860, and February 1, 1861. Beginning in April of that year, it took the Civil War to enforce Lincoln's commitment to maintaining the Union intact under the Constitution. In *Texas v. White* (1869), Chief Justice Salmon P. Chase (1808–73) declared after the war that secession was illegal, stating that even though a presidential reconstruction government was still in place in Texas and the state had not been fully restored to the Union, as far as the law was concerned, Texas had never left the Union.

The opinion referred to the fact that the ARTICLES OF CONFEDERATION (1781) "solemnly declared" the Union of the states to "be perpetual" and that the PREAMBLE of the Constitution that replaced the Articles in 1789 said that the new document was ordained "to form a more perfect Union." *Perpetual* meant no right of secession.

President Andrew Jackson, a native of Tennessee, sympathized with southerners who objected to high tariffs in the 1820s and 1830s. But he also contended that individual states had to recognize federal laws.

When South Carolina in 1832 claimed the right to ignore, or "nullify," a national tariff act, Jackson reacted by threatening to send in troops. He warned that South Carolina was on the brink of treason, and declared, "To say that any State may at pleasure secede from the Union is to say that the United States is not a nation."

The crisis ended in 1833 when Congress agreed to a reduced tariff. But Congress, in a warning to secessionists, also gave Jackson the authority to use military action.

The nullification crisis set a precedent for the Civil War. After the election of Abraham Lincoln in 1860, South Carolina became the first state to secede. Faced with other states seceding as well, Lincoln followed Jackson's precedent and turned to the military.

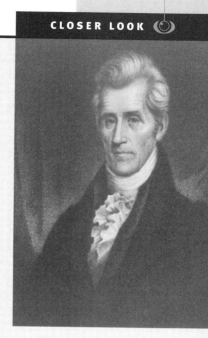

Andrew Jackson
Source: Library of Congress

The question of whether the states could ignore federal law continued to arise even after the Civil War (see STATES' RIGHTS). When the Supreme Court ruled against school SEGREGATION in *BROWN V. BOARD OF EDUCATION OF TOPEKA* (1954), a U.S. senator from Mississippi, James O. Eastland, proclaimed on May 17 of that year that no one was "required to obey any court which passes out such a ruling. In fact, you are obligated to defy it." Some jurisdictions in the South, including Little Rock, Arkansas, refused to comply with orders to integrate public schools, forcing the president to send federal troops to carry out the new desegregation laws.

Today there is little doubt that federal laws act directly on CITIZENS and legal entities such as businesses and not through state governments that once might have seen themselves as unfettered sovereignties. States cannot pick and choose which constitutionally valid federal laws they will obey, although they do have specific rights and powers as guaranteed by the Constitution. According to Article IV, section 4, for example, the federal government must guarantee to the states a REPUBLICAN FORM OF GOVERNMENT. Article V mandates that "no State, without its Consent, shall be deprived of its equal Suffrage in the Senate" (see SENATE). And the Tenth Amendment (1791) acknowledges that any POWERS not granted to the national government or prohibited to the states by the Constitution "are reserved to the States respectively, or to the people."

The strength of the United States lies in its ability to act as a single nation when it counts—in time of war and other emergencies. To allow individual states to secede from the Union every time some of them disagree with national policy would in the long run be as disastrous for those states as for the rest of the nation.

More on this topic:

Supremacy Clause,
p. 526

Second Amendment *See* GUN CONTROL.

Security *See* NATIONAL SECURITY.

Segregation

Segregation is the policy of imposing social separation of races, especially as practiced against nonwhites in a white-dominated society. South Africa's fifty-year policy of apartheid, which finally ended in 1994, placed severe restrictions on its African, Indian, and mixed-race inhabitants, such as where they could live and work. In the United States, the pernicious practice of segregation was legally sanctioned after the Civil War (1861–65), particularly in the former Confederate states that had practiced SLAVERY.

The FRAMERS OF THE CONSTITUTION in 1787 avoided addressing the fact of slavery despite the pronouncement of the DECLARATION OF INDEPENDENCE (1776) that "all Men are created equal." Segregation existed even in many non-slave-owning states. For example, in 1849 Benjamin F. Roberts, a black man, sued the city of Boston to allow his daughter to attend a closer elementary school rather than have to go to the school for blacks across town. Although he lost his case, in 1885 the Massachusetts legislature ended segregation in the state's public schools. After the Civil War, in addition to the Thirteenth Amendment (1865), the Fourteenth (1868) and Fifteenth (1870) Amendments set out to make all African Americans, whether free people or former slaves, equal citizens of the United States.

It was probably overly optimistic to expect that the once-legal institution of slavery would disappear overnight without engendering racial enmity on the part of the whites who had supported it and benefited from it. Even so, it is difficult today to understand how the Supreme Court, which had the power to declare repugnant laws and actions unconstitutional, could have consistently condoned practices such as the segregation of blacks and whites, which were obviously calculated to ensure second-class citizenship for African Americans in many parts of the country. The outright exclusion of black Americans from public facilities was concentrated in the former slave states.

In a series of cases in 1883, known as the Civil Rights Cases, the Supreme Court found that segregating "colored" from white customers in hotels, theaters, and railroads did not violate the Fourteenth Amendment because such DISCRIMINATION was between private individuals and was not instigated or assisted by state government. With its 8–1 decision in *Plessy v. Ferguson* (1896), the Court put its imprimatur on segregation by upholding the principle that "separate but equal" facilities—from public schools and buses to brothels—did not violate the Fourteenth Amendment's EQUAL PROTECTION clause.

The United States was not alone in condoning RACIAL DISCRIMINATION. Before the United Nations' Universal Declaration of Human Rights (1948), there was no well-established international agreement as to whether people of all races, ethnicities, and national origins, as well as both sexes, were entitled to equal treatment under national and INTERNATIONAL LAW. World War II had exposed to the world the horrors of concentration camps and the slavery of so-called inferior races in Europe and Asia by the Nazis and the Japanese, respectively. The resulting movement to establish an international norm of equality for all humans based on equal dignity and equal rights affected many nations, including the United States.

Even in the postwar era, segregation continued to permeate American life. Hospitals were segregated in more than a quarter of the states. In Florida and North Carolina, textbooks used by blacks and whites had to be stored apart. West Virginia and Alabama separated black and white paupers, and many southern states segregated prison chain gangs by race. Circus goers were not immune: in Louisiana and South Carolina they too were kept apart. If whites in Oklahoma wanted separate public telephone booths, the state required that they be provided. A generally unheralded step on the road to desegregation, at least until 2007 when a U.S. postage stamp was issued in its honor, was a U.S. Court of Appeals decision in *Mendez v. Westminister School District* (1946) that opened the way for Mexican American students to attend California public schools.

Another major step toward desegregation in the United States was taken in major league sports when Jackie Robinson was asked to play ball for the Brooklyn Dodgers in 1947. The following year President Harry S. Truman (1884–1972) also desegregated the ARMED FORCES. Bus boycotts began in 1955 when Rosa Parks refused to give up her seat to a white passenger and move to the back of the bus in Montgomery, Alabama. The first sit-in occurred in 1960 when four college students refused to move after being denied service at a Woolworth's lunch counter in Greensboro, North Carolina. By the early 1960s the CIVIL RIGHTS movement was using similar nonviolent protests and demonstrations to urge Congress to enact laws protecting the rights of MINORITIES, which it did in 1964 with passage of the Civil Rights Act. Organizations such as the National Association for the Advancement of Colored People (NAACP)

Major league baseball ended decades of segregation when the Brooklyn Dodgers signed Jackie Robinson, a star infielder in the Negro League.
Source: The Granger Collection, New York

and the Congress of Racial Equality (CORE), along with leaders such as MARTIN LUTHER KING JR., actively worked to end segregation, particularly in business establishments and transportation facilities.

The principle of "separate but equal" was declared unconstitutional in the Supreme Court's watershed decision *BROWN V. BOARD OF EDUCATION OF TOPEKA* (1954), finding a violation of the equal protection clause of the Fourteenth Amendment. School desegregation, including forced busing to integrate schools, continued under federal court supervision for many years, although in *Board of Education of Oklahoma City Public Schools v. Dowell* (1991), the Supreme Court announced that directing compliance with a plan of desegregation could not last forever. In 2001 a $500 million settlement between the Department of Justice and aggrieved Mississippians finally terminated a class-action lawsuit, begun in 1975, calling for desegregation of the state's institutions of higher learning.

Desegregation efforts have led to attempts to achieve racial balancing, particularly in schools, so that the school population is roughly proportional to the racial distribution in the school district. Although courts have been generally suspicious of laws that treat a racial group in a special manner and disadvantage them, such classifications have been upheld to a limited extent to make amends for past discrimination (see AFFIRMATIVE ACTION). However, in *Parents Involved in Community Schools v. Seattle School District No.1* (2007), a still-split Supreme Court rejected racial classification and assignment plans used by public school systems that had not formerly operated as legally segregated schools, because the compelling interest of remedying past intentional discrimination was lacking.

Self-Incrimination

"The guarantee against self-incrimination contained in the Fifth Amendment is not only a protection against conviction and prosecution but a safeguard of conscience and human dignity and freedom of expression as well," suggested Justice William O. Douglas (1898–1980) in his dissent in *Ullmann v. United States* (1956), a case involving a witness jailed for refusing to testify before a grand jury even though granted IMMUNITY from prosecution under federal law. Although Justice Douglas's reading of the Constitution's protection against self-incrimination—often referred to in common parlance as "taking the Fifth"—may have been more expansive than the majority of his brethren on the Supreme Court, any government restriction on the constitutional prohibition against self-incrimination bears a heavy burden that a compelling interest be shown. Based on the old legal maxim "No man is bound to accuse himself," the Fifth Amendment (1791) states, "No person…shall be compelled in any criminal case to be a witness against himself.…"

The right or, as it is sometimes called, the privilege against self-incrimination evolved in English law, in which two systems of criminal justice competed: the inquisitorial and the accusatorial. The dreaded Star Chamber proceedings in the sixteenth and seventeenth centuries, an example of the former method, required a person to take an oath to tell the truth in response to questions, not knowing whether or not he or she was the subject of the inquisition. Under the accusatorial system used in England and the American colonies—based on the presumption of innocence and the prosecution's burden to prove its case independently of the accused—the protection against self-incrimination was narrower than it became under the Fifth Amendment in the BILL OF RIGHTS (1791). The government fails to uphold these principles if it forces people to incriminate themselves.

One legal scholar has suggested that a dozen justifications can be made for the privilege against self-incrimination. The Supreme Court itself has often been expansive in supporting the protection while narrowly interpreting its effect. In *Murphy v. Waterfront Commission* (1964), the Court enumerated some of the rationales behind this right: "It reflects many of our fundamental values and

In 1987 Lieutenant Colonel Oliver North invoked his right against self-incrimination when called to testify before Congress about a scandal involving selling weapons to Iran.
Source: AP Images/Lana Harris

most noble aspirations; our unwillingness to subject those suspected of crime to the cruel trilemma of self-accusation, perjury or contempt; our preference for an accusatorial rather than an inquisitorial system of criminal justice; our fear that self-incriminating statements will be elicited by inhumane treatment and abuses; our sense of fair play which dictates 'a fair state-individual balance by requiring the government to leave the individual alone until good cause is shown for disturbing him and by requiring the government in its contest with the individual to shoulder the entire load,…'; our respect for the inviolability of the human personality and of the right of each individual 'to a private enclave where he may lead a private life,'…, our distrust of self-deprecatory statements; and our realization that the privilege, while sometimes 'a shelter to the guilty,' is often 'a protection to the innocent.'" Yet, in popular opinion and even among strong supporters of the Bill of Rights, a stigma is often attached to those who avail themselves of this right.

Extent of the Privilege

By exercising the privilege against self-incrimination, a person cannot be compelled to testify on the threat of being held in contempt of court and jailed or threatened with other government sanctions, such as the loss of public employment or a business license. But the protection extends only to testimony and personal papers (see SEARCH AND SEIZURE). A witness can still be required to participate in a police lineup of suspects, made to speak to establish voice recognition, or have fingerprints or blood samples taken. Only a person asked to testify can take advantage of the privilege; another party whose interests might be compromised by the testimony cannot claim the privilege. The intent to claim the right against self-incrimination must be formally made before a witness can constitutionally refuse to testify. Once a person begins to testify the privilege will not be granted, and the witness is required to answer any questions on cross-examination based on the testimony given.

A prosecutor cannot comment negatively on a witness's refusal to testify, and a judge may be requested by the defense to instruct the jury to give no weight in their deliberations to a witness's refusal to testify. Safeguards for persons accused of a crime were strengthened in 1966 with the requirement that as soon as suspects are taken into custody they must be advised, among other things, of their Fifth Amendment right to remain silent to avoid incriminating themselves (see MIRANDA V. ARIZONA).

Through a series of cases beginning with *Counselman v. Hitchcock* (1892), the Supreme Court extended the privilege against self-incrimination to federal cases involving WITNESSES testifying before grand JURIES; to civil as well as criminal proceedings; to legislative committees; and to federal ADMINISTRATIVE AGENCIES. In *Malloy v. Hogan* (1964), the Court made the right applicable to the states by incorporating it into the Fourteenth Amendment (1868) (see INCORPORATION DOCTRINE).

More recently, the Supreme Court has had to grapple with the right against self-incrimination and the effect of the rules requiring that suspects be "read" their Miranda rights as mandated by the Court's decision in *Miranda v. Arizona* (1966). For example, in *Chavez v. Martinez* (2003), a split Court held that a confession obtained against a suspect's will is not a constitutional violation if it is never used in a criminal proceeding. Then in *United States v. Patane* (2004), the Court, citing *Chavez*, ruled by a bare majority that a statement taken by the police without giving the suspect his Miranda rights did not require the exclusion of evidence obtained based on noncompelled or noncoerced testimony. But in *Missouri v. Seibert* (2004), four justices and one concurring justice struck down a two-tiered interrogation technique whereby a confession obtained without the Miranda warning being given is later solicited after the warning. Justice David Souter, writing for the plurality, said that "a statement repeated after a warning in such circumstances is inadmissible."

Immunity from Prosecution

Immunity from prosecution alone cannot fully protect a person from the penalties for giving self-incriminating testimony, which can also bring loss of one's reputation, business, community standing, and the respect of friends and family. In the 1892 *Counselman* case, the Supreme Court struck down an attempt to statutorily grant immunity to witnesses to compel their testimony in

More on this topic:

Criminal Law, p. 132

Immunity, p. 289

Witnesses, p. 586

spite of the Fifth Amendment protection. The Court found that the immunity law did not bar the use of direct testimony to seek other evidence with which to prosecute the witness. Congress later passed the Immunity Act (1954), which granted immunity to a witness before a grand jury that was investigating the possibility of NATIONAL SECURITY compromises during a time of heightened concern over the threat of communism. The act conferred "transactional immunity" from prosecution, which is much broader in scope than the old law. Transactional immunity prohibits any state or federal prosecution based on any transactions or other matters arising out of the compelled testimony.

In the 1956 *Ullmann* case, the Supreme Court's seven-member majority held that the Immunity Act did not violate the Fifth Amendment's prohibition against self-incrimination. According to the opinion written by Justice Felix Frankfurter (1882–1965), a witness could be compelled to testify before a grand jury if he or she had been granted transactional immunity from prosecution. Ullmann argued that even with the immunity granted by the statute, he would not be protected from private sanctions such as losing his job or being expelled from his labor union. As Justice Douglas noted in his dissent, "The disclosure that a person is a Communist practically excommunicates him from society."

To some it may appear that the government's power to compel testimony from a witness is a necessary tool in the ongoing fight against crime. One major problem with coerced or compelled testimony, however, is that it may be given falsely simply to avoid PUNISHMENT, as was done in the days of the Spanish Inquisition, authorized by Pope Sixtus IV in 1478, in which the rack and other instruments of torture were routinely used to make a person speak "the truth." If there is a balancing test (see BALANCING TESTS) between the interests of the government and the individual citizen over the extent of the Constitution's protection against self-incrimination, it should be weighted heavily in favor of the citizen. As Justice Douglas noted in *Ullmann*, "[T]he Framers put it beyond the power of Congress to *compel* anyone to confess his crimes.... [They] decreed that the law could not be used to pry open one's lips and make him a witness against himself."

Senate

"No one is to disturb another in his speech by hissing, coughing, spitting, speaking or whispering to another; nor to stand up or interrupt him; nor to pass between the Speaker and the speaking member; nor to go across the house, or to walk up and down it, or to take books or papers from the table, or write there." So states section 17.12, Order in Debate, of *A Manual of Parliamentary Practice for the Use of the Senate of the United States* (1801), compiled by THOMAS JEFFERSON, which is still used by the Senate today. The upper house of CONGRESS, the Senate of the United States—consisting of one hundred members, two from each of the fifty states—has struck some observers as resembling, more than anything else, an exclusive club.

At the beginning of the Roman Republic in 509 B.C.E., the Roman senate included some three hundred highly regarded, upper-class citizens appointed for life. This body, which ruled Rome after the last king was expelled and continued to the end of the Roman Empire, had both legislative and administrative functions. Like the United States, several other nations have drawn from this august body a similar name for the upper house of their national legislature—in France called the *senat* and in Italy the *senato*.

Structure of the Senate

The Senate created by the FRAMERS OF THE CONSTITUTION was intended to have a more aristocratic character than the lower HOUSE OF REPRESENTATIVES, especially in its original form, when senators

Henry Clay addresses the Senate during debates leading to the "Great Compromise" of 1850 in this engraving executed about five years afterward. The Kentucky senator spoke seventy times in favor of the bill to restrict the growth of slave states.
Source: Library of Congress

were chosen by their state legislatures rather than by popular election (changed by the Seventeenth Amendment, ratified in 1913). A product of the "Great Compromise" at the CONSTITUTIONAL CONVENTION OF 1787, the Senate represented a way to recognize the equality of the semisovereign STATES: each state, regardless of size, wealth, or population, could send two members to the Senate, and all senators had an equal vote. Its composition also helped assuage fears of the smaller states that Congress would be dominated by the larger states. Under one original proposal, the Virginia Plan (see pages 622–623), senators would have been selected by the House of Representatives from lists of candidates. Roger Sherman of Connecticut eventually proposed the compromise solution that was adopted. As JAMES MADISON explained in essay 39 of *The Federalist* (1787–88) (see FEDERALIST PAPERS), "The Senate…will derive its powers from the States as political and coequal societies; and these will be represented on the principle of equality in the Senate, as they are now in the existing Congress [under the ARTICLES OF CONFEDERATION]."

Qualifications of Senators. "No Person shall be a Senator," states Article I, section 3, "who shall not have attained to the Age of thirty Years, and been nine Years a Citizen of the United States, and who shall not, when elected, be an Inhabitant of that State for which he shall be chosen." According

COMMITTEES OF THE U.S. SENATE

STANDING COMMITTEES

Standing committees generally have legislative jurisdiction. Their subcommittees are responsible for specific subject areas. The chairs and a majority of members are appointed by the majority party.

Agriculture, Nutrition, and Forestry
Appropriations
Armed Services
Banking, Housing, and Urban Affairs
Budget
Commerce, Science, and Transportation
Energy and Natural Resources
Environment and Public Works
Finance
Foreign Relations
Health, Education, Labor, and Pensions
Homeland Security and Governmental Affairs
Judiciary
Rules and Administration
Small Business and Entrepreneurship
Veterans' Affairs

SELECT COMMITTEES

Select and joint committees conduct primarily oversight or housekeeping responsibilities.

Ethics
Indian Affairs
Intelligence

SPECIAL COMMITTEE

Aging

JOINT COMMITTEES WITH THE HOUSE OF REPRESENTATIVES

Economic
Library
Printing
Taxation

SOURCE: *The World Almanac and Book of Facts.* New York: World Almanac Books, 2002. As updated by author.

to Madison in essay 62 of *The Federalist*, "The term of nine years appears to be a prudent mediocrity between a total exclusion of adopted citizens, whose merits and talents may claim a share in the public confidence, and an indiscriminate and hasty admission of them, which might create a channel for foreign influence on the national councils." The additional five-year age requirement beyond that required for House members reflects the Senate's more conservative and more deliberative nature, as desired by the framers. "The Senators," adds Article VI, "...shall be bound by Oath or Affirmation, to support this Constitution; but no religious Test shall ever be required as a Qualification...."

Elections. Before the Seventeenth Amendment's adoption in 1913, Article I, section 3, provided a different method for selection of senators: "The Senate of the United States shall be composed of Two Senators from each State, chosen by the Legislature thereof, for six Years; and each Senator shall have one Vote." A number of scandals involving payments for seats in the Senate and the fact that most states had decided to elect their senators resulted in the constitutional amendment, which required senators to be "from each State, elected by the people thereof...." The original constitutional requirement that senators' terms be staggered "so that," according to Article I, section 3, "one third may be chosen every second Year" was left unchanged.

"The Times, Places and Manner of holding Elections for Senators and Representatives," states Article I, section 4, "shall be prescribed in each State by the Legislature thereof; but the Congress may at any time by Law make or alter such Regulations, except as to the Places [voting sites] of chusing Senators." As Article I, section 5, specifies, "Each House shall be the Judge of the Elections, Returns and Qualifications of its own Members...." Article V, concerned with procedures for amending the Constitution, guarantees "that no State, without its Consent, shall be deprived of its equal Suffrage in the Senate."

The Seventeenth Amendment provides for filling vacancies in the Senate. "When vacancies happen in the representation of any State in the Senate, the executive authority [governor] of such State shall issue writs of election to fill such vacancies: *Provided,* That the legislature of any State may empower the executive thereof to make temporary appointments until the people fill the vacancies by election as the legislature may direct."

Officers. Article I, section 3, mandates: "The Vice President of the United States shall be President of the Senate, but shall have no Vote, unless they be equally divided." As a rule the VICE

PRESIDENT performs his duties only on ceremonial occasions, such as the president's annual State of the Union speech or when exercising his right to break a tie vote. A number of other national legislatures also give the presiding officer a "casting" vote only in the case of a tie among members. "The Senate shall chuse their other Officers," Section 3 also notes, "and also a President pro tempore, in the Absence of the Vice President, or when he shall exercise the Office of President of the United States."

The role of the president pro tempore (often simply called president pro tem) is limited to presiding over floor debates or selecting a substitute for that purpose. The job is usually given to the member of the majority party with the most seniority, although that senator has no political power in terms of controlling the legislative agenda or other Senate activities. The Senate majority leader, chosen by the members of the political party holding the majority of seats in the Senate, is responsible for the legislative agenda.

Quorum and Rules. Article I, section 4, requires that Congress "assemble at least once in every Year," and pursuant to section 2 of the Twentieth Amendment (1933), "such meeting shall begin at noon on the 3d day of January, unless they shall by law appoint a different day." Article I, section 5, mandates: "Neither House, during the Session of Congress, shall, without the Consent of the other, adjourn for more than three days, nor to any other Place than that in which the two Houses shall be sitting."

A majority, as defined in Article I, section 5, "…shall constitute a Quorum to do Business; but a smaller Number may adjourn from day to day, and may be authorized to compel the Attendance of absent Members, in such Manner, and under such Penalties as each House may provide." This section also permits each house to determine its own rules of procedure and punish "Members for disorderly Behaviour, and, with the Concurrence of two thirds, expel a Member."

"Each House shall keep a Journal of its Proceedings," states Article I, section 5, "and from time to time publish the same, excepting such Parts as may in their judgment require Secrecy; and the Yeas and Nays of the Members of either House on any question shall, at the Desire of one fifth of those Present, be entered on the Journal" (the *Congressional Record*). Until 1795 the Senate held all its sessions in secret, in part because of their lack of any citizen constituency and because of their role in advising the president on nominations and treaties. Criticism by the press led to a change in this policy.

The Senate has a unique rule that perhaps can be rationalized on the grounds that one of its purposes is to be a check on the excesses of majoritarian democracy (see MAJORITY RULE). Called cloture, this procedure is a motion to close debate on a matter and requires the approval of a supermajority of sixty of the one hundred senators. One result of cloture is the filibuster—a tactic by which a senator refuses to yield the floor, continuing to speak for hours on end in hopes of wearing down the opposition. The use of the threat of a filibuster has been growing. In 2007, the first year of the 110th Congress, there were seventy-two motions to stop filibusters, compared to sixty-eight in the two preceding years, and just five such votes in the 1967–1968 session.

Compensation and Immunity. Article I, section 6, provides that senators, like representatives, are entitled to compensation for their services. Currently the base pay is $169,300, which represents more than a fifty percent increase since 1990 (see COMPENSATION OF OFFICIALS); Senate leaders earn $188,100 per annum. Senators are also granted certain privileges and immunities, such as from arrest, except in the case of "Treason, Felony and Breach of the Peace…and for any Speech or Debate in either House, they shall not be questioned in any other Place." Both senators and representatives are prohibited from holding any other national public office during their term of office.

Committees. Like the House, the Senate has committees that are responsible for reviewing proposed measures and reporting on them to the entire body. Standing committees, of which there are eighteen, are assigned specific legislative jurisdiction, while their multiple subcommittees handle

While many senators have considerable tenure, none has ever rivaled Democrat Robert C. Byrd of West Virginia. First elected in 1958, Byrd in 2006 became the longest-serving member in the history of the Senate with more than 17,000 days of service.

Byrd's devotion to the Senate, and the Constitution, is legendary. When Republicans championed their "Contract with America," a list of conservative priorities, in the 1990s, Byrd pulled out a well-worn copy of the Constitution and declared, "This is *my* contract with America."

Byrd has faced criticism for his flowery and long-winded speeches, as well as his zealous pursuit of federal dollars for his home state. He has publically regretted some of his past actions, such as joining the Ku Klux Klan as a young man. But Republicans and Democrats alike admire his mastery of Senate rules and procedures.

During the impeachment trial of President Bill Clinton in 1999, members of both parties looked to Byrd for guidance. Republican Mitch McConnell said, "I'm going to take my cues from Senator Byrd. I think he's the expert."

Robert C. Byrd.
Source: CQ Photo/Scott J. Ferrell

work in specific areas. Committees on appropriations, armed services, foreign relations, and other government concerns review and approve proposed legislation and hold oversight hearings to provide accountability for operations of the executive and judicial branches. Select committees, such as the Senate Select Committee on Intelligence, also provide oversight of targeted government endeavors. The House and Senate additionally cooperate on a number of joint committees, such as on government printing, and ad hoc conference committees to resolve differences in bills passed by each house.

Political Parties. The Senate, also like the House, has evolved a number of procedures not addressed in the Constitution, such as its organization after each election by the majority party or, as happened in 2001, by one party and a newly independent senator no longer affiliated with either major party (see POLITICAL PARTIES). The two major positions in the Senate, in addition to the constitutional positions of president of the Senate (the U.S. vice president) and president pro tempore, are majority leader and minority leader. The majority leader, being able to command a majority of votes, sets the agenda generally in consultation with the senators from his party. Similarly, the majority party picks the committee chairs, who direct the work and tone of their respective committees.

Legislation

The Senate's primary responsibility is to participate in the process of enacting LEGISLATION. Except for "Bills for raising Revenue," according to Article I, section 7 (see TAXATION), the Senate has the same powers as the House of Representatives to introduce bills, add amendments, and pass laws. Bills introduced and passed in the Senate are then sent to the House for its action; bills introduced and passed in the House are similarly sent to the Senate for action. Thereafter, all bills passed by both houses in identical form are transmitted to the PRESIDENT for his signature. The Senate and House may override any presidential veto by a two-thirds vote in each house (see VETOES).

Even the constitutional restriction against introducing tax bills did not stop the Senate in 1982 from introducing the largest peacetime tax increase, by way of an amendment to a relatively minor tax bill passed by the House and sent to the Senate.

Advice and Consent

In addition to carrying out its legislative powers, the Senate must approve certain appointments of the president, including AMBASSADORS, members of the SUPREME COURT, "and all other Officers of the United States whose Appointments are not herein otherwise provided for, and which shall be established by Law," as specified in Article II, section 2 (see APPOINTMENT AND REMOVAL POWER). Congress may, however, permit the president alone to appoint inferior officers. The Senate is given an additional role under Article II, section 2, which provides that the president "shall have Power, by and with the Advice and Consent of the Senate, to make Treaties, provided two thirds of the Senators present concur" (see TREATIES).

The framers of the Constitution believed that the Senate, being further removed from the people and the popular election process as well as being more representative of the states' interests, would be best suited to approve presidential appointments and treaties. The importance of "avoiding entangling alliances," as GEORGE WASHINGTON would later warn against, also led them to require a two-thirds vote by the Senate for RATIFICATION of treaties. Not all treaties require Senate approval, however. The president's power in FOREIGN AFFAIRS and as commander in chief of the ARMED FORCES gives him the authority to make executive agreements that, while they do not supercede existing law as do treaties ratified by the Senate, can accomplish many of the same goals as a formal treaty. Congress may even authorize such agreements and lesser treaties.

Presidential Elections

Article II of the Constitution bases the number of presidential electors on the number of representatives and senators allocated to each state; but, according to Article II, section 1, neither senators nor representatives can serve in the ELECTORAL COLLEGE.

The Twelfth Amendment (1804) changed the procedure for certifying the election of the president and vice president, who now run together on a political party ticket. The votes of the electoral college must be certified and sent to the "President of the Senate;—[who] shall, in the presence of the Senate and House of Representatives, open all the certificates and the votes shall then be counted." The House of Representatives is given the responsibility of electing a president if neither candidate reaches a majority of electoral votes, and the Senate plays the same role for the vice president. In that case, "from the two highest numbers on the list, the Senate shall choose the Vice President; a quorum for the purpose shall consist of two-thirds of the whole number of Senators, and a majority of the whole number shall be necessary to a choice." In section 4, the Twentieth Amendment (1933) authorizes Congress to provide "for the case of the death of any of the persons from whom the Senate may choose a Vice President whenever the right of choice shall have devolved upon them." If the office of vice president becomes vacant, the president, according to the Twenty-fifth Amendment (1967), nominates a candidate who must be confirmed by both the Senate and House. Under this amendment, Gerald R. Ford (1913–2006) and Nelson Rockefeller (1908–79) were appointed vice president in 1973 and 1974, respectively.

Impeachment

"The Senate," instructs Article I, section 3, "shall have the sole power to try all Impeachments" (see IMPEACHMENT). This requirement is similar to the role given the House of Lords in the British Parliament, and the constitutions of a number of other nations have similar provisions. "When sitting for that Purpose, they shall be on Oath or Affirmation. When the President of the United States is tried, the Chief Justice shall preside: And no person shall be convicted without the concurrence of two thirds of the Members present." The Senate has failed to return a verdict of impeachment against the only two presidents ever charged by the House of Representatives: Andrew Johnson (1808–75) in 1868 and Bill Clinton (b. 1946) in 1999.

For better or for worse, the Senate has been a more restraining force in the nation's government. A salutary role in promoting constitutionalism and civil rights has been lacking. However, the framers designed Congress's upper house to act as a brake on overzealous popular legislative initiatives, and in this sense it has generally served its function well.

"Separate but Equal" See BROWN V. BOARD OF EDUCATION OF TOPEKA; RACIAL DISCRIMINATION; SEGREGATION.

Separation of Church and State See RELIGION.

Separation of Powers

Many of the FRAMERS OF THE CONSTITUTION were familiar with the works of Plato, Aristotle, and Montesquieu, all of whom called for government authority to be divided into distinct spheres. A balance of power is needed, said the Greek philosopher Plato (ca. 427–347 B.C.E.) in *The Laws,* to check the possible concentration of power in the hands of one person. Aristotle (384–322 B.C.E.), who studied at Plato's academy, declared in *The Politics*: "All constitutions have three elements…. There is one element which deliberates about public affairs; secondly that is concerned with the magistracies…; and thirdly that which has judicial power." He concluded that "[w]hen they are well-ordered, the constitution is well-ordered…." In *The Spirit of the Laws* (1748), the French jurist Charles-Louis de Secondat, Baron de La Bréde et de Montesquieu (1689–1755), identified legislative, executive, and judicial functions as separate powers of government under the British constitution.

The delegates to the CONSTITUTIONAL CONVENTION OF 1787 had seen that after the DECLARATION OF INDEPENDENCE (1776) was signed, the newly independent states tended to invest their legislatures with the bulk of GOVERNMENT powers, thus diluting the important checks and balances needed to protect against improper acts. JAMES MADISON, called the "Father of the Constitution," quoted Montesquieu in essay 47 of *The Federalist* (1787–88) (see FEDERALIST PAPERS) to the effect that there can be no LIBERTY where a nation's legislative and executive powers are fused in one person or body or where the judicial power is not separated from the other two. Later in essay 51 of *The Federalist,* Madison argued: "Ambition must be made to counteract ambition." This means "supplying, by opposite and rival interests, the defect of better motives…[with] distributions of power where the constant aim is to divide and arrange the several offices in such a manner as that each may be a check on the other."

The Constitution does not state the principle of the separation of government powers in so many words, but the concept is evident throughout the document.

The Constitution does not state the principle of the separation of government powers in so many words, but the concept is evident throughout the document, particularly in the fact that Articles I, II, and III deal with, respectively, CONGRESS (the LEGISLATIVE BRANCH), the PRESIDENT (the EXECUTIVE BRANCH), and the COURTS (the JUDICIAL BRANCH). The framers seem to have addressed these three powers as if they were indeed separate physical entities but ones that nevertheless must interact to implement the will of the people in governing the nation; at the same time they provide checks and balances on one another to prevent anarchy or tyranny. The framers' description of the interaction among the separate powers of government bears some similarity to the previous century's mathematical works of Sir Isaac Newton (1642–1727), in which he described how the balance of gravitational forces of the sun and the planets acts to keep the dynamic solar system stable and functioning harmoniously.

America's federal system of government, which creates another form of separation of powers between the national and the state spheres of SOVEREIGNTY, also contains elements of checks and balances. An example of this is the method used to select the electors of the president through the ELECTORAL COLLEGE, which is placed in the hands of the state legislatures, not with the national government. The states can also act as a check on the federal government through the requirement that the Senate, which represents the states, approves all federal laws; that it gives its ADVICE AND CONSENT to presidential appointments (see APPOINTMENT AND REMOVAL POWER); and that a two-thirds majority approves major TREATIES. The requirement that proposed constitutional AMENDMENTS be approved by the states constitutes another check.

Overlap of Powers

For the checks-and-balances system at the national level to work, there can be no absolute separation of powers. In his dissent in *Springer v. Government of the Philippine Islands* (1928), Justice OLIVER WENDELL HOLMES JR. noted that "however we may disguise it by veiling words we do not and cannot carry out the distinction between the legislative and executive branches with mathematical precision and divide the branches into watertight compartments...." For most of American history the courts have had to arbitrate the drawing of lines between the separate branches of government.

A particularly apt example of how the Constitution changed the traditional concept of national government—as exemplified by the British parliamentary system—is reflected in Article I, section 6, known as the incompatibility clause. In a parliamentary system of government, the executive functions are generally carried out by elected members of the legislature: the prime minister and cabinet ministers. Section 6 of the U.S. Constitution, however, states that "no Person holding any Office under the United States, shall be a Member of either House during his Continuance in Office."

The separation of powers doctrine also restricts the ability of Congress to delegate powers to executive branch officials. The Supreme Court ruled in *Bowsher v. Synar* (1986) that Congress cannot entrust the power to make final BUDGET cuts—an executive function—to the comptroller general, who heads the Government Accountability Office (formerly the General Accounting Office)—part of the legislative branch—but it could authorize the president to do so. Because Article I, section 1, declares, "All legislative Powers herein granted shall be vested in a Congress...," it would appear logical that no one else may have or exercise them. But, although the Court has said that "the legislative power of Congress cannot be delegated," it has in fact upheld broad and poorly defined delegations of power to ADMINISTRATIVE AGENCIES.

Yet the most obvious example of how the powers overlap in the implementation of checks and balances is the president's veto power over LEGISLATION passed by Congress (see VETOES). The British Parliament consists of two chambers—the House of Commons (lower house) and the House of Lords (upper house)—and the monarch. For most acts of Parliament to be effective, the monarch's assent is necessary and thus represents the monarch's theoretical veto power. The presidential veto reflects this historical power of the monarch, although it may be overridden by two-thirds of the members of each house of Congress.

The separation and overlap of powers and functions without many sharp distinctions have permitted the Supreme Court to virtually pick and chose which side to come down on, depending on the disposition of a majority of its members. Some areas, such as the president's supreme role in the conduct of FOREIGN AFFAIRS, have been given wide latitude by the Court. But it has upheld Congress's imposition of restrictions on the president's power to remove members of independent agencies and, more recently, found that a sitting president is not immune from a civil suit while in office.

Court Tests of the Principle

Two important cases involving the separation of powers have involved the "legislative veto" and the line-item veto. In *Immigration and Naturalization Service v. Chadha* (1983), the Supreme Court held that a scheme by Congress to reserve the right to review regulations of administrative agencies violated the separation of legislative and executive functions. And in *Clinton v. City of New York* (1998), an attempt by Congress to authorize the president to exercise a line-item veto in money bills was invalidated as beyond the procedures for enacting legislation expressly set forth in Article I, section 7. More recently, in *United States v. Booker* (2005), the Supreme Court struck down the mandatory aspects of the Federal Sentencing Guidelines, stating that requiring the sentencing factors in the guidelines to be proved to a jury beyond a reasonable doubt would be tantamount to "defining elements of criminal offenses"; and, since the factors were established by the U.S. Sentencing Commission and not Congress directly, the result would be a violation of the separation of powers, because defining "criminal elements" is an "inherently legislative" power.

Court actions are being filed with increasing frequency by one branch against another. However, the extent to which courts should be used to settle political disputes between the executive and legislative branches is an open question. Although the courts can rely on the political question doctrine—that the Constitution contemplates that some disputes are to be settled politically rather than judicially—aggressive courts may seize the opportunity to make a political impact outside the scope of their judicial authority. While opinions of judicial overreach in specific cases often vary according to critics' political allegiances, a case that generated substantial controversy in recent years was BUSH V. GORE (2000). In that case, a bare majority on the Supreme Court determined the winner of the 2000 presidential election, instead of sending the case to the House of Representatives, as allowed for in the Constitution.

In addition to the formal checks and balances in the Constitution, the guarantee of a free press added by the First Amendment (1791) (see THE PRESS) and the growth of the two-party system (see POLITICAL PARTIES) also act as checks on the national and state governments and help balance the powers of the government. The press, for example, can investigate and publish critical findings concerning corruption or abuses of power in government, and the political party out of power can maintain a public debate as to the wisdom and constitutionality of actions by the party in power. The WATERGATE scandal of the 1970s is a good example of how the press and the opposition party uncovered and made public abuses of power by President Richard M. Nixon (1913–94). However, the Supreme Court in *Cheney v. District Court for the District of Columbia* (2004) distinguished its ruling in *United States v. Nixon* (1974) and found that Vice President Dick Cheney did not have to turn over "all documents" relating to meetings he had in 2001 with individuals concerning the formulation of the Bush administration's energy policy. The Court noted that the U.S Court of Appeals should have considered "whether the District Court's actions constituted an unwarranted impairment of another branch in the performance of its constitutional duties."

War on Terror

Several recent cases since the terrorist attacks on the United States on September 11, 2001, and the subsequent declaration of a war on terror have brought into sharp relief the doctrine of the horizontal separation of powers between the three branches of the national government, in particular the separation between the executive and judicial branches. For example, in *Hamdan v.*

Rumsfeld (2006), the U.S. Supreme Court decided what some legal scholars are saying may be the most important constitutional law decision regarding presidential powers during wartime since YOUNGSTOWN SHEET & TUBE CO. V. SAWYER (1952). In *Hamdan*, the Court struck down the president's attempt to remove the trial of prisoners in the war on terror from the courts to military tribunals. A majority of the Court, echoing the opinion of Chief Justice JOHN MARSHALL in *Little v. Barreme* (1804—one of the so-called Quasi-War Cases), found in *Hamdan* that the president could not disregard the constitutionally valid limitation that Congress placed on his authority during wartime.

Time will tell as to how far Congress and the courts will go to either extend or rein in the powers of the presidency during the war on terror. The dynamic tension created by the Constitution with regard to checks and balances and the separation and overlapping nature of the American system of government will continue to evolve in light of both our history and the exigencies of the future.

More on this topic:
Advice and Consent, p. 18
Appointment and Removal Power, p. 39
Federalism, p. 218
Government, p. 258

Seventeenth Amendment *See* SENATE.

Seventh Amendment *See* COMMON LAW; JURIES; TRIALS.

Sex Discrimination

Sex is mentioned only once in the Constitution. The Nineteenth Amendment (1920), ratified after decades of pressure by women's rights proponents such as SUSAN B. ANTHONY, declares: "The right of citizens of the United States to vote shall not be denied or abridged by the United States or by any State on account of sex. Congress shall have power to enforce this article by appropriate legislation." A proposed constitutional amendment granting equal rights to WOMEN in all aspects of their lives—the Equal Rights Amendment, passed by Congress in 1972—failed to obtain approval by a sufficient number of state legislatures, as required under Article V of the Constitution (see AMENDMENTS; RATIFICATION), within the ten-year period allowed by Congress.

Many other national constitutions, including those of Canada (1867, amended 1982), Germany (1949), and Sweden (1975), expressly ban discrimination on the basis of sex, as do some international human rights documents, such as the Universal Declaration of Human Rights (1948) and the Convention on the Elimination of All Forms of Discrimination against Women (1979). According to the latter, "[T]he term 'discrimination against women' shall mean any distinction, exclusion or restriction made on the basis of sex which has the effect or purpose of impairing or nullifying the recognition, enjoyment or exercise by women, irrespective of their marital status, on a basis of equality of men and women, of human rights and fundamental freedoms in the political, economic, social, cultural, civil or any other field."

Equality Denied

In theory, the Constitution is supposed to treat men and women equally, except in certain cases of rational distinctions between them, but in a number of areas women have suffered and continue to suffer from DISCRIMINATION on the basis of their sex. Sex discrimination can take many forms, blatant or subtle, and can be based on male chauvinism, stereotyping, or even overprotection. Women have been discriminated against with respect to political, civil, legal, marital, and parental rights; employment, including in hiring, pay, promotion, job assignments, benefits, and sexual harassment on the job; government programs; education; and sports.

Many of the earlier distinctions drawn by the Supreme Court to rationalize decisions denying women equality with men seem completely irrational today. Rejecting the attempt of Myra Bradwell (1831–94) to be licensed as an attorney in Illinois in 1873, Justice Joseph P. Bradley (1813–92) suggested in the Court's decision in *Bradwell v. Illinois*, "The natural and proper timidity and delicacy which belongs to the female sex evidently unfits it for many of the occupations of civil life." In 1948 Justice Felix Frankfurter (1882–1965) pontificated for the Court in *Goesaert v. Cleary* (1948) on its refusal to allow a woman to be a bartender: "The Constitution does not require legislatures to reflect sociological insight, or shifting social standards, any more than it requires them to keep abreast of the latest scientific standards."

After ratification of the Nineteenth Amendment finally granting women the right to vote and hold public office, the nine male justices of the Supreme Court still could not bring themselves to find equality for women on an equal footing with men. In *Fay v. New York* (1947), the Court concluded that the right to vote was the only right given to women by the Constitution. And in *Hoyt v. Florida* (1961), it held that the state legislature had a rational basis for limiting women to voluntary jury duty and disqualifying them from the same obligation to serve on a jury as men were required to do.

In *Reed v. Reed* (1971), however, the Supreme Court unanimously struck down a state law requiring probate courts to give preference to men to be the administrators of estates of deceased persons. Undoubtedly the justices were responding to the women's rights movement, which was gaining momentum in the country at the time. The Court continued to strike down laws that irrationally discriminated against women in a number of subsequent cases.

Beyond the ERA

Following the lead of the CIVIL RIGHTS movement in the 1960s, the feminist movement became a strong social force in the 1970s. By 1972 women and their supporters had succeeded in pressuring Congress to pass the Equal Rights Amendment, forty-nine years after it was first introduced, to constitutionally prohibit discrimination on the basis of sex. It read simply: "Equality of rights under the law shall not be denied or abridged by the United States or by any State on account of sex." Congress required that the ERA be ratified in seven years by three-fourths of the state legislatures, but when the initial time span expired and the amendment had not garnered the necessary thirty-eight state ratifications, the period was extended for another three years. The amendment still failed to gain ratification, in part because many state legislatures were dominated by more rural and less liberal members whose constituents did not sympathize with the ERA's goals. However, not all constitutional AMENDMENTS

Demonstrators in 1977 protest against ratification of the Equal Rights Amendment.
Source: Library of Congress

carry a similar time limit for approval; the time set was apparently a political, as opposed to legal, decision.

Despite the failure of the Equal Rights Amendment, the women's rights movement continued to have some influence on legislation and the courts' constitutional analysis of cases involving discrimination against women. In 1963 Congress enacted the Equal Pay Act and passed the Civil Rights Act (1964) a year later, Title VII of which expanded prohibitions against EMPLOYMENT DISCRIMINATION on the basis of sex. The Supreme Court would use Title VII as the basis for rejecting policies of private and public employers that discriminated against women. Several cases under Title VII that came before the Supreme Court in the 1980s and 1990s dealt with sexual harassment of women in the workplace. In *Harris v. Forklift Systems, Inc.* (1993), a woman who had been divorced four times was subjected to sexual harassment and other degrading treatment by the company president. In her opinion for the Court, Justice SANDRA DAY O'CONNOR held that it was not necessary to prove psychological damage to establish harassment and the creation of a hostile work environment or even that the victim's work performance had suffered from the treatment—a court could examine the type and frequency of the alleged acts to conclude if sexual discrimination had taken place.

In addition to the provision of Title VII against employment discrimination, an anti-retaliation provision forbids "discriminat[ion] against" an employee or job applicant who, among other things, has "made a charge, testified, assisted, or participated in" a Title VII proceeding or investigation. The Supreme Court, in *Burlington Northern & Santa Fe Railway Co. v. White* (2006), ruled that the anti-retaliation provision was not limited to specific actions or harms as described in the employment discrimination provision, and, therefore, it was reasonable for a jury to conclude that an indefinite suspension could act as a deterrent to filing a discrimination complaint, even if the employee eventually received back pay for the time she was suspended from work.

The new laws and the momentum of the equal rights movement led the Supreme Court in *Craig v. Boren* (1976) to hold that a higher standard of judicial scrutiny—although not as high as STRICT SCRUTINY used in RACIAL DISCRIMINATION cases, however—was needed to analyze the constitutionality of legislation that on its face discriminated against women. The heightened scrutiny was used to determine if any suspect classification or distinction made between men and women substantially furthered some important government objectives. Ironically, in *Craig* the Court struck down a state liquor law that discriminated against males.

Heightened scrutiny gives the courts more flexibility in analyzing sex discrimination cases against either women or men and thus avoids any judicial deference to legislators or any presumption that there is a rational basis for such discrimination. Cases involving statutory classifications on the basis of race or ethnicity, in contrast, are accorded a higher level of scrutiny based on an automatic presumption of discrimination (see MINORITIES).

In addition to using this heightened scrutiny, the Supreme Court also began to look at the impact of seemingly gender-neutral factual classifications. For example, is it discriminatory for a health insurance company to charge women higher rates simply because as a class, on the basis of actuarial tables, they tend to live longer than men and thus will receive benefits for a longer period of time on the average? The Court's ruling in several cases indicates that taking any factors into consideration other than age may be discriminatory. With respect to the ARMED FORCES, however, the Courts have generally upheld discrimination against women in draft registration as well as provision of veterans' benefits that generally favor men.

In *Cleveland Board of Education v. La Fleur* (1974), the Supreme Court held that a law requiring pregnant teachers to leave work after a certain number of months, even though they were willing and able to continue working longer, violated the DUE PROCESS clause of the Fourteenth Amendment (1868). And in *United States v. Virginia* (1996), Justice Ruth Bader

Gussie Ann Lord was one of the first women to attend the Virginia Military Institute after the Supreme Court ruled that the institute could not exclude women.
Source: AP Images/Detroit Free Press, Pauline Lubens

Ginsburg (b. 1933), the second woman appointed to the Supreme Court (joining Sandra Day O'Connor), wrote the majority opinion holding that the Virginia Military Institute could not maintain its single-sex—all-male—status under the Fourteenth Amendment's EQUAL PROTECTION clause.

Discrimination against Men

Men too may be discriminated against on the basis of sex. In *Caban v. Mohammed* (1979), the Supreme Court ruled that a law requiring only an unwed mother's consent for the adoption of her child discriminated against the father. But in the same year, in *Parham v. Hughes*, the Court upheld a law that allowed only an unwed mother to recover damages for the wrongful death of her child, unless the father's parentage has been legitimized by a court order.

A major difficulty with trying to set standards for analyzing sex discrimination cases was reflected in *Michael M. v. Superior Court* (1981). California had enacted a statutory rape law that punished a man for having sexual intercourse with an underage female, but it did not punish a woman for relations with an underage male. The Supreme Court, with no clear majority, upheld the law, with Justice William H. Rehnquist (1924–2005) arguing that men lacked a biological deterrent against having sex, while women are inhibited by nature because they know they will suffer the consequences. Justice William J. Brennan Jr. (1906–97), by contrast, found that the law's classification on the basis of sex "was initially designed to further…outmoded stereotypes" in which women cannot be trusted to consent to sexual intercourse but an underage male can make such a decision for himself.

> **More on this topic:**
> Homosexuals, p. 275

Charges of sex discrimination endure, and the government and the courts will continue to face a difficult challenge in interpreting who is discriminating against whom in future constitutional skirmishes.

Sex Offenders

Alfred Kinsey, the groundbreaking author of *Sexual Behavior in the Human Male* (1948) and *Sexual Behavior in the Human Female* (1953), noted that the law often treated crimes relating to sexual offenses differently than other types of crimes, but it was not until Megan's Law—a federal law requiring all fifty states to set up a community notification system for convicted sex offenders—was passed by Congress in 1996 that the difference became a part of the national consciousness. The major difference with respect to sex offenders—as opposed to other perpetrators of crime who are prosecuted, convicted, and sentenced—is that the law in the United States does not treat sex offenders as exempt from additional restrictions on their freedom after they have fulfilled their punishment.

Historically, the punishment of sex offenders has not been all that consistent. William Blackstone (1723–1780), in his *Commentaries on the Laws of England* (1765–1770), indicated that certain acts of lewdness and offenses against decency were generally punished by fines and imprisonment. But during the days of the English Commonwealth (1649–1660) under Oliver Cromwell, "incest and willful adultery were made capital crimes." The restoration of the monarchy ushered in a period of liberalization such that, according to Blackstone, the courts then took "no cognizance of the crime of adultery, otherwise than as a private injury."

Criminals who commit sex crimes, such as rape, for example, and especially violent rape, have generally been subjected to a special type of social stigma; and those who perpetrate such crimes against children even more so. Part of the impetus for the national movement toward greater restrictions on sex offenders is the pro-victim backlash that began in the 1970s after the Supreme Court's decisions in cases like MAPP V. OHIO (1961) and MIRANDA V. ARIZONA (1966). These cases sought to extend rights to suspects accused of crimes. After several national news stories about particularly gruesome sex crimes involving children, laws relating to sex offenders began to increase punishments, including the addition of postconviction restrictions. Before the 1970s sex offenders were often considered sexual psychopaths because psychiatrists could not consistently explain their behavior, but otherwise they generally received no special treatment.

Examples of the additional punishment or restrictions that now apply to sex offenders include registration in states where they reside, participation in behavior modi-

A sex offender parolee in California wears on his ankle a GPS tracking device issued by the Corrections Department. Constant electronic monitoring is a common restriction placed on such offenders after they are released from prison.
Source: AP Images/Jeff Chiu

fication programs, and civil confinement after serving a criminal sentence. The Supreme Court has generally upheld these restrictions. In *Smith v. Doe* (2003), for example, the Court, in a 6–3 decision, held that it was not an ex post facto punishment (see EX POST FACTO LAWS) for a state to retroactively require sex offenders to register with law enforcement agencies and for a portion of such information to be made available to the public. A part of the purpose of the registry is to allow citizens to be aware of potential sexual predators in their neighborhoods.

The Supreme Court in *McKune v. Lile* (2002), with no majority opinion, found that a Kansas sexual offender treatment program, which the offender is required to attend before being released from prison to avoid loss of various privileges, and in which he is required to admit to "having committed the crime for which he is being treated and other past offenses," did not violate the Constitution's protection against SELF-INCRIMINATION. Noting that the prison setting is different from preconviction conditions, Justice Anthony M. Kennedy (b. 1936), writing for the plurality, said that the threat of the loss of privileges "allows prison administrators to provide to those who need treatment the incentive to seek it."

As for civil confinement, the Court in *Kansas v. Hendricks* (1997) upheld, by a 5–4 majority, the Kansas Sexually Violent Predator Act of 1994, which established procedures for the civil commit-

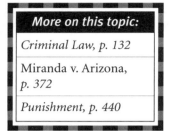

More on this topic:

Criminal Law, p. 132

Miranda v. Arizona, p. 372

Punishment, p. 440

ment of individuals who, because of a "mental abnormality" or a "personality disorder," are likely to engage in "predatory acts of violence." A state law already provided for the involuntary commitment of certain types of mentally ill persons, but the state legislature wanted to strengthen the provisions specifically for sex offenders. Justice Clarence Thomas (b. 1948), in the opinion for the Court, cited *Jacobson v. Massachusetts* (1905) for the proposition that there is no absolute right of liberty under the U.S. Constitution and concluded that involuntary civil commitment did not constitute an additional punishment for Hendricks's crime, but rather was a form of treatment. Justice Kennedy, however, in a concurring opinion, warned states against trying to use civil commitment as "a mechanism for retribution or general deterrence, for example by using civil confinement to increase a sentence that had been reduced as a part of a plea bargain. The Kansas Sexually Violent Predator Act came before the Supreme Court again in 2002 in *Kansas v. Crane*. In that case the Court laid out guidelines for a state seeking to have a sex offender legally determined to be a sexually violent predator.

In 2003 the legislature of Georgia enacted a law that prohibited persons on the state's sex offender registry from living in certain locations, and in 2006 the restrictions were expanded to prohibit such persons from living within 1,000 feet of churches, public or community swimming pools, and school bus stops. The law has been challenged in federal court as a violation of the Constitution on several grounds, including the ex post facto clause, the due process clause, the free exercise of religion clause, the takings clause of the Fifth Amendment (1791), and the Eighth Amendment (1791). A U.S. District Court issued a temporary restraining order to stop the enforcement of the law as it applied to living near churches and school bus stops, pending a decision in the case, titled *Whitaker v. Perdue*.

Florida in 2005 passed the Jessica Lunsford Act to ensure punishment of sex offenders and reduce the possibility of future offenses. The law sets a mandatory minimum sentence of twenty-five years in prison and requires lifetime electronic monitoring of adults convicted of certain sex crimes against victims younger than twelve years old. Jessica's Law was a reaction to the rape and murder of a young Florida girl by a previously convicted sex offender, and it has inspired similar legislation in others states.

Obviously parental fear and moral and social outrage in part have been driving the movement to further restrict convicted sex offenders after they have served their time in prison in order to protect communities from additional sex offenses and to generally deter the commission of such crimes. As indicated here, the law as it is applied to crimes involving sex acts or sexual violence has a long history of being considered a special area in which constitutional guarantees are often less rigorously enforced.

Signers of the Constitution *See* FRAMERS OF THE
CONSTITUTION.

Sixteenth Amendment *See* TAXATION.

Sixth Amendment *See* ASSISTANCE OF COUNSEL; CRIMINAL LAW;
JURIES; TRIALS; WITNESSES.

Slavery

Slavery—legal ownership of another human being as PROPERTY—has until fairly recently been accepted in many cultures, and even today it continues in some forms. The practice existed in ancient Greece, the cradle of DEMOCRACY, and in ancient Rome during the days of the republic and the empire. In fact, the word *liberty* is derived from the Latin *libertas*, which refers to the status of a freed slave (see LIBERTY).

In his draft of the DECLARATION OF INDEPENDENCE (1776), THOMAS JEFFERSON, a slave holder himself, accused George III of England of "violating [the] most sacred rights of life and liberty in the persons of a distant people who never offended him, captivating and carrying them into slavery in another hemisphere...." This language, however, was stricken from the draft at the insistence of the delegates to the Continental Congress from Rhode Island and South Carolina.

Constitutional Compromise

In 1787 the FRAMERS OF THE CONSTITUTION, in order to maintain the union of all thirteen states, compromised on the question of continuing slavery. The language of the Constitution that indirectly reflected this position appears in Article I, section 2: "Representatives and direct Taxes shall be apportioned among the several States which may be included within this Union, according to their respective Numbers, which shall be determined by adding to the whole Number of free Persons, including those bound in Service for a Term of Years, and excluding Indians not taxed, three fifths of all other Persons [slaves]."

In essay 54 of *The Federalist* (1787–88) (see FEDERALIST PAPERS),

Missouri passed an ordinance of emancipation three weeks before the Thirteenth Amendment (1865) was proposed. In this celebratory print a white and an African American child flank the figure of Justice.
Source: Library of Congress

JAMES MADISON, the "Father of the Constitution," explained the basis for the framers' view of the inequality of slaves: "The federal Constitution, therefore, decides with great propriety on the case of our slaves, when it views them in the mixed character of persons and of property. This is in fact their true character. It is the character bestowed on them by the laws under which they live; and it will not be denied that these are the proper criterion; because it is only under the pretext that the laws have transformed the Negroes into subjects of property that a place is disputed them in the computation of numbers; and it is admitted that if the laws were to restore the rights which have been taken away, the Negroes could no longer be refused an equal share of representation with the other inhabitants."

This passage is particularly ambiguous. Madison seems to admit that there is no bar to slaves' becoming CITIZENS of the United States like anyone else, except for the laws that make them slaves. They are human beings like the framers, except that certain laws allow them to be treated other-

EMANCIPATION PROCLAMATION

Whereas on the 22nd day of September, a.d. 1862, a proclamation was issued by the President of the United States, containing, among other things, the following, to wit:

"That on the 1st day of January, a.d. 1863, all persons held as slaves within any State or designated part of a State the people whereof shall then be in rebellion against the United States shall be then, thenceforward, and forever free; and the executive government of the United States, including the military and naval authority thereof, will recognize and maintain the freedom of such persons and will do no act or acts to repress such persons, or any of them, in any efforts they may make for their actual freedom.

"That the executive will on the 1st day of January aforesaid, by proclamation, designate the States and parts of States, if any, in which the people thereof, respectively, shall then be in rebellion against the United States; and the fact that any State or the people thereof shall on that day be in good faith represented in the Congress of the United States by members chosen thereto at elections wherein a majority of the qualified voters of such States shall have participated shall, in the absence of strong countervailing testimony, be deemed conclusive evidence that such State and the people thereof are not then in rebellion against the United States."

Now, therefore, I, Abraham Lincoln, President of the United States, by virtue of the power in me vested as Commander-In-Chief of the Army and Navy of the United States in time of actual armed rebellion against the authority and government of the United States, and as a fit and necessary war measure for supressing said rebellion, do, on this 1st day of January, a.d. 1863, and in accordance with my purpose so to do, publicly proclaimed for the full period of one hundred days from the first day above mentioned, order and designate as the States and parts of States wherein the people thereof, respectively, are this day in rebellion against the United States the following, to wit:

Arkansas, Texas, Louisiana (except the parishes of St. Bernard, Palquemines, Jefferson, St. John, St. Charles, St. James, Ascension, Assumption, Terrebone, Lafourche, St. Mary, St. Martin, and Orleans, including the city of New Orleans), Mississippi, Alabama, Florida, Georgia, South Carolina, North Carolina, and Virginia (except the forty-eight counties designated as West Virginia, and also the counties of Berkeley, Accomac, Northhampton, Elizabeth City, York, Princess Anne, and Norfolk, including the cities of Norfolk and Portsmouth), and which excepted parts are for the present left precisely as if this proclamation were not issued.

And by virtue of the power and for the purpose aforesaid, I do order and declare that all persons held as slaves within said designated States and parts of States are, and henceforward shall be, free; and that the Executive Government of the United States, including the military and naval authorities thereof, will recognize and maintain the freedom of said persons.

And I hereby enjoin upon the people so declared to be free to abstain from all violence, unless in necessary self-defence; and I recommend to them that, in all cases when allowed, they labor faithfully for reasonable wages.

And I further declare and make known that such persons of suitable condition will be received into the armed service of the United States to garrison forts, positions, stations, and other places, and to man vessels of all sorts in said service.

And upon this act, sincerely believed to be an act of justice, warranted by the Constitution upon military necessity, I invoke the considerate judgment of mankind and the gracious favor of Almighty God.

ABRAHAM LINCOLN

SOURCE: The Avalon Project at Yale Law School. Retrieved from www.yale.edu/lawweb/avalon/avalon.htm.

wise. The correctness of those laws, however, is not questioned, and Madison's only intent is to explain why slaves are not counted fully for the purposes of apportionment (see REAPPORTIONMENT) and TAXATION. Clearly the debate over slavery had been settled in the CONSTITUTIONAL CONVENTION OF 1787, and those like Madison who were desperately seeking to have a union of all thirteen states could not rehash this issue before the document's RATIFICATION.

As part of the compromise, however, language was added to the Constitution to allow abolition of the slave trade in the future. Article I, section 9, provides: "The Migration or Importation of such Persons as any of the States now existing shall think proper to admit, shall not be prohibited by the Congress prior to the Year one thousand eight hundred and eight, but a Tax or duty may be imposed on such Importation, not exceeding ten dollars for each Person." Article IV of the original document set forth a duty to "deliver up" any "person held to Service or Labour in one State" who escapes to another, which recognized an unqualified right of a slave owner to repossess his property anywhere in the United States.

The Abolition Movement

Between 1777 and 1804, all of the American states north of Maryland abolished slavery, which was similarly banned in the British Empire in 1807. And then, after a strong plea by President Jefferson, action was taken by Congress on a measure to abolish the slave trade as soon as the Constitution allowed. The Prohibition of the Slave Trade Act (1807), like the Constitution itself, was an ineffective compromise between proslavery and antislavery forces. Later, in 1818 and 1819, stronger measures were taken, but by one informed estimate more than fifty thousand slaves may have been illegally brought into the United States by 1860.

Slavery and the brutal laws applicable only to slaves—who could be treated as animals, beaten and even killed with impunity by slave owners—continued principally in the southern states until the Civil War ended in 1865. Before the war, the federal government did little to effectively address the problem of slavery, and Congress did little to root out the practice. The Fugitive Slave Act (1850) prohibited runaway slaves or any blacks alleged to be slaves from testifying in court or from being granted a jury trial before they were sent back to the slave states, in which they were presumed to be slaves based on their race.

In the infamous Dred Scott case of 1857, *Scott v. Sandford*, the Supreme Court held that no black person, whether free or slave, had any rights under the Constitution. Dred Scott had been taken by his master, a U.S. Army surgeon, to parts of the United States, including Illinois, that prohibited slavery. When he was returned to Missouri, a slave state, he sued in court for his freedom under Missouri legal precedents holding that a slave who had traveled to a free state was consequently emancipated. Increased national activity against slavery changed the complexion of the case, however, and the Missouri Supreme Court summarily rejected the precedents and declared Scott still a slave. The U.S. Supreme Court agreed, saying that "a Negro" was never intended to be included under the word *citizen* in the Constitution and therefore could not claim any of the rights and privileges of U.S. citizenship.

After the war the Thirteenth Amendment (1865) abolished slavery, declaring: "Neither slavery nor involuntary servitude, except as a punishment for crime whereof the party shall have been duly convicted, shall exist within the United States, or any place subject to their jurisdiction." Freed slaves were thereby made citizens of the United States, although adult black women, like white women, were still denied equality with adult male citizens. The Fourteenth Amendment (1868) prohibited the states from abridging the "privileges or immunities" (see PRIVILEGES AND IMMUNITIES) of citizens of the United States or denying "to any person within its jurisdiction the equal protection of the laws" (see EQUAL PROTECTION). The Fifteenth Amendment (1870) expressly protected former male slaves' right to vote, stating: "The right of citizens of the United States to vote shall not be denied or abridged by the United States or by any State on account of race, color, or previous condition of servitude." Many women who had worked for the abolition of slavery had hoped, unsuccessfully, that SEX DISCRIMINATION would similarly be prohibited as a basis for denying any citizen the right to vote. All three amendments authorized Congress to enforce the provisions with appropriate legislation.

Many states in the South continued to find ways to deny African Americans various political, civil (see CIVIL RIGHTS), and social rights. Literacy tests and poll taxes were used to deny blacks voting rights, and "Jim Crow" laws (a reference to a minstrel routine known as "Jump Jim Crow") enforced SEGREGATION of blacks in most public places. In *Plessy v. Ferguson* (1896), the Supreme Court found a way to deny RIGHTS to former slaves and other African Americans by declaring "separate but equal" facilities for blacks to be constitutional. Blatant RACIAL DISCRIMINATION through segregation endured until a new Supreme Court finally reversed its predecessors in *BROWN V. BOARD OF EDUCATION OF TOPEKA* in 1954.

Even after slavery was abolished, black Americans continued to face segregation and other forms of discrimination.
Source: Library of Congress

Not until 1889–90, when a conference was held in Brussels, did the international community act to end the slave trade worldwide. The agreement finally produced, the Slavery Convention (1926), undertook to abolish slave trading and progressively all forms of slavery. Today many international HUMAN RIGHTS agreements and the constitutions of numerous nations—including those of Liberia (1986) and Ecuador (1998), in addition to the United States—expressly prohibit slavery, forced labor, and other forms of involuntary servitude, except as a lawful PUNISHMENT.

The effects of slavery continue to permeate contemporary legal debates about discrimination. Although great strides have been taken to eradicate racial discrimination, highly charged issues such as AFFIRMATIVE ACTION programs, reverse discrimination, and even reparations for the descendants of slaves continue to command a place in public discourse. Sadly, other forms of slavery—prostitution, trafficking in children, and peonage—even today demand attention in the United States and around the world.

Sovereign Immunity   *See* IMMUNITY; SOVEREIGNTY

Sovereignty

The modern concept of sovereignty—the right to govern and set rules for citizens—originated in Europe in the sixteenth and seventeenth centuries with the decline of the Holy Roman Empire and feudalism. In the sixteenth century Jean Bodin (1530–96) of France used Roman law and the development of the French monarchy to expound his theory of the absolute sovereignty of nation-states. Sovereignty, according to Bodin, is "the absolute and perpetual power of a republic, that is to say the active form and personification of the great body of a modern state." It is the power recognized both inside a territorial jurisdiction and outside it by other countries and the international community, representing the right of its rulers, however chosen, to exclusively govern the citizens without being accountable to any other entity.

"Sovereignty in the relation between States signifies independence," explained the arbitrator in the Island of Palmas Case (1928), which involved a dispute between the United States and the Netherlands over the sovereignty of a small island near the Philippines. "Independence in regard to a portion of the globe is the right to exercise therein, to the exclusion of any other State, the functions of a State," he told the Permanent Court of Arbitration.

After World War II and the collapse of the Nazi regime, Germany was occupied by American, British, French, and Soviet forces. But a question arose under INTERNATIONAL LAW: Where did the sovereignty of the defeated and occupied German state reside? Who had authority to exercise it?

In part because of this dilemma—the lack of a valid sovereign authority to act on the country's be-half—no formal peace treaty ever ended the war with Germany.

Some national constitutions expressly mention the concept of sovereignty. "Sovereignty resides in the people, who exercise it through the organs of public power," states the constitution of Ecuador (1998). The preamble to the Indian constitution (1950, amended 1977) proclaims: "We, the people of India, having solemnly resolved to constitute India into a sovereign socialist secular democratic republic...."

Popular Sovereignty

Although not specifically mentioned in the U.S. Constitution, sovereignty plays an important role in our constitutional government. What began as the theoretical underpinning of absolute monarchies centuries ago has evolved into the basis for government of the people, by the people, and for the people. Popular sovereignty was first proclaimed by the DECLARATION OF INDEPENDENCE (1776), which states "that all men are created equal, that they are endowed by their Creator with certain unalienable Rights," adding, "That to secure these rights, Governments are instituted among Men, deriving their just powers from the consent of the governed...." These words closely followed those of GEORGE MASON in the Virginia Declaration of Rights (1776), which asserted that "all power is vested in, and consequently derived from, the people; that magistrates are their trustees and ser-vants, and at all times amenable to them."

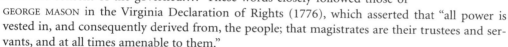

"All power is vested in, and consequently derived from, the people...."

—*George Mason,* in the Virginia Declaration of Rights

At the CONSTITUTIONAL CONVENTION OF 1787, the Pennsylvania delegate James Wilson (see FRAMERS OF THE CONSTITUTION) likewise argued that in the United States sovereignty resides in the people. According to the theory on which the Constitution is based, sovereignty is vested jointly and equally in all citizens, who delegate their sovereign rights and powers to the national and state governments through the national and state constitutions and amendments to them.

The federal system created by the Constitution treats sovereignty as a bundle of RIGHTS and POWERS belonging to the CITIZENS of the United States (see FEDERALISM). For example, sovereign rights or powers to declare WAR and to coin money (see CURRENCY) are delegated to the federal gov-ernment, but the sovereign right to tax citizens is delegated to both the national and state govern-ments (see TAXATION). The sovereign rights to prescribe rules of inheritance, provide public EDU-CATION, and exercise local police and LAW ENFORCEMENT powers, among others, are left up to the STATES. In exchange for receiving funds from the federal government for responsibilities such as schools, however, the states may have to conform to certain federal requirements. "The proposed Constitution," explained ALEXANDER HAMILTON in essay 9 of *The Federalist* (1787–88) (see FEDERAL-IST PAPERS), "so far from implying an abolition of the State governments, makes them constituent parts of the national sovereignty...and leaves in their possession certain exclusive and important portions of sovereign power."

Dual sovereignty is a concept that reflects the separate but equal sovereignty of the national and state governments, much like the concept of federalism itself. For example, states may grant their citizens more extensive rights than does the federal constitution. Such an exercise of state sover-eignty means that the state is in no way subordinate to the federal government within the sphere of its residual sovereignty.

The Ninth and Tenth Amendments (1791), added to the Constitution as part of the BILL OF RIGHTS, reiterate how sovereignty is divided and reserved. "The enumeration in the Constitution, of certain rights," states the Ninth Amendment, "shall not be construed to deny or disparage oth-ers retained by the people." Adds the Tenth Amendment: "The powers not delegated to the United States by the Constitution, nor prohibited by it to the States, are reserved to the States respectively, or to the people." The people can always withdraw some of their sovereign power from institutions of government, and in constitutionally prescribed periodic ELECTIONS and the IMPEACHMENT process, they retain some aspects of the sovereignty of monarchs, including the right to hold their ministers accountable for their stewardship of the people's delegated authority. And as the Declaration of Independence suggested, the people also have the right "to alter or to abolish" their form of government.

National Sovereignty

The question of how to divide up national and state sovereignty was at the heart of the process of creating the CONSTITUTION in 1787. The task was only begun with the Constitution's adoption, however. The SUPREME COURT has since played a major role in establishing the boundaries between national and state sovereignty.

Congress. The Supreme Court held in *GIBBONS V. OGDEN* (1824) that CONGRESS could use its power under the Constitution's COMMERCE clause to invalidate a state law that conflicted with national policy, thereby establishing its national sovereignty over the states. In 1936, in *United States v. Curtiss-Wright Export Corp.*, the Court found that even if the Constitution did not expressly grant a power to a federal agency, it would be implied with respect to FOREIGN AFFAIRS because without such power the United States would simply not be a sovereign nation (see IMPLIED POWERS).

The President. Although the Constitution does not explicitly vest sovereignty in the PRESIDENT, he is generally considered to embody national sovereignty both domestically and internationally because he is the elected head of state with the primary authority to conduct international affairs. In fact, he shares with Congress the right to exercise many sovereign powers. Congress, for example, has the power to declare war and approve appointments of important government officials (see APPOINTMENT AND REMOVAL POWER) and international TREATIES. That the Supreme Court has upheld the president's authority to make treaties on behalf of the nation even without Senate approval indicates that this major aspect of sovereignty is clearly lodged in the chief executive.

State Sovereignty

State sovereignty rests on three key facts: (1) The original thirteen sovereign states created the Constitution itself. (2) Constitutional AMENDMENTS require the approval of a supermajority of the now semisovereign states, confirming the states' power to alter or prevent a change to the Constitution. (3) Government powers within a state's territory that have not been delegated to the federal government or reserved to the citizens are state powers, as confirmed by the Tenth Amendment, and may be exercised by a state to the extent of its sovereign capacity. The Supreme Court has historically protected the rights and powers of the states, only grudgingly conceding an extension of the federal government's powers in certain areas of truly national importance, such as the regulation of commerce and, more recently, the enforcement of CIVIL RIGHTS.

Sometimes labeled STATES' RIGHTS, the sovereignty of the states may be in harmony with national policies or interests or at odds with them. For example, in *Gregory v. Ashcroft* (1991), the Supreme Court, in an opinion by SANDRA DAY O'CONNOR found that a state law requiring the mandatory retirement for most state judges at the age of seventy did not violate the Age Discrimination in Employment Act (1967), because, among other reasons, "congressional interference with the Missouri people's decision to establish a qualification for their judges would upset the usual constitutional balance of federal and state powers" (see AGE DISCRIMINATION). In *United States v. Georgia* (2006), a sharply split Court noted that certain claims against states under the Americans with Disabilities Act of 1990 may not be barred by sovereign immunity, because Congress has power under the Fourteenth Amendment (1868), which incorporates certain other guarantees of the

Constitution (see INCORPORATION DOCTRINE), to enforce its provisions against the states through means that include private suits.

Historically, Native American tribes have been extended sovereign immunity because of the special status of the Indian tribes under the Constitution. As recently as 2003, in *Inyo County v. Paiute-Shoshone Indians*, Justice Ruth Bader Ginsburg (b. 1933), speaking for the Court, noted that for the purposes of the case at bar the Court assumes that Native American tribes are immune from certain civil rights suits due to their separate sovereignty status.

Sovereign Immunity

In an absolute monarchy, the king or queen does not have to suffer the consequences of any of his or her actions or laws. Such sovereign IMMUNITY—based on the notion that because monarchs make the laws, they are above the law—has carried over to the government of a republic like the United States (see REPUBLICAN FORM OF GOVERNMENT). Unless it expressly waives the right of sovereign immunity, therefore, a government's acts cannot be subject to criminal or civil liability.

This doctrine was confirmed by the Supreme Court in *Chisholm v. Georgia* (1793) as an inherent part of our legal system. The sovereign immunity of state governments has been based, somewhat creatively, by the Court on the Eleventh Amendment (1795), which forbids suits "against one of the United States by Citizens of another State, or by Citizens or Subjects of any Foreign State." If a government official acts outside the scope of his or her authority, sovereign immunity does not apply.

The Federal Tort Claims Act (1946) allows citizens to sue the federal government for damages caused by its employees, such as those resulting from automobile accidents. But the Supreme Court confirmed in *United States v. Johnson* (1987) that members of the ARMED FORCES cannot sue the government for injuries they receive while in the military.

The next possible evolutionary step for sovereignty may be the pooling of national sovereignty under INTERNATIONAL LAW, such as European countries have done to form the European Union. This move would permit the formation of a truly global community of nations to secure peace and promote constitutional democracy and HUMAN RIGHTS worldwide.

More on this topic:
Elections, p. 181
Federalism, p. 218
Republican Form of Government, p. 467
Rights, p. 469
States' Rights, p. 520

Speaker of the House

According to Thomas B. "Czar" Reed (1839–1902) (R-Maine), who served as Speaker of the HOUSE OF REPRESENTATIVES for six years between 1889 and 1899, the office of Speaker is "the embodiment of the House, its power and dignity." One of the few federal offices expressly created by the Constitution in addition to the PRESIDENT, VICE PRESIDENT, and CHIEF JUSTICE of the United States and the president pro tempore of the SENATE, the Speaker of the House is second in the line of succession to the presidency after the vice president.

Many other national constitutions create a similar position and title for the presiding officer of the lower (more popularly elected) house of the legislature. The United Kingdom also has a speaker in its Parliament, who presides over the House of Commons, and under the constitutions of Singapore (1974) and Sweden (1975) a speaker is the chief officer of their unicameral national legislatures.

Until the beginning of the nineteenth century, the Speaker of the House of Representatives was not a major power in the federal government. Henry Clay (1777–1852) (D-R, Ky.), who served as

SPEAKERS OF THE HOUSE OF REPRESENTATIVES

Name	Party	State	Tenure
Frederick Muhlenberg	Federalist	Pennsylvania	1789–1791
Jonathan Trumbull	Federalist	Connecticut	1791–1793
Frederick Muhlenberg	Federalist	Pennsylvania	1793–1795
Jonathan Dayton	Federalist	New Jersey	1795–1799
Theodore Sedgwick	Federalist	Massachusetts	1799–1801
Nathaniel Macon	Democratic-Republican	North Carolina	1801–1807
Joseph B. Varnum	Democratic-Republican	Massachusetts	1807–1811
Henry Clay[2]	Democratic-Republican	Kentucky	1811–1814
Langdon Cheves	Democratic-Republican	South Carolina	1814–1815
Henry Clay[2]	Democratic-Republican	Kentucky	1815–1820
John W. Taylor	Democratic	New York	1820–1821
Philip P. Barbour	Democratic-Republican	Virginia	1821–1823
Henry Clay[2]	Democratic-Republican	Kentucky	1823–1825
John W. Taylor	Democratic	New York	1825–1827
Andrew Stevenson	Democratic	Virginia	1827–1834
John Bell	Democratic	Tennessee	1834–1835
James K. Polk	Democratic	Tennessee	1835–1839
Robert M. T. Hunter	Democratic	Virginia	1839–1841
John White	Whig	Kentucky	1841–1843
John W. Jones	Democratic	Virginia	1843–1845
John W. Davis	Democratic	Indiana	1845–1847
Robert C. Winthrop	Whig	Massachusetts	1847–1849
Howell Cobb	Democratic	Georgia	1849–1851
Linn Boyd	Democratic	Kentucky	1851–1855
Nathaniel P. Banks	American	Massachusetts	1856–1857
James L. Orr	Democratic	South Carolina	1857–1859
William Pennington	Republican	New Jersey	1860–1861
Galusha A. Grow	Republican	Pennsylvania	1861–1863
Schuyler Colfax	Republican	Indiana	1863–1869
Theodore M. Pomeroy	Republican	New York	1869
James G. Blaine	Republican	Maine	1869–1875

Speaker from 1811 to 1814, 1815 to 1820, and 1823 to 1825, is credited with significantly increasing the incumbent's power. Increased power, however, led to abuses—preventing legislation from being voted on and appointing cronies as committee chairmen, for example—and members revolted against Speaker Joseph G. Cannon (1836–1926) (R-Ill.) in 1910, seven years after he became Speaker. "Uncle Joe," as Cannon was sometimes called, used his power to make committee assignments to reward loyal cronies and was suspected on occasion of miscounting votes in the House to his advantage. "The 'ayes' make the most noise," he once ruled on a voice vote, "but the 'nays' have it."

The office of Speaker of the House has been filled by a number of men who have served honorably and ably, among them Sam Rayburn (1882–1961) (D-Texas), who was Speaker, except for two two-year periods spent as minority leader, from 1940 until his death in 1961, and Thomas P.

Name	Party	State	Tenure
Michael C. Kerr	Democratic	Indiana	1875–1876
Samuel J. Randall	Democratic	Pennsylvania	1876–1881
Joseph W. Keifer	Republican	Ohio	1881–1883
John G. Carlisle	Democratic	Kentucky	1883–1889
Thomas B. Reed	Republican	Maine	1889–1891
Charles F. Crisp	Democratic	Georgia	1891–1895
Thomas B. Reed	Republican	Maine	1895–1899
David B. Henderson	Republican	Iowa	1899–1903
Joseph G. Cannon	Republican	Illinois	1903–1911
Champ Clark	Democratic	Missouri	1911–1919
Frederick H. Gillett	Republican	Massachusetts	1919–1925
Nicholas Longworth	Republican	Ohio	1925–1931
John N. Garner	Democratic	Texas	1931–1933
Henry T. Rainey	Democratic	Illinois	1933–1935
Joseph W. Byrns	Democratic	Tennessee	1935–1936
William B. Bankhead	Democratic	Alabama	1936–1940
Sam Rayburn[1]	Democratic	Texas	1940–1947
Joseph W. Martin Jr.	Republican	Massachusetts	1947–1949
Sam Rayburn[1]	Democratic	Texas	1949–1953
Joseph W. Martin Jr.	Republican	Massachusetts	1953–1955
Sam Rayburn[1]	Democratic	Texas	1955–1961
John W. McCormack	Democratic	Massachusetts	1962–1971
Carl Albert	Democratic	Oklahoma	1971–1977
Thomas P. O'Neill Jr.[3]	Democratic	Massachusetts	1977–1987
James Wright	Democratic	Texas	1987–1989
Thomas S. Foley	Democratic	Washington	1989–1995
Newt Gingrich	Republican	Georgia	1995–1999
J. Dennis Hastert	Republican	Illinois	1999–2007
Nancy Pelosi	Democrat	California	2007–

SOURCE: *The World Almanac and Book of Facts.* New York: World Almanac Books, 2002. As updated by the author.

1. Longest service (17 years total)
2. Second-longest service (10 years total)
3. Third-longest service (9 years)

"Tip" O'Neill Jr. (1912–94) (D-Mass.), who served from 1977 until his retirement in 1987. Others, however, conducted themselves less than honorably. Jim Wright (b. 1922) (D-Texas) resigned in 1989 under a cloud of financial scandal following a House Ethics Committee report finding sixty-nine violations of House rules. Newt Gingrich (b. 1943) (R-Ga.) removed himself from reelection for the 1999–2000 session to avoid scrutiny concerning his extramarital affair. The "glass dome" of the U.S. Capitol was shattered in 2007 when Nancy Pelosi, the daughter and sister of mayors of Baltimore, Maryland, and a member of Congress from California since 1987, was elected by the House of Representatives as the first woman Speaker of that body.

Every legislative body needs a presiding officer. In Article I, section 2, the Constitution provides that the Speaker of the House of Representatives is to be the presiding officer of the lower house of CONGRESS—the house that the FRAMERS OF THE CONSTITUTION envisioned as being closer

More on this topic:

Legislative Branch, p. 346

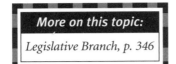

Although enormously powerful, House Speakers are vulnerable to political attacks. In rare cases, they have been forced from office.

Democrat Jim Wright of Texas in 1989 resigned from the speakership amid allegations that he tried to evade congressional rules governing outside earnings. It was the first time in history that a House Speaker was forced by scandal to leave the office in the middle of his term.

One of his main accusers, Rep. Newt Gingrich (R-Ga.), rose to the speakership six years later. But Gingrich, in turn, resigned in 1998 after a series of ethical charges and bruising political battles.

Between those events, Speaker Thomas Foley of Washington suffered a different fate. The Democrat was booted out of office by the voters in 1994—the first time a speaker had been turned out at the polls since the Civil War.

to the people than the upper house: "The House of Representatives shall chuse their Speaker and other Officers...." This selection occurs at the beginning of each two-year session of Congress, starting "at noon on the 3d day of January," according to the Twentieth Amendment (1933) (see LAME DUCKS).

Although not specifically prohibited by the Constitution, no nonmember of the House has ever been named Speaker, who is chosen by the members of the House's majority party (see POLITICAL PARTIES) and then submitted to a formal vote of the whole House. The member who in the last session was the majority or minority leader generally advances to the office of Speaker once that member's party gains a majority in the newly elected House.

The Constitution does not prescribe the Speaker's duties, but they include presiding over sessions of the House, ruling on points of order, referring bills and resolutions to the appropriate committees, setting the agenda for House action on measures including LEGISLATION, and appointing members to select and joint committees, as well as House-Senate conference committees that must reconcile bills when dissimilar acts are passed in each house of Congress on the same subject. Although a Speaker may participate in debate and vote just as any other member of the House, by tradition he or she rarely speaks on the floor of the House, generally votes only in cases of a tie, and does not hold a seat on any House committee.

Under the terms of section 3 of the Twenty-fifth Amendment (1967), which deals with presidential disability, the Speaker of the House, along with the president pro tempore of the Senate, is designated to receive the president's "written declaration that he is unable to discharge the powers and duties of his office." In such a case, the vice president becomes acting president until the Speaker and the president pro tempore receive "a written declaration to the contrary." Under section 4 of the amendment, the Speaker of the House and the president pro tempore are designated to receive any "written declaration that the President is unable to discharge the powers and duties of his office" from "a majority of either the principal officers of the executive departments or of such other body as Congress may by law provide." Again, under such circumstances the vice president becomes acting president until the disability is removed. Thereafter, the Speaker, along with the president pro tempore of the Senate, is designated to receive the declaration of the president "that no inability exists."

Like the other heads of the branches of the national government, success in the office of Speaker of the House depends to a large extent on the incumbent's character and political abilities.

Special Prosecutor *See* INDEPENDENT COUNSEL.

Speech

In his famous funeral speech of 430 B.C.E. commemorating citizens who died in the first year of the Peloponnesian War (431–404 B.C.E.), the Athenian leader Pericles (490–429 B.C.E.), as described by the Greek historian Thucydides (460?–400? B.C.E.), reviewed the requirements for a DEMOCRACY. "Our public men have, besides politics, their private affairs to attend to, and our ordinary citizens, though occupied with their own business, are still fair judges of public matters;

for, unlike any other nation,…we Athenians are at least able to judge,…and instead of looking on discussion as a stumbling-block in the way of action, we think it an indispensable preliminary to any wise action at all."

The faculty of speech sets humans apart from other animals and may be the basis for all of our cognitive functions, including the arts, logic, science, and politics. Clearly the world's first experiment in democracy, as Pericles observed in one of the most famous speeches in history, depended on broad-based discussions of proposals to be carried out by the Athenian government. Such discussions would have been far less productive without the freedom to speak openly and candidly.

The concept of freedom of speech is part of the broader concept of freedom of expression. Freedom of thought or conscience, for example, includes freedom of belief and freedom of religion—as well as the right to be free from religion. Freedom of expression likewise encompasses various modes of communication—oral, written, symbolic, video, and electronic (see COMMUNICATIONS).

The constitutions of many nations contain guarantees of freedom of speech or its equivalent, such as freedom of expression, opinion, or communication. For example, the Declaration of the Rights of Man and of the Citizen (1789), expressly incorporated into France's current constitution (1958), states: "Free communication of ideas and opinions is one of the most precious of the rights of man. Consequently, every citizen may speak, write and print freely; yet he may have to answer for the abuse of that liberty in cases determined by law." The International Covenant on Civil and Political Rights (1966), adopted by the United Nations, guarantees freedom of expression and opinion.

Freedom of Speech

The English Bill of Rights (1688) guaranteed free speech, but only for speech and debate in Parliament. Article I, section 6, of the U.S. Constitution does the same regarding members of CONGRESS: "[F]or any Speech or Debate in either House, they shall not be questioned in any other Place." The guarantee of free speech for the average citizen—at least with respect to the federal government—was added in the First Amendment, made a part of the BILL OF RIGHTS (1791). In addition to rights regarding RELIGION, THE PRESS, public assembly (see ASSEMBLY AND ASSOCIATION), and redress of grievances, the amendment guarantees that "Congress shall make no law…abridging the freedom of speech."

The core right of free speech with regard to the exchange of political ideas is well established in the case law created by the Supreme Court. "The vitality of civil and political institutions in our society depends on free discussion…," Justice William O. Douglas (1898–1980) wrote in his opinion for the Court in *Terminiello v. Chicago* (1949). "The right to speak freely and to promote diversity of ideas and programs is therefore one of the chief distinctions that sets us apart from totalitarian regimes." The Court has also held that the right of free speech includes the right not to speak.

The right of free speech, however, is not absolute. For example, as Justice Oliver Wendell Holmes Jr. explained in *Schenk v. United States* (1919)—a decision that focused on the "clear and present danger" test analysis of limits on freedom of speech—the "most stringent protection of free speech would not protect a man in falsely shouting fire in a theatre and causing a panic." The "clear and present danger" test would be revisited by the Supreme Court in several important cases, including *Gitlow v. New York* (1925) and *Brandenburg v. Ohio* (1969). The Supreme Court has often had to wrestle over which circumstances and government interests provide a basis for infringing freedom of speech. The major battles have been over libel and slander, censorship, prior restraint of publications, obscenity, pornography, symbolic speech, hate speech, broadcasting, and, most recently, the Internet. Also at issue have been the questions of whose freedom of speech is subject to greater restraint and where speech may be con-

> **"[The] most stringent protection of free speech would not protect a man in falsely shouting fire in a theatre and causing a panic."**
>
> **—Justice Oliver Wendell Holmes Jr.,** in *Schenk v. United States* (1919)

stitutionally restricted. The Court has consistently set a higher standard when the government tries to ban or regulate the content of speech than it does when it controls other aspects of speech, such as the time and place where public speech takes place (see PUBLIC FORUMS).

Libel and Slander. Before 1964, the Supreme Court found that COMMON LAW and state laws regarding defamation of character and damage to a person's reputation or business resulting from false or malicious statements, either written (libel) or oral (slander), lay outside the Constitution's free-speech protection. But in NEW YORK TIMES CO. V. SULLIVAN (1964), the Court held that an advertisement in a newspaper criticizing public officials in Montgomery, Alabama, was protected by the First Amendment even though it contained some minor misstatements. The Court's opinion referenced the *Terminiello* case and, citing *N.A.A.C.P. v. Button* (1963), said that where an expression of grievance and protest involved a major public issue of the times—in this case, CIVIL RIGHTS—the constitutional protection does not depend on "the truth, popularity, or social utility of the ideas and beliefs which are offered." However, if a statement is made with actual malice, knowledge that it is false, or reckless disregard for the truth, it loses First Amendment protection.

Censorship and Prior Restraint. CENSORSHIP is the silencing of speech. It is one thing to allow free speech and then punish its abuses; it is another to prevent a person from speaking at all. The long history of American civil disobedience, from the Boston Tea Party in 1773 to the sit-in protests by civil rights advocates in the 1960s, validates the right of conscience, allowing people to speak out or act illegally, knowing full well that such civil disobedience may result in legal PUNISHMENT. Today censorship may involve restraints on employees in sensitive government positions, voluntary codes regarding what is said or shown by the mainstream entertainment industry, blocks on Internet material that may be harmful to children, and removal of publications from libraries and classrooms on the basis that they are deemed unsuitable for students of certain ages.

Prior restraint is a form of censorship in which the government keeps a person from speaking, writing, or publishing certain proscribed material. In *New York Times v. United States* (1971), the PENTAGON PAPERS CASE, the Supreme Court found that the government had not met the "heavy burden" of proving that the country's NATIONAL SECURITY interests outweighed the rights guaranteed under the First Amendment to publish a secret history of the Vietnam War.

Obscenity and Pornography. In *Roth v. United States* (1957)—involving a New York publisher of magazines, photographs, and sexually explicit books by authors such as James Joyce and D.H. Lawrence—the Supreme Court held that OBSCENITY was a form of lower-value speech and thus was not protected by the First Amendment. Obscenity (material that is extremely offensive by contemporary community standards), the justices said, depended or "whether to the average person, applying contemporary community standards, the dominant theme of the material taken as a whole appeals to prurient interest [obsessively interested in improper matters, especially of a sexual nature]."

The Supreme Court has generally held that while hard-core pornography (material depicting erotic behavior that is calculated to cause sexual excitement) can be viewed privately, the state can ban it from being viewed in theaters by adults. In *City of Erie v. Pap's A. M.* (2000), the Court upheld an ordinance in Erie, Pennsylvania, banning public nudity and erotic dancing—expression or symbolic speech—in certain defined public places, in this instance a downtown commercial area. In its opinion the Court referred to the standards set out in *United States v. O'Brien* (1968), in which the justices said that the censoring regulation must further an important or substantial government interest that must be unrelated to the suppression of free expression—content neutral—and the incidental restriction on the freedom must be no greater than necessary to further that interest.

Pornography that may be allowed for adults can be kept out of the hands of minors. An even lower standard of protection is granted to child pornography: the state can outlaw its possession even in the privacy of the home. In 2001 a previously convicted child pornographer was convicted again under an Ohio law for writing down his fantasies about torturing and molesting children, even though they were not disseminated. But in *Ashcroft v. Free Speech Coalition* (2002), the Supreme Court overturned a federal ban on computerized "virtual" child pornography, calling the Child Pornography Protection Act (1996) so broad that it would also prohibit legitimate artistic or political expression.

Symbolic Speech. Because human communication or expression can take many forms, the Supreme Court has had to grapple with which forms of nonverbal speech are protected by the First Amendment. During the Vietnam War, in the *O'Brien* case, the Court upheld a law prohibiting the destruction of draft cards, even by burning them in public to protest the war, because the law's aim of protecting the selective service system was significant enough to override the First Amendment. But in *Tinker v. Des Moines Independent School District* (1969), the Court sanctioned the wearing of black armbands in public schools to protest the war as protected symbolic speech. Burning the American flag in symbolic protest of government policies (see THE FLAG) or otherwise "desecrating the flag" have generally been upheld by the courts because laws forbidding flag desecration have no basis other than to ban the content of the protest. In *Hazelwood School District v. Kuhlmeier* (1988), however, the Court would sidestep the standard set in *Tinker* and hold that a high school newspaper was not a public forum and, therefore, "school officials were entitled to regulate the contents...in any reasonable manner."

In a media-ballyhooed case, *Morse v. Frederick* (2007), a split Supreme Court upheld limitations on students' speech, finding that a school principal who demanded that students participating in a school-authorized event take down a banner that read "BONG HiTS 4 JESUS" did not violate the constitution. Going beyond the Court's analysis in *Tinker*, the opinion in *Morse* focused on the government's policy of educating students against the evils of drug abuse.

Compelled Speech. In a series of cases the Court has had to tackle the questions raised by compelled speech, or the right not to be forced to speak by the government. Beginning with *Minersville School District v. Gobitis* (1940), the Supreme Court found no First Amendment grounds for an exemption from reciting the salute to the flag. But in *West Virginia State Board of Education v. Barnette* (1943), the Court concluded that, indeed, freedom of speech and freedom of worship made the compulsory flag salute and pledge of allegiance unconstitutional. Most recently, in *Rumsfeld v. Forum for Academic and Institutional Rights* (2006), in a unanimous decision, the justices upheld a law that would deny federal funding to institutions of higher learning that prohibit or prevent military recruiting on their campuses on an equal footing with other prospective employers. In the decision, the Court concluded that the law, as a general matter, attempted to regulate conduct and not speech.

Courts have wrestled with the legal issue of whether to require public school students to recite the Pledge of Allegiance.
Source: Library of Congress

Hate Speech. Some states and the federal government have recently sought to legislate against hate crimes and hate speech—speech whose purpose is to express hatred against historically persecuted MINORITIES. How far can such laws go to limit the freedom of speech protected by the First Amendment? In *R.A.V. v. City of St. Paul* (1992), the Supreme Court struck down a city ordinance that made it a crime to place "on public or private property a symbol, object, appellation, characterization or graffiti, including but not limited to, a burning cross, or Nazi swastika, which one knows or has reasonable grounds to know arouses anger, alarm or resentment in others on the basis of race, color, creed, religion or gender...." Although the Court has recognized that "fighting words" used to provoke another person are not protected by the First Amendment, in a 9–0 opinion the justices found that the ordinance in question was unconstitutional, in part because it would affect only the hate speech of a select group. Four justices saw the ordinance as overly broad because it could be used to limit legitimate speech that deserved constitutional protection. In *Virginia v. Black* (2003), in a nonunanimous decision, the justices ruled that a state may make it a crime to burn a cross with the "intent to intimidate a person or group of persons." According to the decision, intimidation is a form of true threat whereby the speaker "directs a threat to a person or group of persons with the intent of placing the victim in fear of bodily harm or death."

Broadcasting. The government's power to regulate broadcasting, as opposed to other forms of COMMUNICATIONS, stems from the limited number of broadcast bands available to be parceled out; in effect they must be rationed among those competing to use them. In 1934 Congress delegated the power to regulate broadcasting to the Federal Communications Commission, saying, however, that "public convenience, interest and necessity" must guide the agency. Because the use of the air waves is considered in some ways a public trust, the FCC initially adopted a "fairness doctrine"— later repealed—which required broadcasters to provide access to the airwaves for such reactions as replies to policy statements.

In *Federal Communications Commission v. Pacifica Foundation* (1978), the Supreme Court declared that radio and television were entitled to a reduced level of First Amendment protection. This case involved a comedian's discussion of obscene language, which was aired in the afternoon when it could be heard by children. The Court held that the right not to be assaulted in public or in the privacy of one's home by indecency outweighed the broadcaster's free-speech rights.

The Internet. The phenomenal growth of this new medium of communication has taken place in less than ten years, making it difficult for the law, and especially constitutional law, to keep pace. Speech problems with other media, from books and magazines to radio and television, similarly affect the INTERNET. Because of the unchecked spread of sexually explicit material on the Internet, Congress passed the Communications Decency Act (1996). However, the Supreme Court found that the act was an overreaching, unconstitutional infringement of the right of free speech that would hamper legitimate communications, such as birth-control information communicated by e-mail between a parent and a child at college. Similarly, in *Ashcroft v. American Civil Liberties Union* (2002 and 2004), the Court struck down another attempt by Congress to censor the Internet by means of the Child Online Protection Act of 1998.

Commercial Speech. Advertising is a form of speech that the government sometimes tries to regulate for various public-policy reasons, especially where dangerous substances or public morality are concerned. For example, in *Posadas de Puerto Rico Associates v. Tourism Company of Puerto Rico* (1986), the Supreme Court upheld a ban on local advertising for legalized casino gambling in Puerto Rico but not for advertising aimed at potential customers on the U.S. mainland. The Court's reasoning included the fact that the government could have banned all advertising if it had wanted to. Later cases have thrown doubt on the wisdom of the Court's deference to the government's assertion in *Posadas* of an important interest as the basis for banning commercial speech.

"At the outset, we must determine whether the expression is protected by the First Amendment," said the Supreme Court in *Board of Trustees, State University of New York v. Fox* (1989), citing an earlier case. "For commercial speech to come within that provision, it at least must concern lawful activity and not be misleading. Next, we ask whether the asserted governmental interest [in regulating it] is substantial. If both inquiries yield positive answers, we must determine whether the regulation directly advances the governmental interest asserted, and whether it is not more extensive than is necessary to serve that interest." In other words, the government may regulate commercial speech, but it must be justified in the eyes of the Court. In *City of Cincinnati v. Discovery Network, Inc.* (1993), the Court found that a city's selective ban on the distribution of "commercial handbills" under the guise of maintaining the safety and attractive appearance of the streets and sidewalks was "not consistent with the dictates of the First Amendment."

More recently, in *Lorillard Tobacco Co. v. Reilly* (2001), the Supreme Court struck down a Massachusetts ban on outdoor truthful advertising of smokeless tobacco and cigars to adult consumers. The Court relied on the test fashioned in *Central Hudson Gas & Electric Corp. v. Public Service Commission of New York* (1980), which requires commercial speech regulation to be "no more extensive than necessary" to serve a substantial government interest and the need for narrow tailoring of regulations developed in *Reno v. American Civil Liberties Union* (1997). In *Thompson v. Western States Medical Center* (2002), again relying on the test in *Hudson*, the Court struck down a U.S. Food and Drug Administration prohibition on advertising compounded drugs, because the sharply divided Court found that the ban violated the commercial freedom of speech of pharmacists.

New Frontiers for Speech

The right of free speech is constantly expanding and shrinking under the interpretations of the Supreme Court. In BUCKLEY V. VALEO (1976), the Court virtually equated the spending of funds on political campaigns with the right of free speech (see CAMPAIGN FINANCING). A Supreme Court case in 2000, *Board of Regents of University of Wisconsin System v. Southworth*, addressed the free-speech implications of a mandatory student activity fee that promoted extracurricular speech activities with which some of the students assessed the fee might not agree. The Court upheld the fee so long as the program was viewpoint neutral and the mandatory fee was used to further the school's educational mission.

"I disapprove of what you say, but I will defend to the death your right to say it."

—Often attributed to Voltaire, but written by Evelyn Beatrice Hall, in her biography *The Friends of Voltaire* (1906)

Because the right of free speech includes the right—some might say the obligation—to criticize the government, it is incongruous for an open, democratic society to penalize citizens for lawfully protesting the acts of government officials or indulging in symbolic speech of a personal nature. The constitutional guarantee of free speech is essential, particularly when it legitimately protects offensive, divisive, or controversial speech that would otherwise be censored.

Speech or Debate Clause *See* CONGRESS; IMMUNITY; SPEECH.

Spending Power *See* BUDGET; CONGRESS; DEBT.

States

The first constituent states of the United States were born out of the thirteen British colonies in America. Although many of the colonists had in common their British heritage and English language, the colonies were settled for different reasons and developed different societies. The Massachusetts Bay Colony, for example, was founded by Pilgrims, members of a Christian religious sect in England known as Puritans. Before landing at Plymouth Rock in 1620, they drew up an agreement, the Mayflower Compact, stating: "[We] combine ourselves together into a civil Body Politick, for our better Ordering and Preservation" (see page 609). Much farther to the south, the Georgia Colony was settled in 1733 by the British humanitarian James Edward Oglethorpe and the earl of Egmont under a land grant from the British Crown for the purpose of "settling poor persons of London" in the New World.

After he traveled across the new nation early in the nineteenth century, the French political observer Alexis de Tocqueville (1805–59) noted, "The Union is a vast body and somewhat vague as the object of patriotism. But," he wrote in *Democracy in America* (1835), "the state has a precise shape and circumscribed boundaries; it represents a [definite] number of familiar things which are dear to those living there." For these and other reasons, he suggested, "interest, custom, and feelings are united in concentrating real political life in the state, and not in the Union."

Today the traditions of New Englanders continue to differ sharply from those of southerners, and both differ in many ways from those of the majority of Californians, for example. Each state also has its own constitution and many laws that differ from those of other states. Supreme Court Justice Louis D. Brandeis (1856–1941) characterized the states essentially as laboratories of democracy because they each, in their own way, experiment with different forms of constitutional democratic government.

State Government

The state governments in existence at the time of the ARTICLES OF CONFEDERATION, from 1781 to 1789, were incorporated into the framework of the Constitution when it went into effect in 1789. Nowhere in the document are any requirements for the form such governments must take. The Constitution instead focuses on the relationship between the states and the federal government and the relationship among the states. In respect to the latter, although the states generally enjoy equality based on their retention of state SOVEREIGNTY in the federal system, there is also some inequality—for example, in the HOUSE OF REPRESENTATIVES and the ELECTORAL COLLEGE, in which representation is weighted in favor of the more populous states.

Role in the Federal Government. The states are an integral part of the federal system created by the Constitution (see FEDERALISM). As sovereign political entities, the states created the federal government, but in the process they also irrevocably relinquished certain aspects of their sovereignty. As ABRAHAM LINCOLN and the Civil War (1861–65) proved, they gave up any right to withdraw from the Union they forged (see SECESSION). And as the Supreme Court has declared in cases reaching back to *GIBBONS V. OGDEN* (1824), they also gave up power over many aspects of COMMERCE, especially as it affects other states and the nation.

> *As sovereign political entities, the states created the federal government, but in the process they also irrevocably relinquished certain aspects of their sovereignty.*

Among the provisions regarding states in the Constitution, Article I, section 4, provides: "The Times, Places and Manner of holding Elections for Senators and Representatives, shall be prescribed in each State by the Legislature thereof...." Article I, section 8, grants CONGRESS the power "To regulate Commerce...among the several States." Article II, section 2, gives the president authority to call up the "Militia of the several States"; and Article III, section 2, gives the federal judiciary jurisdiction over cases involving the states.

Article IV deals with the relationship among the states, requiring in section 1 that FULL FAITH AND CREDIT "shall be given in each State to the public Acts, Records, and judicial Proceedings of every other State" and proclaiming in section 2: "The Citizens of each State shall be entitled to all Privileges and Immunities of Citizens in the several States" (see CITIZENS; PRIVILEGES AND IMMUNITIES). Article IV, section 3, describes the procedures for new states to be admitted to the Union (see ADMISSION OF NEW STATES). Article VI requires an oath of allegiance to the Constitution not just from federal officials but also from state officials such as legislators and all "executive and judicial Officers."

The role of the states in the federal government has evolved under the Constitution, through both amendments and decisions of the federal courts. Today the assumption remains that within their spheres of sovereignty—even if shrunk significantly since the Union began—states can exercise their powers without restrictions other than those imposed by the Constitution. Such residual state sovereignty is guaranteed by the Tenth Amendment (1791), which declares: "The powers not delegated to the United States by the Constitution, nor prohibited by it to the States, are reserved to the States respectively, or to the people."

Form of Government. Article IV, section 4, of the Constitution guarantees "to every state in this Union a Republican Form of Government, and [the United States] shall protect each of them against Invasion; and on Application of the Legislature, or of the Executive (when the Legislature cannot be convened) against domestic Violence." There is no definition of what constitutes a REPUBLICAN FORM OF GOVERNMENT, although clearly a monarchy or a dictatorship without any democratic procedures would not pass muster.

In *Luther v. Borden* (1849), the Supreme Court declared that questions regarding whether a state government met the republican form of government requirement were political in nature, saying that "it rests with Congress to decide what government is the established one in a State…as well as its republican character" (the issues involved rival state governments in Rhode Island). In BAKER V. CARR (1962), however, the Court did not let the *Luther* finding keep it from requiring REAPPORTIONMENT—redistribution of state electoral districts to equalize the contribution of each state's voters, as required under the EQUAL PROTECTION clause of the Fourteenth Amendment (1868).

The chief executive in each of the fifty states is called the governor, and each state except Nebraska has a bicameral legislature. The judicial systems in the states differ as to whether judges are appointed or elected, although in some states both methods of selection may be used.

Restrictions. In Article I, section 10, the Constitution sets out certain prohibitions on the states: "No State shall enter into any Treaty, Alliance, or Confederation; grant Letters of Marque and Reprisal [commissions granted to private individuals to seize the citizens or goods of hostile nations in reprisal for wrongs done by that nation]; coin Money; emit Bills of Credit; make any Thing but gold and silver Coin a Tender in Payment of Debts; pass any Bill of Attainder, ex post facto Law, or Law impairing the Obligation of Contracts, or grant any Title of Nobility" (see ATTAINDER, BILLS OF; CONTRACTS; CURRENCY; EX POST FACTO LAWS; TREATIES). Some of these prohibitions, such as granting titles and passing ex post facto laws, apply to the national government as well.

Other restrictions on the states noted in section 10 include assessing any duties, without the consent of Congress, "on Imports or Exports, except what may be absolutely necessary for executing its inspection Laws…." In addition, "No State shall, without the Consent of Congress, lay any Duty of Tonnage, keep Troops, or Ships of War in time of Peace, enter into any Agreement or Compact with another State, or with a foreign Power, or engage in War, unless actually invaded, or in such imminent Danger as will not admit of delay" (see WAR). The so-called compact clause has been used by the federal government to ensure its input in agreements between states regarding concerns over transportation and the ENVIRONMENT.

Constitutional Amendments. Article V describes the role of the states in ratifying AMENDMENTS to the Constitution, requiring that three-fourths of the state legislatures or state conventions approve amendments passed by Congress; two-thirds of the states may alternatively propose that Congress call a national constitutional convention "for proposing Amendments." (Article VII required the "Ratification of the Conventions of nine States" for the Constitution originally to go into effect.)

Many of the twenty-seven constitutional amendments approved to date—such as the Tenth (1791), Thirteenth (1865), Fifteenth (1870), and Nineteenth (1920)—also directly impact the states. For example, SLAVERY was banned in all states, and all were prohibited from denying to any person due process of law or equal protection of the laws or abridging the right of citizens to vote "on account of race, color, or previous condition of servitude." One of the most important of these changes was the Fourteenth Amendment (1868), which has been the vehicle used by the Supreme Court to make a number of provisions in the BILL OF RIGHTS (1791) applicable to the states (see IN-CORPORATION DOCTRINE), among them the right to ASSISTANCE OF COUNSEL, freedom of SPEECH, and the prohibition against CRUEL AND UNUSUAL PUNISHMENT. The Eleventh Amendment (1795) restored some of the states' IMMUNITY from lawsuits inherent in their semisovereign status in the federal system of government.

State Action

State action is the term given to the legal distinction COURTS have sometimes made between what a state—in the broad sense of the word—does and does not do compared with the actions of private citizens. For example, under the Civil Rights Act of 1875, Congress banned discrimination in public accommodations such as theaters, restaurants, and public transportation (see RACIAL DISCRIMINATION). In the Civil Rights Cases (*United States v. Ryan*, *United States v. Stanley*, and *Robinson v. Memphis and C. R. Co.*)—involving blacks' denial of equal use of hotels, theaters, and railroad trains—the Supreme Court found in 1883 that when a state did not act positively to discriminate on the basis of race in public accommodation, private discriminatory acts were beyond the scope of the Fourteenth Amendment's requirement that no state may take such actions; in these instances, the DISCRIMINATION was found to result only from private infringement of the complainants' rights.

More on this topic:

Admission of New States,
p. 15

Federalism, p. 218

Full Faith and Credit,
p. 246

Incorporation Doctrine,
p. 297

States' Rights, p. 520

Since the Civil Rights Cases the concept of state action has been redefined by the Supreme Court. *BROWN V. BOARD OF EDUCATION OF TOPEKA* (1954) made "separate but equal" public school facilities unconstitutional, and in *United States v. Price* (1966), the Court ruled that even private discrimination could be prohibited if private individuals were found to be conspiring with state authorities. A company town has been held to be liable for state action, but in *Hudgens v. National Labor Relations Board* (1976), the Court would not find that a private shopping mall was capable of state action.

The rich diversity of state laws requires constant Supreme Court review of how those laws relate to the letter and the spirit of the Constitution. The ever-shifting relationship between the federal and state governments can also raise constitutional issues from time to time. The Constitution protects all citizens to a great extent from unjust and unfair acts of state governments, but in a free and open nation there can be no basis for attempting to enforce complete social conformity in the states. If a person does not like the laws of one state, he or she is free to move to another. Yet many citizens of the United States, for better or worse, are deeply rooted in their home state, as Tocqueville noted long ago.

States' Rights

In essay 40 of *The Federalist* (1787–88) (see FEDERALIST PAPERS), JAMES MADISON suggested: "We have seen that in the new government, as in the old [under the ARTICLES OF CONFEDERATION (1781)], the general powers are limited; and that the States, in all unenumerated cases, are left in the enjoyment of their sovereign and independent jurisdiction." Inherent in the concept of FEDERALISM devised by the FRAMERS OF THE CONSTITUTION in 1787, however, was the possibility of clashes between the federal government and the STATES over what might be considered the limits of each other's sovereign powers (see SOVEREIGNTY).

After the Constitution went into effect in 1789, the Federalist Party leader ALEXANDER HAMILTON espoused a broad interpretation of the national government's POWERS, while Madison and THOMAS JEFFERSON, leaders of the Democratic-Republican Party, urged a STRICT CONSTRUCTION (narrow interpretation) of the Constitution regarding those powers vis-á-vis the states. Later the notion of states' rights would become a theme of the southern states that supported SLAVERY, led by Senator John C. Calhoun (1782–1850) of South Carolina. Even today, the term *states' rights* is often perceived as a euphemism for letting some states restrict the rights of MINORITIES despite the guarantees of the Constitution.

Powers Reserved to the States

States' rights is not a constitutional term; it is a political slogan used to connote the exclusive or equal constitutional powers of the states in relation to the federal government. The Constitution, including the BILL OF RIGHTS (1791), expressly defines a number of individual RIGHTS, but, with a few exceptions, there is no similar recitation of states' rights.

The language of the Tenth Amendment (1791), declaring that the "powers not delegated to the United States by the Constitution, nor prohibited by it to the States, are reserved to the States respectively, or to the people," provides no definition of which rights are reserved to the states and which are reserved to the people. It could be argued that the concept of popular sovereignty acknowledged in the DECLARATION OF INDEPENDENCE (1776)—"Governments are instituted among Men, deriving their just Powers from the Consent of the Governed"—makes the states mere vehicles of their CITIZENS, with no independent rights or powers beyond those expressly delegated to them by their inhabitants in state constitutions. However, another view holds that all powers not found in the Constitution are available to the states to use to the extent that they are not prohibited by their own constitutions.

The Constitution does guarantee in Article 1, section 3, that each state is entitled to two senators in CONGRESS and in Article V that no constitutional amendment can deprive a state of its equal representation in the SENATE without its consent. Article I, section 4, guarantees that states can determine the "Places of chusing Senators."

Article IV, section 3, prohibits the formation of a new state from the territory of an existing state and the formation of a state from the "Junction of two or more States, or Parts of States, without the Consent of the Legislatures of the States concerned as well as of the Congress." Article IV, section 4, guarantees "to every State…a Republican Form of Government" and protection "against Invasion…[and] domestic Violence" (see DOMESTIC TRANQUILITY; REPUBLICAN FORM OF GOVERNMENT).

Restrictions on State Power

The leading case affecting states' rights was *MCCULLOCH V. MARYLAND* (1819), in which Chief Justice JOHN MARSHALL asserted the federal government's IMPLIED POWERS—those inherent, but unexpressed, within the language of the Constitution—and the states' lack of power to tax an instrumentality of the national government (see TAXATION). In *Cohens v. Virginia* (1821), Marshall drove home his point that the Constitution made

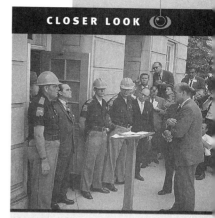

the federal government supreme and the federal judiciary the final arbiter of what the Constitution means (see JUDICIAL REVIEW; SUPREMACY CLAUSE).

After the Civil War (1861–65), the Thirteenth (1865), Fourteenth (1868), and Fifteenth (1870) Amendments attempted to extend the federal government's power to protect the rights of citizens—although not necessarily the rights of WOMEN—against the states in certain matters, particularly with respect to the treatment of former male slaves. Through a number of Supreme Court decisions, however, the potential scope of these amendments, the Fourteenth Amendment in particular, was restricted. Finally, beginning in 1927, the Court began incorporating the federal guarantees of the Bill of Rights (1791) into the Fourteenth Amendment and making them applicable to the states (see INCORPORATION DOCTRINE).

Another avenue through which the national government has reduced states' rights and powers is the COMMERCE clause of the Constitution. Beginning with the Supreme Court's decision in GIBBONS V. OGDEN (1824), which established the preeminence of the federal government's power over interstate commerce, and running through the extension of that power in cases such as *Swift and Co. v. United States* (1905) and *Rice v. Santa Fe Elevator Corp.* (1947), the national power to deal with almost any matter that can conceivably have an impact on interstate commerce has generally been upheld against state challenges.

Today individual states' power is greatly restricted, and they regularly lose in court contests with the federal government when important national interests are involved. Although in *National League of Cities v. Usery* (1976) the Supreme Court struck down a federal regulation extending to state governments the maximum hour and minimum wage provisions of the Fair Labor Standards Act (1938), in *Garcia v. San Antonio Metropolitan Transit Authority* (1985), a 5–4 decision, the Court abandoned any states' rights limitations on Congress's commerce power. In more recent cases, however, such as *United States v. Lopez* (1995) and *Printz v. United States* (1997), the Court invalidated federal laws involving GUN CONTROL as improper impositions on the states.

Recently, in a turnabout of sorts, two states—California and Massachusetts—have, in fact, sued an agency of the federal government to do more in the area of helping the states with their environmental protection efforts (see ENVIRONMENT). California's suit is still pending, but the Supreme Court ruled in favor of Massachusetts in *Massachusetts v. Environmental Protection Agency* (2007).

Strict Construction

The process of JUDICIAL REVIEW of lower court decisions by appellate courts is often conducted in reverse of the generally understood process: first a judge privately makes a decision and then researches the issues to find support for the conclusion. In doing this, a judge's view of the Constitution—either a strict (narrow) construction or interpretation or a liberal (broader) construction—can become the basis for reaching the desired outcome.

A judge's strict construction of a positive power in the Constitution will have a far different effect than a strict construction of a limitation. One example of a positive power is the grant to CONGRESS in Article I, section 8, of authority to "regulate Commerce…among the several States" (see COMMERCE). A constitutional limitation on power is the language in the First Amendment (1791) forbidding Congress from making laws "respecting an establishment of religion" (see RELIGION).

A strict construction of the positive grant of power over interstate commerce would effectively limit the federal government's authority, requiring that control extend only to activities that actually move across state lines. In contrast, a strict construction of the words in the First Amendment limiting the government's power ("Congress shall make no law…") would expand its guarantees by finding unconstitutional any congressional law whatsoever that affected First Amendment freedoms. Over the past two centuries, however, the Supreme Court has generally expanded the powers of the federal government with respect to regulating interstate commerce and found some justifiable exceptions for laws that restrict freedoms under the First Amendment.

The conflict over strict, less strict, and liberal constructions of constitutional provisions has had a long history. JAMES MADISON and THOMAS JEFFERSON both favored a strict construction of Congress's powers when it came to chartering a national bank, while ALEXANDER HAMILTON and JOHN MARSHALL, chief justice from 1801 to 1835, preferred a more flexible reading of Article I, supporting Congress's power to establish a national bank even though this authority was not expressly granted by the Constitution. In his landmark decision in MCCULLOCH V. MARYLAND (1819), Marshall was able to thwart a strict constructionist reading by ruling that the power to create a national bank was a necessary and proper constitutional authority (see NECESSARY AND PROPER CLAUSE) in view of other express powers, such as the power to lay and collect taxes (see TAXATION), borrow money, and regulate commerce.

Supreme Court Justice Clarence Thomas is generally regarded as a strict constructionist of the Constitution.
Source: Supreme Court Historical Society

A strict constructionist's interpretation of any constitutional provision generally reveals an unwillingness to expand a power or a limitation beyond either the ORIGINAL INTENT of the FRAMERS OF THE CONSTITUTION—however that may be determined—or at least no further than current precedent will permit. The term *strict construction* has become loaded with political intent. As a result, labeling court decisions on constitutional questions in terms of strict or liberal construction arguably obfuscates coverage of a case, focusing attention on justices' political leanings rather than clarifying constitutional analysis and interpretation.

Strict Scrutiny

Strict scrutiny of a law to determine if it is constitutional is the highest form of review that COURTS can apply. In using such analysis, courts set aside the normal deference they give to the acts of legislatures and inquire thoroughly as to whether a suspect law violates the Constitution, especially the EQUAL PROTECTION clause of the Fourteenth Amendment (1868). The rationale is that the government's interests must be balanced against citizens' FUNDAMENTAL RIGHTS and particularly that MINORITIES who have historically been discriminated against must be protected. Justice William O. Douglas (1898–1980) was the first to use the term in *Skinner v. Oklahoma* (1942), in a case involving the forced sterilization of certain convicts. "[It is] our view," he wrote, "that strict scrutiny of the classification which a State makes in a sterilization law is essential, lest unwittingly or otherwise invidious discriminations are made against groups or types of individuals in violation of the constitutional guaranty of just and equal laws."

Abortion

In his opinion in *ROE V. WADE* (1973), Justice Harry A. Blackmun (1908–99) gave strict scrutiny to a state law banning ABORTION because of the fundamental nature of the right of PRIVACY involved and the severity of the penalty imposed. The decision required the government to justify the law by showing a "compelling state interest...[which] must be narrowly drawn to express only the legitimate state interests at stake." Balancing the interests of the mother against those of the unborn child was not appropriate, he said, because the term *person*, as used in the Fourteenth Amendment, had not been intended to include persons not yet born. Later, however, a more conservative Supreme Court in *Planned Parenthood of Southeastern Pennsylvania v. Casey* (1992) replaced the strict scrutiny standard with a standard of "undue burden," which is much more deferential to state laws limiting abortion rights.

Privacy, on which the right of abortion is predicated, has been inferred from broader language in the Constitution and is singled out for careful scrutiny when the government asserts a need to infringe it.

First Amendment Rights

First Amendment (1791) rights particularly require strict scrutiny. For example, according to the Supreme Court in *Greer v. Spock* (1976), when the government tries to regulate SPEECH in PUBLIC FORUMS on the basis of its content, such regulation is subject to strict scrutiny. This is not the case where the regulation is content neutral and only indirectly burdens freedom of speech.

In *Simon and Schuster v. Members of the New York State Crime Victims Board* (1991), the Supreme Court, after applying the strict scrutiny standard, struck down New York's "Son of Sam" law, which required that the proceeds from literary works of criminals who write about their crimes go first to the victims and then to the criminal's creditors. The Court noted that the state had a compelling interest in using the fruits of crime to compensate victims but found that the statute in question had to be more narrowly tailored to accomplish its goal without infringing First Amendment rights. In *Arkansas Writers' Project, Inc. v. Ragland* (1987), the Court concluded that the state "faces a heavy burden in attempting to defend its content-based approach to taxation of magazines."

With respect to possible infringement of freedom of association (see ASSEMBLY AND ASSOCIATION), in *Gibson v. Florida Legislative Investigation Committee* (1963) the Supreme Court declared that before a state legislature could require the National Association for the Advancement of Colored People to make its membership list available, the legislature had to "convincingly show a substantial relation between the information sought and…[a] compelling state interest."

Discrimination

Strict scrutiny is especially appropriate for cases of discriminatory legislation (see DISCRIMINATION). In *Romer v. Evans* (1996), the Supreme Court found that a statewide referendum approved by Colorado voters that prohibited any government action to protect HOMOSEXUALS represented an unconstitutional infringement of their fundamental right to participate in the political process. This was true whether a standard of strict scrutiny or "rational relationship" was used, because the law imposed a broad and "undifferentiated disability on a single named group." The second standard requires only some rational relationship between discriminatory treatment and any government interest to be furthered by such treatment.

Laws that classify people on the basis of race or ethnic origin may also be subject to strict scrutiny by the Supreme Court, which said in *Dunn v. Blumstein* (1972) that such cases will require the government to establish that the classification is "necessary to promote a compelling state interest." Strict scrutiny was also employed in *REGENTS OF THE UNIVERSITY OF CALIFORNIA V. BAKKE* (1978), an AFFIRMATIVE ACTION case that prohibited racial quotas or reverse discrimination against nonminorities. More recently, in *Johnson v. California* (2005), the Court, citing *Adarand Constructors, Inc. v. Pena* (1995) to the effect that "*all* racial classifications [imposed by the government]…must be analyzed by a reviewing court under strict scrutiny," held that "strict scrutiny is the proper standard of review for an equal protection challenge" to a state prison policy of "racially segregating prisoners in double cells in reception centers for up to 60 days each time they entered a new correction facility."

Interstate Movement

When a state requires a newcomer to live there a fixed period of time before becoming eligible for benefits that are available to other residents, this type of law has sometimes triggered strict scrutiny and invalidation as a denial of equal protection of the law. In *Memorial Hospital v. Maricopa County* (1974), a residency requirement of one year before an indigent person could obtain public medical treatment was held to be an infringement of the equal protection clause. Residency requirements that do not burden the right of TRAVEL, however, have been upheld.

Elections

Restrictions on voting (see ELECTIONS) or access to the political process have not been treated uniformly by the Supreme Court. In *American Party of Texas v. White* (1974), a requirement that a petition for a minority party be signed by one percent of the voters who had not participated in another party's primary was upheld under the strict scrutiny standard, on the basis that the requirement afforded the minority party a "real and substantial equal opportunity for ballot qualification."

Based on the right of political association, laws that heavily burden the right to vote will incur strict scrutiny, as will state regulation of national POLITICAL PARTIES. Strict scrutiny has also been applied in cases where the government attempts to regulate the content of speech during an election campaign. In contrast, the Supreme Court has denied strict scrutiny over elections related to special interests or districts, such as a local water district that does not exercise general powers of GOVERNMENT.

Other Types of Review

Somewhere between strict scrutiny, involving suspect classifications, and the rational relationship test lie lesser forms of judicial scrutiny such as "intermediate" and "heightened" scrutiny—involving quasi-suspect classifications such as laws making distinctions on the basis of sex—as well as ad hoc BALANCING TESTS in which the interests of the government are balanced against any possible infringement of the Constitution.

Heightened Scrutiny. In *C&A Carbone, Inc. v. Clarkstown* (1994), the majority of the Supreme Court, using heightened judicial scrutiny, struck down by a 6–3 vote a town ordinance that designated one processing station for all solid waste; the dissenters, using a balancing test, would have validated it. In this case, the ordinance was held to be an unconstitutional infringement of interstate COMMERCE, because it discriminated against other solid waste processors. Discrimination against competing commercial facilities would restrict competition, thus requiring heightened review.

Intermediate Scrutiny. In its first case involving discrimination against a male, *Craig v. Boren* (1976), the Supreme Court created a new intermediate scrutiny test, requiring that "classifications by gender must serve important governmental objectives and must be substantially related to achievement of those objectives." The Court found a state law that prohibited the sale of beer with 3.2 percent alcohol to males under twenty-one years of age and women under eighteen to be unconstitutional discrimination based on gender classification (see SEX DISCRIMINATION).

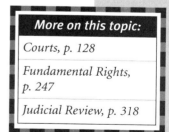

More on this topic:

Courts, p. 128

Fundamental Rights, p. 247

Judicial Review, p. 318

Strict scrutiny and the other levels of judicial scrutiny are not only tools for the courts to use in addressing alleged infringement of rights by the government, they also send a message to legislators that they should take a hard look at proposals that would treat some CITIZENS unfairly for no important government purpose. Rather than blindly resting on tradition, the deference that courts have shown to legislatures is changing toward ensuring that legislators act constitutionally and in the best interests of all the citizens they represent.

Supremacy Clause

According to INTERNATIONAL LAW, SOVEREIGNTY makes all nations equal. Thus the Pacific Island country of Nauru, with eight square miles of territory and some 13,050 people, is theoretically the equal of the United States, with more than 3.7 million square miles of territory and 300 million people. In a federal republic such as Austria, Brazil, or the United States, there are two levels of sovereignty: the national government and the states. Although states may be on an equal footing with one another, national constitutions are generally considered to bestow supreme power over the states, especially in those areas of power delegated exclusively to the national government—for example, control of the ARMED FORCES and FOREIGN AFFAIRS.

The sovereignty of each of the thirteen former British colonies that became STATES after declaring their independence in 1776 was recognized under the ARTICLES OF CONFEDERATION (1781), which governed the United States until 1789. Each state was represented equally in the Continental Congress, having one vote regardless of the number of members in its delegation. The Articles, however, failed to create a strong new nation because individual states retained so much of their sovereignty, including their own power over the regulation of interstate COMMERCE and their own independent judicial systems. The first object of the CONSTITUTIONAL CONVENTION OF 1787 was thus to revise the Articles, but it soon changed to creation of a new truly federal national government with sufficient sovereignty to forge one nation out of many states.

National Government versus the States

The Constitution's supremacy clause, set forth in Article VI, makes the Constitution the nation's supreme law, taking precedence over all other laws that might conflict with it: "This Constitution, and the Laws of the United States which shall be made in Pursuance thereof; and all Treaties made, or which shall be made, under the Authority of the United States, shall be the supreme Law of the Land; and the Judges in every State shall be bound thereby, any Thing in the Constitution or Laws of any State to the Contrary notwithstanding."

The supremacy clause reflected the change in the relationship between the new national government and the component states following termination of the Articles of Confederation. Vis-á-vis one another the states remained politically equal, but vis-á-vis the national government they relinquished some of their sovereignty, becoming semisovereign states in which a number of sovereign attributes were forever lost. One of the Constitution's provisions that reflects this significant change, found in Article I, section 2, is the apportionment of seats in the HOUSE OF REPRESENTATIVES on the basis of each state's population (see REAPPORTIONMENT). States with larger populations have a greater representation in the lower house of Congress.

Some of the delegates to the Constitutional Convention of 1787, including JAMES MADISON, wanted to go even further in extending national supremacy over the states by giving Congress the power to overrule state laws. ALEXANDER HAMILTON, in essay 34 of *The Federalist* (1787–88) (see FEDERALIST PAPERS), rebutted criticism of the supremacy clause by pointing out: "A LAW, by the very meaning of the term, includes supremacy. It is a rule which those to whom it is prescribed are bound to observe."

Article VI also states: "The Senators and Representatives before mentioned, and the Members of the several State Legislatures, and all executive and judicial Officers, both of the United States and of the several States, shall be bound by Oath or Affirmation, to support this Constitution...." Like a feudal vassal's oath of fealty to his lord, this oath is intended to create a primary and overriding loyalty to the national government, not to any state (see OATH OF OFFICE). The officials of the southern states that seceded from the Union during the Civil War (1861–65) (see SECESSION) had to break this oath of loyalty to the supremacy of the Constitution.

Applications by the Supreme Court

The Supreme Court first used the supremacy clause in *Ware v. Hylton* (1796) to invalidate a state law that conflicted with the provisions of the Treaty of Paris (1783), which governed the post–Revolutionary War peace with England. Chief Justice JOHN MARSHALL also relied on it in the Court's landmark decisions in *MCCULLOCH V. MARYLAND* (1819) and *GIBBONS V. OGDEN* (1824). In his opinion in the latter case he wrote: "The appropriate application of that part of the clause which confers the same supremacy on laws and treaties, is to such acts of the State legislatures as do not transcend their powers, but though enacted in the execution of acknowledged State powers, interfere with, or are contrary to the laws of Congress, made in pursuance of the Constitution, or some treaty made under the authority of the United States. In every such case, the act of Congress, or the treaty, is supreme; and the law of the State, though enacted in the exercise of powers not controverted, must yield to it."

To curtail the power of the national government embodied in the supremacy clause, the Supreme Court—after Roger B. Taney (1777–1864) replaced Marshall in 1836—began relying on the concept of the states' POLICE POWER to provide for the WELFARE of their citizens. This general trend, which included the use of economic due process (see ECONOMIC LIBERTY) to elevate PROPERTY and contract rights (see CONTRACTS) over social welfare policies, continued until 1937. After that, the justices began to retreat in the face of federal attempts to counteract the effects of the Great Depression, eventually reverting to rulings more in line with the philosophy espoused by Marshall.

The Supreme Court under Chief Justice William Rehnquist (1924–2005) tried to use state sovereignty to rein in attempts by the federal government to impose general rules on the states. For example, the Court relied on state sovereignty as a basis for striking down a law regulating radioactive waste from nuclear power plants. And in *United States v. Lopez* (1995), the Court held that Congress had exceeded its powers under the commerce clause when it passed the Gun-Free School Zones Act (1990), which made it a crime to knowingly possess a gun within one thousand feet of a school (see GUN CONTROL). The Court would again refer to the supremacy clause in its decision in *Nixon v. Missouri Municipal League* (2004). In interpreting a section of the Telecommunications Act of 1996 that preempted state and local laws that barred "any entity" from providing telecommunications services, the court held the federal law did not preempt similar prohibitions enacted by states regarding their own municipalities and subdivisions.

The real supremacy on which the Constitution's supremacy clause is based is the supremacy of the people—the CITIZENS of all the United States—and not the supremacy of an abstract national government as opposed to state governments. The ORIGINAL INTENT of the FRAMERS OF THE CONSTITUTION was to provide an effective means of dealing with problems that each state alone, or even a few states together, could not deal with effectively on their own.

More on this topic:
Exclusive Powers, p. 204
Federalism, p. 218
Judicial Review, p. 318
States' Rights, p. 520
Treaties, p. 551

Supreme Court

"'Whoever hath an absolute authority to interpret any written or spoken law,'" wrote Felix Frankfurter (1882–1965) in *Mr. Justice Holmes and the Supreme Court* (1965), quoting John Chipman Gray, "'it is he who is truly the lawgiver to all intents and purposes, and not the person who first wrote or spoke them.'" That the Supreme Court is supreme because it is final and not final because it is supreme is only partly true, because the Court's decisions can be changed in some instances by Congress or by constitutional amendment. But to a great extent, as illustrated by the unique case *BUSH V. GORE* (2000)—in which the Court's decision virtually determined the outcome

During the tenure of Fred M. Vinson (1890–1953), center, who was chief justice from 1946 to 1953, the Supreme Court issued more 5–4 decisions than under any other chief justice. He tried to be a peacemaker on his bitterly divided court.
Source: Photograph by Bachrach, Collection of the Supreme Court of the United States

of a presidential election—the Supreme Court often does have the final word on the meaning and constitutionality of the laws of the United States.

The concept of a supreme judicial body that can overrule executive or legislative decisions is at least as old as ancient Athens. For example, in 594 B.C.E. the Athenian lawgiver Solon created a popular court of appeal in which citizens could challenge the decisions of public officials. In contrast, an absolute monarch who made the laws, like the later kings and queens in Europe, was not considered to be subject to the laws or to any court. Even today, in one of the world's last absolute monarchies—Saudi Arabia—the courts still defer to the king and the royal family in judicial matters.

Creation of the Court

In creating the judicial system for the new federal government (see JUDICIAL BRANCH), the FRAMERS OF THE CONSTITUTION could refer to the judicial history of both Great Britain and the thirteen newly independent states of the United States. Britain's highest court was in fact Parliament, and even today a majority vote in Parliament can technically overturn any judicial decision. France—like the United States a republic without a monarch—has a traditional mistrust of the judiciary, and its courts do not have equal status constitutionally with the other branches of government. No constitutional procedure analogous to JUDICIAL REVIEW exists, although the French constitution (1958) provides for a constitutional council to exercise some review of new laws before they become effective. Massachusetts, the last of the thirteen states to adopt a constitution (1780)—but the first to submit it to the people for approval—created a judicial system with a supreme court whose members were appointed and had life tenure. This system would be a model for the framers in designing a federal judiciary.

No national judicial power was established by the ARTICLES OF CONFEDERATION (1781), which the framers saw as a major defect. In essay 22 of *The Federalist* (1787–88) (see FEDERALIST PAPERS),

ALEXANDER HAMILTON explained why a supreme court was necessary for the federal system to be established by the Constitution (see FEDERALISM). "To avoid the confusion which would unavoidably result from the contradictory decisions of a number of independent judicatories," he wrote, "all nations have found it necessary to establish one court paramount to the rest, possessing a general superintendence and authorized to settle and declare in the last resort a uniform rule of civil justice."

The Constitution drafted in 1787 does not contain the word *nation*, but the terms *United States* and *Union* are used, reflecting the framers' intent to create a sovereign federal government comprising semisovereign STATES (see SOVEREIGNTY). The federal government's laws were expected to apply directly to CITIZENS (see SUPREMACY CLAUSE) and not just to the states as independent political jurisdictions, as was the case under the Articles. It was this direct relationship between the national government and the citizens of the United States that underscored the need for a national supreme court to act as a final arbiter of the Union's laws. Although the Supreme Court's jurisdiction—with the exception of its original jurisdiction in cases involving diplomats (see AMBASSADORS) and where a state is a party—is subject to control by CONGRESS, it has become an institution that is nearly synonymous with American constitutional law itself.

Jurisdiction

"The judicial Power of the United States," Article III, section 1, provides, "shall be vested in one supreme Court, and in such inferior Courts as the Congress may from time to time ordain and establish. The Judges, both of the supreme and inferior Courts, shall hold their Offices during good Behaviour, and shall, at stated Times, receive for their Services, a Compensation, which shall not be diminished during their Continuance in Office."

The Supreme Court's jurisdiction is set out in Article III, section 2, which declares: "The judicial Power shall extend to all Cases, in Law and Equity, arising under this Constitution, the Laws of the United States, and Treaties made, or which shall be made, under their Authority;—to all Cases affecting Ambassadors, other public Ministers and Consuls;—to all Cases of admiralty and maritime Jurisdiction;—to Controversies to which the United States will be a Party;—to Controversies between two or more States;—between a State and Citizens of another State;—between Citizens of different States,—between Citizens of the same State claiming Lands under Grants of different States, and between a State, or the Citizens thereof, and foreign States, Citizens or Subjects." This jurisdiction was modified by the Eleventh Amendment (1795), which declares: "The Judicial power of the United States shall not be construed to extend to any suit in law or equity, commenced or prosecuted against one of the United States by Citizens of another State, or by Citizens or Subjects of any Foreign State."

The terms *law* and *equity* refer to a dual court system that developed in England, which had law courts that could order money damages and equity courts that could offer injunctive relief. Under the Constitution, federal courts have both law and equity powers. ADMIRALTY AND MARITIME LAW jurisdiction refers to cases involving the high seas, navigable lakes and rivers, harbors, seamen, and CONTRACTS related to vessels. The phrase "equal justice under law" carved on the facade of the Supreme Court building in Washington, D.C., however, is the invention of the architects and has no precedent in American or English law.

Judicial Power

In the nation's early days, the Supreme Court was not looked to for constitutional analysis or guidance. In fact, in 1789, when a dispute arose over the IMPLIED POWERS of the PRESIDENT to remove EXECUTIVE BRANCH officials (see APPOINTMENT AND REMOVAL POWER), JAMES MADISON argued that Congress was better able to "expound on the Constitution" than the Supreme Court. The Court, however, soon gained recognition and authority, especially under the stewardship of Chief Justice JOHN MARSHALL, who served from 1801 to 1835. His opinions in cases such as *MARBURY V. MADISON*

(1803), MCCULLOCH V. MARYLAND (1819), and GIBBONS V. OGDEN (1824) set the Court on the road to being a coequal branch of the new federal government and the federal government on the road to exercising hegemony over a truly united nation. Although the Court's power of judicial review (determining the constitutionality of federal and state actions) was inherent in the nature of the SEPA-RATION OF POWERS principle on which the Constitution is based and in the Constitution's supremacy over all other law, it was not articulated by the Court until its decision in *Marbury v. Madison*.

The notions that the Supreme Court is the final arbiter of "Cases" and "Controversies" that come before it and that the Constitution is only what the Court says it is have not always been borne out. One reason is that the Court has no enforcement authority of its own and therefore relies on lower courts and the executive branch to carry out its decisions. For example, in 1984 the supreme court of Washington simply ignored a directive of the U.S. Supreme Court in *Washington v. Chrisman* (1982), changed the basis of its reasoning in its prior opinion (which had been reversed on appeal to the Supreme Court), and issued a new opinion concluding that it—not the national tribunal—had been right all along. Congress can also attain the same objective by altering laws found by the Supreme Court to be unconstitutional. In addition to changing the Court's jurisdiction—it withdrew HABEAS CORPUS jurisdiction during the Reconstruction Era after the Civil War (1861–65)—Congress can propose constitutional AMENDMENTS and impeach Supreme Court justices (see IMPEACHMENT); the only one to have been impeached by the HOUSE OF REPRESENTATIVES was Justice Samuel Chase (1741–1811) in 1805, but he was not convicted by the SENATE.

Membership on the Court

The Supreme Court includes the CHIEF JUSTICE of the United States and eight associate justices. Their number is not specified in the Constitution, although other national constitutions prescribe the number of members on their supreme courts; Nigeria, for example, mandates a chief justice and no more than twenty-one others, while Mexico sets the number at eleven. The U.S. Constitution refers only to the chief justice, although not in Article III. The reference occurs in Article I, section 3, which provides, "When the President of the United States is tried [in the Senate on charges of impeachment], the Chief Justice shall preside."

Congress decides how many associate justices there will be. The number was set at five in 1789 but was increased to six in 1807, to eight in 1837, and to nine in 1864. In 1866 Congress reduced the number of associate justices to six but increased it again to eight in 1869. And then, unhappy with decisions thwarting his economic recovery plan for the nation, President Franklin D. Roosevelt (1882–1945) asked Congress to add six more associate justices, but Congress refused his request to "pack the Court." The threat itself, however, had its intended effect on the Supreme Court, and opinions began to uphold Roosevelt's proposals.

The procedures for selecting members of the Supreme Court are included in Article II, section 2, where the Constitution states that the president "shall have Power, by and with the Advice and Consent of the Senate, to…appoint…Judges of the supreme Court…." No qualifications for membership are spelled out in the Constitution; however, members have almost always been lawyers or had some legal training. The chief justice is designated by the president from among one of the members and receives a salary of $217,400, while associate justices are paid $208,100 (as of 2008). All enjoy life tenure. Justice William O. Douglas (1898–1980) served the longest of any justice, retiring in 1975 after more than thirty-six years on the bench; and in 2007 Justice John Paul Stevens, at age 87, became the second longest serving member. At four months served in 1795, John Rutledge (1739–1800) had the shortest tenure.

Candidates for the Supreme Court are often said to be subject to a "litmus test" they must pass on certain issues, such as ABORTION, before being nominated. One school of thought holds that prospective justices should be judged on their ability to perform as a Supreme Court justice in general—not on their personal beliefs—and they should not be asked to prejudge cases for the same reasons that advisory opinions by the Court are unwise. Another school sees the appointment of justices as a reflection of the country's political majority and a mandate to ensure that majority values are fully represented on the Court (see MAJORITY RULE).

Procedures and Decisions

The Supreme Court stands at the apex of the federal court system (see COURTS), which consists of thirteen U.S. courts of appeal and ninety-four U.S. district courts. In addition to having the power to review cases from lower courts in the federal judicial system, the Supreme Court exercises general supervision over them. Its supervisory powers include establishing federal rules of procedures in certain cases and reviewing contempt-of-court actions.

The procedures of the Supreme Court are not spelled out in the Constitution, but the Court itself has refused to give advisory opinions to government officials. Several state constitutions and a number of other national constitutions expressly allow for such advisory opinions. In *Muskrat v. United States* (1911), however, the Supreme Court held that federal judicial power extends only to "Cases" and "Controversies" or, as defined by Chief Justice John Marshall, to suits "instituted according to the regular course of judicial procedure."

This 1937 cartoon shows President Franklin D. Roosevelt trying to pull his Supreme Court reform plan through the Senate.
Source: The Granger Collection, New York

The American government and legal system rest on the proposition that the clash of two highly motivated and interested parties before a neutral arbitrator is the method best calculated to arrive at an acceptable version of the truth. Cases in courts, bills in Congress, and candidates nominated by POLITICAL PARTIES in ELECTIONS are examples of the clash of interested parties that are resolved by contest rather than by resorting to philosopher kings, as proposed by Plato (ca. 427–347 B.C.E.), the ancient Greek philosopher, in *The Republic*, or to actual physical combat between the contending parties. Advisory opinions on what another branch of government should do or what the Supreme Court might do in a future case lack the challenge of a contest by real people with real interests and change the issue instead to a hypothetical contest with, most likely, hypothetical results.

> *The American government and legal system rest on the proposition that the clash of two highly motivated and interested parties before a neutral arbitrator is the method best calculated to arrive at an acceptable version of the truth.*

Cases come to the Supreme Court either by mandatory appeal as determined by Congress or by certiorari—a writ for the removal of a case from an inferior court to a superior court—which allows the Court to decide whether or not to hear the appeal. In 1996, for example, Congress provided for a direct appeal to the Supreme Court in the case of challenges to a law aimed at limiting sexual indecency on the INTERNET and in the law giving the president the power to veto line items in the BUDGET (see VETOES). However, for the most part the Court controls the cases it will review. According to the informal but well-established "rule of four," the Court votes on whether to hear a case on appeal via certiorari and takes the case if at least four members, not a majority, request it.

Decisions of the Supreme Court are generally rendered after an oral hearing, at which the two parties involved in the case are represented by attorneys. Sometimes amicus curiae ("friend of the court") briefs are submitted on behalf of outside parties who have an interest in or who may be affected by the decision's outcome. After the hearing, in which the members of the Court may ask questions of the attorneys, the justices meet in private and discuss the case and a possible decision.

If all nine members participate in reviewing a case—some may not for various reasons including conflicts of interest, or there may be a vacancy on the Supreme Court—a majority of five members is necessary to overrule a lower court decision. If the vote is 4–4, then the lower court ruling is affirmed. One of the justices in the majority is generally selected to write the majority opinion. On occasion, an opinion is issued *per curiam* ("by the court") rather than under the name of a single member. Those justices who disagree with the outcome determined by the majority may write dissenting opinions, and those in the majority may write concurring opinions if they agree with the outcome but do not agree completely with the basis of the majority opinion. Law clerks work for each justice and do most of the research to help them decide cases and write opinions.

The practice of issuing dissenting opinions has been criticized as a detraction from the authoritative nature of the Supreme Court's majority opinions and as ammunition for those who disagree with the ruling. However, over the Court's history some dissenting opinions have paved the way for the Court to later overrule an earlier decision and adopt the dissenter's position. The fact that the Court conducts its discussions about cases in private makes concurring and dissenting opinions an important source of insight into how the justices came to their decisions.

Supreme Court decisions technically have effect only for the parties in each particular case. But because of the Anglo-American legal principles of *stare decisis* and precedent—which require courts to stand by their decisions and apply prior decisions to the same factual situations—courts subordinate to the Supreme Court must enforce such decisions in similar cases that come before them.

Political Questions

In *Marbury v. Madison* (1803), Chief Justice John Marshall inaugurated the Supreme Court's role as the arbiter of the Constitution and its defender even against the other branches of government, but he also announced that "[q]uestions in their nature political, or which are, by the constitution and laws, submitted to the executive can never be [posed] in this court." This doctrine allows the Court to avoid becoming entangled in nonlegal issues that under the Constitution are to be settled by the other branches or by the people at the polls.

Occasions have arisen, however, when the other arenas for determining the rights and interests of individuals or groups have produced manifest injustices—for instance, the failure of state legislatures to redistrict to at least approximate the goal of "one person, one vote" (see REAPPORTIONMENT). In a case addressing that problem, BAKER V. CARR (1962), Justice William J. Brennan (1906–97) said that the political question doctrine was restricted to certain types of situations or outcomes. These include where the Constitution clearly gives authority to another branch, where the courts have no standards with which to resolve a dispute or need a policy decision by another branch, where such action would show great disrespect for another branch, where there is an unusual requirement not to overturn a political decision already made, and where great embarrassment could result from different decisions by different branches of government.

Like the other two branches, the Supreme Court depends on a consensus among the people as to its role in the national government. Granting the justices life tenure was intended to insulate them from public passions and political pandering. To a great extent, however, the opinions of the Supreme Court have reflected the status quo. For all its faults, the Supreme Court nonetheless remains the defender of the Constitution, regardless of how a majority of its members may choose to interpret that responsibility at any particular time.

More on this topic:

Taking of Property   *See* JUST COMPENSATION; PROPERTY.

Taxation

Taxes have been a volatile political issue throughout the nation's history. "No taxation without representation" became the slogan of many British colonists in America at the time of the Revolutionary War (1775–83). English citizens had struggled for centuries to place the power to raise taxes in the hands of their elected representatives in Parliament rather than leave it to the discretion of the monarch, so the colonists naturally resented Parliament's power to tax them when they had no representation in that legislative body. In the Whiskey Rebellion (1794), a response to a national tax on liquor, the home of the regional tax inspector in western Pennsylvania was burned during an armed uprising by small farmers who distilled their own whiskey. Taxes have been especially likely to increase during wartime and other national crises.

Taxes are the means by which governments obtain the resources they need to operate; and in a GOVERNMENT of the people, by the people, and for the people, taxes provide the means "to… establish Justice, insure domestic Tranquility, provide for the common defence, [and] promote the general Welfare"—all goals in the PREAMBLE to the Constitution. "Money is, with propriety, considered as the vital principle of the body politic; as that which sustains its life and motion and enables it to perform its most essential functions," wrote ALEXANDER HAMILTON in essay 30 of *The Federalist* (1787–88) (see FEDERALIST PAPERS). "A complete power, therefore, to procure a regular and adequate supply of revenue, as far as the resources of the community will permit, may be regarded as an indispensable ingredient in every constitution."

At the time of the CONSTITUTIONAL CONVENTION OF 1787, the delegates were acutely aware of the need to provide the new federal government with an adequate source of funds to carry out its responsibilities. But they were also concerned that any taxation be fairly apportioned among the states and that the revenues raised not be excessive. In addition to requiring that direct taxes be apportioned among the states, they also required that revenue bills be initiated in the HOUSE OF REPRESENTATIVES—the more representative house of Congress—and that any revenue bill be approved by Congress and signed by the PRESIDENT, as with any other law (see LEGISLATION).

The Constitution deals with taxes in several sections. Article I, section 8, states in its first item that "Congress shall have Power To lay and collect Taxes, Duties, Imposts and Excises, to pay the Debts and provide for the common Defence and general Welfare of the United States; but all Duties, Imposts and Excises shall be uniform throughout the United States." This key provision resolved the failure of the ARTICLES OF CONFEDERATION (1781) to give Congress the power to tax. Article I, section 9, which authorized a tax on the importation of slaves (see SLAVERY), also provides: "No Tax or Duty shall be laid on Articles exported from any State." The Sixteenth Amendment (1913) provides for a federal income tax, and the Twenty-fourth Amendment (1964) prohibits "any poll tax or other tax" as a requirement for voting.

Several of the Constitution's tax provisions are not of great significance today. For example, Article I, section 2, mandates that "direct Taxes shall be apportioned among the several states" and sets out the basis of this apportionment. Direct taxes were determined by the Supreme Court in *Hylton v. United States* (1796) to mean only taxes on PROPERTY, not on income. This provision, however, was changed by language in the Fourteenth Amendment (1868), which removed the provision regarding "direct Taxes," and by the Sixteenth Amendment, authorizing a federal income tax.

Methods of Taxation

The power to tax is concurrent—both the states and the federal government have this power, subject to constitutional limitations. Such limitations, including the requirement in Article I, section 8, that federal taxes be uniform throughout the United States, have not kept the federal government from taxing almost any object or subject, although the power to tax incomes of citizens necessitated a constitutional amendment.

Income Tax. In 1862, during the Civil War (1861–65), Congress inaugurated an income tax to finance the war and created the office of the commissioner of internal revenue to oversee its collection. The tax was repealed ten years later, but when Congress again enacted an income tax law in 1894, the Supreme Court ruled that it was unconstitutional. Ratification of the Sixteenth Amendment in 1913 finally made a federal income tax constitutional, stating: "The Congress shall have power to lay and collect taxes on incomes, from whatever source derived, without apportionment among the several States, and without regard to any census or enumeration."

Personal income taxes were originally quite low, affecting only a small percentage of the very wealthy. In 1916, for example, the top rate of six percent was levied on incomes of more than $20,000, equivalent to about $300,000 and above today. During World War II a major change resulted in more than thirty-five percent of the population paying income taxes.

Although the Constitution requires that taxes be uniform, the Supreme Court held that this uniformity is geographical in nature and does not apply in the case of differences in rates. Thus, according to *Knowlton v. Moore* (1900), the Constitution does not preclude a progressive income tax in which people with different incomes are taxed at different rates or legislative classification for tax purposes (in this case, categories for estate taxes over a certain dollar amount). More recently, in *Fitzgerald v. Racing Association of Central Iowa* (2003), the Court held that a state scheme to both economically aid racetracks by allowing slot machines and increase state revenue by imposing an escalating tax rate on them, while holding the rate for other slot venues constant, does not violate the equal protection clause of the Constitution.

In several cases the Supreme Court originally excluded taxes on the income of federal judges, on the grounds that such a tax diminished their compensation, contrary to Article III, section 1 (see COMPENSATION OF OFFICIALS). But that reading of the Constitution was overruled in *O'Malley v. Woodrough* (1939), and the Court's determination that state officials' salaries were not subject to federal taxes was overruled in *Graves v. New York ex rel. O'Keefe* (1939).

Estate Tax. Both federal and state governments levy taxes on the estates of citizens when they die if the value of their estate exceeds a certain amount, although the tax-cut package passed by Congress in 2001 proposes to phase out the federal estate tax by 2010. The Supreme Court in *New York Trust Co. v. Eisner* (1921) held that because federal estate taxes are not direct taxes, they do not have to be apportioned among the states. In *Salomon v. State Tax Commission* (1929), the Court held that the DUE PROCESS clause of the Fourteenth Amendment places no restriction on when an inheritance tax can be imposed or on the property to be valued for the purposes of such a tax.

Federal and State Tax Immunity

The concurrent nature of the taxing power, as with federal and state power over COMMERCE, has led to a number of Supreme Court cases involving the respective powers of the state and federal governments. However, the SUPREMACY CLAUSE in Article VI gives the federal government leverage in any such dispute.

Federal Immunity. The leading case in the area of federal immunity from state taxation is MCCULLOCH V. MARYLAND (1819), in which Chief Justice JOHN MARSHALL, relying on the supremacy clause, declared that state taxation of an instrumentality of the national government located in its jurisdiction was unconstitutional because, among other reasons, "the power to tax involves the power to destroy."

State Immunity. In the federal system of government created by the Constitution (see FEDERALISM), state governments retain some sovereign immunity. Over the years the Supreme Court has grappled with determining the extent to which the federal government can impose taxes that affect the "States as States" or in their governmental capacities, as opposed to activities outside the scope of any claim of state sovereignty. In *United States v. Kahriger* (1953), the Court held that "Unless there are provisions, extraneous to any tax needs, courts are without authority to limit the [federal] exercise of the taxing power." But in several later cases, such as *Garcia v. San Antonio Metropolitan Transit Authority* (1985), the Court decided that rather than focus on "predetermined notions of sovereign power…the built-in restraints that our system provides through state participation in federal governmental action [and the] political process ensure that laws that unduly burden the states will not be promulgated." In reviewing the Tax Injunction Act of 1970 that was intended to prohibit federal court interference in state tax collecting efforts, the Supreme Court, in *Hibbs v. Winn* (2004), limited the effect of the law by finding that it did not bar a federal court challenge to the constitutionality of a state taxing scheme when the challenger's own taxes were not at stake.

Standing to Sue

Article III, section 2, limits the federal judicial power to specific "Cases" and "Controversies." Questions thus arise whether a matter brought to a federal court for resolution constitutes a case or a controversy or is not justiciable. As a result, the Supreme Court has variously found that individuals may or may not sue the government over how their taxes are being spent.

CLOSER LOOK

State and local governments have broad leeway under the Constitution to impose sales taxes. But the taxes at times have spawned considerable confusion.

Some states, for example, exempt essential items such as food, medication, and certain clothing from taxes. The reasoning is that such taxes would create a burden on the poor.

But when should an item be considered essential? Some jurisdictions tax snack foods and prepared foods, while leaving most groceries exempt. Others tax toiletry items such as shampoo while exempting similar items with pharmaceutical benefits, such as dandruff shampoo.

To keep the tax code as simple as possible, some states do not exempt essential items. Alabama, for example, has a state sales tax of four percent, which includes groceries.

COST OF SELECTED TAX BREAKS: REVENUE LOSS ESTIMATES FOR SELECTED TAX EXPENDITURES (IN MILLIONS)

Type of tax expenditure	1990	1995	2000	2005	2010
Commerce and housing					
Exclusion of interest on life insurance savings	$7,265	$10,075	$13,460	$17,440	$25,270
Deductibility of interest on consumer credit	1,525	0	0	0	0
Deductibility of mortgage interest on owner-occupied homes	37,580	51,270	60,270	62,160	103,540
Deductibility of property tax on owner-occupied homes	9,520	14,845	22,140	19,110	12,580
Education, training, employment, and social services					
Deductibility of charitable contributions (education)	1,195	1,535	2,130	2,880	5,190
Credit for child and dependent care expenses	3,895	2,900	2,390	3,060	1,570
Health					
Exclusion of employer contributions for medical insurance premiums and medical care	26,360	60,670	76,530	118,420	200,510
Deductibility of medical expenses	2,860	3,660	4,250	6,110	6,840
Social Security and Medicare					
Exclusion of Social Security benefits					
Disability insurance benefits	1,210	1,895	2,640	3,600	6,240
OASI benefits for retired workers	16,040	16,875	18,250	19,110	20,230
Benefits for dependents and survivors	2,995	3,610	3,910	3,940	3,420
Income security					
Exclusion of workmen's compensation benefits	2,735	4,475	5,120	5,770	6,010
Net exclusion of pension contributions and earnings					
Employer plans (includes 401k plans)	45,385	55,540	89,120	88,070	94,900
Individual Retirement Accounts	6,620	6,245	15,200	3,100	7,200
Keogh plans	1,460	4,435	5,500	9,400	14,230
Veterans' benefits and services					
Exclusion of veterans' death benefits and disability compensation[a]	1,580	1,985	3,090	3,321	4,200

SOURCE: Adapted from *Vital Statistics on American Politics, 2007-2008*, pp. 409-410. Washington, D.C.: CQ Press, 2008.
NOTE: The federal tax code includes numerous tax breaks and exemptions for individuals and businesses. This table shows a few major tax provisions and the resulting amount of revenue lost to the federal treasury. Amounts in current dollars. Fiscal year basis. OASI is Old Age and Survivors Insurance. Tax expenditures are defined as revenue losses attributable to provisions of the federal tax laws that allow a special exclusion, exemption, or deduction from gross income or that provide a special credit, a preferential rate of tax, or a deferral of liability. The Internal Revenue Service collected about $1 trillion in 2006 through individual income taxes. Losses shown are those for individuals.
[a] Prior to 2000, veterans' disability compensation only.

In *Frothingham v. Mellon* (1923), the plaintiff had sued the secretary of the Treasury because she did not like the federal government's giving tax dollars to the states to promote the "welfare and hygiene of maternity and infancy," the aim of the Federal Maternity Act (1921). Without any particular justification in the Constitution, the Supreme Court declared: "The party who invokes [the power of the courts] must be able to show that he has sustained or is immediately in danger of sustaining some direct injury as a result of [a] statute's enforcement, and not merely that he suffers in some indefinite way in common with people generally."

In *Flast v. Cohen* (1968), however, the Supreme Court held that a taxpayer had standing to challenge a federal law benefiting parochial schools, alleging that such funding violated the constitutional prohibition against the establishment of RELIGION in the First Amendment (1791). According to the opinion of Chief Justice Earl Warren (1891–1974), a taxpayer suit may be permitted if the legislation questioned directly involves the expenditure of funds and the taxpayer can show that congressional spending exceeds its constitutional powers. The scope of the decision in *Flast*—which resulted in a flood of taxpayer cases, many of which challenged the national government's prosecution of the Vietnam War (1955–75)—has been limited by later cases. The Supreme Court would distinguish challenges under other provisions of the Constitution than the First Amendment in its decision in *DaimlerChrysler Corp. v. Cuno* (2006), which denied standing for a taxpayer suit based on alleged violations of the commerce clause.

Internal Revenue Service

Originally a bureau of the Department of the Treasury, the Internal Revenue Service is the tax-collection agency for the federal government and as such deals directly with more Americans than any other public or private institution. Another major function of the IRS is the enforcement of the nation's tax laws. The bureau's role was expanded as it became necessary to increase revenue to finance American participation in World War I, which the United States entered in 1917. After World War II, the agency was reorganized in the 1950s to remove political patronage jobs in favor of career professional employees, and its name was changed to the Internal Revenue Service.

As a result of allegations that the IRS abused taxpayers, the Taxpayer Bill of Rights 2 was signed into law in 1996 and later codified into the Internal Revenue Code. The act provides a number of procedural rights and safeguards for taxpayers, such as DUE PROCESS protections for taxpayers subject to audit and tax collection actions, as well as relief for innocent spouses and taxpayers unable to manage their own financial affairs.

More on this topic:
Budget, p. 68
Census, p. 85
Debt, p. 146
Exclusive Powers, p. 204

Tenth Amendment *See* STATES; STATES' RIGHTS.

Term Limits *See* TERMS OF OFFICE.

Terms of Office

In ancient Athens, the cradle of DEMOCRACY, the number of citizens eligible to vote—free adult males only—numbered between twenty and forty thousand. Because most of the numerous public offices had a term of one year, a majority of citizens could expect to hold public office sometime during their lifetime.

A basic principle of constitutionalism is public officials' accountability to the people, and regular or periodic ELECTIONS that prevent unlimited terms of office is the primary method of making officials accountable for their actions. Terms for elected officials and judges are thus set or referred to in the constitutions of all democratic governments. Monarchs and dictators, in contrast, do not expose themselves to approval or removal by the citizenry on a regular basis.

The Constitution refers in several places to public officials' terms of office, including members of Congress, the president, and federal judges.

Congress

Article I, section 2, regarding the HOUSE OF REPRESENTATIVES, requires that members be chosen "every second Year. …" Article I, section 3, regarding the SENATE, mandates that senators be elected for six-year terms, one-third every two years.

Article I, section 4, further specifies: "The Congress shall assemble at least once every Year, and such Meeting shall be on the First Monday in December, unless they shall by Law appoint a different Day." The Twentieth Amendment (1933), called the "Lame Duck Amendment" (see LAME DUCKS), changed the date, providing: "The Congress shall assemble at least once in every year, and such meeting shall begin at noon on the 3d day of January, unless they shall by law appoint a different day." Before this amendment, members of CONGRESS took office on March 4 of the odd-numbered year following the election in November of the previous even-numbered year. By assembling in December, any members who had been defeated could vote in the short lame duck session. Now all members of Congress elected in November are sworn in on January 3, when the new congressional session begins.

President and Vice President

Article II, section 1, specifies that the PRESIDENT "shall hold his Office during the Term of four Years, and, together with the Vice President, chosen for the same Term, be elected as follows…" (see VICE PRESIDENT). Under the ARTICLES OF CONFEDERATION (1781), the president, an impotent creature of the Congress, had a term of only one year. The FRAMERS OF THE CONSTITUTION realized that they needed to give the far more powerful president they were creating a greater term in which to serve if he was to be expected to carry out his duties effectively.

In essay 70 of *The Federalist* (1787–88) (see FEDERALIST PAPERS), ALEXANDER HAMILTON noted that the four "ingredients which constitute energy in the executive are unity; duration; an adequate provision for its support; and competent powers." He added in essay 71 that "[d]uration in office…has relation to two objects: to the personal firmness of the executive magistrate in the employment of his constitutional powers, and to the stability of the system of administration which may have been adopted under his auspices." According to Hamilton, a president's success will be "in proportion to the firmness or precariousness of the tenure by which he holds [his office]."

GEORGE WASHINGTON, the first president, took office on April 30, 1789. Thereafter, newly elected presidents and vice presidents were sworn in on March 4 of the year following their election, until this date was changed to January 20 by the Twentieth Amendment.

"Washington Wouldn't. Lincoln Couldn't. Roosevelt Shouldn't."

—Slogan from a 1940 campaign button opposing Franklin D. Roosevelt's bid for a third term as president

Supreme Court

Article III, section 1, provides that "Judges, both of the supreme and inferior Courts, shall hold their Offices during good Behaviour…," meaning for life, unless they resign or are removed by IMPEACHMENT. The tenure of federal judges proposed in the Constitution, said Hamilton in essay 78 of *The Federalist*, "is conformable to the most approved of the State Constitutions [and] in a republic it is a no less excellent barrier to the encroachments and oppressions of the representative body."

Term Limits

By refusing to be a candidate for president for a third term, George Washington set an informal precedent for a century and a half. Franklin D. Roosevelt (1882–1945), however, ignored this custom; he ran and was elected to a third and then a fourth term as president in 1940 and 1944, respectively. His audacity—however popular he may have been during a time of depression and war—resulted in the Twenty-second Amendment (1951), which provides: "No person shall be elected to the office of the President more than twice, and no person who has held the office of President, or acted as President, for more than two years of a term to which some other person was elected President shall be elected to the office of the President more than once…."

Since the early 1990s a movement has been under way to place limits on the terms of members of Congress as well. Even though some state constitutions have imposed term limits on state legislators, the trend has not gained sufficient momentum at the national level for a constitutional amendment, which would be required in light of the Supreme Court's decision in *U.S. Term Limits, Inc. v. Thornton* (1995). In this case, Arkansas voters had adopted an amendment to the state constitution that set term limits for the state's legislature and its congressional delegation. The Court voided such state constitutional limitations on the number of terms

Rep. George Nethercutt, a Republican from Washington, angered supporters of term limits when he decided to run for a fourth term in 1999.
Source: CQ Photo/Scott J. Ferrell

their representatives and senators can serve. In his opinion for the Court, Justice John Paul Stevens (b. 1920) underscored that the Constitution prohibits the states from setting their own qualifications for congressional candidates. Justice Stevens noted that the Articles of Confederation (1781) had included term limits but that the delegates to the CONSTITUTIONAL CONVENTION OF 1787 expressly rejected any such limits.

The relatively high percentage of incumbent members of Congress who are reelected and the entrenched character of those in office have provided impetus for the term-limit movement. However, being returned to office regularly gives a member seniority status, important for committee assignments and chairmanships, and ensures trained leadership for the states they represent. So far, there does not appear to be a public consensus that a wholesale change in members of Congress will solve the perceived problems related to entrenchment or that term limits should be allowed to override the will of the majority of the voters in national elections (see MAJORITY RULE). After all, each election carries the power to limit an unpopular politician's term of office.

Territory

To justify his annexation and invasion of neighboring territory, the Nazi dictator Adolf Hitler (1889–1945) spoke of *Lebensraum*—a term originated by the German geographer and ethnographer Friederich Ratzel (1844–1904)—to provide "living space" for the German people. History is replete with accounts of wars fought for territorial acquisition, although aggressors like Hitler often couched their goals in more euphemistic terms, such as calling them wars of liberation or wars to protect some minority population in a coveted territory.

A nation's territory defines the limits of its jurisdiction under INTERNATIONAL LAW. As Chief Justice JOHN MARSHALL explained in *The Schooner Exchange v. McFaddon* (1812), "The jurisdiction of the nation within its own territory is necessarily exclusive and absolute. It is susceptible of no limitation not imposed by itself." Many national constitutions expressly refer to the nation's territory and its SOVEREIGNTY over it. For example, the Russian constitution (1993) provides in article 4: "1. The sov-

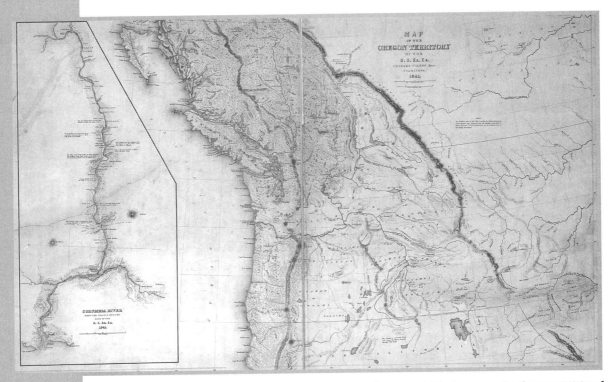

On August 14, 1848, Congress passed a bill creating the Oregon Territory, a tract of land encompassing the present states of Oregon, Idaho, Washington, and western Montana. This map of the region was published around 1879.
Source: Library of Congress

ereignty of the Russian federation shall extend to its entire territory. 2. The constitution of the Russian federation and federal laws shall have priority throughout the territory of the Russian federation. 3. The Russian federation shall ensure the integrity and inviolability of its territory."

The States

The U.S. Constitution sets out two distinct types of territory and methods of governance: states and U.S. territories. The territory of the United States itself was constituted from the thirteen independent STATES that were first joined under the ARTICLES OF CONFEDERATION (1781). The states are named in Article I, section 2, which sets out the apportionment of members for the new HOUSE OF REPRESENTATIVES (see REAPPORTIONMENT), pending the first official CENSUS. Article VII declares that RATIFICATION by just nine of the thirteen states would be "sufficient for the Establishment of this Constitution between the States so ratifying the Same." In the end, by 1790 all thirteen states had ratified the document. Today the territory of the Union comprises the fifty states of the United States, but additional territories that are not a part of any state also come under the nation's jurisdiction.

At the time the Constitution went into effect, additional territories were claimed by some states, mostly to the north and west of the original thirteen. The process of dealing with these lands had begun in 1780, before the adoption of the Articles of Confederation, when the Continental Congress approved the policy that lands ceded to the confederation would "be settled and formed into distinct republican states, which would become members of the Federal Union." A Territorial Ordinance was drafted by THOMAS JEFFERSON and adopted in 1784. And then in July 1787, while the CONSTITUTIONAL CONVENTION OF 1787 was in progress in Philadelphia, the Congress adopted the

Northwest Ordinance. Probably the most important act of the preconstitutional Congress, this law established the basic principles that would be used to convert territories of the United States into states on an equal footing with the other existing states.

Territories

Many of the present fifty states of the Union were created out of former U.S. territories. For example, in addition to the state of Louisiana, a number of states including Missouri and Nebraska were carved out of the territory acquired under the Louisiana Purchase (1803). The last two states to be admitted to the Union were both territories for a period of time before becoming the states of Alaska (1949) and Hawaii (1950). For various reasons both economical and political, however, not all territories can make this transition.

Article IV, section 3, of the Constitution addresses both the ADMISSION OF NEW STATES and the governance of the U.S. territories. With respect to the latter, the Constitution states: "The Congress shall have Power to dispose of and make all needful Rules and Regulations respecting the Territory or other Property belonging to the United States; and nothing in this Constitution shall be so construed as to Prejudice any Claims of the United States, or of any particular State" (see EXCLUSIVE POWERS). The U.S. Supreme Court, in *Nguyen v. United States* (2003), ruled that an Article IV judge from the Commonwealth of the Mariana Islands could not sit on a U.S. district court panel with Article III judges to review an appeal from a territorial court in Guam. *Territory* here refers only to the lands in the possession of the United States and not to any under state jurisdiction. Such territories today include more populous areas such as American Samoa (population 58,000), the Commonwealth of Puerto Rico (3,900,000), the Commonwealth of the Northern Mariana Islands (80,000), Guam (169,000), and the U.S. Virgin Islands (109,000), as well as those with few or no inhabitants, such as Midway Island, Wake Island, Johnston Atoll, Kingman Reef, Palmyra Atoll, Navassa, and Howland, Jarvis, and Baker Islands.

Article I, section 8, gives Congress exclusive authority over the territory of the district set aside from the territory ceded to the national government by Maryland and Virginia for the nation's capital (see CAPITAL, NATIONAL). Land on both sides of the Potomac River, enough for a 100-square-mile tract, was given by Virginia and Maryland for the new city of Washington, D.C., but in 1846 the land south of the Potomac was returned to Virginia.

Any doubt that the Constitution authorized the federal government to acquire new territory was dispelled with the Louisiana Purchase. Westward expansion of the United States continued, impelled by the concept that it was the "manifest destiny" of the United States to reach from sea to sea. Toward the end of the nineteenth century, the United States began acquiring overseas territories. After the Spanish-American War in 1898, for example, in accordance with the Treaty of Paris (1899), Spain ceded Puerto Rico, the Philippine Islands, and Guam to the United States; the Philippines were granted independence in 1946.

Rights of Territorial Inhabitants

The political, civil, and other rights of the inhabitants of the U.S. territories are determined under their own constitutions, organic laws, and local laws and customs. Congress and the federal courts generally determine the effect of the U.S. Constitution on their rights.

Government forms differ in the major territories. American Samoa has a constitution (1967) and elects a governor and a bicameral legislature as well as a delegate to the House of Representatives, who may vote only in committees. Guam is self-governing under a 1950 organic act passed by Congress, and it elects a governor and a unicameral legislature and a nonvoting delegate to the House of Representatives (except in committees). In 2007 the U.S. Supreme Court decided a conflict between the governor and the attorney general of Guam regarding a provision of Guam's organic act, in *Limtiaco v. Camacho*. The Court ruled in favor of the attorney general's position that the debt-limitation provisions of the act had to be based on the assessed rather than appraised value of property. The Commonwealth of the Northern Mariana Islands has a Covenant Agreement with the United States (1986) and elects a governor and a bicameral legislature. Puerto Rico has a constitution (1952) and elects a governor, a bicameral legislature, and a nonvoting delegate to the House of Representatives. The government of the U.S. Virgin Islands operates under an organic act of the Virgin Islands passed by Congress in 1936 and elects a governor and a unicameral legislature and sends a non-voting delegate to the House of Representatives.

In a series of cases known as the Insular Cases, because they involved island territories, the Supreme Court addressed the limits of Congress's power over U.S territories. In the first three cases in 1901, the Court basically held that Congress can determine the constitutional status of U.S. possessions, but constitutional protections apply unless Congress acts otherwise. In later cases in 1903 and 1904, the Court identified FUNDAMENTAL RIGHTS, such as the prohibition against DOUBLE JEOPARDY, that were constitutionally protected, as well as procedural rights, such as trial by jury, that apply only after Congress acts to incorporate the territory into the United States. In 1905 the Court held that because Alaska had been positively incorporated into the United States, the right to a trial by jury as guaranteed by the Sixth Amendment (1791) must apply to its inhabitants (see JURIES; TRIALS). Justice John Marshall Harlan (1833–1911), however, consistently dissented from this incorporation requirement, contending that Congress is bound by all the provisions and guarantees of the Constitution and cannot exempt the territories from its protection.

U.S. territories enjoy considerable self-governance. Here, Felix Camacho, governor of Guam, gives the annual State of the Island address in February 2006.
Source: AP Images/Pacific Daily News, Masako Watanabe

Territorial courts that have jurisdiction in U.S. territories, such as on Guam and in the Virgin Islands, are courts established under the authority of Congress in Article I, section 8, to "constitute Tribunals inferior to the supreme Court." In *American Insurance Co. v. Canter* (1828), the Supreme Court confirmed that the language in Article IV authorizing Congress to "make all needful Rules and Regulations respecting the Territory or other Property belonging to the United States" gave Congress plenary power to acquire and govern territories and permitted the establishment of COURTS other than those expressly authorized under Article III, the judicial article; the decision was made even though this case involved admiralty and maritime jurisdiction, which is expressly placed under the federal courts by Article III (see ADMIRALTY AND MARITIME LAW). In Puerto Rico, however, Congress has created two sets of courts, some of which are constitutionally within the scope of Article III, while others are courts of the Commonwealth of Puerto Rico.

Territorial Seas

"It is now settled in the United States and recognized elsewhere," confirmed the Supreme Court in *Cunard Steamship Co. v. Mellon* (1923), "that the territory subject to its jurisdiction includes the land areas under its dominion and control, the ports, harbors, bays and other enclosed arms of the sea along its coast and a marginal belt of the sea extending from the coast line outward a marine league, or three geographic miles." In 1988, by presidential proclamation, the territorial sea of the United States was extended to twelve miles in accordance with international law allowing the extension of a nation's territorial sovereignty to that limit. In 1999, also by presidential proclamation, the zone contiguous to the territorial waters of the United States, as recognized under international law, was declared to extend "to 24 nautical miles from the baselines of the United States determined in accordance with international law, but in no case within the territorial sea of another nation."

Identification with a particular piece of land or territory is one of a number of ways—together with kinship, culture, and RELIGION—in which people can be united. In addition to enabling national identity, land constitutes a chief source of political power, as noted earlier, with sovereignty over a given area being a key indicator of a functioning state.

> **More on this topic:**
>
> *Sovereignty, p. 506*
>
> *States, p. 517*

Terrorism

Before September 11, 2001, many terrorist attacks had occurred against U.S. citizens overseas: an estimated 250,000 to 300,000 worldwide in the previous twenty years. Of these, the capture of sixty-three American hostages in Iran in 1979 most deeply affected the United States. This terrorist act by militant followers of the Ayatollah Khomeini, leader of a revolutionary movement in Iran, crippled the presidency of Jimmy Carter (b. 1924) and contributed to his defeat for reelection in 1980. But the attacks by Islamic terrorists on the twin towers of the World Trade Center in New York City and the Pentagon outside Washington, D.C., which killed some three thousand persons and caused enormous economic losses, finally brought international terrorism home to American soil.

The roots of terrorism, which probably date to the origins of human history, include certain individuals' frustration at being unable to bring about a desired political or religious goal and hatred of others who do not share the same ideology or who prevent the desired change. In the first century A.D. a religious sect in Palestine called Zealots conducted a campaign of terror against the Roman occupation, and later the Assassins, a messianic religious sect, operated from the eleventh century until being brought under control by the Mongols in the thirteenth century.

A major terrorist act that foreshadowed the tremendous violence of the twentieth century was the 1914 assassination of Archduke Franz Ferdinand, heir to the Austrian throne, an event that precipitated World War I. The Irish Republican Army, established in 1919 and declared illegal in 1931 and 1936, was responsible for a

The terrorist attacks that destroyed New York's World Trade Center and damaged the Pentagon on September 11, 2001, produced the USA PATRIOT Act and other legislation restricting civil liberties of suspects to gain national security.
Source: Reuters/Sean Adair

EXECUTIVE ORDER ESTABLISHING THE OFFICE OF HOMELAND SECURITY AND THE HOMELAND SECURITY COUNCIL (EXCERPTS)

By the authority vested in me as President by the Constitution and the laws of the United States of America, it is hereby ordered as follows:

Section 1. Establishment. I hereby establish within the Executive Office of the President an Office of Homeland Security (the "Office") to be headed by the Assistant to the President for Homeland Security.

Section 2. Mission. The mission of the Office shall be to develop and coordinate the implementation of a comprehensive national strategy to secure the United States from terrorist threats or attacks....

Section 3. Functions. The functions of the Office shall be to coordinate the executive branch's efforts to detect, prepare for, prevent, protect against, respond to, and recover from terrorist attacks within the United States....

(a) National Strategy. The Office shall work with executive departments and agencies, State and local governments, and private entities to ensure the adequacy of the national strategy for detecting, preparing for, preventing, protecting against, responding to, and recovering from terrorist threats or attacks within the United States and shall periodically review and coordinate revisions to that strategy as necessary.

(b) Detection. The Office shall identify priorities and coordinate efforts for collection and analysis of information within the United States regarding threats of terrorism against the United States and activities of terrorists or terrorist groups within the United States. The Office also shall identify, in coordination with the Assistant to the President for National Security Affairs, priorities for collection of intelligence outside the United States regarding threats of terrorism within the United States....

(ii) Executive departments and agencies shall, to the extent permitted by law, make available to the Office all information relating to terrorist threats and activities within the United States....

(c) Preparedness. The Office of Homeland Security shall coordinate national efforts to prepare for and mitigate the consequences of terrorist threats or attacks within the United States....

(d) Prevention. The Office shall coordinate efforts to prevent terrorist attacks within the United States. ...

(e) Protection. The Office shall coordinate efforts to protect the United States and its critical infrastructure from the consequences of terrorist attacks....

(f) Response and Recovery. The Office shall coordinate efforts to respond to and promote recovery from terrorist threats or attacks within the United States....

(g) Incident Management. The Assistant to the President for Homeland Security shall be the individual primarily responsible for coordinating the domestic response efforts of all departments and agencies in the event of an imminent terrorist threat and during and in the immediate aftermath of a terrorist attack within the United States and shall be the principal point of contact for and to the President with respect to coordination of such efforts....

series of bombings in England in 1939 and continued its guerrilla warfare activities for decades afterward, all in protest against British hegemony in Northern Ireland. Hamas, originally a social welfare organization, has for several decades conducted terrorist activities against the civilian population in Israel, as have other militant Palestinian groups. In the Philippines, the Abu Sayyaf terrorists forced the Philippine government in 2001 to begin an all-out offensive against them, with the aid of the United States.

Defining Terrorism

Terrorism is broadly defined as the use or threat of violence to make a statement about ideological, political, religious, or cultural beliefs. It may not have a specific aim, such as coercing a government response to certain demands, but instead may be a display of violence simply for the sake of punishing and frightening the terrorists' perceived enemies. The modern definition of the term *terror* is derived from the period following the French Revolution (1789), called the "Reign of Terror," during which the leaders of the new republic executed thousands of persons suspected of antigovernment activity. Whereas WAR, even civil war, generally has rules observed by recognized

(h) Continuity of Government. The Assistant to the President for Homeland Security, in coordination with the Assistant to the President for National Security Affairs, shall review plans and preparations for ensuring the continuity of the Federal Government in the event of a terrorist attack that threatens the safety and security of the United States Government or its leadership....

(i) Public Affairs. The Office, subject to the direction of the White House Office of Communications, shall coordinate the strategy of the executive branch for communicating with the public in the event of a terrorist threat or attack within the United States. The Office also shall coordinate the development of programs for educating the public about the nature of terrorist threats and appropriate precautions and responses.

(j) Cooperation with State and Local Governments and Private Entities. The Office shall encourage and invite the participation of State and local governments and private entities, as appropriate, in carrying out the Office's functions.

(k) Review of Legal Authorities and Development of Legislative Proposals. The Office shall coordinate a periodic review and assessment of the legal authorities available to executive departments and agencies to permit them to perform the functions described in this order. When the Office determines that such legal authorities are inadequate, the Office shall develop ... proposals for presidential action and legislative proposals for submission to the Office of Management and Budget to en-

hance the ability of executive departments and agencies to perform those functions. ...

(l) Budget Review. The Assistant to the President for Homeland Security ... shall identify programs that contribute to the Administration's strategy for homeland security and, in the development of the President's annual budget submission, shall review and provide advice to the heads of departments and agencies for such programs. ...

Section 5. Establishment of Homeland Security Council.

(a) I hereby establish a Homeland Security Council (the "Council"), which shall be responsible for advising and assisting the President with respect to all aspects of homeland security....

(c) The Council shall meet at the President's direction....

Section 6. Original Classification Authority. I hereby delegate the authority to classify information originally as Top Secret, in accordance with Executive Order 12958 or any successor Executive Order, to the Assistant to the President for Homeland Security.

Section 7. Continuing Authorities. This order does not alter the existing authorities of United States Government departments and agencies. All executive departments and agencies are directed to assist the Council and the Assistant to the President for Homeland Security in carrying out the purposes of this order....

GEORGE W. BUSH
THE WHITE HOUSE
October 8, 2001

---

belligerents, a basic feature of modern terrorism is its anonymity and disregard for any rules of combat or engagement between enemies.

One difficulty in defining terrorism is that the term can mean different things to people on different sides. For example, a Palestinian suicide bomber who explodes a device in a crowded public area in Israel is committing a terrorist act, but reprisals by Israeli armed forces may also seem to Palestinians to be terrorist acts intended to frighten fellow citizens. And although terrorism is usually associated with nongovernmental ("rogue") organizations, death squads run by the Nazis and authoritarian Latin American regimes might also be considered terrorist organizations.

According to the U.S. Code, Title 22, section 2656f(d), *terrorism* "means premeditated, politically motivated violence perpetrated against noncombatant targets by subnational groups or clandestine agents," and *terrorist group* "means any group practicing, or which has significant subgroups which practice, international terrorism." The same section defines *international terrorism* as "terrorism involving citizens or the territory of more than one country."

The International Law Commission defines a terrorist act as "(i) [a]ny act causing death or grievous bodily harm or loss of liberty [assassination or hostage taking] to a Head of State, persons exercising the prerogatives of the head of State, their hereditary or designated successors, the spouse of such persons, or persons charged with public functions or holding public positions when the act is directed against them in their public capacity; (ii) [a]cts calculated to destroy or damage public property...; (iii) [a]ny act likely to imperil human lives through the creation of a public danger, in particular the seizure of aircraft, the taking of hostages and any form of violence directed against persons who enjoy international protection or diplomatic immunity; [and] (iv) [t]he manufacture, obtaining, possession or supplying of arms, ammunition, explosives or harmful substances with a view to the commission of a terrorist act."

Terrorism may be regarded as domestic or international depending on whether it is threatened or perpetrated by nationals within their own country—such as the bombing by Timothy McVeigh of the federal office building in Oklahoma City on April 19, 1995—or by citizens of other nations—as in the case of the September 11 attacks on the United States by the followers of Osama bin Laden. Terrorism is further subdivided into state-sponsored terrorism, state-supported terrorism, and private terrorism. If a country uses terrorism as an extension of its national policy, it is said to sponsor terrorism, but if it only aids terrorists, then such terrorism is considered state supported. Private terrorism is conducted without the official support of any nation.

Constitutional Response

Language that clearly applies to both domestic and international terrorist acts against the United States and its citizens can be found in the PREAMBLE to the Constitution, which speaks of ensuring "domestic Tranquility" (see DOMESTIC TRANQUILITY) and providing "for the common defence" (see ARMED FORCES). In the body of the Constitution, under Article IV, section 4, the U.S. government guarantees to protect the STATES "against Invasion; and on Application of the Legislature, or of the Executive [governor] (when the Legislature cannot be convened) against domestic Violence." Other provisions that can be used to thwart or combat internal and external terrorist activities include the authority granted under Article II, section 2, to the PRESIDENT as commander in chief of the armed forces, including the power to command "the Militia of the several States, when called into the actual Service of the United States."

Terrorist acts can have a ripple effect, leading to fear and anxiety throughout a nation and causing a free society to jettison some of its constitutionally guaranteed rights and liberties (see LIBERTY) while taking measures to protect itself from further attacks (see EMERGENCY POWERS). Freedom of SPEECH, particularly political speech, is the cornerstone of a DEMOCRACY. To curtail free speech even during emergency situations is to strike a blow at the heart of constitutional democracy. After the attacks on the World Trade Center and the Pentagon, complaints from a spokesman for President George W. Bush (b. 1946) resulted in cancellation of a political satirist's television show after he compared the attacks to U.S. military actions that have similarly produced civilian casualties. Freedom of movement is not expressly guaranteed in the Constitution, but it has been affirmed by the Supreme Court on a number of occasions, beginning with *Crandall v. Nevada* (1868) (see TRAVEL). Restrictions on travel and entry into public buildings, increased personal searches (see SEARCH AND SEIZURE), more widespread WIRETAPPING, and the use of military tribunals in lieu of regular TRIALS all impinge on constitutional rights normally taken for granted.

In the wake of the Iranian hostage crisis and subsequent terrorist acts, including the bombings of a U.S. military housing facility in Saudi Arabia in 1996 and the federal office building in Oklahoma City, President Bill Clinton (b. 1946) signed into law the Antiterrorism and Effective Death Penalty Act (1996). This law granted broad powers to LAW ENFORCEMENT agencies to fight domestic terrorism, such as access to certain confidential IMMIGRATION and naturalization files and authorization to arrest and detain certain suspect illegal ALIENS, and imposed stronger PUNISHMENT, including the DEATH PENALTY, for convicted terrorists.

Following the attacks of September 11, 2001, President George W. Bush established an Office of Homeland Security, which later became the cabinet-level Department of Homeland Security, and Congress was asked to approve a number of new laws to counter international terrorism. Quickly approved in 2001, the PATRIOT ACT strengthened criminal laws against terrorism and authorized enhanced domestic security procedures in the areas of surveillance, border protection, investigations, and money laundering and other means of financing terrorism. The act was reauthorized by Congress in 2006, with some changes. The legislation provides additional tools for protecting mass transportation systems and seaports from attack, takes steps to combat the methamphetamine epidemic that is sweeping our country, and closes dangerous loopholes in our ability to prevent terrorist financing. The measure also created in April 2008 a National Security Division at the Department of Justice. Among the more controversial provisions are the "roving wiretap" portion and the "sneak and peek" section. The first allows the government to get a wiretap on every phone a suspect uses, while the second allows federal investigators to get access to library, business, and medical records without a court order. Critics of the new laws have expressed concern that basic rights of persons accused of crimes—such as the right to the ASSISTANCE OF COUNSEL, the presumption of innocence, and the right to face and cross-examine accusers (see WITNESSES)—will be relaxed as a result of overzealous counterterrorist measures. As Justice William J. Brennan (1906–97) noted in *Brown v. Glines* (1980): "The concept of military necessity is seductively broad, and has a dangerous plasticity. Because they invariably have the visage of overriding importance, there is always a temptation to invoke security 'necessities' to justify an encroachment upon civil liberties. For that reason, the military-security argument must be approached with a healthy skepticism."

The balance between a society's freedom and its ability to protect its citizens from any aggression, including terrorist acts, shifts constantly. During World War II the Supreme Court condoned the removal and internment of Japanese Americans, a decision that has since been discredited as antithetical to constitutionally protected rights such as freedom to travel, the presumption of innocence, and the right to a fair trial. Immediately after the 2001 attacks, people of Arabic descent and appearance were likewise singled out for special scrutiny. Persons designated enemies of the United States in the war on terror, including American citizens, have been detained for long periods of time and often subjected to various forms of torture without the benefit of the constitutional guarantees that undergird our American system of justice and liberty. The Supreme Court has had occasion to review some of these measures in several recent cases. For example, in *HAMDI V. RUMSFELD* (2004), the Court rejected the government's contention that a U.S. citizen could be detained in American territory as an "enemy combatant" without being notified as to the basis for such a designation and without being given an opportunity to contest his or her confinement before a neutral decision maker. And in *Rasul v. Bush* (2004), the Court ruled that federal courts had HABEAS CORPUS jurisdiction to entertain applications by persons claiming to be held "in custody in violation of the…laws…of the United States." A more recent case in which the Supreme Court reviewed government responses to terrorism is *Hamdan v. Rumsfeld* (2006). Terrorist acts affecting the United States are testing how far the balance can swing without forfeiting the fundamental principles on which the Constitution is based.

> **More on this topic:**
>
> *Emergency Powers*, p. 187
>
> *Law Enforcement*, p. 338
>
> *National Security*, p. 375
>
> *Search and Seizure*, p. 479

Third Parties See POLITICAL PARTIES.

Thirteenth Amendment See SLAVERY.

Titles of Nobility *See* NOBILITY, TITLES OF.

Travel

Freedom of movement or the right to travel is not expressly guaranteed in the Constitution. The United Nations' Universal Declaration of Human Rights (1948), however, specifically includes freedom of movement, as do the constitutions of some nations. Japan's constitution (1947) provides, "Every person shall have freedom to choose and change his residence," and Sweden's constitution (1975) declares that "[n]o citizen may be deported or refused entry to Sweden."

The Constitution's COMMERCE clause, Article I, section 8, gives Congress the power to regulate interstate commerce, specifically to eliminate trade barriers among the states. If the FRAMERS OF THE CONSTITUTION intended that livestock and goods could move freely across state lines, CITIZENS should be treated no less favorably. Freedom to travel, like freedom of association (see ASSOCIATION AND ASSEMBLY) and the right of PRIVACY, is considered an important civil liberty inferred from the Constitution.

The first Supreme Court case that directly addressed the right of persons to travel freely among the states was *Crandall v. Nevada* (1868). In its decision the Court invalidated a tax on all passengers leaving the state in conveyances for hire—for example, trains or stagecoaches—for several reasons, with some of the justices relying on the commerce clause and others on more general grounds. In his opinion for the Court, Justice Samuel F. Miller (1816–90) wrote: "The question of the taxing power of the States, as its exercise has affected the functions of the Federal government, has been repeatedly considered by this court, and the right of the States in this mode to impede or embarrass the constitutional operations of that government, or the right which the citizens hold under it, has been uniformly denied."

In *Edwards v. California* (1941), a majority of the Supreme Court embraced the commerce clause to invalidate a California law that made it a crime for a citizen of California to knowingly bring into the state an indigent nonresident. But three concurring members of the Court spoke through Justice William O. Douglas (1898–1980), who, reaching for a higher principle, called the "right of free movement…right of national citizenship." To allow the state of California to deny this right to poor citizens would go against the very nature of national unity, Douglas maintained. In *Saenz v. Roe* (1999), Justice John Paul Stevens (b. 1920) noted in his opinion for the Court that while the word *travel* is not found expressly in the Constitution, "the 'constitutional right to travel from one State to another' is firmly embedded in our jurisprudence." He then described three components of the right to travel, saying it "protects the right of a citizen of one State to enter and to leave another State, the right to be treated as a welcome visitor rather than an unfriendly alien when temporarily present in the second State, and, for those travelers who elect to become permanent residents, the right to be treated like other citizens of that State."

In times of crisis or emergency (see EMERGENCY POWERS), the POLICE POWER of the states and the national government, however, may limit a person's freedom of movement within the United States. In *Korematsu v. United States* (1944), for example, the Supreme Court upheld the relocation of Japanese Americans from the West Coast and their internment during World War II— an action now almost universally decried as RACIAL DISCRIMINATION. More recent efforts to prevent terrorist attacks in the United States may impose new restrictions on the right to move freely about the country (see TERRORISM).

"Mobility is basic to any question of freedom of opportunity."

—Justice William O. Douglas, in *Edwards v. California* (1941)

Although the right to travel within the United States may not be infringed by the states, they may, for various reasons, establish a period of residency before extending certain rights to citizens who have recently moved into their jurisdictions. In *Shapiro v. Thompson* (1969), however, the Supreme Court found that a one-year residency requirement before a person became eligible for state WELFARE benefits was an unconstitutional violation of the right to travel. But in *Sosna v. Iowa* (1975), the Court approved of a one-year residency requirement before permitting a divorce to be granted, citing the state's legitimate interest in protecting the rights of the spouse not seeking the divorce and any minor CHILDREN who would be affected.

Before 1918 the U.S. government placed virtually no restrictions on its citizens traveling to another country. As a result of World War I, however, Congress passed a law requiring citizens intending to leave the country to have a passport. The Passport Act (1926) gives the State Department authority to issue or deny travel documents to persons intending to leave the country. Passports are important for travelers in a foreign country because they identify the travelers and their nationality in case they need assistance from their diplomatic representatives and they facilitate reentry into the travelers' country of origin.

Passports may be denied to criminals and to certain persons during periods of international tension. For example, in the early days of the cold war the State Department did not issue passports to members of communist organizations. The Supreme Court's decision in *Kent v. Dulles* (1958), however, rejected the department's authority to deny passports to persons on the basis of their beliefs or associations. In another case, *Aptheker v. Secretary of State* (1964), the Court voided provisions of the McCarran Act (1950) requiring that passports be denied to Communist Party members on the grounds that the law failed to differentiate between knowing and unknowing membership.

The federal government's right to deny travel to certain proscribed countries—Cuba, for example—has been upheld by the Supreme Court in several cases. In *Haig v. Agee* (1981), the justices rejected a former Central Intelligence Agency official's claim that the denial of a passport violated his First Amendment (1791) right to criticize the government. This former employee of the Central Intelligence Agency, who was living in Germany, had embarked on a campaign "to expose CIA officers and agents" around the world. His passport was revoked by the secretary of state under a regulation applying to persons who "are causing or are likely to cause serious damage to the national security or the foreign policy of the United States." In the Court's opinion, a passport is "a document…addressed to foreign powers…, which, by usage and the law of nations, is received as evidence of the fact [that a person is an American citizen]." The Court held that the regulation under the Passport Act of 1926 and subsequent amendments sufficiently empowered the secretary of state to revoke the passport under the circumstances. Furthermore, the revocation did not reduce the plaintiff's ability to criticize the government and thus was not a violation of the First Amendment's guarantee of free SPEECH. "'[W]hile the Constitution protects against invasions of individual rights," said the Court in quoting an earlier case, "it is not a suicide pact.'"

> **More on this topic:**
>
> *Foreign Affairs, p. 226*
>
> *Immigration, p. 286*
>
> *Terrorism, p. 543*

Treason

In his *Commentaries on the Laws of England* (1765–70), William Blackstone (1723–80) said of treason that "this is the highest civil crime which (considered as a member of the community) any man can possibly commit…." Treason would occur, stated Blackstone, when "a man doth compass or imagine the death of our lord the king, of our lady his queen, or of their eldest son and heir."

Julius and Ethel Rosenberg, separated by a wire screen, stare vacantly at the camera as they exit a federal courthouse in 1951. The testimony of Ethel's brother sealed the Rosenbergs' conviction and execution as Soviet spies.
Source: Library of Congress

Today treason is considered any attempt to overthrow one's government or a betrayal of one's country into the hands of a foreign power.

"Treason against the United States," explains Article III, section 3, of the Constitution at some length, "shall consist only in levying War against them, or in adhering to their Enemies, giving them Aid and Comfort. No Person shall be convicted of Treason unless on the Testimony of two Witnesses to the same overt Act, or on Confession in open Court. The Congress shall have Power to declare the Punishment of Treason, but no Attainder of Treason shall work Corruption of Blood, or Forfeiture except during the Life of the Person attainted."

The FRAMERS OF THE CONSTITUTION went to great effort to narrowly define treason and the evidence necessary to convict someone of such a crime against the nation. They were aware of abuses in Great Britain, where—as Blackstone's comment suggests—a person could be found guilty of treason for merely questioning the authority of the monarch. "As treason may be committed against the United States," wrote JAMES MADISON in essay 43 of *The Federalist* (1787–88) (see FEDERALIST PAPERS), "the authority of the United States ought to be enabled to punish it. But as new-fangled and artificial treasons have been the great engines by which violent factions, the natural offspring of free government, have usually wreaked their alternate malignity on each other, the [Constitutional Convention has], with great judgment, opposed a barrier to this peculiar danger, by inserting a constitutional definition of the crime, fixing the proof necessary for conviction of it, and restraining the Congress, even in punishing it, from extending the consequences of guilt beyond the person of its author."

In *Ex parte Bollman* (1807), Chief Justice JOHN MARSHALL confirmed the narrow reading of the treason provisions intended by the framers. "However flagitious [vicious] may be the crime of conspiring to subvert by force the government of our country, such a conspiracy is not treason." Marshall drew a distinction between "the actual enlistment of men to serve against the government" and the "levying of war." Although in this case no war was initiated, he went on to say that "if it be actually levied...all those who performed any part, however minute, or however remote from the scene of action, and who are actually leagued in the general conspiracy, are to be considered as traitors." In *United States v.* [Aaron] *Burr*, in the same year, Marshall virtually limited conviction of treason to the conduct of hostilities or personal participation in actual hostilities.

The Supreme Court first upheld a conviction of treason shortly after World War II, in *Haupt v. United States* (1947). Here the Court somewhat relaxed the restrictions on proving treason to allow the admission of other evidence in addition to the two WITNESSES required by the Constitution. The witnesses could not testify to overt acts of treason. Instead they related that a father sheltered his treasonous son and helped him get a job in a defense plant. Additional evidence was admitted to show that the father knew of his son's treasonous intentions and therefore that his help furthered that cause.

The framers wisely tried to make the crime of treason difficult to prove, so that thoughts, words, and even deeds that fall short of overtly hostile acts against the government cannot be punished.

Recent cases of treason have generally involved people in positions of trust in the government—employees of the Central Intelligence Agency and the Federal Bureau of Investigation, for example—who abuse their positions for personal gain or other reasons.

More on this topic:

Attainder, Bills of, p. 54

Under Article II, section 2, of the Constitution, the PRESIDENT has "Power to grant Reprieves and Pardons for Offences against the United States, except in the Cases of Impeachment" (see IMPEACHMENT; PARDONS). No exception is made for treason. The particularly farsighted rationale for this was explained by ALEXANDER HAMILTON in essay 75 of *The Federalist*: "[I]n seasons of insurrection or rebellion, there are often critical moments when a well-timed offer of pardon to the insurgents or rebels may restore the tranquillity of the commonwealth…." Hamilton concluded that having to take other measures at such a crucial time could jeopardize the opportunity to quell a rebellion and restore order to the nation. Shays's Rebellion in Massachusetts (1786–87), just before the Constitutional Convention met, was undoubtedly fresh in the minds of the men who wrote the Constitution.

In a DEMOCRACY, treason must always be defined narrowly in order to permit open and healthy criticism of the government, its policies, and public officials. The Constitution nonetheless provides PUNISHMENT for traitors, whether their actions are motivated by misguided ideals, greed, or an antipathy toward the American way of life—such as the case of John Walker Lindh, an American citizen who joined the Taliban in Afghanistan and ended up fighting against the United States.

Treaties

According to *A Manual of Parliamentary Practice for the Use of the Senate of the United States* (1801), compiled by THOMAS JEFFERSON: "Treaties are legislative acts. A treaty is a law of the land. It differs from other laws only as it must have the consent of a foreign nation, being but a contract with respect to that nation. In all countries, I believe, except England; treaties are made by the legislative power: and there also, if they touch the laws of the land, they must be approved by Parliament."

Treaties, which are called bilateral if they are between two nations and multilateral if they are among more than two nations, have been used for thousands of years. The ancient city-state of Athens, for example, entered into bilateral treaties with other states to ensure fair treatment in their dealings with each other, and these treaties became a part of the law of each state.

Most national constitutions provide explicit authority and procedures for negotiating and ratifying international treaties. Ireland's constitution (1937) requires that "[e]very international agreement to which the State becomes a party shall be laid before [the lower house of the national legislature]…. No international agreement shall be part of the domestic law of the State save as may be determined by the [parliament]."

Treaty Power

The U.S. Constitution provides in Article II, section 2, that the PRESIDENT "shall have Power, by and with the Advice and Consent of the Senate, to make Treaties, provided two thirds of the Senators present concur." The treaty power under the Constitution is exclusively a national power, given the prohibition in Article I, section 10, that "[n]o State shall enter into any Treaty, Alliance, or Confederation…" (see EXCLUSIVE POWERS).

"The power of making treaties," John Jay (1745–1829), who became the first CHIEF JUSTICE of the United States, wrote in essay 64 of *The Federalist* (1787–88) (see FEDERALIST PAPERS), "is an important one, especially as it relates to war, peace, and commerce; and it should not be delegated but in such a mode, and with such precautions, as will afford the highest security that it will be exercised by men the best qualified for the purpose, and in the manner most conducive to the public good."

CLOSER LOOK

The United States entered into a pair of particularly controversial treaties in 1977, when President Jimmy Carter (b. 1924) agreed to turn over control of the Panama Canal to Panama. The treaties ended a 1904 agreement, in which Panama allowed the United States to build and operate the canal and control five miles of land on either side, in exchange for annual payments.

Conservatives sharply criticized Carter for potentially undermining U.S. security. They worried that the canal, a vital link between the Atlantic and Pacific Oceans, could fall into the hands of a hostile force.

The Carter administration worked closely to assuage Senate concerns. In 1978 the Senate approved the handover by just one vote above the two-thirds requirement.

Like many terms in the Constitution, *treaty* is not defined, but in the United States it generally refers to an international agreement that is ratified (see RATIFICATION) by the president following approval by two-thirds of the SENATE. For giving its ADVICE AND CONSENT to a treaty, the Senate uses a special type of resolution that indicates the two-year session of Congress and the order in which it was submitted, such as Treaty Doc 106-1, meaning the first treaty submitted during the 106th Congress. A treaty resolution is the only type of legislative measure that does not expire with the end of a two-year congressional period; a proposed treaty remains under active consideration until acted upon. Not all treaties are approved by the Senate, however, and many important international agreements—the Convention on the Prevention and Punishment of the Crime of Genocide (1948) and the Convention on the Rights of the Child (1989), among others—have yet to be ratified by the United States.

In *Ware v. Hylton* (1796), the only case that future chief justice JOHN MARSHALL would ever argue before the Supreme Court, the Court established the supremacy of national treaties over conflicting state laws. The Treaty of Paris (1793), which ended the Revolutionary War (1775–83), provided that British creditors be able to recover prewar debts owed them by Americans, but Virginia had tried to extinguish these liabilities through a scheme that allowed the debtors to be discharged of their debts if they paid depreciated currency into the state treasury. Marshall, representing a Virginia debtor, lost the case when the Court held that the treaty nullified the state law.

The scope of the Constitution's treaty power actually allows the government to accomplish acts that otherwise might not be constitutional. The landmark decision on this subject is *Missouri v. Holland* (1920). Under a treaty between the United States and Great Britain regarding protection of migratory birds, both countries were required to pass laws forbidding the killing, capturing, or selling of the birds except in accordance with certain regulations. In accordance with the treaty Congress enacted the necessary legislation, the Migratory Bird Treaty Act (1918), but then Missouri—through which the birds transited—brought suit on the grounds that the legislation was an unconstitutional infringement of the state's SOVEREIGNTY as guaranteed by the Tenth Amendment (1791).

The Supreme Court held in *Holland* that the law passed by Congress was not unconstitutional because the federal government, relying on a valid treaty, could act in ways prohibited to it in the absence of a treaty. "We do not mean to imply," wrote Justice OLIVER WENDELL HOLMES JR. for the Court, "that there are no qualifications to the treaty-making power; but they must be ascertained in a different way. It is obvious that there may be matters of the sharpest exigency for the national well-being that an act of Congress could not deal with but that a treaty followed by such an act could, and it is not lightly to be assumed that, in matters requiring national action, 'a power which must belong to and somewhere reside in every civilized government' is not to be found.... If the treaty is valid," he concluded, "there can be no dispute about the validity of the statute under Article I, Section 8, as a necessary and proper means to execute the powers of the government" (see NECESSARY AND PROPER CLAUSE).

Executive Agreements

Other international agreements that do not rise to the status of a formal treaty, such as executive agreements, are approved by the president under his general authority with respect to FOREIGN AFFAIRS and as commander in chief of the ARMED FORCES. Included are actions such as minor territorial adjustments, fishing agreements, and private claims against a foreign government. The only time they become of constitutional interest is when they tend to set some important future policy

SELECTED U.S. TREATIES

Name	Date	Cosignatories	Subject
Treaty of Paris	1783	Great Britain	Ended the Revolutionary War.
Treaty of Peace	1791	Chiefs and warriors of the Cherokee Nation	Ended the war with the Cherokee and redefined boundaries of their territory.
Treaty of Amity, Commerce, and Navigation (Jay Treaty)	1794	Great Britain	Averted war by resolving conflicts over continued British interests in America's western frontier.
Louisiana Purchase Treaty	1803	France	Transferred the Louisiana Territory to the United States.
Extradition Convention	1856	Austria-Hungary	Provided for the mutual extradition of fugitives from justice.
Treaty Concerning the Cession of the Russian Possessions in North America	1867	Russia	Permitted the U.S. purchase of Alaska.
Treaty of Annexation	1897	Hawaiian Kingdom	Transferred the Hawaiian Islands to the United States.
Treaty of Paris	1898	Spain	Ended the Spanish-American War, giving independence to Cuba and ceding Puerto Rico, Guam, and the Philippine Islands to the United States.
Treaty of Versailles	1919	Germany and various states, including England, France, Italy, Japan, and Brazil	Ended World War I (not approved by the U.S. Senate).
Act of Chapultepec (Inter-American Reciprocal Assistance and Solidarity)	1945	Various states	Affirmed the sovereignty of all states in the American hemisphere, committing members to respond to any act of aggression on any member, whether by an American or non-American state.
United Nations Charter	1945	51 original members	Established the United Nations as an international peacemaking and peacekeeping organization.
Trusteeship Agreement for the Former Japanese Mandated Islands	1947	United Nations	Transferred the trusteeship of the Micronesian Islands from Japan, which had held them under a League of Nations mandate, to the United States.
Charter for the Organization of American States	1948	Various democratic states in the Western Hemisphere	Established the Organization of American States, aimed at promoting economic and cultural cooperation between members, upholding human rights and democracy, and providing for peaceful conflict resolution and collective defense against aggressors.

(continues)

SELECTED U.S. TREATIES (CONTINUED)

Name	Date	Cosignatories	Subject
NATO (The North Atlantic Treaty)	1949	Various states, including Belgium, Canada, France, Luxembourg, the Netherlands, and the United Kingdom	Promoted economic cooperation and mutual defense between democratic member states, concentrated in the North Atlantic region.
Mutual Defense Treaty Between the United States and the Republic of Korea	1953	South Korea	Provided for collective defense against aggressors, affirmed peaceful conflict resolution as desirable, and approved the establishment of U.S. military bases in South Korea, subject to mutual agreement.
Convention Concerning the Protection of the World Cultural and Natural Heritage	1972	Various states	Established a system for collective protection of places and artifacts of outstanding universal value.
Non-Aggression Pact between NATO and Warsaw Pact members	1990	Various states	Affirmed that the members of NATO and the Warsaw Pact, a treaty between communist countries in Central and Eastern Europe, are no longer allied against each other.
START I Treaty (Strategic Arms Reduction Talks)	1991	Russia	Set maximum limits for number of warheads and "strategic offensive delivery vehicles" held by the United States and the successors to the Soviet Union.
International Convention for the Suppression of Terrorist Bombings	1998	Various states	Provided for cooperation to counteract international terrorism.
SORT Treaty (Moscow Treaty/Treaty Between the United States of America and the Russian Federation On Strategic Offensive Reductions)	2002	Russia	Committed both parties to reducing their arsenals of strategic nuclear warheads.
DR-CAFTA (Free Trade Agreement)	2004	Various states	Instituted free trade relationships between the United States and Central American member states.
Strategic Partnership Agreement	2005	Afghanistan	Outlined the objectives of the U.S.-Afghan relationship, including cultural and economic exchanges, integration in international organizations, and cooperation in security and counterterrorism.

Sources: Axelrod, Alan, *American Treaties and Alliances*, Washington, D.C.: CQ Press, 2000; Gibler, Doug, *International Military Alliances*, Washington, D.C.: CQ Press, 2008; *2007 DR-CAFTA Fact Sheets*, Washington, D.C.: Office of the United States Trade Representative, 2007; *Joint-Declaration of the United States-Afghanistan Strategic Partnership*, Washington, D.C.: State Department, 2005; Woolf, Amy F., *Nuclear Arms Control: The U.S.-Russian Agenda*, Washington, D.C.: Congressional Research Service, Foreign Affairs, Defense, and Trade Division, 2005; *DR-CAFTA Final Text*, Washington, D.C.: Office of the U.S. Trade Representative, 2004; *Louisiana Purchase Treaty*, The Avalon Project at Yale Law School, New Haven, 1996–2007.

for the nation. The president may also enter into international agreements to carry out the intent of congressional actions.

The modern power of the president to enter into executive agreements of some consequence began with Franklin D. Roosevelt (1882–1945). His extension of American recognition to the Soviet Union in 1933 included an exchange of pledges by officials on both sides. The incorporation of executive agreements into law—just like treaties approved by the Senate—was recognized by the Supreme Court in *United States v. Belmont* (1937). In *United States v. Curtiss-Wright* (1936), the Court had previously found that the president had broad INHERENT POWERS with respect to entering into international agreements, and while the supremacy of treaties approved by the Senate was expressly established in the Constitution, the same is true "in the case of all international compacts and agreements from the very fact that complete power over international affairs is in the National Government and is not and cannot be subject to any curtailment or interference on the part of the several States."

Termination of Treaties

Treaties generally include provisions stipulating how a nation can withdraw from them. They are typically terminated by the president, either with congressional authorization or on his own. In 1789 Congress abrogated a treaty with France—apparently the only time a treaty has been terminated by an act of Congress—and two days later authorized limited hostilities against the country. On review in *Bas v. Tingy* (1800), the Supreme Court upheld the termination as part of the general declaration of war on France.

President ABRAHAM LINCOLN was probably the first to give notice of a treaty's termination without prior congressional approval, although Congress quickly ratified his action in 1865. In 1899 President William McKinley (1843–1901) became the first to abrogate a treaty, in this case an 1850 agreement with Switzerland, without later approval by Congress, although his action could be justified on the grounds that the treaty conflicted with a subsequent law. The Supreme Court addressed the issue in *Goldwater v. Carter* (1979), deciding that the president had authority to terminate a 1954 mutual defense treaty with Taiwan without Congress's approval.

Treaties with Native Americans

In Article I, section 8, the Constitution empowers Congress to "regulate Commerce…with the Indian Tribes," which were to some extent considered foreign nations existing within the TERRITORY of the United States (see NATIVE AMERICANS). In the Cherokee Cases (1831 and 1832), the Supreme Court first defined the Cherokee people as a domestic dependent nation, not a sovereign nation. But in the second case, the Court held: "The Constitution, by declaring treaties already made, as well as those to be made, to be the supreme law of the land, had adopted and sanctioned the previous treaties with the Indian nations, and consequently admits their rank among those powers who are capable of making treaties. The words 'treaty' and 'nation' are words of our own language, selected in our diplomatic and legislative proceedings, by ourselves, having each a definite and well understood meaning. We have applied them to Indians, as we have applied them to the other nations of the earth. They are applied to all in the same sense."

In another series of cases, the Supreme Court established that STATES could not interfere with the rights created by national treaties with the Indians; as long as the United States acknowledged a tribe's national character, it was under the protection of Congress and immune from TAXATION. However, in the Cherokee Tobacco Case (1871), the Court found that an act of Congress that was incompatible with a prior Indian treaty repealed the treaty. In 1871 Congress passed a law under which Indian tribes or nations were no longer to be treated as independent nations with whom the

More on this topic:

Advice and Consent, p. 18

International Law, p. 304

Native Americans, p. 378

Ratification, p. 451

United States would contract by treaty. In *Choate v. Trapp* (1912), the Court held that PROPERTY rights granted to individual Indians, whether by treaty or congressional action, are protected by the Constitution in the same manner as the rights of other U.S. CITIZENS.

The notion of sovereignty, which forms the basis for treaties among nations, has become blurred as nations seek to cooperate with each other to ensure mutual security and economic progress in the increasingly globalized world. For every major treaty that gains public attention, such as the Strategic Arms Limitations Treaty I (1972) and II (1979), there are hundreds of specialized treaties on subjects ranging from commerce to EXTRADITION of fugitives to narcotics interdiction (see DRUGS), most of which never present any constitutional problems. The Supreme Court basically leaves the matter of treaties in the hands of the EXECUTIVE BRANCH and the LEGISLATIVE BRANCH.

Trials

One of the most famous trials in ancient times was that of Socrates, the Athenian philosopher and teacher of Plato, in 399 B.C.E. Found guilty of crimes against the state religion and of corrupting the youth of Athens with his teachings, Socrates chose suicide rather than a fine as his PUNISHMENT and died by drinking a cup of poison. In the courts of ancient Athens, citizens acted as both judges and jurors at the initial trials and in appeals.

In the American system of justice, trials—hearings of a civil or criminal case in the first instance before a judge, with or without a jury—are derived from the English concept of a contest between two theories of the truth. At a trial both versions of the truth are presented under the applicable rules of legal procedure, and a judge or a jury must decide between the two theories or versions of the truth. One side wins and the other loses; there are no ties. In ancient England, according to William Blackstone (1723–80) in his *Commentaries on the Laws of England* (1765–70), trials might be conducted as ordeals by water or fire. One form of the latter required "walking, barefoot, and blindfold, over nine red-hot ploughshares, laid lengthwise at unequal distances: and if the party escaped unhurt, he was ajudged innocent...." Many of the FRAMERS OF THE CONSTITUTION in 1787 were lawyers, some of whom had been trained in the law in England. They were familiar with English law as applied in colonial America and with Blackstone's *Commentaries*, which were readily available in the states at the time.

Trials are mentioned in Article I (regarding Congress's powers of IMPEACHMENT) and Article III of the Constitution (the judiciary article), and there seems to have been little dispute over these provisions. "The Trial of all Crimes, except in Cases of Impeachment," mandates Article III, section 2, "shall be by Jury; and such Trial shall be held in the State where the said Crimes shall have been committed; but when not committed within any State, the Trial shall be at such Place or Places as the Congress may by Law have directed." The Sixth Amendment, added to the Constitution with the BILL OF RIGHTS (1791), more narrowly defines where a trial is to take place, requiring that it be in "the State and district wherein the crime shall have been committed." In Great Britain criminal trials were held in the "vicinage" or community where the crime was committed, so that jurors could be drawn from nearby. In the United States the districts referred to in the Sixth Amendment correspond to the districts of the federal district COURTS—the lowest level of federal courts in which trials are conducted—which represent a much larger area than a "vicinage."

Fair Trial

When people are put on trial by the government, they should take advantage of every right extended by the Constitution, other laws, and precedents and rules of the courts. The government has many weapons at its command to prove even the innocent guilty of a crime, such as planting incriminating evidence or coercing false or misleading testimony. A criminal trial is a contest in which adherence to the rules should lead to more just results. In contrast, in some totalitarian countries, show trials—unfair trials in which the only outcome in doubt is the severity of the penalty to be imposed—are held not to determine the guilt or innocence of those accused of a crime but to impress on the people the absolute power of the state over their lives.

In the United States the right of a person accused of a crime to a fair trial is addressed principally in the Sixth and Seventh Amendments of the Constitution. "In all criminal prosecutions," states the Sixth Amendment (1791), "the accused shall enjoy the right to a speedy and public trial, by an impartial jury of the State and district wherein the crime shall have been committed, which district shall have been previously ascertained by law, and to be informed of the nature and cause of the accusation; to be confronted with the witnesses against him; to have compulsory process for obtaining witnesses in his favor, and to have the Assistance of Counsel for his defense." According to the Seventh Amendment (1791), "In Suits at common law, where the value in controversy shall exceed twenty dollars, the right of trial by jury shall be preserved, and no fact tried by a jury, shall be otherwise re-examined in any Court of the United States, than according to the rules of the common law."

> *In some totalitarian countries, show trials—unfair trials in which the only outcome in doubt is the severity of the penalty to be imposed—are held not to determine the guilt or innocence of those of accused of crime but to impress on the people the absolute power of the state over their lives.*

A number of elements constitute a fair trial. The COMMON LAW presumption of innocence of those put on trial—although not a part of the written Constitution—is one of a defendant's FUNDAMENTAL RIGHTS. Other elements include the constitutional prohibition against EX POST FACTO LAWS (laws that make an act a crime after the act was committed) in Article I, sections 9 and 10; the ban in the Fifth Amendment (1791) against DOUBLE JEOPARDY and being compelled to be a witness against oneself (see SELF-INCRIMINATION; WITNESSES); the general principles embodied in the DUE PROCESS clauses of the Fifth and Fourteenth Amendments (1868); an impartial judge and jury (see JURIES); a judiciary that is independent from the other major branches of government that make and enforce the laws (see JUDICIAL INDEPENDENCE); and the right to appeal decisions to a higher court.

Another element of a fair trial is the defendant's competence to stand trial and to assist in his or her defense. The burden of proof may be placed on the defendant to prove incompetence, but the standard of proof is a preponderance of the evidence—not the proof beyond a reasonable doubt that is needed to convict a person of a crime. In *Cooper v. Oklahoma* (1996), the Supreme Court pointed out that the right of the defendant to be tried only when competent "outweighs the State's interest in the efficient operation of its criminal justice system."

Speedy Trials. The right to a speedy trial, according to the Supreme Court, is applicable only after a person has been formally accused or arrested. The government may take its time investigating and bringing formal charges without violating the Sixth Amendment. The Court has generally given prosecutors great leeway in delaying a trial, unless there is evidence of bad faith on their part. There is an old legal adage that a delay actually favors the defendant—undoubtedly because time tends to dim the memory and availability of witnesses.

Yet the Supreme Court has found some overly long delays to be unconstitutional. In *Smith v. Hooey* (1969), the justices held that the right to a speedy trial was violated when a state did not attempt to obtain custody of a defendant who was already incarcerated for another crime. And in *Doggett v. United States* (1992), after the federal government "lost" an indicted suspect who lived openly under his own name for six years, the Court ruled that the case must be dismissed, reasoning that the delay was completely the fault of the government and that such a long delay prejudiced the ability of the accused to mount an adequate defense.

NBA basketball star Kobe Bryant leaves a Colorado court after being accused of sexual assault. The constitutional requirement that most legal proceedings be public means that trials frequently generate enormous publicity. In Bryant's case, the charges were eventually dropped.
Source: Reuters/Helen D. Richardson

Public Trials. The Sixth Amendment requirement that a trial be public ensures fairness, but the possibility of excessive publicity or press coverage of the matters to be considered at trial may have the opposite result. The openness of trials has been accepted at both the federal and state levels since the nation's early days. Today trials are almost always open to the public, although there is no right to take still or motion pictures of the proceedings. The Supreme Court has declared that under the First Amendment a criminal trial must be open to the public unless the judge can show an "overriding interest" for closing it to observers. Even closing a preliminary hearing is unconstitutional, unless a substantial possibility exists that publicity would adversely affect the defendant's right to a fair trial.

The Supreme Court, in *Carey v. Musladin* (2006), distinguished between "state sponsored" courtroom practices or actions initiated by the state that may prejudice a defendant at a trial as opposed to private-actor or spectator conduct. In *Carey*, some of the victim's family wore buttons with a photograph of the victim on them in the courtroom. The unanimous decision, written by Justice Clarence Thomas (b. 1948), concluded that the defendant had not shown that the spectators' conduct complained of was "contrary to or involved an unreasonable application of, clearly established Federal law, as determined by [this]…Court."

Nature and Cause of the Accusation. The basis of any defense against charges of wrongdoing lies with the charges themselves. The Supreme Court has held that defendants have the right to insist that indictments apprise them of the crimes for which they are charged with such reasonable certainty that the defendants can make their defense and, after judgments are rendered, be protected against prosecution again for the same crimes. According to *Potter v. United States* (1894), if the statute under which a defendant is being charged is fully descriptive of the offense, then that language can be used in the indictment. But if the elements of the crime must be obtained by reference to common law or other statutes, then such elements must be added to the charges, and the facts required to bring the case within the language of the statute must also be alleged. In 1896, however, the Court let stand an indictment that omitted obscene particulars but that described the accused's conduct in such a way as to reasonably inform him of the nature of the charges being brought against him.

Confrontation of Witnesses. A person accused of a crime has the right to confront and cross-examine WITNESSES that the prosecution is using to prove its case. In *Mattox v. United States* (1895), the Supreme Court spelled out reasons for this right of confrontation. According to the Court, it gives "the accused…an opportunity not only of testing the recollection and sifting the conscience of the witness, but of compelling him [the witness] to stand face to face with the jury in order that they may look at him, and judge by his demeanor…and the manner in which he gives his testimony whether he is worthy of belief."

The right of a defendant to confront witnesses, said the Supreme Court in *Kirby v. United States* (1899), is "[o]ne of the fundamental guarantees of life and liberty...long deemed so essential for the protection of life and liberty that it is guarded against legislative and judicial action by provision in the Constitution of the United States and in the constitutions of most [states]." In 1965, in *Pointer v. Texas*, the Court made the right to confront witnesses applicable to the states.

Compulsory Process for Obtaining Witnesses. Under English common law, an accused might not be allowed to present witnesses in his own defense in felony or treason cases. In *Washington v. Texas* (1967), however, the Supreme Court declared: "Just as an accused has the right to confront the prosecution's witnesses for the purpose of challenging their testimony, he has the right to present his own witnesses to establish a defense. This right is a fundamental element of due process of law."

Several years later the Supreme Court found unconstitutional the strict enforcement of the evidentiary rule against the admission of hearsay statements (what a witness heard rather than what he or she saw) alleging that another person had confessed to the crime with which a defendant is charged. The right to compulsory process (obedience to a court order) has also been relied on to keep a judge from threatening a defense witness with perjury and giving the jury instructions that called into question the testimony of defense witnesses. According to the Supreme Court, due process of law requires fairness in a trial. Just the "probability of unfairness," said the Court in *In re Murchison* (1955), is sufficient to disqualify a judge.

Federal Civil Trials

Compared to criminal trials, the Constitution has less to say about civil trials. From a fundamental rights point of view, there is also less to be concerned about. The Supreme Court has not extended to the states the Constitution's requirement of the right to a jury trial in most civil suits, and it has refused to find that in civil suits indigent people have the same right to the ASSISTANCE OF COUNSEL as in criminal cases. The requirement of a jury in civil trials was actually rejected by the delegates to the CONSTITUTIONAL CONVENTION OF 1787 but became one of the primary concerns over ratification of the document; it was thus added to the Bill of Rights as the Seventh Amendment, as proposed by JAMES MADISON.

The federal right to a jury in civil trials is based on the law as it existed in 1791, including a twelve-person jury under the supervision of a judge and a unanimous verdict. In *Colgrove v. Battin* (1973), the Supreme Court relaxed the Seventh Amendment provision and allowed the use of a six-person jury in civil cases. The parties in a civil trial, however, are free to waive the jury requirement if they wish. In such cases the matter is tried before a judge, who decides questions of fact as well as the law.

State Trials

Each state has its own laws and rules of procedure for civil and criminal trials, but the Supreme Court has incorporated into the Fourteenth Amendment and made applicable to the states many of the requirements for a fair trial guaranteed in the Bill of Rights (see INCORPORATION DOCTRINE). These rights include the protection in the Fourth Amendment (1791) against unreasonable SEARCH AND SEIZURE and the exclusionary rule, which makes illegally obtained evidence inadmissible in a trial; the protection of the Fifth Amendment (1791) against self-incrimination and double jeopardy; the Sixth Amendment right to the assistance of counsel, a public trial, confrontation of witnesses, an impartial jury, compulsory process to obtain witnesses, notice of the accusation, and a unanimous verdict in cases where only six jurors are used in a trial; and the Eighth Amendment's prohibition against CRUEL AND UNUSUAL PUNISHMENT.

The U.S. Supreme Court continually reviews state trial procedures. For example, in *Chambers v. Mississippi* (1973), the Court voided a state rule that prohibited a defendant from impeaching a

More on this topic:

Criminal Law, p. 132

Judicial Branch, p. 312

witness, who, during the trial, had repudiated an earlier confession. And in *Holmes v. South Carolina* (2006), it rejected a state rule of evidence that did not allow a defendant to try to prove that someone else committed the crime if the prosecution "introduced forensic evidence that, if believed, strongly support[ed] a guilty verdict." In *Blakely v. Washington* (2004), the Court held that a state court judge could not increase a sentence beyond the statutory maximum because the decision was not made by a jury.

As it was long ago, a trial is often an ordeal for a defendant. If a person has acted wrongly according to the law, such an ordeal is justified. The purpose of a fair trial, however, is to ensure that wrongdoers are proven guilty in accordance with constitutional and legal standards and procedures so that only those actually guilty of wrongdoing incur punishment.

Twelfth Amendment *See* ELECTIONS; ELECTORAL COLLEGE; PRESIDENT; VICE PRESIDENT.

Twentieth Amendment *See* LAME DUCKS; PRESIDENT; VICE PRESIDENT.

Twenty-fifth Amendment *See* PRESIDENT; VICE PRESIDENT.

Twenty-first Amendment *See* PROHIBITION.

Twenty-fourth Amendment *See* CIVIL RIGHTS; ELECTIONS; RACIAL DISCRIMINATION; TAXATION.

Twenty-second Amendment *See* PRESIDENT; TERMS OF OFFICE.

Twenty-seventh Amendment *See* AMENDMENTS; COMPENSATION OF OFFICIALS.

Twenty-sixth Amendment *See* AGE DISCRIMINATION; ELECTIONS.

Twenty-third Amendment *See* CAPITAL, NATIONAL.

Unions

In 1911 the American labor leader Samuel Gompers (1850–1924) declared that the mission of the country's labor movement was "the protection of the wage-worker, now; to increase his wages; to cut hours off the long workday, which was killing him; to improve the safety and sanitary conditions of the workshop; to free him from the tyrannies, petty or otherwise, which served to make his existence a slavery." Not long afterward, Gompers chaired a commission of delegates from nine countries who met to draft a constitution for a new International Labor Organization. Closely associated with the labor union movement in the United States, the ILO was founded in 1919 as an autonomous intergovernmental organization to promote the rights and interests of workers around the world.

Although the U.S. Constitution does not directly address the rights of workers or UNIONS, several provisions have played a role in Supreme Court cases involving labor. Among them are the requirement in Article I, section 10, that the STATES may not impair the obligation of CONTRACTS; the COMMERCE clause in Article I, section 8; and the First Amendment (1791) rights of assembly and, by court interpretation, of association (see ASSEMBLY AND ASSOCIATION). But for most of the nation's history, the federal government and the Supreme Court in particular have done little to defend the rights of workers or unions.

Labor vs. Management

During the first third of the twentieth century, the Supreme Court used what Justice Hugo L. Black (1886–1971) referred to as the Allgeyer-Lochner-Adair-Coppage Doctrine to strike down state and federal efforts to improve the conditions of American workers. The name was derived from a series of cases beginning with *Allgeyer v. Louisiana* (1897) contesting efforts to restrict child labor, prohibit court-ordered restraints of picketing and strikes, and require arbitration for wage and hour disputes between labor and management.

The Sherman Antitrust Act (1890) articulated a national policy against monopolization or restraint of competition in the economic marketplace (see ANTITRUST LAW; ECONOMIC LIBERTY). In *Loewe v. Lawlor* (1908), known as the Danbury Hatters' Case, the Supreme Court found a violation of the act in a boycott of a hat manufacturer by the United Hatters of North America as well as in a secondary boycott sponsored by the American Federation of Labor aimed at increasing the unionization of workers in the hat-making industry. The justices called the boycotts a restraint of interstate commerce. Then in 1914 Congress passed the Clayton Act, which declared that the "labor of a human being is not a commodity or article of commerce," placing it outside the scope of the Sherman Act. The Supreme Court, however, still found ways to narrowly interpret the Clayton Act, thus frustrating the intent of Congress and union activities.

Congress responded in the 1930s by passing two important acts that gave support to the labor union movement: the Norris-LaGuardia Act (1932), which basically limited federal courts from enjoining strikes and other coercive union activities, and the National Labor Relations Act (1935), also known as the Wagner Act, which allowed workers to organize and required employers to bargain with their representatives. These acts permitted workers to form unions for the purposes of bargaining collectively with employers for wages and other benefits. To have sufficient power to bargain collectively, however, the unions had to monopolize the supply of labor. Otherwise, employers, rather than bargain, could simply hire other workers at a lower wage. This meant that the antitrust laws and the union laws met head on.

The conflict was fairly well settled by the Supreme Court in *United States v. Hutcheson* (1941), a case involving the Anheuser-Busch brewing company. Workers building a new facility for the brewery not only went on strike against the company but also mounted a campaign to boycott the company's products. Anheuser-Busch charged that the union's activities violated the Sherman Act. The Supreme Court had by now seen which way the wind was blowing and reasoned that the Norris-LaGuardia Act, by restricting the situations under which the federal courts could get involved in labor disputes, had given the green light to trade-union activities. Therefore, even though the act did not directly address the case in question, the policy behind it required that a substantial part of the Sherman Act no longer apply to unions.

By 1965 the Supreme Court was again scrutinizing union activities. In *United Mine Workers v. Pennington* (1965), the Court found that a conspiracy between the union and the large mine owners to force smaller owners out of business did violate the antitrust laws. And in *Connell Construction Co. v. Plumbers and Steamfitters Local 100* (1975), the Court drew the line between union activities that reduced competition over wages and benefits for workers—which were not a violation of the antitrust laws—and union activities that reduced competition in the product marketplace—which were.

The Labor Management Relations Act (1947), also known as the Taft-Hartley Act, was passed by Congress over the veto of President Harry S. Truman (1884–1972), who called it a "slave-labor bill." The act declared illegal a closed union shop (a business where only union members could work) and permitted a union shop only after a vote of a majority of the employees. The act also required all union leaders to sign affidavits that they were not members or supporters of the Communist Party, a provision upheld by the Supreme Court in *American Communications Association v. Douds* (1950). Although this provision has not been explicitly overruled, it is doubtful that the Court would find it constitutional today.

In *Railway Employees' Department v. Hanson* (1956), the Supreme Court upheld collective bargaining agreements with unions in which all workers had to abide by the decisions of the union representatives, despite allegations that such agreements violated the freedom of association guarantees of the First Amendment. But in *Machinists v. Street* (1961), the Court held that the First Amendment's guarantee of free SPEECH required that members' compulsory financial contribution to their unions could be used only for collective bargaining activities and not for political or ideological campaigns that a member might disagree with.

To administer the National Labor Relations Act, which is the primary federal law governing unions and employers in the private sector, Congress in 1935 also created the National Labor Relations Board as an independent federal agency (see ADMINISTRATIVE AGENCIES). The board's principal functions are to ensure that employees make free and democratic choices by secret ballot to be represented by a union and to prevent and remedy unfair labor practices by either unions or employers. The board itself consists of five members appointed by the president, with the ADVICE AND CONSENT of the Senate, for five-year terms. The board's general counsel, appointed by the president for a four-year term, independently investigates and prosecutes unfair labor practices. In general, the NLRB has been moving away from upholding union rights. In 2002, however, in *BE & K Construction Co. v. National Labor Relations Board*, the Supreme Court overruled the board's action against an employer for filing what the board determined to be a retaliatory lawsuit against several unions that had tried to hamper the modernization of a steel plant by a contractor using nonunion

Workers participate in a labor rally in Cincinnati in 2007.
Source: AP Images/Tom Uhlman

workers. In its decision, the Court noted that while no one has a constitutional right to file a sham antitrust lawsuit, the meaning of "sham" is narrow, and the board erred in finding that the employer's lawsuit was a sham just because it was dismissed for various reasons. The Court also noted that the right to petition is one of the most precious liberties safeguarded by the BILL OF RIGHTS.

For several decades the union movement has declined in membership and political power, and many unions—especially those in the public sector, such as teachers' unions—have even less power compared to the industrial unions like the United Auto Workers. Many workers in the United States, including managers and supervisors (workers given carefully chosen titles to avoid extending labor law benefits to them), independent contractors, and farm workers, are not unionized.

More on this topic:

Children, p. 90

Health, p. 271

Labor, p. 333

Unit Voting   *See* ELECTORAL COLLEGE.

Unitary System of Government   *See* FEDERALISM.

Vacancies   *See* APPOINTMENT AND REMOVAL POWER.

Vested Rights   *See* RIGHTS.

Vetoes

The power of the PRESIDENT to veto acts of CONGRESS and the power of Congress to override that disapproval, as authorized in Article I, section 7, of the Constitution, has resulted in a number of showdowns between the LEGISLATIVE BRANCH and the EXECUTIVE BRANCH. Andrew Jackson (1767–1845), who served as president from 1829 to 1837, was the first to wield the veto as a way to promote his own legislative goals rather than to register a concern regarding the constitutionality of proposed legislation. In his two terms as president (1885–89, 1893–97), Grover Cleveland (1837–1908) used the veto 584 times, and Franklin D. Roosevelt (1882–1945), who served as president for twelve years (1933–45), exercised the power of the veto 635 times. Congress has overridden the president's veto in only about seven percent of the cases.

The president's veto power bestowed by the FRAMERS OF THE CONSTITUTION—the chief executive's right to convey "Objections" to LEGISLATION—reflects the English monarch's prerogative to refuse to assent to an act of Parliament, thus keeping it from becoming law. At the time of the debate over the Constitution's RATIFICATION, according to ALEXANDER HAMILTON in essay 73 of *The Federalist* (1787–88) (see FEDERALIST PAPERS), "[a] very considerable period [almost eighty years] has elapsed since the negative of the crown has been exercised." Vetoes were also used to nullify proposed legislation in pre-Christian Poland, where clan leaders had to obtain a consensus to make policy; anyone with political rights thus could avail himself of the *liberum veto* simply by saying, "I do not allow," thereby thwarting a proposal.

As Article I, section 7, directs: "Every Bill which shall have passed the House of Representatives and the Senate, shall, before it become a Law, be presented to the President of the United States: If he approve he shall sign it, but if not he shall return it, with his Objections to that House in which it shall have originated, who shall enter the Objections at large on their Journal, and proceed to reconsider it. If after such Reconsideration two thirds of that House shall agree to pass the Bill, it shall be sent, together with the Objections, to the other House, by which it shall likewise be reconsidered, and if approved by two thirds of that House, it shall become a Law. But in all such Cases the Votes of both Houses shall be determined by Yeas and Nays, and the Names of the Persons voting for and against the Bill shall be entered on the Journal of each House respectively." In *Missouri Pacific Railway Co. v. Kansas* (1919), the Supreme Court held that two-thirds, as used in section 7, means only two-thirds of those members present and not two-thirds of the total members of each house.

In a cartoon created around 1915, the House of Representatives is seen as a Democratic circus in which a bill has to clear a presidental veto held by a clownish House speaker.
Source: Library of Congress

"If any Bill shall not be returned by the President within ten Days (Sundays excepted) after it shall have been presented to him," section 7 continues, "the Same shall be a Law, in like Manner as if he had signed it, unless the Congress by their Adjournment prevent its Return, in which Case it shall not be a Law. Every Order, Resolution, or Vote to which the Concurrence of the Senate and House of Representatives may be necessary (except on a question of Adjournment) shall be presented to the President of the United States; and before the Same shall take Effect, shall be approved by him, or being disapproved by him, shall be repassed by two thirds of the Senate and House of Representatives, according to the Rules and Limitations prescribed in the Case of a Bill."

Hamilton discussed the veto power at some length in essay 73, arguing that "[t]he primary inducement to conferring the power in question upon the executive is to enable him to defend himself; the secondary one is to increase the chances in favor of the community against the passing of bad laws, through haste, inadvertence, or design." Originally used sparingly—through 1860 only fifty-two measures were vetoed—the veto power has become a major weapon in the president's battles with Congress: some 2,500 vetoes have been used since then.

Line-Item Veto

The president must either sign a bill presented to him for his signature or veto it in its entirety. With the Line-Item Veto Act (1996), Congress tried to authorize the president to veto individual taxing and spending provisions in certain bills by means of a line-item veto. However, the Supreme Court in *Clinton v. City of New York* (1998) found the new grant of power unconstitu-

VETOES ISSUED AND OVERRIDDEN, 1789–2007

President	All bills vetoed	Regular vetoes	Pocket vetoes	Vetoes overridden
Washington	2	2	0	0
J. Adams	0	0	0	0
Jefferson	0	0	0	0
Madison	7	5	2	0
Monroe	1	1	0	0
J. Q. Adams	0	0	0	0
Jackson	12	5	7	0
Van Buren	1	0	1	0
W. H. Harrison	0	0	0	0
Tyler	10	6	4	1
Polk	3	2	1	0
Taylor	0	0	0	0
Fillmore	0	0	0	0
Pierce	9	9	0	5
Buchanan	7	4	3	0
Lincoln	7	2	5	0
A. Johnson	29	21	8	15
Grant	93[1]	45	48[1]	4
Hayes	13	12	1	1
Garfield	0	0	0	0
Arthur	12	4	8	1
Cleveland (first term)	414	304	110	2
B. Harrison	44	19	25	1
Cleveland (second term)	170	42	128	5
McKinley	42	6	36	0
T. Roosevelt	82	42	40	1
Taft	39	30	9	1
Wilson	44	33	11	6
Harding	6	5	1	0

tional because it in effect allowed the president to amend legislation, a power not granted to him by the Constitution. Many state governors, however, are constitutionally permitted to veto line items in legislation. In 2006 Congress again attempted to give the president limited line-item rescission authority to make cuts in proposed spending up to four times a year during a one-year period after enactment of a spending provision. The proposed rescissions would then have to be voted on by Congress within ten days of introduction. The measure, however, was never acted on by the Senate.

Pocket Veto

A pocket veto occurs when a bill is submitted to the president for his approval and Congress adjourns before the ten-day period prescribed in Article I, section 7, is completed. In effect, the president is precluded from having the full ten days in which to consider and act on the bill, and by simply not approving it before Congress adjourns, the president ensures that it will die. This procedure was upheld by the Supreme Court in the Pocket Veto Case (1929).

All bills President	Regular vetoed	Pocket vetoes	Vetoes vetoes	overridden
Coolidge	50	20	30	4
Hoover	37	21	16	3
F. D. Roosevelt	635	372	263	9
Truman	250	180	70	12
Eisenhower	181	73	108	2
Kennedy	21	12	9	0
L. Johnson	30	16	14	0
Nixon	43[2]	26	17[2]	7
Ford	66	48	18	12
Carter	31	13	18	2
Reagan	78	39	39	9
G. H. W. Bush	44[3]	29	15	1
Clinton	37	36	1	2
G. W. Bush[4]	8	7	1	1

SOURCE: Senate Historical Office.

NOTES:

1. Veto total listed for Grant does not include a pocket veto of a bill that apparently never was placed before him for his signature.

2. Includes Nixon's pocket veto of a bill during the 1970 congressional Christmas recess that was later ruled invalid by the District Court for the District of Columbia and the U.S. Court of Appeals for the District of Columbia.

3. Bush's total number of vetoes, listed here as 44, is controversial. Two additional actions by Bush, involving the pocket-veto procedure, have been described as vetoes. Bush asserted that he had issued pocket vetoes of HJ Res 390, involving thrift bailout rules, on August 16, 1989, and S 1176, involving a foundation named for former Rep. Morris K. Udall, on December 20, 1991. The first came during a congressional recess and the second following adjournment of the first session of the 102nd Congress. Senate experts say Bush's claim that these measures were pocket-vetoed would not stand constitutional scrutiny. The Constitution's veto provisions and Supreme Court cases on the power have established for many constitutional scholars that a true pocket veto can occur only after final adjournment of a Congress and not during recesses or between first and second sessions if Congress has taken certain steps allowing it to receive any veto message the president might send. This view is widely held in Congress but has been challenged by a number of presidents, including Bush. On the two Bush actions in question, HJ Res 390 and S 1176, congressional leaders believe that the measures became law without the president's signature, as occurs under the Constitution if a president takes no action on legislation sent to him before Congress's final adjournment. The issue is further muddied in the case of S 1176 because Congress later repealed it with a new bill, S 2184, which Bush signed while at the same time asserting that although he agreed with the measure he did not accept the congressional disclaimer that S 2184 repealed S 1176.

4. Through December 31, 2007.

Legislative Veto

In the 1930s, when Congress began delegating broad authority to executive branch agencies and officials (see ADMINISTRATIVE AGENCIES), a provision was included in some bills that would allow Congress to pass a concurrent resolution disapproving of actions taken under the authorizing legislation. In some cases the bill required disapproval of only one house of Congress. But in *Immigration and Naturalization Service v. Chadha* (1983), the Supreme Court ruled that such "legislative" veto power was unconstitutional when one house of Congress alone could overturn an executive branch action. The two major problems the Court saw were that such laws violated the bicameral structure of the legislature created by the Constitution and avoided the requirement that legislation be presented to the president.

Congress has continued to exercise some control over authority it has delegated—for example, by conditioning certain executive branch actions on a joint resolution of Congress, which, like bills, must be signed by the president, or by using congressional power to reduce or eliminate funding for executive branch activities that it dislikes.

The involvement in the legislative process of the president—the head of the executive branch, who is charged by the Constitution to "take care that the laws be faithfully executed"—by means of the veto power is one more example of the government's checks and balances (see SEPARATION OF POWERS), in which the executive power may intrude on the legislative power. Some observers have suggested that the veto power is incompatible with the president's duty to enforce the laws, especially when a law is passed over a veto and the president must then enforce it. Justice Hugo L. Black (1886–1971) noted in his opinion in YOUNGSTOWN SHEET AND TUBE CO. V. SAWYER (1952) that the president's constitutional duty "to see that the laws are faithfully executed refutes the idea that he is to be a lawmaker." Despite congressional moves to reduce or eliminate this presidential power, the veto has become an effective tool of presidents in dealing with Congress on proposed legislation and is likely to remain so.

Vice President

As vice president, Theodore Roosevelt automatically succeeded to the presidency on the assassination of William McKinley in 1901. In an illustration from the funeral issue of **Leslie's Weekly**, Roosevelt pays his respects to the fallen president as the body lies in state at Buffalo City Hall.
Source: Library of Congress

In many nations, especially in democratic republics, the head of state or the highest executive official is called the PRESIDENT, and the constitutions of most of these countries create the position of vice president. Some designate several vice presidents; South Africa's constitution (1994) creates the position of deputy president. Some constitutions specify the vice president's responsibilities, while others authorize the president to assign duties to the incumbent. In most cases the vice president succeeds to the office of president when the chief executive can no longer carry out his constitutional duties as a result of death, resignation, removal from office, or a permanent disability that significantly impairs the president's ability to serve.

According to John Nance Garner (1868–1967), vice president from 1933 to 1937, during the first term of Franklin D. Roosevelt (1882–1945), the office of vice president is "not worth a pitcher full of warm spit." Beginning with the first vice president in 1789, John Adams (1735–1826), this has probably been an apt characterization. However, more recent vice presidents—including Richard M. Nixon (1913–94), vice president under Dwight D. Eisenhower (1890–1969); Al Gore (b. 1948), who served Bill Clinton (b. 1946); and Dick Cheney (b. 1941), who has served George W. Bush (b. 1946)—have played a more important and more visible role. Nixon, for example, filled in when Eisenhower had a heart attack that limited his activity for several months and also helped implement foreign policy, including a spontaneous "kitchen debate" on the merits of capitalism versus communism with Soviet President Nikita Khruschev during a 1959 visit to Moscow. Cheney, elected in 2000 and 2004, has displayed enormous influence over White House affairs, leading many observers to describe him as the most powerful vice president in American history. The office's major significance, however, remains the fact that the vice president is "only a heartbeat away" from the presidency.

Vice presidential running mates are generally chosen by presidential candidates to broaden the appeal of the party's ticket. A candidate from the South may choose a running mate from the Northeast, or a more liberal candidate may select a more conservative person. Once elected, the personal chemistry between these candidates often contributes to the extent to which a president uses his vice president to help carry out administrative or policy matters.

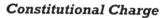

> **The office of vice president is "not worth a pitcher full of warm spit."**
>
> —Vice President John Nance Garner

Constitutional Charge

The delegates to the CONSTITUTIONAL CONVENTION OF 1787 decided to create the office of vice president to solve two problems: (1) providing for a successor to the president in the case of resignation, IMPEACHMENT, or death; and (2) creating a presiding officer of the SENATE, in which each state was to have equal representation. The only affirmative constitutional duty of the vice president is to break tie votes in the Senate.

The Constitution in Article II, section 1, provides that the president "shall hold his Office during the Term of four Years, and, together with the Vice President, chosen for the same Term, be elected as follows...." In 1800, when constitutional procedure specified that the presidential candidate with the second highest number of votes became vice president, there was a tie vote between THOMAS JEFFERSON and his vice presidential running mate, Aaron Burr. After a number of separate votes were taken in the HOUSE OF REPRESENTATIVES, as required under Article II, section 1, Jefferson finally received a majority of the votes. Because of the difficulty encountered in that election, the Twelfth Amendment (1804) was passed to provide that the president and vice president, who run for their respective offices together on a political party ticket, are voted for separately in the ELECTORAL COLLEGE. The presidential candidate with the highest number of electoral votes becomes the new president of the United States, and the vice presidential candidate with the highest number of votes becomes the new vice president.

The Twelfth Amendment authorized the vice president to "act as President" if the president was not selected by March 4—at that time, the date when the new president took office—but this date was changed by the Twentieth Amendment (1933). Under this amendment the term of a new president and vice president begins January 20 of the year following the election. Section 3 of the amendment, regarding the vice president's succession to the presidency or service as acting

Vice President Dick Cheney has had broad influence in George W. Bush's administration.
Source: CQ Photo/Scott J. Ferrell

president under certain circumstances, was changed by the Twenty-fifth Amendment (1967), which specifies the circumstances under which the vice president becomes president and the method of filling a vacancy in the office of the vice president.

VICE PRESIDENTS OF THE UNITED STATES

No.	Name	Political Party	Born	Home State	Inaug.	Died
1.	John Adams	Federalist	1735	Massachusetts	1789	1826
2.	Thomas Jefferson	Democratic-Republican	1743	Virginia	1797	1826
3.	Aaron Burr	Democratic-Republican	1756	New York	1801	1836
4.	George Clinton	Democratic-Republican	1739	New York	1805	1812
5.	Elbridge Gerry	Democratic-Republican	1744	Massachusetts	1813	1814
6.	Daniel D. Tomkins	Democratic-Republican	1774	New York	1817	1825
7.	John C. Calhoun[1]	Democratic-Republican	1782	South Carolina	1825	1850
8.	Martin Van Buren	Democrat	1782	New York	1833	1862
9.	Richard M. Johnson[2]	Democrat	1780	Kentucky	1837	1850
10.	John Tyler	Whig	1790	Virginia	1841	1862
11.	George M. Dallas	Democrat	1792	Pennsylvania	1845	1864
12.	Millard Filmore	Whig	1800	New York	1849	1874
13.	William R. King	Democrat	1786	Alabama	1853	1853
14.	John C. Breckinridge	Democrat	1821	Kentucky	1857	1875
15.	Hannibal Hamlin	Republican	1809	Maine	1861	1891
16.	Andrew Johnson[3]	Democrat	1808	Tennessee	1865	1875
17.	Schuyler Colfax	Republican	1823	Indiana	1869	1885
18.	Henry Wilson	Republican	1812	Massachusetts	1873	1875
19.	William A. Wheeler	Republican	1819	New York	1877	1887
20.	Chester A. Arthur	Republican	1830	New York	1881	1886
21.	Thomas A. Henricks	Democrat	1819	Indiana	1885	1885
22.	Levi P. Morton	Republican	1824	New York	1889	1920
23.	Adlai E. Stevenson[4]	Democrat	1835	Illinois	1893	1914
24.	Garret A. Hobart	Republican	1844	New Jersey	1897	1899
25.	Theodore Roosevelt	Republican	1858	New York	1901	1919
26.	Charles W. Fairbanks	Republican	1852	Indiana	1905	1918

Succession to the Presidency

"In case of the removal of the President from office or of his death or resignation," states section 1 of the Twenty-fifth Amendment, "the Vice President shall become President." With respect to the vice president's succession to the presidency, section 2 states: "Whenever there is a vacancy in the office of the Vice President, the President shall nominate a Vice President who shall take office upon confirmation by a majority vote of both Houses of Congress." This provision was relied on twice during the Nixon administration (1968–74). First, after Vice President Spiro Agnew (1918–96) resigned in the wake of a corruption scandal, Nixon nominated Gerald R. Ford (1913–2006), who was confirmed in 1973. Then in 1974, following Nixon's resignation as a result of the WATERGATE scandal, Ford took office as president—the country's first unelected president (he had been a congressman from Michigan). At the end of 1974 Ford nominated and Congress confirmed Nelson A. Rockefeller (1908–79) to be his vice president.

The Twenty-fifth Amendment also addresses the vice president's role as acting president when the president, according to section 3, "is unable to discharge the powers and duties of his office." Under section 4, the vice president and a majority of the heads of the executive departments or "of such other body as Congress may by law provide" may "transmit to the President pro tempore of the Senate and the Speaker of the House of Representatives their written declaration that the

No.	Name	Political Party	Born	Home State	Inaug.	Died
27.	James S. Sherman	Republican	1855	New York	1909	1912
28.	Thomas R. Marshall	Democrat	1854	Indiana	1913	1925
29.	Calvin Coolidge	Republican	1872	Massachusetts	1921	1933
30.	Charles G. Dawes	Republican	1865	Illinois	1925	1951
31.	Charles Curtis	Republican	1860	Kansas	1929	1936
32.	John Nance Garner	Democrat	1868	Texas	1933	1967
33.	Henry Agard Wallace	Democrat	1888	Iowa	1941	1965
34.	Harry S. Truman	Democrat	1884	Missouri	1945	1972
35.	Alban W. Barkley	Democrat	1877	Kentucky	1949	1956
36.	Richard Milhous Nixon	Republican	1913	California	1953	1994
37.	Lyndon Baines Johnson	Democrat	1908	Texas	1961	1973
38.	Hubert Humphrey	Democrat	1911	Minnesota	1965	1978
39.	Spiro T. Agnew[5]	Republican	1918	Maryland	1969	1996
40.	Gerald Rudolph Ford[6]	Republican	1913	Michigan	1973	2006
41.	Nelson A. Rockefeller[7]	Republican	1908	New York	1974	1979
42.	Walter F. Mondale	Democrat	1928	Minnesota	1977	
43.	George Herbert Walker Bush	Republican	1924	Texas	1981	
44.	Dan Quayle	Republican	1947	Indiana	1989	
45.	Albert Gore Jr.	Democrat	1948	Tennessee	1993	
46.	Dick Cheney	Republican	1941	Wyoming	2001	

[1.] John C. Calhoun resigned December 28, 1832, having been elected to the Senate to fill a vacancy.

[2.] Richard M. Johnson was the only vice president to be chosen by the Senate because of a tie vote in the electoral college.

[3.] Andrew Johnson was nominated as vice president by the Republicans and elected with Lincoln on the National Union Party ticket.

[4.] Adlai E. Stevenson, twenty-third vice president, was the grandfather of the Democratic candidate for president in 1952 and 1956.

[5.] Resigned October 10, 1973.

[6.] First nonelected vice president, chosen under the Twenty-fifth Amendment procedure.

[7.] Second nonelected vice president, chosen under the Twenty-fifth Amendment procedure.

President is unable to discharge the powers and duties of his office." In such a case "the Vice President shall immediately assume the powers and duties of the office as Acting President." Section 4 also establishes the procedure for the president's resumption of duties, including "a written declaration that no inability exists," as well as the procedure for Congress's determination, through a "two-thirds vote of both Houses," that the president is incapable of resuming the duties of the office.

Before the Twenty-fifth Amendment, the country's vice president assumed the office on eight occasions following the incumbent president's death. But the possibility of a president's becoming disabled in office, which arose during the Eisenhower administration (1952–60), argued for a constitutionally established procedure for handling the various types of disability that might befall a president in office. In addition, because seven vice presidents had died in office and one, John C. Calhoun (1782–1850), resigned in 1832 to serve in the Senate, the nation needed a procedure for filling such a vacancy.

In 1947 Congress had enacted a law detailing the order of succession to the presidency, amending it in 1965, 1966, 1977, and 1979. According to the law, the following officers would become president if the vice president were unable to serve: the SPEAKER OF THE HOUSE, president pro tempore of the Senate, secretary of state, secretary of the Treasury, secretary of defense, attorney general, and then the secretaries of the interior, agriculture, commerce, labor, health and human services, housing and urban development, transportation, energy, education, veterans affairs, and homeland security, in that order (see CABINET). To assume the duties of the presidency, the Speaker of the House and the president pro tempore of the Senate must resign their position and their membership in Congress. To date, no official other than a vice president has ever succeeded to the presidency.

President of the Senate

"The Vice President of the United States," states Article I, section 3, "shall be President of the Senate but shall have no Vote, unless they be equally divided. The Senate shall chuse their other Officers, and also a President pro tempore, in the Absence of the Vice President, or when he shall exercise the Office of President of the United States." This constitutional linking of the vice president to the SENATE represents another exception to the principle of strict SEPARATION OF POWERS between the three branches of government.

The vice president's role solves a basic problem for the Senate. Because it is composed of an even number of members—two senators from each state, for a total of one hundred—there is always the possibility of a tie vote. By using the vice president to break ties, the equality and sovereignty of the states are maintained because the vice president is elected by the nation and does not represent any one state. Although the vice president seldom actually presides over the Senate, an ornate ceremonial office is maintained for him in the Capitol in recognition of his constitutional role.

Virginia Plan *See* CONSTITUTIONAL CONVENTION OF 1787. (SEE ALSO DOCUMENT AT THE END OF THE BOOK.)

Voting *See* ELECTIONS.

War

In *On War* (1833), the Prussian military officer Karl von Clausewitz (1780–1831) described war as the continuation "of political intercourse…with the intermixing of other means," which has often been misquoted as "War is the continuation of policy by other means." William Tecumseh Sherman (1820–91), the Union general who captured and burned Atlanta during the Civil War in 1864, is often quoted as having said: "I am tired and sick of war. Its glory is all moonshine…. War is hell." Whether viewed as simply an escalation of policy in the normal relations among nations or as the undoubted horror it can be to those caught up in it, going to war is an extreme step for any nation to take.

According to JAMES MADISON in essay 41 of *The Federalist* (1787–88) (see FEDERALIST PAPERS), "Security against foreign danger is one of the primitive objects of civil society. It is an avowed and essential object of the American Union. The powers requisite for attaining it must be effectually confided to the federal councils. Is the power of declaring war necessary? No man will answer this question in the negative."

The constitutions of most nations lodge the power to declare war, and also peace, in the national legislature. For example, the constitution of the Netherlands (1814, as amended) mandates: "A declaration that the kingdom is in a state of war shall not be made without the prior approval of the states general [parliament]." A few countries, including Italy and Japan, repudiate or renounce war as an option of government policy.

> **"I am tired and sick of war. Its glory is all moonshine…. War is hell."**
>
> **—Gen. William Tecumseh Sherman**

Many important Civil War (1861–65) battles were fought at sea. The dramatic destruction of the **Westfield** *in January 1863 was captured in this illustration published in* **Harper's History of the Great Rebellion.**
Source: Library of Congress

Declared Wars

In the U.S. Constitution, Article I, section 8, grants Congress the power "To declare War…" as well as the authority to raise and support armies, make rules for land and naval forces, and call out the state militias in time of emergency. Yet in Article II the Constitution designates the PRESIDENT as the commander in chief of the ARMED FORCES. To protect against a president's becoming a military dictator, using the armed forces without any checks or balances on his power, the SEPARATION OF POWERS principle on which the Constitution is based splits between the LEGISLATIVE BRANCH and the EXECUTIVE BRANCH the power to declare and fund a war and the power to direct military forces.

Although the United States has been at war on many occasions, Congress has formally declared war in only five cases: the War of 1812 (1812–14) against Great Britain, the Mexican War (1846–48), the Spanish-American War (1898), World War I (1914–18; U.S. declared in 1917), and World War II (1939–45; U.S. declared in 1941). During the two world wars, Congress enacted many laws that tightly controlled the nation's economy and delegated power to the president to take actions necessary for the successful prosecution of the war, such as taking over factories, rail-roads, and the systems of communications, as well as setting prices and regulating factory pro-duction—measures that most likely would be found unconstitutional during peacetime. During the undeclared Korean War (1950–53), the attempt by President Harry S. Truman (1884–1972) to take over the nation's steel mills, without approval by Congress, was held unconstitutional by the

Supreme Court in *YOUNGSTOWN SHEET AND TUBE CO. V. SAWYER* (1952) (see EMERGENCY POWERS). More recently, in *Hamdan v. Rumsfeld* (2006), the Court decided by a 5–3 vote that, absent congressional authorization, the president does not have authority as commander in chief to try Guantanamo Bay detainees in the war on terror by the type of military commissions created by the executive branch for this purpose.

According to the Supreme Court in *Stewart v. Kahn* (1871), the federal government's war powers do not necessarily end with the end of hostilities. In a unanimous decision, the Court said that the war power "carries with it inherently the power to guard against the immediate renewal of the conflict, and to remedy the evils which have arisen from its rise and progress." However, after sufficient time the Court will reject the continuing war powers argument. For example, in *Chastleton Corp. v. Sinclair* (1924), the justices invalidated a rent control law in the District of Columbia, citing the fact that the reason for the wartime emergency—World War I—was over. As Justice OLIVER WENDELL HOLMES JR. wrote for the Court: "In our opinion it is open to inquire whether the exigency still existed upon which the continued operation of the law depended....If about all that remains of war conditions is the increased cost of living that is not in itself a justification of the Act."

But even during peacetime, the threat of war may be used to justify extraordinary measures by the federal government. In *Ashwander v. Tennessee Valley Authority* (1936), the Supreme Court upheld the building of the Wilson Dam (1925) in Muscle Shoals, Alabama, on the grounds that it was constructed under the exercise of the war and commerce powers of the national government during World War I.

Undeclared Wars

The FRAMERS OF THE CONSTITUTION realized that there would be occasions when military force would have to be used without a formal declaration of war. But events since then have shown how important it is that a president who conducts an undeclared war has the support of Congress and the nation's citizens. In 1798–99 the United States engaged in an undeclared war with France. To allow the recapture of American vessels taken by the French, the Supreme Court found in *Bas v. Tingy* (1800) that a war had in fact gone on. But in *Gray v. United States* (1884), the U.S. Court of Claims treated the period as a time of peace.

The Civil War (1861–65) was an undeclared war domestically but constituted a war under INTERNATIONAL LAW, according to the Supreme Court in the Prize Cases (1862). The Court decided that because a state of war existed, the president's blockade of southern ports was a justified measure to subdue forces hostile to the United States.

After the Civil War, the most divisive undeclared war conducted by the United States was the Vietnam War (1955–75). Escalation of American support for South Vietnam in its fight against communist North Vietnam was begun by President John F. Kennedy (1917–63) during his administration (1961–63). After Kennedy's assassination, President Lyndon B. Johnson (1908–73) continued American involvement until in 1967 U.S. troops in Vietnam numbered 389,000. Protests against the war and the draft of young men to fight it also escalated during the 1960s. But in *United States v. O'Brien* (1968), in an 8–1 decision, the Supreme Court upheld the federal draft laws.

War Powers Resolution

President Richard M. Nixon (1913–94) presided over the winding down of the Vietnam War. Nixon, however, was politically weakened by the impending WATERGATE scandal in 1973, and Congress took the opportunity to enact the War Powers Resolution (1973) to restrict a president's power to conduct an undeclared war. The stated purpose of the resolution was "to fulfill the intent of the framers of the Constitution...and insure that the collective judgement of both the Congress and the President will apply to the introduction of United States Armed Forces into

More on this topic:

Armed Forces, p. 42

National Security, p. 375

President, p. 417

hostilities, or into situations where imminent involvement in hostilities is clearly indicated by the circumstances, and to the continued use of such forces in hostilities or in such situations."

The constitutionality of the War Powers Resolution has never been decided by the Supreme Court. In fact, it was simply ignored by President Ronald Reagan (1911–2004) when he sent U.S. troops into Lebanon in 1982. President George H. W. Bush (b. 1924) also ignored the resolution in sending troops into Panama in 1989 to capture Panama's president and later when he began sending troops into the Middle East in 1991 to drive invading Iraqi forces out of Kuwait during the Persian Gulf War (1990–91). Congress, however, did approve this invasion, known as Operation Desert Storm, before it officially began. Similarly, shortly after the terrorist attacks on the United States on September 11, 2001, Congress approved the invasion of Afghanistan in the Authorization for Use of Military Force by joint resolution dated September 18, 2001, and the following year Congress gave the green light to the invasion of Iraq in the Authorization for Use of Military Force Against Iraq Resolution of 2002.

The Constitution's war powers are for the most part exercised by the president, with Congress always having the ultimate power to cut off funds if it is not in accord with the president's actions. However, the very act of assessing the nature of threats to the United States and deciding what military action to take during a time of a declared war or an undeclared war, or even in peacetime probably demands a single decision maker and not a deliberative body such as Congress.

Warrants *See* SEARCH AND SEIZURE.

Washington, George

It is unlikely that anyone was more indispensable to the success of the new United States of America than George Washington (1732–99). A reluctant leader with no particular penchant for politics or political theory, he held the country's three most important positions in its early history: commander in chief of the colonial revolutionary army, president of the CONSTITUTIONAL CONVENTION OF 1787, and first PRESIDENT of the United States under the Constitution drafted in 1787. There is little doubt that Washington's stature at the time of his first inauguration as president in 1789—he was chosen unanimously by the first ELECTORAL COLLEGE—could have propelled a man of lesser character to become a dictator.

Washington was born in Westmoreland County, Virginia, on February 22, 1732. After his father's death, when Washington was eleven years old, he lived alternately with his mother and his half-brother Lawrence in his Mount Vernon home. He attended school irregularly but had a good grasp of functional mathematics, which, combined with his experience surviving in the wild, led to his appointment as official surveyor for Culpeper County in 1749. When Lawrence died of tuberculosis in 1752, Washington inherited Mount Vernon at the age of twenty.

The same year Washington was made a major in the Virginia militia. Although he experienced several defeats during the French and Indian Wars (1754–63), he was made commander of all the Virginia troops—the highest American military rank—at age twenty-three. Resigning his military commission, he married Martha Custis in 1759 and settled down as a gentleman farmer and member of Virginia's colonial legislature, the House of Burgesses. When the American war for independence began in 1775, he was made commander in chief of the Continental Army, in part to ensure Virginia's wholehearted support for the Revolution.

After the successful conclusion of the Revolutionary War, Washington was selected as one of five delegates from Virginia to the Constitutional Convention of 1787 to improve the ARTICLES OF CONFEDERATION (1781), the ineffectual constitution of the thirteen new states. He was unanimously chosen as the convention's president and, although he seldom spoke in debates, wrote urging that the delegates "probe the defects of the [Articles] to the bottom and provide a radical cure."

Washington presided over the Constitutional Convention in Philadelphia for four months and gave the draft document great weight by approving it. His greatest contributions were the force of his character and his prestige, which focused the delegates on the task at hand and facilitated the compromises necessary to obtain agreement on the final document. Afterward, Washington worked hard for RATIFICATION of the Constitution, personally giving out copies of *The Federalist*—essays written in 1787 and 1788 by JAMES MADISON, ALEXANDER HAMILTON, and John Jay to favorably influence ratification (see FEDERALIST PAPERS)—to persuade fellow Virginians to adopt it.

Although not assured of the document's perfection, Washington nevertheless believed that it was the only possible way to save the Union. After its ratification, he contemplated retiring from active public life to his beloved Mount Vernon farm. But the country called Washington again, and again, reluctantly, he answered its call. He was elected its first president in 1789 and then reelected in 1793. He refused to be considered for a third term, thus setting an unwritten precedent for later presidents until 1940, when Franklin D. Roosevelt (1882–1945) ran for a third term and later for a fourth (see TERMS OF OFFICE). Washington's actions in office set further standards for future presidents. Seeing himself as a president of all the people, he eschewed strong partisanship, balancing his first four CABINET appointments with two representatives from each party. Although criticized by the opposition for conducting himself like a king, Washington insisted on solemnity in carrying out his duties, whether in an official capacity or entertaining politicians or dignitaries.

Washington's Farewell Address was written to remove his name for consideration for a third term as president. Never publicly delivered, it was first published in a Philadelphia newspaper on September 19, 1796, and has been read annually in both the Senate and the House of Representatives for many years. In addition to cautioning against "entangl[ing] our peace and prosperity in the toils of European ambition, rivalship, interest, humor, or caprice," he expounded on the people's role in relation to the Constitution: "The basis of our political system is the right of the people to make and to alter their constitutions of government…. But the constitution which at any time exists, until

George Washington was inaugurated on April 30, 1789, on the balcony of Federal Hall on Wall Street in New York City. Almost immediately, patriotic recreations of the event were produced in books for mass consumption in the new nation.
Source: Library of Congress

"[T]o form a Constitution, that will give consistency, stability and dignity to the Union, and sufficient powers to the great Council…is a duty which will be incumbent upon every man …and will meet with my aid as far as it can be rendered in the private walks of life."

—*George Washington,* in a letter to the Marquis de Lafayette, 1783

Even though he had no precedents to guide him, George Washington assembled one of the great cabinets in American history. Left to right: Washington, Secretary of War Henry Knox, Treasury Secretary Alexander Hamilton, Secretary of State Thomas Jefferson, and Attorney General Edmund Randolph.
Source: Library of Congress

changed by an explicit and authentic act of the whole people, is sacredly obligatory upon all. The very idea of power, and the right of the people to establish government, presupposes the duty of every individual to obey the established government."

Shortly after Washington's death, on December 14, 1799, a resolution introduced in the House of Representatives by JOHN MARSHALL, later chief justice of the United States, declared him "first in war, first in peace, and first in the hearts of his countrymen." Of all of America's founders, he is held in the highest esteem in the country and around the world.

Watergate

The Watergate scandal of 1972–74 takes its name from the Watergate complex of apartments and commercial space along the Potomac River in Washington, D.C. During the 1972 presidential election, employees of the campaign committee to reelect Republican president

Richard M. Nixon (1913–94) broke into Democratic National Committee headquarters, located at the Watergate, on June 17. Among other activities, they intended to place a listening device on the telephone of DNC chairman Larry O'Brien. Top aides to the president and the PRESIDENT himself—who won his second term in 1972 against George McGovern—became implicated in a cover-up of the break-in. After a dogged investigation led by the reporters Bob Woodward and Carl Bernstein of the *Washington Post*, involving an unidentified informant known only as "Deep Throat," a special prosecutor (see INDEPENDENT COUNSEL) was appointed to officially investigate the matter. (That informant turned out to be former FBI assistant director W. Mark Felt, who came forward in 2005 at the age of ninety-one, having spent decades denying his involvement.)

Constitutional Crisis

A special Watergate prosecutor, Archibald Cox, was named in May 1973 by Attorney General–designate Elliot Richardson, who had recently replaced Richard Kleindienst, after the Justice Department had closed its investigation into the charges raised by the *Post*. When Cox began to get close to the truth, Nixon had him fired on October 20, 1973, in what has become known as the "Saturday Night Massacre." Nixon maintained publicly that he was not involved, saying, "I am not a crook." Public and political pressure soon forced Nixon to permit the appointment of a new special prosecutor, Leon Jaworski. Citing executive privilege, Nixon withheld in-

This 1973 cartoon by John Pierotti illustrates the damage done to the office of the president by President Nixon's involvement in the Watergate scandal. One legacy of the affair remains wariness of presidential assertions of executive privilege.
Source: The Granger Collection, New York

formation requested by Jaworski, who then asked the SUPREME COURT to intercede. The Court in its opinion in *United States v. Nixon* (1974) forced the president to turn over to the special prosecutor tape recordings of conversations with his subordinates. This evidence directly implicated the president in the cover-up of the Watergate burglary, which had been approved by former attorney general John Mitchell.

The tapes acquired by the special prosecutor became the "smoking gun" that impelled the Judiciary Committee of the HOUSE OF REPRESENTATIVES to begin the IMPEACHMENT process called for under Article II, section 4, of the Constitution and implemented under Article I, sections 2 and 3. The committee voted out a bill of impeachment containing three charges: that the president had prevented, obstructed, and impeded the administration of justice; that he had repeatedly engaged in conduct that violated the rights of citizens; and that he had unlawfully withheld evidence requested under subpoenas issued by the House of Representatives.

Faced with almost inevitable impeachment by the House and almost certain conviction by the SENATE—he would have been the first president so removed from office in the history of the United States—Nixon resigned on August 9, 1974. The powers of the office of the president then passed to Vice President Gerald R. Ford (1913–2006). Under the provisions of the Twenty-fifth

Richard Nixon and his family leave the White House on August 9, 1974, following his resignation.
Source: Nixon Project/NARA

Amendment (1967) governing succession to the office of president and VICE PRESIDENT, Nixon had appointed Ford as vice president following the resignation of Vice President Spiro T. Agnew (1918–96) to avoid punishment in his own corruption scandal. Ford thus became the first unelected vice president to become president, making him also the first unelected president of the United States. Within a month after assuming office, Ford exercised his presidential power to pardon Nixon for all crimes he may have committed in office (see PARDONS).

Constitutional Principles

The Watergate scandal brought to the public's attention seldom-used constitutional procedures created by the nation's founders to protect the country from presidential abuse of power. The checks and balances provisions (see SEPARATION OF POWERS) worked to ensure that illegal attempts to influence an election outcome (see ELECTIONS) were uncovered and the perpetrators punished. (As a result of his pardon, however, Nixon's only punishment was public disgrace and the loss of the presidency.) Watergate also confirmed the importance of a free and aggressive press (see THE PRESS) in ferreting out the cover-up of an illegal operation by top government officials. Supported by the *Post*'s editor, Benjamin C. Bradlee, and its publisher, Katharine Graham, Woodward and Bernstein refused to give up or be intimidated by the "stonewalling" efforts of Nixon and all the president's men. The events also proved the effectiveness of an ad hoc special prosecutor in investigating top officials of the EXECUTIVE BRANCH of the government, including the president himself, and the necessity for an independent judicial system and Supreme Court, which ruled that even the president was not above the law in a criminal investigation.

Watergate proved, among other things, how well the Constitution works in a time of potential crisis. This episode in America's constitutional history led to a reduction in the power of the presidency and the passage of a statute in 1978 to provide for an independent counsel to investigate allegations of wrongdoing by high officials in the executive branch, a position that came into public prominence during the administration (1993–2001) of President Bill Clinton (b. 1946).

⊙ **CLOSER LOOK**

Although Watergate is often regarded as the most serious White House scandal in U.S. history, it is by no means the only one.

One of the worst scandals took place during the administration of Warren G. Harding (1921–1923). Interior Secretary Albert B. Fall leased petroleum reserves in the West to oil companies without public notice or competitive bidding. One of those reserves was known as Teapot Dome, and the scandal became known as the Teapot Dome scandal.

Investigations revealed that Fall had accepted hundreds of thousands of dollars in bribes from the companies. He was sentenced to prison—the first cabinet officer to serve a prison term for illegal activities connected with government service.

The scandal also led to the resignations of the attorney general and the navy secretary.

PRESIDENT RICHARD M. NIXON'S RESIGNATION, AUGUST 8, 1974 (EXCERPTS)

This is the 37th time I have spoken to you from this office, where so many decisions have been made that shaped the history of this Nation. Each time I have done so to discuss with you some matter than I believe affected the national interest.

… In all the decisions I have made in my public life, I have always tried to do what was best for the Nation. Throughout the long and difficult period of Watergate, I have felt it was my duty to persevere, to make every possible effort to complete the term of office to which you elected me.

In the past few days, however, it has become evident to me that I no longer have a strong enough political base in the Congress to justify continuing that effort. As long as there was such a base, I felt strongly that it was necessary to see the constitutional process through to its conclusion, that to do otherwise would be unfaithful to the spirit of that deliberately difficult process and a dangerously destabilizing precedent for the future.

But with the disappearance of that base, I now believe that the constitutional purpose has been served, and there is no longer a need for the process to be prolonged….

I have never been a quitter. To leave office before my term is completed is abhorrent to every instinct in my body. But as President, I must put the interest of America first. America needs a full-time President and a full-time Congress, particularly at this time with problems we face at home and abroad.

To continue to fight through the months ahead for my personal vindication would almost totally absorb the time and attention of both the President and the Congress in a period when our entire focus should be on the great issues of peace abroad and prosperity without inflation at home.

Therefore, I shall resign the Presidency effective at noon tomorrow. Vice President Ford will be sworn in as President at that hour in this office.

As I recall the high hopes for America with which we began this second term, I feel a great sadness that I will not be here in this office working on your behalf to achieve those hopes in the next 2½ years. But in turning over direction of the Government to Vice President Ford, I know, as I told the Nation when I nominated him for that office 10 months ago, that the leadership of America will be in good hands.

In passing this office to the Vice President, I also do so with the profound sense of the weight of responsibility that will fall on his shoulders tomorrow and, therefore, of the understanding, the patience, the cooperation he will need from all Americans.

As he assumes that responsibility, he will deserve the help and the support of all of us. As we look to the future, the first essential is to begin healing the wounds of this Nation, to put the bitterness and divisions of the recent past behind us, and to rediscover those shared ideals that lie at the heart of our strength and unity as a great and as a free people.

By taking this action, I hope that I will have hastened the start of that process of healing which is so desperately needed in America.

I regret deeply any injuries that may have been done in the course of the events that led to this decision. I would say only that if some of my judgments were wrong, and some were wrong, they were made in what I believed at the time to be the best interest of the Nation….

[L]et me say I leave with no bitterness toward those who have opposed me, because all of us, in the final analysis, have been concerned with the good of the country, however our judgments might differ….

I pledge to you tonight that as long as I have a breath of life in my body, I shall continue … to work for the great causes to which I have been dedicated throughout my years as a Congressman, a Senator, a Vice President, and President, the cause of peace not just for America but among all nations, prosperity, justice, and opportunity for all of our people….

I am confident that the world is a safer place today, not only for the people of America but for the people of all nations, and that all of our children have a better chance than before of living in peace rather than dying in war.

This, more than anything, is what I hoped to achieve when I sought the Presidency. This, more than anything, is what I hope will be my legacy to you, to our country, as I leave the Presidency….

SOURCE: www.ukans.edu/carrie/docs/amdocs_index.html.

Weapons *See* GUN CONTROL.

Weights and Measures

In his *Commentaries on the Laws of England* (1765–70), William Blackstone (1723–80) mentioned under the headings Offenses against Public Trade and Cheating "the offence of selling by *false weights and measures.*" Standard references for weights and measures such as pounds and pints were important to any economy built on COMMERCE and trade.

When the thirteen former British colonies drew up the ARTICLES OF CONFEDERATION (1781), which preceded the Constitution, they included in Article IX this language reflecting earlier concerns from the mother country: "The United States, in Congress assembled, shall also have the sole and exclusive right and power of regulating the alloy and value of coin struck by their own authority, or by that of the respective states; [and] fixing the standard of weights and measures throughout the United States...."

Standard references for weights and measures such as pounds and pints were important to any economy built on commerce and trade.

In the new constitution that went into effect in 1789, Article I, section 8, similarly stated: "The Congress shall have Power To...fix the Standard of Weights and Measures." As JAMES MADISON noted in essay 42 of *The Federalist* (1787–88) (see FEDERALIST PAPERS), "The regulation of weights and measures is transferred from the Articles of Confederation, and is founded on like considerations with the preceding power of regulating coin" (see CURRENCY).

In addition to authorizing the federal government to maintain the accuracy, uniformity, and standardization of weights and measures, this constitutional provision also gives Congress the power to change the country's system of weights and measures from the present English system to the metric system, should it ever decide to do so. The Office of Weights and Measures in the National Institute of Standards and Technology implements federal policy in this area. A National Conference on Weights and Measures was established in 1905 as a professional organization representing state and local officials responsible for weights and measures and representatives of business, industry, consumer groups, and federal agencies.

The power of the federal government to regulate weights and measures has not been significantly challenged in the Supreme Court, although the Court has occasionally had to deal with related cases. For example, in *Armour and Co. v. North Dakota* (1916), the justices upheld a state statute that required "[e]very lot of lard compound or lard substitute...[to] be put up in pails or other containers holding one (1), three (3), or five (5), pounds net weight, or some multiple of these numbers, and not any fractions thereof." A meat-packing company did not comply, asserting its inviolable right to sell lard in two-pound, six-ounce containers, but it could not persuade the Court, which found that the statutory requirement was a reasonable consumer protection against deceptive packaging.

Welfare

The term *general welfare* as used in the Constitution—the PREAMBLE states that one of the document's purposes is "to...promote the general Welfare" and Article I, section 8, authorizes Congress to "lay and collect Taxes, Duties, Imposts and Excises, to pay the Debts and provide for the common Defence and general Welfare of the United States"—has meant different things to different people. JAMES MADISON, in essay 41 of *The Federalist* (1787–88) (see FEDERALIST PAPERS), minimized the effect of this language, saying that while it seems excessively broad it is still subject to the enumeration and limitation of national powers elsewhere in the Constitution. ALEXANDER HAMILTON, in contrast, found in the general welfare clause a source of independent power for the federal government. Other national constitutions, including those of India (1950) and the Philippines (1987), specifically require their governments to promote the "general welfare" or the "welfare of the people."

Closely tied to the Constitution's language granting Congress the power to tax (see TAXATION), the welfare clause has given rise to three schools of thought: (1) As Madison had indicated, Congress could tax and spend only to carry out the enumerated powers in the Constitution. (2) As Hamilton argued, Congress could tax and spend for certain general welfare purposes in addition to the enumerated powers. (3) Congress was essentially totally unfettered under the Constitution in its power to spend for the general welfare.

In *United States v. Butler* (1936), the Supreme Court accepted Hamilton's interpretation, saying that Congress could tax and spend beyond the purposes enumerated in the Constitution. However, the Court then found that the tax in question was an attempt to invade a subject under the jurisdiction of the STATES—agricultural production—and therefore held it to be unconstitutional. In later cases the Court confirmed its approval of Hamilton's interpretation by expanding the scope of Congress's power to tax and spend for the general welfare.

This power was again enlarged when the Supreme Court upheld the Social Security Act (1935), which required taxing and spending on a large scale for a major national welfare program. The challenge presented in *Steward Machine Co. v. Davis* (1937) involved the constitutionality of the act, under which Congress taxed employment to create a fund for states to use in administering their unemployment compensation laws. The Court held that the tax was a valid exercise of constitutional power and did not infringe the states' residual powers or rights under the Tenth Amendment (1791), arguing that the state involved, Alabama, was not forced to administer the unemployment relief program under its own laws, which it could repeal at any time.

In *Fullilove v. Klutznick* (1980), the majority opinion by Chief Justice Warren Burger (1907–95) declared that Congress could "further broad policy objectives by conditioning receipt of federal monies upon compliance by the recipient with federal statutory and administrative directives," thus using its spending power "to induce governments and private parties to cooperate voluntarily with federal policy." Today the scope of congressional power to tax and spend for "the general welfare" is virtually unquestioned by the courts. However, according to at least one Supreme Court justice, SANDRA DAY O'CONNOR, if a wholly unrelated condition were imposed by Congress on the states for the receipt of federal funds, this authority might be challenged successfully.

Welfare Rights

In his famous "Four Freedoms" speech in 1941 (see page 248), President Franklin D. Roosevelt (1882–1945) called for "freedom from want—which, translated into world terms, means economic understandings which will secure to every nation a healthy peacetime life for its inhabitants—everywhere in the world." However, so far the Supreme Court has not found a constitutional right of Americans to an adequate standard of living, as enunciated in such international HUMAN RIGHTS documents as the Universal Declaration of Human Rights (1948) and the International Covenant on Economic, Social and Cultural Rights (1966).

Citizens of other nations, including many in Europe, are guaranteed some welfare benefits. Denmark's constitution (1953) assures citizens that "[a]ny person unable to support himself or his dependents shall, where no other per-

"Everyone has the right to a standard of living adequate for the health and well-being of himself and of his family, including food, clothing, housing and medical care and necessary social services."

—Article 25 of the Universal Declaration of Human Rights

son is responsible for his or their maintenance, be entitled to receive public assistance...." The constitution of Brazil (1988) promises "[e]ducation, health, work, leisure, security, social welfare, protection of motherhood and childhood, and assistance to the destitute."

Any right to federal welfare benefits in the United States is dependent on statutory law, which can be changed or simply not fully funded by Congress, depending on the nation's political and economic climate at any particular time. The government's ability to fund Social Security, Medicare (health care for eligible older persons), and Medicaid (health care for people living below the poverty level) (see HEALTH) is a source of constant political debate. In the 2000 presidential election, the term *lockbox* came into vogue as an assertion by presidential candidate Al Gore (b. 1948) that funds earmarked for social security benefits would not be raided for other purposes. Political leaders have tried to ignore the looming problem of how to guarantee future funding for such programs as the population ages and retires while the wage earners who pay the taxes to fund such programs become relatively fewer.

> **"Power has only one duty—to secure the social welfare of the people."**
>
> —British prime minister Benjamin Disraeli

In the 1970s the Supreme Court rejected the assertion of any constitutional right to adequate housing or a minimum level of health care but did indicate that there might be a constitutional right to EDUCATION. CHILDREN have fared somewhat better, as recipients beginning in the 1930s of a federal grant program called Aid to Families with Dependent Children, which by the 1990s had become primarily responsible for providing benefits to poor women who headed a household with minor children. This program was changed by the Personal Responsibility and Work Opportunity Act (1996), which was billed as a move away from public welfare to "workfare."

The United States has tended to reject making constitutional mandates out of social rights programs, arguing that the opportunity for people in the United States to provide for themselves, aided by a minimal "safety net" to tide them over in extreme cases, increases the incentive to work hard and is fairer to those who work at least at low-paying jobs. Yet proponents of programs such as universal health care wonder how the richest nation on earth can defend a policy that denies a large portion of its citizens and residents, including millions of children, adequate food, shelter, and health care, while many other citizens have vast resources to spend on these needs as well as life's luxuries.

Wiretapping

A staple of cold war–era espionage is the wiretap—a concealed listening or recording device attached to a COMMUNICATIONS wire or other transmitter that allows a third party to secretly listen in on a conversation. This surreptitious method of obtaining information and evidence, as well as the new technique of "webtapping" in the age of the INTERNET, has also raised constitutional issues more recently in the war on terror. Government wiretapping of private conversations to obtain evidence in a criminal investigation may raise questions of constitutionality, especially with respect to the prohibitions in the Fourth Amendment (1791) against unreasonable SEARCH AND SEIZURE and in the Fifth Amendment (1791) against SELF-INCRIMINATION, together with the Constitution's more general PRIVACY guarantees.

The invention of the telephone and the microphone created an opportunity for clandestinely wiretapping conversations. The first case involving wiretapping to come before the Supreme Court was *Olmstead v. United States* (1928). Several bootleggers (see PROHIBITION) had been convicted largely on the basis of evidence obtained through telephone taps, which were illegal under Washington state law. In his opinion for the 5–4 Court majority, Chief Justice William Howard Taft (1857–1930) concluded that wiretapping did not violate the "right of the people to be secure in their persons, houses, papers, and effects" under the Fourth Amendment. He rationalized that the protection against unreasonable searches and seizures was aimed at protecting PROPERTY, and because no one had trespassed on the defendant's property—the tap was placed on the external telephone wires—no search of the defendant's premises had occurred. Simply overhearing a conversation, he added, could not qualify as a seizure of evidence, and the fact that the evidence was obtained in violation of a state law did not affect its admissibility in a federal court.

In 1934 Congress passed the Federal Communications Act, which provided in section 605 that "no person not being authorized by the sender shall intercept any communication and divulge or publish the existence, contents, purport, effect, or meaning of such intercepted communication to any person." In *Nardone v. United States* (1939), the Supreme Court decided that if federal officers obtained information through a wiretap, such testimony would violate the statute, so such evidence must be excluded from a federal trial. However, the Court did not require the STATES also to exclude evidence obtained in violation of the act. But according to the Court's decision in *Bananti v. United States* (1957), because the federal government intended to exclusively regulate wiretapping, states could not legalize it in order to use a tap to obtain evidence, even with a court order.

KATZ V. UNITED STATES (1967), a significant wiretapping case, overruled *Olmstead*. In *Silverman v. United States* (1961), the Supreme Court had found that for a violation of the Fourth Amendment's search and seizure provisions to occur, there had to be an intrusion into "a constitutionally protected area." *Katz*, which involved a warrantless wiretap of a public telephone booth, replaced the "constitutionally protected area" test with an "expectation of privacy" test. If citizens have an expectation of privacy at home or in a public telephone booth, they are protected from unreasonable searches and seizures, including wiretaps.

Until 1968, when Congress enacted the Omnibus Crime Control and Safe Streets Act, the only exception to section 605 of the Communications Act was in the case of NATIONAL SECURITY. Title III of the 1968 act allowed state and federal officials to conduct wiretaps if they obtain prior approval by a judge. The Foreign Intelligence Surveillance Act (1978) later set federal requirements, including special judicial warrants permitting wiretaps in the United States, for collecting foreign national security information.

As communications technology has quickly improved, the courts have been trying to keep up. In *Smith v. Maryland* (1979), the Supreme Court found that although LAW ENFORCEMENT officials may not listen in on or secretly record a telephone conversation, they may use a device that records telephone numbers a person dials because there is, according to the court, no expectation of privacy with respect to telephone numbers. The measures taken to counter TERRORISM after the attacks on the United States of September 11, 2001, have brought forth new eavesdropping issues for the Court to address in terms of the Constitution's protection of privacy and its prohibition against unreasonable searches and seizures.

During deliberations in Congress on the PATRIOT ACT, the U.S. Department of Justice advised certain key senators that "[a]s Commander-in-Chief, the President must be able to use whatever means necessary to prevent attacks upon the United States...[; and that] the government's heightened interest in self-

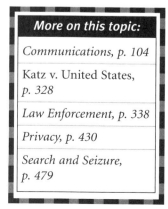

More on this topic:
Communications, p. 104
Katz v. United States, p. 328
Law Enforcement, p. 338
Privacy, p. 430
Search and Seizure, p. 479

defense justifies…warrantless searches." However, the warrantless eavesdropping met resistance, including the 2006 initiative by the American Civil Liberties Union to campaign in twenty states to stop government from monitoring calls and obtaining information from telephone companies. U.S. Attorney General Alberto R. Gonzales, however, defended the data collection citing the *Smith* decision and concluding that because the listening devices were not installed in a person's home, a citizen's privacy was not violated. The Foreign Intelligence Surveillance Act of 1978 permitted wiretapping to gather foreign intelligence without having to show probable cause, if the Foreign Intelligence Surveillance Court approved the request. Congress and the federal courts will undoubtedly continue to address circumvention of this requirement by the executive branch in counterterrorism efforts, as well as other cases involving constitutional protections against unreasonable searches and seizures and invasion of privacy.

Senate Judiciary committee chair Arlen Specter, R-Pa., holds a news conference to discuss possible legislation to withhold funding from the NSA wiretapping program.
Source: CQ Photo/Scott J. Ferrell

Witnesses

"When evidence is needed in court we have to bring as witnesses persons who were actually present, whoever they are [as opposed to] close relatives and intimate friends," said Isaios (ca. 420–350 B.C.E.), an orator and expert on wills and inheritance in ancient Athens. Witnesses were also relied on in ancient Rome to support litigants in the Roman legal system. Magna Carta (1215), the charter of liberties forced on the English King John by his barons, guaranteed that a person could not

An expert witness uses a plastic model of a human head to describe a murder during court testimony.
Source: Reuters/Damian Dovarganes

be placed on trial on the basis of his own testimony; instead, credible witnesses had to testify to the truth of an accused's statement or confession. William Blackstone (1723–80), in his *Commentaries on the Laws of England* (1765–70), declared that "to endeavor to dissuade a witness from giving evidence; to disclose an examination before the Privy Council; or, to advise a prisoner to stand mute (all of which are impediments of justice), are high misprisons and contempts of the sovereign's courts, and punishable by fine and imprisonment."

Today most civilized countries guarantee accused persons the right to confront witnesses against them and to call witnesses on their own behalf. The U.S. legal system is based on using the testimony of lay as well as expert witnesses. The Constitution's Sixth Amendment (1791) provides that in "all criminal prosecutions, the accused shall enjoy the right...to be confronted with the witnesses against him; [and] to have compulsory process for obtaining witnesses in his favor...." The Fifth Amendment (1791) prohibits the government from compelling a person to be a witness against himself (see SELF-INCRIMINATION). The right of those accused of crimes to confront witnesses against them and to compel the appearance of witnesses helps to ensure that TRIALS are conducted fairly.

Confrontation of Witnesses

Persons accused of crimes have the right to confront witnesses against them because this allows them to challenge the reliability and credibility of such witnesses through cross-examination after they have given their testimony in open court under oath. A defendant or his or her attorney can test the witness's ability to observe and recall the facts testified to, as well as the witness's objectivity—his lack of personal bias or prejudice against the defendant. The judge and jury also gain an opportunity to observe the witness's demeanor as a basis for deciding what weight to give to his or her testimony.

The Supreme Court stated in *Mattox v. United States* (1895) that the primary purpose behind the constitutional guarantee of the right to confront witnesses is "to prevent depositions of *ex parte* [one-sided] affidavits...being used against the prisoner in lieu of a personal examination and cross-examination of the witness in which the accused has an opportunity not only of testing the recollection and sifting the conscience of the witness, but of compelling him to stand face to face with the jury in order that they may look at him, and judge by his demeanor upon the stand and the manner in which he gives his testimony whether he is worthy of belief."

In *Kirby v. United States* (1899), the Supreme Court declared that the right to confront witnesses is "[o]ne of the fundamental guarantees of life and liberty...long deemed so essential for the due protection of life and liberty..." (see LIBERTY). The Court also held, in *Motes v. United States* (1900), that a witness, if available, must be called by the prosecution and that pretrial statements made by the witness cannot be substituted for a witness's personal appearance.

In some later cases, however, the Supreme Court retreated from its pronouncement in *Kirby*. In *Baily v. Richardson* (1951), although not a criminal case, the Court upheld the dismissal of a federal government employee on the basis of charges by informants who did not appear at the loyalty board hearing on which her dismissal was based. The lower federal court ruling was upheld by the Court's 4–4 vote—a majority needed to overturn a decision being lacking—and opinions were not filed. Justice William O. Douglas (1898–1980), in a concurring opinion in *Joint Anti-Fascist Refugee Committee v. McGrath*, a case decided on the same day as *Baily*, recounted that in the *Baily* case even counsel's request for the names of the informants against his client was refused. He went on to note that "she was on trial for her reputation, her job, her professional standing." To condemn her "without meticulous regard for the decencies of a fair trial" he argued, "is abhorrent to fundamental justice."

In *Pointer v. Texas* (1965), the Supreme Court confirmed the fundamental importance of allowing confrontation of witnesses in a criminal prosecution, ruling that according to the INCORPORATION DOCTRINE, this Sixth Amendment right applied to the STATES under the DUE PROCESS clause of the Fourteenth Amendment (1868). The Court admitted some exceptions to the right, including the use of dying declarations and the testimony of persons at earlier trials who had since died, even though cross-examination of the witnesses was obviously not possible. In 1992 the Court confirmed a defendant's right to confront any adverse witnesses, not just those who accuse him or her of a crime.

The Supreme Court has had to deal with a number of issues relating to the confrontation clause recently. In 2006, in *Davis v. Washington*, the Court held that a victim's statements in response to a

911 operator's interrogation were not testimonial, and therefore were not subject to the confrontation clause. Two years earlier, the Court unanimously overruled its holding in *Ohio v. Roberts* (1980) that the statement of an unavailable witness could be used at trial if the statement "bears 'particularized guarantees of trustworthiness.' " The Court's decision in *Crawford v. Washington* (2004) found that a statement by the wife of the defendant, herself a possible suspect in the commission of the crime, made to the police that implicated her husband in the crime was not necessarily as "reliable" as the trial court had determined. Thus the rule in *Roberts* had to be abandoned because the Court felt that it could not be applied consistently. The *Crawford* decision would become the basis of the issue before the Court in *Wharton v. Bockting* (2007), which involved determining if the "new rule" in *Crawford* had to be applied retroactively to cases in which the old rule in *Roberts* had been relied on. The Supreme Court found, however, that unlike its decisions in cases like GIDEON V. WAINWRIGHT (1963), which extended the right of counsel to indigent defendants, the risk of an unreliable verdict was not so intolerably high before *Crawford* and *Crawford* did not so "alter our understanding of the *bedrock procedural elements* essential to the fairness of a proceeding" that it had to be applied retroactively.

Compulsory Process

In addition to giving a defendant the ability to mount a defense, his right to use legal procedures to compel witnesses to appear in court was apparently intended to defeat a rule of COMMON LAW that barred the use of witnesses for the defense in TREASON and felony cases. According to the *Commentaries on the Constitution of the United States* (1833) by Justice Joseph Story (1779–1845), "The right to offer the testimony of witnesses, and to compel their attendance, if necessary, is in plain terms the right to present a defense, the right to present the defendant's version of the facts as well as the prosecution's to the jury so it may decide where the truth lies."

The Supreme Court echoed Justice Story's words in *Washington v. Texas* (1967), which extended to the states the Sixth Amendment right to compel the testimony of witnesses. This right, said the Court, includes "the right to present the defendant's version of the facts as well as the prosecution's to the jury so it may decide where the truth lies." The provision of state law that the Court found unconstitutional in *Washington* prohibited testimony for the defense by a person charged with or convicted of being a coparticipant in the same offense.

Coercion of Witnesses

In a case involving a racial incident in Arkansas in which several blacks were sentenced to death for the murder of several whites, the Supreme Court entertained a writ of HABEAS CORPUS on the grounds that a mob had tortured witnesses to coerce their testimony against the defendants. In his opinion for the Court in *Moore v. Dempsey* (1923), Justice OLIVER WENDELL HOLMES JR. declared that mob domination of a state trial violated the Fourteenth Amendment's due process clause. In *Spevak v. Klein* (1967) and *Gardner v. Broderick* (1968), the Court ruled that coercion of a witness to testify by threatening termination of a public job or revocation of a public license violated the Fifth Amendment protection against self-incrimination.

Immunity of Witnesses

On occasion prosecutors grant IMMUNITY to witnesses for testifying when their testimony might incriminate them. After *Counselman v. Hitchcock* (1892), in which the Supreme Court struck down a statute allowing immunity for witnesses in certain situations, Congress enacted a new law allowing "transactional" immunity that protects witnesses from being prosecuted for any part of the transaction or activity to which the witness testified—even if the government independently acquires other evidence that would convict the witness. In *Murphy v. Waterfront Commission* (1964), the Court ruled that the Fifth Amendment's self-incrimination clause protects witnesses granted immunity by states from later federal prosecution for the same matter. In some cases, in order to protect witnesses, the government must help them change identities and even their residency.

Women

The Seneca Falls Declaration of Sentiments and Resolutions drafted by Elizabeth Cady Stanton (1815–1902), a friend and colleague of the women's rights activist SUSAN B. ANTHONY, and issued by a convention of American women held in Seneca Falls, New York, in 1848 proclaims: "[A]ll laws which prevent woman from occupying such a station in society as her conscience shall dictate, or which place her in a position inferior to that of man, are contrary to the great precepts of nature, and therefore of no force or authority."

Glorious histories of the DECLARATION OF INDEPENDENCE (1776) and the Constitution drafted in 1787 often gloss over the fact that a large portion of the American population at the time—women and slaves—received little or no personal benefit from the resounding words of these documents. Whatever the intention of the FRAMERS OF THE CONSTITUTION toward women, the Constitution's language is basically gender neutral—using terms

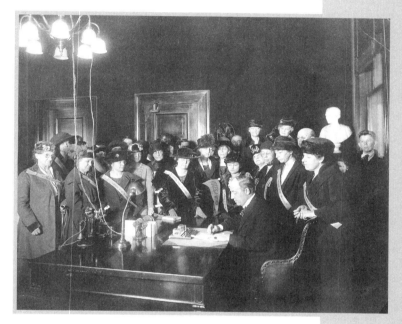

On January 6, 1920, a crowd of women surround Governor Edwin Morrow of Kentucky as he signs the "Anthony Amendment," which granted women the right to vote. Kentucky became the twenty-fourth state to ratify the long-sought Nineteenth Amendment.
Source: Library of Congress

such as *people*, *persons*, and *citizens*. Only in the Fourteenth Amendment (1868) is the term *male inhabitant* used with reference to a denial of voting rights. The framers and those charged with interpreting the Constitution just assumed that women were not to be given any political rights under it.

The legal status of women at the time the Constitution was drafted was a matter of state law, under which women had few if any rights of their own. State constitutions generally used the term *men* in reference to those persons to whom political rights were extended. Many legal disabilities of women were codified in COMMON LAW, including the concept of coverture (incorporation of a woman into the legal person of her husband on marriage), which was controlling as to the rights, or lack thereof, of married women. Unmarried women, however, could generally enter into contracts, own property, and sue and be sued in their own right.

Not for nearly a century and a half, until 1920, were equal political rights extended to women. Today the denial of equal citizenship rights for women seems as irrational as denying the vote to left-handed people or bald men. Yet the struggle of women to be treated equally under the

Constitution and the laws of the land continues in such areas as equal pay for equal work and equality of opportunity in employment.

Political Rights

The Constitution does not in so many words exclude women from equal citizenship, but from the time the document went into effect in 1789 until the ratification of the Nineteenth Amendment on August 18, 1920, women were not allowed to participate in the nation's government by voting or holding political office. According to the amendment, "The right of citizens of the United States to vote shall not be denied or abridged by the United States or by any State on account of sex."

No democracy before the inception of the United States had permitted women to vote. Although the Englishwoman Mary Wollstonecraft (1759–97) first advocated suffrage for women in *A Vindication of the Rights of Woman* (1792), New Zealand became the first country to extend the right to vote to women in 1893.

The movement to abolish SLAVERY before the Civil War (1861–65) had attracted many women, especially in the northern states. The transition to organizing a women's rights movement was sparked by the Seneca Falls Convention and the first national suffrage convention convened by Lucy Stone (1818–93) in 1850 in Worcester, Massachusetts. A second convention in Syracuse, New York, two years later was jointly organized by Stanton and Anthony.

After the war, women who had participated in both the abolition and suffrage causes were disappointed when they were not included in the definition of *citizens* protected by the Fourteenth (1868) and Fifteenth (1870) Amendments and not allowed to vote and run for political office.

By 1914 only eleven states had granted women the right to vote in state and local elections. The courts were no help either. In *Minor v. Happersett* (1875), the Supreme Court ruled unanimously that it was not unconstitutional under the Fourteenth Amendment's PRIVILEGES AND IMMUNITIES clause for a state to deny women the right to vote. As Chief Justice Morrison R. Waite (1816–88) wrote for the Court: "Certainly, if the Courts can consider any question settled, this is one…," he said. "The Constitution, when it conferred citizenship, did not necessarily confer the right of suffrage." Accordingly, Waite reasoned, there was no precedent for extending the right to vote to women, even though they could be considered CITIZENS of the United States.

With the passage of the Nineteenth Amendment, the question of women's political rights was pretty much settled, but there were other areas of the law in which women were still denied equality with men.

Economic Rights

Equal economic rights became the next goal for many women, and the major vehicle for attempting to guarantee such rights was the Equal Rights Amendment (1972), which read: "Equality of rights under the law shall not be denied or abridged by the United States or by any state on account of sex." Congress approved the proposed amendment in 1972—forty-nine years after it was first introduced. Initially it set a deadline of seven years for the ERA's ratification but later extended that by three years to 1982. The proposed amendment still did not receive the required ratification by three-fourths of the states; only thirty-five of the thirty-eight states needed gave their assent in the allotted time (see AMENDMENTS). ERA proponents believed that the amendment's failure was due largely to the fact that many state legislatures were dominated by representatives from conservative rural areas who were averse to giving women rights equal to those of men.

One of the ERA's main objectives was to guarantee equal pay for equal work by women (comparable worth). In *Frontiero v. Richardson* (1973), the Supreme Court reviewed a federal law that awarded a salary supplement to married men, but not to married women, in the military. The basis of the complaint was that although there may be some justification for a distinction between married men and married women with respect to the need for a salary supplement, such discrimination on the basis of sex—like RACIAL DISCRIMINATION—is suspect and sustainable only if the government establishes a compelling justification (see SEX DISCRIMINATION). The Court partly agreed and invalidated the law, but there was no majority for making sex a suspect classification entitled to the same high level of judicial scrutiny as race (see STRICT SCRUTINY).

Early in the twentieth century, an Oregon law made it illegal for women to be employed for more than ten hours a day in factory-like work settings. The Supreme Court in *Muller v. Oregon* (1908) upheld this law, even though it had rejected a similar attempt by New York to set maximum hours for men, because, it said, "as healthy mothers are essential to vigorous offspring, the physical well-being of women becomes an object of public interest and care in order to preserve the strength and vigor of the race."

As for the right to choose an occupation, the Supreme Court on several occasions refused to allow women to be admitted to the bar to practice law. In *Bradwell v. Illinois* (1873), the male justices interpreted the language of an Illinois statute granting eligibility for admission to practice law to any adult "person" of good character and proper training to exclude women. And in *In re Lockwood* (1894), the Court, while noting that Belva Lockwood (1830–1917) was a member of the bar of the U.S. Supreme Court—the first woman permitted to argue a case before that august body—and a member of the bar of the Supreme Court of the District of Columbia, held that she was not entitled to invoke the privileges and immunities clauses of Article IV, section 2, and the Fourteenth Amendment (1868) to challenge the rejection of her application for admission to the Virginia bar because she was a woman. As late as 1948 the Court, in *Goesaert v. Cleary*, denied a woman's right to become a bartender because of the unsavory nature of bartending.

African American women have faced especially severe obstacles in the United States, but that appears to be changing. Here, U.S. Secretary of State Condoleezza Rice testifies during the Senate Foreign Relations hearing on President Bush's strategy for Iraq.
Source: CQ Photo/Scott J. Ferrell

In general, the Supreme Court continued to expand women's rights in the second half of the twentieth century in decisions in cases such as *Meritor Savings Bank v. Vinson* (1986), upholding a sexual harassment complaint under Title VII of the Civil Rights Act of 1964, and beyond. As recently as 2003, in *Nevada Department of Human Resources v. Hibbs*, the Court under Chief Justice William H. Rehnquist (1924–2005) upheld a gender discrimination claim. But under Chief Justice John G.

Roberts, Jr. (b. 1955) the Court rejected a claim based on gender pay discrimination in *Ledbetter v. Goodyear Tire & Rubber Co, Inc.* (2007).

Personal Rights

The right to have an abortion was extended to women in ROE V. WADE (1973) (see ABORTION), based on the right of PRIVACY that the Supreme Court had gleaned from several provisions of the BILL OF RIGHTS (1791), including, according to Justice William O. Douglas (1898–1980) in GRISWOLD V. CONNECTICUT (1965), the First, Third, Fourth, Fifth, and Ninth Amendments. The *Roe* decision acknowledged a woman's right to control the reproductive processes of her own body, thus in part increasing her options with respect to education, occupation, and other aspects of the "pursuit of Happiness" sanctioned by the Declaration of Independence. The Court has also struck down a number of laws that irrationally discriminated against women, such as state laws that prefer men over women as administrators of the estates of deceased persons.

Although the Supreme Court has not yet directly overruled *Roe*, it has generally eroded the right to an abortion. Recently, in *Gonzales v. Carhart* (2007), the Court sustained the constitutionality of the Partial Birth Abortion Act of 2003, although it left the door open for challenges to the constitutionality of its application in individual cases.

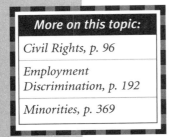

More on this topic:

Civil Rights, p. 96

Employment Discrimination, p. 192

Minorities, p. 369

Major milestones in women's progress toward equality under the law occurred when SANDRA DAY O'CONNOR, who served until retiring in 2006, and Ruth Bader Ginsburg (b. 1933) were appointed to the Supreme Court in 1981 and 1993, respectively.

In the twenty-first century women undoubtedly will continue to press for and attain greater equality with men in all aspects of society. It is not unreasonable to expect that more women will be appointed to the Supreme Court and that one day the nation will have a woman president. Some day women may even be in the majority in many of the political institutions created by the "founding fathers" more than two centuries ago.

Young, Ex Parte

The Supreme Court case *Ex parte Young* (1908) established the proposition that a citizen could go into federal court to protect a constitutional right from infringement by a state, in spite of the prohibition in the Eleventh Amendment (1798) against "any suit in law or equity...against one of the United States by Citizens of another State, or by Citizens or Subjects of any Foreign State." As Justice Rufus W. Peckham (1838–1909) said in the opinion, "The act to be enforced [by the state] is alleged to be unconstitutional, and, if it be so, the use of the name of the state to enforce an unconstitutional act to the injury of the complainants is a proceeding without the authority of, and one which does not affect, the state in its sovereign or governmental capacity." The Court thus concluded in *Young* that states' sovereign IMMUNITY from suits granted by the Eleventh Amendment (1798) was not applicable under such circumstances.

The Eleventh Amendment came about in response to the Supreme Court's decision in *Chisholm v. Georgia* (1793), which held that the Constitution authorized suits against states in federal courts. The amendment restored state immunity except, according to the Court, in cases of JUDICIAL REVIEW of state actions or where the state consents to be sued. In *Osborn v. Bank of the United States* (1824), the Court held that even though a state has sovereign immunity, state officials can be sued in their own right.

Since the beginning of the Republic, one of constitutional law's inexorable trends has been the extension, in fits and starts, of the federal government's power at the expense of the power and SOVEREIGNTY of the STATES (see FEDERALISM; STATES' RIGHTS). Important early cases that reflect this trend include *MCCULLOCH V. MARYLAND* (1819) and *GIBBONS V. OGDEN* (1824). Then in 1908 *Ex parte Young* illustrated how constitutional law can be advanced with the adept use of legal logic.

More on this topic:

Federalism, p. 218

Reapportionment, p. 453

States' Rights, p. 520

In 1907 a Minnesota law sought to reduce the rates charged by railroads and prescribed stiff penalties for any violation. Fearing a loss of revenue from the lower rates, the shareholders of the affected railroads sued in federal court to enjoin both their companies from obeying the law and state officials from enforcing it. The court issued a temporary injunction, but Minnesota's attorney general, Edward T. Young, attempted to enforce the law in state court and was then jailed for contempt of the federal court injunction. To get out of jail, Young sought release by filing a HABEAS CORPUS petition with the Supreme Court.

The Supreme Court, in an 8–1 opinion, with only Justice John Marshall Harlan (1833–1911) dissenting, declared that although Minnesota was protected from a lawsuit by the terms of the Eleventh Amendment, state officials are not entitled to immunity when they commit unconstitutional acts. Young's attempt to enforce an allegedly unconstitutional statute—the law setting the railroad rates—removed any protection that he or the state might have had under the Eleventh Amendment. The importance of enforcing the Constitution prevails over state immunity from a lawsuit, said the justices. Ironically, in *Simpson v. Shepard* (1913), the constitutionality of the Minnesota rates was upheld—the Court finding that Young had not acted unconstitutionally, as it had earlier assumed for the purpose of ruling against him.

In his dissent in *Young*, Justice Harlan argued simply that in law and in fact the suit was against a state and was thus barred by the Eleventh Amendment. The focus on Young as an individual, according to Harlan, was therefore only a legal "fiction."

Ex parte Young nonetheless remains legal precedent. In *Scheuer v. Rhodes* (1974), the Eleventh Amendment was held not to prohibit a suit against Ohio officials for their actions in the deaths of students protesting the Vietnam War at Kent State University. And it is doubtful that without the precedent of *Young*, BAKER V. CARR (1962) and the other REAPPORTIONMENT cases by which the Supreme Court established the principle of "one person, one vote" through state electoral redistricting could have happened. Without *Young*, state legislatures' unfair apportionment could not have been brought before the federal courts, and the EQUAL PROTECTION clause of the Fourteenth Amendment (1868) would have been trumped by the Eleventh Amendment's requirement of state immunity.

Yet the Eleventh Amendment has been found to bar some federal court actions. In *Pennhurst State School and Hospital v. Halderman* (1984), for example, the Supreme Court declared that the amendment prohibited a federal court order directing state officials to conform to state law, because here the state was the party whose interests were involved and no federal rights had to be protected.

To a great extent the problems of state immunity under the Eleventh Amendment have been avoided by waivers of such immunities in CONTRACTS between state agencies and private companies doing business with state governments. But an exception to the *Young* ruling developed in *Edelman v. Jordan* (1974) bars suits against states that would retroactively deplete the state's treasury but not suits that involve prospective remedies, even if such remedies require state expenditures.

Youngstown Sheet and Tube Co. v. Sawyer

Many Supreme Court decisions have dealt with the extent of CONGRESS's powers, but in *Youngstown Sheet and Tube Co. v. Sawyer* (1952) the Court addressed the extent of the PRESIDENT's powers. As Justice Robert H. Jackson (1892–1954) explained in his concurring opinion, the Constitution allows a flexible "zone of twilight" in which the president and Congress share authority.

The powers that would be given to the president under the Constitution were much debated by the delegates to the CONSTITUTIONAL CONVENTION OF 1787. The colonists' bitter experience with the

British monarchy led them to fear allowing the president too much power. However, the lack of a strong chief executive under the ARTICLES OF CONFEDERATION (1781) was one of the basic problems that the convention had been called to solve. "A feeble executive," ALEXANDER HAMILTON wrote in essay 70 of *The Federalist* (1787–88) (see FEDERALIST PAPERS), "implies a feeble execution of the government. A feeble execution is but another phrase for a bad execution; and a government ill executed, whatever it may be in theory, must be, in practice, a bad government." The convention delegates' assumption that GEORGE WASHINGTON, a much-admired and trusted patriot, would be the first president undoubtedly allayed some fears about granting sufficient power to that office.

On December 16, 1950, at the beginning of the Korean War—technically, a United Nations military action in the 1950–53 war between North and South Korea—President Harry S. Truman (1884–72) declared a state of national emergency. On April 8, 1952, fearing that an announced strike of steel workers could disrupt ammunition supplies and thus jeopardize the war effort, Truman ordered Secretary of Commerce William Sawyer to seize and take over operation of the nation's steel mills the day before the proposed strike. He immediately notified Congress of the action, but it did not take any action in response.

The steel companies obtained an injunction from a district court to prevent enforcement of the takeover order. The injunction was stayed (suspended) by a federal court of appeals, after which the Supreme Court, four of whose justices had been appointed by Truman, granted an expedited hearing on the matter. Because the Constitution does not give the president express authority to seize private PROPERTY, three possible grounds existed for upholding the president's executive order: the statutory power of Congress, the power of the commander in chief, or the inherent power of the president. By a 6–3 vote, the Court found that the president had exceeded his constitutional authority in ordering the takeover. Moreover, executive power expressly granted in the Constitution—such as the president's responsibility as commander in chief of the military and his preeminent role in FOREIGN AFFAIRS—were not sufficient to allow him on his own authority, without congressional concurrence, to seize private property, even in times of a national emergency (see EMERGENCY POWERS). In addition, the Court ruled that taking over the steel mills could not be justified on the basis of any statutory authority, which would have indicated that Congress supported the action through passage of a law.

The president's constitutional role to "see that the laws are faithfully executed," Justice Hugo L. Black (1886–1971) explained, "refutes the idea that he is to be a lawmaker." In a concurring opinion, Justice Jackson added that the president's power is greatest when he is acting under Congress's express or implied authorization and weakest when acting in contradiction to Congress's will. In between, he noted, however, is a "zone of twilight" in which the president and Congress share authority and that may allow the president to act as long as Congress does not object. Five years earlier, however, in passing the Taft-Hartley Act (1947), Congress had re-

A steel worker wears flame- and heat-resistant clothing.
Source: The Granger Collection, New York

More on this topic:

Inherent Powers, p. 303

Judicial Review, p. 318

Separation of Powers, p. 494

jected an amendment that would have allowed such seizures by the federal government in an emergency.

Chief Justice Fred M. Vinson (1890–1953) argued in dissent that the president had authority in the current circumstances to take "at least interim action necessary to execute legislative programs essential to survival of the Nation." The Youngstown case has been used as precedent to deny presidential authority in a number of areas, including claims of EXECUTIVE PRIVILEGE and WIRETAPPING and NATIONAL SECURITY activities. However, in *Dames & Moore v. Regan* (1981), the Court was able to distinguish the president's authority to seize foreign assets in the United States in the context of an international claims settlement procedure similar to others previously authorized by Congress and thus find his actions to be constitutional in this case, even without express congressional involvement.

Justice Jackson, in his concurring opinion in *Youngstown*, listed three types of presidential actions: those authorized by Congress, those not expressly authorized or prohibited by Congress, and those expressly prohibited by Congress. This division can be used to analyze more recent challenges to presidential constitutional powers such as in the case of *Hamdan v. Rumsfeld* (2006). While only mentioned in a footnote in the opinion written by Justice John Paul Stevens (b. 1920) in *Hamdan*, the rationale in *Youngstown* is clearly evident in the conclusion that "[w]hether or not the President has independent power, absent congressional authorization, to convene military commissions, he may not disregard limitations the Congress has, in proper exercise of its own war powers, placed on his powers."

Zenger's Case

John Peter Zenger (1697–1746) was thirteen years old in 1710, when he, his mother, and two siblings arrived in New York as refugees from Germany. His father had died on the ill-fated voyage along with many others. Apprenticed to a printer in 1711, he established his own printing business in 1726 and in 1733 began publishing the *New York Weekly Journal*, a newspaper used by the enemies of the colonial governor William Cosby to attack his administration.

After a number of scathing, unsigned articles criticizing the governor appeared in the paper, Cosby had Zenger arrested for seditious libel—criticizing the government—and jailed for nine months, all in an attempt to force him to name the authors. Zenger, in what has since become a journalistic tradition, refused to divulge the names.

On August 4, 1735, Zenger was finally brought to trial. One of the authors behind the attacks offered to represent him, but the judge, a crony of the governor, refused to allow it and summarily disbarred him. A highly reputed lawyer from Philadelphia, Andrew Hamilton (1676?–1741), agreed to represent Zenger.

The law, however, was weighted heavily against the publisher. He could be found guilty of libel if the jury determined that he had uttered or written the words in question and if the judge concluded that they were in fact seditious libel, adversely reflecting on the administration. In a daring maneuver, Hamilton admitted that his client had printed the words, as charged. However, he appealed to the jury to find that the truth of the statements printed constituted a valid defense against a charge of libel. The jury, he said, was entirely competent to decide the truth or falsehood of the statements printed by Zenger. If the people could not freely point out the oppression and abuses of the government, he continued, their LIBERTY and PROPERTY would always be in jeopardy. The jury found Hamilton's novel argument to their liking and returned a general verdict of not guilty.

For some time the case remained an anomaly of little legal significance beyond Zenger and his authors. But it has come to be regarded as an early blow against tyranny and for freedom of THE PRESS. The importance of a free press was recognized when this right became one of the four freedoms enshrined in the Constitution's First Amendment (1791), contained in the BILL OF RIGHTS along with freedom of RELIGION, SPEECH, and assembly (see ASSEMBLY AND ASSOCIATION).

Even after RATIFICATION of the First Amendment, Congress in 1798 criminalized criticism of the government in the Alien and Sedition Acts, which were based on the Federalist Party's narrow interpretation of the First Amendment's guarantee of free speech and freedom of the press. The acts were strongly denounced by THOMAS JEFFERSON and other members of the Democratic-Republican Party, and resentment over them contributed to Jefferson's election as president in 1800. After taking office he pardoned those convicted under the acts, which were allowed to expire shortly thereafter.

> **More on this topic:**
>
> *Bill of Rights, p. 62*
>
> *Censorship, p. 82*
>
> *The Press, p. 425*
>
> *Speech, p. 512*

Zoning

Zoning is the division or designation of areas of land by a government authority for purposes of prescribing the use to which such zoned areas may be put—agricultural, residential, commercial, historic preservation, and so forth—and setting requirements for architectural and structural design in such areas. Local governments make zoning determinations under the POLICE POWER authority to provide for public HEALTH, safety, and WELFARE. The process, which was first introduced just after the turn of the century and is now used in nearly all municipal jurisdictions, grew out of the need to control the development of cities, particularly the proximity of factories to residential areas and ensuing health and safety problems.

The government has an inherent right of eminent domain—the authority to take any PROPERTY for public use. But the question that often arises in zoning cases relates to the requirement under the Fifth Amendment (1791), made applicable to the states through the Fourteenth Amendment (1868), for JUST COMPENSATION to be paid to private property owners for such a taking. As the Fifth Amendment states in part, "…nor shall private property be taken for public use, without just compensation." In matters involving public safety or health, however, the state or federal government may use its police power to take, regulate, or destroy some private property to protect the community as a whole.

Euclidean Zoning

The first major case testing the constitutionality of zoning laws was *Euclid v. Ambler Realty* (1926), in which the Supreme Court upheld a zoning law in Euclid, Ohio, restricting certain property to residential use; a real estate company claimed that the resulting reduction in the value of its land, which was being held for industrial use, constituted a taking without DUE PROCESS as required under the Fourteenth Amendment. The Court, holding that concern for the common good can override an individual's property rights, based its decision on the state's police power to abate a nuisance that would be created by industrial use of the land.

Not all zoning proposals pass constitutional muster, of course. In *Nectow v. City of Cambridge* (1928), just two years after *Euclid*, the Supreme Court ruled against a Cambridge, Massachusetts, zoning determination because it would render a small industrial parcel nearly worthless and no public safety, health, or welfare interest was proven.

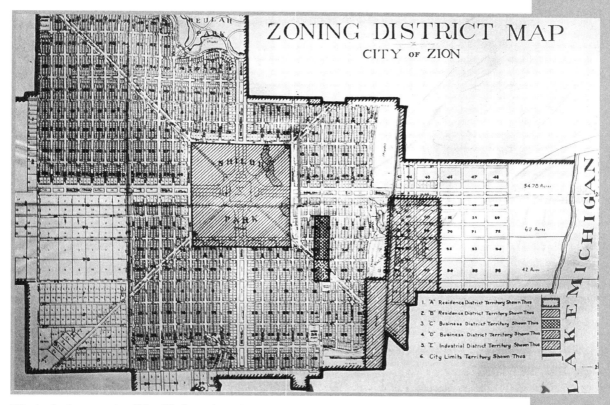

This plan for the community of Zion, Illinois, neatly partitions business away from residential districts. With ever-increasing population density, the battle between zoning laws and private property rights intensified in the early twentieth century.
Source: Courtesy of the Frances Loeb Library, Harvard Graduate School of Design

In *Belle Terre v. Boraas* (1974), the Supreme Court later upheld an ordinance limiting occupancy in single-family dwellings to traditional families or groups of no more than two unrelated persons. According to the opinion of the Court written by Justice William O. Douglas (1898–1980), "A quiet place where yards are wide, people few, and motor vehicles restricted are legitimate guidelines in a land-use project addressed to family needs. The police power is not confined to elimination of filth, stench, and unhealthy places."

In *Young v. American Mini Theaters, Inc.* (1976), the Supreme Court found that a city zoning law aimed at breaking up a concentration of adult theaters could discriminate to some degree as to content—the sexually explicit nature of the activities in this case—and still not run afoul of the First Amendment's guarantee of free SPEECH. Later cases, like *City of Renton v. Playtime Theatres, Inc.* (1986), continued the policy set in *Young*. And, in *City of Los Angeles v. Alameda Books, Inc.* (2002), the Court determined that an ordinance designed to counteract the secondary effect of an increase in crime in areas around aggregations of adult bookstores and other sexually oriented businesses by dispersing them rather than allowing them to concentrate in one part of town was not unconstitutional. Citing the decision in *Renton*, the Court noted that a municipality may rely on any accurate data or logic that is "reasonably believed to be relevant" for proving a connection between the speech being regulated and a substantial government interest—but that *Renton* did not require the city to show that its justification was "necessarily" correct.

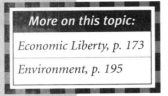

More on this topic:

Economic Liberty, p. 173

Environment, p. 195

Taking of Property?

In a truly landmark zoning case, the Supreme Court in *Penn Central Transportation Co. v. City of New York* (1978) upheld New York City's landmarks preservation law, under which the city denied a request by the owners of Grand Central Terminal to build an office tower on the property because the construction would destroy the historical and architectural integrity of the building. Justice William J. Brennan Jr. (1906–97) concluded for the Court: "[T]he application of New York City's Landmarks Law has not effected a 'taking' of appellants' property. The restrictions imposed are substantially related to the promotion of the general welfare and not only permit reasonable beneficial use of the landmark site but also afford appellants opportunities further to enhance not only the Terminal site proper but also other properties." In this case the Court rejected any set formulas or tests for determining whether zoning-type regulations should be upheld. Rather, the majority found that each case must be determined on the facts and that the property owner's interests must be balanced against the community's interests (see BALANCING TESTS). According to the Court, "Legislation designed to promote the general welfare commonly burdens some more than others."

Subsequent decisions, however, began to find that the Fifth Amendment (1791) requires compensation for substantial losses in property value because of government regulation, even for temporary takings. In *Lucas v. South Carolina Coastal Council* (1992), the Supreme Court ruled that compensation was required whenever "all economically beneficial or productive use" of property is taken by the government, unless such taking could be justified by property and nuisance principles under COMMON LAW. In *First Lutheran Church of Glendale v. Los Angeles County* (1987), the justices also sided with a property owner that was prohibited from rebuilding in a flood plain after a flood destroyed its church buildings, calling the contested zoning ordinance a taking.

But in 2002 the Supreme Court revisited its rulings in the *Penn Central* and *Lucas* cases, announcing in *Tahoe-Sierra Preservation Council, Inc. v. Tahoe Regional Planning Agency* that there were no hard and fast rules regarding when a regulatory taking has occurred. Two moratoriums on development totaling thirty-two months, said the Court, were insufficient to automatically require a finding that compensation was due for a taking of property. Again, the balancing test weighs the burden that private property owners may justifiably bear against the burden that the community as a whole should bear.

The American pioneer Daniel Boone (1734–1820) is said to have moved whenever he could see the smoke rising from a new neighbor's chimney. Today most people live in communities of relatively higher density that require a number of rules and regulations to maintain a balanced, safe, healthy, and otherwise pleasant living and working environment. Zoning has become—and will continue to be into the foreseeable future—a major mechanism for reaching these goals.

◉ CLOSER LOOK

When justices weigh in on a case, they generally cite the Constitution and legal precedents to explain their decisions. But they sometimes point to practical considerations as well.

This happened in 2002, when a majority of justices ruled that a local government agency did not have to compensate landowners for placing two temporary moratoriums on development by Lake Tahoe. That case, *Tahoe-Sierra Preservation Council, Inc. v. Tahoe Regional Planning Agency*, largely turned on such issues as whether the moratoriums deprived landowners of all economic use of the property.

But Justice John Paul Stevens (b. 1920), who wrote the majority opinion, also said that it would be impractical to expect local governments to compensate property owners every time a moratorium was imposed. Such a requirement might cause governments to forgo moratoriums and short-circuit the planning process, Stevens believed.

"A rule that required compensation for every delay in the use of property would render routine government processes prohibitively expensive or encourage hasty decision-making," Stevens wrote.

Reference Material

First Charter of Virginia

April 10, 1606

JAMES, by the Grace of God, King of England, Scotland, France and Ireland, Defender of the Faith, &c. WHEREAS our loving and well-disposed Subjects, Sir Thomas Gales, and Sir George Somers, Knights, Richard Hackluit, Clerk, Prebendary of Westminster, and Edward-Maria Wingfield, Thomas Hanharm and Ralegh Gilbert, Esqrs. William Parker, and George Popham, Gentlemen, and divers others of our loving Subjects, have been humble Suitors unto us, that We would vouchsafe unto them our Licence, to make Habitation, Plantation, and to deduce a colony of sundry of our People into that part of America commonly called VIRGINIA, and other parts and Territories in America, either appertaining unto us, or which are not now actually possessed by any Christian Prince or People, situate, lying, and being all along the Sea Coasts, between four and thirty Degrees of Northerly Latitude from the Equinoctial Line, and five and forty Degrees of the same Latitude, and in the main Land between the same four and thirty and five and forty Degrees, and the Islands "hereunto adjacent, or within one hundred Miles of the Coast thereof;

And to that End, and for the more speedy Accomplishment of their said intended Plantation and Habitation there, are desirous to divide themselves into two several Colonies and Companies; the one consisting of certain Knights, Gentlemen, Merchants, and other Adventurers, of our City of London and elsewhere, which are, and from time to time shall be, joined unto them, which do desire to begin their Plantation and Habitation in some fit and convenient Place, between four and thirty and one and forty Degrees of the said Latitude, alongst the Coasts of Virginia, and the Coasts of America aforesaid: And the other consisting of sundry Knights, Gentlemen, Merchants, and other Adventurers, of our Cities of Bristol and Exeter, and of our Town of Plimouth, and of other Places, which do join themselves unto that Colony, which do desire to begin their Plantation and Habitation in some fit and convenient Place, between eight and thirty Degrees and five and forty Degrees of the said Latitude, all alongst the said Coasts of Virginia and America, as that Coast lyeth:

We, greatly commending, and graciously accepting of, their Desires for the Furtherance of so noble a Work, which may, by the Providence of Almighty God, hereafter tend to the Glory of his Divine Majesty, in propagating of Christian Religion to such People, as yet live in Darkness and miserable Ignorance of the true Knowledge and Worship of God, and may in time bring the Infidels and Savages, living in those parts, to human Civility, and to a settled and quiet Government: Do, by these our Letters Patents, graciously accept of, and agree to, their humble and well-intended Desires;

And do therefore, for Us, our Heirs, and Successors, GRANT and agree, that the said Sir Thomas Gates, Sir George Somers, Richard Hackluit, and Edward-Maria Wingfield, Adventurers of and for our City of London, and all such others, as are, or shall be, joined unto them of that Colony, shall be called the first Colony; And they shall and may begin their said first Plantation and Habitation, at any Place upon the said-Coast of Virginia or America, where they shall think fit and convenient, between the said four and thirty and one and forty Degrees of the said Latitude; And that they shall have all the Lands, Woods, Soil, Grounds, Havens, Ports, Rivers, Mines, Minerals, Marshes, Waters, Fishings, Commodities, and Hereditaments, whatsoever, from the said first Seat of their Plantation and Habitation by the Space of fifty Miles of English Statute Measure, all along the said Coast of Virginia and America, towards the West and Southwest, as the Coast lyeth, with all the Islands within one hundred Miles directly over against the same Sea Coast; And also all the Lands, Soil, Grounds, Havens, Ports, Rivers, Mines, Minerals, Woods, Waters, Marshes, Fishings, Commodities, and Hereditaments, whatsoever, from the said Place of their first Plantation and Habitation for the space of fifty like English Miles, all alongst the said Coasts of Virginia and America, towards the East and Northeast, or towards the North, as the Coast lyeth, together with all the Islands within one hundred Miles, directly over against the said Sea Coast, And also all the Lands, Woods, Soil, Grounds, Havens, Ports, Rivers, Mines, Minerals, Marshes, Waters, Fishings, Commodities, and Hereditaments, whatsoever, from the same fifty Miles every way on the Sea Coast, directly into the main Land by the Space of one hundred like English Miles; And shall and may inhabit and remain there; and shall and may also build and fortify within any the same, for their better Safeguard and Defense, according to their best Discretion, and the Discretion of the Council of that Colony; And that no other of our Subjects shall be permitted, or suffered, to plant or inhabit behind, or on the Backside of them, towards the main Land, without the Express License or Consent of the Council of that Colony, thereunto in Writing; first had and obtained.

And we do likewise, for Us, Our Heirs, and Successors, by these Presents, GRANT and agree, that the said Thomas Hanham, and Ralegh Gilbert, William Parker, and George Popham, and all others of the Town of Plimouth in the County of Devon, or elsewhere which are, or shall be, joined unto them of that Colony, shall be called the second Colony; And that they shall and may begin their said Plantation and Seat of their first Abode and Habitation, at any Place upon the said Coast of Virginia and America, where they shall think fit and convenient, between eight and thirty Degrees of the said Latitude, and five and forty Degrees of the same Latitude; And that they shall have all the Lands, Soils, Grounds, Havens, Ports, Rivers, Mines, Minerals, Woods, Marshes, Waters, Fishings, Commodities, and Hereditaments, whatsoever, from the first Seat of their Plantation and Habitation by the Space of fifty like English Miles, as is aforesaid, all alongst the said Coasts of Virginia and al raerica towards the West and Southwest, or towards the South, as the Coast lyeth, and all the Islands within one hundred Miles, directly over against the said Sea Coast; And also all the Lands, Soils, Grounds, Havens, Ports, Rivers, Mines, Minerals, Woods, Marshes, Waters, Fishings, Commodities, and Hereditaments, whatsoever, from the said Place of their first Plantation and Habitation for the Space of fifty like Miles, all alongst the said Coast of Virginia and America, towards the East and Northeast, or towards the North, as the Coast lyeth, and all the Islands also within one hundred Miles directly over against the same Sea Coast; And also all the Lands, Soils, Grounds, Havens, Ports, Rivers, Woods, Mines, Minerals, Marshes, Waters, Fishings, Commodities, and Hereditaments, whatsoever, from the same fifty Miles every way on the Sea Coast, directly into the main Land, by the Space of one hundred like English Miles; And shall and may inhabit and remain there; and shall and may also build and fortify within any the same for their better Safeguard, according to their best Discretion, and the Discretion of the Council of that Colony; And that none of our Subjects shall be permitted, or suffered, to plant or inhabit behind, or on the back of them, towards the main Land, without express Licence of the Council of that Colony, in Writing thereunto first had and obtained.

Provided always, and our Will and Pleasure herein is, that the Plantation and Habitation of such of the said Colonies, as shall last plant themselves, as aforesaid, shall not be made within one hundred like English Miles of the other of them, that first began to make their Plantation, as aforesaid.

And we do also ordain, establish, and agree, for Us, our Heirs, and Successors, that each of the said Colonies shall have a Council, which shall govern and order all Matters-and Causes, which shall arise, grow, or happen, to or within the same several Colonies, according to such Laws, Ordinances, and Instructions, as shall be, in that behalf, given and signed with Our Hand or Sign Manual, and pass under the Privy Seal of our Realm of England; Each of which Councils shall consist of thirteen Persons, to be ordained, made, and removed, from time to time, according as shall be directed and comprised in the same instructions; And shall have a several Seal, for all Matters that shall pass or concern the same several Councils; Each of which Seals, shall have the King's

Arms engraver on the one Side thereof, and his Portraiture on the other; And that the Seal for the Council of the said first Colony shall have engraver round about, on the one Side, these Words; Sigillum Regis Magne Britanniae, Franciae, & Hiberniae; on the other Side this Inscription round about; Pro Concilio primae Coloniae Virginiae. And the Seal for the Council of the said second Colony shall also have engraven, round about the one Side thereof, the aforesaid Words; Sigillum Regis Magne Britanniae, Franciae, & Hiberniae; and on the other Side; Pro Concilio primae Coloniae Virginiae:

And that also there shall be a Council, established here in England, which shall, in like manner, consist of thirteen Persons, to be for that Purpose, appointed by Us, our Heirs and Successors, which shall be called our Council of Virginia; And shall, from time to time, have the superior Managing and Direction, only of and for all Matters that shall or may concern the Government, as well of the said several Colonies, as of and for any other Part or Place, within the aforesaid Precincts of four and thirty and five and forty Degrees abovementioned; Which Council shall, in like manner, have a Seal, for matters concerning the Council or Colonies, with the like Arms and Portraiture, as aforesaid, with this inscription, engraver round about on the one Side; Sigillum Regis Magne Britanniae, Franciae, & Hiberniae; and round about on the other Side, Pro Concilio fuo Virginiae.

And moreover, we do GRANT and agree, for Us, our Heirs and Successors; that that the said several Councils of and for the said several Colonies, shall and lawfully may, by Virtue hereof, from time to time, without any Interruption of Us, our Heirs or Successors, give and take Order, to dig, mine, and search for all Manner of Mines of Gold, Silver, and Copper, as well within any Part of their said several Colonies, as of the said main Lands on the Backside of the same Colonies; And to HAVE and enjoy the Gold, Silver, and Copper, to be gotten thereof, to the Use and Behoof of the same Colonies, and the Plantations thereof; YIELDING therefore to Us, our Heirs and Successors, the fifth Part only of all the same Gold and Silver, and the fifteenth Part of all the same Copper, so to be gotten or had, as is aforesaid, without any other Manner of Profit or Account, to be given or yielded to Us, our Heirs, or Successors, for or in Respect of the same:

And that they shall, or lawfully may, establish and cause to be made a Coin, to pass current there between the people of those several Colonies, for the more Ease of Traffick and Bargaining between and amongst them and the Natives there, of such Metal, and in such Manner and Form, as the said several Councils there shall limit and appoint.

And we do likewise, for Us, our Heirs, and Successors, by these Presents, give full Power and Authority to the said Sir Thomas Gates, Sir George Somers, Richard Hackluit, Edward-Maria Wingfeld, Thomas Hanham, Ralegh Gilbert, William Parker, and George Popham, and to every of them, and to the said several Companies, Plantations, and Colonies, that they, and every of them, shall and may, at all and every time and times hereafter, have, take, and lead in the said Voyage, and for and towards the said several Plantations, and Colonies, and to travel thitherward, and to abide and inhabit there, in every the said Colonies and Plantations, such and so many of our Subjects, as shall willingly accompany them or any of them, in the said Voyages and Plantations; With sufficient Shipping, and Furniture of Armour, Weapons, Ordinance, Powder, Victual, and all other things, necessary for the said Plantations, and for their Use and Defence there: PROVIDED always, that none of the said Persons be such, as shall hereafter be specially restrained by Us, our Heirs, or Successors.

Moreover, we do, by these Presents, for Us, our Heirs, and Successors, GIVE AND GRANT Licence unto the said Sir Thomas Gates, Sir George Somers, Richard Hackluit, Edward-Maria Wingfield, Thornas Hanham, Ralegh Gilbert, William Parker, and George Popham, and to every of the said Colonies, that they, and every of them, shall and may, from time to time, and at all times forever hereafter, for their several Defences, encounter, expulse, repel, and resist, as well by Sea as by Land, by all Ways and Means whatsoever, all and every such Person or Persons, as without the especial

Licence of the said several Colonies and Plantations, shall attempt to inhabit within the said several Precincts and Limits of the said several Colonies and Plantations, or any of them, or that shall enterprise or attempt, at any time hereafter, the Hurt, Detriment, or Annoyance, of the said several Colonies or Plantations:

Giving and granting, by these Presents, unto the said Sir Thomas Gates, Sir George Somers, Richard Hackluit, Edward-Maria Wingfield, Thomas Hanham, Ralegh Gilbert, William Parker, and George Popham, and their Associates of the said second Colony, and to every of them, from time to time, and at all times for ever hereafter, Power and Authority to take and surprise, by all Ways and Means whatsoever, all and every Person and Persons, with their Ships, Vessels, Goods, and other Furniture, which shall be found trafficking, into any Harbour or Harbours, Creek or Creeks, or Place, within the Limits or Precincts of the said several Colonies and Plantations, not being of the same Colony, until such time, as they, being of any Realms, or Dominions under our Obedience, shall pay, or agree to pay, to the Hands of the Treasurer of that Colony, within whose Limits and Precincts they shall so traffick, two and a half upon every Hundred, of any thing so by them trafficked, bought, or sold; And being Strangers, and not Subjects under our Obeysance, until they shall pay five upon every Hundred, of such Wares and Merchandises, as they shall traffick, buy, or sell, within the Precincts of the said several Colonies, wherein they shall so traffick, buy, or sell, as aforesaid; WHICH Sums of Money, or Benefit, as aforesaid, for and during the Space of one and twenty Years, next ensuing the Date hereof, shall be wholly emploied to the Use, Benefit, and Behoof of the said several Plantations, where such Traffick shall be made; And after the said one and twenty Years ended, the same shall be taken to the Use of Us, our Heires, and Successors, by such Officers and Ministers as by Us, our Heirs, and Successors, shall be thereunto assigned or appointed.

And we do further, by these Presents, for Us, our Heirs and Successors, GIVE AND GRANT unto the said Sir Thomas Gates, Sir George Sommers, Richard Hackluit, and Edward-Maria Wingfield, and to their Associates of the said first Colony and Plantation, and to the said Thomas Hanham, Ralegh Gilbert, William Parker, and George Popham, and their Associates of the said second Colony and Plantation, that they, and every of them, by their Deputies, Ministers, and Factors, may transport the Goods, Chattels, Armour, Munition, and Furniture, needful to be used by them, for their said Apparel, Food, Defence, or otherwise in Respect of the said Plantations, out of our Realms of England and Ireland, and all other our Dominions, from time to time, for and during the Time of seven Years, next ensuing the Date hereof, for the better Relief of the said several Colonies and Plantations, without any Customs, Subsidy, or other Duty, unto Us, our Heirs, or Successors, to be yielded or payed for the same.

Also we do, for Us, our Heirs, and Successors, DECLARE, by these Presents, that all and every the Persons being our Subjects, which shall dwell and inhabit within every or any of the said several Colonies and Plantations, and every of their children, which shall happen to be born within any of the Limits and Precincts of the said several Colonies and Plantations, shall HAVE and enjoy all Liberties, Franchises, and Immunities, within any of our other Dominions, to all Intents and Purposes, as if they had been abiding and born, within this our Realm of England, or any other of our said Dominions.

Moreover, our gracious Will and Pleasure is, and we do, by these Presents, for Us, our Heirs, and Successors, declare and set forth, that if any Person or Persons, which shall be of any of the said Colonies and Plantations, or any other, which shall traffick to the said Colonies and Plantations, or any of them, shall, at any time or times hereafter, transport any Wares, Merchandises, or Commodities, out of any of our Dominions, with a Pretence to land, sell, or otherwise dispose of the same, within any the Limits and Precincts of any of the said Colonies and Plantations, and yet nevertheless, being at Sea, or after he hath landed the same within any of the said Colonies and

Plantations, shall carry the same into any other Foreign Country, with a Purpose there to sell or dispose of the same, without the Licence of Us, our Heirs, and Successors, in that Behalf first had and obtained; That then, all the Goods and Chattels of such Person or Persons, so offending and transporting together with the said Ship or Vessel, wherein such Transportation was made, shall be forfeited to Us, our Heirs, and Successors.

Provided always, and our Will and Pleasure is, and we do hereby declare to all Christian Kings, Princes, and States, that if any Person or Persons which shall hereafter be of any of the said several Colonies and Plantations, or any other, by his, their, or any of their Licence and Appointment, shall, at any Time or Times hereafter, rob or spoil, by Sea or Land, or do any Act of unjust and unlawful Hostility to any the Subjects of Us, our Heirs, or Successors, or any the Subjects of any King, Prince, Ruler, Governor, or State, being then in League or Amitie with Us, our Heirs, or Successors, and that upon such Injury, or upon just Complaint of such Prince, Ruler, Governor, or State, or their Subjects, We, our Heirs, or Successors, shall make open Proclamation, within any of the Ports of our Realm of England, commodious for that purpose, That the said Person or Persons, having committed any such robbery, or Spoil, shall, within the term to be limited by such Proclamations, make full Restitution or Satisfaction of all such Injuries done, so as the said Princes, or others so complaining, may hold themselves fully satisfied and contented; And, that if the said Person or Persons, having committed such Robery or Spoil, shall not make, or cause to be made Satisfaction accordingly, within such Time so to be limited, That then it shall be lawful to Us, our Heirs, and Successors, to put the said Person or Persons, having committed such Robbery or Spoil, and their Procurers, Abettors, and Comforters, out of our Allegiance and Protection; And that it shall be lawful and free, for all Princes, and others to pursue with hostility the said offenders, and every of them, and their and every of their Procurers, Aiders, abettors, and comforters, in that behalf.

And finally, we do for Us, our Heirs, and Successors, and agree, to and with the said Sir Thomas Gates, Sir George Somers, Richard Hackluit, Edward-Maria Wingfield, and all others of the said first colony, that We, our Heirs and Successors, upon Petition in that Behalf to be made, shall, by Letters Patent under the Great Seal of England, GIVE and GRANT unto such Persons, their Heirs and Assigns, as the Council of that Colony, or the most part of then, shall, for that Purpose, nominate and assign all the lands, Tenements, and Hereditaments, which shall be within the Precincts limited for that Colony, as is aforesaid, TO BE HOLDEN of Us, our heirs and Successors, as of our Manor at East-Greenwich, in the County of Kent, in free and common Soccage only, and not in Capite:

And do in like Manner, Grant and Agree, for Us, our Heirs and Successors, to and with the said Thomas Hanham, Ralegh Gilbert, William Parker, and George Popham, and all others of the said second Colony, That We, our Heirs, and Successors, upon Petition in that Behalf to be made, shall, by Letters-Patent, under the Great Seal of England, GIVE and GRANT, unto such Persons, their Heirs and Assigns, as the Council of that Colony, or the most Part of them, shall for that Purpose nominate and assign, all the Lands, Tenements, and Hereditaments, which shall be within the Precincts limited for that Colony, as is aforesaid, TO BE holden of Us, our Heires, and Successors, as of our Manor of East-Greenwich, in the County of Kent, in free and common Soccage only, and not in Capite.

All which Lands, Tenements, and Hereditaments, so to be passed by the said several Letters-Patent, shall be sufficient Assurance from the said Patentees, so distributed and divided amongst the Undertakers for the Plantation of the said several Colonies, and such as shall make their Plantations in either of the said several Colonies, in such Manner and Form, and for such Estates, as shall be ordered and set down by the Council of the said Colony, or the most part of them, respectively, within which the same Lands, Tenements, and Hereditaments shall lye or be; Although express Mention of the true yearly Value or Certainty of the Premises, or any of them, or of any other Gifts or Grants, by Us or any of our Progenitors or Predecessors, to the aforesaid Sir Thomas Gates, Knt. Sir George Somers, Knt. Richard Hackluit, Edward-Maria Wingfield, Thomas Hanham, Ralegh Gilbert, William Parker, and George Popham, or any of them, heretofore made, in these Presents, is not made; Or any Statute, Act, Ordinance, or Provision, Proclamation, or Restraint, to the contrary hereof had, made, ordained, or any other Thing, Cause, or Matter whatsoever, in any wise notwithstanding. IN Witness whereof, we have caused these our Letters to be made Patent; Witness Ourself at Westminster, the tenth Day of April, in the fourth Year of our Reign of England, France, and Ireland, and of Scotland the nine and thirtieth.

LUKIN
Per breve de private Sigillo.

SOURCE: *The Federal and State Constitutions, Colonial Charters, and Other Organic Laws of the States, Territories, and Colonies Now or Heretofore Forming the United States of America.* Compiled and edited under the act of Congress of June 30, 1906, by Francis Newton Thorpe. Washington, D.C.: Government Printing Office, 1909. www.yale.edu/lawweb/avalon/states/va01.htm.

Mayflower Compact

Agreement Between the Settlers at New Plymouth, 1620

IN THE NAME OF GOD, AMEN. We, whose names are underwritten, the Loyal Subjects of our dread Sovereign Lord King James, by the Grace of God, of Great Britain, France, and Ireland, King, Defender of the Faith, &c. Having undertaken for the Glory of God, and Advancement of the Christian Faith, and the Honour of our King and Country, a Voyage to plant the first Colony in the northern Parts of Virginia; Do by these Presents, solemnly and mutually, in the Presence of God and one another, covenant and combine ourselves together into a civil Body Politick, for our better Ordering and Preservation, and Furtherance of the Ends aforesaid: And by Virtue hereof do enact, constitute, and frame, such just and equal Laws, Ordinances, Acts, Constitutions, and Officers, from time to time, as shall be thought most meet and convenient for the general Good of the Colony; unto which we promise all due Submission and Obedience. IN WITNESS whereof we have hereunto subscribed our names at Cape-Cod the eleventh of November, in the Reign of our Sovereign Lord King James, of England, France, and Ireland, the eighteenth, and of Scotland the fifty-fourth, Anno Domini; 1620.

MR. JOHN CARVER,
MR. WILLIAM BRADFORD,
MR EDWARD WINSLOW,
MR. WILLIAM BREWSTER,
ISAAC ALLERTON,
MYLES STANDISH,
JOHN ALDEN,
JOHN TURNER,
FRANCIS EATON,
JAMES CHILTON,
JOHN CRAXTON,
JOHN BILLINGTON,
JOSES FLETCHER,
JOHN GOODMAN,
MR. SAMUEL FULLER,
MR. CHRISTOPHER MARTIN,
MR. WILLIAM MULLINS,
MR. WILLIAM WHITE,
MR. RICHARD WARREN,
JOHN HOWLAND,
MR. STEVEN HOPKINS,

DIGERY PRIEST,
THOMAS WILLIAMS,
GILBERT WINSLOW,
EDMUND MARGESSON,
PETER BROWN,
RICHARD BRITTERIDGE,
GEORGE SOULE,
EDWARD TILLY,
JOHN TILLY,
FRANCIS COOKE,
THOMAS ROGERS,
THOMAS TINKER,
JOHN RIDGDALE,
EDWARD FULLER,
RICHARD CLARK,
RICHARD GARDINER,
MR. JOHN ALLERTON,
THOMAS ENGLISH,
EDWARD DOTEN,
EDWARD LIESTER.

SOURCE: *The Federal and State Constitutions, Colonial Charters, and Other Organic Laws of the States, Territories, and Colonies Now or Heretofore Forming the United States of America.* Compiled and edited under the act of Congress of June 30, 1906, by Francis Newton Thorpe. Washington, D.C.: Government Printing Office, 1909. www.yale.edu/lawweb/avalon/amerdoc/mayflowr.htm.

Declaration and Resolves of the First Continental Congress

October 14, 1774

Whereas, since the close of the last war, the British parliament, claiming a power, of right, to bind the people of America by statutes in all cases whatsoever, hath, in some acts, expressly imposed taxes on them, and in others, under various presences, but in fact for the purpose of raising a revenue, hath imposed rates and duties payable in these colonies, established a board of commissioners, with unconstitutional powers, and extended the jurisdiction of courts of admiralty, not only for collecting the said duties, but for the trial of causes merely arising within the body of a county:

And whereas, in consequence of other statutes, judges, who before held only estates at will in their offices, have been made dependant on the crown alone for their salaries, and standing armies kept in times of peace: And whereas it has lately been resolved in parliament, that by force of a statute, made in the thirty-fifth year of the reign of King Henry the Eighth, colonists may be transported to England, and tried there upon accusations for treasons and misprisions, or concealments of treasons committed in the colonies, and by a late statute, such trials have been directed in cases therein mentioned:

And whereas, in the last session of parliament, three statutes were made; one entitled, "An act to discontinue, in such manner and for such time as are therein mentioned, the landing and discharging, lading, or shipping of goods, wares and merchandise, at the town, and within the harbour of Boston, in the province of Massachusetts-Bay in New England;" another entitled, "An act for the better regulating the government of the province of Massachusetts-Bay in New England;" and another entitled, "An act for the impartial administration of justice, in the cases of persons questioned for any act done by them in the execution of the law, or for the suppression of riots and tumults, in the province of the Massachusetts-Bay in New England;" and another statute was then made, "for making more effectual provision for the government of the province of Quebec, etc." All which statutes are impolitic, unjust, and cruel, as well as unconstitutional, and most dangerous and destructive of American rights:

And whereas, assemblies have been frequently dissolved, contrary to the rights of the people, when they attempted to deliberate on grievances; and their dutiful, humble, loyal, and reasonable petitions to the crown for redress, have been repeatedly treated with contempt, by his Majesty's ministers of state:

The good people of the several colonies of New-Hampshire, Massachusetts-Bay, Rhode Island and Providence Plantations, Connecticut, New-York, New-Jersey, Pennsylvania, Newcastle, Kent, and Sussex on Delaware, Maryland, Virginia, North-Carolina and South-Carolina, justly alarmed at these arbitrary proceedings of parliament and administration, have severally elected, constituted, and appointed deputies to meet, and sit in general Congress, in the city of Philadelphia, in order to obtain such establishment, as that their religion, laws, and liberties, may not be subverted: Whereupon the deputies so appointed being now assembled, in a full and free representation of these colonies, taking into their most serious consideration, the best means of attaining the ends aforesaid, do, in the first place, as Englishmen, their ancestors in like cases have usually done, for asserting and vindicating their rights and liberties, DECLARE,

That the inhabitants of the English colonies in North-America, by the immutable laws of nature, the principles of the English constitution, and the several charters or compacts, have the following RIGHTS:

Resolved, N.C.D. 1. That they are entitled to life, liberty and property: and they have never ceded to any foreign power whatever, a right to dispose of either without their consent.

Resolved, N.C.D. 2. That our ancestors, who first settled these colonies, were at the time of their emigration from the mother country, entitled to all the rights, liberties, and immunities of free and natural-born subjects, within the realm of England.

Resolved, N.C.D. 3. That by such emigration they by no means forfeited, surrendered, or lost any of those rights, but that they were, and their descendants now are, entitled to the exercise and enjoyment of all such of them, as their local and other circumstances enable them to exercise and enjoy.

Resolved, 4. That the foundation of English liberty, and of all free government, is a right in the people to participate in their legislative council: and as the English colonists are not represented, and from their local and other circumstances, cannot properly be represented in the British parliament, they are entitled to a free and exclusive power of legislation in their several provincial legislatures, where their right of representation can alone be preserved, in all cases of taxation and internal polity, subject only to the negative of their sovereign, in such manner as has been heretofore used and accustomed: But, from the necessity of the case, and a regard to the mutual interest of both countries, we cheerfully consent to the operation of such acts of the British parliament, as are bonfide, restrained to the regulation of our external commerce, for the purpose of securing the commercial advantages of the whole empire to the mother country, and the commercial benefits of its respective members; excluding every idea of taxation internal or external, for raising a revenue on the subjects, in America, without their consent.

Resolved, N.C.D. 5. That the respective colonies are entitled to the common law of England, and more especially to the great and inestimable privilege of being tried by their peers of the vicinage, according to the course of that law.

Resolved, N.C.D. 6. That they are entitled to the benefit of such of the English statutes, as existed at the time of their colonization; and which they have, by experience, respectively found to be applicable to their several local and other circumstances.

Resolved, N.C.D. 7. That these, his Majesty's colonies, are likewise entitled to all the immunities and privileges granted and confirmed to them by royal charters, or secured by their several codes of provincial laws.

Resolved, N.C.D. 8. That they have a right peaceably to assemble, consider of their grievances, and petition the king; and that all prosecutions, prohibitory proclamations, and commitments for the same, are illegal.

Resolved, N.C.D. 9. That the keeping a standing army in these colonies, in times of peace, without the consent of the legislature of that colony, in which such army is kept, is against law.

Resolved, N.C.D. 10. It is indispensably necessary to good government, and rendered essential by the English constitution, that the constituent branches of the legislature be independent of each other; that, therefore, the exercise of legislative power in several colonies, by a council appointed, during pleasure, by the crown, is unconstitutional, dangerous and destructive to the freedom of American legislation.

All and each of which the aforesaid deputies, in behalf of themselves, and their constituents, do claim, demand, and insist on, as their indubitable rights and liberties, which cannot be legally taken from them, altered or abridged by any power whatever, without their own consent, by their representatives in their several provincial legislature.

In the course of our inquiry, we find many infringements and violations of the foregoing rights, which, from an ardent desire, that harmony and mutual intercourse of affection and interest may be restored, we pass over for the present, and proceed to state such acts and measures as have been adopted since the last war, which demonstrate a system formed to enslave America.

Resolved, N.C.D. That the following acts of parliament are infringements and violations of the rights of the colonists; and that the repeal of them is essentially necessary, in order to restore harmony between Great Britain and the American colonies, viz.

The several acts of Geo. III. ch. 15, and ch. 34.–5 Geo. III. ch.25.–6 Geo. ch. 52.–7 Geo.III. ch. 41 and ch. 46.–8 Geo. III. ch. 22. which impose duties for the purpose of raising a revenue in America, extend the power of the admiralty courts beyond their ancient limits, deprive the American subject of trial by jury, authorize the judges certificate to indemnify the prosecutor from damages, that he might otherwise be liable to, requiring oppressive security from a claimant of ships and goods seized, before he shall be allowed to defend his property, and are subversive of American rights.

Also 12 Geo. III. ch. 24, intituled, "An act for the better securing his majesty's dockyards, magazines, ships, ammunition, and stores," which declares a new offence in America, and deprives the American subject of a constitutional trial by jury of the vicinage, by authorizing the trial of any person, charged with the committing any offence described in the said act, out of the realm, to be indicted and tried for the same in any shire or county within the realm.

Also the three acts passed in the last session of parliament, for stopping the port and blocking up the harbour of Boston, for altering the charter and government of Massachusetts-Bay, and that which is entitled, "An act for the better administration of justice, etc."

Also the act passed in the same session for establishing the Roman Catholic religion, in the province of Quebec, abolishing the equitable system of English laws, and erecting a tyranny there, to the great danger (from so total a dissimilarity of religion, law and government) of the neighboring British colonies, by the assistance of whose blood and treasure the said country was conquered from France.

Also the act passed in the same session, for the better providing suitable quarters for officers and soldiers in his majesty's service, in North-America.

Also, that the keeping a standing army in several of these colonies, in time of peace, without the consent of the legislature of that colony, in which such army is kept, is against law.

To these grievous acts and measures, Americans cannot submit, but in hopes their fellow subjects in Great Britain will, on a revision of them, restore us to that state, in which both countries found happiness and prosperity, we have for the present, only resolved to pursue the following peaceable measures: 1. To enter into a non-importation, non-consumption, and non-exportation agreement or association. 2. To prepare an address to the people of Great-Britain, and a memorial to the inhabitants of British America: and 3. To prepare a loyal address to his majesty, agreeable to resolutions already entered into.

SOURCE: *Documents Illustrative of the Formation of the Union of the American States*. House Document No. 398. Selected, arranged, and indexed by Charles C. Tansill. Washington, D.C.: Government Printing Office, 1927. www.yale.edu/lawweb/avalon/resolves.htm.

Declaration of Independence

In Congress, July 4, 1776.

The unanimous Declaration of the thirteen united States of America,

When in the Course of human events, it becomes necessary for one people to dissolve the political bands which have connected them with another, and to assume among the powers of the earth, the separate and equal station to which the Laws of Nature and of Nature's God entitle them, a decent respect to the opinions of mankind requires that they should declare the causes which impel them to the separation.

We hold these truths to be self-evident, that all men are created equal, that they are endowed by their Creator with certain unalienable Rights, that among these are Life, Liberty and the pursuit of Happiness.—That to secure these rights, Governments are instituted among Men, deriving their just powers from the consent of the governed,—That whenever any Form of Government becomes destructive of these ends, it is the Right of the People to alter or to abolish it, and to institute new Government, laying its foundation on such principles and organizing its powers in such form, as to them shall seem most likely to effect their Safety and Happiness. Prudence, indeed, will dictate that Governments long established should not be changed for light and transient causes; and accordingly all experience hath shewn, that mankind are more disposed to suffer, while evils are sufferable, than to right themselves by abolishing the forms to which they are accustomed. But when a long train of abuses and usurpations, pursuing invariably the same Object evinces a design to reduce them under absolute Despotism, it is their right, it is their duty, to throw off such Government, and to provide new Guards for their future security.—Such has been the patient sufferance of these Colonies; and such is now the necessity which constrains them to alter their former Systems of Government. The history of the present King of Great Britain is a history of repeated injuries and usurpations, all having in direct object the establishment of an absolute Tyranny over these States. To prove this, let Facts be submitted to a candid world.

He has refused his Assent to Laws, the most wholesome and necessary for the public good.

He has forbidden his Governors to pass Laws of immediate and pressing importance, unless suspended in their operation till his Assent should be obtained; and when so suspended, he has utterly neglected to attend to them.

He has refused to pass other Laws for the accommodation of large districts of people, unless those people would relinquish the right of Representation in the Legislature, a right inestimable to them and formidable to tyrants only.

He has called together legislative bodies at places unusual, uncomfortable, and distant from the depository of their public Records, for the sole purpose of fatiguing them into compliance with his measures.

He has dissolved Representative Houses repeatedly, for opposing with manly firmness his invasions on the rights of the people.

He has refused for a long time, after such dissolutions, to cause others to be elected; whereby the Legislative powers, incapable of Annihilation, have returned to the People at large for their exercise; the State remaining in the mean time exposed to all the dangers of invasion from without, and convulsions within.

He has endeavoured to prevent the population of these States; for that purpose obstructing the Laws for Naturalization of Foreigners; refusing to pass others to encourage their migrations hither, and raising the conditions of new Appropriations of Lands.

He has obstructed the Administration of Justice, by refusing his Assent to Laws for establishing Judiciary powers.

He has made Judges dependent on his Will alone, for the tenure of their offices, and the amount and payment of their salaries.

He has erected a multitude of New Offices, and sent hither swarms of Officers to harrass our people, and eat out their substance.

He has kept among us, in times of peace, Standing Armies without the Consent of our legislatures.

He has affected to render the Military independent of and superior to the Civil power.

He has combined with others to subject us to a jurisdiction foreign to our constitution, and unacknowledged by our laws; giving his Assent to their Acts of pretended Legislation:

For Quartering large bodies of armed troops among us:

For protecting them, by a mock Trial, from punishment for any Murders which they should commit on the Inhabitants of these States:

For cutting off our Trade with all parts of the world:

For imposing Taxes on us without our Consent:

For depriving us in many cases, of the benefits of Trial by Jury:

For transporting us beyond Seas to be tried for pretended offences:

For abolishing the free System of English Laws in a neighbouring Province, establishing therein an Arbitrary government, and enlarging its Boundaries so as to render it at once an example and fit instrument for introducing the same absolute rule into these Colonies:

For taking away our Charters, abolishing our most valuable Laws, and altering fundamentally the Forms of our Governments:

For suspending our own Legislatures, and declaring themselves invested with power to legislate for us in all cases whatsoever.

He has abdicated Government here, by declaring us out of his Protection and waging War against us.

He has plundered our seas, ravaged our Coasts, burnt our towns, and destroyed the lives of our people.

He is at this time transporting large Armies of foreign Mercenaries to compleat the works of death, desolation and tyranny, already begun with circumstances of Cruelty & perfidy scarcely paralleled in the most barbarous ages, and totally unworthy the Head of a civilized nation.

He has constrained our fellow Citizens taken Captive on the high Seas to bear Arms against their Country, to become the executioners of their friends and Brethren, or to fall themselves by their Hands.

He has excited domestic insurrections amongst us, and has endeavoured to bring on the inhabitants of our frontiers, the merciless Indian Savages, whose known rule of warfare, is an undistinguished destruction of all ages, sexes and conditions.

In every stage of these Oppressions We have Petitioned for Redress in the most humble terms: Our repeated Petitions have been answered only by repeated injury. A Prince whose character is thus marked by every act which may define a Tyrant, is unfit to be the ruler of a free people.

Nor have We been wanting in attentions to our Brittish brethren. We have warned them from time to time of attempts by their legislature to extend an unwarrantable jurisdiction over us. We have reminded them of the circumstances of our emigration and settlement here. We have appealed to their native justice and magnanimity, and we have conjured them by the ties of our common kindred to disavow these usurpations, which, would inevitably interrupt our connections and correspondence. They too have been deaf to the voice of justice and of consanguinity. We must, therefore, acquiesce in the necessity, which denounces our Separation, and hold them, as we hold the rest of mankind, Enemies in War, in Peace Friends.

We, therefore, the Representatives of the united States of America, in General Congress, Assembled, appealing to the Supreme Judge of the world for the rectitude of our intentions, do, in the Name, and by Authority of the good People of these Colonies, solemnly publish and declare, That these United Colonies are, and of Right ought to be Free and Independent States; that they are Absolved from all Allegiance to the British Crown, and that all political connection between them and the State of Great Britain, is and ought to be totally dissolved; and that as Free and Independent States, they have full Power to levy War, conclude Peace, contract Alliances, establish Commerce, and to do all other Acts and Things which Independent States may of right do. And for the support of this Declaration, with a firm reliance on the protection of divine Providence, we mutually pledge to each other our Lives, our Fortunes and our sacred Honor.

JOHN HANCOCK
[president]

[Signatories from the thirteen states follow.]

New Hampshire
JOSIAH BARTLETT,
WM. WHIPPLE,
MATTHEW THORNTON.

Massachusetts Bay
SAML. ADAMS,
JOHN ADAMS,
ROBT. TREAT PAINE,
ELBRIDGE GERRY

Rhode Island
STEP. HOPKINS,
WILLIAM ELLERY.

Connecticut
ROGER SHERMAN,
SAM'EL HUNTINGTON,
WM. WILLIAMS,
OLIVER WOLCOTT.

New York
WM. FLOYD,
PHIL. LIVINGSTON,
FRANS. LEWIS,
LEWIS MORRIS.

New Jersey
RICHD. STOCKTON,
JNO. WITHERSPOON,
FRAS. HOPKINSON,
JOHN HART,
ABRA. CLARK.

Pennsylvania
ROBT. MORRIS
BENJAMIN RUSH,
BENJA. FRANKLIN,
JOHN MORTON,
GEO. CLYMER,
JAS. SMITH,
GEO. TAYLOR,
JAMES WILSON,
GEO. ROSS.

Delaware
CAESAR RODNEY,
GEO. READ,
THO. M'KEAN.

Maryland
SAMUEL CHASE,
WM. PACA,
THOS. STONE,
CHARLES CARROLL OF
CARROLLTON.

Virginia
GEORGE WYTHE,
RICHARD HENRY LEE,
TH. JEFFERSON,
BENJA. HARRISON,
THS. NELSON, JR.,
FRANCIS LIGHTFOOT LEE,
CARTER BRAXTON.

North Carolina
WM. HOOPER,
JOSEPH HEWES,
JOHN PENN.

South Carolina
EDWARD RUTLEDGE,
THOS. HAYWARD, JUNR.,
THOMAS LYNCH, JUNR.,
ARTHUR MIDDLETON.

Georgia
BUTTON GWINNETT,
LYMAN HALL,
GEO. WALTON.

SOURCE: *Documents Illustrative of the Formation of the Union of the American States.* House Document No. 398. Selected, arranged, and indexed by Charles C. Tansill. Washington, D.C.: Government Printing Office, 1927. www.yale.edu/lawweb/avalon/declare.htm.

Articles of Confederation

November 15, 1777

To all to whom these Presents shall come, we the undersigned Delegates of the States affixed to our Names send greeting.

Articles of Confederation and perpetual Union between the states of New Hampshire, Massachusetts-bay Rhode Island and Providence Plantations, Connecticut, New York, New Jersey, Pennsylvania, Delaware, Maryland, Virginia, North Carolina, South Carolina and Georgia.

I.

The Stile of this Confederacy shall be
  "The United States of America".

II.

Each state retains its sovereignty, freedom, and independence, and every power, jurisdiction, and right, which is not by this Confederation expressly delegated to the United States, in Congress assembled.

III.

The said States hereby severally enter into a firm league of friendship with each other, for their common defense, the security of their liberties, and their mutual and general welfare, binding themselves to assist each other, against all force offered to, or attacks made upon them, or any of them, on account of religion, sovereignty, trade, or any other pretense whatever.

IV.

The better to secure and perpetuate mutual friendship and intercourse among the people of the different States in this Union, the free inhabitants of each of these States, paupers, vagabonds, and fugitives from justice excepted, shall be entitled to all privileges and immunities of free citizens in the several States; and the people of each State shall have free ingress and regress to and from any other State, and shall enjoy therein all the privileges of trade and commerce, subject to the same duties, impositions, and restrictions as the inhabitants thereof respectively, provided that such restrictions shall not extend so far as to prevent the removal of property imported into any State, to any other State, of which the owner is an inhabitant; provided also that no imposition, duties or restriction shall be laid by any State, on the property of the United States, or either of them.

If any person guilty of, or charged with, treason, felony, or other high misdemeanor in any State, shall flee from justice, and be found in any of the United States, he shall, upon demand of the Governor or executive power of the State from which he fled, be delivered up and removed to the State having jurisdiction of his offense.

Full faith and credit shall be given in each of these States to the records, acts, and judicial proceedings of the courts and magistrates of every other State.

V.

For the most convenient management of the general interests of the United States, delegates shall be annually appointed in such manner as the legislatures of each State shall direct, to meet in Congress on the first Monday in November, in every year, with a power reserved to each State to recall its delegates, or any of them, at any time within the year, and to send others in their stead for the remainder of the year.

No State shall be represented in Congress by less than two, nor more than seven members; and no person shall be capable of being a delegate for more than three years in any term of six years; nor shall any person, being a delegate, be capable of holding any office under the United States, for which he, or another for his benefit, receives any salary, fees or emolument of any kind.

Each State shall maintain its own delegates in a meeting of the States, and while they act as members of the committee of the States.

In determining questions in the United States in Congress assembled, each State shall have one vote.

Freedom of speech and debate in Congress shall not be impeached or questioned in any court or place out of Congress, and the members of Congress shall be protected in their persons from arrests or imprisonments, during the time of their going to and from, and attendence on Congress, except for treason, felony, or breach of the peace.

VI.

No State, without the consent of the United States in Congress assembled, shall send any embassy to, or receive any embassy from, or enter into any conference, agreement, alliance or treaty with any King, Prince or State; nor shall any person holding any office of profit or trust under the United States, or any of them, accept any present, emolument, office or title of any kind whatever from any King, Prince or foreign State; nor shall the United States in Congress assembled, or any of them, grant any title of nobility.

No two or more States shall enter into any treaty, confederation or alliance whatever between them, without the consent of the United States in Congress assembled, specifying accurately the purposes for which the same is to be entered into, and how long it shall continue.

No State shall lay any imposts or duties, which may interfere with any stipulations in treaties, entered into by the United States in Congress assembled, with any King, Prince or State, in pursuance of any treaties already proposed by Congress, to the courts of France and Spain.

No vessel of war shall be kept up in time of peace by any State, except such number only, as shall be deemed necessary by the United States in Congress assembled, for the defense of such State, or its trade; nor shall any body of forces be kept up by any State in time of peace, except such number only, as in the judgement of the United States in Congress assembled, shall be deemed requisite to garrison the forts necessary for the defense of such State; but every State shall always keep up a well-regulated and disciplined militia, sufficiently armed and accoutered, and shall provide and constantly have ready for use, in public stores, a due number of field pieces and tents, and a proper quantity of arms, ammunition and camp equipage.

No State shall engage in any war without the consent of the United States in Congress assembled, unless such State be actually invaded by enemies, or shall have received certain advice of a resolution being formed by some nation of Indians to invade such State, and the danger is so imminent as not to admit of a delay till the United States in Congress assembled can be consulted; nor shall any State grant commissions to any ships or vessels of war, nor letters of marque or reprisal, except it be after a declaration of war by the United States in Congress assembled, and then only against the Kingdom or State and the subjects thereof, against which war has been so declared, and under such regulations as shall be established by the United States in Congress assembled, unless such State be infested by pirates, in which case vessels of war may be fitted out for that occasion, and kept so long as the danger shall continue, or until the United States in Congress assembled shall determine otherwise.

VII.

When land forces are raised by any State for the common defense, all officers of or under the rank of colonel, shall be appointed by the legislature of each State respectively, by whom such forces shall be raised, or in such manner as such State shall direct, and all vacancies shall be filled up by the State which first made the appointment.

VIII.

All charges of war, and all other expenses that shall be incurred for the common defense or general welfare, and allowed by the United States in Congress assembled, shall be defrayed out of a common treasury, which shall be supplied by the several States in proportion to the value of all land within each State, granted or surveyed for any person, as such land and the buildings and improvements thereon shall be estimated according to such mode as the United States in Congress assembled, shall from time to time direct and appoint.

The taxes for paying that proportion shall be laid and levied by the authority and direction of the legislatures of the several States within the time agreed upon by the United States in Congress assembled.

IX.

The United States in Congress assembled, shall have the sole and exclusive right and power of determining on peace and war, except in the cases mentioned in the sixth article—of sending and receiving ambassadors—entering into treaties and alliances, provided that no treaty of commerce shall be made whereby the legislative power of the respective States shall be restrained from imposing such imposts and duties on foreigners, as their own people are subjected to, or from prohibiting the exportation or importation of any species of goods or commodities whatsoever—of establishing rules for deciding in all cases, what captures on land or water shall be legal, and in what manner prizes taken by land or naval forces in the service of the United States shall be divided or appropriated—of granting letters of marque and reprisal in times of peace—appointing courts for the trial of piracies and felonies commited on the high seas and establishing courts for receiving and determining finally appeals in all cases of captures, provided that no member of Congress shall be appointed a judge of any of the said courts.

The United States in Congress assembled shall also be the last resort on appeal in all disputes and differences now subsisting or that hereafter may arise between two or more States concerning boundary, jurisdiction or any other causes whatever; which authority shall always be exercised in the manner following. Whenever the legislative or executive authority or lawful agent of any State in controversy with another shall present a petition to Congress stating the matter in question and praying for a hearing, notice thereof shall be given by order of Congress to the legislative or executive authority of the other State in controversy, and a day assigned for the appearance of the parties by their lawful agents, who shall then be directed to appoint by joint consent, commissioners or judges to constitute a court for hearing and determining the matter in question: but if they cannot agree, Congress shall name three persons out of each of the United States, and from the list of such persons each party shall alternately strike out one, the petitioners beginning, until the number shall be reduced to thirteen; and from that number not less than seven, nor more than nine names as Congress shall direct, shall in the presence of Congress be drawn out by lot, and the persons whose names shall be so drawn or any five of them, shall be commissioners or judges, to hear and finally determine the controversy, so always as a major part of the judges who shall hear the cause shall agree in the determination: and if either party shall neglect to attend at the day appointed, without showing reasons, which Congress shall judge sufficient, or being present shall refuse to strike, the Congress shall proceed to nominate three persons out of each State, and the secretary of Congress shall strike in behalf of such party absent or refusing; and the judgement and sentence of the court to be appointed, in the manner before prescribed, shall be final and conclusive; and if any of the parties shall refuse to submit to the authority of such court, or to appear or defend their claim or cause, the court shall nevertheless proceed to pronounce sentence, or judgement, which shall in like manner be final and decisive, the judgement or sentence and other proceedings being in either case transmitted to Congress, and lodged among the acts of Congress for the security of the parties concerned: provided that every commissioner, before he sits in judgement, shall take an oath to be administered by one of the judges of the supreme or superior court of the State, where the cause shall be tried, 'well and truly to hear and determine the matter in question, according to the best of his judgement, without favor, affection or hope of reward': provided also, that no State shall be deprived of territory for the benefit of the United States.

All controversies concerning the private right of soil claimed under different grants of two or more States, whose jurisdictions as they may respect such lands, and the States which passed such grants are adjusted, the said grants or either of them being at the same time claimed to have originated antecedent to such settlement of jurisdiction, shall on the petition of either party to the Congress of the United States, be finally determined as near as may be in the same manner as is before presecribed for deciding disputes respecting territorial jurisdiction between different States.

The United States in Congress assembled shall also have the sole and exclusive right and power of regulating the alloy and value of coin struck by their own authority, or by that of the respective States—fixing the standards of weights and measures throughout the United States—regulating the trade and managing all affairs with the Indians, not members of any of the States, provided that the legislative right of any State within its own limits be not infringed or violated—establishing or regulating post offices from one State to another, throughout all the United States, and exacting such postage on the papers passing through the same as may be requisite to defray the expenses of the said office—appointing all officers of the land forces, in the service of the United States, excepting regimental officers—appointing all the officers of the naval forces, and commissioning all officers whatever in the service of the United States—making rules for the government and regulation of the said land and naval forces, and directing their operations.

The United States in Congress assembled shall have authority to appoint a committee, to sit in the recess of Congress, to be denominated 'A Committee of the States', and to consist of one delegate from each State; and to appoint such other committees and civil officers as may be necessary for managing the general affairs of the United States under their direction—to appoint one of their members to preside, provided that no person be allowed to serve in the office of president more than one year in any term of three years; to ascertain the necessary sums of money to be raised for the service of the United States, and to appropriate and apply the same for defraying the public expenses—to borrow money, or emit bills on the credit of the United States, transmitting every half-year to the respective States an account of the sums of money so borrowed or emitted—to build and equip a navy—to agree upon the number of land forces, and to make requisitions from each State for its quota, in proportion to the number of white inhabitants in such State; which requisition shall be binding, and thereupon the legislature of each State shall appoint the regimental officers, raise the men and cloath, arm and equip them in a soldier-like manner, at the expense of the United States; and the officers and men so cloathed, armed and equipped shall march to the place appointed, and within the time agreed on by the United States in Congress assembled. But if the United States in Congress assembled shall, on consideration of circumstances judge proper that any State should not raise men, or should raise a smaller number of men than the quota thereof, such extra number shall be raised, officered, cloathed, armed and equipped in the same manner as the quota of each State, unless the legislature of such State shall judge that such extra number cannot be safely spread out in the same, in which case they shall raise, officer, cloath, arm and equip as many of such extra number as they judge can be safely spared. And the officers and men so cloathed, armed, and equipped, shall march to the place appointed, and within the time agreed on by the United States in Congress assembled.

The United States in Congress assembled shall never engage in a war, nor grant letters of marque or reprisal in time of peace, nor enter into any treaties or alliances, nor coin money, nor regulate the value thereof, nor ascertain the sums and expenses necessary for the defense and welfare of the United States, or any of them, nor emit bills, nor borrow money on the credit of the United States, nor appropriate money, nor agree upon the number of vessels of war, to be built or purchased, or the number of land or sea forces to be raised, nor appoint a commander in chief of the army or navy, unless nine States assent to the same: nor shall a question on any other point, except for adjourning from day to day be determined, unless by the votes of the majority of the United States in Congress assembled.

The Congress of the United States shall have power to adjourn to any time within the year, and to any place within the United States, so that no period of adjournment be for a longer duration than the space of six months, and shall publish the journal of their proceedings monthly, except such parts thereof relating to treaties, alliances or military operations, as in their judgement require secrecy; and the yeas and nays of the delegates of each State on any question shall be entered on the journal, when it is desired by any delegates of a State, or any of them, at his or their request shall be furnished with a transcript of the said journal, except such parts as are above excepted, to lay before the legislatures of the several States.

X.

The Committee of the States, or any nine of them, shall be authorized to execute, in the recess of Congress, such of the powers of Congress as the United States in Congress assembled, by the consent of the nine States, shall from time to time think expedient to vest them with; provided that no power be delegated to the said Committee, for the exercise of which, by the Articles of Confederation, the voice of nine States in the Congress of the United States assembled be requisite.

XI.

Canada acceding to this confederation, and adjoining in the measures of the United States, shall be admitted into, and entitled to all the advantages of this Union; but no other colony shall be admitted into the same, unless such admission be agreed to by nine States.

XII.

All bills of credit emitted, monies borrowed, and debts contracted by, or under the authority of Congress, before the assembling of the United States, in pursuance of the present confederation, shall be deemed and considered as a charge against the United States, for payment and satisfaction whereof the said United States, and the public faith are hereby solemnly pleged.

XIII.

Every State shall abide by the determination of the United States in Congress assembled, on all questions which by this confederation are submitted to them. And the Articles of this Confederation shall be inviolably observed by every State, and the Union shall be perpetual; nor shall any alteration at any time hereafter be made in any of them; unless such alteration be agreed to in a Congress of the United States, and be afterwards confirmed by the legislatures of every State.

And Whereas it hath pleased the Great Governor of the World to incline the hearts of the legislatures we respectively represent in Congress, to approve of, and to authorize us to ratify the said Articles of Confederation and perpetual Union. Know Ye that we the undersigned delegates, by virtue of the power and authority to us given for that purpose, do by these presents, in the name and in behalf of our respective constituents, fully and entirely ratify and confirm each and every of the said Articles of Confederation and perpetual Union, and all and singular the matters and things therein contained: And we do further solemnly plight and engage the faith of our respective constituents, that they shall abide by the determinations of the United States in Congress assembled, on all questions, which by the said Confederation are submitted to them. And that the Articles thereof shall be inviolably observed by the States we respectively represent, and that the Union shall be perpetual.

In Witness whereof we have hereunto set our hands in Congress. Done at Philadelphia in the State of Pennsylvania the ninth day of July in the Year of our Lord One Thousand Seven Hundred and Seventy-Eight, and in the Third Year of the independence of America.

Agreed to by Congress 15 November 1777 In force after ratification by Maryland, 1 March 1781

SOURCE: *Documents Illustrative of the Formation of the Union of the American States.* House Document No. 398. Selected, arranged, and indexed by Charles C. Tansill. Washington, D.C.: Government Printing Office, 1927. www.yale.edu/lawweb/avalon/artconf.htm.

Virginia Plan for the U.S. Constitution

Presented by Edmund Randolph to the Constitutional Convention, May 29, 1787

1. Resolved that the Articles of Confederation ought to be so corrected and enlarged, as to accomplish the objects proposed by their institution, namely common Defence Security of Liberty and general welfare.

2. Resolved therefore that the right of Suffrage in the National Legislature ought to be, proportioned to the quotas of Contribution, or to the number of free inhabitants, as the one or the other, may serve best in different cases.

3. Resolved that the National Legislature ought to consist of two branches.

4. Resolved that the Members of the first Branch of the National Legislature, ought to be elected by the people of the several States every _____ for the term of three years, to be of the age of _____ at least. To receive liberal stipends, by which they may be compensated for the devotion ["duration" stricken out] of their time to public service-to be ineligible to any office established by a particular State, or under the authority of the United States, (except those peculiarly belonging to the functions of the first Branch) during the term of service, and for the space of one _____ after the expiration; to be incapable of re-election for the space of after the expiration of their term of service, and to be subject to recal.

5. Resolved, that the members of the second Branch of the Legislature, ought to be elected by the individual Legislatures: to be of the age of _____ years at least; to hold their Offices for a term sufficient to ensure their independency; to receive liberal Stipends by which they may be compensated for the devotion ["devtion" stricken out] of their time to the public service; and to be in-eligible to any office established by a particular State, or under the authority of the United States (except those peculiarly belonging to the functions of the second Branch) during the term of service, and for the space of _____ after the expiration thereof.

6. Resolved that each Branch ought to possess the right of originating acts, that the National Legislature ought to be empowered to enjoy, the Legislative rights vested in Congress, by the Confederation, and moreover to Legislate all cases to which the Separate States are incompetent; or in which the harmony of the United States may be interrupted, by the exercise of individual Legislation-to negative all Laws passed by the several States, contravening, in the opinion of the National Legislature, The articles of Union; or any Treaty subsisting under the Authority of the Union-and to call forth the force of the Union, against any Member of the Union, failing to fulfil its duties under the articles thereof

7th Resolved that a ["the" stricken out] national Executive be insti["consti" stricken out]tuted to consist of a single person, with powers to carry into execution the National Laws, and to appoint to Offices, in cases not otherwise provided for, to be chosen by the National Legislature, for the term of seven years-to receive punctually at stated times a fixed compensation, for the services rendered, in which no increase or diminution shall be made, so as to affect the Magistracy existing at the time of such increase or diminution, and to be in-eligible a second time.

8th Resolved that the Executive and a convenient number of the National Judiciary ought to compose a Council of revision, with authority to examine every act of the National Legislature, before it shall operate, and every act of a particular Legislature before a negative thereon shall be final; and that the dissent of the said council shall amount to a rejection, unless the act of the National Legislature, be again passed, or that of a particular Legislature be again negatived by _____ of the Members of each Branch.

9. Resolved that a National Judiciary be established to Consist of one Supreme Tribunal, to hold their Offices during good behavior, and to receive punctually at stated times fixed compensation for their services, in which no increase or diminution shall be made, so as to affect the persons actually in office at the time of such increase or diminution.

That the jurisdiction of the inferior Tribunals, shall be to hear and determine in the first instance, and of the Supreme Tribunal to hear and determine in the dernier resort; all piracies and felonies on the high Seas, Captures from an Enemy; cases in which Foreigners, or Citizens of other States applying to such jurisdictions, may be interested, or which respect the collection of the national Revenue, Impeachment of any national officer and questions which may involve, the National peace and harmony.

agreed   10. Resolved that provision ought to be made for the admission of States Lawfully arising within the limits of the United States whether from a voluntary junction of Government and Territory or otherwise, with the Consent of a number of Voices in the National Legislatures less than the whole.

agreed   11. Resolved that a republican Government of each State (except in the Voluntary junction of Government and Territory) ought to be guaranteed by the United States to each State.

agreed   12. Resolved that provision ought to be made for the Continuance of a Congress and their authorities, and privileges, until ["untill" stricken out] a given day, after the reform of the Articles of the Union shall be adopted, and for the Completion of all their engagements.

agreed   13. That provision ought to be made for the amendment of the Articles of the Union, whensoever it shall seem necessary (and that the assent of the National Legislature, ought to be required).

14. Resolved that the Legislative, Executive and judicial powers of the several States, ought to be bound by oath to support the Articles of Union.   *agreed*

15. Resolved that the amendments which shall be offered to the Confederation, by the Convention, ought at a proper time, or times, after the approbation of Congress, to be submitted to an assembly or assemblies of representatives, recommended by the several Legislatures, to be expressly chosen by the people to consider and decide thereon.   *postponed*

SOURCE: *Documents Illustrative of the Formation of the Union of the American States.* House Document No. 398. Selected, arranged, and indexed by Charles C. Tansill. Washington, D.C.: Government Printing Office, 1927. www.yale.edu/lawweb/avalon/const/vatextc.htm.

New Jersey Plan for the U.S. Constitution

Presented by William Paterson to the Constitutional Convention, June 15, 1787

1. Resolved, that an union of the states, merely federal, ought to be the sole object of the exercise of the powers vested in this convention.

2. Resolved, that the articles of the confederation ought to be so revised, corrected, and enlarged, as to render the federal constitution adequate to the exigencies of government, and the preservation of the union.

3. Resolved, that in addition to the powers vested in the united states in congress, by the present existing articles of confederation, they be authorized to pass acts for raising a revenue by laying a duty or duties on all goods and merchandise of foreign growth or manufacture, imported into any part of the united states; by imposing stamps on paper, parchment, and vellum; and by a postage on all letters and packages passing through the general post office, to be applied to such federal purposes, as they shall deem proper and expedient; to make rules and regulations for the collection thereof; and the same from time to time to alter and amend in such manner as they shall think proper: provided that all punishments, fines, forfeitures, and penalties, to be incurred for contravening such rules and regulations, shall be adjudged by the common law judiciaries of the state in which any offense, contrary to the true intent and meaning of such rules or regulations, shall be committed or perpetrated; with liberty of commencing all suits or prosecutions for that purpose, in the first instance, in the supreme common law judiciary of such state-subject, nevertheless, to an appeal in the last resort, for the correction of errors, both of law and fact, in rendering judgment, to the judiciary of the united states; and that the united states shall have authority to pass acts for the regulation of trade and commerce, as well with foreign nations, as with each other.

4. Resolved, that should requisitions be necessary, instead of the present rule, the united states in congress be authorized to make such requisitions in proportion to the whole number of white and other free citizens and inhabitants, of every age, sex, and condition, including those bound to servitude for a term of years, and three-fifths of all other persons, not comprehended in the foregoing descriptions (except Indians not paying taxes.)

5. Resolved, that if such requisitions be not complied with, in the time specified therein, the united states in congress shall have power to direct the collection thereof in the non-complying states; and for that purpose to devise and pass acts directing and authorising the same: provided that none of the powers hereby vested in the united states in congress shall be exercised without the consent of at least _____ states; and in that proportion, should the number of confederated states hereafter be increased or diminished.

6. Resolved, that the united states in congress, shall be authorised to elect a federal executive, to consist of _____ person or persons, to continue in office for the term of _____ years, to receive punctually, at stated times, a fixed compensation for the services by him or them to be rendered, in which

no increase or diminution shall be made, so as to affect the executive in office, at the time of such increase or diminution, to be paid out of the federal treasury; to be incapable of holding any other office or appointment during the time of service, and for _____ years after; to be ineligible a second time, and removable on impeachment and conviction for mar-practice, corrupt conduct, and neglect of duty.

7. Resolved, that the executive, besides a general authority to execute the federal acts, ought to appoint all federal officers, not otherwise provided for, and to direct all military operations; provided that the executive shall not on any occasion take command of any troops, so as personally to conduct any military enterprise as general, or in any other capacity.

8. Resolved, that the legislative acts of the united states, made under and in pursuance to the articles of union, and all treaties made and ratified under the authority of the united states, shall be the supreme law of the respective states, as far as those acts or treaties shall relate to the said states or their citizens and inhabitants; and that the judiciaries of the several states shall be bound thereby in their decisions; any thing in the respective laws of the individual states to the contrary notwithstanding.

9. Resolved, that if any state or body of men in any state, shall oppose or prevent the carrying into execution such acts or treaties, the federal executive shall be authorised to call forth the powers of the confederated states, or so much thereof as may be necessary to enforce and compel an obedience to such acts, or an observance of such treaties.

10. Resolved, that a federal judiciary be established, to consist of a supreme tribunal; the judges of which to be appointed by the executive, and to hold their offices during good behaviour; to receive punctually, at stated times, a fixed compensation for their services, to be paid out of the federal treasury; in which no increase or diminution shall be made, so as to affect the persons actually in office, at the time of such increase of diminution. That the judiciary so established, shall have authority to hear and determine, in the first instance, on all impeachments of federal officers, and by way of appeal in the dernier resort in all cases touching the rights and privileges of ambassadors; in all cases of captures from the enemy; in all cases of piracies and felonies committed on the high seas; in all cases in which foreigners may be interested in the construction of any treaty or treaties, or which may arise on any act or ordinance of congress for the regulation of trade, or the collection of the federal revenue; that none of the judiciary officers shall be capable of receiving or holding any other office or appointment, during the time they remain in office, or for _____ years afterwards.

11. Resolved, that the legislative, executive, and judiciary powers within the several states, ought to be bound by oath to support the articles of union.

12. Resolved, that provision ought to be made for hearing and deciding upon all disputes arising between the united states and an individual state, respecting territory.

13. Resolved, that provision ought to be made for the admission of new states into the union.

14. Resolved, that it is necessary to define what offenses, committed in any state, shall be deemed high treason against the united states.

15. Resolved, that the rule for naturalization ought to be the same in every state.

16. Resolved, that a citizen of one state, committing an offense in another state, shall be deemed guilty of the same offense, as if it had been committed by a citizen of the state, in which the offense was committed. Source:

SOURCE: *Documents Illustrative of the Formation of the Union of the American States.* House Document No. 398. Selected, arranged, and indexed by Charles C. Tansill. Washington, D.C.: Government Printing Office, 1927. www.yale.edu/lawweb/avalon/const/njtextc.htm.

Constitution of the United States[1]

September 17, 1787

We the People of the United States, in Order to form a more perfect Union, establish Justice, insure domestic Tranquility, provide for the common defence, promote the general Welfare, and secure the Blessings of Liberty to ourselves and our Posterity, do ordain and establish this Constitution for the United States of America.

ARTICLE. I.

Section. 1. All legislative Powers herein granted shall be vested in a Congress of the United States, which shall consist of a Senate and House of Representatives.

Section. 2. The House of Representatives shall be composed of Members chosen every second Year by the People of the several States, and the Electors in each State shall have the Qualifications requisite for Electors of the most numerous Branch of the State Legislature.

No Person shall be a Representative who shall not have attained to the Age of twenty five Years, and been seven Years a Citizen of the United States, and who shall not, when elected, be an Inhabitant of that State in which he shall be chosen.

Representatives and direct Taxes shall be apportioned among the several States which may be included within this Union, according to their respective Numbers, which shall be determined by adding to the whole Number of free Persons, including those bound to Service for a Term of Years, and excluding Indians not taxed, three fifths of all other Persons.[2] The actual Enumeration shall be made within three Years after the first Meeting of the Congress of the United States, and within every subsequent Term of ten Years, in such Manner as they shall by Law direct. The Number of Representatives shall not exceed one for every thirty Thousand, but each State shall have at Least one Representative; and until such enumeration shall be made, the State of New Hampshire shall be entitled to chuse three, Massachusetts eight, Rhode-Island and Providence Plantations one, Connecticut five, New-York six, New Jersey four, Pennsylvania eight, Delaware one, Maryland six, Virginia ten, North Carolina five, South Carolina five, and Georgia three.

When vacancies happen in the Representation from any State, the Executive Authority thereof shall issue Writs of Election to fill such Vacancies.

The House of Representatives shall chuse their Speaker and other Officers; and shall have the sole Power of Impeachment.

Section. 3. The Senate of the United States shall be composed of two Senators from each State, chosen by the Legislature thereof,[3] for six Years; and each Senator shall have one Vote.

Immediately after they shall be assembled in Consequence of the first Election, they shall be divided as equally as may be into three Classes. The Seats of the Senators of the first Class shall be vacated at the Expiration of the second Year, of the second Class at the Expiration of the fourth Year, and of the third Class at the Expiration of the sixth Year, so that one third may be chosen every second Year; and if Vacancies happen by Resignation, or otherwise, during the Recess of the Legislature of any State, the Executive thereof may make temporary Appointments until the next Meeting of the Legislature, which shall then fill such Vacancies.[4]

No Person shall be a Senator who shall not have attained to the Age of thirty Years, and been nine Years a Citizen of the United States, and who shall not, when elected, be an Inhabitant of that State for which he shall be chosen.

The Vice President of the United States shall be President of the Senate, but shall have no Vote, unless they be equally divided.

The Senate shall chuse their other Officers, and also a President pro tempore, in the Absence of the Vice President, or when he shall exercise the Office of President of the United States.

The Senate shall have the sole Power to try all Impeachments. When sitting for that Purpose, they shall be on Oath or Affirmation. When the President of the United States is tried, the Chief Justice shall preside: And no Person shall be convicted without the Concurrence of two thirds of the Members present.

Judgment in Cases of Impeachment shall not extend further than to removal from Office, and disqualification to hold and enjoy any Office of honor, Trust or Profit under the United States: but the Party convicted shall nevertheless be liable and subject to Indictment, Trial, Judgment and Punishment, according to Law.

Section. 4. The Times, Places and Manner of holding Elections for Senators and Representatives, shall be prescribed in each State by the Legislature thereof; but the Congress may at any time by Law make or alter such Regulations, except as to the Places of chusing Senators.

The Congress shall assemble at least once in every Year, and such Meeting shall be on the first Monday in December,[5] unless they shall by Law appoint a different Day.

Section. 5. Each House shall be the Judge of the Elections, Returns and Qualifications of its own Members, and a Majority of each shall constitute a Quorum to do Business; but a smaller Number may adjourn from day to day, and may be authorized to compel the Attendance of absent Members, in such Manner, and under such Penalties as each House may provide.

Each House may determine the Rules of its Proceedings, punish its Members for disorderly Behaviour, and, with the Concurrence of two thirds, expel a Member.

Each House shall keep a Journal of its Proceedings, and from time to time publish the same, excepting such Parts as may in their Judgment require Secrecy; and the Yeas and Nays of the Members of either House on any question shall, at the Desire of one fifth of those Present, be entered on the Journal.

Neither House, during the Session of Congress, shall, without the Consent of the other, adjourn for more than three days, nor to any other Place than that in which the two Houses shall be sitting.

Section. 6. The Senators and Representatives shall receive a Compensation for their Services, to be ascertained by Law, and paid out of the Treasury of the United States.[6] They shall in all Cases, except Treason, Felony and Breach of the Peace, be privileged from Arrest during their Attendance at the Session of their respective Houses, and in going to and returning from the same; and for any Speech or Debate in either House, they shall not be questioned in any other Place.

No Senator or Representative shall, during the Time for which he was elected, be appointed to any civil Office under the Authority of the United States, which shall have been created, or the Emoluments whereof shall have been encreased during such time; and no Person holding any Office under the United States, shall be a Member of either House during his Continuance in Office.

Section. 7. All Bills for raising Revenue shall originate in the House of Representatives; but the Senate may propose or concur with Amendments as on other Bills.

Every Bill which shall have passed the House of Representatives and the Senate, shall, before it become a Law, be presented to the President of the United States; If he approve he shall sign it, but if not he shall return it, with his Objections to that House in which it shall have originated, who shall enter the Objections at large on their Journal, and proceed to reconsider it. If after such Reconsideration two thirds of that House shall agree to pass the Bill, it shall be sent, together with the Objections, to the other House, by which it shall likewise be reconsidered, and if approved by two thirds of that House, it shall become a Law. But in all such Cases the Votes of both Houses shall be determined by yeas and Nays, and the Names of the Persons voting for and against the Bill shall be entered on the Journal of each House respectively. If any Bill shall not be returned by the President within ten Days (Sundays excepted) after it shall have been presented to him, the Same shall be a Law, in like Manner as if he had signed it, unless the Congress by their Adjournment prevent its Return, in which Case it shall not be a Law.

Every Order, Resolution, or Vote to which the Concurrence of the Senate and House of Representatives may be necessary (except on a question of Adjournment) shall be presented to the President of the United States; and before the Same shall take Effect, shall be approved by him, or being disapproved by him, shall be repassed by two thirds of the Senate and House of Representatives, according to the Rules and Limitations prescribed in the Case of a Bill.

Section. 8. The Congress shall have Power To lay and collect Taxes, Duties, Imposts and Excises, to pay the Debts and provide for the common Defence and general Welfare of the United States; but all Duties, Imposts and Excises shall be uniform throughout the United States;

To borrow Money on the credit of the United States;

To regulate Commerce with foreign Nations, and among the several States, and with the Indian Tribes;

To establish an uniform Rule of Naturalization, and uniform Laws on the subject of Bankruptcies throughout the United States;

To coin Money, regulate the Value thereof, and of foreign Coin, and fix the Standard of Weights and Measures;

To provide for the Punishment of counterfeiting the Securities and current Coin of the United States;

To establish Post Offices and post Roads;

To promote the Progress of Science and useful Arts, by securing for limited Times to Authors and Inventors the exclusive Right to their respective Writings and Discoveries;

To constitute Tribunals inferior to the supreme Court;

To define and punish Piracies and Felonies committed on the high Seas, and Offences against the Law of Nations;

To declare War, grant Letters of Marque and Reprisal, and make Rules concerning Captures on Land and Water;

To raise and support Armies, but no Appropriation of Money to that Use shall be for a longer Term than two Years;

To provide and maintain a Navy;

To make Rules for the Government and Regulation of the land and naval Forces;

To provide for calling forth the Militia to execute the Laws of the Union, suppress Insurrections and repel Invasions;

To provide for organizing, arming, and disciplining, the Militia, and for governing such Part of them as may be employed in the Service of the United States, reserving to the States respectively, the Appointment of the Officers, and the Authority of training the Militia according to the discipline prescribed by Congress;

To exercise exclusive Legislation in all Cases whatsoever, over such District (not exceeding ten Miles square) as may, by Cession of particular States, and the Acceptance of Congress, become the Seat of the Government of the United States, and to exercise like Authority over all Places purchased by the Consent of the Legislature of the State in which the Same shall be, for the Erection of Forts, Magazines, Arsenals, dock-Yards, and other needful Buildings;—And

To make all Laws which shall be necessary and proper for carrying into Execution the foregoing Powers, and all other Powers vested by this Constitution in the Government of the United States, or in any Department or Officer thereof.

Section. 9. The Migration or Importation of such Persons as any of the States now existing shall think proper to admit, shall not be prohibited by the Congress prior to the Year one thousand eight hundred and eight, but a Tax or duty may be imposed on such Importation, not exceeding ten dollars for each Person.

The Privilege of the Writ of Habeas Corpus shall not be suspended, unless when in Cases of Rebellion or Invasion the public Safety may require it.

No Bill of Attainder or ex post facto Law shall be passed.

No Capitation, or other direct, Tax shall be laid, unless in Proportion to the Census or Enumeration herein before directed to be taken.[7]

No Tax or Duty shall be laid on Articles exported from any State.

No Preference shall be given by any Regulation of Commerce or Revenue to the Ports of one State over those of another: nor shall Vessels bound to, or from, one State, be obliged to enter, clear, or pay Duties in another.

No Money shall be drawn from the Treasury, but in Consequence of Appropriations made by Law; and a regular Statement and Account of the Receipts and Expenditures of all public Money shall be published from time to time.

No Title of Nobility shall be granted by the United States: And no Person holding any Office of Profit or Trust under them, shall, without the Consent of the Congress, accept of any present, Emolument, Office, or Title, of any kind whatever, from any King, Prince, or foreign State.

Section. 10. No State shall enter into any Treaty, Alliance, or Confederation; grant Letters of Marque and Reprisal; coin Money; emit Bills of Credit; make any Thing but gold and silver Coin a Tender in Payment of Debts; pass any Bill of Attainder, ex post facto Law, or Law impairing the Obligation of Contracts, or grant any Title of Nobility.

No State shall, without the Consent of the Congress, lay any Imposts or Duties on Imports or Exports, except what may be absolutely necessary for executing it's inspection Laws: and the net Produce of all Duties and Imposts, laid by any State on Imports or Exports, shall be for the Use of the Treasury of the United States; and all such Laws shall be subject to the Revision and Controul of the Congress.

No State shall, without the Consent of Congress, lay any Duty of Tonnage, keep Troops, or Ships of War in time of Peace, enter into any Agreement or Compact with another State, or with a foreign Power, or engage in War, unless actually invaded, or in such imminent Danger as will not admit of delay.

ARTICLE. II.

Section. 1. The executive Power shall be vested in a President of the United States of America. He shall hold his Office during the Term of four Years, and, together with the Vice President, chosen for the same Term, be elected, as follows:

Each State shall appoint, in such Manner as the Legislature thereof may direct, a Number of Electors, equal to the whole Number of Senators and Representatives to which the State may be entitled in the Congress: but no Senator or Representative, or Person holding an Office of Trust or Profit under the United States, shall be appointed an Elector.

The Electors shall meet in their respective States, and vote by Ballot for two Persons, of whom one at least shall not be an Inhabitant of the same State with themselves. And they shall make a List of all the Persons voted for, and of the Number of Votes for each; which List they shall sign and certify, and transmit sealed to the Seat of the Government of the United States, directed to the President of the Senate. The President of the Senate shall, in the Presence of the Senate and House of Representatives, open all the Certificates, and the Votes shall then be counted. The Person having the greatest Number of Votes shall be the President, if such Number be a Majority of the whole Number of Electors appointed; and if there be more than one who have such Majority, and have an equal Number of Votes, then the House of Representatives shall immediately chuse by Ballot one of them for President; and if no Person have a Majority, then from the five highest on the List the said House shall in like Manner chuse the President. But in chusing the President, the Votes shall be taken by States, the Representation from each State having one Vote; A quorum for this Purpose shall consist of a Member or Members from two thirds of the States, and a Majority of all the States shall be necessary to a Choice. In every Case, after the Choice of the President, the Person having the greatest Number of Votes of the Electors shall be the Vice President. But if there should remain two or more who have equal Votes, the Senate shall chuse from them by Ballot the Vice President.[8]

The Congress may determine the Time of chusing the Electors, and the Day on which they shall give their Votes; which Day shall be the same throughout the United States.

No Person except a natural born Citizen, or a Citizen of the United States, at the time of the Adoption of this Constitution, shall be eligible to the Office of President; neither shall any Person be eligible to that Office who shall not have attained to the Age of thirty five Years, and been fourteen Years a Resident within the United States.

In Case of the Removal of the President from Office, or of his Death, Resignation, or Inability to discharge the Powers and Duties of the said Office,[9] the Same shall devolve on the Vice President, and the Congress may by Law provide for the Case of Removal, Death, Resignation or Inability, both of the President and Vice President, declaring what Officer shall then act as President, and such Officer shall act accordingly, until the Disability be removed, or a President shall be elected.

The President shall, at stated Times, receive for his Services, a Compensation, which shall neither be increased nor diminished during the Period for which he shall have been elected, and he shall not receive within that Period any other Emolument from the United States, or any of them.

Before he enter on the Execution of his Office, he shall take the following Oath or Affirmation:— "I do solemnly swear (or affirm) that I will faithfully execute the Office of President of the United States, and will to the best of my Ability, preserve, protect and defend the Constitution of the United States."

Section. 2. The President shall be Commander in Chief of the Army and Navy of the United States, and of the Militia of the several States, when called into the actual Service of the United States; he may require the Opinion, in writing, of the principal Officer in each of the executive Departments, upon any Subject relating to the Duties of their respective Offices, and he shall have Power to grant Reprieves and Pardons for Offences against the United States, except in Cases of Impeachment.

He shall have Power, by and with the Advice and Consent of the Senate, to make Treaties, provided two thirds of the Senators present concur; and he shall nominate, and by and with the Advice and Consent of the Senate, shall appoint Ambassadors, other public Ministers and Consuls, Judges of the supreme Court, and all other Officers of the United States, whose Appointments are not herein otherwise provided for, and which shall be established by Law: but the Congress may by Law vest the Appointment of such inferior Officers, as they think proper, in the President alone, in the Courts of Law, or in the Heads of Departments.

The President shall have Power to fill up all Vacancies that may happen during the Recess of the Senate, by granting Commissions which shall expire at the End of their next Session.

Section. 3. He shall from time to time give to the Congress Information of the State of the Union, and recommend to their Consideration such Measures as he shall judge necessary and expedient; he may, on extraordinary Occasions, convene both Houses, or either of them, and in Case of Disagreement between them, with Respect to the Time of Adjournment, he may adjourn them to such Time as he shall think proper; he shall receive Ambassadors and other public Ministers; he shall take Care that the Laws be faithfully executed, and shall Commission all the Officers of the United States.

Section. 4. The President, Vice President and all civil Officers of the United States, shall be removed from Office on Impeachment for, and Conviction of, Treason, Bribery, or other high Crimes and Misdemeanors.

ARTICLE. III.

Section. 1. The judicial Power of the United States, shall be vested in one supreme Court, and in such inferior Courts as the Congress may from time to time ordain and establish. The Judges, both of the supreme and inferior Courts, shall hold their Offices during good Behaviour, and shall, at stated Times, receive for their Services, a Compensation, which shall not be diminished during their Continuance in Office.

Section. 2. The judicial Power shall extend to all Cases, in Law and Equity, arising under this Constitution, the Laws of the United States, and Treaties made, or which shall be made, under their Authority;—to all Cases affecting Ambassadors, other public Ministers and Consuls;—to all Cases of admiralty and maritime Jurisdiction;—to Controversies to which the United States shall be a Party;—to Controversies between two or more States;—between a State and Citizens of another State;[10]—between Citizens of different States,—between Citizens of the same State claiming Lands under Grants of different States, and between a State, or the Citizens thereof, and foreign States, Citizens or Subjects.

In all Cases affecting Ambassadors, other public Ministers and Consuls, and those in which a State shall be Party, the supreme Court shall have original Jurisdiction. In all the other Cases before mentioned, the supreme Court shall have appellate Jurisdiction, both as to Law and Fact, with such Exceptions, and under such Regulations as the Congress shall make.

The Trial of all Crimes, except in Cases of Impeachment, shall be by Jury; and such Trial shall be held in the State where the said Crimes shall have been committed; but when not committed within any State, the Trial shall be at such Place or Places as the Congress may by Law have directed.

Section. 3. Treason against the United States, shall consist only in levying War against them, or in adhering to their Enemies, giving them Aid and Comfort. No Person shall be convicted of Treason unless on the Testimony of two Witnesses to the same overt Act, or on Confession in open Court.

The Congress shall have Power to declare the Punishment of Treason, but no Attainder of Treason shall work Corruption of Blood, or Forfeiture except during the Life of the Person attainted.

ARTICLE. IV.

Section. 1. Full Faith and Credit shall be given in each State to the public Acts, Records, and judicial Proceedings of every other State. And the Congress may by general Laws prescribe the Manner in which such Acts, Records and Proceedings shall be proved, and the Effect thereof.

Section. 2. The Citizens of each State shall be entitled to all Privileges and Immunities of Citizens in the several States.

A Person charged in any State with Treason, Felony, or other Crime, who shall flee from Justice, and be found in another State, shall on Demand of the executive Authority of the State from which he fled, be delivered up, to be removed to the State having Jurisdiction of the Crime.

No Person held to Service or Labour in one State, under the Laws thereof, escaping into another, shall, in Consequence of any Law or Regulation therein, be discharged from such Service or Labour, but shall be delivered up on Claim of the Party to whom such Service or Labour may be due.[11]

Section. 3. New States may be admitted by the Congress into this Union; but no new State shall be formed or erected within the Jurisdiction of any other State; nor any State be formed by the Junction of two or more States, or Parts of States, without the Consent of the Legislatures of the States concerned as well as of the Congress.

The Congress shall have Power to dispose of and make all needful Rules and Regulations respecting the Territory or other Property belonging to the United States; and nothing in this Constitution shall be so construed as to Prejudice any Claims of the United States, or of any particular State.

Section. 4. The United States shall guarantee to every State in this Union a Republican Form of Government, and shall protect each of them against Invasion; and on Application of the Legislature, or of the Executive (when the Legislature cannot be convened) against domestic Violence.

ARTICLE. V.

The Congress, whenever two thirds of both Houses shall deem it necessary, shall propose Amendments to this Constitution, or, on the Application of the Legislatures of two thirds of the several States, shall call a Convention for proposing Amendments, which, in either Case, shall be valid to all Intents and Purposes, as Part of this Constitution, when ratified by the Legislatures of three fourths of the several States, or by Conventions in three fourths thereof, as the one or the other Mode of Ratification may be proposed by the Congress; Provided that no Amendment which may be made prior to the Year One thousand eight hundred and eight shall in any Manner affect the first and fourth Clauses in the Ninth Section of the first Article; and that no State, without its Consent, shall be deprived of its equal Suffrage in the Senate.

ARTICLE. VI.

All Debts contracted and Engagements entered into, before the Adoption of this Constitution, shall be as valid against the United States under this Constitution, as under the Confederation.

This Constitution, and the Laws of the United States which shall be made in Pursuance thereof; and all Treaties made, or which shall be made, under the Authority of the United States, shall be the supreme Law of the Land; and the Judges in every State shall be bound thereby, any Thing in the Constitution or Laws of any State to the Contrary notwithstanding.

The Senators and Representatives before mentioned, and the Members of the several State Legislatures, and all executive and judicial Officers, both of the United States and of the several States, shall be bound by Oath or Affirmation, to support this Constitution; but no religious Test shall ever be required as a Qualification to any Office or public Trust under the United States.

ARTICLE. VII.

The Ratification of the Conventions of nine States, shall be sufficient for the Establishment of this Constitution between the States so ratifying the Same.

DONE in Convention by the Unanimous Consent of the States present the Seventeenth Day of September in the Year of our Lord one thousand seven hundred and Eighty seven and of the Independence of the United States of America the Twelfth. In witness whereof We have hereunto subscribed our Names,

GO WASHINGTON—Presidt. and deputy from Virginia

New Hampshire
JOHN LANGDON
NICHOLAS GILMAN

Massachusetts
NATHANIEL GORHAM
RUFUS KING

Connecticut
WM. SAML. JOHNSON
ROGER SHERMAN

New York
ALEXANDER HAMILTON

New Jersey
WIL: LIVINGSTON
DAVID BREARLEY.
WM. PATERSON.
JONA: DAYTON

Pennsylvania
B FRANKLIN
THOMAS MIFFLIN
ROBT MORRIS
GEO. CLYMER
THOS. FITZSIMONS
JARED INGERSOLL
JAMES WILSON.
GOUV MORRIS

Delaware
GEO: READ
GUNNING BEDFORD JUN
JOHN DICKINSON
RICHARD BASSETT
JACO: BROOM

Maryland
JAMES MCHENRY
DAN OF ST THOS. JENIFER
DANL CARROLL.

Virginia
JOHN BLAIR
JAMES MADISON JR.

North Carolina
WM BLOUNT
RICHD. DOBBS SPAIGHT.
HU WILLIAMSON

South Carolina
J. RUTLEDGE
CHARLES COTESWORTH
    PINCKNEY
CHARLES PINCKNEY
PIERCE BUTLER.

Georgia
WILLIAM FEW
ABR BALDWIN

ATTEST WILLIAM JACKSON
Secretary

1. This text of the Constitution follows the engrossed copy signed by George Washington and the deputies from twelve states. The Constitution was adopted by a convention of the states on September 17, 1787, and was subsequently ratified by the several states on the following dates: Delaware, December 7, 1787; Pennsylvania, December 12, 1787; New Jersey, December 18, 1787; Georgia, January 2, 1788; Connecticut, January 9, 1788; Massachusetts, February 6, 1788; Maryland, April 28, 1788; South Carolina, May 23, 1788; New Hampshire, June 21, 1788. Ratification was completed on June 21, 1788. The Constitution was subsequently ratified by Virginia, June 25, 1788; New York, July 26, 1788; North Carolina, November 21, 1789; and Rhode Island, May 29, 1790.

2. The part of this clause relating to the mode of apportionment of representatives among the states has been affected by section 2 of the Fourteenth Amendment, and as to taxes on incomes without apportionment by the Sixteenth Amendment.

3. This clause has been affected by clause 1 of the Seventeenth Amendment.

4. This clause has been affected by clause 2 of the Eighteenth Amendment.

5. This clause has been affected by the Twentieth Amendment.

6. This clause has been affected by the Twenty-seventh Amendment.

7. This clause has been affected by the Sixteenth Amendment.

8. This clause has been superseded by the Twelfth Amendment.

9. This clause has been affected by the Twenty-fifth Amendment.

10. This clause has been affected by the Eleventh Amendment.

11. This clause has been affected by the Thirteenth Amendment.

SOURCE: *The Constitution of the United States of America, as Amended.* House Document No. 106–214. Washington, D.C.: Government Printing Office, 2000.

Amendments to the U.S. Constitution[1]

AMENDMENT I

Congress shall make no law respecting an establishment of religion, or prohibiting the free exercise thereof; or abridging the freedom of speech, or of the press; or the right of the people peaceably to assemble, and to petition the government for a redress of grievances. [ratified 1791]

AMENDMENT II

A well regulated militia, being necessary to the security of a free state, the right of the people to keep and bear arms, shall not be infringed. [ratified 1791]

AMENDMENT III

No soldier shall, in time of peace be quartered in any house, without the consent of the owner, nor in time of war, but in a manner to be prescribed by law. [ratified 1791]

AMENDMENT IV

The right of the people to be secure in their persons, houses, papers, and effects, against unreasonable searches and seizures, shall not be violated, and no warrants shall issue, but upon probable cause, supported by oath or affirmation, and particularly describing the place to be searched, and the persons or things to be seized. [ratified 1791]

AMENDMENT V

No person shall be held to answer for a capital, or otherwise infamous crime, unless on a presentment or indictment of a grand jury, except in cases arising in the land or naval forces, or in the militia, when in actual service in time of war or public danger; nor shall any person be subject for the same offense to be twice put in jeopardy of life or limb; nor shall he be compelled in any criminal case to be a witness against himself, nor be deprived of life, liberty, or property, without due process of law; nor shall private property be taken for public use, without just compensation. [ratified 1791]

AMENDMENT VI

In all criminal prosecutions, the accused shall enjoy the right to a speedy and public trial, by an impartial jury of the state and district wherein the crime shall have been committed, which district shall have been previously ascertained by law, and to be informed of the nature and cause of the accusations; to be confronted with the witnesses against him; to have compulsory process for obtaining witnesses in his favor, and to have the assistance of counsel for his defense. [ratified 1791]

AMENDMENT VII

In suits at common law, where the value in controversy shall exceed twenty dollars, the right of trial by jury shall be preserved, and no fact tried by a jury, shall be otherwise re-examined in any court of the United States, than according to the rules of the common law. [ratified 1791]

AMENDMENT VIII

Excessive bail shall not be required, nor excessive fines imposed, nor cruel and unusual punishments inflicted. [ratified 1791]

AMENDMENT IX

The enumeration in the Constitution, of certain rights, shall not be construed to deny or disparage others retained by the people. [ratified 1791]

AMENDMENT X

The powers not delegated to the United States by the Constitution, nor prohibited by it to the states, are reserved to the states respectively, or to the people. [ratified 1791]

AMENDMENT XI

The judicial power of the United States shall not be construed to extend to any suit in law or equity, commenced or prosecuted against one of the United States by citizens of another state, or by citizens or subjects of any foreign state. [ratified 1798]

AMENDMENT XII

The electors shall meet in their respective states, and vote by ballot for President and Vice President, one of whom, at least, shall not be an inhabitant of the same state with themselves; they shall name in their ballots the person voted for as President, and in distinct ballots the person voted for as Vice President, and they shall make distinct lists of all persons voted for as President, and of all persons voted for as Vice President, and of the number of votes for each, which lists they shall sign and certify, and transmit sealed to the seat of the government of the United States, directed to the President of the Senate;—The President of the Senate shall, in the presence of the Senate and House of Representatives, open all the certificates and the votes shall then be counted;—The person having the greatest number of votes for President, shall be the President, if such number be a majority of the whole number of electors appointed; and if no person have such majority, then from the persons having the highest numbers not exceeding three on the list of those voted for as President, the House of Representatives shall choose immediately, by ballot, the President. But in choosing the President, the votes shall be taken by states, the representation from each state having one vote; a quorum for this purpose shall consist of a member or members from two thirds of the states, and a majority of all the states shall be necessary to a choice. And if the House of Representatives shall not choose a President whenever the right of choice shall devolve upon them, before the fourth day of March next following, then the Vice President shall act as President, as in the case of the death or other constitutional disability of the President.[2] The person having the greatest number of votes as Vice President, shall be the Vice President, if such number be a majority of the whole number of electors appointed, and if no person have a majority, then from the two highest numbers on the list, the Senate shall choose the Vice President; a quorum for the purpose shall consist of two-thirds of the whole number of Senators, and a majority of the whole number shall be necessary to a choice. But no person constitutionally ineligible to the office of President should be eligible to that of Vice President of the United States. [ratified 1804]

AMENDMENT XIII

Section 1. Neither slavery nor involuntary servitude, except as a punishment for crime whereof the party shall have been duly convicted, shall exist within the United States, or any place subject to their jurisdiction.

Section 2. Congress shall have power to enforce this article by appropriate legislation. [ratified 1865]

AMENDMENT XIV

Section 1. All persons born or naturalized in the United States, and subject to the jurisdiction thereof, are citizens of the United States and of the state wherein they reside. No state shall make or enforce any law which shall abridge the privileges or immunities of citizens of the United States; nor shall any state deprive any person of life, liberty, or property, without due process of law; nor deny to any person within its jurisdiction the equal protection of the laws.

Section 2. Representatives shall be apportioned among the several states according to their respective numbers, counting the whole number of persons in each state, excluding Indians not taxed. But when the right to vote at any election for the choice of electors for President and Vice President of the United States, representatives in Congress, the executive and judicial officers of a state, or the members of the legislature thereof, is denied to any of the male inhabitants of such state, being twenty-one years of age,[3] and citizens of the United States, or in any way abridged, except for participation in rebellion, or other crime, the basis of representation therein shall be reduced in the proportion which the number of such male citizens shall bear to the whole number of male citizens twenty-one years of age in such state.

Section 3. No person shall be a Senator or representative in Congress, or elector of President and Vice President, or hold any office, civil or military, under the United States, or under any state, who, having previously taken an oath, as a member of Congress, or as an officer of the United States, or as a member of any state legislature, or as an executive or judicial officer of any state, to support the Constitution of the United States, shall have engaged in insurrection or rebellion against the same, or given aid or comfort to the enemies thereof. But Congress may by a vote of two-thirds of each house, remove such disability.

Section 4. The validity of the public debt of the United States, authorized by law, including debts incurred for payment of pensions and bounties for services in suppressing insurrection or rebellion, shall not be questioned. But neither the United States nor any state shall assume or pay any debt or obligation incurred in aid of insurrection or rebellion against the United States, or any claim for the loss or emancipation of any slave; but all such debts, obligations and claims shall be held illegal and void.

Section 5. The Congress shall have power to enforce by appropriate legislation, the provisions of this article. [ratified 1868]

AMENDMENT XV

Section 1. The right of citizens of the United States to vote shall not be denied or abridged by the United States or by any state on account of race, color, or previous condition of servitude.

Section 2. The Congress shall have power to enforce this article by appropriate legislation. [ratified 1870]

AMENDMENT XVI

The Congress shall have power to levy and collect taxes on incomes, from whatever source derived, without apportionment among the several states, and without regard to any census or enumeration. [ratified 1913]

AMENDMENT XVII

The Senate of the United States shall be composed of two Senators from each state, elected by the people thereof, for six years; and each Senator shall have one vote. The electors in each state shall have the qualifications requisite for electors of the most numerous branch of the state legislatures.

When vacancies happen in the representation of any state in the Senate, the executive authority of such state shall issue writs of election to fill such vacancies: *Provided,* That the legislature of any state may empower the executive thereof to make temporary appointment until the people fill the vacancies by election as the legislature may direct.

This amendment shall not be so construed as to affect the election or term of any Senator chosen before it becomes valid as part of the Constitution. [ratified 1913]

AMENDMENT XVIII[4]

Section 1. After one year from the ratification of this article the manufacture, sale, or transportation of intoxicating liquors within, the importation thereof into, or the exportation thereof from the United States and all territory subject to the jurisdiction thereof for beverage purposes is hereby prohibited.

Section 2. The Congress and the several states shall have concurrent power to enforce this article by appropriate legislation.

Section 3. This article shall be inoperative unless it shall have been ratified as an amendment to the Constitution by the legislatures of the several states, as provided in the Constitution, within seven years from the date of the submission hereof to the states by the Congress. [ratified 1919; repealed 1933]

AMENDMENT XIX

The right of citizens of the United States to vote shall not be denied or abridged by the United States or by any state on account of sex.

Congress shall have power to enforce this article by appropriate legislation. [ratified 1920]

AMENDMENT XX

Section 1. The terms of the President and Vice President shall end at noon on the 20th day of January, and the terms of Senators and representatives at noon on the 3rd day of January, of the years in which such terms would have ended if this article had not been ratified; and the terms of their successors shall then begin.

Section 2. The Congress shall assemble at least once in every year, and such meeting shall begin at noon on the 3rd day of January, unless they shall by law appoint a different day.

Section 3. If, at the time fixed for the beginning of the term of the President, the President elect shall have died, the Vice President elect shall become President. If a President shall not have been chosen before the time fixed for the beginning of his term, or if the President elect shall have failed to qualify, then the Vice President elect shall act as President until a President shall have qualified; and the Congress may by law provide for the case wherein neither a President elect nor a Vice President elect shall have qualified, declaring who shall then act as President, or the manner in which one who is to act shall be selected, and such person shall act accordingly until a President or Vice President shall have qualified.

Section 4. The Congress may by law provide for the case of the death of any of the persons from whom the House of Representatives may choose a President whenever the right of choice shall have devolved upon them, and for the case of the death of any of the persons from whom the Senate may choose a Vice President whenever the right of choice shall have devolved upon them.

Section 5. Sections 1 and 2 shall take effect on the 15th day of October following the ratification of this article.

Section 6. This article shall be inoperative unless it shall have been ratified as an amendment to the Constitution by the legislatures of three-fourths of the several states within seven years from the date of its submission. [ratified 1933]

AMENDMENT XXI

Section 1. The eighteenth article of amendment to the Constitution of the United States is hereby repealed.

Section 2. The transportation or importation into any state, territory, or possession of the United States for delivery or use therein of intoxicating liquors, in violation of the laws thereof, is hereby prohibited.

Section 3. This article shall be inoperative unless it shall have been ratified as an amendment to the Constitution by conventions in the several states, as provided in the Constitution, within seven years from the date of the submission hereof to the states by the Congress. [ratified 1933]

AMENDMENT XXII

Section 1. No person shall be elected to the office of the President more than twice, and no person who has held the office of President, or acted as President, for more than two years of a term to which some other person was elected President shall be elected to the office of the President more than once. But this article shall not apply to any person holding the office of President when this article was proposed by the Congress, and shall not prevent any person who may be holding the office of President, or acting as President, during the term within which this article becomes operative from holding the office of President or acting as President during the remainder of such term.

Section 2. This article shall be inoperative unless it shall have been ratified as an amendment to the Constitution by the legislatures of three-fourths of the several states within seven years from the date of its submission to the states by the Congress. [ratified 1951]

AMENDMENT XXIII

Section 1. The District constituting the seat of Government of the United States shall appoint in such manner as the Congress may direct:

A number of electors of President and Vice President equal to the whole number of Senators and Representatives in Congress to which the District would be entitled if it were a State, but in no event more than the least populous State; they shall be in addition to those appointed by the States, but they shall be considered, for the purposes of the election of President and Vice President, to be electors appointed by a State; and they shall meet in the District and perform such duties as provided by the twelfth article of amendment.

Section 2. The Congress shall have power to enforce this article by appropriate legislation. [ratified 1961]

AMENDMENT XXIV

Section 1. The right of citizens of the United States to vote in any primary or other election for President or Vice President, for electors for President or Vice President, or for Senator or Representative in Congress, shall not be denied or abridged by the United States or any State by reason of failure to pay any poll tax or other tax.

Section 2. The Congress shall have power to enforce this article by appropriate legislation. [ratified 1964]

AMENDMENT XXV

Section 1. In case of the removal of the President from office or of his death or resignation, the Vice President shall become President.

Section 2. Whenever there is a vacancy in the office of the Vice President, the President shall nominate a Vice President who shall take office upon confirmation by a majority vote of both houses of Congress.

Section 3. Whenever the President transmits to the President pro tempore of the Senate and the Speaker of the House of Representatives his written declaration that he is unable to discharge the powers and duties of his office, and until he transmits to them a written declaration to the contrary, such powers and duties shall be discharged by the Vice President as acting President.

Section 4. Whenever the Vice President and a majority of either the principal officers of the executive departments or of such other body as Congress may by law provide, transmit to the President pro tempore of the Senate and the Speaker of the House of Representatives their written declaration that the President is unable to discharge the powers and duties of his office, the Vice President shall immediately assume the powers and duties of the office as acting President.

Thereafter, when the President transmits to the President pro tempore of the Senate and the Speaker of the House of Representatives his written declaration that no inability exists, he shall resume the powers and duties of his office unless the Vice President and a majority of either the principal officers of the executive department or of such other body as Congress may by law provide, transmit within four days to the President pro tempore of the Senate and the Speaker of the House of Representatives their written declaration that the President is unable to discharge the powers and duties of his office. Thereupon Congress shall decide the issue, assembling within forty-eight hours for that purpose if not in session. If the Congress, within twenty-one days after receipt of the latter written declaration, or, if Congress is not in session, within twenty-one days after Congress is required to assemble, determines by two-thirds vote of both houses that the President is unable to discharge the powers and duties of his office, the Vice President shall continue to discharge the same as acting President; otherwise, the President shall resume the powers and duties of his office. [ratified 1967]

AMENDMENT XXVI

Section 1. The right of citizens of the United States, who are eighteen years of age or older, to vote shall not be denied or abridged by the United States or by any State on account of age.

Section 2. The Congress shall have power to enforce this article by appropriate legislation. [ratified 1971]

AMENDMENT XXVII

No law, varying the compensation for the services of the Senators and Representatives, shall take effect, until an election of Representatives shall have intervened. [ratified 1992]

1. The first ten amendments to the Constitution (and two others, one of which failed of ratification and the other, which later became the Twenty-seventh amendment) were proposed to the legislatures of the states by the first Congress on September 25, 1789. The first ten amendments were ratified by the following states, and the notifications of ratification by the governors thereof were successively communicated by the president to Congress: New Jersey, November 20, 1789; Maryland, December 19, 1789; North Carolina, December 22, 1789; South Carolina, January 19, 1790; New Hampshire, January 25, 1790; Delaware, January 28, 1790; New York, February 24, 1790; Pennsylvania, March 10, 1790; Rhode Island, June 7, 1790; Vermont, November 3, 1791; and Virginia, December 15, 1791. Ratification was completed on December 15, 1791. The amendments were subsequently ratified by the legislatures of Massachusetts, March 2, 1939; Georgia, March 18, 1939; and Connecticut, April 19, 1939.

2. This sentence has been superseded by section 3 of the Twentieth Amendment.

3. See the Nineteenth Amendment and section 1 of the Twenty-sixth Amendment.

4. Repealed by section 1 of the Twenty-first Amendment.

SOURCE: *The Constitution of the United States of America, as Amended.* House Document No. 106–214. Washington, D.C.: Government Printing Office, 2000.

Resolution of the Constitutional Convention

In Convention Monday September 17th 1787.

Present The States of New Hampshire, Massachusetts, Connecticut, Mr. Hamilton from New York, New Jersey, Pennsylvania, Delaware, Maryland, Virginia, North Carolina, South Carolina and Georgia. Resolved,

That the proceeding Constitution be laid before the United States in Congress assembled, and that it is the Opinion of this Convention, that it should afterwards be submitted to a Convention of Delegates, chosen in each State by the People thereof, under the Recommendation of its Legislature, for their Assent and Ratification; and that each Convention assenting to, and ratifying the Same, should give Notice thereof to the United States in Congress assembled.

Resolved, That it is the Opinion of this Convention, that as soon as the Conventions of nine States shall have ratified this Constitution, the United States in Congress assembled should fix a Day on which Electors should be appointed by the States which shall have ratified the same, and a Day on which the Electors should assemble to vote for the President, and the Time and Place for commencing Proceedings under this Constitution. That after such Publication the Electors should be appointed, and the Senators and Representatives elected: That the Electors should meet on the Day fixed for the Election of the President, and should transmit their Votes certified, signed, sealed and directed, as the Constitution requires, to the Secretary of the United States in Congress assembled, that the Senators and Representatives should convene at the Time and Place assigned; that the Senators should appoint a President of the Senate, for the sole Purpose of receiving, opening and counting the Votes for President; and, that after he shall be chosen, the Congress, together with the President, should, without Delay, proceed to execute this Constitution.

By the Unanimous Order of the Convention

Go Washington Presidt
W. Jackson Secretary.

SOURCE: *Documents Illustrative of the Formation of the Union of the American States.* House Document No. 398. Selected, arranged, and indexed by Charles C. Tansill. Washington, D.C.: Government Printing Office, 1927. www.yale.edu/lawweb/avalon/const/ressub01.htm.

Resolution Transmitting the U.S. Constitution to Congress

Letter of the president of the Constitutional Convention, September 17, 1787, to the president of Congress

In Convention, September 17, 1787

Sir,

We have now the honor to submit to the consideration of the United States in Congress assembled, that Constitution which has appeared to us the most adviseable.

The friends of our country have long seen and desired, that the power of making war, peace, and treaties, that of levying money and regulating commerce, and the correspondent executive and judicial authorities should be fully and effectually vested in the general government of the Union: But the impropriety of delegating such extensive trust to one body of men is evident-Hence results the necessity of a different organization.

It is obviously impracticable in the federal government of these states, to secure all rights of independent sovereignty to each, and yet provide for the interest and safety of all: Individuals entering into society, must give up a share of liberty to preserve the rest. The magnitude of the sacrifice must depend as well on situation and circumstance, as on the object to be obtained. It is at all times diffcult to draw with precision the line between those rights which must be surrendered, and those which may be reserved; and on the present occasion this difficulty was increased by a difference among the several states as to their situation, extent, habits, and particular interests.

In all our deliberations on this subject we kept steadily in our view, that which appears to us the greatest interest of every true American, the consolidation of our Union, in which is involved our prosperity, felicity, safety, perhaps our national existence. This important consideration, seriously and deeply impressed on our minds, led each state in the Convention to be less rigid on points of inferior magnitude, than might have been otherwise expected; and thus the Constitution, which we now present, is the result of a spirit of amity, and of that mutual deference and concession which the peculiarity of our political situation rendered indispensible.

That it will meet the full and entire approbation of every state is not perhaps to be expected; but each will doubtless consider, that had her interest been alone consulted, the consequences might have been particularly disagreeable or injurious to others; that it is liable to as few exceptions as could reasonably have been expected, we hope and believe; that it may promote the lasting welfare of that country so dear to us all, and secure her freedom and happiness, is our most ardent wish.

With great respect, We have the honor to be, Sir,
Your Excellency's most obedient and humble servants,

George Washington, President.
By unanimous Order of the Convention.
His Excellency the President of Congress.

SOURCE: *Documents Illustrative of the Formation of the Union of the American States.* House Document No. 398. Selected, arranged, and indexed by Charles C. Tansill. Washington, D.C.: Government Printing Office, 1927.

Resolution of Congress Submitting the U.S. Constitution to the Several States

Friday Sept. 28. 1787.

Congress assembled present Newhampshire Massachusetts Connecticut New York New Jersey Pensylvania. Delaware Virginia North Carolina South Carolina and Georgia and from Maryland Mr Ross

Congress having received the report of the Convention lately assembled in Philadelphia

Resolved Unanimously that the said Report with the resolutions and letter accompanying the same be transmitted to the several legislatures in Order to be submitted to a convention of Delegates chosen in each state by the people thereof in conformity to the resolves of the Convention made and provided in that case.

Source: *Documents Illustrative of the Formation of the Union of the American States.* House Document No. 398. Selected, Arranged, and Indexed by Charles C. Tansill. Washington, D.C.: Government Printing Office, 1927. www.yale.edu/lawweb/avalon/const/ressub02.htm.

Ratification of the U.S. Constitution by the State of Delaware

We the Deputies of the People of the Delaware State, in Convention met, having taken into our serious consideration the Federal Constitution proposed and agreed upon by the Deputies of the United States in a General Convention held at the City of Philadelphia on the seventeenth day of September in the year of our Lord one thousand seven hundred and eighty seven, Have approved, assented to, ratified, and confirmed, and by these Presents, Do, in virtue of the Power and Authority to us given for that purpose, for and in behalf of ourselves and our Constituents, fully, freely, and entirely approve of, assent to, ratify, and confirm the said Constitution.

Done in Convention at Dover this seventh day of December in the year aforesaid, and in the year of the Independence of the United States of America the twelfth. In Testimony whereof we have hereunto subscribed our Names—

Sussex County	Kent County	New Castle County
JOHN INGRAM	NICHOLAS RIDGELEY	JAS LATIMER, PRESIDENT
JOHN JONES	RICHARD SMITH	JAMES BLACK
WILLIAM MOORE	GEORGE TRUITT	JNO JAMES
WILLIAM HALL	RICHARD BASSETT	GUNNING BEDFORD SENR
THOMAS LAWS	JAMES SYKES	KENSEY JOHNS
ISAAC COOPER	ALLEN MCLANE	THOMAS WATSON
WOODMAN STORKLY	DANIEL CUMMINS SENR	SOLOMON MAXWELL
JOHN LAWS	JOSEPH BARKER	NICHOLAS WAY
THOMAS EVANS	EDWARD WHITE	THOMAS DUFF
ISRAEL HOLLAND	GEORGE MANLOVE	GUNNG BEDFORD JUNR

To all whom these Presents shall come Greeting, I Thomas Collins President of the Delaware State do hereby certify, that the above instrument of writing is a true copy of the original ratification of the Federal Constitution by the Convention of the Delaware State, which original ratification is now in my possession. In Testimony whereof I have caused the seal of the Delaware State to be hereunto an'exed.

THOS COLLINS

SOURCE: *Documents Illustrative of the Formation of the Union of the American States.* House Document No. 398. Selected, arranged, and indexed by Charles C. Tansill. Washington, D.C.: Government Printing Office, 1927. www.yale.edu/lawweb/ avalon/ratde.htm.

Resolution of the First Congress Submitting the Bill of Rights[1]

Congress of the United States, begun and held at the City of New-York, on Wednesday the fourth of March, one thousand seven hundred and eighty nine

THE Conventions of a number of the States, having at the time of their adopting the Constitution, expressed a desire, in order to prevent misconstruction or abuse of its powers, that further declaratory and restrictive clauses should be added: And as extending the ground of public confidence in the Government, will best ensure the beneficent ends of its institution:

RESOLVED by the Senate and House of Representatives of the United States of America, in Congress assembled, two thirds of both Houses concurring, that the following Articles be proposed to the Legislatures of the several States, as Amendments to the Constitution of the United States, all or any of which Articles, when ratified by three fourths of the said Legislatures, to be valid to all intents and purposes, as part of the said Constitution; viz:

ARTICLES in addition to, and Amendment of the Constitution of the United States of America, proposed by Congress, and ratified by the Legislatures of the several States, pursuant to the fifth Article of the original Constitution.

Article the first ... After the first enumeration required by the first Article of the Constitution, there shall be one Representative for every thirty thousand, until the number shall amount to one hundred, after which, the proportion shall be so regulated by Congress, that there shall be not less than one hundred Representatives, nor less than one Representative for every forty thousand persons, until the number of Representatives shall amount to two hundred, after which the proportion shall be so regulated by Congress, that there shall not be less than two hundred Representatives, nor more than one Representative for every fifty thousand persons.

Article the second ... No law, varying the compensation for the services of the Senators and Representatives, shall take effect, until an election of Representatives shall have intervened.

Article the third ... Congress shall make no law respecting an establishment of religion, or prohibiting the free exercise thereof; or abridging the freedom of speech, or of the press; or the right of the people peaceably to assemble, and to petition the Government for a redress of grievances.

Article the fourth ... A well regulated Militia, being necessary to the security of a free State, the right of the people to keep and bear Arms, shall not be infringed.

Article the fifth ... No Soldier shall, in time of peace be quartered in any house, without the consent of the Owner, nor in time of war, but in a manner to be prescribed by law.

Article the sixth ... The right of the people to be secure in their persons, houses, papers, and effects, against unreasonable searches and seizures, shall not be violated, and no Warrants shall issue, but upon probable cause, supported by Oath or affirmation, and particularly describing the place to be searched, and the persons or things to be seized.

Article the seventh ... No person shall be held to answer for a capital, or otherwise infamous crime, unless on a presentment or indictment of a Grand Jury, except in cases arising in the land or naval forces, or in the Militia, when in actual service in time of War or public danger; nor shall any person be subject for the same offense to be twice put in jeopardy of life or limb; nor shall be compelled in any criminal case to be a witness against himself, nor be deprived of life, liberty, or property, without due process of law; nor shall private property be taken for public use, without just compensation.

Article the eighth ... In all criminal prosecutions, the accused shall enjoy the right to a speedy and public trial, by an impartial jury of the State and district wherein the crime shall have been committed, which district shall have been previously ascertained by law, and to be informed of the nature and cause of the accusation; to be confronted with the witnesses against him; to have compulsory process for obtaining witnesses in his favor, and to have the Assistance of Counsel for his defence.

Article the ninth ... In Suits at common law, where the value in controversy shall exceed twenty dollars, the right of trial by jury shall be preserved, and no fact tried by a jury, shall be otherwise re-examined in any Court of the United States, than according to the rules of the common law.

Article the tenth ... Excessive bail shall not be required, nor excessive fines imposed, nor cruel and unusual punishments inflicted.

Article the eleventh ... The enumeration in the Constitution, of certain rights, shall not be construed to deny or disparage others retained by the people.

Article the twelfth ... The powers not delegated to the United States by the Constitution, nor prohibited by it to the States, are reserved to the States respectively, or to the people.

FREDERICK AUGUSTUS MUHLENBERG
Speaker of the House of Representatives.

JOHN ADAMS,
Vice-President of the United States,
and President of the Senate.

ATTEST, JOHN BECKLEY,
Clerk of the House of Representatives.

SAM. A. OTIS
Secretary of the Senate.

1. The proposed amendments were transmitted to the legislatures of the several States, upon which the following action was taken:
By the State of New Hampshire—Agreed to the whole of the said amendments, except the second article.
By the State of New York—Agreed to the whole of the said amendments, except the second article.
By the State of Pennsylvania—Agreed to the second, fourth, fifth, sixth, seventh, eighth, ninth, tenth, eleventh, and twelfth articles of the said amendments.
By the State of Delaware—Agreed to the whole of the said amendments, except the first article.
By the State of Maryland—Agreed to the whole of the said twelve amendments.
By the State of South Carolina—Agreed to the whole said twelve amendments.
By the State of North Carolina—Agreed to the whole of the said twelve amendments.
By the State of Rhode Island and Providence Plantations—Agreed to the whole of the said twelve articles.
By the State of New Jersey—Agreed to the whole of the said amendments, except the second article.
By the State of Virginia—Agreed to the whole of the said twelve articles (*Elliot's Debates*, Vol. I, pp. 339–40.)
No returns were made by the states of Massachusetts, Connecticut, Georgia, and Kentucky.
The amendments thus proposed became a part of the constitution—the first of them excepted: which was not ratified by a sufficient number of the state legislatures.

SOURCE: *Documents Illustrative of the Formation of the Union of the American States.* House Document No. 398. Selected, arranged, and indexed by Charles C. Tansill. Washington, D.C.: Government Printing Office, 1927. www.yale.edu/lawweb/avalon/resolu02.htm.

Guide to the U.S. Constitution

A

ABRIDGED. The privileges or immunities of citizens of the United States shall not be. *Amendment 14:1*

ABSENT MEMBERS, in such manner and under such penalties as it may provide. Each house is authorized to compel the attendance of. *Article 1:5:1*

ACCOUNTS of receipts and expenditures of public money shall be published from time to time. A statement of the. *Article 1:9:7*

ACCUSATION. In all criminal prosecutions the accused shall be informed of the cause and nature of the. *Amendment 6*

ACCUSED shall have a speedy public trial. In all criminal prosecutions the. *Amendment 6*

• He shall be tried by an impartial jury of the state and district where the crime was committed. *Amendment 6*

• He shall be informed of the nature of the accusation. *Amendment 6*

• He shall be confronted with the witnesses against him. *Amendment 6*

• He shall have compulsory process for obtaining witnesses in his favor. *Amendment 6*

• He shall have the assistance of counsel for his defense. *Amendment 6*

ACTIONS at common law involving over twenty dollars shall be tried by jury. *Amendment 7*

ACTS, RECORDS, AND JUDICIAL PROCEEDINGS of another state. Full faith and credit shall be given in each state to the. *Article 4:1*

ACTS. Congress shall prescribe the manner of proving such acts, records, and proceedings. *Article 4:1*

ADJOURN from day to day. A smaller number than a quorum of each house may. *Article 1:5:1*

ADJOURN FOR MORE THAN THREE DAYS, nor to any other place than that in which they shall be sitting. Neither house shall, during the session of Congress, without the consent of the other. *Article 1:5:4*

ADJOURNMENT, the president may adjourn them to such time as he shall think proper. In case of disagreement between the two houses as to. *Article 2:3*

ADMIRALTY and maritime jurisdiction. The judicial power shall extend to all cases of. *Article 3:2:1*

ADMITTED by the Congress into this Union, but no new states shall be formed or erected within the jurisdiction of any other state. New states may be. *Article 4:3:1*

• Nor shall any state be formed by the junction of two or more states, or parts of states, without the consent of the legislatures and of Congress. *Article 4:3:1*

ADOPTION of the Constitution shall be valid. All debts and engagements contracted by the confederation and before the. *Article 6:–:1*

ADVICE AND CONSENT of the Senate. The president shall have power to make treaties by and with the. *Article 2:2:2*

• To appoint ambassadors or other public ministers and consuls by and with the. *Article 2:2:2*

• To appoint all other officers of the United States not herein otherwise provided for by and with the. *Article 2:2:2*

AFFIRMATION. Senators sitting to try impeachments shall be on oath or. *Article 1:3:6*

• To be taken by the president of the United States. Form of the oath or. *Article 2:1:8*

• No warrants shall be issued but upon probable cause and on oath or. *Amendment 4*

• To support the Constitution. Senators and representatives, members of state legislatures, executive and judicial officers, both state and federal, shall be bound by oath or. *Article 6:–:3*

AGE. No person shall be a representative who shall not have attained twenty-five years of. *Article 1:2:2*

• No person shall be a senator who shall not have attained thirty years of. *Article 1:3:3*

• Right of citizens of the United States, who are eighteen years of age or older, to vote shall not be denied or abridged by the United States or any state on account of age. *Amendment 26:1*

AGREEMENT or compact with another state without the consent of Congress. No state shall enter into any. *Article 1:10:3*

AID AND COMFORT. Treason against the United States shall consist in levying war against them, adhering to their enemies, and giving them. *Article 3:3:1*

ALLIANCE or confederation. No state shall enter into any treaty of. *Article 1:10:1*

AMBASSADORS, or other public ministers and consuls. The president may appoint. *Article 2:2:2*

• The judicial power of the United States shall extend to all cases affecting. *Article 3:2:1*

AMENDMENTS to the Constitution. Whenever two-thirds of both houses shall deem it necessary, Congress shall propose. *Article 5*

• On application of the legislatures of two-thirds of the states, Congress shall call a convention to propose. *Article 5*

- Shall be valid when ratified by the legislatures of, or by conventions in, three-fourths of the states. *Article 5*

ANSWER for a capital or infamous crime unless on presentment of a grand jury. No person shall be held to. *Amendment 5*

- Except in cases in the land or naval forces, or in the militia when in actual service. *Amendment 5*

APPELLATE JURISDICTION both as to law and fact, with such exceptions and under such regulations as Congress shall make. In what cases the Supreme Court shall have. *Article 3:2:2*

APPLICATION of the legislature or the executive of a state. The United States shall protect each state against invasion and domestic violence on the. *Article 4:4*

APPLICATION of the legislatures of two-thirds of the states, Congress shall call a convention for proposing amendments to the Constitution. On the. *Article 5*

APPOINTMENT. Of officers and authority to train the militia reserved to the states respectively. *Article 1:8:16*

- Of such inferior officers as they may think proper in the president alone. Congress may by law vest the. *Article 2:2:2*
- In the courts of law or in the heads of departments. Congress may by law vest the. *Article 2:2:2*
- Of presidential and vice-presidential electors. District of Columbia to have power of. *Amendment 23:1*

APPORTIONMENT of representation and direct taxation among the several states. Provisions relating to the. *Article 1:2:3*

- Congress shall have power to lay and collect taxes on incomes, from whatever source derived, without apportionment among the several states. *Amendment 16*
- Of representatives among the several states. Provisions relating to the. *Amendment 14*

APPROPRIATE LEGISLATION. Congress shall have power to make all laws necessary and proper for carrying into execution the foregoing powers, and all other powers vested by the Constitution in the Government of the United States, or in any department or officer thereof. *Article 1:8:18*

- Congress shall have power to enforce the thirteenth article, prohibiting slavery by. *Amendment 13:2*
- Congress shall have power to enforce the provisions of the fourteenth article by. *Amendment 14:5*
- Congress shall have power to enforce the provisions of the fifteenth article by. *Amendment 15:2*

- Congress and the several states shall have concurrent power to enforce the provisions of the eighteenth article. *Amendment 18:2*
- Congress shall have power to enforce the provisions of the nineteenth article. *Amendment 19*
- Congress shall have power to enforce the provisions of the twenty-third article by. *Amendment 23:2*
- Congress shall have power to enforce the provisions of the twenty-fourth article by. *Amendment 24:2*
- Congress shall have power to enforce the provisions of the twenty-sixth article by. *Amendment 26:2*

APPROPRIATION of money for raising and supporting armies shall be for a longer term than two years. But no. *Article 1:8:12*

APPROPRIATIONS made by law. No money shall be drawn from the Treasury but in consequence of. *Article 1:9:7*

APPROVE and sign a bill before it shall become a law. The president shall. *Article 1:7:2*

- He shall return it to the house in which it originated with his objections, if he does not. *Article 1:7:2*

ARMIES. Congress shall make rules for the government and regulation of the land and naval forces. *Article 1:8:14*

ARMIES, but no appropriation for that use shall be for a longer term than two years. Congress shall have power to raise and support. *Article 1:8:12*

ARMS shall not be infringed. A well-regulated militia, being necessary to the security of a free state, the right of the people to keep and bear. *Amendment 2*

ARREST during their attendance at the session of their respective houses, and in going to and returning from the same. Members shall in all cases, except treason, felony, and breach of the peace, be privileged from. *Article 1:6:1*

ARSENALS. Congress shall exercise exclusive authority over all places purchased for the erection of. *Article 1:8:17*

ARTICLES exported from any state. No tax or duty shall be laid on. *Article 1:9:5*

ARTS by securing to authors and inventors their patent rights. Congress may promote the progress of science and useful. *Article 1:8:8*

ASSISTANCE OF COUNSEL for his defense. In all criminal prosecutions the accused shall have the. *Amendment 6*

ASSUMPTION OF THE DEBT or obligations incurred in aid of rebellion or insurrection against the United States. Provisions against the. *Amendment 14:4*

- No person shall be a representative who shall not have attained the age of twenty-five years, and been seven years a. *Article 1:2:2*
- Right of citizens to vote shall not be denied or abridged by the United States or any state on account of sex. *Amendment 19*
- Right to vote shall not be denied or abridged by the United States or any state for failure to pay any poll tax or other tax. *Amendment 24:1*
- Right to vote shall not be denied or abridged by the United States or any state to any citizen eighteen years or older, on account of age. *Amendment 26:1*

CITIZENS OR SUBJECTS of a foreign state. The judicial power of the United States shall not extend to suits in law or equity brought against one of the states by the citizens or another state or by. *Amendment 11*

CITIZENSHIP. Citizens of each state shall be entitled to all the privileges and immunities of citizens of the several states. *Article 4:2:1*
- All persons born or naturalized in the United States, and subject to the jurisdiction thereof, are citizens of the United States and of the state in which they reside. *Amendment 14:1*
- No state shall make or enforce any law which shall abridge the privileges or immunities of citizens of the United States. *Amendment 14:1*
- Nor shall any state deprive any person of life, liberty, or property without due process of law. *Amendment 14:1*
- Nor deny to any person within its jurisdiction the equal protection of the laws. *Amendment 14:1*

CIVIL OFFICERS of the United States shall, on impeachment for and conviction of treason, bribery, and other high crimes and misdemeanors be removed. All. *Article 2:4*

CLAIMS of the United States or any particular state in the territory or public property. Nothing in this Constitution shall be construed to prejudice. *Article 4:3:2*

CLASSIFICATION OF SENATORS. Immediately after they shall be assembled after the first election, they shall be divided as equally as may be into three classes. *Article 1:3:2*
- The seats of the senators of the first class shall be vacated at the expiration of the second year. *Article 1:3:2*
- The seats of the senators of the second class at the expiration of the fourth year. *Article 1:3:2*
- The seats of the senators of the third class at the expiration of the sixth year. *Article 1:3:2*

COIN a tender in payment of debts. No state shall make anything but gold and silver. *Article 1:10:1*

COIN MONEY and regulate the value thereof and of foreign coin. Congress shall have power to. *Article 1:8:5*

COIN OF THE UNITED STATES. Congress shall provide for punishing the counterfeiting the securities and current. *Article 1:8:6*

COLOR, or previous condition of servitude. The right of citizens of the United States to vote shall not be denied or abridged by the United States or any state on account of race. *Amendment 15:1*

COMFORT. Treason against the United States shall consist in levying war against them, and giving the enemies aid and. *Article 3:3:1*

COMMANDER IN CHIEF of the army and navy, and of their militia when in actual service. The president shall be. *Article 2:2:1*

COMMERCE OR REVENUE. No preference shall be given to the ports of one state over those of another by any regulation of. *Article 1:9:6*

COMMERCE with foreign nations, among the states, and with Indian tribes. Congress shall have power to regulate. *Article 1:8:3*
- Vessels clearing from the ports of one state shall not pay duties in those of another. *Article 1:9:6*

COMMISSIONS to expire at the end of the next session. The president may fill vacancies that happen in the recess of the Senate by granting. *Article 2:2:3*

COMMON DEFENSE AND GENERAL WELFARE. Congress shall have power to provide for the. *Article 1:8:1*

COMMON DEFENSE, promote the general welfare, etc. To insure the. *Preamble*

COMMON LAW, where the amount involved exceeds twenty dollars, shall be tried by jury. Suits at. *Amendment 7*
- No fact tried by a jury shall be otherwise reexamined in any court of the United States than according to the rules of the. *Amendment 7*

COMPACT WITH A FOREIGN POWER. No state shall, without the consent of Congress, enter into any agreement or. *Article 1:10:3*

COMPACT WITH ANOTHER STATE. No state shall, without consent of Congress, enter into any agreement or. *Article 1:10:3*

COMPENSATION. Private property shall not be taken for public use without just. *Amendment 5*

COMPENSATION OF SENATORS AND REPRESENTATIVES to be ascertained by law. *Article 1:6:1*

COMPENSATION OF THE JUDGES of the Supreme and inferior courts shall not be diminished during their continuance in office. *Article 3:1*

COMPENSATION OF THE PRESIDENT shall not be increased nor diminished during the period for which he shall be elected. *Article 2:1:7*

COMPULSORY PROCESS for obtaining witnesses in his favor. In criminal prosecutions the accused shall have. *Amendment 6*

CONFEDERATION. No state shall enter into any treaty, alliance, or. *Article 1:10:1*

- All debts contracted and engagements entered into before the adoption of this Constitution shall be valid against the United States under it, as under the. *Article 6:–:1*

CONFESSION in open court. Conviction of treason shall be on the testimony of two persons to the overt act, or upon. *Article 3:3:1*

CONGRESS of the United States. All legislative powers shall be vested in a. *Article 1:1*

- Shall consist of a Senate and House of Representatives. *Article 1:1*
- Shall assemble at least once in every year, which shall be on the first Monday of December, unless they by law appoint a different day. *Article 1:4:2*
- May at any time alter regulations for elections of senators and representatives, except as to the places of choosing senators. *Article 1:4:1*
- Each house shall be the judge of the elections, returns, and qualifications of its own members. *Article 1:5:1*
- A majority of each house shall constitute a quorum to do business. *Article 1:5:1*
- A smaller number may adjourn from day to day and compel the attendance of absent members. *Article 1:5:1*
- Each house may determine the rules of its proceedings, punish its members for disorderly behavior, and, with the concurrence of two-thirds, expel a member. *Article 1:5:2*
- Each house shall keep a journal of its proceedings. *Article 1:5:3*
- Neither house, during the session of Congress, shall, without the consent of the other, adjourn for more than three days. *Article 1:5:4*
- Senators and representatives shall receive a compensation to be ascertained by law. *Article 1:6:1*
- They shall in all cases, except treason, felony, and breach of peace, be privileged from arrest during attendance at their respective houses, and in going to and returning from the same. *Article 1:6:1*
- No senator or representative shall, during his term, be appointed to any civil office which shall have been created, or of which the emoluments

shall have been increased, during such term. *Article 1:6:2*

- No person holding any office under the United States, shall, while in office, be a member of either house of Congress. *Article 1:6:2*
- All bills for raising revenue shall originate in the House of Representatives. *Article 1:7:1*
- Proceedings in cases of bills returned by the president with his objections. *Article 1:7:2*
- Shall have power to lay and collect duties, imposts, and excises, pay the debts, and provide for the common defense and general welfare. *Article 1:8:1*
- Shall have power to borrow money on the credit of the United States. *Article 1:8:2*
- To regulate foreign and domestic commerce, and with the Indian tribes. *Article 1:8:3*
- To establish uniform rule of naturalization and uniform laws on the subject of bankruptcies. *Article 1:8:4*
- To coin money, regulate its value and the value of foreign coin, and to fix the standard of weights and measures. *Article 1:8:5*
- To punish counterfeiting of securities and current coin of the United States. *Article 1:8:6*
- To establish post-offices and post-roads. *Article 1:8:7*
- To promote the progress of science and useful arts. *Article 1:8:8*
- To consitute tribunals inferior to the Supreme Court. *Article 1:8:9*
- To define and punish piracies and felonies on the high seas and to punish offenses against the law of nations. *Article 1:8:10*
- To declare war, grant letters of marque and reprisal, and make rules concerning captures on land and water. *Article 1:8:11*
- To raise and support armies, but no appropriation of money to that use shall be for a longer term than two years. *Article 1:8:12*
- To provide and maintain a Navy. *Article 1:8:13*
- To make rules for the government of the Army and Navy. *Article 1:8:14*
- To call out the militia to execute the laws, suppress insurrections, and repel invasions. *Article 1:8:15*
- To provide for organizing, arming, and equipping the militia. *Article 1:8:16*
- To exercise exclusive legislation over the District fixed for the seat of government, and over forts, magazines, arsenals, and dockyards. *Article 1:8:17*
- To make all laws necessary and proper to carry into execution all powers vested by the Constitu-

tion in the Government of the United States. *Article 1:8:18*

- No person holding any office under the United States shall accept of any present, emolument, office, or title of any kind from any foreign state, without the consent of. *Article 1:9:8*
- May determine the time of choosing the electors for president and vice president and the day on which they shall give their votes. *Article 2:1:4*
- The president may, on extraordinary occasions, convene either house of. *Article 2:3*
- The manner in which the acts, records, and judicial proceedings of the states shall be prescribed by. *Article 4:1*
- New states may be admitted by Congress into this Union. *Article 4:3:1*
- Shall have power to make all needful rules and regulations respecting the territory or other property belonging to the United States. *Article 4:3:2*
- Amendments to the Constitution shall be proposed whenever it shall be deemed necessary by two-thirds of both houses of. *Article 5*
- Shall have power to enforce, by appropriate legislation, the thirteenth amendment. *Amendment 13:2*
- Persons engaged in insurrection or rebellion against the United States disqualified for senators or representatives in. *Amendment 14:3*
- But such disqualification may be removed by a vote of two-thirds of both houses of. *Amendment 14:3*
- Shall have power to enforce, by appropriate legislation, the fourteenth amendment. *Amendment 14:5*
- Shall have power to enforce, by appropriate legislation, the fifteenth amendment. *Amendment 15:2*
- Shall have power to enforce, by appropriate legislation, the nineteenth amendment. *Amendment 19*
- Sessions, time of assembling. *Amendment 20:2*
- To direct appointment of electors for president and vice president by District of Columbia. *Amendment 23:1*
- Shall have power to enforce, by appropriate legislation, the twenty-third amendment. *Amendment 23:2*
- Shall have power to enforce, by appropriate legislation, the twenty-fourth amendment. *Amendment 24:2*
- Confirmation by majority vote of vice president nominated by the president where vacancy in office occurs. *Amendment 25:2*
- Shall decide the issue of the inability of the president to discharge the powers and duties of his office. *Amendment 25:4*
- Shall have power to enforce, by appropriate legislation, the twenty-sixth amendment. *Amendment 26:2*

- No law, varying the compensation for the services of the senators and representatives, shall take effect, until an election of representatives shall have intervened. *Amendment 27*

CONSENT. No state shall be deprived of its equal suffrage in the Senate without its. *Article 5*

CONSENT OF CONGRESS. No person holding any office of profit or trust under the United States shall accept of any present, emolument, office, or title of any kind whatever, from any king, prince, or foreign potentate, without the. *Article 1:9:8*
- No state shall lay any imposts, or duties on imports, except what may be absolutely necessary for executing its inspection laws, without the. *Article 1:10:2*
- No state shall lay any duty of tonnage, keep troops or ships of war in time of peace, without the. *Article 1:10:3*
- No state shall enter into any agreement or compact with another state, or with a foreign power, without the. *Article 1:10:3*
- No state shall engage in war unless actually invaded, or in such imminent danger as will not admit of delay, without the. *Article 1:10:3*
- No new state shall be formed or erected within the jurisdiction of any other state, nor any state be formed by the junction of two or more states, or parts of states, without the consent of the legislatures thereof, as well as the. *Article 4:3:1*

CONSENT OF THE LEGISLATURE OF THE STATE in which the same may be. Congress shall exercise exclusive authority over all places purchased for the erection of forts, magazines, arsenals, dockyards, and other needful buildings by the. *Article 1:8:17*

CONSENT OF THE LEGISLATURES OF THE STATES and of Congress. No states shall be formed by the junction of two or more states or parts of states without the. *Article 4:3:1*

CONSENT OF THE OTHER. Neither house, during the session of Congress, shall adjourn for more than three days, nor to any other place than that in which they shall be sitting, without the. *Article 1:5:4*

CONSENT OF THE OWNER. No soldier shall be quartered in time of peace in any house without the. *Amendment 3*

CONSENT OF THE SENATE. The president shall have power to make treaties, by and with the advice and. *Article 2:2:2*
- The president shall appoint ambassadors, other public ministers and consuls, judges of the Supreme Court, and all other officers created by

law and not otherwise herein provided for, by and with the advice and. *Article 2:2:2*

CONSTITUTION. All officers, legislative, executive, and judicial, of the United States, and of the several states, shall be bound by an oath to support the. *Article 6:–:3*

• But no religious test shall ever be required as a qualification for any office or public trust. *Article 6:–:3*

CONSTITUTION. Done in convention by the unanimous consent of the states present, September 17, 1787. *Article 7:–:2*

CONSTITUTION. The manner in which amendments may be proposed and ratified. *Article 5*

CONSTITUTION. The president, before he enters upon the execution of his office, shall take an oath to preserve, protect, and defend the. *Article 2:1:8*

CONSTITUTION and the laws made in pursuance thereof, and all treaties made, or which shall be made, by the United States, shall be the supreme law of the land. The. *Article 6:–:2*

• The judges in every state, anything in the constitution or laws of a state to the contrary notwithstanding, shall be bound thereby. *Article 6:–:2*

CONSTITUTION, and then engaged in rebellion against the United States. Disqualification for office imposed upon certain class of persons who took an oath to support the. *Amendment 14:3*

CONSTITUTION as under the Confederation shall be valid. All debts and engagements contracted before the adoption of the. *Article 6:–:1*

CONSTITUTION between the states so ratifying the same. The ratification of the conventions of nine states shall be sufficient for the establishment of the. *Article 7*

CONSTITUTION, in the Government of the United States, or in any department or officer thereof. Congress shall have power to pass all laws necessary and proper to the execution of the powers vested by the. *Article 1:8:18*

CONSTITUTION, laws, and treaties of the United States. The judicial power shall extend to all cases arising under the. *Article 3:2:1*

CONSTITUTION, nor prohibited by it to the states, are reserved to the states respectively or to the people. Powers not delegated to the United States by the. *Amendment 10*

CONSTITUTION, of certain rights, shall not be construed to deny or disparage others retained by the people. The enumeration in the. *Amendment 9*

CONSTITUTION, shall be eligible to the office of president. No person except a natural-born citizen, or a citizen at the time of the adoption of the. *Article 2:1:5*

CONSTITUTION shall be so construed as to prejudice any claims of the United States, or of any state (in respect to territory or other property of the United States). Nothing in the. *Article 4:3:2*

CONTRACTS. No state shall pass any ex post facto law, or law impairing the obligation of. *Article 1:10:1*

CONTROVERSIES to which the United States shall be a party: between two or more states; between a state and citizens of another state; between citizens of different states; between citizens of the same state claiming lands under grants of different states; between a state or its citizens and foreign states, citizens, or subjects. The judicial power shall extend to. *Article 3:2:1*

CONVENE CONGRESS or either house, on extraordinary occasions. The president may. *Article 2:3*

CONVENTION, by the unanimous consent of the states present on the 17th of September, 1787. Adoption of the Constitution in. *Article 7:–:2*

CONVENTION for proposing amendments to the Constitution. Congress, on the application of two-thirds of the legislatures of the states, may call a. *Article 5*

CONVENTIONS of nine states shall be sufficient for the establishment of the Constitution. The ratification of the. *Article 7*

CONVICTION in cases of impeachment shall not be had without the concurrence of two-thirds of the members present. *Article 1:3:6*

COPYRIGHTS to authors for limited times. Congress shall have power to provide for. *Article 1:8:8*

CORRUPTION OF BLOOD. Attainder of treason shall not work. *Article 3:3:2*

COUNSEL for his defense. In all criminal prosecutions the accused shall have the assistance of. *Amendment 6*

COUNTERFEITING the securities and current coin of the United States. Congress shall provide for the punishment of. *Article 1:8:6*

COURTS. Congress shall have power to constitute tribunals inferior to the Supreme Court. *Article 1:8:9*

COURTS. The judges of the Supreme and inferior courts shall hold their offices during good behavior. *Article 3:1*

• Their compensation shall not be diminished during their continuance in office. *Article 3:1*

COURTS as Congress may establish. The judicial power of the United States shall be vested in one Supreme Court and such inferior. *Article 3:1*

COURTS OF LAW. Congress may by law vest the appointment of such inferior officers as they think proper in the president alone, in the heads of departments, or in the. *Article 2:2:2*

CREDIT. No state shall emit bills of. *Article 1:10:1*

CREDIT of the United States. Congress shall have power to borrow money on the. *Article 1:8:2*

CREDIT shall be given in every other state to the public acts, records, and judicial proceedings of each state. Full faith and. *Article 4:1*

CRIME, unless on a presentment of a grand jury. No person shall be held to answer for a capital or otherwise infamous. *Amendment 5*

• Except in cases in the military and naval forces, or in the militia when in actual service. *Amendment 5*

CRIMES AND MISDEMEANORS. The president, vice president, and all civil officers shall be removed on impeachment for and conviction of treason, bribery, or other. *Article 2:4*

CRIMES, except in cases of impeachment, shall be tried by jury. All. *Article 3:2:3*

• They shall be tried in the state within which they may be committed. *Article 3:2:3*

• When not committed in a state, they shall be tried at the places which Congress may by law have provided. *Article 3:2:3*

CRIMINAL PROSECUTIONS, the accused shall have a speedy and public trial by jury in the state and district where the crime was committed. In all. *Amendment 6*

• He shall be informed of the nature and cause of the accusation. *Amendment 6*

• He shall be confronted with the witnesses against him. *Amendment 6*

• He shall have compulsory process for obtaining witnesses in his favor. *Amendment 6*

• He shall have the assistance of counsel in his defense. *Amendment 6*

CRUEL AND UNUSUAL PUNISHMENTS inflicted. Excessive bail shall not be required, nor excessive fines imposed, nor. *Amendment 8*

D

DANGER as will not admit of delay. No state shall, without the consent of Congress, engage in war, unless actually invaded, or in such imminent. *Article 1:10:3*

DAY on which they shall vote for president and vice president, which shall be the same throughout the United States. Congress may determine the time of choosing the electors, and the. *Article 2:1:4*

DAY TO DAY, and may be authorized to compel the attendance of absent members. A smaller number than a quorum of each house may adjourn from. *Article 1:5:1*

DEATH, RESIGNATION, OR INABILITY of the president. In case of, powers and duties of his office shall devolve on the vice president. *Article 2:1:6 and Amendment 25*

• Congress may provide by law for the case of the removal. *Article 2:1:6 and Amendment 25*

DEBT of the United States, including debts for pensions and bounties incurred in suppressing insurrection or rebellion, shall not be questioned. The validity of the public. *Amendment 14:4*

DEBTS. No state shall make anything but gold and silver coin a tender in payment of. *Article 1:10:1*

DEBTS and engagements contracted before the adoption of this Constitution shall be as valid against the United States, under it, as under the Confederation. *Article 6:—:1*

DEBTS and provide for the common defense and general welfare of the United States. Congress shall have power to pay the. *Article 1:8:1*

DEBTS or obligations incurred in aid of insurrection or rebellion against the United States, or claims for the loss or emancipation of any slave. Neither the United States nor any state shall assume or pay any. *Amendment 14:4*

DECLARE WAR, grant letters of marque and reprisal, and make rules concerning captures on land and water. Congress shall have power to. *Article 1:8:11*

DEFENSE. In all criminal prosecutions the accused shall have the assistance of counsel for his. *Amendment 6*

DEFENSE and general welfare throughout the United States. Congress shall have power to pay the debts and provide for the common. *Article 1:8:1*

DEFENSE, promote the general welfare, etc. To insure the common. *Preamble*

DELAWARE entitled to one representative in the first Congress. *Article 1:2:3*

DELAY. No state shall, without the consent of Congress, engage in war unless actually invaded, or in such imminent danger as will not admit of. *Article 1:10:3*

DELEGATED to the United States, nor prohibited to the states, are reserved to the states or to the people. The powers not. *Amendment 10*

DENY OR DISPARAGE others retained by the people. The enumeration in the Constitution of certain rights shall not be construed to. *Amendment 9*

DEPARTMENTS. Congress may by law vest the appointment of inferior officers in the heads of. *Article 2:2:2*

DEPARTMENTS upon any subject relating to their duties. The president may require the written opinion of the principal officers in each of the executive. *Article 2:2:1*

DIRECT TAX shall be laid unless in proportion to the census or enumeration. No capitation or other. *Article 1:9:4*

DIRECT TAXES and representatives, how apportioned among the several states. *Article 1:2:3*

DISABILITY. No person shall be a senator or representative in Congress, or presidential elector, or hold any office, civil or military, under the United States, or any state, who having previously taken an oath as a legislative, executive, or judicial officer of the United States, or of any state, to support the Constitution, afterward engaged in insurrection or rebellion against the United States. *Amendment 14:3*

• But Congress may, by a vote of two-thirds of each house, remove such. *Amendment 14:3*

DISABILITY of the president and vice president. Provisions in case of the. *Article 2:1:6 and Amendment 25*

DISAGREEMENT between the two houses as to the time of adjournment, the president may adjourn them to such time as he may think proper. In case of. *Article 2:3*

DISORDERLY BEHAVIOR. Each house may punish its members for. *Article 1:5:2*

• And with the concurrence of two-thirds expel a member. *Article 1:5:2*

DISPARAGE others retained by the people. The enumeration in the Constitution of certain rights shall not be construed to deny or. *Amendment 9*

DISQUALIFICATION. No senator or representative shall, during the time for which he was elected, be appointed to any office under the United States which shall have been created or its emoluments increased during such term. *Article 1:6:2*

• No person holding any office under the United States shall be a member of either house during his continuance in office. *Article 1:6:2*

• No person shall be a member of either house, presidential elector, or hold any office under the United States, or any state, who, having previously sworn to support the Constitution, afterward engaged in insurrection or rebellion. *Amendment 14:3*

• But Congress may, by a vote of two-thirds of each house, remove such disability. *Amendment 14:3*

DISTRICT OF COLUMBIA. Congress shall exercise exclusive legislation in all cases over the. *Article 1:8:17*

• Electors for president and vice president, appointment in such manner as the Congress may direct. *Amendment 23:1*

DOCKYARDS. Congress shall have exclusive authority over all places purchased for the erection of. *Article 1:8:17*

DOMESTIC TRANQUILITY, provide for the common defense, etc. To insure. *Preamble*

DOMESTIC VIOLENCE. THE United States shall protect each state against invasion and. *Article 4:4*

DUE PROCESS OF LAW. No person shall be compelled, in any criminal case, to be a witness against himself, nor be deprived of life, liberty, or property without. *Amendment 5*

• No state shall deprive any person of life, liberty, or property without. *Amendment 14:1*

DUTIES AND POWERS of the office of president, in case of his death, removal, or inability to act, shall devolve on the vice president. *Article 2:1:6 and Amendment 25*

• In case of the disability of the president and vice president, Congress shall declare what officer shall act. *Article 2:1:6 and Amendment 25*

DUTIES, imposts, and excises. Congress shall have power to lay and collect taxes. *Article 1:8:1*

• Shall be uniform throughout the United States. *Article 1:8:1*

DUTIES in another state. Vessels clearing in the ports of one state shall not be obliged to pay. *Article 1:9:6*

• On imports and exports, without the consent of Congress, except where necessary for executing its inspection laws. No state shall lay any. *Article 1:10:2*

• The net produce of all such duties shall be for the use of the Treasury of the United States. *Article 1:10:2*

• All laws laying such duties shall be subject to the revision and control of Congress. *Article 1:10:2*

DUTIES shall be laid on articles exported from any state. No tax or. *Article 1:9:5*

DUTY OF TONNAGE without the consent of Congress. No state shall lay any. *Article 1:10:3*

E

EIGHTEENTH AMENDMENT. Repealed. *Amendment 21:1*

ELECTION of president and vice president. Congress may determine the day for the. *Article 2:1:4*

• Shall be the same throughout the United States. The day of the. *Article 2:1:4*

ELECTIONS. The right of citizens of the United States to vote in shall not be denied or abridged by the United States or any state by reason of failure to pay any poll tax or other tax. *Amendment 24:1*

ELECTIONS FOR SENATORS AND REPRESENTATIVES. The legislatures of the states shall prescribe the times, places, and manner of holding. *Article 1:4:1*

• But Congress may, at any time, alter such regulations, except as to the places of choosing senators. *Article 1:4:1*

• Returns and qualifications of its own members. Each house shall be the judge of the. *Article 1:5:1*

• Senators elected by the people. *Amendment 17:1*

ELECTORS FOR MEMBERS of the House of Representatives. Qualifications of. *Article 1:2:1*

ELECTORS FOR PRESIDENT AND VICE PRESIDENT. Each state shall appoint, in such manner as the legislature thereof may direct, a number of electors equal to the whole number of senators and representatives to which the state may be entitled in the Congress. *Article 2:1:2*

• But no senator or representative, or person holding an office of trust or profit under the United States, shall be appointed an elector. *Article 2:1:2*

• Congress may determine the time of choosing the electors and the day on which they shall give their votes, which day shall be the same throughout the United States. *Article 2:1:4*

• The electors shall meet in their respective states and vote by ballot for president and vice president, one of whom, at least, shall not be an inhabitant of the same state with themselves. *Amendment 12*

• The District of Columbia shall appoint, in such manner the Congress may direct, a number of electors equal to the whole number of senators and representatives to which the District would be entitled if a state. *Amendment 23:1*

ELECTORS FOR SENATORS. Qualifications of. *Amendment 17:1*

ELECTORS shall name, in their ballots, the person voted for as president; and in distinct ballots the person voted for as vice president. *Amendment 12*

• They shall make distinct lists of the persons voted for as president and of persons voted for as vice president, which they shall sign and certify, and transmit sealed to the seat of government, directed to the president of the Senate. *Amendment 12*

• No person having taken an oath as a legislative, executive or judicial officer of the United States, or of any state, and afterwards engaged in insurrection or rebellion against the United States, shall be an elector. *Amendment 14:3*

• But Congress may, by a vote of two-thirds of each house, remove such disability. *Amendment 14:3*

EMANCIPATION of any slave shall be held to be illegal and void. Claims for the loss or. *Amendment 14:4*

EMIT BILLS OF CREDIT. No state shall. *Article 1:10:1*

EMOLUMENT of any kind from any king, prince, or foreign state, without the consent of Congress. No person holding any office under the United States shall accept any. *Article 1:9:8*

ENEMIES. Treason shall consist in levying war against the United States, in adhering to, or giving aid and comfort to their. *Article 3:3:1*

ENGAGEMENTS contracted before the adoption of this Constitution shall be valid. All debts and. *Article 6:–:1*

ENUMERATION in the Constitution of certain rights shall not be construed to deny or disparage others retained by the people. The. *Amendment 9*

ENUMERATION of the inhabitants shall be made within three years after the first meeting of Congress, and within every subsequent term of ten years thereafter. *Article 1:2:3*

• Ratio of representation not to exceed one of every 30,000 until the first enumeration shall be made. *Article 1:2:3*

• Income tax authorized without regard to. *Amendment 16*

EQUAL PROTECTION of the laws. No state shall deny to any person within its jurisdiction the. *Amendment 14:1*

EQUAL SUFFRAGE in the Senate. No state shall be deprived without its consent, of its. *Article 5*

ESTABLISHMENT of this Constitution between the states ratifying the same. The ratification of nine states shall be sufficient for the. *Article 7*

EXCESSIVE BAIL shall not be required, nor excessive fines imposed, nor cruel and unusual punishments inflicted. *Amendment 8*

EXCISES. Congress shall have power to lay and collect taxes, duties, imposts, and. *Article 1:8:1*

• Shall be uniform throughout the United States. All duties, imposts, and. *Article 1:8:1*

EXCLUSIVE LEGISLATION, in all cases, over such district as may become the seat of government. Congress shall exercise. *Article 1:8:17*

• Over all places purchased for the erection of forts, magazines, arsenals, dock-yards and other needful buildings. Congress shall exercise. *Article 1:8:17*

EXECUTIVE OF A STATE. THE United States shall protect each state against invasion and domestic violence, on the application of the legislature or the. *Article 4:4*

EXECUTIVE AND JUDICIAL OFFICERS of the United States and of the several states shall be bound by an oath to support the Constitution. *Article 6:–:3*

EXECUTIVE DEPARTMENTS. On subjects relating to their duties the president may require the written opinions of the principal officers in each of the. *Article 2:2:1*

• Congress may by law vest the appointment of inferior officers in the heads of. *Article 2:2:2*

EXECUTIVE POWER shall be vested in a president of the United States of America. The. *Article 2:1:1*

EXPEL A MEMBER. Each house, with the concurrence of two-thirds, may. *Article 1:5:2*

EXPENDITURES of public money shall be published from time to time. A regular statement of the receipts and. *Article 1:9:7*

EXPORTATIONS from any state. No tax or duty shall be laid on. *Article 1:9:5*

EXPORTS OR IMPORTS, except upon certain conditions. No state shall, without the consent of Congress, lay any duties on. *Article 1:10:2*

• Laid by any state, shall be for the use of the Treasury. The net produce of all duties on. *Article 1:10:2*

• Shall be subject to the revision and control of Congress. All laws of the states laying duties on. *Article 1:10:2*

EX POST FACTO LAW, or law impairing the obligation of contracts. No state shall pass any bill of attainder. *Article 1:10:1*

EX POST FACTO LAW shall be passed. No bill of attainder or. *Article 1:9:3*

EXTRAORDINARY OCCASIONS. The president may convene both houses, or either house of Congress, on. *Article 2:3*

F

FAITH and credit in each state shall be given to the acts, records, and judicial proceedings of another state. Full. *Article 4:1*

FELONIES committed on the high seas. Congress shall have power to define and punish piracies and. *Article 1:8:10*

FELONY, and breach of the peace. Members of Congress shall not be privileged from arrest for treason. *Article 1:6:1*

FINES. Excessive fines shall not be imposed. *Amendment 8*

FOREIGN COIN. Congress shall have power to coin money, fix the standard of weights and measures, and to regulate the value of. *Article 1:8:5*

FOREIGN NATIONS, among the states, and with the Indian tribes. Congress shall have power to regulate commerce with. *Article 1:8:3*

FOREIGN POWER. No state shall, without the consent of Congress, enter into any compact or agreement with any. *Article 1:10:3*

FORFEITURE, except during the life of the person attainted. Attainder of treason shall not work. *Article 3:3:2*

FORMATION of new states. Provisions relating to the. *Article 4:3:1*

FORM OF GOVERNMENT. The United States shall guarantee to every state in this Union a republican. *Article 4:4*

• And shall protect each of them against invasion; and on application of the legislature or of the executive (when the legislature cannot be convened), against domestic violence. *Article 4:4*

FORTS, magazines, arsenals, dock-yards, and other needful buildings. Congress shall exercise exclusive authority over all places purchased for the erection of. *Article 1:8:17*

FREEDOM OF SPEECH OR THE PRESS. Congress shall make no law abridging the. *Amendment 1*

FREE STATE, the right of the people to keep and bear arms shall not be infringed. A well-regulated militia being necessary to the security of a. *Amendment 2*

FUGITIVES from crime found in another state shall, on demand, be delivered up to the authorities of the state from which they may flee. *Article 4:2:2*

FUGITIVES from service or labor in one state, escaping into another state, shall be delivered up to the party to whom such service or labor may be due. *Article 4:2:3*

G

GENERAL WELFARE. Congress shall have power to provide for the common defense and. *Article 1:8:1*

GENERAL WELFARE and secure the blessings of liberty, etc. To promote the. *Preamble*

GEORGIA shall be entitled to three representatives in the first Congress. *Article 1:2:3*

GOLD AND SILVER coin a tender in payment of debts. No state shall make anything but. *Article 1:10:1*

GOOD BEHAVIOR. THE judges of the Supreme and inferior courts shall hold their offices during. *Article 3:1*

GOVERNMENT. The United States shall guarantee to every state in this Union a republican form of. *Article 4:4*

• And shall protect each of them against invasion, and on application of the legislature or of the executive (when the legislature cannot be convened) against domestic violence. *Article 4:4*

GRAND JURY. No person shall be held to answer for a capital or otherwise infamous crime, unless on the presentment of a. *Amendment 5*
- Except in cases arising in the land and naval forces, and in the militia when in actual service. *Amendment 5*

GUARANTEE to every state in this Union a republican form of government. The United States shall. *Article 4:4*
- And shall protect each of them against invasion; and on application of the legislature or of the executive (when the legislature cannot be convened), against domestic violence. *Article 4:4*

H

HABEAS CORPUS shall not be suspended unless in cases of rebellion or invasion. The writ of. *Article 1:9:2*

HEADS OF DEPARTMENTS. Congress may, by law, vest the appointment of inferior officers in the. *Article 2:2:2*
- On any subject relating to their duties, the president may require the written opinion of the principal officers in each of the executive departments. *Article 2:2:1*

HIGH CRIMES AND MISDEMEANORS. The president, vice president, and all civil officers shall be removed on impeachment for and conviction of treason, bribery, or other. *Article 2:4*

HOUSE OF REPRESENTATIVES. Congress shall consist of a Senate and. *Article 1:1*
- Shall be composed of members chosen every second year. *Article 1:2:1*
- Qualifications of electors for members of the. *Article 1:2:1*
- No person shall be a member who shall not have attained the age of twenty-five years, and been seven years a citizen of the United States. *Article 1:2:2*
- The executives of the several states shall issue writs of election to fill vacancies in the. *Article 1:2:4*
- Shall choose their Speaker and other officers. *Article 1:2:5*
- Shall have the sole power of impeachment. *Article 1:2:5*
- Shall be the judge of the elections, returns, and qualifications of its own members. *Article 1:5:1*
- A majority shall constitute a quorum to do business. *Article 1:5:1*
- Less than a majority may adjourn from day to day, and compel the attendance of absent members. *Article 1:5:1*

- May determine its own rules of proceedings. *Article 1:5:2*
- May punish its members for disorderly behavior, and, with the concurrence of two-thirds, expel a member. *Article 1:5:2*
- Shall keep a journal of its proceedings. *Article 1:5:3*
- Shall not adjourn for more than three days during the session of Congress without the consent of the Senate. *Article 1:5:4*
- Members shall not be questioned for any speech or debate in either house or in any other place. *Article 1:6:1*
- No person holding any office under the United States shall, while holding such office, be a member of the. *Article 1:6:2*
- No person, while a member of either house, shall be appointed to an office which shall have been created or the emoluments increased during his membership. *Article 1:6:2*
- All bills for raising revenue shall originate in the. *Article 1:7:1*
- The votes for president and vice president shall be counted in the presence of the Senate and. *Amendment 12*
- If no person have a majority of electoral votes, then from the three highest on the list the House of Representatives shall immediately, by ballot, choose a president. *Amendment 12*
- They shall vote by states, each state counting one vote. *Amendment 12*
- A quorum shall consist of a member or members from two-thirds of the states, and a majority of all the states shall be necessary to the choice of a president. *Amendment 12*
- No person having as a legislative, executive, or judicial officer of the United States, or of any state, taken an oath to support the Constitution, and afterwards engaged in insurrection or rebellion against the United States, shall be a member of the. *Amendment 14:3*
- But Congress may, by a vote of two-thirds of each house, remove such disability. *Amendment 14:3*

I

IMMINENT DANGER as will not admit of delay. No state shall, without the consent of Congress, engage in war, unless actually invaded or in such. *Article 1:10:3*

IMMUNITIES. Members of Congress shall, in all cases except treason, felony, and breach of the peace, be privileged from arrest during their attendance at the session of their respective houses, and in going and returning from the same. *Article 1:6:1*

- No soldier shall be quartered in any house without the consent of the owner in time of peace. *Amendment 3*
- No person shall be twice put in jeopardy of life and limb for the same offense. *Amendment 5*
- All persons born or naturalized in the United States, and subject to the jurisdiction thereof, are citizens of the United States and of the state in which they reside. *Amendment 14:1*
- No state shall make or enforce any law which shall abridge the privileges or immunities of citizens of the United States. *Amendment 14:1*
- Nor shall any state deprive any person of life, liberty, or property without due process of law. *Amendment 14:1*
- Nor deny to any person within its jurisdiction the equal protection of the law. *Amendment 14:1*

IMPEACHMENT. The president may grant reprieves and pardons except in cases of. *Article 2:2:1*
- The House of Representatives shall have the sole power of. *Article 1:2:5*

IMPEACHMENT for and conviction of treason, bribery, and other high crimes and misdemeanors. The president, vice president, and all civil officers shall be removed upon. *Article 2:4*

IMPEACHMENTS. The Senate shall have the sole power to try all. *Article 1:3:6*
- The Senate shall be on oath, or affirmation, when sitting for the trial of. *Article 1:3:6*
- When the president of the United States is tried the Chief Justice shall preside. *Article 1:3:6*
- No person shall be convicted without the concurrence of two-thirds of the members present. *Article 1:3:6*
- Judgment shall not extend beyond removal from office and disqualification to hold office. *Article 1:3:7*
- But the party convicted shall be liable to indictment and punishment according to law. *Article 1:3:7*

IMPORTATION of slaves prior to 1808 shall not be prohibited by the Congress. *Article 1:9:1*
- But a tax or duty of ten dollars for each person may be imposed on such. *Article 1:9:1*

IMPORTS OR EXPORTS except what may be absolutely necessary for executing its inspection laws. No state shall, without the consent of Congress, lay any imposts or duties on. *Article 1:10:2*

IMPORTS OR EXPORTS laid by any state shall be for the use of the Treasury. The net produce of all duties on. *Article 1:10:2*

IMPORTS OR EXPORTS shall be subject to the revision and control of Congress. All laws of states laying duties on. *Article 1:10:2*

IMPOSTS AND EXCISES. Congress shall have power to lay and collect taxes, duties. *Article 1:8:1*
- Shall be uniform throughout the United States. All taxes, duties. *Article 1:8:1*

INABILITY of the president. The powers and duties of his ofrice shall devolve on the vice president. In case of the death, resignation, or. *Article 2:1:6 and Amendment 25*
- The vice president shall succeed to the office of the president. In case of the death, resignation, or removal, or. *Amendment 25*

INABILITY of the president or vice president. Congress may provide by law for the case of the removal, death, resignation, or. *Article 2:1:6 and Amendment 25*

INCOME TAXES. Congress shall have power to lay and collect without apportionment among the several states, and without regard to any census or enumeration. *Amendment 16*

INCRIMINATE HIMSELF. No person as a witness shall be compelled to. *Amendment 5*

INDIAN TRIBES. Congress shall have power to regulate commerce with the. *Article 1:8:3*

INDICTMENT or presentment of a grand jury. No person shall be held to answer for a capital or infamous crime unless on. *Amendment 5*
- Except in cases arising in the land and naval forces, and in the militia when in actual service. *Amendment 5*

INDICTMENT, trial, judgment, and punishment, according to law. The party convicted in case of impeachment shall nevertheless be liable and subject to. *Article 1:3:7*

INFAMOUS CRIME unless on presentment or indictment of a grand jury. No person shall be held to answer for a capital or. *Amendment 5*

INFERIOR COURTS. Congress shall have power to constitute tribunals inferior to the Supreme Court. *Article 1:8:9*

INFERIOR COURTS as Congress may establish. The judicial power of the United States shall be vested in one Supreme Court and such. *Article 3:1*
- The judges of both the Supreme and inferior courts shall hold their offices during good behavior. *Article 3:1*
- Their compensation shall not be diminished during their continuance in office. *Article 3:1*

INFERIOR OFFICERS, Congress, if they think proper, may by law vest the appointment of in the president alone, in the courts of law, or in the heads of departments. *Article 2:2:2*

INHABITANT OF THE STATE for which he shall be chosen. No person shall be a senator who shall not have attained the age of thirty years, been nine years a citizen of the United States, and who shall not, when elected, be an. *Article 1:3:3*

INSURRECTION OR REBELLION against the United States. No person shall be a senator or representative in Congress, or presidential elector, or hold any office, civil or military, under the United States, or any state, who, having taken an oath as a legislative, executive, or judicial officer of the United States, or of a state, afterwards engaged in. *Amendment 14:3*

• But Congress may, by a vote of two-thirds of each house, remove such disabilities. *Amendment 14:3*

• Debts declared illegal and void which were contracted in aid of. *Amendment 14:4*

INSURRECTIONS and repel invasions. Congress shall provide for calling forth the militia to suppress. *Article 1:8:15*

INTOXICATING LIQUORS. Prohibition of manufacture, sale, transportation, importation, or exportation of. *Amendment 18:1*

• Repeal of Eighteenth Amendment. *Amendment 21:1*

• Transportation or importation into any state, Territory or possession, for delivery or use therein in violation of their laws, prohibited. *Amendment 21:2*

INVASION. No state shall, without the consent of Congress, engage in war unless actually invaded, or in such imminent danger as will not admit of delay. *Article 1:10:3*

• The writ of habeas corpus shall not be suspended unless in case of rebellion or. *Article 1:9:2*

INVASION and domestic violence. The United States shall protect each state against. *Article 4:4*

INVASIONS. Congress shall provide for calling forth the militia to suppress insurrections and repel. *Article 1:8:15*

INVENTORS AND AUTHORS in their inventions and writings. Congress may pass laws to secure for limited times exclusive rights to. *Article 1:8:8*

INVOLUNTARY SERVITUDE, except as a punishment for crime, abolished in the United States. Slavery and. *Amendment 13:1*

J

JEOPARDY of life and limb for the same offense. No person shall be twice put in. *Amendment 5*

JOURNAL of its proceedings. Each house shall keep a. *Article 1:5:3*

JUDGES in every state shall be bound by the Constitution, the laws and treaties of the United States, which shall be the supreme law of the land. *Article 6:—:2*

JUDGES of the Supreme and inferior courts shall hold their offices during good behavior. *Article 3:1*

• Their compensation shall not be diminished during their continuance in office. *Article 3:1*

JUDGMENT in cases of impeachment shall not extend further than to removal from office, and disqualification to hold any office of honor, trust, or profit under the United States. *Article 1:3:7*

• But the party convicted shall nevertheless be liable and subject to indictment, trial, judgment, and punishment according to law. *Article 1:3:7*

JUDICIAL AND EXECUTIVE OFFICERS of the United States and of the several states shall be bound by an oath to support the Constitution. *Article 6:—:3*

JUDICIAL POWER OF THE UNITED STATES. Congress shall have power to constitute tribunals inferior to the Supreme Court. *Article 1:8:9*

• The judicial power of the United States shall be vested in one Supreme Court, and in such inferior courts as Congress may from time to time ordain and establish. *Article 3:1*

• The judges of the Supreme and inferior courts shall hold their offices during good behavior. *Article 3:1*

• Their compensation shall not be diminished during their continuance in office. *Article 3:1*

• It shall extend to all cases in law and equity arising under the Constitution, laws, and treaties of the United States. *Article 3:2:1*

• To all cases affecting ambassadors, other public ministers, and consuls. *Article 3:2:1*

• To all cases of admiralty and maritime jurisdiction. *Article 3:2:1*

• To controversies to which the United States shall be a party. *Article 3:2:1*

• To controversies between two or more states. *Article 3:2:1*

• To controversies between a state and citizens of another state. *Article 3:2:1 and Amendment 11*

• To controversies between citizens of different states. *Article 3:2:1*

• To citizens of the same state claiming lands under grants of different states. *Article 3:2:1*

• To controversies between a state or its citizens and foreign states, citizens, or subjects. *Article 3:2:1*

• In all cases affecting ambassadors, other public ministers and consuls, and those in which a state shall be a party, the Supreme Court shall have original jurisdiction. *Article 3:2:2*

- In all other cases before mentioned, it shall have appellate jurisdiction, both as to law and fact, with such exceptions and under such regulations as Congress shall make. *Article 3:2:2*
- The trial of all crimes, except in cases of impeachment, shall be by jury. *Article 3:2:3*
- The trial shall be held in the state where the crimes shall have been committed. *Article 3:2:3*
- But when not committed in a state, the trial shall be at such place or places as Congress may by law have directed. *Article 3:2:3*
- The judicial power of the United States shall not be held to extend to any suit in law or equity commenced or prosecuted against one of the United States by citizens of another state, or by citizens or subjects of any Foreign state. *Amendment 11*

JUDICIAL PROCEEDINGS of every other state. Full faith and credit shall be given in each state to the acts, records, and. *Article 4:1*
- Congress shall prescribe the manner of proving such acts, records, and proceedings. *Article 4:1*

JUDICIARY. The Supreme Court shall have original jurisdiction in all cases affecting ambassadors, other public ministers and consuls, and those in which a state may be a party. *Article 3:2:2*
- The Supreme Court shall have appellate jurisdiction both as to law and fact, with such exceptions and regulations as Congress may make. *Article 3:2:2*

JUNCTION of two or more states or parts of states without the consent of the legislatures and of Congress. No state shall be formed by the. *Article 4:3:1*

JURISDICTION. In all cases affecting ambassadors and other public ministers and consuls, and in cases where a state is a party, the Supreme Court shall have original. *Article 3:2:2*

JURISDICTION, both as to law and fact, with such exceptions and under such regulations as Congress may make. The Supreme Court shall have appellate. *Article 3:2:2*

JURISDICTION of another state. No new state shall, without the consent of Congress, be formed or erected within the. *Article 4:3:1*

JURY. The trial of all crimes, except in cases of impeachment, shall be by. *Article 3:2:2*
- In all criminal prosecutions the accused shall have a speedy and public trial by. *Amendment 6*
- All suits at common law, where the value exceeds twenty dollars, shall be tried by. *Amendment 7*
- Where a fact has been tried by a jury it shall not be reexamined except by the rules of the common law. *Amendment 7*

JUST COMPENSATION. Private property shall not be taken for public use without. *Amendment 5*

JUSTICE, insure domestic tranquility, etc. To establish. *Preamble*

L

LABOR, in one state escaping into another state shall be delivered up to the party to whom such service or labor may be due. Fugitives from service or. *Article 4:2:3*

LAND and naval forces. Congress shall make rules for the government and regulation of the. *Article 1:8:14*

LAW and fact, with exceptions and under regulations to be made by Congress. The Supreme Court shall have appellate jurisdiction as to. *Article 3:2:2*

LAW of nations. Congress shall provide for punishing offenses against the. *Article 1:8:10*

LAW of the land. The Constitution, the laws made in pursuance thereof, and treaties of the United States, shall be the supreme. *Article 6:−:2*
- The judges in every state shall be bound thereby. *Article 6:−:2*

LAWS. Congress shall provide for calling forth the militia to suppress insurrection, repel invasion, and to execute the. *Article 1:8:15*

LAWS AND TREATIES of the United States. The judicial power shall extend to all cases in law and equity arising under the Constitution, or the. *Article 3:2:1*

LAWS necessary to carry into execution the powers vested in the government, or in any department or officer of the United States. Congress shall make all. *Article 1:8:18*

LEGAL TENDER in payment of debts. No state shall make anything but gold and silver coin a. *Article 1:10:1*

LEGISLATION. Congress shall have power to make all laws necessary and proper for carrying into execution all the powers vested by the Constitution in the government of the United States or in any department or officer thereof. *Article 1:8:18*
- Congress shall have power to enforce the Thirteenth Amendment, prohibiting slavery, by appropriate. *Amendment 13:2*
- Congress shall have power to enforce the Fourteenth Amendment by appropriate. *Amendment 14:5*
- Congress shall have power to enforce the Fifteenth Amendment by appropriate. *Amendment 15:2*
- Congress and the several states shall have concurrent power to enforce the Eighteenth Amendment by appropriate. *Amendment 18:2*
- Congress shall have power to enforce the Nineteenth Amendment by appropriate. *Amendment 19*

- Congress shall have power to enforce the Twenty-third Amendment by appropriate. *Amendment 23:2*
- Congress shall have power to enforce the Twenty-fourth Amendment by appropriate. *Amendment 24:2*
- Congress shall have power to enforce the Twenty-sixth Amendment by appropriate. *Amendment 26:2*

LEGISLATION in all cases over such district as may become the seat of government. Congress shall exercise exclusive. *Article 1:8:17*
- Over all. places purchased for the erection of forts, magazines, arsenals, dock-yards, and other needful buildings. Congress shall exercise exclusive. *Article 1:8:17*

LEGISLATIVE powers herein granted shall be vested in Congress. All. *Article 1:1*

LEGISLATURE, OR THE EXECUTIVE (when the legislature cannot be convened). The United States shall protect each state against invasion and domestic violence, on the application of the. *Article 4:4*

LEGISLATURES of two-thirds of the states, Congress shall call a convention for proposing amendments to the Constitution. On the application of the. *Article 5*

LETTERS of marque and reprisal. Congress shall have power to grant. *Article 1:8:11*
- No state shall grant. *Article 1:10:1*

LIBERTY TO ourselves and our posterity, etc. To secure the blessings of. *Preamble*

LIFE, LIBERTY, AND PROPERTY without due process of law. No person shall be compelled in any criminal case to be a witness against himself, nor be deprived of. *Amendment 5*
- No state shall abridge the privileges or immunities of citizens of the United States, nor deprive any person of. *Amendment 14:1*

LIFE or limb for the same offense. No person shall be twice put in jeopardy of. *Amendment 5*

Loss or emancipation of any slave shall be held illegal and void. Claims for the. *Amendment 14:4*

M

MAGAZINES, arsenals, deck-yards, and other needful buildings. Congress shall have exclusive authority over all places purchased for the erection of. *Article 1:8:17*

MAJORITY of each house shall constitute a quorum to do business. A. *Article 1:5:1*
- But a smaller number may adjourn from day to day and may be authorized to compel the attendance of absent members. *Article 1:5:1*

MAJORITY of all the states shall be necessary to a choice. When the choice of a president shall devolve on the House of Representatives, a quorum shall consist of a member or members from two-thirds of the states; but a. *Amendment 12*
- When the choice of a vice president shall devolve on the Senate, a quorum shall consist of two-thirds of the whole number of senators, and a majority of the whole number shall be necessary to a choice. *Amendment 12*

MARITIME JURISDICTION. The judicial power shall extend to all cases of admiralty and. *Article 3:2:1*

MARQUE and reprisal. Congress shall have power to grant letters of. *Article 1:8:11*
- No state shall grant any letters of. *Article 1:10:1*

MARYLAND entitled to six representatives in the first Congress. *Article 1:2:3*

MASSACHUSETTS entitled to eight representatives in the first Congress. *Article 1:2:3*

MEASURES. Congress shall fix the standard of weights and. *Article 1:8:5*

MEETING OF CONGRESS. The Congress shall assemble at least once in every year, and such meeting shall be on the first Monday in December, unless they shall by law appoint a different day. *Article 1:4:2*

MEETING OF ELECTORS. The electors shall meet in their respective states and vote by ballot for president and vice president, one of whom, at least, shall not be an inhabitant of the same state with themselves. *Amendment 12*
- District of Columbia, electors for president and vice president appointed by District. *Amendment 23:1*

MEMBERS of Congress and of state legislatures shall be bound by oath or affirmation to support the Constitution. *Article 6:−:3*

MILITIA to execute the laws, suppress insurrections, and repel invasions. Congress shall provide for calling forth the. *Article 1:8:15*
- Congress shall provide for organizing, arming, and disciplining the. *Article 1:8:16*
- Congress shall provide for governing such part of them as may be employed by the United States. *Article 1:8:16*
- Reserving to the states the appointment of the officers and the right to train the militia according to the discipline prescribed by Congress. *Article 1:8:16*
- A well-regulated militia being necessary to the security of a free state, the right of the people to keep and bear arms shall not be infringed. *Amendment 2*

MISDEMEANORS. The president, vice president, and all civil officers shall be removed on impeachment for and conviction of treason, bribery, or other high crimes and. *Article 2:4*

MONEY on the credit of the United States. Congress shall have power to borrow. *Article 1:8:2*

- Regulate the value thereof and of foreign coin. Congress shall have power to coin. *Article 1:8:5*
- Shall be drawn from the Treasury but in consequence of appropriations made by law. No. *Article 1:9:7*
- Shall be published from time to time. A regular statement and account of receipts and expenditures of public. *Article 1:9:7*
- For raising and supporting armies. No appropriation of money shall be for a longer term than two years. *Article 1:8:12*

N

NATIONS. Congress shall have power to regulate commerce with foreign. *Article 1:8:3*

- Congress shall provide for punishing offenses against the law of. *Article 1:8:10*

NATURAL-BORN CITIZEN, or a citizen at the adoption of the Constitution, shall be eligible to the office of president. No person except a. *Article 2:1:5*

NATURALIZATION. Congress shall have power to establish a uniform rule of. *Article 1:8:4*

NATURALIZED in the United States, and subject to their jurisdiction, shall be citizens of the United States and of the states in which they reside. All persons born, or. *Amendment 14:1*

NAVAL FORCES. Congress shall make rules and regulations for the government and regulation of the land and. *Article 1:8:14*

NAVY. Congress shall have power to provide and maintain a. *Article 1:8:13*

NEW HAMPSHIRE entitled to three representatives in the first Congress. *Article 1:2:3*

NEW JERSEY entitled to four representatives in the first Congress. *Article 1:2:3*

NEW STATES may be admitted by Congress into this Union. *Article 4:3:1*

- But no new state shall be formed within the jurisdiction of another state without the consent of Congress. *Article 4:3:1*
- Nor shall any state be formed by the junction of two or more states or parts of states, without the consent of the legislatures and of Congress. *Article 4:3:1*

NEW YORK entitled to six representatives in the first Congress. *Article 1:2:3*

NOBILITY shall be granted by the United States. No title of. *Article 1:9:8*

- No state shall grant any title of. *Article 1:10:1*

NOMINATIONS FOR OFFICE by the president. The president shall nominate, and, by and with the advice and consent of the Senate, shall appoint ambassadors and other public officers. *Article 2:2:2*

- He may grant commissions to fill vacancies that happen in the recess of the Senate, which shall expire at the end of their next session. *Article 2:2:3*
- The president shall nominate a successor to the vice president whenever a vacancy in office occurs. *Amendment 25:2*

NORTH CAROLINA entitled to five representatives in the first Congress. *Article 1:2:3*

NUMBER OF ELECTORS for president and vice president in each state shall be equal to the number of senators and representatives to which such state may be entitled in Congress. *Article 2:1:2*

O

OATH OF OFFICE of the president of the United States. Form of the. *Article 2:1:8*

OATH OR AFFIRMATION. No warrants shall be issued but upon probable cause supported by. *Amendment 4*

OATH OR AFFIRMATION to support the Constitution. Senators and representatives, members of state legislatures, executive and judicial officers of the United States and of the several states, shall be bound by. *Article 6:—:3*

- But no religious test shall ever be required as a qualification for office. *Article 6:—:3*
- The senators when sitting to try impeachment shall be on. *Article 1:3:6*

OBJECTIONS. If he shall not approve it, the president shall return the bill to the house in which it originated with his. *Article 1:7:2*

OBLIGATION OF CONTRACTS. No state shall pass any ex post facto law, or law impairing the. *Article 1:10:1*

OBLIGATIONS incurred in aid of insurrection or rebellion against the United States to be held illegal and void. All debts or. *Amendment 14:4*

OFFENSE. No person shall be twice put in jeopardy of life or limb for the same. *Amendment 5*

OFFENSES against the law of nations. Congress shall provide for punishing. *Article 1:8:10*

- Against the United States, except in cases of impeachment. The president may grant reprieves or pardons for. *Article 2:2:1*

OFFICE OF PRESIDENT, in case of his removal, death, resignation, or inability, shall devolve on the vice president. The powers and duties of the. *Article 2:1:6 and Amendment 25*

- During the term of four years. The president and vice president shall hold. *Article 2:1:1*

• Of trust or profit under the United States shall be an elector for president and vice president. No person holding an. *Article 2:1:2*

OFFICE UNDER THE UNITED STATES. No person shall be a member of either house while holding any civil. *Article 1:6:2*

• Civil or military under the United States, or any state, who had taken an oath as a legislative, executive, or judicial officer of the United States, or of any state, and afterward engaged in insurrection or rebellion. No person shall be a senator, representative or presidential elector, or hold any. *Amendment 14:3*

• No senator or representative shall be appointed to any office under the United States which shall have been created, or its emoluments increased, during the term for which he is elected. *Article 1:6:2*

• Or title of any kind from any king, prince, or foreign state, without the consent of Congress. No person holding any office under the United States shall accept of any present, emolument. *Article 1:9:8*

OFFICERS in the president alone, in the courts of law, or in the heads of departments. Congress may vest the appointment of inferior. *Article 2:2:2*

• Of the United States shall be removed on impeachment for and conviction of treason, bribery, or other high crimes and misdemeanors. The president, vice president, and all civil. *Article 2:4*

• The House of Representatives shall choose their Speaker and other. *Article 1:2:5*

• The Senate, in the absence of the vice president, shall choose a president pro tempore, and also their other. *Article 1:3:5*

OFFICES becoming vacant in the recess of the Senate may be filled by the president, the commissions to expire at the end of the next session. *Article 2:2:3*

ONE-FIFTH of the members present, be entered on the journal of each house. The yeas and nays shall, at the desire of. *Article 1:5:3*

OPINION of the principal officers in each of the executive departments on any subject relating to their duties. The president may require the written. *Article 2:2:1*

ORDER, resolution, or vote (except on a question of adjournment) requiring the concurrence of the two houses, shall be presented to the president. Every. *Article 1:7:3*

ORIGINAL JURISDICTION, in all cases affecting ambassadors, other public ministers, and consuls, and in which a state may be a party. The Supreme Court shall have. *Article 3:2:2*

OVERT ACT, or on confession in open court. Conviction of treason shall be on the testimony of two witnesses to the. *Article 3:3:1*

P

PARDONS, except in cases of impeachment. The president may grant reprieves and. *Article 2:2:1*

PATENT RIGHTS TO inventors. Congress may pass laws for securing. *Article 1:8:8*

PEACE. Members of Congress shall not be privileged from arrest for treason, felony, and breach of the. *Article 1:6:1*

• No state shall, without the consent of Congress, keep troops or ships of war in time of. *Article 1:10:3*

• No soldier shall be quartered in any house without the consent of the owner in time of. *Amendment 3*

PENNSYLVANIA entitled to eight representatives in the first Congress. *Article 1:2:3*

PENSIONS AND BOUNTIES shall not be questioned. The validity of the public debt incurred in suppressing insurrection and rebellion against the United States, including the debt for. *Amendment 14:4*

PEOPLE. The enumeration of certain rights in the Constitution shall not be held to deny or disparage others retained by the. *Amendment 9*

• Powers not delegated to the United States, nor prohibited to the states, are reserved to the states or to the. *Amendment 10*

PEOPLE, peaceably to assemble and petition for redress of grievances, shall not be abridged by Congress. The right of the. *Amendment 1*

• To keep and bear arms shall not be infringed. A wellregulated militia, being necessary to the security of a free state, the right of the. *Amendment 2*

• To be secure in their persons, houses, papers, and effects, against unreasonable searches and seizures shall not be violated. The right of the. *Amendment 4*

PERFECT UNION, etc. To establish a more. *Preamble*

PERSONS, as any state may think proper to admit, shall not be prohibited prior to 1808. The migration or importation of such. *Article 1:9:1*

• But a tax or duty of ten dollars shall be imposed on the importation of each of such. *Article 1:9:1*

PERSONS, houses, papers, and effects against unreasonable searches and seizures. The people shall be secure in their. *Amendment 4*

PETITION for the redress of grievances. Congress shall make no law abridging the right of the people peaceably to assemble and to. *Amendment 1*

PIRACIES AND FELONIES committed on the high seas. Congress shall define and punish. *Article 1:8:10*

PLACE than that in which the two houses shall be sitting. Neither house during the session shall, without the consent of the other, adjourn for more than three days, nor to any other. *Article 1:5:4*

PLACES OF CHOOSING SENATORS. Congress may by law make or alter regulations for the election of senators and representatives, except as to the. *Article 1:4:1*

POLL TAX. The right of citizens of the United States to vote shall not be denied or abridged by the United States or any state by reason of failure to pay. *Amendment 24:1*

PORTS of one state over those of another. Preference shall not be given by any regulation of commerce or revenue to the. *Article 1:9:6*

• Vessels clearing from the ports of one state shall not pay duties in another. *Article 1:9:6*

POST OFFICES AND POST ROADS. Congress shall establish. *Article 1:8:7*

POWERS and duties of the office shall devolve on the vice president, on the removal, death, resignation, or inability of the president. The. *Article 2:1:6 and Amendment 25*

POWERS herein granted shall be vested in Congress. All legislative. *Article 1:1*

POWERS not delegated to the United States nor prohibited to the states are reserved to the states and to the people. *Amendment 10*

• The enumeration of certain rights in this Constitution shall not be held to deny or disparage others retained by the people. *Amendment 9*

POWERS vested by the Constitution in the Government or in any department or officer of the United States. Congress shall make all laws necessary to carry into execution the. *Article 1:8:18*

PREFERENCE, by any regulation of commerce or revenue, shall not be given to the ports of one state over those of another. *Article 1:9:6*

PREJUDICE any claims of the United States or of any particular state in the territory or property of the United States. Nothing in this Constitution shall. *Article 4:3:2*

PRESENT, emolument, office, or title of any kind whatever from any king, prince, or foreign state. No person holding any office under the United States shall, without the consent of Congress, accept any. *Article 1:9:8*

PRESENTMENT or indictment of a grand jury, except in cases arising in the land or naval forces, or in the militia when in actual service. No person shall be held to answer for a capital or otherwise infamous crime unless on a. *Amendment 5*

PRESIDENT OF THE SENATE, but shall have no vote unless the Senate be equally divided. The vice president shall be. *Article 1:3:4*

PRESIDENT OF THE UNITED STATES. The Senate shall choose a president pro tempore when the vice president shall exercise the office of. *Article 1:3:5*

• Additional provision for succession through act of Congress. *Amendment 20:4*

• Succession in case of death. *Amendment 20:3*

• Succession in case of failure to be chosen or qualified. *Amendment 20:3*

• Term of office, beginning and ending. *Amendment 20:1*

• The chief justice shall preside upon the trial of the. *Article 1:3:6*

• Shall approve and sign all bills passed by Congress before they shall become laws. *Article 1:7:2*

• Shall return to the house in which it originated, with his objections, any bill which he shall not approve. *Article 1:7:2*

• If not returned within ten days (Sundays excepted), it shall become a law, unless Congress shall adjourn before the expiration of that time. *Article 1:7:2*

• Every order, resolution, or vote which requires the concurrence of both Houses, except on a question of adjournment, shall be presented to the. *Article 1:7:3*

• If disapproved by him, shall be returned and proceeded on as in the case of a bill. *Article 1:7:3*

• The executive power shall be vested in a. *Article 2:1:1*

• He shall hold his office during the term of four years. *Article 2:1:1*

• In case of the removal of the president from office, or of his death, resignation, or inability to discharge the duties of his office, the vice president shall perform the duties of. *Article 2:1:6 and Amendment 25*

• Congress may declare, by law, in the case of the removal, death, resignation, or inability of the president, what officer shall act as. *Article 2:1:6 and Amendment 25*

• The president shall receive a compensation which shall not be increased nor diminished during his term, nor shall he receive any other emolument from the United States. *Article 2:1:7*

• Before he enters upon the execution of his office he shall take an oath of office. *Article 2:1:8*

• Shall be commander in chief of the army and navy and of the militia of the states when called into actual service. *Article 2:2:1*

- He may require the opinion, in writing, of the principal officer in each of the executive departments. *Article 2:2:1*
- He may grant reprieves or pardons for offenses, except in cases of impeachment. *Article 2:2:1*
- He may make treaties by and with the advice and consent of the Senate, two-thirds of the senators present concurring. *Article 2:2:2*
- He may appoint, by and with the advice and consent of the Senate, ambassadors, other public ministers and consuls, judges of the Supreme Court, and all other officers whose appointments may be authorized by law and not herein provided for. *Article 2:2:2*
- Congress may vest the appointment of inferior officers in the. *Article 2:2:2*
- He may fill up all vacancies that may happen in the recess of the Senate by commissions which shall expire at the end of their next session. *Article 2:2:3*
- He shall give information to Congress of the state of the Union, and recommend measures. *Article 2:3*
- On extraordinary occasions he may convene both houses or either. *Article 2:3*
- In case of disagreement between the two houses as to the time of adjournment, he may adjourn them to such time as he may think proper. *Article 2:3*
- He shall receive ambassadors and other public ministers. *Article 2:3*
- He shall take care that the laws be faithfully executed. *Article 2:3*
- He shall commission all the officers of the United States. *Article 2:3*
- On impeachment for, and conviction of, treason, bribery, or other high crimes and misdemeanors, shall be removed from office. The. *Article 2:4*
- No person except a natural-born citizen, or a citizen of the United States at the adoption of the Constitution, shall be eligible to the office of. *Article 2:1:5*
- No person shall be elected to office more than twice. *Amendment 22*
- No person who shall not have attained the age of thirty-five years and been fourteen years a resident of the United States shall be eligible to the office of. *Article 2:1:5*
- Congress to decide the issue of the president's ability to discharge the powers and duties of his office. *Amendment 25:4*
- Declaration of his inability to discharge the powers and duties of his office *Amendment 25:3*
- Nomination of successor to the vice president whenever a vacancy in the office of the vice president occurs. *Amendment 25:2*

- Succession of vice president to office in case of death, resignation, removal, or inability of president to discharge the powers and duties of his office. *Amendment 25*
- President and vice president, manner of choosing. Each state, by its legislature, shall appoint a number of electors equal to the whole number of senators and representatives to which the state may be entitled in the Congress. *Article 2:1:2*
- No senator or representative or person holding an office of trust or profit under the United States shall be an elector. *Article 2:1:2*
- Congress may determine the time of choosing the electors and the day on which they shall give their votes, which day shall be the same throughout the United States. *Article 2:1:4*
- The electors shall meet in their respective states and vote by ballot for president and vice president, one of whom, at least, shall not be an inhabitant of the same state with themselves. *Amendment 12*
- They shall name in distinct ballots the person voted for as president and the person voted for as vice president. *Amendment 12*
- They shall make distinct lists of the persons voted for as president and as vice president, which they shall sign and certify and transmit sealed to the president of the Senate at the seat of government. *Amendment 12*
- The president of the Senate shall, in the presence of the Senate and House of Representatives, open all the certificates, and the votes shall then be counted. *Amendment 12*
- The person having the greatest number of votes shall be the president, if such number be a majority of the whole number of electors appointed. *Amendment 12*
- If no person have such majority, then from the persons having the highest numbers, not exceeding three, on the list of those voted for as president, the House of Representatives shall choose immediately, by ballot, the president. *Amendment 12*
- In choosing the president, the votes shall be taken by states, the representation from each state having one vote. *Amendment 12*
- A quorum for this purpose shall consist of a member or members from two-thirds of the states, and a majority of all the states shall be necessary to a choice. *Amendment 12*
- But if no choice shall be made before the 4th of March next following, then the vice president shall act as president, as in the case of the death or disability of the president. *Amendment 12*

- The District of Columbia shall appoint, in such manner as the Congress may direct, a number of electors equal to the whole number of senators and representatives to which the District would be entitled if a state. *Amendment 23:1*

PRESIDENT PRO TEMPORE. In the absence of the vice president the Senate shall choose a. *Article 1:3:5*
- When the vice president shall exercise the office of president of the United States, the Senate shall choose a. *Article 1:3:5*
- President to transmit his declaration of inability to discharge the powers and duties of his office to. *Amendment 25:3*
- Vice president and a majority of the principal officers of the executive departments to transmit their declaration of the president's inability to discharge the powers and duties of his office to. *Amendment 25:4*

PRESS. Congress shall pass no law abridging the freedom of speech or of the. *Amendment 1*

PREVIOUS CONDITION OF SERVITUDE. The right of citizens of the United States to vote shall not be denied or abridged by the United States, or by any state, on account of race, color, or. *Amendment 15:1*

PRIMARY ELECTIONS. The right of citizens of the United States to vote in shall not be denied or abridged by the United States or any state by reason of failure to pay any poll tax or other tax. *Amendment 24:1*

PRIVATE PROPERTY shall not be taken for public use without just compensation. *Amendment 5*

PRIVILEGE. Senators and representatives shall, in all cases except treason, felony, and breach of the peace, be privileged from arrest during their attendance at the session of their respective houses, and in going to and returning from the same. *Article 1:6:1*
- They shall not be questioned for any speech or debate in either house in any other place. *Article 1:6:1*

PRIVILEGES AND IMMUNITIES OF CITIZENS OF THE UNITED STATES. The citizens of each state shall be entitled to all the privileges and immunities of the citizens of the several states. *Article 4:2:1*
- No soldier shall be quartered in any house without the consent of the owner in time of peace. *Amendment 3*
- No person shall be twice put in jeopardy of life and limb for the same offense. *Amendment 5*
- All persons born or naturalized in the United States, and subject to the jurisdiction thereof, are citizens of the United States and of the state in which they reside. *Amendment 14:1*

- No state shall make or enforce any law which shall abridge the privileges or immunities of citizens of the United States. *Amendment 14:1*
- No state shall deprive any person of life, liberty, or property without due process of law. *Amendment 14:1*
- Nor deny to any person within its jurisdiction the equal protection of its laws. *Amendment 14:1*

PRIZES captured on land or water. Congress shall make rules concerning. *Article 1:8:11*

PROBABLE CAUSE. The right of the people to be secure in their persons, houses, papers, and effects, against unreasonable searches and seizures, shall not be violated. And no warrant shall issue for such but upon. *Amendment 4*

PROCESS OF LAW. No person shall be compelled in any criminal case to be a witness against himself, nor be deprived of life, liberty, or property, without due. *Amendment 5*
- No state shall deprive any person of life, liberty, or property, without due. *Amendment 14:1*

PROCESS for obtaining witnesses in his favor. In all criminal prosecutions the accused shall have. *Amendment 6*

PROGRESS of science and useful arts. Congress shall have power to promote the. *Article 1:8:8*
- Property of the United States. Congress may dispose of and make all needful rules and regulations respecting the territory or. *Article 4:3:3*

PROPERTY, without due process of law. No person shall be compelled in any criminal case to be a witness against himself; nor shall he be deprived of his life, liberty, or. *Amendment 5*
- No state shall abridge the privileges or immunities of citizens of the United States; nor deprive any person of his life, liberty, or. *Amendment 14:1*

PROSECUTIONS. The accused shall have a speedy and public trial in all criminal. *Amendment 6*
- He shall be tried by a jury in the state or district where the crime was committed. *Amendment 6*
- He shall be informed of the nature and cause of the accusation. *Amendment 6*
- He shall be confronted with the witnesses against him. *Amendment 6*
- He shall have compulsory process for obtaining witnesses. *Amendment 6*
- He shall have counsel for his defense. *Amendment 6*

PROTECTION of the laws. No state shall deny to any person within its jurisdiction the equal. *Amendment 14:1*

PUBLIC DEBT of the United States incurred in suppressing insurrection or rebellion shall not be questioned. The validity of the. *Amendment 14:4*

PUBLIC SAFETY must require it. The writ of *habeas corpus* shall not be suspended, unless when in cases of rebellion or invasion the. *Article 1:9:2*

PUBLIC TRIAL by jury. In all criminal prosecutions the accused shall have a speedy and. *Amendment 6*

PUBLIC USE. Private property shall not be taken for, without just compensation. *Amendment 5*

PUNISHMENT according to law. Judgment in cases of impeachment shall not extend further than to removal from, and disqualification for, office; but the party convicted shall nevertheless be liable and subject to indictment, trial, judgment, and. *Article 1:3:7*

PUNISHMENTS inflicted. Excessive bail shall not be required nor excessive fines imposed nor cruel and unusual. *Amendment 8*

Q

QUALIFICATION FOR OFFICE. No religious test shall ever be required as a. *Article 6:—:3*

QUALIFICATIONS of electors of members of the House of Representatives shall be the same as electors for the most numerous branch of the state legislature. *Article 1:2:1*

QUALIFICATIONS of electors of senators shall be the same as electors of the most numerous branch of the state legislature. *Amendment 17:1*

QUALIFICATIONS of members of the House of Representatives. They shall be twenty-five years of age, seven years a citizen of the United States, and an inhabitant of the state in which chosen. *Article 1:2:2*

• Of senators. They shall be thirty years of age, nine years a citizen of the United States, and an inhabitant of the state in which chosen. *Article 1:3:3*

• Of its own members. Each house shall be the judge of the election, returns, and. *Article 1:5:1*

• Of the president. No person except a natural-born citizen, or a citizen of the United States at the time of the adoption of the Constitution, shall be eligible to the office of president. *Article 2:1:5*

• Neither shall any person be eligible to the office of president who shall not have attained the age of thirty-five years and been fourteen years a resident within the United States. *Article 2:1:5*

• Of the vice president. No person constitutionally ineligible to the office of president shall be eligible to that of vice president. *Amendment 12*

QUARTERED in any house without the consent of the owner in time of peace. No soldier shall be. *Amendment 3*

QUORUM to do business. A majority of each house shall constitute a. *Article 1:5:1*

• But a smaller number than a quorum may adjourn from day to day and may be authorized to compel the attendance of absent members. *Article 1:5:1*

• Of the House of Representatives for choosing a president shall consist of a member or members from two-thirds of the states, and a majority of all the states shall be necessary to a choice. *Amendment 12*

QUORUM to elect a vice president by the Senate. Two-thirds of the whole number of senators shall be a. *Amendment 12*

• A majority of the whole number shall be necessary to a choice. *Amendment 12*

R

RACE, color, or previous condition of servitude. The right of citizens of the United States to vote shall not be denied or abridged by the United States or by any state on account of. *Amendment 15:1*

RATIFICATION of amendments to the Constitution shall be by the legislatures of three-fourths of the several states or by conventions in three-fourths of the states, accordingly as Congress may propose. *Article 5*

RATIFICATION of the conventions of nine states shall be sufficient to establish the Constitution between the states so ratifying the same. *Article 7*

RATIO OF REPRESENTATION shall be apportioned among the several states according to their respective numbers, counting the whole number of persons in each state, excluding Indians not taxed. *Amendment 14:2*

• But when the right to vote for presidential electors or members of Congress, or the legislative, executive, and judicial officers of the state, except for engaging in rebellion or other crime, shall be denied or abridged by a state, the basis of representation shall be reduced therein in the proportion of such denial or abridgment of the right to vote. *Amendment 14:2*

RATIO OF REPRESENTATION until the first enumeration under the Constitution shall be made not to exceed one for every thirty thousand. *Article 1:2:3*

REBELLION against the United States. Persons who, while holding certain federal and state offices, took an oath to support the Constitution, afterward engaged in insurrection or rebellion, disabled from holding office under the United States. *Amendment 14:3*

- But Congress may by a vote of two-thirds of each house remove such disability. *Amendment 14:3*
- Debts incurred for pensions and bounties for services in suppressing the rebellion shall not be questioned. *Amendment 14:4*
- All debts and obligations incurred in aid of the rebellion, and all claims for the loss or emancipation of slaves, declared and held to be illegal and void. *Amendment 14:4*

REBELLION or invasion. The writ of *habeas corpus* shall not be suspended except when the public safety may require it in cases of. *Article 1:9:2*

RECEIPTS and expenditures of all public money shall be published from time to time. A regular statement of. *Article 1:9:7*

RECESS OF THE SENATE. The president may grant commissions, which shall expire at the end of the next session, to fill vacancies that may happen during the. *Article 2:2:3*

RECONSIDERATION OF A BILL returned by the president with his objections. Proceedings to be had upon the. *Article 1:7:2*

RECORDS, and judicial proceedings of every other state. Full faith and credit shall be given in each state to the acts. *Article 4:1*
- Congress shall prescribe the manner of proving such acts, records, and proceedings. *Article 4:1*

REDRESS OF GRIEVANCES. Congress shall make no law abridging the right of the people peaceably to assemble and to petition for the. *Amendment 1*

REGULATIONS, except as to the places of choosing senators. The time, places, and manner of holding elections for senators and representatives shall be prescribed by the legislatures of the states, but Congress may at any time by law make or alter such. *Article 1:4:1*

REGULATIONS of commerce or revenue. Preference to the ports of one state over those of another shall not be given by any. *Article 1:9:6*

RELIGION or prohibiting the free exercise thereof. Congress shall make no law respecting the establishment of. *Amendment 1*

RELIGIOUS test shall ever be required as a qualification for any office or public trust under the United States. No. *Article 6:—:3*

REMOVAL of the president from office. The same shall devolve on the vice president. In case of the. *Article 2:1:6 and Amendment 25*
- The vice president shall succeed to the office of the president. In case of the death, resignation, inability, or. *Amendment 25*

REPRESENTATION. No state, without its consent, shall be deprived of its equal suffrage in the Senate. *Article 5*

REPRESENTATION among the several states shall be according to their respective numbers, counting the whole number of persons in each state, excluding Indians not taxed. The ratio of. *Amendment 14:2*
- But where the right to vote in certain federal and state elections is abridged for any cause other than rebellion or other crime, the basis of representation shall be reduced. *Amendment 14:2*

REPRESENTATION and direct taxation, how apportioned among the several states. *Article 1:2:3*

REPRESENTATION in any state. The executive thereof shall issue writs of election to fill vacancies in the. *Article 1:2:4*

REPRESENTATION until the first enumeration under the Constitution not to exceed one for every thirty thousand. The ratio of. *Article 1:2:3*

REPRESENTATIVES. Congress shall consist of a Senate and House of. *Article 1:1*
- Qualifications of electors of members of the House of. *Article 1:2:1*
- No person shall be a representative who shall not have attained the age of twenty-five years, been seven years a citizen of the United States, and an inhabitant of the state in which he shall be chosen. *Article 1:2:2*
- And direct taxes, how apportioned among the several states. *Article 1:2:3*
- Executives of the state shall issue writs of election to fill vacancies in the House of. *Article 1:2:4*
- Shall choose their Speaker and other officers. The House of. *Article 1:2:5*
- Shall have the sole power to impeachment. The House of. *Article 1:2:5*
- The times, places, and manner of choosing representatives shall be prescribed by the legislatures of the states. *Article 1:4:1*
- But Congress may make by law at any time or alter such regulations except as to the places of choosing senators. *Article 1:4:1*
- And senators shall receive a compensation, to be ascertained by law. *Article 1:6:1*
- Shall in all cases, except treason, felony, and breach of the peace, be privileged from arrest during attendance at the session of the House, and in going to and returning from the same. *Article 1:6:1*
- Shall not be questioned in any other place for any speech or debate. Members of the House of. *Article 1:6:1*

- No member shall be appointed during his term to any civil office which shall have been created, or the emoluments of which shall have been increased, during such term. *Article 1:6:2*
- No person holding any office under the United States shall, while holding such office, be a member of the House of. *Article 1:6:2*
- All bills for raising revenue shall originate in the House of. *Article 1:7:1*
- No senator or representative shall be an elector for president or vice president. *Article 2:1:2*
- No law, varying the compensation for the services of the senators and representatives, shall take effect, until an election of representatives shall have intervened. *Amendment 27*

REPRESENTATIVES among the several states. Provisions relative to the apportionment of. *Amendment 14:2*

REPRESENTATIVES AND SENATORS. Prescribing certain disqualifications for office as. *Amendment 14:3*
- But Congress may, by a vote of two-thirds of each house, remove such disqualification. *Amendment 14:3*

REPRESENTATIVES shall be bound by an oath or affirmation to support the Constitution of the United States. The senators and. *Article 6:—:3*

REPRIEVES and pardons except in cases of impeachment. The president may grant. *Article 2:2:1*

REPRISAL. Congress shall have power to grant letters of marque and. *Article 1:8:11*
- No state shall grant any letters of marque and. *Article 1:10:1*

REPUBLICAN FORM OF GOVERNMENT. The United States shall guarantee to every state in this Union a. *Article 4:4*
- And shall protect each of them against invasion; and on the application of the legislature, or of the executive (when the legislature cannot be convened), against domestic violence. *Article 4:4*

RESERVED RIGHTS of the states and the people. The enumeration in the Constitution of certain rights shall not be construed to deny or disparage others retained by the people. *Amendment 9*
- The powers not delegated to the United States by the Constitution, nor prohibited by it to the states, are reserved to the states respectively, or to the people. *Amendment 10*

RESIGNATION OF THE PRESIDENT. The duties and powers of his office shall devolve on the vice president. In case of the death. *Amendment 25*
- Congress may by law provide for the case of the removal, death. *Article 2:1:6*

- The vice president shall succeed to the office of the president. In case of the death, removal, inability, or. *Amendment 25*

RESOLUTION, or vote (except on a question of adjournment) requiring the concurrence of the two houses shall, before it becomes a law, be presented to the president. Every order. *Article 1:7:3*

REVENUE. Preference shall not be given to the ports of one state over those of another by any regulations of commerce or. *Article 1:9:6*

REVENUE shall originate in the House of Representatives. All bills for raising. *Article 1:7:1*

RHODE ISLAND entitled to one representative in the first Congress. *Article 1:2:3*

RIGHT OF PETITION. Congress shall make no law abridging the right of the people peaceably to assemble and to petition for the redress of grievances. *Amendment 1*

RIGHT TO KEEP AND BEAR ARMS. A well-regulated militia, being necessary to the security of a free state, the right of the people to keep and bear arms shall not be infringed. *Amendment 2*

RIGHTS in the Constitution shall not be construed to deny or disparage others retained by the people. The enumeration of certain. *Amendment 9*

RIGHTS NOT DELEGATED to the United States nor prohibited to the states are reserved to the states or to the people. *Amendment 10*

RULES AND REGULATIONS respecting the territory or other property of the United States. Congress shall dispose of and make all needful. *4:3:2*

RULES of its proceedings. Each house may determine the. *Article 1:5:2*

RULES OF THE COMMON LAW. All suits involving over twenty dollars shall be tried by jury according to the. *Amendment 7*
- No fact tried by a jury shall be re-examined except according to the. *Amendment 7*

S

SCIENCE AND USEFUL ARTS by securing to authors and inventors the exclusive right to their writings and discoveries. Congress shall have power to promote the progress of. *Article 1:8:8*

SEARCHES AND SEIZURES shall not be violated. The right of the people to be secure against unreasonable. *Amendment 4*
- And no warrants shall be issued but upon probable cause, on oath or affirmation, describing the place to be searched and the persons or things to be seized. *Amendment 4*

SEAT OF GOVERNMENT. Congress shall exercise exclusive legislation in all cases over such district as may become the. *Article 1:8:17*

SECURITIES and current coin of the United States. Congress shall provide for punishing the counterfeiting of the. *Article 1:8:6*

SECURITY OF A FREE STATE, the right of the people to keep and bear arms shall not be infringed. A well-regulated militia being necessary to the. *Amendment 2*

SENATE AND HOUSE OF REPRESENTATIVES. The Congress of the United States shall consist of a. *Article 1:1*

SENATE OF THE UNITED STATES. The Senate shall be composed of two senators from each state, chosen by the legislature for six years. *Article 1:3:1*

- The Senate shall be composed of two senators from each state, elected by the people thereof, for six years. *Amendment 17:1*
- Qualifications of electors of senators. *Amendment 17:1*
- If vacancies happen during the recess of the legislature of a state, the executive thereof may make temporary appointments until the next meeting of the legislature. *Article 1:3:2*
- When vacancies happen the executive authority of the state shall issue writs of election to fill such vacancies; provided, that the legislature of any state may empower the executive thereof to make temporary appointment until the people fill the vacancies by election as the legislature may direct. *Amendment 17:2*
- The vice president shall be president of the Senate, but shall have no vote unless the Senate be equally divided. *Article 1:3:4*
- The Senate shall choose their other officers, and also a president pro tempore in the absence of the vice president or when he shall exercise the office of president. *Article 1:3:5*
- The Senate shall have the sole power to try all impeachments. When sitting for that purpose they shall be on oath or affirmation. *Article 1:3:6*
- When the president of the United States is tried the Chief Justice shall preside; and no person shall be convicted without the concurrence of two-thirds of the members present. *Article 1:3:6*
- It shall be the judge of the elections, returns, and qualifications of its own members. *Article 1:5:1*
- A majority shall constitute a quorum to do business but a smaller number may adjourn from day to day, and may be authorized to compel the attendance of absent members. *Article 1:5:1*

- It may determine the rules of its proceedings, punish a member for disorderly behavior, and with the concurrence of two-thirds expel a member. *Article 1:5:2*
- It shall keep a journal of its proceedings and from time to time publish the same, except such parts as may in their judgment require secrecy. *Article 1:5:3*
- It shall not adjourn for more than three days during a session without the consent of the other house. *Article 1:5:4*
- It may propose amendments to bills for raising revenue, but such bills shall originate in the House of Representatives. *Article 1:7:1*
- The Senate shall advise and consent to the ratification of all treaties, provided two-thirds of the members present concur. *Article 2:2:2*
- It shall advise and consent to the appointment of ambassadors, other public ministers and consuls, judges of the Supreme Court, and all other officers not herein otherwise provided for. *Article 2:2:2*
- It may be convened by the president on extraordinary occasions. *Article 2:3:2*
- No state, without its consent, shall be deprived of its equal suffrage in the Senate. *Article 5*

SENATORS. They shall, immediately after assembling under their first election, be divided into three classes, so that the seats of one-third shall become vacant at the expiration of every second year. *Article 1:3:2*

- No person shall be a senator who shall not be thirty years of age, nine years a citizen of the United States, and an inhabitant when elected of the state for which he shall be chosen. *Article 1:3:3*
- The times, places, and manner of choosing senators may be fixed by the legislature of a state, but Congress may by law make or alter such regulations, except as to the places of choosing. *Article 1:4:1*
- If vacancies happen during the recess of the legislature of a state, the executive thereof may make temporary appointments until the next meeting of the legislature. *Article 1:3:2*
- If vacancies happen the executive authority of the state shall issue writs of election to fill such vacancies; provided, that the legislature of any state may empower the executive thereof to make temporary appointment until the people fill the vacancies by election as the legislature may direct. *Amendment 17:2*
- They shall in all cases, except treason, felony, and breach of the peace, be privileged from arrest dur-

ing their attendance at the session of the Senate and in going to and returning from the same. *Article 1:6:1*

- Senators and representatives shall receive a compensation to be ascertained by law. *Article 1:6:1*
- Senators and representatives shall not be questioned for any speech or debate in either house in any other place. *Article 1:6:1*
- No senator or representative shall, during the time for which he was elected, be appointed to any civil office under the United States which shall have been created, or of which the emoluments shall have been increased during such term. *Article 1:6:2*
- No person holding any office under the United States shall be a member of either house during his continuance in office. *Article 1:6:2*
- No senator or representative or person holding an office of trust or profit under the United States shall be an elector for president and vice president. *Article 2:1:2*
- Senators and representatives shall be bound by an oath or affirmation to support the Constitution. *Article 6:—:3*
- No person shall be a senator or representative who, having, as a federal or state officer, taken an oath to support the Constitution, afterward engaged in rebellion against the United States. *Amendment 14:3*
- But Congress may, by a vote of two-thirds of each house, remove such disability. *Amendment 14:3*
- No law, varying the compensation for the services of the senators and representatives, shall take effect, until an election of representatives shall have intervened. *Amendment 27*

SERVICE OR LABOR in one state, escaping into another state, shall be delivered up to the party to whom such service or labor may be due. Fugitives from. *Article 4:2:3*

SERVITUDE. The right of citizens of the United States to vote shall not be denied or abridged by the United States or by any state, on account of race, color, or previous condition of. *Amendment 15:1*

SERVITUDE, except as a punishment for crime, whereof the party shall have been duly convicted, shall exist in the United States or any place subject to their jurisdiction. Neither slavery nor involuntary. *Amendment 13:1*

SEX. Right of citizens to vote shall not be denied or abridged by the United States or any state on account of. *Amendment 19*

SHIPS OF WAR in time of peace, without the consent of Congress. No state shall keep troops or. *Article 1:10:3*

SILVER COIN a tender in payment of debts. No state shall make anything but gold and. *Article 1:10:1*

SLAVE. Neither the United States nor any state shall assume or pay any debt or obligation incurred in aid of insurrection or rebellion, or any claim for the loss or emancipation of any. *Amendment 14:4*

SLAVERY nor involuntary servitude, except as a punishment for crime, whereof the party shall have been duly convicted, shall exist in the United States, or any places subject to their jurisdiction. Neither. *Amendment 13:1*

SOLDIERS shall not be quartered, in time of peace, in any house without the consent of the owner. *Amendment 3*

SOUTH CAROLINA entitled to five representatives in the first Congress. *Article 1:2:3*

SPEAKER and other officers. The House of Representatives shall choose their. *Article 1:2:5*

SPEAKER OF THE HOUSE OF REPRESENTATIVES. president to transmit his declaration of inability to discharge the powers and duties of his office to. *Amendment 25:3*

- Vice president and a majority of the principal officers of the executive departments to transmit their declaration of the president's inability to discharge the powers and duties of his office to. *Amendment 25:4*

SPEECH OR OF THE PRESS. Congress shall make no law abridging the freedom of. *Amendment 1*

SPEEDY AND PUBLIC TRIAL by a jury. In all criminal prosecutions the accused shall have a. *Amendment 6*

STANDARD OF WEIGHTS and measures. Congress shall fix the. *Article 1:8:5*

STATE OF THE UNION. The president shall, from time to time, give Congress information of the. *Article 2:3*

STATE LEGISLATURES, and all executive and judicial officers of the United States, shall take an oath to support the Constitution. All members of the several. *Article 6:—:3*

STATES. When vacancies happen in the representation from any state, the executive authority shall issue writs of election to fill such vacancies. *Article 1:2:4*

- When vacancies happen in the representation of any state in the Senate, the executive authority shall issue writs of election to fill such vacancies. *Amendment 17:2*
- Congress shall have power to regulate commerce among the several. *Article 1:8:3*
- No state shall enter into any treaty, alliance, or confederation. *Article 1:10:1*

- Shall not grant letters of marque and reprisal. *Article 1:10:1*
- Shall not coin money. *Article 1:10:1*
- Shall not emit bills of credit. *Article 1:10:1*
- Shall not make anything but gold and silver coin a tender in payment of debts. *Article 1:10:1*
- Shall not pass any bill of attainder, *ex post facto* law, or law impairing the obligation of contracts. *Article 1:10:1*
- Shall not grant any title of nobility. *Article 1:10:1*
- Shall not, without the consent of Congress, lay any duties on imports or exports, except what may be absolutely necessary for executing its inspection laws. *Article 1:10:1*
- Shall not, without the consent of Congress, lay any duty of tonnage, keep troops or ships of war in time of peace, enter into any agreement or compact with another state or with a foreign power, or engage in war unless actually invaded or in such imminent danger as will not admit of delay. *Article 1:10:3*
- Full faith and credit in every other state shall be given to the public acts, records, and judicial proceedings of each state. *Article 4:1*
- Congress shall prescribe the manner of providing such acts, records, and proceedings. *Article 4:1*
- Citizens of each state shall be entitled to all privileges and immunities of citizens in the several states. *Article 4:2:1*
- New states may be admitted by Congress into this Union. *Article 4:3:1*
- But no new state shall be formed or erected within the jurisdiction of another state. *Article 4:3:1*
- Nor any state formed by the junction of two or more states or parts of states, without the consent of the legislatures as well as of Congress. *Article 4:3:1*
- No state shall be deprived, without its consent, of its equal suffrage in the Senate. *Article 5*
- Three-fourths of the legislatures of the states, or conventions of three-fourths of the states, as Congress shall prescribe, may ratify amendments to the Constitution. *Article 5*
- The United States shall guarantee a republican form of government to every state in the Union. *Article 4:4*
- They shall protect each state against invasion. *Article 4:4*
- And on application of the legislature, or the executive (when the legislature cannot be convened), against domestic violence. *Article 4:4*
- The ratification by nine states shall be sufficient to establish the Constitution between the states so ratifying the same. *Article 7*
- When the choice of president shall devolve on the House of Representatives, the vote shall be taken by states. *Amendment 12*
- But in choosing the president the vote shall be taken by states, the representation from each state having one vote. *Amendment 12*
- A quorum for choice of president shall consist of a member or members from two-thirds of the states, and a majority of all the states shall be necessary to a choice. *Amendment 12*

STATES OR THE PEOPLE. Powers not delegated to the United States, nor prohibited to the states, are reserved to the. *Amendment 10*

SUCCESSION to the offices of the president and vice president. *Amendment 25*

SUFFRAGE in the Senate. No state shall be deprived without its consent of its equal. *Article 5*
- No denial of right to vote on account of sex. *Amendment 19*
- The right of citizens who are eighteen years or older to vote shall not be denied or abridged by the United States or by any state. *Amendment 26*

SUITS at common law, where the value in controversy shall exceed $20, shall be tried by jury. *Amendment 7*
- In law or equity against one of the states, by citizens of another state, or by citizens of a foreign state. The judicial power of the United States shall not extend to. *Amendment 11*

SUPPRESS insurrections and repel invasions. Congress shall provide for calling forth the militia to execute the laws. *Article 1:8:15*

SUPPRESSION of insurrection or rebellion shall not be questioned. The public debt, including the debt for pensions and bounties, incurred in the. *Amendment 14:4*

SUPREME COURT. Congress shall have power to constitute tribunals inferior to the. *Article 1:8:9*
- And such inferior courts as Congress may establish. The judicial power of the United States shall be vested in one. *Article 3:1*
- The judges of the Supreme Court and inferior courts shall hold their offices during good behavior. *Article 3:1*
- The compensation of the judges shall not be diminished during their continuance in office. *Article 3:1*
- Shall have original jurisdiction. In all cases affecting ambassadors, other public ministers and consuls, and in which a state may be a party, the. *Article 3:2:2*

- Shall have appellate jurisdiction, both as to law and fact, with such exceptions and regulations as Congress may make. The. *Article 3:2:2*

SUPREME LAW of the land. This Constitution, the laws made in pursuance thereof, and the treaties of the United States, shall be the. *Article 6:—:2*

- The judges in every state shall be bound thereby. *Article 6:—:2*

T

TAX. The right of citizens of the United States to vote shall not be denied or abridged by the United States or any state by reason of failure to pay. *Amendment 24:1*

TAX ON INCOMES authorized without apportionment among the several states, and without regard to any census or enumeration. *Amendment 16*

TAX or duty shall be laid on articles exported from any state. No. *Article 1:9:5*

TAX shall be laid unless in proportion to the census or enumeration. No capitation or other direct. *Article 1:9:4*

TAXES (direct) and representatives, how apportioned among the several states. *Article 1:2:3*

TAXES, duties, imposts, and excises. Congress shall have power to lay. *Article 1:8:1*

- They shall be uniform throughout the United States. *Article 1:8:1*

TEMPORARY APPOINTMENTS until the next meeting of the legislature. If vacancies happen in the Senate in the recess of the legislature of a state, the executive of the state shall make. *Article 1:3:2*

TENDER in payment of debts. No state shall make anything but gold and silver coin a. *Article 1:10:1*

TERM for which he is elected. No senator or representative shall be appointed to any office under the United States which shall have been created or its emoluments increased during the. *Article 1:6:2*

TERM OF OFFICE. president, not more than twice. *Amendment 22*

TERMS OF FOUR YEARS. The president and vice president shall hold their offices for the. *Article 2:1:1*

TERRITORY or other property of the United States. Congress shall dispose of and make all needful rules and regulations respecting the. *Article 4:3:2*

TEST as a qualification to any office or public trust shall ever be required. No religious. *Article 6:—:3*

TESTIMONY of two witnesses to the same overt act, or on confession in open court. No person shall be convicted of treason except on the. *Article 3:3:1*

THREE-FOURTHS OF THE LEGISLATURES of the states, or conventions in three-fourths of the states, as Congress shall prescribe, may ratify amendments to the Constitution. *Article 5*

TIE. The vice president shall have no vote unless the Senate be equally divided. *Article 1:3:4*

TIMES, PLACES, AND MANNER of holding elections for senators and representatives shall be prescribed in each state by the legislature thereof. *Article 1:4:1*

- But Congress may at any time by law make or alter such regulations, except as to the places of choosing senators. *Article 1:4:1*

TITLE of any kind, from any king, prince, or foreign state, without the consent of Congress. No person holding any office under the United States shall accept of any. *Article 1:9:8*

TITLE OF NOBILITY. The United States shall not grant any. *Article 1:9:8*

- No state shall grant any. *Article 1:10:1*

TONNAGE without the consent of Congress. No state shall lay any duty of. *Article 1:10:3*

TRANQUILITY, provide for the common defense, etc. To insure domestic. *Preamble*

TREASON against the United States shall consist only in levying war against them, or in adhering to their enemies, giving them aid and comfort. *Article 3:3:1*

- No person shall, unless on the testimony of two witnesses to the same overt act, or on confession in open court, be convicted of. *Article 3:3:1*

- Congress shall have power to declare the punishment of. *Article 3:3:2*

- Shall not work corruption of blood. Attainder of. *Article 3:3:2*

- Shall not work forfeiture, except during the life of the person attainted. Attainder of. *Article 3:3:2*

TREASON, BRIBERY, or other high crimes and misdemeanors. The president, vice president, and all civil officers shall be removed from office on impeachment for and conviction of. *Article 2:4:1*

TREASON, FELONY, AND BREACH OF THE PEACE. Senators and representatives shall be privileged from arrest while attending or while going to or returning from the sessions of Congress, except in cases of. *Article 1:6:1*

TREASURY, but in consequence of appropriations made by law. No money shall be drawn from the. *Article 1:9:7*

TREATIES. The president shall have power, with the advice and consent of the Senate, provided two-thirds of the senators present concur, to make. *Article 2:2:2*

- The judicial power shall extend to all cases arising under the Constitution, laws, and. *Article 3:2:1*

VALIDITY of the public debt incurred in suppressing insurrection against the United States, including debt for pensions and bounties, shall not be questioned. *Amendment 14:4*

VESSELS bound to or from the ports of one state, shall not be obliged to enter, clear, or pay duties in another state. *Article 1:9:6*

VETO of a bill by the president. Proceedings of the two houses upon the. *Article 1:7:2*

VICE PRESIDENT of the United States shall be president of the Senate. *Article 1:3:4*

• He shall have no vote unless the Senate be equally divided. *Article 1:3:4*

• The Senate shall choose a president pro tempore in the absence of the. *Article 1:3:5*

• He shall be chosen for the term of four years. *Article 2:1:1*

• The number and the manner of appointing electors for president and. *Article 2:1:2*

• In case of the removal, death, resignation, or inability of the president, the powers and duties of his office shall devolve on the. *Article 2:1:6 and Amendment 25*

• Congress may provide by law for the case of the removal, death, resignation, or inability both of the president and. *Article 2.1.6 and Amendment 25*

• On impeachment for and conviction of treason, and other high crimes and misdemeanors, shall be removed from office. The. *Article 2:4*

VICE PRESIDENT. THE MANNER OF CHOOSING THE. The electors shall meet in their respective states and vote by ballot for president and vice president, one of whom, at least, shall not be an inhabitant of the same state with themselves. *Amendment 12*

• Additional provision for succession through act of Congress. *Amendment 20:4*

• Nomination by president in case of vacancy in office. *Amendment 25:2*

• Term of office, beginning and ending. *Amendment 20:1*

• The electors shall name, in distinct ballots, the person voted for as vice president. *Amendment 12*

• They shall make distinct lists of the persons voted for as vice president, which lists they shall sign and certify, and send sealed to the seat of Government, directed to the president of the Senate. *Amendment 12*

• The president of the Senate shall, in the presence of the Senate and House of Representatives, open all the certificates, and the votes shall be then counted. *Amendment 12*

• The person having the greatest number of votes shall be vice president, if such number be a majority of the whole number of electors. *Amendment 12*

• If no person have a majority, then from the two highest numbers on the list the Senate shall choose the vice president. *Amendment 12*

• A quorum for this purpose shall consist of two-thirds of the whole number of senators; and a majority of the whole number shall be necessary to a choice. *Amendment 12*

• But if the house shall make no choice of a president before the 4th of March next following, then the vice president shall act as president, as in the case of the death or other constitutional disability of the president. *Amendment 12*

• No person constitutionally ineligible as president shall be eligible as. *Amendment 12*

• In case of the removal, death, resignation, or inability of the president, the powers and duties of his office shall devolve upon the. *Amendment 25*

• Nomination by president of successor in event of vacancy in office of. *Amendment 25:2*

VIOLENCE. The United States shall guarantee to every state a republican form of government, and shall protect each state against invasion and domestic. *Article 4:4*

VIRGINIA entitled to ten representatives in the first Congress. *Article 1:2:3*

VOTE. Each senator shall have one. *Article 1:3:1*

• The vice president, unless the Senate be equally divided, shall have no. *Article 1:3:4*

• Requiring the concurrence of the two houses (except upon a question of adjournment) shall be presented to the president. Every order, resolution, or. *Article 1:7:3*

• Shall not be denied or abridged by the United States or by any state on account of race, color, or previous condition of servitude. The right of citizens of the United States to. *Amendment 15:1*

• Right of citizens to vote shall not be denied or abridged by the United States or any state on account of sex. *Amendment 19*

• Shall not be denied or abridged by the United States or any state by reason of failure to pay any poll tax or other tax. The right of citizens of the United States to. *Amendment 24:1*

• Right of citizens who are eighteen years of age or older to vote shall not be denied or abridged by the United States or any state, on account of age. *Amendment 26:1*

VOTE OF TWO-THIRDS. Each house may expel a member by a. *Article 1:5:2*

- A bill vetoed by the president may be repassed in each house by a. *Article 1:7:2*
- No person shall be convicted on an impeachment except by a. *Article 1:3:6*
- Whenever both houses shall deem it necessary, Congress may propose amendments to the Constitution by a. *Article 5*
- The president may make treaties with the advice and consent of the Senate, by a. *Article 2:2:2*
- Disabilities incurred by participation in insurrection or rebellion, may be relieved by Congress by a. *Amendment 14:3*

W

WAR against the United States, adhering to their enemies, and giving them aid and comfort. Treason shall consist only in levying. *Article 3:3:1*

WAR, grant letters of marque and reprisal, and make rules concerning captures on land and water. Congress shall have power to declare. *Article 1:8:11*
- For governing the land and naval forces. Congress shall have power to make rules. *Article 1:8:14*
- No state shall, without the consent of Congress, unless actually invaded, or in such imminent danger as will not admit of delay, engage in. *Article 1:10:3*

WARRANTS shall issue but upon probable cause, on oath or affirmation, describing the place to be searched, and the person or things to be seized. No. *Amendment 4*

WEIGHTS AND MEASURES. Congress shall fix the standard of. *Article 1:8:5*

WELFARE. Congress shall have power to provide for the common defense and general. *Article 1:8:1*

WELFARE and to secure the blessings of liberty, etc. To promote the general. *Preamble*

WITNESS against himself. No person shall, in a criminal case, be compelled to be a. *Amendment 5*

WITNESSES against him. In all criminal prosecutions the accused shall be confronted with the. *Amendment 6*

WITNESSES in his favor. In all criminal prosecutions the accused shall have compulsory process for obtaining. *Amendment 6*

WITNESSES to the same overt act, or on confession in open court. No person shall be convicted of treason unless on the testimony of two. *Article 3:3:1*

WRIT OF HABEAS CORPUS shall not be suspended unless in case of rebellion or invasion the public safety may require it. *Article 1:9:2*

WRITS of election to fill vacancies in the representation of any state. The executives of the state shall issue. *Article 1:2:4*

WRITTEN opinion of the principal officer in each of the executive departments on any subject relating to the duties of his office. The president may require the. *Article 2:2:1*

Y

YEAS AND NAYS of the members of either house shall, at the desire of one-fifth of those present, be entered on the journals. *Article 1:5:3*
- The votes of both houses upon the reconsideration of a bill returned by the president with his objections shall be determined by. *Article 1:7:2*

SOURCE: *The Constitution of the United States of America, as Amended.* House Document No. 106–214. Washington, D.C.: Government Printing Office, 2000.

Table of Cases

Selected Bibliography

Abbell, Michael. *Extradition to and from the United States*. Ardsley, N.Y.: Transnational, 2001.

Abramson, Jeffery B. *We, the Jury: The Jury System and the Ideal of Democracy*. Cambridge: Harvard University Press, 2000.

Ackerman, Bruce A., and Ian Ayres. *Voting with Dollars: A New Paradigm for Campaign Finance*. New Haven: Yale University Press, 2002.

Adams, Arlin M., and Charles J. Emmerich. *A Nation Dedicated to Religious Liberty: The Constitutional Heritage of the Religion Clauses*. Philadelphia: University of Pennsylvania Press, 1990.

Adler, David Gray, and Michael A. Genovese, eds. *The Presidency and the Law: The Clinton Legacy*. Lawrence: University Press of Kansas, 2002.

Agel, Jerome, and Mort Gerberg. *The U.S. Declaration of Independence for Everyone*. New York: Perigee, 2001.

Albelda, Randy P., et al. *Unlevel Playing Fields: Understanding Wage Inequality and Discrimination*, 2d ed. Boston: Economic Affairs Bureau, Inc., 2004.

Alexander, Yonah, and Edgar H. Brenner, eds. *Terrorism and Law*. Ardsley, N.Y.: Transnational, 2001.

American Bar Association. *The ABA Complete and Easy Guide to Health Care Law: Your Guide to Protecting Your Rights as a Patient, Dealing with Hospitals, Health Insurance, Medicare, and More*. New York: Three Rivers Press, 2001.

———. *The American Bar Association Guide to Workplace Law: Everything Every Employer and Employee Needs to Know about the Law and Hiring, Firing, Discrimination, as an Employee or Employer*, 2d ed. New York: Random House, 2006.

Anderson, Margo J., ed. *Encyclopedia of the U.S. Census*. Washington, D.C.: CQ Press, 2000.

Aristotle. *The Politics*. Stephen Everson, ed. New York: Cambridge University Press, 1993.

Armor, David J. *Forced Justice: School Desegregation and the Law*. New York: Oxford University Press, 1995.

Axtmann, Roland, ed. *Balancing Democracy*. New York: Continuum, 2001.

Baird, Douglas G. *The Elements of Bankruptcy*, 4th ed. Westbury, N.Y: Foundation Press, 2005.

Baker, Ross K. *House and Senate*, 3d ed. New York: Norton, 2001.

Ball, Howard. *The Bakke Case: Race, Education, and Affirmative Action*. Lawrence: University of Kansas, 2000.

Banner, Stuart. *The Death Penalty: An American History*. Cambridge: Harvard University Press, 2002.

Barbour, Scott, ed. *Free Speech*. San Diego: Greenhaven Press, 2000.

Barlow, Hugh D. *Criminal Justice in America*. Upper Saddle River, N.J.: Prentice Hall, 2000.

Barron, Jerome A., and C. Thomas Dienes. *Constitutional Law in a Nutshell*, 6th ed. St. Paul, Minn.: West Group, 2005.

Barry, Kathleen. *Susan B. Anthony: A Biography of a Singular Feminist*. New York: New York University Press, 1988.

Barry, Norman P. *Welfare*. Minneapolis: University of Minnesota Press, 1999.

Barton, David. *Original Intent: The Courts, the Constitution and Religion*, 3d ed. Aledo, Texas: WallBuilder Press, 2004.

Baum, Lawrence. *American Courts: Process and Policy*, 6th ed. Boston: Houghton Mifflin, 2007.

_____. *The Supreme Court*, 9th ed. Washington, D.C.: CQ Press, 2007.

Beahm, Donald L. *Conceptions of and Corrections to Majoritarian Tyranny*. Lanham, Md.: Lexington Books, 2002.

Becker, Carl L. *The Declaration of Independence: A Study in the History of Political Ideas*. New York: Random House, 1958.

Bell, David, and Jon Binnie. *The Sexual Citizen: Queer Politics and Beyond*. Malden, Mass: Polity Press, 2000.

Benenson, Bob, ed. *Elections A to Z*, 3d ed. Washington, D.C.: CQ Press, 2008.

Bennett, Anthony J. *The American President's Cabinet: From Kennedy to Bush*. New York: St. Martin's Press, 1996.

Bennett, James T., and Bruce E. Kaufman, eds. *The Future of Private Sector Unionism in the United States*. Armonk, N.Y.: M. E. Sharpe, 2002.

Ben-Yehuda, Nachman. *Betrayals and Treason: Violations of Trust and Loyalty*. Boulder, Colo.: Westview Press, 2001.

Bergen, Peter L. *Holy War Inc.: Inside the Secret World of Osama bin Laden*. New York: Free Press, 2001.

Berger, Raoul. *The Fourteenth Amendment and the Bill of Rights*. Norman: University of Oklahoma Press, 1989.

Bernstein, Carl, and Bob Woodward. *All the President's Men*. New York: Simon and Schuster, 1974.

Binder, Sarah A. *Minority Rights, Majority Rule: Partisanship and the Development of Congress*. New York: Cambridge University Press, 1997.

Birnbaum, Jeffrey H. *The Money Men: The Real Story of Fund-raising's Influence on Political Power in America*. New York: Crown, 2000.

Biskupic, Joan, and Elder Witt. *The Supreme Court and the Powers of the American Government*. Washington, D.C.: Congressional Quarterly Inc., 1997.

Black, Charles L., Jr. *Impeachment: A Handbook*. New Haven: Yale University Press, 1998.

Blackstone, William. *Commentaries on the Laws of England*, Vol. 4. Chicago: University of Chicago Press, 1979.

Bogus, Carl T., ed. *The Second Amendment in Law and History: Historians and Constitutional Scholars on the Right to Bear Arms*. New York: New Press, 2001.

Bollinger, Lee C., and Geoffrey R. Stone, eds. *Eternally Vigilant: Free Speech in the Modern Era*. Chicago: University of Chicago Press, 2002.

Borjesson, Kristina, ed. *Into the Buzzsaw: Leading Journalists Expose the Myth of a Free Press*. Amherst, N.Y.: Prometheus Books, 2002.

Bosmajian, Haig A. *The Freedom Not to Speak*. New York: New York University Press, 1999.

Bowers, James R. *Pro-Choice and Anti-Abortion: Constitutional Theory and Public Policy*. Westport, Conn.: Praeger, 1997.

Bowman, Ann O'M., and Richard C. Kearney. *State and Local Government*, 7th ed. Boston: Houghton Mifflin, 2008.

Bradford, Melvin E. *Founding Fathers: Brief Lives of the Framers of the United States Constitution*, 2d ed., rev. Lawrence: University Press of Kansas, 1994.

Bridwell, R. Randall. *The Power: Government by Consent and Majority Rule in America*. San Francisco: Austin and Winfield, 1999.

Brookhiser, Richard. *Alexander Hamilton, American*. New York: Free Press, 1999.

Brown, Ken. *The Right to Learn: Alternatives for a Learning Society*. London: RoutledgeFalmer, 2002.

Buchanan, James M., and Roger D. Congleton. *Politics by Principle, Not Interest: Towards Nondiscriminatory Democracy*. New York: Cambridge University Press, 1998.

Burns, Robert P. *A Theory of the Trial*. Princeton: Princeton University Press, 1999.

Cameron, Charles M. *Veto Bargaining: Presidents and the Politics of Negative Power*. New York: Cambridge University Press, 2000.

Carey, John M., and Matthew S. Shugart, eds. *Executive Decree Authority*. New York: Cambridge University Press, 1998.

Carp, Robert A., Ronald Stidham, and Kenneth L. Manning. *Judicial Process in America*, 7th ed. Washington, D.C.: CQ Press, 2007.

Carson, Clayborne, ed. *The Autobiography of Martin Luther King, Jr.* New York: Warner Books, 1998.

Cass, Ronald A. *The Rule of Law in America*. Baltimore: Johns Hopkins University Press, 2001.

Chapin, Bradley. *American Law of Treason: Revolutionary and Early National Origins.* Seattle: University of Washington Press, 1964.

Charleton, James H., et al., eds. *Framers of the Constitution.* Washington, D.C.: National Archives and Records Administration, 1986.

Cheney, Timothy D. *Who Makes the Law: The Supreme Court, Congress, the States, and Society.* Upper Saddle River, N.J.: Prentice Hall, 1998.

Clark, David S., and Tugrul Ansay, eds. *Introduction to the Law of the United States,* 2d rev. ed. Boston: Kluwer Law International, 2001.

Cohen, Jeffrey E., Richard Fleisher, and Paul Kantor, eds. *American Political Parties: Decline or Resurgence?* Washington, D.C.: CQ Press, 2001.

Cohen, Joshua, and Archon Fung, eds. *Constitution, Democracy, and State Power: The Institutions of Justice,* 4 vols. Brookfield, Mass.: Elgar, 1996.

Congressional Quarterly. *Cabinets and Counselors: The President and the Executive Branch,* 2d ed. Washington, D.C.: Congressional Quarterly Inc., 1997.

Cooter, Robert, and Thomas Ulen. *Law and Economics,* 5th ed. Reading, Mass.: Addison-Wesley, 2007.

Copeland, Pamela C., and Richard K. MacMaster. *The Five George Masons: Patriots and Planters of Virginia and Maryland.* Board of Regents of Gunston Hall. Charlottesville: University Press of Virginia, 1989.

Corwin, Edward S. *John Marshall and the Constitution.* New Haven: Yale University Press, 1919.

———. *The President: Office and Powers, 1787–1957,* 4th rev. ed. New York: New York University Press, 1957.

Currie, David P. *The Constitution of the United States: A Primer for the People,* 2d ed. Chicago: University of Chicago Press, 2000.

Darling, Marsha J. Tyson, ed. *Race, Voting and Redistricting, and the Constitution: Sources and Explorations on the Fifteenth Amendment.* New York: Routledge, 2001.

Dean, John W. *Blind Ambition: The White House Years.* New York: Simon and Schuster, 1976.

Deats, Richard L. *Martin Luther King, Jr., Spirit-Led Prophet: A Biography,* rev. ed. New York: New City Press, 2003.

Dempsey, James X., and David Cole. *Terrorism and the Constitution: Sacrificing Civil Liberties in the Name of National Security,* rev. ed. New York: New Press, 2006.

Dershowitz, Alan M. *Supreme Injustice: How the High Court Hijacked Election 2000.* New York: Oxford University Press, 2001.

Dietze, Gottfried. *The Federalist: A Classic on Federalism and Free Government.* Baltimore: Johns Hopkins University Press, 1960.

Donald, David Herbert. *Lincoln.* New York: Simon and Schuster, 1995.

Donkin, Richard. *Blood, Sweat and Tears: The Evolution of Work.* New York: Texere, 2001.

Doron, Gideon, and Michael Harris. *Term Limits.* Lanham, Md.: Lexington Books, 2001.

Drake, Frederick D., and Lynn R. Nelson, eds. *States' Rights and American Federalism: A Documentary History.* Westport, Conn.: Greenwood Press, 1999.

Dubois, Philip L., and Floyd Feeny. *Lawmaking by Initiative: Issues, Options, and Comparisons.* New York: Agathon Press, 1998.

Dudley, Robert L., and Alan R. Gitelson. *American Elections: The Rules Matter.* New York: Longman, 2002.

Durham, Alan L. *Patent Law Essentials: A Concise Guide,* 2d ed. Westport, Conn.: Praeger, 2004.

Eisaguirre, Lynne. *Sexual Harassment: A Reference Handbook,* 2d ed. Santa Barbara, Calif.: ABC-CLIO, 1997.

Ellis, Joseph J. *Founding Brothers: The Revolutionary Generation.* New York: Knopf, 2000.

Ellis, Richard J. *Democratic Delusions: The Initiative Process in America.* Lawrence: University Press of Kansas, 2002.

Ely, James W., Jr., ed. *The Contract Clause in American History.* New York: Garland, 1997.

———. *The Guardian of Every Other Right: A Constitutional History of Property Rights,* 2d ed. New York: Oxford University Press, 1998.

Epstein, Richard A. *Takings: Private Property and the Power of Eminent Domain.* Reprint. Cambridge: Harvard University Press, 1989.

Falk, Gerhard. *Sex, Gender, and Social Change: The Great Revolution.* Lanham, Md.: University Press of America, 1998.

Fallon, Richard H., Jr. *Implementing the Constitution.* Cambridge: Harvard University Press, 2001.

Farrand, Max. *The Framing of the Constitution of the United States.* Buffalo, N.Y.: W. S. Hein, 2000.

Fehrenbacher, Don E., ed. *Abraham Lincoln: Speeches and Writings, 1832–1858.* New York: Library of America, 1989.

Feinberg, Barbara Silberdick. *Next in Line: The American Vice Presidency.* New York: Franklin Watts, 1996.

Feldman, Leslie D. *Freedom as Motion.* Lanham, Md.: University Press of America, 2001.

Ferejohn, John A., and Barry R. Weingast, eds. *The New Federalism: Can the States Be Trusted?* Stanford, Calif.: Hoover Institution Press, 1997.

Finer, Samuel E. *The History of Government from the Earliest Times*, 3 vols. New York: Oxford University Press, 1997.

Fireside, Harvey. *New York Times v. Sullivan: Affirming Freedom of the Press.* Springfield, N.J.: Enslow, 1999.

Fletcher, George P. *Our Secret Constitution: How Lincoln Redefined American Democracy.* New York: Oxford University Press, 2001.

Frankfurter, Felix. *The Commerce Clause under Marshall, Taney and Waite.* Chapel Hill: University of North Carolina Press, 1937.

Freeman, Eric M. *Habeas Corpus: Rethinking the Great Writ of Liberty.* New York: New York University Press, 2001.

Freeman, Joanne B. *Affairs of Honor: National Politics in the New Republic.* New Haven: Yale University Press, 2001.

———, ed. *Hamilton: Writings.* New York: Library of America, 2001.

Frey, Lou, Jr., and Michael T. Hayes, eds. *Inside the House: Former Members Reveal How Congress Really Works.* Lanham, Md.: University Press of America, 2001.

Furrow, Barry R., et al. *Health Law: Cases, Materials, and Problems*, 5th ed. Eagan, Minn.: West Group, 2004.

Gagné, Patricia, and Richard Tewksbury, eds. *The Dynamics of Inequality: Race, Class, Gender, and Sexuality in the United States.* Upper Saddle River, N.J.: Prentice Hall, 2002.

Gerhardt, Michael J. *The Federal Impeachment Process: A Constitutional and Historical Analysis*, 2d ed. Chicago: University of Chicago Press, 2000.

Glendon, Mary Ann. *A World Made New: Eleanor Roosevelt and the Universal Declaration of Human Rights.* New York: Random House, 2001.

Goldwin, Robert. *From Parchment to Power: How James Madison Used the Bill of Rights to Save the Constitution.* Washington, D.C.: American Enterprise Institute, 1997.

Goode, Judith, and Jeff Maskovsky, eds. *New Poverty Studies: The Ethnography of Power, Politics, and Impoverished People in the United States.* New York: New York University Press, 2001.

Gregg, Gary L., II, ed. *Securing Democracy: Why We Have an Electoral College*, rev. ed. Wilmington, Del.: Intercollegiate Studies Institute, 2008.

Gregory, Raymond F. *Age Discrimination in the American Workplace: Old at a Young Age.* New Brunswick, N.J.: Rutgers University Press, 2001.

Gutman, Amy, ed. *Freedom of Association.* Princeton: Princeton University Press, 1998.

Haley, James, ed. *Work.* San Diego: Greenhaven Press, 2002.

Hall, John Wesley. *Search and Seizure*, 3d ed. Charlottesville, Va.: LEXIS Law, 2000.

Hall, Kermit L. *The Oxford Guide to United States Supreme Court Decisions.* New York: Oxford University Press, 1999.

———, ed. *Judicial Review and Judicial Power in the Supreme Court.* New York: Garland, 2000.

Harris, Leslie J., Lee E. Teitelbaum, and June Carbone. *Family Law*, 3d ed. Gaithersburg, Md.: Aspen Law and Business, 2005.

Harrison, Maureen, and Steve Gilbert. *Obscenity and Pornography Decisions of the United States Supreme Court.* Carlsbad, Calif.: Excellent Books, 2000.

Haskell, John. *Direct Democracy or Representative Government? Dispelling the Populist Myth.* Boulder, Colo.: Westview Press, 2000.

Hensley, Thomas R., ed. *The Boundaries of Freedom of Expression and Order in American Democracy.* Kent, Ohio: Kent State University Press, 2001.

Herring, George C., ed. *The Pentagon Papers* (abridged). New York: McGraw-Hill, 1993.

Herrnson, Paul S., and John C. Green, eds. *Multiparty Politics in America: Prospects and Performance.* Lanham, Md.: Rowman and Littlefield, 2002.

Higginbottom, Don, ed. *George Washington Reconsidered.* Charlottesville, Va.: University Press of Virginia, 2001.

Hobson, Charles F. *The Great Chief Justice: John Marshall and the Rule of Law.* Lawrence: University Press of Kansas, 1996.

Hoebeke, C. H. *The Road to Mass Democracy: Original Intent and the Seventeenth Amendment.* New Brunswick, N.J.: Transaction, 1995.

Hoffman, John. *Sovereignty.* Minneapolis: University of Minnesota Press, 1998.

Holmes, Oliver Wendell. *The Common Law*, 1881. Reprint. New York: Dover, 1991.

How Our Laws Are Made. Washington, D.C.: U.S. Government Printing Office, 2003.

Hudson, David L., Jr. *The Fourteenth Amendment: Equal Protection under the Law.* Berkely Heights, N.J.: Enslow, 2002.

Hull, Mary E. *Censorship in America: A Reference Handbook.* Santa Barbara, Calif.: ABC-CLIO, 1999.

Hull, N. E. H., and Peter C. Hoffer. *Roe v. Wade: The Abortion Rights Controversy in American History.* Lawrence: University Press of Kansas, 2001.

Inciardi, James A. *The War on Drugs III: The Continuing Saga of the Mysteries and Miseries of Intoxication, Addiction, Crime, and Public Policy.* Boston: Allyn and Bacon, 2002.

Jasper, Margaret C. *The Americans with Disability Act,* 2d ed. Dobbs Ferry, N.Y.: Oceana, 2008.

Jensen, Merrill. *The Articles of Confederation: An Interpretation of the Social-Constitutional History of the American Revolution, 1774–1781.* Madison: University of Wisconsin Press, 1970.

Johnson, Charles A., and Danette Brickman. *Independent Counsel: The Law and the Investigations.* Washington, D.C.: CQ Press, 2001.

Johnson, Frank M. *Defending Constitutional Rights.* Athens: University of Georgia Press, 2001.

Jost, Kenneth, ed. *The Supreme Court A to Z*, 4th ed. Washington, D.C.: CQ Press, 2007.

Kang, Jerry. *Communications Law and Policy: Cases and Materials*, 2d ed. New York: Foundation Press, 2005.

Keefe, William J., and Morris S. Ogul. *The American Legislative Process: Congress and the States*, 10th ed. Upper Saddle River, N.J.: Prentice Hall, 2001.

Kemp, Thomas Jay. *The American Census Handbook.* Wilmington, Del.: Scholarly Resources, 2001.

Keynes, Edward. *Liberty, Property, and Privacy: Towards a Jurisprudence of Substantive Due Process.* State College: Pennsylvania State University Press, 1996.

Kimmel, Michael S., and Amy Aronson, eds. *The Gendered Society Reader.* New York: Oxford University Press, 2000.

Klein, Irving J. *The Law of Arrest, Search, Seizure, and Liability Issues: Principles, Cases, and Comments.* South Miami, Fla.: Coral Gables Company, 1994.

Konvitz, Milton R. *Fundamental Rights: History of a Constitutional Doctrine.* New Brunswick, N.J.: Transaction, 2001.

Kraus, Samuel, ed. *The Milligan Case.* Holmes Beach, Fla.: Gaunt, 1997.

Kura, Alexandra, ed. *Electoral College and Presidential Elections.* Huntington, N.Y.: Nova Science, 2001.

Kura, N. O., ed. *Congress of the United States: Powers, Structure, and Procedures.* Huntington, N.Y.: Nova Science, 2001.

Lerner, Max, and Robert Schmuhl. *Thomas Jefferson: America's Philosopher King.* New Brunswick, N.J.: Transaction, 1995.

Lessig, Lawrence. *Code and Other Laws of Cyberspace.* New York: Basic Books, 1999.

Levinson, Isabel Simone. *Gibbons v. Ogden: Controlling Trade between States.* Springfield, N.J.: Enslow, 1999.

Levinson, Sanford. *Responding to Imperfection: The Theory and Practice of Constitutional Amendment.* Princeton: Princeton University Press, 1995.

Levy, Leonard W. *Origins of the Bill of Rights.* New Haven: Yale University Press, 1999.

_____. *Origins of the Fifth Amendment: The Right against Self-Incrimination.* Chicago: Ivan R. Dee, 1999.

_____, and Kenneth L. Karst. *Encyclopedia of the American Constitution*, 2d ed., 6 vols. New York: Macmillan Reference, 2000.

Lewis, Anthony. *Gideon's Trumpet.* New York: Random House, 1964.

Lieberman, Jethro K. *A Practical Companion to the Constitution: How the Supreme Court Has Ruled on Issues from Abortion to Zoning.* Berkeley: University of California Press, 1999.

Loss, Richard, ed. *Corwin on the Constitution*, 3 vols. Ithaca, N.Y.: Cornell University Press, 1981–88.

Loury, Glenn C. *The Anatomy of Racial Inequality.* Cambridge: Harvard University Press, 2002.

Lynch, Joseph M. *Negotiating the Constitution: The Earliest Debate over Original Intent.* Ithaca, N.Y.: Cornell University Press, 1999.

Lynn, Barry W., Marc D. Stern, and Oliver S. Thomas. *The Right to Religious Liberty: The Basic ACLU Guide to Religious Rights*, 2d ed. Carbondale: Southern Illinois University Press, 1995.

Maddex, Robert L. *Constitutions of the World*, 3d ed. Washington, D.C.: CQ Press, 2008.

_____. *Encyclopedia of Sexual Behavior and the Law.* Washington, D.C.: CQ Press, 2006.

_____. *The Illustrated Dictionary of Constitutional Concepts.* Washington, D.C.: Congressional Quarterly Inc., 1996.

_____. *International Encyclopedia of Human Rights: Freedoms, Abuses, and Remedies.* Washington, D.C.: CQ Press, 2000.

_____. *State Constitutions of the United States*, 2d ed. Washington, D.C.: CQ Press, 2006.

Malone, Dumas. *Jefferson and the Rights of Man.* Boston: Little, Brown, 1951.

Maraist, Frank L., and Thomas C. Gallgan. *Admiralty in a Nutshell*, 5th ed. St. Paul, Minn.: West Group, 2005.

Mathis, William S., ed. *Presidency of the United States: History, Analyses, Bibliography.* Huntington, N.Y.: Nova Science, 2002.

May, Christopher N., and Allan Ides. *Constitutional Law—National Power and Federalism: Examples and Explanations*, 4th ed. Gaithersburg, Md.: Aspen Law and Business, 2006.

Mayer, David N. *The Constitutional Thought of Thomas Jefferson*. Charlottesville: University Press of Virginia, 1994.

McCullough, David. *John Adams*. New York: Simon and Schuster, 2001.

McGlen, Nancy E., et al. *Women, Politics, and American Society*, 4th ed. New York: Longman, 2005.

McGuire, Kevin T. *Understanding the Supreme Court: Cases and Controversies*. Boston: McGraw-Hill, 2002.

Melanson, Philip H. *Secrecy Wars: National Security, Privacy, and the Public's Right to Know*. Washington, D.C.: Potomac Books, 2001.

Melton, Buckner F., Jr. *Aaron Burr: Conspiracy to Treason*. New York: Wiley, 2002.

Middleton, Kent R., and William E. Lee. *The Law of Public Communication*, 7th ed. Boston: Allyn and Bacon, 2007.

Mikva, Abner J., and Eric Lane. *Legislative Process*, 2d ed. New York: Aspen Law and Business, 2002.

Mitchell, Hayley R., ed. *The Death Penalty*. San Diego: Greenhaven Press, 2001.

Mitchell, Ralph. *CQ's Guide to the U.S. Constitution*, 2d ed. Washington, D.C.: Congressional Quarterly Inc., 1998.

Moon, Gay, ed. *Race Discrimination: Developing and Using a New Legal Framework*. Portland, Ore.: Hart, 2001.

Morgan, Edmund S. *Inventing the People: The Rise of Popular Sovereignty in England and America*. New York: Norton, 1988.

Morison, Samuel Eliot. *The Oxford History of the American People*, Vol. 1. New York: Oxford University Press, 1972.

Morris, Irwin L. *Congress, the President, and the Federal Reserve: The Politics of American Monetary Policy-Making*. Ann Arbor: University of Michigan Press, 2000.

Moynihan, Daniel P. *On the Law of Nations*. Cambridge: Harvard University Press, 1996.

Murphy, Paul L. *Rights of Assembly, Petition, Arms and Just Compensation*. The Bill of Rights and American Legal History. New York: Garland, 1990.

Neely, Mark E., Jr. *The Fate of Liberty: Abraham Lincoln and Civil Liberties*. New York: Oxford University Press, 1992.

Newmyer, R. Kent. *John Marshall and the Heroic Age of the Supreme Court*. Baton Rouge: Louisiana State University Press, 2001.

O'Connor, Sandra Day, and H. Alan Day. *Lazy B: Growing Up on a Cattle Ranch in the American Southwest*. New York: Random House, 2002.

Page, Benjamin I., and James R. Simmons. *What Government Can Do: Dealing with Poverty and Inequality*. Chicago: University of Chicago Press, 2000.

Pardeck, John T. *Children's Rights: Policy and Practice*, 2d ed. New York: Routledge, 2006.

Paust, Jordan J. *International Law as Law of the United States*, 2d ed. Durham, N.C.: Carolina Academic Press, 2003.

Peabody, James Bishop. *John Adams: A Biography in His Own Words*. New York: Newsweek Books, Harper and Row, 1973.

Peak, Kenneth J. *Justice Administration: Police, Courts, and Corrections Management*, 5th ed. Upper Saddle River, N.J.: Prentice Hall, 2006.

Peters, Gerhard, John T. Wooley, and Michael Nelson, eds. *The Presidency A to Z*, 4th ed. Washington, D.C.: CQ Press, 2008.

Peters, Ronald M., Jr., ed. *The Speaker: Leadership in the U.S. House of Representatives*. Washington, D.C.: Congressional Quarterly, 1995.

Phelps, Glenn A. *George Washington and American Constitutionalism*. Lawrence: University Press of Kansas, 1993.

Plato. *The Laws*. Trevor J. Saunders, trans. London: Penguin Books, 1975.

Pohlman, H. L. *Constitutional Debate in Action: Governmental Powers*, 2d ed. Lanham, Md.: Rowman and Littlefield, 2005.

Proceedings of the United States Senate in the Impeachment Trial of President William Jefferson Clinton. Washington, D.C.: U.S. Government Printing Office, 1999.

Prucha, Francis Paul. *American Indian Treaties: The History of a Political Anomaly*. Berkeley: University of California Press, 1997.

Pyle, Christopher H. *Extradition, Politics, and Human Rights*. Philadelphia: Temple University Press, 2001.

Rakove, Jack N. *James Madison and the Creation of the American Republic*, 3d ed. The Library of American Biography, Mark C. Carnos, ed. New York: Longman, 2006.

Randall, Kenneth C. *Federal Courts and the International Human Rights Paradigm*. Durham, N.C.: Duke University Press, 1991.

Riley, Gail Blasser. *Miranda v. Arizona: Rights of the Accused*. Hillside, N.J.: Enslow, 1994.

Roach, Kent. *Due Process and Victims' Rights: The New Law and Politics of Criminal Justice*. Toronto: University of Toronto, 1999.

Robinson, Marlyn, and Christopher Simoni. *The Flag and the Law: A Documentary History of the*

Treatment of the American Flag by the Supreme Court and Congress, 3 vols. Buffalo, N.Y.: W. S. Hein, 1993.

Rodley, Nigel S. *The Treatment of Prisoners under International Law*, 2d ed. New York: Oxford University Press, 1999.

Roleff, Tamara L., ed. *Censorship: Opposing Viewpoints*. San Diego: Greenhaven Press, 2002.

Roshwald, Mordecai. *Liberty: Its Meaning and Scope*. Westport, Conn.: Greenwood Press, 2000.

Rossiter, Clinton, ed. *The Federalist Papers*. New York: New American Library, Mentor, 1999.

Rozell, Mark J. *Executive Privilege: The Dilemma of Secrecy and Democratic Accountability*. Baltimore: John Hopkins University Press, 1994.

Rozell, Mark J., William D. Pederson, and Frank J. Williams, eds. *George Washington and the Origins of the American Presidency*. Westport, Conn.: Praeger, 2000.

Rudenstine, David. *The Day the Presses Stopped: A History of the Pentagon Papers Case*. Berkeley: University of California Press, 1996.

Rutland, Robert A. *George Mason: Reluctant Statesman*. Baton Rouge: Louisiana State University Press, 1961.

Saltzburg, Stephen A., et al. *Criminal Law: Cases and Materials*, 2d ed. New York: Lexis, 2000.

Schick, Allen. *The Federal Budget: Politics, Policy, Process*, 3d ed. Washington, D.C.: Brookings Institution Press, 2007.

Schoenbaum, Thomas J. *Admiralty and Maritime Law*, 4th ed. St. Paul, Minn.: West Group, 2004.

Scott, James Brown. *James Madison's Notes of the Debates in the Federal Convention of 1787 and Their Relation to a More Perfect Society of Nations*. Union, N.J.: Lawbook Exchange, 2001.

Sense, Donald J., ed. *George Mason and the Legacy of Constitutional Liberty: An Examination of the Influence of George Mason and the Bill of Rights*. Fairfax, Va.: Fairfax County History Commission, 1989.

Shapiro, Ian, ed. *The Rule of Law*. New York: New York University Press, 1994.

Sherr, Lynn. *Failure Is Impossible: Susan B. Anthony in Her Own Words*. New York: Times Books, 1995.

Siebold, Thomas, ed. *Martin Luther King, Jr.* San Diego: Greenhaven Press, 2000.

Simon, James F. *What Kind of Nation: Thomas Jefferson, John Marshall, and the Epic Struggle to Create a United States*. New York: Simon and Schuster, 2002.

Simon, Paul. *Advice and Consent: Clarence Thomas, Robert Bork, and the Intriguing History of the Supreme Court's Nomination Battles*. Washington, D.C.: National Press Books, 1992.

Solimine, Michael E., and James L. Walker. *Respecting State Courts: The Inevitability of Judicial Federalism*. Westport, Conn.: Greenwood Press, 1999.

Spohn, Cassia C. *How Do Judges Decide? The Search for Fairness and Justice in Punishment*. Thousand Oaks, Calif.: Sage, 2002.

Statsky, William P. *Family Law*, 5th ed. Albany, N.Y.: West, Thomson Learning, 2001.

Sterba, James P., ed. *Justice: Alternative Political Perspectives*, 4th ed. Belmont, Calif.: Wadsworth, 2003.

Stiehm, Judith Hicks, ed. *It's Our Military, Too!: Women and the U.S. Military*. Philadelphia: Temple University Press, 1996.

Story, Joseph. *A Familiar Exposition of the Constitution of the United States*, special ed. Birmingham, Ala.: Palladium Press, 2001.

Strauss, Steven D. *Debt and Bankruptcy*. New York: Norton, 1998.

Stuart, Peter C. *Isles of Empire: The United States and Its Overseas Possessions*. Lanham, Md.: University Press of America, 1999.

Stumpf, Felix F. *Inherent Powers of the Courts: Sword and Shield of the Judiciary*. Reno, Nev.: National Judicial College, 1994.

Sullivan, Harold J. *Civil Rights and Liberties: Provocative Questions and Evolving Answers*, 2d ed. Upper Saddle River, N.J.: Prentice Hall, 2004.

Sullivan, Kathleen M., and Gerald Gunther. *Constitutional Law*, 16th ed. New York: Foundation Press, 2007.

Summers, Robert S., et al. *Law: Its Nature, Functions and Limits*, 3d ed. St. Paul, Minn.: West, 1986.

Sunstein, Cass R., and Richard A. Epstein, eds. *The Vote: Bush, Gore, and the Supreme Court*. Chicago: University of Chicago, 2001.

Syrett, Harold C., and Jacob E. Cooke, eds. *The Papers of Alexander Hamilton*, 27 vols. New York: Columbia University Press, 1961–87.

Tarr, David R., ed. *Congress A to Z*, 5th ed. Washington, D.C.: CQ Press, 2008.

Thierer, Adam D. *The Delicate Balance: Federalism, Interstate Commerce, and Economic Freedom in the Technological Age*. Washington, D.C.: Heritage Foundation, 1999.

Thomas, George C. *Double Jeopardy: The History, The Law*. New York: New York University Press, 1998.

Tocqueville, Alexis de. *Democracy in America*. J. P. Mayer, ed. New York: HarperCollins, 2000.

Toobin, Jeffrey. *The Nine: Inside the Secret World of the Supreme Court*. New York: Doubleday, 2007.

Troy, Daniel E. *Retroactive Legislation*. Washington, D.C.: American Enterprise Institute Press, 1998.

Tunick, Mark. *Punishment: Theory and Practice*. Berkeley: University of California Press, 1992.

Tushnet, Mark, ed. *Thurgood Marshall: His Speeches, Writings, Arguments, Opinions, and Reminiscences*. Chicago: Lawrence Hill Books, 2001.

Uhlman, Michael M., ed. *Last Rights? Assisted Suicide and Euthanasia Debated*. Ethics and Public Policy Center. Grand Rapids, Mich.: William B. Eerdmans, 1998.

Vandenberg, Andrew, ed. *Citizenship and Democracy in a Global Era*. New York: St. Martin's, 2000.

Van Tassel, Emily Field, and Paul Finkelman. *Impeachable Offenses: A Documentary History from 1787 to the Present*. Washington, D.C.: CQ Press, 1999.

Vieira, Norman. *Constitutional Civil Rights in a Nutshell*. St. Paul, Minn.: West Group, 1998.

Vile, M. J. C. *Constitutionalism and the Separation of Powers*, 2d ed. Indianapolis: Liberty Fund, 1998.

Warren, Charles. *The Supreme Court in United States History*. Boston: Little, Brown, 1932.

Waters, M. Dane, ed. *The Battle over Citizen Lawmaking: A Collection of Essays*. Durham, N.C.: Carolina Academic Press, 2001.

Wattson, Peter S. *Redistricting in the 1990s: A Review of U.S. Supreme Court Decisions*. St Paul, Minn.: Senate Counsel, State of Minnesota, 1997.

Weber, Lynn. *Understanding Race, Class, Gender, and Sexuality: A Conceptual Framework*. Boston: McGraw-Hill, 2001.

Weddington, Sarah Ragle. *A Question of Choice*. New York: Putnam, 1992.

Weil, Alan, and Kenneth Finegold, eds. *Welfare Reform: The Next Act*. Washington, D.C.: Urban Institute Press, 2002.

Weisberger, Bernard A. *America Afire: Jefferson, Adams, and the Revolutionary Election of 1800*. New York: William Morrow, 2000.

Wells, Tom. *Wild Man: The Life and Times of Daniel Ellsberg*. New York: Palgrave, 2001.

West, Robin, ed. *Rights*. Burlington, Vt.: Ashgate, 2001.

Westervelt, Saundra D., and John A. Humphrey, eds. *Wrongly Convicted: Perspectives on Failed Justice*. New Brunswick, N.J.: Rutgers University Press, 2001.

White, G. Edward. *Justice Oliver Wendell Holmes: Law and the Inner Self*. New York: Oxford University Press, 1993.

Whitehead, John S. *Completing the Union: The Alaska and Hawaii Statehood Movements*. Anchorage: Alaska Historical Commission, 1986.

Whittington, Keith E. *Constitutional Construction: Divided Powers and Constitutional Meaning*. Cambridge: Harvard University Press, 1999.

Wiecek, William M. *The Guarantee Clause of the U.S. Constitution*. Ithaca, N.Y.: Cornell University Press, 1972.

Wildavsky, Aaron B. *Budgeting and Governing*, 2d ed. New Brunswick, N.J.: Transaction, 2006.

Wilkinson, Charles F. *American Indians, Time, and the Law: Native Societies in a Modern Constitutional Democracy*. New Haven: Yale University Press, 1987.

Williams, Juan. *Thurgood Marshall: American Revolutionary*. New York: Times Books, 1998.

Wills, Garry. *James Madison*. American Presidents Series. Arthur M. Schlesinger Jr., ed. New York: Times Books, 2002.

Wilson, Paul E. *A Time to Lose: Representing Kansas in Brown v. Board of Education*. Lawrence: University Press of Kansas, 1995.

Winters, Paul A., ed. *The Death Penalty: Opposing Viewpoints*, 3d ed. San Diego: Greenhaven Press, 1997.

Yalof, David Alistair, and Kenneth Dautrich. *The First Amendment and the Media in the Court of Public Opinion*. New York: Cambridge University Press, 2002.

Zelezny, John D. *Communications Law: Liberties, Restraints, and the Modern Media*, 3d ed. Belmont, Calif.: Wadsworth, Thomson Learning, 2001.

Zimmerman, Joseph F., and Wilma Rule, eds. *The U.S. House of Representatives: Reform or Rebuild?* Westport, Conn.: Praeger, 2000.

Internet Resources

A number of Internet sites offer information on the Constitution and related topics. Here are some of the best:

The Constitution
www.law.cornell.edu/constitution/constitution.overview.html
The Constitution presented by article and section with amendments.

The Constitution of the United States
www.archives.gov/national-archives-experience/charters/constitution_transcript.html
A National Archives and Records Administration transcription of the text of the Constitution in its original form with amended or superseded provisions highlighted in hypertext, plus links to biographies of the framers.

The Constitution of the United States
www.aboutgovernment.org/print_historicaldocuments_constitution.htm
An online version of the Constitution that contains links within the text to definitions for students and to supplementary historical material.

Documents in Law, History, and Diplomacy
www.yale.edu/lawweb/avalon/avalon.htm
The Avalon Project at the Yale Law School contains materials relevant for research on the Constitution and the related fields of law, history, economics, politics, diplomacy, and government.

Facts About the Constitution
www.constitutionfacts.com
Varied information about the Constitution.

Library of Constitutional Classics
www.constitution.org
More than 150 entries relating to constitutional government from the eighteenth-century B.C.E. Code of Hammurabi to state constitutions and many national constitutions.

National Constitution Center

www.constitutioncenter.org

Established to promote awareness and understanding of the Constitution.

Supreme Court Cases

www.findlaw.com/casecode/constitution/

Key cases and other legal materials.

Note: For specific queries relating to the Constitution, the search engine at www.google.com may be helpful.

Index

Encyclopedia entries are listed in bold type. Page numbers in italics refer to illustrations.